T0185547

Practical Database Programming with Java

IEEE Press
445 Hoes Lane
Piscataway, NJ 08854

Practical Database Programming with Java

Ying Bai
Department of Computer Science and Engineering
Johnson C. Smith University
Charlotte, North Carolina

IEEE PRESS

A John Wiley & Sons, Inc., Publication

Published by John Wiley & Sons, Inc., Hoboken, New Jersey
Published simultaneously in Canada

Library of Congress Cataloging-in-Publication Data:
Bai, Ying, 1956-
Practical database programming with Java / Ying Bai.
p. cm.
ISBN 978-0-470-88940-4 (pbk.)
1. Database management–Computer programs. 2. Database design. 3. Java (Computer program language) 4. Computer software–Development. I. Title.
QA76.9.D3B314 2011
005.13'3–dc22
2011009323

obook ISBN 9781118104651
ePDF ISBN 9781118104668
ePub ISBN 9781118104699

Printed in the United States of America

10 9 8 7 6 5 4 3 2 1

This book is dedicated to my wife, Yan Wang,
and to my daughter, Xue Bai.

Contents

Section II Insert, Update and Delete Data Using Java Runtime Objects Method 488

Preface

Databases have become an integral part of our modern day life. We are an information-driven society. Database technology has a direct impact on our daily lives. Decisions are routinely made by organizations based on the information collected and stored in databases. A record company may decide to market certain albums in selected regions based on the music preference of teenagers. Grocery stores display more popular items at the eye level and reorders are based on the inventories taken at regular intervals. Other examples include patients' records in hospitals, customers' account information in banks, book orders by the libraries, club memberships, auto part orders, winter cloth stock by department stores, and many others.

In addition to database management systems, in order to effectively apply and implement databases in real industrial or commercial systems, a good graphic user interface (GUI) is needed to enable users to access and manipulate their records or data in databases. NetBeans IDE is an ideal candidate to be selected to provide this GUI functionality. Unlike other programming languages, Java is a kind of language that has advantages, such as easy to earn and easy to be understood, with little learning curves. Beginning from Java 1.0, Sun has integrated a few programming languages, such as C++, JavaFX, and PHP, with some frameworks into dynamic models that make Internet and Web programming easy and simple, and any language integrated in this model can be used to develop professional and efficient Web applications that can be used to communicate with others via Internet.

This book is mainly designed for college students and software programmers who want to develop practical and commercial database programming with Java and relational databases, such as Microsoft Access, SQL Server 2008, and Oracle Database 10g XE. The book provides a detailed description about the practical considerations and applications in database programming with Java and authentic examples and detailed explanations. More important, a new writing style is developed and implemented in this book, combined with real examples, to provide readers with a clear picture as how to handle the database programming issues in NetBeans IDE environment.

The outstanding features of this book include but are not limited to the following.

1. A novel writing style is adopted to attract students or beginning programmers who are interested in learning and developing practical database programs, with the hope of avoiding the headaches caused by huge blocks of codes found in traditional database programming books.
2. A real completed sample database, CSE_DEPT, with three versions (Microsoft Access 2007, SQL Server 2008, and Oracle Database 10g XE Release 2), is provided and used for the entire book. A step-by-step, detailed description about how to design and build a practical relational database is provided.

3. Both fundamental and advanced database programming techniques are covered, for the convenience of both beginning students and experienced programmers.
4. Updated Java database programming techniques, such as Java Persistence API, Java Enterprise Edition 6, JavaServer Pages, JavaServer Faces, and Enterprise Java Beans, are discussed and analyzed with real projects to enable readers to have a clear picture and easy-to-learn path for Java database applications.
5. More than 30 real sample database programming projects are covered, with detailed illustrations and explanations to help students to understand key techniques and programming technologies.
6. Three types of popular databases are covered and discussed in detail with practical sample examples: Microsoft Access, SQL Server 2008, and Oracle Database 10g Express Edition (XE).
7. The various actual JDBC APIs and JDBC drivers are discussed and presented with real example coding explanations. The working structure and principle of using a JDBC driver to establish a valid database connection, build an SQL statement, and process the query results are introduced in detail with example codes. JDBC RowSet, a useful tool, is also discussed and analyzed with some example codes.
8. Problems and selected solutions are provided for each chapter to strengthen and improve understanding of the topics.
9. Power Point teaching slides are also provided to help instructors.

I sincerely hope that this book will be useful to all who adopt it, as a textbook for college students, as well as a reference book for programmers, software engineers, and academic researchers. I would be more than happy to know that you have been able to develop and build professional and practical database applications with the help of this book.

Ying Bai

Acknowledgments

First, I thank my wife, Yan Wang, in particular. I could not have finished this book without her sincere encouragement and support.

I also thank Satish Bhalla, who made important contributions to Chapter 2. Dr. Bhalla is a specialist in database programming and management, in particular, in SQL Server, Oracle, and DB2. Dr. Bhalla spent much time preparing materials for the first part of Chapter 2, and this is gratefully acknowledged.

Many thanks also go to Mary Mann at Wiley, who helped to make this book available to the public, and for her deep perspective and hard work. The same thanks are extended to the editorial team, without whose contributions the book would not have been published.

Thanks should also be extended to the following book reviewers for their important feedback on the manuscript:

- Dr. Jifeng Xu, Research Scientist, Boeing Company
- Dr. Xiaohong Yuan, Associate Professor, Department of Computer Science, North Carolina A&T State University
- Dr. Daoxi Xiu, Application Analyst Programmer, North Carolina Administrative Office of the Courts
- Dr. Dali Wang, Assistant Professor, Department of Physics and Computer Science, Christopher Newport University

Finally, thanks should be given to all of the people who supported me in the completion of this book.

Chapter 1

Introduction

For years while teaching database programming, I found it difficult to find a good textbook for this topic, so I had to combine a few different books together in order to teach the course. Most of those books are designed for programmers or software engineers, which cover a lot of programming strategies and huge blocks of coding, a headache to college students or beginning programmers who are new to programming. I dreamed that one day I would find a good textbook that is suitable for college students or beginning programmers, and that would help them to learn and master database programming easily and conveniently. Finally, I decided to realize this dream myself.

Another reason to write this book was the job market. Most companies in the United States, such as manufacturers, retailers, banks, and hospitals, use database applications extensively. The majority need professionals to develop and build database-related applications, but not necessarily database management and design. To enable our students to be good candidates for those jobs, a book such as this one is needed.

Unlike most database programming books on the current market, which discuss and present database programming techniques with huge blocks of programming codes from the first page to the last page, this book uses a new writing style to show readers, especially the college students, how to develop professional and practical database programs with Java, by using Java Persistence API (JAPI), Java Enterprise Edition (J2EE), Enterprise Java Beans (EJB), and plug-in tools related to NetBeans IDE, and to apply codes that are autogenerated by using those tools. Thus, the huge blocks of programming codes can be removed, and, instead, a simple and easy way to create database programs using plug-in tools can be developed to attract students' interests, and furthermore to enable students to build professional and practical database programming in more efficient and interesting ways.

To meet the needs of some experienced or advanced students or software engineers, the book contains two programming methods: the interesting fundamental database programming method (JAPI and plug-in tools method) and the advanced database programming method (runtime object method). In the second method, all database-related objects are created and applied during or when your project is running by utilizing quite a few blocks of codes.

Practical Database Programming with Java, First Edition. Ying Bai.

WHAT THIS BOOK COVERS

The contents of each chapter can be summarized as follows. Chapter 1 provides an introduction to the book. Chapter 2 provides a detailed discussion and analysis of the structure and components about relational databases. Some key technologies in developing and designing databases are also given and discussed. The procedure and components used to develop a practical relational database with three database versions, such as Microsoft Access, SQL Server 2008, and Oracle Database 10g XE, are analyzed in detail with some real data tables in our sample database CSE_DEPT.

Chapter 3 provides an introduction to JDBC APIs and JDBC drivers. A detailed introduction to components and architecture of JDBC is given with step-by-step illustrations. Four popular types of JDBC drivers are discussed and analyzed with their advantages and disadvantages in actual database applications. The working structure and operational principle of using JDBC drivers to establish a valid database connection, build a SQL statement, and process the query results are discussed and presented in detail. JDBC RowSet, a useful tool, is also discussed and analyzed with some example codes.

Chapter 4 provides a detailed discussion and analysis of JDBC design and actual application considerations. The fundamentals of using JDBC to access and manipulate data against databases are discussed and introduced with example codes. Different JDBC interfaces, including the ResultSet, ResultSetMetaData, DatabaseMetaData, and ParameterMetaData, are introduced and discussed with example codes.

Chapter 5 provides a detailed description of the NetBeans IDE, including the components and architecture. This topic is necessary for college students who have no knowledge of NetBeans IDE. Starting with an introduction to installing NetBeans IDE, this chapter goes through each aspect of NetBeans IDE, including the NetBeans Platform, NetBeans Open Source, and all plug-in tools. Different projects built with NetBeans IDE are discussed and presented in detail with 14 example projects.

Starting with Chapter 6, the real database programming techniques with Java, query data from database, are provided and discussed. Two parts are covered in this chapter: Part I contains detailed descriptions of how to develop professional data-driven applications with the help of the JAPI and plug-in tools with some real projects, and this part contains a lot of hiding codes that are created by NetBeans IDE automatically when using those tools and wizards. Therefore, the coding for this part is very simple and easy. Part II covers an advanced technique, the runtime object method, in developing and building professional data-driven applications. Detailed discussions and descriptions of how to build professional and practical database applications using this runtime method are provided combined with two real projects. In addition to basic query techniques, advanced query methods, such as PreparedStatement, CallableStatement, and stored procedure, are also discussed and implemented in this chapter with some real sample projects.

Chapter 7 provides detailed discussions and analyses of how to insert, update, and delete data from three popular databases: Microsoft Access, SQL Server 2008, and Oracle.

This chapter is also divided into two parts: In Part I, JAPI and plug-in tools to perform data manipulations are discussed. Part II covers the technique to manipulate data in our sample database using the runtime object method. Four real projects illustrate how to perform the data manipulations against three different databases: Microsoft Access, SQL Server 2008, and Oracle Database 10g XE. Professional and practical data validation methods are also discussed in this chapter to confirm the data manipulations. Some advanced data manipulation techniques, such as using Updatable ResultSet and Callable Statements to perform data actions, are also discussed with some real sample projects.

Chapter 8 discusses the developments and implementations of three-tier Java Web applications in the NetBeans IDE environment. At the beginning of this chapter, a detailed historical review of Java Web application development is provided, which is especially useful to students or programmers who lack knowledge or background in Java Web application development and implementation. Then different techniques used in building Java Web applications are introduced and discussed in detail. Starting with Section 8.4, the detailed development and building process of Java Web applications using J2EE and EJB to access databases is discussed with six real Web application projects. Two popular databases, SQL Server and Oracle, are utilized as the target databases for those development and building processes. JavaServer Pages and JavaServer Faces techniques are also discussed and involved in those real Web application projects.

Chapter 9 discusses the development and implementation of Java Web services in the NetBeans IDE environment. A detailed analysis of the structure and components of Java Web services is provided. Two popular databases, SQL Server and Oracle, are discussed and used for two example Web service projects, which include WebServiceSQLApp and WebServiceOracleApp. Each Web service contains different operations that can be used to access different databases and perform the desired data actions, such as Select, Insert, Update, and Delete, via the Internet. To consume those Web services, different Web service client projects are also developed in this chapter. Both Windows-based and Web-based Web service client projects are discussed and built for each kind of Web service. Eight projects in total, including the Web service projects and the associated Web service client projects, are developed. All projects have been debugged and tested and can be run in any Windows compatible operating system, such as Windows 95, 98, 2000, XP, and Windows 7.

HOW THIS BOOK IS ORGANIZED AND HOW TO USE THIS BOOK

This book is designed for both college students who are new to database programming with Java and professional database programmers who have experience in this topic.

Chapters 2 and 3 provide the fundamentals on database structures and components, JDBC API and components it covered. Chapter 4 covers an introduction to JDBC design and application considerations. Chapter 5 provides a detailed introduction to NetBeans IDE and its working environment. Chapters 6 and 7 are divided into two parts: a fundamental part and an advanced part. The data-driven applications developed with JAPI and plug-in tools provided by NetBeans IDE, which can be considered as the fundamental part, have less coding loads and therefore are more suitable to students or programmers who are new to the database programming with Java. Part II contains the runtime object method and covers many coding developments to perform the different data actions against the database; this method is more flexible and convenient to experienced programmers when a lot of coding is involved.

Chapters 8 and 9 give a full discussion and analysis of the development and implementation of Java Web applications and Web services. These technologies are necessary

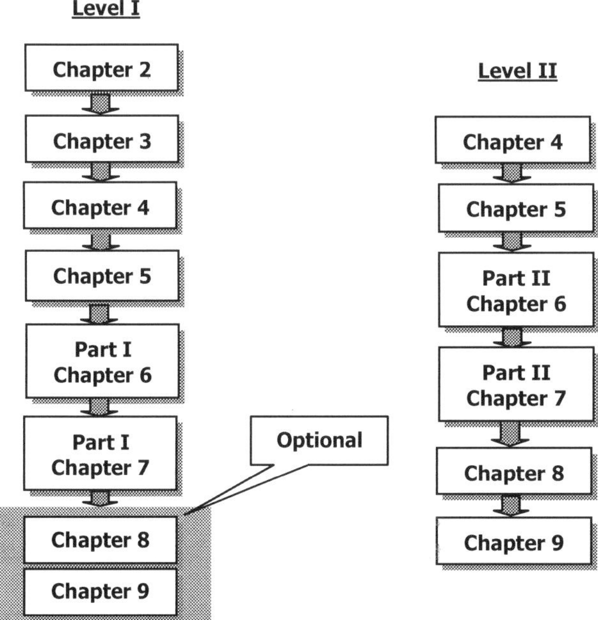

Figure 1.1. Two levels in this book.

to students and programmers who want to develop and build Web applications and Web services to access and manipulate data via the Internet.

Based on the organization of this book as described above, this book can be used in two ways, Level I or Level II, as shown in Figure 1.1. For undergraduate college students or beginning software programmers, it is highly recommended to learn and understand the contents of Chapters 2–5 and Part I of Chapters 6 and 7, since those are fundamental to database programming with Java. Chapters 8 and 9 are optional.

In Chapter 2, a detailed introduction about how to design and build a practical relational sample database, CSE_DEPT, with three database versions, is provided. A step-by-step detailed description is given to illustrate how to design and set up relationships between parent and child tables using the primary and foreign keys for Microsoft Access 2007, SQL Server 2008, and Oracle Database 10g XE Release 2 databases. In Part I of Chapters 6 and 7, JAPI, plug-in tools, and wizards are discussed and analyzed to show readers how to use them to design and build professional database programs with Java easily and conveniently.

For experienced college students or software programmers who have already some knowledge and technique in database programming, it is recommended to learn and understand the contents of Part II of Chapters 6 and 7, as well as Chapters 4, 5, 8, and 9, since the runtime data objects method and some sophisticated database programming techniques such as Java RowSet object, Callable Statements, stored procedures, and Oracle Package are discussed and illustrated with real examples. Also, the Java Web applications and Java Web services are discussed and analyzed with eight real database program examples for SQL Server 2008 and Oracle Database 10g XE database systems.

HOW TO USE THE SOURCE CODE AND SAMPLE DATABASES

All source codes of each real project developed in this book are available on the Web. All projects are categorized into the associated chapters that are located in the folder DBProjects, on the site ftp://ftp.wiley.com/public/sci_tech_med/practical_database_java. You can copy or download those codes into your computer and run each project as you like. To successfully run those projects on your computer, the following conditions must be met:

- NetBeans IDE 6.8 or higher versions must be installed in your computer.
- Three database' management systems, Microsoft Access 2007 (Microsoft Office 2007), Microsoft SQL Server 2008 Management Studio, and Oracle Database 10g Express Edition (XE) must be installed in your computer.
- Three versions of sample databases, CSE_DEPT.accdb, CSE_DEPT.mdf, and Oracle version of CSE_DEPT, must be installed in your computer in the appropriate folders.
- To run projects developed in Chapters 8 and 9, in addition to conditions listed above, a Web server such as Glassfish v3 and J2EE must be installed in your computer.

The following appendixes are useful when one needs some references and practical knowledge to install database management systems and develop actual database application projects:

Appendix A: Data Type Mappings between SQL Statements and Java Applications.

Appendix B: Basic java.sql Package Class Reference.

Appendix C: Basic java.sql Package Interface References.

Appendix D: Download and Install SQL Server 2008 Database Express and SQL Server 2008 Management Studio.

Appendix E: Download and Install Oracle Database 10g Express Edition.

Appendix F: Build Oracle Databases Using Load and Unload Methods.

Appendix G: How to Use Sample Databases Provided with the Book.

Appendix H: Build a SQL Server 2008 Stored Procedure dbo.FacultyInfo.

Appendix I: Install Java EE 6 SDK Software and Configure GlassFish v3 Server.

Appendix J: A Complete SQL Commands Reference.

Appendix K: Build a Java EE 6 Database Application with SQL Server Database.

All of these appendixes can be found in the folder named **Appendix** that is located at the site ftp://ftp.wiley.com/public/sci_tech_med/practical_database_java.

Three sample database files, **CSE_DEPT.accdb**, **CSE_DEPT.mdf,** and the Oracle version of **CSE_DEPT**, are located in the different folders, such as **Access**, **SQLServer,** and **Oracle**, which are sub-folders and under the folder **Database** at the site ftp://ftp.wiley.com/public/sci_tech_med/practical_database_java. To use these databases for your applications or sample projects, refer to Appendix G.

INSTRUCTOR AND CUSTOMER SUPPORT

The teaching materials for all chapters have been extracted and represented by a sequence of Microsoft Power Point files, one file for each chapter. Interested instructors can find those teaching materials in the folder TeachingPPT that is located at the site http://www.wiley.com, and those instructor materials are available on request from the book's listing on http://www.wiley.com (see Fig. 1.2).

FOR INSTRUCTORS:

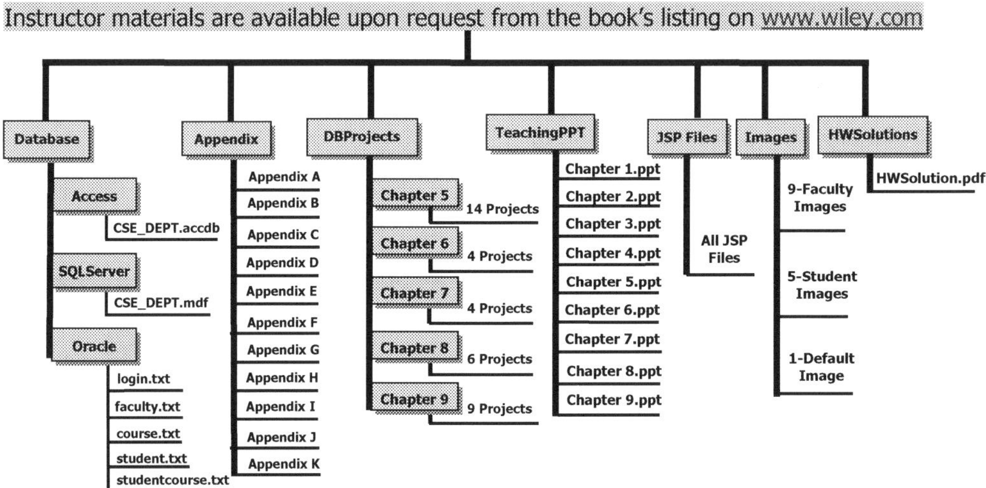

FOR STUDENTS:

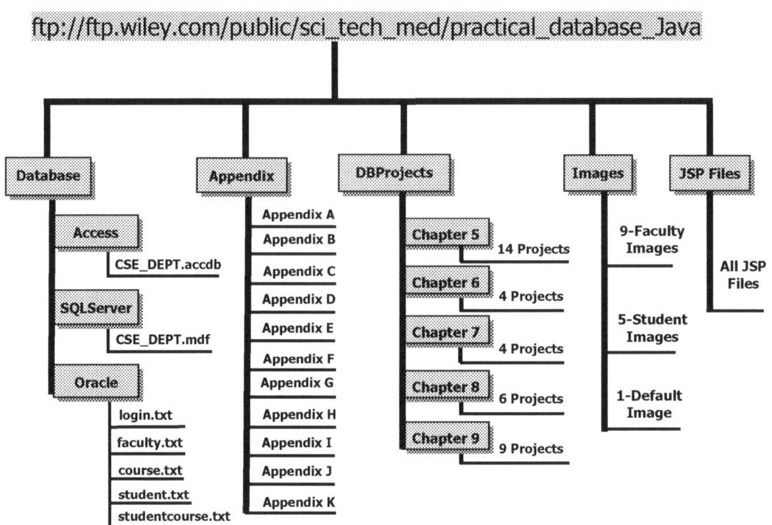

Figure 1.2. Book related materials on the Web sites.

E-mail support is available to readers of this book. When you send email to us, please provide the following information:

A detailed description about your problem, including the error message and debug message, as well as the error or debug number, if it is provided.

Your name, job title, and company name.

Please send all questions to the email address: baidbbook@bellsouth.net.

HOMEWORK SOLUTIONS

A selected homework solution is available on request from the book's listing on http://www.wiley.com.

Chapter 2

Introduction to Databases

SATISH BHALLA AND YING BAI

Databases have become an integral part of our modern-day life. We are an information-driven society. We generate large amounts of data that is analyzed and converted into information. A recent example of biological data generation is the Human Genome Project, which was jointly sponsored by the Department of Energy and the National Institute of Health. Many countries in the world participated in this venture for 10 years. The project was a tremendous success. It was completed in 2003 and resulted in the generation of a huge amount of genome data, currently stored in databases around the world. The scientists will be analyzing this data in years to come.

Database technology has a direct impact on our daily lives. Decisions are routinely made by organizations based on the information collected and stored in the databases. A record company may decide to market certain albums in selected regions based on the music preference of teenagers. Grocery stores display more popular items at the eye level, and reorders are based on the inventories taken at regular intervals. Other examples include book orders by the libraries, club memberships, auto part orders, winter cloth stock by department stores, and many others.

Database management programs have been in existence since the 1960s. However, it was not until the seventies when E. F. Codd proposed the then revolutionary relational data model that database technology really took off. In the early eighties, it received a further boost with the arrival of personal computers and microcomputer-based data management programs like dBase II (later followed by dBase III and IV). Today we have a plethora of vastly improved programs for PCs and mainframe computers, including Microsoft Access, IBM DB2, Oracle, Sequel Server, My SQL, and others.

This chapter covers the basic concepts of database design followed by implementation of a specific relational database to illustrate the concepts discussed here. The sample database, CSE_DEPT, is used as a running example. The database creation is shown in detail using Microsoft Access, SQL Server, and Oracle. The topics discussed in this chapter include:

Practical Database Programming with Java, First Edition. Ying Bai.

- What are databases and database programs?
  - File processing system
  - Integrated databases
- Various approaches to developing a database
- Relational data model and entity-relationship model (ER)
- Identifying keys
  - Primary keys, foreign keys and referential integrity
- Defining relationships
- Normalizing the data
- Implementing the relational database
  - Create a Microsoft Access sample database
  - Create a Microsoft SQL Server 2008 sample database
  - Create an Oracle sample database

2.1 WHAT ARE DATABASES AND DATABASE PROGRAMS?

A modern-day database is a structured collection of data stored in a computer. The term structured implies that each record in the database is stored in a certain format. For example, all entries in a phone book are arranged in a similar fashion. Each entry contains a name, an address, and a telephone number of a subscriber. This information can be queried and manipulated by database programs. The data retrieved in answer to queries become information that can be used to make decisions. The databases may consist of a single table or related multiple tables. The computer programs used to create, manage, and query databases are known as database management systems (DBMS). Just like the databases, the DBMS vary in complexity. Depending on the need of a user, one can use either a simple application or a robust program. Some examples of these programs were given earlier.

2.1.1 File Processing System

The file processing system is a precursor of the integrated database approach. The records for a particular application are stored in a file. An application program is needed to retrieve or manipulate data in this file. Thus, various departments in an organization will have their own file processing systems with their individual programs to store and retrieve data. The data in various files may be duplicated and not available to other applications. This causes redundancy and may lead to inconsistency, meaning that various files that supposedly contain the same information may actually contain different data values. Thus, duplication of data creates problems with data integrity. Moreover, it is difficult to provide access to multiple users with the file processing systems without granting them access to the respective application programs, which manipulate the data in those files.

The file processing system may be advantageous under certain circumstances. For example, if data is static and a simple application will solve the problem, a more expensive DBMS is not needed. For example, in a small business environment, you want to keep track of the inventory of the office equipment purchased only once or twice a year. The data can be kept in an Excel spreadsheet and manipulated with ease from time to time. This avoids the need to purchase an expensive database program and hiring a knowledgeable database administrator. Before the DBMS became popular, the data was kept in files, and application programs were developed to delete, insert, or modify records in the files. Since specific application programs were developed for specific data, these programs lasted for months or years before modifications were necessitated by business needs.

2.1.2 Integrated Databases

A better alternative to a file processing system is an integrated database approach. In this environment, all data belonging to an organization is stored in a single database. The database is not a mere collection of files; there is a relation between the files. Integration implies a logical relationship, usually provided through a common column in the tables. The relationships are also stored within the database. A set of sophisticated programs known as DBMS is used to store, access and manipulate the data in the database. Details of data storage and maintenance are hidden from the user. The user interacts with the database through the DBMS. A user may interact either directly with the DBMS or via a program written in a programming language, such as C++, Java, or Visual Basic. Only the DBMS can access the database. Large organizations employ Database Administrators (DBAs) to design and maintain large databases.

There are many advantages to using an integrated database approach over that of a file processing approach:

1. **Data Sharing:** The data in the database is available to a large numbers of users who can access the data simultaneously and create reports and manipulate the data given proper authorization and rights.
2. **Minimizing Data Redundancy:** Since all the related data exists in a single database, there is a minimal need of data duplication. The duplication is needed to maintain relationship between various data items.
3. **Data Consistency and Data Integrity:** Reducing data redundancy will lead to data consistency. Since data is stored in a single database, enforcing data integrity becomes much easier. Further more, the inherent functions of the DBMS can be used to enforce the integrity with minimum programming.
4. **Enforcing Standards:** DBAs are charged with enforcing standards in an organization. DBA takes into account the needs of various departments and balances it against the overall need of the organization. DBA defines various rules, such as documentation standards, naming conventions, update and recovery procedures, and so on. It is relatively easy to enforce these rules in a Database System, since it is a single set of programs that is always interacting with the data files.
5. **Improving Security:** Security is achieved through various means, such as controlling access to the database through passwords, providing various levels of authorizations, data encryption, providing access to restricted views of the database, and so on.
6. **Data Independence:** Providing data independence is a major objective for any database system. Data independence implies that even if the physical structure of a database changes, the applications are allowed to access the database as before the changes were implemented.

In other words, the applications are immune to the changes in the physical representation and access techniques.

The downside of using an integrated database approach has mainly to do with exorbitant costs associated with it. The hardware, the software, and maintenance are expensive. Providing security, concurrency, integrity, and recovery may add further to this cost. Furthermore, since DBMS consists of a complex set of programs, trained personnel are needed to maintain it.

2.2 DEVELOP A DATABASE

Database development process may follow a classical Systems Development Life Cycle.

1. **Problem Identification:** Interview the user, identify user requirements. Perform preliminary analysis of user needs.
2. **Project Planning:** Identify alternative approaches to solving the problem. Does the project need a database? If so, define the problem. Establish scope of the project.
3. **Problem Analysis:** Identify specifications for the problem. Confirm the feasibility of the project. Specify detailed requirements.
4. **Logical Design:** Delineate detailed functional specifications. Determine screen designs, report layout designs, data models, and so on.
5. **Physical Design:** Develop physical data structures.
6. **Implementation:** Select DBMS. Convert data to conform to DBMS requirements. Code programs; perform testing.
7. **Maintenance:** Continue program modification until desired results are achieved.

An alternative approach to developing a database is through a phased process, which will include designing a conceptual model of the system that will imitate the real-world operation. It should be flexible and change when the information in the database changes. Furthermore, it should not be dependent upon the physical implementation. This process follows the following phases:

1. **Planning and Analysis:** This phase is roughly equivalent to the first three steps mentioned above in the Systems Development Life Cycle. This includes requirement specifications, evaluating alternatives, determining input, output, and reports to be generated.
2. **Conceptual Design:** Choose a data model and develop a conceptual schema based on the requirement specification that was laid out in the planning and analysis phase. This conceptual design focuses on how the data will be organized without having to worry about the specifics of the tables, keys, and attributes. Identify the entities that will represent tables in the database; identify attributes that will represent fields in a table; and identify each entity attribute relationship. Entity–relationship diagrams provide a good representation of the conceptual design.
3. **Logical Design:** Conceptual design is transformed into a logical design by creating a roadmap of how the database will look before actually creating the database. Data model is identified; usually it is the relational model. Define the tables (entities) and fields (attributes). Identify primary and foreign key for each table. Define relationships between the tables.

4. **Physical Design:** Develop physical data structures; specify file organization, and data storage and so on. Take into consideration the availability of various resources, including hardware and software. This phase overlaps with the implementation phase. It involves the programming of the database taking into account the limitations of the DBMS used.
5. **Implementation:** Choose the DBMS that will fulfill the user needs. Implement the physical design. Perform testing. Modify if necessary or until the database functions satisfactorily.

2.3 SAMPLE DATABASE

We will use CSE_DEPT database to illustrate some essential database concepts. Tables 2.1–2.5 show sample data tables stored in this database.

The data in CSE_DEPT database is stored in five tables—LogIn, Faculty, Course, Student, and StudentCourse. A table consists of row and columns (Fig. 2.1). A row represents a record and the column represents a field. A row is called a tuple and a column is called an attribute. For example, the Student table has seven columns or fields—student_id, name, gpa, major, schoolYear, and email. It has five records or rows.

Table 2.1. LogIn table

user_name	pass_word	faculty_id	student_id
abrown	america	B66750	
ajade	tryagain		A97850
awoods	smart		A78835
banderson	birthday	A52990	
bvalley	see		B92996
dangles	tomorrow	A77587	
hsmith	try		H10210
jerica	excellent		J77896
jhenry	test	H99118	
pjking	goodman	K69880	
sbhalla	india	B86590	
sjohnson	jermany	J33486	
ybai	reback	B78880	

Table 2.2. Faculty table

faculty_id	faculty_name	office	phone	college	title	email
A52990	Black Anderson	MTC-218	750-378-9987	Virginia Tech	Professor	banderson@college.edu
A77587	Debby Angles	MTC-320	750-330-2276	University of Chicago	Associate Professor	dangles@college.edu
B66750	Alice Brown	MTC-257	750-330-6650	University of Florida	Assistant Professor	abrown@college.edu
B78880	Ying Bai	MTC-211	750-378-1148	Florida Atlantic University	Associate Professor	ybai@college.edu
B86590	Satish Bhalla	MTC-214	750-378-1061	University of Notre Dame	Associate Professor	sbhalla@college.edu
H99118	Jeff Henry	MTC-336	750-330-8650	Ohio State University	Associate Professor	jhenry@college.edu
J33486	Steve Johnson	MTC-118	750-330-1116	Harvard University	Distinguished Professor	sjohnson@college.edu
K69880	Jenney King	MTC-324	750-378-1230	East Florida University	Professor	jking@college.edu

Table 2.3. Course table

course_id	course	credit	classroom	schedule	enrollment	faculty_id
CSC-131A	Computers in Society	3	TC-109	M-W-F: 9:00-9:55 AM	28	A52990
CSC-131B	Computers in Society	3	TC-114	M-W-F: 9:00-9:55 AM	20	B66750
CSC-131C	Computers in Society	3	TC-109	T-H: 11:00-12:25 PM	25	A52990
CSC-131D	Computers in Society	3	TC-109	M-W-F: 9:00-9:55 AM	30	B86590
CSC-131E	Computers in Society	3	TC-301	M-W-F: 1:00-1:55 PM	25	B66750
CSC-131I	Computers in Society	3	TC-109	T-H: 1:00-2:25 PM	32	A52990
CSC-132A	Introduction to Programming	3	TC-303	M-W-F: 9:00-9:55 AM	21	J33486
CSC-132B	Introduction to Programming	3	TC-302	T-H: 1:00-2:25 PM	21	B78880
CSC-230	Algorithms & Structures	3	TC-301	M-W-F: 1:00-1:55 PM	20	A77587
CSC-232A	Programming I	3	TC-305	T-H: 11:00-12:25 PM	28	B66750
CSC-232B	Programming I	3	TC-303	T-H: 11:00-12:25 PM	17	A77587
CSC-233A	Introduction to Algorithms	3	TC-302	M-W-F: 9:00-9:55 AM	18	H99118
CSC-233B	Introduction to Algorithms	3	TC-302	M-W-F: 11:00-11:55 AM	19	K69880
CSC-234A	Data Structure & Algorithms	3	TC-302	M-W-F: 9:00-9:55 AM	25	B78880
CSC-234B	Data Structure & Algorithms	3	TC-114	T-H: 11:00-12:25 PM	15	J33486
CSC-242	Programming II	3	TC-303	T-H: 1:00-2:25 PM	18	A52990
CSC-320	Object Oriented Programming	3	TC-301	T-H: 1:00-2:25 PM	22	B66750
CSC-331	Applications Programming	3	TC-109	T-H: 11:00-12:25 PM	28	H99118
CSC-333A	Computer Arch & Algorithms	3	TC-301	M-W-F: 10:00-10:55 AM	22	A77587
CSC-333B	Computer Arch & Algorithms	3	TC-302	T-H: 11:00-12:25 PM	15	A77587
CSC-335	Internet Programming	3	TC-303	M-W-F: 1:00-1:55PM	25	B66750
CSC-432	Discrete Algorithms	3	TC-206	T-H: 11:00-12:25 PM	25	B86590
CSC-439	Database Systems	3	TC-206	M-W-F: 1:00-1:55 PM	18	B86590
CSE-138A	Introduction to CSE	3	TC-301	T-H: 1:00-2:25 PM	15	A52990
CSE-138B	Introduction to CSE	3	TC-109	T-H: 1:00-2:25 PM	35	J33486
CSE-330	Digital Logic Circuits	3	TC-305	M-W-F: 9:00-9:55 AM	26	K69880
CSE-332	Foundations of Semiconductors	3	TC-305	T-H: 1:00-2:25 PM	24	K69880
CSE-334	Elec. Measurement & Design	3	TC-212	T-H: 11:00-12:25 PM	25	H99118
CSE-430	Bioinformatics in Computer	3	TC-206	Thu: 9:30-11:00 AM	16	B86590
CSE-432	Analog Circuits Design	3	TC-309	M-W-F: 2:00-2:55 PM	18	K69880
CSE-433	Digital Signal Processing	3	TC-206	T-H: 2:00-3:25 PM	18	H99118
CSE-434	Advanced Electronics Systems	3	TC-213	M-W-F: 1:00-1:55 PM	26	B78880
CSE-436	Automatic Control and Design	3	TC-305	M-W-F: 10:00-10:55 AM	29	J33486
CSE-437	Operating Systems	3	TC-303	T-H: 1:00-2:25 PM	17	A77587
CSE-438	Advd Logic & Microprocessor	3	TC-213	M-W-F: 11:00-11:55 AM	35	B78880
CSE-439	Special Topics in CSE	3	TC-206	M-W-F: 10:00-10:55 AM	22	J33486

Table 2.4. Student table

student_id	student_name	gpa	credits	major	schoolYear	email
A78835	Andrew Woods	3.26	108	Computer Science	Senior	awoods@college.edu
A97850	Ashly Jade	3.57	116	Information System Engineering	Junior	ajade@college.edu
B92996	Blue Valley	3.52	102	Computer Science	Senior	bvalley@college.edu
H10210	Holes Smith	3.87	78	Computer Engineering	Sophomore	hsmith@college.edu
J77896	Erica Johnson	3.95	127	Computer Science	Senior	ejohnson@college.edu

Table 2.5. StudentCourse table

s_course_id	student_id	course_id	credit	major
1000	H10210	CSC-131D	3	CE
1001	B92996	CSC-132A	3	CS/IS
1002	J77896	CSC-335	3	CS/IS
1003	A78835	CSC-331	3	CE
1004	H10210	CSC-234B	3	CE
1005	J77896	CSC-234A	3	CS/IS
1006	B92996	CSC-233A	3	CS/IS
1007	A78835	CSC-132A	3	CE
1008	A78835	CSE-432	3	CE
1009	A78835	CSE-434	3	CE
1010	J77896	CSC-439	3	CS/IS
1011	H10210	CSC-132A	3	CE
1012	H10210	CSC-331	2	CE
1013	A78835	CSC-335	3	CE
1014	A78835	CSE-438	3	CE
1015	J77896	CSC-432	3	CS/IS
1016	A97850	CSC-132B	3	ISE
1017	A97850	CSC-234A	3	ISE
1018	A97850	CSC-331	3	ISE
1019	A97850	CSC-335	3	ISE
1020	J77896	CSE-439	3	CS/IS
1021	B92996	CSC-230	3	CS/IS
1022	A78835	CSE-332	3	CE
1023	B92996	CSE-430	3	CE
1024	J77896	CSC-333A	3	CS/IS
1025	H10210	CSE-433	3	CE
1026	H10210	CSE-334	3	CE
1027	B92996	CSC-131C	3	CS/IS
1028	B92996	CSC-439	3	CS/IS

2.3.1 Relational Data Model

A data model is like a blue print for developing a database. It describes the structure of the database and various data relationships and constraints on the data. This information is used in building tables, keys, and defining relationships. Relational model implies that a user perceives the database as made up of relations, a database jargon for tables. It is imperative that all data elements in the tables are represented correctly. In order to achieve these goals, designers use various tools. The most commonly used tool is entity–relationship model (ER). A well-planned model will give consistent results and will allow changes if needed later on. The following section further elaborates on the ER Model.

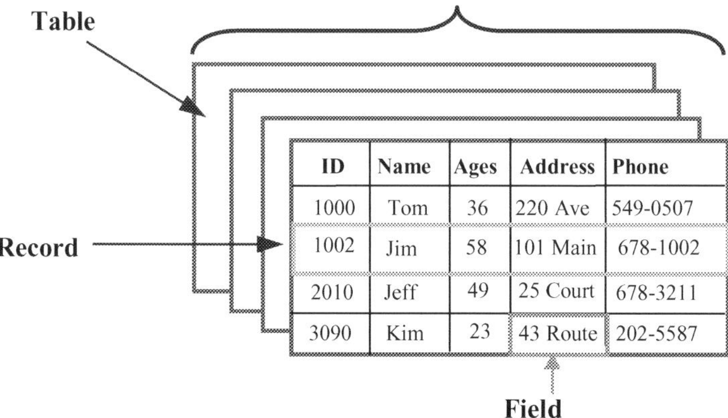

Figure 2.1. Records and fields in a table.

2.3.2 Entity–Relationship Model

The ER model was first proposed and developed by Peter Chen in 1976. Since then, Charles Bachman and James Martin have added some refinements; the model was designed to communicate the database design in the form of a conceptual schema. The ER model is based on the perception that the real world is made up of entities, their attributes, and relationships. The ER model is graphically depicted as entity–relationship diagrams (ERD). The ERD are a major modeling tool; they graphically describe the logical structure of the database. ERD can be used with ease to construct the relational tables, and are a good vehicle for communicating the database design to the end user or a developer. The three major components of ERD are entities, relationships, and the attributes.

Entities: An entity is a data object, either real or abstract, about which we want to collect information. For example, we may want to collect information about a person, a place, or a thing. An entity in an ER diagram translates into a table. It should preferably be referred to as an entity set. Some common examples are departments, courses, and students. A single occurrence of an entity is an instance. There are four entities in the CSE_Dept database, LogIn, Faculty, Course, and Student. Each entity is translated into a table with the same name. An instance of the Faculty entity will be Alice Brown and her attributes.

Relationships: A database is made up of related entities. There is a natural association between the entities; it is referred to as relationship. For example,

- Students take courses
- Departments offer certain courses
- Employees are assigned to departments

The number of occurrences of one entity associated with single occurrence of a related entity is referred to as **cardinality**.

Attributes: Each entity has properties or values called attributes associated with it. The attributes of an entity map into fields in a table. *Database processing* is one attribute of an entity called *Courses*. The domain of an attribute is a set of all possible values from which an attribute can derive its value.

2.4 IDENTIFYING KEYS

2.4.1 Primary Key and Entity Integrity

An attribute that uniquely identifies one and only one instance of an entity is called a primary key. Sometimes, a primary key consists of a combination of attributes. It is referred to as a *composite key. Entity integrity rule* states that no attribute that is a member of the primary (composite) key may accept a null value.

A FacultyID may serve as a primary key for the Faculty entity, assuming that all faculty members have been assigned a unique FaultyID. However, caution must be exercised when picking an attribute as a primary key. Last Name may not make a good primary key because a department is likely to have more than one person with the same last name. Primary keys for the CSE_DEPT database are shown in Table 2.6.

Primary keys provide a tuple-level addressing mechanism in the relational databases. Once you define an attribute as a primary key for an entity, the DBMS will enforce the uniqueness of the primary key. Inserting a duplicate value for primary key field will fail.

2.4.2 Candidate Key

There can be more than one attribute which uniquely identifies an instance of an entity. These are referred to as *candidate keys.* Any one of them can serve as a primary key. For example, ID Number as well as Social Security Number may make a suitable primary key. Candidate keys that are not used as primary key are called *alternate keys.*

2.4.3 Foreign Keys and Referential Integrity

Foreign keys are used to create relationships between tables. It is an attribute in one table whose values are required to match those of primary key in another table. Foreign keys are created to enforce *referential integrity*, which states that you may not add a record to a table containing a foreign key unless there is a corresponding record in the related table to which it is logically linked. Furthermore, the referential integrity rule also implies that every value of a foreign key in a table must match the primary key of a related table or

Table 2.6. Faculty table

faculty_id	faculty_name	office	phone	college	title	email
A52990	Black Anderson	MTC-218	750-378-9987	Virginia Tech	Professor	banderson@college.edu
A77587	Debby Angles	MTC-320	750-330-2276	University of Chicago	Associate Professor	dangles@college.edu
B66750	Alice Brown	MTC-257	750-330-6650	University of Florida	Assistant Professor	abrown@college.edu
B78880	Ying Bai	MTC-211	750-378-1148	Florida Atlantic University	Associate Professor	ybai@college.edu
B86590	Satish Bhalla	MTC-214	750-378-1061	University of Notre Dame	Associate Professor	sbhalla@college.edu
H99118	Jeff Henry	MTC-336	750-330-8650	Ohio State University	Associate Professor	jhenry@college.edu
J33486	Steve Johnson	MTC-118	750-330-1116	Harvard University	Distinguished Professor	sjohnson@college.edu
K69880	Jenney King	MTC-324	750-378-1230	East Florida University	Professor	jking@college.edu

be null. MS Access also makes provision for cascade update and cascade delete, which imply that changes made in one of the related tables will be reflected in the other of the two related tables.

Consider two tables Course and Faculty in the sample database, CSE_DEPT. The Course table has a foreign key entitled faculty_id, which is a primary key in the Faculty table. The two tables are logically related through the faculty_id link. Referential integrity rules imply that we may not add a record to the Course table with a faculty_id, which is not listed in the Faculty table. In other words, there must be a logical link between the two related tables. Second, if we change or delete a faculty_id in the Faculty table, it must reflect in the Course table, meaning that all records in the Course table must be modified using a cascade update or cascade delete (Table 2.7).

2.5 DEFINE RELATIONSHIPS

2.5.1 Connectivity

Connectivity refers to the types of relationships that entities can have. Basically it can be *one-to-one, one-to-many*, and *many-to-many*. In ER diagrams, these are indicated by placing 1, M, or N at one of the two ends of the relationship diagram. Figure illustrates the use of this notation.

- A ***one-to-one*** (**1:1**) relationship occurs when one instance of entity A is related to only one instance of entity B. For example, **user_name** in the LogIn table and **user_name** in the Student table (Fig. 2.2).

Table 2.7. The Faculty and the Course Partial Data

course_id	course	faculty_id
CSC-132A	Introduction to Programming	J33486
CSC-132B	Introduction to Programming	B78880
CSC-230	Algorithms & Structures	A77587
CSC-232A	Programming I	B66750
CSC-232B	Programming I	A77587
CSC-233A	Introduction to Algorithms	H99118
CSC-233B	Introduction to Algorithms	K69880
CSC-234A	Data Structure & Algorithms	B78880

faculty_id	faculty_name	office
A52990	Black Anderson	MTC-218
A77587	Debby Angles	MTC-320
B66750	Alice Brown	MTC-257
B78880	Ying Bai	MTC-211
B86590	Satish Bhalla	MTC-214
H99118	Jeff Henry	MTC-336
J33486	Steve Johnson	MTC-118
K69880	Jenney King	MTC-324

LogIn

user_name	pass_word
ajade	tryagain
awoods	smart
bvalley	see
hsmith	try
jerica	excellent

Student

user_name	gpa	credits	student_id
ajade	3.26	108	A97850
awoods	3.57	116	A78835
bvalley	3.52	102	B92996
hsmith	3.87	78	H10210
jerica	3.95	127	J77896

Figure 2.2. One to one relationship in the LogIn and the Student tables.

Faculty

faculty_id	faculty_name	office
A52990	Black Anderson	MTC-218
A77587	Debby Angles	MTC-320
B66750	Alice Brown	MTC-257
B78880	Ying Bai	MTC-211
B86590	Satish Bhalla	MTC-214
H99118	Jeff Henry	MTC-336
J33486	Steve Johnson	MTC-118
K69880	Jenney King	MTC-324

Course

course_id	course	faculty_id
CSC-132A	Introduction to Programming	J33486
CSC-132B	Introduction to Programming	B78880
CSC-230	Algorithms & Structures	A77587
CSC-232A	Programming I	B66750
CSC-232B	Programming I	A77587
CSC-233A	Introduction to Algorithms	H99118
CSC-233B	Introduction to Algorithms	K69880
CSC-234A	Data Structure & Algorithms	B78880

Figure 2.3. One-to-many relationship between Faculty and Course tables.

- A ***one-to-many*** **(1:M)** relationship occurs when one instance of entity A is associated with zero, one, or many instances of entity B. However, entity B is associated with only one instance of entity A. For example, one department can have many faculty members; each faculty member is assigned to only one department. In CSE_DEPT database, One-to-many relationship is represented by **faculty_id** in the Faculty table and **faculty_id** in the Course table, **student_id** in the Student table and **student_id** in the StudentCourse table, **course_id** in the Course table and **course_id** in the StudentCourse table (Fig. 2.3).
- A ***many-to-many*** **(M:N)** relationship occurs when one instance of entity A is associated with zero, one, or many instances of entity B. And one instance of entity B is associated with zero, one, or many instance of entity A. For example, a student may take many courses, and one course may be taken by more than one student.

In CSE_DEPT database, a many-to-many relationship can be realized by using the third table. For example, in this case, the StudentCourse that works as the third table, set a many-to-many relationship between the Student and the Course tables (Fig. 2.4).

This database design assumes that the course table only contains courses taught by all faculty members in this department for one semester. Therefore, each course can only be taught by a unique faculty. If one wants to develop a Course table that contains courses taught by all faculty in more than one semester, the third table, say FacultyCourse table, should be created to set up a many-to-many relationship between the Faculty and the Course table, since one course may be taught by the different faculty for the different semester.

The relationships in CSE_DEPT database are summarized in Figure 2.5.

Database name: **CSE_DEPT**

Five entities are:

- LogIn
- Faculty
- Course
- Student
- StudentCourse

The relationships between these entities are shown below. **P.K.** and **F.K** represent the primary key and the foreign key, respectively.

Student

student_id	student_name	gpa	credits
A78835	Andrew Woods	3.26	108
A97850	Ashly Jade	3.57	116
B92996	Blue Valley	3.52	102
H10210	Holes Smith	3.87	78
J77896	Erica Johnson	3.95	127

Course

course_id	course	faculty_id
CSC-132A	Introduction to Programming	J33486
CSC-132B	Introduction to Programming	B78880
CSC-230	Algorithms & Structures	A77587
CSC-232A	Programming I	B66750
CSC-232B	Programming I	A77587
CSC-233A	Introduction to Algorithms	H99118

StudentCourse

s_course_id	student_id	course_id	credit	major
1000	H10210	CSC-131D	3	CE
1001	B92996	CSC-132A	3	CS/IS
1002	J77896	CSC-335	3	CS/IS
1003	A78835	CSC-331	3	CE
1004	H10210	CSC-234B	3	CE
1005	J77896	CSC-234A	3	CS/IS
1006	B92996	CSC-233A	3	CS/IS

Figure 2.4. Many-to-many relationship between Student and Course tables.

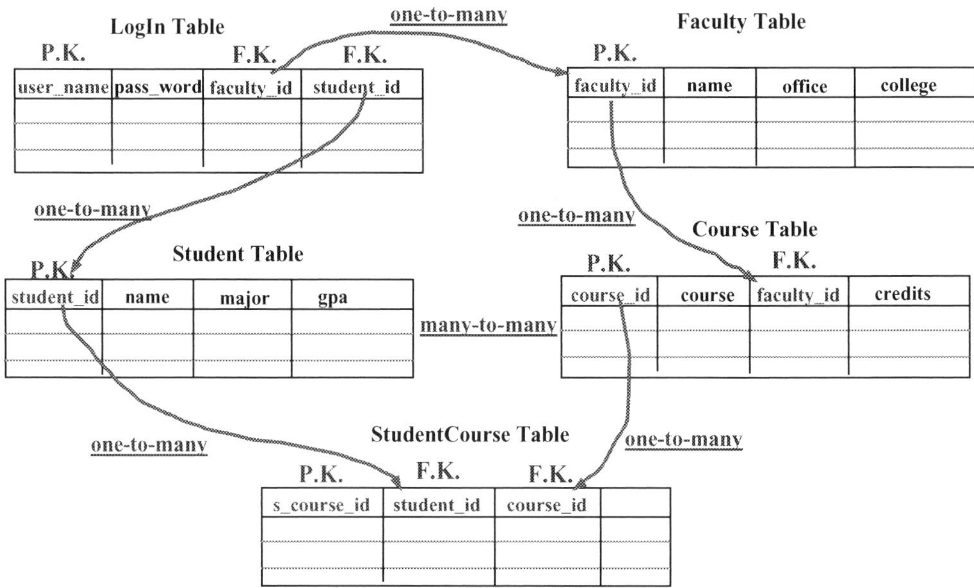

Figure 2.5. Relationships in CSE_DEPT database.

Figure 2.6 displays the Microsoft Access relationships diagram among various tables in the CSE_Dept database. One-to-many relationships are indicated by placing 1 at one end of the link and ∞ at the other. The many-to-many relationship between the Student and the Course table was broken down to two 1-to-many relationships by creating a new StudentCourse table.

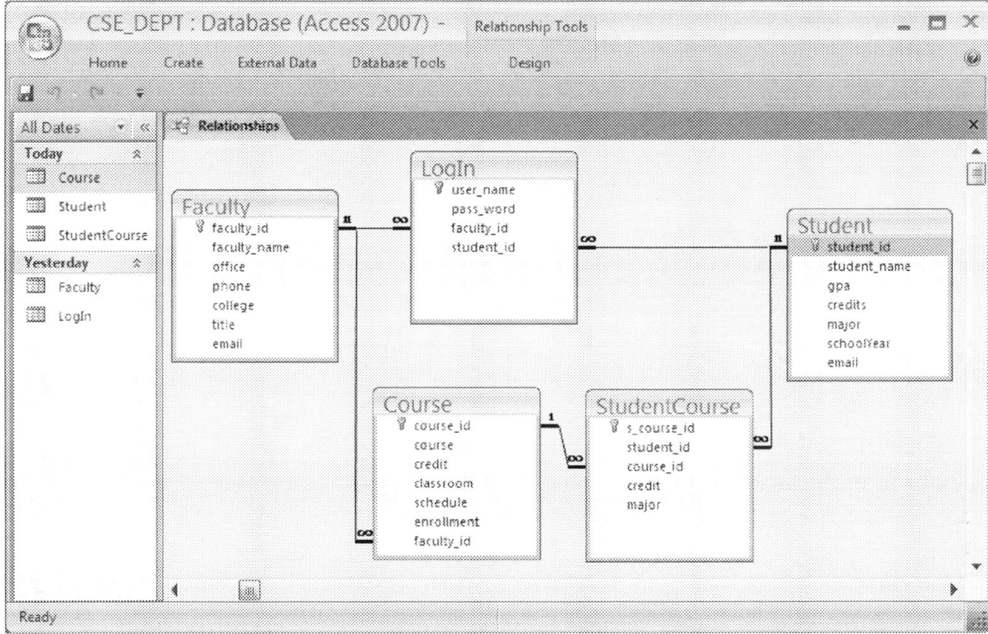

Figure 2.6. Relationships are illustrated using MS Access in the CSE_DEPT database.

2.6 ER NOTATION

There are a number of ER notations available, including Chen's, Bachman, Crow's foot, and a few others. There is no consensus on the symbols and the styles used to draw ERDs. A number of drawing tools are available to draw ERDs. These include ER Assistant, Microsoft Visio, and Smart Draw among others. Commonly used notations are shown in Figure 2.7.

2.7 DATA NORMALIZATION

After identifying tables, attributes, and relationships, the next logical step in database design is to make sure that the database structure is optimum. Optimum structure is achieved by eliminating redundancies, various inefficiencies, and update and deletion anomalies that usually occur in the unnormalized or partially normalized databases. Data normalization is a progressive process. The steps in the normalization process are called normal forms. Each normal form progressively improves the database and makes it more efficient. In other words, a database that is in second normal form is better than the one in the first normal form, and the one in third normal form is better than the one in second normal form. To be in the third normal form, a database has to be in the first and second normal form. There are fourth and fifth normal forms, but for most practical purposes, a database meeting the criteria of third normal form is considered to be of good design.

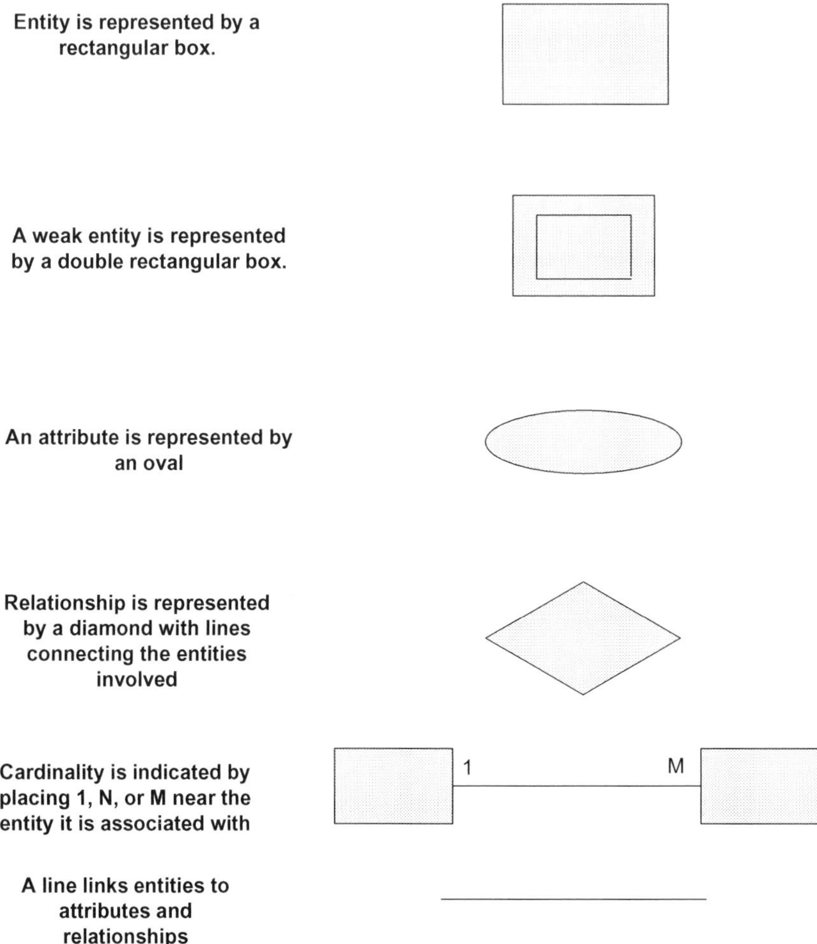

Figure 2.7. Commonly used symbols for ER notation.

2.7.1 First Normal Form (1NF)

A table is in first normal form if values in each column are atomic, that is, there are no repeating groups of data.

The following Faculty table (Table 2.8) is not normalized. Some faculty members have more than one telephone number listed in the phone column. These are called repeating groups.

In order to convert this table to the First Normal Form (INF), the data must be atomic. In other words, the repeating rows must be broken into two or more atomic rows. Table 2.9 illustrates the Faculty table in 1NF, where repeating groups have been removed. Now, it is in INF.

Table 2.8. Unnormalized Faculty table with repeating groups

faculty_id	faculty_name	office	phone
A52990	Black Anderson	MTC-218, SHB-205	750-378-9987, 555-255-8897
A77587	Debby Angles	MTC-320	750-330-2276
B66750	Alice Brown	MTC-257	750-330-6650
B78880	Ying Bai	MTC-211, SHB-105	750-378-1148, 555-246-4582
B86590	Satish Bhalla	MTC-214	750-378-1061
H99118	Jeff Henry	MTC-336	750-330-8650
J33486	Steve Johnson	MTC-118	750-330-1116
K69880	Jenney King	MTC-324	750-378-1230

Table 2.9. Normalized Faculty table

faculty_id	faculty_name	office	phone
A52990	Black Anderson	MTC-218	750-378-9987
A52990	Black Anderson	SHB-205	555-255-8897
A77587	Debby Angles	MTC-320	750-330-2276
B66750	Alice Brown	MTC-257	750-330-6650
B78880	Ying Bai	MTC-211	750-378-1148
B78880	Ying Bai	SHB-105	555-246-4582
B86590	Satish Bhalla	MTC-214	750-378-1061
H99118	Jeff Henry	MTC-336	750-330-8650
J33486	Steve Johnson	MTC-118	750-330-1116
K69880	Jenney King	MTC-324	750-378-1230

2.7.2 Second Normal Form (2NF)

A table is in second normal form if it is already in 1NF, and every nonkey column is fully dependent upon the primary key.

This implies that if the primary key consists of a single column, then the table in 1NF is automatically in 2NF. The second part of the definition implies that if the key is composite, then none of the nonkey columns will depend upon just one of the columns that participate in the composite key.

The Faculty table in Table 2.9 is in first normal form. However, it has a composite primary key, made up of faculty_id and office. The phone number depends on a part of the primary key, the office, and not on the whole primary key. This can lead to update and deletion anomalies mentioned above.

By splitting the old Faculty table (Fig. 2.8) into two new tables, Faculty and Office, we can remove the dependencies mentioned earlier. Now the faculty table has a primary key, faculty_id, and the Office table has a primary key, office. The nonkey columns in both tables now depend only on the primary keys only.

Old Faculty table in 1NF

faculty_id	faculty_name	office	phone
A52990	Black Anderson	MTC-218	750-378-9987
A52990	Black Anderson	SHB-205	555-255-8897
A77587	Debby Angles	MTC-320	750-330-2276
B66750	Alice Brown	MTC-257	750-330-6650
B78880	Ying Bai	MTC-211	750-378-1148
B78880	Ying Bai	SHB-105	555-246-4582
B86590	Satish Bhalla	MTC-214	750-378-1061
H99118	Jeff Henry	MTC-336	750-330-8650
J33486	Steve Johnson	MTC-118	750-330-1116
K69880	Jenney King	MTC-324	750-378-1230

New Faculty table

faculty_id	faculty_name
A52990	Black Anderson
A52990	Black Anderson
A77587	Debby Angles
B66750	Alice Brown
B78880	Ying Bai
B78880	Ying Bai
B86590	Satish Bhalla
H99118	Jeff Henry
J33486	Steve Johnson
K69880	Jenney King

New Office table

office	phone	faculty_id
MTC-218	750-378-9987	A52990
SHB-205	555-255-8897	A52990
MTC-320	750-330-2276	A77587
MTC-257	750-330-6650	B66750
MTC-211	750-378-1148	B78880
SHB-105	555-246-4582	B78880
MTC-214	750-378-1061	B86590
MTC-336	750-330-8650	H99118
MTC-118	750-330-1116	J33486
MTC-324	750-378-1230	K69880

Figure 2.8. Converting Faulty table into 2NF by decomposing the old table in two, Faculty and Office.

2.7.3 Third Normal Form (3NF)

A table is in third normal form if it is already in 2NF, and every nonkey column is nontransitively dependent upon the primary key. In other words, all nonkey columns are mutually independent, but at the same time, they are fully dependent upon the primary key only.

Another way of stating this is that in order to achieve 3NF, no column should depend upon any nonkey column. If column B depends on column A, then A is said to functionally determine column B; hence, the term determinant. Another definition of 3NF says that the table should be in 2NF, and only determinants it contains are candidate keys.

For the Course table in Table 2.10, all nonkey columns depend on the primary key—course_id. In addition, name and phone columns also depend on faculty_id. This table is

Table 2.10. The old Course table

course_id	course	classroom	faculty_id	faculty_name	phone
CSC-131A	Computers in Society	TC-109	A52990	Black Anderson	750-378-9987
CSC-131B	Computers in Society	TC-114	B66750	Alice Brown	750-330-6650
CSC-131C	Computers in Society	TC-109	A52990	Black Anderson	750-378-9987
CSC-131D	Computers in Society	TC-109	B86590	Satish Bhalla	750-378-1061
CSC-131E	Computers in Society	TC-301	B66750	Alice Brown	750-330-6650
CSC-131I	Computers in Society	TC-109	A52990	Black Anderson	750-378-9987
CSC-132A	Introduction to Programming	TC-303	J33486	Steve Johnson	750-330-1116
CSC-132B	Introduction to Programming	TC-302	B78880	Ying Bai	750-378-1148

Table 2.11. The new Course table

course_id	course	classroom
CSC-131A	Computers in Society	TC-109
CSC-131B	Computers in Society	TC-114
CSC-131C	Computers in Society	TC-109
CSC-131D	Computers in Society	TC-109
CSC-131E	Computers in Society	TC-301
CSC-131I	Computers in Society	TC-109
CSC-132A	Introduction to Programming	TC-303
CSC-132B	Introduction to Programming	TC-302

Table 2.12. The new instructor table

faculty_id	faculty_name	phone
A52990	Black Anderson	750-378-9987
B66750	Alice Brown	750-330-6650
A52990	Black Anderson	750-378-9987
B86590	Satish Bhalla	750-378-1061
B66750	Alice Brown	750-330-6650
A52990	Black Anderson	750-378-9987
J33486	Steve Johnson	750-330-1116
B78880	Ying Bai	750-378-1148
A77587	Debby Angles	750-330-2276

in second normal form but it suffers from update, addition, and deletion anomalies because of transitive dependencies. In order to conform to third normal form, we can split this table into two tables, Course and Instructor (Tables 2.11 and 2.12). Now we have eliminated the transitive dependencies that are apparent in the Course table in Table 2.10.

2.8 DATABASE COMPONENTS IN SOME POPULAR DATABASES

All databases allow for storage, retrieval, and management of the data. Simple databases provide basic services to accomplish these tasks. Many database providers, like Microsoft SQL Server and Oracle, provide additional services that necessitate storing many components in the database other than data. These components, such as views, stored procedures, and so on, are collectively called database objects. In this section, we will discuss various objects that make up MS Access, SQL Server, and Oracle databases.

There are two major types of databases, *File Server* and *Client Server:*

In a File Server database, data is stored in a file, and each user of the database retrieves the data, displays the data, or modifies the data directly from or to the file. In a Client Server database, the data is also stored in a file, however, all these operations are mediated through a master program, called a server. MS Access is a File Server database, whereas Microsoft SQL Server and Oracle are Client Server databases. The Client Server databases have several advantages over the File Server databases. These include, minimizing chances of crashes, provision of features for recovery, enforcement of security, better performance, and more efficient use of the network compared with the file server databases.

2.8.1 Microsoft Access Databases

Microsoft Access Database Engine is a collection of information stored in a systematic way that forms the underlying component of a database. Also called a Jet (Joint Engine Technology), it allows the manipulation of relational database. It offers a single interface that other software may use to access Microsoft databases. The supporting software is developed to provide security, integrity, indexing, record locking, and so on. By executing MS Access program, MSACCESS.EXE, you can see the database engine at work and the user interface it provides. Figure 2.9 shows how a Java application accesses the MS Access database via ACE OLE database provider.

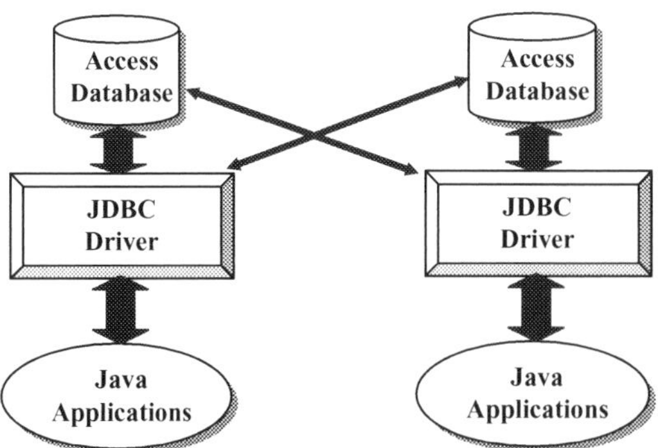

Figure 2.9. Microsoft Access database illustration.

2.8.1.1 Database File

Access database is made up of a number of components called objects, which are stored in a single file referred to as *database file*. As new objects are created or more data is added to the database, this file gets bigger. This is a complex file that stores objects like tables, queries, forms, reports, macros, and modules. The Access files have an .mdb (Microsoft DataBase) extension. Some of these objects help user to work with the database, others are useful for displaying database information in a comprehensible and easy to read format.

2.8.1.2 Tables

Before you can create a table in Access, you must create a database container and give it a name with the extension .mdb. Database creation is simple process and is explained in detail with an example, later in this chapter. Suffice it to say that a table is made up of columns and rows. Columns are referred to as fields, which are attributes of an entity. Rows are referred to as records also called tuples.

2.8.1.3 Queries

One of the main purposes of storing data in a database is that the data may be retrieved later as needed, without having to write complex programs. This purpose is accomplished in Access and other databases by writing SQL statements. A group of such statements is called a query. It enables you to retrieve, update, and display data in the tables. You may display data from more than one table by using a Join operation. In addition, you may insert or delete data in the tables.

Access also provides a visual graphic user interface to create queries. This bypasses writing SQL statements and makes it appealing to beginning and not so savvy users, who can use wizards or GUI interface to create queries. Queries can extract information in a variety of ways. You can make them as simple or as complex as you like. You may specify various criteria to get desired information, perform comparisons, or you may want to perform some calculations and obtain the results. In essence, operators, functions, and expressions are the building blocks for Access operation.

2.8.2 SQL Server Databases

The Microsoft SQL Server Database Engine is a service for storing and processing data in either a relational (tabular) format or as XML documents. Various tasks performed by the Database Engine include:

- Designing and creating a database to hold the relational tables or XML documents.
- Accessing and modifying the data stored in the database.
- Implementing websites and applications
- Building procedures
- Optimizing the performance of the database.

The SQL Server database is a complex entity made up of multiple components. It is more complex than MS Access database, which can be simply copied and distributed. Certain procedures have to be followed for copying and distributing an SQL server database.

SQL Server is used by a diverse group of professionals with diverse needs and requirements. To satisfy different needs, SQL Server comes in five editions, Enterprise edition, Standard edition, Workgroup edition, Developer edition, and Express edition. The most common editions are Enterprise, Standard, and Workgroup. It is noteworthy that the database engine is virtually the same in all of these editions.

SQL Server database can be stored on the disk using three types of files—primary data files, secondary data files, and transaction log files. Primary data files are created first and contain user defined objects, like tables and views, and system objects. These file have an extensions of .mdf. If the database grows too big for a disk, it can be stored as secondary files with an extension .ndf. The SQL Server still treats these files as if they are together. The data file is made up of many objects. The transaction log files carry .ldf extension. All transactions to the database are recorded in this file.

Figure 2.10 illustrates the structure of the SQL Server Database. Each Java application has to access the server, which in turn accesses the SQL database.

2.8.2.1 Data Files

A data file is a conglomeration of objects, which includes tables, keys, views, stored procedures, and others. All these objects are necessary for the efficient operation of the database.

2.8.2.2 Tables

The data in a relational database resides in tables. These are the building blocks of the database. Each table consists of columns and rows. Columns represent various attributes or fields in a table. Each row represents one record. For example, one record in the Faculty

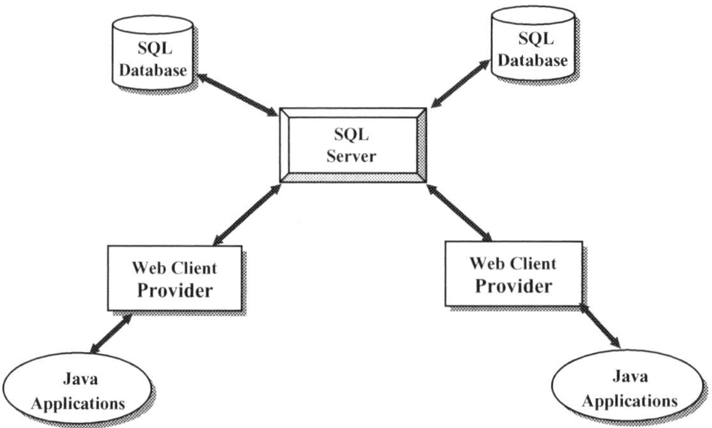

Figure 2.10. SQL Server database structure.

table consists of name, office, phone, college, title, and email. Each field has a distinct data type, meaning that it can contain only one type of data such as numeric or character. Tables are the first objects created in a database.

2.8.2.3 Views

Views are virtual tables, meaning that they do not contain any data. They are stored as queries in the database, which are executed when needed. A view can contain data from one or more tables. The views can provide database security. Sensitive information in a database can be excluded by including nonsensitive information in a view and providing user access to the views instead of all tables in a database. The views can also hide the complexities of a database. A user can be using a view that is made up of multiple tables, whereas it appears as a single table to the user. The user can execute queries against a view just like a table.

2.8.2.4 Stored Procedures

Users write queries to retrieve, display, or manipulate data in the database. These queries can be stored on the client machine or on the server. There are advantages associated with storing SQL queries on the server rather than on the client machine. It has to do with the network performance. Usually, users use the same queries over and over again; frequently, different users are trying to access the same data. Instead of sending the same queries on the network repeatedly, it improves the network performance and executes queries faster if the queries are stored on the server where they are compiled and saved as stored procedures. The users can simply call the stored procedure with a simple command, like *execute stored_procedure* A.

2.8.2.5 Keys and Relationships

A *primary key* is created for each table in the database to efficiently access records and to ensure *entity integrity*. This implies that each record in a table is unique in some way. Therefore, no two records can have the same primary key. It is defined as globally unique identifier. Moreover, a primary key may not have null value that is missing data. SQL server creates a unique index for each primary key. This ensures fast and efficient access to data. One or columns can be combined to designate a primary key.

In a relational database, relationships between tables can be logically defined with the help of *foreign keys*. A foreign key of one record in a table points specifically to a primary key of a record in another table. This allows a user to join multiple tables and retrieve information from more than one table at a time. Foreign keys also enforce *referential integrity*, a defined relationship between the tables that does not allow insertion or deletion of records in a table unless the foreign key of a record in one table matches a primary key of a record in another table. In other words, a record in one table cannot have a foreign key that does not point to a primary key in another table. Additionally, a primary key may not be deleted if there are foreign keys in another table pointing to it. The foreign key values associated with a primary key must be deleted first. Referential integrity protects related data from corruption, stored in different tables.

2.8.2.6 Indexes

The indexes are used to find records, quickly and efficiently, in a table just like one would use an index in a book. SQL server uses two types of indexes to retrieve and update data—clustered and nonclustered.

Clustered index sorts the data in a table so that the data can be accessed efficiently. It is akin to a dictionary or a phone book, where records are arranged alphabetically. So one can go directly to a specific alphabet, and from there search sequentially for the specific record. The clustered indexes are like an inverted tree. The index a structure is called a B-tree for binary tree. You start with the root page at the top and find the location of other pages further down at the secondary level, following to tertiary level and so on until you find the desired record. The very bottom pages are the leaf pages and contain the actual data. There can be only one clustered index per table because clustered indexes physically rearrange the data.

Nonclustered indexes do not physically rearrange the data as do the clustered indexes. They also consist of a binary tree with various levels of pages. The major difference, however, is that the leaves do not contain the actual data as in the clustered indexes; instead, they contain pointers that point to the corresponding records in the table. These pointers are called row locators.

The indexes can be unique where the duplicate keys are not allowed, or not unique, which permit duplicate keys. Any column that can be used to access data can be used to generate an index. Usually, the primary and the foreign key columns are used to create indexes.

2.8.2.7 Transaction Log Files

A transaction is a logical group of SQL statements that carry out a unit of work. Client server database use log file to keep track of transactions that are applied to the database. For example, before an update is applied to a database, the database server creates an entry in the transaction log to generate a before picture of the data in a table, and then applies a transaction and creates another entry to generate an afterpicture of the data in that table. This keeps track of all the operations performed on a database. Transaction logs can be used to recover data in case of crashes or disasters. Transaction logs are automatically maintained by the SQL Server.

2.8.3 Oracle Databases

Oracle was designed to be platform independent, making it architecturally more complex than the SQL Server database. The Oracle database contains more files than the SQL Server database.

The Oracle DBMS comes in three levels: Enterprise, Standard, and Personal. Enterprise edition is the most powerful and is suitable for large installations using a large number of transactions in a multiuser environment. Standard edition is also used by high-level multiuser installations. It lacks some of the utilities available in Enterprise edition. Personal edition is used in a single-user environment for developing database applications. The database engine components are virtually the same for all three editions.

Oracle architecture is made up of several components, including an Oracle server, Oracle instance and an Oracle database. The Oracle server contains several files, processes, and memory structures. Some of these are used to improve the performance of the database and ensure database recovery in case of a crash. The Oracle server consists of an Oracle instance and an Oracle database. An Oracle instance consists of background processes and memory structures. Background processes perform input/output, and monitor other Oracle processes for better performance and reliability. Oracle database consists of data files that provide the actual physical storage for the data.

2.8.3.1 Data Files

The main purpose of a database is to store and retrieve data. It consists of a collection of data that is treated as a unit. An Oracle database has a logical and physical structure. The logical layer consists of table spaces, necessary for the smooth operation of an Oracle installation. Data files make up the physical layer of the database. These consist of three types of files: *data files* that contain actual data in the database, *redo logfiles*, which contain records of modifications made to the database for future recovery in case of failure, and *control files*, which are used to maintain and verify database integrity. Oracle server uses other files that are not part of the database. These include a *parameter file*, which defines the characteristics of an Oracle instance, a *password file* used for authentication, and *archived redo log* files, which are copies of the redo log files necessary for recovery from failure. A partial list of some of the components follows.

2.8.3.2 Tables

Users can store data in a regular table, partitioned table, index-organized table, or clustered table. A *regular table* is the default table as in other databases. Rows can be stored in any order. A *partitioned table* has one or more partitions where rows are stored. Partitions are useful for large tables, which can be queried by several processes concurrently. *Index-organized tables* provide fast key-based access for queries involving exact matches. The table may have an index on one or more of its columns. Instead of using two storage spaces for the table and a B-tree index, a single storage space is used to store both the B-tree and other columns. A *clustered table* or group of tables share the same block called a cluster. They are grouped together because they share common columns and are frequently used together. Clusters have a cluster key for identifying the rows that need to be stored together. Cluster keys are independent of the primary key and may be made up of one or more columns. Clusters are created to improve performance.

2.8.3.3 Views

Views are like virtual tables and are used in a similar fashion as in the SQL Server databases discussed above.

2.8.3.4 Stored Procedures

In Oracle, functions and procedures may be saved as stored program units. Multiple-input arguments (parameters) may be passed as input to functions and procedures; however,

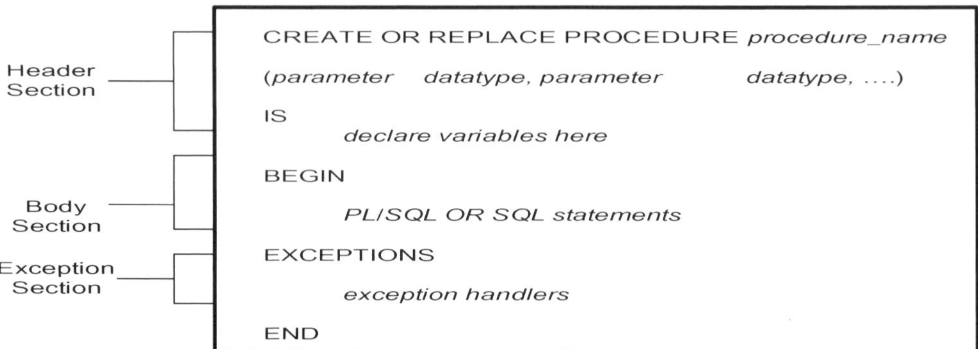

Figure 2.11. Syntax for creating a stored procedure in Oracle.

functions return only one value as output, whereas procedures may return multiple values as output. The advantages to creating and using stored procedures are the same as mentioned above for SQL server. By storing procedures on the server, individual SQL statements do not have to be transmitted over the network, thus reducing the network traffic. In addition, commonly used SQL statements are saved as functions or procedures, and may be used again and again by various users, thus saving rewriting the same code over and over again. The stored procedures should be made flexible so that different users are able to pass input information to the procedure in the form of arguments or parameters and get the desired output.

Figure 2.11 shows the syntax to create a stored procedure in Oracle. It has three sections—a header, a body, and an exception section. The procedure is defined in the header section. Input and output parameters, along with their data types, are declared here and transmit information to or from the procedure. The body section of the procedure starts with a key word BEGIN and consists of SQL statements. The exceptions section of the procedure begins with the keyword EXCEPTION and contains exception handlers, which are designed to handle the occurrence of some conditions that changes the normal flow of execution.

2.8.3.5 Indexes

Indexes are created to provide direct access to rows. An index is a tree structure. Indexes can be classified on their logic design or their physical implementation. Logical classification is based on application perspective, whereas physical classification is based on how the indexes are stored. Indexes can be partitioned or nonpartitioned. Large tables use partitioned indexes, which spreads an index to multiple table spaces, thus decreasing contention for index look up and increasing manageability. An index may consist of a single column or multiple columns; it may be unique or nonunique. Some of these indexes are outlined below.

Function-based indexes precompute the value of a function or expression of one or more columns and store it in an index. It can be created as a B-tree or as a bitmap. It can improve the performance of queries performed on tables that rarely change.

Domain indexes are application specific and are created and managed by the user or applications. Single-column indexes can be built on text, spatial, scalar, object, or LOB data types.

B-tree indexes store a list of row IDs for each key. Structure of a *B-tree* index is similar to the ones in the SQL Server described above. The leaf nodes contain indexes that point to rows in a table. The leaf blocks allow scanning of the index in either ascending or descending order. Oracle server maintains all indexes when insert, update, or delete operations are performed on a table.

Bitmap indexes are useful when columns have low cardinality and a large number of rows. For example, a column may contain few distinct values like Y/N for marital status, or M/F for gender. A bitmap is organized like a B-tree, where the leaf nodes store a bitmap instead of row IDs. When changes are made to the key columns, bit maps must be modified.

2.8.3.6 Initialization Parameter Files

The Oracle server must read the initialization parameter file before starting an oracle database instance. There are two types of initialization parameter files: static parameter file and a persistent parameter file. An initialization parameter file contains a list of instance parameters, and the name of the database the instance is associated with, name and location of control files, and information about the undo segments. Multiple initialization parameter files can exist to optimize performance.

2.8.3.7 Control Files

A control file is a small binary file that defines the current state of the database. Before a database can be opened, the control file is read to determine if the database is in a valid state or not. It maintains the integrity of the database. Oracle uses a single control file per database. It is maintained continuously by the server and can be maintained only by the Oracle server. It cannot be edited by a user or database administrator. A control file contains: database name and identifier, time stamp of database creation, tablespace name, names and location of data files and redo logfiles, current log files sequence number, and archive and backup information.

2.8.3.8 Redo log Files

Oracle's redo log files provide a way to recover data in the event of a database failure. All transactions are written to a redo log buffer and passed on to the redo log files.

Redo log files record all changes to the data, provide a recovery mechanism, and can be organized into groups. A set of identical copies of online redo log files is called a redo log file group. The Oracle server needs a minimum of two online redo logfile groups for normal operations. The initial set of redo log file groups and members are created during the database creation. Redo log files are used in a cyclic fashion. Each redo log file group is identified by a log sequence number and is overwritten each time the log is reused. In other words, when a redo log file is full, then the log writer moves to the second redo log file. After the second one is full, the first one is reused.

2.8.3.9 Password Files

Depending upon whether the database is administered locally or remotely, one can choose either operating system or password file authentication to authenticate database administrators. Oracle provides a password utility to create a password file. Administrators use the GRANT command to provide access to the database using the password file.

2.9 CREATE MICROSOFT ACCESS SAMPLE DATABASE

In this section, you will learn how to create a sample Microsoft Access database `CSE_DEPT.mdb` and its database file. As we mentioned in the previous sections, the Access is a file-based database system, which means that the database is composed of a set of data tables that are represented in the form of files.

Open the Microsoft Office Access 2007. Select `Blank Database` item and enter **CSE_DEPT** into the `File Name` box as the database name and keep the extension **accdb** unchanged. Click the small file folder icon that is next to the `File Name` box to open the `File New Database` dialog to select the desired destination to save this new database. In our case, select the `C:\Database` and then click the `OK` button. Now click the `Create` button to create this new database.

2.9.1 Create the LogIn Table

After a new blank database is created, click the drop-down arrow of the `View` button from the Toolbar, and select the `Design View` item to open the database in the design view. Enter **LogIn** into the `Table Name` box of the pop-up dialog as the name of our first table, LogIn. Click the OK button to open this table in the design view. Enter the following data, which are shown in Figure 2.12, into this design view to build our LogIn table.

> Starting from Office 2007, Microsoft released a new Access database format, **accdb**, which is different with old formats and contains a quite few new functionalities that the old Access formats do not have, such as allowing you to store file attachments as parts of your database files, use multivalued fields, integrate with SharePoint and Outlook, and perform encryption improvements. You can convert the old formats, such as Access 2000, Access 2002–2003, with the **.mdb** extension to this new format with the extension **.accdb** if you like.

Three columns are displayed in this `Design view: Field Name, Data Type`, and `Description`. Since the first table you want to create is the `LogIn` table with four columns: `user_name`, `pass_word`, `faculty_id`, and `student_id`. Enter `user_name` into the first `Field Name` box. The data type for this `user_name` should be `Text`, so click the drop-down arrow of the `Data Type` box and select the `Text`. You can enter some comments in the `Description` box to indicate the purpose of this data. In this

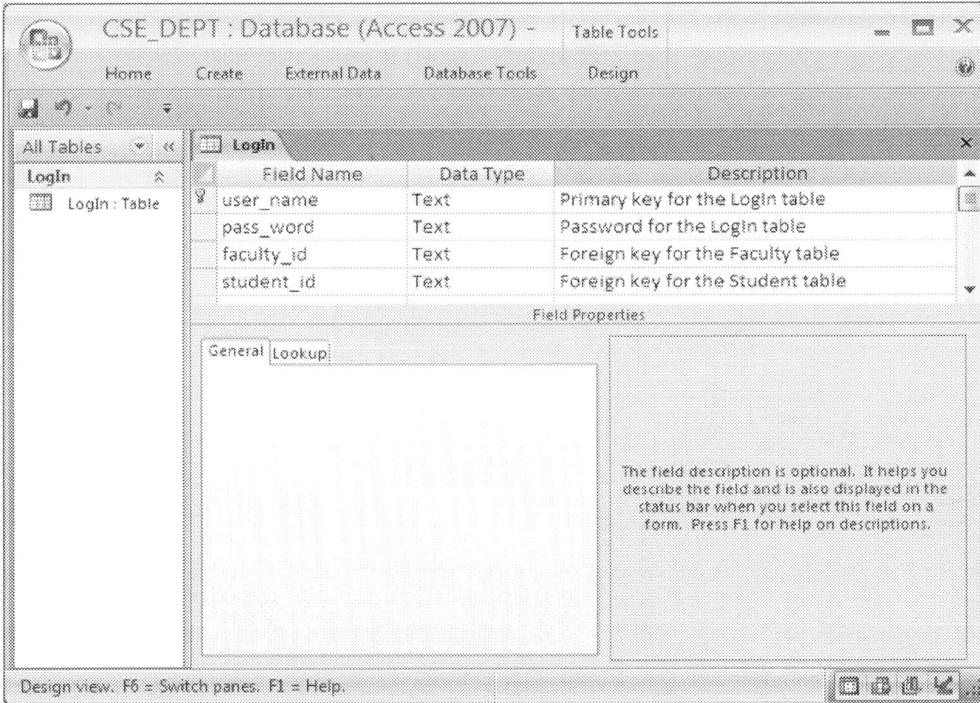

Figure 2.12. The Design view of the LogIn table.

case, just enter: `Primary key` for the LogIn table, since you need this column as the primary key for this table.

In the similar way, enter the `pass_word`, `faculty_id` and `student_id` into the second, third and fourth fields with the data type as `Text` for those fields. Now you need to assign the `user_name` column as the primary key for this table. In the previous versions of the Microsoft Office Access, such as Office 2003 or XP, you need to click and select the first row `user_name` from the table, and then go to the Toolbar and select the `Primary key` tool that is displayed as a key. But starting from Office 2007, you do not need to do that since the first column has been selected as the primary key by default, which is represented as a key sign and is shown in Figure 2.12.

Click the Save button on the Toolbar to save the design for this table. Your finished `Design view` of the `LogIn` table should match one that is shown in Figure 2.12.

Next, you need to add the data into this LogIn table. To do that, you need to open the `Data Sheet view` of the table. You can open this view by clicking the drop-down arrow of the `View` tool on the Toolbar, which is the first tool located on the Toolbar, then select the `Data Sheet view`.

Four data columns, `user_name`, `pass_word`, `faculty_id`, and `student_id`, are displayed when the `DataSheet view` of this `LogIn` table is opened. Enter the data shown in Table 2.13 into this table. Your finished `LogIn` table is shown in Figure 2.13.

Your finished `LogIn` table should match one that is shown in Figure 2.13. Click the Save button on the Toolbar to save this table. Then click the `Close` button that is located on the upper-right corner of the table to close this `LogIn` table.

Table 2.13. The data in the LogIn table

user_name	pass_word	faculty_id	student_id
abrown	america	B66750	
ajade	tryagain		A97850
awoods	smart		A78835
banderson	birthday	A52990	
bvalley	see		B92996
dangles	tomorrow	A77587	
hsmith	try		H10210
jerica	excellent		J77896
jhenry	test	H99118	
jking	goodman	K69880	
sbhalla	india	B86590	
sjohnson	jermany	J33486	
ybai	reback	B78880	

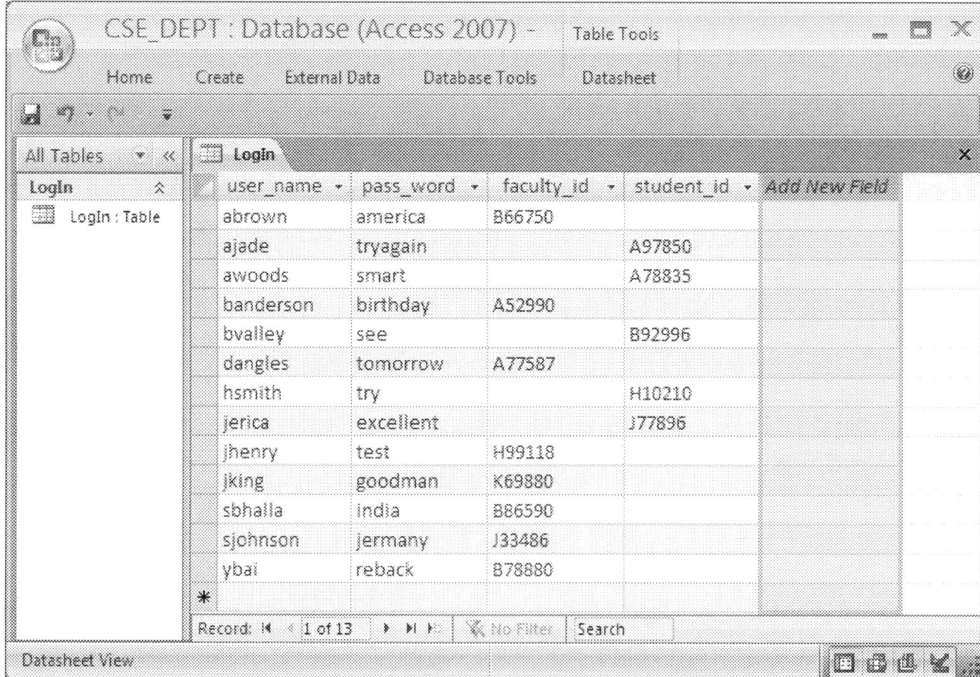

Figure 2.13. The completed LogIn table.

2.9.2 Create the Faculty Table

Now let's continue to create the second table `Faculty`. Click the `Create` menu item from the menu bar and select the `Table` icon from the Toolbar to create a new table. Click the Home menu item and select the `Design View` by clicking the drop-down arrow

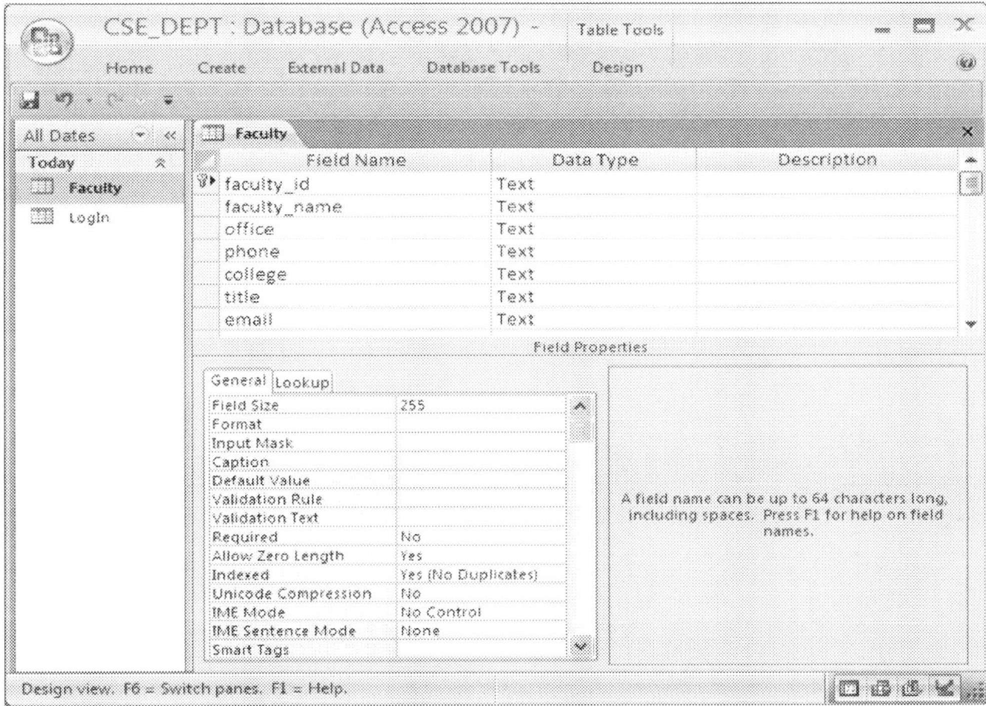

Figure 2.14. The Design view of the Faculty table.

from the `View` tool on the Toolbar. Enter **Faculty** into the `Table Name` box `of the pop-up dialog as the name for this new table, and click the OK button.`

Seven columns are included in this table; they are: `faculty_id`, `faculty_name`, `office`, `phone`, `college`, `title`, and `email`. The data types for all columns in this table are `Text`, since all of them are string variables. You can redefine the length of each Text string by modifying the Field Size in the Field Properties pane located below of the table, which is shown in Figure 2.14. The default length for each text string is 255.

Now you need to assign the primary key for this table. As we discussed in the last section, you do not need to do this in Office 2007 Access, since the first column, faculty_id, has been selected as the Primary key by default. Click the Save tool on the Toolbar to save this table. The finished `Design View` of the `Faculty` table is shown in Figure 2.14.

Now open the `DataSheet view` of the `Faculty` table by clicking the Home menu item, and then the drop-down arrow of the View tool, and select the Datasheet View item. Enter the data that is shown in Table 2.14 into this opened `Faculty` table. The finished `Faculty` table should match one that is shown in Figure 2.15.

2.9.3 Create the Other Tables

In a similar way, you need to create the following three tables: `Course`, `Student`, and `StudentCourse`. Select the `course_id`, `student_id`, and `s_course_id` columns as

Table 2.14. The data in the Faculty table

faculty_id	faculty_name	office	phone	college	title	email
A52990	Black Anderson	MTC-218	750-378-9987	Virginia Tech	Professor	banderson@college.edu
A77587	Debby Angles	MTC-320	750-330-2276	University of Chicago	Associate Professor	dangles@college.edu
B66750	Alice Brown	MTC-257	750-330-6650	University of Florida	Assistant Professor	abrown@college.edu
B78880	Ying Bai	MTC-211	750-378-1148	Florida Atlantic University	Associate Professor	ybai@college.edu
B86590	Satish Bhalla	MTC-214	750-378-1061	University of Notre Dame	Associate Professor	sbhalla@college.edu
H99118	Jeff Henry	MTC-336	750-330-8650	Ohio State University	Associate Professor	jhenry@college.edu
J33486	Steve Johnson	MTC-118	750-330-1116	Harvard University	Distinguished Professor	sjohnson@college.edu
K69880	Jenney King	MTC-324	750-378-1230	East Florida University	Professor	jking@college.edu

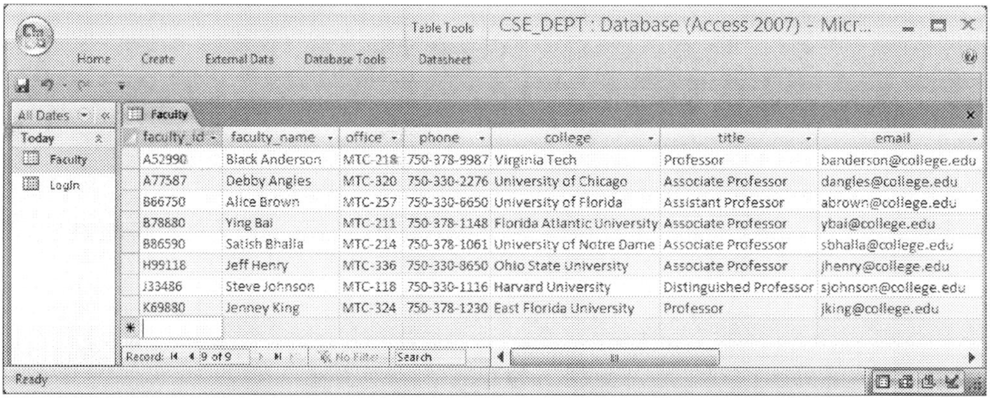

Figure 2.15. The completed Faculty table.

the primary key for the `Course`, `Student`, and `StudentCourse` tables (refer to Tables 2.15–2.17). For the data type selections, follow the directions below:

The data type selections for the `Course` table:

- `course_id`—`Text`
- credit—`Number`
- enrolment—`Number`
- All other columns—`Text`

The data type selections for the `Student` table:

- `student_id`—`Text`
- credits—`Number`
- All other columns—`Text`

The data type selections for the `StudentCourse` table:

- `s_course_id`—`Number`
- credit—`Number`
- All other columns—`Text`

Table 2.15. The data in the Course table

course_id	course	credit	classroom	schedule	enrollment	faculty_id
CSC-131A	Computers in Society	3	TC-109	M-W-F: 9:00-9:55 AM	28	A52990
CSC-131B	Computers in Society	3	TC-114	M-W-F: 9:00-9:55 AM	20	B66750
CSC-131C	Computers in Society	3	TC-109	T-H: 11:00-12:25 PM	25	A52990
CSC-131D	Computers in Society	3	TC-109	M-W-F: 9:00-9:55 AM	30	B86590
CSC-131E	Computers in Society	3	TC-301	M-W-F: 1:00-1:55 PM	25	B66750
CSC-131I	Computers in Society	3	TC-109	T-H: 1:00-2:25 PM	32	A52990
CSC-132A	Introduction to Programming	3	TC-303	M-W-F: 9:00-9:55 AM	21	J33486
CSC-132B	Introduction to Programming	3	TC-302	T-H: 1:00-2:25 PM	21	B78880
CSC-230	Algorithms & Structures	3	TC-301	M-W-F: 1:00-1:55 PM	20	A77587
CSC-232A	Programming I	3	TC-305	T-H: 11:00-12:25 PM	28	B66750
CSC-232B	Programming I	3	TC-303	T-H: 11:00-12:25 PM	17	A77587
CSC-233A	Introduction to Algorithms	3	TC-302	M-W-F: 9:00-9:55 AM	18	H99118
CSC-233B	Introduction to Algorithms	3	TC-302	M-W-F: 11:00-11:55 AM	19	K69880
CSC-234A	Data Structure & Algorithms	3	TC-302	M-W-F: 9:00-9:55 AM	25	B78880
CSC-234B	Data Structure & Algorithms	3	TC-114	T-H: 11:00-12:25 PM	15	J33486
CSC-242	Programming II	3	TC-303	T-H: 1:00-2:25 PM	18	A52990
CSC-320	Object Oriented Programming	3	TC-301	T-H: 1:00-2:25 PM	22	B66750
CSC-331	Applications Programming	3	TC-109	T-H: 11:00-12:25 PM	28	H99118
CSC-333A	Computer Arch & Algorithms	3	TC-301	M-W-F: 10:00-10:55 AM	22	A77587
CSC-333B	Computer Arch & Algorithms	3	TC-302	T-H: 11:00-12:25 PM	15	A77587
CSC-335	Internet Programming	3	TC-303	M-W-F: 1:00-1:55 PM	25	B66750
CSC-432	Discrete Algorithms	3	TC-206	T-H: 11:00-12:25 PM	20	B86590
CSC-439	Database Systems	3	TC-206	M-W-F: 1:00-1:55 PM	18	B86590
CSE-138A	Introduction to CSE	3	TC-301	T-H: 1:00-2:25 PM	15	A52990
CSE-138B	Introduction to CSE	3	TC-109	T-H: 1:00-2:25 PM	35	J33486
CSE-330	Digital Logic Circuits	3	TC-305	M-W-F: 9:00-9:55 AM	26	K69880
CSE-332	Foundations of Semiconductors	3	TC-305	T-H: 1:00-2:25 PM	24	K69880
CSE-334	Elec Measurement & Design	3	TC-212	T-H: 11:00-12:25 PM	25	H99118
CSE-430	Bioinformatics in Computer	3	TC-206	Thu: 9:30-11:00 AM	16	B86590
CSE-432	Analog Circuits Design	3	TC-309	M-W-F: 2:00-2:55 PM	18	K69880
CSE-433	Digital Signal Processing	3	TC-206	T-H: 2:00-3:25 PM	18	H99118
CSE-434	Advanced Electronics Systems	3	TC-213	M-W-F: 1:00-1:55 PM	26	B78880
CSE-436	Automatic Control and Design	3	TC-305	M-W-F: 10:00-10:55 AM	29	J33486
CSE-437	Operating Systems	3	TC-303	T-H: 1:00-2:25 PM	17	A77587
CSE-438	Advd Logic & Microprocessor	3	TC-213	M-W-F: 11:00-11:55 AM	35	B78880
CSE-439	Special Topics in CSE	3	TC-206	M-W-F: 10:00-10:55 AM	22	J33486

Enter the data that are shown in Tables 2.15–2.17 into each associated table, and save each table as `Course`, `Student`, and `StudentCourse`, respectively.

The finished Course table is shown in Figure 2.16. The completed `Student` and `StudentCourse` tables are shown in Figures 2.17 and 2.18.

2.9.4 Create Relationships among Tables

All five tables are completed, and now we need to set up the relationships between these five tables by using the primary and foreign keys. Go to the `Database Tools|`

Table 2.16. The data in the Student table

student_id	student_name	gpa	credits	major	schoolYear	email
A78835	Andrew Woods	3.26	108	Computer Science	Senior	awoods@college.edu
A97850	Ashly Jade	3.57	116	Information System Engineering	Junior	ajade@college.edu
B92996	Blue Valley	3.52	102	Computer Science	Senior	bvalley@college.edu
H10210	Holes Smith	3.87	78	Computer Engineering	Sophomore	hsmith@college.edu
J77896	Erica Johnson	3.95	127	Computer Science	Senior	ejohnson@college.edu

Table 2.17. The data in the StudentCourse table

s_course_id	student_id	course_id	credit	major
1000	H10210	CSC-131D	3	CE
1001	B92996	CSC-132A	3	CS/IS
1002	J77896	CSC-335	3	CS/IS
1003	A78835	CSC-331	3	CE
1004	H10210	CSC-234B	3	CE
1005	J77896	CSC-234A	3	CS/IS
1006	B92996	CSC-233A	3	CS/IS
1007	A78835	CSC-132A	3	CE
1008	A78835	CSE-432	3	CE
1009	A78835	CSE-434	3	CE
1010	J77896	CSC-439	3	CS/IS
1011	H10210	CSC-132A	3	CE
1012	H10210	CSC-331	3	CE
1013	A78835	CSC-335	3	CE
1014	A78835	CSE-438	3	CE
1015	J77896	CSC-432	3	CS/IS
1016	A97850	CSC-132B	3	ISE
1017	A97850	CSC-234A	3	ISE
1018	A97850	CSC-331	3	ISE
1019	A97850	CSC-335	3	ISE
1020	J77896	CSE-439	3	CS/IS
1021	B92996	CSC-230	3	CS/IS
1022	A78835	CSE-332	3	CE
1023	B92996	CSE-430	3	CE
1024	J77896	CSC-333A	3	CS/IS
1025	H10210	CSE-433	3	CE
1026	H10210	CSE-334	3	CE
1027	B92996	CSC-131C	3	CS/IS
1028	B92996	CSC-439	3	CS/IS

course_id	course	cred	classroor	schedule	enrollment	faculty_id
CSC-131A	Computers in Society	3	TC-109	M-W-F: 9:00-9:55 AM	28	A52990
CSC-131B	Computers in Society	3	TC-114	M-W-F: 9:00-9:55 AM	20	B66750
CSC-131C	Computers in Society	3	TC-109	T-H: 11:00-12:25 PM	25	A52990
CSC-131D	Computers in Society	3	TC-109	M-W-F: 9:00-9:55 AM	30	B86590
CSC-131E	Computers in Society	3	TC-301	M-W-F: 1:00-1:55 PM	25	B66750
CSC-131I	Computers in Society	3	TC-109	T-H: 1:00-2:25 PM	32	A52990
CSC-132A	Introduction to Programming	3	TC-303	M-W-F: 9:00-9:55 AM	21	J33486
CSC-132B	Introduction to Programming	3	TC-302	T-H: 1:00-2:25 PM	21	B78880
CSC-230	Algorithms & Structures	3	TC-301	M-W-F: 1:00-1:55 PM	20	A77587
CSC-232A	Programming I	3	TC-305	T-H: 11:00-12:25 PM	28	B66750
CSC-232B	Programming I	3	TC-303	T-H: 11:00-12:25 PM	17	A77587
CSC-233A	Introduction to Algorithms	3	TC-302	M-W-F: 9:00-9:55 AM	18	H99118
CSC-233B	Introduction to Algorithms	3	TC-302	M-W-F: 11:00-11:55 AM	19	K69880
CSC-234A	Data Structure & Algorithms	3	TC-302	M-W-F: 9:00-9:55 AM	25	B78880
CSC-234B	Data Structure & Algorithms	3	TC-114	T-H: 11:00-12:25 PM	15	J33486
CSC-242	Programming II	3	TC-303	T-H: 1:00-2:25 PM	18	A52990
CSC-320	Object Oriented Programming	3	TC-301	T-H: 1:00-2:25 PM	22	B66750
CSC-331	Applications Programming	3	TC-109	T-H: 11:00-12:25 PM	28	H99118
CSC-333A	Computer Arch & Algorithms	3	TC-301	M-W-F: 10:00-10:55 AM	22	A77587
CSC-333B	Computer Arch & Algorithms	3	TC-302	T-H: 11:00-12:25 PM	15	A77587

Figure 2.16. The completed Course table.

student_id	student_name	gpa	credits	major	schoolYear	email
A78835	Andrew Woods	3.26	108	Computer Science	Senior	awoods@college.edu
A97850	Ashly Jade	3.57	116	Information System Engineering	Junior	ajade@college.edu
B92996	Blue Valley	3.52	102	Computer Science	Senior	bvalley@college.edu
H10210	Holes Smith	3.87	78	Computer Engineering	Sophomore	hsmith@college.edu
J77896	Erica Johnson	3.95	127	Computer Science	Senior	ejohnson@college.edu

Figure 2.17. The completed Student table

`Relationships` menu item to open the Show Table dialog. Keep the default tab `Tables` selected, and select all five tables by pressing and holding the `Shift` key on the keyboard and clicking the last table—`StudentCourse`. Click the `Add` button, and then the `Close` button to close this dialog box. All five tables are added and displayed in the Relationships dialog box. The relationships we want to add are shown in Figure 2.19.

The P.K and F.K. in Figure 2.19 represent the Primary and Foreign keys, respectively. For example, the `faculty_id` in the Faculty table is a primary key, and it can be

CSE_DEPT : Database (Access 2007) - Table Tools

Home Create External Data Database Tools Datasheet

All Dates

Today: Course, Student, StudentCourse

Yesterday: Faculty, LogIn

StudentCourse | Course | Student

s_course_id	student_id	course_id	credit	major	Add New Field
1000	H10210	CSC-131D	3	CE	
1001	B92996	CSC-132A	3	CS/IS	
1002	J77896	CSC-335	3	CS/IS	
1003	A78835	CSC-331	3	CE	
1004	H10210	CSC-234B	3	CE	
1005	J77896	CSC-234A	3	CS/IS	
1006	B92996	CSC-233A	3	CS/IS	
1007	A78835	CSC-132A	3	CE	
1008	A78835	CSE-432	3	CE	
1009	A78835	CSE-434	3	CE	
1010	J77896	CSC-439	3	CS/IS	
1011	H10210	CSC-132A	3	CE	
1012	H10210	CSC-331	3	CE	
1013	A78835	CSC-335	3	CE	
1014	A78835	CSE-438	3	CE	
1015	J77896	CSC-432	3	CS/IS	
1016	A97850	CSC-132B	3	ISE	
1017	A97850	CSC-234A	3	ISE	
1018	A97850	CSC-331	3	ISE	
1019	A97850	CSC-335	3	ISE	
1020	J77896	CSE-439	3	CS/IS	

Record: 30 of 30 No Filter Search

Datasheet View

Figure 2.18. The completed StudentCourse table.

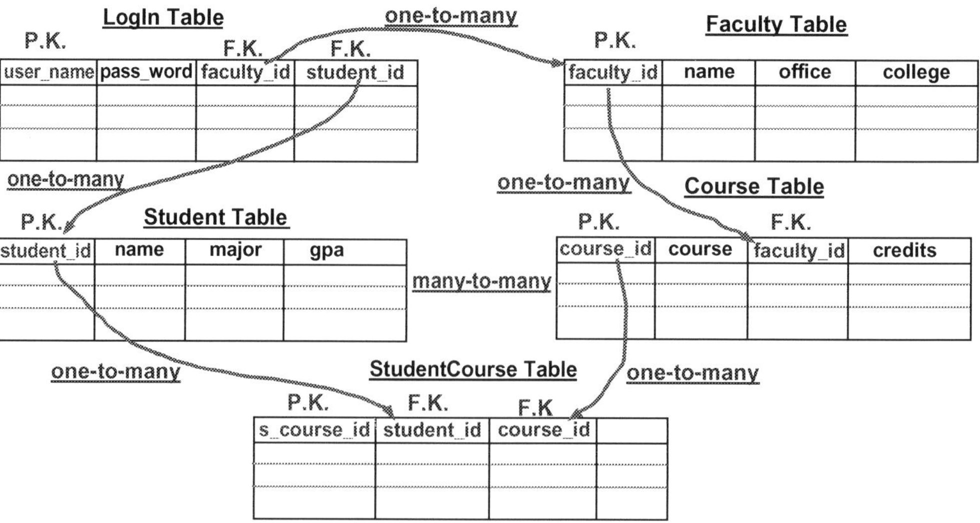

Figure 2.19. Relationships between tables.

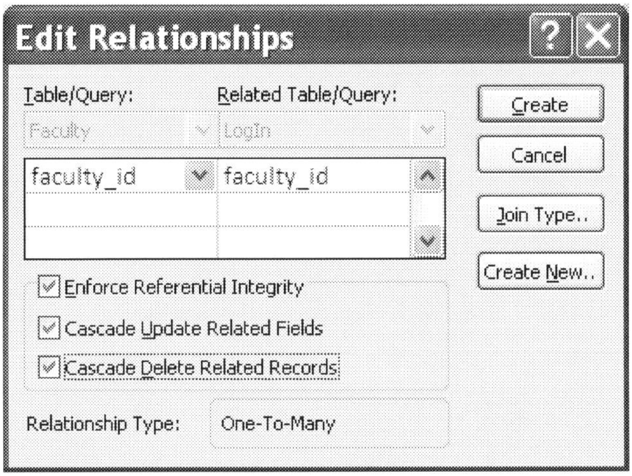

Figure 2.20. Edit Relationships dialog box.

connected with the `faculty_id` that is a foreign key in the LogIn table. The relationship between these two tables are one-to-many, since the unique primary key `faculty_id` in the Faculty table can be connected to multiple foreign key that is `faculty_id` located in the LogIn table.

To set this relationship between these two tables, click faculty_id from the Faculty table and drag to the faculty_id in the LogIn table. The `Edit Relationships` dialog box is displayed, which is shown in Figure 2.20.

Select the `Enforce Referential Integrity` checkbox to set up this reference integrity between these two fields. Also check the following two checkboxes:

- Cascade Update Related Fields
- Cascade Delete Related Records

The purpose of checking these two checkboxes is that all fields or records in the cascaded or child tables will be updated or deleted when the related fields or records in the parent tables are updated or deleted. This will greatly simplify the updating and deleting operations for a given relational database that contains a lot of related tables. Refer to Chapters 6 and 7 for more detailed discussions about the data updating and deleting actions.

Click the `Create` button to create this relationship. In the similar way, you can create all other relationships between these five tables. One point you need to remember when you perform this dragging operation is that always starting this drag from the Primary key in the parent table and ending it with the Foreign key in the child table. As shown in Figure 2.20, the table located in the left of the `Edit Relationships` dialog is considered as the parent table, and the right of this dialog is the child table. Therefore, the faculty_id in the left is the Primary key, and the faculty_id in the right is the Foreign key, respectively.

The finished relationships dialog should match the one that is shown in Figure 2.21.

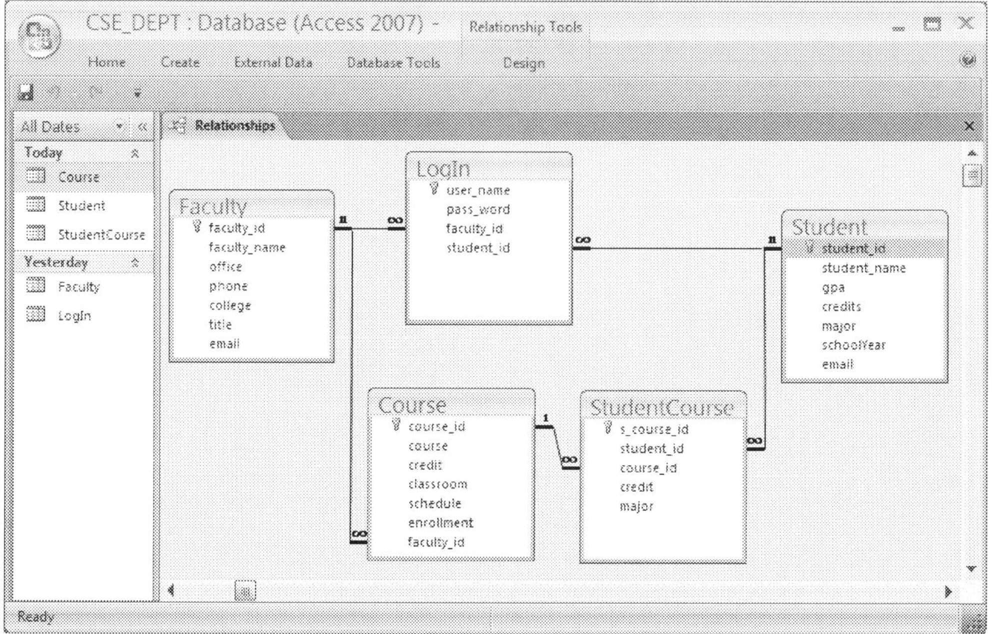

Figure 2.21. The completed relationships for tables.

During the process of creating relationships between tables, sometimes, an error message may be displayed to indicate that some of tables are used by other users and are not locked to allow you to perform this relationship creation. In that case, just save your current result, close your database, and exit the Access. This error will be solved when you restart Access and open your database again. The reason for that is because some tables are considered to be used by you when you finished creating those tables and continue to perform the creating of the relationships between them.

A completed Microsoft Access 2007 database file **`CSE_DEPT.accdb`** can be found from the folder **Database\Access** that is located at the Wiley ftp site. Refer to Appendix G if you want to use this sample database in your applications.

2.10 CREATE MICROSOFT SQL SERVER 2008 SAMPLE DATABASE

After you finished the installation of SQL Server 2008 Management Studio (refer to Appendix D), you can begin to use it to connect to the server and build your database. To start, go to **Start|All Programs|Microsoft SQL Server 2008** and select **SQL Server Management Studio**. A connection dialog is opened, as shown in Figure 2.22.

Your computer name followed by your server name should be displayed in the Server name: box. In this case, it is `SMART\SQL2008EXPRESS`. The Windows NT default

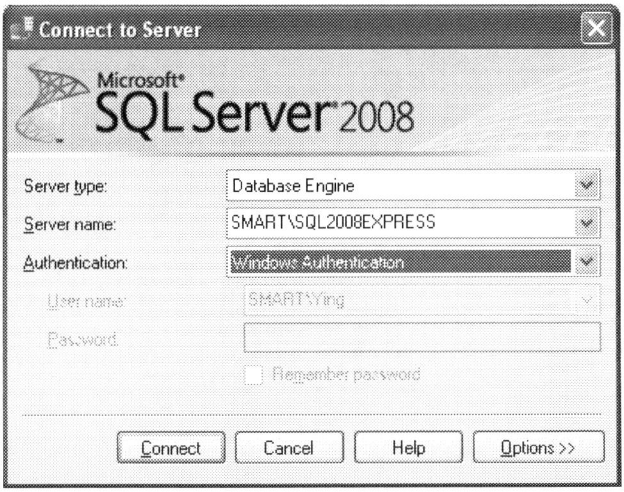

Figure 2.22. Connect to the SQL Server 2008.

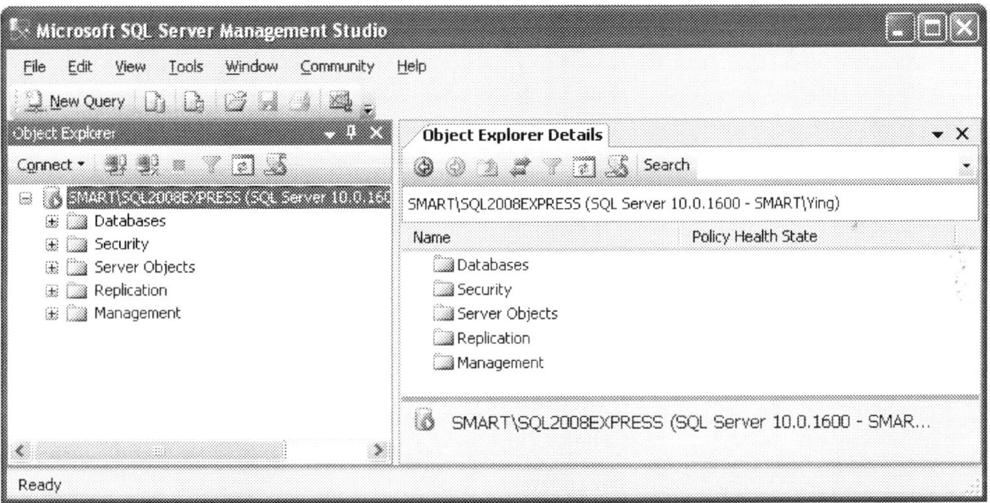

Figure 2.23. The opened server management studio.

security engine is used by selecting the **Windows Authentication** method from the `Authentication` box. The User name box contains the name you entered when you register for your computer. Click the **Connect** button to connect your client to your server.

The server management studio is opened when this connection is completed, which is shown in Figure 2.23.

To create a new database, right click on the Databases folder from the Object Explorer window, and select the `New Database` item from the popup menu. Enter `CSE_DEPT` into the Database name box in the New Database dialog as the name of our

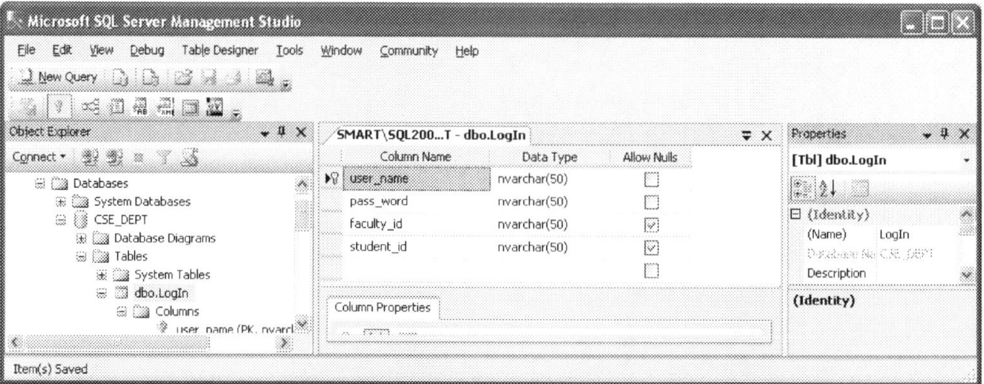

Figure 2.24. The new table window.

database, keep all other settings unchanged, and then click the `OK` button. You can find that a new database named `CSE_DEPT` is created, and it is located under the `Database` folder in the Object Explorer window.

Then you need to create data tables. For this sample database, you need to create five data tables: `LogIn, Faculty, Course, Student`, and `StudentCourse`. Expand the `CSE_DEPT` database folder by clicking the plus symbol next to it. Right click on the `Tables` folder and select the `New Table` item; a new table window is displayed, which is shown in Figure 2.24.

2.10.1 Create the LogIn Table

A default data table named `dbo`.Table_1 is created, as shown in Figure 2.24. Three columns are displayed in this new table: `Column Name, Data Type`, and `Allow Nulls`, which allows you to enter the name, the data type, and check mark for each column. You can check the checkbox if you allow that column to be empty, otherwise do not check it if you want that column to must contain a valid data. Generally, for the column that has been selected to work as the primary key, you should not check for the checkbox associated with that column.

The first table is the `LogIn` table, which has four columns with the following column names: `user_name, pass_word, faculty_id`, and `student_id`. Enter those four names into four `Column Names` columns. The data types for these four columns are all `nvarchar(50)`, which means that this is a varied char type with a maximum letters of 50. Enter those data types into each Data Type column. The first column `user_name` is selected as the primary key, so leave the checkbox blank for that column and check other three checkboxes.

To make the first column `user_name` as a primary key, click on the first row and then go to the Toolbar and select the `Primary Key` (displayed as a key) tool. In this way, a symbol of primary key is displayed on the left of this row, which is shown in Figure 2.24.

Before we can continue to finish this LogIn table, we need first to save and name this table. Go to `File|Save Table_1` and enter the **LogIn** as the name for this new table.

Click the `OK` button to finish this saving. A new table named **`dbo.LogIn`** is added into the new database under the `Tables` folder in the Object Explorer window.

To add data into this `LogIn` table, right click on this table and select Edit Top 200 Rows item from the pop-up menu. Enter all login data that is shown in Table 2.18 into this table. Your finished `LogIn` table should match one that is shown in Figure 2.25.

Table 2.18. The data in the LogIn table

user_name	pass_word	faculty_id	student_id
abrown	america	B66750	NULL
ajade	tryagain	NULL	A97850
awoods	smart	NULL	A78835
banderson	birthday	A52990	NULL
bvalley	see	NULL	B92996
dangles	tomorrow	A77587	NULL
hsmith	try	NULL	H10210
jerica	excellent	NULL	J77896
jhenry	test	H99118	NULL
jking	goodman	K69880	NULL
sbhalla	india	B86590	NULL
sjohnson	jermany	J33486	NULL
ybai	reback	B78880	NULL

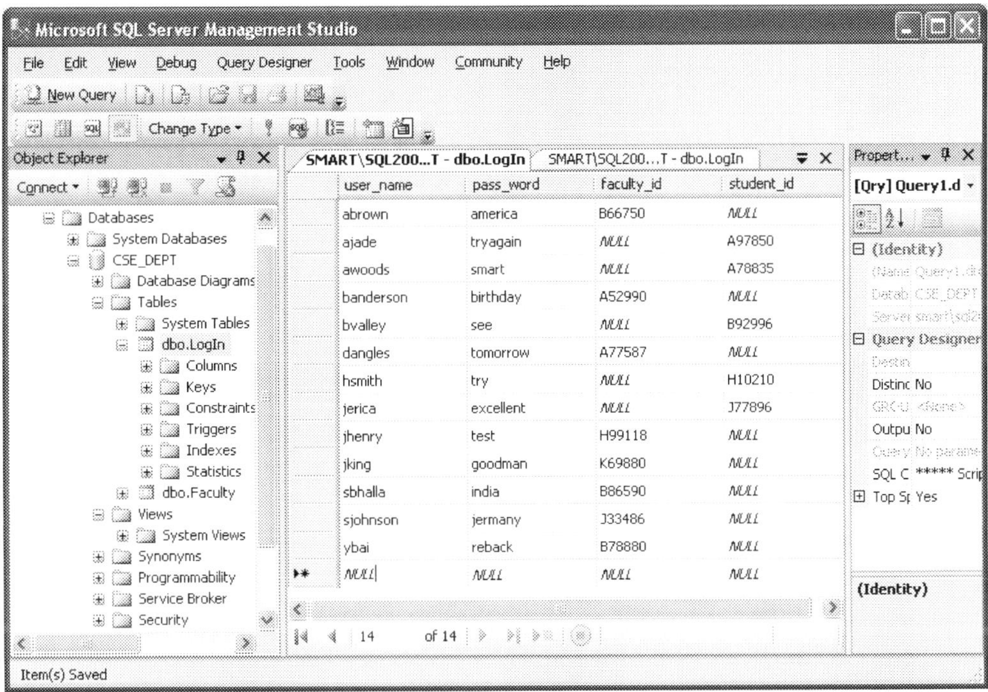

Figure 2.25. The finished LogIn table.

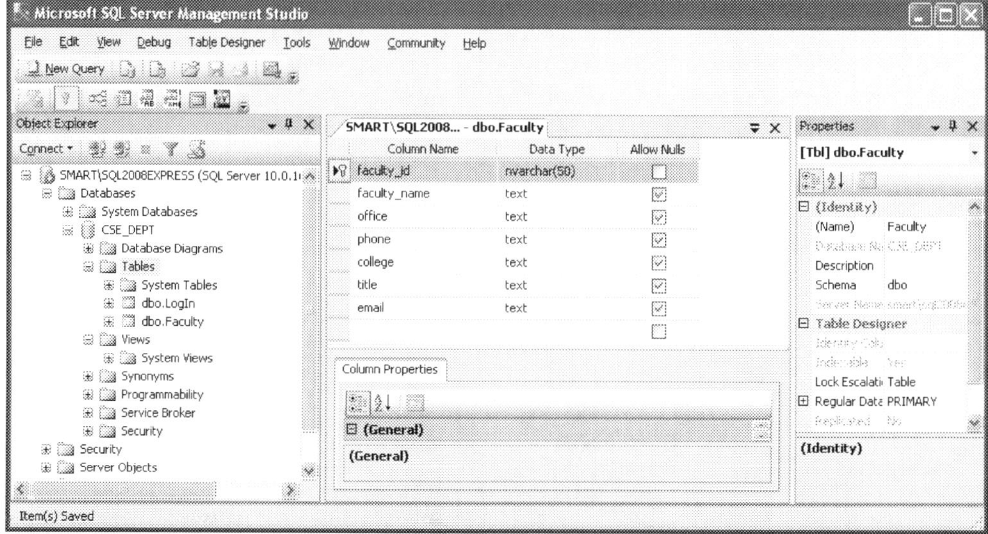

Figure 2.26. The design view of the Faculty table.

One point to be noted is that you must place a NULL for any field that has no value in this LogIn table, since it is different for the blank field between the Microsoft Access and the SQL Server database. Go to the File|Save All item to save this table. Now let's continue to create the second table `Faculty`.

2.10.2 Create the Faculty Table

Right click on the Tables folder under the CSE_DEPT database folder and select the **New Table** item to open the design view of a new table, which is shown in Figure 2.26.

For this table, we have seven columns: `faculty_id`, `faculty_name`, `office`, `phone`, `college`, `title`, and `email`. The data types for the columns faculty_id and faculty_name are nvarchar(50), and all other data types can be either text or nvarchar(50), since all of them are string variables. The reason we selected the nvarchar(50) `as the` data type for the `faculty_id` is that a primary key can work for this data type, but it does not work for the `text`. The finished design view of the `Faculty` table should match one that is shown in Figure 2.26.

Since we selected the `faculty_id` column as the primary key, click on that row and then go to the Toolbar and select the `Primary Key` tool. In this way, the `faculty_id` is chosen as the primary key for this table, which is shown in Figure 2.26.

Now go to the `File` menu item and select the `Save Table_1`, and enter `Faculty` into the box for the `Choose Name` dialog as the name for this table; click `OK` to save this table.

Next you need to enter the data into this `Faculty` table. To do that, first open the table by right clicking on the `dbo.Faculty` folder under the `CSE_DEPT` database folder in the Object Explorer window, and then select `Open Table` item to open this table. Enter the data that is shown in Table 2.19 into this `Faculty` table.

Table 2.19. The data in the Faculty table

faculty_id	faculty_name	office	phone	college	title	email
A52990	Black Anderson	MTC-218	750-378-9987	Virginia Tech	Professor	banderson@college.edu
A77587	Debby Angles	MTC-320	750-330-2276	University of Chicago	Associate Professor	dangles@college.edu
B66750	Alice Brown	MTC-257	750-330-6650	University of Florida	Assistant Professor	abrown@college.edu
B78880	Ying Bai	MTC-211	750-378-1148	Florida Atlantic University	Associate Professor	ybai@college.edu
B86590	Satish Bhalla	MTC-214	750-378-1061	University of Notre Dame	Associate Professor	sbhalla@college.edu
H99118	Jeff Henry	MTC-336	750-330-8650	Ohio State University	Associate Professor	jhenry@college.edu
J33486	Steve Johnson	MTC-118	750-330-1116	Harvard University	Distinguished Professor	sjohnson@college.edu
K69880	Jenney King	MTC-324	750-378-1230	East Florida University	Professor	jking@college.edu

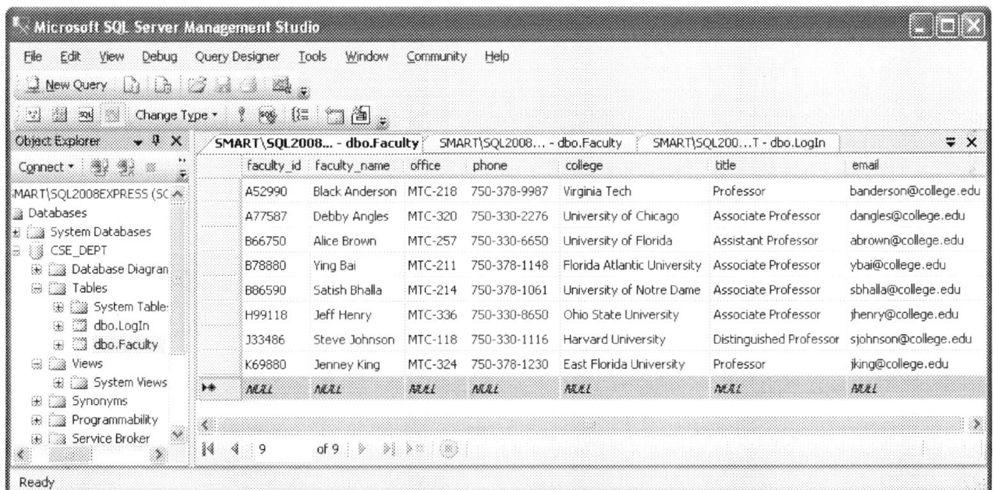

Figure 2.27. The completed Faculty table.

Your finished `Faculty` table should match one that is shown in Figure 2.27.

Now go to the `File` menu item and select `Save All` to save this completed `Faculty` data table. Your finished `Faculty` data table will be displayed as a table named `dbo.Faculty` that has been added into the new database `CSE_DEPT` under the folder `Tables` in the Object Explorer window.

2.10.3 Create Other Tables

In the similar way, you need to create the rest of three tables: `Course`, `Student`, and `StudentCourse`. Select `course_id`, `student_id`, and `s_course_id` as the primary keys for these three tables (refer to Tables 2.20–2.22). For the data type selections, follow the directions below:

The data type selections for the `Course` table:

- `course_id`—`nvarchar(50)` (Primary key)
- credit—`smallint`

Table 2.20. The data in the Course table

course_id	course	credit	classroom	schedule	enrollment	faculty_id
CSC-131A	Computers in Society	3	TC-109	M-W-F: 9:00-9:55 AM	28	A52990
CSC-131B	Computers in Society	3	TC-114	M-W-F: 9:00-9:55 AM	20	B66750
CSC-131C	Computers in Society	3	TC-109	T-H: 11:00-12:25 PM	25	A52990
CSC-131D	Computers in Society	3	TC-109	M-W-F: 9:00-9:55 AM	30	B86590
CSC-131E	Computers in Society	3	TC-301	M-W-F: 1:00-1:55 PM	25	B66750
CSC-131I	Computers in Society	3	TC-109	T-H: 1:00-2:25 PM	32	A52990
CSC-132A	Introduction to Programming	3	TC-303	M-W-F: 9:00-9:55 AM	21	J33486
CSC-132B	Introduction to Programming	3	TC-302	T-H: 1:00-2:25 PM	21	B78880
CSC-230	Algorithms & Structures	3	TC-301	M-W-F: 1:00-1:55 PM	20	A77587
CSC-232A	Programming I	3	TC-305	T-H: 11:00-12:25 PM	28	B66750
CSC-232B	Programming I	3	TC-303	T-H: 11:00-12:25 PM	17	A77587
CSC-233A	Introduction to Algorithms	3	TC-302	M-W-F: 9:00-9:55 AM	18	H99118
CSC-233B	Introduction to Algorithms	3	TC-302	M-W-F: 11:00-11:55 AM	19	K69880
CSC-234A	Data Structure & Algorithms	3	TC-302	M-W-F: 9:00-9:55 AM	25	B78880
CSC-234B	Data Structure & Algorithms	3	TC-114	T-H: 11:00-12:25 PM	15	J33486
CSC-242	Programming II	3	TC-303	T-H: 1:00-2:25 PM	18	A52990
CSC-320	Object Oriented Programming	3	TC-301	T-H: 1:00-2:25 PM	22	B66750
CSC-331	Applications Programming	3	TC-109	T-H: 11:00-12:25 PM	28	H99118
CSC-333A	Computer Arch & Algorithms	3	TC-301	M-W-F: 10:00-10:55 AM	22	A77587
CSC-333B	Computer Arch & Algorithms	3	TC-302	T-H: 11:00-12:25 PM	15	A77587
CSC-335	Internet Programming	3	TC-303	M-W-F: 1:00-1:55 PM	25	B66750
CSC-432	Discrete Algorithms	3	TC-206	T-H: 11:00-12:25 PM	20	B86590
CSC-439	Database Systems	3	TC-206	M-W-F: 1:00-1:55 PM	18	B86590
CSE-138A	Introduction to CSE	3	TC-301	T-H: 1:00-2:25 PM	15	A52990
CSE-138B	Introduction to CSE	3	TC-109	T-H: 1:00-2:25 PM	35	J33486
CSE-330	Digital Logic Circuits	3	TC-305	M-W-F: 9:00-9:55 AM	26	K69880
CSE-332	Foundations of Semiconductors	3	TC-305	T-H: 1:00-2:25 PM	24	K69880
CSE-334	Elec. Measurement & Design	3	TC-212	T-H: 11:00-12:25 PM	25	H99118
CSE-430	Bioinformatics in Computer	3	TC-206	Thu: 9:30-11:00 AM	16	B86590
CSE-432	Analog Circuits Design	3	TC-309	M-W-F: 2:00-2:55 PM	18	K69880
CSE-433	Digital Signal Processing	3	TC-206	T-H: 2:00-3:25 PM	18	H99118
CSE-434	Advanced Electronics Systems	3	TC-213	M-W-F: 1:00-1:55 PM	26	B78880
CSE-436	Automatic Control and Design	3	TC-305	M-W-F: 10:00-10:55 AM	29	J33486
CSE-437	Operating Systems	3	TC-303	T-H: 1:00-2:25 PM	17	A77587
CSE-438	Advd Logic & Microprocessor	3	TC-213	M-W-F: 11:00-11:55 AM	35	B78880
CSE-439	Special Topics in CSE	3	TC-206	M-W-F: 10:00-10:55 AM	22	J33486

Table 2.21. The data in the student table

student_id	student_name	gpa	credits	major	schoolYear	email
A78835	Andrew Woods	3.26	108	Computer Science	Senior	awoods@college.edu
A97850	Ashly Jade	3.57	116	Information System Engineering	Junior	ajade@college.edu
B92996	Blue Valley	3.52	102	Computer Science	Senior	bvalley@college.edu
H10210	Holes Smith	3.87	78	Computer Engineering	Sophomore	hsmith@college.edu
J77896	Erica Johnson	3.95	127	Computer Science	Senior	ejohnson@college.edu

Table 2.22. The data in the StudentCourse table

s_course_id	student_id	course_id	credit	major
1000	H10210	CSC-131D	3	CE
1001	B92996	CSC-132A	3	CS/IS
1002	J77896	CSC-335	3	CS/IS
1003	A78835	CSC-331	3	CE
1004	H10210	CSC-234B	3	CE
1005	J77896	CSC-234A	3	CS/IS
1006	B92996	CSC-233A	3	CS/IS
1007	A78835	CSC-132A	3	CE
1008	A78835	CSE-432	3	CE
1009	A78835	CSE-434	3	CE
1010	J77896	CSC-439	3	CS/IS
1011	H10210	CSC-132A	3	CE
1012	H10210	CSC-331	2	CE
1013	A78835	CSC-335	3	CE
1014	A78835	CSE-438	3	CE
1015	J77896	CSC-432	3	CS/IS
1016	A97850	CSC-132B	3	ISE
1017	A97850	CSC-234A	3	ISE
1018	A97850	CSC-331	3	ISE
1019	A97850	CSC-335	3	ISE
1020	J77896	CSE-439	3	CS/IS
1021	B92996	CSC-230	3	CS/IS
1022	A78835	CSE-332	3	CE
1023	B92996	CSE-430	3	CE
1024	J77896	CSC-333A	3	CS/IS
1025	H10210	CSE-433	3	CE
1026	H10210	CSE-334	3	CE
1027	B92996	CSC-131C	3	CS/IS
1028	B92996	CSC-439	3	CS/IS

- enrolment—`int`
- `faculty_id`—`nvarchar(50)`
- All other columns—either `nvarchar(50)` or `text`

The data type selections for the `Student` table:

- `student_id`—`nvarchar(50)` (Primary key)
- `student_name`—`nvarchar(50)`
- gpa—`float`

- credits—`int`
- All other columns—either `nvarchar(50)` or `text`

The data type selections for the `StudentCourse` table:

- `s_course_id`—`int` (Primary key)
- `student_id`—`nvarchar(50)`
- `course_id`—`nvarchar(50)`
- credit—`int`
- `major`—either `nvarchar(50)` or `text`

Enter the data that are shown in Tables 2.20–2.22 into each associated table, and save each table as `Course`, `Student`, and `StudentCourse`, respectively.

The finished Course table should match one that is shown in Figure 2.28.

The finished `Student` table should match one that is shown in Figure 2.29. The finished StudentCourse table should match one that is shown in Figure 2.30.

One point you need to note is that you can copy the content of the whole table from the Microsoft Access database file to the associated data table opened in the Microsoft SQL Server environment if the Microsoft Access database has been developed.

To make these copies and pastes, first you must select a whole blank row from your destination table—table in the Microsoft SQL Server database, and then select all data rows from your source table—Microsoft Access database file by highlighting them, and

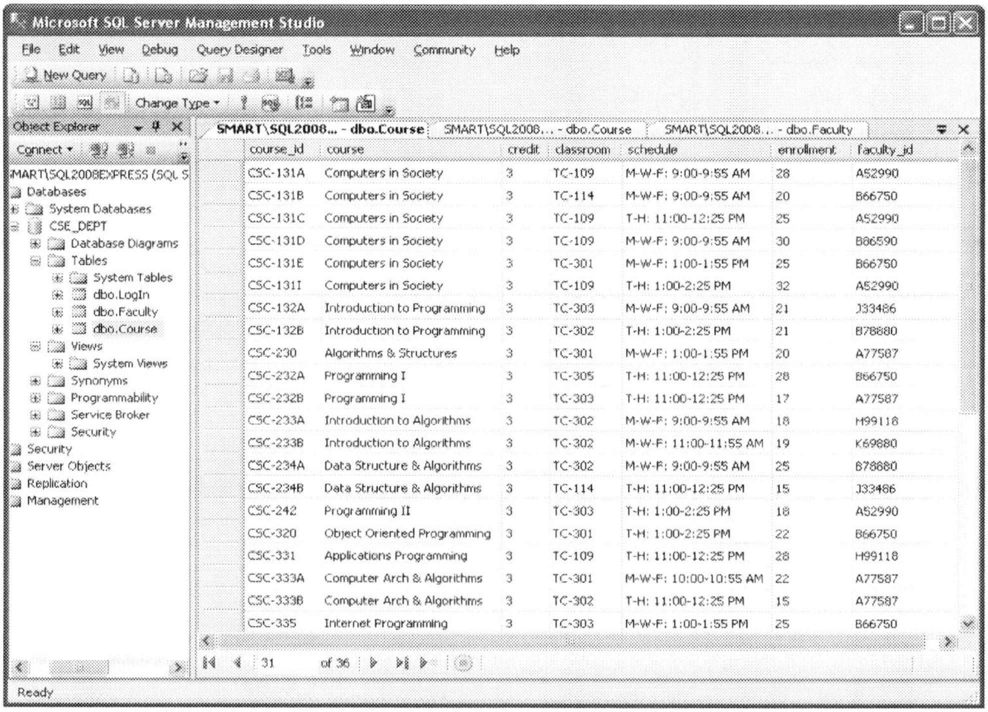
Microsoft SQL Server Management Studio
File Edit View Debug Query Designer Tools Window Community Help
New Query
Change Type
Object Explorer
Connect
MART\SQL2008EXPRESS (SQL S
Databases
System Databases
CSE_DEPT
Database Diagrams
Tables
System Tables
dbo.LogIn
dbo.Faculty
dbo.Course
Views
System Views
Synonyms
Programmability
Service Broker
Security
Security
Server Objects
Replication
Management
SMART\SQL2008... - dbo.Course
SMART\SQL2008... - dbo.Course
SMART\SQL2008... - dbo.Faculty
course_id course credit classroom schedule enrollment faculty_id
CSC-131A Computers in Society 3 TC-109 M-W-F: 9:00-9:55 AM 28 A52990
CSC-131B Computers in Society 3 TC-114 M-W-F: 9:00-9:55 AM 20 B66750
CSC-131C Computers in Society 3 TC-109 T-H: 11:00-12:25 PM 25 A52990
CSC-131D Computers in Society 3 TC-109 M-W-F: 9:00-9:55 AM 30 B86590
CSC-131E Computers in Society 3 TC-301 M-W-F: 1:00-1:55 PM 25 B66750
CSC-131I Computers in Society 3 TC-109 T-H: 1:00-2:25 PM 32 A52990
CSC-132A Introduction to Programming 3 TC-303 M-W-F: 9:00-9:55 AM 21 J33486
CSC-132B Introduction to Programming 3 TC-302 T-H: 1:00-2:25 PM 21 B78880
CSC-230 Algorithms & Structures 3 TC-301 M-W-F: 1:00-1:55 PM 20 A77587
CSC-232A Programming I 3 TC-305 T-H: 11:00-12:25 PM 28 B66750
CSC-232B Programming I 3 TC-303 T-H: 11:00-12:25 PM 17 A77587
CSC-233A Introduction to Algorithms 3 TC-302 M-W-F: 9:00-9:55 AM 18 H99118
CSC-233B Introduction to Algorithms 3 TC-302 M-W-F: 11:00-11:55 AM 19 K69880
CSC-234A Data Structure & Algorithms 3 TC-302 M-W-F: 9:00-9:55 AM 25 B78880
CSC-234B Data Structure & Algorithms 3 TC-114 T-H: 11:00-12:25 PM 15 J33486
CSC-242 Programming II 3 TC-303 T-H: 1:00-2:25 PM 18 A52990
CSC-320 Object Oriented Programming 3 TC-301 T-H: 1:00-2:25 PM 22 B66750
CSC-331 Applications Programming 3 TC-109 T-H: 11:00-12:25 PM 28 H99118
CSC-333A Computer Arch & Algorithms 3 TC-301 M-W-F: 10:00-10:55 AM 22 A77587
CSC-333B Computer Arch & Algorithms 3 TC-302 T-H: 11:00-12:25 PM 15 A77587
CSC-335 Internet Programming 3 TC-303 M-W-F: 1:00-1:55 PM 25 B66750
31 of 36
Ready

Figure 2.28. The completed Course table.

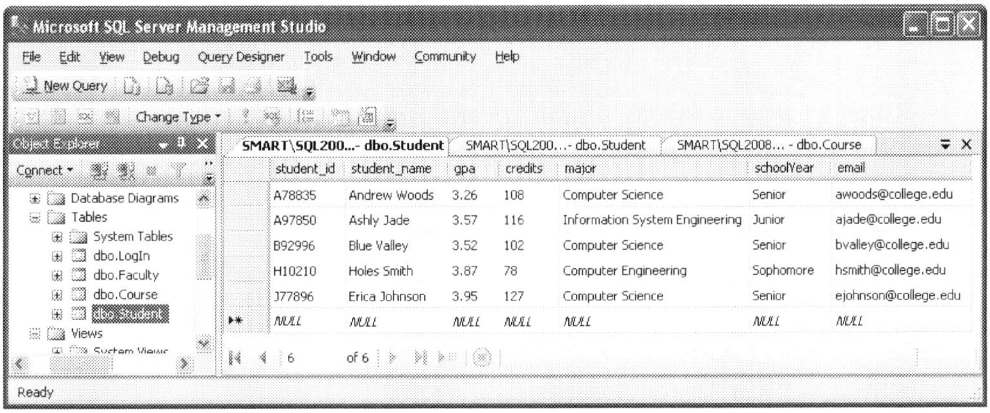
Microsoft SQL Server Management Studio
File Edit View Debug Query Designer Tools Window Community Help
New Query
Change Type
Object Explorer
Connect
Database Diagrams
Tables
System Tables
dbo.LogIn
dbo.Faculty
dbo.Course
dbo.Student
Views
SMART\SQL200...- dbo.Student
SMART\SQL200...- dbo.Student
SMART\SQL2008... - dbo.Course
student_id student_name gpa credits major schoolYear email
A78835 Andrew Woods 3.26 108 Computer Science Senior awoods@college.edu
A97850 Ashly Jade 3.57 116 Information System Engineering Junior ajade@college.edu
B92996 Blue Valley 3.52 102 Computer Science Senior bvalley@college.edu
H10210 Holes Smith 3.87 78 Computer Engineering Sophomore hsmith@college.edu
J77896 Erica Johnson 3.95 127 Computer Science Senior ejohnson@college.edu
NULL NULL NULL NULL NULL NULL NULL
6 of 6
Ready

Figure 2.29. The completed Student table.

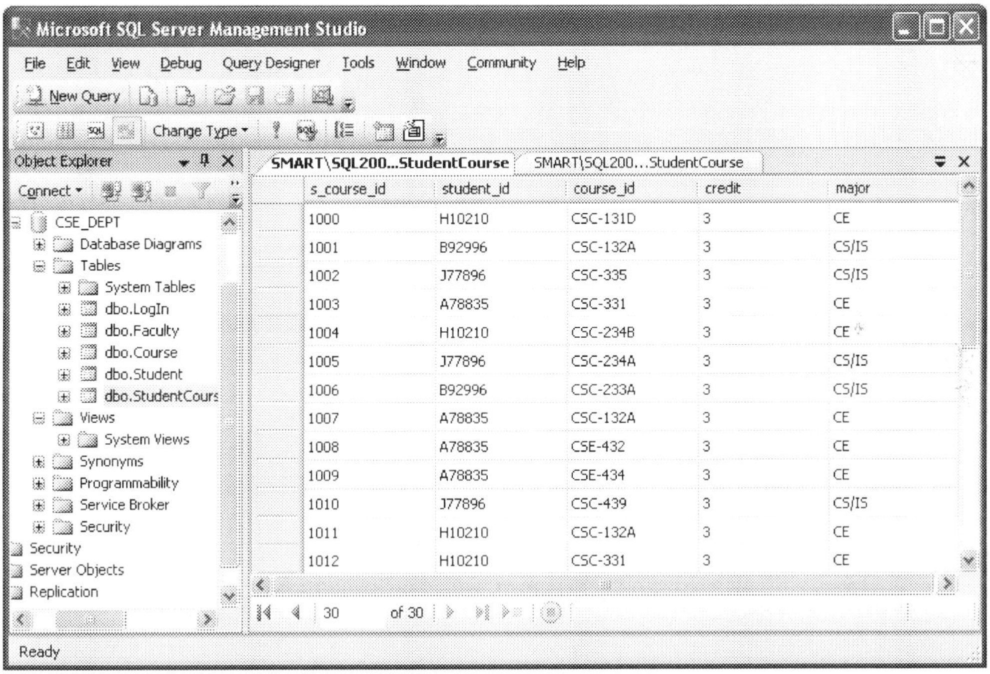
Microsoft SQL Server Management Studio
File Edit View Debug Query Designer Tools Window Community Help
New Query
Change Type
Object Explorer
Connect
CSE_DEPT
Database Diagrams
Tables
System Tables
dbo.LogIn
dbo.Faculty
dbo.Course
dbo.Student
dbo.StudentCours
Views
System Views
Synonyms
Programmability
Service Broker
Security
Security
Server Objects
Replication
SMART\SQL200...StudentCourse
SMART\SQL200...StudentCourse
s_course_id student_id course_id credit major
1000 H10210 CSC-131D 3 CE
1001 B92996 CSC-132A 3 CS/IS
1002 J77896 CSC-335 3 CS/IS
1003 A78835 CSC-331 3 CE
1004 H10210 CSC-234B 3 CE
1005 J77896 CSC-234A 3 CS/IS
1006 B92996 CSC-233A 3 CS/IS
1007 A78835 CSC-132A 3 CE
1008 A78835 CSE-432 3 CE
1009 A78835 CSE-434 3 CE
1010 J77896 CSC-439 3 CS/IS
1011 H10210 CSC-132A 3 CE
1012 H10210 CSC-331 3 CE
30 of 30
Ready

Figure 2.30. The completed StudentCourse table.

choose the `Copy` menu item. Next, you need to paste those rows by clicking that blank row in the Microsoft SQL Server database and then click the `Paste` item from the `Edit` menu item. An error message may be displayed as shown in Figure 2.31.

Just click the `OK` button and your data will be pasted to your destination table without problem. The reason for that error message is because of the primary key, which cannot be an NULL value. Before you can finish this paste operation, the table cannot identify whether you will have a non-null value in your source row that will be pasted in this column or not.

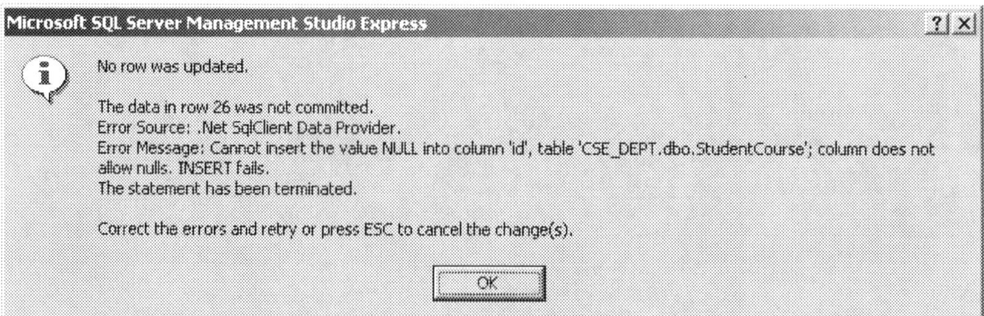
Microsoft SQL Server Management Studio Express

No row was updated.

The data in row 26 was not committed.
Error Source: .Net SqlClient Data Provider.
Error Message: Cannot insert the value NULL into column 'id', table 'CSE_DEPT.dbo.StudentCourse'; column does not allow nulls. INSERT fails.
The statement has been terminated.

Correct the errors and retry or press ESC to cancel the change(s).

OK

Figure 2.31. An error message when performing a paste job.

2.10.4 Create Relationships among Tables

Next, we need to set up relationships among these five tables using the Primary and Foreign Keys. In the Microsoft SQL Server 2008 Express database environment, the relationship between tables can be set by using the Keys folder under each data table from the Object Explorer window. Now let's begin to set up the relationship between the LogIn and the Faculty tables.

2.10.4.1 Create Relationship between the LogIn and the Faculty Tables

The relationship between the Faculty and the LogIn table is one-to-many, which means that the `faculty_id` is a primary key in the `Faculty` table, and it can be mapped to many `faculty_id` that are foreign keys in the `LogIn` table. To set up this relationship, expand the `LogIn` table and the `Keys` folder that is under the `LogIn` table. Currently, only one primary key, `PK_LogIn`, is existed under the Keys folder.

To add a new foreign key, right click on the `Keys` folder and select the `New Foreign Key` item from the pop-up menu to open the `Foreign Key Relationships` dialog, which is shown in Figure 2.32.

The default foreign relationship is `FK_LogIn_LogIn*`, which is displayed in the `Selected Relationship` box. Right now, we want to create the foreign relationship between the `LogIn` and the `Faculty` tables, so change the name of this foreign relationship to `FK_LogIn_Faculty` by modifying its name in the (Name) box that is under the Identity pane, and then press the `Enter` key from your keyboard. Then select two tables by clicking on the `Tables And Columns Specification` item that is under the General pane. Click the expansion button ▪ that is located on the right of the `Tables And Columns Specification` item to open the `Tables and Columns` dialog, which is shown in Figure 2.33.

Click the drop-down arrow from the `Primary key table` combo box and select the Faculty table, since we need the primary key `faculty_id` from this table, then click the blank row that is just below the `Primary key table` combo box and select the `faculty_id` column. You can see that the `LogIn` table has been automatically selected and displayed in the `Foreign key table` combo box. Click the drop-down arrow from the box that is just under the `Foreign key table` combo box and select the faculty_id

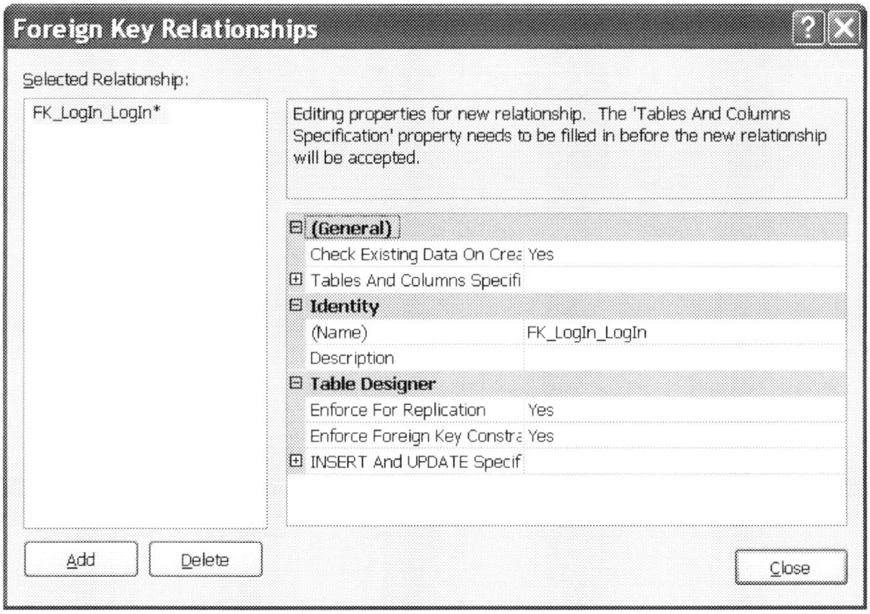

Figure 2.32. The opened Foreign Key Relationships dialog box.

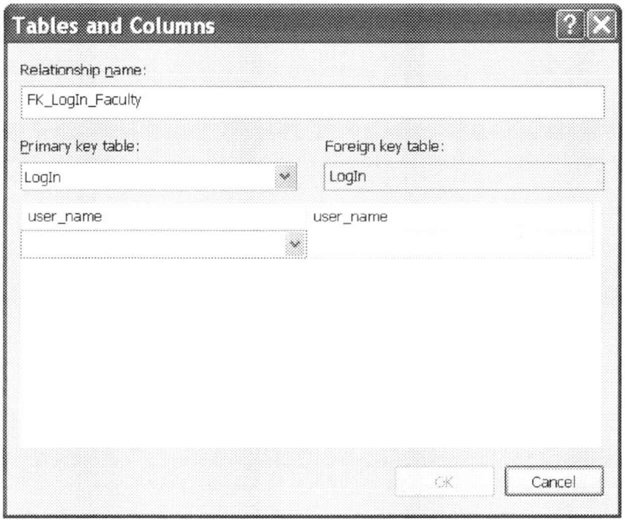

Figure 2.33. The opened Tables and Columns dialog box.

as the foreign key for the LogIn table. Your finished `Tables and Columns` dialog should match one that is shown in Figure 2.34.

Click the `OK` button to close this dialog.

Before we can close this dialog, we need to do one more thing, which is to set up a cascaded relationship between the Primary key (faculty_id) in the parent table Faculty and the Foreign keys (faculty_id) in the child table LogIn. The reason we need to do this

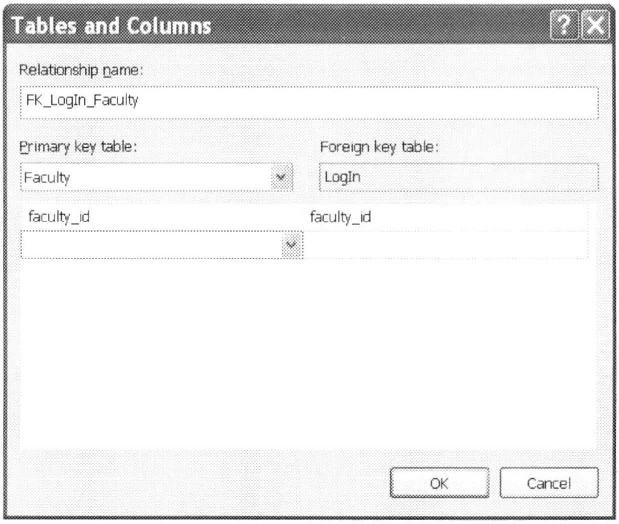

Figure 2.34. The finished Tables and Columns dialog box.

is because we want to simplify the data updating and deleting operations between these tables in a relational database, such as CSE_DEPT. You will have a better understanding about this cascading later on when you learn how to update and delete data against a relational database in Chapter 7.

To do this cascading, scroll down along this Foreign Key Relationships dialog and expand the item Table Designer. You find the INSERT And UPDATE Specifications item. Expand this item by clicking the small plus icon; two subitems are displayed, which are:

- Delete Rule
- Update Rule

The default value for both subitems is No Action. Click the No Action box for the Delete Rule item, and then click the drop-down arrow and select the Cascade item from the list. Perform the same operation for the Update Rule item. Your finished Foreign Key Relationships dialog should match one that is shown in Figure 2.35.

In this way, we established the cascaded relationship between the Primary key in the parent table and the Foreign keys in the child table. Later on, when you update or delete any Primary key from a parent table, the related foreign keys in the child tables will also be updated or deleted without other additional operations. It is convenient! Click the Close button to close this dialog.

Go to the `File|Save LogIn` menu item to open the `Save` dialog and click the `Yes` button to save this relationship. You can select `Yes` or `No` to the `Save Change Script` dialog box if it appears.

Now right click on the `Keys` folder under the `LogIn` table from the Object Explorer window, and select the `Refresh` item from the popup menu to refresh this `Keys` folder. Immediately, you can find a new foreign key named `FK_LogIn_Faculty`, which appears

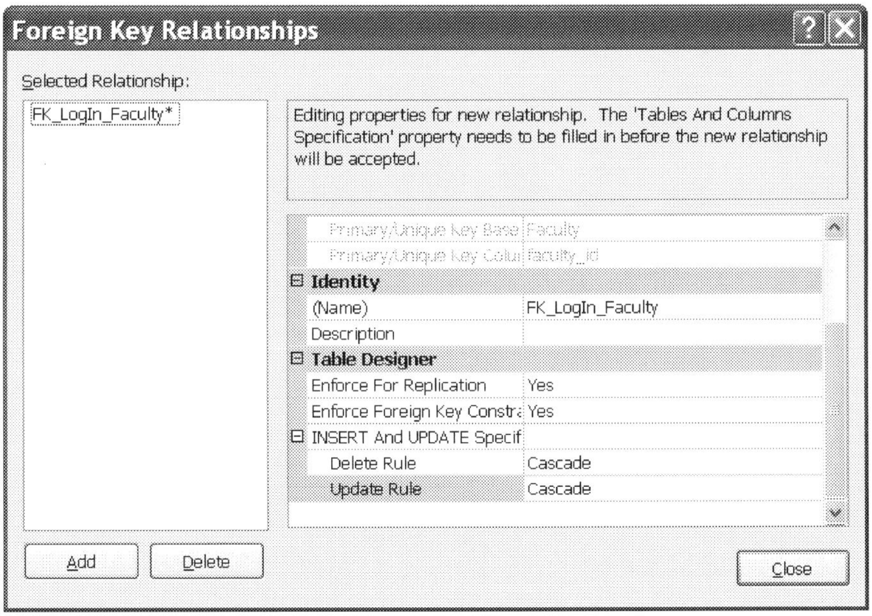

Figure 2.35. The finished Foreign Key Relationships dialog.

under this `Keys` folder. This is our new created foreign key that sets the relationship between our `LogIn` and `Faculty` tables. You can confirm and find this new created foreign key by right clicking on the `Keys` folder that is under the `Faculty` table.

2.10.4.2 Create Relationship between the LogIn and the Student Tables

In a similar way, you can create a foreign key for the LogIn table and set up a one-to-many relationship between the Student and the LogIn tables.

Right click on the `Keys` folder that is under the `dbo.LogIn` table and select the `New Foreign Key` item from the popup menu to open the `Foreign Key Relationships` dialog. Change the name to `FK_LogIn_Student` and press the Enter key from your keyboard. Go to the `Tables And Columns Specification` item to open the `Tables and Columns` dialog, then select the `Student` table from the `Primary key table` combo box and `student_id` from the box that is under the `Primary key table` combo box. Select the `student_id` from the box that is under the `Foreign key table` combo box. Your finished `Tables and Columns` dialog should match one that is shown in Figure 2.36.

Click the OK button to close this dialog box. Do not forget to establish the cascaded relationship for Delete Rule and Update Rule items by expanding the Table Designer and the INSERT And UPDATE Specifications items, respectively. Click the Close button to close the `Foreign Key Relationships` dialog box.

Go to the `File|Save LogIn` menu item to save this relationship. Click `Yes` for the following dialog box to finish saving. Now, right click on the `Keys` folder that is under the

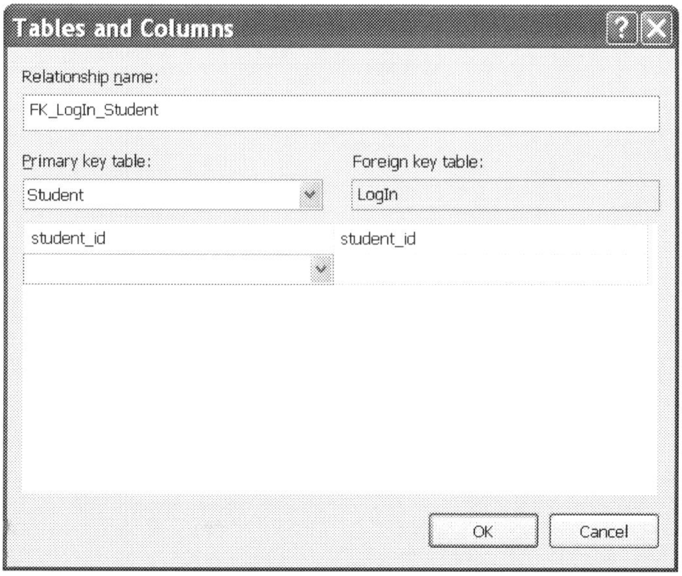

Figure 2.36. The completed Tables and Columns dialog.

dbo.LogIn table, and select Refresh item to show our new created foreign key FK_LogIn_Student.

2.10.4.3 Create Relationship between the Faculty and the Course Tables

The relationship between the Faculty and the Course tables is one-to-many, and the faculty_id in the Faculty table is a Primary key, and the faculty_id in the Course table is a Foreign key.

Right click on the Keys folder under the dbo.Course table from the Object Explorer window and select the New Foreign Key item from the popup menu. On the opened Foreign Key Relationships dialog, change the name of this new relationship to FK_Course_Faculty in the (Name) box and press the Enter key from the keyboard. In the opened Tables and Columns dialog box, select the Faculty table from the Primary key table combo box and select the faculty_id from the box that is just under the Primary key table combo box. Then select the faculty_id from the box that is just under the Foreign key table combo box. Your finished Tables and Columns dialog should match one that is shown in Figure 2.37.

Click the OK to close this dialog and set up the cascaded relationship for the Delete Rule and the Update Rule items, and then click the Close button to close the Foreign Key Relationships dialog box. Go to the File|Save Course menu item and click Yes for the following dialog box to save this setting.

Now right click on the Keys folder under the dbo.Course table, and select the Refresh item. Immediately, you can find our new created relationship key FK_Course_Faculty.

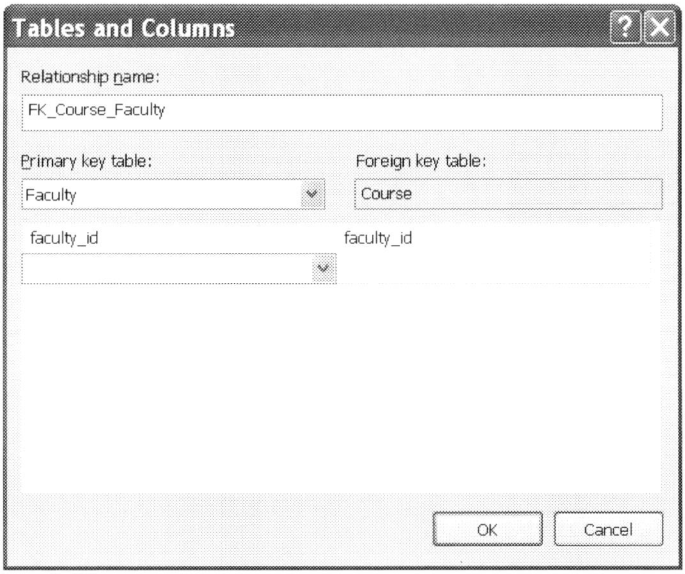

Figure 2.37. The finished Tables and Columns dialog.

2.10.4.4 Create Relationship between the Student and the StudentCourse Tables

The relationship between the Student and the StudentCourse tables is one-to-many, and the student_id in the Student table is a Primary key and the student_id in the StudentCourse table is a Foreign key.

Right click on the Keys folder under the dbo.StudentCourse table from the Object Explorer window and select the New Foreign Key item from the popup menu. On the opened Foreign Key Relationships dialog, change the name of this new relationship to FK_StudentCourse_Student in the (Name) box and press the Enter key from the keyboard. In the opened Tables and Columns dialog box, select the Student table from the Primary key table combo box, and select the student_id from the box that is just under the Primary key table combo box. Then select the student_id from the box that is just under the Foreign key table combo box. The finished Tables and Columns dialog should match one that is shown in Figure 2.38.

Click the OK button to close this dialog and set up the cascaded relationship for Delete Rule and the Update Rule items, and then click the Close button to close the Foreign Key Relationships dialog box. Go to the File|Save StudentCourse menu item and click Yes for the following dialog box to save this relationship.

Now right click on the Keys folder under the dbo.StudentCourse table, and select the Refresh item. Immediately you can find our new created relationship key FK_StudentCourse_Student.

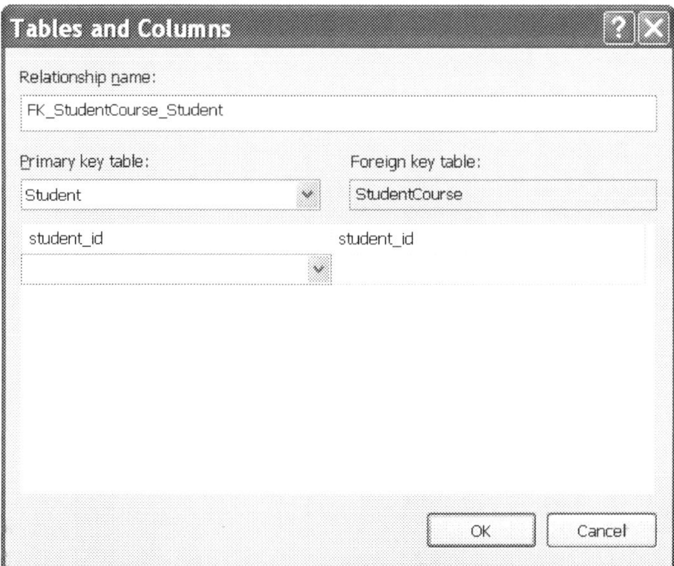

Figure 2.38. The finished Tables and Columns dialog.

2.10.4.5 Create Relationship between the Course and the StudentCourse Tables

The relationship between the Course and the StudentCourse tables is one-to-many, and the course_id in the Course table is a Primary key and the course_id in the StudentCourse table is a Foreign key.

Right click on the Keys folder under the dbo.StudentCourse table from the Object Explorer window and select the New Foreign Key item from the popup menu. On the opened Foreign Key Relationships dialog, change the name of this new relationship to FK_StudentCourse_Course in the (Name) box and press the Enter key from the keyboard. In the opened Tables and Columns dialog box, select the Course table from the Primary key table combo box and select the course_id from the box that is just under the Primary key table combo box. Then select the course_id from the box that is just under the Foreign key table combo box. Your finished Tables and Columns dialog should match one that is shown in Figure 2.39.

Click the OK button to close this dialog and do not forget to establish a cascaded relationship for the Delete Rule and the Update Rule items, and then click the Close button to close the Foreign Key Relationships dialog box. Then go to the File | Save StudentCourse menu item and click Yes for the following dialog box to save this relationship.

Now right click on the Keys folder under the dbo.StudentCourse table, and select the Refresh item. Immediately, you can find our new created relationship key FK_StudentCourse_Course.

At this point, we complete setting the relationships among our five data tables.

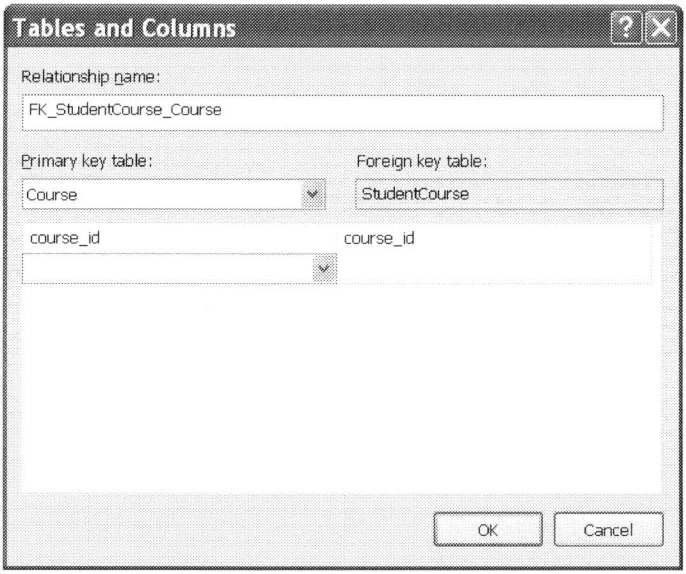

Tables and Columns

Relationship name:

FK_StudentCourse_Course

Primary key table: Course

Foreign key table: StudentCourse

course_id course_id

OK Cancel

Figure 2.39. The finished Tables and Columns dialog.

A completed Microsoft SQL Server 2008 sample database file `CSE_DEPT.mdf` can be found from the folder **SQLServer** that is located at the website: http://www.xxx.org/bai/database. The completed relationships for these tables are shown in Figure 2.40.

2.11 CREATE ORACLE 10G XE SAMPLE DATABASE

After you download and install Oracle Database 10g XE (refer to Appendix E), you need to create a customer Oracle database. To do that, you need to start this job from the Oracle Home page in the server. To connect your computer to your Oracle server, go to `Start|All Programs|Oracle Database 10g Express Edition|Go To Database Home Page` to open the Login page, which is shown in Figure 2.41.

You can login as an Administrator by entering `SYSTEM` into the `Username` box and password you selected during your download and installation of the `Oracle Database 10g XE` into the Password box if you want to use the whole system. But if you want to create customer databases, you must create a new user and login as that user. We will concentrate on creating a customer database, CSE_DEPT, in this section only. If you want to work as an Administrator to create and manage all data sources, just log on yourself as an Administrator. There is no difference between the Administrator and a specific database user in creating and manipulating tables in Oracle Database 10g XE, and the only difference is that the Administrator has more control abilities than any specific database user has.

In Oracle database 10g XE, only a single database instance is allowed to be created and implemented for any database applications. To make the database simple and easy, each database object is considered as a schema, and each schema is related to a user or

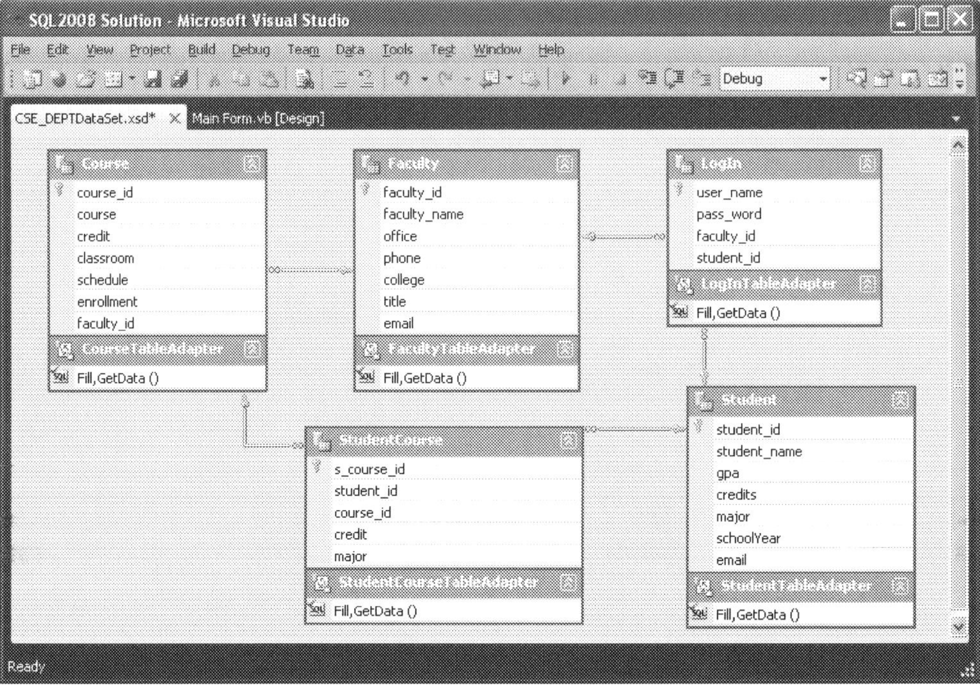

Figure 2.40. Relationships among tables.

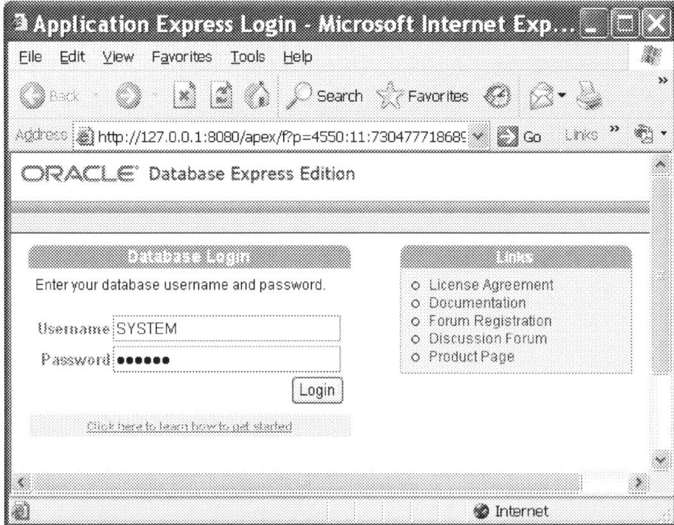

Figure 2.41. The opened Login page.

a user account. When you create a new user and assign a new account to that user, you create a new schema. A schema is a logical container for the database objects (such as tables, views, triggers, etc.) that the user creates. The schema name is the same as the user name, and can be used to unambiguously refer to objects owned by the user.

After you download and install Oracle Database 10g XE, by default, that database contains a lot of default utility tables, and most of them are not related to our special applications. In order to specify a database for our applications, we need to create a user database or a schema to meet our specific requirements in our applications. Next, we will use the CSE_DEPT database as an example to illustrate how to create a user database in Oracle Database 10g XE.

2.11.1 Create an Oracle User Database

To create a schema or a new user database, we need to create a new user account with the following steps:

1. Log on to the Oracle Database 10g XE as the Administrator using the user ID SYSTEM and your password
2. Create a new user account using the `Administration|Database Users|Create User` items
3. Enter the desired Username and Password
4. Click the `Create` button to create a new user account

Now let's follow these four steps to create our new user account or user database named CSE_DEPT.

Open the Oracle Database 10g XE home page, log in as an Administrator, and click the Administration button and go to Administration|Database Users|Create User. On the opened dialog box, enter "CSE_DEPT" into the Username and "reback" into the Password and the Confirm Password textboxes, respectively. Keep the "Unlocked" in the Account Status box unchanged and check the following checkboxes:

- CONNECT
- RESOURCE
- CREATE DATABASE LINK
- CREATE TABLE
- CREATE TYPE

The purpose of checking these checkboxes is to allow this new created user to be able to set up a connection (CONNECT) with this user database, use all data sources, set up database links, create tables as well as the data types as a new instance of this database is created in an application.

Your finished creating new user dialog box should match one that is shown in Figure 2.42. Click the Create button to create this new user.

After a new user is created, a new schema or a database is also created with the same name as the user's name, CSE_DEPT. Next, we can add new data tables into this new database. To do that, first, we need to log out from the current Administrator account and

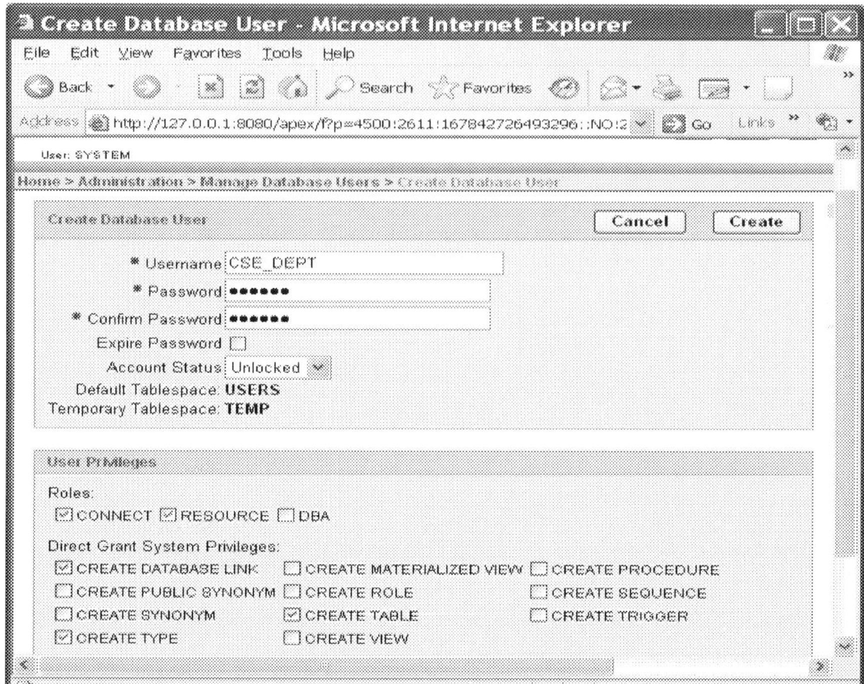

Figure 2.42. Create new user dialog box.

log in as our new user account CSE_DEPT. Click the Logout icon on the upper-right corner of this window and click the Login icon to open the homepage again.

Enter **CSE_DEPT** into the Username and **reback** into the Password textboxes to log in as a CSE_DEPT user.

Now we can create five data tables, such as LogIn, Faculty, Course, Student, and StudentCourse in this CSE_DEPT user account or user database as we did in the last part. Also we need to define the constraints relationships between those five tables as we did in the last section to set up relationships between these five tables.

2.11.2 Add New Data Tables into the Oracle User Database

You need to use the Object Browser to create, access, and manipulate the data in this database via the Oracle Database 10g Express server. Now click the Object Browser icon to open the Object Browser window, which is shown in Figure 2.43.

Since we just created a new database CSE_DEPT without any table attached with this database, therefore, a blank table list is displayed under the Tables item, as shown in Figure 2.43. We need to create and add five new tables, `LogIn`, `Faculty`, `Course`, `Student`, and `StudentCourse`, into this new database.

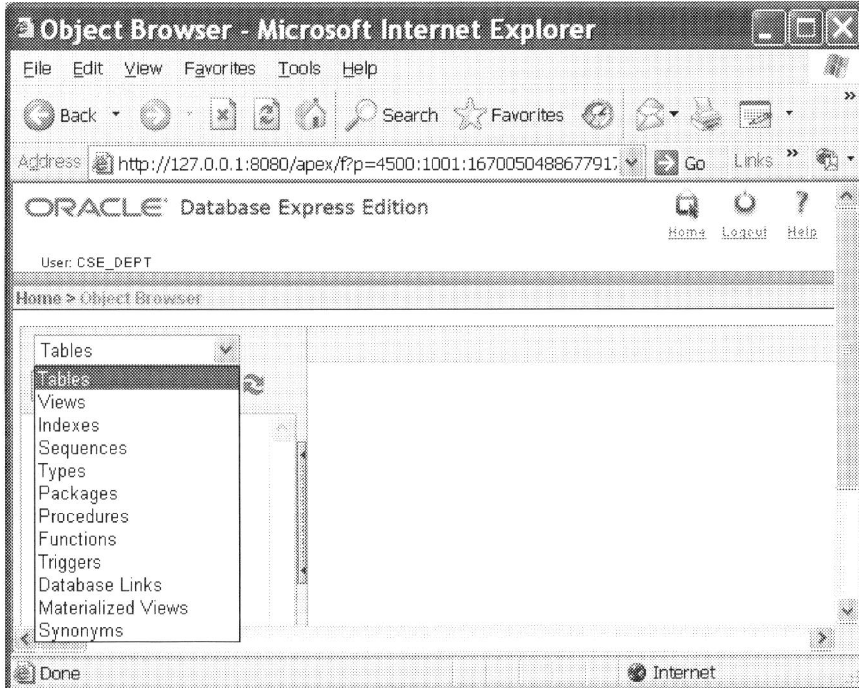

Figure 2.43. The opened Object Browser window.

2.11.2.1 Create the LogIn Table

Make sure that the content of the textbox in the left column is Tables, which is the default value; click the drop-down arrow of the `Create` button and select `Tables` to create our first new table, `LogIn`, which is shown in Figure 2.44.

A flowchart of developing the table is shown in the left pane. This means that you need to follow these five steps to finish the creation of your data table, and each step is mapped to one page. The middle pane contains the most components that allow us to create and edit our data table. Enter LogIn as the table name into the Table Name box.

The first step in the flowchart is the `Columns`, which means that you need to create each column based on the information of your data table, such as the Column Name, Type, Precision, Scale, and Not Null. For our `LogIn` table, we have four columns: `user_name`, `pass_word`, `faculty_id`, and `student_id`. The data type for all columns is VARCHAR2(15), since this data type is flexible, and it can contain varying-length characters. The upper bound of the length is 15, which is determined by the number you entered in the Scale box, and it means that each column can contain up to 15 characters. Since the `user_name` is selected as the primary key for this table, check the Not Null checkbox next to this column to indicate that this column cannot contain a blank value.

Your finished first step is shown in Figure 2.44.

Click the `Next` button to go to the next page to assign the primary key for this table, which is shown in Figure 2.45.

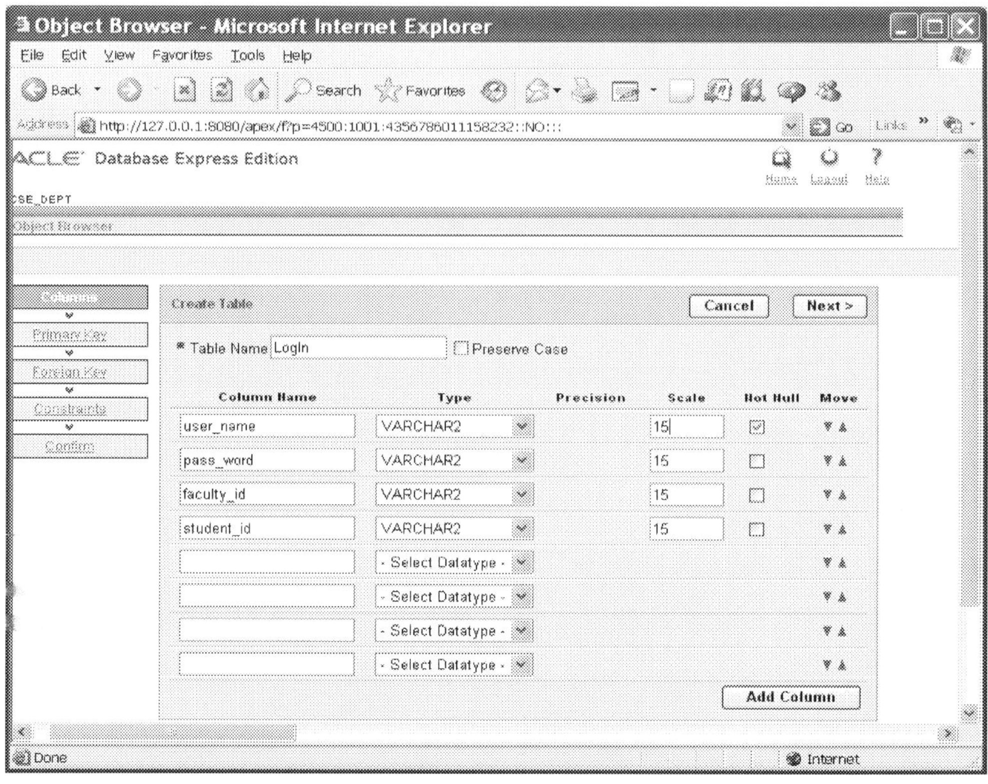

Figure 2.44. Create a new table.

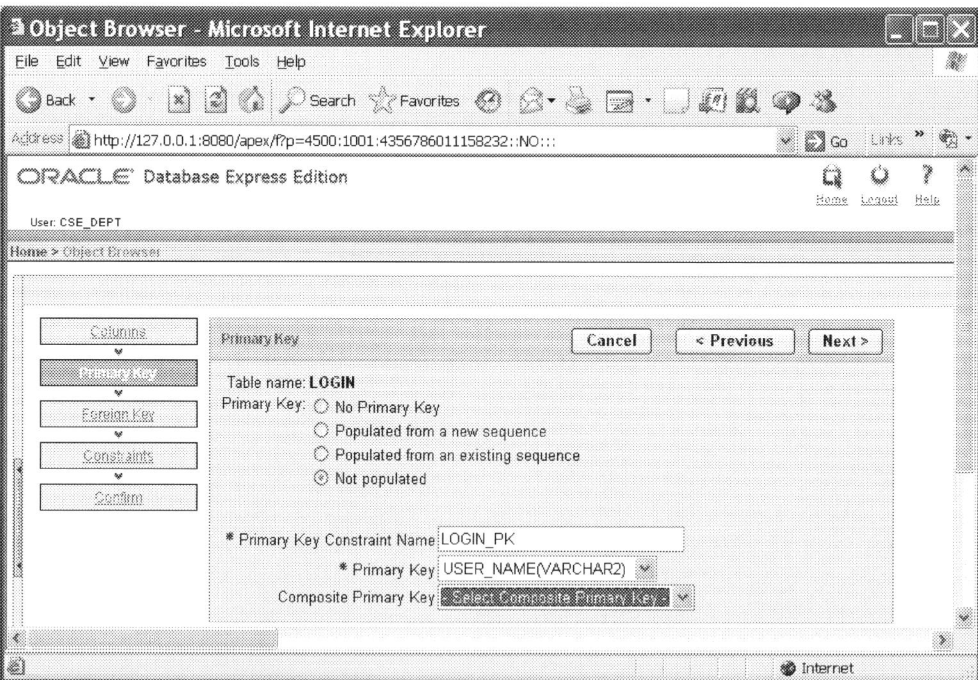

Figure 2.45. The second step—assign the primary key.

To assign a primary key to our new LogIn table, select the `Not Populated` from `the Primary Key` selection list because we don't want to use any Sequence object to assign any sequence to our primary key. The Sequence object in Oracle is used to automatically create a sequence of numeric number for the primary key. In our case, our primary key is a string, and therefore we cannot use this object. Keep the Primary Key Name, `LOGIN_PK`, unchanged, and select the `USER_NAME(VARCHAR2)` from the `Primary Key` box. In this way, we select the `user_name` as the primary key for this table. Since we do not have any Composite Primary Key for this table, just keep this box unchanged. Your finished second step should match one that is shown in Figure 2.45. Click the `Next` button to continue to the next page—Set the foreign key page.

Since we have not created any other table, therefore, we cannot select our foreign key for this LogIn table right now. We leave this job to be handled later. Click the `Next` button to go to the next page. The next page allows you to set up some constraints on this table, which is shown in Figure 2.46.

No constraint is needed for this sample database at this moment, so you can click the Finish button to go to the last page to confirm our `LogIn` table. The opened `Confirm` page is shown in Figure 2.47.

Click the `Create` button to create and confirm this new `LogIn` table. Your created LogIn table should match one that is shown in Figure 2.48 if it is successful. The new created `LogIn` table is also added into the left pane.

After the `LogIn` table is created, the necessary editing tools are attached with this table and displayed at the top of this table. The top row of these tools contains object

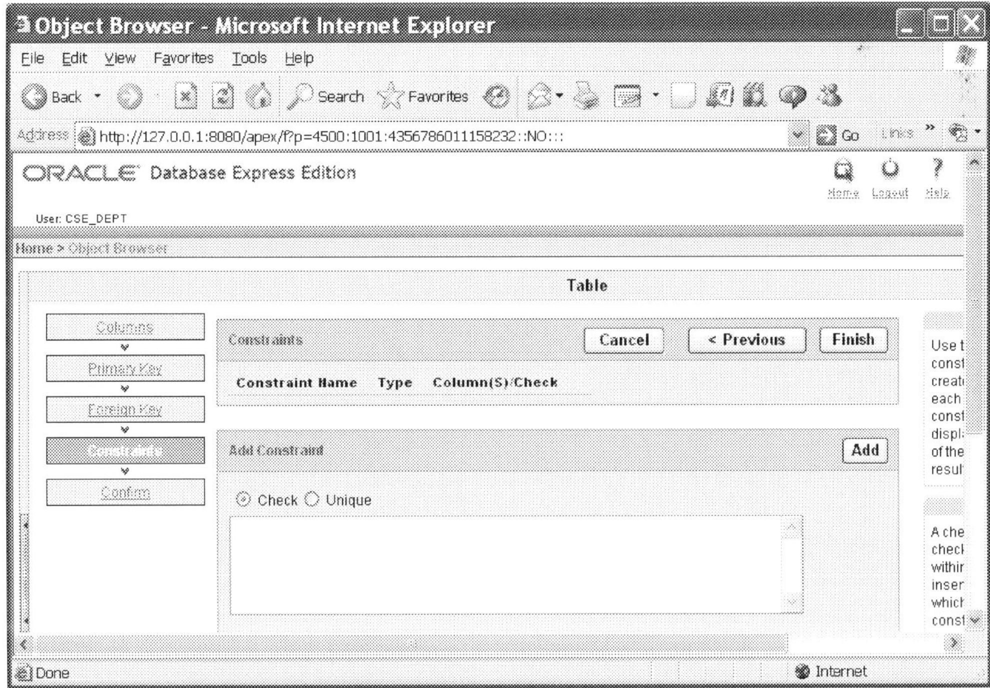

Figure 2.46. The fourth step—setup constraints.

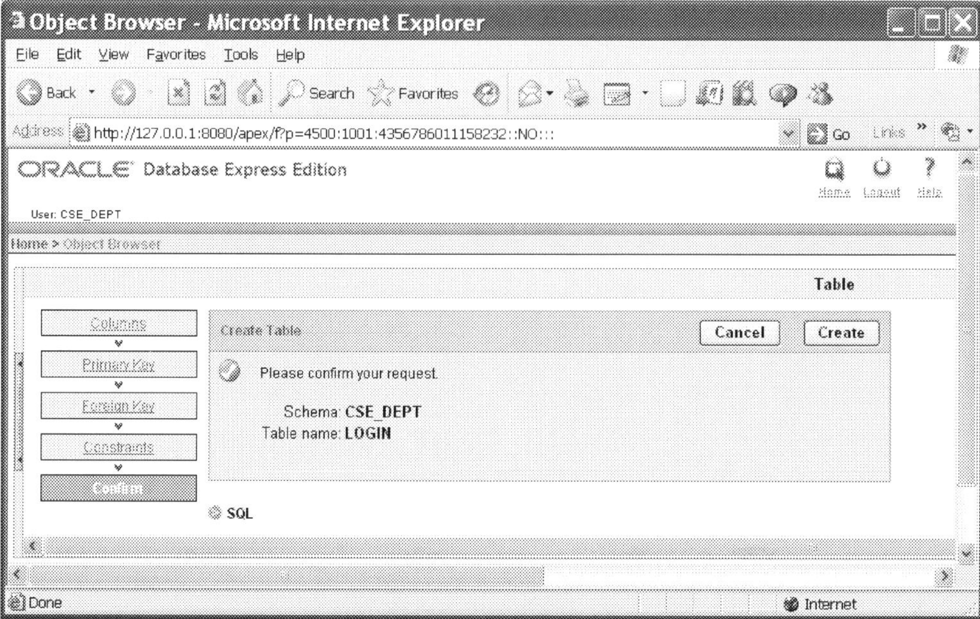

Figure 2.47. The last step—confirmation.

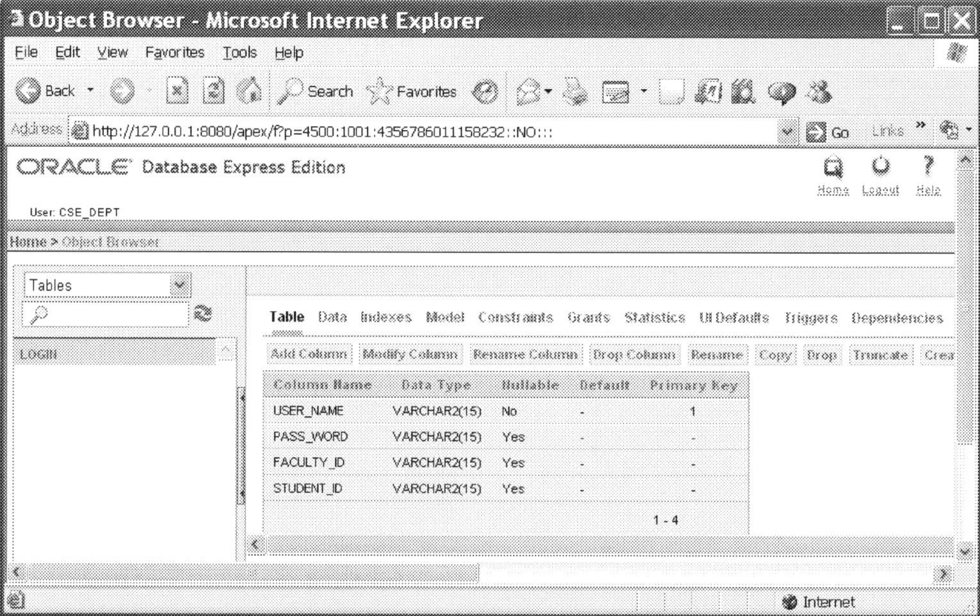

Figure 2.48. The created LogIn table.

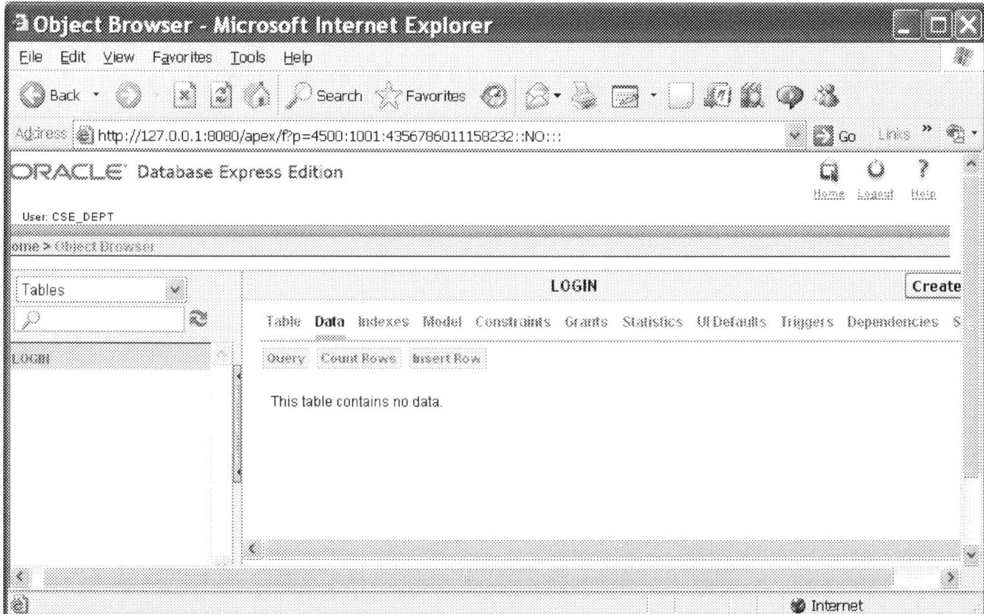

Figure 2.49. The opened Data page.

editing tools, and the bottom line includes the actual editing methods. The editing methods include Add Column, Modify Column, Rename Column, and Drop Column, and these methods are straightforward in meaning without question.

To add data into this new LogIn table, you need to use and open the Data object tool in the top row. Click the Data tool to open the Data page, which is shown in Figure 2.49.

Click the `Insert Row` button to open the data sheet view of the LogIn table, which is shown in Figure 2.50.

Add the following data into the first row: User Name—`abrown`, Pass Word—`America`, Faculty Id—B66750. Since this user is a faculty, leave the Student Id column blank (**don't place a NULL in here, otherwise you will have trouble when you create a foreign key for this table later!**). Your finished first row is shown in Figure 2.50.

Click the `Create and Create Another` button to create the next row. In the similar way, add each row that is shown in Table 2.23 into each row on the LogIn table.

You can click the `Create` button after you add the final row into your table. Your finished `LogIn` table should match one that is shown in Figure 2.51.

Next, let's create our second table—Faculty table.

2.11.2.2 Create the Faculty Table

Click the `Table` tool on the top raw and click the `Create` button to create another new table. Select the `Table` item to open a new table page. Enter `Faculty` into the `Table Name` box as the name for this new table, and enter the following columns into this new table:

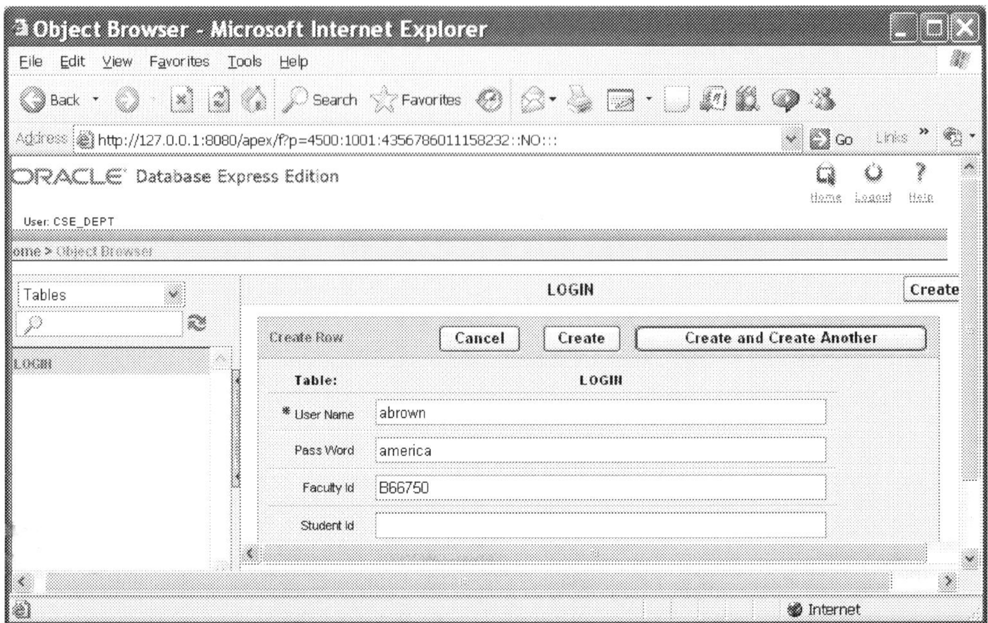

Figure 2.50. The opened data sheet view of the LogIn table.

Table 2.23. The data in the LogIn table

user_name	pass_word	faculty_id	student_id
abrown	america	B66750	
ajade	tryagain		A97850
awoods	smart		A78835
banderson	birthday	A52990	
bvalley	see		B92996
dangles	tomorrow	A77587	
hsmith	try		H10210
jerica	excellent		J77896
jhenry	test	H99118	
jking	goodman	K69880	
sbhalla	india	B86590	
sjohnson	jermany	J33486	
ybai	reback	B78880	

- faculty_id—VARCHAR2(10)
- faculty_name—VARCHAR2 (20)
- office—VARCHAR2 (10)
- phone—CHAR(12)
- college—VARCHAR2 (50)

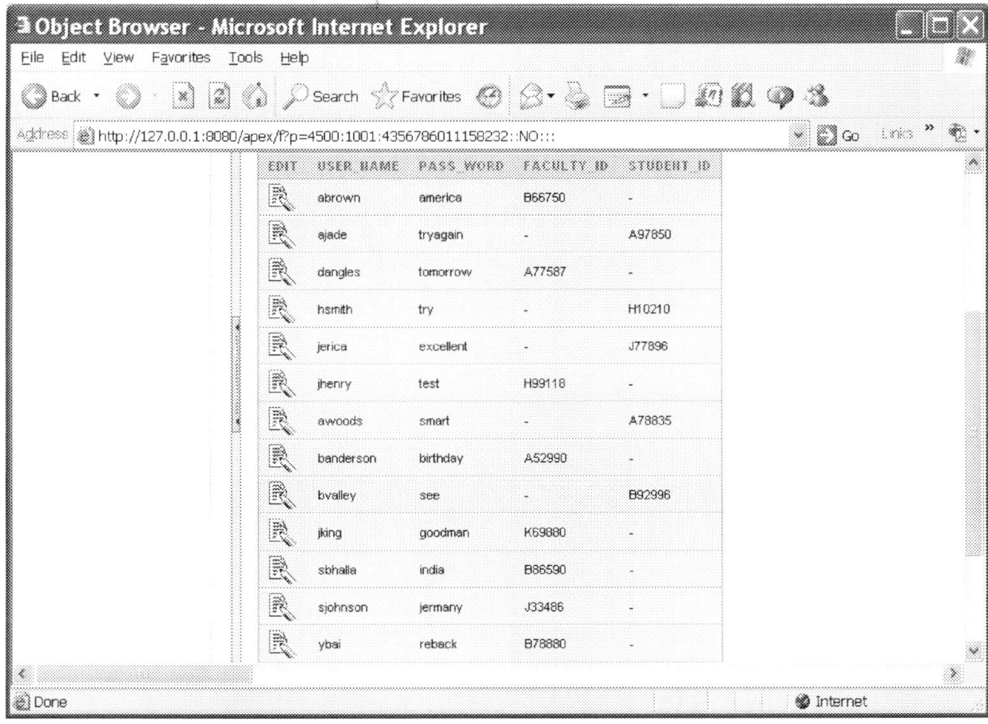

EDIT	USER NAME	PASS WORD	FACULTY ID	STUDENT ID
	abrown	america	B66750	-
	ajade	tryagain	-	A97850
	dangles	tomorrow	A77587	-
	hsmith	try	-	H10210
	jerica	excellent	-	J77896
	jhenry	test	H99118	-
	awoods	smart	-	A78835
	banderson	birthday	A52990	-
	bvalley	see	-	B92996
	jking	goodman	K69880	-
	sbhalla	india	B86590	-
	sjohnson	jermany	J33486	-
	ybai	reback	B78880	-

Figure 2.51. The completed LogIn table.

- title—VARCHAR2 (30)
- email—VARCHAR2 (30)

The popular data types used in the Oracle database include NUMBER, CHAR, and VARCHAR2. Each data type has its upper bound and low bound. The difference between the CHAR and the VARCHAR2 is that the former is used to store a fixed-length string, and the latter can provide a varying-length string, which means that the real length of the string depends on the number of real letters entered by the user. The data types for all columns are VARCHAR2 with one exception, which is the phone column that has a CHAR type with an upper bound of 12 letters, since our phone number is composed of 10 digits, and we can extend this length to 12 with two dashes. For all other columns, the length varies with the different information, so the VARCHAR2 is selected for those columns.

The finished design view of your Faculty table is shown in Figure 2.52. You need to check the `Not Null` checkbox for the faculty_`id` column, since we selected this column as the primary key for this table.

Click the `Next` button to go to the next page to add the primary key for this table, which is shown in Figure 2.53.

Check the `Not Populated from the Primary Key` list since we don't want to use any Sequence object to automatically generate a sequence of numeric number as our primary key, and then select the `FACULTY_ID(VARCHAR2)` from the `Primary Key`

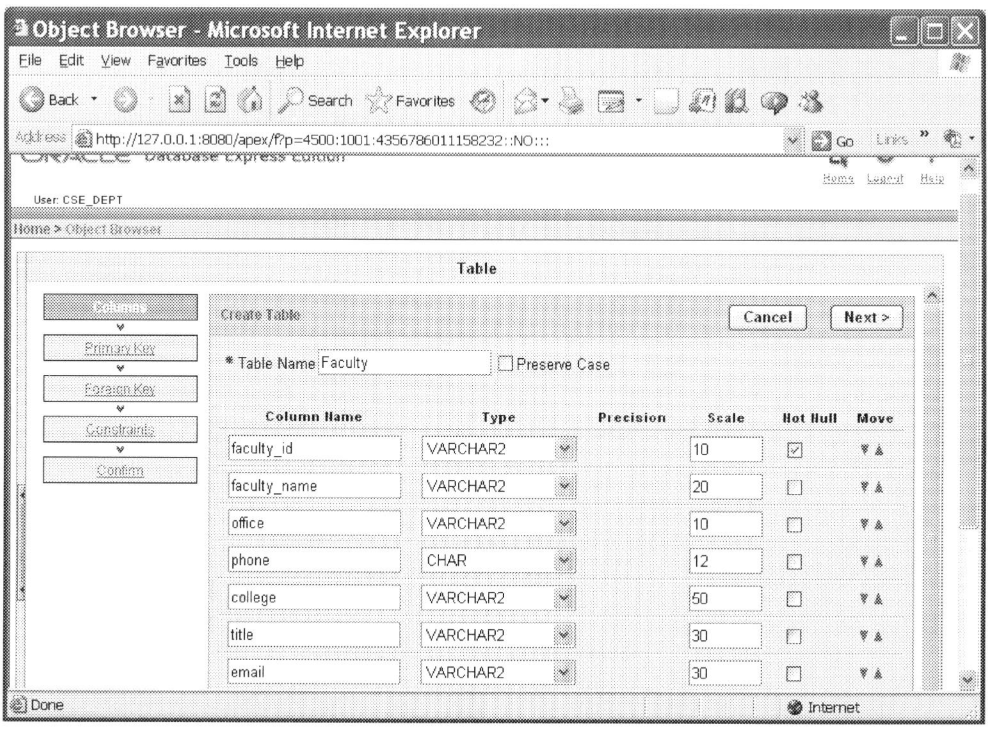

Figure 2.52. The finished design view of the Faculty table.

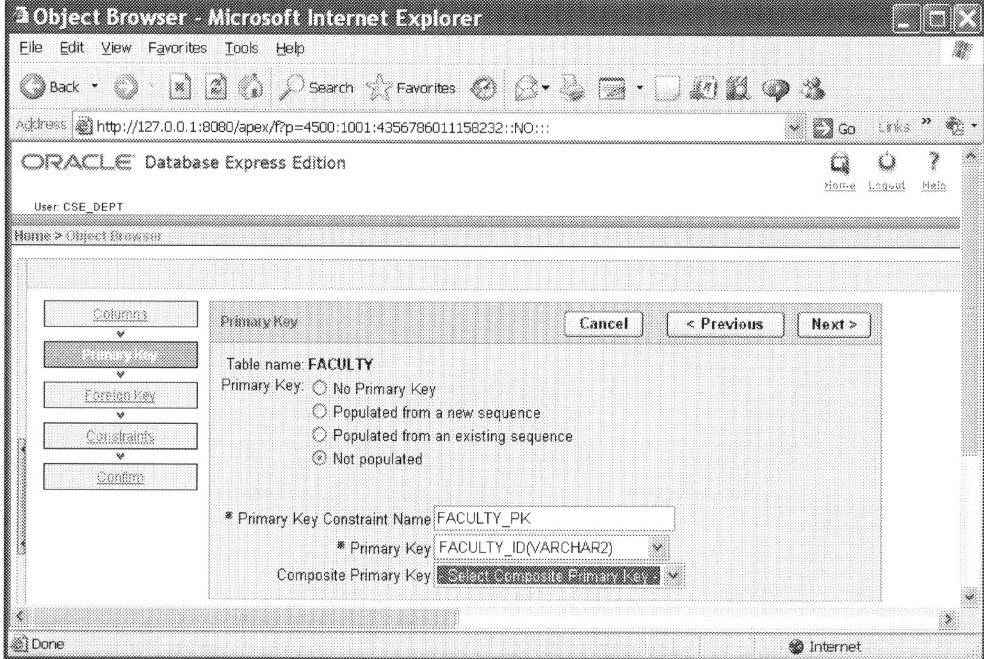

Figure 2.53. The opened Primary Key window.

textbox. In this way, the `faculty_id` column is selected as the primary key for this table. Keep the Composite Primary Key box untouched, since we do not have that kind of key in this table, and click the Next button to go to the next page.

Since we have not created all other tables to work as our reference tables for the foreign key, click the Next to continue and we will do the foreign key for this table later. Click the Finish button to go to the Confirm page. Finally, click the Create button to create this new Faculty table. Your completed columns in the Faculty table are shown in Figure 2.54.

Now click the `Data` object tool to add the data into this new table. Click the `Insert Row` button to add all rows that are shown in Table 2.24 into this table.

Click the `Create and Create Another` button when the first row is done, and continue to create all rows with the data shown in Table 2.24. You may click the Create

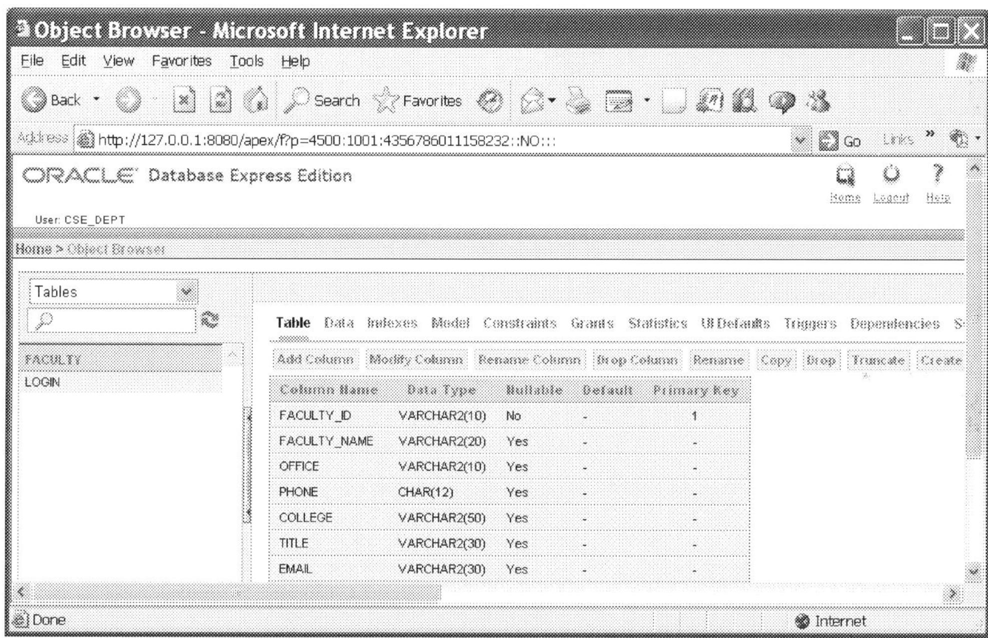

Figure 2.54. The completed columns in the Faculty table.

Table 2.24. The data in the Faculty table

faculty_id	faculty_name	office	phone	college	title	email
A52990	Black Anderson	MTC-218	750-378-9987	Virginia Tech	Professor	banderson@college.edu
A77587	Debby Angles	MTC-320	750-330-2276	University of Chicago	Associate Professor	dangles@college.edu
B66750	Alice Brown	MTC-257	750-330-6650	University of Florida	Assistant Professor	abrown@college.edu
B78880	Ying Bai	MTC-211	750-378-1148	Florida Atlantic University	Associate Professor	ybai@college.edu
B86590	Satish Bhalla	MTC-214	750-378-1061	University of Notre Dame	Associate Professor	sbhalla@college.edu
H99118	Jeff Henry	MTC-336	750-330-8650	Ohio State University	Associate Professor	jhenry@college.edu
J33486	Steve Johnson	MTC-118	750-330-1116	Harvard University	Distinguished Professor	sjohnson@college.edu
K69880	Jenney King	MTC-324	750-378-1230	East Florida University	Professor	jking@college.edu

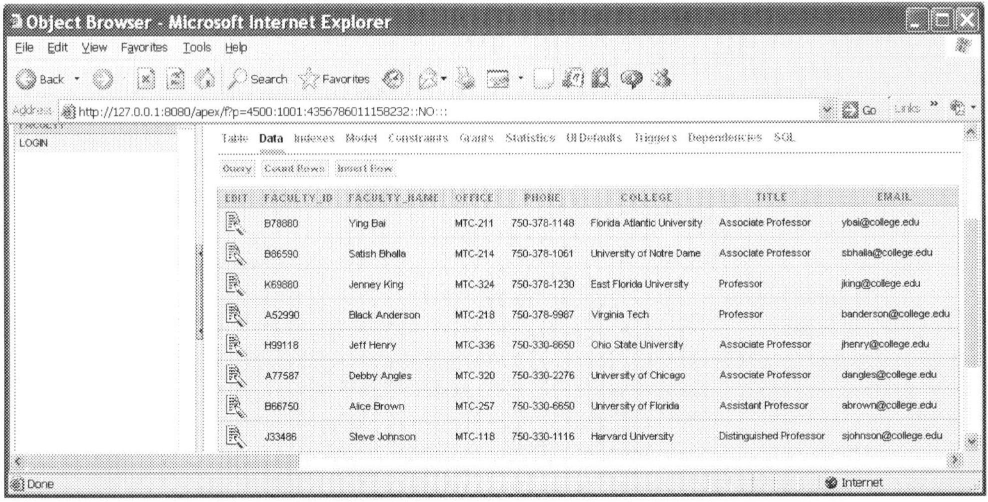

FACULTY_ID	FACULTY_NAME	OFFICE	PHONE	COLLEGE	TITLE	EMAIL
B78880	Ying Bai	MTC-211	750-378-1148	Florida Atlantic University	Associate Professor	ybai@college.edu
B86590	Satish Bhalla	MTC-214	750-378-1061	University of Notre Dame	Associate Professor	sbhalla@college.edu
K69880	Jenney King	MTC-324	750-378-1230	East Florida University	Professor	jking@college.edu
A52990	Black Anderson	MTC-218	750-378-9987	Virginia Tech	Professor	banderson@college.edu
H99118	Jeff Henry	MTC-336	750-330-8650	Ohio State University	Associate Professor	jhenry@college.edu
A77587	Debby Angles	MTC-320	750-330-2276	University of Chicago	Associate Professor	dangles@college.edu
B66750	Alice Brown	MTC-257	750-330-6650	University of Florida	Assistant Professor	abrown@college.edu
J33486	Steve Johnson	MTC-118	750-330-1116	Harvard University	Distinguished Professor	sjohnson@college.edu

Figure 2.55. The finished Faculty table.

button for your last row. Your finished Faculty table should match one that is shown in Figure 2.55.

2.11.2.3 Create Other Tables

In the similar way, you can continue to create the following three tables: `Course`, `Student`, and `StudentCourse` based on the data shown in Tables 2.25–2.27.

The data types used in the Course table are:

- course_id: VARCHAR2(10)—Primary Key
- course: VARCHAR2(40)
- credit: NUMBER(1, 0)—precision = 1, scale = 0 (1-bit integer)
- classroom: CHAR(6)
- schedule: VARCHAR2(40)
- enrollment: NUMBER(2, 0)—precision = 2, scale = 0 (2-bit integer)
- faculty_id VARCHAR2(10)

The data types used in the Student table are:

- student_id: VARCHAR2(10)—Primary Key
- student_name: VARCHAR2(20)
- gpa: NUMBER(3, 2)—precision = 3, scale = 2 (3-bit floating point data with 2-bit after the decimal point)
- credits: NUMBER(3, 0)—precision = 3, scale = 0 (3-bit integer)
- major: VARCHAR2(40)

Table 2.25. The data in the Course table

course_id	course	credit	classroom	schedule	enrollment	faculty_id
CSC-131A	Computers in Society	3	TC-109	M-W-F: 9:00-9:55 AM	28	A52990
CSC-131B	Computers in Society	3	TC-114	M-W-F: 9:00-9:55 AM	20	B66750
CSC-131C	Computers in Society	3	TC-109	T-H: 11:00-12:25 PM	25	A52990
CSC-131D	Computers in Society	3	TC-119	M-W-F: 9:00-9:55 AM	30	B86590
CSC-131E	Computers in Society	3	TC-301	M-W-F: 1:00-1:55 PM	25	B66750
CSC-131F	Computers in Society	3	TC-109	T-H: 1:00-2:25 PM	32	A52990
CSC-132A	Introduction to Programming	3	TC-303	M-W-F: 9:00-9:55 AM	21	J33486
CSC-132B	Introduction to Programming	3	TC-302	T-H: 1:00-2:25 PM	21	B78880
CSC-230	Algorithms & Structures	3	TC-301	M-W-F: 1:00-1:55 PM	20	A77587
CSC-232A	Programming I	3	TC-305	T-H: 11:00-12:25 PM	28	B66750
CSC-232B	Programming I	3	TC-303	T-H: 11:00-12:25 PM	17	A77587
CSC-233A	Introduction to Algorithms	3	TC-302	M-W-F: 9:00-9:55 AM	18	H99118
CSC-233B	Introduction to Algorithms	3	TC-302	M-W-F: 11:00-11:55 AM	19	K69880
CSC-234A	Data Structure & Algorithms	3	TC-302	M-W-F: 9:00-9:55 AM	25	B78880
CSC-234B	Data Structure & Algorithms	3	TC-114	T-H: 11:00-12:25 PM	15	J33486
CSC-242	Programming II	3	TC-303	T-H: 1:00-2:25 PM	18	A52990
CSC-320	Object Oriented Programming	3	TC-301	T-H: 1:00-2:25 PM	22	B66750
CSC-331	Applications Programming	3	TC-109	T-H: 11:00-12:25 PM	28	H99118
CSC-333A	Computer Arch & Algorithms	3	TC-301	M-W-F: 10:00-10:55 AM	22	A77587
CSC-333B	Computer Arch & Algorithms	3	TC-302	T-H: 11:00-12:25 PM	15	A77587
CSC-335	Internet Programming	3	TC-303	M-W-F: 1:00-1:55 PM	25	B66750
CSC-432	Discrete Algorithms	3	TC-206	T-H: 11:00-12:25 PM	20	B86590
CSC-439	Database Systems	3	TC-206	M-W-F: 1:00-1:55 PM	18	B86590
CSE-138A	Introduction to CSE	3	TC-301	T-H: 1:00-2:25 PM	15	A52990
CSE-138B	Introduction to CSE	3	TC-109	T-H: 1:00-2:25 PM	35	J33486
CSE-330	Digital Logic Circuits	3	TC-305	M-W-F: 9:00-9:55 AM	26	K69880
CSE-332	Foundations of Semiconductors	3	TC-305	T-H: 1:00-2:25 PM	24	K69880
CSE-334	Elec Measurement & Design	3	TC-212	T-H: 11:00-12:25 PM	25	H99118
CSE-430	Bioinformatics in Computer	3	TC-206	Thu: 9:30-11:00 AM	16	B86590
CSE-432	Analog Circuits Design	3	TC-309	M-W-F: 2:00-2:55 PM	18	K69880
CSE-433	Digital Signal Processing	3	TC-206	T-H: 2:00-3:25 PM	18	H99118
CSE-434	Advanced Electronics Systems	3	TC-213	M-W-F: 1:00-1:55 PM	26	B78880
CSE-436	Automatic Control and Design	3	TC-305	M-W-F: 10:00-10:55 AM	29	J33486
CSE-437	Operating Systems	3	TC-303	T-H: 1:00-2:25 PM	17	A77587
CSE-438	Advd Logic & Microprocessor	3	TC-213	M-W-F: 11:00-11:55 AM	35	B78880
CSE-439	Special Topics in CSE	3	TC-206	M-W-F: 10:00-10:55 AM	22	J33486

Table 2.26. The data in the student table

student_id	student_name	gpa	credits	major	schoolYear	email
A78835	Andrew Woods	3.26	108	Computer Science	Senior	awoods@college.edu
A97850	Ashly Jade	3.57	116	Information System Engineering	Junior	ajade@college.edu
B92996	Blue Valley	3.52	102	Computer Science	Senior	bvalley@college.edu
H10210	Holes Smith	3.87	78	Computer Engineering	Sophomore	hsmith@college.edu
J77896	Erica Johnson	3.95	127	Computer Science	Senior	ejohnson@college.edu

Table 2.27. The data in the StudentCourse table

s_course_id	student_id	course_id	credit	major
1000	H10210	CSC-131D	3	CE
1001	B92996	CSC-132A	3	CS/IS
1002	J77896	CSC-335	3	CS/IS
1003	A78835	CSC-331	3	CE
1004	H10210	CSC-234B	3	CE
1005	J77896	CSC-234A	3	CS/IS
1006	B92996	CSC-233A	3	CS/IS
1007	A78835	CSC-132A	3	CE
1008	A78835	CSE-432	3	CE
1009	A78835	CSE-434	3	CE
1010	J77896	CSC-439	3	CS/IS
1011	H10210	CSC-132A	3	CE
1012	H10210	CSC-331	3	CE
1013	A78835	CSC-335	3	CE
1014	A78835	CSE-438	3	CE
1015	J77896	CSC-432	3	CS/IS
1016	A97850	CSC-132B	3	ISE
1017	A97850	CSC-234A	3	ISE
1018	A97850	CSC-331	3	ISE
1019	A97850	CSC-335	3	ISE
1020	J77896	CSE-439	3	CS/IS
1021	B92996	CSC-230	3	CS/IS
1022	A78835	CSE-332	3	CE
1023	B92996	CSE-430	3	CE
1024	J77896	CSC-333A	3	CS/IS
1025	H10210	CSE-433	3	CE
1026	H10210	CSE-334	3	CE
1027	B92996	CSC-131C	3	CS/IS
1028	B92996	CSC-439	3	CS/IS

- schoolYear: VARCHAR2(20)
- email: VARCHAR2(20)

The data types used in the StudentCourse table are:

- s_course_id: NUMBER(4, 0)—precision = 4, scale = 0 (4-bit integer) Primary Key
- student_id: VARCHAR2(10)
- course_id: VARCHAR2(10)
- credit: NUMBER(1, 0)—precision = 1, scale = 0 (1-bit integer)
- major: VARCHAR2(40)

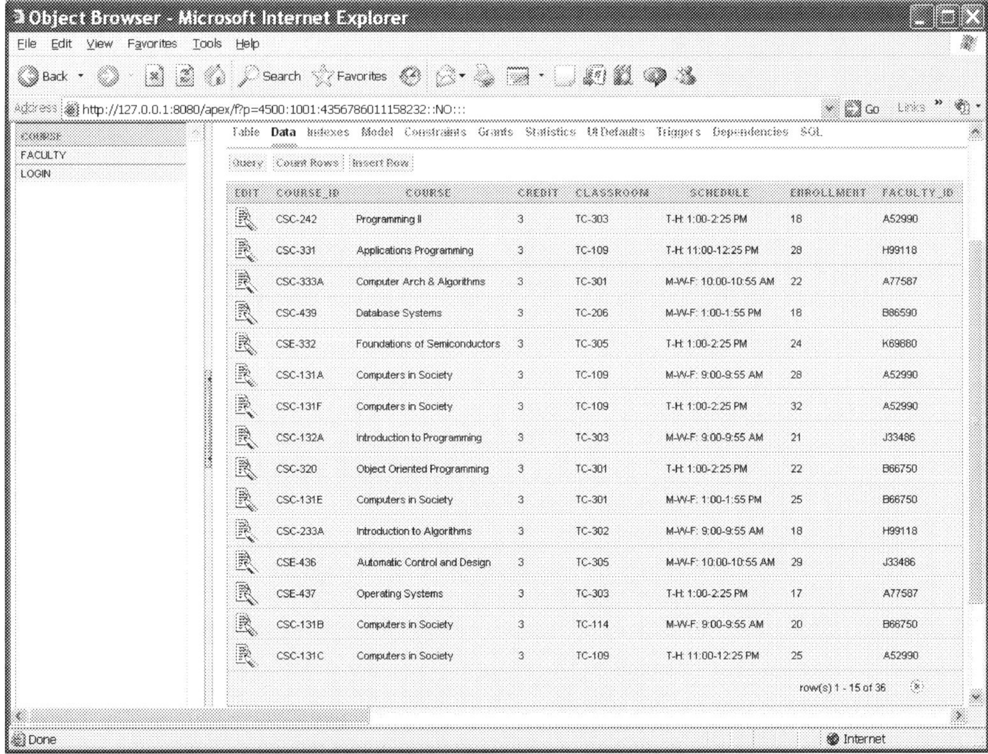

EDIT	COURSE_ID	COURSE	CREDIT	CLASSROOM	SCHEDULE	ENROLLMENT	FACULTY_ID
	CSC-242	Programming II	3	TC-303	T-H: 1:00-2:25 PM	18	A52990
	CSC-331	Applications Programming	3	TC-109	T-H: 11:00-12:25 PM	28	H99118
	CSC-333A	Computer Arch & Algorithms	3	TC-301	M-W-F: 10:00-10:55 AM	22	A77587
	CSC-439	Database Systems	3	TC-206	M-W-F: 1:00-1:55 PM	18	B86590
	CSE-332	Foundations of Semiconductors	3	TC-305	T-H: 1:00-2:25 PM	24	K69880
	CSC-131A	Computers in Society	3	TC-109	M-W-F: 9:00-9:55 AM	28	A52990
	CSC-131F	Computers in Society	3	TC-109	T-H: 1:00-2:25 PM	32	A52990
	CSC-132A	Introduction to Programming	3	TC-303	M-W-F: 9:00-9:55 AM	21	J33486
	CSC-320	Object Oriented Programming	3	TC-301	T-H: 1:00-2:25 PM	22	B66750
	CSC-131E	Computers in Society	3	TC-301	M-W-F: 1:00-1:55 PM	25	B66750
	CSC-233A	Introduction to Algorithms	3	TC-302	M-W-F: 9:00-9:55 AM	18	H99118
	CSE-436	Automatic Control and Design	3	TC-305	M-W-F: 10:00-10:55 AM	29	J33486
	CSE-437	Operating Systems	3	TC-303	T-H: 1:00-2:25 PM	17	A77587
	CSC-131B	Computers in Society	3	TC-114	M-W-F: 9:00-9:55 AM	20	B66750
	CSC-131C	Computers in Society	3	TC-109	T-H: 11:00-12:25 PM	25	A52990

Figure 2.56. The completed Course table.

Your finished `Course`, `Student`, and `StudentCourse` tables are shown in Figures 2.56–2.58, respectively.

2.11.3 Create the Constraints Between Tables

Now it is the time for us to set up the relationships between our five tables using the Primary and Foreign keys. Since we have already selected the Primary key for each table when we create and build those tables, therefore, we only need to take care of the Foreign keys and connect them with the associated Primary keys in the related tables. Let's start from the first table, LogIn table.

2.11.3.1 Create the Constraints between the LogIn and Faculty Tables

Now let's create the constraints between the LogIn and the Faculty tables by using a foreign key. Exactly, create a foreign key for the LogIn table and connect it to the primary key in the Faculty table. The faculty_id is a foreign key in the LogIn table but it is a primary key in the Faculty table. A one-to-many relationship is existed between the faculty_id in the Faculty table and the faculty_id in the LogIn table.

EDIT	STUDENT_ID	STUDENT_NAME	GPA	CREDITS	MAJOR	SCHOOLYEAR	EMAIL
	J77896	Erica Johnson	3.95	127	Computer Science	Senior	ejohnson@college.edu
	A78835	Andrew Woods	3.26	108	Computer Science	Senior	awoods@college.edu
	A97850	Ashly Jade	3.57	116	Information System Engineering	Junior	ajade@college.edu
	B92996	Blue Valley	3.52	102	Computer Science	Senior	bvalley@college.edu
	H10210	Holes Smith	3.87	78	Computer Engineering	Sophomore	hsmith@college.edu

row(s) 1 - 5 of 5

Figure 2.57. The completed Student table.

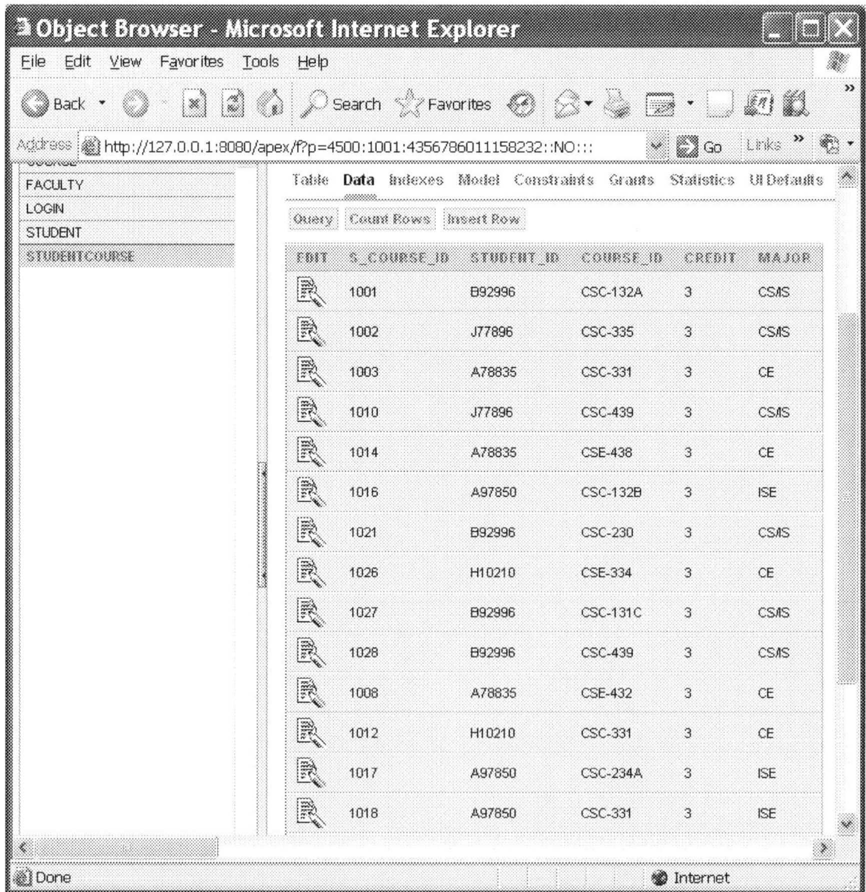

EDIT	S_COURSE_ID	STUDENT_ID	COURSE_ID	CREDIT	MAJOR
	1001	B92996	CSC-132A	3	CS/IS
	1002	J77896	CSC-335	3	CS/IS
	1003	A78835	CSC-331	3	CE
	1010	J77896	CSC-439	3	CS/IS
	1014	A78835	CSE-438	3	CE
	1016	A97850	CSC-132B	3	ISE
	1021	B92996	CSC-230	3	CS/IS
	1026	H10210	CSE-334	3	CE
	1027	B92996	CSC-131C	3	CS/IS
	1028	B92996	CSC-439	3	CS/IS
	1008	A78835	CSE-432	3	CE
	1012	H10210	CSC-331	3	CE
	1017	A97850	CSC-234A	3	ISE
	1018	A97850	CSC-331	3	ISE

Figure 2.58. The completed StudentCourse table.

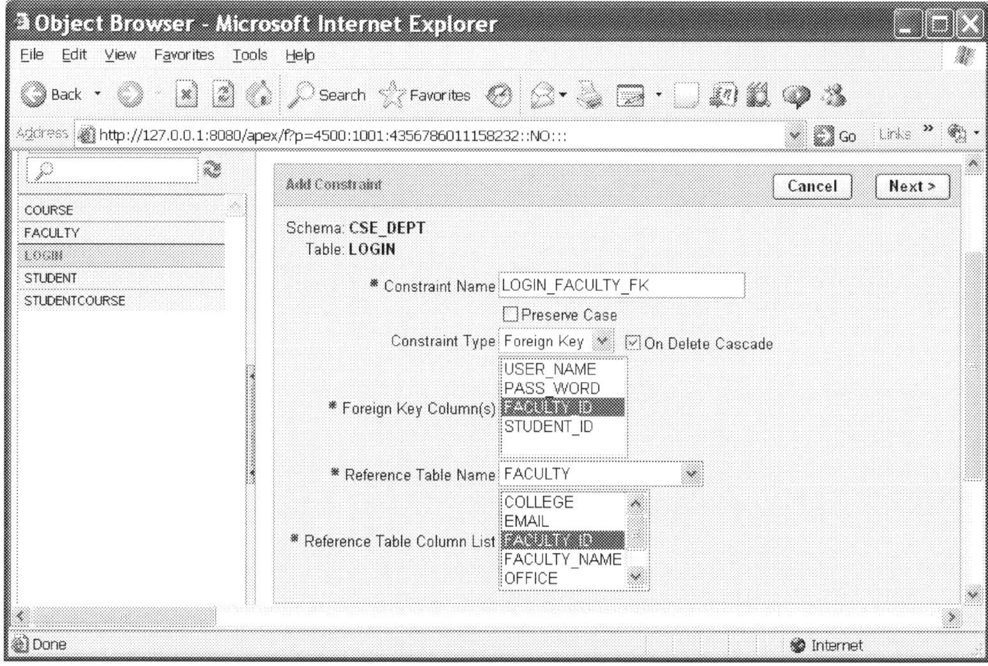

Figure 2.59. Create the foreign key between the LogIn and the Faculty table.

Log on the Oracle Database 10g XE using the customer username, CSE_DEPT and the customer database password, and then open the home page of the Oracle Database 10g XE. Click the Object Browser icon and select Browse|Table to list all tables. Select the LogIn table from the left pane to open it, click the Constraints tab, and then click the Create button that is the first button in the second row. Enter LOGIN_FACULTY_FK into the Constraint Name box, and select the Foreign Key from the Constraint Type box, which is shown in Figure 2.59. Check the `On Delete Cascade` checkbox. Then select the FACULTY_ID from the LogIn table as the foreign key column. Select the FACULTY table from the Reference Table Name box as the reference table, and select the FACULTY_ID from the Reference Table Column List as the reference table column. Your finished Add Constraint window should match one that is shown in Figure 2.59.

Click the Next button to go to the next window, and then click the Finish button to confirm this foreign key's creation.

2.11.3.2 Create the Constraints between the LogIn and Student Tables

The relationship between the Student table and the LogIn table is a one-to-many relationship. The student_id in the Student table is a primary key, but the student_id in the LogIn table is a foreign key. Multiple student_id can be existed in the LogIn table, but only one or unique student_id can be found from the Student table.

To create a foreign key from the LogIn table and connect it to the primary key in the Student table, open the LogIn table if it is not opened, and click the Constraints tab, and then click the Create button that is the first button in the second row to open the

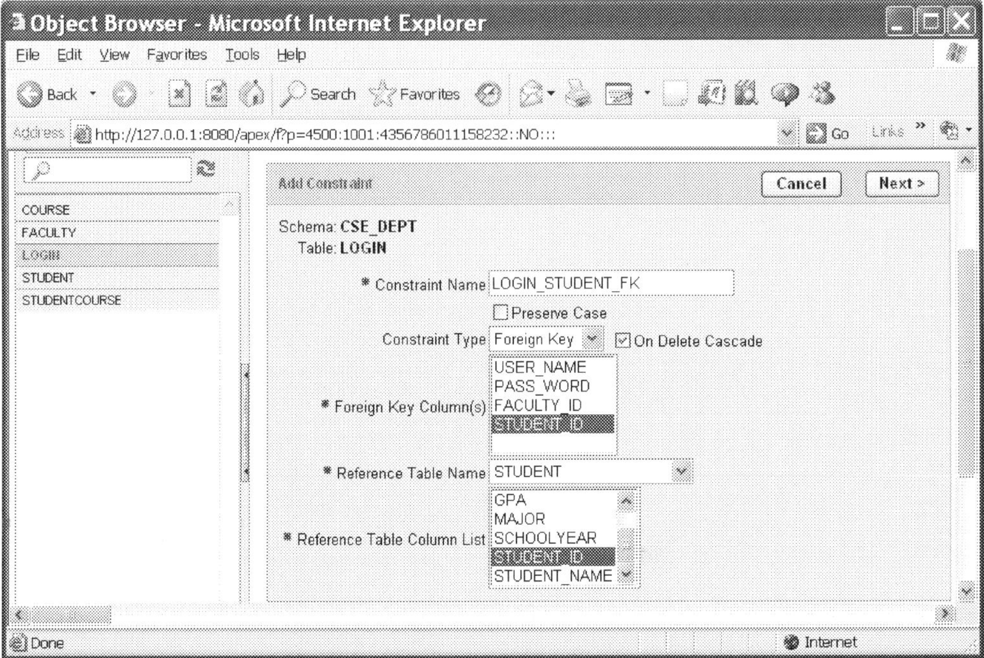

Figure 2.60. Create the foreign key between the LogIn and the Student table.

Add Constraint window. Enter LOGIN_STUDENT_FK into the Constraint Name box, and select the Foreign Key from the Constraint Type box, which is shown in Figure 2.60. Check the `On Delete Cascade` checkbox. Then select the STUDENT_ID from the LogIn table as the foreign key column. Select the STUDENT table from the Reference Table Name box as the reference table, and select the STUDENT_ID from the Reference Table Column List as the reference table column. Your finished Add Constraint window should match one that is shown in Figure 2.60.

Recall that when we created the LogIn table in Section 2.11.2.1, we emphasized that for the blank fields in both faculty_id and student_id columns, don't place a NULL into these fields and just leave those fields blank. The reason for this is that an ALTER TABLE command will be issued when you create a foreign key for the LogIn table, and the NULL cannot be recognized by this command; therefore, an error ORA-02298 occurs, and your creation of foreign key will fail.

Click the Next button to go to the next window, and then click the Finish button to confirm this foreign key's creation. Your finished foreign key creation window for the LogIn table should match one that is shown in Figure 2.61.

2.11.3.3 Create the Constraints between the Course and Faculty Tables

The relationship between the Faculty table and the Course table is a one-to-many relationship. The faculty_id in the Faculty table is a primary key, but it is a foreign key in the Course table. This means that only unique faculty_id is existed in the Faculty table but

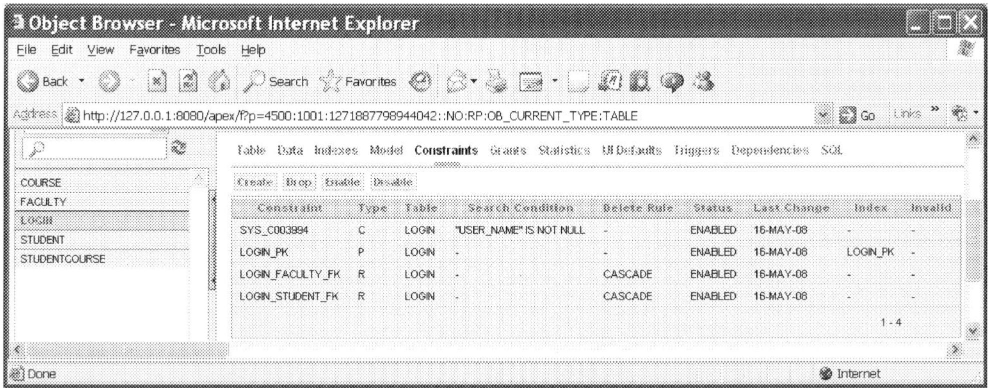

Figure 2.61. The finished foreign key creation window for the LogIn table.

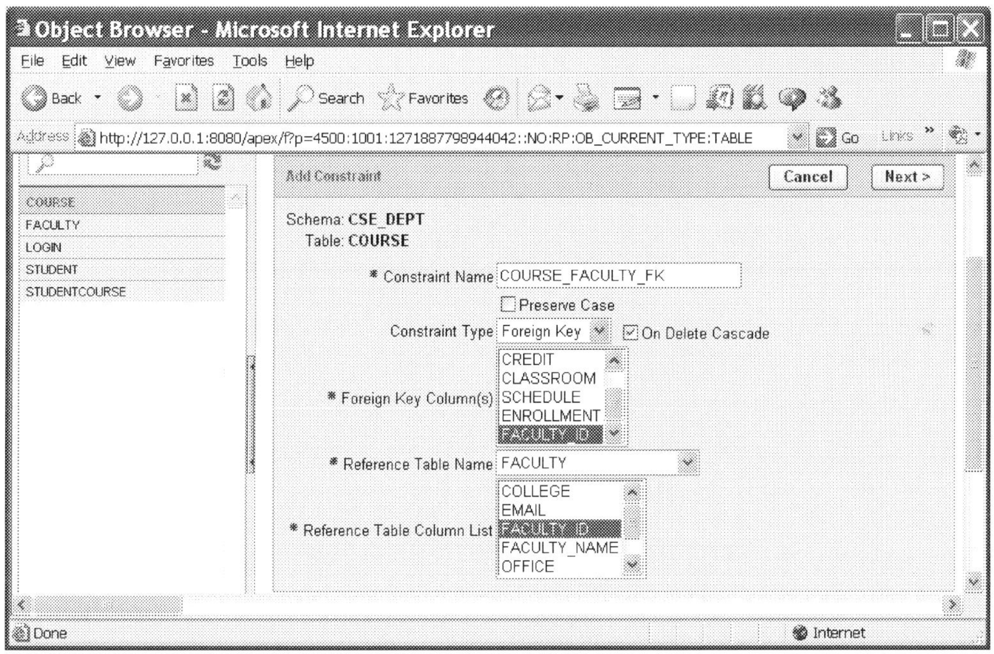

Figure 2.62. Create the foreign key between the Course and the Faculty table.

multiple faculty_id can be existed in the Course table since one faculty can teach multiple courses.

Open the Course table by clicking it from the left pane. Click the Constraints tab and then click the Create button. Enter COURSE_FACULTY_FK into the Constraint Name box, and select the Foreign Key from the Constraint Type box, which is shown in Figure 2.62. Check the `On Delete Cascade` checkbox. Then select the FACULTY_ID from the Course table as the foreign key column. Select the FACULTY table from the Reference Table Name box as the reference table, and select the FACULTY_ID from the Reference

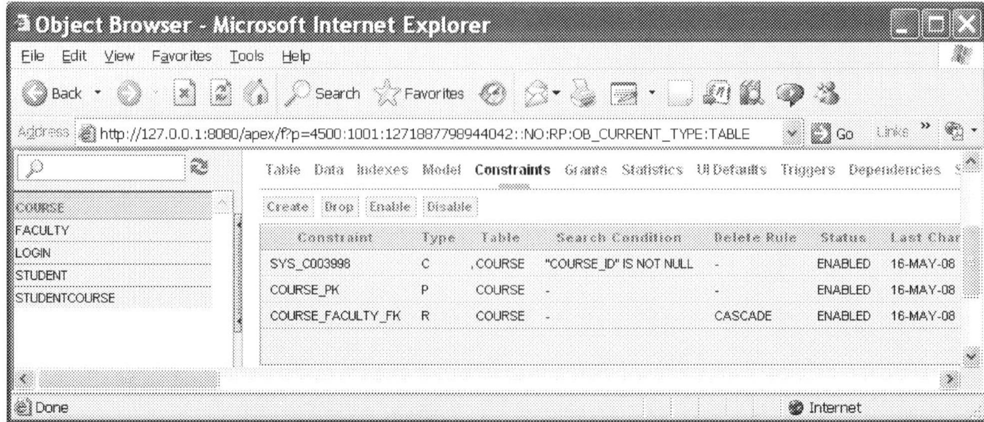

Figure 2.63. The finished foreign key creation window for the Course table.

Table Column List as the reference table column. Your finished Add Constraint window should match one that is shown in Figure 2.62.

Click the Next button to go to the next window, and then click the Finish button to confirm this foreign key's creation. Your finished foreign key creation window for the Course table should match one that is shown in Figure 2.63.

2.11.3.4 Create the Constraints between the StudentCourse and Student Tables

The relationship between the Student table and the StudentCourse table is a one-to-many relationship. The primary key student_id in the Student table is a foreign key in the StudentCourse table, since one student can take multiple different courses. In order to create this relationship by using the foreign key, first, let's open the StudentCourse table.

Click the Constraints tab and then click the Create button that is the first button on the second row. Enter STUDENTCOURSE_STUDENT_FK into the Constraint Name box, and select the Foreign Key from the Constraint Type box, which is shown in Figure 2.64. Check the `On Delete Cascade` checkbox. Then select the STUDENT_ID from the StudentCourse table as the foreign key column. Select the STUDENT table from the Reference Table Name box as the reference table, and select the STUDENT_ID from the Reference Table Column List as the reference table column. Your finished Add Constraint window should match one that is shown in Figure 2.64.

Click the Next button to go to the next window, and then click the Finish button to confirm this foreign key's creation.

2.11.3.5 Create the Constraints between the StudentCourse and Course Tables

The relationship between the Course table and the StudentCourse table is one-to-many relationship. The primary key course_id in the Course table is a foreign key in the

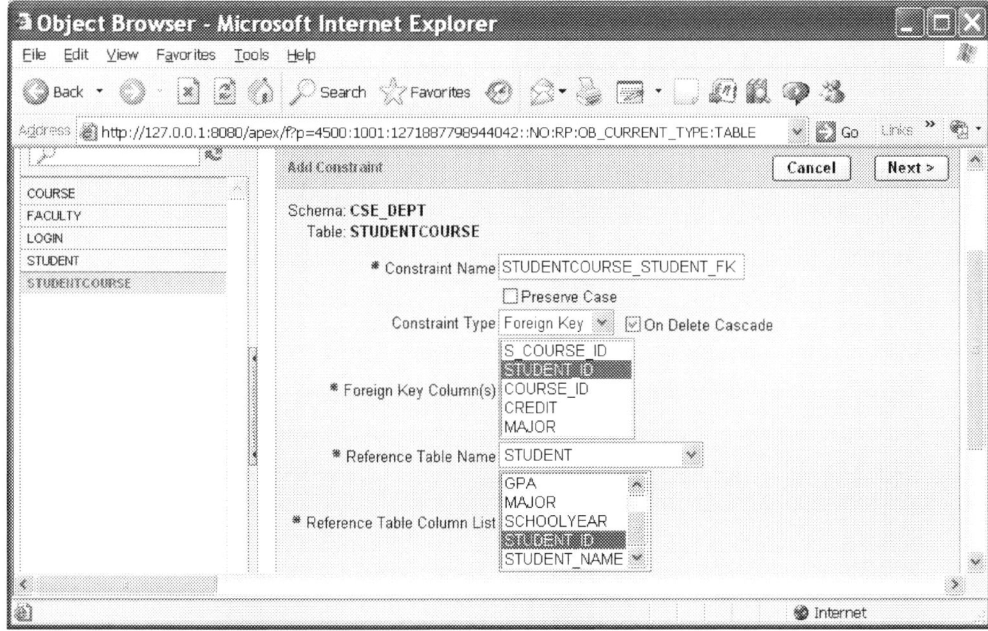

Figure 2.64. Create the foreign key between the StudentCourse and the Student table.

StudentCourse table, since one course can be taken by multiple different students. By using the StudentCourse table as an intermediate table, a many-to-many relationship can be built between the Student table and the Course table.

To create this relationship by using the foreign key, open the StudentCourse table by clicking it from the left pane. Click the Constraints tab and then click the Create button, which is the first button on the second row. Enter STUDENTCOURSE_COURSE_FK into the Constraint Name box, and select the Foreign Key from the Constraint Type box, which is shown in Figure 2.65. Check the `On Delete Cascade` checkbox. Then select the COURSE_ID from the StudentCourse table as the foreign key column. Select the COURSE table from the Reference Table Name box as the reference table, and select the COURSE_ID from the Reference Table Column List as the reference table column. Your finished Add Constraint window should match one that is shown in Figure 2.65.

Click the Next button to go to the next window, and then click the Finish button to confirm this foreign key's creation. Your finished foreign key creation window for the StudentCourse table should match one that is shown in Figure 2.66.

Our customer database creation for Oracle Database 10g Express Edition is completed. A completed Oracle 10g XE sample database CSE_DEPT that is represented by a group of table files can be found from the folder **Oracle** that is located at the site http://www.xxxxxx.org/bai/database.

At this point, we have finished developing and creating all sample databases we need to use later. All of these sample databases will be utilized for the different applications we will develop in this book.

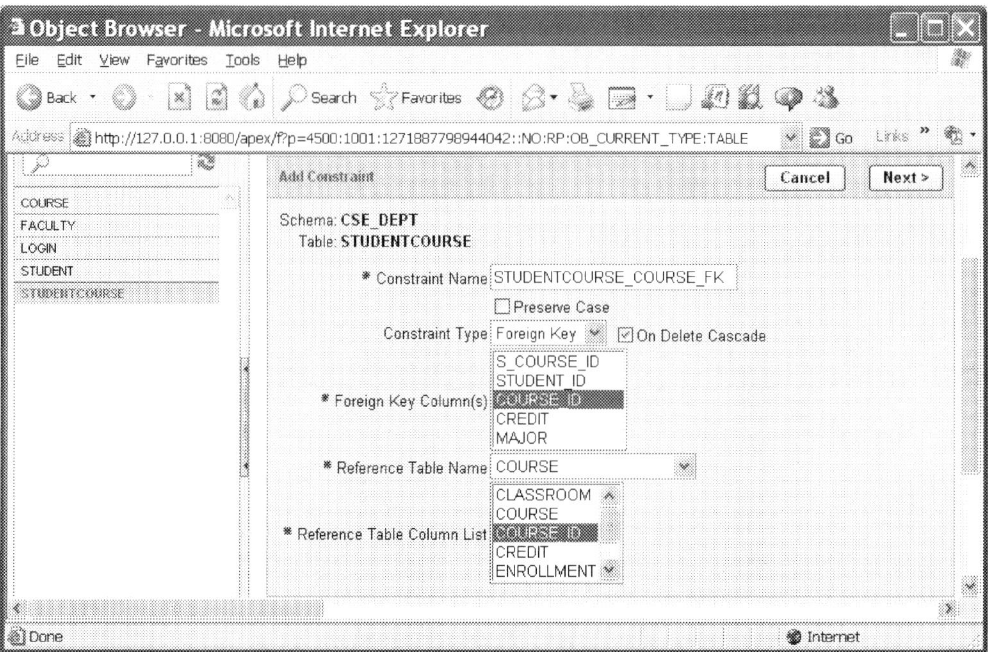

Figure 2.65. Create the foreign key between the StudentCourse and the Course table.

Object Browser - Microsoft Internet Explorer

Address http://127.0.0.1:8080/apex/f?p=4500:1001:1271887798944042::NO:RP:OB_CURRENT_TYPE:TABLE

Table Data Indexes Model **Constraints** Grants Statistics UI Defaults Triggers Dependencies SQL

Create Drop Enable Disable

Constraint	Type	Table	Search Condition	Delete Rule	Status	Last Change	Index	Invalid
SYS_C004002	C	STUDENTCOURSE	"S_COURSE_ID" IS NOT NULL	-	ENABLED	16-MAY-08	-	-
STUDENTCOURSE_PK	P	STUDENTCOURSE	-	-	ENABLED	16-MAY-08	STUDENTCOURSE_PK	-
STUDENTCOURSE_STUDENT_FK	R	STUDENTCOURSE	-	CASCADE	ENABLED	16-MAY-08	-	-
STUDENTCOURSE_COURSE_FK	R	STUDENTCOURSE	-	CASCADE	ENABLED	16-MAY-08	-	-

1 - 4

Figure 2.66. The finished foreign key creation window for the StudentCourse table.

Since the Oracle Database 10g XE is very different with other databases, such as Microsoft Access and SQL Server 2008, you need to refer to Appendix G to get a clear picture about how to use this CSE_DEPT Oracle database files. Refer to Appendix F to get the knowledge in how to use the Utilities of Oracle Database 10g XE to Unload the five tables to five Text files, and how to Load those five table files into a new customer Oracle database to create a new customer Oracle database easily.

2.12 CHAPTER SUMMARY

A detailed discussion and analysis of the structure and components about databases are provided in this chapter. Some key technologies in developing and designing database are also given and discussed in this part. The procedure and components to develop a relational database are analyzed in detail with some real data tables in our sample database CSE_DEPT. The process in developing and building a sample database is discussed in detailed with the following points:

- Defining relationships
- Normalizing the data
- Implementing the relational database

In the second part of this chapter, three sample databases that are developed with three popular database management systems, such as Microsoft Access 2007, SQL Server 2008, and Oracle Database 10g XE are provided in detail. All of these three sample databases will be used in the following chapters throughout the whole book.

HOMEWORK

I. True/False Selections

_____**1.** Database development process involves project planning, problem analysis, logical design, physical design, implementation, and maintenance

_____**2.** Duplication of data creates problems with data integrity.

_____**3.** If the primary key consists of a single column, then the table in 1NF is automatically in 2NF.

_____**4.** A table is in first normal form if there are no repeating groups of data in any column.

_____**5.** When a user perceives the database as made up of tables, it is called a Network Model.

_____**6.** *Entity integrity rule* states that no attribute that is a member of the primary (composite) key may accept a null value.

_____**7.** When creating data tables for the Microsoft Access database, a blank field can be kept as a blank without any letter in it.

_____**8.** To create data tables in SQL Server database, a blank field can be kept as a blank without any letter in it.

_____**9.** The name of each data table in SQL Server database must be prefixed by the keyword dbo.

____**10.** The Sequence object in Oracle database is used to automatically create a sequence of numeric numbers that work as the primary keys.

II. Multiple Choices

1. There are many advantages to using an integrated database approach over that of a file processing approach. These include

a. Minimizing data redundancy

b. Improving security

c. Data independence
d. All of the above

2. Entity integrity rule implies that no attribute that is a member of the primary key may accept _______
   a. Null value
   b. Integer data type
   c. Character data type
   d. Real data type
3. Reducing data redundancy will lead to _____
   a. Deletion anomalies
   b. Data consistency
   c. Loss of efficiency
   d. None of the above
4. ______ keys are used to create relationships among various tables in a database
   a. Primary keys
   b. Candidate keys
   c. Foreign keys
   d. Composite keys
5. In a small university, the department of Computer Science has six faculty members. However, each faculty member belongs to only the computer science department. This type of relationship is called ________
   a. One-to-one
   b. One-to-many
   c. Many-to-many
   d. None of the above
6. The Client Server databases have several advantages over the File Server databases. These include ________
   a. Minimizing chances of crashes
   b. Provision of features for recovery
   c. Enforcement of security
   d. Efficient use of the network
   e. All of the above
7. One can create the foreign keys between tables ______
   a. Before any table can be created
   b. When some tables are created
   c. After all tables are created
   d. With no limitations
8. To create foreign keys between tables, first, one must select the table that contains a _______ key, and then select another table that has a _______ key.
   a. Primary, foreign
   b. Primary, primary
   c. Foreign, primary
   d. Foreign, foreign

9. The data type VARCHAR2 in Oracle database is a string variable with ______
   a. Limited length
   b. Fixed length
   c. Certain number of letters
   d. Varying length
10. For data tables in Oracle Database 10g XE, a blank field must be _______
   a. Indicated by NULL
   b. Kept as a blank
   c. Either by NULL or a blank
   d. Avoided

III. Exercises

1. What are the advantages to using an integrated database approach over that of a file processing approach?
2. Define entity integrity and referential integrity. Describe the reasons for enforcing these rules.
3. Entities can have three types of relationships. It can be *one-to-one, one-to-many*, and *many-to-many*. Define each type of relationship. Draw ER diagrams to illustrate each type of relationship.
4. List all steps to create Foreign keys between data tables for SQL Server database in the SQL Server Management Studio Express. Illustrate those steps by using a real example. For instance, how to create foreign keys between the LogIn and the Faculty table.
5. List all steps to create Foreign keys between data tables for Oracle database in the Oracle Database 10g XE. Illustrate those steps by using a real example. For instance, how to create foreign keys between the StudentCourse and the Course table.

Chapter 3

JDBC API and JDBC Drivers

This chapter discusses the fundamentals of JDBC and JDBC API, which include an overview of the JDBC and JDBC API, JDBC drivers, and related components used in JDBC API.

3.1 WHAT ARE JDBC AND JDBC API?

JDBC is a standard *Java Database Connectivity*, and JDBC API can be considered as a *Java Database Connectivity Application Programming Interface* (JDBC API). All components and techniques of JDBC are embedded and implemented in JDBC API. Basically, the JDBC API is composed of a set of classes and interfaces used to interact with databases from Java applications.

Generally, the JDBC API performs the following three functions:

1. Establish a connection between your Java application and related databases
2. Build and execute SQL statements
3. Process the results

Different database vendors provide various JDBC drivers to support their applications to different databases. The most popular JDBC components are located at the following packages:

- java.sql: contains the standard JDBC components
- javax.sql: contains the Standard Extension of JDBC, which provides additional features, such as Java Naming and Directory Interface (JNDI) and Java Transaction Service (JTS).
- oracle.jdbc: contains the extended functions provided by the java.sql and javax.sql interfaces.
- oracle.sql: contains classes and interfaces that provide Java mappings to SQL data types.

All of these parts are combined together to provide necessary components and classes to build database applications using Java.

Practical Database Programming with Java, First Edition. Ying Bai.

Generally, JDBC API enables users to access virtually any kind of tabular data source, such as spreadsheets or flat files from a Java application. It also provides connectivity to a wide scope of SQL or Oracle databases. One of the most important advantages of using JDBC is that it allows users to access any kind of relational database in a same coding way, which means that the user can develop one program with the same coding to access either a SQL Server database or an Oracle database, or MySQL database without coding modification.

The JDBC 3.0 and JDBC 4.0 specifications contain additional features, such as extensions to the support to various data types, MetaData components, and improvements on some interfaces.

3.2 JDBC COMPONENTS AND ARCHITECTURE

The JDBC API is the only part of the entire JDBC product line.

The core of JDBC API is called a JDBC driver, which implements all JDBC components, including the classes and interfaces, to build a connection and manipulate data between your Java application and selected database. Exactly a JDBC driver, which is a class that is composed of a set of methods, builds a connection and accesses databases through those methods.

The JDBC API contains two major sets of interfaces: the first is the JDBC API for application writers (interface to your Java applications), and the second is the lower-level JDBC driver API for driver writers (interface to your database). JDBC technology drivers fit into one of four categories. Applications and applets can access databases via the JDBC API using pure Java JDBC technology-based drivers, as shown in Figure 3.1.

As we mentioned, the JDBC API is composed of a set of classes and interfaces used to interact with databases from Java applications. Table 3.1 lists all classes defined in the JDBC API and their functions, and Table 3.2 shows all interfaces defined in the JDBC API.

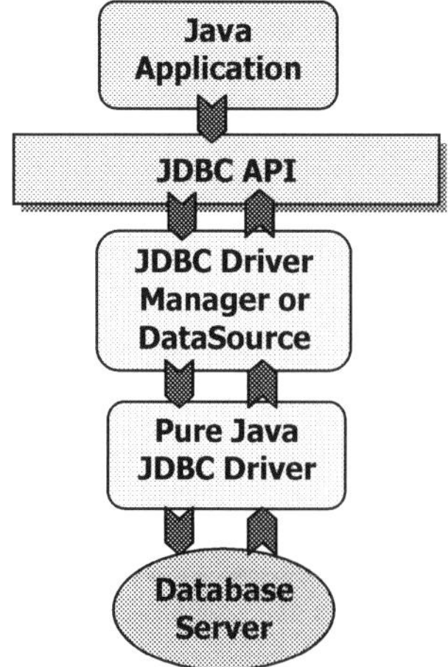

Figure 3.1. The components and architecture of a JDBC API.

Table 3.1. Classes defined in the JDBC API

Classes	Function
DriverManager	Handle loading and unloading of drivers and establish a connection to a database
DriverPropertyInfo	All methods defined in this class are used to setup or retrieve properties of a driver. The properties can then be used by the Connection object to connect to the database
Type	The Type class is only used to define the constants used for identifying of the SQL types
Date	This class contains methods to perform conversion of SQL date formats and Java Date objects
Time	This class is similar to the Date class, and it contains methods to convert between SQL time and Java Time object
TimeStamp	This class provides additional precision to the Java Date object by adding a nanosecond field

Table 3.2. Interfaces defined in the JDBC API

Interface	Function
Driver	The primary use of the Driver interface is to create the Connection objects. It can also be used for the collection of JDBC driver meta data and JDBC driver status checking
Connection	This interface is used for the maintenance and status monitoring of a database session. It also provides data access control through the use of transaction locking
Statement	The Statement methods are used to execute SQL statements and retrieve data from the ResultSet object
PreparedStatement	This interface is used to execute precompile SQL statements. Precompile statements allow for faster and more efficient statement execution, and more important, it allows running dynamic query with querying parameters' variation. This interface can be considered as a subclass of the Statement
CallableStatement	This interface is mainly used to execute SQL stored procedures. Both IN and OUT parameters are supported. This interface can be considered as a subclass of the Statement
ResultSet	The ResultSet object contains the queried result in rows and columns format. This interface also provides methods to retrieve data returned by an SQL statement execution. It also contains methods for SQL data type and JDBC data type conversion
ResultSetMetaData	This interface contains a collection of metadata information or physical descriptions associated with the last ResultSet object
DatabaseMetaData	This interface contains a collection of metadata regarding to the database used, including the database version, table names, columns, and supported functions

It can be found from Table 3.1 that the most popular classes in JDBC API are top three classes: DriverManager, DriverPropertyInfo, and Type, and they are widely implemented in the Java database programming applications.

All interfaces listed in Table 3.2 are popular and widely implemented in the Java database applications. More detailed discussion and example applications of these interfaces will be provided in Chapter 6 with real project examples.

The core of the JDBC API is the JDBC Driver that can be accessed and called from the DriverManager class method. Depends on the different applications, a JDBC driver can be categorized into four types: Type I, Type II, Type III, and Type IV. A more detailed discussion about the JDBC Driver and its types will be given in Section 3.4. An optional way to access the database is to use the DataSource object, which is a better way to identify and connect to a data source, and makes code even more portable and easier to maintain.

3.3 HOW DOES JDBC WORK?

As we mentioned in the last section, the JDBC API has three functions: (1) setup a connection between your Java application and your database; (2) build and execute SQL statements; and (3) process results. We will discuss these functions in more details in this section based on the JDBC architecture shown in Figure 3.1.

3.3.1 Establish a Connection

JDBC Driver class contains six methods, and one of the most important methods is the connect() method, which is used to connect to the database. When using this Driver class, a point to be noted is that most methods defined in the Driver class never be called directly; instead, they should be called via the DriverManager class methods.

3.3.1.1 Using DriverManager to Establish a Connection

The DriverManager class is a set of utility functions that work with the Driver methods together and manage multiple JDBC drivers by keeping them as a list of drivers loaded. Although loading a driver and registering a driver are two steps, only one method call is necessary to perform these two operations. The operational sequence of loading and registering a JDBC driver is:

1. Call class methods in the DriverManager class to load the driver into the Java interpreter.
2. Register the driver using the registerDriver() method.

When loaded, the driver will execute the DriverManager.registerDriver() method to register itself. The above two operations will never be performed until a method in the DriverManager is executed, which means that even both operations have been coded in an application; however, the driver cannot be loaded and registered until a method such as connect() is first executed.

To load and register a JDBC driver, two popular methods can be used:

1. Use Class.forName() method:

```
Class.forName("com.microsoft.sqlserver.jdbc.SQLServerDriver");
```

2. Create a new instance of the Driver class: Driver sqlDriver = new com.microsoft.sqlserver.jdbc.SQLServerDriver;

Relatively speaking, the first method is more professional, since the driver is both loaded and registered when a valid method in the DriverManager class is executed. The second method cannot guarantee that the driver has been registered by using the DriverManager.

3.3.1.2 Using DataSource Object to Establish a Connection

Another and better way to establish a connection is to use the DataSouce object.

The DataSource interface, introduced in the JDBC 2.0 Standard Extension API, is a better way to connect to a data source to perform data actions. In JDBC, a data source is a class that implements the interface javax.sql.DataSource to connect to more than one desired databases. The `getConnection()` method is always used to setup this connection.

A DataSource object is normally registered with a JNDI naming service. This means that an application can retrieve a DataSource object by name from the naming service independently of the system configuration.

Perform the following three operations to deploy a DataSource object:

1. Create an instance of the DataSource class
2. Set its properties using setter methods
3. Register it with a JNDI naming service

After a valid connection has been setup using the DataSource object, one can use any data query methods listed in Tables 3.3 and 3.4 to perform data actions against the desired database.

Table 3.3. The function of three SQL statements execution methods

Method	Function
executeQuery()	This method performs data query and returns a ResultSet object that contains the queried results
executeUpdate()	This method does not perform data query, instead it only performs either a data updating, insertion, or deleting action against the database and returns an integer that equals to the number of rows that have been successfully updated, inserted, or deleted
execute()	This method is a special method, and it can be used either way. All different data actions can be performed by using this method, such as data query, data insertion, data updating, and data deleting. The most important difference between the execute() method and two above methods is that this method can be used to execute some SQL statements that are unknown at the compile time or return multiple results from stored procedures. Another difference is that the execute() method does not return any result itself, and one needs to use getResultSet() or getUpdateCount() method to pick up the results. Both methods belong to the Statement class

Table 3.4. The desired method used to pick up the SQL execution results

Execution Method	Picking up Method
executeQuery()	getResultSet(), getXXX(), where XXX equals to the desired data type of returned result
executeUpdate()	getUpdateCount() This method will returns an integer that equals to the number of rows that have been successfully updated, inserted, or deleted
execute()	getResultSet(), getUpdateCount() This method does not return any result itself, and one needs to use getResultSet() or getUpdateCount() method to pick up the results. Both methods belong to the Statement class

3.3.2 Build and Execute SQL Statements

Once a valid connection is established and a Connection object is created, the JDBC driver is responsible for ensuring that an application has consistent and uniform access to any database. It is also responsible for ensuring that any requests made the application are presented to the database in a way that can be recognized by the database.

To build a SQL statement, one needs to call the method createStatement() that belongs to the Connection class to create a new Statement object. Regularly, there are three type of Statement objects widely implemented in the JDBC API: Statement, PreparedStatement, and CallableStatement. The relationship among these three classes is: the PreparedStatement and CallableStatement classes are the subclasses of the Statement class.

To execute a SQL statement, one of the following three methods can be called:

1. executeQuery()
2. executeUpdate()
3. execute()

All of these methods belong to the Statement and the PreparedStatement classes and used to access database to perform different data actions.

The differences between these three methods are dependents on the different data operations and actions. Table 3.3 lists the function for each method and the situation under which the appropriate method should be utilized. Mode-detailed discussion about these three methods and their implementations can be found in Section 6.4.2.3 in Chapter 6.

3.3.3 Process Results

After the desired SQL statement is executed, you need to retrieve the execution results. Depends on the different execution methods you called, you need to use the different methods to pick up the results.

Table 3.4 lists some necessary methods used to pick up the appropriate results based on the different execution methods utilized.

3.3.3.1 Using ResultSet Object

A ResultSet object will be created after the `executeQuery()` method is executed or a `getResultSet()` method is executed. A ResultSet object is a data structure that presents rows and columns returned by a valid query. It maintains a cursor pointing to its current row of data. Initially, the cursor is positioned before the first row. One can use the `next()` method to move the cursor to the next row, and continue this moving one can scan the entire ResultSet. With a loop, one can use the appropriate `getXXX()` method of the ResultSet class to pick up each row in the ResultSet object. The XXX indicates the corresponding Java data type of the selected row. A more detailed discussion about these methods will be provided in Chapter 4.

3.3.3.2 Using RowSet Object

A RowSet object contains a set of rows from a result set or some other source of tabular data, like a file or spreadsheet. Because a RowSet object follows the JavaBeans model for properties and event notification, it is a JavaBeans component that can be combined with other components in an application. As is compatible with other Beans, application developers can probably use a development tool to create a RowSet object and set its properties.

RowSets may have many different implementations to fill different needs. These implementations fall into two broad categories, connected and disconnected:

1. A connected RowSet is equivalent to a ResultSet, and it maintains a connection to a data source as long as the RowSet is in use.
2. A disconnected RowSet works as a DataSet in Visual Studio.NET, and it can connect to a data source to perform the data updating periodically. Most time, it is disconnected with the data source and uses a mapping memory space as a mapped database.

While a RowSet is disconnected, it does not need a JDBC driver or the full JDBC API, so its footprint is very small. Thus, a RowSet is an ideal format for sending data over a network to a thin client.

Because it is not continually connected to its data source, a disconnected RowSet stores its data in memory. It needs to maintain metadata about the columns it contains and information about its internal state. It also needs a facility for making connections, for executing commands, and for reading and writing data to and from the data source. A connected RowSet, by contrast, opens a connection and keeps it open for as long as the RowSet is being used.

A more detailed discussion about the RowSet object and its implementation will be given in Sections 6.4.6.1 and 6.4.6.2 in Chapter 6.

Since the JDBC driver is a core for entire JDBC API, we will have a more detailed discussion about this component in the next section.

3.4 JDBC DRIVER AND DRIVER TYPES

The JDBC driver builds a bridge between your Java applications and your desired database, and works as an intermediate-level translator to perform a double-direction conversion: convert your high-level Java codes to the low-level native codes to interface to the database, and convert the low-level native commands from the database to your high-level Java codes.

As we discussed in the last section, a JDBC driver class contains six method and one of the most important methods is the connect() method, which is used to connect to the database. When using this Driver class, a point to be noted is that most methods defined in the Driver class can never be called directly; instead, they should be called via the DriverManager class methods.

Generally, the JDBC API will not contain any JDBC driver, and you need to download a desired JDBC driver from the corresponding vendor if you want to use a specified driver. Based on the different configurations, JDBC drivers can be categorized into the following four types.

3.4.1 Type I: JDBC-ODBC Bridge Driver

Open Database Connectivity (ODBC) is a Microsoft-based database Application Programming Interface (API), and it aimed to make it independent of programming languages, database systems, and operating systems. In other words, the ODBC is a database and operating system independent API, and it can access any database in any platform without problem at all.

Figure 3.2 shows a typical architecture of JDBC-ODBC Bridge Driver application. Figure 3.2a is for a Java standard-alone application, and Figure 3.2b is a Java 2-tire application.

Basically, ODBC is built and based on various Call Level Interface (CLI) specifications from the SQL Access Group and X/Open techniques. To access an ODBC to interface to a desired database, a JDBC-ODBC Bridge is needed, and this bridge works just like a translator or a converter, that interprets the JDBC requests to the CLI in ODBC when a request is sent from the JDBC to the ODBC, and perform an inverse translation (from CLI in ODBC to JDBC) when a result is returned from the database. The advan-

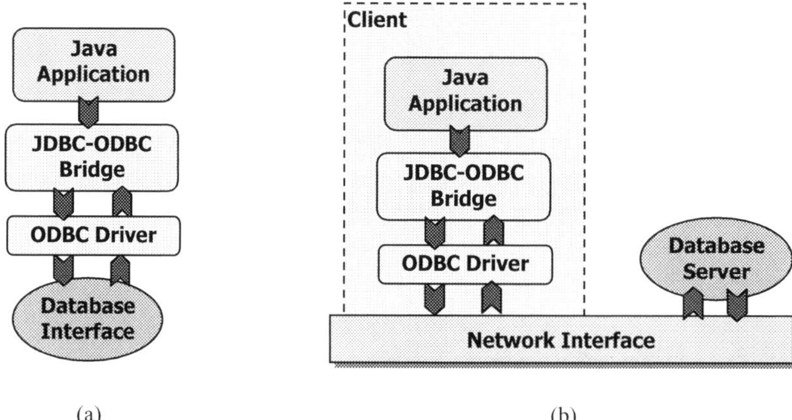

Figure 3.2. JDBC-ODBC Bridge Driver.

tage of using Type I driver is simplicity, since we do not need to know the details inside ODBC and transactions between the ODBC and DBMS. Refer to Figure 3.2a, it is a typical Java standalone application that uses JDBC-ODBC Bridge Driver to access a local database, and it will work fine. However, a problem will be exposed if applying this JDBC-ODBC Bridge Driver in a two-tier application that is shown in Figure 3.2b. The problem is that the network standard security manager will not allow the ODBC that is downloaded as an applet to access any local files when you build a Java Applet application to access a database located in a database server. Therefore, it is impossible to build a Java Applet application with this JDBC-ODBC Bridge Driver configuration.

3.4.2 Type II: Native-API-Partly-Java Driver

The Native-API-Partly-Java driver makes use of local native libraries to communicate with the database. The driver does this by making calls to the locally installed native call level interface (CLI) using a native language, either C or C++, to access the database. The CLI libraries are responsible for the actual communications with the database server. When a client application makes a database accessing request, the driver translates the JDBC request to the native method call and passes the request to the native CLI. After the database processed the request, results will be translated from their native language back to the JDBC and presented to the client application. Figure 3.3 shows a Type II driver configuration.

Compared with Type I driver, the communications between the driver and the database are performed by using the native CLI without needing any translation between JDBC and ODBC driver; therefore, the speed and efficiency of Type II driver is higher than that of Type I driver. When available, Type II drivers are recommended over Type I drivers.

3.4.3 Type III: JDBC-Net-All-Java Driver

Basically, the Type III drivers are similar with Type II drivers, and the only difference between them is the replacement of the native database access libraries.

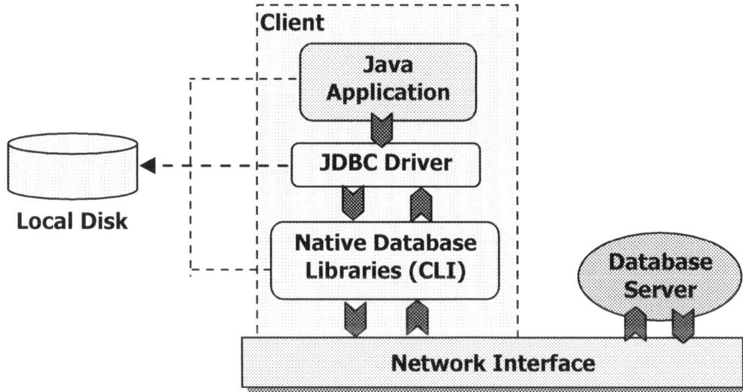

Figure 3.3. Type II Driver.

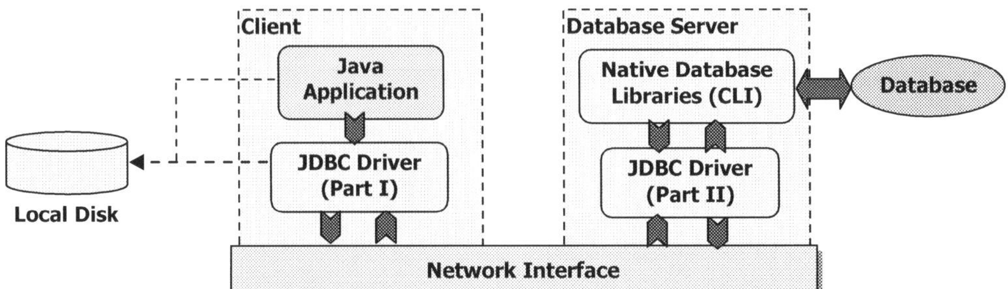

Figure 3.4. Type III Driver configuration.

For both Type I and Type II drivers, either the ODBC driver or the native CLI libraries must be installed and located on the client machine. All communications between the server processes and the JDBC driver have been through native program interface. However, in Type III driver configuration, the native CLI libraries are placed on a server and the driver uses a network protocol to facilitate communications between the application and the driver. The result of this modification is to separate the driver into two parts: (1) a part of JDBC driver that is an all-Java portion can be downloaded to the client; and (2) a server portion containing both another part of JDBC driver and native CLI methods. All communications between the application and the database server are 100% Java to Java. However, the communication between the database and the server is still done via a native database CLI. Figure 3.4 shows this configuration.

It can be found from Figure 3.4 that the client does not need to perform either database-specified protocol translation or a Java-to-CLI translation by using Type III drivers, and this will greatly reduce the working loads for the client machine, and the client piece of a Type III driver only needs to translate requests into the network protocol to communicate with the database server. Another advantage of using a Type III driver is that the second part of the Type III driver, which is used to communicate with the database native libraries, does not need to be downloaded to the client, and as a result of this fact, Type III drivers are not subject to the same security restrictions found as Types I and II did. Since all database-related codes reside on the server side, a large driver that is capable of connecting to many different databases can be built.

3.4.4 Type IV: Native-Protocol-All-Java Driver

Type IV drivers are totally different with any drivers we have discussed so far. These types of drivers are capable of communicating directly with the database without the need for any type of translation since they are 100% Java without using any CLI native libraries. Figure 3.5 shows a typical Type IV driver configuration.

The key issue in use of a Type IV driver is that the native database protocol will be rewritten to converts the JDBC calls into vendor specific protocol calls, and the result of this rewritten is that the driver can directly interact with the database without needing any other translations. Therefore, Type IV drivers are the fastest drivers compared with all other three-type drivers, Types I~III. By using a Type IV driver, it will greatly simplify database access for applets by eliminating the need for native CLI libraries.

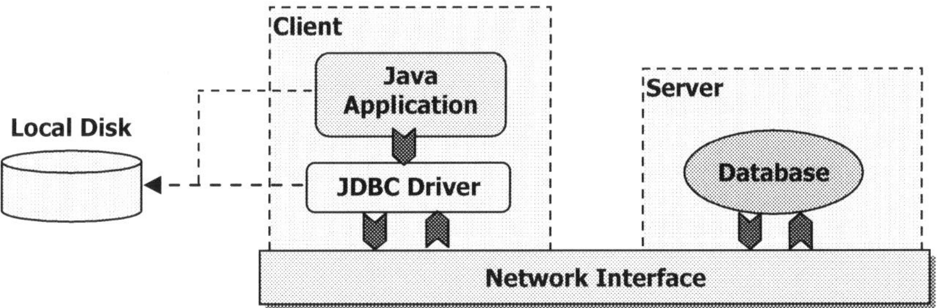

Figure 3.5. Type IV driver configuration.

3.5 JDBC STANDARD EXTENSION API

Besides the standard JDBC API (or core API), Sun added an extension package called JDBC 2.0 Standard Extension API to support extended database operations. This package contains the following components:

1. JDBC DataSource
2. JDBC driver-based connection pooling
3. JDBC RowSet
4. Distributed transactions

We will take a close look at these components and provide a more detailed discussion about these elements in the following sections.

3.5.1 JDBC DataSource

In Section 3.3.3.2, we have had a brief discussion about the DataSource object. Because of its specialty and advantage over JDBC drivers and DriverManagers, we will provide a more detailed discussion about this interface in this part.

As we know, the DataSource interface is introduced in the JDBC 2.0 Standard Extension API, and it is a better way to connect to a data source to perform data actions. In JDBC, a data source is a class that implements the interface `javax.sql.DataSource` to connect to more than one desired databases. The `getConnection()` method is always used to setup this connection.

As we discussed in Section 3.3.1, to establish a connection by using a JDBC driver, you need to use the DriverManager to load a desired driver and register that driver to the driver list. You also need to know exactly the driver name and the driver URLs to complete this connection. In fact, the DataSource can provide an alternative and better way to do that connection in fast and more efficient way.

The advantage of using a DataSource to perform this database connection is: a DataSource object is normally registered with a Java Naming and Directory Interface (JNDI) naming service. This means that an application can retrieve a DataSource object by the name of that DataSource only, without needing to know the driver name, database name, and driver URLs, even without needing to register any drivers. In other words, this naming service is independent of the system configurations and databases.

Table 3.5. The most popular methods used in the Context interface

Method	Function
bind(string name, object obj)	Binds a name to an object
createSubcontext(string name)	Creates and binds a new context
destroySubcontext(string name)	Destroys the named context and removes it from the namespace
listBindings(string name)	Enumerates the names bound in the named context, along with the objects bound to them
lookup(string name)	Retrieves the named object
unbind(string name)	Unbinds the named object
close()	Closes this context

3.5.1.1 Java Naming and Directory Interface

The Java Naming and Directory Interface (JNDI) provides naming and directory functionality and service to Java applications. It is defined to be independent of any specific directory service implementation so that different directories can be accessed in a common way.

Exactly, the JNDI can be analogous to a file directory that allows users to find and work with files by name. In this way, the JNDI is used to find the DataSource using the logical name assigned to it when it is registered with the JNDI.

The association of a name with an object is called a binding process. A DataSource object stores the attributes that tell it how to connect to a database and those attributes are assigned when you bind the DataSource instance to its JNDI directory. The core JNDI interface that performs looking up, binding, unbinding, renaming objects, creating, and destroying subcontexts is the Context interface.

The Context interface represents a naming context, which consists of a set of name-to-object bindings. It contains methods for examining and updating these bindings. Table 3.5 shows some most popular methods used by this interface.

In fact, using JNDI can significantly improve the portability of a Java application by removing the need to hard code a driver name and database name, and it is very similar to a file directory to improve file accessing by overcoming the need to reference disk cylinders and sectors. To establish a valid database connection using the JNDI, the only information you need is the name of the DataSource; yes, that is all you need, and it is so simple and easy, is it not?

3.5.1.2 Deploy and Use a Basic Implementation of DataSource

In this section, we will use a piece of codes to illustrate the implementation of a DataSource object. Perform the following three operations to deploy a DataSource object:

1. Create an instance of the DataSource class.
2. Set its properties using setter methods.
3. Register it with a JNDI naming service.

```
Vendor_DataSource ds = new Vendor_DataSource();

ds.setServerName("localhost");
ds.setDatabaseName("CSE_DEPT");
ds.setDescription("CSE_DEPT Database");

Context ctx = new InitialContext();
ctx.bind("jdbc/CSE_DEPT", ds);
```

Figure 3.6. An example coding for the creation of a new DataSource object.

```
Context ctx = new InitialContext();
DataSource ds = (DataSource)ctx.lookup("jdbc/CSE_DEPT");
Connection con = ds.getConnection("myUserName", "myPassWord");

// Execute the SQL statements to perform data actions via database......
```

Figure 3.7. An example coding for execution of the database connection via DataSource.

The first step is to create a DataSource object, set its properties, and register it with a JNDI naming service. A DataSource object is usually created, deployed, and managed separately from the Java applications that use it. A point to be noted is that a DataSource object for a particular data source is created and deployed by a developer or system administrator, not the user. Figure 3.6 shows a piece of example codes to create a new DataSource object with some properties setting by using some setters. The class `Vendor_DataSource` would most likely be supplied by a driver vendor.

In Figure 3.6, the first coding line is to create a new DataSource object based on the data source provided by the vendor. The following three lines are used to set up different properties using a setter. The last two lines are used to create an InitialContext object and to bind and register the new DataSource object `ds` to the logical name `jdbc/CSE_DEPT` with a JNDI naming service.

The JNDI namespace consists of an initial naming context and any number of subcontexts under it. It is hierarchical, similar to the directory/file structure in many file systems, with the initial context being analogous to the root of a file system, and subcontexts being analogous to subdirectories. The root of the JNDI hierarchy is the initial context, here represented by the variable `ctx`. There may be many subcontexts under the initial context, one of which is jdbc, the JNDI subcontext reserved for JDBC data sources. The logical data source name may be in the subcontext jdbc, or in a subcontext under jdbc. The last element in the hierarchy is the object being registered, analogous to a file, which in this case is a logical name for a data source.

The codes shown in Figure 3.7 show how an application uses this to connect to a data source.

To get a connection using a DataSource object, create a JNDI Context instance, and use the name of the DataSource object to its `lookup()` method to try to find it from a JNDI subcontext `jdbc`. The returned DataSource object will call its `getConnection()` method to establish a connection to the database.

As soon as a database connection has been established, you can execute any SQL statements as you want to perform any desired data action against the connected database.

3.5.2 JDBC Driver-Based Connection Pooling

By using a DataSource object, you can easily setup a connection with your database and perform any data operation you want. Sound good! Yes, this kind of operation is good for two-tier database applications without problem. However, a problem would come if you apply this operation in a three-tier database application. The main issue is the overhead in transactions between the application server and client. If you are running in a three-tier database application, each time when you communicate between your application server and your database via a database server to perform a connection or a disconnection, there would be quite a few communication traffic running between your server and your database, and this will introduce multiple opening and closing operations to your database and greatly reduce the efficiency of the database.

To solve this overhead problem, a Connection Pooling API has been provided by JDBC Standard Extension API. The pooling implementations do not actually close connections when the client calls the close() method, but instead return the connections to a pool of available connections for other clients to use. This avoids any overhead of repeatedly opening and closing connections, and allows a large number of clients to share a small number of database connections.

The connection pooling API is an extension of the regular connection API. The working principle of using a connection pooling is: when a resource or connection is no longer needed after a task has been completed, it is not destroyed but is added into a resource pool instead, making it available when required for a subsequent operation. In other words, we can temporarily store all unused connections to a connection pool, and reuse them as soon as a new data action is required for the target database. In this way, we can greatly improve the database performance by cutting down on the number of new connections that need to be created.

The JDBC API provides a client and a server interface for connection pooling. The client interface is javax.sql.DataSource, which is what application code will typically use to acquire a pooled database connection. The server interface is javax.sql.ConnectionPoolDataSource, which is how most application servers will interface with the PostgreSQL JDBC driver. Both interfaces are defined in the JDBC 2.0 Standard Extension (also known as the JDBC 2.0 Optional Package).

The server interface for connection pooling, `ConnectionPoolDataSource` object, is a factory for `PooledConnection` objects. All Connection objects that implement this interface are registered with a JNDI naming service.

To implement a DataSource object to create pooled connections, you need to perform the following operations:

- Create a `ConnectionPoolDataSource` object.
- Set its properties to the data source that produced connections.
- Register `ConnectionPoolDataSource` object with the JNDI naming service.

```
ConnectionPoolDataSource  cpds = new ConnectionPoolDataSource();

cpds.setServerName("localhost");
cpds.setDatabaseName("CSE_DEPT");
cpds.setPortNumber(5000);
cpds.setDescription("CSE_DEPT Database");

Context ctx = new InitialContext();
ctx.bind("jdbc/pool/CSE_DEPT", cpds);

PooledDataSource  ds = new PooledDataSource();
ds.setDescription("CSE_DEPT database pooled connection source");
ds.setDataSourceName("jdbc/pool/CSE_DEPT");

Context  ctx = new InitialContext();
ctx.bind("jdbc/CSE_DEPT", ds);
```

Figure 3.8. An example coding for the connection pooling DataSource.

- Create a DataSource object.
- Set properties to the DataSource object by using setter.

Figure 3.8 shows a piece of example codes to illustrate how to use the connection pooling API to create and deploy a DataSource object that an application can use to get pooled connections to the database.

The first coding line is used to create a new `ConnectionPoolDataSource` object, and this object is equivalent to a pool body to hold unused data sources later.

The following four lines are used to set appropriate properties to this created object. Then, in the sixth and seventh lines, the created `ConnectionPoolDataSource` object is registered with the JNDI naming service. The logical name associated with `cpds` has a subcontext pool added under the subcontext `jdbc`, which is similar to adding a subdirectory to another subdirectory in a file system.

Now we need to create our DataSource object implemented to work with it, or in other words, we can add this DataSource object into our pool, the `ConnectionPoolDataSource` object, when it is temporarily unused in an application. The coding lines between the eighth and the tenth are used to create our DataSource object `ds` with the `PooledDataSource` class. Note in the tenth coding line, the name of the DataSource is `jdbc/pool/CSE_DEPT`, which is identical with the logical name of our `ConnectionPoolDataSource` object we created before.

The last two coding lines are used to register our DataSource object with the JNDI naming service.

Now you can use this connection pooling for your data source object. The point is that when you finished a task to your current database, you must call the `close()` method from your client to inform the server that this database connection will be temporarily unused, and this will allow the Connection Pooling API to add this unused connection to the `ConnectionPoolDataSource` object. Later on, if you want to reuse this database, you need to use the codes shown in Figure 3.9 to get that connection from the pool.

Another situation to use a DataSource object is when you need to implement distributed transactions, which means that you need to use multiple databases synchronously in your applications. In that case, use of a DataSource object with built-in distributed transaction capabilities is the best solution.

```
Connection con = null;
 try {
      con = ds.getConnection();
      // use connection
      }
catch(SQLException e)
    {
      // log error
      }
finally
    {
         if(con != null)
           try {con.close();}catch(SQLException e) {}
    }
```

Figure 3.9. An example coding for the retrieving and reusing a connection.

3.5.3 Distributed Transactions

A *distributed transaction*, sometimes referred to as a *global transaction*, is a set of two or more related transactions that must be managed in a coordinated way. The transactions that constitute a distributed transaction might be in the same database, but more typically are in different databases and often in different locations. Each individual transaction of a distributed transaction is referred to as a *transaction branch*.

In the JDBC 2.0 extension API, distributed transaction functionality is built on top of connection pooling functionality, which we have discussed in the last section. This distributed transaction functionality is also built upon the open XA standard for distributed transactions. (XA is part of the X/Open standard and is not specific to Java.)

3.5.3.1 Distributed Transaction Components and Scenarios

A typical distributed transaction can be composed of the following components and scenarios:

- A distributed transaction system typically relies on an external transaction manager, such as a software component that implements standard Java Transaction API (JTA) functionality, to coordinate the individual transactions. Many vendors will offer XA-compliant JTA modules. This includes Oracle, which is developing a JTA module based on the Oracle implementation of XA.
- XA functionality is usually isolated from a client application, being implemented instead in a middle-tier environment such as an application server. In many scenarios, the application server and transaction manager will be together on the middle tier, possibly together with some of the application code as well.
- The term resource manager is often used in discussing distributed transactions. A resource manager is simply an entity that manages data or some other kind of resource. Wherever the term is used in this chapter, it refers to a database.

By definition, XA is a standard protocol that allows coordination, commitment, and recovery between transaction managers (e.g., CICS, Tuxedo, and even BEA Web Logic

Server) and resource managers (e.g., databases, message queuing products such as JMS or Web Sphere MQ, mainframe applications, ERP packages).

As with connection pooling API, two classes must be used for a distributed transaction:

- A XADataSource that produces XAConnections supporting distributed transactions.
- A DataSource object that is implemented to work with it.

The transaction manager is responsible for making the final decision either to `commit` or `rollback` any distributed transaction. A commit decision should lead to a successful transaction; rollback leaves the data in the database unaltered. JTA specifies standard Java interfaces between the transaction manager and the other components in a distributed transaction: the application, the application server, and the resource managers.

3.5.3.2 The Distributed Transaction Process

The transaction manager is the primary component of the distributed transaction infrastructure; however, the JDBC driver and application server components should have the following characteristics:

- The driver should implement the JDBC 2.0 API (including the Optional Package interfaces XADataSource and XAConnection) or higher and the JTA interface XAResource.
- The application server should provide a DataSource class that is implemented to interact with the distributed transaction infrastructure and a connection pooling module.

The first step of the distributed transaction process is to send a request to the transaction manager by the application. Although the final commit/rollback decision treats the transaction as a single logical unit, there can be many transaction branches involved. A transaction branch is associated with a request to each resource manager involved in the distributed transaction. Requests to three different RDBMSs, therefore, require three transaction branches. Each transaction branch must be committed or rolled back by the local resource manager. The transaction manager controls the boundaries of the transaction, and is responsible for the final decision as to whether or not the total transaction should commit or rollback. This decision is made in two phases, called the two-phase commit protocol.

In the first phase, the transaction manager polls all of the resource managers (RDBMSs) involved in the distributed transaction to see if any of them is ready to commit. If a resource manager cannot commit, it responds negatively and rolls back its particular part of the transaction so that data is not altered.

In the second phase, the transaction manager determines if any of the resource managers have responded negatively, and, if so, rolls back the whole transaction. If there are no negative responses, the translation manager commits the whole transaction, and returns the results to the application.

The DataSource implemented to produce connections for distributed transactions are almost always implemented to produce connections that are pooled as well. The XAConnection interface extends the PooledConnection interface.

To begin a distributed transaction, a XADataSource object should be created first, and this can be done by creating a new instance of the XATransactionIDS and setting its properties. Figure 3.10 shows an example coding for a distributed transaction.

```
XATransactionIDS  xads = new XATransactionIDS ();

xads.setServerName("localhost");
xads.setDatabaseName("CSE_DEPT");
xads.setPortNumber(5000);
xads.setDescription("CSE_DEPT Database");

Context ctx = new InitialContext();
ctx.bind("jdbc/xa/CSE_DEPT", xads);

TransactionIDS  ds  = new  TransactionIDS();
ds.setDescription("CSE_DEPT distributed transaction connection source");
ds.setDataSourceName("jdbc/xa/CSE_DEPT");

Context  ctx = new InitialContext();
ctx.bind("jdbc/CSE_DEPT", ds);
```

Figure 3.10. An example coding for the distributed transaction implementation.

The first coding line is used to create a new `XADataSource` object, and it produces XAConnections supporting distributed transactions.

The following four lines are used to set appropriate properties to this created object.

Then, in the sixth and seventh lines, the created `XADataSource` object is registered with the JNDI naming service. The logical name associated with `xads` has a subcontext `xa` added under the subcontext `jdbc`, which is similar to adding a subdirectory to another subdirectory in a file system.

Finally, the DataSource object is created to interact with `xads`, and other `XADataSource` objects are deployed.

Now that instances of the `TransactionlDS` and `XATransactionlDS` classes have been created, an application can use the DataSource to get a connection to the CSE_DEPT database, and this connection can then be used in any distributed transactions.

3.5.4 JDBC RowSet

A JDBC RowSet object is one of the JavaBeans components with multiple supports from JavaBeans, and it is a new feature in the `java.sql` package. By using the RowSet object, a database query can be performed automatically with the data source connection and a query statement creation. In this section, we will provide a brief introduction about this new feature to reduce the coding load and improve the efficiency of the data query with the help of this RowSet object. A more detailed discussion with real project examples will be given in Section 6.4.6 in Chapter 6.

3.5.4.1 Introduction to Java RowSet Object

A RowSet object contains a set of rows from a result set or some other source of tabular data, like a file or spreadsheet. Because a RowSet object follows the JavaBeans model for properties and event notification, it is a JavaBeans component that can be combined with other components in an application. As it compatible with other Beans, application developers can probably use a development tool to create a RowSet object and set its properties.

RowSets may have many different implementations to fill different needs. These implementations fall into two broad categories, connected and disconnected:

1. A connected RowSet is equivalent to a ResultSet, and it maintains a connection to a data source as long as the RowSet is in use.
2. A disconnected RowSet works as a DataSet in Visual Studio.NET, and it can connect to a data source to perform the data updating periodically. Most time, it is disconnected with the data source and uses a mapping memory space as a mapped database.

While a RowSet is disconnected, it does not need a JDBC driver or the full JDBC API, so its footprint is very small. Thus, a RowSet is an ideal format for sending data over a network to a thin client.

To make writing an implementation easier, the Java Software division of Sun Microsystems, Inc. plans to provide reference implementations for five different styles of RowSets in the future. Among them, two components are very popular and widely implemented in Java database applications:

1. A CachedRowSet class—a disconnected RowSet that caches its data in memory; not suitable for very large data sets, but an ideal way to provide thin Java clients, such as a Personal Digital Assistant (PDA) or Network Computer (NC), with tabular data.
2. A JDBCRowSet class—a connected RowSet that serves mainly as a thin wrapper around a ResultSet object to make a JDBC driver look like a JavaBeans component.

To effectively apply RowSet objects to perform data actions against desired databases, the following operational sequence should be adopted.

3.5.4.2 Implementation Process of a RowSet Object

Generally, the operational procedure of using a RowSet object to query data can be divided into the following four steps:

1. Set up and configure a RowSet object.
2. Register the RowSet Listeners.
3. Set input and output parameters for the query command.
4. Traverse through the result rows from the ResultSet.

The first step is used to setup and configure the static or dynamic properties of a RowSet object, such as the connection `url`, username, password, and running command, to allow the RowSet object to connect to the data source, pass user parameters into the data source, and perform the data query.

The second step allows users to register different Listeners for the RowSet object with different event sources. The RowSet feature supports multiple listeners to be registered with the RowSet object. Listeners can be registered using the addRowSetListener() method and unregistered through the removeRowSetListener() method. A listener should implement the `javax.sql.RowSetListener` interface to register itself as the RowSet listener. Three types of events are supported by the RowSet interface:

1. cursorMoved event : Generated whenever there is a cursor movement, which occurs when the next() or previous() methods are called.

2. rowChanged event : Generated when a new row is inserted, updated, or deleted from the row set.

3. rowsetChanged event : Generated when the whole row set is created or changed.

In this book, the NetBeans IDE 6.8 is used, and the event-listener model has been set up by NetBeans IDE. So we can skip this step and do not need to take care of this issue during our coding process in the following chapters.

Step 3 allows users to set up all static or dynamic parameters for the query statement of the RowSet object. Depending on the data type of the parameters used in the query statement, suitable setXXX() methods should be used to perform this parameter setup process.

The fourth step is used to retrieve each row from the ResultSet object.

3.6 CHAPTER SUMMARY

This chapter discusses the fundamentals of JDBC and JDBC API, which include an overview of the JDBC and JDBC API, JDBC drivers and related components used in JDBC API.

The JDBC components and architecture are discussed and analyzed in detailed in the first part of this chapter. All classes and interfaces defined in a JDBC API are discussed and presented with a sequence tables. With some basic idea on JDBC and its components, the function and operational procedure of using JDBC API to perform data actions are described by three key steps:

1. Establish a connection between your Java application and related databases.

2. Build and execute SQL statements.

3. Process the results.

To setup a valid database connection, two popular connection methods are introduced: using the DriverManager class method and using the DataSource object. Relatively speaking, the second method is simple and easy to be used in real applications, since no detailed data source information is needed for this database connection.

To build and execute a typical SQL statement, the Statement, PreparedStatement, and CallableStatement components are discussed and introduced. Both PreparedStatement and CallableStatement classes are subclasses of the Statement class; however, both of them have more flexibility compared with the Statement component.

To process returned query results, different objects, such as ResultSet and RowSet, are introduced and discussed to provide users a clear picture about those objects and their functionalities.

Following the JDBC API and JDBC driver discussion, a detailed discussion about the types of JDBC Drivers is provided. Four popular types of drivers are analyzed and compared with architectures and their implementations.

Finally, four important components defined in the JDBC Standard Extension API, DataSource, Connection Pooling, Distributed Transactions, and RowSet are introduced and discussed with example coding.

The topics discussed in this chapter are prerequisite for the next chapter, and some components will be discussed and analyzed in more detailed to give users a deeper understanding and a better picture about their roles in real Java database applications.

HOMEWORK

I. True/False Selections

____**1.** JDBC is a standard *Java Database Connectivity*, and JDBC API can be considered as a *Java Database Connectivity Application Programming Interface*.

____**2.** JDBC API is not the only component included in a JDBC.

____**3.** JDBC API is composed of a set of classes and interfaces used to interact with databases from Java applications.

____**4.** JDBC Drivers are implementation dependent, which means that different applications need different drivers.

____**5.** The core of JDBC 2.0 API provides standard JDBC components that are located at the `java.sql` package, and some additional components such as JNDI and JTS are defined in JDBC 2.0 Standard Extension that is located at the `javax.sql` package.

____**6.** One can establish a database connection by directly calling the Driver class method `connect()`.

____**7.** To load and register a JDBC driver, two popular methods can be used: using either Class.forName() method or to create a new instance of the Driver class.

____**8.** Three components can be used to build a SQL statement: Statement, Prepared-Statement, and CallableStatement.

____**9.** To pick up the execution results, one can use the executeQuery() and executeUpdate() methods. The former returns an integer and the latter returns a ResultSet.

___**10.** There are four types of JDBC drivers, and Type IV driver is a pure Java driver with fast running speed and high efficiency in data actions.

II. Multiple Choices

1. Generally, the JDBC API perform the following three functions _____

- **a.** Connect to database, load JDBC driver, perform the query
- **b.** Perform the query, connect to database, load JDBC driver
- **c.** Get result from ResultSet, connect to database, load JDBC driver
- **d.** Establish a connection to database, execute SQL statements, and get running results

2. To establish a connection with a DataSource object, you need to ________

- **a.** Create a DataSource object, set properties and use this object
- **b.** Set properties, setup a connection, and perform queries
- **c.** Create a DataSource object, set properties, and register it with JNDI naming service
- **d.** Register a DataSource object, set properties, and create a DataSource object

3. To build and run a SQL statement, following components can be utilized ______

- **a.** Statement
- **b.** Statement, PreparedStatement
- **c.** Statement, PreparedStatement, CallableStatement
- **d.** None of them

4. To execute a SQL statement to get a query result, ________ method(s) should be used.

- **a.** executeQuery()
- **b.** executeUpdate()

c. execute() and executeUpdate()
d. executeQuery() and execute()

5. To perform an insert, update or delete operation, the _______ method(s) should be used.
   a. executeUpdate()
   b. executeQuery()
   c. executeQuery() and execute()
   d. executeQuery() and executeUpdate()
6. The _______ method can be used to either pick up a query result or update a datum.
   a. executeUpdate()
   b. execute()
   c. executeQuery()
   d. None of them
7. A *distributed transaction* is defined as to access ________ data source(s) at ______ location(s).
   a. Single, single
   b. Multiple, same
   c. Multiple, different
   d. Single, multiple
8. The execute() method can ____________.
   a. Not return any result
   b. Return some results
   c. Be used either to return a result or not return any result
   d. None of above
9. A CachedRowSet class is a _________ that caches its data in _________.
   a. Connected RowSet, database
   b. Disconnected RowSet, database
   c. Connected RowSet, memory
   d. Disconnected RowSet, memory
10. The ResultSet object can be created by either executing the __________ or _________ method, which means that the ResultSet instance cannot be created or used without executing a query operation first.
    a. executeQuery(), getResultSet()
    b. getResultSet(), execute()
    c. createResultSet(), getResultSet()
    d. buildResultSet(), executeQuery()

III. Exercises

1. Provide a detailed description about the JDBC API, which includes:
   a. The definition of the JDBC and JDBC API
   b. The components defined in a JDBC API, including all classes and interfaces
   c. The architecture of the JDBC API
   d. The regular functions of a JDBC API performed
   e. The packages of the JDBC API is involved

2. Provide a brief discussion about database connection using JDBC API, which includes:
   a. Two popular methods used to establish a connection
   b. Operational procedure to establish a connection
   c. How to use a DataSource object to establish a connection
   d. Compare two popular method with the DataSource method in establishing a database connection
3. Explain the function of three different statement execution methods: executeQuery(), executeUpdate(), and execute(). For each method, provides a way to retrieve the execution result.
4. Provides a brief introduction about four types of JDBC drivers and their architecture.
5. Provides a brief introduction about the connection pooling API.

Chapter 4

JDBC Application Design Considerations

This chapter discusses the application fundamentals of JDBC and JDBC API, which include the application models and operational procedures of the JDBC API implemented in Java database applications.

4.1 JDBC APPLICATION MODELS

JDBC API supports both two-tier and three-tier models for database accesses. In a two-tier model, a Java application or an applet can communicate directly with the database.

In a three-tier model, commands are sent to a middle-tier, which sends the messages to the database. In return, the result of the database query is sent to the middle tier that finally directs it to the application or applet. The presence of a middle tier has a number of advantages, such as a tight control over changes done to the database.

4.1.1 Two-Tier Client-Server Model

In a two-tier client–server model, a Java application can directly communicate with the database. In fact, the so-called two-tier model means that the Java application and the target database can be installed in two components with two layers:

- Application layer, which includes the JDBC driver, user interface, and the whole Java application, installed in a client machine.
- Database layer, which includes the RDBMS and the database, installed in a database server.

Figure 4.1 shows a typical configuration of a two-tier model.

It can be found from Figure 4.1 that both Java application and JDBC API are located at the first layer, or the client machine and the DBMS and database are located at the second layer or the database server. A DBMS-Related protocol is used as a tool to communicate between these two layers. The interface to the database is handled by a JDBC driver that is matched to the particular database management system being used. The JDBC driver has double-side functionality; it passes SQL statement to the database when

Practical Database Programming with Java, First Edition. Ying Bai.

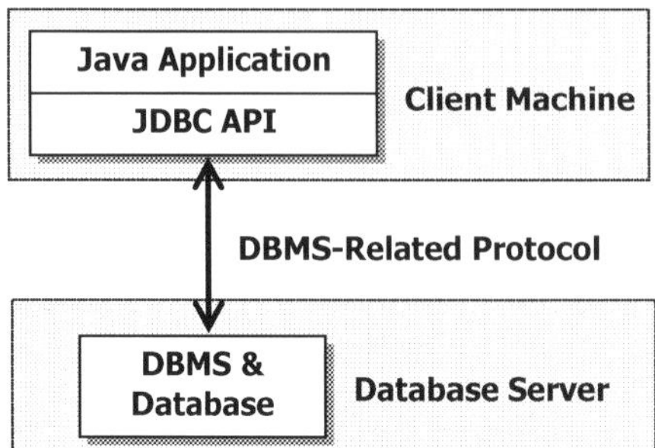

Figure 4.1. A typical configuration of a two-tier model.

a data action request is sent from the client, and returns the results of executing those statements to the client when the data action is done.

A client–server configuration is a special case of the two-tier model, where the database is located on another machine called the database server. The Java application program runs on the client machine that is connected to the database server through a network.

Most topics discussed in Chapters 6–8 in this book are about two-tier model applications. The Java application projects are built in the client machine and communicate with the database server through the network to perform all kinds of data actions. The inherent flexibility of Java JDBC approach to develop database applications enables you to access a variety of RDBMS systems, including Microsoft Access 2007, SQL Server, and Oracle.

4.1.2 Three-Tier Client–Server Model

In a three-tier client-server model, a data action request is coming from an application GUI and sent to the application server that can be considered as a middle tier, and the application server that contains the JDBC API then sends SQL statements to the database located on a database server. When the data action is processed, the database sends the results back to the application server, which then sends them to the client. In fact, the so-called three-tier model is common in Web applications, in which the client tier is implemented in a Web browser, the middle tier is a Web server, and the database management system runs on a database server. This model can be represented by the following three layers:

- Client layer, which includes a Web browser with some language-specified virtual machines, installed in a client machine.
- Application server layer, which includes Java Web applications or Java Web services, installed in a Web server. This layer is used to handle the business logic or application logic. This may be implemented using Java Servlet engines, Java Server Pages, or Java Server Faces. The JDBC driver is also located in this layer.
- Database layer, which includes the RDBMS and the database, installed in a database server.

Figure 4.2 shows a typical configuration of a three-tier model.

Advantages of using a three-tier configuration over two-tier counterpart include:

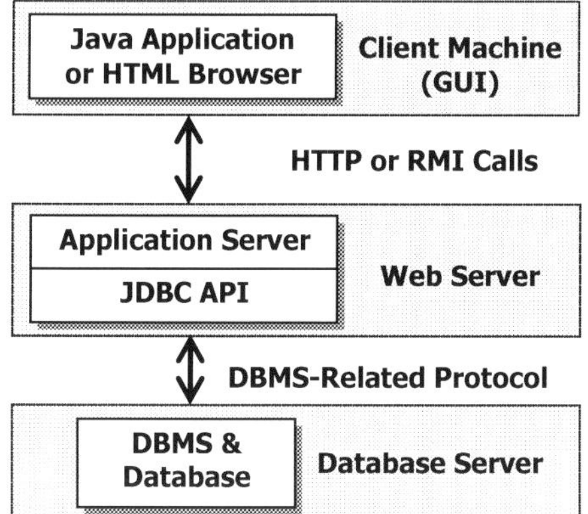

Figure 4.2. A typical configuration of a three-tier model.

- Application performance can be greatly improved by separating the application server and database server.
- Business logic is clearly separated from the database.
- Client application can then use a simple protocol to access the server.

Topics discussed in Chapters 8 and 9 in this book are about three-tier applications that use a Web browser as the client, a Java Server Face (JSF) or Java Server Page (JSP) as the middle tier, and a relational database management system as the database server.

Now that we have a clear picture about the Java application running models, next we need to dig a little deeper about the Java database applications.

4.2 JDBC APPLICATIONS FUNDAMENTALS

As we discussed in Section 3.1 in Chapter 3, to run a Java database application to perform data actions against the selected database, a JDBC API needs to perform the following operations:

1. Establish a connection between your Java application and related databases.
2. Build and execute SQL statements.
3. Process the results.

In fact, to successfully develop and run a Java database application, the above three operational steps need to be further divided into the following seven steps:

1. Import necessary Java packages, such as `java.awt`, `java.util`, `javax.swing`, `java.sql`, and `javax.sql`.
2. Load and register the JDBC driver.
3. Establish a connection to the database server.
4. Create a SQL statement.
5. Execute the built statement.

6. Retrieve the executing results.
7. Close the statement and connection objects.

In all steps listed above, step 1 is a prerequisite step since all JDBC-related components and interfaces are defined in the `java.sql` and `javax.sql` packages. All GUI-related components are defined in the `java.awt` and `javax.swing` packages, and all other application-related components are defined in the `java.util` package. In order to use any component defined in those packages, you must first import those packages into your program to provide namespaces and locations for those components. Otherwise, a compiling error may be encountered, since the compiler cannot find and identify those components when you used them but without providing the related packages.

In this and the following sections, we will provide a deeper and more detailed discussion about the data actions on Java database applications based on these seven fundamental steps.

4.2.1 Loading and Registering Drivers

As we studied in Chapter 3, to establish a valid database connection, first you need to load and register a JDBC driver. Then you can call the `connect()` method to establish a database connection to your desired database.

We provided a brief discussion about the JDBC Driver and DriverManager components in Chapter 3. In fact, the core of the JDBC API is the JDBC Driver that can be accessed and called from the DriverManager class method. However, the Driver class in under the control of the DriverManager class, and the DriverManager is exactly a manager for the Driver class. When using this Driver class, you cannot call and run any method defined in the Driver class; instead, you need to call them via the DriverManager class methods.

The DriverManager class is a set of utility functions that work with the Driver methods together and manage multiple JDBC drivers by keeping them as a list of drivers loaded. Although loading a driver and registering a driver are two steps, only one method call is necessary to perform these two operations. The operational sequence of loading and registering a JDBC driver is:

1. Call class methods in the DriverManager class to load the driver into the Java interpreter.
2. Register the driver using the **registerDriver()** method.

When loaded, the driver will execute the **DriverManager.registerDriver()** method to register itself. The above two operations will never be performed until a method in the DriverManager is executed, which means that even both operations have been coded in an application; however, the driver cannot be loaded and registered until a method such as **connect()** is first executed.

To load and register a JDBC driver, two popular methods can be used;

1. Use Class.forName() method:

   Class.forName("com.microsoft.sqlserver.jdbc.SQLServerDriver");

2. Create a new instance of the Driver class:

   Driver sqlDriver = new com.microsoft.sqlserver.jdbc.SQLServerDriver;

```
import java.sql.*;
try
{
    //Load and register SQL Server driver
    Class.forName("com.microsoft.sqlserver.jdbc.SQLServerDriver");
}
catch (Exception e) {
    System.out.println("Class not found exception!" + e.getMessage());
}
```

Figure 4.3. A sample coding for the driver loading and registering.

Relatively speaking, the first method is more professional since the driver is both loaded and registered when a valid method in the DriverManager class is executed. The second method cannot guarantee that the driver has been registered by using the DriverManager.

A piece of sample codes that are used to load and register a Microsoft SQL Server JDBC driver using the first method is shown in Figure 4.3.

In Figure 4.3, the first coding line is used to import the JDBC API package java.sql.*.

Then a `try.....catch` block is used to load and register a Microsoft SQL Server JDBC Driver. The **Class.forName()** method is utilized to make sure that our JDBC Driver is not only loaded, but also registered when it is connected by running the **getConnection()** method later. The argument of this method, `com.microsoft.sqlserver.jdbc.SQLServerDriver`, is the name of this Microsoft SQL Server JDBC Driver class, and it is created by the NetBeans when it is added to a Java database application project.

The `catch` block is used to track any possible error for this loading and registering. The related exception information will be displayed if any error occurred.

You can use the second method to replace this method to perform the same driver loading and registering operation if you like.

4.2.2 Getting Connected

To establish a connection to the desired database, two methods can be used:

1. Using `DriverManager.getConnection()` method
2. Using `Driver.connect()` method

Before we can take a closer look at these two methods, first, let's have a quick review for all methods defined in these two classes, `DriverManager` and `Driver`.

4.2.2.1 The DriverManager and Driver Classes

All 12 methods defined in the DriverManager class are shown in Table 4.1.

Four methods in the DriverManager class are widely applied in most database applications; `getConnection()`, `getDriver()`, `registerDriver()`, and `deregisterDriver()`. Note that the `getConnection()` method has two more overloading methods with different arguments.

Table 4.1. Methods defined in the DriverManager class

Method	Function
deregisterDriver(Driver dr)	Remove a Driver from the driver list
getConnection(String url, Properties login)	Attempt to establish a connection to the referenced database
getConnection(String url, String user, String pswd)	Attempt to establish a connection to the referenced database
getConnection(String url)	Attempt to establish a connection to the referenced database
getDriver(String url)	Locate an appropriate driver for the referenced URL from the driver list
getDrivers()	Get a list of all drivers currently loaded and registered
getLoginTimeout()	Get the maximum time (in seconds) a driver will wait for a connection
getLogStream()	Get the current PrintStream being used by the DriverManager.
Println(String msg)	Print a message to the current LogStream.
registerDriver(Driver dr)	Add the driver to the driver list. This is normally done automatically when the driver is instantiated
setLoginTimeout(int seconds)	Set the maximum time (in seconds) that a driver can wait when attempting to connect to a database before giving up
setLogStream(PrintStream out)	Set the PrintStream to direct logging message to

Table 4.2. Methods defined in the Driver class

Method	Function
acceptsURL(String url)	Return a true if the driver is able to open a connection to the database given by the URL
connect(String url, Properties login)	Check the syntax of the URL and the matched drivers in the driver list. Attempt to make a database connection to the given URL
getMajorVersion()	Determine the minor revision number of the driver
getMinorVersion()	Determine the major revision number of the driver
getPropertyInfo(String url, Properties login)	Return an array of DriverPropertyInfo objects describing login properties accepted by the database
jdbcCompliant()	Determine if the driver is JDBC COMPLIANT

All six methods defined in the Driver class are shown in Table 4.2.

Most popular methods in the Driver class are `acceptsURL()` and `connect()`.

Most methods defined in the Driver class will not be called directly in most Java database applications, instead, they will be called indirectly by using the DriverManager class.

Now let's have a closer look at these two methods.

4.2.2.2 Using the DriverManager.getConnection() Method

When using the first method `DriverManager.getConnection()` to establish a database connection, it does not immediately try to do this connection; instead, in order to make this connection more robust, it performs a two-step process. The `getConnection()` method first checks the driver and Uniform Resource Locator (URL) by running a method called `acceptsURL()`via DriverManager class to test the first driver in the driver list; if no matched driver returns, the `acceptURL()`method will go to test the next driver in the list. This process continues until each driver is tested or until a matched driver is found. If a matched driver is found, the `Driver.connect()` method will be executed to establish this connection. Otherwise, a SQLException is raised.

It looks like that this two-step connection is not efficient enough; however, a more robust connection can be set if more than one driver is available in the driver list.

The purpose of the `acceptsURL()` method is to check whether the current driver is able to open a valid connection to the given URL or not. This method does not create a real connection or test the actual database connections; instead, it merely examines the subprotocol of the URL and determine if it understands its syntax. In this way, it can effectively reduce the chance of the misconnection and make sure the correctness of an established connection.

4.2.2.3 Using the Driver.connect() Method

The `Driver.connect()`method enable you to create a actual connection to the desired database and returns an associated Connection object. This method accepts the database URL string and a Properties object as its argument. An URL indicates the protocol and location of a data source, while the properties object normally contains the user login information. One point to be noted is that the only time you can use this `Driver.connect()`method directly is when you have created a new instance of the Driver class.

A null will be returned if an exception occurs when this `Driver.connect()` method is executed, which means that something went wrong during this connection operation.

Comparing the `DriverManager.getConnection()` method with this `Driver.connect()` method, the following conclusions can be obtained:

- The `DriverManager.getConnection()` method can perform checking and testing each driver in the driver list automatically for all loaded drivers. As soon as a matched driver is found, it can be connected to the database directly by using `Driver.connect()` method. This automatic process will greatly reduce the processing time.
- The `DriverManager.getConnection()`method has looser requirements for the arguments passed with this method. When applying the `Driver.connect()`method, you have to pass two arguments, the URL as a string, and the login properties as a Properties object with strict syntax and grammar requirements. However, when using the `DriverManager.getConnection()`method, you can define login properties as either String, a Properties object, or even a null string, since the DriverManager can handle the converting these arguments to the appropriate Properties object when it is applied.

From this comparison, it can be found that the `DriverManager.getConnection()`method is over the `Driver.connect()`method; therefore, we will use this method to do our database connection in all example projects in this book.

After a driver has been loaded and registered, the next step is to establish a database connection using a URL. Before we can continue on the database connection, we need to have a clear picture and understanding about the JDBC connection URL.

4.2.2.4 The JDBC Connection URL

The JDBC URL provides all information for applications to access to a special resource, such as a database. Generally, a URL contains three parts or three segments: protocol name, sub-protocol and subname for the database to be connected. Each of these three segments has different function when they worked together to provide unique information for the target database.

The syntax for a JDBC URL can be presented as:

protocol:sub-protocol:subname

The protocol name works as an identifier or indicator to show what kind of protocol should be adopted when connected to the desired database. For a JDBC driver, the name of the protocol should be **jdbc**. The protocol name is used to indicate what kind of items to be delivered or connected.

The subprotocol is generally used to indicate the type of the database or data source to be connected, such as **sqlserver** or **oracle**.

The subname is used to indicate the address to which the item is supposed to be delivered or the location of the where database resides. Generally, a subname contains the following information for an address of a resource:

- Network host name/IP address
- The database server name
- The port number
- The name of the database

An example of a subname for our SQL Server database is:

localhost\\SQLEXPRESS:5000

The network host name is **localhost**, and the server name is **SQLEXPRESS**, and the port number the server used is **5000**. You need to use a double slash, either forward or back, to represent a normal slash in this URL string since this is a DOS-style string.

By combining all three segments together, we can get a full JDBC URL. An example URL that is using a SQL Server JDBC driver is:

jdbc:sqlserver//localhost\\SQLEXPRESS:5000

The database's name works as an attribute of the connected database.

Now that we have a clear picture about the JDBC URL, next, let's connect our application to our desired database.

4.2.2.5 Establish a Database Connection

Now, we have a clear picture and understanding about the fundamentals in `DriverManager` and Driver classes, as well as related database connection methods. As we discussed in

```
........
//A driver has been successfully loaded and registered

String url = "jdbc:sqlserver://localhost\\SQLEXPRESS:5000;databaseName=CSE_DEPT;";
//String url = "jdbc:sqlserver://localhost\\SQLEXPRESS:5000;
//              databaseName=CSE_DEPT;user=cse;password=mack8000";

//Establish a connection
try {
     con = DriverManager.getConnection(url,"cse","mack8000");
     //con = DriverManager.getConnection(url);
     con.close();
   }
   catch (SQLException e) {
     System.out.println("Could not connect! " + e.getMessage());
     e.printStackTrace();
   }
```

Figure 4.4. An example coding for the database connection.

the previous sections, to connect to a database, two methods, `DriverManager.getConnection()` and `Driver.connect()`, can be used. However, as we know, the first method is better than the second one; therefore, in this section, we will concentrate on the use of the first method to establish a database connection.

Figure 4.4 shows a piece of example codes to establish a connection using the `DriverManager.getConnection()` method. This piece of codes should be a follow-up of the codes shown in Figure 4.3; in other words, a valid driver has been loaded and registered before the following connection can be established.

Since the `DriverManager.getConnection()` method is an overloading method with three different signatures, here we used two of them, and the first one is highlighted in bold and the second one is commented out.

To establish a database connection, a valid JDBC URL is defined in the first coding line with the following components:

- The protocol name **jdbc**
- The subprotocol **sqlserver**
- The subname **localhost\\SQLEXPRESS:5000**
- The database name **CSE_DEPT**

Then, a `try...catch` block is used to try to establish a connection using the `getConnection()` method with three arguments: URL, username and password. After a valid connection is established, a Connection object is returned, and this returned object has the following functions and properties:

1. The Connection object represents an SQL session with the database.
2. The Connection object provides methods for the creation of Statement objects that will be used to execute SQL statements in the next step.
3. The Connection object also contains methods for the management of the session, such as transaction locking, catalog selection, and error handling.

Table 4.3. Methods defined in the Connection interface

Method	Function
close()	Close the connection to the database
createStatement()	Create a Statement object for the execution of static SQL statements
getMetaData()	Retrieve all database-related information stored in the DatabaseMetaData object for the current connection
isClosed()	Determine if the referenced Connection has been closed—True = closed
prepareCall(String sqlString)	Create a CallableStatement object for use with SQL stored procedures
prepareStatement(String sqlString)	Create a PreparedStatement object for use with SQL dynamic queries
commit()	Immediately commits all transactions to the database. All updates and changes are made permanent

By definition, the responsibility of a Connection object is to establish a valid database connection with your Java application, and that is all. The Connection object has nothing to do with the SQL statement execution. The SQL statement execution is the responsibility of the Statement, PreparedStatement, and CallableStatement objects. As we mentioned, both PreparedStatement and CallableStatement are subclasses of the Statement class, and they play different roles for the statement execution.

In the next coding line in Figure 4.4, a `close()` method that belongs to the Connection class is called to try to close a connection. In fact, it is unnecessary to close a connected database in actual applications. However, we used this method here to show users a complete picture of using the Connection object, which means that you must close a connection when it is no longer to be used in your application (even in the connection pooling situation, but it will not be really closed instead it is placed into a pool), otherwise a running error may be encountered when you reuse this connection in the future. Therefore, this coding line is only for the testing purpose, and should be removed in a real application.

The `catch` block is used to detect any possible exception and display them if any of them occurred.

A Connection class contains 19 methods, and Table 4.3 lists the seven most popular methods.

Now that a valid database connection has been established, the next step is to execute the SQL statements to perform data actions against our connected database.

4.2.3 Executing Statements

To successfully execute an appropriate Statement object to perform SQL statements, the following operational sequence should be followed:

1. Creating a `Statement` object based on the requirement of the data actions
2. Calling the appropriate execution method to run the SQL statements

In a simple word, the `Statement` object is used for executing a static SQL statement and returning the results stored in a ResultSet object.

4.2.3.1 Overview of Statement Objects and Their Execution Methods

By using the Connection object, three separate statement objects can be created, and they are:

- Statement object
- PreparedStatement object
- CallableStatement object

The `Statement` object is used to execute static SQL queries. The so-called static statements do not include any IN or OUT parameters in the query string and do not contain any parameters passing to or from the database.

The `Statement` interface contains more than 18 methods, and Table 4.4 lists the 10 most popular methods.

Among those 10 methods in the `Statement` interface, three execution methods, including the `executeQuery()`, `executeUpdate()` and `execute()`, and `getResultSet()` method, are often used in Java database applications.

Table 4.4. Methods defined in the Statement interface

Method	Function
close()	Close the Statement and release all resources including the ResultSet associated with it
execute(String sqlString)	Execute an SQL statement that may have an unknown number of results. A return of True means that the first set of results from the sqlString execution is a ResultSet. If the execution resulted in either no results or an update count, a False is returned
executeQuery(String sqlString)	Execute an SQL Select statement. A ResultSet object that contained the query results from the database will be returned
executeUpdate(String sqlString)	Execute an SQL Update, Insert or Delete statement. An integer will be returned to indicate the number of rows that have been affected
getMaxRows()	Determine the maximum number of rows that can be returned in a ResultSet object
getMoreResults()	Move to the Statements next result. Only in conjunction with the execute statement and where multiple results are returned by the SQL statement. A False is returned if the next result is null or the results are an update count
getResultSet()	Return the current result set for the Statement. Only used in conjunction with execute() method. The current ResultSet object will be returned
getUpdateCount()	Return the number of rows affected by the last SQL statement. Is only meaningful for INSERT, UPDATE, or DELETE statements
setCursorName(String name)	Set the cursor name to be used by the Statement. Only useful for databases that support positional updates and deletes
setMaxRows(int rows)	Set the maximum number of rows that can be returned in a ResultSet. If more results are returned by the query, they are truncated

Table 4.5. Methods defined in the PreparedStatement interface

Method	Function
clearParameters()	Clear all parameters associated with a PreparedStatement. After execution of this method, all parameters have the value null
execute()	Execute the associated SQL Statement when the number of results returned is unknown. A False is returned if the returned result is null
executeQuery()	Execute an SQL Select statement. A ResultSet object that contained the query results from the database will be returned
executeUpdate()	Execute an SQL Update, Insert, or Delete statement. An integer will be returned to indicate the number of rows that have been affected
getMetaData()	Return a set of metadata for the returned ResultSet object
getParameterMetaData()	Return the number, types and properties of this PreparedStatement object's parameters
setBoolean(int index, Boolean value)	Bind a Boolean value to an input parameter
setByte(int index, Byte value)	Bind a byte value to an input parameter
setDouble(int index, double value)	Bind a double value to an input parameter
setFloat(int index, float value)	Bind a floating point value to an input parameter
setInt(int index, int value)	Bind an integer value to an input parameter
setLong(int index, long value)	Bind a long value to an input parameter
setNull(int index, int sqlType)	Bind a null value to an input parameter
setObject(int index, Object obj)	Bind an Object to an input parameter. The Object will be converted to an SQL data type before being sent to the database
setShort(int index, short value)	Bind a short value to an input parameter
setString(int index, String value)	Bind a String value to an input parameter
setTime(int index, Time value)	Bind a Time value to an input parameter

The `PreparedStatement` is a subclass of the `Statement`, and it is mainly used to execute dynamic SQL queries with IN parameter involved. These kind of statements can be preparsed and precompiled by the database, and therefore have faster processing speed and lower running loads for the database server.

The `PreparedStatement` interface contains more than 20 methods, and Table 4.5 lists 17 most popular methods.

It can be found from Table 4.5 that three execution methods, `execute()`, `executeQuery()`, and `executeUpdate()`, look like a duplication with those methods defined in the Statement interface. However, a significant difference is: all of these three methods defined in the Statement interface have their query strings as an argument when these methods are executed, which means that the SQL statements have to be defined in those query strings, and should be passed into the database as the arguments of those methods. In contrast, all three methods defined in the PreparedStatement interface have no any argument to be passed into the database when they are executed. This means that the SQL statements have been built and passed into the database by using the PreparedStatement object before these three methods are executed.

Two methods belong to the getters that are used to retrieve the metadata for the ResultSet and the ParameterMetaData objects. Both methods are very useful when the developer wants to get more detailed structure and properties information about a returned ResultSet object or ParameterMetaData object.

More than 10 methods defined in the PreparedStatement interface are setter method, which means that these methods are used to set up an appropriate value to an input parameter with different data types. These methods are especially useful when a dynamic query is built, with one or more dynamic input parameters need to be determined in the SQL statements.

The CallableStatement is also a subclass of the Statement and the PreparedStatement classes, and it is mainly used to execute the stored procedures with both IN and OUT parameters involved. As we know, stored procedures are built and developed inside databases, and therefore have higher running and responding efficiency in data queries and processing.

This interface is used to execute SQL stored procedures. The JDBC API provides a stored procedure SQL escape syntax that allows stored procedures to be called in a standard way for all RDBMSs. This escape syntax has one form that includes a result parameter, and one that does not. If used, the result parameter must be registered as an OUT parameter. The other parameters can be used for input, output, or both. Parameters are referred to sequentially, by number or position, with the first parameter being 1.

```
{?= call <procedure-name>[(<arg1>,<arg2>, . . . )]}
{call <procedure-name>[(<arg1>,<arg2>, . . . )]}
```

The IN parameter values are set using the **setXXX()** methods inherited from the interface PreparedStatement. The type of all OUT parameters must be registered prior to executing the stored procedure; their values are retrieved after execution via the **getXXX()** methods defined in this CallableStatement interface.

A CallableStatement can return one ResultSet object or multiple ResultSet objects. Multiple ResultSet objects are handled using operations inherited from the Statement interface.

The CallableStatement interface contains more than 30 methods, and Table 4.6 lists 15 most popular methods.

The registerOutParameter() method is an overloading method with two signatures, and these methods are used to declare what SQL type the OUT parameter will return when a CallableStatement method is executed.

By default, only one ResultSet object per Statement object can be open at the same time. Therefore, if the reading of one ResultSet object is interleaved with the reading of another, each must have been generated by different Statement objects. All execution methods in the Statement interface implicitly close a Statement's current ResultSet object if an open one exists.

The Statement interface contains three important query methods with different functions; **executeQuery()**, **executeUpdate()**, and **execute()**. For each method, different operations can be performed, and different results will be returned.

Generally, the query methods can be divided into two categories; (1) the query method that needs to perform data query, such as **executeQuery()**, which returns an

Table 4.6. Methods defined in the CallableStatement interface

Method	Function
getBigDecimal(int index, int scale)	Return the value of parameter specified by the parameter index number as a BigDecimal
getBoolean(int index)	Return the value of parameter specified by the parameter index number as a Boolean
getByte(int index)	Return the value of parameter specified by the parameter index number as a byte
getBytes(int index)	Return the value of parameter specified by the parameter index number as an array of bytes
getDouble(int index)	Return the value of parameter specified by the parameter index number as a double
getFloat(int index)	Return the value of parameter specified by the parameter index number as a floating point number
getInt(int index)	Return the value of parameter specified by the parameter index number as an integer
getLong(int index)	Return the value of parameter specified by the parameter index number as a long integer
getObject(int index)	Return the value of parameter specified by the parameter index number as an Object. The object type is determined by the default mapping of the SQL data type to Java data type
getShort(int index)	Return the value of parameter specified by the parameter index number as a short integer
getString(int index)	Return the value of parameter specified by the parameter index number as a String object
getTime(int index)	Return the value of parameter specified by the parameter index number as a Time object
registerOutParameter(int index, int slqType)	Register the specified output parameter to receive the SQL data type indicated by the argument passed.
registerOutParameter(int index, int slqType, int scale)	Register the specified output parameter to receive the SQL data type indicated by the argument passed. If the output is registered as either DECIMAL or NUMERIC, the scale of the value may also be specified
wasNull()	Determine if the last value read by a **getXXX()** method was a SQL null value. A True is returned if the last read value contained a null value

instance of **ResultSet** that contained the queried results, and (2) the query method that does not perform data query and only return an integer, such as **executeUpdate()**. An interesting method is the **execute()**, which can be used in either ways.

Let's first concentrate on the creation of the Statement objects based on the different requirements of data actions.

4.2.3.2 Using the Statement Object

As we discussed in the last section, three separate statement objects can be created based on three different data actions: `Statement`, `PreparedStatement` and `CallableStatement`. Let's discuss how to create a `Statement` object first.

4.2.3.2.1 Creating the Statement Object The `Statement` object is the most common type of object and is easy to use in a static data query. The shortcoming of using this `Statement` object is that all SQL statements must be predefined with definite parameters when a Statement object is created. In other words, by using a Statement object to execute a SQL statement, no parameter can be passed into or from the database.

The `Statement` object is created by using the `createStatement()` method defined in the `Connection` interface (refer to Table 4.3). Figure 4.5 shows an example coding for the creation of a `Statement` object.

The coding line that is used to create a `Statement` object has been highlighted in bold. All other lines are prerequisite codes that are used to load and register a driver, establish a connection using the URL, and build a SQL query string.

4.2.3.2.2 Executing the Statement Object To execute the created `Statement` object to perform a data action, you need to call one of the execution methods defined in the `Statement` interface shown in Table 4.4. Figure 4.6 shows an example coding for the execution of an SQL query with this `Statement` object.

The coding line that is used to execute a `Statement` object has been highlighted in bold. All other lines are prerequisite codes that are used to load and register a driver, establish a connection using the URL, build a SQL query string, and create a `Statement` object. It can be found from this piece of codes that no parameter can be passed to or from the database when this query is executed. Therefore the `Statement` object can only be used to perform static queries.

To overcome this shortcoming, we need to use `PreparedStatement` objects to perform dynamic queries with varied input parameters.

4.2.3.3 Using the PreparedStatement Object

To perform dynamic SQL statements, we need to use a `PreparedStatement` object. Generally to use a `PreparedStatement` object to perform a dynamic SQL statement includes the following steps:

```
String url = "jdbc:sqlserver://localhost\\SQLEXPRESS:5000;databaseName=CSE_DEPT;";
//Establish a connection
try {
      con = DriverManager.getConnection(url,"cse","mack8000");
}
catch (SQLException e) {
      System.out.println("Could not connect! " + e.getMessage()); }
String query = "SELECT user_name, pass_word FROM LogIn";
try{
      Statement stmt = con.createStatement();
}
catch (SQLException e) {
      System.out.println("Error in Statement! " + e.getMessage()); }
```

Figure 4.5. An example coding for the creation of a Statement object.

```
import java.sql.*;
static Connection con;
try {
        //Load and register SQL Server driver
        Class.forName("com.microsoft.sqlserver.jdbc.SQLServerDriver");
}
catch (Exception e) {
        System.out.println("Class not found exception!" + e.getMessage()); }
String url = "jdbc:sqlserver://localhost\\SQLEXPRESS:5000;databaseName=CSE_DEPT;";
//Establish a connection
try {
        con = DriverManager.getConnection(url,"cse","mack8000");
}
catch (SQLException e) {
        System.out.println("Could not connect! " + e.getMessage()); }
String query = "SELECT user_name, pass_word FROM LogIn";
try{
        Statement  stmt = con.createStatement();
        ResultSet rs = stmt.executeQuery(query);
}
catch (SQLException e) {
        System.out.println("Error in Statement! " + e.getMessage()); }
```

Figure 4.6. An example coding for the execution of a Statement object.

1. Create a `PreparedStatement` object
2. Set data types and values to the associated input parameters in the query string
3. Call appropriate execution method to perform this dynamic query

Let's first concentrate on the creation of a `PreparedStatement` object.

4.2.3.3.1 Creating the PreparedStatement Object Refer to Table 4.3; the `prepare Statement()` method defined in the Connection interface is used to create a `PreparedStatement` object. An example code to create a PreparedStatement object looks like:

```
PreparedStatement pstmt = con.prepareStatement(query);
```

Unlike Statement objects, the `PreparedStatement` object takes the SQL statement to be executed as an argument. For dynamic SQL statements that contain input parameters to be passed into the database, you need to define a position for each input parameter in the query string. Regularly, a placeholder is used to inform the database that it can expect a variable in that position. Each placeholder that holds a position for a variable in the query string is represented by a question mark "?", which holds a place for the associated variable during compiling time. When compiled, the placeholder is part of the statement and therefore appears static to the compiler. In this way, no matter what value is later assigned to the variable, the database does not need to recompile the statement. At the runtime, you can assign values to the variables by using any **setXXX()** method defined in the `PreparedStatement` interface shown in Table 4.5.

Before we can call an execution method to run the `PreparedStatement` to perform a dynamic query, let's first take a look at how to use **setXXX()** method to reserve a place for the input parameter with the correct data type settings.

4.2.3.3.2 Setting the Input Parameters All input parameters used for a PreparedStatement interface must be clearly bound to the associated IN parameters in a dynamic query string by using a **setXXX()** method. This **setXXX()** method can be divided into three categories based on the different data types,

1. The primitive data type method
2. The object method
3. The stream method

For the primitive and the object method, the syntax is identical, and the difference between them is the type of value that is assigned. For the stream method, both the syntax and the data types are different.

Set Primitive Data Type and Object IN Values

The primitive data type means all built-in data types used in Java programming language. The syntax of setting a primitive data type or an object value method is,

```
setXXX(int position, data_type value);
```

where **XXX** means the associated value type to be assigned, the **position** is an integer that is used to indicate the relative position of the IN parameter in the SQL statement or the SQL stored procedure, and the **value** is the actual data value to be assigned to the IN parameter.

Some popular **setXXX()** methods defined in the `PreparedStatement` interface can be found from the Table 4.5.

An example of using the **setXXX()** method is:

```
String query = "SELECT product, order_date FROM Order " +
"WHERE order_id = ? AND customer = ?";
PreparedStatement pstmt = con.prepareStatement(query);
setInt(1, 101);
setString(2, "Tom Johnson");
```

Two dynamic parameters are used in the query string, and both of them are IN parameters. The data type of first IN parameter is an integer and the second one is a String, and both are represented by a placeholder "?". The first setting method, **setInt(1, 101)** is to assign an integer value of 101 to the first IN parameter, which is indicated with a position number of 1, and the second setting method, **setString(2, "Tom Johnson")** is to assign a String value "**Tom Johnson**" to the second IN parameter, which is indicated with a position number of 2.

From this example, you can find that there is no difference between setting a primitive parameter and an object value to the IN parameters in a SQL statement.

Set Object Methods

The **setObject()** method has three protocols, which are:

```
setObject(int position, object_type object_value);
setObject(int position, object_type object_value, data_type
        desired_data_type);
```

```
setobject(int position, object_type object_value, data_type
          desired_data_type, int scale);
```

The first one is straightforward, and it contains two parameters; the first one is the relative position of the IN parameter in the SQL statement, and the second one is the value of a desired object to be assigned to the IN object.

The second one adds one more input parameter, **desired_data_type**, and it is used to indicate a data type to which to convert the object to.

The third one adds the fourth input parameter, **scale**, and it is used to make sure that the object conversion result contains a certain number of digits.

An example of the **setObject()** method is shown here:

```
pstmt.setObject(2, 101);
pstmt.setObject(2, 101, Type.FLOAT);
pstmt.setObject(2, 101, Type.FLOAT, 2);
```

The first method is to set an input parameter, which is the second one in a SQL statement, to an object (here is an integer) with a value of 101. The next method is to set the same input to the same object; however, it needs to convert the object (integer) to a float data type. The final method performs the same operation as the previous one, but it indicates that the conversion result should contain at least two digits.

Since set stream IN methods are not very popular in Java database applications, we skip this part in this section. If you want to get more detailed information for these methods, refer to Section 6.4.5.2.3 in Chapter 6.

Now let's begin to call some appropriate execution methods to run this PreparedStatement object to perform dynamic queries.

4.2.3.3.3 Executing the PreparedStatement Object As we discussed in Section 3.3.2 in Chapter 3, three execution methods can be called to perform the data action against the database. Refer to Tables 4.4 and 4.5; it can be found that both `Statement` and `PreparedStatement` interfaces contain these three methods:

- executeQuery()
- executeUpdate()
- execute()

The difference between these three methods in both interfaces is that all three execution methods defined in the Statement interface need an argument, which works as a query statement passed into the database. However, all three methods defined in the `PreparedStatement` interface have no any argument, which means that the query statement has been built and passed to the database by using the `PreparedStatement` object when it is created.

Figure 4.7 shows a piece of example codes for calling of the `executeQuery()`method to perform a login process.

First, the query statement `query` is created in which two placeholders (?) are used since we have two dynamic parameters, username, and password, to be passed into our sample database CSE_DEPT.

```
String url = "jdbc:sqlserver://localhost\\SQLEXPRESS:5000;databaseName=CSE_DEPT;";
//Establish a connection
try {
      con = DriverManager.getConnection(url,"cse","mack8000");
}
catch (SQLException e) {
      System.out.println("Could not connect! " + e.getMessage()); }
String query = "SELECT user_name, pass_word FROM LogIn " +
               "WHERE user_name = ? AND pass_word = ?";
try{
      PreparedStatement pstmt = con.prepareStatement(query);
      pstmt.setString(1, "cse");
      pstmt.setString(2, "mack8000");
      ResultSet rs = pstmt.executeQuery();
}
catch (SQLException e) {
      System.out.println("Error in PreparedStatement! " + e.getMessage()); }
```

Figure 4.7. An example coding for the execution of a PreparedStatement.

Then, with a `try...catch` block, a `PreparedStatement` object is created with the `query` statement as an argument. Two `setString()` methods defined in the `PreparedStatement` interface are used to initialize these two dynamic parameters (username = "`cse`", password = "`mack8000`"). Finally, the `executeQuery()` method defined in the `PreparedStatement` interface is called to run this query statement, and the results are returned and stored in a `ResultSet` object.

In addition to using the `executeQuery()` method, the `PreparedStatement` object can also use another two methods, `executeUpdate()` and `execute()` to perform a data action. However, those methods have different functionalities, and should be applied in the different situations. For more detailed information about these methods, refer to Section 4.2.3.8.

Compared with the `Statement` interface, the advantage of using a `PreparedStatement` interface is that it can perform a dynamic query, with some known or unknown dynamic parameters as inputs. Most time, those dynamic parameters are input parameters and can be defined as IN variables. However, you do not need to specify those parameters with an IN keyword when using a `PreparedStatement` interface.

4.2.3.4 Using the CallableStatement Object

As we discussed in the early part of this chapter, the `CallableStatement` is a subclass of both `Statement` and `PreparedStatement`, and this interface is mainly used to call stored procedures to perform a group data actions. The JDBC `CallableStatement` method provides a way to allow us to perform a complicated query. The speed and efficiency of a data query can be significantly improved by using the stored procedure, since it is built in the database side.

The difference between a `PreparedStatement` and a `CallableStatement` interface is: unlike the `PreparedStatement` interface, the `CallableStatement` interface has both input and output parameters, which are indicated with IN and OUT keywords, respectively. In order to setup values for input parameters or get values from the output parameters, you have to use either a **setXXX()** method inherited from the `PreparedStatement` or a **getXXX()** method to do that. However, the point is that before you can use any **getXXX()** method to pick up the values of output parameters, you must first register the output parameters to allow the `CallableStatement` interface to know them.

Generally, the sequence to run a `CallableStatement` to perform a stored procedure is:

1. Build a `CallableStatement` query string.
2. Create a `CallableStatement` object.
3. Set the input parameters.
4. Register the output parameters.
5. Execute `CallableStatement`.
6. Retrieve the running result by using different **getXXX()** method.

Let's discuss this issue one by one in more details in the following sections.

4.2.3.4.1 Building a CallableStatement Query String The `CallableStatement` interface is used to execute SQL stored procedures. The JDBC API provides a stored procedure SQL escape syntax that allows stored procedures to be called in a standard way for all RDBMSs. This escape syntax has one form that includes an output parameter and one that does not. If used, the output parameter must be registered as an OUT parameter. The other parameters can be used for input, output, or both. Parameters are referred to sequentially, by number, with the first parameter being 1.

```
{?= call <procedure-name>[<arg1>,<arg2>, ...]}
{call <procedure-name>[<arg1>,<arg2>, ...]}
```

Two syntaxes are widely used to formulate a CallableStatement string: the SQL92 syntax and the Oracle syntax. The SQL92 syntax is more popular in most applications. We will concentrate on the SQL92 syntax in this section, and take care of the Oracle syntax later when we build data queries for the Oracle database.

For a standard alone stored procedure or packaged procedure, the SQL92 syntax can be represented as:

```
{call [schema.][package.]procedure_name[(?, ?, ...)]}
```

For standard alone functions or packaged functions, the SQL92 syntax looks like:

```
{? = call [schema.][package.]function_name[(?, ?, ...)]}
```

The definition and meaning of elements used in these syntaxes are:

- All elements enclosed inside the square brackets [] means that they are optional.
- The curly braces {} are necessary in building a `CallableStatement` string, and they must be used to cover the whole string.

- The schema indicates the schema in which the stored procedure is created.
- The package indicates the name of the package if the stored procedure is involved in a package.
- The *procedure_name* or the *function_name* indicate the name of the stored procedure or the function.
- The question mark ? is the placeholder for either an IN, IN/OUT, or OUT parameters used in the stored procedure, or the returned value of a function. The order of these placeholders, which starts from 1, is very important, and it must be followed exactly when using either a **setXXX()** method to set up input parameters or register the output parameters for the built CallableStatement string later.

A `CallableStatement` can either return a `ResultSet` object and multiple `ResultSet` objects by using **executeQuery()** method or return nothing by using **execute()** method. Multiple `ResultSet` objects are handled using operations inherited from the `Statement` interface. A suitable **getXXX()** method is needed to pick up the running result of a `CallableStatement`.

Now that we have built a `CallableStatement` query string, next we need to create a `CallableStatement` object to execute the associated method to run stored procedures.

4.2.3.4.2 Creating the CallableStatement Object To create a `CallableStatement` object, you need to use one of methods defined in the `Connection` class (refer to Table 4.3), **prepareCall()**, to do that. When the SQL92 syntax is used to create this `CallableStatement` object, it will look like:

```
CallableStatement cstmt = null;
try{

String query = "{call dbo.FacultyCourse(?, ?)}";
cstmt = con.prepareCall(query);
```

The operation sequence of this piece of codes to create a new `CallableStatement` object is:

1. A new null `CallableStatement` object **cstmt** is first declared.
2. A `try` block is used to create the query string with the SQL92 syntax. The name of the stored procedure to be called is **dbo.FacultyCourse()**, with two arguments: the first one is an input parameter, **faculty_name**, and the second one is an output parameter used to store all **course_id** taught by the selected faculty. Both parameters are represented by placeholders, and they are positional parameters.
3. The `CallableStatement` object is created by calling the **prepareCall()** method, which belongs to the `Connection` class, with the query string as the argument.

Next, let's take a look at how to setup the input parameter for this object.

4.2.3.4.3 Setting the Input Parameters We have provided a very detailed introduction in setting the input parameters for the PreparedStatement object in Section 4.2.3.3.2. Refer to that section to get more detailed description about setting the input parameters for a query string in the CallableStatement object. Figure 4.8 shows a piece of example codes to set input parameters for two dynamic parameters, *faculty_name* and *class_name*,

```
String query = "{call dbo.FacultyCourse(?, ?)}";
cstmt = con.prepareCall(query);
cstmt.setString(1, "Jones");
cstmt.setString(2, "CSC-132B");
```

Figure 4.8. An example coding for the setting input parameters.

```
String query = "{call dbo.FacultyCourse(?, ?)}";
cstmt = con.prepareCall(query);
cstmt.setString(1, "Jones");
cstmt.setString(2, "CSC-132B");

cstmt.registerOutParameter(2, java.sql.Types.VARCHAR);
```

Figure 4.9. An example coding for the registering of the output parameters.

the data type for both input parameters is String. Therefore, a `setString()` method is used.

Now let's take a look at how to register output parameters for a query string when using the `CallableStatement` object to perform a stored procedure call.

4.2.3.4.4 Registering the Output Parameters

After a `CallableStatement` interface is executed, you need to use the associated **getXXX()** method to pick up the running result from the `CallableStatement` object, since it cannot return any result itself. However, before you can do that, you must first register any output parameter in the SQL statement to allow the `CallableStatement` to know that the output result is involved and stored in the related output parameters in the SQL statement.

Once an output parameter is registered, the parameter is considered an OUT parameter, and it can contain running results that can be picked up by using the associated **getXXX()** method.

To register an output parameter, the **registerOutParameter()** method that belongs to the `CallableStatement` interface, should be used to declare what SQL type the OUT parameter will return. A point to be noted is that a parameter in a SQL statement can be defined both as an IN and an OUT at the same time, which means that you can setup this parameter as an IN by using the **setXXX()** method, and also you can register this parameter as an OUT using the **registerOutParameter()** method at the same time. In this way, this parameter can be considered as an IN/OUT parameter with both the input and the output functions.

The syntax to register an output parameter is:

```
registerOutParameter(int position, data_type SQL_data_type);
```

where the **position** is still the relative position of the OUT parameter in the SQL statement, and the **SQL_data_type** is the SQL data type of the OUT parameter, which can be found from the JDBC API class, **java.sql.TYPE**.

An example of using this method is shown in Figure 4.9.

There are two parameters in this `CallableStatement` interface in this example. The first one is an IN parameter, which is set by using the **setString()** method. The second one is an IN/OUT parameter, which is first setup by using the **setString()** method and then registered by using the **registerOutParameter()** method with the data type of VARCHAR. The SQL data type VARCHAR can be mapped to a data type of String in Java. Refer to Appendix A to get more detailed information about the data type mapping between the SQL and Java.

An interesting point to this **registerOutParameter()** method is that all OUT parameters can be registered by using this syntax except those OUT parameters with the NUMERIC and DECIMAL data types. The syntax to register those OUT parameters looks like:

```
registerOutParameter(int position, data_type SQL_data_type,
                     int scale);
```

The only difference is that a third parameter **scale** is added, and it is used to indicate the number of digits to the right of the decimal point for the OUT parameter.

4.2.3.4.5 Executing the CallableStatement Object To run a `CallableStatement` object, three execution methods can be used; **executeQuery()**, **executeUpdate()** and **execute()**. As we discussed in Section 4.2.3.1, the **executeQuery()** method can return a `ResultSet` object that contains the running or query results, and the **executeUpdate()** method can return an integer to indicate the number of rows that have been inserted, updated, or deleted against the target database. However, the **execute()** method cannot return any running result with itself, and you need to use associated **getXXX()** methods to pick up the query or running result. Another important point of using the **execute()** method is that it can handle an unknown result with undefined data type. Refer to Section 4.2.3.5 to get more detailed information about the **execute()** method.

An example of using the **execute()** method to run the `CallableStatement` object is shown in Figure 4.10.

After finishing building the query string, creating the `CallableStatement` object, and setting and registering input and output parameters, the `execute()` method is called to execute this `CallableStatement` object to perform a stored procedure processing.

Before we can continue in how to retrieve the running result from the execution of a `Statement`, `PreparedStatement`, or `CallableStatement` object, we need to have a closer look at three execution methods.

4.2.3.5 More about the Execution Methods

The three statement objects are used to perform different data actions against the target database, and the type of statement object to be used is determined by the parameters

```
String query = "{call dbo.FacultyCourse(?, ?)}";
cstmt = con.prepareCall(query);
cstmt.setString(1, "Jones");
cstmt.setString(2, "CSC-132B");
cstmt.registerOutParameter(2, java.sql.Types.VARCHAR);
cstmt.execute();
```

Figure 4.10. An example coding for running of the CallableStatement object.

of the SQL statement. To make it simple, the following strategy should be adopted for the given situation:

- For static statements without needing to pass any parameter into the database, a Statement object can be used to perform this kind of data action.
- For dynamic statements with some input parameters that are needed to be passed into the target database, a PreparedStatement object should be used to perform this kind of data action.
- For stored procedures with both input and output parameters needed to be passed into the target database, a CallableStatement object can be used to perform this kind of data action.

Similarly to statement objects, the execute method to be used is determined by the expected output of the SQL statement. There are three types of output that can be expected from a SQL statement:

- A ResultSet containing data in tabular format with certain rows and columns
- An integer indicating the number of rows affected by the SQL statement
- A combination of a ResultSet and an integer

Each of these output types requires its own special output handling. Accordingly, three execute methods, `executeQuery()`, `executeUpdate()`, and `execute()`, can be used for each type of statement object.

Generally, the execute methods can be divided into two categories: (1) the execute method that needs to perform a data query, such as the **executeQuery()**, which returns an instance of **ResultSet** that contained the queried results, and (2) the execute method that does not perform a data query and only return an integer, such as the **executeUpdate()**. An interesting method is the **execute()**, which can be used in either ways. In conclusion, the following points should be noted when using any of these execute methods:

- The **executeQuery()** method performs data query and returns a **ResultSet** object that contains the queried results.
- The **executeUpdate()** method does not perform data query, instead it only performs either a data updating, insertion, or deleting action against the database and returns an integer that equals to the number of rows that have been successfully updated, inserted, or deleted.
- The **execute()** method is a special method, and it can be used either way. All different data actions can be performed by using this method, such as data query, data insertion, data updating, and data deleting. The most important difference between the **execute()** method and two above methods is that the former can be used to execute some SQL statements that are unknown at the compile time or return multiple results from stored procedures. Another difference is that the **execute()** method does not return any result itself, and one needs to use **getResultSet()** or **getUpdateCount()** method to pick up the results. Both methods belong to the `Statement` interface.

A confusion issue may come with the using of the **execute()** method. As we mentioned, since any SQL statement, either known or unknown at the compile time, can be used with this **execute()** method, how do we know the execution results? Yes, that indeed is a problem. However, fortunately, we can solve this problem by using some testing methods indirectly.

In fact, we can call either **getResultSet()** or **getUpdateCount()** method to try to pick up the running results from execution of the **execute()** method. The key point is:

```
PreparedStatement pstmt = con.prepareStatement(query);
pstmt.setString(1, "faculty_name");
pstmt.execute();

int updateCount = pstmt.getUpdateCount();
if (updateCount == -1)
    System.out.println("execute() method returned a ResultSet object!");
else
    System.out.println("execute() method returned an integer!");
```

Figure 4.11. An example coding to distinguish the returned result.

- The **getResultSet()** method will return a null if the running result is an integer, which is a number of rows that have been affected, either inserted, updated, or deleted.
- The **getUpdateCount()** method will return a –1 if the running result is a `ResultSet`.

Based on these two key points, we can easily determine whether a result is a `ResultSet` or an integer. Figure 4.11 shows a piece of example codes to illustrate how to distinguish what kind of result is returned by using these two methods.

A `PreparedStatement` object is created, and the input parameter is initialized using the `setString()` method, and then the `execute()` method is called to run the SQL statement. In order to distinguish the running result, first, we use the `getUpdateCount()` method to pick up the returned result. A `ResultSet` object is returned if a –1 is returned for the execution of the `getUpdateCount()` method. Otherwise, an integer is returned to indicate that a data update, insert, or delete action has been executed, and the integer value is equal to the number of rows that have been affected.

Now that we have known how to create and execute different execute methods, let's have a closer look at the creation and execution of SQL statements by using those methods.

4.2.3.6 Creating and Executing SQL Statements

To execute any execution method we discussed in the previous sections, exactly it is to execute a string representing an SQL statement. In fact, the SQL statement and the JDBC representation are exactly the same thing from the point of view of the terminal execution results. However, in some cases, you have to modify the JDBC string to make sure that the database can receive the correct SQL statement.

All SQL statements can be divided into two categories:

- Data definition language (DDL) statements
- Data manipulation language (DML) statements

The DDL statements are used to create and modify the structure of your database tables and other objects related to the database. The DML statements are used to work and manipulate with data in the database tables.

Let's discuss the creation and execution of SQL statements based on these two categories in the following sections.

```
String sqlString = (" CREATE TABLE LogIn"
                    + "(user_name VARCHAR2(10), "
                    + " pass_word VARCHAR2(10), "
                    + " login_ID int )";
Statement stmt = con.createStatement();
stmt.execute(sqlString);
```

Figure 4.12. An example coding to create a LogIn table using JDBC statement.

4.2.3.6.1 Creating and Executing the DDL Statements Since DDL statements are mainly used for the creation and modification of the structure of the database tables and related objects, therefore, they do not perform any query, and do not affect any rows in the database-related tables. Of course, they will never return any `ResultSet` object, either. However, in order to keep DDL statements consistent with other types of SQL statements, the DDL statements always return a 0 in an actual application.

A standard DDL protocol used to create the structure of a table is:

```
CREATE TABLE <table name>
(<attribute name 1> <data type 1>,
<attribute name n> <data type n>);
```

Figure 4.12 shows a piece of example codes to illustrate how to create a `LogIn` table using the JDBC statement.

First, the protocol used to create the `Login` table is assigned to a JDBC statement string `sqlString`. The data type for both `user_name` and `pass_word` columns are `VARCHAR2`, which is a varied-length char. The argument 10 is used to define the length of those chars. The `login_ID` is an integer. Then a `Statement` object is created, and the `execute()`method is called to perform the creation of this table with the `sqlString` as the argument that is passed to the database.

To add data into a created table, you need to use the DML statements to do that job.

4.2.3.6.2 Creating and Executing the DML Statements The DML statements are used to build and complete the body of the database tables. These statements include the data query statements, insert, update, and delete statements. All of these statements need to return some execution results, either a ResultSet object or an integer.

A standard DML statement used to insert data into the created data table looks like:

```
INSERT INTO <table name>
VALUES (<value 1>, <value 2>, ...<value n>);
```

A standard DML statement used to update data from a created data table looks like:

```
UPDATE <table name>
SET <attribute> = <expression>
WHERE <condition>;
```

Figure 4.13 shows a piece of example codes to illustrate how to add some data items to the created `LogIn` table using the JDBC statement.

```
String sqlString = ("INSERT INTO LogIn"
                  + "VALUES ('Tom Baker', 'come123', 100078, 'David Tim', 'test55', 100080)";

Statement stmt = con.createStatement();
stmt.execute(sqlString);
```

Figure 4.13. An example coding to insert data into the LogIn table using JDBC statement.

```
String query = "SELECT user_name, pass_word FROM LogIn " +
               "WHERE user_name = ? AND pass_word = ?";
try{
      PreparedStatement pstmt = con.prepareStatement(query);
      pstmt.setString(1, "cse");
      pstmt.setString(2, "mack8000");
      ResultSet rs = pstmt.executeQuery();
}
catch (SQLException e) {
       System.out.println("Error in PreparedStatement! " + e.getMessage()); }
```

Figure 4.14. An example coding to perform a SQL query using JDBC statement.

Figure 4.14 shows a piece of example codes to illustrate how to perform a select query to retrieve the desired username and password from the LogIn table.

4.2.3.6.3 JDBC Escape Syntax When JDBC perform a SQL statement, it does not check the SQL grammar, and you can send any SQL statement to your database. This gives you flexibility to allow you to use some extended functions that are not included in the entry level SQL92 standard and provided by particular vendors. To support these extensions in a database independent manner, JDBC implements an ODBC-style escape syntax for many of these extensions. By using escape syntax, applications can achieve total database independence and still take advantages of the additional functionalities provided by those extensions.

Escape syntax works much like the escape character, which contains a keyword and parameters all enclosed in curly braces.

```
{ keyword [parameter], ....}
```

As JDBC finds a set of curly braces in an executable string, the driver maps the enclosed keyword and parameters to the database-specified syntax, and the mapped syntax is then sent to the database for execution.

JDBC escape syntax supports seven keywords; each of them indicates the type of extension that is enclosed within the braces. Table 4.7 shows a collection of the keywords and their syntax.

So far, we have discussed most Statement components and interfaces in JDBC data actions and applications; now let's take care of the retrieving the execution results.

Table 4.7. Keywords and their syntax supported by JDBC escape syntax

Keyword	Function	Syntax
Call	Execute stored procedures	{ call procedure_name [arg1, . . .]}
? = call	Execute stored functions	{ ? = call function_name [arg1, . . .] }
d	Define a date	{ d 'yyy-mm-dd' }
escape	Define the databases escape character	{ escape 'escape character' }
fn	Execute a scalar function	{ 'fn function [arg1, . . .] }
oj	Define an outer join	{ oj outer-join }
t	Define a time	{ 'hh:mm:ss' }
ts	Define a time stamp	{ 'yyyy-mm-dd hh:mm:ss.f....' }

4.2.4 Retrieving Results

Based on the different SQL statements, three execution methods can be used to run an associated SQL statement. As we discussed in Section 4.2.3.1, each execution method performs different data actions:

- The `executeQuery()`method is used to run a data query, and the expected returning result is a result set stored in a `ResultSet` object.
- The `executeUpdate()` method is used to perform a insert, update, or delete data action, and the returning result should be an integer that equals to the number of rows that have been affected by running this data manipulation.
- The `execute()`method can be used in either way, but this method never returns any result, and you need to use special methods to pick up the running results.

To pick up the running results for different methods, the following rules should be followed:

1. For the `executeQuery()`method, the `getResultSet()`method defined in the `Statement` interface should be used, since the running result is a result set stored in a `ResultSet` object.
2. For the `executeUpdate()`method, the `getUpdateCount()`method defined in the `Statement` interface should be used since the running result is an integer that equals to the number of rows that have been affected.
3. For the `execute()`method, since this method can handle both `ResultSet` and integer, it also never returns any result, you need to use special methods to retrieve the running result for the execution of this method.

Relatively speaking, for the first two methods, it is relatively easy to pick the running result since the result is known and definite. The challenge is the third method, `execute()`, since the result of execution of this method can be either a `ResultSet` or an integer. Another challenge is that this method can be used where the SQL statement to be executed is not known at the compile time or there is a possibility of multiple results being returned by a stored procedure. Unlike the first two methods, the `execute()`method never returns any result, and you must use either the `getResultSet()`or `getUpdateCount()` method to retrieve the running results.

Table 4.8. Methods used to determine the types of returned result

Method	Return Value	Testing Result
getUpdateCount()	>0	The result is an update count
getUpdateCount()	=–1	The result is not an update count
getUpdateCount()	=0	Either the update count is zero or a data definition language (DDL) statement is executed, such as CREATE TABLE.
getResultSet()	=null	The result is not a ResultSet
getResultSet()	=–1	The result is a ResultSet
getUpdateCount()	! = null	

To distinguish what kind of result is returned, we can use the method we discussed in the last section to do that. To handle multiple results, we need to use the `getMoreResults()` method defined in the `Statement` interface (refer to Table 4.4). When executing this method, a `True` will be returned if a `ResultSet` object is returned. If the result retrieved is an integer, then the `getMoreResults()` method returns a `False`. The confusing issue is that this method will also return a `False` if no result is received. In order to solve this confusion, you must use the `getUpdateCount()` method to test the possible results. Table 4.8 shows a full picture with associated testing condition and possible testing results.

It is easy to get the result of the execution of the `executeUpdate()`method since only an integer is returned as the result for this method. However, it needs more work to do for the result of the execution of the `executeQuery()`and `execute()`methods since a `ResultSet` object that contains a tabular set is returned. We will concentrate on the methods used to retrieve and process the actual data contained in the `ResultSet` object. First, let's have a closer look at the `ResultSet` interface.

4.2.4.1 The ResultSet Interface

Data stored in a `ResultSet` are returned by the database in a tabular format. Each field of the database can be described by a unique combination of a row ID and a column ID. A column can be mapped to an array, since all data in a single column have the same data type. Similarly, a row can be mapped to a Vector since all elements in a single row may have the different data types.

The `ResultSet` interface has more than 25 methods, and Table 4.9 lists some most often used methods.

All `getXXX()`methods defined in this `ResultSet` interface, except the `getMetaData()`, are overloading methods with two signatures, which means that all of those methods can pass two types of arguments, either a column index that is an integer or a column name that is a String. To save space, here we only list the first signature for each of those methods.

Now that we have a clear picture about the `ResultSet` interface, next we need to get the running results from the execution of an execute method. First, let's take care of how to get a `ResultSet` object after an execute method has been done.

Table 4.9. Methods defined in the ResultSet interface

Method	Function
close()	Close the ResultSet and release all resources associated with it
findColumn(String colName)	Return the column index number corresponding to the column name argument
getAsciiStream(int index)	Retrieve the value of the specified column from the current row as an ASCII stream. The column can be represented by either the column index or the column name
getBigDecimal(int index)	Return the value of the referenced column from the current row as a BigDecimal object
getBoolean(int index)	Return the value of the referenced column from the current row as a Boolean
getByte(int index)	Return the value of the referenced column from the current row as a byte
getBytes(int index)	Return the value of the referenced column from the current row as an array of bytes
getDouble(int index)	Return the value of the referenced column from the current row as a double
getFloat(int index)	Return the value of the referenced column from the current row as a floating point number
getInt(int index)	Return the value of the referenced column from the current row as an integer
getLong(int index)	Return the value of the referenced column from the current row as a long integer
getObject(int index)	Return the value of the referenced column from the current row as an Object. The object type is determined by the default mapping of the SQL data type
getShort(int index)	Return the value of the referenced column from the current row as a short integer
getString(int index)	Return the value of the referenced column from the current row as a String object
getTime(int index)	Return the value of the referenced column from the current row as a java.sql.Time object
getMetaData()	Return a metadata object from the ResultSet object
next()	Move the ResultSet row cursor to the next row
wasNull()	Determine if the last value read by a getXXX() method was a SQL null value. A True is returned if the last read value contained a null value

4.2.4.2 Getting and Processing the ResultSet Object

When a SQL data query is executed, the returned result is stored in a `ResultSet` object, and this `ResultSet` object can be created by one of the following two methods:

- The `executeQuery()` method
- The `getResultSet()` method

When an `executeQuery()`method is executed, the result of the queried data is stored in a `ResultSet` object and returned. However, when an `execute()`method is used to retrieve a data query result, it will not return any result directly; instead, you need to use the `getResultSet()` method to create a `ResultSet` to pick up the returned result.

Once the `ResultSet` object is created by using either method, an appropriate `getXXX()` method defined in the ResultSet interface can be used to access and retrieve data. Since the data is in a tabular format, any data can be retrieved by using the column and row ordinals. Two different ways can be used to select and access each column and row in a `ResultSet` object:

1. Using either column index or column name to select the desired column
2. Using the cursor that points to the current row to select a desired row

In order to scan the entire table in a `ResultSet` object, you can use the `next()`method defined in the `ResultSet` interface to move the cursor row by row until the last record. To pick up a specified column from a given row, you can use an appropriate `getXXX()`method defined in the `ResultSet` interface with a column index or column name as the argument.

Let's have a closer look at accessing and processing each row and column from a `ResultSet` object with a little more discussion in the following sections.

4.2.4.2.1 Fetching by Row In a `ResultSet` object, a cursor is used as a pointer to point to each row, and each row of data must be processed in the order in which they can be returned. At the beginning time, after an execution method is executed and a `ResultSet` object is returned, the cursor points the initial row, which is an empty row (refer to Fig.4.15). To move the cursor to point to the first row of data, as we mentioned, the `next()`method can be used. Then, an appropriate `getXXX()`method can be used to pick up the desired column from the current row based on the column index or the column name as the argument of that method. Figure 4.15 shows a structure of a `ResultSet` object with a row pointer positioning diagram.

Figure 4.15a shows an initial cursor position of a `ResultSet` object, in which an execution method is just completed and a `ResultSet` object is created. The cursor now points to the initial row, row 0, and it is an empty row with no data included.

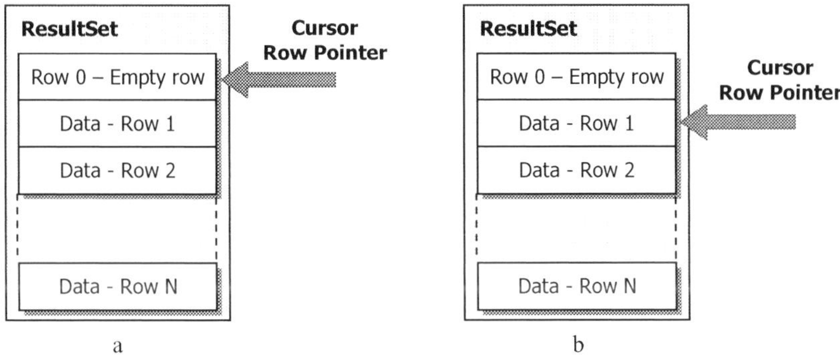

Figure 4.15. The structure of a ResultSet with a row pointer positioning diagram.

```
String query = "SELECT user_name, pass_word FROM LogIn " +
               "WHERE user_name = ? AND pass_word = ?";
PreparedStatement pstmt = con.prepareStatement(query);
pstmt.setString(1, "cse");
pstmt.setString(2, "mack8000");
ResultSet rs = pstmt.executeQuery();
while (rs.next()){
    username = rs.getString(1);          // username = rs.getString("user_name");
    password = rs.getString(2);          // password = rs.getString("pass_word");
}
```

Figure 4.16. An example coding of using the looped next() method.

To access and retrieve a row of data, the `next()`method is executed to move the cursor to point to the next row, row 1 (shown in Fig.4.15b), in which the first row of data is stored. An appropriate `getXXX()` method can be used to retrieve the desired column with the column index or column name as the argument. To navigate through the entire `ResultSet` and process each row, you can use the `next()` method again until the last row. A `true` will be returned from this `next()` method if it points to a row containing data, and a `false` will be returned if the cursor points to a null row, which means that the bottom of the `ResultSet` has arrived, and no more data are available in this object.

In an actual program development and coding process, a `while` loop can be used to execute the `next()` method to advance the cursor from the current row to point to the next row, until a `false` is returned, which means that the bottom of the `ResultSet` object has arrived.

Figure 4.16 shows a piece of example codes to illustrate how to use a `while` loop with the `next()` method to retrieve the related username and password from the LogIn table in our sample database CSE_DEPT.

Those nonhighlighted codes are prerequisite codes used to create an SQL statement query string, create a `PreparedStatement` object, and set input parameters for the query string. The codes in bold are key codes used to create a `ResultSet` object and perform a `while` loop with the `next()` method to retrieve all related username and password from the LogIn table in our sample database. Since most `getXXX()` methods defined in the `ResultSet` interface are overloading methods, alternatively, you can use the column name as an argument to pick up the desired column. Those alternative codes are shown in the right side with the comment out symbol in front of them.

4.2.4.2.2 Fetching by Column When a valid data row has been retrieved, we need to get each column from that row. To do that, a different `getXXX()`method should be used based on the different data type of the returned data. One can use either the name of a column or the index of that column to get the data value. Inside the `while` loop in Figure 4.16, we used a column index as the argument for the `getString()` method to retrieve the username and password columns from our LogIn table. As you know, the data type for both the **user_name** and the **pass_word** are String in our LogIn table; therefore, a `getString()`method is used with the index of each column. A point to be noted is that the first column has an index of 1, not 0. If the name of each column, not an index, is used for the `getString()`method in this `while` loop, the codes can be re-written as

```
while (rs.next()){
username = rs.getString("user_name");
password = rs.getString("pass_word");
}
```

One of the most important methods in `ResultSet` class is the `getObject()`. The advantage of using this method is that a returned datum, which is stored in a `ResultSet` object and its data type is unknown (a datum is dynamically created), can be automatically converted from its SQL data type to the ideal Java data type. This method outperform any other `getXXX()`method, since the data type of returned data must be known before a suitable `getXXX()`method can be used to fetch the returned data.

The `findColumn()`method is used to find the index of a column if the name of that column is given, and the `close()`method is used to close a `ResultSet` instance.

The `getMetaData()`method is a very good and convenient method, and it allows users to have a detailed and clear picture about the structure and properties of data returned to a `ResultSet`. A `ResultSetMetaData` object, which contains all pieces of necessary information about the returned data stored in a `ResultSet` instance, is returned when this method is executed. By using different methods of the `ResultSetMetaData` interface, we can obtain a clear picture about the returned data. For example, by using the `getColumnCount()`method, we can know totally how many columns have been retrieved and stored in the `ResultSet`. By using `getTableName()`, `getColumnName()`, and `getColumnType()`, we can know the name of the data table we queried, the name of column we just fetched, and the data type of that column. A more detailed discussion about the `ResultSetMetaData` component will be given in the following sections.

4.2.5 Using JDBC MetaData Interfaces

In addition to general and popular data information provided by three statement interfaces and execution methods, JDBC also provides useful and critical information and descriptions about the database, running result set and parameters related to the JDBC drivers and database applications. All of these properties, structures and descriptions can be categorized into three interfaces of so-called metadata interfaces, or

1. ResultSetMetaData interface
2. DatabaseMetaData interface
3. ParameterMetaData interface

In the following sections, we will concentrate on these three interfaces to illustrate how to use these interfaces to retrieve detailed descriptions and structures, as well as properties related to the data action components, such as `ResultSet`, database, and parameters to facilitate database applications.

Let's start from the ResultSetMetaData interface.

4.2.5.1 Using the ResultSetMetaData Interface

In Section 4.2.4, we discussed how to retrieve running result stored in a `ResultSet` object and important methods of this interface. By using different fetching methods, either fetching by rows or columns, we can easily retrieve a whole set of returned results stored in a

ResultSet object. However, in some applications, we may need more detailed information and properties about the returned result set, such as the total number of columns returned, each column name and data type, as well as some other structure information related to the returned result set. By using these structure information and properties, we can get a clear and full picture about the returned ResultSet, and furthermore enable us to retrieve our desired data information more directly and conveniently. With the help of the metadata provided by the ResultSetMetaData, you can develop entire database applications without even knowing what RDBMS, table, or type of data to be accessed.

The ResultSetMetaData interface provides a collection of information about the structure and properties related to the returned ResultSet object, and this give us a possibility to perform the functions we described above.

The ResultSetMetaData interface contains more than 20 methods, and Table 4.10 shows 16 most popular methods.

It can be found from Table 4.10 that the top 10 methods in a ResultSetMetaData object are mainly used to retrieve the structure and properties for the specified column with the column index as an argument. The rest of methods that return a Boolean value are used to determine some important properties that describe special functions provided by the database engine for the selected column. One of the advantages of using this metadata is that you can build dynamic applications that are independent of the data source. One possible way to achieve this is to remove the need for all direct column name references.

Table 4.10. Methods defined in the ResultSetMetaData interface

Method	Function
getCatalogName(int index)	Determine the name of the catalog that contains the referenced column
getColumnCount()	Return the total number of columns contained in the ResultSet object
getColumnDisplaySize(int index)	Return the maximum display width for the selected column
getColumnLabel(int index)	Return the preferred display name for the selected column
getColumnName(int index)	Return the name of the column for the selected column
getColumnType(int index)	Return the SQL data type for the selected column
getPrecision(int index)	Return the precision used for the selected column
getScale(int index)	Return the scale used for the selected column
getSchemaName(int index)	Return the name of the schema that contains the selected column
getTableName(int index)	Return the name of the table that contains the selected column
isAutoIncrement(int index)	Determine if the column is automatically numbered by the database (autonumber)
isCurrency(int index)	Determine if the column represents currency
isNullable(int index)	Determine if the column is able to accept null values
isSigned(int index)	Determine if the column contains signed numbers
isWritable(int index)	Determine if the column is writable by the user
isReadOnly(int index)	Determine if the column is read-only

```
ResultSet rs = pstmt.executeQuery();
ResultSetMetaData  rsmd = rs.getMetaData();

While (rs.next()){
   for (int m = 1; m< rsmd.getColumnCount(); m ++)
   {
      System.out.println( rs.getString(m));
   }
}
```

Figure 4.17. An example coding of using the getColumnCount() method.

Because of the space limitation, we can only provide a brief discussion for some important methods that are widely implemented in most database applications.

After a data query is executed and a `ResultSet` object is returned, before we can retrieve our desired data from the `ResultSet`, we may need to get some structure information and properties related to columns we preferred. One of the most important properties is the total number of columns returned in the `ResultSet` object. By using the `getColumnCount()` method, we can get not only the total number of columns, but also the content of each column easily. Figure 4.17 shows a piece of example codes to illustrate how to use this method to scan the entire `ResultSet` to retrieve each column from it.

The first coding line is used to create a ResultSet object by executing the `executeQuery()` method. Then a `ResultSetMetaData` object `rsmd` is created by calling the `getMetaData()` method defined by the `ResultSet` interface. To pick up each returned column, a `while` loop is used combined with the `next()`method. By using this piece of codes, you even do not need to know how many columns returned in that `ResultSet`, and what are the names for each column; in other words, you do not have to have prior knowledge about the table and database—you can retrieve all columns with their exact names! Yes, that is easy and fancy.

In some applications, you may need to know some other useful information about the columns, such as the data type of each column, the width of each column, the precision and scale of the selected column if a floating point or double data is stored in that column. To get those properties, you can call the appropriate methods, such as `getColumnType()`, `getColumn-DisplaySize()`, `getPrecision()` and `getScale()`.

Besides to get some important information and properties about the returned ResultSet, sometimes, we may need to get similar information for the connected database. In that case, you may need to use the `DatabaseMetaData` interface.

4.2.5.2 Using the DatabaseMetaData Interface

Compared with other metadata interfaces, the `DatabaseMetaData` is the largest metadata interface, with over 150 methods. This interface is mainly used for by those developers who are building database applications that need to be fully RDBMS independent, which means that the developers do not need to know anything about the database or do not have prior knowledge about the database they are using. In this way, the users can discover and retrieve structures and properties of the RDBMS dynamically as the application runs.

To create a `DatabaseMetaData` object, one needs to call the `getMetaData()` method defined in the `Connection` interface.

Relatively speaking, the `ResultSetMetaData` interface allows you to discover the structure of tables and properties of columns, but the `DatabaseMetaData` interface enables you to dynamically determine properties of the RDBMS. Table 4.11 shows some 16 most popular and important methods widely implemented by the `DatabaseMetaData` interface.

These 16 methods can be divided into seven groups based on their functionalities:

1. Catalog Identification Methods
2. Database Identification Methods
3. Driver Identification Methods
4. Stored Procedure-Related Methods
5. Schema Identification Methods
6. Table Identification Methods
7. Database-Related Parameters Methods

To get the name and version of the current database being used, the `getDatabaseProduct-Name()` and `getDatabaseProductVersion()` methods can

Table 4.11. Popular methods defined in the DatabaseMetaData interface

Method	Function
getCatalogs()	Return a ResultSet containing a list of all catalogs available in the database
getCatalogTerm()	Determine what the database specific name for Catalog is
getDatabaseProductName()	Return the name of the database product
getDatabaseProductVersion()	Return the database revision number
getDriverName()	Return the name of the driver
getDriverVersion()	Return the revision number of the driver
getPrimaryKeys(String catalog, String schema, String table)	Return a ResultSet describing all of the primary keys within a table
getProcedures(string catalog, String schPatt, String proPatt)	Return a ResultSet describing all stored procedures available in the catalog
getProcedureTerm()	Determine the database specific term for procedure
getSchemas()	Return a ResultSet containing a list of all schemas available in the database
getSchemaTerm()	Determine the database specific term for schema
getTables(String catalog, String schePatt, String tablePatt, String[] types)	Return a ResultSet containing a list of all tables available matching the catalog, schema, and table type selection criteria
getTableTypes()	Return a ResultSet listing the table types available
getTypeInfo()	Return a ResultSet describing all of the standard SQL types supported by the database
getURL()	Return the current URL for the database
getUserName()	Return the current user name used by the database

be used. Similarly, to get the name and revision number of the JDBC driver being used, the `getDriverName()` and `getDriverVersion()` methods can be executed.

In fact, the `DatabaseMetaData` interface provides methods that allow you to dynamically discover properties of a database as the project runs. Many methods in the `DatabaseMetaData` return information in the `ResultSet` component, and one can get those pieces of information from `ResultSet` object by calling related methods, such as **getString()**, **getInt()**, and **getXXX()**. A SQLException would be thrown out if the queried item is not available in the `MetaData` interface.

Overall, the `DatabaseMetaData` interface provides an easy and convenient way to allow users to identify and retrieve important structure and properties information about the database dynamically.

4.2.5.3 Using the ParameterMetaData Interface

The detailed information about the parameters passed into or from the database can be obtained by calling the `getParameterMetaData()`method that is defined in the `PreparedStatement` interface. Although this interface is not as popular as `ResultSetMetaData` and `DatabaseMetaData`, it is useful in some special applications.

Basically, the `ParameterMetaData` interface can be defined as: an object that can be used to get information about the types and properties of the parameters in a PreparedStatement object. For some queries and driver implementations, the data that would be returned by a ParameterMetaData object may not be available until the PreparedStatement has been executed. Some driver implementations may not be able to provide information about the types and properties for each parameter marker in a CallableStatement object.

The `ParameterMetaData` interface contains seven fields and nine methods. Table 4.12 shows some most popular methods that are widely implemented in most database applications.

Figure 4.18 shows a piece of example codes to illustrate how to retrieve the total number of parameters related to a `PreparedStatement` object.

After a `PreparedStatement` instance is created, the `getParameterMetaData()` method is executed to retrieve the total number of parameters returned in the `ParameterMetaData` object.

Finally, let's handle the closing the connection object and releasing used resources, including the statement objects.

4.2.6 Closing the Connection and Statements

After a set of data actions has been performed and the desired data have been acquired, the Connection object that is used to connect to our target database should be closed, and the related data operational resources including all opened statement objects used for these data actions should also be released. Otherwise, you may encounter some possible exceptions when you try to open a database that has been opened but without being closed in the previous applications. To these cleanup jobs, it is very easy with a piece of codes shown in Figure 4.19.

Table 4.12. Popular methods defined in the ParameterMetaData interface

Method	Function
getParameterCount()	Return the number of parameters in the PreparedStatement object for which this ParameterMetaData object contains information
getPrecision(int param)	Return the designated parameter's number of decimal digits
getScale(int param)	Return the designated parameter's number of digits to right of the decimal point
getParameterType(int param)	Return the designated parameter's SQL type
getParameterTypeName(int param)	Return the designated parameter's database-specific type name
getParameterMode(int param)	Return the designated parameter's mode
isNullable(int param)	Determine whether null values are allowed in the designated parameter
isSigned(int param)	Determine whether values for the designated parameter can be signed numbers

```
String query = "SELECT user_name, pass_word FROM LogIn " +
               "WHERE user_name = ? AND pass_word = ?";
PreparedStatement pstmt = con.prepareStatement(query);
pstmt.setString(1, "cse");
pstmt.setString(2, "mack8000");
ResultSet rs = pstmt.executeQuery();
ParameterMetaData pmmd = pstmt.getParameterMetaData();
System.out.println( "The total number of parameter is " + pmmd.getParameterCount());
```

Figure 4.18. An example coding of using the getParameterCount() method.

```
try{
     stmt.close();
     if (!con.isClosed())
        con.close();
}
catch(SQLException e){
    System.out.println("Could not close!" + e.getMessage());
}
```

Figure 4.19. An example coding of closing the Connection and Statement objects.

To do a closing operation, a `try...catch` block had better be used to track and monitor this closing process with possible exceptions warning.

4.3 CHAPTER SUMMARY

The application fundamentals of JDBC and JDBC API, which include the application models and operational procedures of the JDBC API implemented in Java database applications, are discussed in detailed in this chapter.

Starting with an introduction to two JDBC application models, two-tier and three-tier models, a detailed illustration and description about these two models are given in the first part of this chapter. A typical two-tier model contains an application server and a database server, in which a Java database application project residents in an application server, and the target database is located at the database server. The so-called three-tier model places the application onto an application server that can be considered as a mid-tier, and installs database in a database server. To run this three-tier model application, the user needs to communicate with the application server by using a Web browser that can be considered as a top tier, with a GUI being installed in this browser. Then the application server can process requests sent from the browser via the target database via the database server. Finally, when requests have been done, results will be returned to the browser by the application server.

Following the application models, a complete operational procedure to perform a standard Java database application is discussed with some example codes, which includes:

- Load and register a JDBC Driver.
- Connect to the target database using either `DriverManager.getConnection()` method or `Driver.connect()`method.
- Execute an SQL statement by creating and calling an appropriate `Statement` object, which include:
  - `Statement` object
  - `PreparedStatement` object
  - `CallableStatement` object
- Distinguish different queries by running associated execute method.
- Execute DDL and DML SQL statements.
- Retrieve the running result by creating and getting a ResultSet object.
- Develop sophisticated Java database applications using different JDBC metadata interfaces, including the ResultSetMetaData, DatabaseMetaData, and ParameterMetaData interfaces.
- Close the connected database and opened statement objects to release data resource used for the application.

Combining the contents in this chapter and the last chapter, you should have had a complete and clear picture about the JDBC fundamentals and application procedure. Beginning from the next chapter, we will introduce and discuss some development tools and actual techniques used in Java database applications.

HOMEWORK

I. True/False Selections

____**1.** JDBC applications are made of two models: two-tier and three-tier models.

____**2.** In a three-tier model, the application is located at a Web server, and the database is installed in a database server. The user can access the application server through a Web browser with a GUI being installed in the browser.

____**3.** To load and register a driver, the `creating a new instance of the Driver class` method is a better method compared with the `Class.forName()` method.

____**4.** When establishing a database connection, the `DriverManager.getConnection()` method is a better method compared with the `Driver.connect()` method.

____**5.** A JDBC URL is composed of three parts: network host name, the database server name, and the port number.

____**6.** By using three methods defined in the Connection interface, `createStatement()`, `prepareStatement()`, and `prepareCall()`, one can create three statement objects: `Statement`, `PreparedStatement`, and `CallableStatement`.

____**7.** The `Statement` object can be used to perform both static and dynamic data queries.

____**8.** To create a `ResultSet` object, you can use either the `getResultSet()` method or call the `executeQuery()` method.

____**9.** The `executeQuery()` method returns an integer that equals to the number of rows that have been returned, and the `executeUpdate()` method returns a `ResultSet` object containing the running result.

___**10.** The `next()` method defined in the `ResultSet` interface can be used to move the cursor that points to the current row to the next row in a `ResultSet`.

II. Multiple Choices

1. The _________ object provides methods for the creation of Statement objects that will be used to execute SQL statements in the next step.

a. Statement
b. Connection
c. DriverManager
d. Driver

2. The relationship between three statement objects are: the ___________ is a subclass of the _________ that is a subclass of the _________.

a. CallableStatement, PreparedStatement, Statement
b. Statement, CallableStatement, PreparedStatement
c. PreparedStatement, Statement, CallableStatement
d. Statement, PreparedStatement, CallableStatement

3. The _________ method returns a(n) _________, and the ________ method returns a(n) _________.

a. execute(), ResultSet, executeQuery(), integer
b. executeQuery(), integer, execute(), nothing
c. executeUpdate(), integer, executeQuery(), ResultSet
d. execute(), integer, executeUpdate(), ResultSet

4. The _________ object is used to execute a static SQL query, but the ________ object is used to execute a dynamic SQL query with IN and OUT parameters.

   a. PreparedStatement, Statement
   b. Statement, PreparedStatement
   c. CallableStatement, Statement
   d. Statement, CallableStatement

5. Both interfaces, PreparedStatement and CallableStatement, are used to perform dynamic SQL statements; however, the ________ performs queries with only _____ parameters, but the _______ calls stored procedures with both ______ and _______ parameters.

   a. CallableStatement, OUT, PreparedStatement, IN, OUT
   b. PreparedStatement, IN, CallableStatement, IN, OUT
   c. CallableStatement, IN, PreparedStatement, IN, OUT
   d. PreparedStatement, OUT, CallableStatement, IN, OUT

6. By using _________ method, we can get a collection of information about the structure and properties of the returned ResultSet object.

   a. getResultSetMetaData()
   b. getResultSet()
   c. getMetaData()
   d. ResultSetMetaData()

7. To create a ______________ object, one needs to call the _____________ method defined in the `Connection` interface.

   a. ResultSet, getMetaData()
   b. Statement, getStatement()
   c. PreparedStatement, getPreparedStatement()
   d. DatabaseMetaData, getMetaData()

8. The _______________ interface allows you to discover the structure of tables and properties of columns, but the __________________ interface enables you to dynamically determine properties of the RDBMS.

   a. ResultSet, DatabaseMetaData
   b. ParameterMetaData, ResultMetaData
   c. DatabaseMetaData, ParameterMetaData
   d. DatabaseMetaData, ResultSet

9. When using a CallableStatement object to run a stored procedure, you need to register the _________ parameters by using the ____________ method.

   a. IN/OUT, getParameters()
   b. IN, registerINParameter()
   c. OUT, registerOUTParameter()
   d. IN/OUT, registerINOUTParameter()

10. The placeholder used in the `setXXX()` and the `registerOUTParameter()` methods is used to __________________.

    a. Indicate the location of the input or output parameters
    b. Reserve spaces for input or output parameters
    c. Inform the compiler to hold memory spaces for those parameters
    d. All of them

III. Exercises

1. Provide a brief description about seven basic steps to use JDBC.
2. Translate the above seven steps to Java codes.
3. Provide a detailed description about JDBC three-tier model and its function.
4. Provides a brief description about the JDBC URL.
5. Explain the operational sequence of retrieving results from a returned `ResultSet` object.
6. Explain the relationship between three Statement objects, and illustrate why and how the `CallableStatement` object can use `setXXX()` methods defined in the `PreparedStatement` interface.
7. Explain the advantages of using JDBC metadata for Java database applications.

Chapter 5

Introduction to NetBeans IDE

Java was originally created by Sun Microsystems to try to overcome some complexities in C++ and try to simplify the structure and architecture of applications developed by using object-oriented programming (OOP) languages such as C++. In the early days, Java developers need to use separate tools to build, develop, and run a Java application. The following tools are most popular used when building a Java application:

- NotePad or WordPad—used to develop the Java source codes
- Java Compiler—used to compile the Java source codes to the Java byte codes
- Java Interpreter—used to convert the byte codes to the machine codes

There is no any graphical user interface (GUI) tool available in the early days and developers have to use the Java layout manager to design and build the GUI by using different layouts with different components, such as buttons, labels, text fields, checkboxes, and radio buttons. Even Web-related Java applications, such as Applets, must be built by using different tools, too. This brought a significant inconvenience and complicated development environment for Java developers in that age.

As more sophisticated and advanced techniques were developed, the Java development environment and tools have been greatly improved. By combining Java Software Development Kits (SDK) and GUI components, such as Abstract Windowing Toolkit (AWT) and Swing API, Sun integrated those components and tools together to establish and build an Integrated Development Environment (IDE). This IDE is very similar to Visual Studio.NET, in which all program development tools and components have been integrated together and categorized into the different packages. Developers can design, develop, build, and run a Java standalone or a Web application easily and conveniently inside this IDE without needing to use different tools.

The NetBeans IDE is one of the most current and updated IDEs and widely implemented in a wide spectrum of Java applications. The NetBeans IDE is actually written in Java and runs everywhere a Java Virtual Machine (JVM) is installed, including Windows, Mac OS, Linux, and Solaris. A Java Development Kits (JDK) is required for

Practical Database Programming with Java, First Edition. Ying Bai.

Java development functionality, but is not required for development in other programming languages.

The NetBeans project consists of an open-source IDE and an application platform that enable developers to rapidly create web, enterprise, desktop, and mobile applications using the Java platform, as well as JavaFX, PHP, JavaScript and Ajax, Ruby and Ruby on Rails, Groovy and Grails, and C/C++.

NetBeans IDE, which is released by Sun Microsystems, is a modular, standards-based integrated development environment (IDE) written in the Java programming language. The NetBeans project consists of a full-featured open source IDE written in the Java programming language and a rich client application platform, which can be used as a generic framework to build any kind of application.

5.1 OVERVIEW OF THE NETBEANS IDE 6.8

The current version of the NetBeans IDE is 6.8, and it is the first IDE to offer complete support for the entire Java Enterprise Edition (EE) 6 spec with improved support for JSF 2.0/Facelets, Java Persistence 2.0, Enterprise JavaBean (EJB) 3.1 including using EJBs in web applications, RESTful web services, and GlassFish v3. It is also recommended for developing with the latest JavaFX SDK 1.2.1, and for creating PHP web applications with the new PHP 5.3 release or with the Symfony Framework.

Table 5.1 shows some most popular features provided by NetBeans IDE 6.8.

Table 5.2 shows the most popular techniques supported by the NetBeans IDE 6.8 and application servers adopted by the NetBeans 6.8.

Table 5.1. Most popular features supported by NetBeans IDE 6.8

Project Category	Features
Java Enterprise Edition 6	• Web Projects with Java EE 6 and Java EE 6 Web profiles, EJBs in web applications. • EJB 3.1 support, EJB project file wizard also supports Singleton session type. • RESTful web services (JAX-RS 1.1), GlassFish Metro 2.0 web services (JAX-WS 2.2), JAXB 2.2. • Java Persistence JPA 2.0, deployment, debugging, and profiling with GlassFish v3 application server.
Web Projects with JavaServer Faces 2.0 (Facelets)	• Code completion, error hints, namespace completion, documentation pop-ups, and tag auto-import for Facelets. • Editor support for Facelets libraries, composite components, expression language, including generators for JSF and HTML forms. • Customizable JSF components palette generates JSF forms and JSF data tables from entities. • New File wizard generates customizable CRUD (create/read/update/delete) JSF pages from entities. • Broader usage of annotations instead of deployment descriptors.

Table 5.1. (*Continued*)

Project Category	Features
JavaFX	• Added support for the latest JavaFX SDK 1.2.1. • Improved code completion. • Editor Hints: Fix Imports, Surround With, Implements Abstract Methods, and more. • Improved navigation: Hyperlinks, Go to Type, Find Usages.
http://Kenai.com: Connected Developer	• Full JIRA support (plug-in from update center). • Project dashboard with more member and project details, improved search and navigation, easier project sharing. • Improved instant messenger integration: Online presence, private and group chat with Kenai members, easy to add links to code/files/issues/stack traces to messages. • Improved issue tracker integration.
PHP	• Full PHP 5.3 support: namespaces, lambda functions and closures, syntax additions: NOWDOC, ternary conditions, jump labels, __callStatic(). • Symfony Framework support: Symfony projects, Symfony commands, shortcuts, PHP syntax coloring in YAML files. • Create a PHP project from a remote PHP application. • PHPUnit, Code Coverage, FTP/SFTP integration improvements, exclude PHP project folders from scanning/indexing.
Maven	• New Project from Maven archetype catalog and improved support for Java EE 6, Groovy, Scala projects. • Customizable dependency exclusion in dependency graph. • Maven CheckStyle plug-in. • "Update from Kenai" action for Kenai.com-hosted Maven projects.
Ruby	• Support for creating Rails 2.3.4 apps with dispatchers, JRuby 1.4, Ruby 1.9 debugging, and RSpec 1.2.7 • Improved rename refactoring, type inference, and navigation • Specifying arguments for Rails servers • Run/Debug File with arguments, also for files not part of a project
C and C++	• Profiling: New Microstate Accounting indicator, Thread Map view, Hot Spots view, Memory Leaks view, Sync Problems view • Faster synchronization during remote development • Support for gdbserver attach and easier attaching to already running processes
Miscellaneous Improvements	• Java Debugger: Mark an object in the variables tree with a name to refer to it in expressions • Database integration: Code completion in SQL Editor now also for DELETE, DROP, UPDATE statements, and for reserved keywords • Groovy 1.6.4 & Grails: Improved code completion, including methods introduced via AST Transformations

Table 5.2. Most popular techniques and application servers supported by NetBeans 6.8

Category	Supported Techniques and Application Servers
Supported technologies	Java EE 5, Java EE 6 and J2EE 1.4 JavaFX SDK 1.2.1 Java ME SDK 3.0 Struts 1.3.8 Spring 2.5 Hibernate 3.2.5 Java API for RESTful Web Services (JAX-RS) 1.1 PHP 5.3, 5.2, 5.1 Ruby 1.9, 1.8 JRuby 1.4 Rails 2.3.4 Groovy 1.6.4 Grails 1.1 VCS • CVS: 1.11.x, 1.12.x • Subversion: 1.4.x, 1.5.x, 1.6.x • Mercurial: 1.x • ClearCase V7.0
Tested application servers	• GlassFish v3 • Sun Java System Application Server PE 8.2 • WebLogic 11g (10.3.1.0) • Tomcat 6.0.20 • Tomcat 5.5 • JBoss 5.0

As we know, the NetBeans projects are composed of an open-source IDE and an application platform that enable developers to rapidly create web, enterprise, desktop, and mobile applications. Let's have a closer look at these two components to have a deeper understanding about this IDE.

5.1.1 The NetBeans Platform

The NetBeans Platform is a broad Swing-based framework on which you can base large desktop applications. The IDE itself is based on the NetBeans Platform. The Platform contains APIs that simplify the handling of windows, actions, files, and many other things typical in applications.

Each distinct feature in a NetBeans Platform application can be provided by a distinct NetBeans module, which is comparable with a plug-in. A NetBeans module is a group of Java classes that provides an application with a specific feature.

You can also create new modules for NetBeans IDE itself. For example, you can write modules that make your favorite cutting-edge technologies available to users of NetBeans IDE. Alternatively, you might create a module to provide an additional editor feature.

The NetBeans platform offers reusable services common to desktop applications, allowing developers to focus on the logic specific to their application. Among the features of the platform are:

- User interface management (e.g., menus and toolbars)
- User settings management
- Storage management (saving and loading any kind of data)
- Window management
- Wizard framework (supports step-by-step dialogs)
- NetBeans Visual Library

Let's take a look at the second part of a NetBeans project, the NetBeans open source IDE.

5.1.2 The NetBeans Open Source IDE

The NetBeans IDE is an open-source integrated development environment, and it supports development of all Java application types, such as Java Standard Edition (Java SE), including JavaFX, Java Mobile Edition (Java ME), Web, Enterprise JavaBean (EJB), and mobile applications, out of the box. Among other features are an Ant-based project system, Maven support, refactorings, and version control.

All the functions of the IDE are provided by modules. Each module provides a well-defined function, such as support for the Java language, editing, or support for the Concurrent Versions System (CVS) versioning system, and Java Subversion (SVN). NetBeans contains all the modules needed for Java development in a single download, allowing the user to start working immediately. Modules also allow NetBeans to be extended. New features, such as support for other programming languages, can be added by installing additional modules. For instance, Sun Studio, Sun Java Studio Enterprise, and Sun Java Studio Creator from Sun Microsystems are all based on the NetBeans IDE.

Three main modules included in the NetBeans IDE and most often used are shown in Table 5.3.

Users can choose to download NetBeans IDE bundles tailored to specific development needs.

Users can also download and install all other features at a later date directly through the NetBeans IDE. A complete set of bundles that can be used by users when they download and install NetBeans IDE onto their computers is shown below:

- NetBeans Base IDE
- Java SE, JavaFX
- Web & Java EE
- Java ME
- Ruby

Table 5.3. Three main modules included in the NetBeans IDE 6.8

Module Name	Functions
NetBeans Profiler	This is a tool for the monitoring of Java applications: It helps you find memory leaks and optimize speed. Formerly downloaded separately, it is integrated into the core IDE since version 6.0. The Profiler is based on a Sun Laboratories research project that was named JFluid. That research uncovered specific techniques that can be used to lower the overhead of profiling a Java application. One of those techniques is dynamic bytecode instrumentation, which is particularly useful for profiling large Java applications. Using dynamic bytecode instrumentation and additional algorithms, the NetBeans Profiler is able to obtain runtime information on applications that are too large or complex for other profilers. NetBeans also support Profiling Points that let you profile precise points of execution and measure execution time.
GUI design tool	The GUI design tool enables developers to prototype and design Swing GUIs by dragging and positioning GUI components. The GUI builder also has built-in support for JSR 296 (Swing Application Framework) and JSR 295 (Beans Binding technology).
NetBeans JavaScript Editor	This module provides extended support for Javascript, Ajax, and Cascading Style Sheets (CSS). JavaScript editor features comprise syntax highlighting, refactoring, code completion for native objects and functions, generation of JavaScript class skeletons, generation of Ajax callbacks from a template, and automatic browser compatibility checks. CSS editor features comprise code completion for styles names, quick navigation through the navigator panel, displaying the CSS rule declaration in a List View and file structure in a Tree View, sorting the outline view by name, type or declaration order (List & Tree), creating rule declarations (Tree only), refactoring a part of a rule name (Tree only).

- C/C++
- PHP (Version 6.5 and later)
- GlassFish
- Apache Tomcat

Figure 5.1 shows a typical structure and architecture of the NetBeans IDE 6.8.

Now that we have had a clear picture and understanding about the NetBeans IDE 6.8, next we need to download, install, and configure the NetBeans 6.8 in our computers.

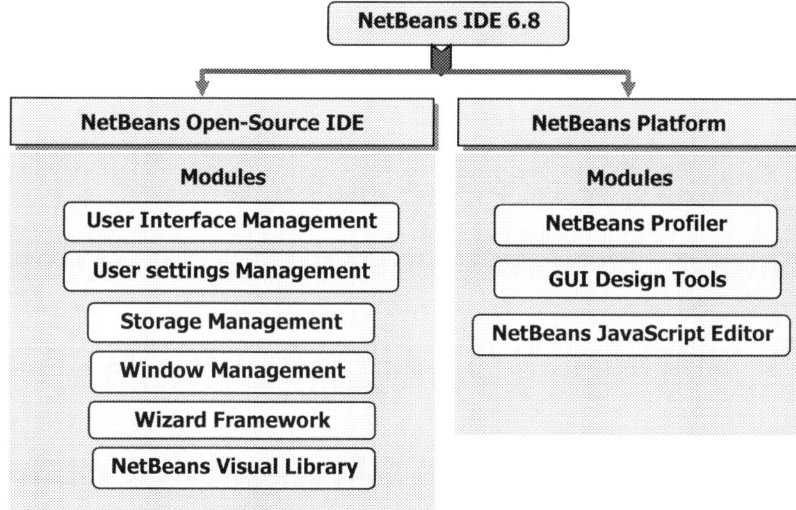

Figure 5.1. A typical structure of the NetBeans IDE 6.8.

5.2 INSTALLING AND CONFIGURING THE NETBEANS IDE 6.8

To download and install the NetBeans IDE 6.8, go to the website:

http://java.sun.com/javase/downloads/widget/jdk_netbeans.jsp

On the opened `java.sun/javase/downloads` homepage, click on the `Download` button to begin this download process, which is shown in Figure 5.2.

On the next page, which is a login and registration page, click on the `Skip this Step` link to continue this download process, which is shown in Figure 5.3.

Click on the **Run** button to begin to download this NetBeans IDE 6.8, and then click on the **Run** button to begin to install the NetBeans IDE 6.8 to your machine.

When the `Java SE Development Kit and NetBeans IDE Installer` appears, click on the **Next** to continue the installation, as shown in Figure 5.4.

Confirm that both `Java JDK 1.6.0_17` and `NetBeans 6.8` will be installed to the correct folders in your machine, and then click on the **Install** button to begin this installation, as shown in Figure 5.5.

Follow the instructions on the following dialog boxes to complete this installation, and click on the **Finish** button to complete this installation process when it is done.

Next, we need to configure the installed NetBeans IDE 6.8 to make it our desired development environment.

To launch the installed NetBeans IDE 6.8, double click on the NetBeans 6.8 icon from the desktop and click on the **Install Plugins** item to install some necessary Web components used in the Java Web Applications, as shown in Figure 5.6.

As the `Plugins` dialog box appears, select the desired components by checking them one by one. The following components are needed for our projects:

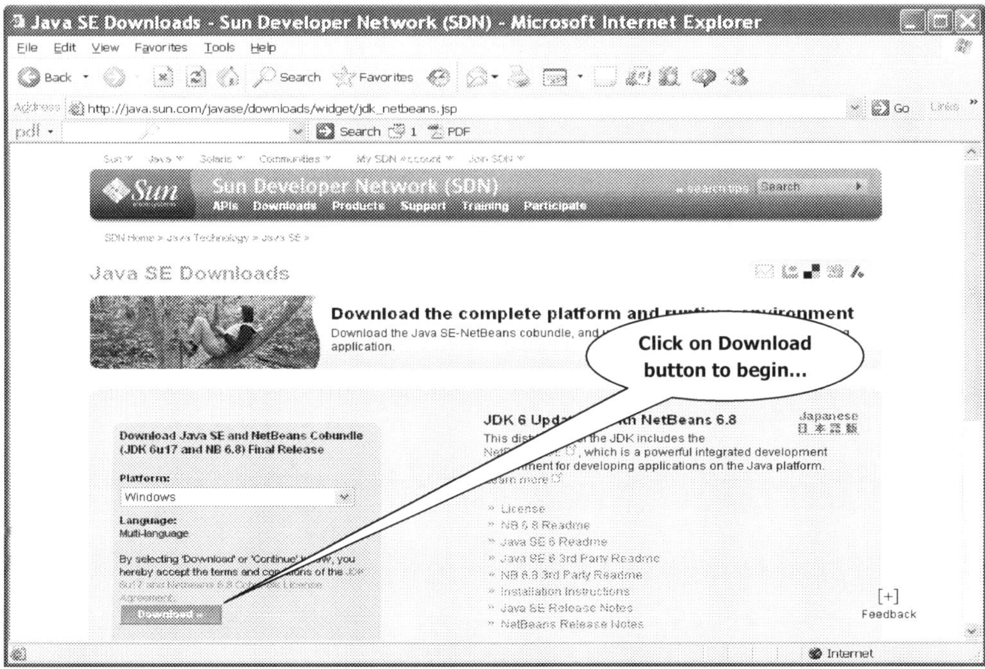

Figure 5.2. The opened `java.sun/javase/downloads` home page.

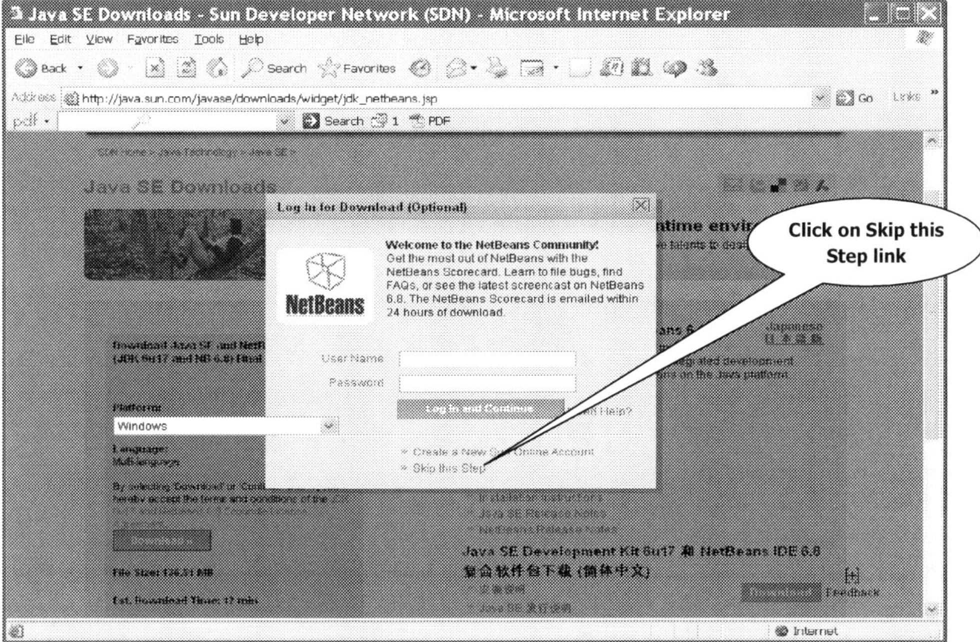

Figure 5.3. The login and registration page.

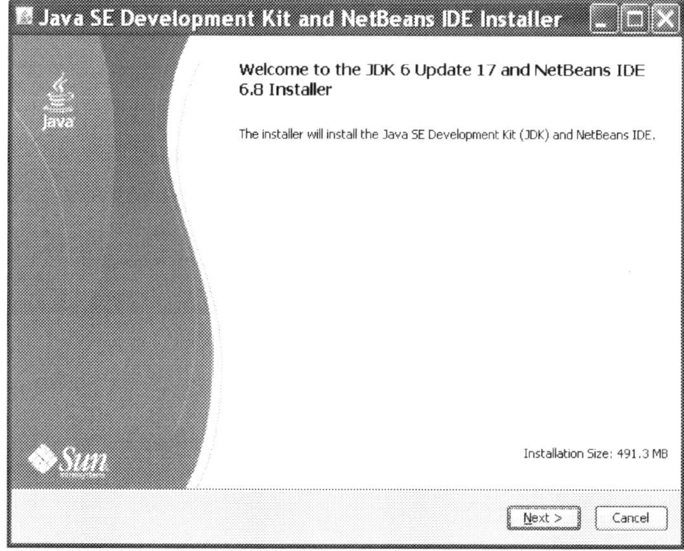

Figure 5.4. The Java SE Development Kit and NetBeans IDE Installer dialog—1.

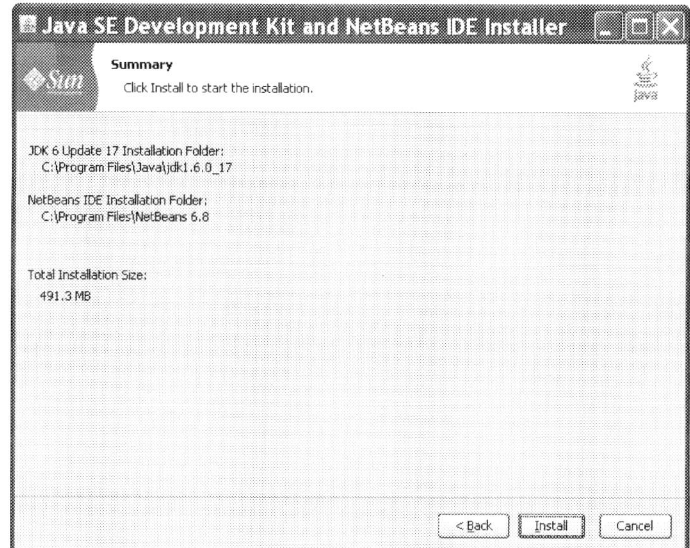

Figure 5.5. The Java SE Development Kit and NetBeans IDE Installer dialog—2.

- NetBeans API Documentation
- Module Manager
- Groovy and Grails
- JavaFX Composer
- JavaFX Kit
- Spring Web MVC

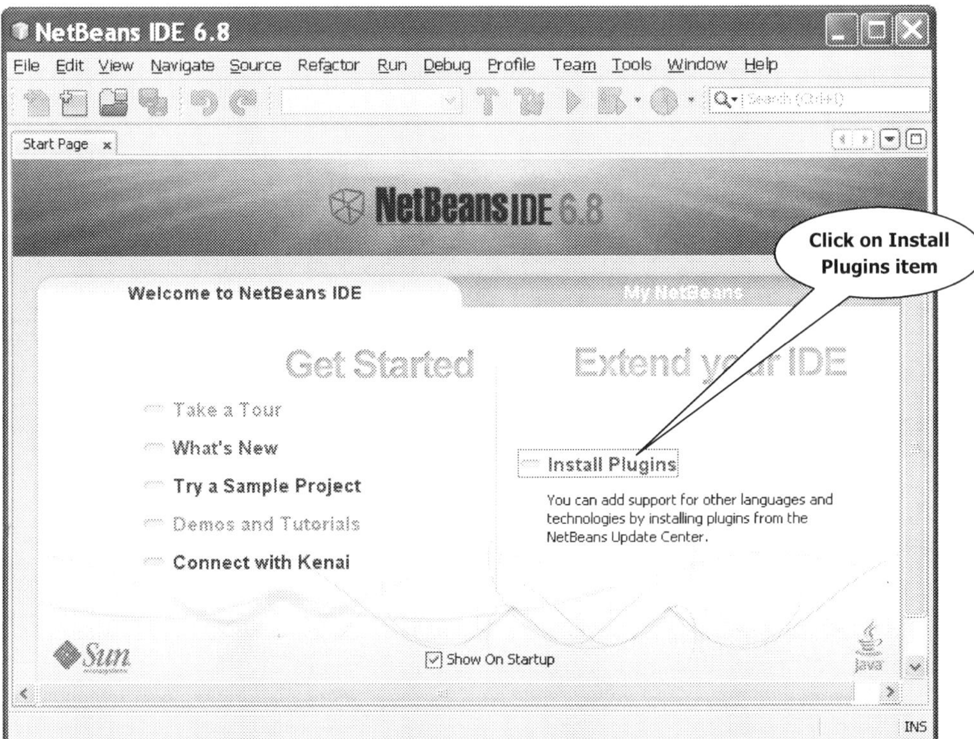

Figure 5.6. The launched NetBeans IDE 6.8.

- SOAP Web Services
- Java Web applications
- Sun Java System Web Server 7.0
- EJB and EAR
- Struts
- JSF
- Web preview

Your finished `Plugins` dialog box should match one that is shown in Figure 5.7. Click on the **Install** button to install these `plug-ins` into the NetBeans 6.8.

Follow the instructions on the following dialog boxes to complete this installation.

Now that we have installed and configured the NetBeans IDE 6.8, next, we need to explorer it to find all useful features we will use to build our professional database applications in this integrated development environment.

5.3 EXPLORING NETBEANS IDE 6.8

By using NetBeans IDE 6.8, the developers can design and build Java related applications with different categories that are shown below:

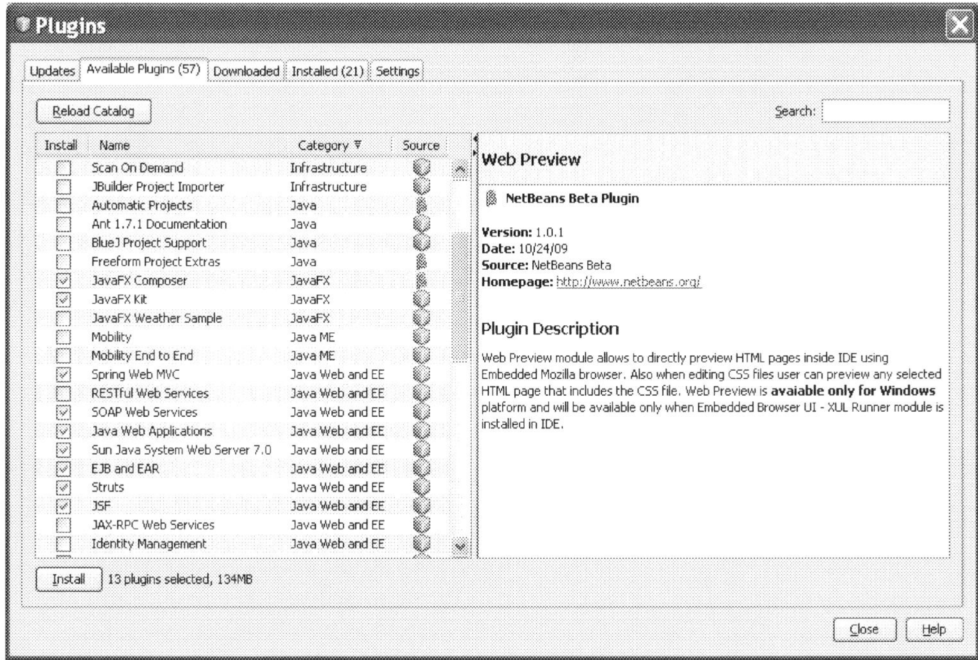

Figure 5.7. The finished Plugins window.

- Java applications
- JavaFX applications
- Java Web applications
- Java Enterprise applications
- Maven applications
- Grails applications
- NetBeans modules

To get a clear picture and detailed description about this IDE, first, let's have a work through overview for this product and its functionalities.

5.3.1 An Overview of NetBeans IDE 6.8 GUI

When you launch for first time the NetBeans IDE 6.8, a main menu and some default windows are displayed, as shown in Figure 5.8.

The first window or pane located at the upper-left corner is called Projects|Files|Services window, which contains three different kinds of items:

1. All opened projects
2. All created files
3. All database services

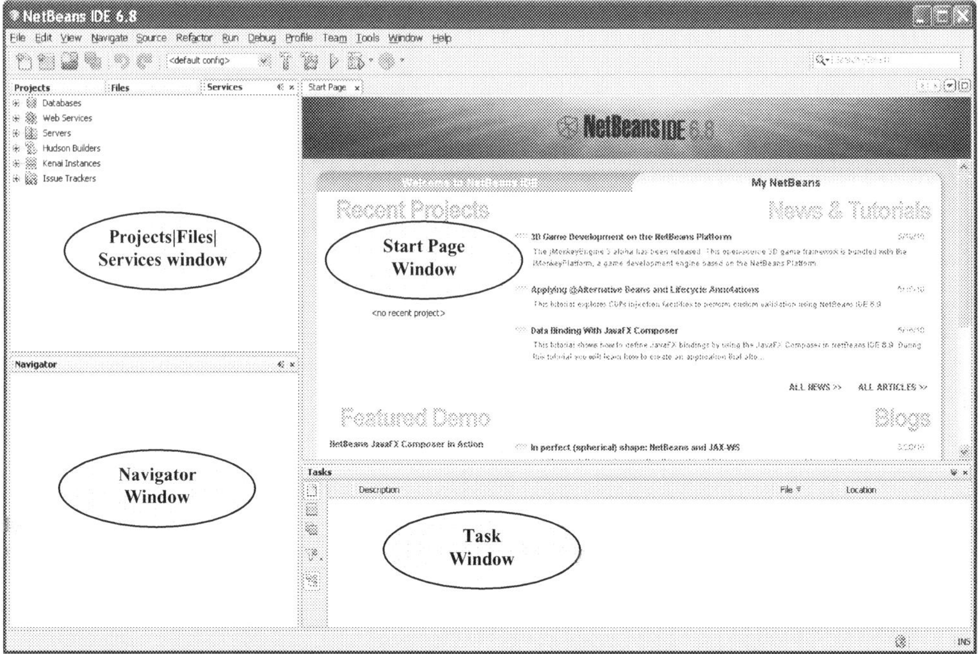

Figure 5.8. The opened NetBeans IDE 6.8.

These three different items can be displayed and switched by clicking on the corresponded tab on the top of this window.

The second window located at the lower-left corner is called Navigator window that contains all components to enable users to scan and go through all different objects or parts of a file. In fact, the Navigator window provides structured views of the file you are working with and lets you quickly navigate between different parts of the file.

The Tasks window is located at the bottom and it is mainly used to list all methods in your projects and allow you to enter the codes into those methods at any time when you building your project.

The Start Page is a main window when the IDE is opened and this window displays all recent projects you developed. All updated news and tutorials related to the NetBeans will also be displayed in this window.

Refer to Figure 5.8; among all menu items, the following items are special items with the specific functionalities in the NetBeans IDE:

- **Navigate:** the NetBeans Navigator is used to navigate to any object, file, type of objects, and symbol you created and built in your projects. With the name of each object or file, you can navigate to any of them at the development stage. Another important property of using the Navigate menu item is to enable you to inspect any member and hierarchy of those members defined in your project. In fact, the Inspect submenu item is used to inspect the members and hierarchy of any Java class in a convenient popup window that displays base classes, derived classes, and interfaces. Use filters to control the level of detail that is displayed.
- **Source:** the NetBeans Source is used to facilitate your source coding development by allowing you to insert codes, fix codes, fix Imports, show method parameters, shift and move codes in your projects.

- **Refactor:** the NetBeans Refactor allows you to restructure code in your project without breaking it. For example, when you rename an identifier or move a class to another package, you do not need to use Search and Replace; instead, the IDE can identify and update all occurrences instantly.
- **Profile:** the NetBeans Profiler is a tool for the monitoring of Java applications. It helps you find memory leaks and optimize speed. The Profiler is based on a Sun Laboratories research project that was named JFluid. That research uncovered specific techniques that can be used to lower the overhead of profiling a Java application. One of those techniques is dynamic bytecode instrumentation, which is particularly useful for profiling large Java applications. Using dynamic bytecode instrumentation and additional algorithms, the NetBeans Profiler is able to obtain runtime information on applications that are too large or complex for other profilers. NetBeans also support Profiling Points that let you profile precise points of execution and measure execution time.
- **Team:** the NetBeans Team provides the source code management and connected developer services to enable developers to perform the following functions:
  - Source code management (Subversion, Mercurial, CVS)
  - Local file history
  - Integrated Connected Developer features for projects hosted on http://Kenai.com:
    - ✓ Source code management (Subversion, Mercurial, and Git)
    - ✓ Issue tracking (Jira and Bugzilla)
    - ✓ Team wiki, forums, mailing lists
    - ✓ Document and downloads hosting

In the NetBeans IDE, you always work inside of a project. In addition to source files, an IDE project contains metadata about what belongs on the Classpath, how to build and run the project, and so on. The IDE stores project information in a project folder, which includes an Ant build script and properties file that control the building and running settings, and a project.xml file that maps Ant targets to IDE commands.

The Apache Ant is a Java-based building tool used to standardize and automate building and running environments for development. The IDE's project system is based directly on Ant. All of the project commands, like Clean and Build Project and Debug, call targets in the project's Ant script. You can therefore build and run your project outside the IDE exactly as it is built and run inside the IDE.

It is not necessary to know Ant to work with the IDE. You can set all the basic compilation and runtime options in the project's Project Properties dialog box, and the IDE automatically updates your project's Ant script. If you are familiar with Ant, you can customize a standard project's Ant script or write your own Ant script for a project.

Now let's have a closer look at different components and tools in NetBeans IDE 6.8 to help us to create, build, and run our desired Java application projects.

5.3.2 Build a New Java Project

To create a new project under the NetBeans IDE 6.8, go to `File|New Project` menu item.

A `New Project` wizard is displayed and shown in Figure 5.9.

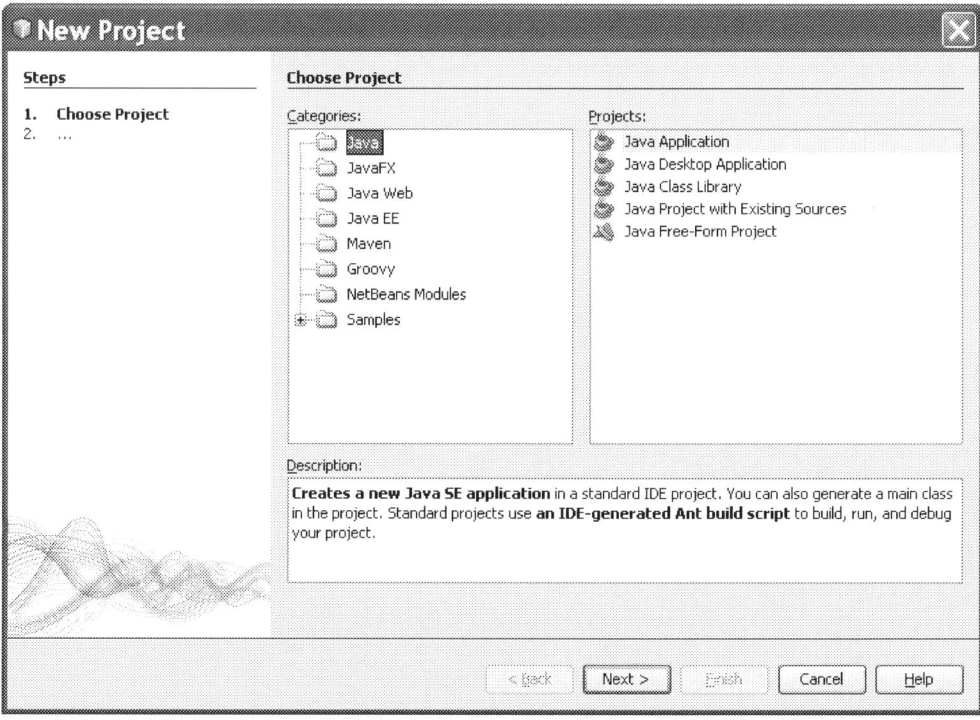

Figure 5.9. The opened create New Project dialog box.

The NetBeans IDE allows you to create and build different projects based on different categories by selecting the right template for your project and completing the remaining wizard steps. First, let's take care of creating a new Java project.

Under the `Java` category, the IDE contains the following standard project templates for Java desktop and Web applications:

- `Java Application`: Creates a skeleton Java Standard Edition (SE) project with a main class.
- `Java Desktop Application`: Creates an application based on the Swing Application Framework. Skeletons are offered for a basic desktop application and a database application that makes use of the Beans Binding and Java Persistence API (JPA) libraries.
- `Java Class Library`: Creates a skeleton Java class library without a main class.
- `Java Project with Existing Sources`: Creates a Java SE project based on your own Java sources.
- `Java Free-Form Project`: The free-form templates enable you to use an existing Ant script for a project but require manual configuration.

Let's give a more detailed discussion for each of these projects one by one.

5.3.2.1 Build a Java Application Project

On the opened `New Project` wizard, select the Java from the `Categories` pane and click on the `Java Application` node from the `Projects` pane to create a new Java

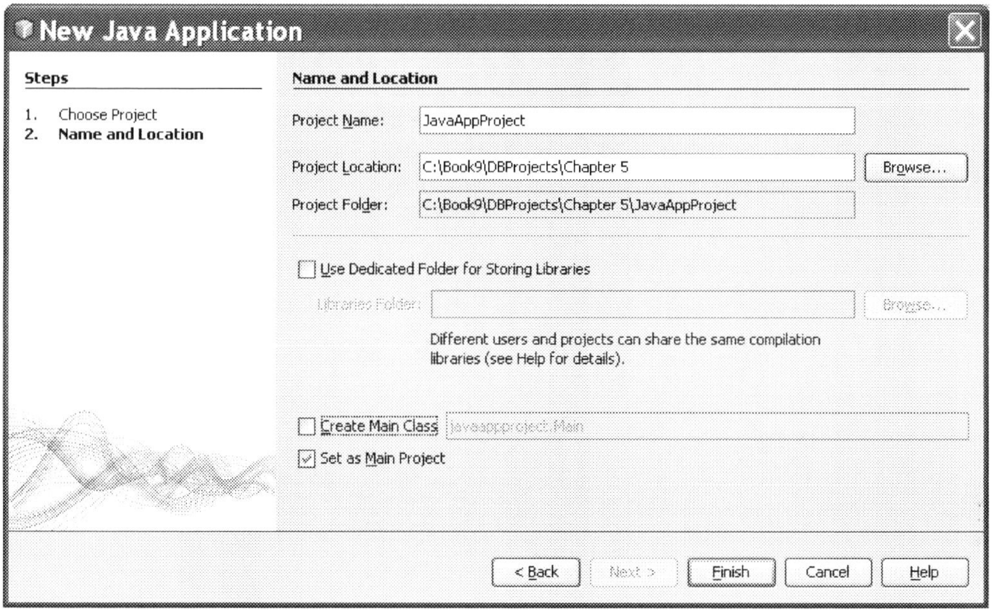

Figure 5.10. The New Java Application wizard.

Application Project. Click on the `Next` to open the `New Java Application` wizard, which is shown in Figure 5.10.

Perform the following operation to set up properties for this new project:

- Enter a desired project name, such as `JavaAppProject` in this example, into the `Project Name` box as the name for this project.
- Select a desired location to save this project. In this example, our desired location is `C:\Book9\DBProjects\Chapter 5`. You can select any other valid folder to save your project.
- Uncheck the `Create Main Class` checkbox since we do not want to use this class in this application.
- Keep all other default settings and click on the `Finish` button.

When you finish creating a project, it opens in the IDE with its logical structure displayed in the `Projects` window and its file structure displayed in the `Files` window, as shown in Figure 5.11.

1. The `Projects` window is the main entry point to your project sources. It shows a logical view of important project contents, such as Java packages and web pages. You can right click on any project node to access a popup menu of commands for building, running, and debugging the project, as well as opening the `Project Properties` dialog box. The `Projects` window can be opened by choosing `Window > Projects (Ctrl-1)`.
2. The `Files` window shows a directory-based view of your projects, including files and folders that are not displayed in the `Projects` window. From the `Files` window, you can open and edit your project configuration files, such as the project's build script and properties file. You can also view build output like compiled classes, JAR files, WAR files, and

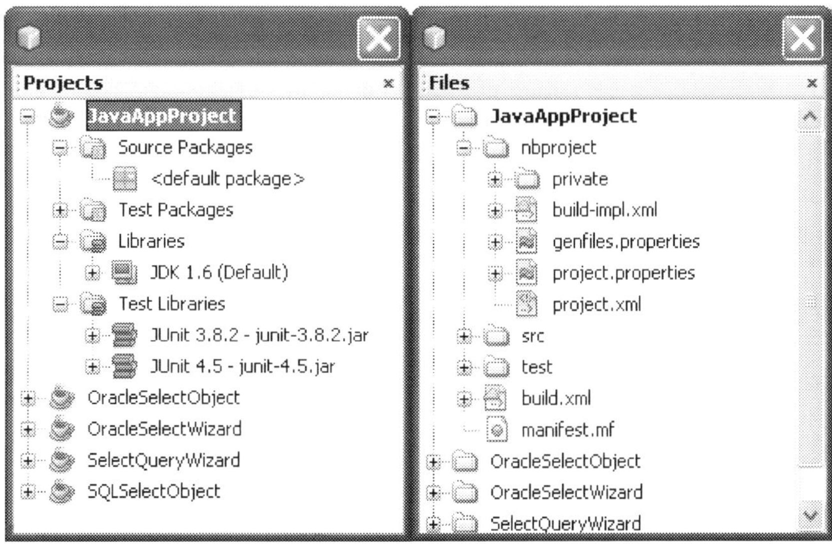

Figure 5.11. The logical and file structures displayed in the Projects and the Files windows.

generated Javadoc documentation. The `Files` window can be opened by choosing `Window > Files (Ctrl-2)`.

If you need to access files and directories that are outside of your project directories, you can use the `Favorites` window. You open the `Favorites` window by choosing `Window > Favorites` (`Ctrl-3`). You add a folder or file to the `Favorites` window by right clicking in the `Favorites` window and choosing the `Add to Favorites` menu item.

It can be found from Figure 5.11 that the `Java JDK 1.6` has been installed with the NetBeans IDE 6.8 and located in the `Libraries` folder in this project. If you want to use other Software Development Kits (SDK), JDK, project, or library with your projects, you can load them first, and then add them into your library by right clicking on the `Libraries` node and select the associated operational menu item from the popup menu.

Next, we need to add a graphical user interface (GUI) with other necessary GUI components to our project, and use it as a user interface to communicate with our project during the project runs.

5.3.2.1.1 Add a Graphical User Interface To proceed with building our interface, we need to create a Java container within which we will place the other required GUI components. Generally, the most popular Java GUI containers include:

- JFrame Form (Java Frame Form window)
- JDialog Form (Java Dialog Box Form window)
- JPanel Form (Java Panel Form window)

In this step, we'll create a container using the JFrame component. We will place the container in a new package, which will appear within the `Source Packages` node.

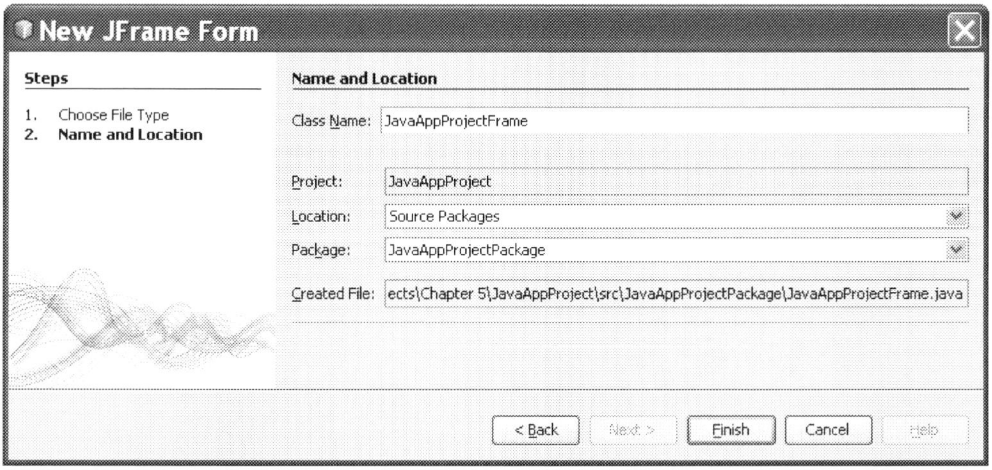

Figure 5.12. The finished New JFrame Form wizard.

Perform the following operations to complete this GUI adding process:

1. In the `Projects` window, right click on our newly created project `JavaAppProject` node and choose the `New > JFrame Form` menu item.
2. Enter `JavaAppProjectFrame` into the `Class Name` box as the class name.
3. Enter `JavaAppProjectPackage` into the `Package` box as the package name.
4. Click on the `Finish` button.

Your finished `New JFrame Form` wizard should match one that is shown in Figure 5.12.

The IDE creates the `JavaAppProjectFrame` form and the `JavaAppProjectFrame` class within the `JavaAppProject` application, and opens the `JavaAppProjectFrame` form in the GUI Builder. The `JavaAppProjectPackage` package replaces the default package.

When we added the `JFrame` container, the IDE opened the newly created `ContactEditorUI` form in an `Editor` tab with a toolbar containing several buttons, as shown in Figure 5.13. The `ContactEditor` form opened in the GUI Builder's Design view, and three additional windows appeared automatically along the IDE's edges, enabling you to navigate, organize, and edit GUI forms as you build them.

The GUI Builder's various windows include:

- **Design Area:** The GUI Builder's primary window for creating and editing Java GUI forms. The toolbar's `Source` and `Design` toggle buttons enable you to view a class's source code or a graphical view of its GUI components. The additional toolbar buttons provide convenient access to common commands, such as choosing between Selection and Connection modes, aligning components, setting component auto-resizing behavior, and previewing forms.
- **Inspector Window:** Provides a representation of all the components, both visual and nonvisual, in your application as a tree hierarchy. The Inspector also provides visual feedback

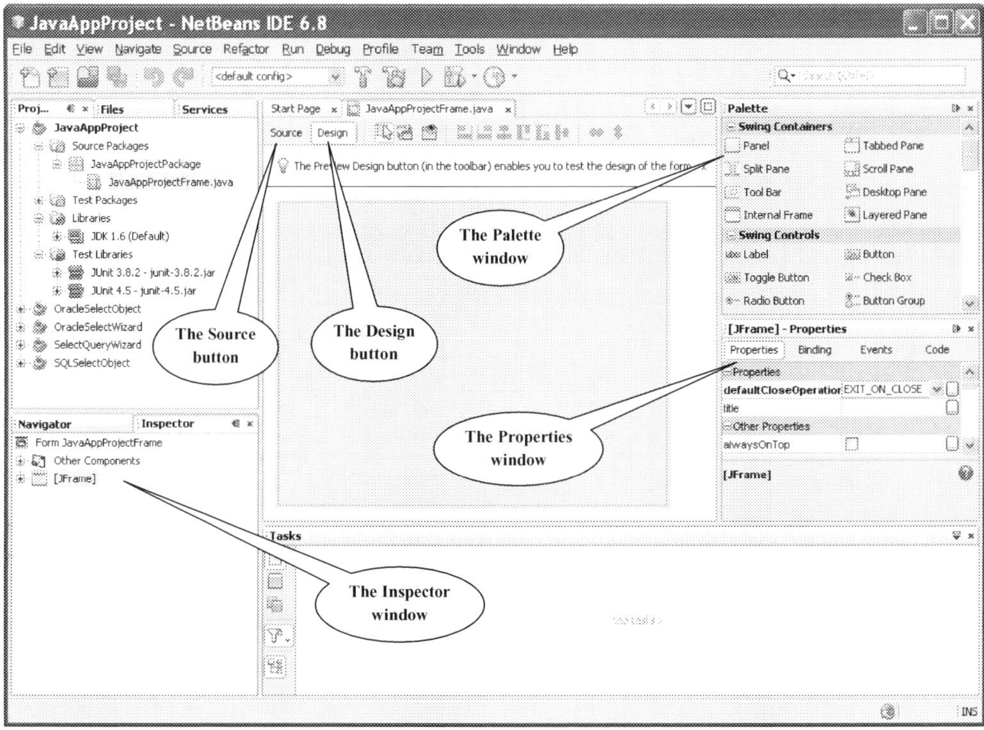

Figure 5.13. The opened ContactEditor form.

about what component in the tree is currently being edited in the GUI Builder, as well as allows you to organize components in the available panels.

- **Palette Window:** A customizable list of available components containing tabs for JFC/Swing, AWT, and JavaBeans components, as well as layout managers. In addition, you can create, remove, and rearrange the categories displayed in the `Palette` using the customizer.
- **Properties Window:** Displays the properties of the component currently selected in the `GUI Builder`, `Inspector` window, `Projects` window, or `Files` window.

Two more points to be emphasized are about the `Palette` and the `Properties` windows.

All Java GUI-related components are located in the Palette window and distributed in the different packages or namespaces. This Palette window contains the following GUI-related components based on the different packages:

- Swing Containers: contains all Java container classes
- Swing Controls: contains all Swing-related GUI components
- Swing Menus: contains all Swing-related menu items
- Swing Windows: contains all Swing-related window classes
- AWT: contains all AWT-related GUI components
- Beans: contains all JavaBeans-related GUI components
- Java Persistence: contains all Java Persistence-related components

Relatively speaking, AWT related GUI components are older compared with those components defined in the Swing package, in which all components are defined in a model view controller (MVC) style. The `java.awt` package contains all basic and fundamental graphic user interface components (AWT). However, the `javax.swing` package contains extensions of `java.awt`, which means that all components in the `javax.swing` package have been built into a model-view-controller (MVC) mode with more object oriented properties (Swing).

The `Properties` window is used to set up and display all properties about GUI components you added into the container, such as appearances and physical descriptions. Let's illustrate how to use this window to set up and show each property for added GUI-related components on this container in the next section.

5.3.2.1.2 Add Other GUI-Related Components Next, let's finish this GUI by adding some GUI-related components into this GUI container. For this application, we want to add:

1. One JPanel object that can be considered as a kind of container.
2. Two JTextField objects to retrieve and hold the user's first and the last name.
3. Four JLabel objects to display the caption for each JTextFields and the user's full name as the Display button is clicked.
4. Three JButton objects, Display, Clear, and Exit. The Clear button is used to clean up all contents on two JTextField objects (user's first and last name), and the Exit button is used to exit the application.

Now let's begin to add those components one by one by dragging them from the `Palette` window. If you did not see the `Palette` window in the upper-right corner of the IDE, choose the `Windows > Palette` menu item to open it.

Let's add the JPanel object first in the following operational sequence:

1. Start by selecting a JPanel from the `Palette` window and drop it onto the JFrame.
2. While the JPanel is highlighted, go to the `Properties` window and click on the ellipsis (. . .) button next to the `Border` property to choose a border style.
3. In the `Border` dialog, select `TitledBorder` from the list, and type in `Display Full Name` in the `Title` field, and click on the `OK` to save the changes and exit the dialog.
4. You should now see an empty titled JFrame that says `Display Full Name` JPanel object. Now add the rest of GUI-related components, including four JLabels, two JTextFields, and three JButtons, into this JPanel object as you see in Figure 5.14.

Next, let's rename all added components and modify JLabel4 by setting the appropriate property for that label in the `Properties` window.

Perform the following operational sequence:

1. Double click on jLabel1 and change the text property to First Name.
2. Double click on jLabel2 and change the text to Last Name.
3. Double click on jLabel3 and change the text to Full Name.
4. Click on jLabel4 and click on the ellipsis (. . .) button next to the `Border` property to choose a border style. In the `Border` dialog, select `Line Border` from the list, and change the border color to dark blue by clicking on the ellipsis (. . .) button next to the

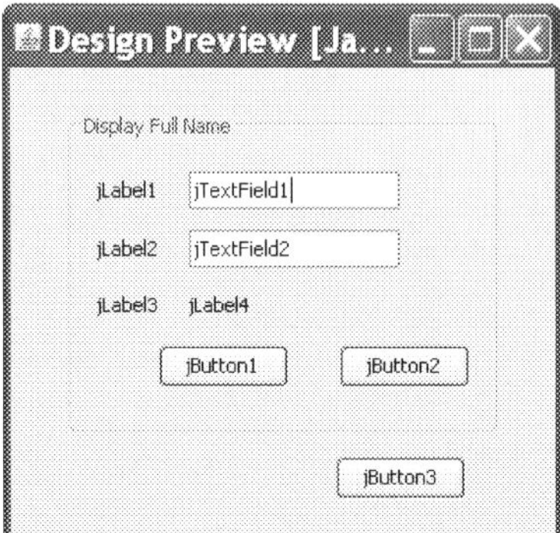

Figure 5.14. A Design Preview of the GUI Window Form.

Color property, and click on the OK to save the changes and exit the dialog. Then go to the Text property to delete the default text JLabel4 to make this an empty label.

5. Delete the sample text from jTextField1. You can make the display text editable by clicking on the Text field, pausing, and then clicking the Text field again. You may have to resize the jTextField1 to its original size. Repeat this step for jTextField2.
6. Change the name of jTextField1 to FirstTextField. To do that change, right click on the jTextField1 object and select Change Variable Name menu item from the popup menu, then enter FirstTextField into the New Name box. Click on the OK button to complete this rename operation.
7. Perform a similar operation to change the Name property of the jTextField2 to LastTextField, and the Name property of the jLabel4 to FullNameLabel.
8. Rename the display text of jButton1 to Display. You can edit a button's Text property by right clicking on the button and choosing the Edit Text menu item from the popup menu. Or you can click on the button, pause, and then click again.
9. Rename the display text of jButton2 to Clear.
10. Rename the display text of jButton3 to Exit.
11. Change the Name property of the jButton1 to DisplayButton, jButton2 to ClearButton, and jButton3 to ExitButton, respectively.

Your finished GUI should now look like one that is shown in Figure 5.15.

Next, let's develop the coding for each component to connect our GUI related components with our coding to process and response user's input and display the running result.

5.3.2.1.3 Develop the Codes In fact, only three JButton objects need the coding process since both TextField objects are used to retrieve and hold the user's input without any other actions in this application. A similar situation happened to the JLabel4, which is used to display the running result of this application.

In order to give function to the buttons, we have to assign an event handler to each to respond to events. In our case, we want to know when the button is pressed, either by mouse click or via keyboard. So we will use ActionListener responding to ActionEvent.

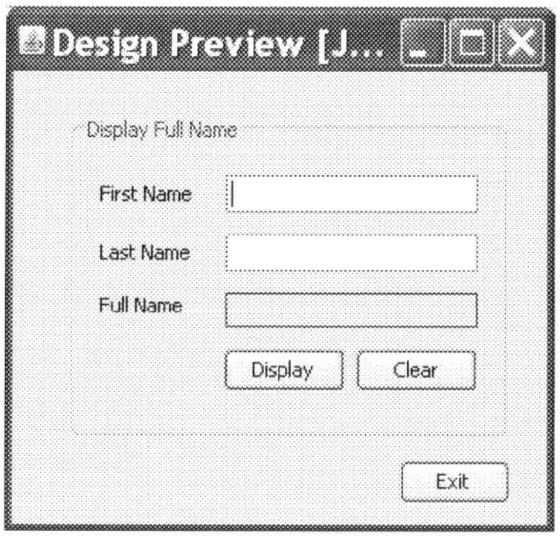

Design Preview [J...
Display Full Name
First Name
Last Name
Full Name
Display Clear
Exit

Figure 5.15. The finished GUI design window.

```
private void DisplayButtonActionPerformed(java.awt.event.ActionEvent evt) {
    // TODO add your handling code here:
    FullNameLabel.setText(FirstTextField.getText() + " " + LastTextField.getText());
}
```

Figure 5.16. The coding for the DisplayButtonActionPerformed() event handler.

In the early days, the developers must do the connection between the `ActionListener` and `ActionEvent` manually in an application. Thanks to NetBeans IDE, this Listener and Event model has been set up and configured. To set up that connection, what the developer needs to do is just to perform a double click on the selected button. Is that easy? Yes, it is. Now let's do this Event-Listener action connection with our first button—`DisplayButton`.

5.3.2.1.3.1 Coding for the Display Button: The function of the `Display` button is to concatenate the first and the last names entered by the user and stored in the `FirstTextField` and the `LastTextField` TextFields, and display it in the `FullNameLable` when this `Display` button is clicked by the user as the project runs.

Double clicking on the `Display` button, you can open its callback method or event handler, `DisplayButtonActionPerformed()`. Enter the codes shown in Figure 5.16 into this event handler to concatenate the first and the last names entered by the user and display it in the `FullNameLabel`.

Regularly, for most events and the associated event handler methods, you can do that connection by right clicking on the source object (`DisplayButton` in this application), and select the `Events` menu item from the popup menu. All events that can be triggered by this source object will be displayed in a pop-up menu. By moving your cursor to the desired event, all event handlers responding to this event will be displayed in a popup submenu, and you can select the desired event handler to open it, and a connection between that event and event handler has been set up simultaneously.

The coding for this Display button `ActionPerformed()` event handler is simple, and the `setText()` method is used to display the concatenated first and last name with a plus symbol.

```
private void ClearButtonActionPerformed(java.awt.event.ActionEvent evt) {
    // TODO add your handling code here:
    FirstTextField.setText(null);
    LastTextField.setText(null);
    FullNameLabel.setText(null);
}
```

Figure 5.17. The coding for the ClearButtonActionPerformed() event handler.

```
private void ExitButtonActionPerformed(java.awt.event.ActionEvent evt) {
    // TODO add your handling code here:
    System.exit(0);
}
```

Figure 5.18. The coding for the ExitButtonActionPerformed() event handler.

5.3.2.1.3.2 Coding for the Clear Button: The function of this `Clear` button is to clean up all contents in two TextFields, `FirstTextField` and `LastTextField`, respectively, to allow the user to enter a new name. Double click on the `Clear` button to open its event handler, and enter the codes shown in Figure 5.17 into this event handler.

When this button is clicked by the user, the `setText()` method is executed with a `null` as the argument to clean up three objects' contents, the `FirstTextField`, `LastTextField`, and `FullNameLabel`.

5.3.2.1.3.3 Coding for the Exit Button: The function of this button is to stop the running of this project and exit from this application. To open its event handler, this time, we use another way to do that. Perform the following operations to finish this coding process.

1. Right click on the `Exit` button. From the pop-up menu, choose `Events > Action > ActionPerformed`. Note that the menu contains many more events you can respond to! When you select the `actionPerformed` event, the IDE will automatically add an `ActionListener` to the `Exit` button and generate a handler method for handling the listener's `actionPerformed` method.
2. The IDE will open up the Source Code window and scroll to where you implement the action you want the button to do when the button is pressed.
3. Enter the codes that are shown in Figure 5.18 into this event handler.

A system method, `exit()`, is executed as this button is clicked by the user, and a 0 is used as an argument to be returned to the operating system to indicate that the application has been completed successfully. A returned nonzero value indicates that some exceptions may have been encountered when the application runs.

Before we can run the project to test functions we have built, we need to do one more coding, which is to locate the GUI window in the center when the project runs.

The NetBeans IDE has a default location for each GUI window, the upper-left corner, and will display those windows in that location as the project runs. To make our GUI window located in the center of the screen as the project runs, we need to put one line

```
public class JavaAppProjectFrame extends javax.swing.JFrame {

   /** Creates new form JavaAppProjectFrame */
   public JavaAppProjectFrame() {
      initComponents();
      this.setLocationRelativeTo(null);          // set the GUI form at the center
   }
   ........
}
```

Figure 5.19. The coding for the constructor of the class JavaAppProjectFrame.

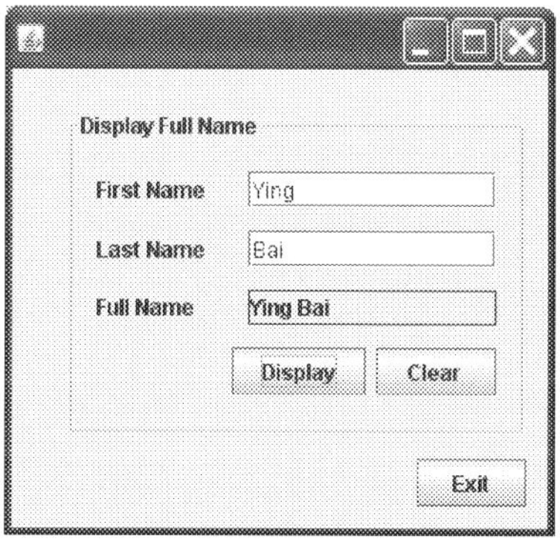

Figure 5.20. The running result of our project.

coding into the constructor of this class since the first thing we need to do is to display our GUI window after the project runs. Open the code window by clicking on the `Source` button and enter one coding line into the constructor of this class, which is shown in Figure 5.19.

A system method `setLocationRelativeTo()` is used to set this form at the center of the screen as the project runs. A `null` argument means that no object can be referenced or relative to, and the JFrame Form is set to the center.

Now we have finished the building process for this project, and we are ready to run it to test functions we have built.

5.3.2.1.4 Run the Project

Perform the following operations to run our project:

- Click on the `Clean and Build Main Project` button to compile and build our project.
- Choose the `Run > Run Main Project` menu item.
- If you get a window informing you that Project `JavaAppProject` does not have a main class set, then you should select `JavaAppProjectPackage.JavaAppProjectFrame` as the main class in the same window and click the `OK` button.

A sample of our running project is shown in Figure 5.20.

Enter your first and last name into the `First Name` and `Last Name` TextFields, respectively, and click on the `Display` button. Your full name will be displayed in the

`Full Name` label, as shown in Figure 5.20. Try to click on the `Clear` button to see what happened. Then you can click on the `Exit` button to stop our project.

Yes, that is all for a typical Java Application project.

A complete Java Application project `JavaAppProject` can be found from the folder `DBProjects\Chapter 5` that is located at the Wiley ftp site (refer to Figure 1.2 in Chapter 1).

5.3.2.2 Build a Java Desktop Application

As we mentioned in the last section, a `Java Desktop Application` is an application based on the Swing Application Framework. Skeletons are offered for a basic desktop application and a database application that makes use of the Beans Binding and JPA libraries. By using JPA, all components developed in a relational database can be mapped to the associated objects, and developers only need to take care of those mapped objects in the entity classes to perform desired data actions with their connected databases without worrying about any real staff in the database.

Three important components are critical to develop a Java Desktop Application project:

- The JPA, which helps you use Java code to interact with databases.
- Beans Binding, which provides a way for different JavaBeans components to have property values that are synchronized with each other. For example, you can use beans binding to keep the values of cells in a JTable visual component in synch with the values of fields in an entity class. (In turn, the entity class represents the database table.)
- The Swing Application Framework, which provides some useful building blocks for quickly creating desktop applications.
- First, let's set up a database to be used in this project.

5.3.2.2.1 Set Up the Database To simplify this database setup process and save time, we can use a default Java DB Server and a sample database that has been installed when the NetBeans IDE 6.8 is installed into your computer. Perform the following operations to complete this database setup:

- Launch the NetBeans IDE 6.8 and open the `Services` window.
- Right click on the `Databases > Java DB` node and choose `Properties`.

If a default Java DB server is registered, the Java DB Installation and Database Location fields will be filled in, as shown in Figure 5.21.

Click on the `OK` button to close this dialog box.

Now let's start the Java DB Server in the NetBeans by right clicking on the `Databases > Java DB` and choose the `Start Server` menu item. Once the server is started, Java DB Database Process tab opens in the `Output` window and displays a message similar the following:

```
Security manager installed using the Basic server security policy.
Apache Derby Network Server - 10.4.2.1 - (706043) started and ready to
accept connections on port 1527 at 2010-05-24 22:38:21.187 GMT
```

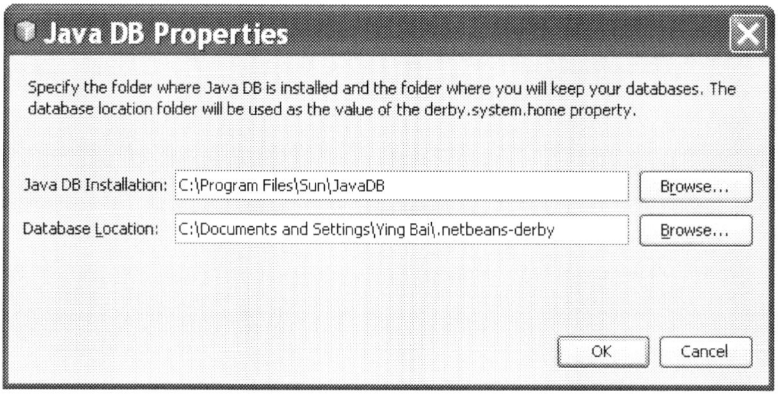

Java DB Properties

Specify the folder where Java DB is installed and the folder where you will keep your databases. The database location folder will be used as the value of the derby.system.home property.

Java DB Installation: C:\Program Files\Sun\JavaDB Browse...

Database Location: C:\Documents and Settings\Ying Bai\.netbeans-derby Browse...

OK Cancel

Figure 5.21. The opened Java DB Server location and default database location.

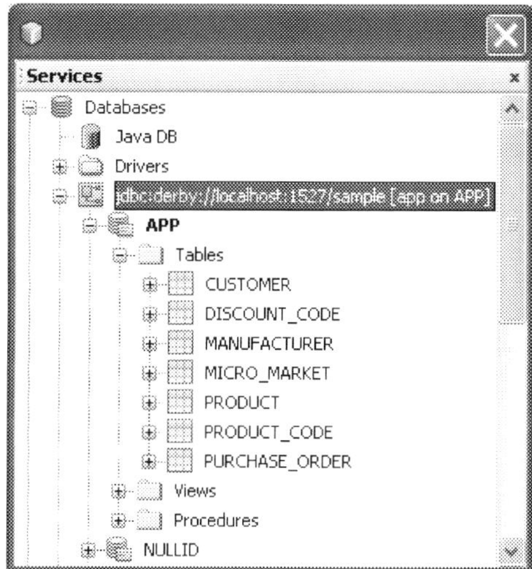

Figure 5.22. The connected Sample database and tables in the Services window.

Now let's connect to the sample database to complete this database setup.

- Right click on the default sample database connection node `jdbc:derby://localhost:1527/sample[app on APP]` and choose Connect.
- Expand that connected node and the APP and Table subnodes, and you can find all tables built under this sample database, as shown in Figure 5.22.
- Expand each table, such as the `CUSTOMER` table, and you can find all columns defined in that table. The primary key is highlighted with the red color.

Next, let's create a new Java Desktop Application project named `JavaDeskApp` to connect to this database to perform data actions.

5.3.2.2.2 Create the Java Desktop Application Perform the following operations to create a new Java Desktop Application project:

1. Choose the `File > New Project` menu item to open the `New Project` wizard.
2. In the first panel of the wizard, expand the `Java` category and select the `Java Desktop Application` template, then click on the `Next` button. The `Java Desktop Application` template provides many basics of a visual application, including basic menu items and commands.
3. In the `Project Name` field, type `JavaDeskApp`. The value of this field sets the display name for the project in the `Projects` window.
4. In the `Project Location` field, enter a valid folder to store this project. In this application, we used `C:\Book9\DBProjects\Chapter 5` folder to do that.
5. Check the `Set As Main Project` checkbox.
6. In the `Choose Application Shell` field, select the `Database Application` item.
7. Click on the `Next` button to continue. Your finished `Name and Location` page should match one that is shown in Figure 5.23.
8. In the `Master Table` page of the wizard, select the `Database Connection` for the Sample database we just set up in the last section. The listing for the database should look something like: `jdbc:derby://localhost:1527/sample[app on APP]`.
9. After the connection to the database is established, the `Database Table` field should display the first table `CUSTOMER`, and the `Columns to Include` list should include

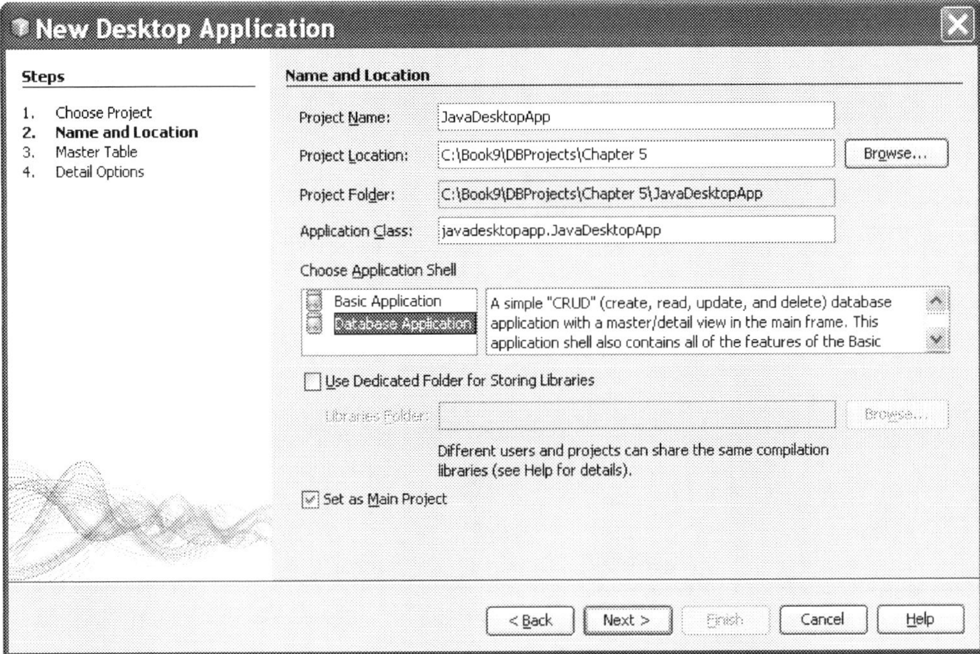

Figure 5.23. The finished Name and Location page.

the names of all 12 columns for the CUSTOMER table. For now, we will use this CUSTOMER table with only seven columns in this application.

Remove the following five columns from the `Columns to Include` list by clicking on each of them one by one (you can hold the `Ctrl` key to do that): `DISCOUNT_CODE`, `FAX`, `ADDRESSLINE2`, `EMAIL`, and `CREDIT_LIMIT`, and click the < button to move them to the left column, `Available Columns` list. Then click on the `Next` button.

In the `Detail Options` panel, just keep the default settings and click on the `Finish` button, since we want to display these columns in a `TextFields` format. Your `Detail Options` panel should match one that is shown in Figure 5.24.

The wizard then generates a basic user interface with a table and a database connection. This might take a few seconds as the IDE generates the project and the code.

Now click on the `Clean and Build Main Project` button on the toolbar to compile and build our project. After this new `Java Desktop Application` project is created, five folders with related files are created and added into the `Source Packages` folder in the `Projects` window, which is shown in Figure 5.25.

Let's take a closer look at these folders and related files.

The `META-INF` folder: this folder contains the `persistence.xml` file and it is used to define a connection between the database and the entity class. This file is also known as the persistence unit.

The `META-INF.services` folder: this folder contains the `org.jdesktop.application. Application` file that is a subclass inherited from the base class `java.lang.Object`. This class provides all necessary attributes and behaviors (fields and methods) used to build a standard Java desktop application projects.

The `javadesktopapp` folder has the following four files:

1. Customer.java
2. JavaDesktopAboutBox.java

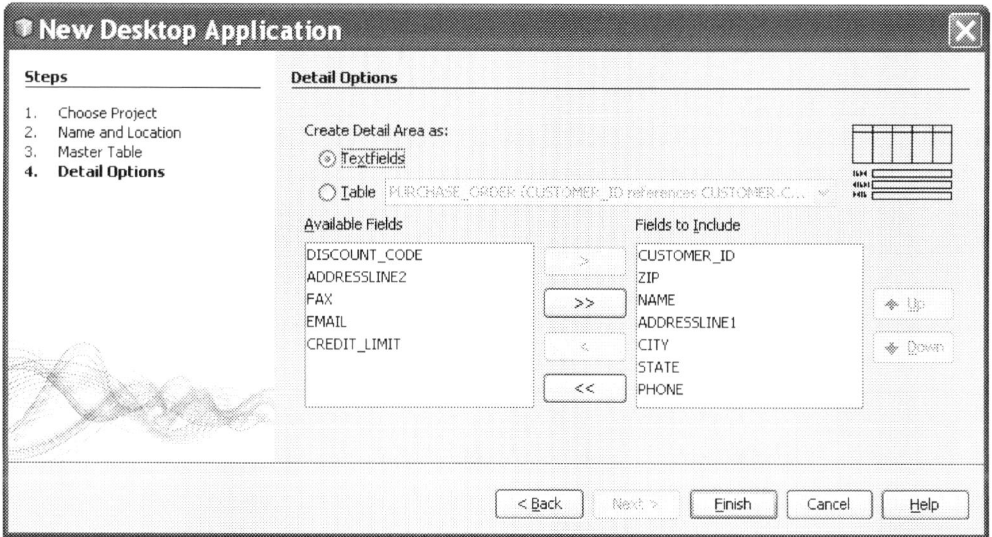

Figure 5.24. The finished Detail Options page.

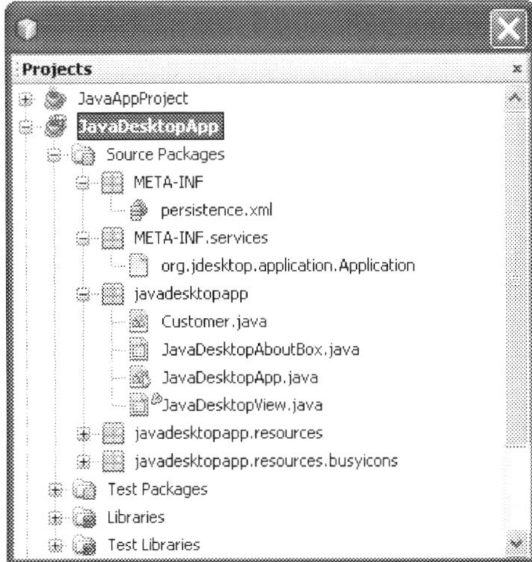

Figure 5.25. Four new files are created and added into the Projects window.

3. JavaDesktopApp.java
4. JavaDesktopView.java

The first file `Customer.java` is an Entity class that is used to map all components defined the CUSTOMER table in the Sample database to the associated objects using JPA. If you open this file by double clicking on it, you can find all mapping definitions between each column and the associated object (string object for most columns), as well as the setter and getter methods used to pick up and set up for each object. All static or named queries are defined at the beginning part of this file. With the help of this Entity class and those mappings, we can directly access those objects to perform data actions with our database during the project runs.

The second file, `JavaDesktopAboutBox.java`, provides a default `About` dialog box for this project with the version, vendor, and homepage involved to give users a basic introduction to this project.

The third file, `JavaDesktopApp.java`, is the main program or main thread of this project that contains the main frame and skeleton of this project. Also, this file provides an entry point of this project, since the `main()` method is included in this file.

The last file, `JavaDesktopView.java`, provides a `View` class for this project with prebuilt GUI components, such as a `JTable`, a menu, seven `TextFields`, and four `JButtons`, to allow users to access and manipulate data in the connected Sample database via this GUI window as the project runs.

The `javadesktopapp.resources` folder: this folder contains five files:

1. JavaDesktopAboutBox.properties
2. JavaDesktopApp.properties
3. JavaDesktopView.properties
4. about.png
5. splash.png

The first three files contain all physical descriptions and properties for the `AboutBox`, the main thread, and the View classes. The last two are image files used in the `About` dialog box.

The `javadesktopapp.resources.busyicons` folder: this folder contains all image files related to the icons used in the applications.

At this point, we have a basic Java desktop running application with a GUI that has the following features:

- Ability to view and modify values in seven columns of the Sample database.
- Basic menu items.
- Persistence of its window state between sessions. When you close the application, the window position and size are remembered. So when you reopen the application, the window opens in the same position as it was when you closed it.
- An About dialog box, which you can easily customize.
- Properties files containing the labels in the user interface. Using .properties files is a good way to keep the logic of your code separate from the text that appears in the user interface of your application. Such separation is useful for making it easier to localize your program, among other reasons.

Now let's run our project to see how to access and modify data in the CUSTOMER table by using this Java desktop application.

5.3.2.2.3 Run the Project Click on the `Run Main Project` button (green arrow) on the toolbar to start our application, and an example of our running project is shown in Figure 5.26. You can enlarge this GUI window by dragging it to either left or up to enable all seven columns to be displayed.

As you can see, as the project runs, all seven columns in the CUSTOMER table are displayed in the upper part of this GUI window. If you click on any row on the table, a detailed record is displayed in the seven TextFields located at the bottom of this GUI window, as shown in Figure 5.26.

You can modify this table by adding a new record, by deleting a record and saving these modifications to the table by using three buttons. If you want to add a new record, click on the `New` button and a blank row will be attached to the bottom of the table to allow you to do that. When you finish adding a new record, click on the `Save` button to write it into the database. To delete a record, just click on that record and click on the `Delete` button. Click on the `Save` button, so you can save all modifications you have made.

Click on the `Close` button on the upper-right corner of this window, so you can stop and close the project.

A complete Java Desktop Application project `JavaDesktopApp` can be found from the folder `DBProjects\Chapter 5` that is located at the Wiley ftp site (refer to Figure 1.2 in Chapter 1).

5.3.2.3 Build a Java Class Library

As we mentioned, a Java Class Library is only a skeleton Java class library without a main class, and it cannot be executed by itself; instead, it must be called or used by other Java

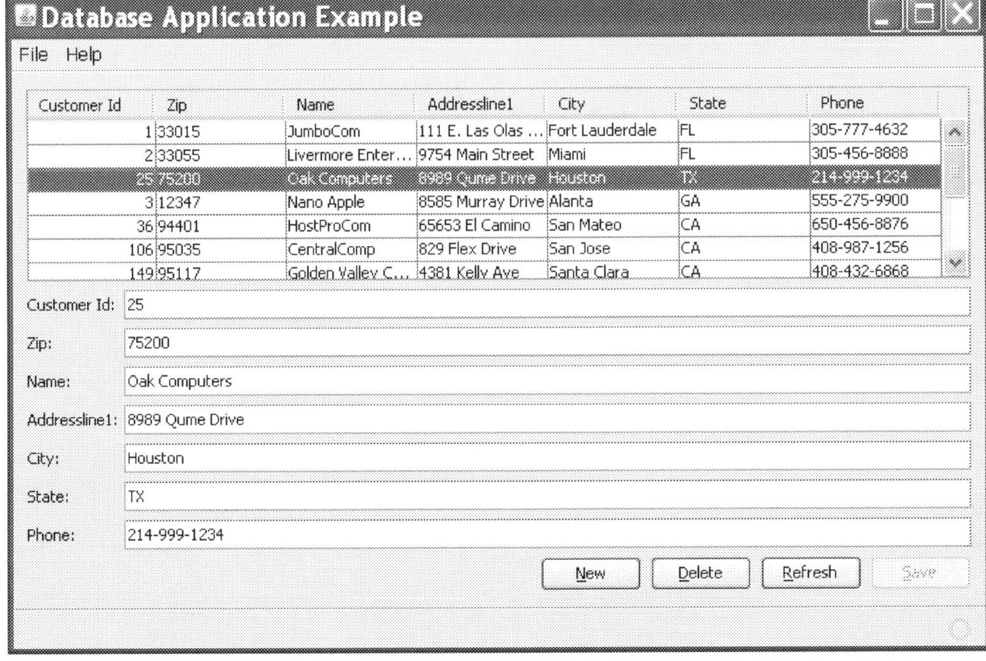

Figure 5.26. The running status of our Java desktop application.

applications. Similar to other general libraries, a Java Class Library can be statically or dynamically bound or connected with an application and to be used as a utility class.

Since a Java class library cannot be executed by itself, we need to create a Java Application project to call or use that Java class library. Therefore, we need to create two projects to illustrate how to use a Java class library from a Java application:

- A Java Class Library project in which you will create a utility class.
- A Java Application project with a main class that implements a method from the library project's utility class.

The function of this Java class library is simple, which is just to add two integers together and return the sum result to the Java application project, and the result will be displayed in the application project by calling some methods defined in the Java application project.

First, let's create a Java Class Library project named `SumLib()`.

5.3.2.3.1 Create a Java Class Library Project Perform the following operations to create this new Java Class Library project:

- Choose the `File > New Project` menu item. Under the `Categories`, select `Java`. Under `Projects`, select `Java Class Library`, and then click on the `Next` button.
- Enter `SumLib` into the `Project Name` field as the name of this class library. Change the `Project Location` to any directory as you want on your computer. From now on, this directory is `C:\Book9\DBProjects\Chapter 5`.

```
public class SumLibClass {
   public static int sumapp(String args) {
      int sum = 0;

      String[] temp;
      temp = args.split(",");
      int num[] = new int[temp.length];
      for(int i = 0; i < temp.length ; i++){
         System.out.println(temp[i]);
         num[i] = java.lang.Integer.parseInt(temp[i]);
         sum = sum + num[i];
      }
      return sum;
   }
}
```

Figure 5.27. The coding for the class method sumapp().

- Click the `Finish` button. The `SumLib` project opens in both the `Projects` window and the `Files` window.

Next, we need to create a new Java package and our class file. The Java package is used as a container or a namespace to hold the class file.

Perform the following operations to finish this Java package and class file:

1. Right click on the `SumLib` project node from the `Projects` window and choose the `New > Java Class` item. Type `SumLibClass` as the name for the new class, type `org.me.sumlib` in the `Package` field as the package name for this class file, and click on the `Finish` button. The `SumLibClass.java` opens in the `Source Editor`.
2. In the opened `SumLibClass.java` file, place the cursor on the line after the class declaration, `public class SumLibClass {`.
3. Type or paste in the method code shown in Figure 5.27.
4. If the code that you pasted in is not formatted correctly, press Alt-Shift-F to reformat the entire file.
5. Go to `File > Save All` menu item to save this file.

This coding is simple and straightforward. The input argument to this method should be a sequence of integers separated with commas (,), which can be considered as a String entered by the user as the project runs.

Let's have a closer look at this piece of codes to see how it works.

First, a temporary String array `temp` is created, and it is used to hold the split input integers. Then, the `split()` method is executed to separate the input argument into each separate number string. A `for` loop is used to display each separated number string and convert each of them to the associated integer using the `parseInt()` method. Since this method is defined in the `java.lang.Integer` package, so a full name of the method must be used. A summarization operation is performed to add all integers together and returned to the `main()` method in the Java application project `SumApp`.

Now that a Java class library project has been created and a Java class file has been coded, next, we need to create our `Java Application` project to call or use that class library to perform a two-integer addition operation.

5.3.2.3.2 Create a Java Application Project Perform the following operations to create a new Java Application project:

- Choose the `File > New Project` menu item. Under `Categories`, select `Java`. Under `Projects`, select `Java Application`. Then click on the `Next` button.
- Enter `SumApp` into the `Project Name` field. Make sure the `Project Location` is set to `C:\Book9\DBProjects\Chapter 5`.
- Enter `sumapp.Main` as the main class.
- Ensure that the `Set as Main Project` and `Create Main Class` checkboxes are checked.
- Click the `Finish` button. The `SumApp` project is displayed in the `Projects` window and `Main.java` opens in the `Source Editor`.

Now we have finished creating two Java projects.

After these two projects have been created, you need to add the Java class library project to the *classpath* of the Java application project. Then you can code the application. The library project will contain a utility class with a `sumapp()` method. This method takes two integers as arguments, and then generates a sum based on those integers. The `SumApp` project will contain a main class that calls the `sumapp()` method and passes the integers that are entered as arguments when the application is run.

Now let's configure the compilation classpath in the Java application project to enable the application to know the location of the class library and execute it to perform the integer addition operation during the project runs.

5.3.2.3.3 Configure the Compilation Classpath Since the `SumApp` Java application is going to depend on a class in `SumLib`, you have to add `SumLib` to the classpath of `SumApp`. Doing so also ensures that classes in the `SumApp` project can refer to classes in the `SumLib` project without causing compilation errors. In addition, this enables you to use code completion in the `SumApp` project to fill in code based on the `SumLib` project. In the NetBeans IDE 6.8, the classpath is visually represented by the `Libraries` node.

Perform the following operations to add the `SumLib` library's utility classes to the application `SumApp` project classpath:

1. In the `Projects` window, right click the `Libraries` node for the `SumApp` project and choose `Add Project` as shown in Figure 5.28.
2. Browse to `C:\Book9\DBProjects\Chapter 5` and select the SumLib project folder, as shown in Figure 5.29. The `Project JAR Files` pane shows the JAR files that can be added to the project. Notice that a JAR file for `SumLib` is listed even though you have not actually built the JAR file yet. This JAR file will get built when you build and run the `SumApp` project.
3. Click on the `Add Project JAR Files` button.
4. Now expand the `Libraries` node. The `SumLib` project's JAR file has been added to the `SumApp` project's classpath.

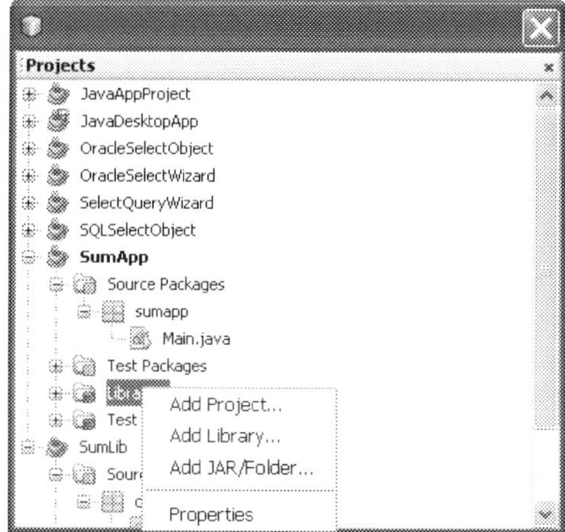

Figure 5.28. To add the SumLib class to the classpath of the SumApp project.

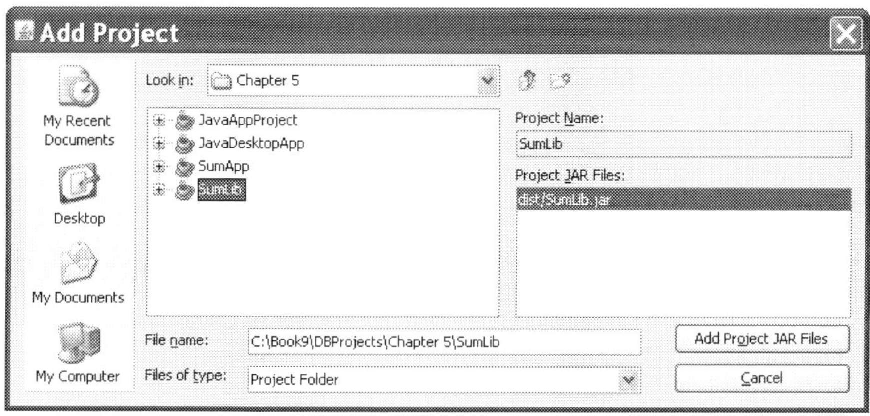

Figure 5.29. The Add Project dialog box.

Before we can run our Java application project to call the Java class library, we need to add some codes to the Main.java tab in our Java application project.

5.3.2.3.4 Add Codes to the Main.java tab in the Java Application Project Now we need to add some code to `Main.java`. In doing so, you will see the Source Editor's code completion and code template (abbreviation) features.

1. Select the `Main.java` tab in the Source Editor. If it isn't already open, expand `SumApp` > `Source Packages` > `sumapp` in the `Projects` window and double click on the item `Main.java`.
2. Inside the `main()` method, replace the comment `//TODO code application logic here` with the following:

```
int result = Sum
```

3. Leave the cursor immediately after `Sum`. In the next step, you will use code completion to turn `Sum` into `SumLibClass`.
4. Press Ctrl-Space to open the code completion box. A short list of possible ways to complete the word appears. However, the class that you want, `SumLibClass`, might not be there.
5. Press Ctrl-Space again to display a longer list of possible matches. The `SumLibClass` should be in this list.
6. Select the `SumLibClass` and press the `Enter` key. The NetBeans IDE 6.8 fills in the rest of the class name and also automatically creates an import statement for the class.

Note: The IDE also opens a box above the code completion box that displays Javadoc information for the selected class or package. Since there is no Javadoc information for this package, the box displays a "Cannot find Javadoc" message.

7. In the main method, type a period (.) after `SumLibClass`. The code completion box opens again.
8. Select the `sumapp(String args) int` method and press the `Enter` key. The IDE fills in the `sumapp()` method and highlights the input parameters.
9. Press the `Enter` key to accept the `null` as the parameter, and change this `null` to `args[0]`. Type a semicolon (;) at the end of this coding line. The final line should look like the following line.

```
int result = SumLibClass.sumapp(args[0]);
```

10. Press the `Enter` key to start a new line. Then type the following coding line.

```
System.out.println("The sum = " + result);
```

11. Go to the `File > Save All` menu item to save the file.

At this point, we are ready to run our Java application project `SumApp` to test its calling function to our Java library file `SumLibClass`.

5.3.2.3.5 Run the Application Project to Call the Java Library The output of this application program `SumApp.java` is based on arguments that you provide when you run the application. As arguments, you can provide two or more integers, from which the adding result of those input integers will be generated. The adding process will be executed by the Java library file `sumapp()` located in the `SumLibClass` library, and the execution result will be returned to and displayed in the `main()` method in the Java application project `SumApp.java`.

Now let's run the application. Since this application needs arguments as inputs to the `main()` method, therefore we have to use an alternative way to run it. First, let's perform the following operations to add the arguments for the IDE to use when running the application:

- Right click on the SumApp project node, choose the `Properties` item, and select the Run node in the dialog's left pane. The main class should already be set to sumapp.Main.

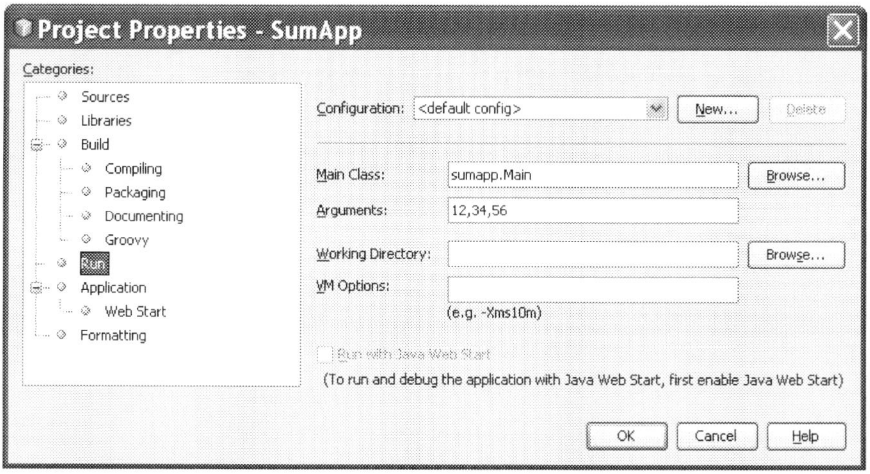

Figure 5.30. The completed Project Properties window.

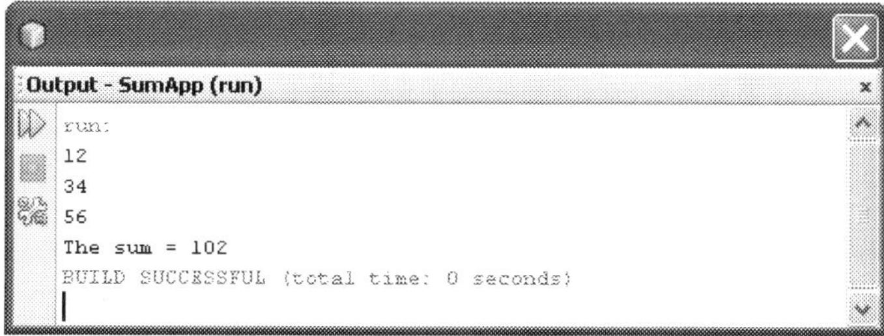

Figure 5.31. The running result shown in the Output window.

- Enter some integers as input arguments to the `Arguments` field, and each integer should be separated with a comma, such as `12,34,56`, and click on the `OK` button.

Your finished `Project Properties` window should match one that is shown in Figure 5.30.

Now that we have created the application and provided runtime arguments for the application, we can test and run the application in two ways: run the application inside the NetBeans IDE 6.8, or run the application outside the NetBeans IDE 6.8.

To run the application inside the NetBeans IDE 6.8:

Choose the `Run > Run Main Project` menu item (or F6 key).

In the `Output` window shown in Figure 5.31, you should see both the input arguments (`12`, `34` and `56`) and the output result from the program (The sum =102).

To run this application outside of the NetBeans IDE 6.8, you need first to build and deploy the application into a JAR file and then run the JAR file from the command line.

5.3.2.3.6 Build and Deploy the Application The main build command in the NetBeans IDE is the `Clean and Build Main Project` command. The `Clean and Build Main Project` command deletes previously compiled classes and other build artifacts, and then rebuilds the entire project from scratch.

Notes: There is also a Build Main Project command, which does not delete old building artifacts, but this command is disabled by default.

Perform the following operations to build the application:

1. Click on the `Run > Clean and Build Main Project` button (Shift-F11).
2. Output from the Ant build script appears in the `Output` window. If the `Output` window does not appear, you can open it manually by choosing `Window > Output > Output`.
3. When you clean and build your project, the following things occur:
   - **A.** Output folders that have been generated by previous build actions are deleted ("cleaned"). In most cases, these are the `build` and `dist` folders.
   - **B.** The `build` and `dist` folders are added to your project folder, or hereafter referred to as the `PROJECT_HOME` folder.
   - **C.** All of the sources are compiled into `.class` files, which are placed into the `PROJECT_HOME/build` folder.
   - **D.** A JAR file `SumApp.jar` containing your project is created inside the `PROJECT_HOME/dist` folder.
   - **E.** If you have specified any libraries for the project (`SumLib.jar` in this case), a `lib` folder is created in the `dist` folder. The libraries are copied into `dist/lib` folder.
   - **F.** The manifest file in the JAR is updated to include entries that designate the main class and any libraries that are on the project's classpath.

Note: You can view the contents of the manifest in the IDE's Files window. After you have built your project, switch to the Files window and navigate to dist/SumApp.jar. Expand the node for the JAR file, expand the META-INF folder, and double click MANIFEST.MF to display the manifest in the Source Editor.

```
Manifest-Version: 1.0
Ant-Version: Apache Ant 1.7.1
Created-By: 14.3-b01 (Sun Microsystems Inc.)
Main-Class: sumapp.Main
Class-Path: lib/SumLib.jar
X-COMMENT: Main-Class will be added automatically by build
```

After building and deploying the application, now we can run this application outside the NetBeans IDE. To do that, perform the following operations:

1. On your system, open up a command prompt or terminal window.
2. In the command prompt, change directories to the `SumApp/dist` directory.

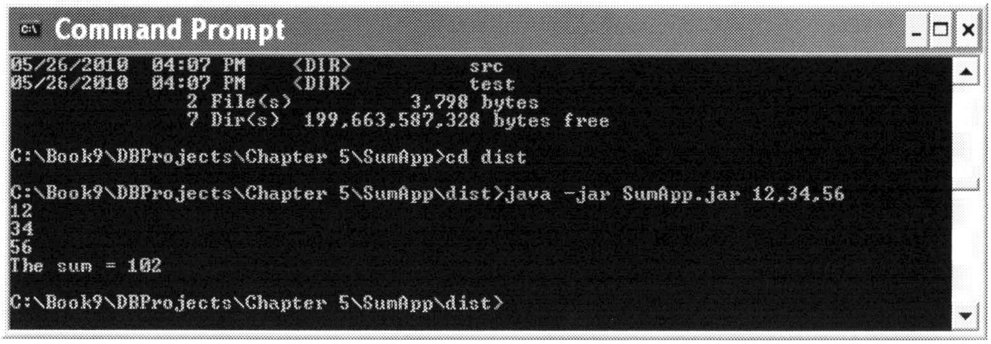

```
Command Prompt
05/26/2010  04:07 PM    <DIR>          src
05/26/2010  04:07 PM    <DIR>          test
               2 File(s)          3,798 bytes
               7 Dir(s)  199,663,587,328 bytes free

C:\Book9\DBProjects\Chapter 5\SumApp>cd dist

C:\Book9\DBProjects\Chapter 5\SumApp\dist>java -jar SumApp.jar 12,34,56
12
34
56
The sum = 102

C:\Book9\DBProjects\Chapter 5\SumApp\dist>
```

Figure 5.32. The running result shown in the Command window.

3. At the command line, type the following statement:

```
java -jar SumApp.jar 12,34,56
```

The application then executes and returns the outputs as shown in Figure 5.32.

5.3.2.3.7 Distribute the Application to Other Users Now that you have verified that the application works outside of the IDE, you are ready to distribute the application and allow other users to use it.

To distribute the application, perform the following operations:

1. On your system, create a zip file that contains the application JAR file (`SumApp.jar`) and the accompanying lib folder that contains `SumLib.jar`.
2. Send the file to the people who will use the application. Instruct them to unpack the zip file, making sure that the `SumApp.jar` file and the `lib` folder are in the same folder.
3. Instruct the users to follow the steps listed in the last section above to run this application outside the NetBeans IDE 6.8.

Two complete Java projects, Java Class Library project `SumLib` and Java Application project `SumApp`, can be found from the folder `DBProjects\Chapter 5` that is located at the site `ftp://ftp.wiley.isbn/JavaDB`. You can download these two projects and test them by calling the Java class library `SumLib` from the Java application project `SumApp`.

Next, let's develop and build a Java project with existing sources.

5.3.2.4 Build a Java Project with Existing Sources

To build a Java project with existing sources is mainly used for development of a new Java project, but some existing sources, either GUIs or source codes that had been built in early Java or current Java JDK, must be involved in this new Java project to save developing efforts or the time. For Java projects developed outside of NetBeans, you can use an "Existing Sources" template in the New Project wizard to make a NetBeans project. In the wizard, you identify the location of the sources and specify a location for the NetBeans project metadata. You then use the `Project Properties` dialog box to configure the project.

Perform the following operations to set up a NetBeans project for an existing Java application:

1. Choose `File > New Project` (Ctrl-Shift-N).
2. Choose `Java > Java Project with Existing Sources`, then click on the `Next` button.
3. In the `Name and Location` page of the wizard, follow these steps:
   - **A.** Type a project name.
   - **B.** (Optional) Change the location of the project folder.
   - **C.** (Optional) Change the name of the build script used by the IDE. This might be desirable if there is already a build script called build.xml that is used to build the sources.
   - **D.** (Optional) Select the `Use Dedicated Folder for Storing Libraries` checkbox, and specify the location for the libraries folder.
   - **E.** Select the `Set as Main Project` checkbox. When you select this option, keyboard shortcuts for commands such as `Clean and Build Main Project` (Shift-F11) apply to this project.
4. Click on the `Next` to advance to the `Existing Sources` page of the wizard.
5. In the `Source Packages Folder` pane and click `Add Folder`. Then navigate to your sources and select the source roots.
6. When you add a folder containing source code, you must add the folder that contains the highest folder in your package tree. For example, in the `com.mycompany.myapp.ui` package, you add the folder that contains the `com` folder.
7. (Optional) In the Test Package Folders pane, click Add Folder to select the folder containing the JUnit package folders.
8. (Optional) In the Includes & Excludes page of the wizard, enter file name patterns for any files that should be included or excluded from the project. By default, all files in your source roots are included.
9. Click on the `Finish` button to complete this process.

The newly created project is displayed in both the `Projects` window and the `Files` window.

Because of the simplicity of this kind of Java projects, no example project is involved in this chapter.

5.3.2.5 Build a Java Free-Form Project

There are also project templates available for Java free-form projects. In so-called free-form projects, the NetBeans IDE uses targets in an existing Ant script to build, run, clean, test, and debug your application. If the Ant script does not contain targets for some of these functions, the functions are unavailable for the project. To implement these functions, you write targets either in your Ant script or in a secondary Ant script.

In general, it is better to use standard "With Existing Sources" project templates for importing projects. For Eclipse projects, it is best to use the Import Project feature, which creates and configures a standard project for you. Standard projects are easier to maintain in the long term. However, the free-form project templates can be useful if you have an existing Ant-based project with a complex or idiosyncratic configuration that cannot be replicated within a standard project. For example, if you are importing a project with multiple source roots, each of which has a different classpath, and you cannot split the source roots into different projects, it might be necessary to use a free-form project template.

Because the scope of this book is about database programming with Java, for more detailed information to set up free-form projects, refer to Advanced Free-Form Project Configuration.

5.3.3 Build a JavaFX Application Project

JavaFX is a Java platform for creating and delivering rich Internet applications that can run across a wide variety of connected devices. By using the JavaFX, developers can design and build applications for desktop, browser, and mobile phones.

5.3.3.1 Overview of JavaFX

JavaFX builds on Java technology. To build JavaFX applications, developers use a statically typed, declarative language called JavaFX Script; Java code can be integrated into JavaFX programs and compiled to Java bytecodes, so JavaFX applications run on any desktop and browser that runs the Java Runtime Environment (JRE) and on top of mobile phones running Java ME.

JavaFX is the best software for creating feature-rich applications that deliver secure and expressive cross-platform user experiences. With the JavaFX SDK, developers and designers now have the essential set of technologies, tools, and resources to easily create and deploy their content across browsers, desktops, mobile devices, TVs, and other connected devices.

Regularly, a JavaFX contains the following components:

1. **JavaFX Composer—Preview**
   The JavaFX Composer is a visual layout tool for JavaFX applications, like the NetBeans GUI Builder is for Java SE applications. The JavaFX Composer is a plug-in for NetBeans IDE 6.8. It provides:
   - Visual editor for a form-like UI using components in JavaFX 1.2.1 SDK
   - Dynamic design editing based on states
   - Data access to Web Services, databases, and local storages
   - Support for JavaFX binding
   - Simple animation editor
   - Multiscreen-size editing
2. **JavaFX Script Editor**
   The JavaFX Script Editor brings you improved semantic and syntactic highlighting, source navigation, faster code completion, code folding, javadoc pop-ups, refactoring, and error detection and hints, such as fixing import statements and packages. You can `Go to Types`, `Find Usages`, and navigate through code with hypertext links. The Palette allows you to drag and drop JavaFX structures for transformations, effects, animation, and more to your project. You can also let the code snippet generator surround selected lines or implement abstract methods, then use the Preview button to display the output of your visual code live.

3. **Full JavaFX Mobile Support**
   The JavaFX SDK 1.2.x supports JavaFX Mobile and comes with a JavaFX Mobile Emulator. JavaFX Mobile applications run directly on the Java Micro Edition platform: Benefit from Java ME's ubiquity, security, and advanced APIs, including support for media, GPS, cameras, file system, networking, and Bluetooth.
4. **JavaFX Debugging and Profiling**
   The improved Debugger uses the common debugger infrastructure so you benefit from better extensibility and performance. Use the integrated Profiler for standard CPU or memory profiling, or simple monitoring to optimize your JavaFX application's speed and memory usage. The options have been preset to default values by experts, but you can customize settings for a specific application.

All of these components are included in the JavaFX SDK.

In addition to these components, you also need JavaFX Compiler and JavaFX Runtime to compile your source codes to the bytecodes and run them in your machine using the Java Virtual Machine (JVM or Java Interpreter). However, because we are using NetBeans IDE as our JavaFX development environment, these two components have been installed automatically by NetBeans IDE when we use plug-in to add JavaFX components into this IDE at the beginning time.

5.3.3.2 JavaFX SDK

The JavaFX Software Development Kits (SDK) includes the following components (also included when you download NetBeans IDE for JavaFX):

- JavaFX Desktop Runtime
- JavaFX Mobile & TV Emulators (for Windows & Mac OS X)
- JavaFX APIs
- JavaFX Compiler
- JavaFX API documentation
- Samples

When you add JavaFX components into the NetBeans IDE by using plug-in, those components will be organized by the functionality to the different bundles based on different applications. Figure 5.33 shows an example bundle for applications developed in NetBeans IDE.

The developer bundle contains the following tools:

- **NetBeans IDE for JavaFX**
  The JavaFX technology is integrated with the NetBeans IDE, a mature and powerful development environment that makes it easy to build, preview, and debug JavaFX applications. The NetBeans IDE for JavaFX is easy to learn, and it comes bundled with the JavaFX SDK and lots of sample applications. The NetBeans editor features a drag-and-drop palette to quickly add JavaFX statements, including transformations, effects, and animation. The new JavaFX Composer adds a visual editor for form-like user interfaces, along with support for animation, multiple screen sizes, and more.
- **JavaFX Plug-In for NetBeans**
  If you are already using the NetBeans IDE, you can add the JavaFX plug-in to include support for developing JavaFX applications.

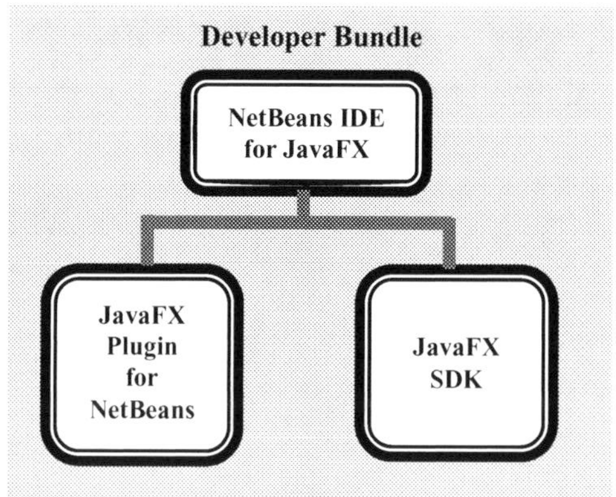

Figure 5.33. An example bundle for applications built in NetBeans IDE.

To develop and build a JavaFX application, you need to use the JavaFX Script programming language. Let's have a closer look at this kind of language.

5.3.3.3 JavaFX Script Language

JavaFX Script is a scripting language designed by Sun Microsystems, forming part of the JavaFX family of technologies on the Java Platform. JavaFX targets the Rich Internet Application domain (competing with Adobe Flex and Microsoft Silverlight), specializing in rapid development of visually rich applications for the desktop and mobile markets. JavaFX Script works with integrated development environments, such as NetBeans and Eclipse. JavaFX is released under the GNU General Public License, via the Sun sponsored OpenJFX project.

JavaFX Script used to be called `F3` for `Form Follows Function`. Its name was changed to JavaFX Script, and it became open sourced at JavaOne in 2007.

JavaFX Script language has the following important properties:

- Statically typed—when type checking is performed during compile time as opposed to run time.
- Declarative programming—a programming paradigm that expresses the logic of a computation without describing its control flow.

Like other OOP languages, JavaFX Script can be used to develop various targeting applications. The syntax used to create and apply variables, functions, and objects are similar to most other OOP languages. In the following sections, we will use an example to illustrate how easy it is to use JavaFX Script language to build a JavaFX application in NetBeans IDE 6.8.

5.3.3.4 Build a JavaFX Script Application

In this section, we will develop a JavaFX Script application project `JavaFXScriptCounter`. The function of this project is simple and easy; it is used to perform simple counting between 0 and 9, and the output is the count result displayed in a single LED.

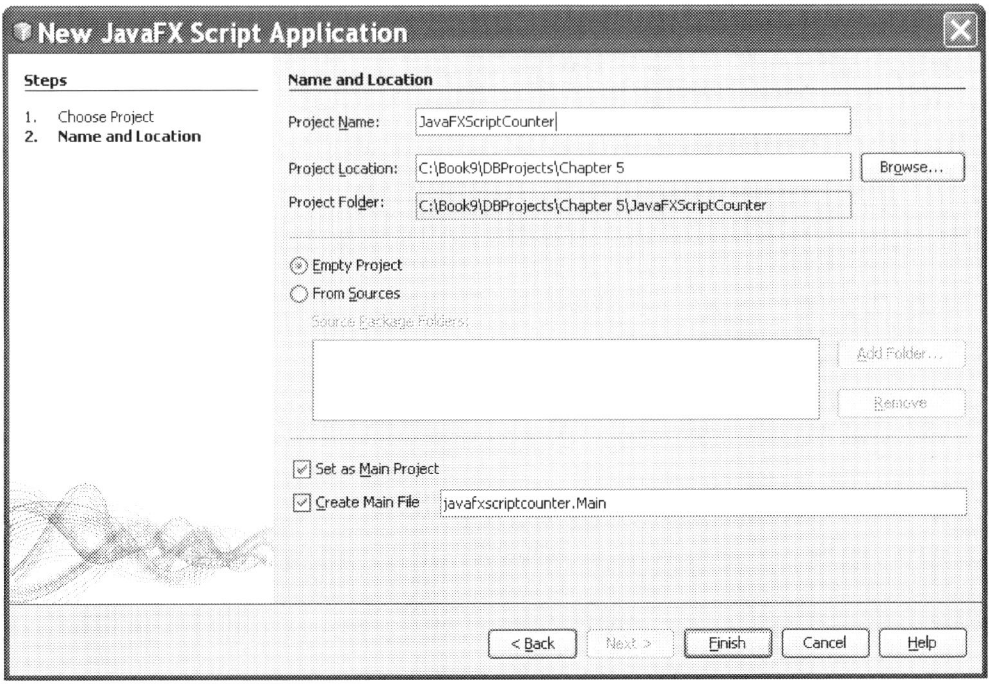

Figure 5.34. The finished Name and Location page.

Let's first create a new JavaFX Script application project under NetBeans IDE 6.8.

5.3.3.4.1 Create a JavaFX Script Application Project Launch the NetBeans IDE and choose File|New Project. When the new project wizard appears, choose JavaFX as the category and press the Next button to continue.

On the `Name and Location` page, type `JavaFXScriptCounter` for the `Project Name`, specify your desired location for the project's files in the `Project Location` text field, and leave all the other default settings unchanged, as shown in Figure 5.34.

Click on the `Finish` button to complete this new project creation process.

The `JavaFXScriptCounter` project opens in both the `Projects` window and the `Files` window, and the `Main.fx` file opens in the source editor, as shown in Figure 5.35.

Notice that all JavaFX Script codes, including the codes created by the system or codes developed by the developer, are included within the `Main.fx` file by default. These codes include all operations to successfully perform a JavaFX Script application with declaring variables, creating functions and objects, and invoking functions. Several import statements and object literals such as Stage and Scene have been prewritten in this `Main.fx` file. These Object literals represent key concepts within the JavaFX application, and are described in Table 5.4.

It can be found from Figure 5.35 that four import statements are coded at the beginning of this script file to indicate the locations of associated packages that contain the related classes and components to be used in this project. Then the Stage and Scene

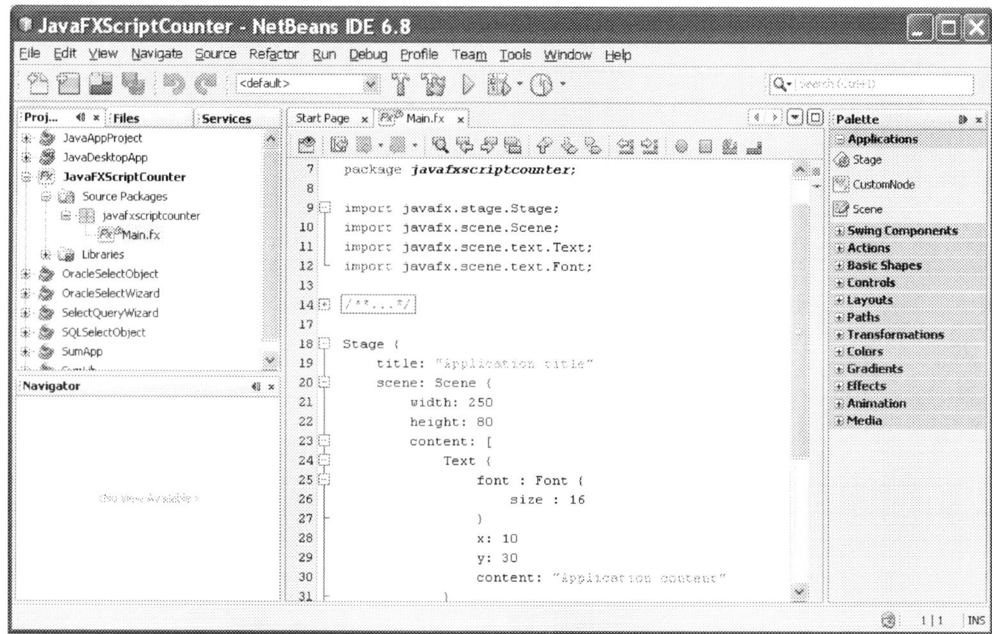

Figure 5.35. The opened Main.fx file.

Table 5.4. Object literals created by default JavaFX Script projects

Object Literals	Functions
Stage	The top-level container window required to display any visible JavaFX objects. The default instance variables title, width, and height define the text that appears on the window's top border and its height and width. The scene variable defines an instance of the Scene object literal which sets the area in which you can place the JavaFX objects.
Scene	Similar to a drawing surface for the graphical content of your application. The scene instance variable has a content variable that is used to hold JavaFX graphical elements and defines the graphical content of your application. The instance variables, width, and height, define the width and height of the content area.
Text	Defines the graphical element that displays text in the scene.
Font	Defines the font used to display the text in the scene.

objects are created and initialized with some default values, such as the title, width, height, and content of the Scene object. Also, the text font and starting values for both horizontal and vertical axes, *x* and *y*, are also set up for the Scene object.

Refer to Table 5.4 to get a more detailed description about these four components and their functionalities.

In addition to those components, JavaFX Script utilized different variables, functions, and objects. Table 5.5 lists syntax used to declare and create most popular variables, objects, and functions using JavaFX Script language.

Table 5.5. Syntax used to declare and create JavaFX script variables and objects

Syntax	Functions
var variable_name; var num1, num2;	var keyword is used to declare a new script variable without assigning any initial value, which means that this variable's value can be assigned later.
def variable_name = value; def num1 = 10;	def keyword is used to define a new variable with an initial value. The difference between the var and the def is that the variable's value cannot be changed if it is declared with the def keyword.

class_name{
instance variable: value;
instance method: name;
}
	To create a new object based on an existing class, use this syntax. The point is that the definition of the class must have been created and located at a package, and the package has been imported into the project file.

function f_name() {
function body…
}
function add() {
var result = num1+num2; }
	Declare a new script function.
	You can pass arguments to any script function. The syntax used to pass arguments to a function is: (arg_name: arg_type). For example, function add(num1:integer, num2:double) {…}

f_name(); add();	To invoke a JavaFX script function. Just call that function with its name.

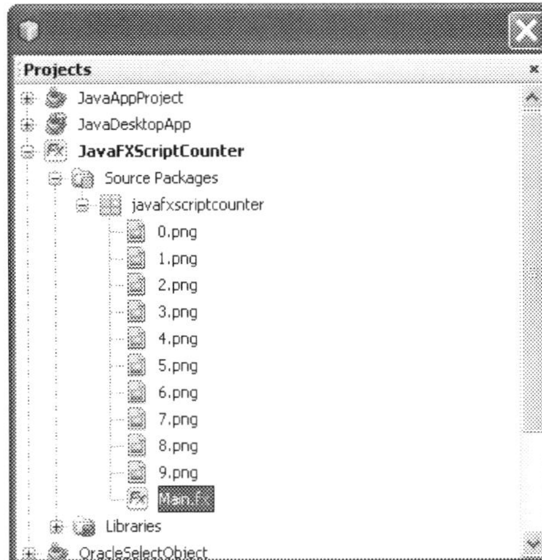

Figure 5.36. The stored 10-digit image files.

5.3.3.4.2 Add Graphical Images into the JavaFX Script Project Since we need to use 0~9 images to display the counting number for the single LED, we need to download those images and save them in our project. The popular way to do that is to use a `resources` folder under our project folder to store any image or other resource files. To save time and space, we can download those 10-digit image files and directly store them in our current project folder.

Download the `0.png` ~ `9.png` image files from the folder `Images` that is located at the Wiley ftp site (refer to Figure 1.2 in Chapter 1), and save them in our project folder `javafxscriptcounter` in which our `Main.fx` file is located, as shown in Figure 5.36.

```
import javafx.stage.Stage;
import javafx.scene.Scene;
import javafx.scene.text.Text;
import javafx.scene.text.Font;

def images = for(i in [0..9]){Image {url: "{__DIR__}{i}.png"};}

Stage {
   title: "Application title"
   scene: Scene {
      width: 250
      height: 80
      content: [ ImageView {image: images[0]}
```

Figure 5.37. The newly added codes to the Main.fx file.

Now we are ready to develop our JavaFX Script project using the JavaFX Script programming language in the `Main.fx` window.

5.3.3.4.3 Develop JavaFX Script Language Codes Double click on our `Main.fx` project file from the `Projects` window to open it. Add code lines that are shown in Figure 5.37 into this file. The newly added coding lines have been highlighted in bold.

The purpose of this added coding line is to display the counting number in the single LED. As you know, to work with images in JavaFX applications, you need to use the `Image` and `ImageView` classes. The `Image` class loads the image from the specified location, and the `ImageView` class displays the image in your application. Create a variable `images` to display 10-digit images, `0.png` ~ `9.png`.

A script `for` loop is used to continuously display 10 counting numbers. The location of those images is represented using a URL.

An error flag appears as soon as we added this coding line since we have not imported the associated packages to tell the compiler where those image components are located. To fix this error and import the desired package, perform the following operations:

1. Right click in any white space in the editor and select `Fix Imports` from the popup menu to remove the error flag. You need to select the type of `Image` by double clicking the `javafx.scene.image.Image` line
2. Similarly, select the type of `ImageView` by double clicking the `javafx.scene.image.ImageView` line.

Two import statements have been added into the project file after you completed these two operations, which are:

```
import javafx.scene.image.Image;
import javafx.scene.image.ImageView;
```

If you run the project in this way, the number displayed in LED cannot be changed as you click on it since we need to set up a binding between each image file. On the opened `Main.fx` window, perform the modifications that are shown in Figure 5.38.

```
  ......
  import javafx.scene.text.Text;
  import javafx.scene.text.Font;
  import javafx.scene.image.Image;
  import javafx.scene.image.ImageView;
A import javafx.scene.input.MouseEvent;
B var count = 0;
  def images = for(i in [0..9]){Image {url: "{__DIR__}{i}.png"};}
C var currImg = images[count];
  Stage {
     title: "Application title"
     scene: Scene {
        width: 250
D       height: 100
E       content: [ImageView {image: bind currImg
F              onMouseClicked:
                  function(e: MouseEvent) {
                     println("Click number {++count} ...");
                     currImg = images[count];
               }
           }
           Text {
              font : Font {
                 size : 16
              }
G             x: 65
              y: 30
H             content: "Click on the LED to Begin"
           }
        ]
     }
  }
```

Figure 5.38. The modified codes for the Main.fx file.

Let's take a closer look at this piece of codes to see how it works.

A. In order to set up a connection between each click on the LED and the click event, we need to import the `MouseEvent` package in which a mouse click event source and event listener are involved.

B. The variable `count` is initialized to 0 as the starting number.

C. By assigning the image with the current count number to the current image variable, the current image with the current clicking number can be displayed.

D. By enlarging this number, we can make the height of the scene a little big.

E. By using the `bind` control, we bind the image object with the current image object together to enable the current image to be displayed in this image object.

F. If the `onMouseClicked` event occurs, which means that the mouse has been clicked by the user, and the listener function will be triggered to display the current clicking number and the current digit in the current image object.

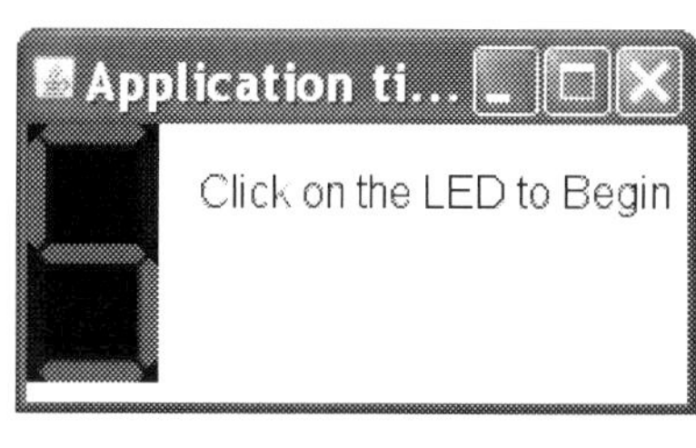

(a)

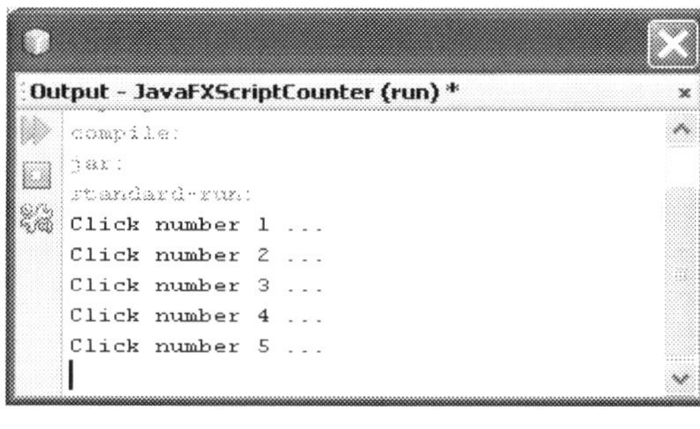

(b)

Figure 5.39. The running status of our JavaFX Script project.

G. We move the starting point to display the content of this project horizontally to make it in the center of the script window.

H. The content is changed to work as a prompt to remind users to perform a click as the project runs.

Now we are ready to compile, build, and run our project to test its functionality. Click on the `Clean and Build Main Project` button to build our project.

5.3.3.4.4 Run the JavaFX Script Project After building and compiling our project, right click on the `Main.fx` file from the projects window and click on the `Run File` item to run our JavaFX Script project. A running example of our project is shown in Figure 5.39a.

Click on the LED and you can find that the number displayed in the LED will increase one by one for each clicking. The output result is also displayed in the `Output` window, as shown in Figure 5.39b.

Our JavaFX Script project is very successful!

Click on the `Close` button that is located at the upper-right corner of this window to close our project.

A complete JavaFX Script application project `JavaFXScriptCounter` can be found from the folder `DBProjects\Chapter 5` that is located at the Wiley ftp site (refer to Figure 1.2 in Chapter 1). You can download this project from that site and run it in your computer with the following plug-in components in your NetBeans IDE:

- JavaFX Composer
- JavaFX Kit (including the JavaFX SDK)
- JavaScript Debugger

You can add those plug-in components by selecting the `Tools > Plugins` menu item and select the `Available Plugins` tab, and then checking those components.

5.3.3.5 Build a JavaFX Desktop Business Application

JavaFX Desktop Business Application is exactly based on the JavaFX Script Application template, and it uses the Standard Execution mode as the default running mode.

Additionally, it creates a design file with preset Desktop profile and a 480 × 320 screen-size.

Relatively, the difference between a JavaFX Script Application and a JavaFX Desktop Business Application is that the former runs the application using command-line JavaFX executable with a default scene, and the latter uses a Standard Execution mode with a define view or scene. Since the JavaFX Script Application does not provide any scene or view window as the project runs, a default scene window will be provided as the project runs. However, the JavaFX Desktop Business Application provides a design file with a design view scene to allow users to design and build this scene view using the JavaFX Composer; therefore, it is more professional compared with the former.

Now let's create a new JavaFX Desktop Business Application project.

5.3.3.5.1 Create a JavaFX Desktop Business Application Project In this JavaFX Desktop Business Application, we want to illustrate how to develop a simple but professional JavaFX Desktop application to access a JavaDB Sample database named `Sample` and retrieve different columns from the `CUSTOMER` table in the `Sample` database.

To access a data source from a JavaFX Desktop Business Application, one needs to use the JDBC Data Source in the JavaFX Data Sources tool in the JavaFX composer. In fact, the JavaFX Composer, which is very similar to the Java Swing component, is a visual layout or container that contains all JavaFX GUI components to enable users to build a JavaFX Desktop application with a preset design scene or view.

To create a new JavaFX Desktop Business Application project, launch the NetBeans IDE 6.8 and choose `File > New Project` menu item and select the `JavaFX` from the `Categories` list and the `JavaFX Desktop Business Application` item from the `Projects` list, and then click on the `Next` button to continue.

In the `Name and Location` page, enter `JavaFXDeskDSApp` into the `Project Name` field as the name for this project. You can set up the desired location to save this project in the `Project Location` field as you want. In this application, we still use our default folder, which is `C:\Book9\DBProjects\Chapter 5`. Keep all other settings unchanged and click on the `Finish` button. Your finished `Name and Location` page should match one that is shown in Figure 5.40.

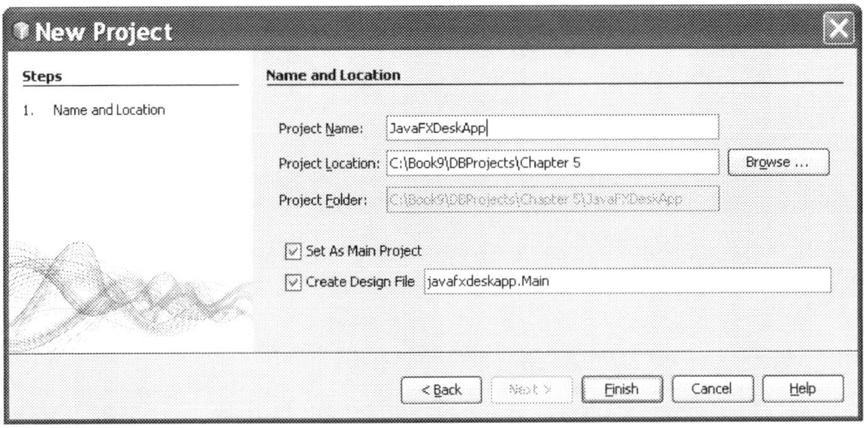

Figure 5.40. The finished Name and Location page.

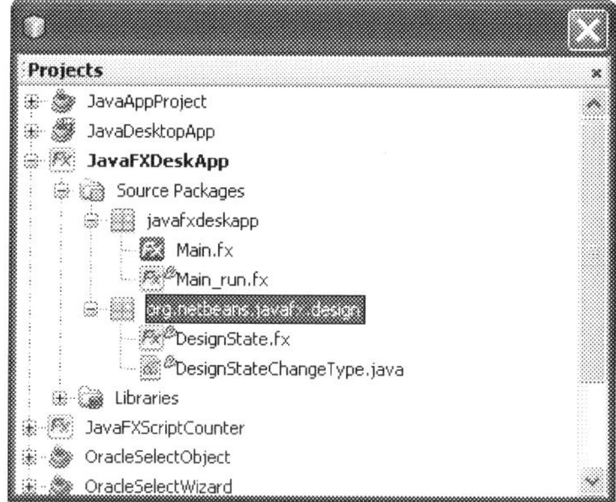

Figure 5.41. The newly created JavaFX Desktop Business Application project.

As a new JavaFX Desktop Business Application is created, two new folders are created and added into the new project, the `javafxdesktop` and the `org.netbeans.javafx.design`, as shown in Figure 5.41.

The `javafxdesktop` is the package that contains two new files, the `Main.fx` and the `Main_run.fx`. The former is the main project file for this application, and the latter is a runtime `Stage` object that is used to start the scene of the project.

The `org.netbeans.javafx.design` is a class container that contains all GUI components related to JavaFX composer. Two files are created and added into this folder when a new JavaFX Desktop application is created: `DesignState.fx` and `DesignStateChangeType.java`. The former is used to represent a container of a single state variable in a design, and the latter is used to take care of the changing of the States in the design and the running time of the project.

A `state` can be considered as a set of property values of all or part GUI components located at the scene or design file at a time, and these properties can be used to describe appearances of all or part GUI component at that time interval. A JavaFX Desktop project can contain many states; each of them can have different sets of properties or appearances at a time. Additionally, the project can start with a starting state and change from one state to other states at different times. In other words, the state can be thought as a snapshot of the design view or scene at a time, and this snapshot can be changed from one to the other at a time sequence. This provides a good foundation for the animation of the JavaFX Desktop applications.

Now let's take a global look at our new project, which is shown in Figure 5.42.

Two new windows are added into our project, the `States` and the `Design` scene. As we mentioned, the state present a set of properties of all GUI components at the design scene at a time, and a project can contain many different states. The States window allows users to add, delete, and manipulate states to the project, and the Design scene window enable users to design a user-desired GUI-like scene by adding JavaFX composer components located at the `JavaFX Container` at the right side of this project global view.

The white rectangular box in the Design scene window is the scene and the default size is 480 by 320, which can be found from the size field that is next to the `Design` button on the top of this view. If you want to change this default size, you can click on the scene

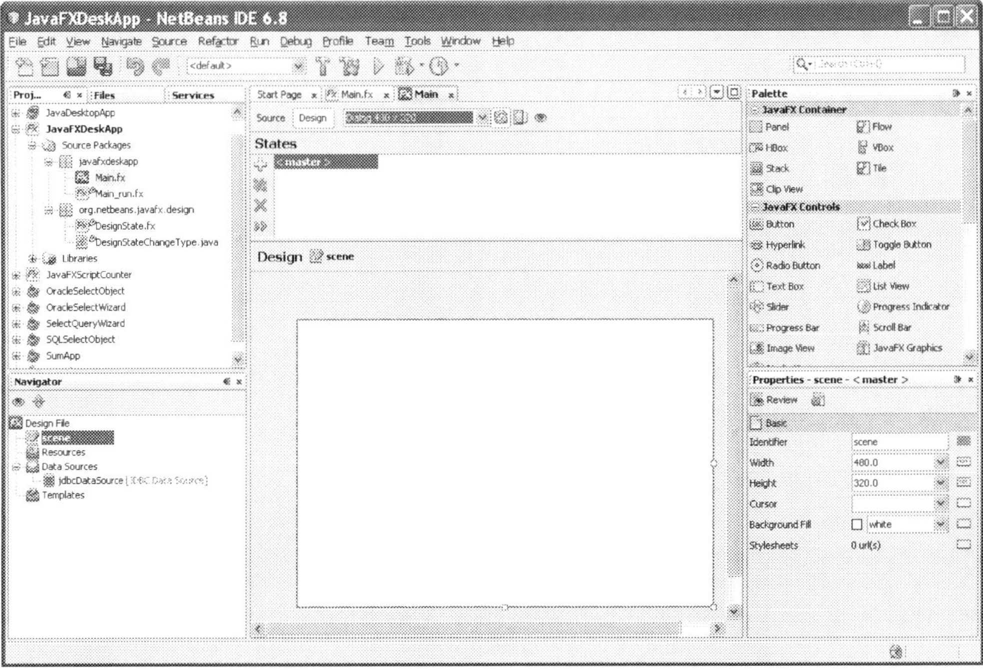

Figure 5.42. The global view of our new project.

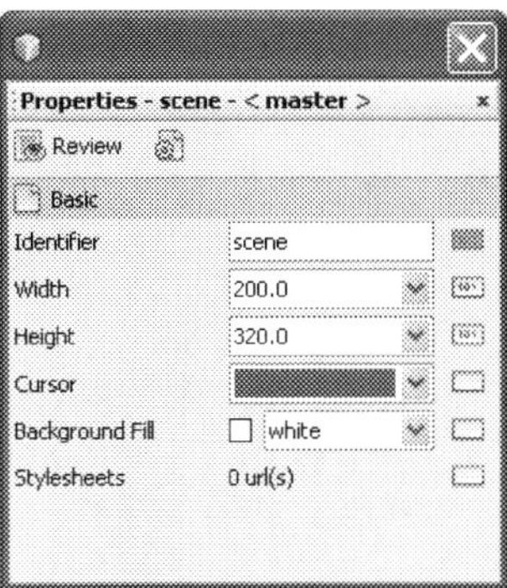

Figure 5.43. The Properties window of the scene.

icon from the `Navigator` window, and go to the `Properties - scene - <master>` window that is located at the upper-right corner of the window to change the width and height data by typing some new values into those fields, as shown in Figure 5.43.

You can also change the name and the background color of this scene. To do that, just modify the content of the `Identifier` field and click on the drop-down arrow from the `Background Fill` combo box and select your desired color from that box.

Now change the name of this scene to `Customer` by entering `Customer` to the `Identifier` field.

Before we can build our design scene by adding JavaFX Controls into the scene object, we need first to connect the JavaDB default sample database `Sample` with our NetBeans IDE. In other words, we need to connect our JavaFX Desktop Business application to a data source. Let's have a clear and global picture about the Data Source in JavaFX composer first.

5.3.3.5.2 Data Source in JavaFX Composer To access to data coming from various sources in various formats, we have unified the data format on the client side so that it is easier for people to start using a remote data source. There are two basic aspects of each data source:

- Actual source of data (HTTP server, database, file, etc.)
- Format of data (XML, JSON, etc.)

JavaFX Composer data source framework defines a specialized DataSource class for each source of data (HttpDataSource, FileDataSource, etc.) and defines a set of parsers for each supported data format (Parsers.XML_PARSER, etc.).

When a DataSource object retries the data, it typically passes the raw stream to a Parser, which understands the format and produces a RecordSet, a common data format of JavaFX Composer. To summarize, common data source framework consists of three fundamental entities (classes):

1. **DataSource**: responsible for fetching raw data from the source.
2. **Parser**: responsible for parsing raw data and producing RecordSets and Records.
3. **RecordSet**: groups Records into an array, maintaining a cursor over it.
4. **Record**: set of (name→value) pairs holding actual data.

A Data Source object holds basic properties needed to fetch data from a source. For example, for HTTP Data Source, this is URL, Authentication method, and so on. For JDBC Data Source, this is a connection string, credentials, and SQL query. For File Data Source, this is a file path.

Refer to Table 5.6 for an overview of JavaFX Composer supported data sources.

In this section, we will concentrate on the data query using JDBC data source, `DbDataSource` and `DataSource`; therefore, let's have a closer look at this kind of data source.

All JavaFX JDBC-related data source components are located at the package `org.netbeans.javafx.datasrc`, and the `DbDataSource` is a class stored in that package. Table 5.7 lists some popular variables defined in that class. Table 5.8 shows most popular functions defined in the `DbDataSource` class and the `DataSource` class (inherited functions).

To have a clear picture about these variables and functions defined in the JDBC-related classes, we will use some of them to build our JavaFX Desktop Business application to access the Sample database to perform data query in the following sections. First, let's set up our JavaDB Sample database.

5.3.3.5.3 Set Up the JavaDB Sample Database In Section 5.3.2.2.1 in this chapter, we have provided a detailed discussion about this database connection to our IDE. You

Table 5.6. An overview of JavaFX Composer supported data sources

Name	Class	Supported Data Format	Description
HTTP	HttpDataSource	XML, JSON, LINE, PROPERTIES	Fetches data from HTTP and HTTPS servers. Supports BASIC authentication.
JDBC	DbDataSource	SQL Table	Fetches data from a JDBC compliant database by executing an SQL query
File	FileDataSource	XML, JSON, LINE, PROPERTIES	Reads a file on the local filesystem
JavaFx Storage	StorageDataSource	XML, JSON, LINE, PROPERTIES	Uses javafx.io.Storage API to load data
Resources	ClasspathDataSource	XML, JSON, LINE, PROPERTIES	Reads data from runtime classpath using java Classloader. getResourceAsStream

Table 5.7. Most popular variables defined in the DbDataSource class

Access	Name	Description
Public	connectionString	Standard JDBC connection string (URL)
Public	driverParams	Additional driver parameters or null
Public-init	lazyLoading	Lazy loading is useful for large tables with lots of rows when fetching data at once would cause performance issues
Public	password	Password for authentication purposes or null if authentication is not used or required
Public	user	Username for authentication purposes or null if authentication is not used or required
Public	query	SQL query to be used when fetching data

may refer to that section to finish this connection. For your convenience, some key steps are listed here again to facilitate this connection.

- Open the `Services` window, expand the `Databases` node and right click on the `Java DB` node, and choose the `Properties`.
- If a default Java DB server is registered, the Java DB Installation and Database Location fields will be filled in.
- Click on the `OK` button to close this dialog box.
- Start the Java DB Server in the NetBeans by right clicking on the `Java DB` and choose the `Start Server` menu item. Once the server is started, Java DB Database Process tab opens in the `Output` window and displays a message similar the following:

  Security manager installed using the Basic server security policy.

  Apache Derby Network Server - 10.4.2.1 - (706043) started and ready to accept connections on port 1527 at 2010-05-24 22:38:21.187 GMT

Table 5.8. Most popular functions defined in the DbDataSource and DataSource classes

Access	Name	Description
Public	void fetchData()	Perform data fetching operation with no data returned
Public	RecordSetMetaData metaData()	Return RecordSetMetaData object
Protected	RecordSet dataFetched(RecordSet)	Callback function that data source classes call when they successfully fetch data in response to fetchData() call
Protected	RecordSet dataFetchError(exception)	Callback function that data source classes call when they fail to fetch data in response to fetchData() call
Protected abstract	void fetchData()	A derived class overrides this to fetch data. When it succeeds, it calls the dataFetched() callback function. When it fails, it calls the dataFetchError callback. Derived classes are free to fetch data asynchronously
public bound	DataSource getDataSource(expression)	Filter data from this data source according to the given expression
public bound	RecordSet getRecordSet()	Retrieve data from this data source, and the returned data stored in a RecordSet
public abstract	RecordSetMetaData metaData()	Return RecordSetMetaData object or null if data has not yet been fetched
public	void refresh()	Force this data source to refetch all data

- Connect to the `Sample` database with the steps listed below:
  - Right click on the default sample database connection node `jdbc:derby://localhost:1527/sample[app on APP]` and choose the Connect.
  - Expand that connected node, the `APP` and `Table` subnodes, and you can find all tables built under this sample database.
  - Expand each table, such as the `CUSTOMER` table, so you can find all columns defined in that table. The primary key is highlighted with the red color.

Now let's set up and configure the data source, the JavaDB Sample database, with our JavaFX Desktop application.

Open the design scene by clicking on it and pick up the `JDBC Data Source` control from the `JavaFX Data Sources` group from the `Palette` window, and place it to the design scene. Click on the `OK` to the message box to allow required data source files to be copied to the project.

On the opened `Data Source Customizer` window, perform the following operations to complete this database setup and testing:

- Click on the `Browse` button to open the `Browse Database Connections` dialog box and select our connected JavaDB sample database URL `jdbc:derby://localhost:1527/sample [app on APP]` by clicking on it. Click on the `OK` to close this connection.

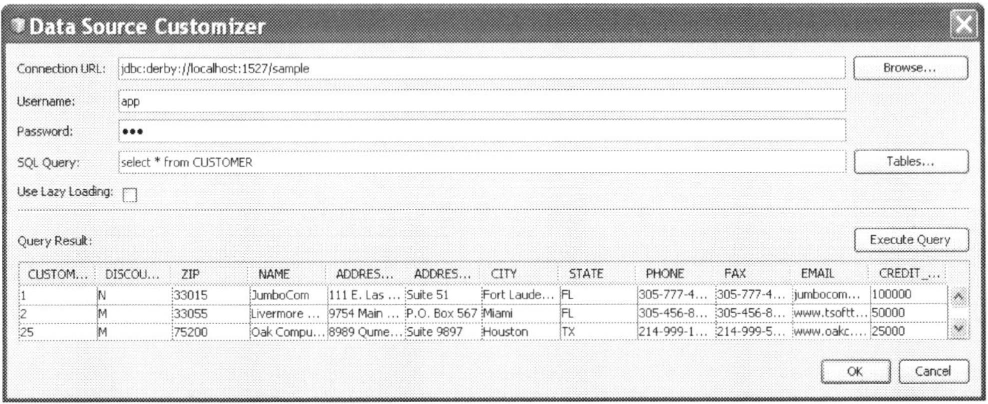

Figure 5.44. The running result of executing a query.

- The `Username` and `Password` fields will be filled automatically by the IDE, as shown in Figure 5.44.
- You can test this database setup by executing a SQL query. To do that, click on the `Create` button to open all available tables in this sample database.
- On the opened `Browse Tables` dialog box, select the `CUSTOMER` table and check the `Generate SELECT clause` checkbox. Click on the `OK` button to continue.
- Click on the `Execute Query` button to run this query.

A sample running result is shown in Figure 5.44.

Click on the `OK` button to close this setup process.

Now that we have finished the set up for our data source, next let's start to build our design scene by inserting our desired JavaFX GUI components into this scene.

5.3.3.5.4 Build the Design Scene by Adding JavaFX GUI Components Double click on the `Main.fx` file to open its JavaFX GUI design window. Drag and place the following JavaFX Controls to the scene:

- Desktop Form
- Label
- Textbox
- ListView
- Button

Let's do these dragging and placing operations one by one.

We need a Template to display our query results from the CUSTOMER table, since the `scene` is just a View window that does not contain any template, so we need to add either a `Desktop Form` or a `Mobile Form` as a template for this application.

To add a `Desktop Form`, go to the `Palette` window and drag the `Desktop Form` from the `Templates` group and place it in the scene.

In the opened `Customize Template` dialog box, click on the drop-down arrow for the `Data Source` combo box, and select the `jdbcDataSource` we just added in the last

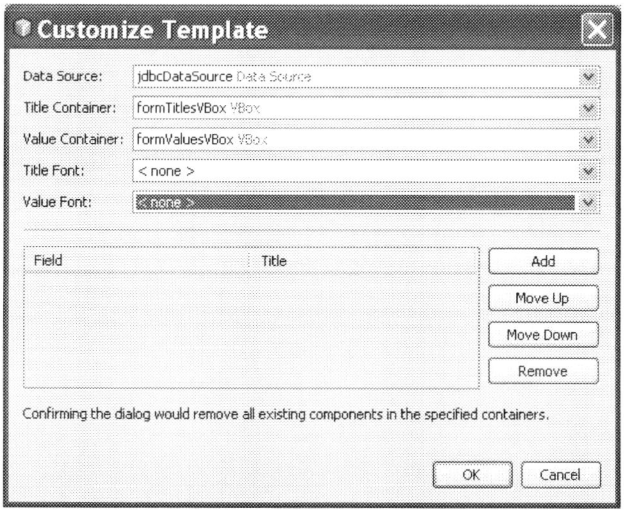

Figure 5.45. The finished Customer Template for the Desktop Form.

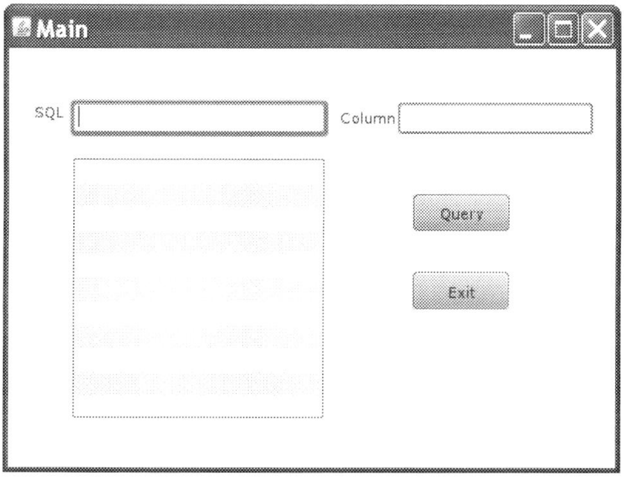

Figure 5.46. The finished design scene for project JavaFXDeskApp.

section. Your finished `Customize Template` dialog box should match one that is shown in Figure 5.45.

Click on the `OK` button to close this setup.

Perform the following operations to complete this design scene development:

1. Add two labels as indicators for two Textboxes to this `Desktop Form`. Go to the `Palette` window and drag the `Label` item and place it into the `Desktop Form`.
2. Go to the `Properties` window and change the `Text` of this newly added label to `SQL`.
3. Perform a similar operation to add the second label and set its `Text` property to `Column`.
4. Add two TextBoxes into this Form and place each of them in the next to each label, as shown in Figure 5.46.

5. Change the names for both TextBoxes by entering `txtQuery` and `txtColumn` into the `Identifier` field in the `Properties` window of each Text Box.
6. Add two Button controls into this Form by dragging them one by one and place them into this scene, as shown in Figure 5.46.
7. Change the names of two buttons by entering `QueryButton` and `ExitButton` into the `Identifier` field in the `Properties` window of each button.
8. Change the captions of two buttons by entering `Query` and `Exit` into the `Text` field in the `Properties` window of each button.

In this way, we complete the building of our design scene for this project. Next, let's develop the codes for two buttons to access our connected data source and perform our desired data query.

5.3.3.5.5 Develop Codes for the Project The function of this project is: as the project runs, users can perform any data query by entering a SQL statement into the `SQL` TextBox, and then users also need to enter a column name into the `Column` TextBox to enable the application to know which column the users want to query. When the user clicks on the `Query` button, the query result will be returned and displayed in the ListView box. Click on the `Exit` button so you can exit the project.

The coding job we need to do is for two buttons; the `QueryButton` and the `ExitButton`. First, let's do the coding for the `QueryButton` control.

Select the `QueryButton` control and in its property sheet, click on the pen icon next to the `Action` property and let it generate an empty function. Enter the codes that are shown in Figure 5.47 into this empty function.

Let's have a closer look at this piece of codes to see how it works.

A. First, a script integer variable `i` is created, and it is used as a loop counter later to retrieve each record from the selected column.

```
  function QueryButtonAction(): Void {
      //TODO
A     var i = 0;
B     var ds = jdbcDataSource;
C     ds.query = txtQuery.text;
D     ds.fetchData();
E     var rs = ds.getRecordSet();
F     while(rs.hasNext())
      {
G        var r = rs.current();
         var s:String;
H        s = r.getString(txtColumn.text);
I        listView.items[i]= s;
J        i++;
K        println("{s}");
L        rs.next();
      }
  }
```

Figure 5.47. The coding for the QueryButton function.

B. A script object variable `ds` is created, and the configured data source `jdbcDataSource` is assigned to this object.

C. The query variable defined in the JDBC Data Source, `DbDataSource`, is initialized with the content of the TextBox `txtQuery`, which is a SQL statement and entered by the user as the project runs. The `text` property of the TextBox `txtQuery` is used to get the query string from this TextBox.

D. The `fetchData()` function defined in the `DataSource` class (refer to Table 5.8) is executed to perform this data query by running the SQL statement. The query result is stored in a `RecordSet` object.

E. The `getRecordSet()` function defined in the `DataSource` class is executed to pick up the returned query result and assigned to the script variable `rs`.

F. A `while` loop is used to scan the whole `RecordSet` to pick up each record from that `RecordSet` object one by one. The `hasNext()`method, which returns a `true` if more records available in the RecordSet and `false` if no more available record in the RecordSet object, is used as the condition variable.

G. The `current()` method is used to pick up the current row pointed by the cursor in the RecordSet and assign it to the script variable `r`.

H. The `getString()` method is utilized to pick up the selected column, which is the content of the TextBox `txtColumn` and entered by the user as the project runs. The selected column is assigned to a script variable `s` that is a String variable.

I. The selected column is also assigned to the ListView object with the loop counter `i` as the index of the ListView control. To add a value to a ListView control, the `items[]` property must be used.

J. The loop counter is increased by one to point to the next position in the ListView control.

K. The query result is also displayed in the `Output` window by calling the JavaFX function `println()`. The point to be noted is that you have to use curly braces to cover the displayed string in JavaFX, otherwise, you would get a compiling error.

L. Finally, the `next()` method is used to move the cursor in the RecordSet to the next position to point to the next row.

The coding for the `QueryButton` control is complete. Next, let's do the coding for the `ExitButton` control. Open its empty method and enter one line of code into this method, as shown in Figure 5.48.

By calling the `System.exit()` method defined in the `java.lang` package, we can exit the project.

At this point, we have finished the coding for our project. Now we are ready to run our project to test the data query function from the CUSTOMER table.

However, before we can run our project, we need to confirm that the JDBC Data Source has been added to the same classpath as our project located. To do that checking,

```
function ExitButtonAction(): Void {
     //TODO
     java.lang.System.exit(0);
 }
```

Figure 5.48. The coding for the ExitButton control.

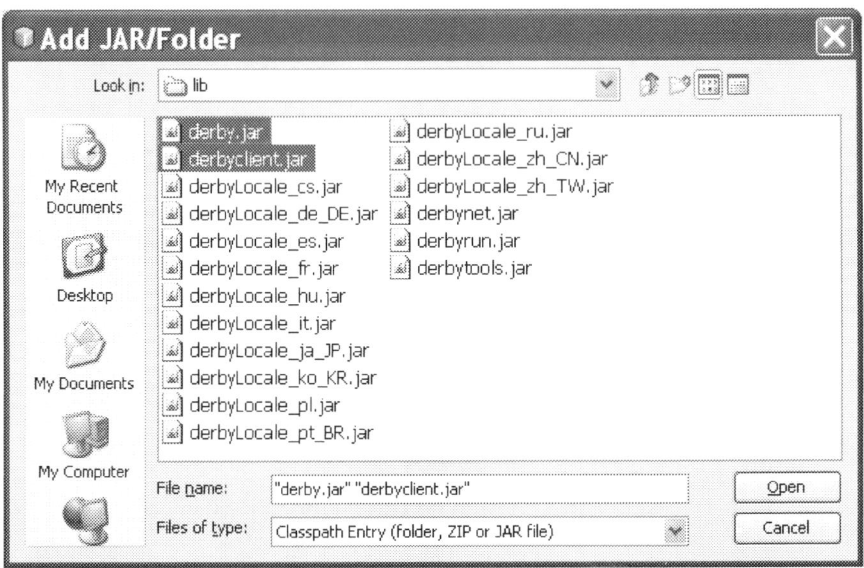

Figure 5.49. The finished Add JAR/Folder dialog box.

right click on our project `JavaFXDeskApp` from the `Projects` window and click on the `Properties` item to open the `Project Properties` window.

On the opened Project Properties window, click on the `Libraries` node and click on the `Add JAR/Folder` button to open the `Add JAR/Folder` dialog box. From the `Look in` combo box, browse to the default folder where all Java libraries are located in your computer, which generally should be `C:\Program Files\Sun\JavaDB\lib`. Select top two JAR files, `derby.jar` and `derbyclient.jar` by clicking on them, and click on the `Open` button to add them into our project classpath as shown in Figure 5.49.

Make sure to check the `Build Projects on Classpath` checkbox and then click on the `OK` button to complete this step.

Now let's run our project to test the data query function.

5.3.3.5.6 Run the JavaFX Desktop Business Project Now click on the `Clean and Build Main Project` button to compile and build our project. If everything is fine, click on the `Run Main Project` button to run the project. The running status of our project is shown in Figure 5.50.

Enter `select * from CUSTOMER` into the `SQL` TextBox as the SQL query statement, and `NAME` into the `Column` TextBox as the query column. Then click on the `Query` button to perform this query. Immediately, you can find that the query result is returned and displayed in the ListView control, which is shown in Figure 5.50.

The query result is also displayed in the `Output` window, as shown in Figure 5.51.

You can try to enter different query statements and different column names to test this project, such as the `WHERE` clause and some limitations. The point is that you may get some running exceptions when you try to get the `CREDIT_LIMIT` column. The key issue is that you can only get those columns that have a String data type from this data source since we used a `getString()` method in line **H** in our coding (refer to Fig. 5.47) to pick

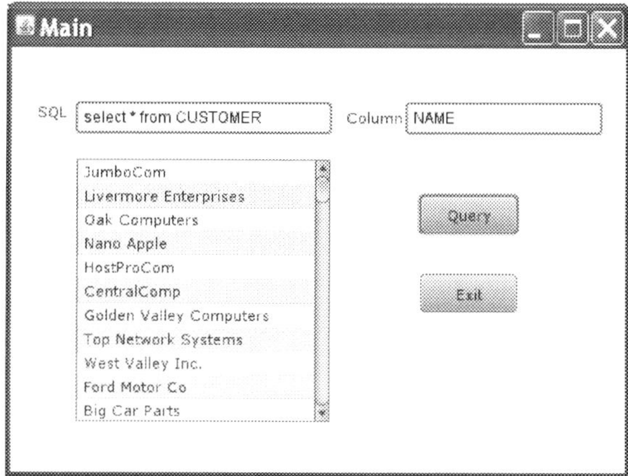

Figure 5.50. The running result of the project.

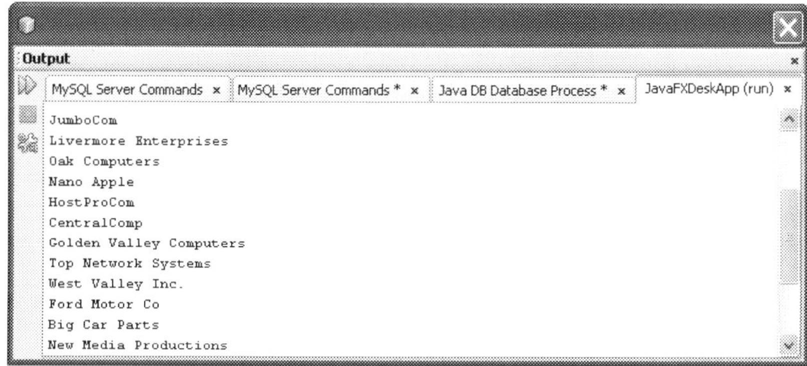

Figure 5.51. The running result displayed in the Output window.

up the query result. However, the data type for the `CREDIT_LIMIT` column in the `CUSTOMER` table is an integer. If you want to fix this kind of error to avoid this exception, you need to figure out how to distinguish between the columns that have either String or Integer data type, and use a different fetch method, such as `getString()` and `get(column_name)` method, to pick up the query result.

Click on the `Exit` button to exit the project.

Yes, our project is very successful! Wait a moment, here is a problem or bug that may be found when a careful developer builds and runs this project.

Note: The bug is that only 12 customer names were queried and displayed when running this project. The trick is that inside the while loop, when it detects the next record in the RecordSet is null, which means that no more record available in the RecordSet, the loop is exited even the current cursor points to a valid record and that record cannot be queried and displayed.

How to fix this bug and make the project run correctly to query and display all 13 entities from the `CUSTOMER` table? We leave this as a homework for students.

A complete JavaFX Desktop Business project `JavaFXDeskApp` can be found from the folder `DBProjects\Chapter 5` that is located at the Wiley ftp site (refer to Figure 1.2 in Chapter 1). You can download this project and run it in your computer. However, you need to perform the following two jobs after you download this project and before you can run it in your computer:

1. Start the JavaDB Server
2. Connect to the JavaDB `Sample` database

Now you are ready to run the project on your computer.

5.3.3.6 Build JavaFX Mobile Business Application

Generally, there is no significant difference between a JavaFX Desktop Business application and a JavaFX Mobile Business application, and the only difference between them is the target device type the application will be applied. Both applications are built and developed in the similar design scene and components with the JavaFX script language. We will not provide a very detailed discussion for this kind of application in this section because of the similarity between these two kinds of applications. Refer to discussions in the last section, one can easily build and develop a JavaFX Mobile Business application without problem at all.

Next let's take care of building and developing Java Web Application projects to perform data access and query between clients and application servers.

5.3.4 Build a Java Web Application Project

Java Platform, either Standard Edition (SE) or Enterprise Edition (EE), provides rich and flexible tools and components to support Web applications and Web Services developments. With Java EE, developers can build professional, multitier and portable applications that can be run at cross-platform environments with improved efficiency.

We will provide a detailed discussion about the Java Web Applications development in Chapter 8 with real project examples. Refer to that chapter to get more detailed information for building this kind of application in NetBeans IDE.

5.3.5 Build a Java Enterprise Edition Project

Java Platform, Enterprise Edition or Java EE is a widely used platform for server programming in the Java programming language. The Java EE differs from the Java Standard Edition Platform (Java SE) in that it adds libraries that provide functionality to deploy fault-tolerant, distributed, multi-tier Java software, based largely on modular components running on an application server.

Although Java EE is closely related to Java Web applications, it is so important to Java application developments, and therefore we prefer to provide a detailed discussion in this section to give readers a preintroduction about this critical component.

5.3.5.1 Overview of Java Enterprise Edition 6

The aim of the Java EE platform is to provide developers with a powerful set of APIs while reducing development time, reducing application complexity, and improving application performance. The Java EE platform uses a simplified programming model. XML deployment descriptors are optional. Instead, a developer can simply enter the information as an annotation directly into a Java source file, and the Java EE server will configure the component at deployment and runtime. These annotations are generally used to embed in a program data that would otherwise be furnished in a deployment descriptor. With annotations, the specification information is put directly in your code next to the program element that it affects.

Java EE is a widely used platform containing a set of coordinated technologies that significantly reduce the cost and complexity of developing, deploying, and managing multitier, server-centric applications. Java EE builds upon the Java SE platform and provides a set of APIs for developing and running portable, robust, scalable, reliable, and secure server-side applications.

Some of the fundamental components of Java EE include:

- **Enterprise JavaBeans (EJB):** a managed, server-side component architecture used to encapsulate the business logic of an application. EJB technology enables rapid and simplified development of distributed, transactional, secure, and portable applications based on Java technology.
- **JPA:** a framework that allows developers to manage data using object-relational mapping (ORM) in applications built on the Java Platform.

5.3.5.1.1 Java EE Application Model Java EE is designed to support applications that implement enterprise services for customers, employees, suppliers, partners, and others who make demands on or contributions to the enterprise. Such applications are inherently complex, potentially accessing data from a variety of sources and distributing applications to a variety of clients.

The Java EE application model defines an architecture for implementing services as multitier applications that deliver the scalability, accessibility, and manageability needed by enterprise-level applications. This model partitions the work needed to implement a multitier service into two parts: the business and presentation logic to be implemented by the developer, and the standard system services provided by the Java EE platform. The developer can rely on the platform to provide solutions for the hard systems-level problems of developing a multitier service.

Java EE is defined by its specification. As with other Java Community Process specifications, providers must meet certain conformance requirements in order to declare their products as Java EE compliant, which is shown in Figure 5.52.

5.3.5.1.2 Distributed Multitiered Applications The Java EE platform uses a distributed multitiered application model for enterprise applications. Application logic is divided into components according to function, and the various application components that make up a Java EE application are installed on different machines depending on the tier in the multitiered Java EE environment to which the application component belongs.

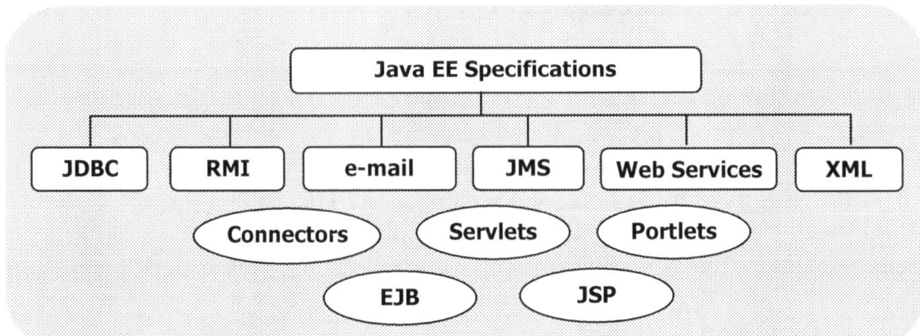

Figure 5.52. Java EE Specifications.

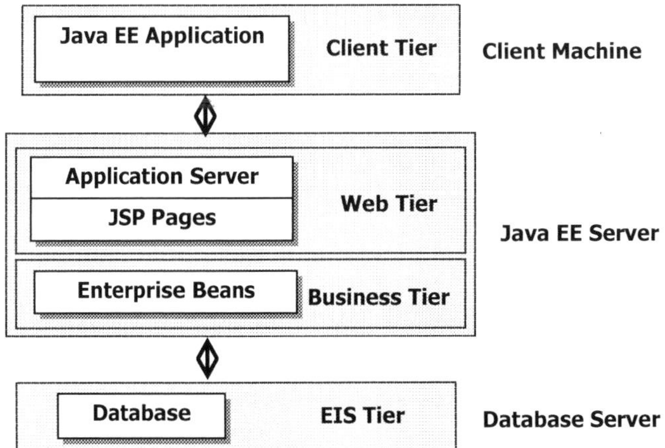

Figure 5.53. A multitiered Java EE application.

Figure 5.53 shows a multitiered Java EE application divided into the tiers described in the following list. The Java EE application parts shown in Figure 5.53 are presented in Java EE Components.

- Client-tier components run on the client machine.
- Web-tier components run on the Java EE server.
- Business-tier components run on the Java EE server.
- Enterprise information system (EIS)-tier software runs on the EIS server.

The enterprise information system tier handles EIS software and includes enterprise infrastructure systems, such as enterprise resource planning (ERP), mainframe transaction processing, database systems, and other legacy information systems. For example, Java EE application components might need access to enterprise information systems for database connectivity.

Although a Java EE application can consist of the three or four tiers shown in Figure 5.53, Java EE multitiered applications are generally considered to be three-tiered applications because they are distributed over three locations: client machines, the Java EE server machine, and the database or legacy machines at the back end. Three-tiered applications that run in this way extend the standard two-tiered client and server model by placing a multithreaded application server between the client application and back-end storage.

5.3.5.1.3 Java EE Components

Java EE applications are made up of components. A Java EE component is a self-contained functional software unit that is assembled into a Java EE application with its related classes and files and that communicates with other components.

The Java EE specification defines the following Java EE components:

- Application clients and Applets are components that run on the client machine.
- Java Servlet, JavaServer Faces, and JavaServer Pages (JSP) technology components are web components that run on the server.
- Enterprise JavaBeans (EJB) components are business components that run on the server.

Java EE components are written in the Java programming language and are compiled in the same way as any program in the language. The difference between Java EE components and standard Java classes is that Java EE components are assembled into a Java EE application, are verified to be well formed and in compliance with the Java EE specification, and are deployed to production, where they are run and managed by the Java EE server.

A Web client consists of two parts:

1. Dynamic web pages containing various types of markup language (HTML, XML, and so on), which are generated by Web components running in the Web tier.
2. A Web browser, which renders the pages received from the server.

A Web client is sometimes called a `thin client`. Thin clients usually do not query databases, execute complex business rules, or connect to legacy applications. When you use a thin client, such heavyweight operations are off-loaded to enterprise beans executing on the Java EE server, where they can leverage the security, speed, services, and reliability of Java EE server-side technologies.

An Application client runs on a client machine and provides a way for users to handle tasks that require a richer user interface than can be provided by a markup language. It typically has a GUI created from the Swing or the Abstract Window Toolkit (AWT) API, but a command-line interface is certainly possible.

Application clients directly access enterprise beans running in the business tier. However, if application requirements warrant it, an application client can open an HTTP connection to establish communication with a Servlet running in the Web tier. Application clients written in languages other than Java can interact with Java EE servers, enabling the Java EE platform to interoperate with legacy systems, clients, and non-Java languages.

Java EE Web components are either Servlets or web pages created using JavaServer Faces technology and/or JSP technology (JSP pages). Servlets are Java programming language classes that dynamically process requests and construct responses. JSP pages are text-based documents that execute as Servlets but allow a more natural approach to creating static content. JavaServer Faces technology builds on Servlets and JSP technology, and provides a user interface component framework for Web applications.

Static HTML pages and applets are bundled with Web components during application assembly but are not considered Web components by the Java EE specification. Server-side utility classes can also be bundled with Web components, and, like HTML pages, are not considered Web components.

A Java EE application is packaged into one or more standard units for deployment to any Java EE platform-compliant system. Each unit contains:

- A functional component or components (such as an enterprise bean, webpage, servlet, or applet)
- An optional deployment descriptor that describes its content

Once a Java EE unit has been produced, it is ready to be deployed. Deployment typically involves using a platform's deployment tool to specify location-specific information, such as a list of local users that can access it and the name of the local database. Once deployed on a local platform, the application is ready to run.

5.3.5.1.4 Java EE Packaging Applications A Java EE application is delivered in either a Java Archive (JAR) file, a Web Archive (WAR) file, or an Enterprise Archive (EAR) file. A WAR or EAR file is a standard JAR (.jar) file with a .war or .ear extension. Using JAR, WAR, and EAR files and modules makes it possible to assemble a number of different Java EE applications using some of the same components. No extra coding is needed; it is only a matter of assembling (or packaging) various Java EE modules into Java EE JAR, WAR, or EAR files.

An EAR file that is shown in Figure 5.54 contains Java EE modules, and, optionally, deployment descriptors. A deployment descriptor is an XML document with an `.xml` extension that describes the deployment settings of an application, a module, or a component. Because deployment descriptor information is declarative, it can be changed without the need to modify the source code. At runtime, the Java EE server reads the deployment descriptor and acts upon the application, module, or component accordingly.

A Java EE module consists of one or more Java EE components for the same container type, and, optionally, one component deployment descriptor of that type. An

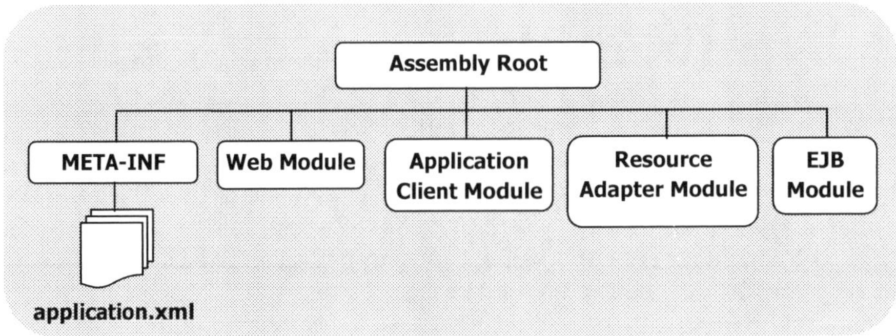

Figure 5.54. EAR file structure.

enterprise bean module deployment descriptor, for example, declares transaction attributes and security authorizations for an enterprise bean. A Java EE module can be deployed as a standalone module.

The four types of Java EE modules are listed as follows:

1. EJB modules, which contain class files for enterprise beans and an EJB deployment descriptor. EJB modules are packaged as JAR files with a `.jar` extension.
2. Web modules, which contain Servlet class files, Web files, supporting class files, GIF and HTML files, and a Web application deployment descriptor. Web modules are packaged as JAR files with a `.war` (Web ARchive) extension.
3. Application client modules, which contain class files and an application client deployment descriptor. Application client modules are packaged as JAR files with a `.jar` extension.
4. Resource adapter modules, which contain all Java interfaces, classes, native libraries, and other documentation, along with the resource adapter deployment descriptor. Together, these implement the Connector architecture for a particular EIS. Resource adapter modules are packaged as JAR files with a `.rar` (resource adapter archive) extension.

5.3.5.1.5 Java EE 6 APIs An EJB component, or enterprise bean, is a body of code having fields and methods to implement modules of business logic. You can think of an enterprise bean as a building block that can be used alone or with other enterprise beans to execute business logic on the Java EE server.

There are two kinds of enterprise beans: session beans and message-driven beans.

1. A `session bean` represents a transient conversation with a client. When the client finishes executing, the session bean and its data are gone.
2. A `message-driven bean` combines features of a session bean and a message listener, allowing a business component to receive messages asynchronously. Commonly, these are Java Message Service (JMS) messages.

Java EE includes several API specifications, such as JDBC, RMI, email, JMS, Web services, XML, etc, and defines how to coordinate them. Java EE also features some specifications unique to Java EE for components. These include Enterprise JavaBeans (EJB), Connectors, Servlets, portlets (following the Java Portlet specification), JavaServer Pages, and several web service technologies. This allows developers to create enterprise applications that are portable and scalable, and that integrate with legacy technologies. A Java EE application server can handle transactions, security, scalability, concurrency and management of the components that are deployed to it in order to enable developers to concentrate more on the business logic of the components rather than on infrastructure and integration tasks.

The Java EE APIs includes several technologies that extend the functionality of the base Java SE APIs. Table 5.9 shows most components included in Enterprise Edition 6 API Specification.

5.3.5.1.6 Java EE 6 APIs Included in the Java SE 6 Several APIs that are required by the Java EE 6 platform are included in the Java SE 6 platform and are thus available to Java EE applications. Table 5.10 lists these APIs.

Table 5.9. Most components defined in Enterprise Edition 6 API Specification

Component Name	Description
javax.ejb.*	The EJB specification defines a set of lightweight APIs that an object container (the EJB container) will support in order to provide Java Transaction API (JTA) remote procedure calls using Remote Method Invocation (RMI), concurrency control, dependency injection, and access control for business objects. This package contains the EJB classes and interfaces that define the contracts between the enterprise bean and its clients, and between the enterprise bean and the EJB container
javax.enterprise.context.*	These packages define the context (scope) annotations and interfaces for the Contexts and Dependency Injection (CDI) API
javax.enterprise.inject.*	These packages define the injection annotations for the Contexts and Dependency Injection (CDI) API
javax.jms.*	This package defines the Java Message Service (JMS) API. The JMS API provides a common way for Java programs to create, send, receive, and read an enterprise messaging system's messages
javax.faces.*	This package defines the root of the JavaServer Faces (JSF) API. JSF is a technology for constructing user interfaces out of components
javax.faces.component.*	This package defines the component part of the JavaServer Faces (JSF) API. Since JSF is primarily component oriented, this is one of the core packages. The package overview contains a UML diagram of the component hierarchy
javax.persistence	This package contains the classes and interfaces that define the contracts between a persistence provider and the managed classes and the clients of the Java Persistence API (JPA)
javax.xml.stream	This package contains readers and writers for XML streams
javax.resource.*	This package defines the Java EE Connector Architecture API. Java EE Connector Architecture (JCA) is a Java-based technology solution for connecting application servers and enterprise information systems (EIS) as part of enterprise application integration (EAI) solutions

5.3.5.1.7 Java EE 6 Application Servers To build a Java EE application, developers can use some certified Application Servers provided by Sun. Here are some popular Java EE6 related application servers. The servers are categorized based on the following groups:

1. Java EE 6 certified servers
   - Sun GlassFish Enterprise Server v3 based on the open source GlassFish application server
   - JEUS 7, an application server from TmaxSoft. According to their website, "JEUS 7 is scheduled to be released at the end of 2010."
2. In development for full Java EE 6
   - JBoss Application Server 6

Table 5.10. Java Enterprise Edition 6 APIs included in Java Standard Edition 6 API

API Name	Description
Java Database Connectivity API	The Java Database Connectivity (JDBC) API lets you invoke SQL commands from Java programming language methods. You use the JDBC API in an enterprise bean when you have a session bean access the database. You can also use the JDBC API from a Servlet or a JSP page to access the database directly without going through an enterprise bean.
	The JDBC API has two parts: an application-level interface used by the application components to access a database, and a service provider interface to attach a JDBC driver to the Java EE platform
Java Naming and Directory Interface	The Java Naming and Directory Interface (JNDI) provides naming and directory functionality, enabling applications to access multiple naming and directory services, including existing naming and directory services such as LDAP, NDS, DNS, and NIS. It provides applications with methods for performing standard directory operations, such as associating attributes with objects and searching for objects using their attributes. Using JNDI, a Java EE application can store and retrieve any type of named Java object, allowing Java EE applications to coexist with many legacy applications and systems
JavaBeans Activation Framework	The JavaBeans Activation Framework (JAF) is used by the JavaMail API. JAF provides standard services to determine the type of an arbitrary piece of data, encapsulate access to it, discover the operations available on it, and create the appropriate JavaBeans component to perform those operations
Java API for XML Processing	The Java API for XML Processing (JAXP), part of the Java SE platform, supports the processing of XML documents using Document Object Model (DOM), Simple API for XML (SAX), and Extensible Style sheet Language Transformations (XSLT). JAXP enables applications to parse and transform XML documents independent of a particular XML processing implementation
Java Architecture for XML Binding (JAXB)	The Java Architecture for XML Binding (JAXB) provides a convenient way to bind an XML schema to a representation in Java language programs. JAXB can be used independently or in combination with JAX-WS, where it provides a standard data binding for web service messages. All Java EE application client containers, web containers, and EJB containers support the JAXB API.
SOAP with Attachments API for Java	The SOAP with Attachments API for Java (SAAJ) is a low-level API on which JAX-WS and JAXR depend. SAAJ enables the production and consumption of messages that conform to the SOAP 1.1 and 1.2 specifications and SOAP with Attachments note. Most developers do not use the SAAJ API, instead using the higher-level JAX-WS API

(*Continued*)

Table 5.10. (*Continued*)

API Name	Description
Java API for XML Web Services (JAX-WS)	The JAX-WS specification provides support for web services that use the JAXB API for binding XML data to Java objects. The JAX-WS specification defines client APIs for accessing web services, as well as techniques for implementing web service endpoints. The Implementing Enterprise Web Services specification describes the deployment of JAX-WS-based services and clients. The EJB and Java Servlet specifications also describe aspects of such deployment. It must be possible to deploy JAX-WS-based applications using any of these deployment models
Java Authentication and Authorization Service (JAAS)	The Java Authentication and Authorization Service (JAAS) provides a way for a Java EE application to authenticate and authorize a specific user or group of users to run it. JAAS is a Java programming language version of the standard Pluggable Authentication Module (PAM) framework, which extends the Java Platform security architecture to support user-based authorization

3. In development for Java EE 6 Web Profile
   - Caucho Resin 4.0. Discussion

Next, let's build a Java EE 6 project to illustrate how to use some important components we have discussed, such as Java EJB, JPA, and JFS, to develop a three-tier application to access a sample database via application server to perform data actions.

5.3.5.2 Install and Configure Java EE 6 Software and Tools

To build and develop a Java EE 6 Web application, the following software and tools are needed:

- Java EE 6 Software Development Kit (SDK)
- Apache Ant

Since most Java EE 6 Web applications are three-tier applications, which mean:

- Web browser works as the top tier
- Enterprise server works as the mid-tier
- Database server works as the third tier

Sun GlassFish Enterprise Server v3 is targeted as the build and runtime environment for the Java EE 6 Web applications. To build, deploy, and run a Java EE 6 project, you need a copy of the Enterprise Server. To obtain the Enterprise Server, you must install the Java EE 6 Software Development Kit (SDK), which you can download from http://java.sun.com/javaee/downloads/. Make sure you download the Java EE 6 SDK, not the Java EE 6 Web Profile SDK.

Let's first take care of downloading the Java EE 6 SDK.

5.3.5.2.1 Install Java EE 6 SDK Software Go to the site http://java.sun.com/javaee/downloads/ to open the `GlassFish and Java EE 6` page. Select `Windows` and `English` from the `Platform` and `Language` combo box, and click on the `Download` button under the Java EE 6 SDK column to begin this downloading process.

On the opened `Download` dialog, click on the `Continue to Download` button to skip this registration step. Click on the `Save` button to temporarily save this software to the `Temp` folder under the root (`C:/`) driver in your computer.

When the download is done, you can click on the `Run` button to install it to your computer. Follow the installation instructions to complete this process.

During the installation of the SDK, pay special attention to the following steps:

1. Configure the Enterprise Server administration Username as the default setting (admin). You can select and enter any password as you like (reback is used in our application).
2. Accept the default port values for the Admin Port (**4848**) and the HTTP Port (**8080**), unless the Port has been occupied. In that case, change the Port number to enable system to use other Port. In our application, change the HTTP Port to **8082** since the Port **8080** has been used by some other devices.
3. Allow the installer to download and configure the Update Tool. If you access the Internet through a firewall, provide the proxy host and port.

Click on the `Install` button to begin this installation process, as shown in Figure 5.55.

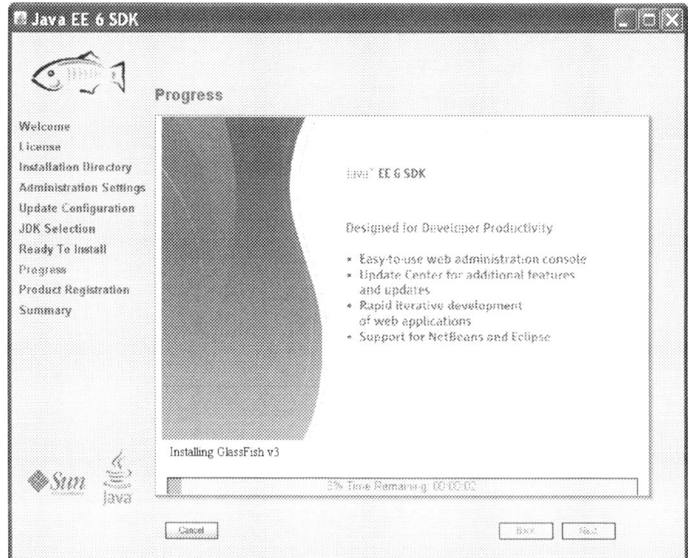

Figure 5.55. The installation process of Java EE 6 SDK.

In the Registration step, click on the Skip Registration radio button if you do not want to perform this registration. Click on the Next button to continue.

When the installation is complete, a Summary page is displayed to provide a detailed installation and configuration report for this installation. Click on the Exit button to complete this installation if everything looks fine. Refer to Appendix I for more details on this installation.

5.3.5.2.2 Add Enterprise Server as a Server in the NetBeans IDE To run the Java EE 6 Web applications in the NetBeans IDE, you must register your Enterprise Server installation as a NetBeans Server Instance. Follow these instructions to register the Enterprise Server in the NetBeans IDE.

1. Launch the NetBeans IDE 6.8.
2. Select the Tools > Servers menu item to open the Servers dialog.
3. Click on the Add Server button.
4. In the opened Add Server Instance dialog, select the GlassFish v3, as shown in Figure 5.56, and click on the Next button.
5. Under Server Location, enter the location of your Enterprise Server installation, which is C:\glassfishv3, and click on the Next button.
6. Select the Register Local Domain radio button
7. Click on the Finish button.

Your finished installed GlassFish v3 server window should match one that is shown in Figure 5.57. Click on the Close button to complete this adding process.

Now let's create a new Java EE 6 Web application project.

5.3.5.3 Create a Java EE 6 Web Application Project

In this section, we will build a Java EE 6 Web application, combined with a brief introduction to some features introduced as part of Java EE 6 specification we discussed in the

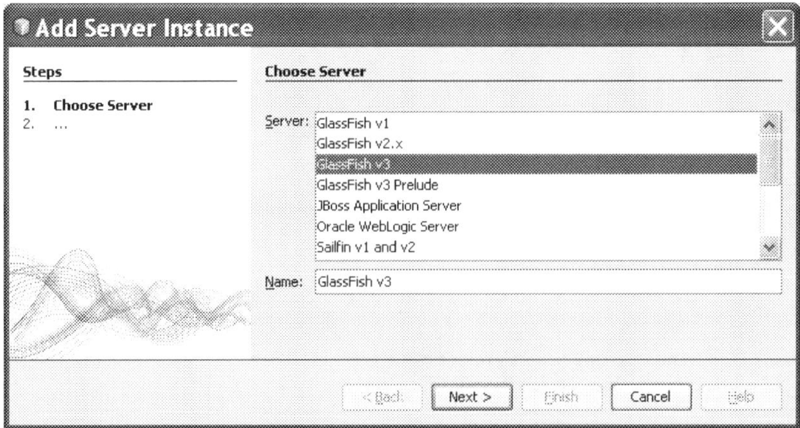

Figure 5.56. Add the GlassFish v3 Enterprise Server into the NetBeans IDE.

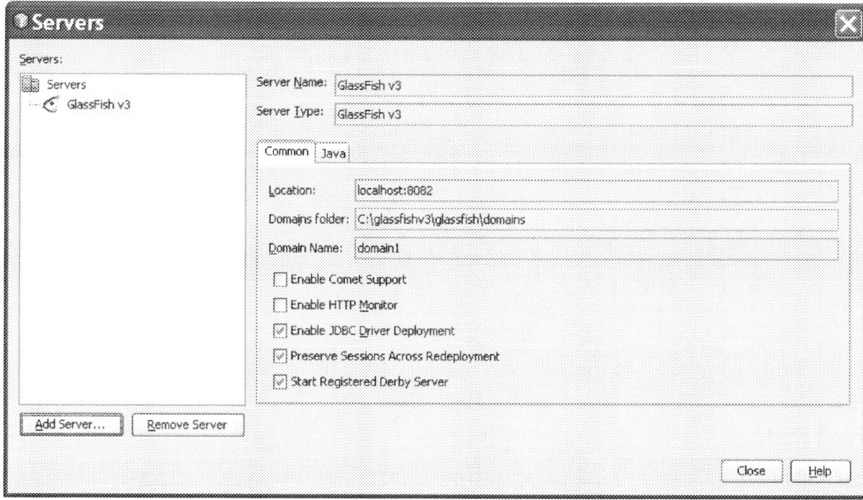

Figure 5.57. The finished adding glassfish v3 server into the NetBeans IDE window.

previous sections. To illustrate the new features, we will demonstrate how to create a simple Java EE 6 Web application that contains an EJB 3.1 stateless session bean facade for an entity class. We will use wizards in the NetBeans IDE to generate the entity class and the session bean. The code generated by the wizard uses queries that are defined in the Criteria API that is part of JPA 2.0 and contained in the Java EE 6 specification. We will then create a named managed bean that accesses the session facade and a presentation layer that uses the Facelets view framework as specified in JSF 2.0.

This project is based on technologies in the Java EE 6 specification, such as JavaServer Faces 2.0 (JSF), Enterprise Java Beans 3.1 (Session Bean and Message-Driven Bean), and JPA, with the help of NetBeans IDE 6.8 as the tool. We will creates a Java EE 6 Web application called `JavaEEDBManufacturer` that performs only the retrieving function on the manufacturer records in the `Manufacturer` table provided by the NetBeans sample database served by the Glassfish built-in database server, JavaDB.

The objective of this project is to demonstrate the ease of using several Java EE 6 technologies like JSF2.0, EJB3, and JPA with the help of NetBeans IDE, and putting them together to create an enterprise-ready Web-based application.

Figure 5.58 shows a structure diagram of this Web application project.

Perform the following operations to create a new Java EE 6 Web application project named `JavaEEWebDBApp`:

1. Launch the NetBeans IDE 6.8.
2. Choose `File > New Project` (`Ctrl-Shift-N`) from the main menu.
3. Select `Enterprise Application` from the `Java EE` category and click on the `Next` button.
4. Type `JavaEEDBManufacturer` for the project name and set the desired project location.

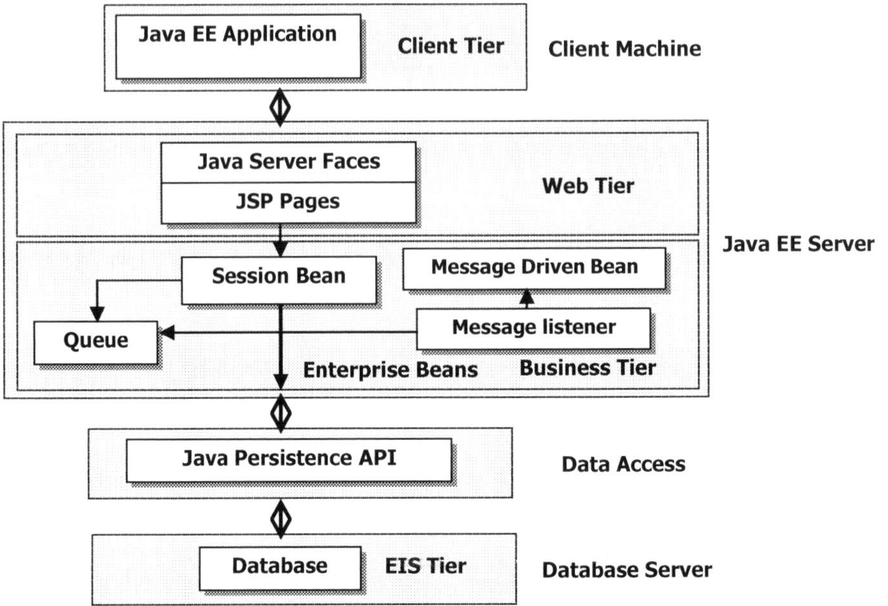

Figure 5.58. The structure diagram of the Java EE 6 Web application project.

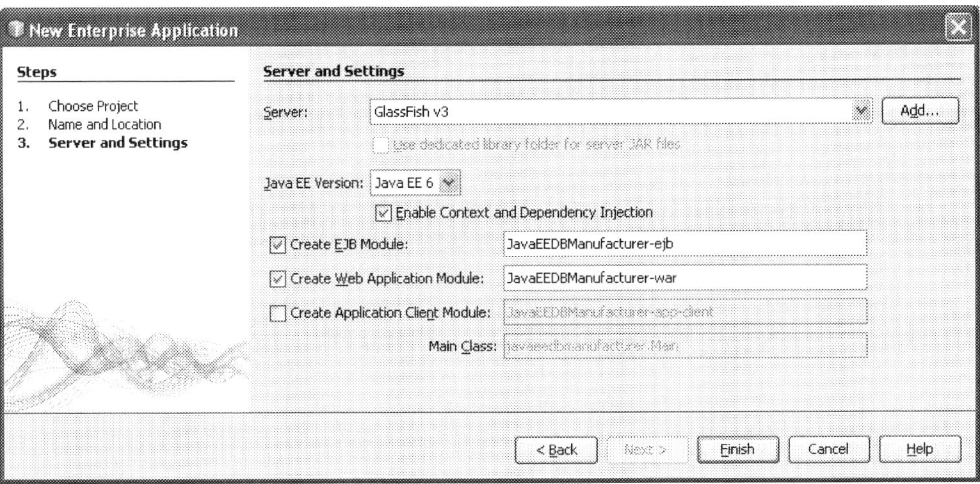

Figure 5.59. The finished New Enterprise Application window.

5. Deselect the `Use Dedicated Folder` option, if selected. Click on the `Next` button. For this application, there is little reason to copy project libraries to a dedicated folder because we will not need to share libraries with other users or projects.
6. Set the server to `GlassFish v3`, and set the Java EE Version to `Java EE 6`. Keep all other default settings and click on the `Finish` button.

Your finished `New Enterprise Application` window should match one that is shown in Figure 5.59.

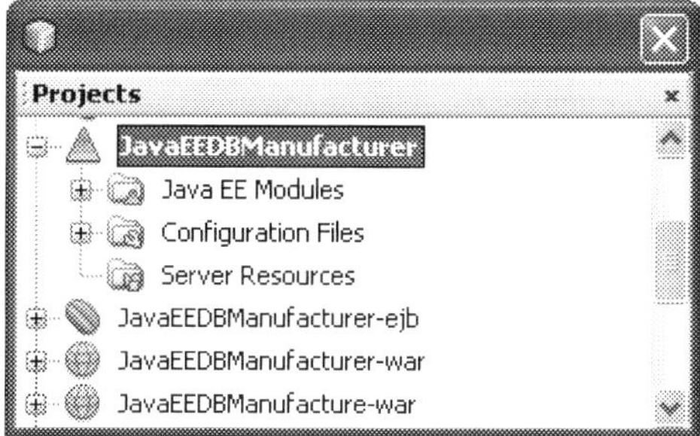

Figure 5.60. Created three projects by NetBeans IDE.

NetBeans will create three projects, namely `JavaEEDBManufacturer` (Enterprise Application project), `JavaEEDBManufacturer-ejb` (EJB project), and `JavaEEDBManufacturer-war` (Web project), as shown in Figure 5.60.

Next, let's create our entity classes to map our sample database and tables, since the Session Beans are responsible for manipulating the data, and they will be created in the EJB project (refer to Fig. 5.58).

5.3.5.4 Creating the Entity Classes from the Database

Perform the following operations to create our entity classes for our sample database:

1. In the `Projects` window, right click on the `JavaEEDBManufacturer-ejb` project and select the `New > Entity Classes from Database` item from the pop-up menu.
2. Check the `Data Source` Radio button, click on the dropdown arrow, and select the `New Data Source` from the corresponding dropdown list.
3. On the opened `Create Data Source` dialog, enter `jdbc/sample` into the JNDI Name field and click on the dropdown arrow on the `Database Connection` combo box, and select the default JavaDB sample database connection URL `jdbc:derby://localhost:1527/sample [app on APP]`. Click on the `OK` button to close this dialog box.
4. Under the `Available Tables` list box, select MANUFACTURER and click on Add button so that it appears in the `Selected Tables` list box. Your `New Entity Classes from Database` window should match one that is shown in Figure 5.61. Click on the `Next` button to continue.

Note: You do not need to create a new Data Source; instead, you can directly select the jdbc/sample from the existing data source if this default database has been installed and set up in your NetBeans IDE.

5. Click on the `Create Persistence Unit` button and select `jdbc/sample` as the `Data Source`. Leave the rest as default as shown in Figure 5.62, and click on the `Create` button to continue.

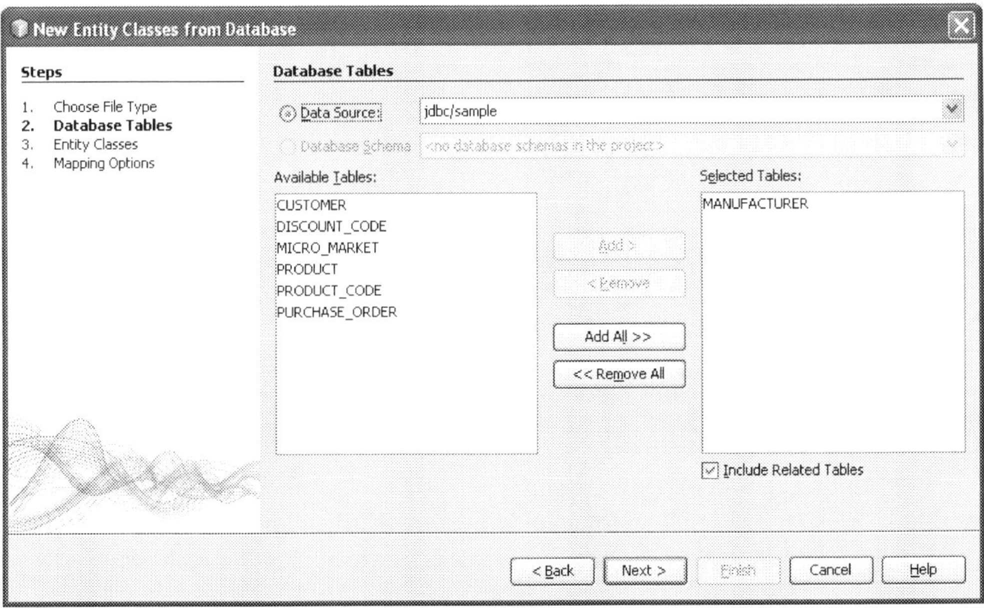

Figure 5.61. The New Entity Classes from Database window.

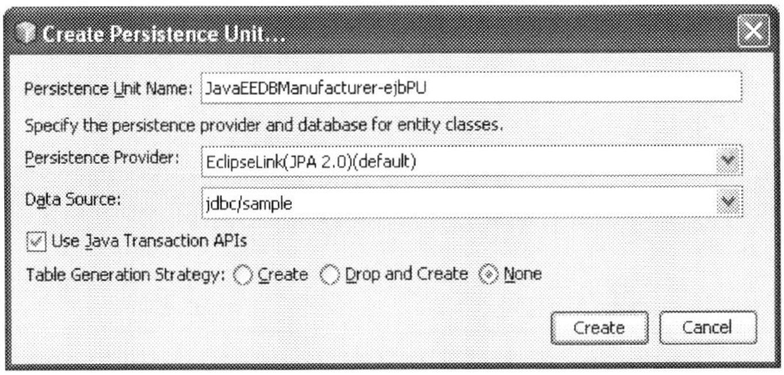

Figure 5.62. The Create Persistence Unit dialog.

6. Provide a package name, `com.javaeedbmanufacturer.entity`, in the `Package` field and click on the `Next` button.
7. Change the `Collection Type` to `java.util.List` and click on the `Finish` button to complete this entity class creation process.

You can find that one entity class, `Manufacturer.java`, has been created under the `Source Packages`, `com.javaeedbmanufacturer.entity`, in the `Projects` window, which is shown in Figure 5.63.

Next, let's create the Java Beans to perform communication functions between the JSF pages and JPA to make the data actions against our sample database.

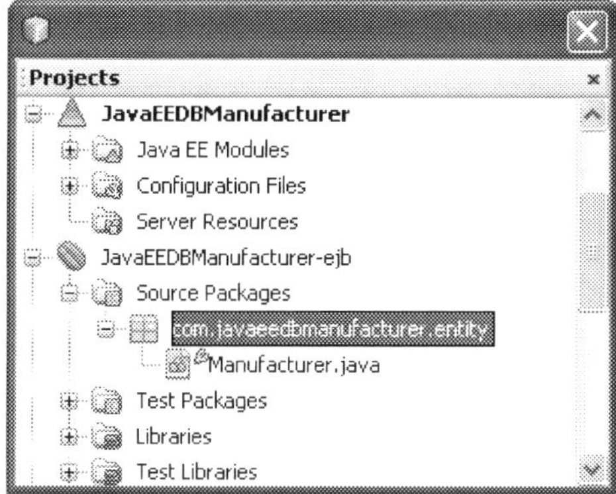

Figure 5.63. The newly created entity class `Manufacturer`.java.

5.3.5.5 Creating Enterprise Java Beans

Now that we have the Entity classes, the next step is to create the Session (Stateless) Bean, `ManufacturerSession`, that will manipulate and provide the Retrieving functionality on the `Manufacturer` object. In this application, the client that uses this function is the JSF pages. One of the benefits of doing this (i.e., to provide the functionalities in the EJB layer) is reusability, because the same functions can be used by more than one JSF pages, other EJBs, Enterprise Application Clients, and Web Services Clients when exposed as Web services. Other benefits include scalability because the EJB container can easily be tuned and scaled up when load increases.

Perform the following operations to create this Enterprise Java Bean:

1. From the `Projects` window, right click on the `JavaEEDBManufacturer-ejb` project and select the `New > Session Bean` menu item.
2. In the opened `New Session Bean` dialog, specify the `EJB Name` as `ManufacturerSession`, the `Package` as `com.javaeedbmanufacturer.ejb`, the `Session Type` as `Stateless` and leave two `Create Interface` checkboxes unchecked. Your finished `New Session Bean` dialog box should match one that is shown in Figure 5.64. Click on the `Finish` button to complete this creation of Session Bean process.
3. From the `Projects` window, navigate to the source of the newly created `Session Bean` (skeleton) by double clicking on the `ManufacturerSession` item that is under the `Enterprise Beans` folder, as shown in Figure 5.65.
4. In the opened code window, right click in any place in this window, and select the `Persistence > Use Entity Manager` menu item from the popup menu, and then you can find that the `@PersistenceContext` notation is inserted automatically into this code window, so now the `EntityManager`, with variable name `em`, is ready to be used. The autocreated codes by the NetBeans have been highlighted in bold and shown in Figure 5.66.
5. Create a business method for the Session Bean: **Retrieve**() since we need to use this method to perform data query from the Manufacturer table later; right click in the `Insert Code > Add Business Method` section in the code window, and select the `Insert`

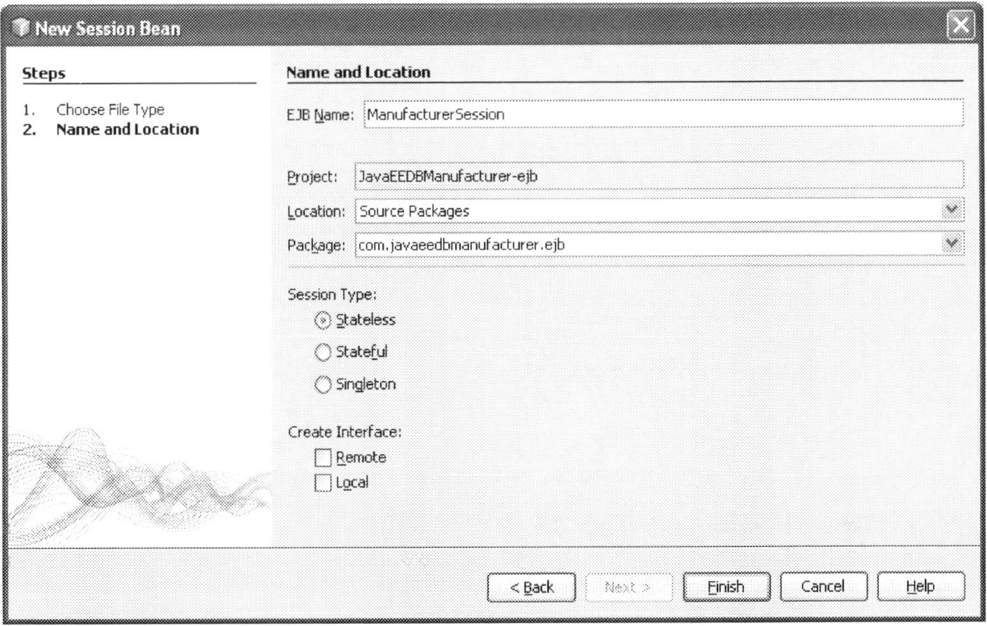

Figure 5.64. The finished New Session bean dialog box.

Figure 5.65. The newly created ManufacturerSession Bean.

Code menu item from the pop-up menu; under the `Generate` list, select the `Add Business Method` menu item.

6. In the opened `Add Business Method` dialog, provide `Retrieve` to the `Name` field as the name of this method. Click on the `Browse` button that is next to the `Return Type` combo box and type the `list` on the `List Name` field from the `Find Type` dialog to scan the available type list. Select the item `List(java.util)` from the list and click on the `OK` button in the `Find Type` dialog to select this type. Your finished `Add Business Method` dialog should match one that is shown in Figure 5.67.

Click on the `OK` button to close this adding method process.

```
package com.javaeedbmanufacturer.ejb;
import javax.ejb.Stateless;
import javax.ejb.LocalBean;
import javax.persistence.EntityManager;
import javax.persistence.PersistenceContext;
@Stateless
@LocalBean
public class ManufacturerSession {
    @PersistenceContext(unitName = "JavaEEDBManufacturer-ejbPU")
    private EntityManager  em;
    public void persist(Object object) {
        em.persist(object);
    }
    // Add business logic below. (Right-click in editor and choose
    // "Insert Code > Add Business Method")
}
```

Figure 5.66. The inserted codes for the Entity Manager.

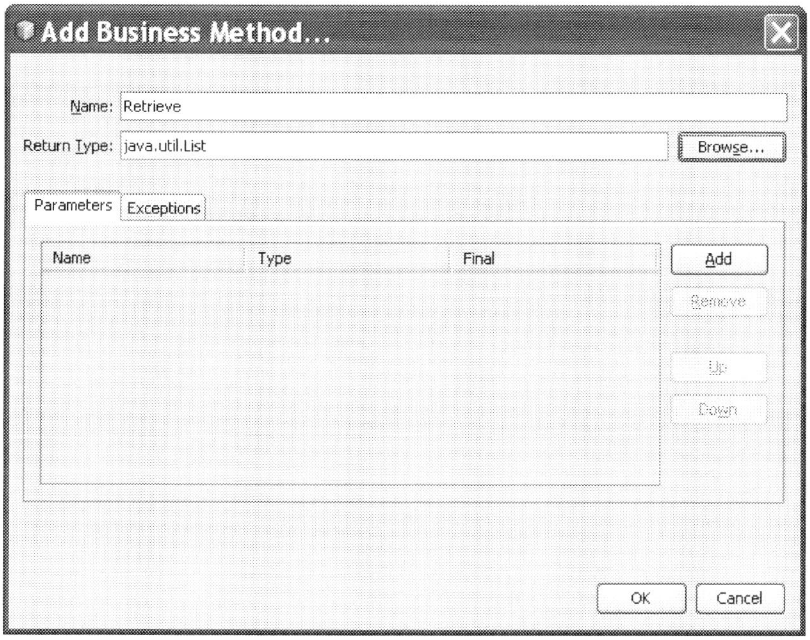

Figure 5.67. The finished Add Business Method dialog box.

Now let's develop the codes for this `Retrieve()` methods to implement the intended function. Edit this method by adding the codes that are shown in Figure 5.68 into this method.

The edited codes have been highlighted in bold, and let's have a closer look at this piece of codes to see how it works.

```
  @Stateless
  @LocalBean
  public class ManufacturerSession {
     @PersistenceContext(unitName = "JavaEEDBManufacturer-ejbPU")
     private EntityManager em;

     public void persist(Object object) {
        em.persist(object);
     }

     public List<Manufacturer> Retrieve() {
A       Query query = em.createNamedQuery("Manufacturer.findAll");
B       return query.getResultList();
     }
```

Figure 5.68. The edited coding for both business methods.

A. Inside the `Retrieve()` method, first we create a JPA query instance `query` and execute a named or static query to pick up all columns from the `Manufacturer` entity. The query result is returned and stored to the `query` instance.

B. The `getResultList()` method is executed to get the query result and return it to the `List` object.

After you finish adding this piece of codes into the `Retrieve()` method, you may encounter some in-time compiling errors for some class and interface, such as the `Manufacturer` class and `Query` interface. The reason for that is because those classes and interfaces are defined in the different packages, and you need to involve those packages into this project file. Perform the following import operations to add those packages to the top of this project file:

```
import javax.persistence.Query;
import com.javaeedbmanufacturer.entity.Manufacturer;
```

Your complete code window for this `ManufacturerSession` class file should match one that is shown in Figure 5.69. The newly inserted codes have been highlighted in bold.

Now you can build and compile the project files we have developed so far by clicking on the `Clean and Build Main Project` button. Up to this point, we have completed the tasks required to be done in the EJB project, and we will move on to the next tier, JSF pages.

5.3.5.6 Using JavaServer Faces (JSF) 2.0

Before we can create the web pages for this project, ensure that the JavaServer Faces framework is added to the Web project, `JavaEEDBManufacturer-war`. Perform the following operations to confirm this addition.

1. In the `Projects` window, right click on the Web project, `JavaEEDBManufacturer-war`, and select the `Properties` menu item from the popup menu.
2. Under the `Categories` items, select `Frameworks`, and ensure that the `JavaServer Faces` has been added into the `Used Frameworks` list. If not, click on the Add button

```
package com.javaeedbmanufacturer.ejb;

import java.util.List;
import javax.ejb.Stateless;
import javax.ejb.LocalBean;
import javax.persistence.EntityManager;
import javax.persistence.PersistenceContext;
import javax.persistence.Query;
import com.javaeedbmanufacturer.entity.Manufacturer;
@Stateless
@LocalBean
public class ManufacturerSession {
    @PersistenceContext(unitName = "JavaEEDBManufacturer-ejbPU")
    private EntityManager em;

    public void persist(Object object) {
        em.persist(object);
    }

    public  List<Manufacturer> Retrieve() {
        Query  query = em.createNamedQuery("Manufacturer.findAll");
        return  query.getResultList();
    }

    // Add business logic below. (Right-click in editor and choose
    // "Insert Code > Add Business Method")
}
```

Figure 5.69. The complete codes for the ManufacturerSession class.

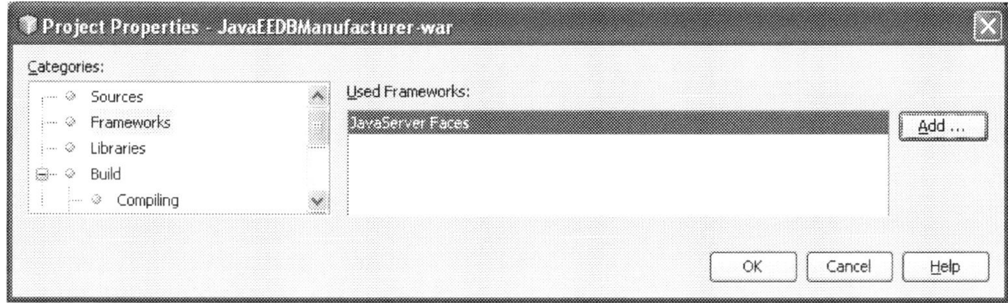

Figure 5.70. The finished Project Properties window.

to open the `Add a Framework` dialog to add the `JavaServer Faces` to the project by selecting it and clicking on the `OK` button. Your finished `Project Properties` window should match one that is shown in Figure 5.70. Click on the `OK` button to complete this confirmation process.

Now we need to create the JSF pages to present the screens to perform the **R**ead function. To achieve this, we will be creating two web pages:

- **ManufacturerList**: listing of all Manufacturer records in our sample database in a tabular form.
- **ManufacturerDetails**: view/edit the details of the selected Manufacturer record.

However, before creating the JSF pages, we first need to create the managed bean that will be providing the required services for the JSF pages that will be created later.

5.3.5.7 Creating the Manufacturer Managed Bean

Perform the following operations to create the managed bean that provides message communications between the web pages and the JPA.

1. In the `Projects` window, right click on the Web project, `JavaEEDBManufacturer-war`, and select the `New > JSF Managed Bean` item by clicking on it to open the `New JSF Managed Bean` dialog.
2. Specify the `ManufacturerMBean` as the `Class Name`, and `com.javaeedbmanufacturer.web` as the `Package Name`, `manufacturer` as the `Name`, and the `Scope` to be `session`. Your finished `New JSF Managed Bean` dialog should match one that is shown in Figure 5.71. Click on the `Finish` button to complete this creation of a new JSF managed bean process.
3. Open the code window of the newly created class, `ManufacturerMBean.java`, by double clicking on this file folder in the `Projects` window, right click inside the constructor of this class and select the `Insert Code` menu item, and select the `Call Enterprise Bean` item under the `Generate` list.
4. In the opened `Call Enterprise Bean` dialog, expand the `JavaEEDBManufacturer-ejb` project and select the `ManufacturerSession` and select the `No Interface` option. Also, disable the `Local and Remote` options because we created the Session Bean with no interface for `Referenced Interface`, and then click on the `OK` button.

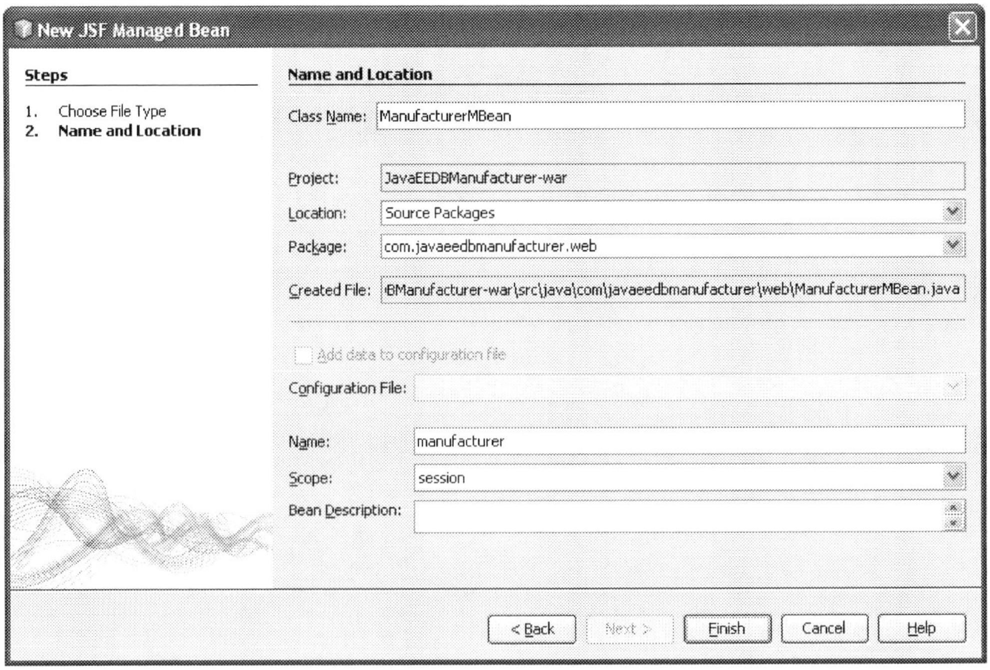

Figure 5.71. The finished New JSF Managed Bean dialog.

5. Notice the automatically generated variable, `manufacturerSession`, which represents an instance of the session bean, at the beginning of the class declaration.

Now let's do the coding jobs for this class file.

First, we need to add the following import packages statements into this class to enable the compiler to correctly locate and identify related objects we will use in this class:

```
import com.javaeedbmanufacturer.entity.Manufacturer;
import java.util.List;
```

Second, let's add the rest of the methods, properties and action handlers, and its implementations to the class as shown in Figure 5.72, which will be used by the JSF pages later. The new added codes have been highlighted in bold.

Let's have a closer look at this new added piece of codes to see how it works.

A. Two packages have been added into this class file since we need to use the `Manufacturer` entity and the `List` class in this file, and both of them are defined in those two different packages.

B. In order to use the `Manufacturer` entity to access the `Manufacturer` table in our sample database, we need to create a new instance of this class, `manufacturer`.

C. The `getManufacturers()` method is defined to pick up a list of manufacturer objects to be displayed in the data table. Exactly the `Retrieve()` method defined in our `ManufacturerSession` bean will be executed to perform this retrieving operation.

D. The `getDetails()` method is defined to return the selected `Manufacturer` object.

E. The `showDetails()` method is exactly a handler to handle the users' selection from the list.

F. The `list()` method is a event handler used to direct this event to open the Manufacturer List page we will create in the next section.

At this point, we have finished editing and modifying the codes for our `Manufacturer Managed Bean` code window. Your finished code window should match one that is shown in Figure 5.72.

Now, let's create the first webpage that lists the Manufacturer records in the database in a tabular form.

5.3.5.8 Creating the Manufacturer Listing Web Page

Perform the following operations to create this Manufacturer Listing web page:

1. In the `Projects` window, right click on our Web project, `JavaEEDBManufacturer-war`, and select the `New > JSF Page` item from the popup menu. On the opened the `New JSF File` dialog, specify `ManufacturerList` as the `File Name` and check the `JSP File` radio button under the `Options` group. Your finished `New JSF File` dialog should match one that is shown in Figure 5.73. Click on the `Finish` button to continue.
2. In the opened code window, drag the item, `JSF Data Table from Entity` from the `Palette` window and drop it in between the <body> </body> tags of the newly generated file, `ManufacturerList.jsp`, as shown in Figure 5.74. If the `Palette`

```
  package com.javaeedbmanufacturer.web;

  import com.javaeedbmanufacturer.ejb.ManufacturerSession;
  import javax.ejb.EJB;
  import javax.faces.bean.ManagedBean;
  import javax.faces.bean.SessionScoped;
A import com.javaeedbmanufacturer.entity.Manufacturer;
  import java.util.List;

  @ManagedBean(name="manufacturer")
  @SessionScoped

  public class ManufacturerMBean {
     @EJB
     private ManufacturerSession manufacturerSession;
B    private Manufacturer manufacturer;

     /** Creates a new instance of ManufacturerMBean */
     public ManufacturerMBean() {

     }
     /* Returns list of manufacturer objects to be displayed in the data table */
C    public List<Manufacturer> getManufacturers() {
       return manufacturerSession.Retrieve();
     }

     /* Returns the selected Manufacturer object */
D    public Manufacturer getDetails() {
       //Can either do this for simplicity or fetch the details again from the
       //database using the Manufacturer ID
       return manufacturer;
     }

     /* Action handler - user selects a manufacturer record from the list */
E    public String showDetails(Manufacturer manufacturer) {
       this. manufacturer = manufacturer;
       return "DETAILS";
     }

     /* Action handler - goes to the Manufacturer listing page */
F    public String list(){
       System.out.println("###LIST###");
       return "LIST";
     }
  }
```

Figure 5.72. The modified Manufacturer Managed Bean code window.

window is not opened, go to the `Window` menu item and click on the `Palette` item to open it.

You can use this dragged `JSF Data Table from Entity` item to replace the original instruction:

```
<h1><h:outputText value="Hello World!"/></h1>
```

Or you can leave the original instruction at the bottom of this new inserted item.

3. A dialog with the title, `JSF Table from Entity` appears; from the `Entity` combo box, select the `com.javaeedbmanufacturer.entity.Manufacturer` as the

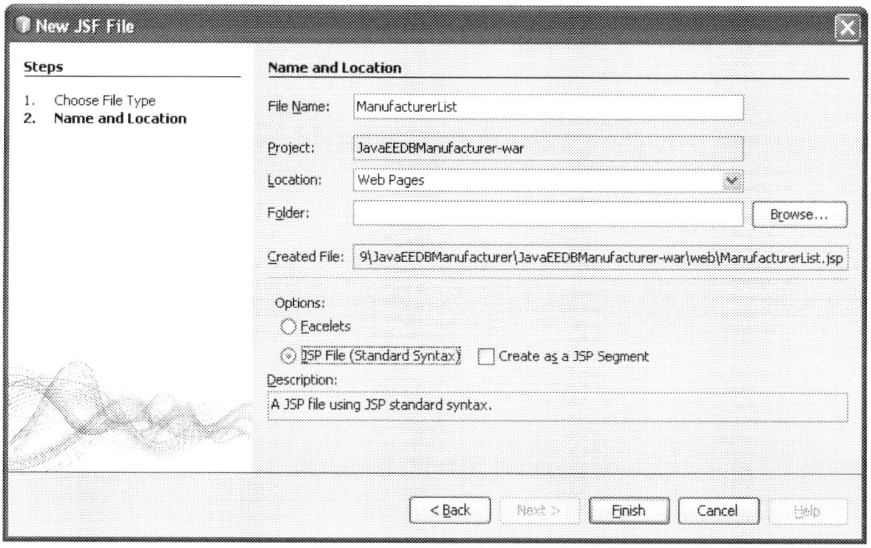

Figure 5.73. The finished New JSF File dialog box.

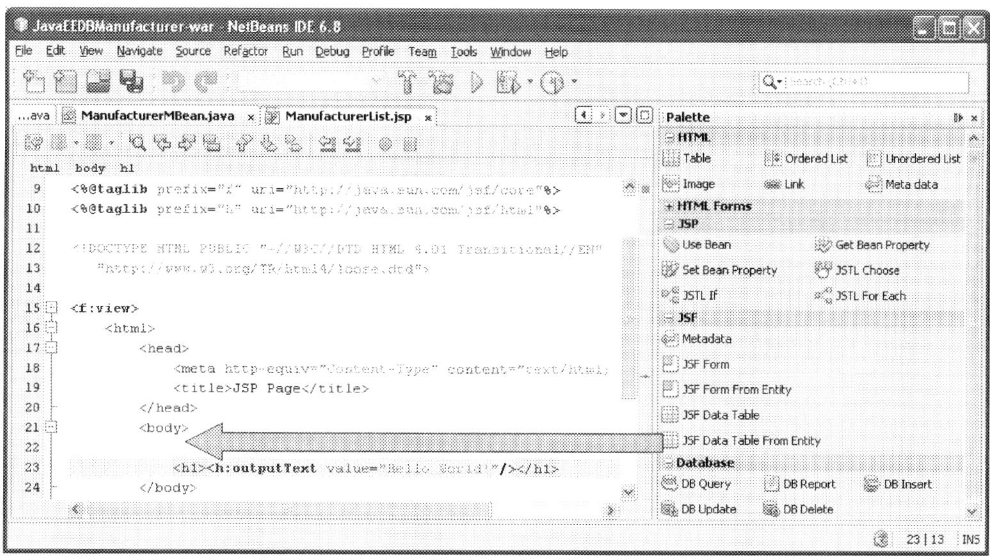

Figure 5.74. The inserted JSF Data Table from Entity item.

`Entity Bean`, and the `manufacturer.manufacturers` as the `Managed Bean Property`, as shown in Figure 5.75, and click on the `OK` button.

Notice that the results of this operation are lines of codes automatically generated to display a default list of the Manufacturer objects.

At this point, we are ready to see the result of the first web page created so far.

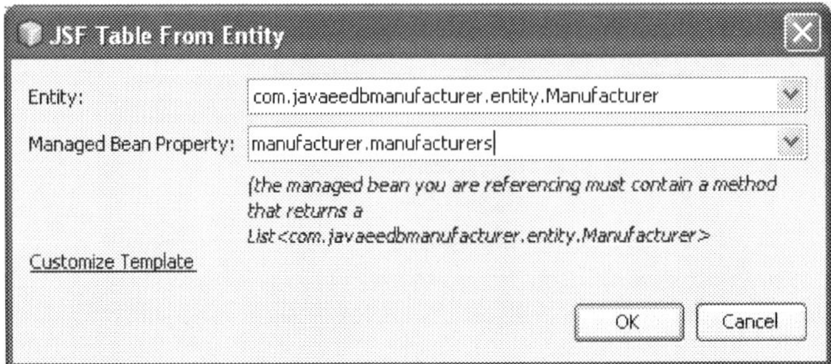

Figure 5.75. The finished JSF Table From Entity dialog box.

Figure 5.76. The deployed JavaEEDBManufacturer project.

5.3.5.9 Building and Running the First Java EE 6 Web Page

Perform the following operations to build and run this JSP web page:

1. In the `Projects` window, right click on our `JavaEEDBManufacturer` project and select the `Clean and Build` menu item from the pop-up menu to build our project. If everything is fine, right click on our project `JavaEEDBManufacturer` again and select `Deploy`. Enter the username and password you used when you installed the Java Glassfish v3 Server in Section 5.3.5.2.1 to the `Authentication Required` dialog box if it is displayed. In this application, we used `admin` and `reback` as the username and password for the Java Glassfish v3 Server in this installation.
2. To confirm that the deployment is successful, navigate to the `Applications` folder in the Glassfish server under the `Services` view, as shown in Figure 5.76, and check if the application `JavaEEDBManufacturer` exists.

Now open the browser and go to URL: http://localhost:8082/JavaEEDBManufacturer-war/faces/ManufacturerList.jsp, and you should see the opened `Manufacturer` data table in the sample database, which is shown in Figure 5.77. The port we have used for our Glassfish v3 server is 8082, since the default port 8080 has been occupied by some other device.

Two issues to be noted here are: in some cases, (1) your project deployment may not be successful by executing the `Deploy` command in the `Projects` window, and (2) the

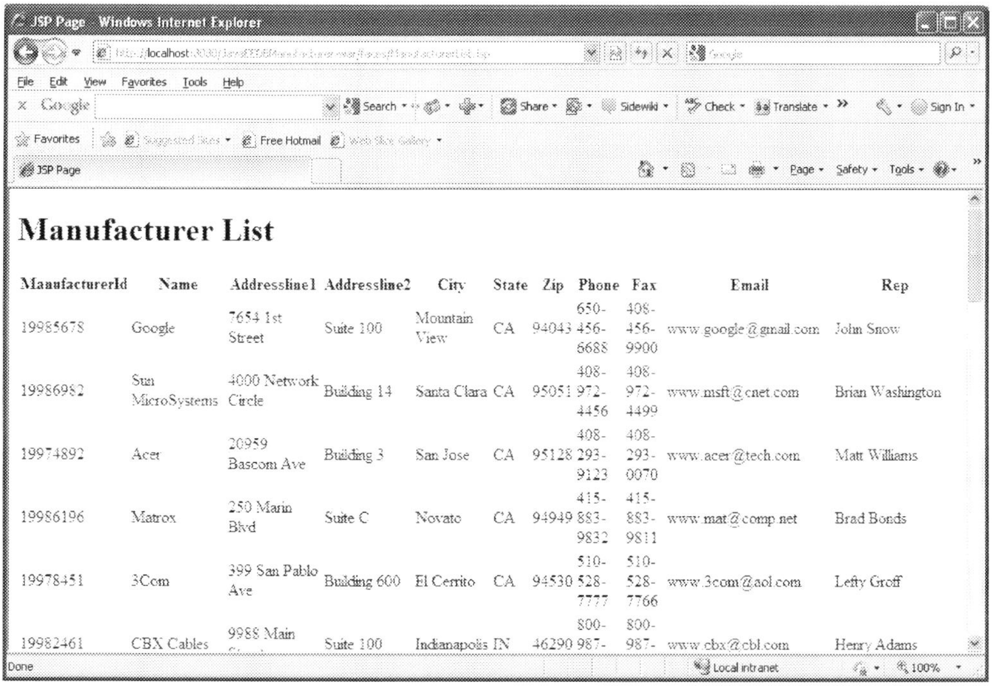
JSP Page - Windows Internet Explorer
File Edit View Favorites Tools Help
Favorites
Free Hotmail
JSP Page
Page Safety Tools
Manufacturer List
ManufacturerId Name Addressline1 Addressline2 City State Zip Phone Fax Email Rep
19985678 Google 7654 1st Street Suite 100 Mountain View CA 94043 650-456-6688 408-456-9900 www.google@gmail.com John Snow
19986982 Sun MicroSystems 4000 Network Circle Building 14 Santa Clara CA 95051 408-972-4456 408-972-4499 www.msft@cnet.com Brian Washington
19974892 Acer 20959 Bascom Ave Building 3 San Jose CA 95128 408-293-9123 408-293-0070 www.acer@tech.com Matt Williams
19986196 Matrox 250 Marin Blvd Suite C Novato CA 94949 415-883-9832 415-883-9811 www.mat@comp.net Brad Bonds
19978451 3Com 399 San Pablo Ave Building 600 El Cerrito CA 94530 510-528-7777 510-528-7766 www.3com@aol.com Lefty Groff
19982461 CBX Cables 9988 Main Suite 100 Indianapolis IN 46290 800-987- 800-987- www.cbx@cbl.com Henry Adams
Done
Local intranet
100%

Figure 5.77. The opened web page contained the Manufacturer data table.

screen is very raw and without any beautification. We will discuss these two issues and solutions in the following sections. First let's take care of the deployment of your project, and then we can make this display better by showing only some selected columns in the `Faculty` table.

5.3.5.10 Deploying the Project Using the Administration Console

Because of the complexity in building Java EE projects, in some cases, you may need to use different tools to help you to deploy your Java EE projects. A good candidate is the Administration Console tool provided by Java EE 6 SDK.

To administer the Enterprise Server and manage users, resources, and Java EE applications, you can use the Administration Console. One of the most important features provided by this tool is to deploy your Java EE project. One of the advantages of using the Administration Console tool to deploy Java EE applications is that more detailed and clear debug information can be obtained by using this tool compared with the `Deploy` process in the NetBeans IDE.

Perform the following operations to deploy your Java EE project using the Administration Console:

1. Make sure that the Java EE 6 SDK has been installed in your computer since the Administration Console is a part of this SDK. Refer to Section 5.3.5.2.1 in this Chapter to complete this installation if the SDK has not been installed.

2. Before you can run the Administration Console tool, make sure that the Enterprise Server—here we used Glassfish v3—has been started. To start the Enterprise Server in Windows, go to `Start > All Programs > Java EE 6 SDK Web Profile > Start Application Server`.
3. As the server started, you can start the Administration Console by going to `Start > All Programs > Java EE 6 SDK Web Profile > Administration Console`.
4. In the `Login` window, enter your Java EE Server username and password. In this application, they are `admin` and `reback`, and click on the `Login` button to continue.
5. In the `Common Tasks` window, click on the `Deploy an Application` button to start this deployment process.
6. In the opened `Deploy Application` window, check the `Local Packaged File or Directory That Is Accessible from the Enterprise Server` radio button.
7. Click on the `Browse Files` button to scan and find our target application file, `JavaEEDBManufacturer.ear`, which is located at the folder `C:\Book9\DBProjects\Chapter 5\JavaEEDBManufacturer\dist`. Click on the `Choose File` button to select this file.
8. Check any desired checkboxes, such as `Force Redeploy` and `Java Web Start` to set up your desired deploying environment.
9. Click on the `OK` button to begin this deployment process.

If this deployment is successful, the successful deployment page should be displayed, and check the deployment application `JavaEEDBManufacturer` from the Name column, the detailed deployment result is displayed, as shown in Figure 5.78.

Now let's do some sophisticated jobs to make our data query result look better.

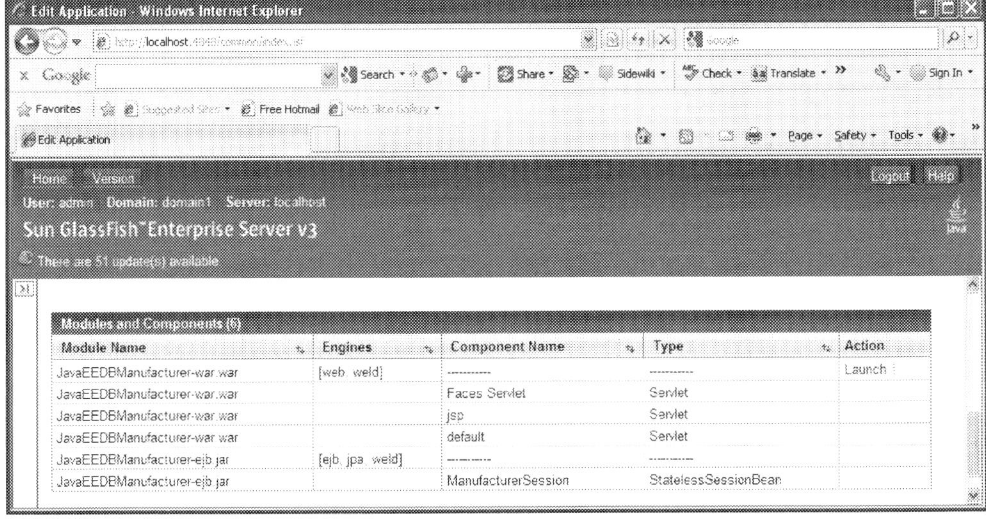

Module Name	Engines	Component Name	Type	Action
JavaEEDBManufacturer-war.war	[web, weld]	----------	----------	Launch
JavaEEDBManufacturer-war.war		Faces Servlet	Servlet	
JavaEEDBManufacturer-war.war		jsp	Servlet	
JavaEEDBManufacturer-war.war		default	Servlet	
JavaEEDBManufacturer-ejb.jar	[ejb, jpa, weld]	----------	----------	
JavaEEDBManufacturer-ejb.jar		ManufacturerSession	StatelessSessionBean	

Figure 5.78. The deployment result.

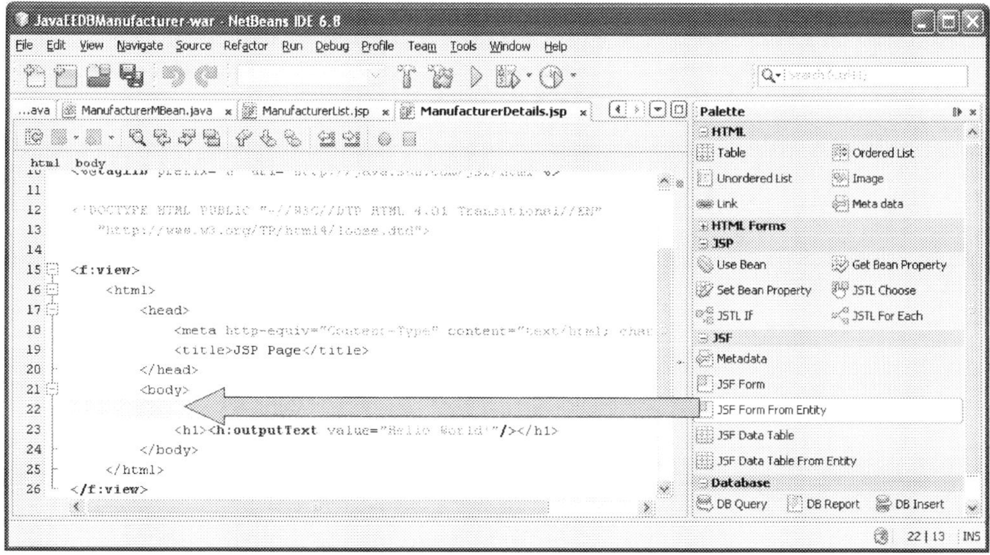

Figure 5.79. Drag the JSF Form From Entity from the Palette window.

5.3.5.11 Creating the Manufacturer Details Web Page

Now we will handle the second issue to create the page where the details of the selected manufacturer are displayed. Perform the following operations to complete this displaying:

1. In the `Projects` window, right click on the Web project, `JavaEEDBManufacturer-war`, and select `New > JSF Page`, specify `ManufacturerDetails` as the `File Name` and `JSP File` under the `Options`. Click on the `Finish` button to complete this process.
2. In the code window, drag the item, `JSF Form from Entity` from the `Palette` window and drop it in between the <body> </body> tags of the newly generated file, `ManufacturerDetails.jsp`, as shown in Figure 5.79.
3. In the `JSF Form From Entity` dialog, select our entity class file `com.javaeedb-manufacturer.entity.Manufacturer` from the `Entity` combo box and `manufacturer.details` from the `Managed Bean Property` combo box, as shown in Figure 5.80. Click on the `OK` button to complete this process. Notice the result of this are lines of codes automatically generated to display label and input field of all the attributes in Manufacturer object in a two-column grid.

To enable the navigation from the `Listing` page to the `Details` and vice versa, we need to create and edit the `faces-config.xml` with the `PageFlow` editor and connect these two pages together.

First, let's have a clear picture and idea about the `faces-config.xml` file and the `PageFlow` editor.

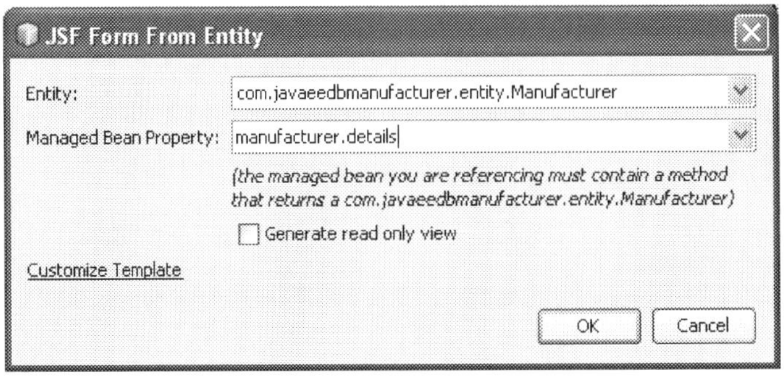

Figure 5.80. The finished JSF Form From Entity dialog box.

5.3.5.12 *Creating and Editing the faces-config.xml Configuration File*

When you create a new Java EE Web application with JSF, the JSF also creates some configuration files, and all Web-related and JSF-related components are included in the following two configuration files:

- `web.xml`—Contains general Web application configuration file.
- `faces-config.xml`—Contains the configuration of the JSF application.

The detailed functions for these two configuration files are:

- **web.xml:** JSF requires the central configuration list `web.xml` in the directory `WEB-INF` of the application. This is similar to other web applications which are based on Servlets. You must specify in `web.xml` that a `FacesServlet` is responsible for handling JSF applications. `FacesServlet` is the central controller for the JSF application, and it receives all requests for the JSF application and initializes the JSF components before the JSP is displayed.
- **faces-config.xml:** The `faces-config.xml` file allows the JSF to configure the application, managed beans, convertors, validators, and navigation.

The NetBeans IDE provides two distinct views for the faces-config.xml file: the `XML View`, which displays the XML source code, and the `PageFlow view`, which is a graphical interface that depicts JSF navigation rules defined in the faces-config.xml file.

The `PageFlow view` displays the navigation relationships between JSF pages, indicating that navigation from one JSF page to another JSF page occurs when response is passed to JSF's NavigationHandler.

Double clicking on components in the `PageFlow view` enables you to navigate directly to the source file. Likewise, if you double click on the arrow between the two components, the editor will focus on the navigation rule defined in the faces-config.xml XML view.

Now let's first create a `faces-config.xml` file for our `JavaEEDBManufacturer` application. Perform the following operations to create this configuration file:

1. Right click on our Web application `JavaEEDBManufacturer-war` and select the `New > Other` item from the pop-up menu to open the `New File` dialog.

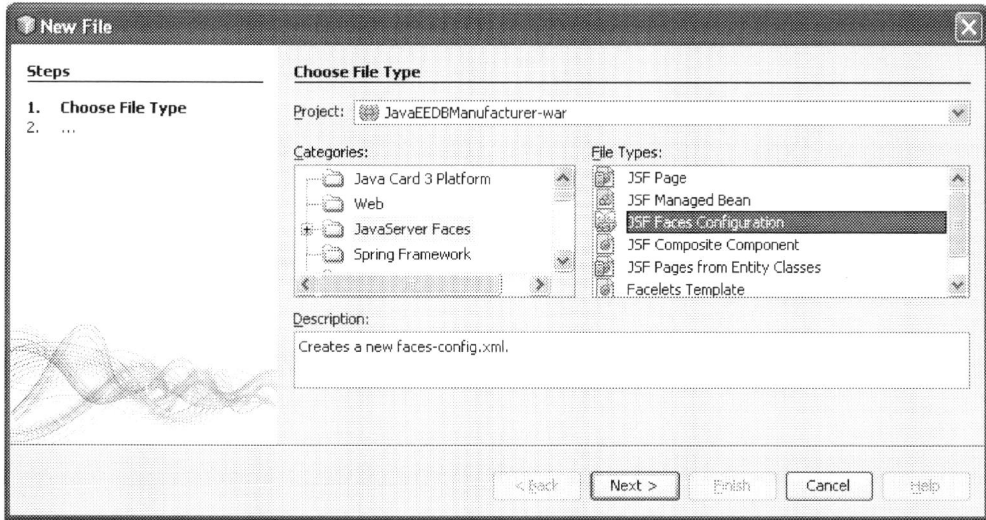

Figure 5.81. The New File dialog box.

Figure 5.82. The created faces-config.xml file.

2. Select the `JavaServer Faces` from the `Categories` list and `JSF Faces Configuration` from the `File Types` list, as shown in Figure 5.81. Click on the `Next` button to continue.
3. In the opened `New JSF Faces Configuration` dialog, enter `faces-config` into the `File Name` field as the name of this file, and click on the `Finish` button.

The newly created `faces-config.xml` file is opened and shown in Figure 5.82.

First, let's add our managed bean into this `faces-config.xml` file by perform the following operations:

1. Right click on any location inside the opened `faces-config.xml` file, and select `Insert > Managed Bean` item from the popup menu. In some cases, you may need to close and re-open the NetBeans IDE to have this `Insert` menu item available.
2. In the opened `Add Managed Bean` dialog, enter `manufacturer` into the `Bean Name` field, and click the `Browse` button to open the `Find Type` dialog. Type `Manufacturer`

Figure 5.83. The finished Add Managed Bean dialog box.

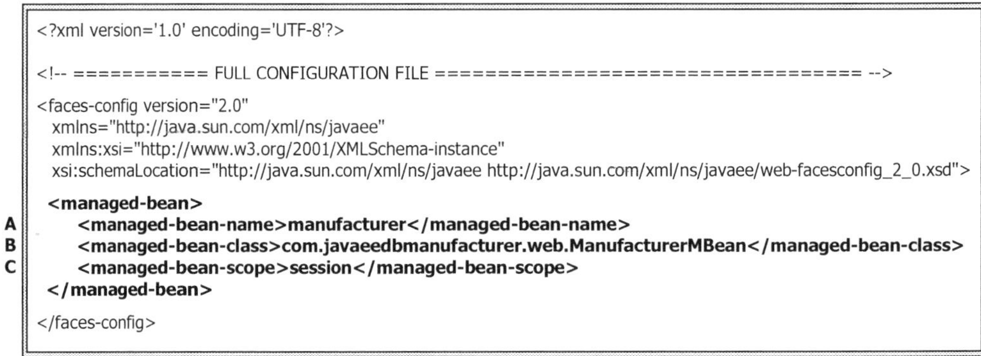

```
  <?xml version='1.0' encoding='UTF-8'?>

  <!-- =========== FULL CONFIGURATION FILE ==================================== -->

  <faces-config version="2.0"
    xmlns="http://java.sun.com/xml/ns/javaee"
    xmlns:xsi="http://www.w3.org/2001/XMLSchema-instance"
    xsi:schemaLocation="http://java.sun.com/xml/ns/javaee http://java.sun.com/xml/ns/javaee/web-facesconfig_2_0.xsd">
   <managed-bean>
A      <managed-bean-name>manufacturer</managed-bean-name>
B      <managed-bean-class>com.javaeedbmanufacturer.web.ManufacturerMBean</managed-bean-class>
C      <managed-bean-scope>session</managed-bean-scope>
   </managed-bean>
  </faces-config>
```

Figure 5.84. The added managed bean to the faces-config.xml file.

to the `Type Name` field and select the `ManufacturerMBean` item from the list, and click on the `OK` button.

3. Select the `session` from the `Scope` combo box.
4. You can enter some description for this managed bean into the `Bean Description` box if you like.

Your finished `Add Managed Bean` dialog box should match one that is shown in Figure 5.83.

Click on the `Add` button to add this `ManufacturerMBean` as our managed bean into this configuration file. Now you can find that the related XML tags have been added into this `faces-config.xml` file, which is shown in Figure 5.84. The new added codes have been highlighted in bold.

Let's have a closer look at this piece of new added codes to see how it works.

A. The name of our managed bean, `manufacturer`, is added to the managed-bean name tag.

B. The class of our managed bean, `ManufacturerMBean`, with its namespace, is added under the `managed-bean-class` tag to indicate the managed bean class used in this application.

C. The scope of this managed bean is session and has been added under the managed-bean scope tag.

Note: This faces-config.xml **file may be located at two locations: (1)** under the Web Pages\WEB-INF **folder, and (2) under the** Configuration Files **folder. It is the same file that just resides at the different locations.**

To set up navigation relationship between JSF pages, especially between the `ManufacturerList` and `ManufacturerDetails` pages in this application, we need to edit this configuration file using the `PageFlow` editor.

Now click on the `Clean and Build Main Project` button to build our modified project to cover the newly added `faces-config.xml` file.

Then double click on our new added and edited `faces-config.xml` file from either location to open this file. Click on the `PageFlow` button to open its page flow view.

Note: In some cases, you may need to close and restart the NetBeans to make this new added faces-config.xml **to have the PageFlow view.**

In the opened PageFlow view, in total, there are four JSF pages that are displayed in this configuration view: `index.jsp`, `index.xhtml`, `ManufacturerList.jsp`, and `ManufacturerDetails.jsp`, as shown in Figure 5.85.

To set up the navigation relationships between the `ManufacturerList` and `ManufacturerDetails` JSF pages, perform the following operations:

1. Move your cursor to the starting arrow location as shown in Figure 5.85 until a square appears in the `ManufacturerList.jsp` page object. Then click on this square and drag this stating arrow and point to and stop at the center of the `ManufacturerDetails.`

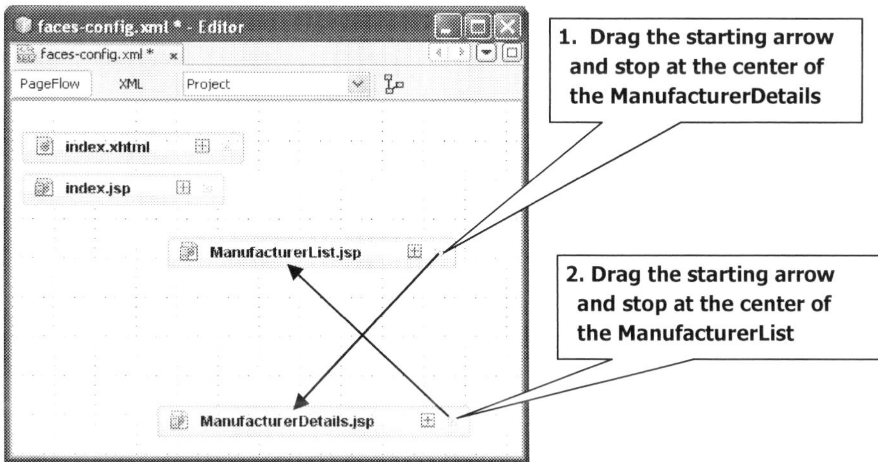

Figure 5.85. The opened PageFlow view of the faces-config.xml file.

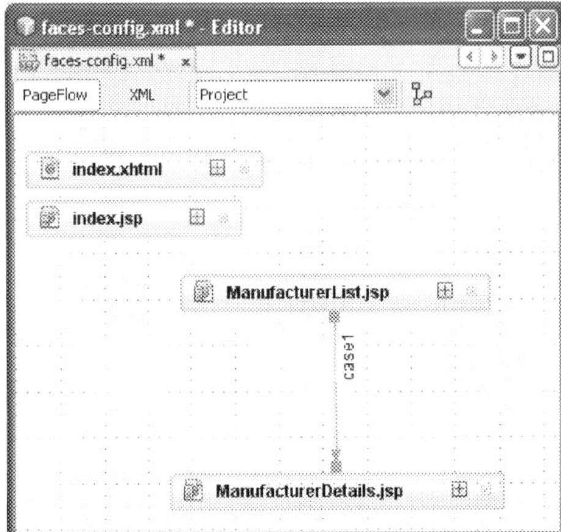

Figure 5.86. The established default navigation link.

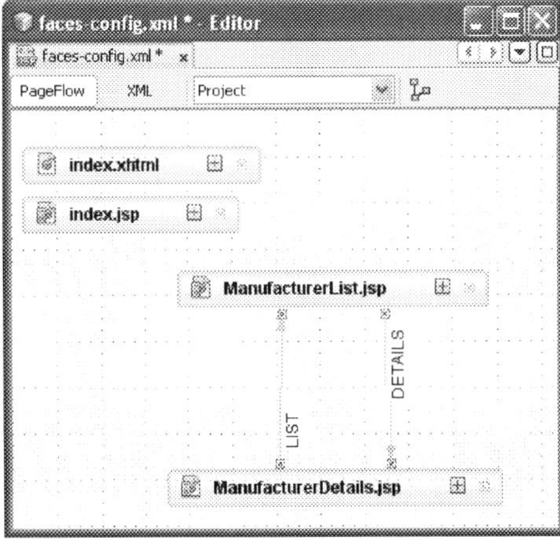

Figure 5.87. The finished PageFlow view of the JSF page objects.

`jsp`, as shown in Figure 5.85-1. A navigation link is established with the default name `case1`, as shown in Figure 5.86.

2. Double click on the default navigation link `case1` and change its name to `DETAILS`.
3. Perform a similar operation to create another navigation link from the `ManufacturerDetails` to the `ManufacturerList`, as shown in Figure 5.85-2.
4. Double click on the new established link and change its name to `LIST`. Your finished PageFlow view of two JSF page objects should match one that is shown in Figure 5.87.

Now if you click on the XML button to open the XML view of this `faces-config.xml` file, you can find that the navigation rules shown in Figure 5.88 have been added into this file. The new added codes have been highlighted in bold.

As shown in Figure 5.88, two navigation rules, which are indicted by A and B, have been added into this configuration file. The first one is from the `FacultyList` to the `FacultyDetails`, and the second is from the `FacultyDetails` to the `FacultyList`.

```
<?xml version='1.0' encoding='UTF-8'?>
<!-- =========== FULL CONFIGURATION FILE ==================================== -->
<faces-config version="2.0"
  xmlns="http://java.sun.com/xml/ns/javaee"
  xmlns:xsi="http://www.w3.org/2001/XMLSchema-instance"
  xsi:schemaLocation="http://java.sun.com/xml/ns/javaee http://java.sun.com/xml/ns/javaee/web-facesconfig_2_0.xsd">
  <!-- a normal Managed Bean -->
   <managed-bean>
      <managed-bean-name>CustomerMBean</managed-bean-name>
      <managed-bean-class>view.CustomerMBean</managed-bean-class>
      <managed-bean-scope>session</managed-bean-scope>
   </managed-bean>
A  <navigation-rule>
      <from-view-id>/ManufacturerList.jsp</from-view-id>
      <navigation-case>
         <from-outcome>DETAILS</from-outcome>
         <to-view-id>/ManufacturerDetails.jsp</to-view-id>
      </navigation-case>
   </navigation-rule>
B  <navigation-rule>
      <from-view-id>/ManufacturerDetails.jsp</from-view-id>
      <navigation-case>
         <from-outcome>LIST</from-outcome>
         <to-view-id>/ManufacturerList.jsp</to-view-id>
      </navigation-case>
   </navigation-rule>
</faces-config>
```

Figure 5.88. The newly added navigation rules.

Notes: the <from-outcome> strings LIST and DETAILS must match the return String of the list() and showDetails() methods defined in the CustomerMBean.

5.3.5.13 Editing the General Web Application Configuration File web.xml

As we mentioned in the last section, the `web.xml` file contains the central configuration list, including all configuration descriptions about the JSF pages built in the project. To include our new added `faces-config.xml` configuration file into our project, we need to add some XML tags to this `web.xml` file to enable system to know that a new edited `faces-config.xml` file has been added and will be implemented in this project.

Perform the following operations to complete this addition process:

1. Open the `web.xml` file by double clicking on it from the `Projects` window. Regularly, this file should be located at the `WEB-INF` folder or the `Configuration Files` folder.
2. On the opened `web.xml` file, add the XML tags that are shown in Figure 5.89 into this configuration file. The new added XML tags have been highlighted in bold.

Your completed `web.xml` configuration file should match one that is shown in Figure 5.89

Next, let's modify our `ManufacturerList.jsp` page to set up a connection relationship with our `ManufacturerDetails.jsp` page.

```
<?xml version="1.0" encoding="UTF-8"?>
<web-app version="3.0" xmlns="http://java.sun.com/xml/ns/javaee" xmlns:xsi="http://www.w3.org/2001/XMLSchema-
instance" xsi:schemaLocation="http://java.sun.com/xml/ns/javaee http://java.sun.com/xml/ns/javaee/web-app_3_0.xsd">
  <context-param>
    <param-name>javax.faces.PROJECT_STAGE</param-name>
    <param-value>Development</param-value>
  </context-param>
  <context-param>
    <param-name>javax.faces.CONFIG_FILES</param-name>
    <param-value>/WEB-INF/faces-config.xml</param-value>
  </context-param>
  <servlet>
    <servlet-name>Faces Servlet</servlet-name>
    <servlet-class>javax.faces.webapp.FacesServlet</servlet-class>
    <load-on-startup>1</load-on-startup>
  </servlet>
  <servlet-mapping>
    <servlet-name>Faces Servlet</servlet-name>
    <url-pattern>/faces/*</url-pattern>
  </servlet-mapping>
  <session-config>
    <session-timeout>
      30
    </session-timeout>
  </session-config>
  <welcome-file-list>
    <welcome-file>faces/index.xhtml</welcome-file>
  </welcome-file-list>
</web-app>
```

Figure 5.89. The modified general Web configuration file web.xml.

5.3.5.14 Modifying the JSF Pages to Perform Page Switching

In the last section, we have established the navigation relationships between the `ManufacturerList` and the `ManufacturerDetails` JSF pages using the navigation rules in the `faces-config.xml` file. In order to trigger those rules and switch from the `ManufacturerList` to the `ManufacturerDetails` page, we need to modify some part of the `ManufacturerList` page to accomplish this navigation. We want to use the `manufacturerID` as a connection key or link to display the detailed record for only one manufacturer based on the `manufacturerID`.

To do this modification, open the `ManufacturerList.jsp` page from the `Projects` window and replace the coding line

```
<h:outputText value="#{item. manufacturerId}"/>
```

With the following coding lines

```
<h:commandLink action="#{manufacturer.showDetails(item)}"
value="#{item.manufacturerId}"/>
```

Your modified part on the `ManufacturerList.jsp` is shown in Figure 5.90.

Next, open the `ManufacturerDetails.jsp` page and add one JSF tag to the end of this page, as shown in Figure 5.91. The newly added tag has been highlighted in bold. This command button will enable users to switch the `ManufacturerDetails` page back to the `ManufacturerList` page, and it has a similar function as that of `Back` button on a Web browser.

```
<f:view>
  <html>
    <head>
      <meta http-equiv="Content-Type" content=
      <title>JSP Page</title>
    </head>
    <body>
      <h:form>
        <h1><h:outputText value="Manufacturer Listing"/>
        <h:dataTable value="#{manufacturer.manufact        em">
          <h:column>
            <f:facet name="header">
              <h:outputText value="Manu        erId"/>
            </f:facet>

            <h:outputText value="#{item.manufacturerId}"/>

            </h:column>
          <h:column>
            <f:facet name="header">
              <h:outputText value="Name"/>
            </f:facet>
            <h:outputText value="#{item.name}"/>
          </h:column>
          ............
```

Using the following codes to replace the outputText to navigate to the ManufacturerDetails page

```
<h:commandLink action="#{manufacturer.showDetails(item)}"
               value="#{item.manufacturerId}"/>
```

Figure 5.90. The modified codes in the ManufacturerList.jsp page.

```
          ............
          <h:outputLabel value="Email:" for="email" />
          <h:inputText id="email" value="#{manufacturer.details.email}" title="Email" />
          <h:outputLabel value="Rep:" for="rep" />
          <h:inputText id="rep" value="#{manufacturer.details.rep}" title="Rep" />
        </h:panelGrid>
        <h:commandButton id="list" value="List" action="#{manufacturer.list}" />
      </h:form>

      <h1><h:outputText value="Hello World!"/></h1>
    </body>
  </html>
</f:view>
```

Figure 5.91. The modified codes for the ManufacturerDetails page.

Now we can build and run the project to test the functions of this project.

5.3.5.15 Building and Running the Entire Java EE 6 Project

At this point, we have completed all coding jobs for this project. To see the running result, first let's build the application by right clicking on our project `JavaEEDBManufacturer` and select the `Clean and Build` item, and deploy the application by right clicking on our project `JavaEEDBManufacturer`, and select the `Deploy` item.

If everything is fine, open a Web browser and go to the Manufacturer listing page at URL, http://localhost:8082/JavaEEDBManufacturer-war/faces/ManufacturerList.jsp. You can find that all manufacturer IDs have been underscored. Click on the `Manufacturer ID` on the first row in the table to open the `ManufacturerDetails` page to query and display the detailed record for this manufacturer ID only.

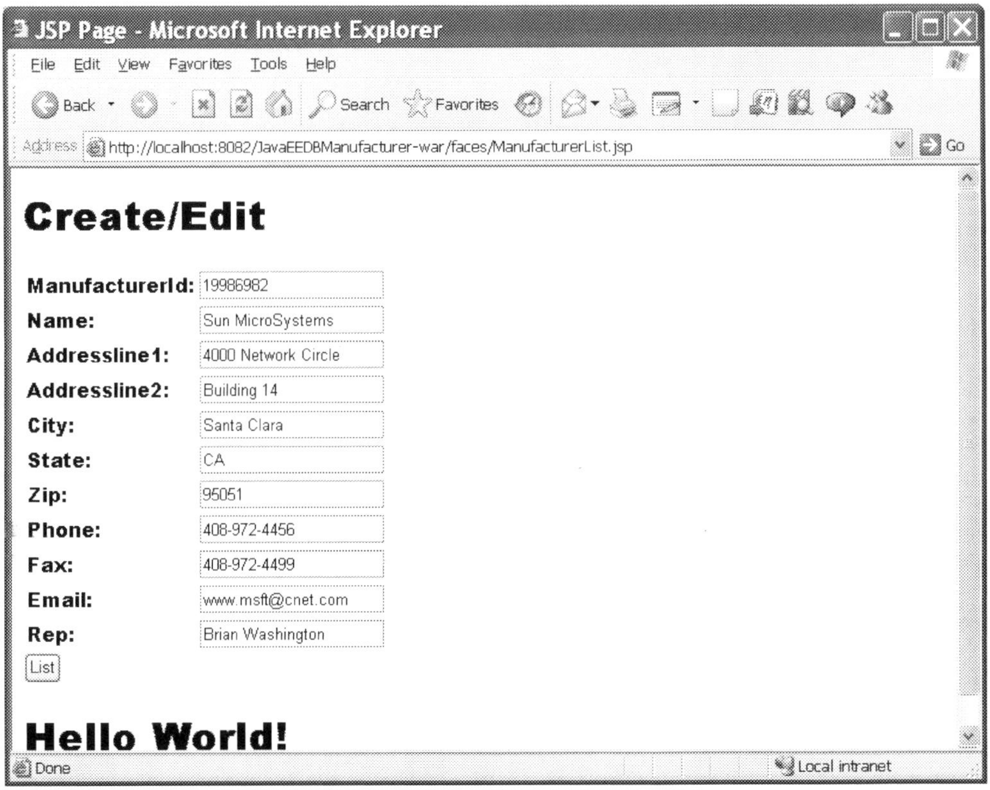

Figure 5.92. A running result of the project JavaEEDBManufacturer.

A running result of this project with a manufacturer ID of 19986982 is shown in Figure 5.92. You can click on the `List` button to return to the `ManufacturerList` page and reselect some other manufacturerID to see more results.

A complete Java EE 6 Database-related project `JavaEEDBManufacturer` can be found from the folder `DBProjects\Chapter 5` that is located at the Wiley ftp site (refer to Figure 1.2 in Chapter 1).

You can download this project from that site and run it on your computer. However, you have to make sure that you have installed all required software before you can run this project on your computer:

1. Java Enterprise Edition 6
2. Glassfish v3
3. NetBeans IDE 6.8 or higher version of IDE.

For your convenience, another complete Java EE 6 application project `JavaEEDBFaculty` has been built and can be found from the folder `DBProjects\Chapter 5` that is located at the Wiley ftp site (refer to Figure 1.2 in Chapter 1). The difference between this `JavaEEDBFaculty` project and the `JavaEEDBManufacturer` project is that a SQL Server database `CSE_DEPT` we built in Chapter 2 is used as the data source for the `JavaEEDBFaculty` project.

To use a different data source in Java EE 6 applications, the only point to be noted is that you have to add the associated database driver to the Web application file; in that application, it is `JavaEEDBFaculty-war`. Refer to Appendix K to get a more detailed description about the development process for this kind of application.

Next let's take care of building and implementing a Java Maven project.

5.3.6 Build a Maven Project

The Maven is exactly a project building and management tool and widely implemented in portable and cross-platform applications. In this section, we try to develop a Maven-based application to illustrate how to use this kind of application to access a data source to perform data actions against different databases.

5.3.6.1 Introduction to Maven

Apache Maven is a tool used to build and manage software projects. Based on the concept of a project object model (POM), Maven can manage a project's building, reporting, and documentation from a central piece of information with the plug-ins strategies. When you use Maven, you describe your project using a well-defined POM, Maven can then apply cross-cutting logic from a set of shared or custom-built plug-in.

Based on the definition of the Maven, it has two major functionalities: project building and project management.

Like other traditional project building tools, such as ASP.NET, ADO.NET, and Apache Ant, Maven has all of those functionalities to help developers to build and develop a professional application without problem. However, compared with those tools, Maven has the advantage in managing projects using a common interface. By using this common interface, the developers can save significant time to build and manage new projects with the help of the dependency management and reuse of common build logic through plug-ins.

Another benefit of using the Maven to build projects is that the Maven provides a so-called convention over configuration technique. By using this technique, all components and files you built in your project can be placed in certain default locations. For example, the source code is assumed to be in `${basedir}/src/main/java`, and resources are assumed to be in `${basedir}/src/main/resources`. Tests are assumed to be in `${basedir}/src/test`, and a project is assumed to produce a JAR file. Maven's adoption of convention over configuration goes farther than just simple directory locations; Maven's core plug-ins apply a common set of conventions for compiling source code, packaging distributions, generating web sites, and many other processes.

Maven has plug-ins for everything from compiling Java code, to generating reports, to deploying to an application server. Maven has abstracted common build tasks into plug-ins which are maintained centrally and shared universally. Most of the intelligence of Maven is implemented in the plug-ins, and the plug-ins are retrieved from the Maven Repository. In fact, when you first time run the mvn install command with a brand-new Maven installation, the Maven will retrieve most of the core Maven plug-ins from the Central Maven Repository.

Maven maintains a model of a project. When you build a Maven project, you are not just compiling source code into byte codes; instead, you are developing a description of a software project and assigning a unique set of coordinates to a project. With a model of a project, the following benefits can be obtained:

- **Dependency Management**
  Since a project is defined by a unique set of coordinates consisting of a group identifier, an artifact identifier, and a version, therefore projects can now use these coordinates to declare dependencies.
- **Remote Repositories**
  We can use the coordinates defined in the Maven POM to create repositories of Maven artifacts.
- **Universal Reuse of Build Logic**
  Plug-ins contain logic that works with the descriptive data and configuration parameters defined in POM; they are not designed to operate upon specific files in known locations.
- **Tool Portability/Integration**
  Tools like Eclipse and NetBeans now have a common place to find information about a project. Before the Maven, every IDE had a different way to store what was essentially a custom POM. Maven has standardized this description, while each IDE continues to maintain custom project files.

An artifact can be considered as an interface that contains all descriptions and properties of a project dependency built by the system or developers, and it can be stored in either local or remote repositories.

The first thing you will do when creating a Maven project is to select a `group ID` and an `artifact ID`. A `group ID` is used to describe the entire product, and `artifact ID`s are the basis of filenames for each item you distribute. The `artifact ID` may or may not overlap the `group ID`.

A typical Maven project structure or convention over configuration is shown in Figure 5.93.

```
/
+- src/
|   +- main/
|   |  +- java/
|   |  |  +- ...
|   |  +- resources/
|   |     +- ...
|   +- test/
|   |  +- java/
|   |  |  +- ...
|   |  +- resources/
|   |     +- ...
|   +- site/
|      +- xdoc/
|         +- ...
+- target/
|   +- ...
+- project.xml
+- README.txt
+- LICENSE.txt
```

Figure 5.93. A typical Maven project structure.

There are just two subdirectories of this structure: src and target. The only other directories are metadata like CVS or .svn, and any subprojects in a multiproject build.

The src directory contains all source materials for building the project, its site, and so on. It also contains a subdirectory for each type: main for the main build artifact, test for the unit test code and `resources`, site, and so on.

The target directory is used to house all outputs of the build.

Within artifact-producing source directories, such as main and test, there is one directory for the language java under which the normal package hierarchy exists, and one for resources under which the structure that is copied to the target *classpath* provides the default resource definition.

At the top-level files descriptive of the project, there is a project.xml file and any properties, maven.xml or build.xml if using Ant. In addition, there are textual documents meant for the user to be able to read immediately on receiving the source: README.txt, LICENSE.txt, and BUILDING.txt, and so on.

Generally, a Maven project should have the key files or components in the following structure:

- **src/main/java:** Contains handwritten Java code.
- **src/main/resources:** All non-Java handwritten code, including Workflow and Xtext grammar.
- **target/generated/java:** Contains generated code.

In the following sections, we want to use NetBeans IDE to create a Java Swing application from a Maven archetype. The application uses the Hibernate framework as the persistence layer to retrieve plain old Java objects (POJOs) from a sample relational database. We try to demonstrate how to use wizards provided in the IDE to help you create the necessary Hibernate files and add Hibernate dependencies to the POM. After creating the Java objects and configuring the application to use Hibernate, you can add a GUI interface for searching and displaying the data from the Customer table in the JavaDB default sample database.

Before we can start to build a Maven project to access a data source to perform certain data actions against databases, first we need to install and configure the building and developing environment for Maven applications.

5.3.6.2 Introduction to Hibernate Framework

Hibernate is an object-relational mapping (ORM) library for the Java language, and it provides a framework for mapping an object-oriented domain model to a traditional relational database. Unlike the JPA, Hibernate solves object-relational impedance mismatch problems by replacing direct persistence-related database accesses with high-level object handling functions.

One of the most primary features of using Hibernate is the mapping from Java classes to database tables and from Java data types to SQL data types. Hibernate also provides data query and retrieval facilities. Hibernate generates the SQL calls and relieves the developer from manual result set handling and object conversion, keeping the application portable to all supported SQL databases, with database portability delivered at very little performance overhead.

Hibernate provides the ORM operational functions with the following properties:

1. Mapping
2. Persistence
3. Hibernate Query Language (HQL)
4. Integration
5. Entities and Components
6. Application Programming Interface (API)

5.3.6.2.1 Mapping Mapping Java classes to database tables is accomplished through the configuration of an XML file or by using Java Annotation. When using an XML file, Hibernate can generate skeletal source code for the persistence classes. This is unnecessary when annotation is used. Hibernate can use the XML file or the annotation to maintain the database schema.

Facilities to arrange one-to-many and many-to-many relationships between classes are provided. In addition to managing association between objects, Hibernate can also manage reflexive associations where an object has a one-to-many relationship with other instances of its own type.

Hibernate supports the mapping of custom value types. This makes the following scenarios possible:

- Overriding the default SQL type that Hibernate chooses when mapping a column to a property.
- Mapping Java Enum to columns as if they were regular properties.
- Mapping a single property to multiple columns.

5.3.6.2.2 Persistence Hibernate provides transparent persistence for Plain Old Java Objects (POJOs). The only strict requirement for a persistent class is a no-argument constructor, not necessarily `public`. Proper behavior in some applications also requires special attention to the `equals()` and `hashCode()` methods.

Collections of data objects are typically stored in Java collection objects, such as Set and List. Java generics, introduced in Java 5, are supported. Hibernate can be configured to lazy load associated collections. Lazy loading is the default as of Hibernate 3.

Related objects can be configured to `cascade` operations from one to the other. For example, a parent such as an Album object can be configured to cascade its save and/or delete operation to its child Track objects. This can reduce development time and ensure referential integrity. A `dirty checking` feature avoids unnecessary database write actions by performing SQL updates only on the modified fields of persistent objects.

5.3.6.2.3 Hibernate Query Language (HQL) Hibernate provides a SQL-inspired language called Hibernate Query Language (HQL) that allows SQL-like queries to be written against Hibernate's data objects. `Criteria Queries` are provided as an object-oriented alternative to HQL.

5.3.6.2.4 Integration Hibernate can be used both in Java standalone applications and in Java EE applications using Servlets or EJB session beans. It can also be included as a feature in other programming languages. For example, Adobe integrated Hibernate into version 9 of ColdFusion that runs on J2EE app servers with an abstraction layer of new functions and syntax added into ColdFusion Markup Language (CFML).

5.3.6.2.5 Entities and Components In Hibernate jargon (jargon is terminology which is especially defined in relationship to a specific activity, profession, or group), an `entity` is a standalone object in Hibernate's persistent mechanism that can be manipulated independently of other objects. In contrast, a `component` is subordinate to other entities and can be manipulated only with respect to other entities. For example, an Album object may represent an entity, but the Tracks object associated with the Album objects would represent a `component` of the Album entity if it is assumed that Tracks can only be saved or retrieved from the database through the Album object.

5.3.6.2.6 Application Programming Interface (API) The Hibernate API is provided in the Java package `org.hibernate`.

1. The `org.hibernate.SessionFactory` interface.
   References immutable and thread-safe object creating new Hibernate sessions. Hibernate-based applications are usually designed to make use only of a single instance of the class implementing this interface and often exposed using a singleton design pattern.
2. The `org.hibernate.Session` interface
   Represents a Hibernate session, such as the main point of the manipulation, performed on the database entities. The latter activities include (among the other things) managing the persistence state (transient, persisted, detached) of the objects, fetching the persisted ones from the database, and the management of the transaction demarcation.

A session is intended to last as long as the logical transaction on the database. Due to the latter feature, Session implementations are not expected to be thread-safe, nor to be used by multiple clients.

5.3.6.3 Installing and Configuring the Apache Maven

Since Maven is a Java tool, so before you can download and install Maven in your computer, you must have Java installed in order to proceed. More precisely, you need a JDK, since the JRE is not sufficient to support Maven.

The current version of Maven is 2.2.1, and it is distributed in several formats for your convenience. As you know, the Maven stored and distributed its artifacts in different repositories, either local or remote ones. Regularly, you can develop and build your own custom repositories inside your projects and with those sharing your project easily to get the right settings out of the box. However, you may need to use an alternative mirror for a particular repository without changing the project files. In that case, we encourage you to configure a Maven repository mirror closer to their location.

Some reasons to use a mirror are:

1. There is a synchronized mirror on the Internet that is geographically closer and faster.
2. You want to replace a particular repository with your own internal repository which you have greater control over.
3. You want to run maven proxy to provide a local cache to a mirror and need to use its URL instead.

To configure a mirror of a given repository, you can provide it in your settings file `${user.home}/.m2/settings.xml`, give the new repository its own `id` and `URL`, and specify the `mirrorOf` setting that is the `ID` of the repository you are using a mirror of.

We recommend downloading and installing Maven with its zip format since it is one of the most popular styles in traditional software installation.

To begin this downloading, go to the site http://maven.apache.org/ and click on the `Download` item from the left column under the `Get Maven` category. Select the apache-maven-2.2.1-bin.zip file under the `Mirrors` column. Click and select the suggested mirror to start.

It is highly recommended to first save this file to your `Temp` folder, and then you can unzip and install this software to your computer.

Perform the following operations to install Maven to your computer:

1. Unzip the distribution archive, that is, `apache-maven-2.2.1-bin.zip` to the directory you wish to install Maven 2.2.1. This installation assumes that you chose the `C:\Program Files\Apache Software Foundation` as this directory. The subdirectory `apache-maven-2.2.1` will be created from the archive. Perform the following operations to complete this unzip process:

   A. Open the Windows Explorer and create a new folder `Apache Software Foundation` under the `C:\Program Files` folder.

   B. Go to the folder you just downloaded the Maven software; in this case, it is `Temp` folder. Right click on the downloaded `apache-maven-2.2.1-bin.zip` and select the `Extract All...` menu item from the popup menu.

   C. Browse to the folder `C:\Program Files\Apache Software Foundation` and click on the `Extract` button.

2. Add the `M2_HOME` environment variable by performing the following operations:

   A. Open the `Control Panel` and click on the `Performance and Maintenance` link, and double click on the `System` icon to open the `System Properties` window

   B. Select the `Advanced` tab and the `Environment Variables` button. Click on the `New` button under the `User variables` list. On the opened `New User Variable` dialog, enter M2_HOME to the `Variable name` field and `C:\Program Files\Apache Software Foundation\apache-maven-2.2.1` to the `Variable value` field. Be sure to omit any quotation marks around the path even if it contains spaces. Your finished `New User Variable` dialog box should match one that is shown in Figure 5.94.

   C. Click on the `OK` button to complete this process.

3. In the same dialog, add the `M2` environment variable in the user variables with the value `%M2_HOME%\bin`, as shown in Figure 5.95. Click on the `OK` buttons to complete this process.

New User Variable

Variable name: M2_HOME

Variable value: C:\Program Files\Apache Software Foundal

OK Cancel

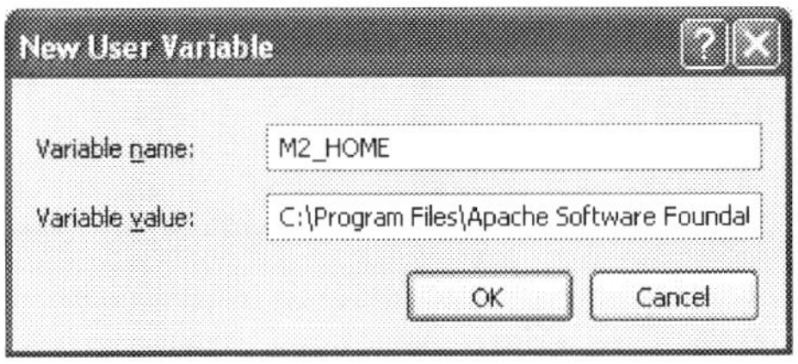

Figure 5.94. The finished New User Variable dialog box.

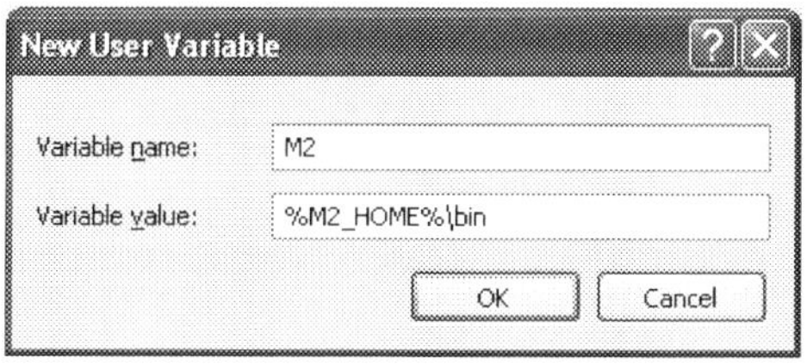

Figure 5.95. The added M2 environment variable.

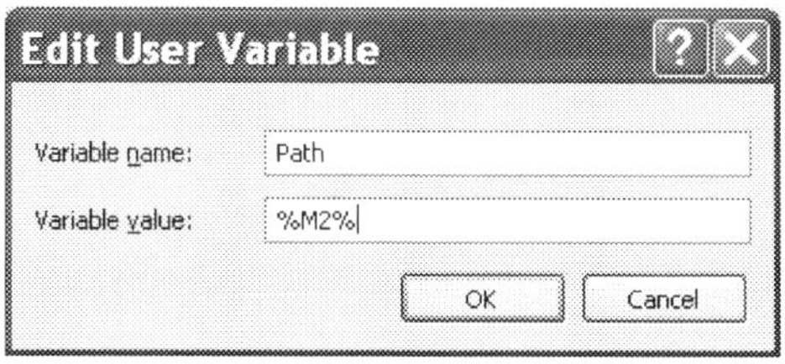

Figure 5.96. The added Path environment variable.

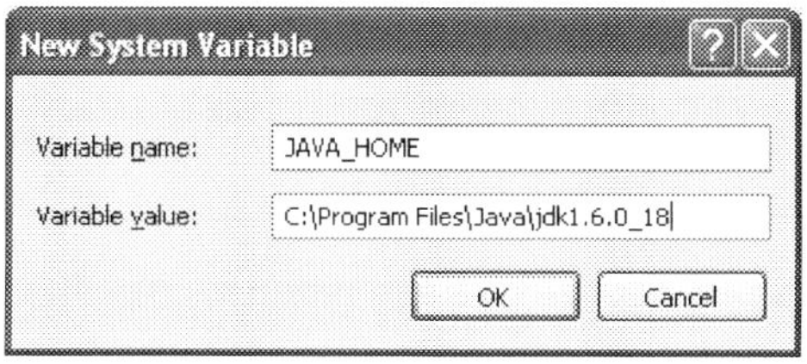

Figure 5.97. The newly added JAVA_HOME path.

4. *Optional:* In the same dialog, add the MAVEN_OPTS environment variable in the user variables to specify JVM properties, such as the value `-Xms256m` or `-Xmx512m`.. This environment variable can be used to supply extra options to Maven.
5. In the same dialog, update or create the `Path` environment variable in the user variables and prepend the value %M2% to add Maven available in the command line, as shown in Figure 5.96.
6. In the same dialog, make sure that JAVA_HOME exists in your `User variables` or in the `System variables`, and it is set to the default location of your Java JDK, `C:\Program Files\Java\jdk1.6.0_17`, and that %JAVA_HOME%`\bin` is in your `Path` environment variable. To do that check, select the `Path` variable from either the `User variables` or `System variables` list, and click on the `Edit` button to open the whole path. If you cannot find those path variables, perform the following operations to add them:
   - **A.** From the `System variables` list, select the `Path` variable and click on the `New` button to open the `New System Variable` dialog box.
   - **B.** Enter JAVA_HOME into the `Variable name` field and `C:\Program Files\Java \jdk1.6.0_17` to the `Variable value` field, as shown in Figure 5.97.
   - **C.** Click on the `OK` button to close this dialog box.

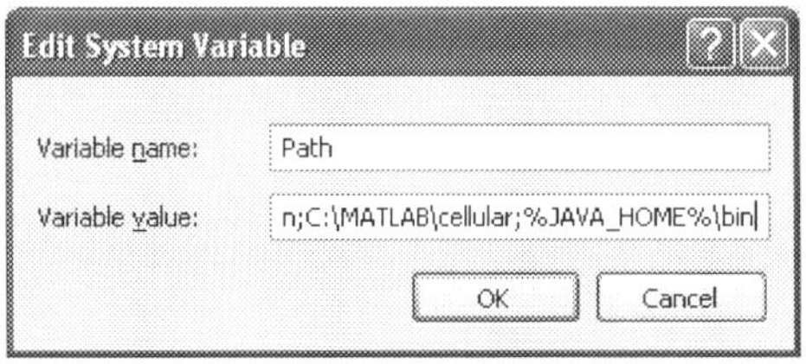

Edit System Variable

Variable name: Path

Variable value: n;C:\MATLAB\cellular;%JAVA_HOME%\bin

OK Cancel

Figure 5.98. The added JAVA_HOME path variable.

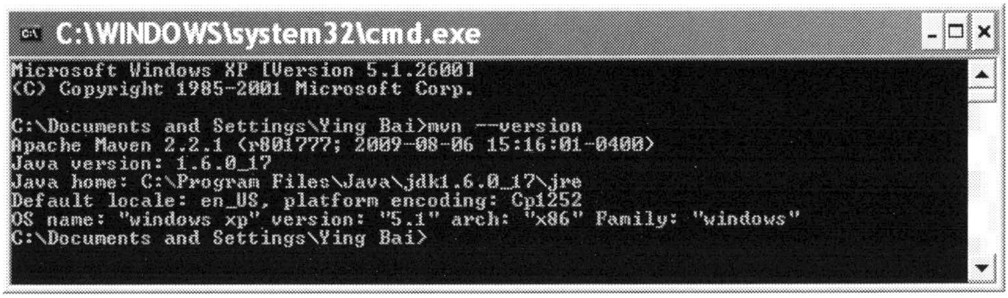

```
C:\WINDOWS\system32\cmd.exe
Microsoft Windows XP [Version 5.1.2600]
(C) Copyright 1985-2001 Microsoft Corp.

C:\Documents and Settings\Ying Bai>mvn --version
Apache Maven 2.2.1 (r801777; 2009-08-06 15:16:01-0400)
Java version: 1.6.0_17
Java home: C:\Program Files\Java\jdk1.6.0_17\jre
Default locale: en_US, platform encoding: Cp1252
OS name: "windows xp" version: "5.1" arch: "x86" Family: "windows"
C:\Documents and Settings\Ying Bai>
```

Figure 5.99. A running result of the checking of the installed Maven tool.

D. To add the %JAVA_HOME%\bin to the Path environment variable under the System variables list, select the Path from the System variables list and click on the Edit button to open the Edit System Variable dialog. Move your cursor to the end of the path environment variable, and type a semicolon (;) and enter %JAVA_HOME%\bin, as shown in Figure 5.98.

E. Click on the OK buttons to close this dialog and the System Properties window.

At this point, we have finished installing and configuring the Maven in your computer. Before we can continue, let's first test this installation and configuration. Open a new command prompt and run mvn -version to verify that it is correctly installed. A sample of running result is shown in Figure 5.99.

5.3.6.4 Configuring Maven Inside the NetBeans IDE

If this is your first Maven project, you need to check the Maven configuration settings in the Options item under the Tools menu item in the NetBeans IDE 6.8. To complete this configuration, you should have Maven installed on your local system. Refer to the last section to complete this installation if you have not done that.

Another point to be noted is the Hibernate component, since we need to use this framework as the persistence to access the data in a data source. Perform the following operations to check and configure Maven and Hibernate framework:

1. Go to Tools > Options menu item to open the Options dialog box.
2. Click on the Maven tab from the opened dialog box.
3. Make sure that your Local Repository is the default location.
4. Click on the OK button to close this dialog box.

5. Go to `Tools > Plugins` menu item to open the `Plugins` dialog box.
6. Click on the `Installed` tab to open a list that contains all installed components for your NetBeans IDE. Make sure that the following components are in this list, which means that they have been installed in your IDE:

   A. Maven
   B. Ant
   C. Hibernate

   If any component is missed from this list, you need to perform another `Plugin` operation to add each of the missed component.
7. To add a missed component, click on the `Available Plugins` tab to open all available components that can be plug-ined.
8. Browse down the list and select the missed component by checking the associated checkbox, and click on the `Install` button to add this component to the system.
9. Follow the instructions on the screens to finish this installation.

The artifacts that are used by Maven to build all your projects are stored in your local Maven repository. When an artifact is declared as a project dependency, the artifact is downloaded to your local repository from one of the registered remote repositories.

Several well-known indexed Maven repositories are registered and listed in the repository browser by default. The registered repositories contain most of the public artifacts necessary for users to build their projects. In most cases, it does not need to register any additional repositories unless your project requires artifacts found only in a private repository.

You can use the `Maven Repository Browser` to view the contents of your local and remote repositories. Any artifact that is in your local or remote repositories can be added as a project dependency. You can expand the `Local Repository` node to see the artifacts that are present locally. The artifacts listed under the remote repository nodes can be added as project dependencies, but not all of them are present locally. They are only added to the `Local Repository` when they are declared as project dependencies.

Perform the following operations to open the `Maven Repository Browser`:

1. Choose `Window > Other > Maven Repository Browser` from the main menu.
2. When your cursor is over an artifact, the IDE displays a tooltip with the artifact's coordinates, as shown in Figure 5.100. You can view additional details about an artifact by double clicking the artifact's JAR file in the browser.
3. You can search for an artifact by clicking the `Find` button in the toolbar of the `Maven Repository Browser` or by using the `Quicksearch` textfield in the main toolbar.

A sample of using the `Maven Repository Browser` to view the default local repository is shown in Figure 5.100.

Now let's start to build a Maven project that can be used to access some data source to perform certain data actions against databases.

5.3.6.5 Creating a Maven Database Application Project

Support for Maven is fully integrated in starting in NetBeans IDE 6.8. You can create applications from the bundled Maven archetypes or from archetypes in remote

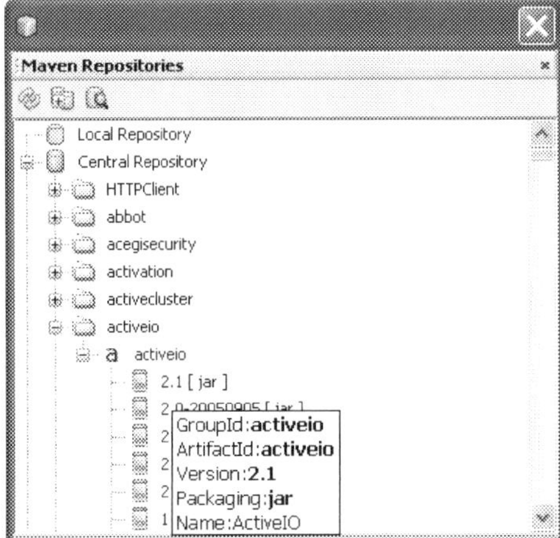

Figure 5.100. A sample view the default local repository.

repositories in the `New Project` wizard. The `Maven Repository Browser` enables you to explore your local and remote Maven repositories, examine artifacts, and add project dependencies to the project's POM.

In this section, we will create a simple Java Swing application project `JavaMavenDBApp`. We will create the project from one of the bundled Maven archetypes and then modify the default project settings.

We can use the `New Project` wizard to create a Maven project from a Maven archetype. The NetBeans IDE includes several archetypes for common NetBeans project types, but we can also locate and choose archetypes in remote repositories in the wizard. In this application, we will use the Maven Quickstart Archetype as the project template.

Perform the following operations to create this new Maven project:

1. Choose `File > New Project` (Ctrl-Shift-N).
2. Select `Maven Project` from the `Maven` category.
3. Click on the `Next` button to continue.
4. Select `Maven Quickstart Archetype` from the opened `New Project` dialog box, and click on the `Next` button.
5. Type `JavaMavenDBApp` for the project name and set the project location.
6. Change the default `Group Id` to `com.mymaven` and keep the `Version` unchanged.
7. The `Group Id` and `Version` will be used as the coordinates for the artifact in the local repository when we build the project.
8. Keep the default Package unchanged and click on the `Finish` button to complete this creation of the new Maven project process.

Your finished new Maven project `JavaMavenDBApp` should match one that is shown in Figure 5.101.

After we create a Maven project using the wizard, the default project properties are based on the archetype. In some cases, we may need to modify the default properties

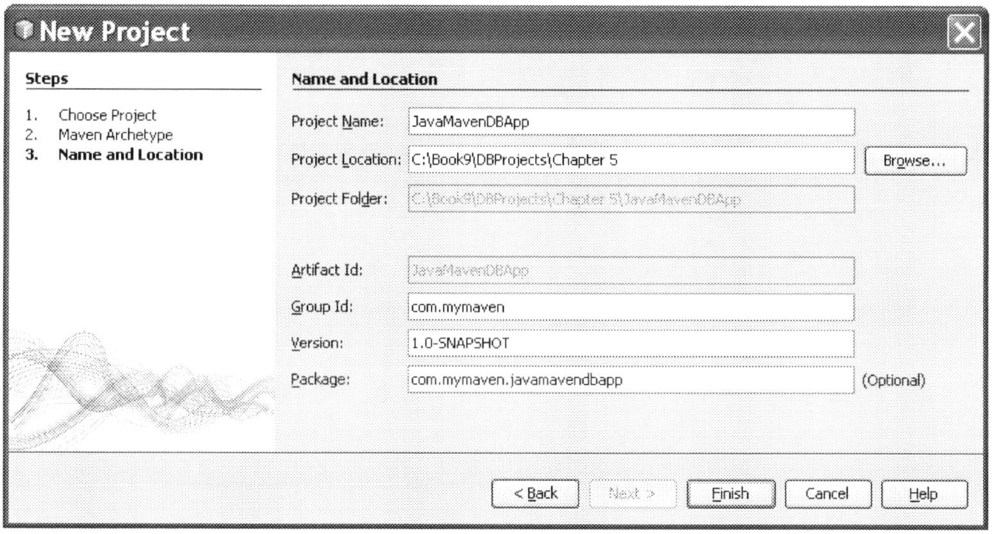

Figure 5.101. The completed dialog of creation of new Maven project.

according to our system and the project's requirements. For example, for this project, we want to make sure that the Source level is set to 1.5 because the project uses annotations.

Perform the following operations to set up this source level:

1. Right click on our new project node and choose the `Properties` menu item.
2. Select the `Sources` category from the `Properties` window.
3. Select `1.5` from the drop-down list at the `Source/Binary Format` property.
4. Select `UTF-8` from the drop-down list at the `Encoding` property.
5. Click on the `OK` button to close this dialog.

Next, let's handle adding the Hibernate framework to our project since we need it to interface to our data source.

5.3.6.6 Adding Hibernate Files and Dependencies

To add support for Hibernate, we need to make the Hibernate libraries available by declaring the necessary artifacts as dependencies in the POM. The NetBeans IDE includes wizards to help us to create the Hibernate files we need in our project. We can use the wizards provided by the NetBeans IDE to create a Hibernate configuration file and a utility helper class. If we create the Hibernate configuration file using a wizard, the NetBeans IDE will automatically update the POM to add the Hibernate dependencies to the project.

We can add dependencies to the project in the `Projects` window or by editing `pom.xml` directly.

To add a dependency in the `Projects` window,

1. Right click on the `Libraries` node from the `Projects` window.
2. Choose the `Add Dependency` item from the pop-up menu to open the `Add Dependency` dialog box.
3. When a dependency is added into the project, the IDE updates the POM and downloads any required artifacts to the local repository that are not already present locally.

To add a dependency by editing the `pom.xml` file directly,

1. Open the file by expanding the `Project Files` node in the `Projects` window.
2. Double clicking on the `pom.xml` item.

First, let's create the Hibernate configuration file for our project.

5.3.6.6.1 Creating the Hibernate Configuration File The Hibernate configuration file, hibernate.cfg.xml, contains information about the database connection, resource mappings, and other connection properties. When we create a Hibernate configuration file using a wizard, we need to specify the database connection by choosing our data source from a list of database connection registered with the NetBeans IDE. When generating the configuration file, the NetBeans IDE automatically adds the connection details and dialect information based on the selected database connection. The NetBeans IDE also automatically modifies the POM to add the required Hibernate dependencies. After creating the configuration file, we can edit the file using the multiview editor, or edit the XML directly in the XML editor.

Perform the following operations to complete this editing:

1. Open the `Services` window and right click on the JavaDB Sample database connection URL `jdbc:derby://localhost:1527/sample [app on APP]`, and choose the `Connect` item.
2. Right click on the `Source Packages` node from the `Projects` window and choose `New > Other` to open the `New File` wizard.
3. Select `Hibernate` from the `Categories` list, and `Hibernate Configuration Wizard` from the `File Types` list. Click on the `Next` button to continue.
4. Keep the default file name hibernate.cfg unchanged.
5. Click on the `Browse` button and specify the src/main/resources directory as the `Folder` location. Click on the `Next` button to continue.
6. Select the `jdbc/sample` database connection URL in the `Database Connection` drop down list, and then click on the `Finish` button.

Your finished `New Hibernate Configuration Wizard` should match one that is shown in Figure 5.102.

When you click on the `Finish` button, the NetBeans IDE opens the `hibernate.cfg.xml` in the editor. The configuration file contains information about a single database.

By expanding the `Libraries` node in the `Projects` window, you can see that the NetBeans IDE added the required Hibernate artifacts as dependencies, as shown in Figure 5.103. The NetBeans IDE lists all direct and transitive dependencies required to

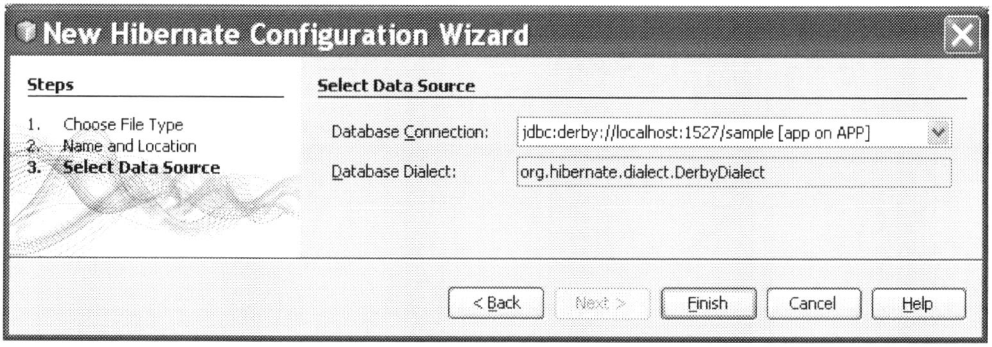

Figure 5.102. The finished New Hibernate Configuration Wizard.

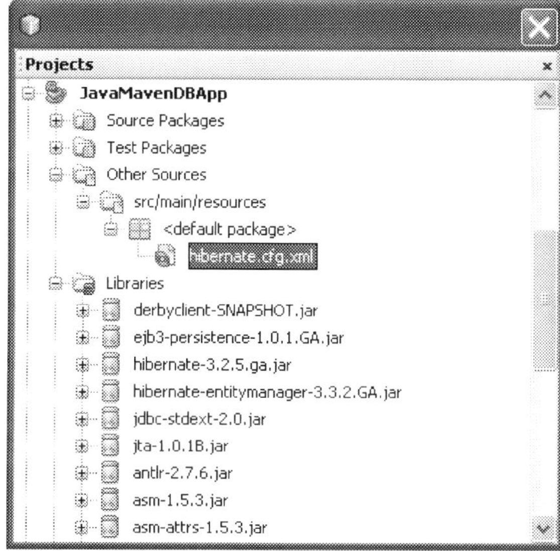

Figure 5.103. The added Hibernate artifacts by NetBeans IDE.

compile the project under the `Libraries` node. The artifacts that are direct dependencies, which mean that those dependencies are specified in the project's POM, are indicated by color JAR icons. An artifact is in gray color if it is a transitive dependency, or an artifact that is the dependency of one or more direct dependency.

We can also view details of artifacts by right clicking a JAR and choosing `View Artifact Details`. The `Artifact Viewer` contains tabs that provide details about the selected artifact. For example, the `Basic` tab provides details about the artifact's coordinates and available versions. The `Graph` tab provides a visual representation of the dependencies of the selected artifact. An example of a detailed view of `hibernate-3.2.5.ga.jar` is shown in Figure 5.104.

Next, let's modify the Hibernate configuration file to make it match to our application.

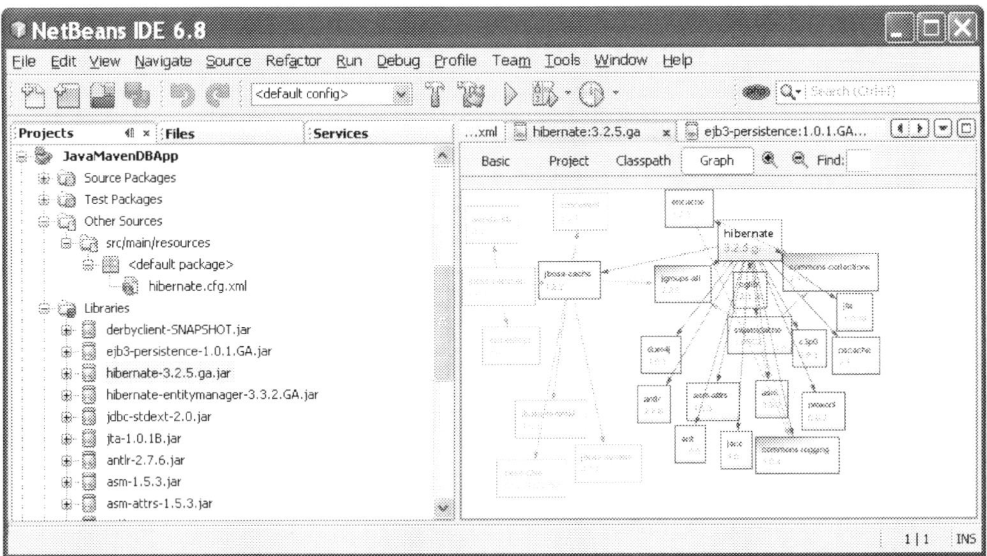

Figure 5.104. An example detailed view of the `hibernate-3.2.5.ga.jar` artifact.

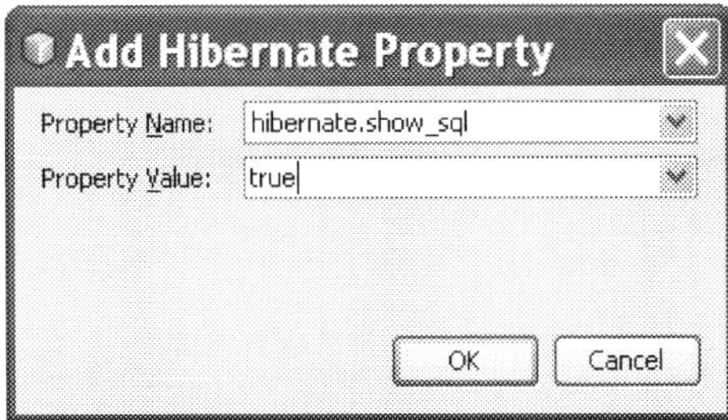

Figure 5.105. The finished Add Hibernate Property dialog box.

5.3.6.6.2 Modifying the Hibernate Configuration File In this section, we will edit the default properties specified in `hibernate.cfg.xml` file to enable debug logging for SQL statements.

Perform the following operations to complete this modification:

1. Open `hibernate.cfg.xml` in the `Design` tab by expanding the file nodes `src > main > resources` in the `Files` window and double clicking on the `hibernate.cfg.xml`.
2. Expand the `Configuration Properties` node under `Optional Properties`.
3. Click on the Add button to open the `Add Hibernate Property` dialog box.
4. In the dialog box, select the `hibernate.show_sql` property and set the value to `true`. Your finished dialog should match one that is shown in Figure 5.105.

This will enable the debug logging of the SQL statements.

If you click on the `XML` tab in the editor, you can see the file in XML view. Your modified Hibernate configuration file should look like that shown in Figure 5.106. You

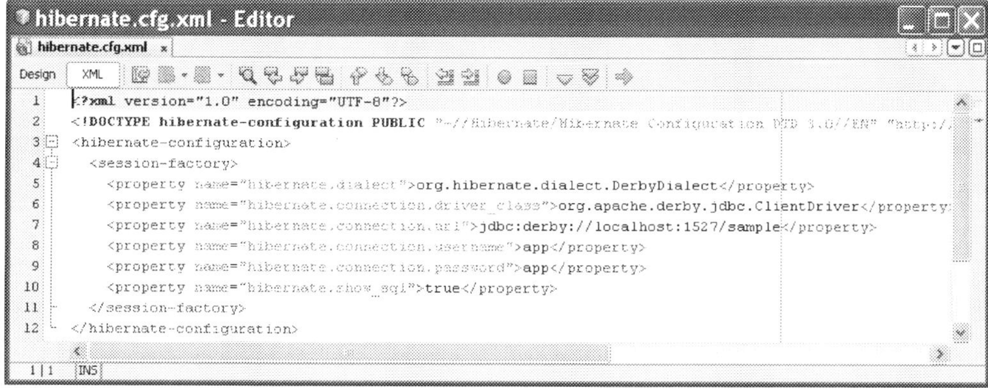

Figure 5.106. The modified Hibernate configuration file.

can save all changes and modifications to the file by selecting the `File > Save All` menu item.

Later, on when you run this project, you will be able to see the SQL query printed in the NetBeans IDE's Output window.

Now let's create the Hibernate helper class file to handle startup and accessing Hibernate's `SessionFactory` to obtain a Session object.

5.3.6.6.3 Creating the HibernateUtil.java Helper File To use the Hibernate framework, we need to create a helper class that handles startup and that accesses Hibernate's SessionFactory to obtain a Session object. The class calls Hibernate's configure() method, loads the hibernate.cfg.xml configuration file, and then builds the SessionFactory to obtain the Session object.

In this section, we will use the `New File` wizard to create the helper class file HibernateUtil.java. Perform the following operations to create this helper class file:

1. Right click on the `Source Packages` node in the `Projects` window and select `New > Other` menu item to open the `New File` wizard.
2. Select `Hibernate` from the `Categories` list and `HibernateUtil.java` from the `File Types` list, and then click on the `Next` button.
3. Type `HibernateUtil` for the class name and `customer.util` as the package name, as shown in Figure 5.107. Click on the `Finish` button.

Next, let's create Hibernate mapping files and related Java classes to perform the data actions against the default JavaDB sample database.

5.3.6.7 Generating Hibernate Mapping Files and Java Classes

In this section, we will use a plain old Java object (POJO), `Customer.java`, to represent the data in the table `Customer` in the JavaDB sample database. The class specifies the fields for the columns in the tables and uses simple setters and getters to retrieve and write the data. To map `Customer.java` to the `Customer` table, we can use a Hibernate mapping file or use annotations in the class.

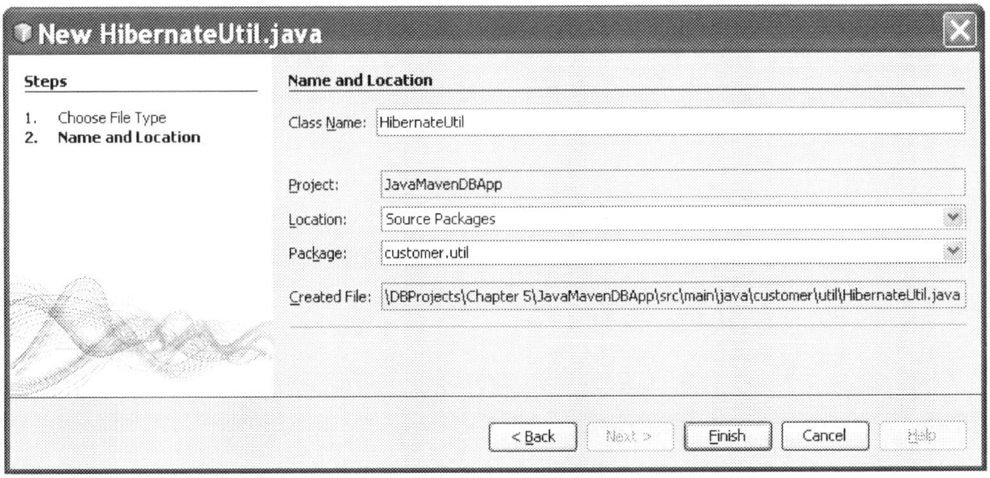

Figure 5.107. The finished New HibernateUtil.java dialog box.

We can use the `Reverse Engineering` wizard and the `Hibernate Mapping Files and POJOs from a Database` wizard to create multiple POJOs and mapping files based on database tables that we selected. Alternatively, we can use wizards provided by the NetBeans IDE to help us to create individual POJOs and mapping files from scratch.

A point to be noted is that if you want to create mapping files for multiple tables, you may most likely want to use the wizards. In this application, you only need to create one POJO and one mapping file so it is fairly easy to create the files individually.

5.3.6.7.1 Creating Reverse Engineering File To use the POJOs and Mapping Files from Database wizard, we need to first create the `reveng.xml` reverse engineering file in the `src/main/resources` directory where we created our `hibernate.cfg.xml`.

Perform the following operations to create this reverse engineering file:

1. Right click on the `Source Packages` node from the `Projects` window and select the `New > Other` menu item to open the `New File` wizard.
2. Select `Hibernate` from the `Categories` list and `Hibernate Reverse Engineering Wizard` from the `File Types` list. Click on the `Next` button to continue.
3. Type `hibernate.reveng` for the file name.
4. Specify `src/main/resources` as the `Folder` location, and then click on the `Next` button.
5. Select `CUSTOMER` in the `Available Tables` pane and click on the `Add` button to add this data table. The related table `DISCOUNT_CODE` is also added, as shown in Figure 5.108.
6. Click on the `Finish` button to complete this process.

The wizard generates a `hibernate.reveng.xml` reverse engineering file.

Now let's create Hibernate mapping files and POJOs from the JavaDB sample database.

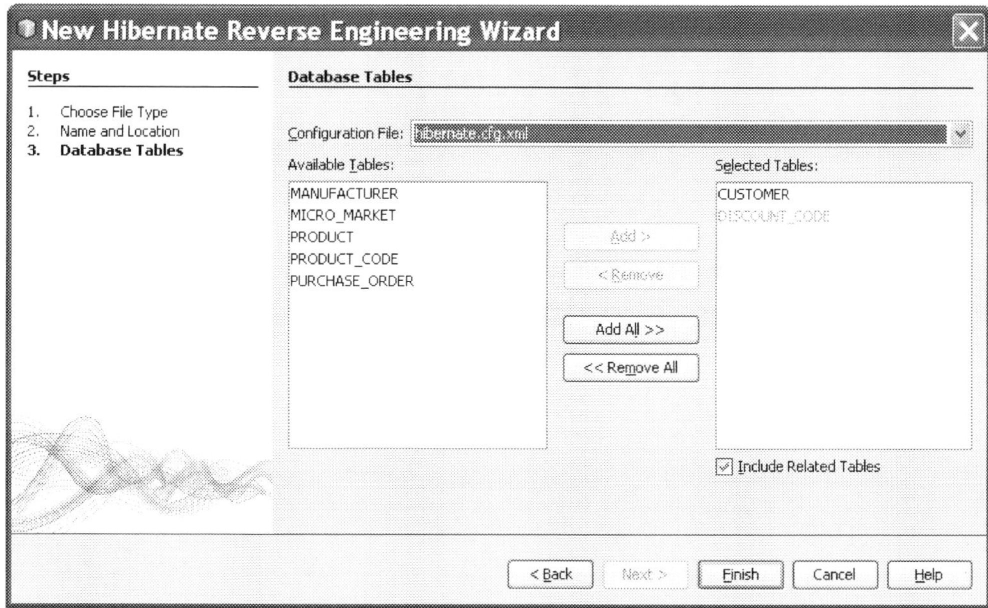

Figure 5.108. The added data table CUSTOMER.

5.3.6.7.2 Creating Hibernate Mapping Files and POJOs from a Database The Hibernate Mapping Files and POJOs from a Database wizard generates files based on tables in the connected database. When using the wizard, the NetBeans IDE generates POJOs and mapping files for us based on the database tables specified in `hibernate.reveng.xml` and then adds the mapping entries to `hibernate.cfg.xml`. When we use the wizard, we can choose the files that we want the NetBeans IDE to generate, for example, only the POJOs, and select code generation options, for example, generate code that uses EJB 3 annotations.

Perform the following operations to create mapping files and POJOs:

1. Right click on the `Source Packages` node in the `Projects` window and choose `New > Other` menu item to open the `New File` dialog.
2. Select `Hibernate` from the `Categories` list and `Hibernate Mapping Files and POJOs from a Database` from the `File Types` list. Click on the `Next` button to continue.
3. Select `hibernate.cfg.xml` from the `Hibernate Configuration File` dropdown list, if not selected.
4. Select `hibernate.reveng.xml` from the `Hibernate Reverse Engineering File` dropdown list, if not selected.
5. Ensure that the `Domain Code` and `Hibernate XML Mappings` options are selected.
6. Type `customer.entity` for the Package name. The finished `New Hibernate Mapping Files and POJOs from Database` wizard is shown in Figure 5.109.
7. Click on the `Finish` button to complete this creation process.

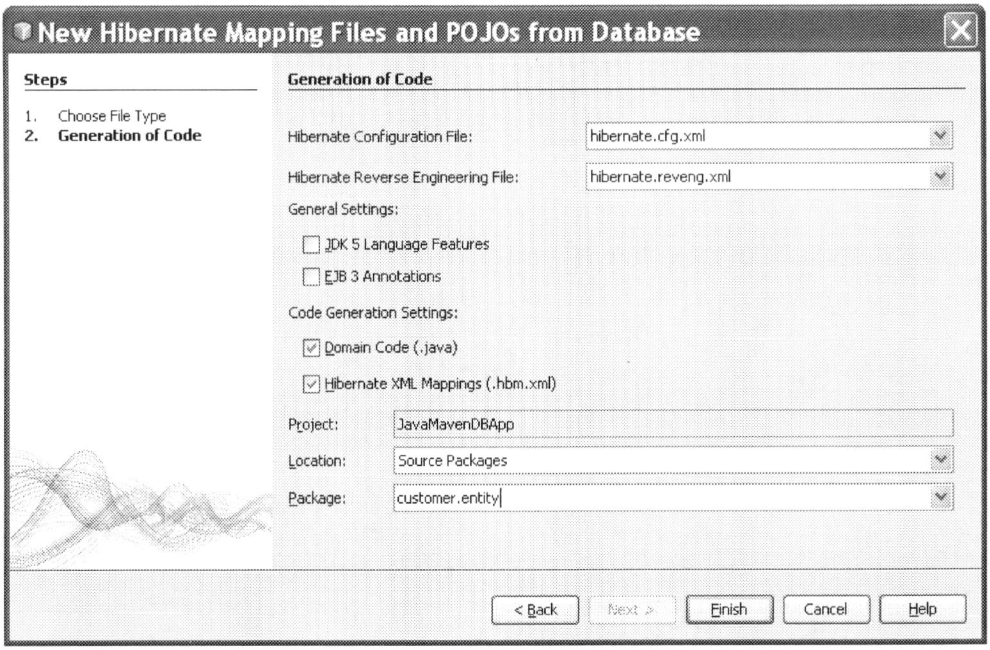

Figure 5.109. The finished New Hibernate Mapping Files and POJOs from Database wizard.

When clicking on the `Finish` button, the NetBeans IDE generates the POJO `Customer.java` with all the required fields in the `src/main/java/customer/entity` directory. The NetBeans IDE also generates a Hibernate mapping file in the `src/main/resources/customer/entity` directory and adds the mapping entry to `hibernate.cfg.xml`.

Now that we have the POJO and necessary Hibernate-related files, we can now create a simple Java GUI front end for our application. We will also create and then add an HQL query that queries the database to retrieve the data. In this process, we also use the HQL editor to build and test the query.

5.3.6.8 Creating the Application GUI

In this section, we will create a simple JFrame Form with some fields for entering and displaying data. We will also add a button that will trigger a database query to retrieve the data from the `Customer` table.

To create a new JFrame Form, perform the following operations:

1. Right click on our project node `JavaMavenDBApp` in the `Projects` window and choose `New > JFrame Form` to open the `New JFrame Form` wizard.
2. Type `JavaMavenDBApp` for the `Class Name` and type `customer.ui` for the `Package`. Click on the `Finish` button to create this new JFrame Form.

The NetBeans IDE will create the JFrame class and opens the JFrame Form in the Design view of the editor when you click on the `Finish` button.

When the form is open in Design view in the editor, the `Palette` window appears in the right side of the IDE. To add an element to the form, drag the element from the `Palette` window into the form area. After adding an element to the form, you need to modify the default value of the `Variable Name` property for that element.

In this application, we want to query and display details for some columns, such as the customer names and credit limit of the customers in the `Customer` table in the JavaDB sample database. Add the following components to this JFrame Form:

1. Drag a Label element from the `Palette` window and change the text to `Customer Profile`.
2. Drag a Label element from the `Palette` window and change the text to `Customer Name`.
3. Drag a Text Field element next to the `Customer Name` label and delete the default text.
4. When deleting the default text, the text field will collapse. You can resize the text field later to adjust the alignment of the form elements.
5. Drag a Label element from the `Palette` window and change the text to `Credit Limit`.
6. Drag a Text Field element next to the `Credit Limit` label and delete the default text.
7. Drag a Button element from the `Palette` window and change the text to `Query`.
8. Drag a Table element from the `Palette` window into the form.
9. Modify the `Variable Name` values of the following UI elements according to the values shown in Table 5.11.

Your finished JFrame Form window should match one that is shown in Figure 5.110.

You may perform the following operations to improve the appearance of this JFrame Form:

1. Modify the `Variable Name` value of an element by right clicking the element in the Design view and then choosing `Change Variable Name`. Alternatively, you can change the `Variable Name` directly in the `Inspector` window.
2. Resize the text fields and align the form elements.
3. Enable the `Horizontal Resizable` property for the text fields to ensure that the text fields resize with the window and that the spacing between elements remains constant.
4. Save all changes and modifications by selecting the `File > Save All` menu item.

Now that we have created a form we need to query and display the query result, now we need to create the code to assign events to the form elements.

In the next section, we will construct queries based on Hibernate Query Language to retrieve data from the `Customer` table in the default JavaDB sample database. After

Table 5.11. The modified elements in the JFrame form

GUI Component	Modified Variable Name
Customer name text field	NameTextField
Credit limit text field	CreditLimitTextField
Query button	QueryButton
Table	ResultTable

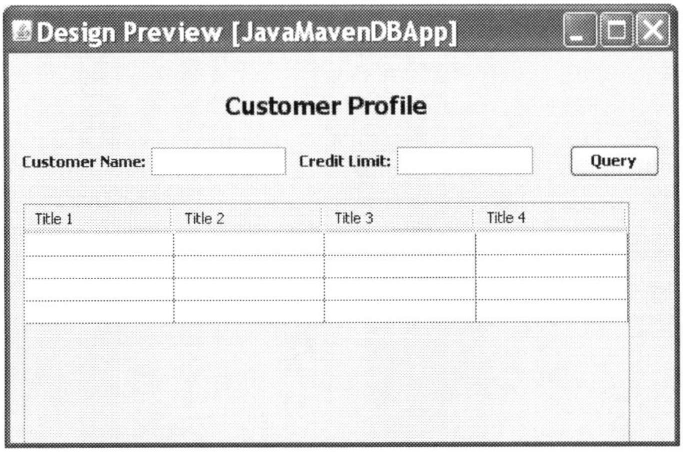

Figure 5.110. The Design View of the JFrame Form.

we construct the queries, we will add methods to the form to invoke the appropriate query when the `Query` button is pressed as the project runs.

5.3.6.9 Creating the Query in the HQL Query Editor

In the NetBeans IDE, we can construct and test queries based on the HQL using the `HQL Query Editor`. As we type the query, the editor shows the equivalent or translated SQL query. When clicking on the `Run HQL Query` button in the toolbar, the NetBeans IDE executes the query and shows the results at the bottom of editor.

In this application, we will use the HQL Editor to construct simple HQL queries that retrieve a list of Customer' details based on matching the first name or the last name. Before we can add the query to the class, we need to use the HQL Query Editor to test and confirm that the connection is working correctly, and that the query produces the desired results.

Perform the following operations to create and test this query in a HQL Editor:

1. Expand the `<default package>` node under the `src/main/resources` node that is under the `Other Sources` node in the `Projects` window.
2. Right click on the `hibernate.cfg.xml` file folder and choose `Run HQL Query` to open the HQL Editor.
3. Test the connection by typing `from Customer` in the HQL Query Editor. Click the `Run HQL Query` button ( ) in the toolbar.
4. When clicking on the `Run HQL Query` button, you should see the query results in the bottom pane of the HQL Query Editor, as shown in Figure 5.111.

If you click on the `SQL` button that is above the results shown in Figure 5.111, you should see the following equivalent SQL query:

```
select customer0_.CUSTOMER_ID as col_0_0_ from APP.CUSTOMER customer0_
```

HQL Query0 - Editor

Session: hibernate.cfg

from Customer

Result SQL — Set Max. Row Count: 100

0 row(s) updated.; 13 row(s) selected.

Email	CustomerId	DiscountCode	Zip	Addressline1	Addressline2	City	Phone	Fax	CreditLi...	Name
jumbocom@gmail.com	1	N	33015	111 E. Las Olas Blvd	Suite 51	Fort Lauderdale	305-777-4632	305-777-4635	100000	JumboCom
www.tsoftt.com	2	M	33055	9754 Main Street	P.O. Box 567	Miami	305-456-8888	305-456-8889	50000	Livermore Ent
www.oakc.com	25	M	75200	8989 Qume Drive	Suite 9897	Houston	214-999-1234	214-999-5432	25000	Oak Computer
www.nanoapple.net	3	L	12347	8585 Murray Drive	P.O. Box 456	Alanta	555-275-9900	555-275-9911	90000	Nano Apple
www.hostprocom.net	36	H	94401	65653 El Camino	Suite 2323	San Mateo	650-456-8876	650-456-1120	65000	HostProCom
www.centralcomp.com	106	L	95035	829 Flex Drive	Suite 853	San Jose	408-987-1256	408-987-1277	26500	CentralComp
www.gvc.net	149	L	95117	4381 Kelly Ave	Suite 77	Santa Clara	408-432-6868	408-432-6899	70000	Golden Valley
www.hpsys.net	863	N	94401	456 4th Street	Suite 45	Redwood City	650-345-5656	650-345-4433	25000	Top Network S
www.westv.com	777	L	48128	88 North Drive	Building C	Dearborn	313-563-9900	313-563-9911	100000	West Valley In
www.parts@ford.com	753	H	48128	2267 Michigan Ave	Building 21	Dearborn	313-787-2100	313-787-3100	5000000	Ford Motor Co
www.sparts.com	722	N	48124	52963 Outer Dr	Suite 35	Detroit	313-788-7682	313-788-7600	50000	Big Car Parts
www.nymedia.com	409	L	10095	4400 22nd Street	Suite 562	New York	212-222-5656	212-222-5600	10000	New Media Pr
www.nycomp@repair.com	410	M	10096	9653 33rd Ave	Floor 4	New York	212-535-7000	212-535-7100	25000	Yankee Compu

Figure 5.111. A sample running result of executing the HQL Query.

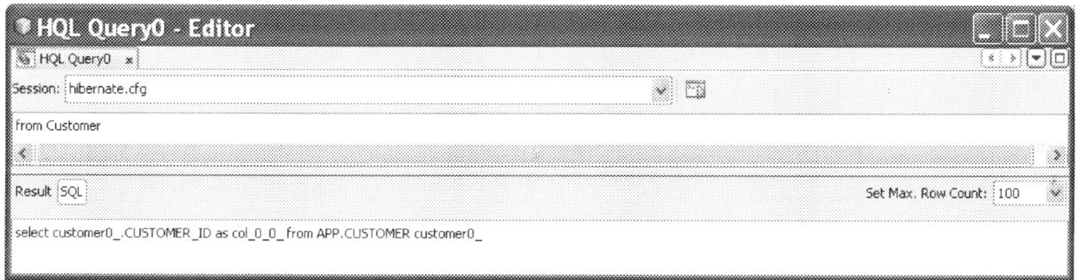

Figure 5.112. The mapped HQL query statement.

This is a mapped HQL query statement and is shown in Figure 5.112.

To further confirm and test the other query actions using the HQL Editor, perform the following two more query tests:

1. Type the following query in the HQL Query Editor and click `Run HQL Query` to check the query results when the credit limit is in the range of 50,000 and 150,000.

   ```
   from Customer c where c.creditLimit between 50000 and 150000
   ```

   The query returns a list of customers whose credit limits are between 50,000 and 150,000.

2. Open a new HQL Query Editor tab and type the following query in the editor pane. Click the `Run HQL Query` button to execute this HQL query.

   ```
   from Customer c where c.name like 'N%'
   ```

   The query returns a list of customers' details for those customers whose names begin with the letter N.

Notes: when typing a HQL query in the HQL Query Editor, for each column name you used in your query, you must use the mapped column name, or it is called the property in the HQL language, not the original column name in the relational data table. All mapped column names are located in the mapped entity file; in this application, its Customer.java is located under the customer.entity node. To check and use the appropriate mapped column name, you need to open that file and use mapped columns in that file.

Our testing query results show that the queries return the desired results.

Our next step is to implement the queries in the application so that the appropriate query is invoked by clicking the `Query` button in the form.

5.3.6.10 Adding the Query to the GUI Form

We now need to modify our main GUI file `JavaMavenDBApp.java` to add the query strings and create the methods to construct and invoke a query that incorporates the input variables. We also need to modify the `Query` button event handler to invoke the correct query and add a method to display the query results in the table.

Perform the following operations to add the query strings and create the associated query responding methods:

1. Open the GUI code file `JavaMavenDBApp.java` from the `customer.ui` node by double clicking on it and click the `Source` tab.
2. Add the codes shown in Figure 5.113 into to the class. The new added codes have been highlighted in bold.

Let's have a closer look at this piece of newly added codes to see how it works.

A. Some necessary packages are first imported into this code file since we need to use related classes and components, and they are defined in those packages.

B. A system method `setLocationRelativeTo()` is called to locate our GUI Form in the center of the screen as the project runs.

C. Two static or named query strings are defined here with the HQL language. The first query string is used to query a detailed customer record based on the customer's name, and the second is to query a detailed record based on the credit limit.

D. Inside the `Query` button's event handler, an `if-else` selection structure is used to check if a query criterion is stored in the `NameTextField` or in the `CreditLimitTextField`. If any of them is not empty, the associated query function, either `runQueryBasedOn-Name()` or `runQueryBasedOnCreditLimit()`, is executed.

E. The detailed definition of the function `runQueryBasedOnName()` is shown here; it calls another function, `executeHQLQuery()`, with the static query string QUERY_BASED_ON_NAME and the content of the `NameTextField` as the final query string argument.

F. The body of the function `runQueryBasedOnCreditLimit()` is shown here; it calls another function `executeHQLQuery()` with the static query string QUERY_BASED_

```
    package customer.ui;
A   import org.hibernate.Query;
    import org.hibernate.Session;
    import org.hibernate.HibernateException;
    import javax.swing.table.*;
    import java.util.*;                                  // for List & Vector classes
    public class JavaMavenDBApp extends javax.swing.JFrame {
      /** Creates new form JavaMavenDBApp */
      public JavaMavenDBApp() {
        initComponents();
B       this.setLocationRelativeTo(null);                 // set the GUI Form at the center
      }
C     private static String QUERY_BASED_ON_NAME = "from Customer c where c.name like '";
      private static String QUERY_BASED_ON_CREDITLIMIT = "from Customer c where c.creditLimit >= ";
      private void QueryButtonActionPerformed(java.awt.event.ActionEvent evt) {
D       if(!NameTextField.getText().trim().equals("")) {
          runQueryBasedOnName();
        } else if(!CreditLimitTextField.getText().trim().equals("")) {
          runQueryBasedOnCreditLimit();
        }
      }
E     private void runQueryBasedOnName() {
        executeHQLQuery(QUERY_BASED_ON_NAME + NameTextField.getText() + "%'");
      }
F     private void runQueryBasedOnCreditLimit() {
        executeHQLQuery(QUERY_BASED_ON_CREDITLIMIT + CreditLimitTextField.getText());
      }
G     private void executeHQLQuery(String hql) {
        try {
H           Session session = customer.util.HibernateUtil.getSessionFactory().openSession();
I           session.beginTransaction();
J           Query q = session.createQuery(hql);
K           List resultList = q.list();
L           displayResult(resultList);
M           session.getTransaction().commit();
N         } catch (HibernateException he) {
            he.printStackTrace();
          }
      }
O     private void displayResult(List resultList) {
        Vector<String> tableHeaders = new Vector<String>();
        Vector tableData = new Vector();
        tableHeaders.add("CustomerId");
        tableHeaders.add("Name");
        tableHeaders.add("CreditLimit");
        tableHeaders.add("Email");
P       for(Object o : resultList) {
          customer.entity.Customer customer = (customer.entity.Customer)o;
          Vector<Object> oneRow = new Vector<Object>();
          oneRow.add(customer.getCustomerId());
          oneRow.add(customer.getName());
          oneRow.add(customer.getCreditLimit());
          oneRow.add(customer.getEmail());
          tableData.add(oneRow);
        }
Q       ResultTable.setModel(new DefaultTableModel(tableData, tableHeaders));
      }
```

Figure 5.113. The newly added codes for the GUI class JavaMavenDBApp.

ON_CREDITLIMIT and the content of the CreditLimitTextField as the final query string argument.

G. The detailed definition of the function executeHQLQuery() is given here.

H. A try-catch block is used here to perform this query function. A java session bean is created by calling the method openSession() that is the running result of the method getSessionFactory(), which is defined in the customer.util.HibernateUtil helper class.

I. The system method beginTransaction() is executed to begin performing this query.

J. The createQuery() method is called to create this HQL query string.

K. A List object, resultList, is created to hold the returned list query result.

L. A local function displayResult() is executed to display the list query result in our GUI Form, exactly in our added Table object.

M. The commit() method is executed to terminate this transaction.

N. The catch block is used to track and collect any possible exception that occurred during this transaction, and print them out if exceptions occurred.

O. The local function displayResult() is defined here. The main function of this method is to display four columns in the Customer table, CustomerId, Name, CreditLimit, and Email, with certain tabular format.

P. An extended for loop is used to pick up the contents for four columns in the Customer table. One point to be noted is that you have to use the full name, including the package and class names, to create this new customer instance. Here this full name is: customer.entity.Customer.

Q. Finally the setModel() method is executed to display this table with the selected format.

At this point, we have finished all coding development for this project. Now let's build and run our project to see the running result.

Click on the Clean and Build Main Project button from the toolbar to compile and build our project. If everything is fine, perform the following operations to launch our application:

1. Right click on our main project node JavaMavenDBApp in the Projects window and choose the Properties item from the popup menu.
2. Select the Run category in the Project Properties dialog box.
3. Click on the Browse button and choose the class customer.ui.JavaMavenDBApp from the Main classes list, as shown in Figure 5.114.

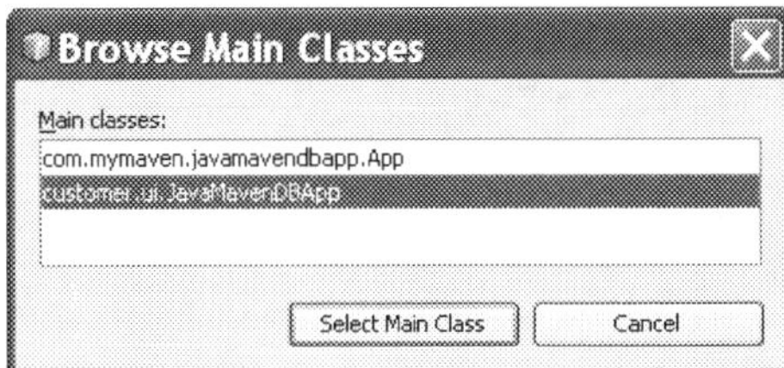

Figure 5.114. The selected main class for our project.

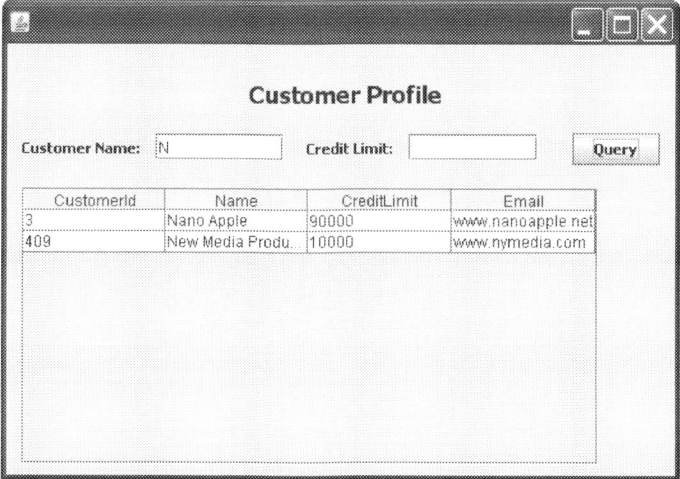

Figure 5.115. A sample running result of our Maven project.

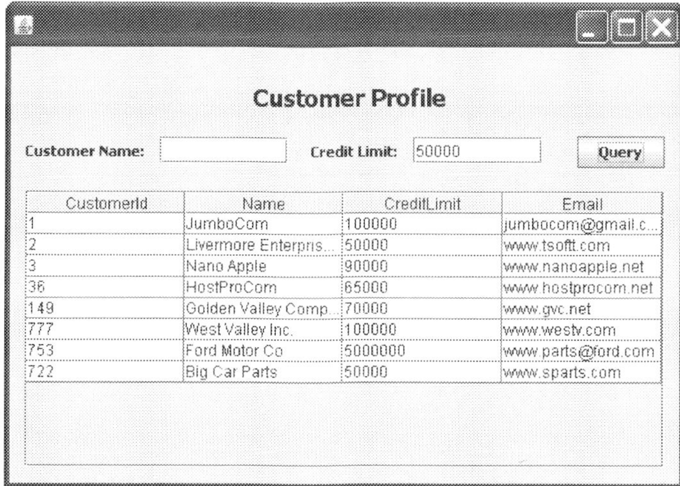

Figure 5.116. Another running result of our Maven project.

4. Click on the `Select Main Class` button to close this dialog box, and click on the `OK` button to finish this main class selection process.
5. Click on the `Run Main Project` button in the main toolbar to launch the application.
6. Type `N` to the `Customer Name` TextField and click on the `Query` button to try to retrieve all customers whose names start with `N`. The running result is shown in Figure 5.115.
7. Remove `N` from the `Customer Name` TextField and enter `50000` to the `Credit Limit` TextField. Click on the `Query` button to perform this query. The function of this query is to retrieve all customers whose credit limits are greater than or equal to 50,000. The running result of this query is shown in Figure 5.116.

A complete Java Maven application project `JavaMavenDBApp` can be found from the folder `DBProjects\Chapter 5` that is located at the Wiley ftp site (refer to Figure 1.2 in Chapter 1). You can download and run this application in your computer. However, before you can run this application in your computer, you need to have the following conditions met:

1. All related software have been installed in your computer, which include Apache Maven 2.2.1 or higher, NetBeans IDE 6.8 or higher, Java SDK 1.6 or higher.
2. The default JavaDB sample database has been connected and run in your computer. This can be done by right clicking on the sample database connection URL and selecting the `Connect` item from the popup menu in the `Services` window.

Next, let's handle how to build PHP applications with NetBeans IDE 6.8.

5.3.7 Build a PHP Project

Personal Home Page (PHP) is a scripting language that is designed to develop dynamic web pages. The codes of PHP are embedded into the source document of HTML, and are able to be interpreted through a Web server into a processor module for PHP, and this creates the web page. When this is used as a programming language for general programming purposes, it is processed by an interpreter application that performs the operations of a selected operating system and creates output for the program through its regular channel for output. PHP is also able to work in a graphical form as a GUI. Today, PHP is there as a processor for the majority of Web servers, as well as an interpreter for the majority of operating systems and platforms of computing. This program was originally made by Rasmus Lerdorf in 1995. It has continued to develop since that time. It is now currently produced by what is called the PHP Group. This is free software, and it has been released through the PHP License.

5.3.7.1 Introduction to PHP

As we mentioned, PHP is a scripting language that is particularly useful for server-side development of the Web application, in which PHP will run on a Web server. The PHP code in a file that is requested is utilized by the PHP runtime. This is often used to create content for dynamic web pages. Additionally, it can be utilized for command-line scripting, as well as GUI applications for the client. Since PHP is able to be deployed on the majority of Web servers, the majority of operating platforms and systems are able to be used along with the database management systems. This program is fortunately free, and the PHP Group that develops it will provide the total source code for the users to build on-their-own applications, make it custom, and extend PHP for their own purpose.

The main purpose of the PHP is to mostly act like a filter as it takes input from a stream or from a file that has text or PHP instructions, and will then put out another group of data, and most often this data will be HTML. Today, PHP is primarily focused on providing server side scripting. This is close to other types of server side scripting languages, such as JavaFX and Java Scripts, to provide dynamic content through a Web server and to the client. This program has also lead to the development of a number of frameworks that will create a structure of design in order to provide for the rapid application development.

PHP only parses code within its delimiters. Anything outside its delimiters is sent directly to the output and is not processed by PHP, although non-PHP text is still subject to control structures described within PHP code. The most common delimiters are <?php to open and ?> to close PHP sections. <script language="php"> and </script> delimiters are also available, as are the shortened forms <? or <?=, which is used to echo back a string or variable, and ?>, as well as ASP-style short forms <% or <%= and %>. While short delimiters are used, they make script files less portable as their purpose, and this can be disabled in the PHP configuration, and so they are discouraged. The purpose of all these delimiters is to separate PHP code from non-PHP code, including HTML.

The first form of delimiters, <?php and ?>, in XHTML and other XML documents, creates correctly formed XML "processing instructions." This means that the resulting mixture of PHP code and other markup in the server-side file is itself well-formed XML.

Variables are prefixed with a dollar sign, and a type does not need to be specified in advance. Unlike function and class names, variable names are case sensitive. Both double-quoted ("") and heredoc strings allow the ability to embed a variable's value into the string. PHP treats newlines as whitespace in the manner of a free-form language (except when inside string quotes), and statements are terminated by a semicolon.

PHP has three types of comment syntax: /* */ marks block and inline comments; // as well as # are used for one-line comments. The echo statement is one of several facilities PHP provides to output text, such as to a Web browser.

In terms of keywords and language syntax, PHP is similar to most high-level languages that follow the C style syntax. *If* conditions, *for* and *while* loops, and function returns are similar in syntax to languages such as C, C++, Java, and Perl.

5.3.7.2 Downloading and Installing Apache HTTP Web Server

Generally, you need the following software to build and run a PHP project in the NetBeans IDE:

- NetBeans IDE 6.8 or higher
- A PHP Engine (`PHP 5` or higher)
- A Web Server (`Apache HTTP Server 2.2` is recommended)
- A PHP Debugger (`XDebug 2.0` or later)

You can install the PHP engine, Web server and database separately or use AMP (Apache, MySQL, PHP) packages. In this application, we want to install them separately since we want to use the default JavaDB sample database attached with the NetBeans IDE.

Let's start to download an `Apache HTTP Server` by going to the site: http://httpd.apache.org/download.cgi and select a download source mirror that is close to us. Click on that mirror to begin the downloading process. The current version is 2.2.15 for Windows applications. Therefore, click on the link: `Win32 Binary without crypto (no mod_ssl) (MSI Installer)`: httpd-2.2.15-win32-x86-no_ssl.msi to begin this process. It is recommended to first save this file to your `Temp` folder in your root driver. Try to avoid downloading a zip server file since you need to compile the downloaded file if you did that.

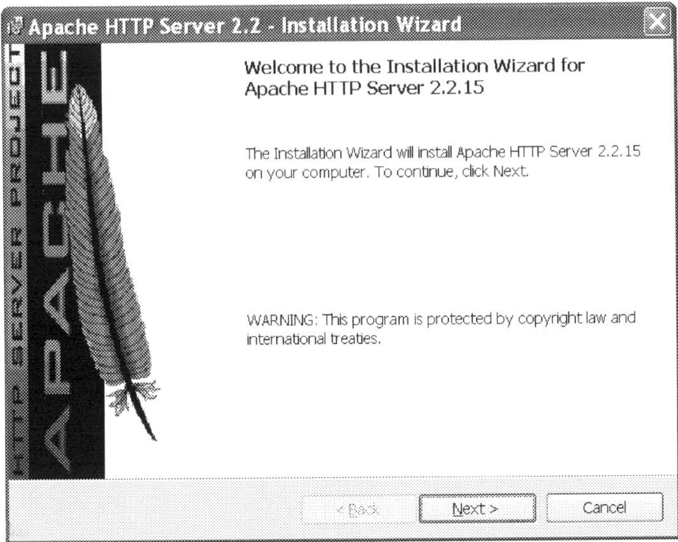

Figure 5.117. The Installation wizard.

After the downloading is complete, open the `Temp` folder and double click on the downloaded server file `httpd-2.2.15-win32-x86-no_ssl.msi` to install it. Click on the `Run` button to begin this installation. An `Installation Wizard` appears, as shown in Figure 5.117.

Click on the `Next` button to continue.

Click on the `Accept the Terms` radio button and the `Next` button to go to the next page.

In the next page, the installer displays the following information:

- Network Domain
- Server Name
- Administrator's Email Address
- HTTP Server shortcut

You can modify these settings if you like others to access your site. However, we just want to use this server as our local server and do not want to expose it to others, therefore to make it simple, we just keep the default settings for this wizard, which are shown in Figure 5.118.

Click on the `Next` button to continue.

Select the Typical radio button for the set up type, and click on the Next button again to continue.

On the next wizard, make sure that the location you want to install this HTTP Server is: `C:\Program Files\Apache Software Foundation\Apache 2.2`, and click on the `Next` and `Install` button to begin this installation process.

Click on the `Finish` button to close this process when the installation is complete.

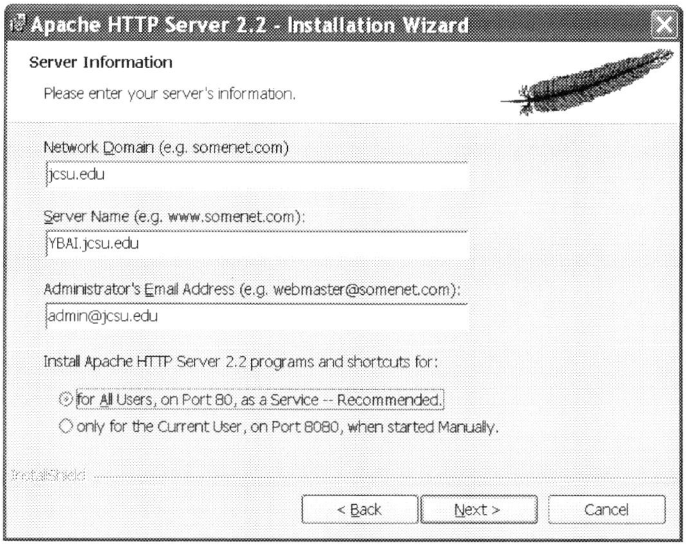

Figure 5.118. Default settings for the HTTP Server.

5.3.7.3 Configuring and Testing the Installed Apache HTTP Web Server

Now let's configure and test our installed Apache HTTP Server. The main configuring jobs are executed inside the configure file named `httpd.conf` that is located at the folder `C:\Program Files\Apache Software Foundation\Apache 2.2\conf`. This configuration is not necessary if your installed HTTP Server can work on your computer without any problem. To test this server, first let's start it by going to `Start\All Programs\Apache HTTP Server 2.2\Control Apache Server\Start` menu item. If the server can start without any problem, or you cannot find any debug or error information from the pop-up command window, which means that your server does not need to be configured and you can use it without problem.

However, if you did get some error information from the popup command window, you need to correct them by modifying your `httpd.conf` file. The most common problem is the port number you are using, and it may be used by some other devices. The reason for that is because in most situations, the default Web server, Internet Information Services (IIS), will be installed in your computer when you installed your Windows operating system, and this server will use port 80 as the default port. Therefore, our installed Apache HTTP Server cannot use the same port.

To solve this problem, we need to configure the Apache HTTP server by modifying the server configuring file, `httpd.conf`, which is located at the folder `C:\Program Files\Apache Software Foundation\Apache2.2\conf`. Go to that folder and double click on the configuring file `httpd.conf` to open it. In normal case, we can open it in the NotePad format.

On the opened file, browse down the file and try to find the command line like

```
Listen 80
```

Change the port number from 80 to any other available port number, such as 800. Then save this configuring file. Open a Web browser and enter http://localhost:800 to the

Figure 5.119. The successful server page.

Address field. Press the Enter key and you will find that the successful Apache HTTP Server welcome page is displayed, as shown in Figure 5.119.

5.3.7.4 Downloading and Installing the PHP Engine

Download the current PHP engine by going to the site: http://www.php.net/downloads.php. The current PHP engine version is PHP 5.3.2. Click on the link http://windows.php.net/download/ to begin this downloading process, since we need to download a Windows Binaries package that can be installed later on when the downloading is complete.

On the next page, you can select a Non Thread Safe or Thread Safe version to download. In our case, we prefer to select Thread Safe version. Click on the Installer from the VC9 x86 Thread Safe group to begin this downloading process. It is recommended to first save this package to your Temp folder, and then you can click the downloaded file to being the installation process.

When the saving process is complete, click on the Open Folder button to open the Temp folder, then double click on the downloaded file php-5.3.2-Win32-VC9-x86.msi and click on the Run button to begin the installation process.

A PHP 5.3.2 Setup dialog is displayed, as shown in Figure 5.120.

Click on the Next button to continue.

Check the Accept Items checkbox and the Next button to go to the next wizard. Keep the default location, C:\Program Files\PHP\ unchanged and click on the Next button to continue.

In the next wizard, check the Apache 2.2x Module radio button from the server group to make this as our default Web server. Click on the Next button to continue.

In the next opened wizard, click on the Browse button to browse to our default HTTP Server configuration folder, C:\Program Files\Apache Software Foundation\Apache 2.2\conf, and we need to use this folder to store the configuration file for the PHP engine. Your finished wizard should match one that is shown in Figure 5.121.

Click on the Next button to go to the next wizard.

In the next wizard, select all icons from the available sources since we want to install all of components, as shown in Figure 5.122.

Click on the Next and Install button to begin this installation process. Then click on the Finish button to close this wizard when the installation is complete.

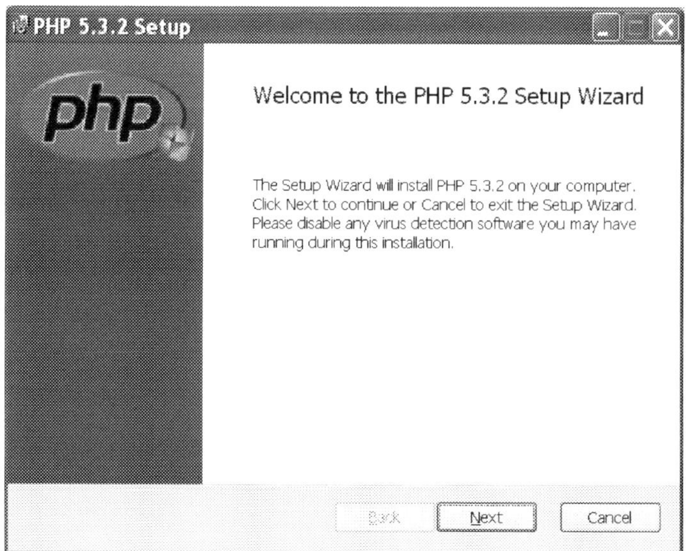

Figure 5.120. The PHP 5.2.3 Setup dialog box.

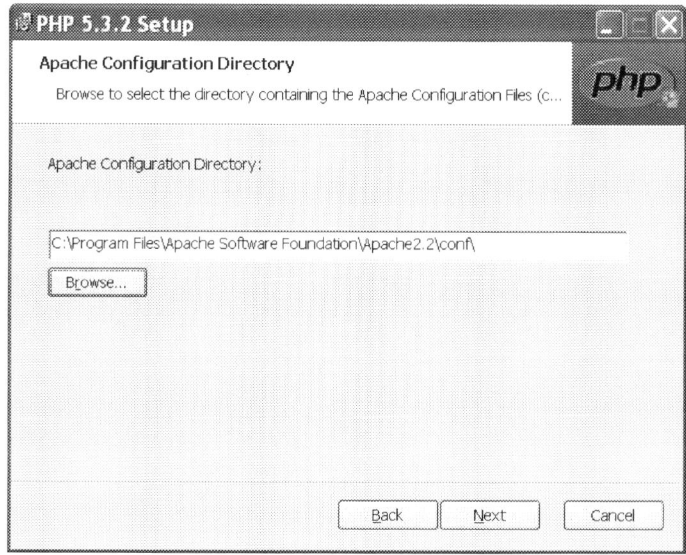

Figure 5.121. The selected Apache configuration directory.

Before we can continue to use this installed PHP engine, we need to test it to confirm that this installation is fine and the installed engine will work.

5.3.7.5 Testing the Installed PHP Engine

To check that the PHP engine has been installed successfully and PHP processing has been enabled in the Apache configuration, we need to test this engine by performing the following operations:

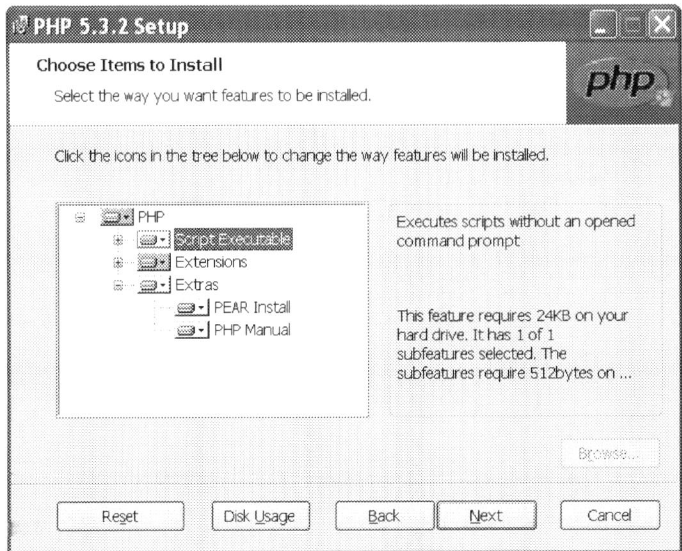

Figure 5.122. Select all components.

```
<?php
    echo "PHP has been installed successfully!";
?>
```

Figure 5.123. The coding for the testing file.

1. Start the Apache HTTP Server by going to `Start\All Programs\Apache HTTP Server 2.2\Control Apache Server\Start` menu item and click on the Start item.
2. Open a new NotePad file and enter the codes that are shown in Figure 5.123 into this file.
3. Save this file as the name of `test.php` to the folder: C:\Program Files\Apache Software Foundation\Apache2.2\htdocs.

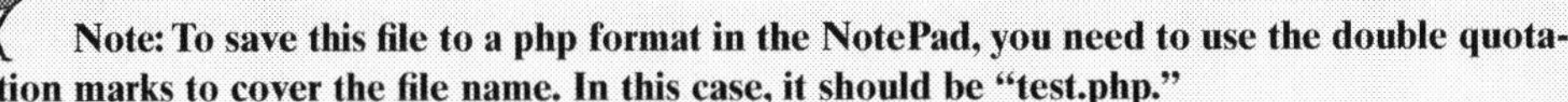

Note: To save this file to a php format in the NotePad, you need to use the double quotation marks to cover the file name. In this case, it should be "test.php."

4. Open the Internet Explorer and enter the URL: http://localhost:800/test.php into the `Address` field. A successful PHP engine running result should be displayed, as shown in Figure 5.124.

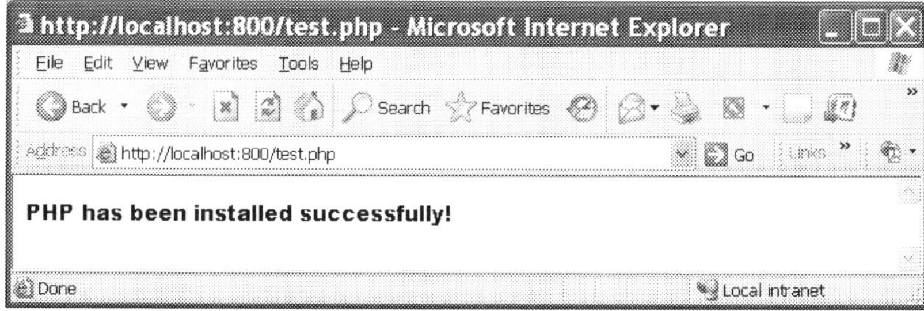

Figure 5.124. The successful testing result for the installed PHP engine.

```
#AddEncoding x-compress .Z
#AddEncoding x-gzip .gz .tgz
#
# If the AddEncoding directives above are commented-out, then you
# probably should define those extensions to indicate media types:
#
AddType  application/x-compress .Z
AddType  application/x-gzip .gz .tgz
AddType  Application/x-httpd-php .php
#
# AddHandler allows you to map certain file extensions to "handlers":
# actions unrelated to filetype. These can be either built into the server
# or added with the Action directive (see below)
```

Figure 5.125. The modified httpd.conf file.

Note: If you cannot open this page, which means that your PHP engine cannot start or work properly. The solution is to modify the httpd.conf **file to add one more command:** AddType Application/x-httpd-php .php **under two** AddType **commands that are located about line 380. To track this file with the line number, click on the** View **menu item in the NotePad and check the** Status Bar.

An example of adding this command is shown in Figure 5.125. The added command has been highlighted in bold.

At this point, we have successfully installed and configured Apache HTTP Server and PHP engine in our computer. Next, let's start to develop and build our PHP project to perform data actions between our project and our desired databases.

5.3.7.6 Creating a PHP Project

In this section, we will create and set up a PHP project in NetBeans IDE 6.8. Perform the following operations to complete this creation and setup:

1. Start the NetBeans IDE 6.8 and switch to the `Projects` window.
2. Choose `File > New Project`. The `Choose Project` panel opens.
3. Select `PHP` from the `Categories` list, and `PHP Application` from the `Projects` list since we want to create a new PHP project without using any existing source. Click on the `Next` button to continue.
4. In the opened `New PHP Project` wizard, enter `PHPCustomer` into the `Project Name` field, keep all default settings unchanged, and click on the `Next` button to continue.
5. In the `Run Configuration` wizard, we can select the following three different running configurations for this project:

   A. Local Web site
   B. Remote Web site (FTP)
   C. Script

   The *Local Web site* configuration is to run this project in our local Web site using the Apache HTTP server. By using this configuration, it involves a copy of your PHP source folders in the Web folder of the Apache web server installed on your machine.

   The *Remote Web site* configuration is to run your project in a remote Web site with a hosting account on a remote server and an FTP account on that server. You need to deploy and upload your complete project to the Web server on which your project will run.

   The *Script* configuration does not require that a Web server be installed and running on your computer. You only need a PHP engine to run your project.
6. To make it simple, in this application, we just want to run our project in our local Web site. Therefore, select the `Local Web site` from the `Run As` combo box and enter `http://localhost:800/PHPCustomer/` into the `Project URL` combo box. Keep the `Copy files from Sources Folder to another location` checkbox unchecked since we do not want to save our project files to other location. Your finished `Run Configuration` wizard should match one that is shown in Figure 5.126. Click on the `Next` button to continue.
7. Click on the `Finish` button on the next wizard to complete this creation process.

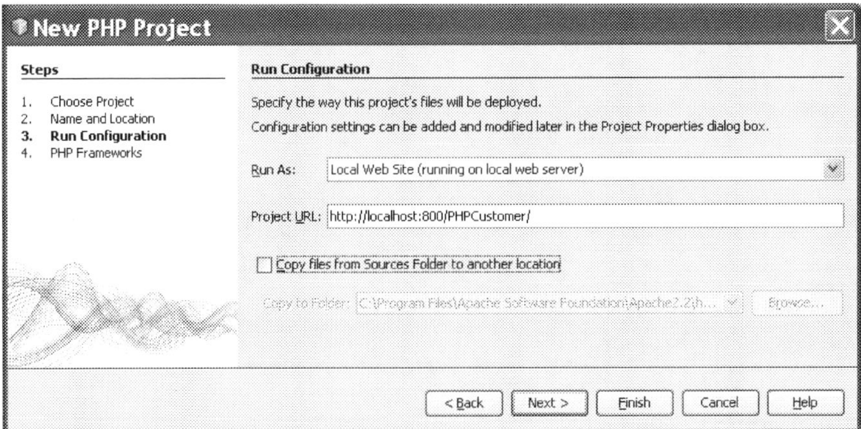

Figure 5.126. The finished Run Configuration wizard.

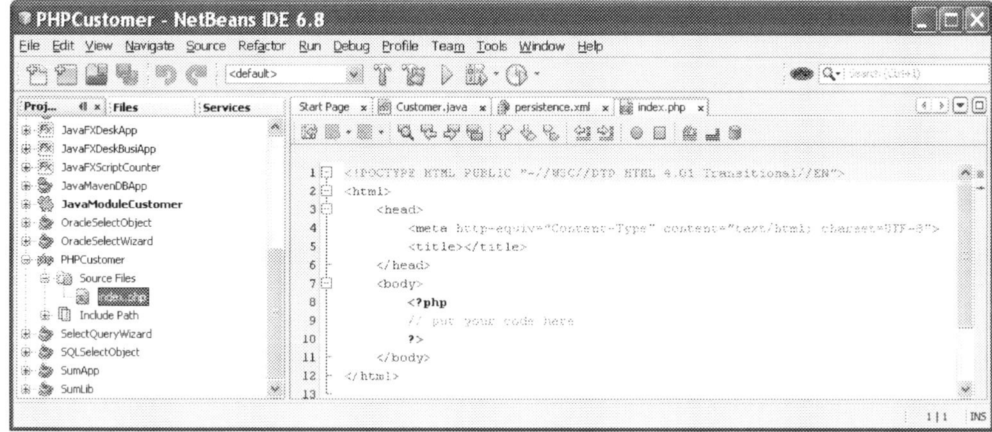

Figure 5.127. The default starting page of the new PHP project.

As a new PHP project is created, the starting page, `index.php`, is displayed with the default php codes, as shown in Figure 5.127.

Next, let's handle our target database server issue since we need to connect to our database via server to perform data actions between our PHP project and that database.

5.3.7.7 Downloading and Configuring MySQL Database Server

As we know, the most popular database used in PHP is MySQL database. Currently, the only Web server database supported by PHP is MySQL. Therefore, we need to first download a MySQL database server and use it in this PHP application.

Go to the site http://www.mysql.com/downloads/mysql/ to begin this downloading process.

On the opened page, select the first item, **Windows (x86, 32-bit), MSI Installer Essentials,** and click on the `Download` button to go to the next page.

In the next page, click on the `No Thanks, just take me to the downloads` link to continue. Select a source mirror that is close to you and click on the related `HTTP` link to save this program to the `Temp` folder in your computer. When this download is complete, open the `Temp` folder and double click on the downloaded file to install it.

Click on the `Next` button to continue.

Select the `Typical` radio button and click on the `Next` button to continue. Click on the `Install` button to begin this installation process. The installation starts, as shown in Figure 5.128.

Click on the `Next` buttons and the `Finish` button to complete this process.

The `MySQL Server Instance Configuration Wizard` is appeared. Click on the `Next` button to go to the next wizard. Select the `Detailed Configuration` item in the next wizard, as shown in Figure 5.129, and the `Next` button to continue.

Select the `Developer Machine` item in the next wizard since we need to develop our PHP applications and run them in our local machine. Click on the `Next` button to continue.

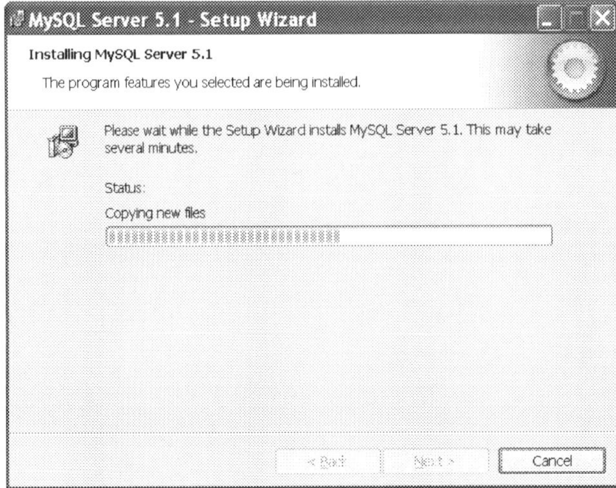

Figure 5.128. The installation process of the MySQL database.

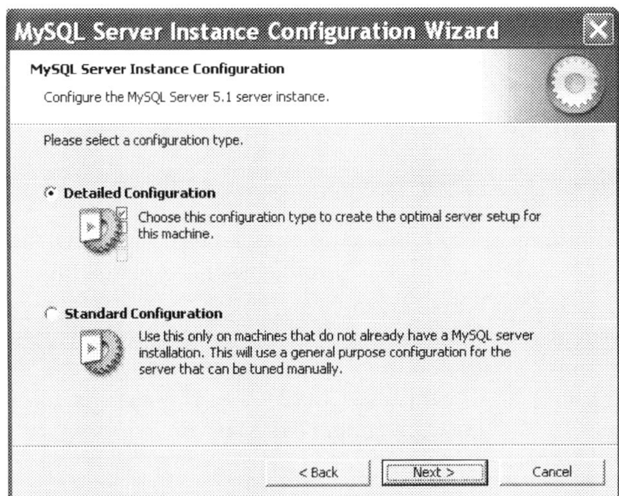

Figure 5.129. The server configuration selection process.

In the next wizard, keep the default selection, `Multifunctional Database`, unchanged, and click on the `Next` button to continue.

In the next wizard, select `\MySQL Datafiles\` as the directory to save the `InnoDB tablespace`. Click on the `Next` button to continue.

Keep the default settings for the next two wizards, including the default port of 3306, and click on the `Next` button to continue.

In the next wizard, select the `Best Support For Multilingualism` item to make all default character sets as `UTF8`, as shown in Figure 5.130. Click on the `Next` button to continue.

In the next wizard, keep all default settings unchanged and check the `Include Bin Directory in Windows PATH` checkbox, as shown in Figure 5.131, since we may need

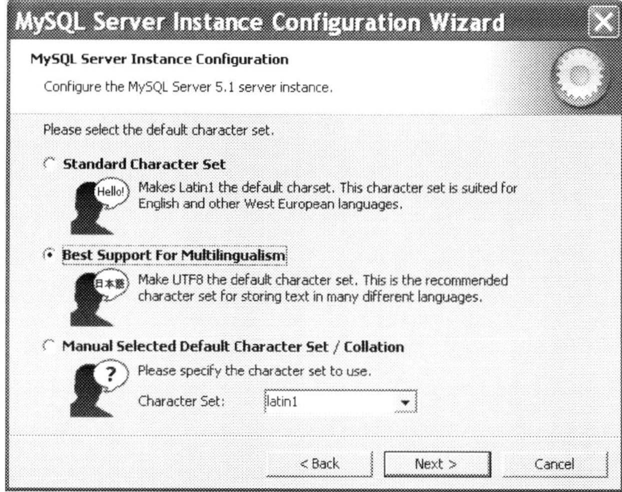

Figure 5.130. The character set selection.

Figure 5.131. Install the MySQL as a window server.

to start this server from the command window later. Click on the `Next` button to continue.

In the next wizard, you need to provide a new root password. You can use any valid password if you like. In this application, we used `reback` as our new root password. You need to remember this password since you need to use it later to start this server.

Enter this root password `reback` to both `root password` and `Confirm` fields, and check the `Enable root access from remote machines` checkbox. Your finished root password selection wizard should match one that is shown in Figure 5.132.

Click on the `Next` button to continue.

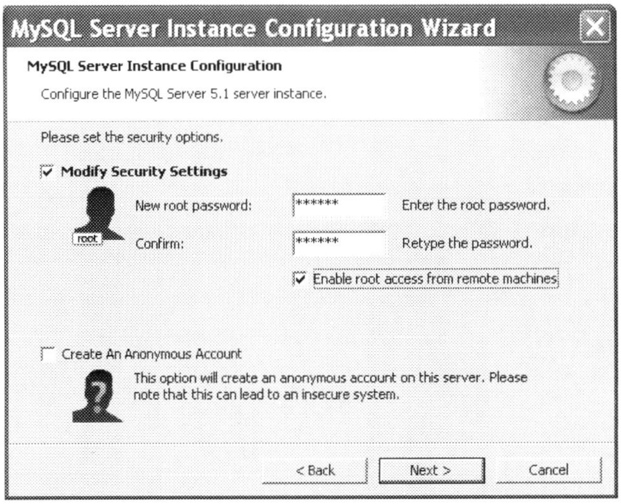

Figure 5.132. The finished root password selection wizard.

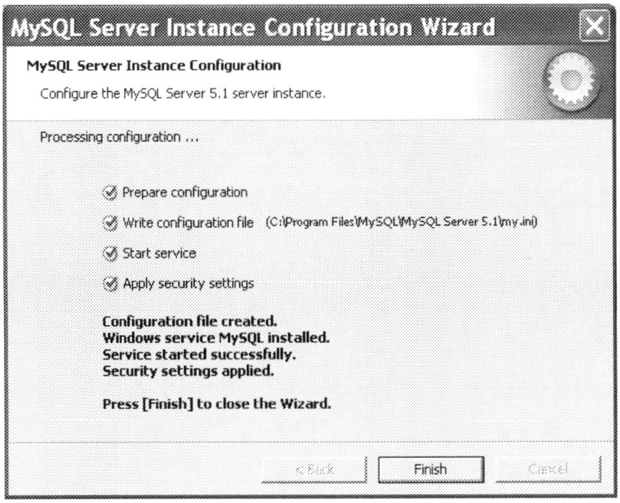

Figure 5.133. The successful configuration dialog box.

In the opened next wizard, click on the `Execute` button to start this configuration process. If everything is fine, a successful configuration dialog box is displayed, as shown in Figure 5.133.

Click on the `Finish` button to complete this installation and configuration process.

5.3.7.8 Configuring the MySQL Server in NetBeans IDE

To configure our installed MySQL database server in NetBeans IDE 6.8 and create a new user for MySQL database to be created later, perform the following operations:

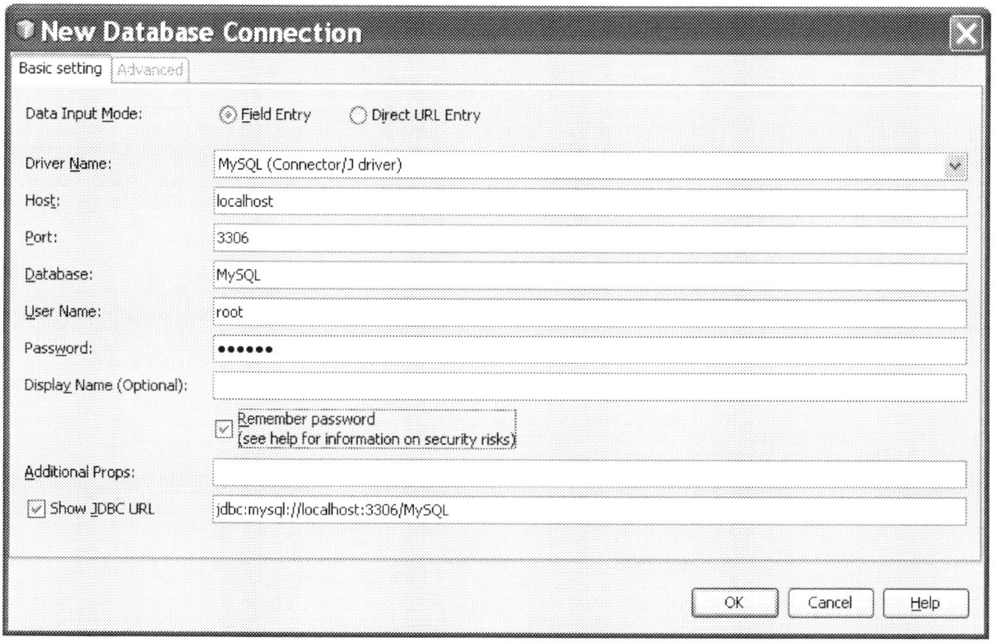

Figure 5.134. The connection information.

1. Launch NetBeans IDE and open the `Services` window.
2. Expand the `Drivers` node and right click on MySQL icon; select the `Connect Using` item from the pop-up menu to open the `New Database Connection` wizard.
3. On the opened wizard, enter the MySQL database-related information into the associated fields, as shown in Figure 5.134. Make sure to check both `Show JDBC URL` and `Remember password` checkboxes. The password you need to enter to the `Password` field is `reback`, which is created when we downloaded and configured the MySQL database in the last section.

   Click on the OK button to complete this process. Immediately, you can find a new connection URL `jdbc:mysql://localhost:3306/MySQL [root on Default schema]` added into the `Services` window.
4. Right click on that connection URL and select the `Execute Command` item from the pop-up menu to open the SQL Command window.
5. In the opened SQL Command window, enter the codes shown below into this window:

   ```
   CREATE USER 'php_user'@'localhost'
   IDENTIFIED BY '!php_user'
   ```
6. Highlight two lines of codes above and right click on them, and choose the `Run Selection` item from the popup menu to run these two coding lines. If the command is executed successfully, the Status bar shows the message: "`SQL Statement(s) executed successfully`". If another message is displayed, check the syntax and follow the message hints.

Step 6 is necessary since you must create a user before you can create a MySQL database. The user can grant the right to perform any operations on the database.

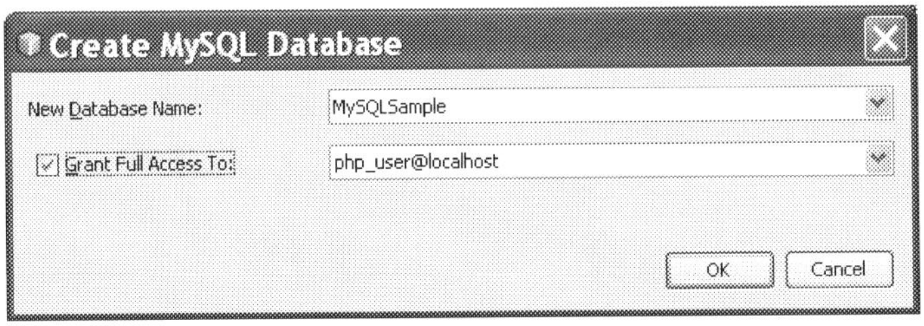

Figure 5.135. The opened Create MySQL Database wizard.

Note: To run SQL statements in the SQL Command window, you can only run them one time. An error may be encountered if you try to run statements more than one time.

Now we have created our database user named `php_user` identified by `!php_user`, next, we need to create our MySQL sample database `MySQLSample` to be used in this PHP application project.

5.3.7.9 Creating Our Sample Database MySQLSample

Perform the following operations to create this sample database MySQLSample:

1. Navigate to the MySQL Server at localhost:3306 [root] node, which is under the `Databases` icon in the `Services` window, and from the context menu choose `Create Database` item. The `Create MySQL Database` dialog box appears, as shown in Figure 5.135. Fill in the fields:

   A. In the Database Name field, enter `MySQLSample`.
   B. Switch on the `Grant Full Access To` checkbox, and from the drop-down list select `php_user@localhost`, and then click on the OK button.

   Your finished Create MySQL Database wizard should match one that is shown in Figure 5.135.

2. A new database connection URL, `jdbc:mysql://localhost:3306/MySQLSample [root on Default schema]` has been created and added into the `Services` window.

We need to create two tables in this sample database: LogIn and Customer. The relationship between these two tables is shown in Figure 5.136.

Now let's create these two tables in NetBeans IDE.

Right click on our `MySQLSample` database URL `jdbc:mysql://localhost:3306/MySQLSample [root on Default schema]` from the Services window and select `Execute Command` from the pop-up menu to open a blank SQL Command window. Enter the codes that are shown in Figure 5.137 into this SQL Command window. Click on the `Run SQL` button on the toolbar to execute this piece of SQL command to create our `LogIn` table.

In a similar way, create the second table `Customer` by entering the codes that are shown in Figure 5.138 into the blank SQL Command window.

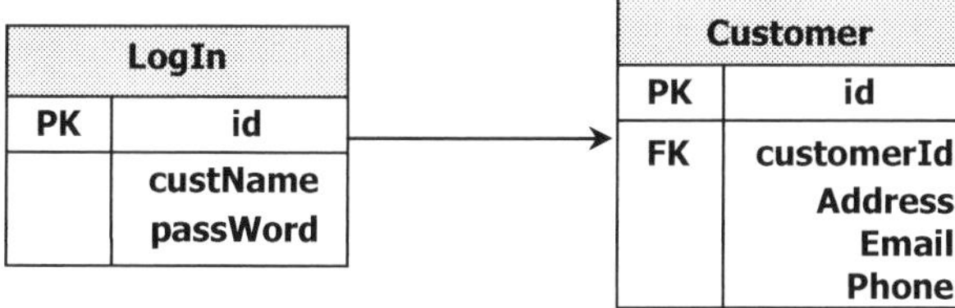

Figure 5.136. The relationship between two tables.

```
CREATE TABLE LogIn(
     id INT NOT NULL AUTO_INCREMENT PRIMARY KEY,
     custName CHAR(50) CHARACTER SET utf8 COLLATE utf8_general_ci NOT NULL UNIQUE,
     passWord CHAR(50) CHARACTER SET utf8 COLLATE utf8_general_ci NOT NULL
)
```

Figure 5.137. The codes used to create the Login table.

```
CREATE TABLE Customer(
     id INT NOT NULL AUTO_INCREMENT PRIMARY KEY,
     customerId INT NOT NULL,
     Address CHAR(50) CHARACTER SET utf8 COLLATE utf8_general_ci NOT NULL,
     Email CHAR(50) CHARACTER SET utf8 COLLATE utf8_general_ci  NOT NULL,
     Phone CHAR(50) CHARACTER SET utf8 COLLATE utf8_general_ci NOT NULL,
     FOREIGN KEY (customerId) REFERENCES LogIn(id)
)
```

Figure 5.138. The codes used to create the Customer table.

Click on the `Run SQL` button on the toolbar to execute this piece of SQL command to create our `Customer` table.

Now let's enter data into these two tables to complete this table creation process. Perform the following operations to insert data for these two tables:

1. On the `jdbc:mysql://localhost:3306/MySQLSample [root on Default schema]` connection, click the right mouse button and choose `Execute Command` to open an empty SQL Command window.
2. Enter the codes shown below into this empty window:

```
INSERT INTO LogIn(custName, passWord)
VALUES ('White', 'tomorrow');
INSERT INTO LogIn(custName, passWord)
VALUES ('Jerry', 'test');
INSERT INTO LogIn(custName, passWord)
VALUES ('CameraBuyer', '12345');
```

3. Click on the `Run SQL` button on the toolbar to execute this piece of SQL command to insert these data into the `LogIn` table.

These statements do not contain a value for the id field in the LogIn table, since these id values are entered automatically by the database engine because the field type is specified as AUTO_INCREMENT (refer to Fig. 5.137).

4. Perform a similar operation to insert the codes shown below into the Customer table:

```
INSERT INTO Customer (customerId, Address, Email, Phone)
VALUES (1, '101 Main Street', 'product@coming.org', '750-380-5577');
INSERT INTO Customer (customerId, Address, Email, Phone)
VALUES (1, '205 Morone Street', 'forsale@cat.net', '800-777-7788');
INSERT INTO Customer (customerId, Address, Email, Phone)
VALUES (2, '501 DeerField Beach', 'fish@see.net', '800-799-7600');
INSERT INTO Customer (customerId, Address, Email, Phone)
VALUES (3, '353 Linkfield Dr', 'field@vetcory.com', '700-777-2255');
```

5. Click on the Run SQL button on the toolbar to execute this piece of SQL command to insert these data into the Customer table.

Now go to the Services window and you should find two tables, LogIn and Customer, which have been added into our sample database MySQLSample. If not, right click on our sample database mysqlsample under the URL jdbc:mysql://localhost:3306/MySQLSample [root on Default schema] and select the Refresh item to get these two tables.

To see the detailed content of these two tables, right click on each of them and select the View Data item from the pop-up menu to open each of them. An opened Customer table is shown in Figure 5.139.

Next, let's add the functions to this PHP project to perform desired data actions between our PHP project and our sample database MySQLSample we created in this section.

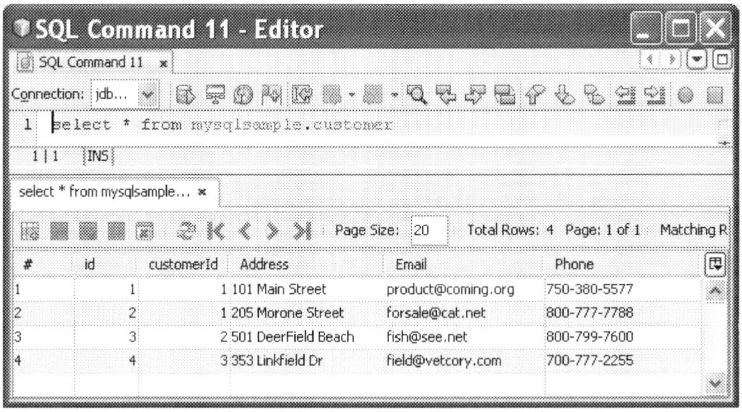

#	id	customerId	Address	Email	Phone
1	1	1	101 Main Street	product@coming.org	750-380-5577
2	2	1	205 Morone Street	forsale@cat.net	800-777-7788
3	3	2	501 DeerField Beach	fish@see.net	800-799-7600
4	4	3	353 Linkfield Dr	field@vetcory.com	700-777-2255

Figure 5.139. The content of the Customer table.

5.3.7.10 Building the Functions for the PHP Project

In this PHP project, we want to use the `index.php` file and create another PHP file, `customerDetails.php`, to perform the following functions:

1. By using the `index.php` file, we can enter a desired customer name to try to find a matched customer ID in the `Customer` table in our sample database.
2. By using the `customerDetails.php` file, we can retrieve all details about the selected `customerID` from the `index.php` file.
3. An error message will be given if no matched `customerID` can be found from the `Customer` table.

By using these two files, we can

- Displaying a page with controls for entering customer ID.
- Transferring the entered data to the `customerDetails.php` page.

Now let's create our next PHP file `customerDetails.php`. Perform the following operations to complete this creation process:

1. Start the NetBeans IDE 6.8 if it is not started.
2. In the `Projects` window, browse to our new PHP project `PHPCustomer`, and right click on the folder `Source Files` that is under our `PHPCustomer` project and choose `New > PHP File` menu item from the popup menu.
3. On the opened `New PHP File` wizard, enter `customerDetails` into the `File Name` field and click on the `Finish` button.

Now that a new PHP file has been created, next, let's handle the data transferring between the `index.php` page and the `customerDetails.php` page.

5.3.7.10.1 Transferring Data from index.php to the customerDetails.php The data (`customerID`) is received and processed on the destination page, `customerDetails.php`. In this application, the data is entered on the index page (`index.php`) and transferred to the `customerDetails.php` page. We need to implement data transferring in `index.php` and data reception in `customerDetails.php`.

Enter the codes that are shown in Figure 5.140 into the body of the `index.php` file. The newly added codes have been highlighted in gray background.

Let's take a closer look at this piece of newly added codes to see how it works.

- The opening `<form>` tag that contains the `action` field for entering the name of the file where the data must be transferred (`customerDetails.php`) and the method to be applied to transferring data (GET). PHP will creates a special array $_GET and populate there values of the fields from the original form.
- The text that appears on the page: `Show customer Name of:`
- A text input field for entering the `customer name` that will be matched to a `customerID` in the `Customer` table. The name "`user`" is the key to pick up the data on the destination form.

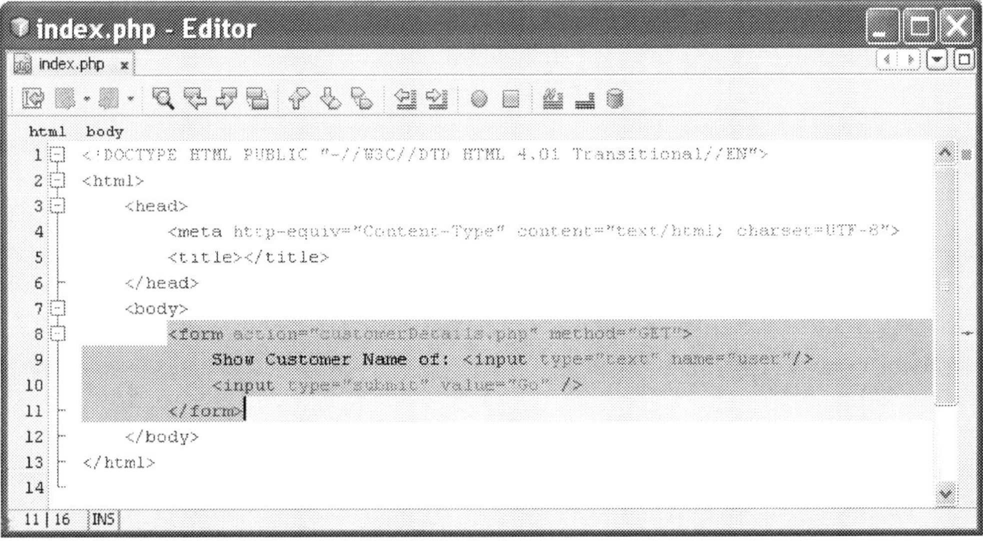

Figure 5.140. The added codes to the index.php file.

Figure 5.141. The running result of the index.php page.

- An input field of the `submit` type with the text `Go`. The type of `submit` means that the input field appears on the page as a button, and the data is transferred when exactly this control is affected.

Now let's test this starting page by right clicking on the `index.php` in the `Projects` window, and select the `Run` item from the popup menu. The running result is shown in Figure 5.141.

In the `Show Customer Name of:` edit box, enter `Tom`, and click on `Go`. An empty page with the following URL appears: http://localhost:800/PHPCustomer/customerDetails.php?user=Tom. This URL indicates that your main page works properly.

5.3.7.10.2 Receiving and Processing Data in the customerDetails.php Page As you can see from Figure 5.140, the `index.php` file did not contain any PHP code, so we have removed the codes inside the `<?php ... ?>` block and replaced them with a set

```
  <html>
A   <body>Customer Name of <?php echo $_GET["user"]."<br/>";?>
      <?php
B     $con = mysql_connect("localhost", "php_user", "!php_user");
C     if (!$con) {
         die('Could not connect: ' . mysql_error());
      }
D     mysql_query("SET NAMES 'utf8'");
E     mysql_select_db("MySQLSample", $con);
F     $custId = mysql_query("SELECT id FROM LogIn WHERE custName='".mysql_real_escape_string($_GET["user"])."'");
G     if (mysql_num_rows($custId)<1) {
         die("The person " .$_GET["user"]. " is not found. Please check the spelling and try again" );
      }
H     $customerID = mysql_result($custId, 0);
      ?>
    </body>
  </html>
```

Figure 5.142. The codes for the customerDetails.php page.

of HTML codes in a form. This means that all functions in the index.php page can be fulfilled by using the HTML codes.

However, in the destination page, `customerDetails.php`, we need to use PHP and HTML codes together to perform the receiving data (`customer ID`) and retrieving the details related to the received customer ID and displaying them in this page.

Perform the following operations to complete the coding for this page:

1. Double click the `customerDetails.php` file from the `Projects` window. The template that opens is different from `index.php`. Begin and end the file with `<html> </html>` and `<body></body>` tags as the file will contain HTML code, too.
2. Enter the codes that are shown in Figure 5.142 into this page.

Let's have a closer look at this piece of newly added codes to see how it works.

A. Starting from an HTML code block, the title of this page is displayed first. The `echo` and `GET[]` PHP commands are used to display the transferred customer name from the `index.php` page. This piece of PHP codes is embedded inside the HTML codes.

B. The database connection is executed inside a PHP block with the `mysql_connect()` PHP function being called. The returned connection is assigned to a PHP local variable `$con`. The point is that all variables in PHP start with a $ sign symbol. In fact, you can use the username and password to replace the last two arguments of this function to perform this connection, such as:

```
$con = mysql_connect("localhost", "root", "reback");
```

C. If any error occurred during this connection process, the PHP `die()` function is called to display this situation and exit this script. Generally, the functionality of the `die()` function is to print a message and exits the current script. The PHP function `mysql_error()` is called to display the error source.

D. The PHP function `mysql_query()` is executed to perform a query to set up the customer's name in a utf8 format.

E. The PHP function `mysql_select_db()` is executed to select our target database `MySQLSample` we built in Section 5.3.7.9.

F. A MySQL query is executed to get matched id from the LogIn table based on the customer name entered by the user in the index.php page. A PHP MySQL-related function, mysql_real_escape_string(), is executed to pick up the customer name using the GET[] function. The mysql_real_escape_string() function escapes special characters in a string for use in an SQL statement. Since this function returns a string, a single quotation mark must be used to cover this string. The returned id is assigned to a local variable $cusId.

G. If this execution returns nothing, the PHP function mysql_num_rows() will return a 0, which means that this query has something wrong, the die() function is called to display this situation.

H. The queried id is assigned to another local variable $customerID if this query is successful.

For more detailed information about PHP and related MySQL functions in PHP, refer to the site: http://www.w3schools.com/php/default.asp.

You can compile and build the project by clicking on the Clean and Build Main Project button from the toolbar. A successful building result will be displayed in the Output window if everything is fine.

Now let's add the additional codes to this page to display the running result for this data transferring. Insert the codes that are shown in Figure 5.143 into this customerDetails.php, exactly, between the PHP ending mark ?> and the body ending mark </body>, as shown in Figure 5.143. The newly inserted codes have been highlighted in bold.

Let's have a closer look at this piece of inserted codes to see how it works.

A. A table HTML tab is used to create a table with the black color as the border.

B. This table has four columns with headers of CustomerID, Address, Email, and Phone, which are matched to four columns in our Customer table in our MySQLSample database.

C. Starting a PHP block, the mysql_query() function is executed to perform a query to select and pick up all records from our Customer table based on the customerID retrieved from the top part of this page. The returned query result is assigned to a local variable $result.

D. A while loop is used to pick up each row based on each column's name. The PHP function mysql_fetch_array() returns a row from a recordset as an associative array and/or a numeric array. This function gets a row from the mysql_query() function and returns an array if it is success, or FALSE on failure or when there are no more rows.

E. The <tr></tr> tags form rows, the <td></td> tags form cells within rows, and \n starts a new line. The echo script and strip_tags() functions are used to display each column in a normal table format. The strip_tags() function removes any HTML tags from the displayed columns. Note that <br>, <p>, and <h1> tags are allowed in all columns. The strip_tags() function cannot accept a variable passed as a reference, which is why the variables $cID, $addr, $email, and $phone are created and used here.

F. The mysql_close() function is called to close this database connection.

G. The ending tag of </table> indicates that the table is complete.

Compile and build the project by clicking on the Clean and Build Main Project button from the toolbar. A successful building result will be displayed in the Output window if everything is fine. Next, let's run our PHP project to test its functionalities.

```
  html>
    <body>Customer Name of <?php echo $_GET["user"]."<br/>";?>
      <?php
      $con = mysql_connect("localhost", "php_user", "!php_user");
      if (!$con) {
         die('Could not connect: ' . mysql_error());
      }
      mysql_query("SET NAMES 'utf8'");
      mysql_select_db("MySQLSample", $con);
      $custId = mysql_query("SELECT id FROM LogIn WHERE custName='".mysql_real_escape_string($_GET["user"])."'");
      if (mysql_num_rows($custId)<1) {
         die("The person " .$_GET["user"]. " is not found. Please check the spelling and try again" );
      }
      $customerID = mysql_result($custId, 0);
      ?>
A     <table border="black">
        <tr>
B         <th>CustomerID</th>
          <th>Address</th>
          <th>Email</th>
          <th>Phone</th>
        </tr>
        <?php
C       $result = mysql_query("SELECT * FROM Customer WHERE customerId=". $customerID);
D       while($row = mysql_fetch_array($result)) {
              $cID = $row["customerId"];
              $addr = $row["Address"];
              $email = $row["Email"];
              $phone = $row["Phone"];
E             echo "<tr><td>" . strip_tags($cID,'<br><p><h1>')."</td>";
              echo "<td>". strip_tags($addr,'<br><p><h1>')."</td>";
              echo "<td>". strip_tags($email,'<br><p><h1>')."</td>";
              echo "<td>". strip_tags($phone)."</td></tr>\n";
          }
F         mysql_close($con);?>
G     </table>
    </body>
  </html>
```

Figure 5.143. The newly inserted codes to the customerDetails.php page.

5.3.7.11 Running and Testing the PHP Project

First, make sure that the Apache HTTP Server has been started and run on your computer. If not, go to the `Start\All Programs\Apache HTTP Server 2.2\Control Apache Server\Start` menu item to start this Web server. Then from the `Projects` window, right click on the `index.php` page and select the `Run` menu item from the popup menu to run the project.

In the opened page, enter `White` into the `Customer Name` field, and click on the `Go` button. The `customerDetails.php` page is called and the running result is shown in Figure 5.144.

Click on the `Back` button to return to the `index.php` page and replace `White` with `Jerry` in the Customer Name field, and click on the `Go` button again. The running result for the customer name `Jerry` is shown in Figure 5.145.

You can also try to enter other customer name, such as `Tom`, to this field in the `index.php` page. A running page that displays "`cannot find the person`" would be displayed since the customer name `Tom` is not existed in our `LogIn` table.

http://localhost:800/PHPCustomer/customerDetails.php?user=White

Customer Name of White

CustomerID	Address	Email	Phone
1	101 Main Street	product@coming.org	750-380-5577
1	205 Morone Street	forsale@cat.net	800-777-7788

Figure 5.144. The running result for the customer name of White.

Figure 5.145. The running result for the customer name of Jerry.

Our PHP project is successful.

A complete PHP project `PHPCustomer` can be found from the folder `DBProjects\Chapter 5` that is located at the Wiley ftp site (refer to Figure 1.2 in Chapter 1). You can download and run this application in your computer. However, before you can run this application in your computer, you need to have the following conditions met:

- An Apache HTTP Web Server has been installed in your computer at the default location, `C:\Program Files\Apache Software Foundation\Apache 2.2`.
- A PHP engine has been installed in your computer at the default location, `C:\Program Files\PHP`.
- The MySQL Server has been installed and run in your computer.
- The MySQL sample database `MySQLSample` has been created and connected.
- The Apache HTTP Web Server has been started and run in your computer.
- Make sure that both Apache HTTP Web Server and PHP engine have been successfully tested and run in your computer.
- Copy and save the PHP project `PHPCustomer` to the default location, `C:\Program Files\Apache Software Foundation\Apache 2.2\htdocs\`.

Next, let's take care of creating and building a NetBeans Module project.

5.3.8 Build a NetBeans Module

A module can be considered as an independent object or unit that can be combined or bound together to form a big and more complex application. In fact, a NetBeans module enables NetBeans to be extended dynamically. All of the Open APIs are designed to be used for purposes of implementing modules. Modules can be ranged in complexity from a single Java class, properly packaged to do something elementary such as add a menu item to the Edit menu to display the contents of the clipboard, to a full-scale integration of a major external application, such as a Java profiling suite.

All modules are distributed and installed as JAR files. The basic format should be rather familiar; classes constituting the module are archived in the JAR, and special entries in the manifest file are recognized.

To the greatest extent possible, NetBeans has designed the module system to reuse standard technologies when they are sufficient, and to follow the style of others when not.

The basic idea for the format of modules is taken from the Java Extension Mechanism. The basic idea behind the Package Versioning Specification is used to handle dependencies both between modules and of modules to the system.

All modules have some set of basic properties that indicate: which types of features they provide, which Java classes implement these features, and what special option settings should be used when installing these features. Some of this information is listed in the manifest file using the customary format and NetBeans-specific attributes. The Java Activation Framework, as well as JDK-internal features, such as support for executable JAR files, is used as a model for how to specify the useful contents of a JAR in a data-driven fashion: many modules will need no special installation code other than attributes in the manifest and an XML layer giving additional more specific deployment information.

All module implementation classes must reside in a JAR file when they are finished in building. If you want to split up a large application into several pieces, perhaps so as to make independent upgrades possible, you should do so by creating multiple modules and relating them using versioning.

The so-called module versioning provides a way for modules to be specified in:

- Which module they are (i.e., that one JAR is an upgrade from another);
- Which version they are;
- Whether they have introduced incompatible API changes since a previous version;
- Whether they depend on other modules or system features.

While very simple modules may not require special versioning support, this system should be used for any module published on a general release schedule, or where it is expected other modules may want to make use of.

A module is recognized as such by NetBeans, by virtue of its having a special magic tag in the global section of the manifest file. Modules can do three things with versioning:

1. Specify what they are. This is done by the special `OpenIDE-Module` tag, whose value should be a unique (programmatic) identifier for the module, as mentioned above. Not be

confused with the display name, which is free form and may be changed at will, this code name should not be changed arbitrarily—pick a name and stick with it throughout module releases.

2. Specify which version they are. In line with the Java Versioning Specification, modules can indicate two pieces of version information about themselves using the `OpenIDE-Module-Specification-Version` and the `OpenIDE-Module-Implementation-Version` tags. Modules are also permitted to use `OpenIDE-Module-Build-Version` to give information about when or by whom they were physically built, in case there is more specialized semantics given to the implementation version.
3. Specify which features they depend on. Again, this is done using the Versioning Specification—modules can request general or specific versions of other modules (`OpenIDE-Module-Module-Dependencies`), Java packages (`OpenIDE-Module-Package-Dependencies`), or Java itself (`OpenIDE-Module-Java-Dependencies`).

In the following sections, we will build a real NetBeans application to wrap three modules together to illustrate how to use the NetBeans Module to build and implement modules to develop a big and more complex application.

5.3.8.1 Create a New NetBeans Module Project

In this section, we will create a new NetBeans Module application `JavaModuleCustomer`, and then we will develop some other units and convert them to the associated modules. Finally, we will combine all associated modules with our main module `JavaModuleCustomer` together to make a big application.

The operation steps required for building this application are:

1. Create our main module application `JavaModuleCustomer`
2. Create an entity class for the `Customer` table in the JavaDB sample database and wrap that entity class into a module—module 2 in this application.
3. Wrap the system library `EclipseLink`, which works as a persistence library for our persistence API, and the database connector into another two modules—modules 3 and 4 in this application.
4. Create a new module that provides the user interface for our application. The new module gives the user a tree hierarchy showing data from the database—module 5 in this application.
5. Create another module that lets the user edit the data displayed by module 5.

By separating the viewer from the editor in distinct modules, we will enable the user to install a different editor for the same viewer, since different editors could be created by external vendors, some commercially and some for free. It is this flexibility that the modular architecture of the NetBeans Platform makes possible.

The software requirements for building this application are: NetBeans 6.8 or higher, and Java Developer Kit (JDK) 6.0 or higher.

Now let's first create a new NetBeans Module application project `JavaModuleCustomer`.

Launch NetBeans IDE 6.8 and go to `File > New Project`. In the opened `New Project` wizard, select `NetBeans Modules` from the `Categories` list and `NetBeans`

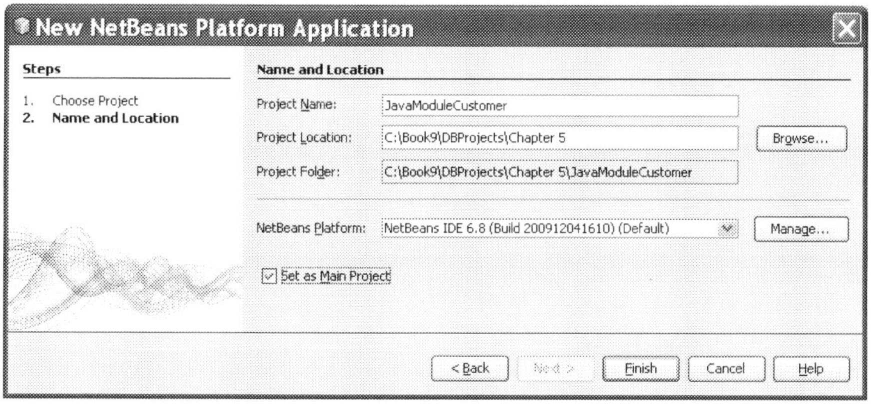

Figure 5.146. The finished New Project wizard.

Platform Application from the Projects list, and then click on the Next button to continue.

Enter JavaModuleCustomer into the Project Name field and a desired location into the Project Location field. Make sure that the Set as Main Project checkbox is checked. Your finished New Project wizard should match one that is shown in Figure 5.146. Click on the Finish button to complete this creation process.

Next, let's create the entity class for the Customer table in the JavaDB sample database and wrap it into a module.

5.3.8.2 Create the Customer Entity Class and Wrap It into a Module

Since we will not include this entity class into our new project, instead, we need to create a new entity class for the Customer table and wrap it into a new module. So perform the following operations to create this Customer entity class and wrap it into a module:

1. In the opened NetBeans IDE 6.8, go to File > New Project menu item to open the New Project wizard.
2. Select Java from the Categories list and Java Class Library from the Projects list. Click on the Next button to continue.
3. Enter CustomerLibrary into the Project Name field, and click on the Finish button to close this process.
4. In the Projects window, right click on the CustomerLibrary project and choose New > Entity Classes from Database.
5. In the opened wizard, select the JavaDB sample database by choosing its URL from the Database Connection field, jdbc:derby://localhost:1527/sample[app on APP].
6. Select the Customer table from the Available Tables list and click on the Add button to add it into the Selected Tables list. The Discount Code table is also added automatically since there is a relationship between these two tables. Click on the Next button to continue.

7. Click on the `Create Persistence Unit` button to open the `Create Persistence Unit` wizard, since we need to use this persistence later. Keep all default settings unchanged and click on the `Create` button to create this persistence.
8. Enter `CustomerPackage` into the `Package` field as the package name, and click on the `Next` button to continue. Your finished `New Entity Classes from Database` wizard should match one that is shown in Figure 5.147.
9. Click on the `Finish` button to close this process.

Once you have completed this step, look at the generated code and notice that, among other things, you now have a `persistence.xml` file in a folder called `META-INF`, as well as entity class `Customer.java` for the `Customer` table, as shown in Figure 5.148.

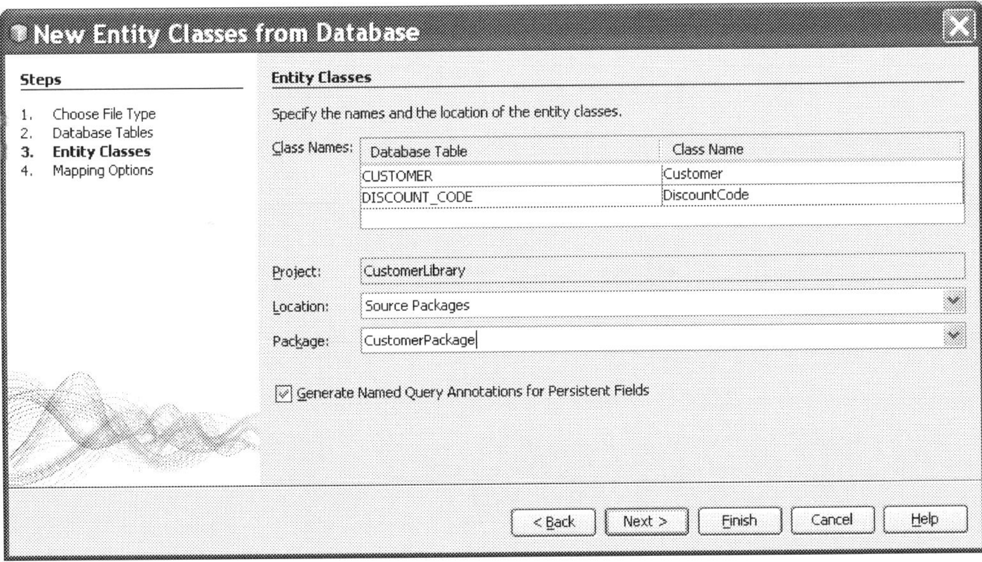

Figure 5.147. The finished New Entity Classes from Database wizard.

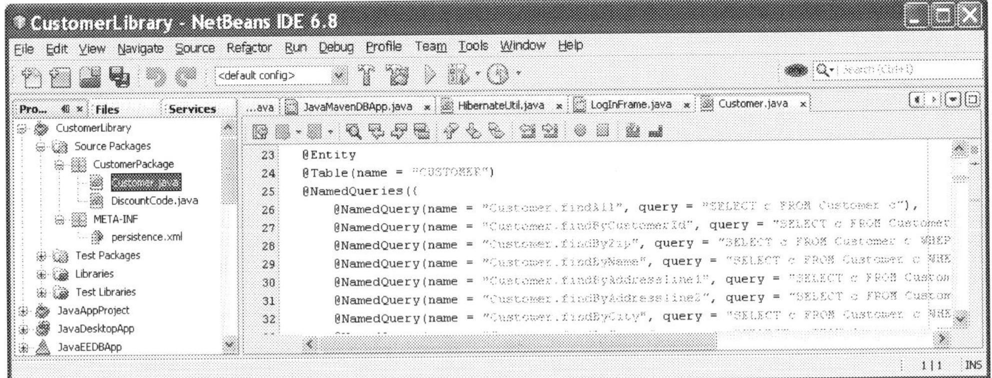

Figure 5.148. The created entity class for the Customer table.

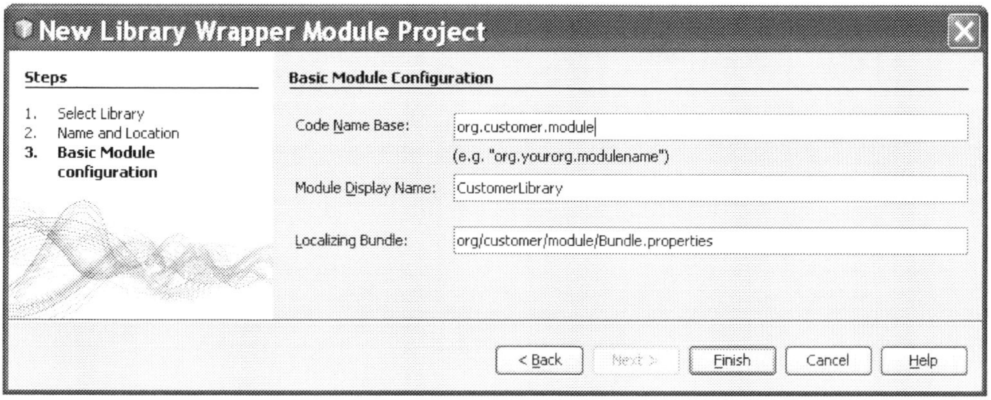

Figure 5.149. The finished New Library Wrapper Module Wizard.

Now open the `Files` window and you can find our library JAR file, `CustomerLibrary.jar`, in the library project's `dist` folder.

Next, we need to wrap this library module into our main module application `JavaModuleCustomer` we created before.

Perform the following operations to finish this wrapping:

1. Right click on `JavaModuleCustomer`'s `Modules` node in the `Projects` window and choose `Add New Library` from the popup menu.
2. On the opened wizard, click on the `Browse` button that is next to the `Library` field to locate the folder in which our `CustomerLibrary.jar` file is located. In this application, it is `C:\Book 9\DBProjects\Chapter 5\CustomerLibrary\dist`. Click this file to select it and click on the `Select` button. Leave the `License` field empty and click on the `Next` button to continue.
3. Click on the `Next` button to the next wizard.
4. Enter `org.customer.module` into the `Code Name Base` field and click on the `Finish` button to complete this process. Your finished wizard should match one that is shown in Figure 5.149.

Now you can find that a wrapped module `CustomerLibrary` has been added into our main project `JavaModuleCustomer` under the `Modules` node, as shown in Figure 5.150.

Next, let's create another two modules to wrap the system library `EclipseLink`, which works as a persistence library for our persistence API, and the database connector into another two modules.

5.3.8.3 Create Other Related Modules

Perform the following operations to create and wrap these two libraries into the first module:

1. Right click on the `Modules` node under our project `JavaModuleCustomer` from the `Projects` window and select the `Add New Library` item from the popup menu to open the `New Library Wrapper Module Project` wizard.

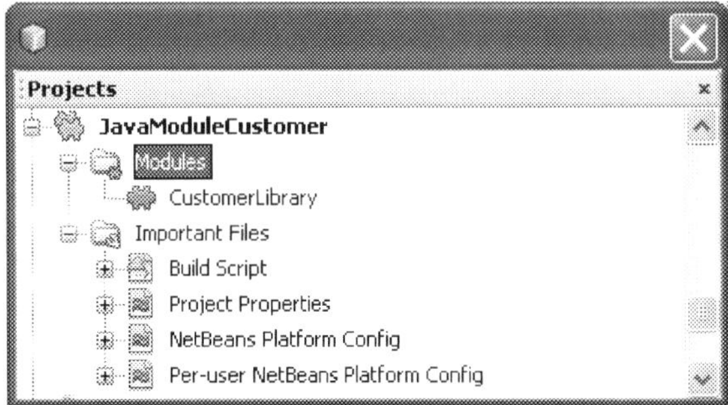

Figure 5.150. The newly wrapped module CustomerLibrary.

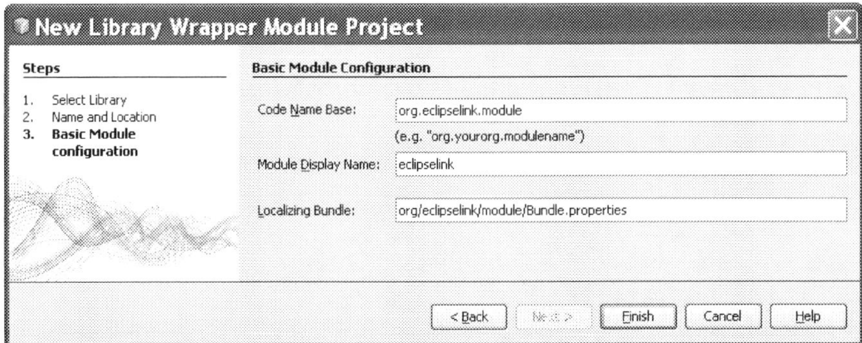

Figure 5.151. The finished New Library Wrapper Module Project wizard.

2. Click on the `Browse` button that is next to the `Library` field and browse to the location where the system library `EclipseLink` is located; it is `CustomerLibrary\dist\lib`. Select two library files, `eclipselink-2.0.0.jar` and `eclipselink-javax.persistence-2.0.jar`, and click on the `Select` button.
3. Leave the `License` field empty and click on the `Next` button to continue.
4. In the `Name and Location` wizard, keep all default settings unchanged and click on the `Next` button to continue.
5. In the `Basic Module configuration` wizard, enter `org.eclipselink.module` into the `Code Name Base` field and keep all other default settings unchanged. Your finished `Basic Module configuration` wizard should match one that is shown in Figure 5.151.
6. Click on the `Finish` button to complete this process.

Immediately after you complete this creation and wrapper process, you can find that a new module `eclipselink` has been added into our project `JavaModuleCustomer` under the `Modules` node in the `Projects` window. If you open the `Files` window and expand the project folder to `CustomerLibrary\dist\lib`, you can find those two wrapper module files have been there, as shown in Figure 5.152.

Now let's create another library wrapper module to make our database connector to another module.

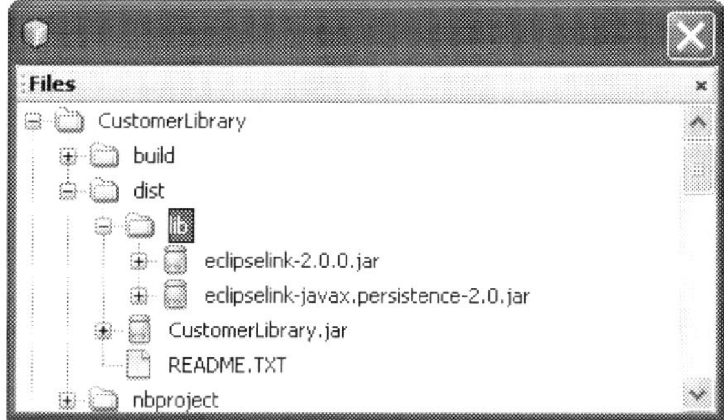

Figure 5.152. Two created wrapper module files.

Figure 5.153. The finished wrapper module derbyclient.

Perform the following operations to create this wrapper module:

1. Right click on the `Modules` node under our project `JavaModuleCustomer` from the `Projects` window, and select the `Add New Library` item from the popup menu to open the `New Library Wrapper Module Project` wizard.
2. Click on the `Browse` button that is next to the `Library` field and browse to the location where the `Java DB client` JAR is located in this application, which is `C:\Program Files\Sun\JavaDB\lib`. Select file, `derbyclient.jar`, and click on the `Select` button.
3. Leave the `License` field empty and click on the `Next` button to continue.
4. In the `Name and Location` wizard, keep all default settings unchanged and click on the `Next` button to continue.
5. In the `Basic Module configuration` wizard, enter `org.derbyclient.module` into the `Code Name Base` field and keep all other default settings unchanged. Your finished `Basic Module configuration` wizard should match one that is shown in Figure 5.153.
6. Click on the `Finish` button to complete this process.

Immediately, you can find that a new module `derbyclient` has been added into our project `JavaModuleCustomer` under the `Modules` node in the `Projects` window.

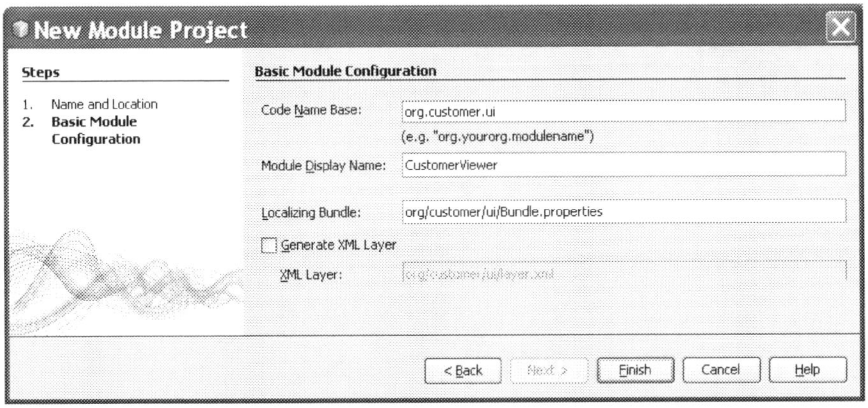

Figure 5.154. The finished New Module Project wizard.

Next, let's create a user interface to display the retrieved data from the `Customer` table in the JavaDB sample database.

5.3.8.4 Create the User Interface Module

In this section, we will create a user interface module and use it to display our retrieved data from the Customer table. Perform the following operations to complete this process:

1. Right click on the `Modules` node under our project `JavaModuleCustomer` from the `Projects` window, and select the Add New item from the popup menu to open the New `Module Project` wizard.
2. Enter `CustomerViewer` into the `Project Name` field and keep all default settings unchanged. Click on the `Next` button to continue.
3. In the `Basic Module configuration` wizard, enter `org.customer.ui` into the `Code Name Base` field and keep all other default settings unchanged. Your finished `Basic Module configuration` wizard should match one that is shown in Figure 5.154.
4. Click on the `Finish` button to complete this process.
5. In the `Files` window, right click on the newly created module `CustomerViewer`, and select `New > Window Component` item from the pop-up menu.
6. In the opened `New Window` wizard, select the `editor` from the `Window Position` combo box and check the `Open on Application Start` checkbox. Click on the `Next` button to continue.
7. Enter `Customer` into the `Class Name Prefix` field and keep all other default settings unchanged. Your finished `New Window` wizard should match one that is shown in Figure 5.155. Click on the `Finish` button to complete this GUI creation process.
8. Use the Palette to drag and drop a `Label` to the top of this GUI window. Change the **text** of this label to `The Details in the Customer Table`.
9. Use the Palette to drag and drop a `Text Area` on this GUI window. Right click on this newly added `Text Area` and select the `Change Variable Name` item to change

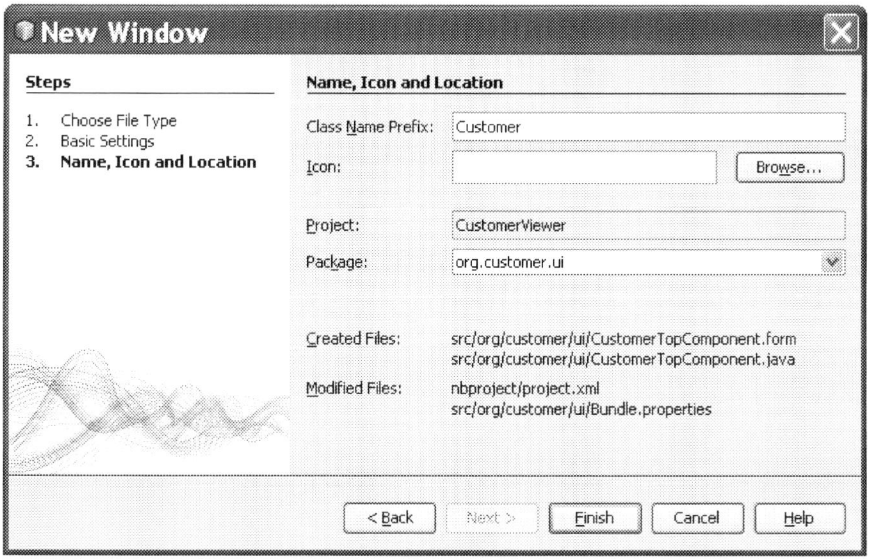

Figure 5.155. The finished New Window wizard.

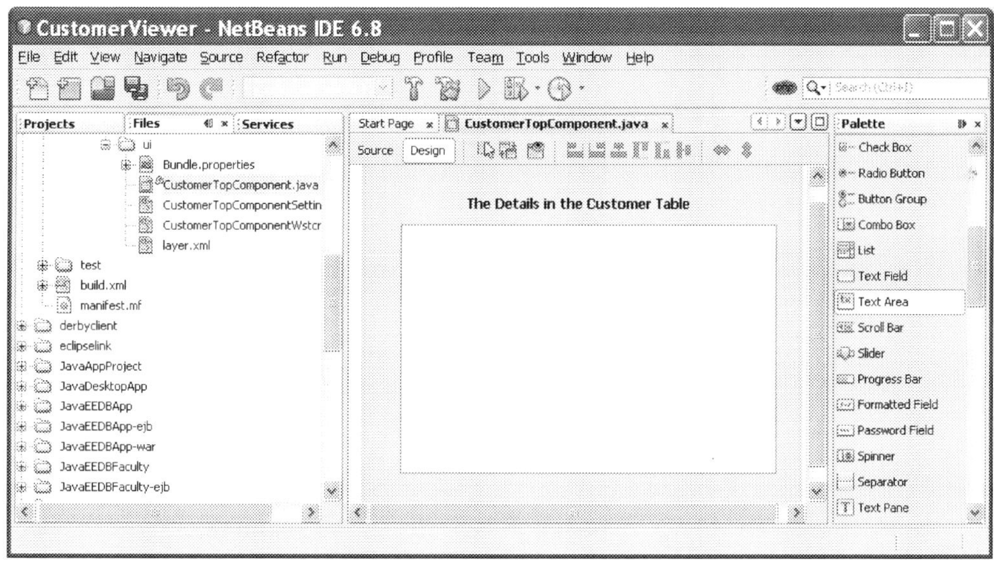

Figure 5.156. The finished GUI Window.

its name to `CustomerTextArea`. Your finished GUI window should match one that is shown in Figure 5.156.

10. Click on the `Source` button to open the code window of this GUI Window, and add the codes that are shown in Figure 5.157 to the end of the `TopComponent()` constructor.

Let's have a closer look at this piece of newly added codes to see how it works.

```
.........
public CustomerTopComponent() {
      initComponents();
      setName(NbBundle.getMessage(CustomerTopComponent.class, "CTL_CustomerTopComponent"));
      setToolTipText(NbBundle.getMessage(CustomerTopComponent.class, "HINT_CustomerTopComponent"));
      // setIcon(ImageUtilities.loadImage(ICON_PATH, true));

A    EntityManager entityManager = Persistence.createEntityManagerFactory("CustomerLibraryPU").createEntityManager();
B    Query query = entityManager.createQuery("SELECT c FROM Customer c");
C    List<Customer> resultList = query.getResultList();
D    for (Customer c : resultList) {
        CustomerTextArea.append(c.getName() + " (" + c.getCity() + ")" + "\n");
      }
}
```

Figure 5.157. The added codes to the end of the constructor.

A. A new entity manager instance is created since we need to use it to create and execute some queries to our `Customer` table in the JavaDB sample database later.

B. A Java persistence query is performed to pick up all columns from the `Customer` table.

C. The `getResultList()` method is executed to pick up returned columns stored in a Query collection, and assign them to a local variable `resultList` that has a `List` collection format.

D. An extended Java `for` loop is executed to get all names and cities for all customers in the `Customer` table. The `append()` method is used to attach each record to the end of the Text Area control.

Since we have not set dependencies on the modules that provide the `Customer` object and the persistence JARs, the statements above will be marked with red error underlines. These will be fixed in the next section.

5.3.8.5 Set Dependencies between Modules

In this section, we will enable some modules to use code from some of the other modules. We can do this very explicitly by setting intentional contracts between related modules, that is, as opposed to the accidental and chaotic reuse of code that tends to happen when we do not have a strict modular architecture such as that provided by the NetBeans Platform.

The dependencies used in this application can be described as:

1. The entity class module needs to have dependencies on the `derbyclient` module, as well as on the `eclipselink` module. To set up these dependencies, right click on the `CustomerLibrary` module and choose the `Properties`, to open the Project Properties wizard. Select the `Libraries` tab and click on the `Add Dependency` button. On the opened wizard, select the `derbyclient` and `eclipselink` modules from the `Modules` list, as shown in Figure 5.158, and click on the `OK` button to set dependencies on the two modules that the `CustomerLibrary` module needs.

   Your finished `Project Properties` wizard should match one that is shown in Figure 5.159.

   Click on the `OK` button to finish these dependencies setup process.

2. The `CustomerViewer` module needs a dependency on the `eclipselink` module, as well as on the entity class module. To set up these dependencies, right click on the `CustomerViewer` module, and choose `Properties`, and use the `Libraries` tab to set dependencies (`eclipselink` and `CustomerLibrary`) on those two modules that the `CustomerViewer` module needs.

3. Open the `CustomerTopComponent` in the `Source` view, right click in the editor, and choose "`Fix Imports`" to open the `Fix All Imports` wizard and click the `OK` button to try to fix any missed package and dependency. The IDE is now able to add the required import statements, because the modules that provide the required classes are now available to the `CustomerTopComponent`.

4. A possible unsolved component may be encountered, which is the `Query` class. There are two `Query` classes located at the different packages: the `javax.management` and `javax.persistence` packages. In this application, we need the `Query` class that is located at the second package. To fix this problem, just prefix the package name `javax.`

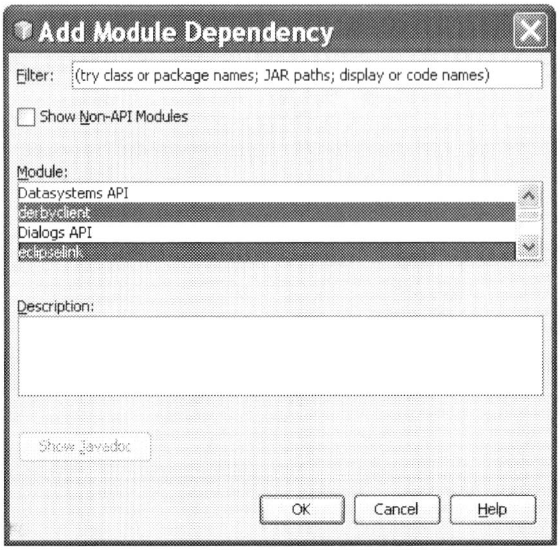

Figure 5.158. The Add Module Dependency wizard.

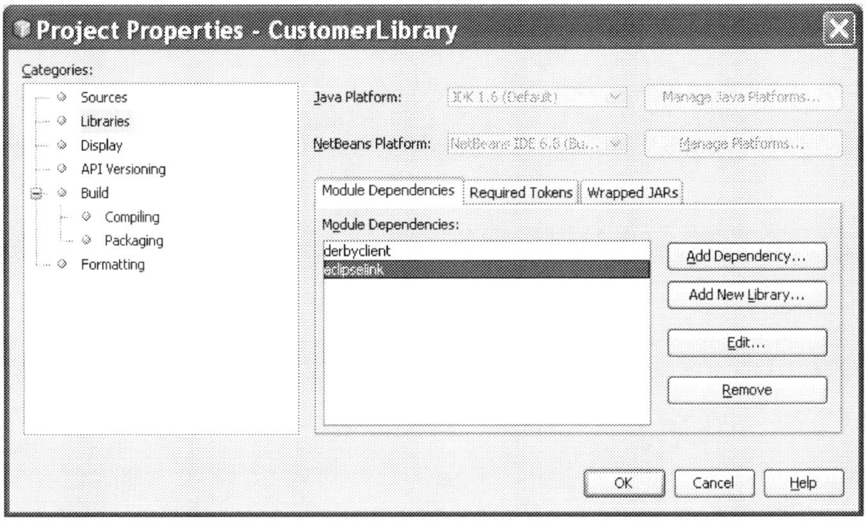

Figure 5.159. The finished Project Properties wizard.

persistence before the Query class, as shown in step **A** in Figure 5.160. The prefixing part has been highlighted in bold.

We now have set contracts between the modules in our application, giving our control over the dependencies between distinct pieces of code.

Now we are ready to build and run our module project to test its functionality.

```
.........
public CustomerTopComponent() {
      initComponents();
      setName(NbBundle.getMessage(CustomerTopComponent.class, "CTL_CustomerTopComponent"));
      setToolTipText(NbBundle.getMessage(CustomerTopComponent.class, "HINT_CustomerTopComponent"));
      // setIcon(ImageUtilities.loadImage(ICON_PATH, true));

    EntityManager entityManager = Persistence.createEntityManagerFactory("CustomerLibraryPU").createEntityManager();
A   javax.persistence.Query query = entityManager.createQuery("SELECT c FROM Customer c");
    List<Customer> resultList = query.getResultList();
    for (Customer c : resultList) {
        CustomerTextArea.append(c.getName() + " (" + c.getCity() + ")" + "\n");
      }
  }
```

Figure 5.160. The modified codes for the CustomerTopComponent class.

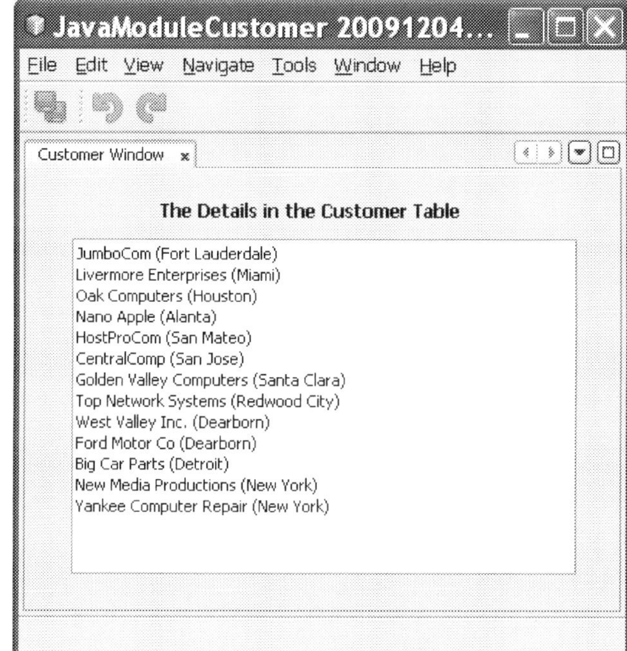

Figure 5.161. A running example of the project JavaModuleCustomer.

5.3.8.6 Build and Run the NetBeans Module Project

Click on the `Clean and Build Main Project` button to build our project. A successful building message should be displayed in the `Output` window if everything is fine.

First, let's run our database server by right clicking on the JavaDB sample database connection URL `jdbc:derby://localhost:1527/sample [app on APP]`from the `Services` window and select the `Connect` item from the popup menu. Then right click on our project `JavaModuleCustomer` from the `Projects` window, and select the `Run` item from the popup menu to run the project. A running result is shown in Figure 5.161.

A complete NetBeans Module project `JavaModuleCustomer` can be found from the folder `DBProjects\Chapter 5` that is located at the Wiley ftp site (refer to Figure 1.2 in Chapter 1). You can download and run this application in your computer.

5.4 CHAPTER SUMMARY

The basic and fundamental knowledge and implementations of NetBeans IDE 6.8 are discussed and presented with a lot of real examples projects in this chapter. The components and architecture of NetBeans IDE 6.8 are introduced and analyzed in detail at the beginning of this chapter. Following an overview of NetBeans IDE 6.8, a detailed discussion and introduction of the NetBeans IDE 6.8 platform is given. A detailed introduction and illustration in how to download and install NetBeans IDE 6.8 are provided in this chapter.

Most popular technologies and applications supported by NetBeans IDE 6.8 are discussed, which include:

- Java Applications
- Java Desktop Applications
- Java Class Library
- JavaFX Script Applications
- JavaFX Desktop Business Applications
- JavaFX Mobile Business Applications
- Java Enterprise Edition Applications
- Java Enterprise Edition 6 Web Applications
- Apache Maven Applications
- PHP Applications
- NetBeans Module Applications

Each of these technologies and implementations is discussed and analyzed in detailed with real project examples, and line-by-line coding illustrations and explanations. Each real sample project has been compiled and built in NetBeans IDE, and can be downloaded and run at user's computer easily and conveniently.

The main application Web and database servers, as well as databases involved in those example projects, include:

1. JavaDB Sample Database Server
2. Glassfish Enterprise Web Server v3
3. Apache HTTP Web Server
4. MySQL Database Server
5. Hibernate Query Language (HQL)
6. MySQL Database and MySQL Query Language

All of these technologies and their implementations are discussed and illustrated by using real project examples in this chapter step by step and line by line. By following these example projects, users can learn and master those key techniques easily and conveniently with lower learning curves.

All actual example projects discussed and developed in this chapter have been compiled and built successfully, and stored in the folder `DBProjects\Chapter 5` that is located at the Wiley ftp site (refer to Figure 1.2 in Chapter 1).

HOMEWORK

I. True/False Selections

____**1.** The NetBeans Platform is a broad Swing-based framework on which you can base large desktop applications.

____**2.** Each distinct feature in a NetBeans Platform application can be provided by a distinct NetBeans module, which is comparable with a plug-in.

____**3.** A NetBeans module is a group of Java classes that provides an application with a specific feature.

____**4.** The NetBeans IDE is an open-source integrated development environment, and it only supports development of all Java application types.

____**5.** Three main modules included in the NetBeans IDE are: NetBeans Profiler, GUI Design Tool, and NetBeans JavaScript Editor.

____**6.** NetBeans IDE is mainly composed of NetBeans Open-Source IDE and NetBeans Platform.

____**7.** A Java Class Library is only a skeleton Java class library without a main class, but it can be executed by itself.

____**8.** JavaFX, which is a kind of script language, is a Java platform for creating and delivering rich Internet applications that can run across a wide variety of connected devices.

____**9.** The difference between a JavaFX Script Application and a JavaFX Desktop Business Application is that the former runs the application using command-line JavaFX executable with a default scene, and the latter uses a Standard Execution mode with a definite view or scene.

____**10.** The Java EE differs from the Java SE in that it adds libraries that provide functionality to deploy fault-tolerant, distributed, multi-tier Java software, based largely on modular components running on an application server.

II. Multiple Choices

1. Some of the fundamental components of Java EE include: ________________.

- **a.** Java SE and NetBeans IDE
- **b.** NetBeans IDE platform and open source
- **c.** Java EE Application model and specifications
- **d.** Enterprise JavaBeans (EJB) and Java Persistence API (JPA)

2. A Java EE application is delivered in either a Java Archive (JAR) file, a(n) __________, or a(n) ______________.

- **a.** Application file, deployment file
- **b.** Web file, Desktop application file
- **c.** Web Archive (WAR) file, Enterprise Archive (EAR) file
- **d.** Deployment file, Web Archive (WAR) file

3. The most often used Java EE 6 Application server is ________________.
   a. JEUS 7 application server
   b. JBoss Application Server 6
   c. Caucho Resin 4.0
   d. GlassFish application server
4. The major Java Bean used to handle or process a message is called ___________.
   a. Session Bean
   b. Notification Bean
   c. Message-Driven Bean
   d. Manager Bean
5. The ____________ just work as a View for the Glassfish application server and set up a connection between the application server and the Session Bean in the Web tier.
   a. Java EE 6
   b. Enterprise Java Beans (EJB)
   c. Java Server Faces (JSF)
   d. Java Persistence API
6. Based on the definition of the Maven, it has two major functionalities: __________ and ______________.
   a. Project development, project implementation
   b. Project building, project management
   c. Project deployment, project implementation
   d. Project implementation, project debugging
7. When typing a HQL query in the HQL Query Editor, for each column name you used in your query, you must use the _________ column name, not the __________ column name in the relational data table.
   a. Original, modified
   b. Modified, original
   c. SQL, mapped
   d. Mapped, original
8. PHP is a scripting language that is particularly useful for server side development of the Web application, in which PHP will run on a Web server.
   a. Script, server
   b. Procedure-oriented, client
   c. Web programming, server
   d. Object-oriented, server
9. A PHP project can run in a ___________.
   a. Local website
   b. Remote website (FTP)
   c. script
   d. all of above
10. A module can be considered as a(n) __________ object or unit that can be combined or bound together to form a __________________ application.
   a. Dependent, big and complex
   b. Dependent, small and easier

c. Independent, big and complex
d. Independent, small and easier

III. Exercises

1. Provide a brief description about the Java EE 6 and its multi-tier application model.
2. Provide a brief discussion about Java EE 6 three-tier application layers.
3. Provide a brief description about JavaFX script language.
4. List the most popular application servers used by Java EE 6.
5. Refer to Section 5.3.2.2; build a similar Java Desktop Application named `JavaDesktopDB` and use the `Manufacturer` table as the target table.
6. Explain the advantages of using NetBeans Module for Java project development.

PART I
Building Two-Tier Client–Server Applications

Chapter 6

Query Data from Databases

Similarly to querying data in Visual Studio.NET, when querying data in the Java NetBeans IDE environment, two query modes or methods can be utilized; Java Persistence API (JPA) Wizards and runtime object codes. Traditional Java codes (SDK 1.x) only allow users to access databases with a sequence of codes, starting from creating a DriverManager to load the database driver, setting up a connection using the Driver, creating a query statement object, running the executeQuery object and processing the received data using a ResultSet object. This coding is not a big deal to the experienced programmers; however, it may be a headache to the college students or beginners who are new to the Java database programming. In order to effectively remove the headache caused by the huge blocks of coding and reduce the learning curve, in this Chapter, we introduce two methods to perform the database queries: JPA Wizards attached with the NetBeans IDE 6.8 and regular Java runtime object method.

SECTION I QUERY DATA USING JAVA PERSISTENCE API WIZARDS

JPA is a new component added to EE 5 and attached to the NetBeans IDE 6.8. With the help of JPA, a database query operation can be built and developed with a few lines of codes as soon as a connection has been set up by entity manager. Thanks to the JPA, which provides a significant improvement in database programming, and makes the database programming a simpler issue. You would find how easy it is to make a database query using this JPA in this Chapter, and I bet you that you will like it!

6.1 JAVA PERSISTENCE APIS

JPA is the standard API used for the management of the persistent data and object/relational mapping. Java Persistence API is added into Java EE 5 platform. Each application server compatible with Java EE 5 supports the Java Persistent APIs. Java Persistence API ensures the management of persistence and object-relational (O-R) mapping. These are helpful while using the JPA in the development of applications using the platform for

Practical Database Programming with Java, First Edition. Ying Bai.

Java EE 5. It provides O-R mapping facility to manage relational data in java applications.

The JPA contains the following components:

- JPA
- Mapping metadata
- The query language

6.1.1 Features of JPA

JPA is a lightweight framework based on Plain Old Java Objects (POJO) for O-R mapping. Java language metadata annotations and/or XML deployment descriptor is used for the mapping between Java objects and a relational database. It allows the SQL-like query language that works for both static as well as dynamic queries. It also allows the use of the pluggable persistence API. JPAs are mainly depends on metadata annotations. API includes the following components:

- JPA
- Metadata annotations
- Java Persistence query language

6.1.2 Advantages of JPA

JPA is build upon the best ideas from the persistence technologies like TopLink, Java Data objects (JDO) and Hibernate. JPA is compatible with Java Standard Edition (SE) environment, as well as Java Enterprise Edition (EE), and allows developers to take advantages of the standard persistence API.

Persistency of data is not so easy for most of the enterprise applications because for this, they require access to the relational database like SQL Server or Oracle 10g. It is the users' responsibility to update and retrieve the database by writing the code using SQL and JDBC. While several O-R frameworks, such as JBoss Hibernate and OracleTopLink, make persistence challenges simpler and popular. They let the java developer free from writing JDBC code and concentrate only on the development logic. In Enterprise JavaBeans (EJB) 2.x, container manage persistence (CMP) try to solve the persistence challenges but is not completely successful.

Persistence tier of the application can be developed in several ways, but Java platform does not follow any standard that can be used by both Java EE and Java SE environment. But the JPA (JPA) part of EJB 3.0 spec (JSR-220) makes the persistence API standard for the Java platform. O-R mapping vendors like Hibernate and TopLink, as well as JDO vendors and other leading application server vendors, are receiving the JSR-220.

6.1.3 Architecture and Function of JPA

While developing an enterprise application, first we need to design the domain object model to persist the data in the database. Domain model represents the persistence

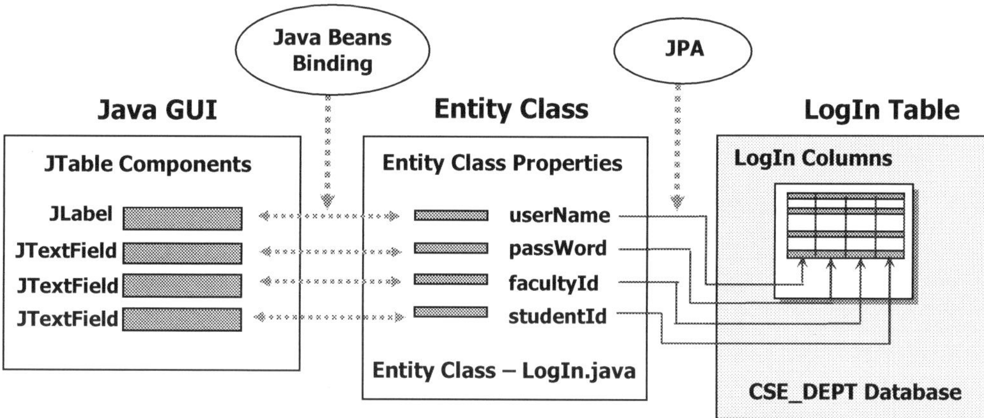

Figure 6.1. Architecture of JPA.

objects or entities in the database. An entity can be mapped to a data table in a database, and properties of an entity can be mapped to columns in that table. Architecture of JPA is shown in Figure 6.1.

The LogIn table in our sample database CSE_DEPT developed in Chapter 2 is used as an example to illustrate the mapping relationship between a domain model and a real database. In the domain model, each column in the database table LogIn is mapped to a property in the entity class, and the whole LogIn table is mapped to the entity class LogIn.java. The Java Beans Binding set a connection between each GUI component in the Java GUI and each associated entity property in the Entity class. Similarly, the JPA set up a connection between each property in the Entity class and each column in the LogIn table in our real database. The real mapping between each object in the entity class and each column in the relation database is established by the JPA.

When JPA works, the Entity Manager provides managements in the set and the get data between the entity class and database. The Query object provides a way or definition in how to get data from the Entity Manager, and the Query Result object provides a temporary location to hold and store the data coming from the Query in a certain format.

Now that we have a clear picture about the JPA, let's start to use it in our real project to perform the data query from our sample database. First, we introduce how to query data from our database using the JPA Wizards method.

6.2 QUERY DATA USING JAVA PERSISTENCE API WIZARDS (JPA)

In order to use JPA to set a map between our database and entity classes, we need first to connect our database to NetBeans IDE. By using the NetBeans IDE connection functions, we can connect to different databases, such as Microsoft Access 2007, SQL Server 2008, or Oracle Database 10g XE. This kind of connection belongs to project-independent connection, which means that no matter whether a project has been created or not, or whether any project will use this connection or not, the connection can be made for the entire IDE.

6.2.1 Connect to Different Databases and Drivers Using JPA Wizards

First, let's connect to our Microsoft Access 2007 sample database CSE_DEPT.accdb.

6.2.1.1 Connect to the Microsoft Access Database CSE_DEPT

NetBeans 6.8 does provide drivers for JDBC-ODBC Bridge Driver, such as Microsoft Access/MSSQL), MySQL, Java, and PostgreSQL database. Therefore, we do not need to install a third-party driver for these databases as in version 6.8.

The first thing we need to do is to set up a connection between the NetBeans IDE and our sample Microsoft Access 2007 database CSE_DEPT.accdb we developed in Chapter 2. Following the step listed below to make this connection:

1. Launch NetBeans IDE 6.8 to open its Start Page
2. Go to Window|Services menu item to open the Services pane shown in Figure 6.2.
3. Expand the Databases and Drivers folders, which are shown in Figure 6.2. You can find that five types of database drivers, Java DB (Embedded), Java DB (Network), JDBC-ODBC Bridge, MySQL, and PostgreSQL, have been installed with this IDE.
4. To connect to our sample Microsoft Access database CSE_DEPT, right click on the JDBC-ODBC Bridge item and select the Connect Using ... tab to open the New Database Connection dialog box, which is shown in Figure 6.3.
5. Enter the following information to start this connection:
   - **A.** Your computer name, which is YBAI in this project.
   - **B.** Your password, which is reback in this project.
   - **C.** Display Name, which is an optional and a blank, is used for this project.

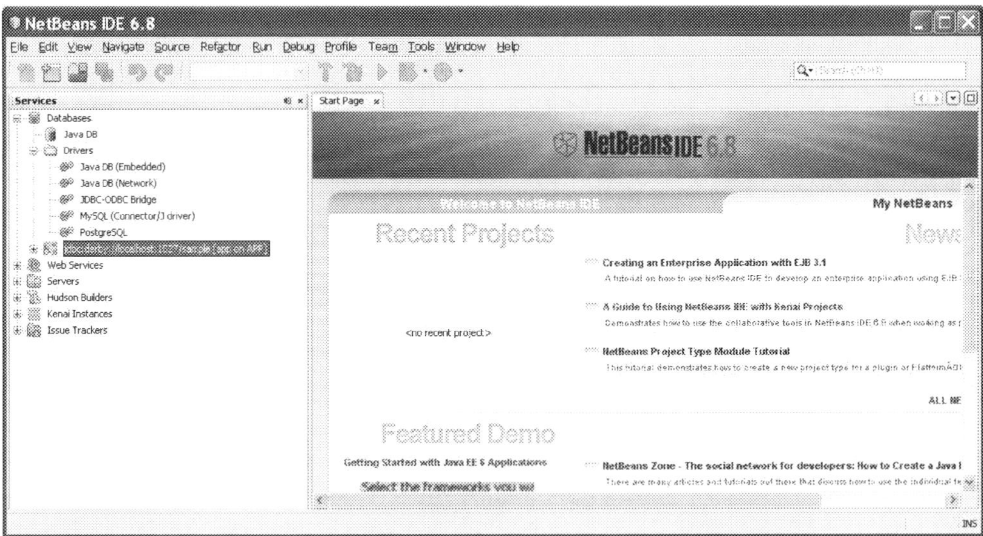

Figure 6.2. The opened Services pane in NetBeans IDE 6.8.

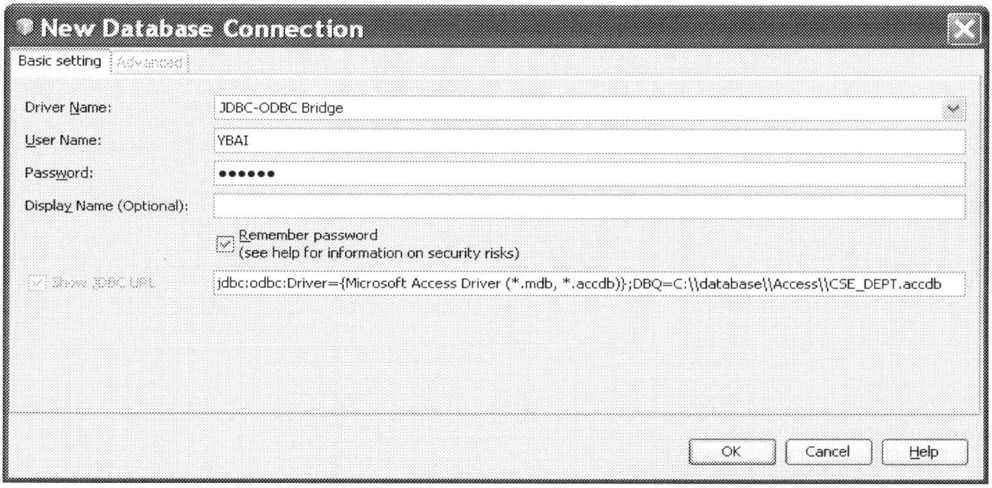

Figure 6.3. The New Database Connection dialog box.

D. A valid JDBC URL. Enter the following string into this textbox as the URL (our sample database CSE_DEPT.accdb is located at the folder C:\database\Access)

jdbc:**odbc**:Driver={Microsoft Access Driver (*.mdb, *.accdb)};DBQ=C:\\database\\Access\\CSE_DEPT.accdb

One point to be noted when typing this connection URL is that this string is a single line, and a space exists between the Driver and the opening parenthesis (, and between the *.mdb and the *.accdb. An error message would be displayed if these spaces are missed.

6. Click on the OK button to set up this connection.
7. Now we have connected to our sample database and a connection node can be found from the Services pane, which is shown in Figure 6.4.
8. Now you can expand this connection node, our sample database and five tables, LogIn, Faculty, Course, Student, and StudentCourse, as shown in Figure 6.5.

You can go to Window|Reset Windows menu item to recover the original settings with the Start Page as a default page to be displayed as the NetBeans IDE 6.8 is launched.

6.2.1.2 Connect to the Microsoft SQL Server 2008 Express Database CSE_DEPT

This connection can be divided into the following four sections:

1. Download and install Microsoft SQL Server JDBC Driver
2. Configure TCP/IP protocol and set up for SQL Server Express

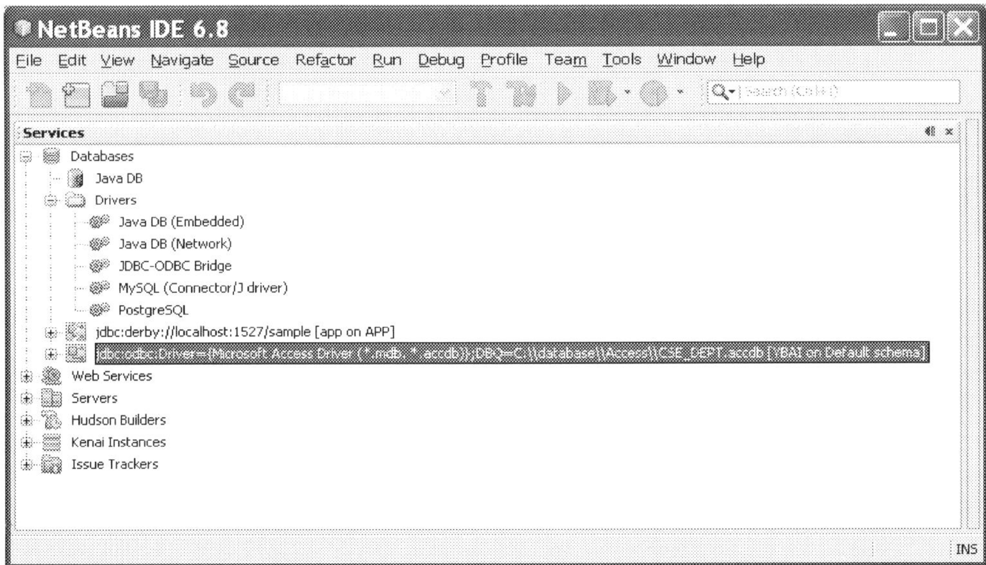

Figure 6.4. The connected database.

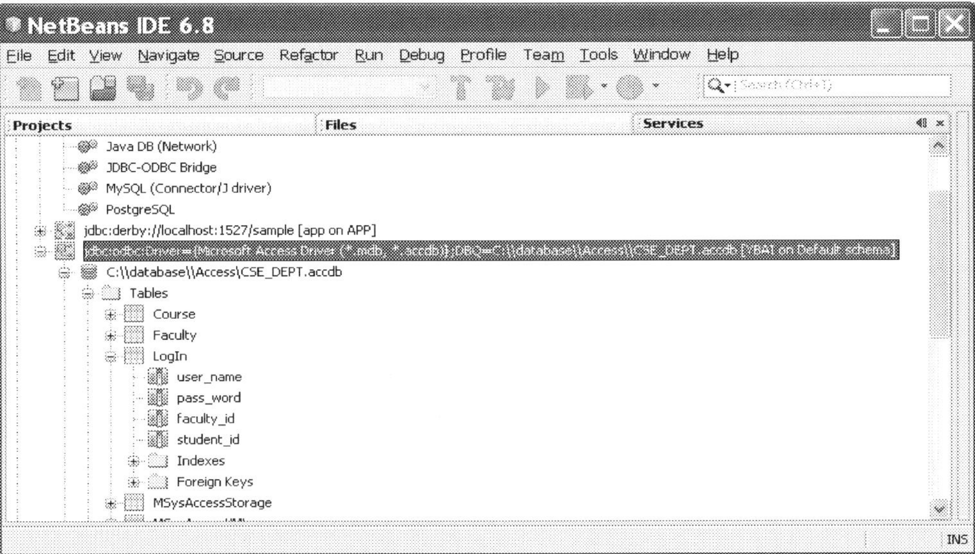

Figure 6.5. The connected database and five tables.

3. Configure Authentication Mode for SQL Server 2008 Express
4. Use NetBeans IDE 6.8 New Database Connection to set up a connection

Now let's start from the first section.

6.2.1.2.1 Download and Install Microsoft SQL Server JDBC Driver Go to the site http://msdn.microsoft.com/data/jdbc/ and click on the link Microsoft SQL Server JDBC

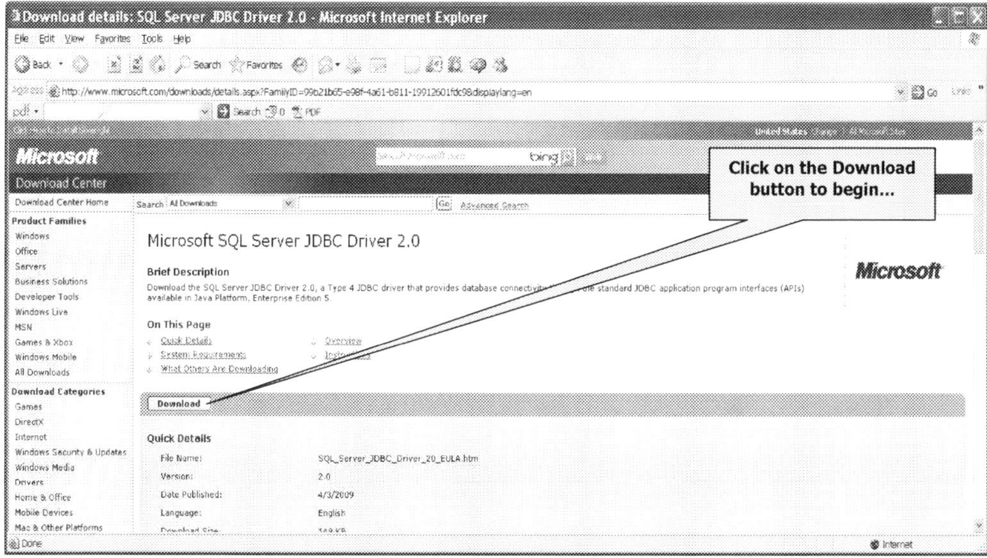

Figure 6.6. The opened download site.

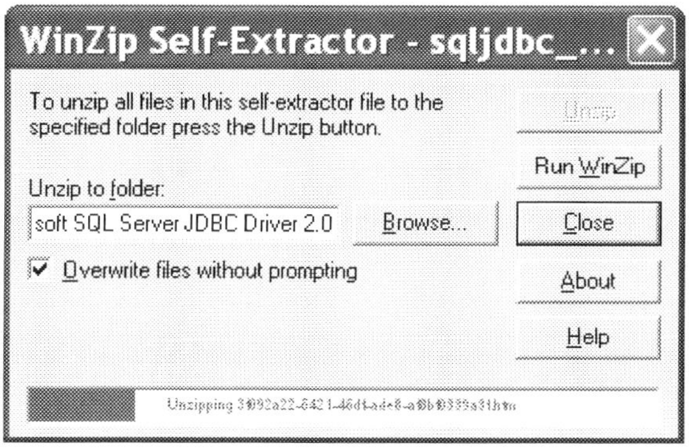

Figure 6.7. The unzipping process.

Driver 2.0 to begin this download process. Click on the Download button to begin this process, which is shown in Figure 6.6.

Click on the Open button from the `File Download` dialog box to open the Microsoft Download Agreement page and click on the `Accept` link to continue.

Click on the Run buttons to begin this process, and click on the Unzip button to begin to unzip the download zip files, which is shown in Figure 6.7. Click on the OK and the Close buttons when this unzipping process is complete.

The SQL Server JDBC Driver is created in the folder Microsoft SQL Server JDBC Driver 2.0 in the `Temp` folder at your root drive. It is recommended to move this folder to the folder C:\Program Files. Two drive files, sqljdbc.jar and sqljdbc4.jar, can be found from the subfolder enu, and we will use the latter since it is an updated one.

6.2.1.2.2 Configure TCP/IP Protocol and Setup for SQL Server Express By default, the TCP/IP for *SQL Server Express* 2008 is disabled when an SQL Server Express server is installed in your machine, therefore the JDBC cannot directly connect to it when a connection command is issued. Also, the port used for TCP/IP to listen to the network has not been established when the SQL Server Express 2008 server is installed in your machine. In order to fix these problems and make the TCP/IP work properly, we need to perform the following operations to meet our connection requirements:

1. Open the SQL Server Configuration Manager by going to **Start|All Programs|Microsoft SQL Server 2008|Configuration Tools|SQL Server Configuration Manager**.
2. Expand the **SQL Server Network Configuration** folder to get **Protocols for SQL2008EXPRESS** item, as shown in Figure 6.8. Click on that item to open all four protocols used for this SQL2008EXPRESS server on the right pane. Right click on the **TCP/IP** protocol and select **Enable** to enable it. Click on the **OK** button to allow server to restart to make this enable take effect.
3. Double click on the **TCP/IP** protocol we just enabled on the right pane to open the **TCP/IP Properties** dialog box, which is shown in Figure 6.9.
4. Click on the `IP Address` tab to display all valid IP Addresses used for this machine. By default, no TCP/IP port number has been assigned for SQL Server Express 2008, and all three TCP Port under three categories, `IP1`, `IP2`, and `IPAll`, are blanks. Therefore we need to set up this port number ourselves manually. To do that, select any port number you want and enter it into three TCP Port boxes, as shown in Figure 6.9. Here we used 5000 as our desired port number. Regularly, a big number should be used to avoid any possible conflict with some other port numbers that have been used by the system.
5. To make this TCP/IP port effective, you should stop the SQL 2008 Server and then restart it. To do that, click on the SQL Server Services icon and right click on the SQL Server (SQL2008EXPRESS) item from the right list and select the Stop item to stop the server. Then right click on this server again and select the Start item to restart the server.
6. To test this TCP Port number, open a command window and type: netstat –an. A running TCP/IP result window is displayed, as shown in Figure 6.10. You can find that one of TCP/IP Ports, port 5000, is working, and it is displayed as a test result as:
   TCP 0.0.0.0:5000 0.0.0.0:0 LISTENING
   Close the SQL Server Configuration Manager to complete this TCP/IP configuration.

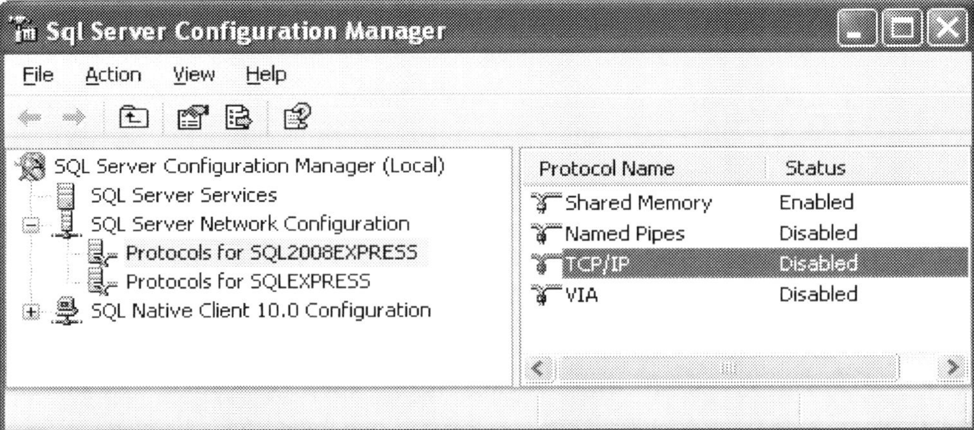

Figure 6.8. Enable TCP/IP protocol for SQL Server Express 2008.

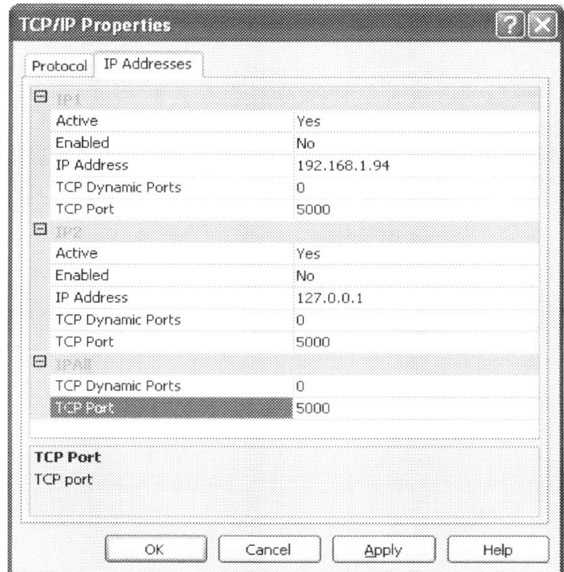

Figure 6.9. The opened TCP/IP Properties dialog box.

```
Command Prompt
C:\>netstat -an

Active Connections

  Proto  Local Address          Foreign Address        State
  TCP    0.0.0.0:25             0.0.0.0:0              LISTENING
  TCP    0.0.0.0:80             0.0.0.0:0              LISTENING
  TCP    0.0.0.0:135            0.0.0.0:0              LISTENING
  TCP    0.0.0.0:443            0.0.0.0:0              LISTENING
  TCP    0.0.0.0:445            0.0.0.0:0              LISTENING
  TCP    0.0.0.0:1025           0.0.0.0:0              LISTENING
  TCP    0.0.0.0:1029           0.0.0.0:0              LISTENING
  TCP    0.0.0.0:1030           0.0.0.0:0              LISTENING
  TCP    0.0.0.0:1521           0.0.0.0:0              LISTENING
  TCP    0.0.0.0:2814           0.0.0.0:0              LISTENING
  TCP    0.0.0.0:5000           0.0.0.0:0              LISTENING
  TCP    127.0.0.1:1027         0.0.0.0:0              LISTENING
  TCP    127.0.0.1:1034         0.0.0.0:0              LISTENING
  TCP    127.0.0.1:1494         0.0.0.0:0              LISTENING
  TCP    127.0.0.1:4664         0.0.0.0:0              LISTENING
  TCP    127.0.0.1:5152         0.0.0.0:0              LISTENING
  TCP    127.0.0.1:5152         127.0.0.1:4007         CLOSE_WAIT
  TCP    127.0.0.1:8080         0.0.0.0:0              LISTENING
  TCP    127.0.0.1:62514        0.0.0.0:0              LISTENING
  TCP    192.168.1.95:139       0.0.0.0:0              LISTENING
```

Figure 6.10. Testing the TCP/IP Port number.

6.2.1.2.3 Configure Authentication Mode for SQL Server 2008 Express By default, *SQL Server 2008 Express* uses *Windows Authentication Mode* to authenticate connections when it is installed in your machine. However, the SQL Authentication Mode is used by SQL Server JDBC Driver as it is connected to the NetBeans IDE 6.8. A connection errors, such as

> Login failed for user '<User name>'. The user is not associated with a trusted SQL Server connection

may be encounted if this default authentication mode is used for the connection. Perform the following operations to change the authentication to a mixed mode:

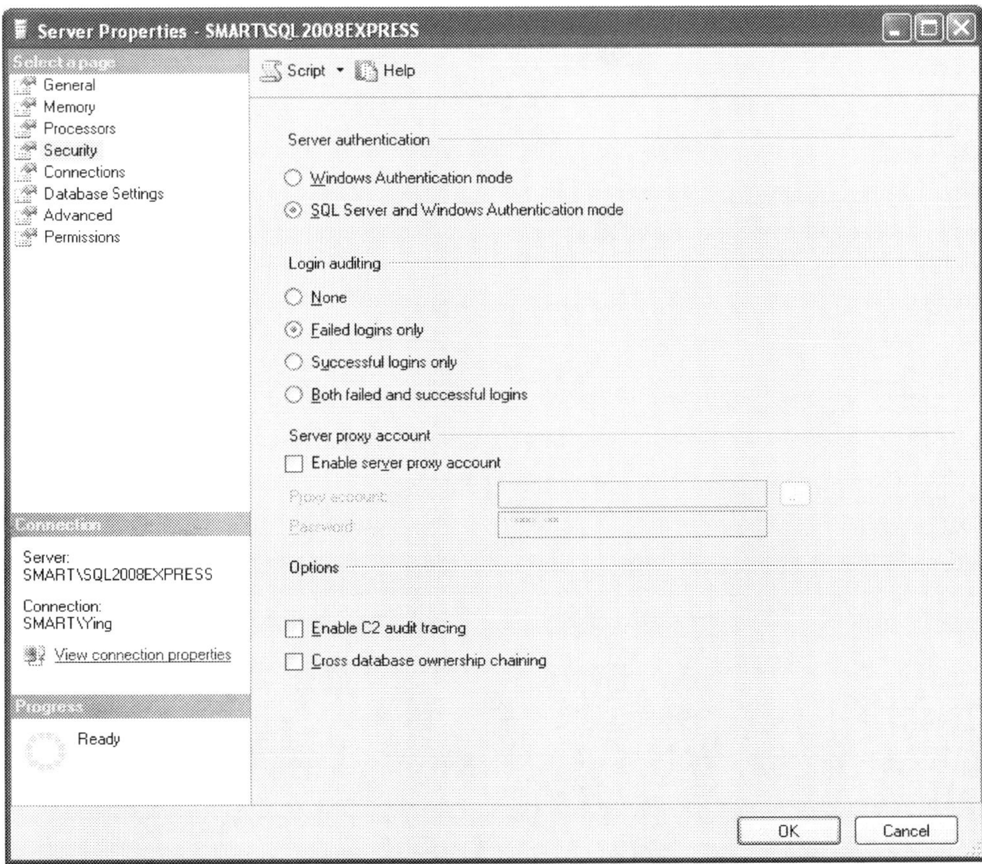

Figure 6.11. The Server Properties dialog box.

1. Launch Microsoft SQL Server Management Studio Express by going to Start|All Programs|Microsoft SQL Server 2008|SQL Server Management Studio item. Login and connect to your SQL Server using the Window Authentication mode.
2. Right click on our server icon SMART\SQL2008EXPRESS at the top of the Object Explorer window and click on the Properties from the pop up menu to open the Server Properties dialog box, which is shown in Figure 6.11.
3. Click on the Security item to open the Security page, and check the SQL Server and Windows Authentication mode radio button to select this mixed mode. Then click on the OK button to close this configuration.
4. In the *Object Explorer* pane, expand Security/Logins node. Now we want to add a new user to access this database via the SQL Server Express server.
5. Right click on the Logins folder and select `New Login` to open the Login–New dialog box, which is shown in Figure 6.12.
6. Enter a desired username, such as ybai, into the Login name box and check the SQL Server authentication radio button, since we need to use this mode to connect to the NetBeans using SQL Server JDBC driver. Enter a desired password, such as reback1956,

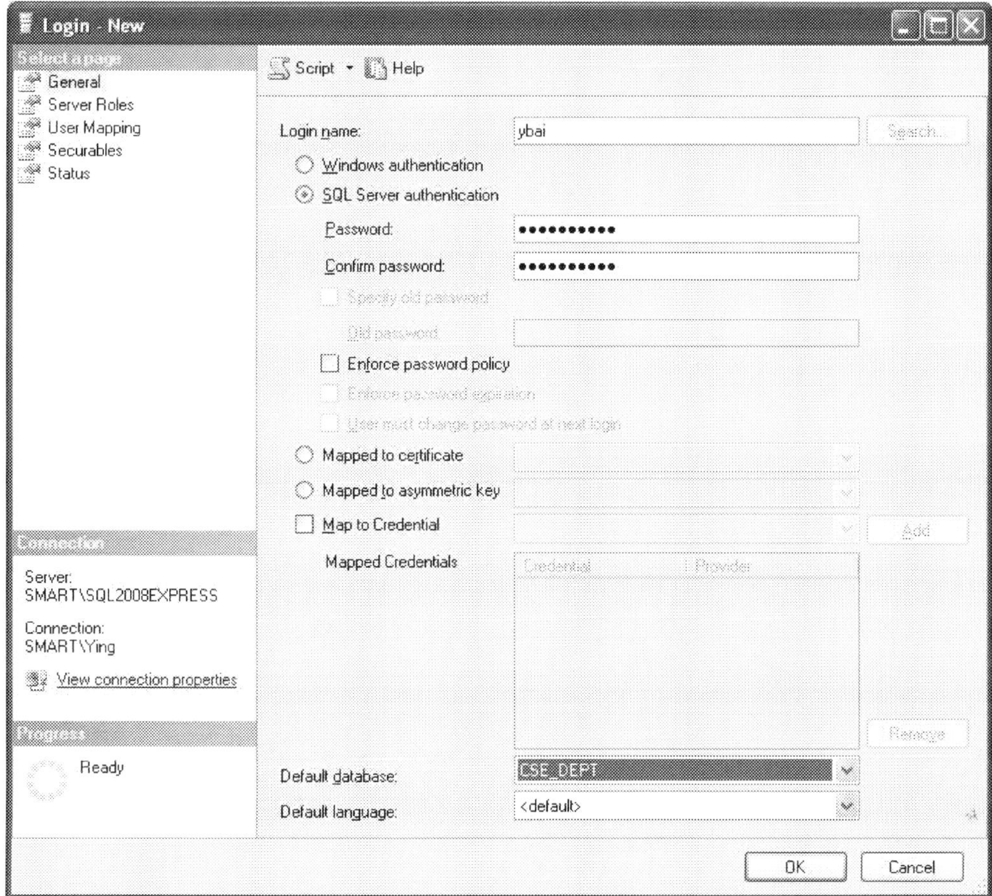

Figure 6.12. Login New dialog box.

into the Password and Confirm password boxes. Uncheck all four checkboxes under the Confirm password box and select our sample database CSE_DEPT that we developed in Chapter 2 from the Default database combo box.

7. Click on the Server Roles icon from the left pane to open the `Server Roles` page, which is shown in Figure 6.13. Check the sysadmin checkbox to make this new user as a system administrator to access this database (refer to Fig. 6.13).
8. Click on the Status icon from the left pane to open the `Status` page, and then check the Enabled radio button under the Login item to enable this new user.
9. Click on the OK button to complete this authentication configuration.

Now let's connect our sample database from NetBeans IDE 6.8 using Microsoft SQL Server JDBC Driver.

6.2.1.2.4 Use NetBeans IDE 6.8 New Database Connection to Set Up a Connection Before we can start NetBeans IDE 6.8, make sure that the following jobs have been performed, and the following required components have been configured:

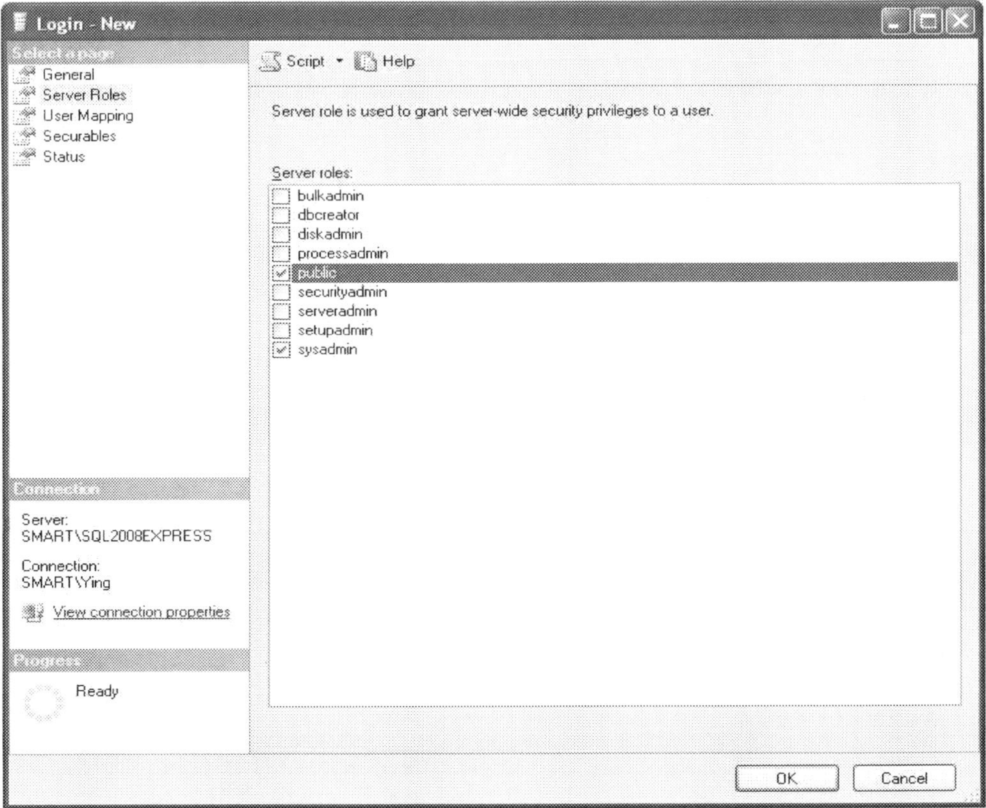

Figure 6.13. The opened Server Roles page.

- Make sure that the SQL Server 2008 Express has been running in your host computer.
- Make sure that the SQL Server 2008 Express Browser has been running in your host computer.

To do that checking, open the Microsoft SQL Server Configuration Manager, and then click on the SQL Server 2008 Services item from the left pane. Make sure that both SQL Server and SQL Server Browser in the right pane are in running status under the State tab. Close this Configuration Manager when this checking is finished.

Now let's launch NetBeans IDE 6.8 to begin this database connection.

1. Click on the Services tab on the opened NetBeans and expand the Databases icon from the Object Explorer window. Now we need to add the Microsoft SQL Server JDBC Driver we downloaded in step 1 into the NetBeans IDE system.
2. Right click on the Drivers folder and select New Driver item to open the New JDBC Driver dialog box, which is shown in Figure 6.14. Click on the Add button to browse to our driver's location, which is C:\Program Files\Microsoft SQL Server JDBC Driver 2.0\sqljdbc_2.0\enu, and click on our driver sqljdbc4.jar, and then click on the Open button to add it into our NetBeans system. Your finished New JDBC Driver dialog box should match one that is shown in Figure 6.14.
3. Click on the OK button to complete this process. Immediately, you can find that a new driver named Microsoft SQL Server 2008 has been added into the Drivers folder.

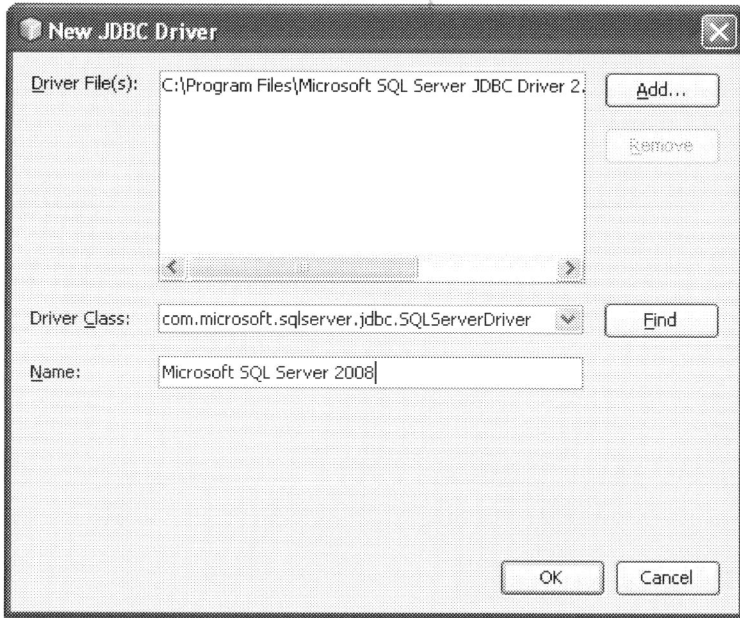

Figure 6.14. The finished New JDBC Driver dialog box.

4. Now right click on the newly added driver Microsoft SQL Server 2008 and select the Connect Using item to open the New Database Connection dialog box, as shown in Figure 6.15.
5. Enter the following connection parameters into the associated boxes:
   - **A.** localhost to the Host box since we are using a server that is installed in our local computer as our database server.
   - **B.** 5000 into the Port box since we set up this number as our TCP/IP communication port number.
   - **C.** CSE_DEPT into the Database box since we developed this SQL Server database in Chapter 2.
   - **D.** SQL2008EXPRESS into the Instance Name box since the SQL2008EXPRESS is a default instance name when we install SQL Server 2008 Express server in our machine.
   - **E.** ybai and reback1956 into the User Name and Password boxes, respectively, since we added a new user with this username and password when we configure our SQL Server 2008 server in the previous steps.
   - **F.** Check on the Show JDBC URL checkbox to display a full URL that will be used to set up this connection.
6. Your finished New Database Connection dialog box is shown in Figure 6.15.
7. Click on the OK button to set up this connection.
8. If this connection is successful, a Connection Established dialog box is displayed, as shown in Figure 6.16. Select the dbo from the Select schema combo box.
9. Click on the OK button to confirm this connection.

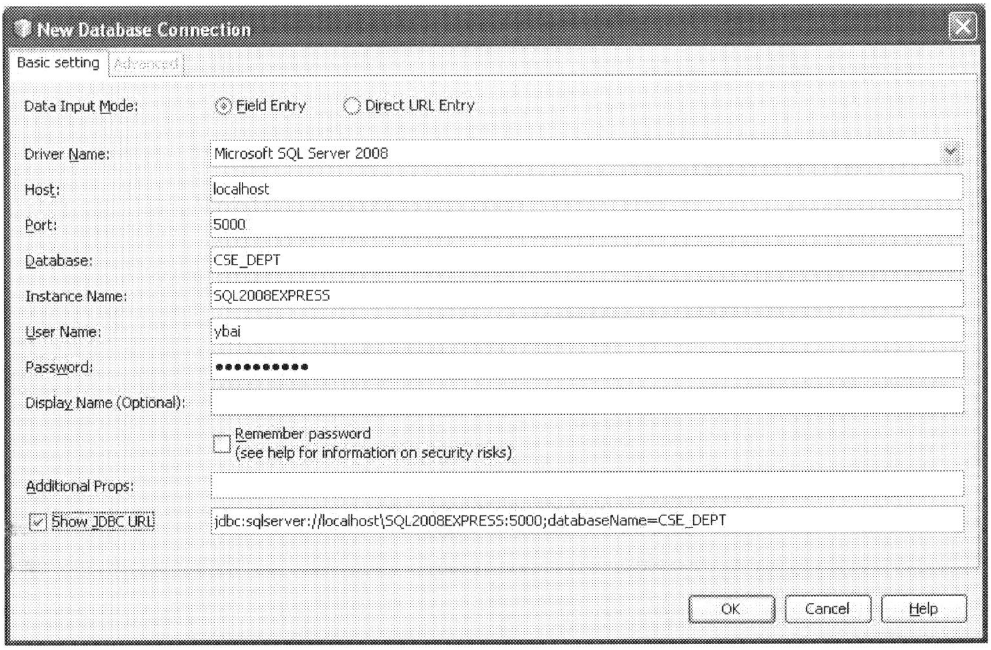

Figure 6.15. Finished New Database Connection dialog box.

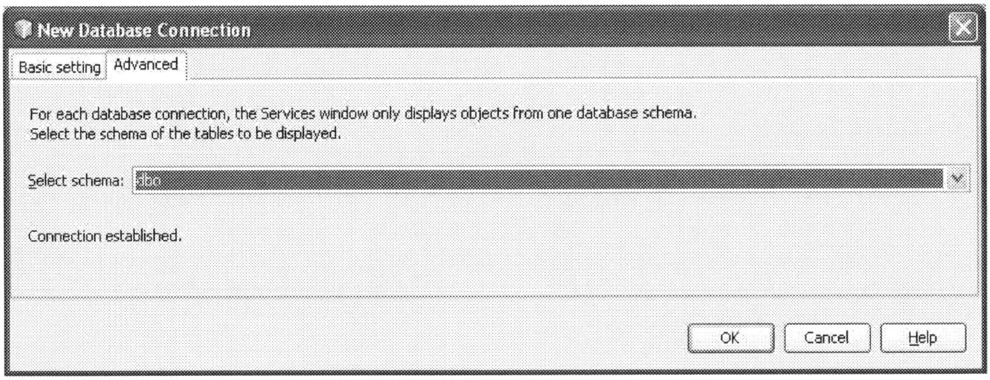

Figure 6.16. The Connection Established dialog box.

Immediately, you can find that a new database connection URL icon named

jdbc:sqlserver://localhost\SQL2008EXPRESS:5000;databaseName=CSE_DEPT [ybai on dbo]

has been added into the Drivers folder in the Object Explorer window in the NetBeans IDE 6.8.

The contents inside the square bracket indicate that the user who set ups and uses this connection is ybai, and the dbo is the database schema when we built our sample database CSE_DEPT in Chapter 2.

Note: If you cannot make this connection or an error is returned, try to restart or reboot your computer to disconnect to the SQL Server 2008 Express since the NetBeans IDE cannot connect to that database if it is still being used by the SQL Server 2008.

Next, let's do the connection to the Oracle Database 10g Express Edition in the NetBeans IDE 6.8 environment.

6.2.1.3 Connect to the Oracle Database 10g Express Edition CSE_DEPT

The first thing we need to do is to download an Oracle JDBC thin driver since we need this driver to connect to our sample database CSE_DEPT.

The Oracle JDBC thin driver is a Type IV JDBC driver, meaning that it is platform-independent and does not require any extra Oracle software on the client side to interact with an Oracle database. So you can download the JAR file containing the classes of an appropriate thin driver version from the JDBC Driver Downloads page and then install the driver on your machine without having to install and upgrade any other Oracle software.

Go to the site: http://www.oracle.com/technology/software/tech/java/sqlj_jdbc/htdocs/jdbc_111060.html?rssid=rss_otn_soft and click on the Accept License Agreement radio button to begin this downloading process (Fig. 6.17).

Then select our Oracle JDBC driver ojdbc6.jar by clicking on it to open the Oracle login page. You need to enter your username and password to begin this downloading process even it is free (you need to create your username and password if you have never downloaded any driver from the Oracle page and finish this login process). You also need

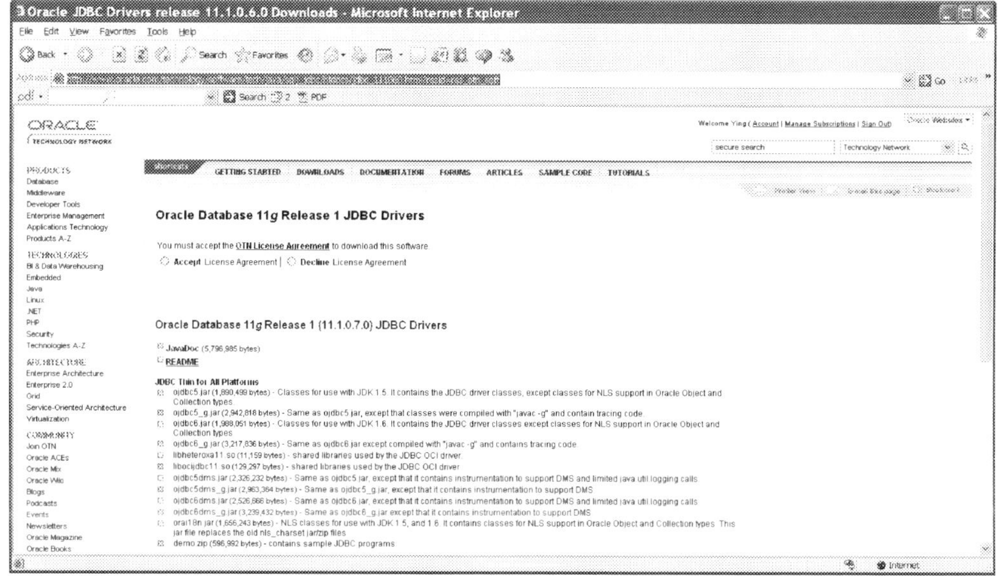

Figure 6.17. Oracle JDBC driver download page.

to enter your email address from which you can activate your account after you finished the login process.

You need to select a default folder to store this driver. Regularly, the Temp folder under your root is selected, and it is highly recommended to first save this driver file to the Temp folder. Click the Save button from the File Download dialog box to finish this downloading process.

Next, we need to set up a connection between the NetBeans IDE and our sample oracle database CSE_DEPT we developed in Chapter 2 via the Oracle JDBC driver we just downloaded. Following the step listed below to make this connection:

1. Launch NetBeans IDE 6.8 to open its Start Page
2. Go to Window|Services menu item to open the Services pane shown in Figure 6.18.
3. Right click on the Databases icon and select New Connection... menu item to open the New Database Connection dialog box, which is shown in Figure 6.19.
4. Click on the drop-down arrow from the Driver Name textbox and select the New Driver item from the driver list to open the New JDBC Driver dialog box.
5. Click on the Add button to scan and browse to the folder under which our new downloaded Oracle JDBC driver ojdbc6.jar is located (Fig. 6.20), and select that driver file and click on the Open button to add this driver into our driver list. Your finished New JDBC Driver dialog box should match one that is shown in Figure 6.21.
6. Click on the OK button to complete this adding new driver process.
7. Enter the following parameters into the associated textbox as the connection elements (refer to Fig. 6.22):

   A. Select Oracle Thin from the Driver Name textbox.
   B. Enter localhost to the Host box as the host name since we are using our local machine as the database server.

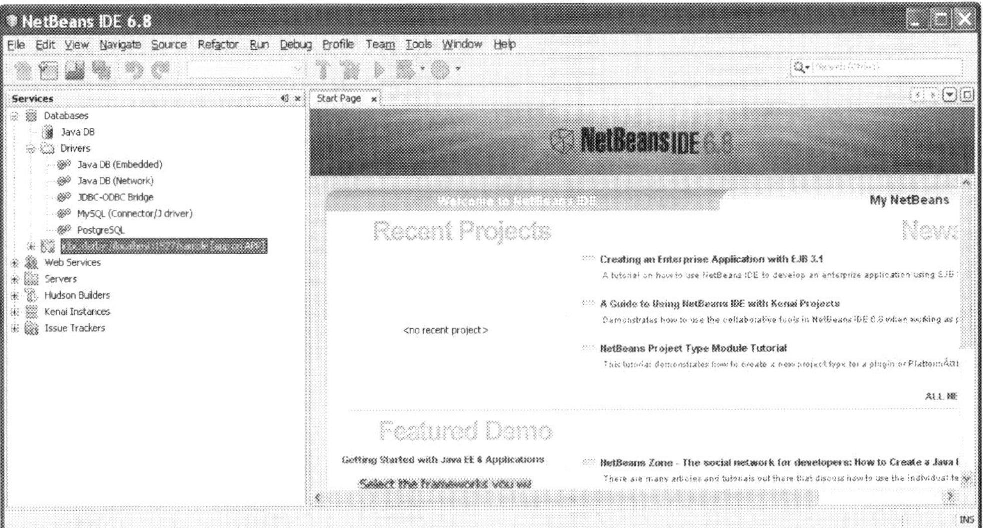

Figure 6.18. The opened Services pane in NetBeans IDE 6.8.

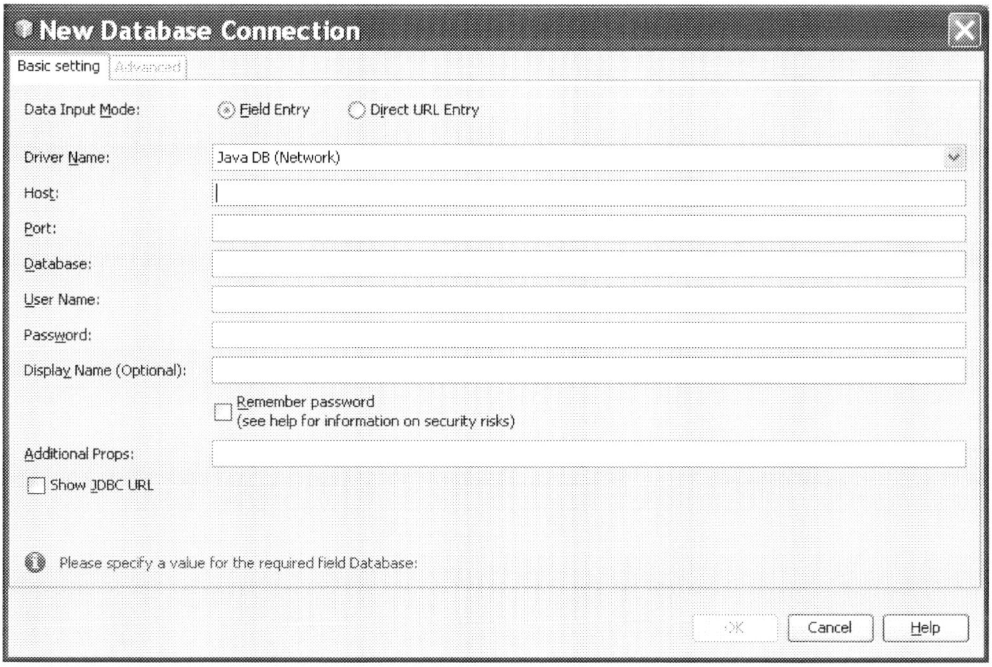

Figure 6.19. New Database Connection dialog box.

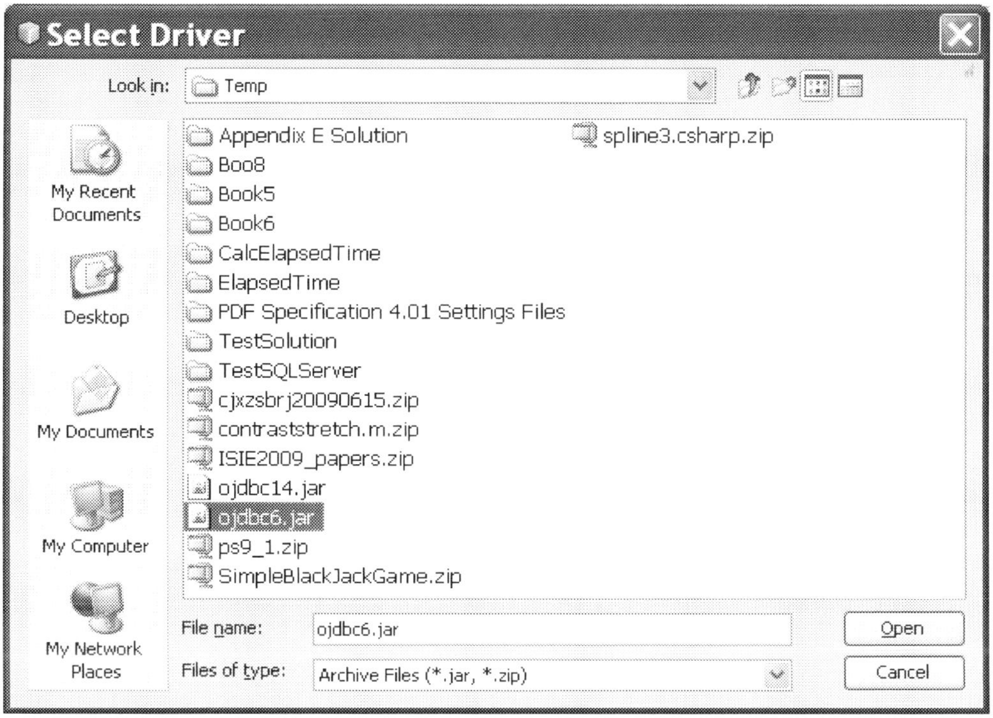

Figure 6.20. Select the downloaded Oracle JDBC driver.

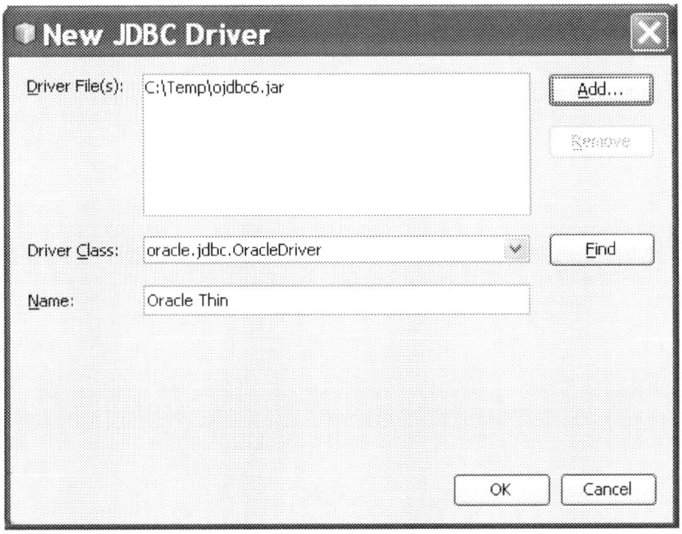

Figure 6.21. Finished New JDBC Driver dialog box.

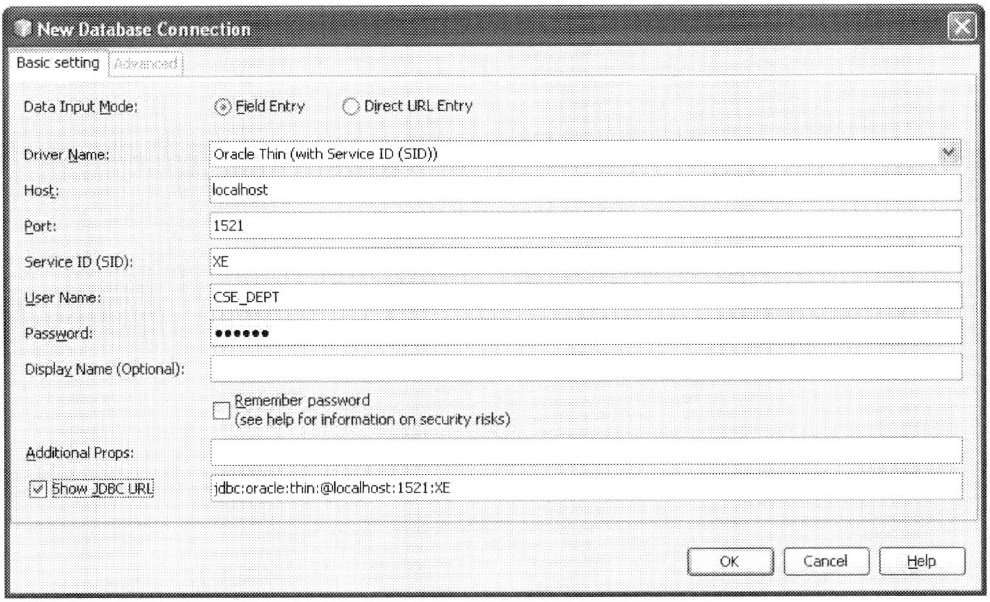

Figure 6.22. New Database Connection dialog box.

C. Enter 1521 to the Port box since we have used this as our port number when we installed our Oracle 10g database XE (refer to the tnsnames.ora file that is located at the folder: `C:\oraclexe\app\oracle\product\10.2.0\server\NETWORK\ADMIN)`.

D. Enter XE to the Service ID box since we used this as our service name (refer to the tnsnames.ora file, and this file provided a description for the Oracle database after it is installed in our machine).

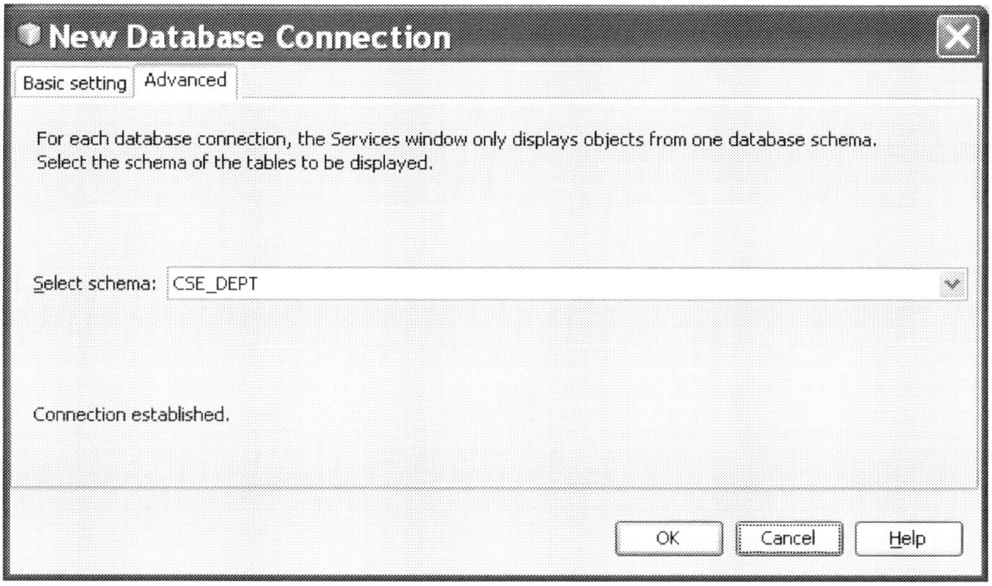

Figure 6.23. A connection is established dialog box.

E. Enter CSE_DEPT, which is the name of our database created in Chapter 2, to the User Name box.
F. Enter reback to the Password box since we used this as our password when we created our sample Oracle database CSE_DEPT (refer to Chapter 2).
G. Click Show JDBC URL checkbox to display the full URL for this connection.
H. Click the OK button to set up this connection.

A connection established dialog box is shown up if this connection is successful, which is shown in Figure 6.23.

To test and check this connection, click on the OK button to return to the Service pane.

Immediately, you can find that a new Oracle database connection URL icon, jdbc:oracle:thin:@localhost:1521:XE [CSE_DEPT on CSE_DEPT], has been set up in this pane, which is shown in Figure 6.24. Expand this icon and our sample database CSE_DEPT, as well as one of our tables, LogIn; you can find that all columns we created for this table are displayed under that table folder. You can expand all our five tables, such as Faculty, Course, Student, and StudentCourse, to check them and confirm the correctness of each of them.

Our Oracle database connection is successful, as shown in Figure 6.24.

Expand this URL and our sample database CSE_DEPT; you can find all five tables we created in Chapter 2, which is shown in Figure 6.24.

Now we have finished connecting to different database using NetBeans IDE 6.8 Services. Next, let's create a new Java Application project to query data from connected database via JPA.

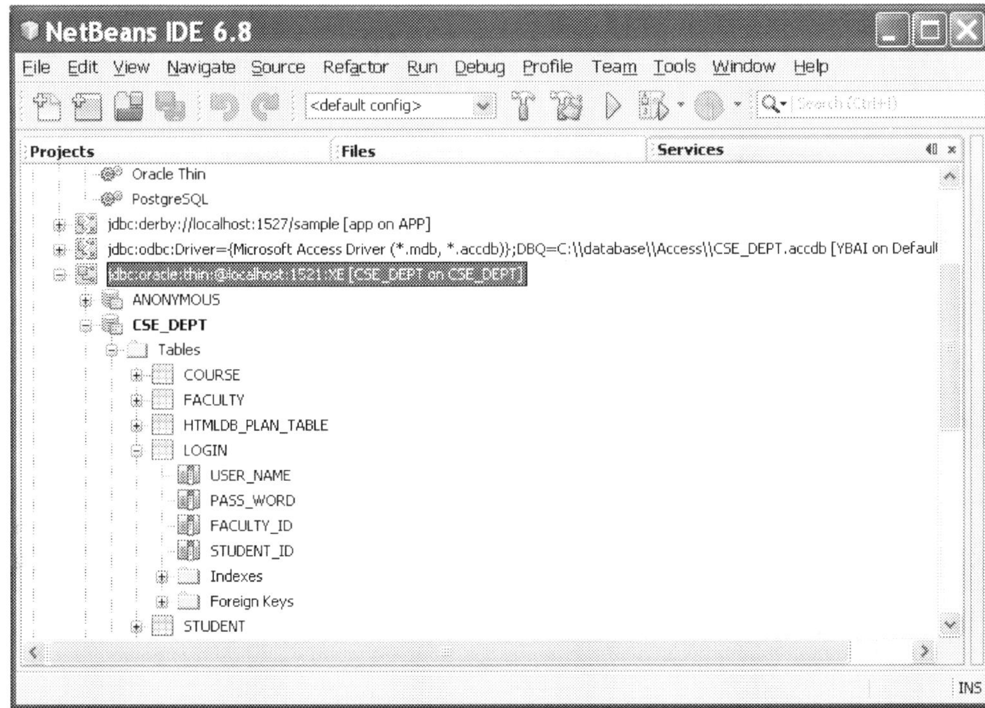

Figure 6.24. A connected Oracle database with all tables.

6.2.2 Create a Java Application Project to Query SQL Server Database

Launch NetBeans IDE 6.8 and go to File|New Project menu item to open New Project dialog box, which is shown in Figure 6.25. Select Java from the Categories list and Java Application from the Projects list. There are five kinds of project templates available for the Java Standard Applications under the Java Categories. As we discussed in Chapter 5, these templates serves for the different applications. Refer to Chapter 5 to get a clear picture for the differences for those project templates. The reason we selected the Java Application, instead of the Java Desktop Application, as our template, is that the latter provides a full set of application files, including a default menu-based Java Windows GUI that is not desired for our application.

Click on the Next button to open the New Java Application dialog box. Perform the following operations to create this new project:

- Enter SelectQueryWizard into the Project Name box as our new project's name.
- Select an appropriate folder as the location to save this project by entering a desired folder to the project location. In this example, we used C:\Book9\DBProjects\Chapter 6 as our project location.
- Uncheck the Create Main Class checkbox since we do not want to use this as our main class file.

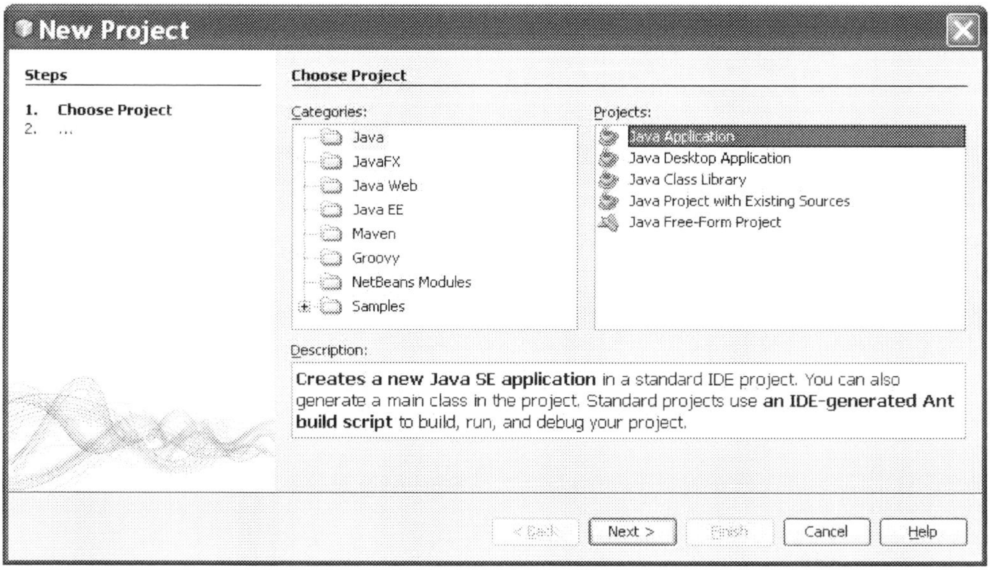

Figure 6.25. The New Project dialog box.

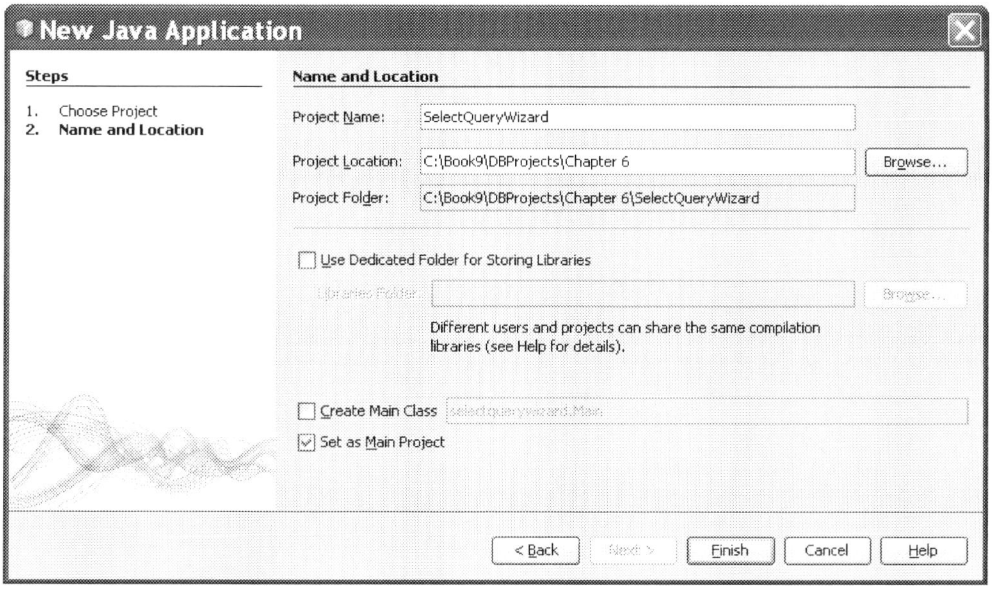

Figure 6.26. The New Java Project dialog box.

- Make sure to check the Set as Main Project checkbox, and your finished New Java Project dialog box should match one that is shown in Figure 6.26. Click on the Finish button to create this new project.

A new Java Application project SelectQueryWizard is created with four file folders: Source Packages, Test Packages, Libraries, and Test Libraries in the Project Windows. Refer to Chapter 5 to get a clear picture for the function of each folder.

Now let's create a set of Java GUIs as our user interfaces to access and query data from our sample database. Generally, each GUI is associated with a data table in our sample database, except the Student GUI, which is associated with two tables. Table 6.1 shows this relationship.

First let's create our LogIn GUI.

6.2.3 Use Java JPA Wizards to Query the LogIn Table

Right click on our new project SelectQueryWizard from the Project windows and select the submenu items New|JFrame Form to open the New JFrame Form dialog box, which is shown in Figure 6.27.

Change the Class Name of the JFrame to LogInFrame and enter LogInFrame into the Package box as the name of our Package. Your finished New JFrame Form dialog box is shown in Figure 6.27. Click on the **Finish** button to add this new JFrame Form to our project.

A new blank JFrame Form named LogInFrame is created and displayed in the Design Windows. Add the following GUI components with the appropriate properties shown in Table 6.2 into this Form. You need to drag each component from the Palette Windows and place it to the LogInFrame Form, and set up each property in the Properties Windows.

Table 6.1. Relationship between the GUI and data table

Java GUI	Tables in Sample Database
LogIn	LogIn
Faculty	Faculty
Course	Course
Student	Student, StudentCourse

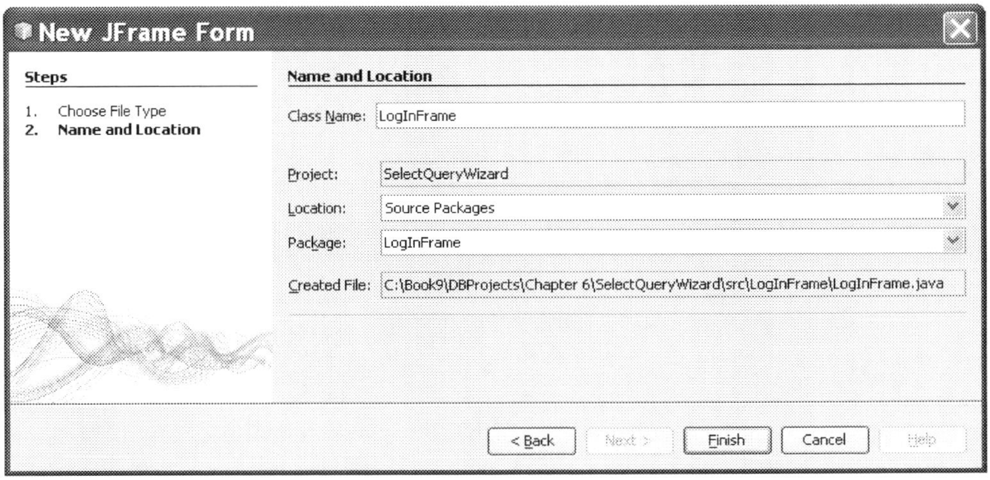

New JFrame Form

Steps

1. Choose File Type
2. Name and Location

Name and Location

Class Name: LogInFrame

Project: SelectQueryWizard

Location: Source Packages

Package: LogInFrame

Created File: C:\Book9\DBProjects\Chapter 6\SelectQueryWizard\src\LogInFrame\LogInFrame.java

< Back | Next > | Finish | Cancel | Help

Figure 6.27. New JFrame Form dialog box.

Table 6.2. Objects and controls in the LogIn form

Type	Variable Name	Text
Label	Label1	Welcome to CSE department
Label	Label2	Username
Text field	UserNameField	
Label	Label3	Password
Text field	PassWordField	
Button	LogInButton	LogIn
Button	CancelButton	Cancel
Title		CSE DEPT LogIn

Figure 6.28. The finished LogInFrame Form.

When setting up property for each component, you need first to click on that component to select it and then go the Property Windows to set up an appropriate property for that component. To set up a Variable Name for each component, you need to right click on that component and select Change Variable Name item from the pop-up menu, and then enter a desired name into the New Name box for that object.

Your finished LogInFrame Form is shown in Figure 6.28.

6.2.4 Use Java Persistence API to Build Entity Classes from Databases

In this section, we will use a real example to illustrate what is the JPA and how to use the JPA Wizards to create Entity classes, map objects in the Entity class to the columns in our database table, and access our sample database via Entity classes. To do that, we need first to build Entity classes for our new project. Right click on our new project

SelectQueryWizard from the Project Windows and select New|Entity Classes from Database to open New Entity Classes from Database dialog box, which is shown in Figure 6.29. Perform the following operations to complete this Entity classes-building process.

1. Click on the dropdown arrow from the Database Connection combo box and select our SQL Server sample database URL we connected in Section 6.2.1.2, which is represented by a connection node jdbc:sqlserver://localhost\SQL2008EXPRESS:5000;databaseName=CSE_DEPT [ybai on dbo].
2. Select all tables from the Available Tables box and click on the Add All button to add all five tables to the Selected Tables box.
3. Make sure that the Include Related Tables checkbox is checked.
4. Your finished New Entity Classes from Database dialog box should match one that is shown in Figure 6.29. Click on the Next button to continue.
5. The next dialog box allows you to select desired names and locations for the created Entity classes, which is shown in Figure 6.30.
6. Keep all default settings and click on the Create Persistence Unit button to open the Create Persistence Unit dialog box, which is shown in Figure 6.31.
7. Keep the default Persistence Unit Name unchanged and select the TopLink item from the Persistence Library combo box. Also make sure that the None radio button under the `Table Generation Strategy` is checked. Click on the Create button to create this Persistence Unit and add it into our project.
8. Click on the Next button to go to the last dialog box, which is shown in Figure 6.32.

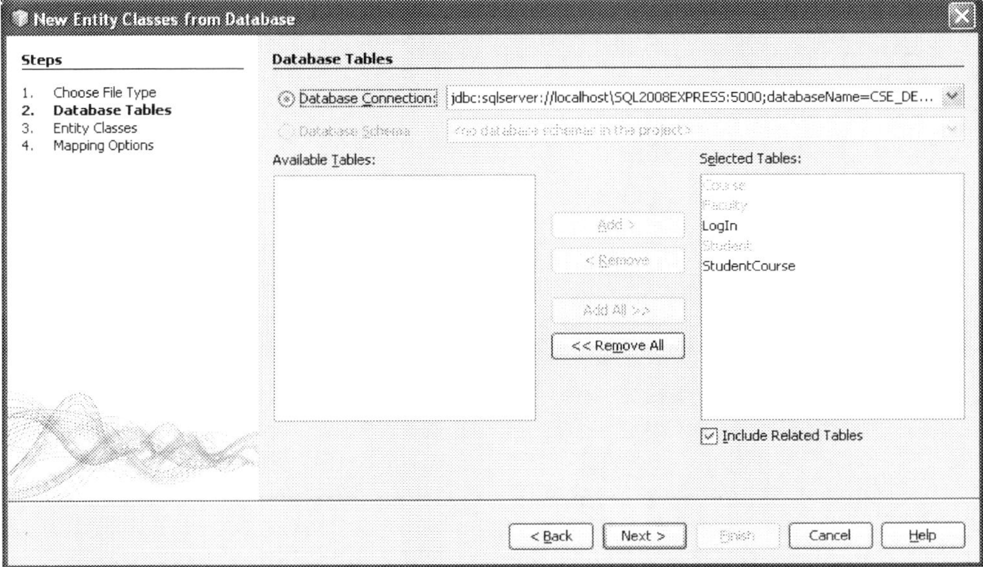

Figure 6.29. New Entity Classes from database dialog box.

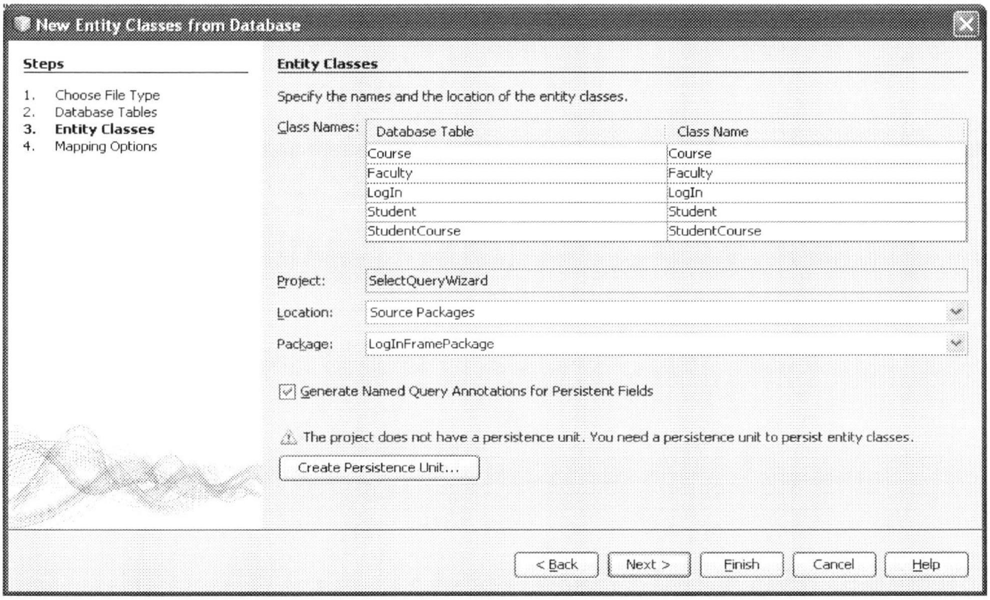

Figure 6.30. Selecting names and locations for the created Entity classes.

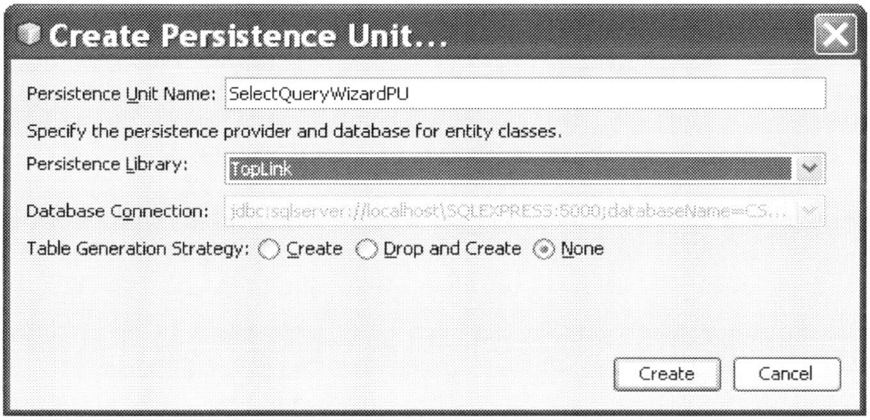

Figure 6.31. The Create Persistence Unit dialog box.

9. Select java.util.List from the Collection Type combo box and click on the Finish button to complete this building of new entity classes from the database process.

Immediately you can find that five Entity classes, named LogIn.java, Fcaulty.java, Course.java, Student.java, and StudentCourse.java, are generated under the LogInFrame Package folder in the Project Windows.

Now you can build and run our new project to test the LogInFrame Form. Click on the Clean and Build Main Project icon in the toolbar to build our project, and then click on the Run icon to run our project. Click on the OK to the Select the main class dialog box to select our LogInFrame as the main class to run the project.

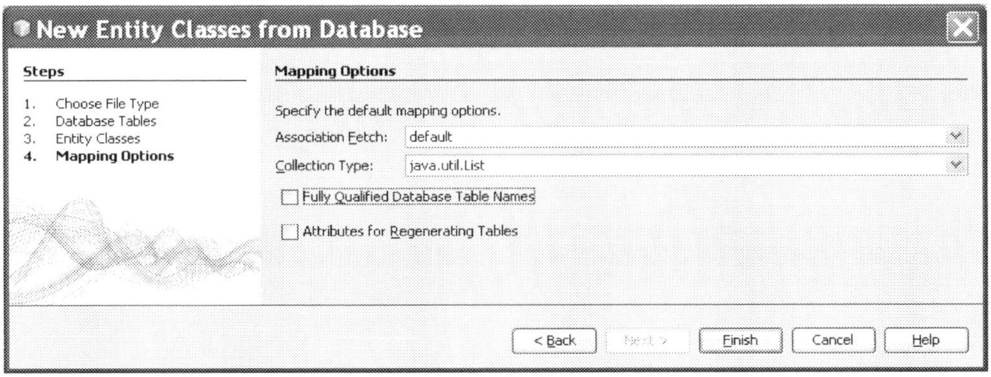

Figure 6.32. The Mapping Options dialog box.

The running result should be identical with one shown in Figure 6.28. Click the Close button on the upper-right corner of the LogInFrame window to close the project. Now that a mapping has been set up using the JPA, next let's begin to use it to build and perform our data query operations.

6.2.5 Add LogIn Entity Manager and JPA Components into the Project

Before we can start our query process, we need to physically add the Entity Manager that will control all Entity classes and all JPA components, such as Query and Query Result (List in this project since we selected java.util.List in step 9 in the last section) we created in the last section into the LogInFrame Form window. In this way, we can use the Entity Manager to manage all Entity classes to set up mapping relations between components in our Java GUI Forms and all five tables in our sample database and perform all query-related operations. Perform the following operations to complete this adding process:

1. Expand our connected SQL Server database in the Services Window to the dbo node and then the Tables folder. Drag our LogIn table and place it onto our LogInFrame Form.
2. Immediately you can find that one Entity Manager class entityManager and two JPA components, logInQuery and logInList, have been added into our project in the Other Components folder in the Inspector Window.

Now we can start to perform the query to access our sample database using the added Entity Manager; two points must be paid a special attention before we can do that:

- How the data columns in our real database can be mapped to the objects in the Entity class, and what the mapped objects look like in the Entity class
- How to construct a query string to access the mapped objects in the Entity class, and further to access the data columns in our real sample database

As we know, the JPA has mapped all data columns in our LogIn table to an Entity class LogIn.java, therefore, we cannot directly access our real LogIn table in our database; instead, we have to use the Entity class, or, exactly, use the mapped objects in the Entity class, to access our LogIn table. To do that, we need first to have a clear picture about the mapped objects in the Entity class, and, second, we need also to find a way to use those mapped objects in a JPA compatible language.

Let's first concentrate on the first part.

6.2.5.1 Entity Classes Mapping Files

As we mentioned, each data table in our sample database, such as LogIn, has been mapped to a unique Entity class, LogIn.java. Each column in the LogIn table has also been mapped to an associated property using JPA. In order to perform any query based on those mapped objects, first let's have a look at mapped objects in our Entity class to see what those columns have been mapped to and how to use them to perform a query. An example of Entity class file is shown in Figure 6.33, which is our LogIn Entity class LogIn.java.

It can be found from this Entity class that all components in the relational database have been mapped to the associated objects, and all queries have been changed to the named queries. Both columns and relations between columns have also been mapped to the different objects. Two mapped columns, userName and passWord, have been highlighted in this file.

When the project runs, all queries are performed based on objects mapped in this Entity class file instead of columns in our sample database.

Now that we have an understanding about the mapped objects in the Entity class, next, let's have a closer look at how to use those objects to perform a query. As you know, all data columns in our relational database has been converted to the associated objects in our Entity class by using JPA, therefore a JPA-matched language that can be compatible to those mapped objects should be used to construct our query to access the Entity

```
@Entity
@Table(name = "LogIn")

@NamedQueries({
    @NamedQuery(name = "LogIn.findAll", query = "SELECT l FROM LogIn l"),
    @NamedQuery(name = "LogIn.findByUserName", query = "SELECT l FROM LogIn l WHERE l.userName = :userName"),
    @NamedQuery(name = "LogIn.findByPassWord", query = "SELECT l FROM LogIn l WHERE l.passWord = :passWord")})

public class LogIn implements Serializable {
    @Transient
    private PropertyChangeSupport changeSupport = new PropertyChangeSupport(this);
    private static final long serialVersionUID = 1L;
    @Id
    @Basic(optional = false)
    @Column(name = "user_name")
    private String userName;
    @Column(name = "pass_word")
    private String passWord;
    @JoinColumn(name = "faculty_id", referencedColumnName = "faculty_id")
    @ManyToOne
    private Faculty facultyId;
    @JoinColumn(name = "student_id", referencedColumnName = "student_id")
    @ManyToOne
    private Student studentId;
```

Figure 6.33. An example of the Entity class LogIn.java.

class to perform a query. A popular language called Java Persistence Query Language (JPQL) is used for that purpose.

6.2.5.2 Use Java Persistence Query Language Statement

The Java Persistence Query Language (JPQL) is a platform-independent object-oriented query language that is defined as part of the JPA specification. JPQL is used to make queries against entities stored in a relational database. It is heavily inspired by SQL, and its queries resemble SQL queries in syntax, but operate against JPA entity objects rather than directly with database tables.

In addition to retrieving objects (SELECT queries), JPQL supports bulk UPDATE and DELETE queries.

The execution of JPQL is directly dependent on the mapping objects (name and type) stored in the JPA Entity classes. For example, in our LogIn Entity class LogIn.java, all columns in that table have been mapped to the different String object. Such as, user_name is mapped to userName, pass_word is mapped to passWord, and so on.

Now let's take a closer look at a query string example built using JPQL, and we will use this query string in the next section to perform a data query, which is:

```
"SELECT q.userName, q.passWord FROM LogIn q " +
"WHERE q.userName=:UserName AND q.passWord=:PassWord";
```

The difference between this JPQL and standard SQL query string is that an abstract schema q is used and prefixed for each clause. Also, the real column name has been replaced by the mapped String object in the Entity class file. The abstract schema is defined as a persistent schema abstraction (persistent entities, their state, and their relationships) over which queries operate. The query language translates queries over this persistent schema abstraction into queries that are executed over the database schema to which entities are mapped. The major advantage of using this abstract schema is that it makes the query more type-safe and easy in coding. An abstract schema used in a JPQL string can be any letter or word. For more detailed information about the JPQL, refer to http://java.sun.com/javaee/5/docs/tutorial/doc/bnbth.html.

Now that we have a clear picture about the JPQL, let's get a little more detail in the query string: how to build and use a JPQL query.

6.2.5.3 Static and Dynamic JPA Query API

The EntityManager serves as manager classes to get a reference to the query objects. The query string built in Java Persistent Query Language or JPQL is used to locate entity objects. The current version of the JPQL is 2.0, and it is more robust flexible and object-oriented than SQL. The persistence engine will parse the query string and translate the JPQL to the native SQL before executing it.

According to the functionality, JPA queries can be divided into two categories: static query and dynamic query.

A static query is also called a Named Query, and it is defined statically with the help of annotation or XML before the entity class is created. A name is usually given to the query definition so that other components in the same persistent unit can refer the query using the same. In most cases, static queries are defined inside the Entity classes. An example of static queries or named queries is shown in the top section in Figure 6.34, which is the Entity class Course that is mapped to the Course table in our sample database. The bottom section shows an example in how to call the named query "Course.findByEnrollment."

Each query is defined as a named query using the annotation @NamedQury() with a definite query name that is in bold and enclosed with quotation marks. Following the query name, a real JPA query string written in JPQL is attached. The advantage of using a named query is that you can directly call the desired query with the name of that query in your project when you want to use it, and you do not need to touch any real query string. An example of calling the named query "Course.findByEnrollment" is shown in the bottom part in Figure 6.34. Another advantage is that the executing speed for this kind of query is relative higher, since it should be compiled before it can be used when your project runs. The disadvantage is that a static or named query is not flexible compared with the dynamic one, since it must be written and compiled before your project runs, and no modification can be performed during the project runs.

Dynamic queries belong to queries in which the query strings are provided at runtime or created dynamically. All calls to EntityManager.createQuery(queryString) are actually creating dynamic query objects. The advantage of using dynamic queries is that this kind of query is more flexible, since it can be created or modified during the project runs. However, any good thing is always coming with bad staff, too. By defining query objects in this way, we lose the efficiency, and from the performance point of view, the query execution may be slower compared with the static query, since the persistence engine has to do all the parsing and validation stuffs, along with mapping the JPQL to the SQL during the runtime of your project.

An example of creating and calling a dynamic query is shown in Figure 6.35.

```
@Entity
@Table(name = "Course")
@NamedQueries({
  @NamedQuery(name = "Course.findAll", query = "SELECT c FROM Course c"),
  @NamedQuery(name = "Course.findByCourseId", query = "SELECT c FROM Course c WHERE c.courseId = :courseId"),
  @NamedQuery(name = "Course.findByCredit", query = "SELECT c FROM Course c WHERE c.credit = :credit"),
  @NamedQuery(name = "Course.findByEnrollment", query = "SELECT c FROM Course c WHERE c.enrollment = :enrollment")

  Query courseQuery = SelectQueryWizardPUEntityManager.createNamedQuery("Course.findByEnrollment");
```

Figure 6.34. An example of static or named JPA query.

```
String query = "SELECT q.userName, q.passWord FROM LogIn q " +
               "WHERE q.userName=:UserName AND q.passWord=:PassWord";
logInQuery = SelectQueryWizardPUEntityManager.createQuery(query);
logInQuery.setParameter("UserName", UserNameField.getText());
logInQuery.setParameter("PassWord", PassWordField.getText());
```

Figure 6.35. An example of creating and calling a dynamic query.

This is an example of querying the username and password from our LogIn entity object, and the createQuery() method is exactly used to create our dynamic query.

6.2.5.4 Positional Parameters and Named Parameters

When building either a static or a dynamic JPA query, some dynamic parameters are sometimes necessarily involved into the query string. An example of dynamic parameters, UserName and PassWord, are shown in Figure 6.35. A nominal value, such as UserName or PassWord, is given in the query string. However, the real values for those parameters must be provided by using the setParameter() method to replace those nominal values as the project runs, which is shown in the last two coding lines in Figure 6.35. The nominal values, UserName and PassWord, are replaced by the real values obtained by calling the getText() method for two text fields, UserNameField and PassWordField, respectively, as the project runs.

There are two ways to set up a real parameter for a nominal parameter: positional parameter and named parameter.

The so-called positional parameters mean that the nominal parameters will be replaced by the real parameters based on the locations or positions they are located in the query string. A question mark followed by an index indicates a dynamic parameter and its location in a query string. For example, in our LogIn query string, we can represent two dynamic parameters, UserName and PassWord, in a positional parameter, as shown in Figure 6.36.

In the query string, ?1 and ?2 represent two nominal parameters, UserName and PassWord, and the index always starts from 1. When using setParameter() method to set up the real parameter values to replace those nominal parameters, the same index is used to indicate the position of those nominal parameters are located. In the positional parameter setup process, the position of the nominal parameter must be indicated by the index in the same order as that appeared in the query string.

However, in a named parameter style, each nominal parameter in the query string is indicated with a unique name, and, therefore, the position or the order of those parameters is not important. An example of named parameter setup process is shown in Figure 6.35. Both nominal parameters are represented by the named parameter, :UserName and :PassWord. A colon is prefixed before each nominal parameter to indicate that this is a named parameter. When replacing these nominal parameters using the setParameter() method, the nominal parameters' name (note, no colon should be prefixed for those nominal parameters) must be used as a string to indicate the related nominal parameter to be replaced.

```
String query = "SELECT q.userName, q.passWord FROM LogIn q " +
               "WHERE q.userName= ?1 AND q.passWord= ?2";
logInQuery = SelectQueryWizardPUEntityManager.createQuery(query);
logInQuery.setParameter( 1, UserNameField.getText());
logInQuery.setParameter( 2, PassWordField.getText());
```

Figure 6.36. An example of query using positional parameters.

Now we have a basic understanding about the JPA and JPQL. Let's start to use Entity class to build our query to perform the data query from the LogIn table in our real database.

6.2.5.5 Use Entity Classes to Build a Query to Perform the Login Process

Open the Design View of our LogInFrame Form and double click on the LogIn button to open its event handler, since we need to start and perform the login process when this LogIn button is clicked. Enter the following codes into this event handler, which is shown in Figure 6.37.

```
  package LogInFramePackage;
A import java.util.*;

  public class LogInFrame extends javax.swing.JFrame {

     /** Creates new form LogInFrame */
     public LogInFrame() {
        initComponents();
B       this.setLocationRelativeTo(null);        // set the LogIn Form at the center
     }
     @SuppressWarnings("unchecked")

     private void LogInButtonActionPerformed(java.awt.event.ActionEvent evt) {
        // TODO add your handling code here:
C       String username="", password="";

D       String query = "SELECT q.userName, q.passWord FROM LogIn q " +
                       "WHERE q.userName=:UserName AND q.passWord=:PassWord";
E       logInQuery = entityManager.createQuery(query);
F       logInQuery.setParameter("UserName", UserNameField.getText());
        logInQuery.setParameter("PassWord", PassWordField.getText());

G       List<Object[]> QueryResult = logInQuery.getResultList();
H       for (Object[]  resultElement : QueryResult)
        {
           username = (String)resultElement[0];
           password = (String)resultElement[1];
        }
I       if (UserNameField.getText().isEmpty() || PassWordField.getText().isEmpty())
        {
           System.out.println("Enter the LogIn Information...");
        }
J       else if (username.equals(UserNameField.getText()) && password.equals(PassWordField.getText()))
        {
           System.out.println("LogIn is successful!");
        }
K       else
        {
           System.out.println("LogIn is failed!");
        }

     }
```

Figure 6.37. The codes for the LogIn button event handler.

Let's have a closer look at this piece of codes to see how it works.

A. A Java util package is imported since we need to use the List component that is located at that package.

B. The setLocationRelativeTo() method is called to set up this LogInFrame Form at the center of the screen as the project runs. A null argument means that no object can be referenced or relative to and the JFrame Form is set to the center.

C. Two local String variables are created since we need to use them to temporarily hold the queried username and password from the LogIn table.

D. A JPQL query string, as we discussed in the last section, is declared here. Please note that this query string is a little different with the standard SQL query string, since we are using the JPA, not database connection engine, to connect to our sample database. A mapping has been made by JPA, and therefore we have to use a query language called Java Persistence query language (JPQL) that can be recognized by the JPA to access our sample database in an Entity class LogIn.java. Another point to be noted is the columns' names used in this query string, which are not identical with those columns' names in out LogIn table in our sample database CSE_DEPT. The column named user_name and pass_word in our LogIn table have been changed to userName and passWord, respectively, in this query string. This is also because of a mapping between each column in our LogIn table in our database and each property in the Entity class LogIn.java.

E. The logInQuery, which is a Query object created by the JPA when we drag our LogIn table to the LogInFrame Form to add the JPA components into the project, is used to create a new dynamic query by calling the method CreateQuery() with the query string we built in step D as an argument.

F. The setParameters() method of the logInQuery class is executed to set up two dynamic parameters in the WHERE clause in the query string. These two dynamic parameters are obtained from two TextField boxes, `UserNameField` and `PassWordField`, and entered by the user as the project runs. The getText() method is used to retrieve two dynamic parameters in real time.

G. The Query Result class is used to create a new QueryResult object that is used to hold the returned querying data from calling the method getResultList(). The returned username and password are stored in the list in a List format, which is a single line with two units.

H. Since our query string contains multiple SELECT clauses and returned data are wrapped and stored in the QueryResult in a List array. In order to retrieve that kind of query result, an **enhanced for loop** in Java is used to scan and retrieve all elements from the QueryResult list. Here, the variable resultElement is used to point to the current instance of Object in the List collection.

I. First, we need to check whether any input TextField is empty, which means that the user forgets to enter valid username or password. A warning message will be given if this situation occurred.

J. Next, we need to check whether the retrieved username and password match to the user's inputs. Here, we used the equals() method instead of the equal operator (==). The advantage of using this method is to avoid some possible bugs as the project runs. A login successful message will be displayed if the condition is true.

K. Otherwise, no matched username and password can be found from the LogIn table, and the login process is failed. A warning message is shown up for that situation.

We can build and run our project now; however, we want do a little modification to our project to make it more professional before we can run it.

6.2.5.6 Use a JDialog as a MessageBox

As you know, unlike Visual Studio.NET, a MessageBox is not provided in the Java programming environment. In order to display some running status or warning messages, we need to use a MessageBox. In this section, we show users how to build one using a Java Dialog box class, JDialog.

On the opened project, right click on our project **SelectQueryWizard** from the Projects window, and select the **New|OK/Cancel Dialog Sample Form** item from the pop-up menu to open the New JDialog Form dialog box. Enter **MsgDialog** to the Class Name box as our dialog box's name and select **LogInFramePackage** from the Package box to select it as our package in which our **MsgDialog** will be developed. Your finished New JDialog Form dialog box should match one that is shown in Figure 6.38.

Click on the Design tab from the top to open the Design View of our newly created **MsgDialog** box. Reduce the size to an appropriate one, and add one label control to this dialog by dragging a Label control from the Palette window and place it onto our dialog box. Right click on this label and select **Change Variable Name** item from the pop-up menu to change it to **MsgLabel**. Go to the text property to remove the default text. A preview of this dialog box is shown in Figure 6.39.

In order to use this dialog box as our MessageBox, we need to add some codes to this class. First, we need to add codes into the constructor of this class to make this dialog to be displayed at the center of the screen as the project runs. To do that, open the Code Window by clicking on the **Source** tab from the top and enter **this.setLocationRelativeTo(null);** just under the **initComponents();** method in the constructor.

Then move your cursor just under the line: **@SuppressWarnings("unchecked")**, and enter the codes shown in Figure 6.40 to create a new method, **setMessage()**. Your finished codes for these two code adding, which have been highlighted, is shown in Figure 6.40.

Now we need to add some codes to our main LogInFrame project to call this dialog box to display the login information to replace those command println method.

Open the Code Window of the LogInFrame class by clicking on the **Source** tab from the top, and move your cursor just under two String variables declaration, and enter the

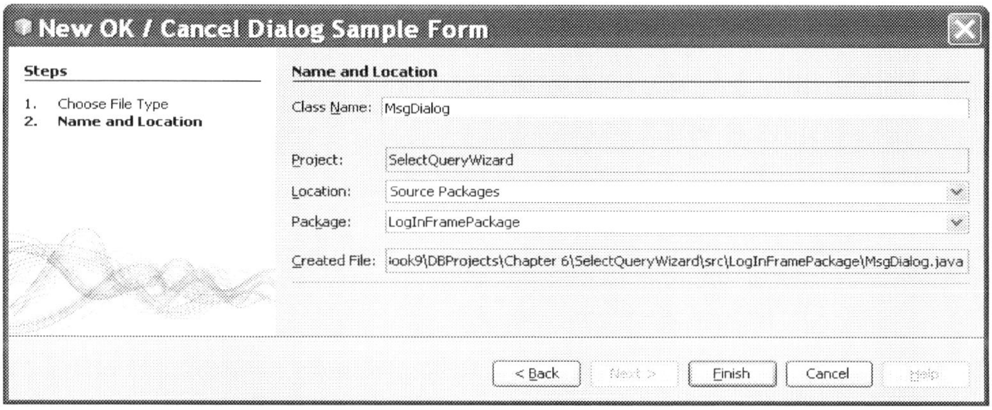

Figure 6.38. Finished New OK/Cancel Dialog Sample Form.

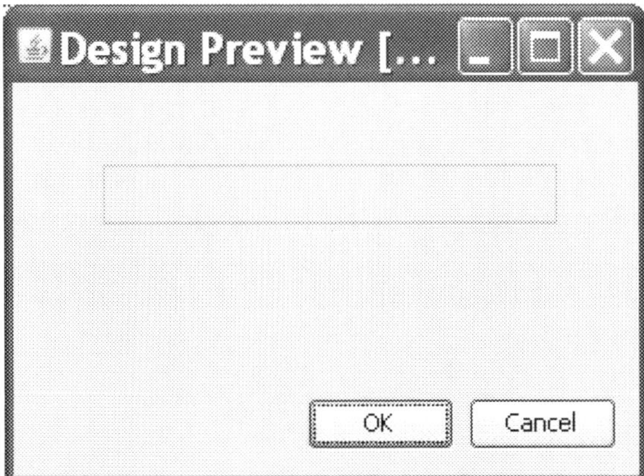

Figure 6.39. A preview of the designed MessageBox.

```
public MsgDialog(java.awt.Frame parent, boolean modal) {
        super(parent, modal);
        initComponents();
        this.setLocationRelativeTo(null);
    }
public void setMessage(String msg){
    MsgLabel.setText(msg);
}
```

Figure 6.40. Codes for the constructor and the setMessage() method.

following code to create a new instance of our dialog box MsgDialog, which is shown in Figure 6.41. Also, replace those command println coding lines with the associated Dialog calling operations, which have been highlighted in Figure 6.41.

Let's have a closer look at these added parts to see how they work.

A. Before we can use our built dialog box, first we need to create a new instance dialog with two arguments: the first one is the parent class name, and the second is a Boolean value to indicate whether this dialog is a model or modeless dialog.

B. If neither username nor password is presented, we need to call our dialog box to set up a message "Enter the Login Information" to the MsgLabel, also to call a method setVisible(true) to display this message.

C. Similarly, if a matched username and password have been found from our LogIn Table, a successful login message should be displayed.

D. Finally, if no matched username and password have been found, a login fail message should be displayed.

The last coding is for the Cancel button event handler. Open the Design View by clicking on the Design tab from the top, and double click on the Cancel button to open its event handler, enter the following codes into this event handler, which is shown in Figure 6.42.

The coding for this part is simple; the LogIn Form should be invisible and the LogIn class should be disposed if the Cancel button is clicked by the user. The keyword *this* means the current Form object, LogInFrame Form.

```
package LogInFramePackage;
import java.util.*;

public class LogInFrame extends javax.swing.JFrame {

    /** Creates new form LogInFrame */
    public LogInFrame() {
        initComponents();
        this.setLocationRelativeTo(null);
    }
    @SuppressWarnings("unchecked")

    private void LogInButtonActionPerformed(java.awt.event.ActionEvent evt) {
        // TODO add your handling code here:
        String username="", password="";
A       MsgDialog dialog = new MsgDialog(new javax.swing.JFrame(), true);
        String query = "SELECT q.userName, q.passWord FROM LogIn q " +
                       "WHERE q.userName=:UserName AND q.passWord=:PassWord";
        logInQuery = entityManager.createQuery(query);
        logInQuery.setParameter("UserName", UserNameField.getText());
        logInQuery.setParameter("PassWord", PassWordField.getText());

        List<Object[]> QueryResult = logInQuery.getResultList();
        for (Object[]  resultElement : QueryResult)
        {
            username = (String)resultElement[0];
            password = (String)resultElement[1];
        }
        if (UserNameField.getText().isEmpty() || PassWordField.getText().isEmpty())
        {
B           dialog.setMessage ("Enter the LogIn Information...");
            dialog.setVisible(true);
        }
        else if (username.equals(UserNameField.getText()) && password.equals(PassWordField.getText()))
        {
C           dialog.setMessage ("LogIn is successful!");
            dialog.setVisible(true);
        }
        else
        {
D           dialog.setMessage ("LogIn is failed!");
            dialog.setVisible(true);
        }
    }
```

Figure 6.41. Modified codes for the LogInFrame class.

```
private void CancelButtonActionPerformed(java.awt.event.ActionEvent evt) {
        this.setVisible(false);
        this.dispose();
    }
```

Figure 6.42. The codes for the Cancel button event handler.

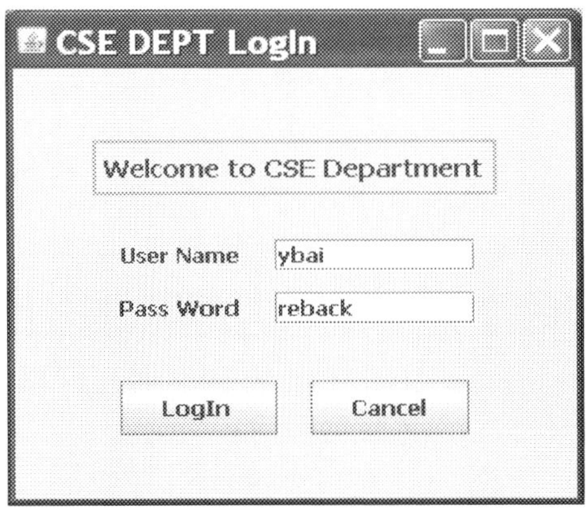

a

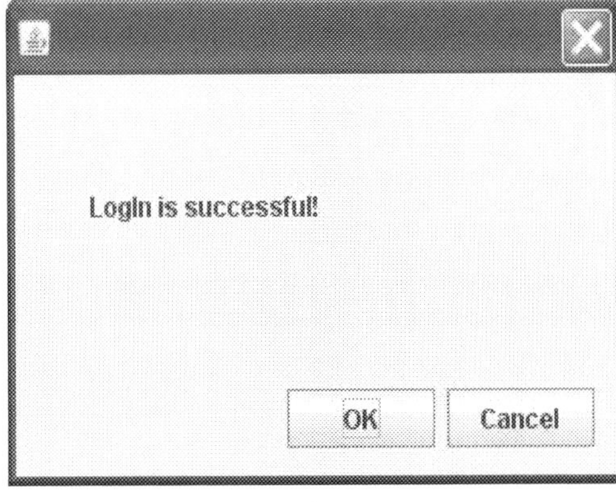

b

Figure 6.43. The running example of the LogInFrame Form.

Now that we have finished all coding for this LogIn JFrame Form, let's build and run the project to test its functionality.

Click on the Clean and Build Main Project icon on the toolbar, and a successful building message should be displayed in the Output window if our project is fine. Then click on the Run Main Project icon on the toolbar to run our project. You can try entering different username and password either correctly or incorrectly, or even leave both boxes blank to test the project.

A running example for successful login process is shown in Figure 6.43a,b. Figure 6.43a shows a login form, and Figure 6.43b shows a successful login message.

Click on the OK button on the dialog box and the Cancel button on the LogIn form to close our project. Our LogIn Form and login process are successful!

As the login process is successful, the next job is to enable users to select different functions to perform data query from the different data tables in our sample database. We need to build a Selection Form to enable users to make this kind of selections.

6.2.6 Use Java JPA Wizards to Create Selection Window

This form allows users to select the different form windows to connect to the different data tables, and furthermore to browse data from the associated table. No data table is connected to this form.

The function of the Select Form is: as this form is shown up, a combo box is displayed with three selections: Faculty Information, Course Information, and Student Information. Users can select any one of them to go to the associated Form window to access the selected data table to query required information by clicking on the OK button. When the Exit button is clicked by the user, the project is exited

6.2.6.1 Add a New JFrame as the SelectionFrame Form

As we did for the LogIn Form, to create a JFrame Form, right click on our project SelectQueryWizard from the Projects window and select New|JFrame Form item from

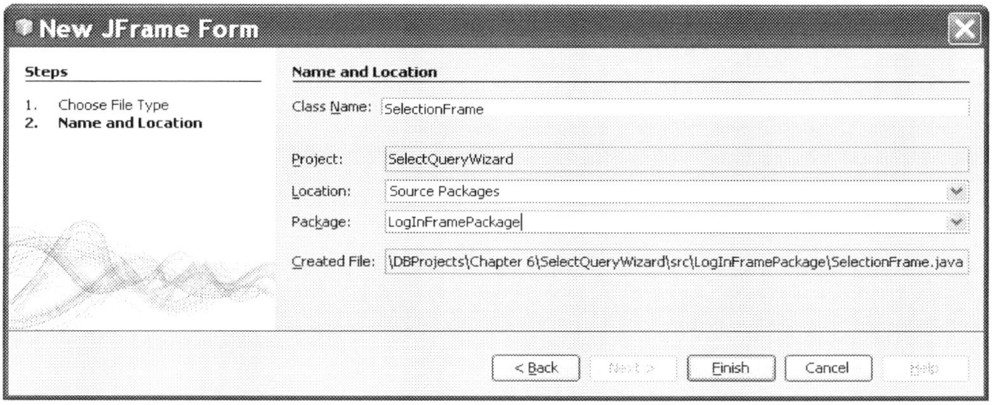

Figure 6.44. The completed New JFrame Form dialog box.

Table 6.3. Objects and controls in the SelectionFrame form

Type	Variable Name	Text	Model	Title
Label	Label1	Make Your Selection		
ComboBox	ComboSelection			
Button	cmdOK	OK		
Button	cmdExit	Exit		
SelectionFrame				CSE DEPT Selection

the pop-up menu to open New JFrame Form dialog box, which is shown in Figure 6.44. Enter **SelectionFrame** into the Class Name box as the name of our new Frame Form class, and select **LogInFramePackage** from the Package box. Your finished New JFrame Form dialog box should match one that is shown in Figure 6.44. Click on the **Finish** button to complete this creation.

Add the following objects and controls, which are shown in Table 6.3, into this SelectionFrame Form.

One point to be noted is that you need to remove all default items located inside the model property of the Combo Box **ComboSelection**. To do that, click on the **ComboSelection** combo box from the Design view, and then go the model property, and click on the three-dot button to open the model dialog box. Select all four default items, click on the Delete button from the keyboard to remove all of those items. A preview of the completed SelectionFrame Form should match one that is shown in Figure 6.45.

When defining the variable name, right click on each object and select **Change Variable Name** item from the pop-up menu to do that.

Now let's perform the coding for this SelectionFrame Form. The first coding is to add the initialization codes to the constructor of this SelectionFrame Form class to initialize the Combo box **ComboSelection** to allow users to make their desired selection as the project runs. Open the Code Window by clicking on the **Source** tab from the top and enter the codes that are in bold and are shown in Figure 6.46 into the constructor.

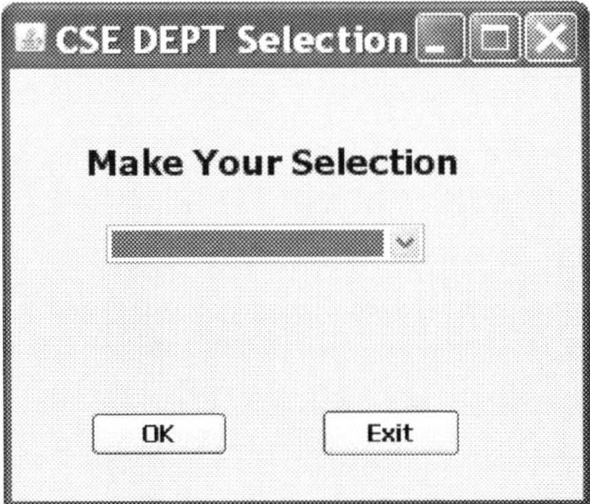

Figure 6.45. A preview of the created SelectionFrame Form.

```
package LogInFramePackage;
public class SelectionFrame extends javax.swing.JFrame {

    /** Creates new form SelectionFrame */
    public SelectionFrame() {
       initComponents();
A      this.setLocationRelativeTo(null);
B      this.ComboSelection.addItem("Faculty Information");
       this.ComboSelection.addItem("Course Information");
       this.ComboSelection.addItem("Student Information");
    }
```

Figure 6.46. Codes for the constructor of the SelectionFrame Form.

Let's have a closer look at this piece of codes to see how it works.

A. The setLocationRelativeTo() method is called to locate this SelectionFrame Form at the center of the screen as the project runs. A null argument means that no any object can be referenced or relative to, and the JFrame Form is set to the center.

B. The addItem() method is executed to add three pieces of information into the Combo Box ComboSelection to allow users to choose one of them as the project runs. Another method to add these three pieces of information is to directly add those pieces of information into the model box under the Combo Box Model Editor, which can be considered as a static adding (before the project runs). In that way, you do not need to enter these three lines of codes in this constructor. However, we prefer to call the addItem() method to add those pieces of information, since it belongs to a dynamic adding.

Next let's do the coding for the OK and Exit command buttons, exactly for the event handlers of those buttons. The function for the SelectionFrame Form is: as the user selected a desired choice from the combo box and click the OK button to query the related information, the related information frame, such as FacultyFrame Form, CourseFrame Form, or StudentFrame Form, will be displayed to enable users to make related queries. However, at this moment of time, we have not built those Frame Forms. To make our project be able to be run and tested in that sequence, we temporarily use a dialog box we developed in Section 6.2.5.6 to indicate the normal progress.

```
  private void cmdOKActionPerformed(java.awt.event.ActionEvent evt) {
      // TODO add your handling code here:
A     MsgDialog dialog = new MsgDialog(new javax.swing.JFrame(), true);

B     if (ComboSelection.getSelectedItem()== "Faculty Information"){
         dialog.setMessage("Faculty Information is selected\n");
         dialog.setVisible(true);
      }
      else if (ComboSelection.getSelectedItem()== "Course Information"){
         dialog.setMessage("Course Information is selected\n");
         dialog.setVisible(true);
      }
      else {
         dialog.setMessage("Student Information is selected\n");
         dialog.setVisible(true);
      }
  }
```

Figure 6.47. Codes for the OK button Click event handler.

```
A public SelectionFrame getSelectionFrame(){
     return this;
  }
  private void cmdExitActionPerformed(java.awt.event.ActionEvent evt) {
      // TODO add your handling code here:
B     this.setVisible(false);
      this.dispose();
C     System.exit(0);
  }
```

Figure 6.48. Codes for the getter method and the Exit button Click event handler.

Now let's open the Design View of the project by clicking on the Design tab from the top and double clicking on the OK button to open its event handler. Enter the codes that are shown in Figure 6.47 into this handler.

Let's have a closer look at this piece of codes to see how it works.

A. A new instance of the MsgDialog class is created at the beginning of this handler.

B. An if selection structure is used to identify each selected item from the Combo Box. Also, the selected item is displayed using our dialog box by calling the setMessage() method and setVisible() method.

The rest of the coding includes two parts: coding for the Exit button Click event handler and coding for creating a getter method. As you know, in the object-oriented programming, in order to use the unique object created in a project, a popular way is to create a setter and a getter method in the target class. In this way, when other objects such as JFrames, JDialogs, or JWindows in the same project want to use the target object, they can call this getter to get the desired target object.

Let's create codes for both the getter method and the Exit button click event handler by entering the codes that are shown in Figure 6.48 into this SelectionFrame class.

Let's have a closer look at this piece of codes to see how it works.

A. The function of the codes for the getter method is simple; as this method is called, the current SelectionFrame object is obtained by returning this component that is a pointer point to the current Frame object to the calling object. A point to be noted is that the accessing mode of this method must be public, since we want this method to be called by any other objects to get this SelectionFrame object as the project runs.

B. In the Exit button Click event handler, close the SelectionFrame Form object by calling setVisible() method with a false as the argument. The object this indicates the current Frame Form object, and a dispose() method is executed to throw out and dispose this object.

C. A system exit method is called to allow the project to be officially exited from the current process. An argument 0 means that no error for this exit operation.

6.2.6.2 Modify Codes to Coordinate Operations in SelectionFrame and LogInFrame

Before we can run our project to test the login and selection function, we need to do some modifications or adding codes to both LogInFrame and SelectionFrame classes. As we mentioned, when the user clicks on the Exit button on the SelectionFrame Form, the whole project should be exited. One issue is that how we can close the LogInFrame Form object from the SelectionFrame object as the Exit button is clicked. Another word is that how we can access the LogInFrame object from the SelectionFrame object as the project runs. One possible solution is to create another getter method in the LogInFrame class, and in this way, we can pick up the LogInFrame object from the SelectionFrame object by calling this method as the project runs.

Now let's create a getter in the LogInFrame class. Open the Code Window of the LogInFrame class by clicking on the Source tab from the top of the window, and add the codes that are in bold and shown in Figure 6.49 into the LogInFrame class to create this getter method. In fact, you can add this method in any location inside the class. However, we prefer to add it just under the constructor.

Next, we need to add some codes into the LogIn button Click event handler to direct the project to open the SelectionFrame Form window if the login process is successful. Open the LogIn button event handler and add the following codes into this handler, which is shown in Figure 6.50.

Let's have a closer look at these modified codes to see how they work.

A. A new instance of the SelectionFrame class selFrame is created. However, the getter method getSelectionFrame() we built for the SelectionFrame class is called to retrieve

```
public class LogInFrame extends javax.swing.JFrame {

   /** Creates new form LogInFrame */
   public LogInFrame() {
      initComponents();
      this.setLocationRelativeTo(null);   // set the LogIn Form at the center
   }
   public LogInFrame getLogInFrame(){
      return this;
   }
   ......
```

Figure 6.49. Create a getter method for the LogInFrame class.

```
  private void LogInButtonActionPerformed(java.awt.event.ActionEvent evt) {
      // TODO add your handling code here:
      String username="", password="";
      MsgDialog msgDlg = new MsgDialog(new javax.swing.JFrame(), true);
A     SelectionFrame  selFrame = new SelectionFrame().getSelectionFrame();
      String query = "SELECT q.userName, q.passWord FROM LogIn q " +
                     "WHERE q.userName=:UserName AND q.passWord=:PassWord";
      logInQuery = entityManager.createQuery(query);
      logInQuery.setParameter("UserName", UserNameField.getText());
      logInQuery.setParameter("PassWord", PassWordField.getText());

      List<Object[]> QueryResult = logInQuery.getResultList();
      for (Object[] resultElement : QueryResult)
      {
         username = (String)resultElement[0];
         password = (String)resultElement[1];
      }
      if (UserNameField.getText().isEmpty() || PassWordField.getText().isEmpty())
      {
         msgDlg.setMessage("Enter the LogIn Information...");
         msgDlg.setVisible(true);
      }
      else if (username.equals(UserNameField.getText()) && password.equals(PassWordField.getText()))
      {
B        selFrame.setVisible(true);
         this.setVisible(false);
         this.dispose();
      }
      else
      {
         msgDlg.setMessage("LogIn is failed!");
         msgDlg.setVisible(true);
      }
  }
```

Figure 6.50. Modified codes for the LogIn button Click event handler.

the original SelectionFrame instance and assign it to the newly created instance. In this way, we did not create any new instance of the SelectionFrame; instead, we are still using the original SelectionFrame instance, and it is a unique instance in this project.

B. Replace the old codes by using the code line selFrame.setVisible(true) to display our SelectionFrame Form window if the login process is successful. Also, close and dispose this LogInFrame Form window since we have finished the login process.

Now we need to modify some codes in the SelectionFrame class to allow it to access the LogInFrame object and close it as the Exit button is clicked by the user. Open the Exit button Click event handler by double clicking on the Exit button from the Design View of the SelectionFrame Form window and enter the codes that are shown in Figure 6.51 into this event handler. All newly added codes have been highlighted with bold.

The functionality of this piece of new added code is:

A. First, an instance of the LogInFrame class logFrame is created, and the method getLogInFrame() is called to get the current instance of that class and assign it to the instance logFrame. This makes sure that we are using the original instance, instead of creating a new instance of that class.

B. If the LogInFrame Form window is active, the setVisible() method will be called to close it, and the dispose() method is used to dispose the LogInFrame Form.

```
  private void cmdExitActionPerformed(java.awt.event.ActionEvent evt) {
      // TODO add your handling code here:
A     LogInFrame logFrame = new LogInFrame().getLogInFrame();

B     if (logFrame.isActive()){
        logFrame.setVisible(false);
        logFrame.dispose();
      }
      this.setVisible(false);
      this.dispose();
      System.exit(0);
  }
```

Figure 6.51. The new added codes to the Exit button Click event handler.

At this point, we have finished all coding jobs for the SelectionFrame. In the following sections, we will design and build FacultyFrame, CourseFrame, and StudentFrame classes to replace those temporary codes in three branches in the if selection structure in Section 6.2.6.1.

6.2.7 Use Java JPA Wizards to Query the Faculty Table

We divide this section into the following four parts:

1. Create a new FacultyFrame class and add it into our project.
2. Use JPA Wizards to build Entity class for our Faculty table in our sample database.
3. Develop codes to perform the data query from the Faculty table.
4. Modify the codes in FacultyFrame and SelectionFrame classes to coordinate the operations between both components.

First, let's create a new FacultyFrame class and add it into our project.

6.2.7.1 Create a New FacultyFrame Class and Add It into Our Project

As we did for the LogIn Form, to create a JFrame Form, right click on our project SelectQueryWizard from the Projects window and select New|JFrame Form item from the pop-up menu to open New JFrame Form dialog box, which is shown in Figure 6.52. Enter FacultyFrame into the Class Name box as the name of our new Frame Form class, and then select the item LogInFramePackage from the Package box. Your finished New JFrame Form dialog box should match one that is shown in Figure 6.52. Click on the Finish button to complete this creation.

Add the following objects and controls, which are shown in Table 6.4, into this FacultyFrame Form. One point to be noted is that you need to remove all default items located inside the model property of the Combo Box ComboName and ComboMethod. To do that, click on the ComboName combo box from the Design view, and then go the model property, click on the three-dot extension button to open the model dialog box. Select all four default items, click on the Delete button from the keyboard to remove all of those items. Perform the similar operations for the

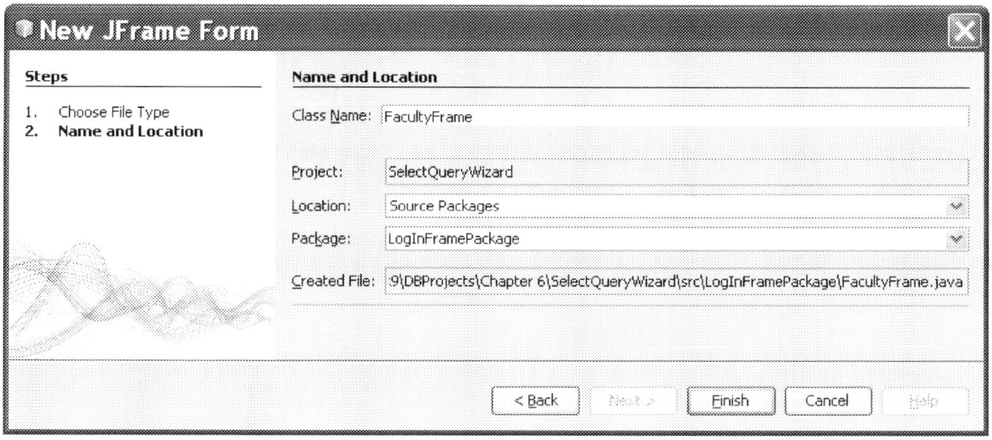

Figure 6.52. The finished FacultyFrame Form window.

Table 6.4. Objects and controls in the FacultyFrame form

Type	Variable Name	Text	Border	Title
Canvas	ImageCanvas			
Panel	jPanel1		Titled Border	Faculty Name and Query Method
Label	Label1	Faculty Name		
ComboBox	ComboName			
Label	Label2	Query Method		
ComboBox	ComboMethod			
Panel	jPanel2		Titled Border	Faculty Information
Label	Label3	Title		
Label	Label4	Office		
Label	Label5	Phone		
Label	Label6	College		
Label	Label7	Email		
Text Field	TitleField			
Text Field	OfficeField			
Text Field	PhoneField			
Text Field	CollegeField			
Text Field	EmailField			
Button	cmdSelect	Select		
Button	cmdInsert	Insert		
Button	cmdUpdate	Update		
Button	cmdDelete	Delete		
Button	cmdBack	Back		
FacultyFrame Form	FacultyFrame			CSE DEPT Faculty Form

ComboMethod. A preview of the completed FacultyFrame Form should match one that is shown in Figure 6.53.

A point to be noted is that when you drag a Canvas control from the Palette and place it into the FacultyFrame Form window, first, you need to click on the Canvas from the Palette. Then you need to click a location where you want to place it in the

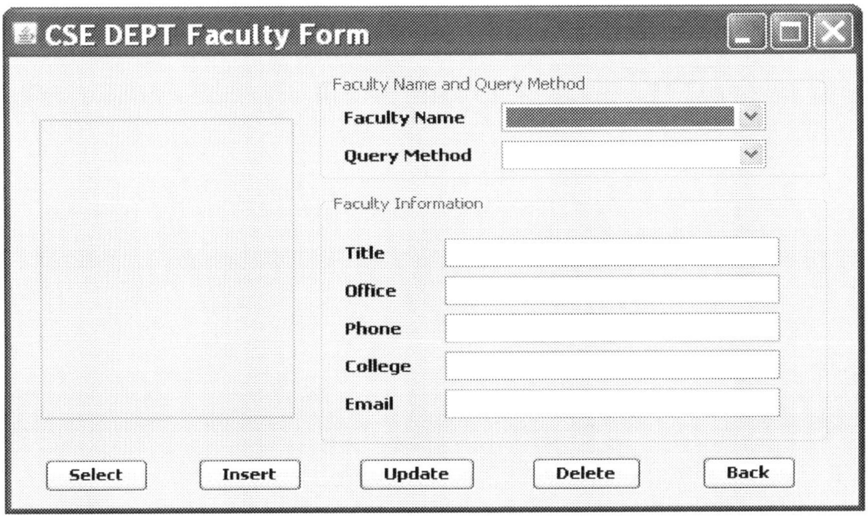

CSE DEPT Faculty Form

Faculty Name and Query Method

Faculty Name

Query Method

Faculty Information

Title

Office

Phone

College

Email

Select Insert Update Delete Back

Figure 6.53. A preview of the finished FacultyFrame Form window.

FacultyFrame. A Canvas icon is displayed in that location you clicked. You must drag this Canvas icon to the upper-left direction—never drag it to the lower-right direction—to enlarge it.

The function of this FacultyFrame object is:

1. When the user selected the Faculty Information item from the SelectionFrame Form, the FacultyFrame Form window is displayed to allow users to query detailed information for the selected faculty from the Faculty Name combo box.
2. The Query Method combo box enables users to select a different query method, such as JPA Wizards method, Java Code method, Precompiled Method, or Callable Method, to perform the data query. In this project, we only concentrate on the JPA Wizards method.
3. The Canvas and five Text Field boxes are used to display the retrieved detailed information related to the selected faculty member, including a picture of selected faculty, as the Select button is clicked by the user.
4. When the Back button is clicked by the user, which means that the data query for the Faculty table is done, and the current FacultyFrame Form window should be closed, and the control is returned to the SelectionFrame Form window to allow users to perform other information query.

In this project, we only use Select and Back buttons, and all other buttons will be used later for the following projects.

6.2.7.2 Add Faculty Entity Manager and JPA Components into the Project

Before we can start our query process, we need to add the Entity Manager, which will control all Entity classes and all JPA components, such as Query and Query Result that we created in Section 6.2.4 into the FacultyFrame Form window. In this way, we can use the Entity Manager to manage the Entity class to set up mapping relations between components in our Java GUI Forms and the Faculty table in our sample database, and perform all query-related operations. Perform the following operations to complete this adding process:

1. Expand the Databases icon in the Services Window to find our connected SQL Server database jdbc:sqlserver://localhost\SQL2008EXPRESS:5000;databaseName=CSE_DEPT [ybai on dbo]. If it has not been connected, right click on this icon and select Connect item from the pop-up menu to connect it.
2. Expand our connected database icon to our database CSE_DEPT and to the dbo node, and then the Tables folder. Drag our Faculty table and place it onto our FacultyFrame Form.
3. Immediately, you can find that one Entity Manager class entityManager and two JPA components, facultyQuery and facultyList, have been added into our project in the Other Components folder in the Inspector Window.

Now we can start to perform the query to access our sample database using the added Entity Manager and JPA components.

6.2.7.3 Use Entity Classes to Perform Data Query from the Faculty Table

After the Entity class, Entity Manager, and JPA components have been built and added in our project, we can perform the data query to our Faculty table. The development of this query can be divided into the following five parts:

1. Adding some necessary java packages and coding for the constructor of the FacultyFrame class to perform some initialization processes.
2. Coding for the Select button Click event handler to perform the data query operation to the Faculty table in our sample database.
3. Adding a new user-defined method ShowFaculty() to display an image for the selected faculty in the FacultyFrame Form window.
4. Coding for the Back button Click event handler to close the FacultyFrame Form window and return the control to the SelectionFrame Form.
5. Modifying the codes in the SelectionFrame class to allow a smooth switching from the SelectionFrame to the FacultyFrame if the user selected the Faculty Information item.

Now let's start with the first part.

6.2.7.3.1 Add Java Package and Coding for the Constructor of the FacyltyFrame Class Since we used a List as our query result holder, therefore, we need to add the java.util.* package into our project because the List class is located at that package. Also, we need to display an image of the selected faculty when a data query is executed; the java.awt.* package should be imported since some image related classes, such as Image, Graphics, and MediaTracker, are located at that Abstract Windowing Tools (AWT) package.

```
  package LogInFramePackage;
A import java.awt.*;        // added in January 9, 2010
  import java.util.*;

  public class FacultyFrame extends javax.swing.JFrame {

     /** Creates new form FacultyFrame */
     public FacultyFrame() {
        initComponents();
B       this.setLocationRelativeTo(null);   // set the faculty Form at the center
        // add all query methods
C       ComboMethod.addItem("JPA Wizards Method");
        ComboMethod.addItem("Java Codes Method");
        ComboMethod.addItem("Precompiled Method");
        ComboMethod.addItem("Callable Method");
        // add all faculty members
D       ComboName.addItem("Ying Bai");
        ComboName.addItem("Satish Bhalla");
        ComboName.addItem("Black Anderson");
        ComboName.addItem("Steve Johnson");
        ComboName.addItem("Jenney King");
        ComboName.addItem("Alice Brown");
        ComboName.addItem("Debby Angles");
        ComboName.addItem("Jeff Henry");
     }
```

Figure 6.54. Initialization codes for the FacultyFrame class.

Open the Code Window of the FacultyFrame class by clicking on the Source tab from the top of the window, and add the codes that are shown in Figure 6.54 into this source file.

Let's have a closer look at this piece of codes to see how it works.

A. Two java packages, java.awt.* and java.util.* are imported at the beginning of this file since we need to use some classes defined in those packages.

B. The setLocationRelativeTo() method is called to set up this FacultyFrame Form at the center of the screen as the project runs. A null argument means that no any object can be referenced or relative to, and the JFrame Form is set to the center.

C. The addItem() method is used to add all four query methods into the Query Method combo box.

D. Also the addItem() method is utilized to add all eight faculty members into the Faculty Name combo box.

Now let's develop codes for the Select button click event handler to perform the data query.

6.2.7.3.2 Coding for the Select Button Click Event Handler to Perform the Data Query Open the Design View of the FacultyFrame Form window by clicking on the Design tab from the top of the window, and double click on the Select button to open its event handler. Enter the codes that are shown in Figure 6.55 into this event handler.

```
  private void cmdSelectActionPerformed(java.awt.event.ActionEvent evt) {
      // TODO add your handling code here:
A     MsgDialog msgDlg = new MsgDialog(new javax.swing.JFrame(), true);

B     if (ComboMethod.getSelectedItem()=="JPA Wizards Method"){
C        String query = "SELECT f.title, f.office, f.phone, f.college, f.email " +
                        "FROM Faculty f WHERE f.facultyName=:FacultyName";
D        facultyQuery = entityManager.createQuery(query);
E        facultyQuery.setParameter("FacultyName", ComboName.getSelectedItem());
F        java.util.List<Object[]> QueryResult = facultyQuery.getResultList();
G        for (Object[] resultElement : QueryResult)
         {
           TitleField.setText((String)resultElement[0]);
           OfficeField.setText((String)resultElement[1]);
           PhoneField.setText((String)resultElement[2]);
           CollegeField.setText((String)resultElement[3]);
           EmailField.setText((String)resultElement[4]);
         }
      }
  }
```

Figure 6.55. The codes for the Select button Click event handler.

Let's have a closer look at this piece of codes to see how it performs the data query function.

A. First, a new instance of the JDialog class is created since we may use this dialog box to display some warning information to monitor the running status of the data query.

B. Next, we need to check which query method has been selected by the user to perform this data query. In this part, we only take care of the first method, `JPA Wizards Method`.

C. A Java Persistence Query statement is declared for this faculty information query. Five columns, Title, Office, Phone, College, and Email, are queried based on the Faculty Name selected from the combo box ComboName by the user. One point to be noted is that the protocol of this query statement is not a standard SQL statement; instead, it is based on the Java Persistence Query Language (JPQL) and the Entity-mapping file Faculty.java. An abstract schema and mapped column names have been used in this statement. Refer to Sections 6.2.5.1 and 6.2.5.2 to get more detailed information on Entity class mapping file and JPQL.

D. The createQuery() method in the EntityManager class is executed to create this query with the query statement we built in the last step as the argument.

E. The setParameter() method is called to replace the nominal name of the dynamic parameter FacultyName with a real faculty name selected by the user from the combo box ComboName using the method getSelectedItem() method.

F. The query is executed by calling the getResultList() method. One point to be noted is that both java.awt and java.util packages contain List class with two different definitions in the constructor. Therefore, in order to clearly indicate which List class we are suppose to use, a full path of this class is defined, which means that both the package and the class names are involved in this definition. In this example, we prefer to use the List class in the java.util package.

G. An enhanced for loop is used to retrieve the queried columns from the QueryResult list and assign them one by one to the associated Text Fields to display them.

Now, let's consider to add an image for the selected faculty member to make our project more professional.

6.2.7.3.3 Display an Image for the Selected Faculty There are different ways to store and display images in a database-related project. One professional way is to store all images as binary files in a database with all queried data together. However, the shortcoming of this kind of image storage is that both a huge block of memory spaces will be occupied by those huge binary files, and a slow retrieving speed is expected by the query mechanism. To effectively overcome those disadvantages and make our project simple, in this book, we prefer to store all image files in the current project folder. In this way, the image-retrieving process and speed can be significantly simplified and improved.

Unlike Visual Studio.NET, such as Visual Basic.NET and Visual C#.NET, there is no PictureBox class available in the Java to display an image or a picture. One needs to use a Canvas object as an image holder, a Graphics object as a tool to display an image, and a MediaTracker class as a monitor to coordinate the image processing. In Java, the main package containing the key image processing classes, such as Image, Toolkit, Graphics, and MediaTracker, is java.awt. Currently, Sun's Java graphics programming library (AWT) supports GIF and JPEG images. Format considerations include local color palettes, feature restrictions (compression, color depth, and interlacing, for example), and dithering.

We divide this section into the following three parts to make the image displaying in Java more illustrative and straightforward:

1. Operation sequence to display an image in Java
2. Creating a new user-defined method ShowFaculty to select desired faculty image
3. Developing the additional codes to coordinate this image displaying

Now let's start with the first part.

6.2.7.3.3.1 Operation Sequence to Display an Image in Java: Regularly, to display an image in Java, two steps are necessary to be performed:

1. Loading an image from an image file
2. Displaying that image by drawing it in a Graphics context

For example, to load an image named "**faculty.jpg**," use the **getImage()** method that belongs the Toolkit class as:

```
Image img = myWindow.getToolkit().getImage("faculty.jpg");
```

where **MyWindow** is the Java GUI container, such as a JFrame, JDialog, or a JWindow, in which the image will be displayed. The **getToolkit()** method that belongs to the Java GUI container is used to get the Toolkit object. One point to be noted when this instruction is executed is that both Image and Toolkit classes are abstract classes, which means that you cannot directly create new instances by invoking those classes' constructors. Instead, you have to use some methods related to those abstract classes to do that.

After an image is loaded, display the image by drawing it in a Graphics context by using

```
g.drawImage(img, x, y, width, height, imageObserver);
```

where object g is an instance of the Graphics class.

As you know, every AWT component object has a Graphics context, and the real drawing is done in the paint() method of a component, because paint() is called by AWT automatically when the image is finished in loading. However, an important issue is that the image loading is asynchronous process, which means that the loading does not necessarily occur until you attempt to display the image via drawImage(). The last parameter to drawImage() specifies which component to repaint when the image is finally ready. This is normally the component that calls drawImage() in the Java GUI container.

In fact, when the first step—loading an image starts, the getImage() method kicks off a new thread to load and fetch the image, and this thread does not start immediately or synchronously as you run this loading method. Instead, this thread will not begin its process until the drawImage() method is called. Therefore, it is no guaranteed that the required image will be loaded and ready to be displayed as the drawImage() is executed.

In order to solve this asynchronous problem in the image loading and displaying, another image-related class, MediaTracker, should be used to monitor and track the running status of the image-loading process. The MediaTracker is a utility class designed to track the status of media objects. In theory, media objects could include audio clips and other media, as well as images. You can use a media tracker object by instantiating an instance of MediaTracker for the component that you want to have monitored, and invoking its addImage() method for each image that you want to track. Each image can be assigned a unique identifier starting from 1, or groups of images can be assigned the same identifier. You can determine the status of an image or group of images by invoking one of several methods on the MediaTracker object and passing the identifier as a parameter to the method.

Another way you can use the MediaTracker object is that you can cause MediaTracker to block and wait until a specified image or group of images completes loading. We will use this approach in this project to make certain that a desired faculty image has completed loading before we attempt to draw it.

Before we can start this image displaying process with codes, we need first to create a user-defined method to identify and select the desired faculty image in terms of the selected faculty member.

6.2.7.3.3.2 Create a User-Defined Method to Select Desired Faculty Image: Open the Code Window of the FacultyFrame class by clicking on the Source tab from the top of the window, and enter the codes that are shown in Figure 6.56 to create this new method ShowFaculty().

Let's have a closer look at this piece of codes to see how it works.

A. Some local variables and objects used in this method are declared and defined first. The imgId and timeout are used as the ID of the tracked image and the maximum waiting time

```
  private boolean ShowFaculty(){
A     Image  img;
      int  imgId = 1, maxNumber = 7, timeout = 1000;
      MediaTracker  tracker = new MediaTracker(this);
      MsgDialog  msgDlg = new MsgDialog(new javax.swing.JFrame(), true);

B     String  fImage = null;
C     String[] fname = { "Ying Bai", "Black Anderson", "Satish Bhalla", "Steve Johnson",
                         "Jenney King", "Alice Brown", "Debby Angles", "Jeff Henry"};
D     String[] fimage = { "Bai.jpg", "Anderson.jpg", "Satish.jpg", "Johnson.jpg",
                          "King.jpg", "Brown.jpg", "Angles.jpg", "Henry.jpg"};
E     for (int i=0; i<=maxNumber; i++){
          if (fname[i].equals((String)ComboName.getSelectedItem())){
            fImage = fimage[i];
            break;
          }
      }
F     if (fImage != null){
        img = this.getToolkit().getImage(fImage);
        Graphics g = ImageCanvas.getGraphics();
G       tracker.addImage(img, imgId);
H       try{
          if(!tracker.waitForID(imgId, timeout)){
            msgDlg.setMessage("Failed to load image");
            msgDlg.setVisible(true);
            }//end if
I       }catch(InterruptedException e){
          msgDlg.setMessage(e.toString()); msgDlg.setVisible(true); }
J       g.drawImage(img, 0, 0, ImageCanvas.getWidth(), ImageCanvas.getHeight(), this);
        return true;
      }
K     else{
          return false;
      }
  }
```

Figure 6.56. The codes for the user-defined method ShowFaculty.

for that tracking process. Two new instances, one for MediaTracker class tracker and another one for MsgDialog class msgDlg, are created since we need to use them in this ShowFaculty() method.

B. A local String object fImage, which is used to temporarily hold the identified faculty image, is created and initialized to null.

C. A 2D String array fname is created and initialized with the names of all eight faculty members.

D. Similarly a 2D String array fimage is also created and initialized with all eight faculty images. The reason we used these two 2D arrays to store faculty names and associated images is that there is a one-to-one relationship existed between these two arrays, and we can easily get the associated faculty image by using the index if a matched faculty member is identified.

E. A for loop is used to repeatedly look for the matched faculty member between the faculty name in the array fname and the faculty name selected by the user from the combo box ComboName. An equals() method, instead of an equal operator (==), is used to make this comparison between two Strings since the former is more formal and safer to get the matched result. If a matched faculty name is found, the associated faculty image, which can be identified by using the index of the matched faculty array, is assigned to the local variable fImage, and the for loop is done and broken to the next step.

F. If a matched faculty image has been found, which is indicated by a non-null in the local variable fImage, the getImage() method that belongs to the abstract class Toolkit is executed to load the matched image. Since the Toolkit class is an abstract class, we used a method getToolkit() to create it instead of generating it by invoking its constructor. The getGraphics() method is called to get a Graphics context, and our ImageCanvas works as a holder for this faculty image.

G. The addImage() method that belongs to the MediaTracker class is called to add our image with its ID into the tracking system.

H. A try catch block is used to begin this tracking process and the waitForID() method is called to execute this tracking. If a timeout occurred for this tracking process, which means that the matched faculty image has not been loaded into the project, a warning message is displayed using our MsgDialog object.

I. Any possible exception or error will be caught by the catch block and displayed.

J. If no timeout error happened, which means that the matched faculty image has been loaded into our project and ready to be displayed, the drawImage() method is executed to display it in the FacultyFrame Form window. We want to display this image starting from the origin of the Canvas object, which is the upper-left corner of the canvas (0, 0), with a width and height that are identical with those of the canvas. Therefore, the getWidth() and getHeight() methods are called to get both of them from the canvas object. A true is returned to the main program to indicate that the execution of this ShowFaculty() method is successful.

K. Otherwise, if the local variable fImage contained a null, which means that no matched faculty image has been found, a false is returned to the main program to indicate this error.

Now we have finished coding process for the ShowFaculty() method. Next let's finish this faculty image displaying and the coding process for this FacultyFrame class by adding the additional codes into our project.

6.2.7.3.3.3 Develop Additional Codes to Coordinate This Image Displaying: Open the Design View of our FacultyFrame Form by clicking on the Design tab from the top of the window, and double click on the Select button to open its the event handler. Add the codes that are in bold and shown in Figure 6.57 into this handler.

The function of this newly added piece of codes is simple: if the returned value from calling the ShowFaculty() method is false, which means that no matched faculty image can be found, a warning message is displayed to indicate this to the user.

The final coding job we need to do for this FacultyFrame class is the Back button Click event handler. This coding is very easy, and the FacultyFrame object should be closed and disposed as the user clicks on this button, and the control should be directed to the SelectionFrame Form to allow users to continue selecting other functions.

From the Design View of the FacultyFrame Form window, double click on the Back button to open its event handler, and enter the codes that shown in Figure 6.58 into this handler.

The codes are simple; as soon as the user clicks on this Back button, the FacultyFrame Form window is closed and the control should be directed to return to the SelectionFrame Form window to allow users to select other information.

```
private void cmdSelectActionPerformed(java.awt.event.ActionEvent evt) {
    // TODO add your handling code here:
    MsgDialog msgDlg = new MsgDialog(new javax.swing.JFrame(), true);

    if (ComboMethod.getSelectedItem()=="JPA Wizards Method"){
        String query = "SELECT f.title, f.office, f.phone, f.college, f.email " +
                       "FROM Faculty f WHERE f.facultyName=:FacultyName";
        facultyQuery = entityManager.createQuery(query);
        facultyQuery.setParameter("FacultyName", ComboName.getSelectedItem());
        java.util.List<Object[]> QueryResult = facultyQuery.getResultList();
        for (Object[] resultElement : QueryResult)
        {
            TitleField.setText((String)resultElement[0]);
            OfficeField.setText((String)resultElement[1]);
            PhoneField.setText((String)resultElement[2]);
            CollegeField.setText((String)resultElement[3]);
            EmailField.setText((String)resultElement[4]);
        }
    }
    if (!ShowFaculty()){
        msgDlg.setMessage("No matched faculty image found!");
        msgDlg.setVisible(true);
    }
}
```

Figure 6.57. The newly added codes to the Select button Click event handler.

```
private void cmdBackActionPerformed(java.awt.event.ActionEvent evt) {
    // TODO add your handling code here:
    this.setVisible(false);
    this.dispose();
}
```

Figure 6.58. Codes for the Back button Click event handler.

We have finished all coding jobs for this FacultyFrame class. One point to be noted is that before you can run and test it, you must copy and paste all faculty and student image files that are located at the folder Images in the accompanying ftp site (see Chapter 1) to your project folder. In this case, it is C:\Chapter 6\SelectQuryWizard to allow the compiler to know where those image files are located as the project runs.

Now you can build and test this FacultyFrame object, not the whole project, by right clicking on the FacultyFrame.java from the Project window, and select the Run File item to run it. Select the JPA Wizards Method from the Query Method combo box and select the faculty member Ying Bai from the Faculty Name combo box. Click on the Select button to try to retrieve the detailed information with the faculty image for this faculty. A running result is shown in Figure 6.59.

Close this running result by clicking on the Close button located at the upper-right corner on this form window.

Next, we need to integrate this FacultyFrame object with our project together to build and test the whole project. The only class we need to add some codes is the SelectionFrame. Open the Code Window of that class and move your cursor to the first if block inside the

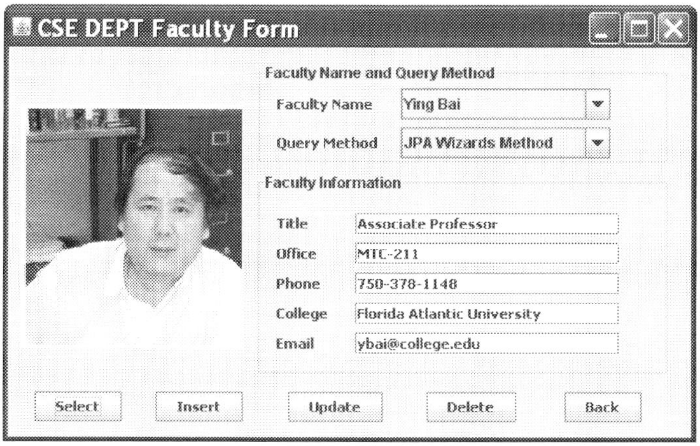

Figure 6.59. Running result of the FacultyFrame object.

```
  private void cmdOKActionPerformed(java.awt.event.ActionEvent evt) {
      // TODO add your handling code here:
      MsgDialog dialog = new MsgDialog(new javax.swing.JFrame(), true);
A     FacultyFrame facultyFrame = new FacultyFrame();
      if (ComboSelection.getSelectedItem()== "Faculty Information"){
         //dialog.setMessage("Faculty Information is selected\n");
B        facultyFrame.setVisible(true);
      }
      else if (ComboSelection.getSelectedItem()== "Course Information"){
         dialog.setMessage("Course Information is selected\n");
         dialog.setVisible(true);
      }
      else {
         dialog.setMessage("Student Information is selected\n");
         dialog.setVisible(true);
      }
  }
```

Figure 6.60. The modified codes for the SelectionFrame Form window.

OK button Click event handler, enter the codes that are in bold and shown in Figure 6.60 to replace the original code line:

```
dialog.setMessage("Faculty Information is selected\n");
```

The function of this new added code is:

A. A new instance of the FacultyFrame Form class is created since we need to display this form if the user selected the Faculty Information from the combo box control.

B. The setVisible() method is called to display the FacultyFrame Form window to allow users to query the detailed information for the selected faculty.

Now we can build and test our whole project. Click on the Clean and Build Main Project button from the toolbar on the top of this window and click on the Run Main Project (green arrow) button to run our project. Enter the correct login information, such as yabi to the username and reback to the password box, respectively. Click on the LogIn button to complete the login process. Select Faculty Information from the SelectionFrame Form window to open the FacultyFrame Form window. Select a desired faculty member and click on the **Select** button to query and get detailed information for the selected faculty. Click on the **Back** button to return to the SelectionFrame Form window, and then the **Exit** button to exit our project.

Next, let's concentrate on the Course Information item to develop and build the CourseFrame class to enable users to browse the detailed course information for the selected faculty member.

6.2.8 Use Java JPA Wizards to Query the Course Table

We divide this section into the following four parts:

1. Create a new CourseFrame class and add it into our project.
2. Use JPA Wizards to build Entity class for our Course table in our sample database.
3. Develop codes to perform the data query from the Course table.
4. Modify the codes in CourseFrame and SelectionFrame classes to coordinate the operations between both components.

First, let's add a new JFrame as our CourseFrame Form.

6.2.8.1 Create a New CourseFrame Class and Add It into Our Project

Right click on our project **SelectQueryWizard** from the **Project** window, and then select **New|JFrame Form** item from the pop-up menu to open New JFrame Form dialog box. Enter **CourseFrame** into the Class Name box as the name for our new class, and select the **LogInFramePackage** from the Package box, and click on the **Finish** button to create this new **CourseFrame** class.

Add the following objects and controls shown in Table 6.5 into this CourseFrame Form window to finish the GUI design for this form.

Your finished CourseFrame Form window should match one that is shown in Figure 6.61.

The function of this CourseFrame Form class is:

1. The CourseFrame Form window will be displayed if the user selected the Course Information from the SelectionFrame Form window to query the detailed course information for a selected faculty. The user can select the desired faculty and query method from the Faculty Name and Query Method combo boxes, respectively.
2. As the Select button is clicked by the user, all courses, exactly all **course_id**, taught by the selected faculty will be displayed in the Course ID List ListBox.
3. When the user clicks on one **course_id** from the Course ID List box, the detailed information for the selected **course_id** is displayed in five Text Fields.
4. The **Back** button allows users to close the current CourseFrame Form window and return to the SelectionFrame Form window to perform other queries.

In this part, only two buttons, **Select** and **Back**, are used for this CourseFrame Form, and the **Insert** button will be used later for the data insertion query.

Table 6.5. Objects and controls in the CourseFrame form

Type	Variable Name	Text	Border	Title
Panel	jPanel1		Titled Border	Faculty Name and Query Method
Label	Label1	Faculty Name		
ComboBox	ComboName			
Label	Label2	Query Method		
ComboBox	ComboMethod			
Panel	jPanel2		Titled Border	Course ID List
ListBox	CourseList			
Panel	jPanel3		Titled Border	Course Information
Label	Label3	Course		
TextField	CourseField			
Label	Label4	Schedule		
TextField	ScheduleField			
Label	Label5	Classroom		
TextField	ClassRoomField			
Label	Label6	Credits		
TextField	CreditField			
Label	Label7	Enrollment		
TextField	EnrollField			
Button	cmdSelect	Select		
Button	cmdInsert	Insert		
Button	cmdBack	Back		
JFrame	CourseFrame			CSE DEPT Course Form

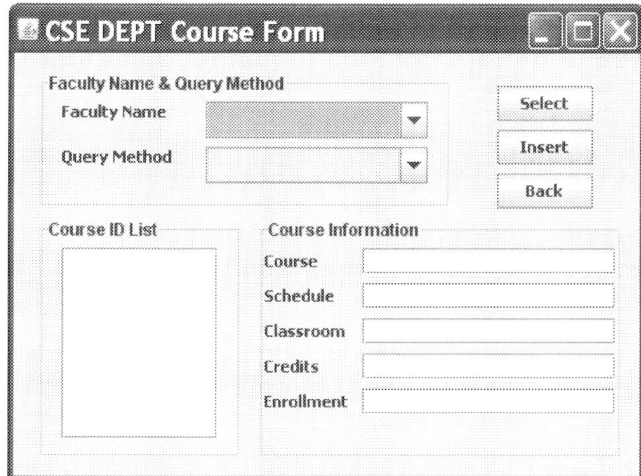

Figure 6.61. Finished CourseFrame Form window.

6.2.8.2 Add Course Entity Manager and JPA Components into the Project

Before we can start our query process, we need to add the Entity Manager that controls all Entity classes and all JPA components, such as Query and Query Result, into the CourseFrame Form window. In this way, we can use the Entity Manager to manage the Course Entity class to set up mapping relations between components in our Java GUI

Forms and the Course table in our sample database, and to perform all query-related operations. Perform the following operations to complete this adding process:

1. Expand the Databases icon in the Services Window to find our connected SQL Server database jdbc:sqlserver://localhost\SQL2008EXPRESS:5000;databaseName=CSE_DEPT [ybai on dbo]. If it has not been connected, right click on this icon and select Connect item from the pop-up menu to connect it.
2. Expand our connected database icon to our database CSE_DEPT and to the dbo node, and then the Tables folder. Drag our Course table and place it onto our CourseFrame Form.
3. As you may know, there is no faculty_name column that exist in the Course table in our sample database, and the only relationship between the Course and the Faculty tables is the faculty_id, which is a primary key in the Faculty table, but a foreign key in the Course table. In order to fetch all courses taught by the selected faculty, the faculty_id works as a unique query criterion. However, in this project, we need to use the faculty name as a query criterion; therefore, we need to perform two queries from two tables first query is used to get the faculty_id based on the selected faculty name, and the second query is to fetch all courses taught by the selected faculty based on the faculty_id queried from the first query. Therefore, we also need the Faculty table in this CourseFrame Form window. Drag our Faculty table and place it onto our CourseFrame Form, too.
4. Besides the Entity Manager and query components, we also need to perform a static query from our Course Entity object Course.java. Therefore, we need to drag the Course.java and place it onto our CourseFrame Form window.
5. You can find that one Entity Manager class, SelectQueryWizardPUEntityManager, and five JPA components, courseQuery, courseList, facultyQuery, facultyList, and course1, have been added into our project in the Other Components folder in the Inspector Window.

Now we can start to perform the query to access our sample database using the added Entity Manager and JPA components.

6.2.8.3 Use Entity Classes to Perform Data Query from the Course Table

After the Entity class, Entity Manager and JPA components have been built and added in our project, we can perform the data query to our Course table. Two query types can be developed for this query: static query and dynamic query. We will use two types of queries in this course query process. The development of queries can be divided into the following six parts:

1. Importing some necessary Java packages and coding for the constructor of the CourseFrame class to perform some initialization processes.
2. Static query—creating a static or named query string in the Course Entity class Course.java to perform the join column query for the foreign key faculty_id that is a Faculty object mapped in the Entity class Course.java.
3. Dynamic query—coding for the Select button Click event handler to perform either a static or a dynamic data query operation to the Course table in our sample database.
4. Coding for the CourseList box to allow an event to occur when a course_id in that ListBox is selected or changed to display the detailed information in five text fields for the selected course_id.

```
A   import java.util.*;
    public CourseFrame() {
        initComponents();
B       this.setLocationRelativeTo(null);
C       ComboMethod.addItem("JPA Wizards Method");
        ComboMethod.addItem("Java Codes Method");
        ComboMethod.addItem("Precompiled Method");
        ComboMethod.addItem("Callable Method");
D       ComboName.addItem("Ying Bai");
        ComboName.addItem("Satish Bhalla");
        ComboName.addItem("Black Anderson");
        ComboName.addItem("Steve Johnson");
        ComboName.addItem("Jenney King");
        ComboName.addItem("Alice Brown");
        ComboName.addItem("Debby Angles");
        ComboName.addItem("Jeff Henry");
    }
```

Figure 6.62. The coding for the constructor of the CourseFrame class.

5. Coding for the Back button Click event handler to close the CourseFrame Form window and return the control to the SelectionFrame Form.
6. Modifying the codes in the SelectionFrame class to allow a smooth switching from the SelectionFrame to the CourseFrame if the user selected the Course Information item.

Now let's start with the first part.

6.2.8.3.1 Import Java Packages and Coding for the CourseFrame Constructor

Open the Code Window of the CourseFrame class by clicking on the Source tab from the top of the window and add the codes that are shown in Figure 6.62 into this source file.

Let's have a closer look at this piece of codes to see how it works.

A. The java.util.* package is added into this file since we need to use the List class that is located in that package.
B. The setLocationRelativeTo() method is called to set up this CourseFrame Form at the center of the screen as the project runs. A null argument means that no any object can be referenced or relative to and the JFrame Form is set to the center.
C. Four query methods are added into the Query Method combo box to enable users to perform different query with desired method. In this project, we only take care of the first method, JPA Wizards Method.
D. Eight faculty members are also added into the Faculty Name combo box to allow users to select all courses taught by the different faculty members.

As we mentioned, there is no faculty_name column available in the Course table, and the only relationship between our Faculty and Course tables is the faculty_id, which is a primary key in the Faculty table, but a foreign key in the Course table. After the mapping process by JPA, the faculty_id has been mapped to a Faculty object in the Course Entity class, not a String as we defined in our Course table. This mapping allows a many-to-one relationship between the Course and the Faculty class can be built. However, this mapping also brings a trouble for us to make our query string using JPQL. As we know, all query criteria defined in the WHERE clause are built-in variable's values, either String, integer, Boolean, or other single data type; no any object data type can be used for this WHERE clause. But the faculty_id, which is a String, has been mapped to a Faculty object in the Course Entity class, we have to figure out how to perform a JPA query using this object as the query criterion.

6.2.8.3.2 Create a Static Query String to Perform Join Column Query Open the Course Entity class file Course.java by double clicking on it from the Project window. Browse down and you can find this many-to-one relationship mapping after the columns mapping, which is shown in Figure 6.63.

Take a closer look at those three bold coding lines. The String faculty_id we defined in the Course table has been mapped into a Faculty object, and it works as a join column in this Course Entity class to build a many-to-one connection between the Course and the Faculty Entity classes. It is not easy to create a JPA query string to perform a data query using this object as a query criterion. In order to solve this problem and make our coding easy, we need to build a static or named query inside the Course Entity class to perform this query.

Keep inside this Course Entity class and move up, and you can find all four static or named JPA queries, which are shown at top four queries in Figure 6.64.

```
@Lob
@Column(name = "schedule")
private String schedule;
@Column(name = "enrollment")
private Integer enrollment;

@JoinColumn(name = "faculty_id", referencedColumnName = "faculty_id")
@ManyToOne
private Faculty facultyId;

@OneToMany(mappedBy = "courseId")
private List<StudentCourse> studentCourseList;
```

Figure 6.63. A mapping between a String and an object.

```
  @Entity
  @Table(name = "Course")
  @NamedQueries({
   @NamedQuery(name ="Course.findAll", query = "SELECT c FROM Course c"),
   @NamedQuery(name ="Course.findByCourseId", query = "SELECT c FROM Course c WHERE c.courseId = :courseId"),
   @NamedQuery(name ="Course.findByCredit", query = "SELECT c FROM Course c WHERE c.credit = :credit"),
   @NamedQuery(name ="Course.findByEnrollment", query = "SELECT c FROM Course c WHERE c.enrollment = :enrollment"),

A  @NamedQuery(name ="Course.findByFacultyId", query = "SELECT c.courseId FROM Course c WHERE c.facultyId = :facultyID")})
```

Figure 6.64. Creating a static or named query in the Course entity class.

Each named query starts with an annotation @NamedQuery with two arguments. The first argument is the name of that query, and the second is the real JPA query string. Similar to those four static queries, enter the fifth query as our named query (indicated with A) into this class file. Remember, the name of our query is Course.findByFacultyId, and the nominal name for our only dynamic parameter is facultyID. We need to call this named JPA query later in our CourseFrame Form to execute this query to fetch all courses taught by the selected faculty based on the facyltyId.

Go to File|Save All item to save this Entity class file.

Next, let's develop the codes for the Select button click event handler to perform either a static query or a dynamic query and display all courses taught by the selected faculty member.

6.2.8.3.3 Coding the Select Button Click Event Handler to Perform Static and Dynamic Query First let's develop the codes to perform a static query.

From the Design view of the CourseFrame Form window, double click on the Select button to open its event handler and enter the codes shown in Figure 6.65 into that event handler.

Let's have a closer look at this piece of codes to see how it works.

A. First, we need to perform a dynamic query from the Faculty Entity class to get the faculty_id based on the selected faculty member by the user from the Faculty Name combo box.

B. The createQuery() method is called to create a dynamic query.

C. The setParameter() method is executed to replace the nominal parameter FacultyName in the dynamic query string with a real faculty member that is obtained from the Faculty Name combo box with the getSelectedItem() method.

D. The created dynamic query is executed by calling the getSingleResult() method, since we only need to query a single item faculty_id from the Faculty table. Also, this queried faculty_id works as an argument to create a new Faculty object cFaculty based on the

```
  private void cmdSelectActionPerformed(java.awt.event.ActionEvent evt) {
      // TODO add your handling code here:
      if (ComboMethod.getSelectedItem()=="JPA Wizards Method"){
A       String fQuery = "SELECT f.facultyId FROM Faculty f WHERE f.facultyName=:FacultyName";
B       facultyQuery = SelectQueryWizardPUEntityManager.createQuery(fQuery);
C       facultyQuery.setParameter("FacultyName", ComboName.getSelectedItem());
D       Faculty cFaculty = new Faculty((String)facultyQuery.getSingleResult());
E       course1.setFacultyId(cFaculty);
F       courseQuery = SelectQueryWizardPUEntityManager.createNamedQuery("Course.findByFacultyId");
G       courseQuery.setParameter("facultyID", cFaculty);
H       courseList = courseQuery.getResultList();
I       CourseList.setListData(courseList.toArray());
      }
  }
```

Figure 6.65. Codes for the Select button Click event handler—static query.

Faculty Entity class, since we need to use this object and assign it to the nominal parameter facultyID in the named query string we built in the Course.java Entity class in the last section to perform the course query.

E. The setFacultyId() method in the Course Entity class is executed to set the queried faculty_id to the newly created Faculty object cFaculty. A point to be noted is that it looks like that steps D and E are duplicated; however, in the real programming, it is necessary to do that to make sure that the newly created Faculty object cFaculty is initialized with the desired faculty_id.

F. A static or named query is created by calling the method createNamedQuery() with the name of our named query, Course.findByFacultyId, which we built in the Course.java Entity class in the last section, as the argument.

G. The setParameter() method is executed to replace the nominal parameter facultyID, which is a Faculty object, with our newly created Faculty object cFaculty whose faculty_id equals to the desired faculty_id obtained from the first dynamic query.

H. The static query is executed by calling the getResultList() method, and the result is a collection of all courses (exactly all course_id) taught by the selected faculty in a List format.

I. The setListData() method that belongs to the List class is executed to add all queried courses into the CourseList box. The point is that all courses are stored in a List, and they must be converted to an array format before that can be added into the ListBox using the setListData() method.

Now let's continue to develop a dynamic query to perform the same query.

To build a dynamic query, just replace the step F in Figure 6.65 with the two coding lines that are shown in steps **A** and **B** in Figure 6.66, and both lines have been highlighted in bold.

Next, we need to develop the codes for the ValueChanged() method of the CourseList box to display detailed information for the selected course in five text field boxes.

6.2.8.3.4 Coding the CourseList Box to Display Detailed Information for the Selected Course The function of this method is that the detailed information of the

```
private void cmdSelectActionPerformed(java.awt.event.ActionEvent evt) {
    // TODO add your handling code here:
    if (ComboMethod.getSelectedItem()=="JPA Wizards Method"){
      String fQuery = "SELECT f.facultyId FROM Faculty f WHERE f.facultyName=:FacultyName";
      facultyQuery = SelectQueryWizardPUEntityManager.createQuery(fQuery);
      facultyQuery.setParameter("FacultyName", ComboName.getSelectedItem());
      Faculty cFaculty = new Faculty((String)facultyQuery.getSingleResult());
      course1.setFacultyId(cFaculty);
A     String cQuery = "SELECT c.courseId FROM Course c WHERE c.facultyId = :facultyID";
B     courseQuery = SelectQueryWizardPUEntityManager.createQuery(cQuery);
      courseQuery.setParameter("facultyID", cFaculty);
      courseList = courseQuery.getResultList();
      CourseList.setListData(courseList.toArray());
    }
}
```

Figure 6.66. Codes for the Select button Click event handler—dynamic query.

selected course, exactly the course_id, such as the course title, course schedule, credits, classroom, and enrollment, should be displayed in five text fields under the Course Information panel when the user clicks on a course_id from the CourseList Box. Unlike the standard Java JDK, in which the users have to create and build event sources and event listeners using different interfaces, in NetBeans 6.8, all of these jobs can be done by the NetBeans engine.

First, let's open the CourseListValueChanged() method by:

1. Opening the Design View of the CourseFrame Form window by clicking on the Design tab from the top of the window.
2. Right clicking on the CourseList box, then selecting Events|ListSelection|valueChanged item by clicking on it.

On the opened CourseListValueChanged() method, enter the codes that are shown in Figure 6.67 into this method.

Let's have a closer look at this piece of codes to see how it works.

A. Since the JList component belongs to the javax.swing package, not java.awt package, therefore, a clicking on an entry in the CourseList box causes the itemStateChanged() method to fire twice: once when the mouse button is depressed, and once again when it is released. Therefore, the selected course_id will be appear twice when it is selected. To prevent this from occurring, the getValueIsAdjusting() method is used to make sure that no any item has been adjusted to be displayed twice. Then the selected course_id is assigned to a local String variable courseid by calling the getSelectedValue() method of the CourseList Box class.

B. Before we can proceed to the query operation, first we need to confirm that the selected courseid is not a null value. A null value would be returned if the user did not select any

```
  private void CourseListValueChanged(javax.swing.event.ListSelectionEvent evt) {
      // TODO add your handling code here:
A     if( !CourseList.getValueIsAdjusting() ){
         String courseid = (String)CourseList.getSelectedValue();
B        if (courseid != null){
            String cidQuery = "SELECT c.course, c.schedule, c.classroom, " +
                              "c.credit, c.enrollment FROM Course c WHERE c.courseId = :courseid";
C           courseQuery = SelectQueryWizardPUEntityManager.createQuery(cidQuery);
D           courseQuery.setParameter("courseid", courseid);
E           List<Object[]> courselist = courseQuery.getResultList();
F           for (Object[] result : courselist){
               CourseField.setText((String)result[0]);
               ScheduleField.setText((String)result[1]);
               ClassroomField.setText((String)result[2]);
               CreditField.setText(result[3].toString());
               EnrollField.setText(result[4].toString());
            }
         }
      }
  }
```

Figure 6.67. Codes for the CourseListValueChanged() method.

course_id from the CourseList box; instead, the user just clicked on the Select button to try to find all courses taught by other faculty members. Even the user only clicked on the Select button without touching any course_id in the CourseList box; however, the system still considers that a null course_id has been selected, and thus a null value will be returned. To avoid that situation from occurring, an if selection structure is used to make sure that no null value has been returned from the CourseList box. A JPA query string is created if no null value has been returned.

C. The createQuery() method is used to create a dynamic query.

D. The setParameter() method is executed to use the real query criterion coursed to replace the nominal parameter.

E. The dynamic query is actually executed by calling the getResultList() method, and the query result is returned in a List format.

F. An enhanced for loop is used to retrieve the queried columns from the courselist, and assign them one by one to the associated five Text Fields to display them.

Next, we need to take care of the coding for the Back button Click event handler to switch from the CourseFrame Form back to the SelectionFrame Form to allow users to perform other query operations.

6.2.8.3.5 Coding for the Back Button Click Event Handler When this Back button is clicked, the CourseFrame Form should be closed, and the control will be returned to the SelectionFrame Form. Open the Design View of the CourseFrame Form window by clicking on the Design tab from the top of the window and double click on the Back button to open its event handler. Enter the codes that are shown in Figure 6.68 into this event handler.

The function of this piece of codes is straightforward; the CourseFrame Form will be closed by calling the setVisible() method with a false argument, and the dispose() method is used to remove the CourseFrame Form from the screen.

At this point, we have finished almost all coding jobs for the CourseFrame Form object. Before we can run our project to test its function, we need to do one more coding, modifying codes in the SelectionFrame Form object to enable a smooth switching from the SelectionFrame Form to the CourseFrame Form if the user selected the Course Information item from the ComboSelection combo box.

6.2.8.3.6 Modify Codes in the SelectionFrame Class to Switch to CourseFrame Form Open the Design View of the SelectionFrame Form window by clicking on the Design tab from the top of the window, and double click on the OK button to open its

```
private void cmdBackActionPerformed(java.awt.event.ActionEvent evt) {
    // TODO add your handling code here:
    this.setVisible(false);
    this.dispose();
}
```

Figure 6.68. Coding for the Back button Click event handler.

```
  private void cmdOKActionPerformed(java.awt.event.ActionEvent evt) {
      // TODO add your handling code here:
      MsgDialog dialog = new MsgDialog(new javax.swing.JFrame(), true);
      FacultyFrame facultyFrame = new FacultyFrame();
A     CourseFrame courseFrame = new CourseFrame();
      if (ComboSelection.getSelectedItem()== "Faculty Information"){
         //dialog.setMessage("Faculty Information is selected\n");
         facultyFrame.setVisible(true);
      }
      else if (ComboSelection.getSelectedItem()== "Course Information"){
         //dialog.setMessage("Course Information is selected\n");
         //dialog.setVisible(true);
B        courseFrame.setVisible(true);
      }
      else {
         dialog.setMessage("Student Information is selected\n");
         dialog.setVisible(true);
      }
  }
```

Figure 6.69. Modified codes for the SelectionFrame class.

event handler. Replace the original codes located inside the first else if block, which indicates that the Course Information item in the ComboSelection combo box has been selected, with the codes that are in bold and shown in Figure 6.69.

Let's have a closer look at this piece of modified codes to see how it works.

A. A new instance of the CourseFrame class is created that will be used later.

B. The setVisible() method is executed to display the CourseFrame Form if the user selected the Course Information item from the ComboSelection combo box.

Now let's build and run our project. Click on the Clean and Build Main Project button on the toolbar to build the project, and then click on the Run Main Project button to run the project. Enter a suitable username and password, such as jhenry and test, to complete the login process. Select the Course Information from the SelectionFrame Form window to open the CourseFrame Form. Select any faculty member from the Faculty Name combo box, and all courses taught by the selected faculty will be displayed in the CourseList box. Then click on any course_id from the CourseList box; detailed information of the selected course_id will be displayed in five text fields, which is shown in Figure 6.70.

Click on the Back and Exit buttons to close our project.

A complete project SelectQueryWizard can be found from the folder DBProjects\Chapter 6 that is located at the accompanying ftp site (see Chapter 1).

6.2.9 Use Java JPA Wizards to Query Oracle Database

There is no significant difference in querying an SQL Server and an Oracle database using JPA Wizard in NetBeans 6.8. The whole project, SelectQueryWizard, we built in the last section can be used to query an Oracle database with a little modification. Two modifications are important and listed below:

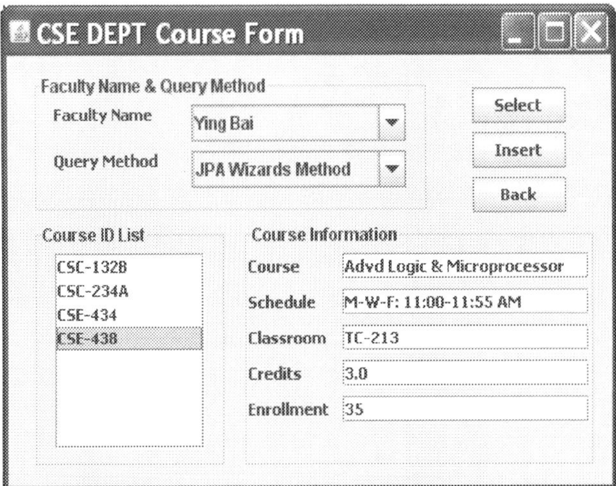

Figure 6.70. A running example of our project.

1. The data table name used in the query strings. There is a little difference for the table names used in SQL Server database and Oracle database in the JPA-mapped Entity classes. For example, the LogIn table in our sample SQL Server database CSE_DEPT is still mapped to LogIn in the LogIn.java Entity class; however, it is mapped to Login in the Login.java Entity class for the Oracle database. Make sure to check the Entity classes to confirm and use the correct table names when different databases are utilized.
2. The query components used in the data query operations. These is a little difference for the names of the JPA query components used in SQL Server database and Oracle database when they are added into each Frame Form window. For example, the LogIn JPA query object used in SQL Server database is named logInQuery; however, it is named loginQuery when is created for the Oracle database. Make sure to check the added query components to confirm and use the correct query components for each Frame.

Another point to be noted is that do not forget to copy all image files, including both faculty and student image files, from the Images folder that is located at the accompanying ftp site (see Chapter 1), and paste them to your current project folder. In this case, it should be C:\Chapter 6\OracleSelectWizard. You need also to remember to connect to our sample Oracle database we loaded in Section 6.2.1.3 when you create Entity classes for each tables in that Oracle database. Follow steps listed below to complete this database connection and mapping:

1. Click on the Services tab to open the Services window.
2. Extend the Databases node and you can find our load in Oracle sample database jdbc:oracle:thin:@localhost:1251:XE [CSE_DEPT on CSE_DEPT].
3. Right click on that load in database node and select the Connect item from the pop-up menu to connect to this sample database.

Now you can use JPA Wizard to create Entity classes and set up a mapping between our relational database and the Entity objects.

A complete sample project OracleSelectWizard that can be used to query data from Oracle Database 10g XE can be found from the folder DBProjects\Chapter 6 that is located at the accompanying ftp site (see Chapter 1).

SECTION II QUERY DATA USING JAVA RUNTIME OBJECTS METHOD

The topic we discussed in Section I is mainly about the database query using JPA Wizards. With the help of JPA Wizards, a professional and practical database query project can be easily built and implemented with a few of coding lines. It is a simple and efficient way to enable students and beginners to effectively learn basic theoretical knowledge in Java database programming, build professional database accessing projects, master, and practice what they learned from this process. The most important is that the students' study and learning curves of Java database programming can be significantly reduced by using this method.

Any good thing is always accompanying with some side effects, which is also true to the JPA Wizard method. The disadvantages of using JPA Wizard include:

1. The details of the Java database programming is not clear as that of the Java runtime object method we will discuss in this section. Since most codes are created by JPA Wizards, quite a few details would be hidden to the users, and a complete and clear picture of Java database programming, especially for the structure and organization, is hard to be obtained and understood.
2. It is not as flexible as that of the Java runtime object method we will discuss in this section. All of the codes must be created and developed before the project runs, or, statically, no modification can be performed during the project runs.
3. The compatibility is not desired as we expected. Since all projects are built based on NetBeans IDE and J2EE 5, they are not easy to be run at a different platform when other IDE is utilized.

To solve those shortcomings, in this section, we discuss how to use Java runtime object method to improve the global and detailed views in Java database programming and to make database queries more flexible and powerful.

6.3 INTRODUCTION TO RUNTIME OBJECT METHOD

The so-called Java runtime object method is to develop and build database-accessing operations using runtime Java codes without touching JPA Wizards and Entity classes. In other words, no object-to-relational database mapping is needed, and the project can directly access the database using Java codes.

As we discussed in Chapter 4, to access a database to perform data query, the following operational sequence should be followed:

1. Load and register the database driver using DriverManager class and Driver methods.
2. Establish a database connection using the Connection object.
3. Create a data query statement using the createStatement() method.

4. Execute the data query statement using the executeQuery() method.
5. Retrieve the queried result using the ResultSet object.
6. Close the statement and connection using the close() method.

In JPA Wizards method, the first and the second operations are combined together using JPA Entity classes. The Query Manager and Query components are also used in steps 3 through 5 to simplify the query operations. However, in Java runtime object method, all those operations are performed by developing the Java codes without touching any JPA Wizards. In the following sections, we will use two example projects, SQLSelectObject and OracleSelectObject, to illustrate how to use Java runtime object method to develop and build database query projects to access both SQL Server database and Oracle database, respectively. To make these developments easy, we still use NetBeans 6.8 as our development IDE.

6.4 CREATE A JAVA APPLICATION PROJECT TO ACCESS THE SQL SERVER DATABASE

Go to File|New Project to open the New Project pane. Keep the default selection Java in the Categories box, and select Java Application from the Projects box. Click on the Next button to open the New Java Application pane. Enter SQLSelectObject into the Project Name box and uncheck the Create Main Class checkbox. Click on the Finish button to create this new Java Application project.

Next, we need to create four JFrame Form windows as our graphical user interfaces, LogInFrame, SelectionFrame, FacultyFrame, and CourseFrame, to perform the data queries to three data tables in our sample database. We also need to create a JDialog as our message box.

6.4.1 Create Graphic User Interfaces

First let's create the LogInFrame Form window.

Right click on our new project SQLSelectObject and select New|JFrame Form item from the pop-up menu to open a New JFrame Form pane. Enter the following values to this pane to create this new JFrame Form:

1. LogInFrame to the Class Name box.
2. SQLSelectObjectPackage into the Package box.
3. Click on the Finish button.

Add the following GUI components with the appropriate properties shown in Table 6.6 into this Form. You need to drag each component from the Palette Windows and place it to the LogInFrame Form, and set up each property in the Properties Windows.

When set up property for each component, you need first to click on that component to select it and then go the Property Windows to set up an appropriate property for that component. To set up a Variable Name for each component, you need to right click on that component and select Change Variable Name item from the pop-up menu, and then enter a desired name into the New Name box for that object.

Table 6.6. Objects and controls in the LogIn form

Type	Variable Name	Text
Label	Label1	Welcome to CSE Department
Label	Label2	User Name
Text Field	UserNameField	
Label	Label3	Pass Word
Text Field	PassWordField	
Button	LogInButton	LogIn
Button	CancelButton	Cancel
Title		CSE DEPT LogIn

Figure 6.71. The finished LogInFrame Form.

Your finished LogInFrame Form is shown in Figure 6.71.

Now let's create the SelectionFrame Form window.

As we did for the LogIn Form, right click on our project SQLSelectObject from the Projects window and select New|JFrame Form item from the pop-up menu to open New JFrame Form pane. Enter SelectionFrame into the Class Name box as the name of our new Frame Form class, and select SQLSelectObjectPackage from the Package box. Click on the Finish button to complete this creation.

Add the following objects and controls, which are shown in Table 6.7, into this SelectionFrame Form. One point to be noted is that you need to remove all default items located inside the model property of the combo box ComboSelection. To do that, click on the ComboSelection combo box from the Design View, and then go the model property, and click on the three-dot button to open the model pane. Select all four default items, and press the Delete button from the keyboard to remove all of those items. A preview of the completed SelectionFrame Form should match one that is shown in Figure 6.72.

Next, let's create our FacultyFrame Form window.

Table 6.7. Objects and controls in the SelectionFrame form

Type	Variable Name	Text	Model	Title
Label	Label1	Make Your Selection		
ComboBox	ComboSelection			
Button	cmdOK	OK		
Button	cmdExit	Exit		
SelectionFrame				CSE DEPT Selection

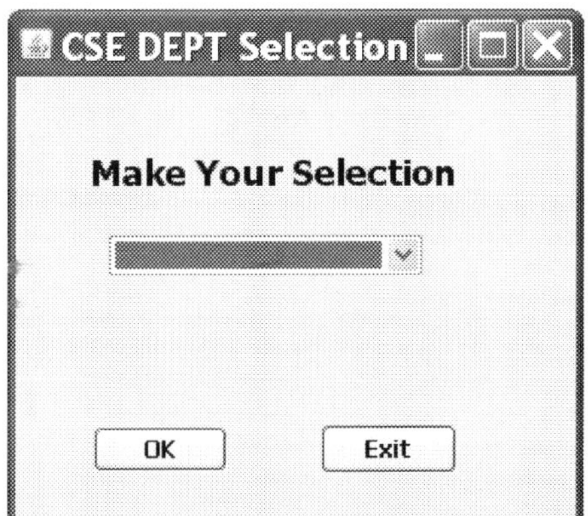

Figure 6.72. A preview of the created SelectionFrame Form.

As we did for the LogIn Form, to create a JFrame Form, right click on our newly created project SQLSelectObject from the Projects window and select New|JFrame Form item from the pop-up menu to open New JFrame Form pane. Enter FacultyFrame into the Class Name box as the name of our new Frame Form class, and then select the item SQLSelectObjectPackage from the Package box. Click on the Finish button to complete this creation.

Add the following objects and controls, which are shown in Table 6.8, into this FacultyFrame Form. One point to be noted is that you need to remove all default items located inside the model property of the Combo Box ComboName and ComboMethod. To do that, click on the ComboName combo box from the Design View, and then go to the model property, and click on the three-dot extension button to open the model pane. Select all four default items, and then press the Delete button from the keyboard to remove all of those items. Perform the similar operations for the ComboMethod. A preview of the completed FacultyFrame Form should match one that is shown in Figure 6.73.

A point to be noted is that when you drag a Canvas control from the Palette and places it into the FacultyFrame Form window, first, you need to click on the Canvas from the Palette. Then you need to click a location where you want to place it in the FacultyFrame. A Canvas icon is displayed in that location you clicked. You must drag this Canvas icon to the upper-left direction; never drag it to the lower-right direction, to enlarge it.

Table 6.8. Objects and controls in the FacultyFrame form

Type	Variable Name	Text	Border	Title
Canvas	ImageCanvas			
Panel	jPanel1		Titled Border	Faculty Name and Query Method
Label	Label1	Faculty Name		
ComboBox	ComboName			
Label	Label2	Query Method		
ComboBox	ComboMethod			
Panel	jPanel2		Titled Border	Faculty Information
Label	Label3	Title		
Label	Label4	Office		
Label	Label5	Phone		
Label	Label6	College		
Label	Label7	Email		
Text Field	TitleField			
Text Field	OfficeField			
Text Field	PhoneField			
Text Field	CollegeField			
Text Field	EmailField			
Button	cmdSelect	Select		
Button	cmdInsert	Insert		
Button	cmdUpdate	Update		
Button	cmdDelete	Delete		
Button	cmdBack	Back		
FacultyFrame Form	FacultyFrame			CSE DEPT Faculty Form

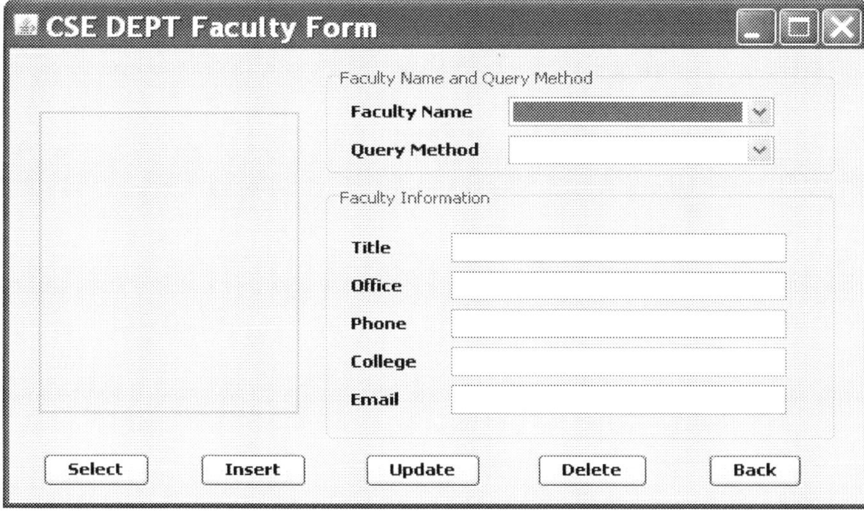

Figure 6.73. A preview of the finished FacultyFrame Form window.

Table 6.9. Objects and controls in the CourseFrame form

Type	Variable Name	Text	Border	Title
Panel	jPanel1		Titled Border	Faculty Name and Query Method
Label	Label1	Faculty Name		
ComboBox	ComboName			
Label	Label2	Query Method		
ComboBox	ComboMethod			
Panel	jPanel2		Titled Border	Course ID List
ListBox	CourseList			
Panel	jPanel3		Titled Border	Course Information
Label	Label3	Course		
TextField	CourseField			
Label	Label4	Schedule		
TextField	ScheduleField			
Label	Label5	Classroom		
TextField	ClassRoomField			
Label	Label6	Credits		
TextField	CreditField			
Label	Label7	Enrollment		
TextField	EnrollField			
Button	cmdSelect	Select		
Button	cmdInsert	Insert		
Button	cmdBack	Back		
JFrame	CourseFrame			CSE DEPT Course Form

Next, let's build our CourseFrame Form window.

Right click on our project SQLSelectObject from the Projects window, select New|JFrame Form item to open New JFrame Form pane. Enter CourseFrame into the Class Name box, and select the SQLSelectObjectPackage from the Package box. Click on the Finish button to create this new CourseFrame class.

Add the objects and controls shown in Table 6.9 into this CourseFrame Form window to finish the GUI design for this form.

Your finished CourseFrame Form window should match one that is shown in Figure 6.74.

Finally, we need to create a JDialog box to work as our message box to display any except or error information. Refer to Section 6.2.5.6 to create this JDialog, and name it as MsgDialog.

At this point, we have completed building in all graphical user interfaces we need in this project. Next, let's concentrate on the coding development to perform the data query for each different data table in our sample SQL Server database.

6.4.2 Perform the Data Query for the LogIn Table

The function of this LogInFrame Form is to check and confirm the username and password entered by the user to make sure that both are correct. The user needs to enter both

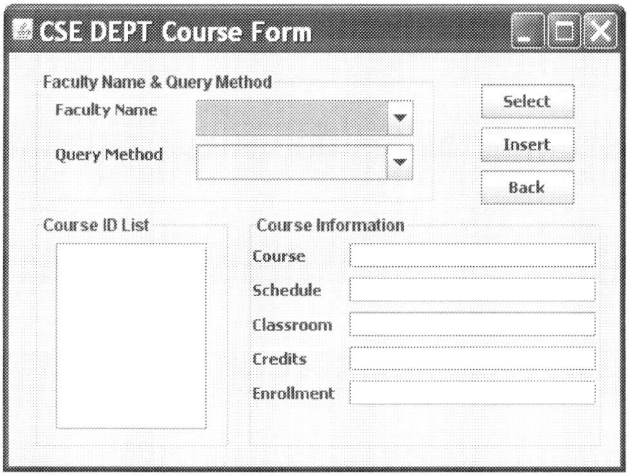

Figure 6.74. Finished CourseFrame Form window.

username and password, and then click on the LogIn button to begin this login process. An error message will be displayed if either an invalid username/password pair has been entered, or both boxes are kept empty.

First, let's start from loading and registering the database driver using DriverManager class and Driver methods. In this section, we want to use Microsoft SQL Server database as the target database; therefore, we will concentrate on the Microsoft SQL Server JDBC Driver.

6.4.2.1 Load and Register Database Drivers

As we discussed in Chapter 3, the core component or interface of accessing databases in Java is Java Database Connectivity API (JDBC API), which is composed of two parts in two packages: JDBC 2.0 core API in java.sql and JDBC Standard Extension in javax.sql. Both parts are combined together to provide necessary components and classes to build database applications using Java.

Generally, JDBC API enables users to access virtually any kind of tabular data source, such as spreadsheets or flat files from a Java application. It also provides connectivity to a wide scope of SQL or Oracle databases. One of the most important advantages of using JDBC is that it allows users to access any kind of relational database in a same coding way, which means that the user can develop one program with the same coding to access either an SQL Server database or an Oracle database, or MySQL database without coding modification.

The JDBC 3.0 and JDBC 4.0 specifications contain additional features, such as extensions to the support to various data types, metadata components, and improvements on some interfaces.

Exactly, the JDBC API is composed of a set of classes and interfaces used to interact with databases from Java applications. As we discussed in Chapter 3, the basic components of JDBC is located at the package java.sql, and the Standard Extension of JDBC, which provides additional features, such as Java Naming and Directory Interface (JNDI) and Java Transaction Service (JTS), is in the javax.sql package.

6.4.2.1.1 Add Microsoft SQL Server JDBC Driver to the Project Before we can load and register a JDBC driver, first we need to add the Microsoft SQL Server JDBC Driver we downloaded and installed in Section 6.2.1.2.1 as a library file into our current project Libraries node to enable our project to locate and find it when it is loaded and registered. To do that, follow steps below to finish this adding process:

1. Right click on our project SQLSelectObject from the Projects window and select Properties item from the pop-up menu to open Project Properties pane.
2. In the Categories box, select the Libraries item by clicking on it.
3. Click on the Add JAR/Folder button and browse to the location in which we installed the Microsoft SQL Server JDBC Driver, which is C:\Program Files\Microsoft SQL Server JDBC Driver 2.0\sqljdbc_2.0\enu. Click on the driver sqljdbc4.jar, and click on the Open and OK buttons to add this driver to our project Libraries node.

6.4.2.1.2 Load and Register Microsoft SQL Server JDBC Driver The first step to build a Java database application is to load and register a JDBC driver. Two important components, DriverManager and Driver, are used for this process. As we discussed in Chapter 3, Driver class contains six method and one of the most important methods is the connect() method, which is used to connect to the database. When using this Driver class, a point to be noted is that most methods defined in the Driver class is never be called directly; instead, they should be called via the DriverManager class methods.

The DriverManager class is a set of utility functions that work with the Driver methods together and manage multiple JDBC drivers by keeping them as a list of drivers loaded. Although loading a driver and registering a driver are two steps, only one method call is necessary to perform these two operations. The operational sequence of loading and registering a JDBC driver is:

1. Call class methods in the DriverManager class to load the driver into the Java interpreter.
2. Register the driver using the registerDriver() method.

When loaded, the driver will execute the DriverManager.registerDriver() method to register itself. The above two operations will never be performed until a method in the DriverManager is executed, which means that even both operations have been coded in an application; however, the driver cannot be loaded and registered until a method such as connect() is first executed.

To load and register a JDBC driver, two popular methods can be used;

1. Use Class.forName() method:

   ```
   Class.forName("com.microsoft.sqlserver.jdbc.SQLServerDriver");
   ```

2. Create a new instance of the Driver class:

   ```
   Driver sqlDriver = new com.microsoft.sqlserver.jdbc.SQLServerDriver;
   ```

Relatively speaking, the first method is more professional since the driver is both loaded and registered when a valid method in the DriverManager class is executed. The

```
  package SQLSelectObjectPackage;
A import java.sql.*;

  public class LogInFrame extends javax.swing.JFrame {
B    static Connection con;
     MsgDialog msgDlg = new MsgDialog(new javax.swing.JFrame(), true);
     /** Creates new form LogInFrame */
     public LogInFrame() {
        initComponents();
C       this.setLocationRelativeTo(null);
        try
        {
           //Load and register SQL Server driver
D          Class.forName("com.microsoft.sqlserver.jdbc.SQLServerDriver");
        }
E       catch (Exception e) {
           msgDlg.setMessage("Class not found exception!" + e.getMessage());
           msgDlg.setVisible(true);
        }
F       String url = "jdbc:sqlserver://localhost\\SQL2008EXPRESS:5000;databaseName=CSE_DEPT;";
        //String url = "jdbc:sqlserver://localhost\\SQL2008EXPRESS:5000;
        //                databaseName=CSE_DEPT;user=ybai;password=reback1956";
        //Establish a connection
G       try {
        con = DriverManager.getConnection(url,"ybai","reback1956");
        //con = DriverManager.getConnection(url);
H       con.close();
        }
I       catch (SQLException e) {
           msgDlg.setMessage("Could not connect! " + e.getMessage());
           msgDlg.setVisible(true);
J          e.printStackTrace();
        }
  }
```

Figure 6.75. Codes for loading and registering a JDBC Driver.

second method cannot guarantee that the driver has been registered by using the DriverManager.

Now let's develop the codes to load and register the Microsoft SQL Server JDBC Driver in our LogInFrame class. Open the Code Window of the LogInFrame by clicking on the Source tab from the top of the window, and enter the codes that are shown in Figure 6.75 into this window.

Let's have a closer look at this piece of codes to see how it works.

A. Since all JDBC related classes and interfaces are located in the java.sql package, we need first to import this package.

B. A class instance con is declared here since we need to use this connection object in our whole project. An MsgDialog object is also created and we need to use it in this form.

C. The setLocationRelativeTo() method is called to set up this LogInFrame Form at the center of the screen as the project runs. A null argument means that no any object can be referenced or relative to, and the JFrame Form is set to the center.

D. A try . . . catch block is used to load and register our Microsoft SQL Server JDBC Driver. The Class.forName() method is utilized to make sure that our JDBC Driver is not only loaded but also registered when it is connected by running the getConnection() method in step G later. The argument of this method is the name of our Microsoft SQL Server JDBC Driver class, and it is created by the NetBeans when we add this driver to our project in Section 6.2.1.2.4.

E. The catch block is used to track any possible error for this loading and registering. The related exception information will be displayed if any error occurred.

F. The connection url, which includes the protocol, subprotocol, and subname of the data source, is created to define a full set of the information for the database to be connected. An alternative url that has been commented out is another way to build this connection url.

G. A try . . . catch block is used to perform the database connection by calling the getConnection() method. Three arguments are passed into this method: url, username, and password. Another way to call this method, which has been commented out, has only one argument that has combined three arguments together to make it simple.

H. The connected database is disconnected by calling the close() method. This instruction is only for the testing purpose for this LogInFrame Form, and it will be removed later when we build the formal project, since we need to keep this single database connection for all our four JFrame Form windows until the project is terminated.

I. Any possible exception occurred during this connection will be displayed by using the catch block.

J. Prints this `Throwable` and its backtrace to the standard error stream. This method prints a stack trace for this `Throwable` object on the error output stream that is the value of the field `System.err`. The first line of output contains the result of the `toString()` method for this object. Remaining lines represent data previously recorded by the method `fillInStackTrace()`.

The reason we put this coding that includes the loading, registering, and connection to our JDBC Driver inside the constructor of this LogInFrame class is that we need to set up and complete these operations first, or before other data actions can be performed, since a valid database connection is a prerequisite for any database query operation.

Before we can continue to discuss database connection, first let's have a clear picture about the JDBC URLs.

6.4.2.1.3 The JDBC Uniform Resource Locators (URLs) The JDBC url provides all information for applications to access to a special resource, such as a database. Generally, a url contains three parts or three segments: protocol name, subprotocol, and subname for the database to be connected. Each of these three segments has different function when they worked together to provide unique information for the target database.

The syntax for a JDBC url can be presented as:

```
protocol:sub-protocol:subname
```

The protocol name works as an identifier or indicator to show what kind of protocol should be adopted when connect to the desired database. For a JDBC driver, the name of the protocol should be jdbc. The protocol name is used to indicate what kind of items to be delivered or connected.

The subprotocol is generally used to indicate the type of the database or data source to be connected, such as sqlserver or oracle.

The subname is used to indicate the address to which the item supposed to be delivered or the location of the database is resided. Generally, a subname contains the following information for an address of a resource:

- Network host name/IP address
- The database server name
- The port number
- The name of the database

An example of a subname for our SQL Server database is:

localhost\\SQL2008EXPRESS:5000

The network host name is localhost, and the server name is SQL2008EXPRESS, and the port number the server used is 5000. You need to use a double slash, either forward or back, to represent a normal slash in this url string, since this is a DOS-style string.

By combining all three segments together, we can get a full JDBC url. An example url that is using an SQL Server JDBC driver is:

jdbc:sqlserver//localhost\\SQL2008EXPRESS:5000

The database's name works as an attribute of the connected database.

Now that we have a clear picture about the JDBC url, next, let's connect our application to our desired database.

6.4.2.2 Connect to Databases and Drivers

In step **G** of Figure 6.75, we showed how to call the getConnection() method that belongs to the DriverManager class to connect to our sample database from our Java application. In fact, the retuned Connection object is not only used as a connection between our application and database, but also used for providing different ways to create SQL statements and methods for the different session managements, such as transaction locking, catalog selection, and except handling. The statement execution is performed by the associated components, such as Statement, PreparedStatement and CallableStatement.

The Statement object is used to execute static SQL queries. The so-called static statements do not include any IN or OUT parameters in the query string, and do not contain any parameters passing to or from the database.

The PreparedStatement is used to execute dynamic SQL queries with IN parameter involved. These kind of statements can be preparsed and precompiled by the database, and therefore have faster processing speed and lower running loads for the database server.

The CallableStatement is used to execute the stored procedures with both IN and OUT parameters involved. As we know, stored procedures are built and developed inside databases, and therefore have higher running and responding efficiency in data queries and processing.

6.4.2.3 Create and Manage Statement Object

The Statement class contains three important query methods with different functions; executeQuery(), executeUpdate(), and execute(). For each method, both different operations will be performed, and different results can be returned. Generally, the execute methods can be divided into two categories: (1) the execute method that needs to perform a data query, such as executeQuery(), which returns an instance of ResultSet that contained the queried results, and (2) the execute method that does not perform a data query and only return an integer, such as the executeUpdate(). An interesting method is the execute(), which can be used in either ways.

- The executeQuery() method performs data query and returns a ResultSet object that contains the queried results.
- The executeUpdate() method does not perform data query; instead it only performs either a data updating, insertion, or deleting action against the database and returns an integer that equals to the number of rows that have been successfully updated, inserted, or deleted.
- The execute() method is a special method, and it can be used either way. All different data actions can be performed by using this method, such as data query, data insertion, data updating, and data deleting. The most important difference between the execute() method and two above methods is that the former can be used to execute some SQL statements that are unknown at the compile time, or return multiple results from stored procedures. Another difference is that the execute() method does not return any result itself, and one needs to use getResultSet() or getUpdateCount() method to pick up the results. Both methods belong to the `Statement` interface.

A confusion issue may come with the using of the execute() method. As we mentioned, since any SQL statement, either known or unknown at the compile time, can be used with this execute() method, how do we know the execution results? Yes, that indeed is a problem. However, fortunately, we can solve this problem by using some testing methods indirectly.

In fact, we can call either getResultSet() or getUpdateCount() method to try to pick up the running results from execution of the execute() method. The key point is that:

- The getResultSet() method will return a null if the running result is an integer, which is a number of rows that have been affected, either inserted, updated, or deleted.
- The getUpdateCount() method will return a –1 if the running result is a ResultSet.

Based on these two key points, we can easily determine whether a result is a ResultSet or an integer.

Now let's first use the executeQuery() method to perform our data query from the LogIn table in our sample database. We will illustrate how to use the execute() method to perform the data query for the FacultyFrame Form in Section 6.4.4.3.

As we mentioned, a static statement does not contain any parameter passing into or from the database;, therefore, this kind of statement does not met our requirement since we need to pass two parameters, username, and password, into our sample database to perform the login process. To make a data query to our LogIn table to perform the login process, we need to use the second type of statement, PreparedStatement.

The advantages of using a PreparedStatement object to build and perform a dynamic query is that both the query flexibility can be increased, and the query execution speed

```
  private void LogInButtonActionPerformed(java.awt.event.ActionEvent evt) {
      // TODO add your handling code here:
A     String username = null, password = null;
B     String query = "SELECT user_name, pass_word FROM LogIn " +
                     "WHERE user_name = ? AND pass_word = ?";
C     try{
          PreparedStatement pstmt = con.prepareStatement(query);
D         pstmt.setString(1, UserNameField.getText());
          pstmt.setString(2, PassWordField.getText());
E         ResultSet rs = pstmt.executeQuery();
F         while (rs.next()){
             username = rs.getString(1);
             password = rs.getString(2);
          }
      }
G     catch (SQLException e) {
         msgDlg.setMessage("Error in Statement! " + e.getMessage());
         msgDlg.setVisible(true);
      }
H     if (UserNameField.getText().isEmpty() || PassWordField.getText().isEmpty()) {
         msgDlg.setMessage("Enter the LogIn Information...");
         msgDlg.setVisible(true);
      }
I     else if (username.equals(UserNameField.getText()) && password.equals(PassWordField.getText())) {
         msgDlg.setMessage("LogIn is Successful! ");
         msgDlg.setVisible(true);
         this.setVisible(false);
         this.dispose();
      }
J     else {
         msgDlg.setMessage("LogIn is failed!");
         msgDlg.setVisible(true);
      }
  }
```

Figure 6.76. The codes for the LogIn button Click event handler.

and efficiency can be significantly improved since the prepared statement can be precompiled and rerun again for a multiple query situation.

6.4.2.4 Use PreparedStatement Object to Perform Dynamic Query

In the Design View of the LogInFrame Form window, double click on the LogIn button to open its event handler, and enter the codes that are shown in Figure 6.76 into this event handler.

Let's have a closer look at this piece of codes to see how it works.

A. Two local string variable, username and password, are declared first since we need to use them to hold the returned queries result later.

B. The query string is created with two dynamic parameters that are represented by using the positional parameter mode.

C. A try . . . catch block is used to perform the data query. First, a PreparedStatement object is created based on the Connection object we obtained from the database connection in the constructor of this LogInFrame class.

D. The setString() method of the PreparedStatement class is used to set up two dynamic parameters. The position of each parameter is indicated with the associated index of each parameter. The getText() method is used to get the username and password entered by the user from two text fields, UserNameField and PassWordField, respectively. A point to be noted is that a different setXXX() method should be used to perform this setup operation for the different types of the dynamic parameter. For example, here, both username and password are String, so the setString() method is used. If the type of the parameter is integer, the setInt() method should be used to finish this parameter setting, where XXX means the data type used for the dynamic parameter.

E. The executeQuery() method that belongs to the Statement class is called to perform this data query, and the query result is returned to the ResultSet object rs.

F. The next() method of the ResultSet class is utilized with a while loop to point to the next available queried row. This method returned a Boolean value, and a true indicates that more queried rows are in the ResultSet. A false means that no more queried row in the ResultySet. The getString() method is used to pick up each column from the ResultSet until a false is returned from the next() method. Similarly to the setString() method discussed in step D, different getXXX() method should be used to pick up queried column with different data type. The argument index in the getString() method is used to indicate the position of the queried column in the ResultSet, which starts from 1, not 0.

G. The catch block is used to catch and display any possible error for this data query process.

H. If both UserName and PassWord text fields are empty, a warning message should be displayed to allow user to enter valid login information.

I. If both queried username and password match to those entered by the user, which means that the login process is successful. A successful message is displayed to indicate this. This message only works as a testing purpose, and it will be removed later for the formal development of this project.

J. A login failed message will be displayed if any error occurred.

Before we can run this piece of codes to test it, make sure to remove or comment out the code in step **H** in Figure 6.75, which is to close the connection to our sample database. Because when we make connection coding in Figure 6.75, we need to close any connection to our sample database if a connection is successful made to avoid possible multiple connections to our database. However, now we want to perform data queries, therefore we need to connect to our database to do that since no data query can be performed if no database connection has been made.

After remove or comment out that close() coding, now we can build and run this LogInFrame Form to test our coding. Click on the Clean and Build Main Project button from the toolbar to build our project. Then right click on our LogInFrame.java file from the Projects window, and select the Run File item to run this object. A sample of running result is shown in Figure 6.77.

Enter valid username and password, such as ybai and reback, and click on the LogIn button to begin this login process. A login successful message should be displayed if this process is fine.

Before we can move to the next section, we need to finish developing the codes for the Cancel button Click event handler. The function of the coding for this button is to close the LogInFrame Form window, and the database connection if this button is clicked

Figure 6.77. A running sample of the LogInFrame Form.

```
  private void CancelButtonActionPerformed(java.awt.event.ActionEvent evt) {
A         this.setVisible(false);
          this.dispose();
B         try {
              con.close();
          }
C         catch (SQLException e) {
             msgDlg.setMessage("Could not close!" + e.getMessage());
             msgDlg.setVisible(true);
          }
  }
```

Figure 6.78. The codes for the Cancel button Click event handler.

by the user. Open the Design View of the LogInFrame Form and double click on the Cancel button to open its event handler, and enter the codes that are shown in Figure 6.78 into this event handler.

Let's have a closer look at this piece of codes to see how it works.

A. The setVisible() and dispose() methods are called to remove the LogInFrame Form window from the screen when this button is clicked by the user.

B. Also, a try . . . catch block is used to try to close the database connection. A point to be noted is that a try . . . catch block must be used if one wants to perform a close action to a connected database.

C. The catch block will track and display any possible exception occurred for this close action.

Next, let's discuss how to retrieve the query result by calling ResultSet object.

6.4.2.5 Use ResultSet Object

The ResultSet class contains 25 methods, and the most popular methods to be used are:

- getXXX()
- getMetaData()
- next()
- findColumn()
- close()

The ResultSet object can be created by either executing the executeQuery() or getResultSet() method, which means that the ResultSet instance cannot be created or used without executing a query operation first. Similar to a Statement object, a Connection object must be first created, and then the Statement component can be created and implemented to perform a query.

The queried result or queried data are stored in the ResultSet with a certain format, and generally in a 2D tabular form with columns and rows. Each column can be mapped into an array and each row can be considered as a Vector. Therefore, the easiest way to map a ResultSet is to create an array of Vectors.

When a query operation is performed and a ResultSet instance is created, next, we need to retrieve the queried result from the ResultSet object by using a suitable getXXX() method. As we mentioned in step D in Figure 6.76, depending on the returned data type of the queried result, different method should be used, such as getInt(), getString(), getByte(), getDouble(), getShort(), and getObject().

Two different ways can be used to get returned data from a ResultSet instance: fetching by row and fetching by column.

6.4.2.5.1 Fetching by Row Since the returned data can be stored in a ResultSet in a tabular form, the data can be picked up in row by row. The next() method in the ResultSet class is specially used for this purpose. Each row can be selected by using a cursor that can be considered as a pointer to point to each row. The next() method can move the row pointer from the current position to the next row. As we discussed in steps E and F in Figure 6.76, when a login query is executed, a ResultSet instance rs is created and returned. Initially, the cursor pointed to a row that is just above the first row, and you have to run the next() method once to allow it to point to the first data row, and then you can repeat to run this method by using a while loop to scan the whole table until the last row. A true will be returned by the next() method if a valid row has been found and pointed to, and a false is returned if the cursor points to null row, which means that no more valid row can be found and the bottom of the ResultSet has been touched.

6.4.2.5.2 Fetching by Column When a valid data row has been retrieved, we need to get each column from that row. To do that, a different getXXX() method should be used based on the different data type of the returned data. One can use either the name of a column or the index of that column to get the data value. In step F in Figure 6.76, for our LogIn table, both the user_name and the pass_word are String, therefore a getString() method is used with the index of each column. A point to be noted is that the first column has an index of 1, not 0. If the name of each column, not an index, is used for the getString() method in step F in Figure 6.76, the codes can be rewritten as

```
while (rs.next()){
                    username = rs.getString("user_name");
                    password = rs.getString("pass_word");
                  }
```

One of the most important methods in ResultSet class is the getObject(). The advantage of using this method is that a returned datum, which is stored in a ResultSet object and its data type is unknown (a datum is dynamically created), can be automatically converted from its SQL data type to the ideal Java data type. This method outperform any other getXXX() method, since the data type of returned data must be known before a suitable getXXX() method can be used to fetch the returned data.

The findColumn() method is used to find the index of a column if the name of that column is given, and the close() method is used to close a ResultSet instance.

The getMetaData() method is a very good and convenient method, and it allows users to have a detailed and clear picture about the structure and properties of data returned to a ResultSet. A ResultSetMetaData object, which contains all pieces of necessary information about the returned data stored in a ResultSet instance, is returned when this method is executed. By using different methods of the ResultSetMetaData class, we can obtain a clear picture about the returned data. For example, by using the getColumnCount() method, we can know totally how many columns have been retrieved and stored in the ResultSet. By using getTableName(), getColumnName(), and getColumnType(), we can know the name of the data table we queried, the name of column we just fetched, and data type of that column. A more detailed discussion about the ResultSetMetaData component will be given in Sections 6.4.4.2.2 and 6.4.4.2.5.

Now that we have finished the coding development for the LogIn table, we are ready to perform the data query for the Faculty table using the FacultyFrame Form window. We need first to develop the codes for the SelectionFrame Form window to allow users to select the desired data query.

6.4.3 Develop the Codes for the SelectionFrame Form

Select the SelectionFrame class by clicking on it from the Projects window and open its Code Window by clicking on the Source tab from the top of the window. Enter the codes that are shown in Figure 6.79 into the constructor of this class.

Let's have a closer look at this piece of codes to see how it works.

A. The Java JDBC Driver package is imported first, since we need to use some classes located in that package to perform the data query.

B. A class-level object of the JDialog class dialog is created here since we need to use this dialog to display some debug and warning messages during the project runs.

C. The setLocationRelativeTo() method is called to locate this SelectionFrame Form at the center of the screen as the project runs. A null argument means that no any object can be referenced or relative to and the JFrame Form is set to the center.

D. The addItem() method is executed to add three pieces of information into the combo box ComboSelection to allow users to choose one of them as the project

```
  package SQLSelectObjectPackage;
A import java.sql.*;
  public class SelectionFrame extends javax.swing.JFrame {
B   MsgDialog dialog = new MsgDialog(new javax.swing.JFrame(), true);
    public SelectionFrame() {
      initComponents();
C     this.setLocationRelativeTo(null);
D     this.ComboSelection.addItem("Faculty Information");
      this.ComboSelection.addItem("Course Information");
      this.ComboSelection.addItem("Student Information");
    }
```

Figure 6.79. The codes for the constructor of the SelectionFrame class.

runs. Another method to add these three pieces of information is to direct add those pieces of information into the model box under the Combo Box Model Editor, which can be considered as a static adding (before the project runs). In that way, you do not need to enter these three lines of codes in this constructor. However, we prefer to call the addItem() method to add those pieces of information since it belongs to a dynamic adding.

Next, let's do the coding for the OK and Exit command buttons, exactly for the event handlers of those buttons. The function for the SelectionFrame Form is: as the user selected a desired choice from the Combo Box and click the OK button to query the related information, the related information frame, such as FacultyFrame Form, CourseFrame Form, or StudentFrame Form, will be displayed to enable users to make related queries.

Now let's open the Design View of the SelectionFrame Form by clicking on the Design tab from the top and double click on the OK button to open its event handler. Enter the codes that are shown in Figure 6.80 into this handler.

Let's have a closer look at this piece of codes to see how it works.

A. Two objects are created at the beginning of this handler, which include the FacultyFrame and CourseFrame, since we need to direct the program to the different frame when an associated frame is selected by the user.

B. An if selection structure is used to identify each selected item from the ComboSelection combo box. The MsgDialog is used if the Student Information item is selected since we have not built that frame.

The rest coding includes two parts; coding for the Exit button Click event handler and coding for the creating a getter method. As you know, in the object oriented programming, in order to use the unique object created in a project, a popular way is to create a setter and a getter method in the target class. In this way, when other objects such as JFrames, JDialogs, or JWindows in the same project want to use the target object, they can call this getter to get the desired target object.

Let's create codes for both the getter method and the Exit button Click event handler by entering the codes that are shown in Figure 6.81 into this SelectionFrame class.

Let's have a closer look at this piece of codes to see how it works.

A. The function of the getter method is simple: as this method is called, the current SelectionFrame object is obtained by returning this component that is a pointer point to

```
   private void cmdOKActionPerformed(java.awt.event.ActionEvent evt) {
       // TODO add your handling code here:
A      FacultyFrame facultyFrame = new FacultyFrame();
       CourseFrame courseFrame = new CourseFrame();

B      if (ComboSelection.getSelectedItem()== "Faculty Information"){
          facultyFrame.setVisible(true);
       } else if (ComboSelection.getSelectedItem()== "Course Information"){
          courseFrame.setVisible(true);
       } else {
          dialog.setMessage("Student Information is selected\n");
          dialog.setVisible(true);
       }
   }
```

Figure 6.80. Codes for the OK button Click event handler.

```
A  public SelectionFrame getSelectionFrame(){
      return this;
   }
   private void cmdExitActionPerformed(java.awt.event.ActionEvent evt) {
        // TODO add your handling code here:
B       try{
             if (!LogInFrame.con.isClosed()){ LogInFrame.con.close(); }
        }
C       catch(SQLException e){
           dialog.setMessage("Could not close!" + e.getMessage());
           dialog.setVisible(true);
           }
D       this.setVisible(false);
        this.dispose();
        System.exit(0);
   }
```

Figure 6.81. Codes for the getter method and the Exit button Click event handler.

the current Frame object to the calling object. A point to be noted is that the accessing mode of this method must be public since we want this method to be called by any other objects to get this SelectionFrame object as the project runs.

B. In the Exit button Click event handler, a try . . . catch block is used to check whether the database connection we created in the LogInFrame Form window is still connected to our database by using the isClosed() method. A true will be returned if that connection has been closed, otherwise a false is returned to indicate that the connection is still active. The close() method of the Connection class is called to close this connection if a false is returned. As you may remember, the Connection object con we created in the LogInFrame class is a class instance; therefore, we can directly use the class name to access that instance without needing to create a new instance.

C. The catch block is used to track and display any error for this close process.

D. Then the SelectionFrame Form object is removed from the screen by calling the setVisible() and dispose() methods. The object this indicates the current Frame Form object, which is the SelectionFrame. A system exit() method is called to allow the project to be officially exited from the current process. An argument 0 means that no error for this exit operation.

At this point, we have completed all coding for the SelectionFrame Form window. Before we can continue to the next section, we need to modify some codes in both SelectionFrame and the LogInFrame classes to allow a smooth switching from either of them.

6.4.3.1 Modify Codes to Coordinate between SelectionFrame and LogInFrame

First, we need to add some codes into the LogIn button Click event handler in the LogInFrame class to direct the project to open the SelectionFrame Form window if the login process is successful. Open the LogIn button event handler and add the following codes into this handler, which is shown in Figure 6.82.

```
  private void LogInButtonActionPerformed(java.awt.event.ActionEvent evt) {
      // TODO add your handling code here:
      String username = null, password = null;
A     SelectionFrame selFrame = new SelectionFrame().getSelectionFrame();
      String query = "SELECT user_name, pass_word FROM LogIn " +
                     "WHERE user_name = ? AND pass_word = ?";
      try{
        PreparedStatement pstmt = con.prepareStatement(query);
        pstmt.setString(1, UserNameField.getText());
        pstmt.setString(2, PassWordField.getText());
        ResultSet rs = pstmt.executeQuery();
        while (rs.next()){
          username = rs.getString(1);
          password = rs.getString(2);
        }
      }
      catch (SQLException e) {
        msgDlg.setMessage("Error in Statement!" + e.getMessage());
        msgDlg.setVisible(true);
      }
      if (UserNameField.getText().isEmpty() || PassWordField.getText().isEmpty()) {
        msgDlg.setMessage("Enter the LogIn Information...");
        msgDlg.setVisible(true);
      } else if (username.equals(UserNameField.getText()) && password.equals(PassWordField.getText())) {
B       selFrame.setVisible(true);
C       //msgDlg.setMessage("LogIn is Successful! ");
        //msgDlg.setVisible(true);
        this.setVisible(false);
        this.dispose();
      } else {
        msgDlg.setMessage("LogIn is failed!");
        msgDlg.setVisible(true);
      }
  }
```

Figure 6.82. Modified codes for the LogIn button Click event handler.

Let's have a closer look at these modified codes to see how they work.

A. A new instance of the SelectionFrame class selFrame is created. However, the getter method getSelectionFrame() we built for the SelectionFrame class is called to retrieve the original SelectionFrame instance and assign it to the newly created instance. In this way, we did not create any new instance of the SelectionFrame; instead, we are still using the original SelectionFrame instance, and it is a unique instance in this project.

B. Replace the old codes by using the code line selFrame.setVisible(true) to display our SelectionFrame Form window if the login process is successful. Also, close and dispose this LogInFrame Form window since we have finished the login process.

C. Comment out all messages displayed by using the msgDlg object, since those are only used for the testing purpose.

At this point, we have finished all coding jobs for the LogInFrame and the SelectionFrame. In the following sections, we will discuss how to perform data query to our Faculty table using the FacultyFrame class.

6.4.4 Perform the Data Query for the Faculty Table

The function of this form is: as the user selected a faculty member from the ComboName combo box and click the Select button, the detailed information with an image for the selected faculty should be displayed in five text fields and a canvas. The development of this query can be divided into the following five parts:

1. Adding some necessary java packages and coding for the constructor of the FacultyFrame class to perform some initialization processes.
2. Coding for the Select button Click event handler to run the executeQuery() method to query data from the Faculty table in our sample database using the DatabaseMetaData interface and ResultSetMetaData interface.
3. Coding for the Select button Click event handler to run the execute() method to query data from our Faculty table in our sample database.
4. Adding a user-defined method ShowFaculty() to display an image for the selected faculty in the FacultyFrame Form window.
5. Coding for the Back button Click event handler to close the FacultyFrame Form window and return the control to the SelectionFrame Form.

Now let's start with the first part.

6.4.4.1 Add Java Package and Coding for the Constructor

Since we used to display an image of the selected faculty when a data query is executed, the java.awt.* package should be imported since some image-related classes, such as Image, Graphics and MediaTracker, are located at that Abstract Windowing Tools (AWT) package.

Open the Code Window of the FacultyFrame class by clicking on the Source tab from the top of the window and add the codes that are shown in Figure 6.83 into this source file.

```
  package SQLSelectObjectPackage;
A import java.awt.*;
  import java.sql.*;
  /**
   *
   * @author Ying Bai
   */
B public class FacultyFrame extends javax.swing.JFrame {
     MsgDialog msgDlg = new MsgDialog(new javax.swing.JFrame(), true);
     /** Creates new form FacultyFrame */
     public FacultyFrame() {
        initComponents();
        this.setLocationRelativeTo(null);   // set the faculty Form at the center
C       ComboMethod.addItem("JPA Wizards Method");
        ComboMethod.addItem("Runtime Object Method");
        ComboMethod.addItem("Java execute() Method");
        ComboMethod.addItem("Java Callable Method");
D       ComboName.addItem("Ying Bai");
        ComboName.addItem("Satish Bhalla");
        ComboName.addItem("Black Anderson");
        ComboName.addItem("Steve Johnson");
        ComboName.addItem("Jenney King");
        ComboName.addItem("Alice Brown");
        ComboName.addItem("Debby Angles");
        ComboName.addItem("Jeff Henry");
     }
```

Figure 6.83. Initialization codes for the FacultyFrame class.

Let's have a closer look at this piece of codes to see how it works.

A. Two java packages, java.awt.* and java.sql.*, are imported at the beginning of this file since we need to use some classes defined in those packages.

B. A JDialog object msgDlg is created here as a class-level object because we need to use it in the whole class of the FacultyFrame to display some debug or warning messages.

C. The addItem() method is used to add all four query methods into the Query Method combo box. In this section, we only use the Runtime Object Method and the execute() method.

D. Also, the addItem() method is utilized to add all eight faculty members into the Faculty Name combo box.

Now let's develop codes for the Select button Click event handler to perform the data query.

6.4.4.2 Query Data using JDBC MetaData Interface

In Section 6.4.2.5, we discussed how to use ResultSet component to retrieve the queried result. Relatively speaking, there are some limitations on using the ResultSet object to get the returned query result. In other words, it is hard to get a clear and detailed picture about the queried result, such as the structure and properties of the data stored in the ResultSet. For example, no information about the returned result, such as the name of the data table, the total number of columns, each column's name, and the data type, would be available when using ResultSet object to pick up the queried result. In order to solve that problem to get detailed prior knowledge of the data table structure, we need to use the ResultSetMetaData component.

The JDBC MetaData Interface provides detailed information about the database and its contents made available by the JDBC API, and it can be divided into the following three categories:

1. The DatabaseMetaData interface
2. The ResultSetMetaData interface
3. The ParameterMetaData interface

Each class has its special functions and operation sequences, and some of them are related when they are utilized in some specific ways.

6.4.4.2.1 The DatabaseMetaData Interface The DatabaseMetaData interface contains more than 150 methods and provides detailed information about the database as a whole body, such as:

- General information about the database
- Data source limitations
- Levels of transaction support
- Feature support
- Information about the SQL objects that source includes

In fact, the DatabaseMetaData interface provides methods that allow you to dynamically discover properties of a database as the project runs. Many methods in the DatabaseMetaData return information in the ResultSet component, and one can get those pieces of information from ResultSet object by calling related methods, such as getString(), getInt(), and getXXX(). A SQLException would be thrown out if the queried item is not available in the MetaData interface.

6.4.4.2.2 The ResultSetMetaData Interface The detailed information about the structure of a queried data table can be obtained by calling the getMetaData() method that belongs to the ResultSetMetaData class, and a ResultSetMetaData object will be created when the getMetaData() method is executed. Some popular methods included in the ResultSetMetaData class are:

- getColumnCount()—returns the total number of columns in the ResultSet
- getColumnName()—returns the column name
- getColumnType()—returns the column data type
- getTableName()—returns the data table name

Similar to DatabaseMetaData interface, the ResultSetMetaData interface allows users to discover the structure of data tables and properties of columns in tables.

6.4.4.2.3 The ParameterMetaData Interface The detailed information about the parameters passed into or from the database can be obtained by calling the getParameterMetaData() method that belongs to the PreparedStatement class. Although this interface is not as popular as ResultSetMetaData and DatabaseMetaData, it is useful in some special applications.

In this section, we will use the DatabaseMetaData and the ResultSetMetaData interfaces to illustrate how to improve the data query for our Faculty table.

6.4.4.2.4 Use DatabaseMetaData Interface to Query Database Related Information Open the Select button Click event handler of the FacultyFrame class and enter the codes that are shown in Figure 6.84 into this event handler.

Let's have a closer look at this piece of codes to see how it works.

A. An if selection structure is used to identify the desired data query method, Runtime Object Method, which will be used in this section. A prepared query statement is then created to query the detailed information for the selected faculty member.

B. First, a try . . . catch block is utilized to perform the database-related information query using the DatabaseMetaData interface. A DatabaseMetaData object dbmd is created by calling the getMetaData() method that belongs to the Connection class, and detailed information about the connected database is also returned and assigned to the dbmd object.

C. Two methods, getDriverName() and getDriverVersion(), are executed to pick up the retrieved driver name and version and assign them to the associated String variables.

D. The msgDlg is used to display retrieved driver name and version.

Here, the msgDlg is only used for the testing purpose, and it can be commented out as the project is finally built and deployed later. From this example, it is shown that some useful database-related information can be easily obtained by using the DatabaseMetaData interface.

6.4.4.2.5 Use ResultSetMetaData Interface to Query Table Related Information Still, in the Select button Click event handler of the FacultyFrame class, add the codes

```
  private void cmdSelectActionPerformed(java.awt.event.ActionEvent evt) {
       // TODO add your handling code here:
A      String query = "SELECT title, office, phone, college, email " +
                      "FROM Faculty WHERE faculty_name = ?";
       if (ComboMethod.getSelectedItem()=="Runtime Object Method"){
         try{
B             DatabaseMetaData dbmd = LogInFrame.con.getMetaData();
C             String drName = dbmd.getDriverName();
              String drVersion = dbmd.getDriverVersion();
D             msgDlg.setMessage("DriverName is: " + drName + ", Version is: " + drVersion);
              msgDlg.setVisible(true);
            }
         }
         catch (SQLException e) {
            msgDlg.setMessage("Error in Statement!" + e.getMessage());
            msgDlg.setVisible(true);
         }
       }
  }
```

Figure 6.84. The codes for the Select button Click event handler.

```
  private void cmdSelectActionPerformed(java.awt.event.ActionEvent evt) {
      // TODO add your handling code here:
      String query = "SELECT title, office, phone, college, email " +
                     "FROM Faculty WHERE faculty_name = ?";
      if (ComboMethod.getSelectedItem()=="Runtime Object Method"){
        try{
            DatabaseMetaData dbmd = LogInFrame.con.getMetaData();
            String drName = dbmd.getDriverName();
            String drVersion = dbmd.getDriverVersion();
            msgDlg.setMessage("DriverName is: " + drName + ", Version is: " + drVersion);
            msgDlg.setVisible(true);
A           PreparedStatement pstmt = LogInFrame.con.prepareStatement(query);
B           pstmt.setString(1, ComboName.getSelectedItem().toString());
C           ResultSet rs = pstmt.executeQuery();
D           ResultSetMetaData rsmd = rs.getMetaData();
E           msgDlg.setMessage("Faculty Table has " + rsmd.getColumnCount() + " Columns");
            msgDlg.setVisible(true);
            }
        }
        catch (SQLException e) {
            msgDlg.setMessage("Error in Statement!" + e.getMessage());
            msgDlg.setVisible(true);
        }
     }
  }
```

Figure 6.85. The codes of using the ResultSetMetaData interface.

that are in bold and shown in Figure 6.85 into this handler to apply ResultSetMetaData interface to obtain the Faculty table related information.

Let's take a closer look at this added piece of codes to see how it works.

A. A PreparedStatement object pstmt is created by calling the prepareStatement() method with the prepared query string as the argument.

B. The setString() method is used to set up the dynamic positional parameter in the prepared query statement. The actual value of this parameter, which is the selected faculty member by the user from the ComboName combo box, can be obtained by calling the getSelectedItem() method.

C. The executeQuery() method is called to perform the prepared statement to get the queried result. The returned result is assigned to the ResultSet object rs.

D. The getMetaData() method is executed to query the detailed information about the structure of the Faculty table and properties of the columns in that table. The returned result is assigned to the ResultSetMetaData object rsmd.

E. The msgDlg is used to test and display the number of columns in the Faculty table.

Although we only use the getColumnCount() method to get the total number of columns in the Faculty table, in fact, you can use any other method to get more detailed description about the Faculty table as you like. Also, as we mentioned before, here, the msgDlg is only for the testing purpose and it can be commented out when the final project is debugged and implemented.

Next let's use this number of columns in our Faculty table to retrieve the detailed information for the selected faculty member.

```
  private void cmdSelectActionPerformed(java.awt.event.ActionEvent evt) {
      // TODO add your handling code here:
A     javax.swing.JTextField[] f_field = {TitleField, OfficeField, PhoneField, CollegeField, EmailField};
      String query = "SELECT title, office, phone, college, email " +
                     "FROM Faculty WHERE faculty_name = ?";
      if (ComboMethod.getSelectedItem()=="Runtime Object Method"){
        try{
          DatabaseMetaData dbmd = LogInFrame.con.getMetaData();
          String drName = dbmd.getDriverName();
          String drVersion = dbmd.getDriverVersion();
          msgDlg.setMessage("DriverName is: " + drName + ", Version is: " + drVersion);
          //msgDlg.setVisible(true);
          PreparedStatement pstmt = LogInFrame.con.prepareStatement(query);
          pstmt.setString(1, ComboName.getSelectedItem().toString());
          ResultSet rs = pstmt.executeQuery();
          ResultSetMetaData rsmd = rs.getMetaData();
          msgDlg.setMessage("Faculty Table has " + rsmd.getColumnCount() + " Columns");
          //msgDlg.setVisible(true);
B         while (rs.next()){
C           for (int i=1; i <=rsmd.getColumnCount(); i++) {
              f_field[i-1].setText(rs.getString(i));
            }
          }
        }
        catch (SQLException e) {
           msgDlg.setMessage("Error in Statement!" + e.getMessage());
           msgDlg.setVisible(true);
        }
      }
  }
```

Figure 6.86. The codes for the ResultSetMetaData query method.

Open the Select button Click event handler if it has not been opened, and enter the codes that are in bold and shown in Figure 6.86 into this event handler.

Let's take a closer look at this added piece of codes to see how it works.

A. First a TextField array is created since we need to combine all five TextField objects, TitleField, OfficeField, PhoneField, CollegeField, and EmailField, into this array and assign the queried results to these TextField objects one by one later to improve the assignment efficiency. Because the definition of the TextField class is different in the basic java.awt package and the javax.swing package, therefore we need to clearly indicate that this TextField belongs to the latter by using the whole package path.

B. As we did before, a while loop is used with the next() method as the argument to move the data table cursor from the initial position to the first row position in the ResultSet object, to allow us to pick up each row.

C. A for loop is then used to pick up each column from the returned row and assign each of them to the associated TextField object in the TextField array f_field. The upper bound of the columns we used for this for loop is obtained from the calling of the getColumnCount() method that belongs to the ResultSetMetaData interface. A point to be noted is that the index used to indicate each column in the ResultSet object is different with that used in the TextField array. The former starts from 1; however, the latter starts from 0. Therefore an i=1 is used for the index in the TextField array.

Now let's develop codes to display an image for the selected faculty.

6.4.4.2.6 Display an Image for the Selected Faculty The coding in this section is very similar to that we developed in Section 6.2.7.3.3. Refer to that section to complete this coding. A point to be noted is that you have to copy all image files, including both faculty and student image files, from the Images folder that is located at the accompanying ftp site (see Chapter 1), and paste them to our current project folder, which is, in this case, C:\Chapter 6\SQLSelectObject. Otherwise, you may encounter a runtime error and the required image file cannot be found by the compiler.

6.4.4.2.7 Develop the Codes for the Back Button Click Event Handler The coding for this event handler is simple. The FacultyFrame Form window should be closed and removed from the screen as this button is clicked by the user. Open the Back button Click event handler and enter the codes that are shown in Figure 6.87 into this event handler.

Both the setVisible() and the dispose() methods are called to close and remove this FacultyFrame Form window as this button is clicked.

Before you can build and run the project to test it, it is highly recommended to comment out two tested msgDlg methods, which have been highlighted in Figure 6.86, to speed up the process of the project.

Now we can build and run our project to test the functionalities of the LogInFrame Form, SelectionFrame Form, and FacultyFrame Form. Click on the Clean and Build Main Project button on the toolbar to build our project, and click on the Run Main Project button from the toolbar to run our project. Select SQLSelectObjectPackage. LogInFrame as the main class set for our project, and click on the OK button to run our project.

Enter the correct username and password, such as jhenry and test to the LogInFrame to complete the login process. Select the Faculty Information from the SelectionFrame Form window to open the FacultyFrame Form window. Select the default faculty member Ying Bai from the Faculty Name combo box and the Runtime Object Method from the Query Method combo box, and click on the Select button to get detailed information for this selected faculty. Immediately, the detailed information of the selected faculty is displayed in five text fields with the faculty image, which is shown in Figure 6.88. You can try to select other faculty members to perform different query to test the function of this form.

Click on the Back and the Exit buttons to terminate our project. Our project is very successful!

But wait a moment, the story is not finished. As we discussed in Section 6.4.2.3, both the executeQuery() and execute() method can be used to perform a data query operation; however, the execute() method is more popular since it can perform not only a query-related action, but also a nonquery-related action. In the next section, we will

```
private void cmdBackActionPerformed(java.awt.event.ActionEvent evt) {
    // TODO add your handling code here:
    this.setVisible(false);
    this.dispose();
}
```

Figure 6.87. The codes for the Back button Click event handler.

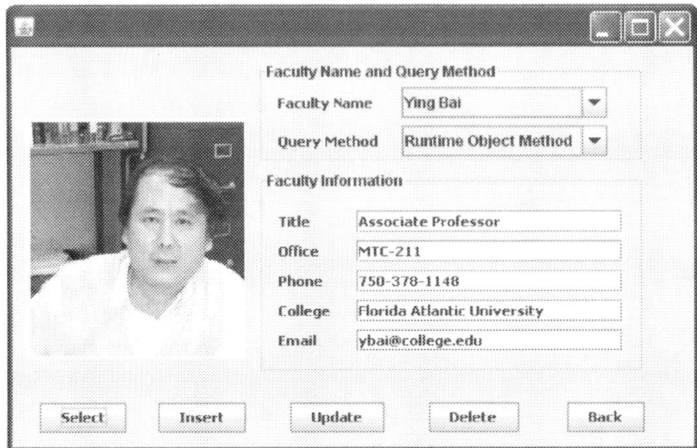

Figure 6.88. A running result of the project.

discuss how to use the execute() method to perform a query-related action against our sample database.

6.4.4.3 Query Data Using the execute() Method to Perform a Query-Related Action

As we mentioned in Section 6.4.2.3, the execute() method will not return any result itself, and one needs to use either getResultSet() or getUpdateCount() method to pick up the results. Both methods belong to the Statement class. The key point is:

- The getResultSet() method will return a null if the running result is an integer, which is a number of rows that have been affected, either inserted, updated, or deleted.
- The getUpdateCount() method will return a –1 if the running result is a ResultSet.

Based on these two key points, we can easily determine whether a result is a ResultSet or an integer.

Now let's modify the codes in the Select button Click event handler to use the execute() method to perform this data query. Open the Select button Click event handler and add the codes that are in bold and shown in Figure 6.89 into this event handler.

Let's have a closer look at this piece of newly added codes to see how it works.

A. If the user selected the Java execute() Method from the Query Method combo box, a try . . . catch block is used to create a prepared statement using the prepareStatement() method with the query string as the argument. Then the setString() method is used to set up the positional dynamic parameter, which is obtained from the ComboName combo box and selected by the user.

B. The execute() method is called to perform this data query. The advantage of using this method is that both a query-related action and a nonquery-related action can be performed by using this method. The disadvantage of using this method is that the running result cannot be determined when this method is done since this method can execute either a data query and return a ResultSet object or an updating, insertion, and deleting action and return an integer.

```
private void cmdSelectActionPerformed(java.awt.event.ActionEvent evt) {
      // TODO add your handling code here:
      javax.swing.JTextField[] f_field = {TitleField, OfficeField, PhoneField, CollegeField, EmailField};
      String query = "SELECT title, office, phone, college, email " +
                     "FROM Faculty WHERE faculty_name = ?";
      if (ComboMethod.getSelectedItem()=="Runtime Object Method"){
         try{
              DatabaseMetaData dbmd = LogInFrame.con.getMetaData();
              String drName = dbmd.getDriverName();
              String drVersion = dbmd.getDriverVersion();
              msgDlg.setMessage("DriverName is: " + drName + ", Version is: " + drVersion);
              //msgDlg.setVisible(true);
              PreparedStatement pstmt = LogInFrame.con.prepareStatement(query);
              pstmt.setString(1, ComboName.getSelectedItem().toString());
              ResultSet rs = pstmt.executeQuery();
              ResultSetMetaData rsmd = rs.getMetaData();
              msgDlg.setMessage("Faculty Table has " + rsmd.getColumnCount() + " Columns");
              //msgDlg.setVisible(true);
              while (rs.next()){
                 for (int i=1; i <=rsmd.getColumnCount(); i++) {
                    f_field[i-1].setText(rs.getString(i));
                 }
              }
           }
           catch (SQLException e) {
              msgDlg.setMessage("Error in Statement!" + e.getMessage());
              msgDlg.setVisible(true);
           }
      }
A     if (ComboMethod.getSelectedItem()=="Java execute() Method"){
        try{
             PreparedStatement pstmt = LogInFrame.con.prepareStatement(query);
             pstmt.setString(1, ComboName.getSelectedItem().toString());
B            pstmt.execute();
C            int updateCount = pstmt.getUpdateCount();
D            if (updateCount == -1){
                ResultSet rs = pstmt.getResultSet();
                ResultSetMetaData rsmd = rs.getMetaData();
E               while (rs.next()){
                   for (int i=1; i <=rsmd.getColumnCount(); i++){
                     f_field[i-1].setText(rs.getString(i));
                   }
                }
             }
F            else{
                msgDlg.setMessage("execute() method returned an integer!");
                msgDlg.setVisible(true);
             }
        }
G       catch (SQLException e) {
             msgDlg.setMessage("Error in Statement!" + e.getMessage());
             msgDlg.setVisible(true);
        }
      }
      if (!ShowFaculty()){
         msgDlg.setMessage("No matched faculty image found!");
         msgDlg.setVisible(true);
      }
}
```

Figure 6.89. The codes for the execute() method.

C. Suppose we do not know what kind of data will be returned by running this execute() method, we assume that a nonquery-related action has been performed by calling this method. So we try to use the getUpdateCount() method to pick up the running result, which is supposed to be an integer.

D. If the returned result of calling of the getUpdateCount() method is –1, which means that the running result of the execute() method is not an integer; instead, it is a ResultSet object. The getResultSet() method will be called to pick up that result.

E. A while loop combined with the next() method is used to move the cursor to point to the first row of the data stored in the returned ResultSet object. Also, a for loop is used to pick up each column obtained from the Faculty table and assign each of them to the associated text field to display them.

F. If the returned result from running of the execute() method is not –1, which means that a nonquery-related action has been performed, the msgDlg is used to display this situation.

G. The catch block is used to track and monitor any possible error occurred during this query operation.

Now you can rebuild our project and run it to test this piece of newly added codes. Select the Java execute() Method from the Query Method combo box as the FacultyFrame Form is opened, and click on the Select button to test the function of this new coding.

Next, let's move to the CourseFrame class to build some data actions using the Callable Statement method to query detailed information for the courses taught by the selected faculty and related course information.

6.4.4.4 Query Data Using the CallableStatement Method

The JDBC CallableStatement method provides a way to allow us to call a stored procedure to perform a complicated query. The speed and efficiency of a data query can be significantly improved by using the stored procedure since it is built in the database side. An example of using the CallableStatement method to query detailed information for a selected faculty is provided in this FacultyFrame class with an SQL stored procedure named dbo.FacultyInfo. Refer to Appendix H to get more details in building this stored procedure. A more detailed discussion of developing and implementing the CallableStatement method will be given in the next section for the CourseFrame class.

6.4.5 Perform the Data Query for the Course Table

As we discussed, the function of this CourseFrame Form is to allow users to get all courses taught by the selected faculty member and detailed information for each course. First, all courses, exactly all course_id, taught by the selected faculty member from the Faculty Name combo box, will be displayed in the Course ID List listbox as the user clicks on the Select button. Second, the detailed information for each course (course_id) selected from the Course ID List listbox will be displayed in five text fields as each course_id is clicked by the user.

In this section, only two buttons, Select and Back, are used for this CourseFrame Form, and the Insert button will be used later for the data insertion query.

The codes development in this section can be divided into the following four parts:

1. Importing some necessary Java packages and coding for the constructor of the CourseFrame class to perform some initialization processes.
2. Coding for the Select button Click event handler to perform a CallableStatement to run a stored procedure to query data from the Course table in our sample database.
3. Coding for the CourseList box to handle an event when a course_id in the CourseList box is selected to display the detailed information for that course_id in five text fields.
4. Coding for the Back button Click event handler to close the CourseFrame Form window and return the control to the SelectionFrame Form.

Now let's start with the first part.

6.4.5.1 Import Java Packages and Coding for the CourseFrame Constructor

Open the Code Window of the CourseFrame class by clicking on the Source tab from the top of the window and add the codes that are shown in Figure 6.90 into this source file.

Let's have a closer look at this piece of codes to see how it works.

A. The java.sql.* package is added into this file since we need to use some JDBC API classes and interfaces that are located in that package.

B. A class-level object msgDlg, which is an instance of the JDialog class, is created since we need to use it to display some debug and exception information to track and monitor the running status of our project during its running.

C. Four query methods are added into the Query Method combo box to enable users to perform a different query with desired method. In this project, we only take care of the fourth method, JPA Callable Method.

```
  package SQLSelectObjectPackage;
A import java.sql.*;
  public class CourseFrame extends javax.swing.JFrame {
B    MsgDialog msgDlg = new MsgDialog(new javax.swing.JFrame(), true);
     /** Creates new form CourseFrame */
     public CourseFrame() {
        initComponents();
        this.setLocationRelativeTo(null);
C       ComboMethod.addItem("JPA Wizards Method");
        ComboMethod.addItem("Runtime Object Method");
        ComboMethod.addItem("Java execute Method");
        ComboMethod.addItem("Java Callable Method");
D       ComboName.addItem("Ying Bai");
        ComboName.addItem("Satish Bhalla");
        ComboName.addItem("Black Anderson");
        ComboName.addItem("Steve Johnson");
        ComboName.addItem("Jenney King");
        ComboName.addItem("Alice Brown");
        ComboName.addItem("Debby Angles");
        ComboName.addItem("Jeff Henry");
     }
```

Figure 6.90. The coding for the constructor of the CourseFrame class.

D. Eight faculty members are also added into the Faculty Name combo box to allow users to select all courses taught by the different faculty members.

Next, let's have a detailed discussion about the CallableStatement method.

6.4.5.2 Query Data from Course Table Using CallableStatements

When a faculty member has been selected from the Faculty Name combo box and the Select button is clicked by the user, all courses (course_id) taught by the selected faculty member should be displayed in the Course ID List listbox. As we know, there is no faculty_name column available in the Course table; instead, the only connection between each course and the faculty who teaches that course is the faculty_id, which is a foreign key in the Course table. Therefore, in order to get the course_id that is taught by the selected faculty, two queries are needed to be performed: first, we need to perform a query to the Faculty table to get the faculty_id based on the selected faculty name, and, second, we can perform another query to the Course table to get all course_id based on the faculty_id obtained from the first query.

To save time and space, a good solution for these two queries is to combine both of them into a stored procedure. As you know, stored procedures are developed and built inside a database. The execution speed and efficiency of stored procedures can be significantly improved compared with a normal query. In JDBC API, a CallableStatement interface is used for this purpose.

As we discussed in the last section, compared with the Statement interface, the advantage of using a PreparedStatement interface is that it can perform a dynamic query with some known or unknown dynamic parameters as inputs. Most time, those dynamic parameters are input parameters and can be defined as IN variables. However, you do not need to specify those parameters with an IN keyword when using a PreparedStatement interface.

The difference between the PreparedStatement and the CallableStatement interfaces is: unlike the PreparedStatement interface, the CallableStatement interface has both input and output parameters, which are indicated with IN and OUT keywords, respectively. In order to set up values for input parameters, or get values for the output parameters, you have to use either a setXXX() method or a getXXX() method to do that. However, the point is that before you can use any getXXX() method to pick up the values of output parameters, you must first register the output parameters to allow the CallableStatement interface to know them.

Generally, the sequence to run a CallableStatement to perform a stored procedure is:

1. Build and formulate the CallableStatement query string.
2. Create a CallableStatement object.
3. Set the input parameters.
4. Register the output parameters.
5. Execute CallableStatement.
6. Retrieve the running result by using different getXXX() method.

Let's discuss this issue in more details in the following sections.

6.4.5.2.1 Build and Formulate the CallableStatement Query String The CallableStatement interface is used to execute SQL stored procedures. The JDBC API provides a stored procedure SQL escape syntax that allows stored procedures to be called in a standard way for all RDBMSs. This escape syntax has one form that includes an output parameter and one that does not. If used, the output parameter must be registered as an OUT parameter. The other parameters can be used for input, output, or both. Parameters are referred to sequentially, by number, with the first parameter being 1.

```
{?= call <procedure-name>[<arg1>,<arg2>, ...]}
{call <procedure-name>[<arg1>,<arg2>, ...]}
```

Two syntaxes are widely used to formulate a CallableStatement string: the SQL92 syntax and the Oracle syntax. The SQL92 syntax is more popular in most applications. We will concentrate on the SQL92 syntax in this section, and take care of the Oracle syntax in later when we build data queries for the Oracle database.

For a standalone stored procedure or packaged procedure, the SQL92 syntax can be represented as:

```
{call [schema.][package.]procedure_name[(?, ?,...)]}
```

For standalone functions or packaged functions, the SQL92 syntax looks like:

```
{? = call [schema.][package.]function_name[(?, ?,...)]}
```

The definition and meaning of elements used in these syntaxes are:

- All elements enclosed inside the square brackets [] means that they are optional.
- The curly braces {} are necessary in building a CallableStatement string, and they must be used to cover the whole string.
- The schema indicates the schema in which the stored procedure is created.
- The package indicates the name of the package if the stored procedure is involved in a package.
- The procedure_name or the function_name indicate the name of the stored procedure or the function.
- The question make ? is the place holder for either an IN, IN/OUT, or OUT parameters used in the stored procedure, or the returned value of a function. The order of these place holders, which starts from 1, is very important, and it must be followed exactly when using either a setXXX() method to set up input parameters or register the output parameters for the built CallableStatement string later.

A CallableStatement can either return a ResultSet object and multiple ResultSet objects by using executeQuery() method or return nothing by using execute() method. Multiple ResultSet objects are handled using operations inherited from Statement. A suitable getXXX() method is needed to pick up the running result of a CallableStatement.

6.4.5.2.2 Create a CallableStatement Object To create a CallableStatement object, you need to use one of the methods defined in the Connection class, prepareCall(), to do that. When the SQL92 syntax is used to create this CallableStatement object, it will looks like:

```
CallableStatement cstmt = null;
try{
      String query = "{call dbo.FacultyCourse(?, ?)}";
      cstmt = LogInFrame.con.prepareCall(query);
   ........
```

The operation sequence of this piece of codes to create a new CallableStatement object is:

1. A new null CallableStatement object cstmt is first declared.
2. A try block is used to create the query string with the SQL92 syntax. The name of the stored procedure to be called is dbo.FacultyCourse() with two arguments: the first one is an input parameter, faculty_name, and the second one is an output parameter used to store all course_id taught by the selected faculty. Both parameters are represented by place holders, and they are positional parameters.
3. The CallableStatement object is created by calling the prepareCall() method, which belongs to the Connection class, with the query string as the argument.

Next let's take a look at how to set up the input parameter for this object.

6.4.5.2.3 Set the Input Parameters All input parameters used for a CallableStatement interface must be clearly bound to the associated IN parameters in a stored procedure by using a setXXX() method. This setXXX() method can be divided into three categories based on the different data types,

1. The primitive data type method
2. The object method
3. The stream method

For the primitive and the object method, the syntax is identical, and the difference between them is the type of value that is assigned. For the stream method, both the syntax and the data types are different.

Set Primitive Data Type and Object IN Values

The primitive data type means all built-in data types used in Java programming language. The syntax of setting a primitive data type or an object value method is,

```
setXXX(int position, data_type value);
```

where XXX means the associated value type to be assigned, the position that is an integer is used to indicate the relative position of the IN parameter in the SQL statement or the SQL stored procedure, and the value is the actual data value to be assigned to the IN parameter.

Some popular setXXX() methods are:

```
   setBoolean(), setByte(), setInt(), setDouble(), setFloat(),
setLong(), setShort(), setString(), setObject(), setDate(),
setTime() and setTimeStamp()
```

An example of using the setXXX() method is:

```
String query = "SELECT product, order_date FROM Order " +
               "WHERE order_id = ? AND customer = ?";
```

```
PreparedStatement pstmt = con.prepareStatement(query);
setInt(1, 101);
setString(2, "Tom Johnson");
```

Two dynamic parameters are used in the query string, and both of them are IN parameters. The data type of first IN parameter is an integer, and the second one is a String, and both are represented by a placeholder "?". The first setting method, setInt(1, 101), is to assign an integer value of 101 to the first IN parameter, which is indicated with a position number of 1, and the second setting method, setString(2, "Tom Johnson") is to assign a String value "Tom Johnson" to the second IN parameter, which is indicated with a position number of 2.

From this example, you can find that there is no difference between setting a primitive parameter and an object value to the IN parameters in an SQL statement.

Set Object Methods

The setObject() method has three protocols, which are:

```
setObject(int position, object_type object_value);
setObject(int position, object_type object_value, data_type
        desired_data_type);
setobject(int position, object_type object_value, data_type
        desired_data_type, int scale);
```

The first one is straightforward, and it contains two parameters: the first one is the relative position of the IN parameter in the SQL statement, and the second one is the value of a desired object to be assigned to the IN object.

The second one adds one more input parameter, desired_data_type, and it is used to indicate a data type to which to convert the object to.

The third one adds the fourth input parameter, scale, and it is used to make sure that the object conversion result contains a certain number of digits.

An example of the setObject() method is shown here,

```
pstmt.setObject(2, 101);
pstmt.setObject(2, 101, Type.FLOAT);
pstmt.setObject(2, 101, Type.FLOAT, 2);
```

The first method is to set an input parameter, which is the second one in an SQL statement, to an object (here is an integer) with a value of 101. The next method is to set the same input to the same object; however, it needs to convert the object (integer) to a float data type. The final method performs the same operation as the previous one, but it indicates that the conversion result should contain at least 2 digits.

Set Stream IN Methods

When transferring images between an application and a database, it needs a large size for the IN parameters. In that situation, an InputStream() method should be used to perform that kind of operation. The syntax of using this method is:

```
setXXXStream(int position, data_type input_stream, int
        number_of_bytes);
```

where XXX means the InputStream type: ASCII, Binary or Unicode. The first parameter is the relative position of the IN parameter in the SQL statement, and the second parameter is the data stream to be read from. The third parameter indicates the number of bytes to be read from the data stream at a time.

A simple example of using the InputStream() method is:

```
FileInputStream picFile = new FileInputStraem("new_file");
String query = "INSERT INTO picture (image) VALUES (?) WHERE
               pic_id = 101 ";
PreparedStatement pstmt = prepareStatement(query);
pstmt.setUnicodeStream(1, picFile, 2048);
```

This piece of codes is used to set the first IN parameter to read a 2KB bytes from a picture file, which is Unicode file, named picFile at a time.

6.4.5.2.4 Register the Output Parameters As we discussed in Section 6.4.5.2, after a CallableStatement interface is executed, you need to use the associated getXXX() method to pick up the running result from the CallableStatement object, since it cannot return any result itself. However, before you can do that, you must first register any output parameter in the SQL statement to allow the CallableStatement to know that the output result is involved and stored in the related output parameters in the SQL statement.

Once an output parameter is registered, the parameter is considered an OUT parameter, and it can contain running results that can be picked up by using the associated getXXX() method.

To register an output parameter, the registerOutParameter() method that belongs to the `CallableStatement` interface should be used to declare what SQL type the OUT parameter will return. A point to be noted is that a parameter in an SQL statement can be defined both an IN and an OUT at the same time, which means that you can set up this parameter as an IN by using the setXXX() method, and also you can register this parameter as an OUT using the registerOutParameter() method at the same time. In this way, this parameter can be considered as an IN/OUT parameter with both the input and the output functions.

The syntax to register an output parameter is:

```
registerOutParameter(int position, data_type SQL_data_type);
```

where the position is still the relative position of the OUT parameter in the SQL statement, and the SQL_data_type is the SQL data type of the OUT parameter, which can be found from the JDBC API class, java.sql.TYPE.

An example of using this method is shown here:

```
String query = "{call dbo.FacultyCourse(?, ?)}";
cstmt = LogInFrame.con.prepareCall(query);
cstmt.setString(1, ComboName.getSelectedItem().toString());
cstmt.setString(2, "CSC-132B");
cstmt.registerOutParameter(2, java.sql.Types.VARCHAR);
```

There are two parameters in this CallableStatement interface in this example. The first one is an IN parameter, which is set by using the setString() method. The second one is an IN/OUT parameter, which is first set up by using the setString() method, and then registered by using the registerOutParameter() method with the data type of VARCHAR. The SQL data type VARCHAR can be mapped to a data type of String in Java. Refer to Appendix A to get more detailed information about the data type mapping between the SQL and Java.

An interesting point to this registerOutParameter() method is that all OUT parameters can be registered by using this syntax except those OUT parameters with the

NUMERIC and DECIMAL data types. The syntax to register those OUT parameters look like:

```
registerOutParameter(int position, data_type SQL_data_type, int scale);
```

The only difference is that a third parameter **scale** is added, and it is used to indicate the number of digits to the right of the decimal point for the OUT parameter.

6.4.5.2.5 Execute CallableStatement To run a CallableStatement object, three methods can be used: **executeQuery()**, **executeUpdate()**, and **execute()**. As we discussed in Section 6.4.2.3, the **executeQuery()** method can return a ResultSet object that contains the running or query results; however, the **execute()** method cannot return any running result with itself, and you need to use associated **getXXX()** methods to pick up the query or running result. Another important point of using the **execute()** method is that it can handle an unknown result with undefined data type. Refer to Sections 6.4.2.3 and 6.4.4.3 to get more detailed information about the **execute()** method.

An example of using the **execute()** method to run the CallableStatement object is:

```
String query = "{call dbo.FacultyCourse(?, ?)}";
cstmt = LogInFrame.con.prepareCall(query);
cstmt.setString(1, ComboName.getSelectedItem().toString());
cstmt.registerOutParameter(2, java.sql.Types.VARCHAR);
cstmt.execute();
```

Now let's handle how to retrieve the running result from the execution of a CallableStatement object.

6.4.5.2.6 Retrieve the Running Result To pick up the running results from the execution of a CallableStatement object, one needs to use an associated **getXXX()** method to do that. Two popular ways to get back a running result from a CallableStatement are: **getXXX()** method and **getObject()** method. The former is based on the returned data type of the result, and the latter is more general to get any kind of result.

All of the **getXXX()** methods and **getObject()** use the same syntax, which looks like:

```
getXXX(int position);
getObject(int position);
```

where XXX indicates the OUT value Java data type, and the position is the relative position of the OUT parameter in the SQL statement. Same syntax is used for the **getObject()** method.

An example of using **getXXX()** method to pick up the running result from the execution of a CallableStatement object is shown below:

```
String query = "{call dbo.FacultyCourse(?, ?)}";
cstmt = LogInFrame.con.prepareCall(query);
cstmt.setString(1, ComboName.getSelectedItem().toString());
cstmt.registerOutParameter(2, java.sql.Types.VARCHAR);
cstmt.execute();
String cResult = cstmt.getString(2);
```

Since the OUT parameter is a String and is located at position of 2, therefore, an argument of 2 is used in the **getString()** method to pick up the running result. An alternative way to get the same running result is to use the getObject() method, which looks like:

```
String cResult = (String)cstmt.getObject(2);
```

The returned result must be casted by using the String data type, since an object can be any data type.

Ok, that is enough for the theoretical discussion, now let's go to our real staff, developing the codes for the Select button Click event handler to perform this CallableStatement object to call an SQL stored procedure to make the course query from our Course table in our sample database.

6.4.5.3 Coding for the Select Button Click Event Handler to Perform CallableStatement Query

Open the CourseFrame Form window by clicking on the Design tab from the top of the window, and then open the Select button Click event handler by double clicking on the Select button. Enter the codes that are shown in Figure 6.91 into this event handler.

Let's have a closer look at this piece of codes to see how it works.

A. First, we need to check whether a Java Callable Method has been selected or not. If it is, a new null object of the CallableStatement class, cstmt, is created.

B. A try . . . catch block is used to perform this CallableStatement query. A SQL92 syntax is used to build a query string to try to call an SQL stored procedure dbo.FacultyCourse, which will be developed in the next section, to query all courses, exactly all course_id, taught by the selected faculty member. Two parameters are used in this SQL statement; the first one is an IN parameter, faculty_name obtained from the Faculty Name combo box ComboName, and the second one is an OUT parameter that contains all course_id taught by the selected faculty member.

```
    private void cmdSelectActionPerformed(java.awt.event.ActionEvent evt) {
        // TODO add your handling code here:
A       if (ComboMethod.getSelectedItem()=="Java Callable Method"){
            CallableStatement cstmt = null;
            try{
B               String query = "{call dbo.FacultyCourse(?, ?)}";
C               cstmt = LogInFrame.con.prepareCall(query);
D               cstmt.setString(1, ComboName.getSelectedItem().toString());
E               cstmt.registerOutParameter(2, java.sql.Types.VARCHAR);
F               cstmt.execute();
G               String cResult = cstmt.getString(2);
H               //String cResult = (String)cstmt.getObject(2);
I              String[] result = cResult.split(",");
J              CourseList.setListData(result);
             }
K           catch (SQLException e){
               msgDlg.setMessage("Error in CallableStatement! " + e.getMessage());
               msgDlg.setVisible(true);
             }
        }
    }
```

Figure 6.91. The codes for the Select button Click event handler.

C. The real CallableStatement object is created by calling the prepareCall() method and assigned to the null object cstmt we created in step A. One point to be noted is that the prepareCall() method belongs to the Connection class; therefore, we need to call our Connection object con, which is a class instance defined in the LogInFrame class, to perform this creation.

D. The first parameter in this SQL statement is a String faculty_name, which is an IN parameter and bound using the setString() method. The value of this input parameter is obtained by calling the getSelectedItem() method from the Faculty Name combo box ComboName.

E. The second parameter in this query string, which is an OUT parameter and contains all queried course_id taught by the selected faculty member, is registered using the registerOutParameter() method. The SQL data type of this OUT parameter is VARCHAR.

F. The CallableStatement object is executed by calling the execute() method.

G. The getString() method is used to pick up the running result with a position of 2. The SQL data type VARCHAR can be mapped to a String in Java.

H. An alternative way to pick up this running result is to use the getObject() method. However, it must be casted to a String object before it can be picked up.

I. The running result stored in the cResult contains all course_id that are separated by a comma, so the split() method is executed to separate each of course_id and assign them to a String array result.

J. The setListData() method is used to add all course_id that are stored in the String array result into the Course ID List listbox, CourseList, to display them.

K. The catch block is used to catch any possible errors and display them if they indeed occurred.

Now that we have a clear picture about the coding for the CallableStatement in the Java side, let's begin to deal with the stored procedure in the SQL side.

6.4.5.4 Build the SQL Stored Procedure dbo.FacultyCourse

Stored Procedures are nothing more than functions or procedures applied in any project developed in any programming language. This means that stored procedures can be considered as functions or subroutines, and they can be called easily with any arguments, and they can also return any data with a certain type. One can integrate multiple SQL statements into a single stored procedure to perform multiple queries at a time, and those statements will be precompiled by the SQL Server to form an integrated target body. In this way, the precompiled body is insulated with your coding developed in Java environment. You can easily call the stored procedure from your Java application project as the project runs. The result of using the stored procedure is that the performance of your data-driven application can be greatly increased, and the data query's speed can be significantly improved. Also, when you develop a stored procedure, the database server automatically creates an execution plan for that procedure, and the developed plan can be updated automatically whenever a modification is made to that procedure by the database server.

Regularly, there are three types of stored procedures: System-stored procedures, extended stored procedures, and custom-stored procedures. The system-stored procedures are developed and implemented for administrating, managing, configuring, and monitoring the SQL server. The extended stored procedures are developed and applied in the dynamic linked library (dll) format. This kind of stored procedures can improve the running speed and save the running space since they can be dynamically linked to your project. The custom-stored procedures are developed and implemented by users for their applications.

Six possible ways can be used to create a stored procedure.

1. Using SQL Server Enterprise Manager
2. Using Query Analyzer
3. Using ASP Code
4. Using Visual Studio.NET—Real Time Coding Method
5. Using Visual Studio.NET—Server Explorer
6. Using Enterprise Manager Wizard

For our current application, I prefer to use the Server Explorer in Visual Studio.NET. A more complicated but flexible way to create the stored procedure is to use the real-time coding method from Visual Studio.NET. In this section, we will concentrate on the fifth method listed above.

6.4.5.4.1 Structure and Syntax of an SQL Stored Procedure The prototype or syntax of creating an SQL stored procedure is shown in Figure 6.92.

For SQL Server database, the name of the stored procedure is always prefixed by the schema dbo. A sample stored procedure `StudentInfo` is shown in Figure 6.93.

The parameters declared inside the braces are either input or output parameters used for this stored procedure, and an @ symbol must be prefixed before the parameter in the SQL Server database. Any argument sent from the calling procedure to this stored procedure should be declared in here. The other variables, which are created by using the

```
CREATE PROCEDURE Stored Procedure's name
{
        @Param1's name    Param1's data type Input/Output,
        @Param2's name    Param2's data type Input/Output
        .......
}
AS
    (DECLARE Your local variables.... If you have)
    (Your SQL Statements)
    RETURN
```

Figure 6.92. The structure and syntax of an SQL stored procedure.

```
CREATE PROCEDURE dbo.StudentInfo
{
    @StudentName VARCHAR(50)
}
AS
    SELECT student_id FROM Student
    WHERE name LIKE @StudentName
    RETURN
```

Figure 6.93. An example of an SQL stored procedure.

keyword DECLARE located after the keyword AS, are local variables, and they can only be used in this stored procedure. The keyword RETURN is used to return the queried data columns.

6.4.5.4.2 Return Multiple Rows from an SQL Stored Procedure to the Java CallableStatement As we know, in an SQL stored procedure, regularly, only one piece of data or one row can be returned to the calling procedure. In order to return multiple rows, a cursor must be used to hold those multiple data rows. A cursor works as a data table, and it can hold data in a certain format. A problem is that there is no a mapped data type for the cursor in the Java environment! Therefore, we cannot use the cursor to return the queried result from an SQL stored procedure to our Java applications. When we perform a query to our Course table to get multiple courses taught by the selected faculty, we need to return multiple rows or multiple course_id to our Java CourseFrame class.

In JDBC API 4.0, it indeed added more components to facilitate the interface between the SQL Server database and Java applications, however, unfortunately, it still have not covered this topic.

To solve this problem and allow multiple rows to be returned from an SQL stored procedure to the Java applications, we need to perform the following operations:

1. The data type of the OUT parameter in the SQL statement or in the SQL stored procedure should be defined as a VARCHAR, which can be mapped to a String in the Java code.
2. Inside the SQL stored procedure, we need to declare a local cursor variable and use that local cursor to collect the queried multiple rows or multiple course_id.
3. Fetch each queried row from the cursor into the each associated local variable.
4. Combine all fetched rows into the OUT parameter that has a data type of VARCHAR.

A key point to build this SQL stored procedure is that our sample database CSE_DEPT.mdf should have been built and located at the default location, which is C:\Program Files\Microsoft SQL Server\MSSQL10.SQL2008EXPRESS\MSSQL\DATA. Refer to Chapter 2 to build this sample database if it has not been built.

Now open the Microsoft Visual Studio.NET 2010 and open the Server Explorer by going to the View|Server Explorer menu item. Make sure that our sample database CSE_DEPT.mdf has been connected to the Visual Studio.NET 2010. If not, you need to use the Data Source window to first connect it by adding a new data source. The point to be noted is that you need to check the `Data Source` you are connecting is SQL2008EXPRESS. To do this checking, click on the Advanced button in the `Add Connection` wizard and then the `Data Source` property.

Expand our sample database CSE_DEPT.mdf from the Server Explorer window, and right click on the Stored Procedures folder, select `Add New Stored Procedure` item from the pop-up menu to open the `New Stored Procedure` window, which is shown in Figure 6.94.

Remove all comment out marks and replace the name of this stored procedure with the dbo.FacultyCourse. Add the codes that are shown in Figure 6.95 into this stored procedure to make it as our target stored procedure. Go to File|Save StoredProcedure1 menu item to save this stored procedure. Let's have a closer look at this new added piece of codes to see how it works.

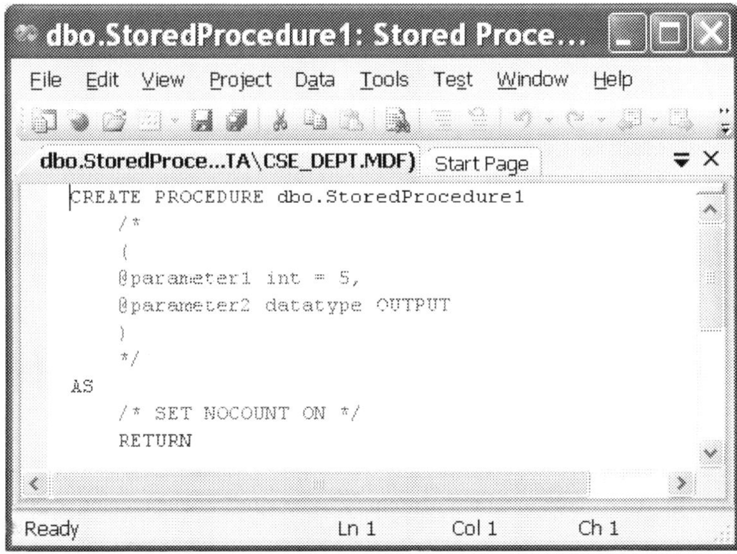

Figure 6.94. The opened New Stored Procedure window.

```
  CREATE PROCEDURE dbo.FacultyCourse
  (
A         @facultyName VARCHAR(50),
          @result VARCHAR(800) OUTPUT
  )
  AS
B         DECLARE @courseID CURSOR
          DECLARE @facultyID VARCHAR(50)
C         DECLARE @courseid1 VARCHAR(100)
          DECLARE @courseid2 VARCHAR(100)
          DECLARE @courseid3 VARCHAR(100)
          DECLARE @courseid4 VARCHAR(100)
          DECLARE @courseid5 VARCHAR(100)
D         DECLARE @message VARCHAR(800)
E         SET @facultyID = (SELECT faculty_id FROM Faculty
          WHERE faculty_name LIKE @facultyName)
F         SET @courseID = CURSOR FOR (SELECT course_id FROM Course WHERE faculty_id LIKE @facultyID)
G         OPEN @courseID
H         FETCH NEXT FROM @courseID INTO @courseid1
          FETCH NEXT FROM @courseID INTO @courseid2
          FETCH NEXT FROM @courseID INTO @courseid3
          FETCH NEXT FROM @courseID INTO @courseid4
I         IF @@FETCH_STATUS = 0
          FETCH NEXT FROM @courseID INTO @courseid5
J         IF @@FETCH_STATUS = -1
             SET @result = @courseid1 + ',' + @courseid2 + ',' + @courseid3 + ',' + @courseid4
K         ELSE IF @@FETCH_STATUS = 0
             SET @result = @courseid1 + ',' + @courseid2 + ',' + @courseid3 + ',' + @courseid4 + ',' + @courseid5
L         CLOSE @courseID
    PRINT ' '
M   SELECT @message = '----- ResultSet =: ' + @result
N   PRINT @message
    RETURN
```

Figure 6.95. The codes for the stored procedure dbo.FacultyCourse.

A. Both IN and OUT parameters are first declared in the parameter section. The @faculty-Name is an input parameter with a data type of VARCHAR(50), and the @result is an output parameter with a data type of VARCHAR(800). The keyword OUTPUT must be attached after the OUT parameter to indicate that this is an output parameter in this stored procedure.

B. Two local variables, @facultyID and @courseID, are declared here since we need to use them inside this stored procedure only. The first one is a VARCHAR variable, and the second is a cursor variable since we need to query multiple rows by using this cursor later.

C. Another five local variables are created, and each of them is related to one course_id queried from this stored procedure. As we know, all faculty members in this CSE dept teach either four or five courses, so the maximum number of course_id should be five.

D. The local variable @message is used for the testing purpose of this stored procedure.

E. As we remember, there is no faculty_name column available in our Course table, and the only relationship between each faculty and each course is made by the faculty_id column, which is a primary key in the Faculty table, but a foreign key in the Course table. In order to get the faculty_id, we need to perform a query to the Faculty table based on the faculty_name, which is an input to this stored procedure. Then we can perform another query to the Course table to get all courses taught by the selected faculty_id obtained from the first query. So you can see that we need to perform two queries to get our desired course_id. To save the time and space, here we used a stored procedure to combine these two queries together to speed up this query process.

F. Here we used a cursor @courseID to collect multiple rows (course_id) returned from this query. To perform an assignment operation in SQL, a SET instruction must be used.

G. After a query is performed and the result has been stored into the cursor. To fetch each row from the cursor, the cursor must be first opened.

H. A FETCH command is used to fetch the first four courses into four local variables, @ courseid1 and @courseid4.

I. By checking the global variable @@FETCH_STATUS, we can know whether the last fetch operation is successful or not. If this status returned a 0, which means that the last fetch is fine, and then we can try to fetch the fifth course into the local variable @courseid5. Because all faculty members in this CSE dept teach either four or five courses, therefore, the maximum number of queried courses should be five.

J. If the fetch status @@FETCH_STATUS returned a –1, which means that the last fetch is unsuccessful or there is no fifth course to be fetched, we need to combine only the first four fetched courses into the OUT parameter @result. In order to make it convenient to separate this combined string in the Java application, we combine these fetched rows with a comma mark as a separator.

K. If the fetch status @@FETCH_STATUS returned a 0, which means that the last fetch is successful or the fifth course is indeed existed, we can combine all five fetched courses together into the OUT parameter @result, and separate them with a comma mark.

L. After all fetches have been completed, the cursor is closed.

M. To test this stored procedure, we use a SELECT statement to collect the values of the OUT parameter and

N. Use the PRINT command to display it.

Now let's test this stored procedure by right click on any place in this stored procedure, and select the Execute item from the pop-up menu to open the Run Stored Procedure dialog, which is shown in Figure 6.96.

Enter Ying Bai and CSC-333 into the Value box as the input and the output parameters, and click on the OK button to run this stored procedure. The running result is shown in the Output window, which is shown in Figure 6.97.

Our SQL stored procedure is successful!

Before we can call this stored procedure from our CourseFrame Form to test the CallableStatement interface, make sure that you have closed the connection between our sample database CSE_DEPT.mdf and the Visual Studio.NET 2010. To do that, right click on our sample database CSE_DEPT.mdf from the Server Explorer window, and select the Close Connection item from the pop-up menu. Otherwise, you may encounter a connection exception when you run our Java application project.

Now we can test the CallableStatement object we built in our CourseFrame class. Open our project and the CourseFrame Form window, click on the Clean and Build

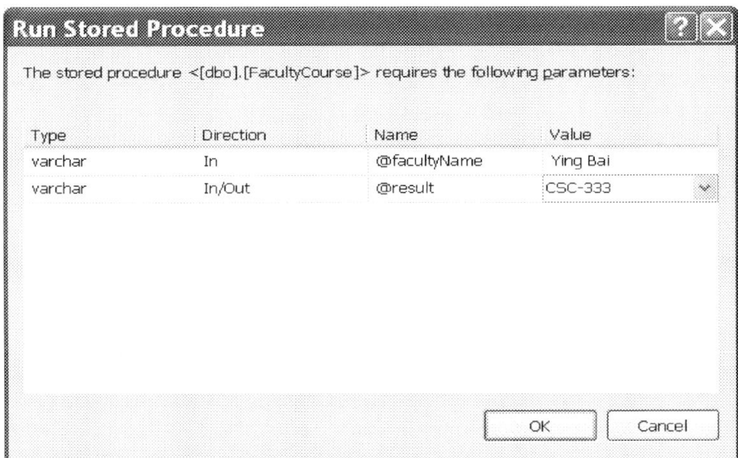

Figure 6.96. The running status of the stored procedure.

```
Output
Show output from: Database Output
Running [dbo].[FacultyCourse] ( @facultyName = Ying Bai, @result = CSC-333 ).


----- ResultSet =: CSC-132B,CSC-234A,CSE-434,CSE-438
No rows affected.
(0 row(s) returned)
@result = CSC-132B,CSC-234A,CSE-434,CSE-438
@RETURN_VALUE = 0
Finished running [dbo].[FacultyCourse].
```

Figure 6.97. The running result of the stored procedure.

Main Project button from the toolbar to build our project. Then click on the Run Main Project button to run our project.

Enter the suitable username and password, such as jhenry and test, to complete the login process. Then select the Course Information from the SelectionFrame Form window to open the CourseFrame Form window. Select the Java Callable Method from the Query Method combo box, and click on the Select button to run our CallableStatement object to query all course_id taught by the default faculty member Ying Bai. A sample running result is shown in Figure 6.98.

Click on the Close button that is located at the upper-right corner of this CourseFrame Form window to terminate our project.

Next, let's develop the codes to display the detailed information for each course shown in the Course ID List listbox.

6.4.5.5 Coding for the CourseList Box to Display Detailed Information for the Selected Course

The function of this event handler is simple, which is listed below:

1. After the user selected a faculty member from the Faculty Name combo box, a Java Callable Method from the Query Method combo box, and clicked on the Select button, all courses, exactly all course_id, taught by the selected faculty should be displayed in the Course ID List listbox.
2. As the user clicks on a course_id from the Course ID List listbox, the detailed information for the selected course_id should be displayed in five text fields.

Based on the function description listed above, the coding for this event handler is easy and straightforward. Open the Design View of the CourseFrame Form window by clicking on the Design tab on the top of the window, and right click on the CourseList listbox and select the Events|ListSelection|valueChanged item to open its

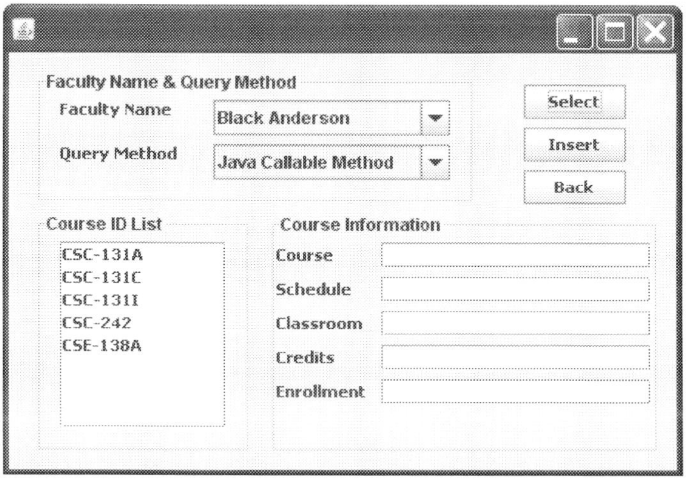

Figure 6.98. The running result of the CourseFrame Form.

CourseListValueChanged() event handler. Enter the codes that are shown in Figure 6.99 into this event handler.

Let's have a closer look at this piece of codes to see how it works.

A. A text field array c_field is created here since we need to assign the queried detailed course information to five text fields to display them; therefore it is easy to use an array to do that assignment.

B. Since JList component belongs to the javax.swing package, not java.awt package, therefore, a clicking on an entry in the CourseList box causes the itemStateChanged() method to fire twice: once when the mouse button is depressed, and once again when it is released. Therefore, the selected course_id will be appearing twice when it is selected. To prevent this from occurring, the getValueIsAdjusting() method is used to make sure that no item has been adjusted to be displayed twice. Then the selected course_id is assigned to a local String variable courseid by calling the getSelectedValue() method of the CourseList Box class.

C. Before we can proceed to the query operation, first we need to confirm that the selected courseid is not a null value. A null value would be returned if the user did not select any course_id from the CourseList box; instead, the user just clicked on the Select button to try to find all course_id taught by other faculty members. Even the user only clicked on the Select button without touching any course_id in the CourseList box; however, the system still considers that a null course_id has been selected, and thus a null value will be returned. To avoid that situation from occurring, an if selection structure is used to make sure that no null value has been returned from the CourseList box. A SQL query string is created if no null value has been returned.

```
  private void CourseListValueChanged(javax.swing.event.ListSelectionEvent evt) {
     // TODO add your handling code here:
A    javax.swing.JTextField[] c_field = {CourseField, ScheduleField, ClassroomField, CreditField, EnrollField};
B    if(!CourseList.getValueIsAdjusting() ){
       String courseid = (String)CourseList.getSelectedValue();
C      if (courseid != null){
          String cQuery = "SELECT course, schedule, classroom, credit, "
                      + "enrollment FROM Course WHERE course_id = ?";
D      try{
          PreparedStatement pstmt = LogInFrame.con.prepareStatement(cQuery);
E         pstmt.setString(1, courseid);
F         ResultSet rs = pstmt.executeQuery();
G         ResultSetMetaData rsmd = rs.getMetaData();
H         while (rs.next()){
             for (int i=1; i <=rsmd.getColumnCount(); i++) {
                c_field[i-1].setText(rs.getString(i));
             }
          }
       }
I      catch (SQLException e) {
          msgDlg.setMessage("Error in Statement!" + e.getMessage());
          msgDlg.setVisible(true);
       }
      }
     }
  }
```

Figure 6.99. The coding for the CourseListValueChanged() event handler.

D. A try . . . catch block is used to perform this PreparedStatement query operation. First, a PreparedStatement object is created with the query string as the argument.

E. The setString() method is executed to use the real query criterion courseid to replace the nominal position parameter.

F. The dynamic query is actually executed by calling the executeQuery() method, and the query result is returned and stored in a ResultSet object.

G. The getMetaData() method is called to return the detailed information about the returned ResultSet object, including the column number, column name, and data type.

H. A while and for loops are used to retrieve the queried columns from the ResultSet object, and assign them one by one to the associated Text Field to display them.

I. The catch block is used to track and monitor the running status of this piece of codes. An error message will be displayed if any exception is occurred.

Next, we need to take care of the coding for the Back button Click event handler to switch from the CourseFrame Form back to the SelectionFrame Form to allow users to perform other query operations.

6.4.5.6 Coding for the Back Button Click Event Handler

When this Back button is clicked, the CourseFrame Form should be closed, and the control will be returned to the SelectionFrame Form. Open the Design View of the CourseFrame Form window by clicking on the Design tab from the top of the window, and double click on the Back button to open its event handler. Enter the codes that are shown in Figure 6.100 into this event handler.

The function of this piece of codes is straightforward, the CourseFrame Form will be closed by calling the setVisible() method with a false argument, and the dispose() method is used to remove the CourseFrame Form from the screen.

At this point, we have finished all coding jobs for the CourseFrame Form object. Now we can build and run our project to test its function. Click on the Clean and Build Main Project button on the top of the window to build our project. Then click on the Run Main Project button to run the project.

Enter suitable username and password, such as jhenry and test, to the LogInFrame Form to complete the login process. Select the Course Information item from the SelectionFrame Form window to open the CourseFrame Form window. Then select the Java Callable Method from the Query Method combo box, keep the default faculty member Ying Bai from the Faculty Name combo box, and click on the Select button. All courses, exactly all course_id, taught by the selected faculty member are shown in the Course ID List listbox, which is shown in Figure 6.101.

```
private void cmdBackActionPerformed(java.awt.event.ActionEvent evt) {
    // TODO add your handling code here:
    this.setVisible(false);
    this.dispose();
}
```

Figure 6.100. Coding for the Back button Click event handler.

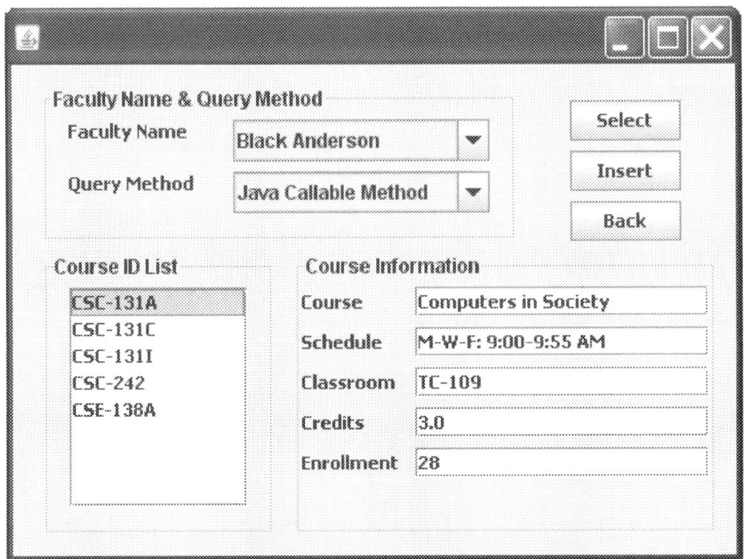

Figure 6.101. The running result of the CourseFrame Form window.

Click on any course_id from the Course ID List listbox, the detailed course information about the selected course_id is displayed in five text fields, which is also shown in Figure 6.101. Our course query using the CallableStatement with the stored procedure is successful!

Click on the Back and then Exit buttons to terminate our project.

A complete project SQLSelectObject can be found from the folder DBProjects\Chapter 6 that is located at the accompanying ftp site (see Chapter 1).

Next, let's discuss how to perform data queries from the Student table in our sample database using the RowSet object.

6.4.6 Query Data from the Student Table Using the Java RowSet Object

A RowSet object is one of the JavaBeans components with multiple supports from JavaBeans, and it is a new feature in the `java.sql` package. By using the RowSet object, a database query can be performed automatically with the data source connection and a query statement creation. In this section, we will show readers how to use this new feature to reduce the coding load and improve the efficiency of the data query with the help of this RowSet object.

6.4.6.1 Introduction to Java RowSet Object

The JDBC 2.0 API includes many new features in the java.sql package, as well as the new Standard Extension package, javax.sql. This new JDBC API moves Java applications into the world of heavy-duty database computing. One of important features is the RowSet object.

A RowSet object contains a set of rows from a result set or some other source of tabular data, like a file or spreadsheet. Because a RowSet object follows the JavaBeans model for properties and event notification, it is a JavaBeans component that can be combined with other components in an application. As it compatible with other Beans, application developers can probably use a development tool to create a RowSet object and set its properties.

RowSets may have many different implementations to fill different needs. These implementations fall into two broad categories, connected and disconnected:

1. A connected RowSet is equivalent to a ResultSet, and it maintains a connection to a data source as long as the RowSet is in use.
2. A disconnected RowSet works as a DataSet in Visual Studio.NET, and it can connect to a data source to perform the data updating periodically. Most time, it is disconnected with the data source, and uses a mapping memory space as a mapped database.

While a RowSet is disconnected, it does not need a JDBC driver or the full JDBC API, so its footprint is very small. Thus, a RowSet is an ideal format for sending data over a network to a thin client.

Because it is not continually connected to its data source, a disconnected RowSet stores its data in memory. It needs to maintain metadata about the columns it contains and information about its internal state. It also needs a facility for making connections, for executing commands, and for reading and writing data to and from the data source. A connected RowSet, by contrast, opens a connection and keeps it open for as long as the RowSet is being used.

To make writing an implementation easier, the Java Software division of Sun Microsystems, Inc. plans to provide reference implementations for five different styles of RowSets in the future. The following list of planned implementations gives you an idea of some of the possibilities.

1. A CachedRowSet class—a disconnected RowSet that caches its data in memory; not suitable for very large datasets, but an ideal way to provide thin Java clients, such as a Personal Digital Assistant (PDA) or Network Computer (NC), with tabular data
2. A JDBCRowSet class—a connected RowSet that serves mainly as a thin wrapper around a ResultSet object to make a JDBC driver look like a JavaBeans component
3. A WebRowSet class—a connected RowSet that uses the HTTP protocol internally to talk to a Java Servlet that provides data access; used to make it possible for thin web clients to retrieve and possibly update a set of rows.
4. A FilteredRowSet is an extension to WebRowSet that provides programmatic support for filtering its content. This enables you to avoid the overhead of supplying a query and the processing involved. The SQL implementation of FilteredRowSet is javax.sql.rowset.FilteredRowSet. The Oracle implementation of FilteredRowSet is oracle.jdbc.rowset.OracleFilteredRowSet. The OracleFilteredRowSet class in the ojdbc14.jar file implements the standard JSR-114 interface javax.sql.rowset.FilteredRowSet.
5. A JoinRowSet is another extension to WebRowSet that consists of related data from different RowSets. There is no standard way to establish an SQL JOIN between disconnected RowSets without connecting to the data source. A JoinRowSet addresses this issue. The SQL implementation of JoinRowSet is the javax.sql.rowset.JoinRowSet class. The Oracle

implementation of JoinRowSet is the oracle.jdbc.rowset. OracleJoinRowSet class. This class, which is in the ojdbc14.jar file, implements the standard JSR-114 interface javax.sql.rowset. JoinRowSet. Any number of RowSet objects, which implement the Joinable interface, can be added to a JoinRowSet object, provided they can be related in an SQL JOIN. All five types of RowSet support the Joinable interface. The Joinable interface provides methods for specifying the columns based on which the JOIN will be performed, that is, the match columns.

Next, let's have a closer look at the operational sequence for the RowSet object.

6.4.6.2 The Operational Procedure of Using the JDBC RowSet Object

A compliant JDBC RowSet implementation must implement one or more standard interfaces specified in this package, and may extend the BaseRowSet abstract class. For example, a CachedRowSet implementation must implement the CachedRowSet interface and extend the BaseRowSet abstract class. The BaseRowSet class provides the standard architecture on which all RowSet implementations should be built, regardless of whether the RowSet objects exist in a connected or disconnected environment. The BaseRowSet abstract class provides any RowSet implementation with its base functionality, including property manipulation and event notification that is fully compliant with JavaBeans component requirements. As an example, all implementations provided in the reference implementations (contained in the com.sun.rowset package) use the BaseRowSet class as a basis for their implementations.

Table 6.10 illustrates the features that the BaseRowSet abstract class provides.

In this application, we will concentrate on the implementation of the CachedRowSet component, since we preferred to use a disconnected RowSet.

Generally, the operational procedure of using a RowSet object to query data can be divided into the following four steps:

Table 6.10. Features of the BaseRowSet abstract class

Feature	Details
Properties	Provides standard JavaBeans property manipulation mechanisms to allow applications to get and set RowSet command and property values. Refer to the documentation of the javax.sql.RowSet interface (available in the JDBC 3.0 specification) for more details on the standard RowSet properties.
Event notification	Provides standard JavaBeans event notifications to registered event listeners. Refer to the documentation of javax.sql.RowSetEvent interface (available in the JDBC 3.0 specification) for more details on how to register and handle standard RowSet events generated by compliant implementations.
Setters for a RowSet object's command	Provides a complete set of setter methods for setting RowSet command parameters.
Streams	Provides fields for storing of stream instances in addition to providing a set of constants for stream type designation

1. Set up and configure a RowSet object.
2. Register the RowSet Listeners.
3. Set input and output parameters for the query command.
4. Traverse through the result rows from the ResultSet.

The first step is used to set up and configure the static or dynamic properties of a RowSet object, such as the connection URL, username, password, and running command, to allow the RowSet object to connect to the data source, pass user parameters into the data source, and perform the data query.

The second step allows users to register different Listeners for the RowSet object with different event sources. The RowSet feature supports multiple listeners to be registered with the RowSet object. Listeners can be registered using the addRowSetListener() method and unregistered through the removeRowSetListener() method. A listener should implement the javax.sql.RowSetListener interface to register itself as the RowSet listener. Three types of events are supported by the RowSet interface:

1. cursorMoved event: Generated whenever there is a cursor movement, which occurs when the next() or previous() methods are called.
2. rowChanged event: Generated when a new row is inserted, updated, or deleted from the row set.
3. rowsetChanged event: Generated when the whole row set is created or changed.

In our applications, the NetBeans IDE 6.8 is used and the event-listener model has been set up by NetBeans IDE. So we can skip this step and do not need to take care of this issue during our coding process.

Step 3 allows users to set up all static or dynamic parameters for the query statement of the RowSet object. Depends on the data type of the parameters used in the query statement, suitable setXXX() method should used to perform this parameter setup process.

The fourth step is used to retrieve each row from the ResultSet object.

A point to be noted when using any RowSet object to perform data query is that most RowSet classes are abstract classes, and they cannot be instantiated directly. One needs to use a suitable RowSet Implementation class to create a RowSet implementation object to perform a data query.

Now let's follow four steps listed above to develop a data query operation using the CachedRowSet object to query data from the Student table in our sample database CSE_DEPT.mdf. First, let's build a GUI named StudentFrame Form using NetBeans 6.8.

6.4.6.3 Build a Graphical User Interface StudentFrame Form

As we did for the other JFrame Forms, right click on our project SQLSelectObject from the Projects window, and then select New|JFrame Form item from the pop-up menu to open New JFrame Form dialog box. Enter StudentFrame into the Class Name box as the name for our new class, and select the SQLSelectObjectPackage from the Package box, and click on the Finish button to create this new StudentFrame class.

Add the following objects and controls shown in Table 6.11 into this StudentFrame Form window to finish the GUI design for this form.

Table 6.11. Objects and controls in the StudentFrame form

Type	Variable Name	Text	Border	Title
Canvas	ImageCanvas			
Panel	jPanel1		Titled Border	Student Name and Query Method
Label	Label1	Student Name		
ComboBox	ComboName			
Label	Label2	Query Method		
ComboBox	ComboMethod			
Panel	jPanel2		Titled Border	Course Selected
ListBox	CourseList			
Panel	jPanel3		Titled Border	Student Information
Label	Label3	Student ID		
Text Field	StudentIDField			
Label	Label4	School Year		
Text Field	SchoolYearField			
Label	Label5	GPA		
Text Field	GPAField			
Label	Label6	Major		
Text Field	MajorField			
Label	Label7	Credits		
Text Field	CreditsField			
Label	Label8	Email		
Text Field	EmailField			
Button	cmdSelect	Select		
Button	cmdInsert	Insert		
Button	cmdExit	Exit		
StudentFrame Form	StudentFrame			CSE DEPT Student Form

Your finished StudentFrame Form window should match one that is shown in Figure 6.102.

The function of this StudentFrame Form class is:

1. As this StudentFrame Form runs, the user can select the desired student and query method from the Student Name and Query Method combo boxes, respectively. As the Select button is clicked by the user, all courses, exactly all course_id, taken by the selected student will be displayed in the Course Selected ListBox. Also the detailed information about the selected student will be displayed in six text fields.
2. When the user clicks on the Exit button, the StudentFrame Form project will be terminated and the database related connection will be closed, too.
3. In this section, we only use the Java JDBC RowSet Method as our data query method, and the Select and the Exit buttons as our coding objectives.

A point to be noted is that when you drag a Canvas control from the Palette and place it into the StudentFrame Form window, first you need to click on the Canvas from the Palette. Then you need to click a location where you want to place it in the StudentFrame. A Canvas icon is displayed in that location you clicked. You must drag this Canvas icon to the upper-left direction—never drag it to the lower-right direction—to enlarge it.

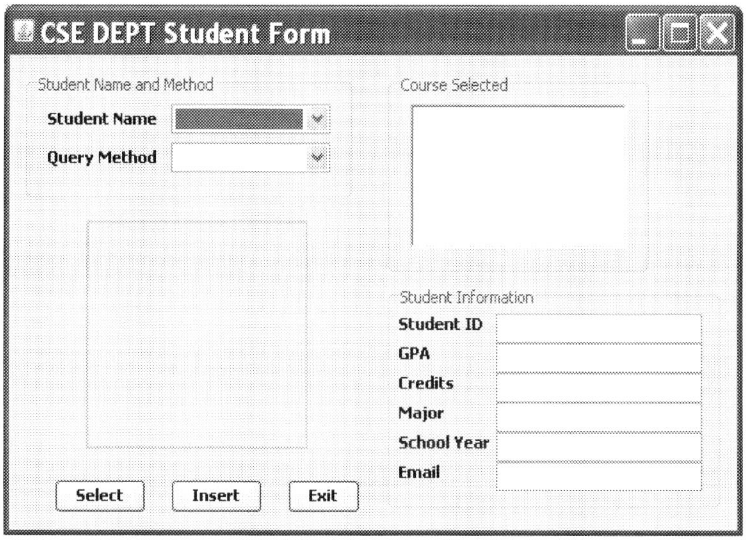

Figure 6.102. A sample window of the StudentFrame Form.

Another point to be noted is that you need to remove all default items located inside the model property of the combo boxes ComboName and ComboMethod. To do that, click on each combo box from the Design View, and then go to the model property, click on the three-dot button to open the model pane. Select all four default items, and press the Delete button from the keyboard to remove all of those items.

6.4.6.4 Coding for the Constructor of the StudentFrame Class

Open the Code Window of the StudentFrame class by clicking on the Source tab from the top of the window and enter the codes that are shown in Figure 6.103 into the top of this window and the constructor of this class.

Let's have a closer look at this piece of codes to see how it works.

A. Three useful java packages are added first since we need to utilize some classes defined in those packages. The first package, java.sql.*, provides all classes and interfaces used in JDBC API for SQL Server database. The next two packages contain all related classes and interfaces used for the CachedRowSet component and CachedRowSet Implementation classes. As we mentioned, the CachedRowSet is an abstract class, and we have to use its implementation class to perform any data query.

B. Two class-level, not class, variables are declared here since we need to use them in our whole class. The msgDlg is used to track and display any debug and warning information if any error is encountered during our project runs. The rowSet object is a null instance of the CachedRowSet class and will be used later for our data query performance.

C. Three query methods are added into the Query Method combo box. In this application, we only use the third one, CachedRowSet Method.

D. Five students' names are added into the Student Name combo box.

```
  package SQLSelectObjectPackage;
A import java.sql.*;
  import javax.sql.rowset.CachedRowSet;
  import com.sun.rowset.CachedRowSetImpl; // Sun's CachedRowSet implementation
  public class StudentFrame extends javax.swing.JFrame {
B    MsgDialog msgDlg = new MsgDialog(new javax.swing.JFrame(), true);
     CachedRowSet rowSet = null;
     /** Creates new form StudentFrame */
     public StudentFrame() {
        initComponents();
        this.setLocationRelativeTo(null);
C       ComboMethod.addItem("JPA Wizards Method");
        ComboMethod.addItem("Runtime Object Method");
        ComboMethod.addItem("CachedRowSet RowSet Method");
D       ComboName.addItem("Erica Johnson");
        ComboName.addItem("Ashly Jade");
        ComboName.addItem("Holes Smith");
        ComboName.addItem("Andrew Woods");
        ComboName.addItem("Blue Valley");
E       try
        {
           //Load and register SQL Server driver
           Class.forName("com.microsoft.sqlserver.jdbc.SQLServerDriver");
        }
F       catch (Exception e) {
           msgDlg.setMessage("Class not found exception!" + e.getMessage());
           msgDlg.setVisible(true);
        }
  }
```

Figure 6.103. The coding for the constructor of the StudentFrame class.

E. A try . . . catch block is used to load and register the JDBC driver for SQL Server database.

F. The catch block is used to track and catch any exception occurred during this driver loading and registration process.

Next, let's figure out the coding for the Select button Click event handler. When this button is clicked, the detailed information about the selected student should be displayed in both six text fields and the Course Selected listbox.

6.4.6.5 Coding for the Select Button Event Handler to Query Data Using the CachedRowSet

Open this event handler and enter the codes that are shown in Figure 6.104 into this event handler. Let's have a closer look at this new added piece of codes to see how it works.

A. As we know, there is no student_name column available in the StudentCourse table, and the only relationship between a student and a course taken by that student is the student_id, which is a primary key in the Student table and a foreign key in the StudentCourse table. In order to pick up all courses taken by the selected student, we need to perform

```
  private void cmdSelectActionPerformed(java.awt.event.ActionEvent evt) {
      // TODO add your handling code here:
A     String strStudent = "SELECT student_id, gpa, credits, major, schoolYear, email FROM Student " +
                          "WHERE student_name = ?";
B     String strStudentCourse = "SELECT course_id FROM StudentCourse WHERE student_id = ?";
      if (ComboMethod.getSelectedItem()== "CachedRowSet Method"){
C        try{
            String url = "jdbc:sqlserver://localhost\\SQL2008EXPRESS:5000;databaseName=CSE_DEPT;";
D           rowSet = new CachedRowSetImpl();
            rowSet.setUrl(url); // set database URL
            rowSet.setUsername("ybai"); // set username
            rowSet.setPassword("reback1956"); // set password
            rowSet.setCommand(strStudent);
E           rowSet.setString(1, ComboName.getSelectedItem().toString());
F           rowSet.execute();
G           while ( rowSet.next() ){
               StudentIDField.setText(rowSet.getString(1));
               GPAField.setText(rowSet.getString(2));
               CreditsField.setText(rowSet.getString(3));
               MajorField.setText(rowSet.getString(4));
               SchoolYearField.setText(rowSet.getString(5));
               EmailField.setText(rowSet.getString(6));
            } // end while
H           rowSet.setCommand(strStudentCourse);
I           rowSet.setString(1, StudentIDField.getText().toString());
J           rowSet.execute();
            int i = 0;
K           String Result[] = {null, null, null, null, null, null, null, null};
L           while (rowSet.next()){
               String sResult = rowSet.getString(1);
               Result[i] = sResult;
               i++;
            }
M           CourseList.setListData(Result);
N           rowSet.close();
         }
O        catch(SQLException e){
            msgDlg.setMessage("RowSet is wrong!" + e.getMessage());
            msgDlg.setVisible(true);
            System.exit( 1 );
         } // end catch
      } // end if
  }
```

Figure 6.104. The coding for the Select button Click event handler.

two queries: first we need to perform a query to the Student table to get a student_id based on the selected student_name, and then we can perform another query to the StudentCourse table based on the student_id to get all courses taken by the selected student. The first SQL query string, strStudent, is created here with a positional parameter, student_name.

B. The second SQL query string strStudentCourse is also created with another positional parameter, student_id.

C. If the user selected the CachedRowSet Method, a try . . . catch block is used to perform this query using the CachedRowSet implementation component. First a database connection url is declared.

D. Then a CachedRowSet implementation object is created with the CachedRowSetImpl() constructor. Also, the new CachedRowSetImpl instance is initialized by calling a sequence of setter methods. The setCommand() method is used to create a executable command object with the first query string as the argument.

E. The setString() method is used to set up the real value for the positional parameter, student_name, which is obtained from the Student Name combo box, ComboName.

F. The query is actual executed by calling the execute() method to perform the first query using the CachedRowSetImpl instance.

G. A while loop is used to repeatedly pick up all six piece of information related to the selected student. The next() method works as the loop condition, and it returns a true as long as a valid row can be found from the returned data for the execution of the CachedRowSetImpl object. The result of running this next() method is to move the cursor that points to the initial position to the first row in the returned data stored in the ResultSet. In fact, only one row is returned and stored in the ResultSet object for the first query, and a sequence of getString() method is used to pick up each column from the ResultSet and assign each of them to the associated text field to display them.

H. To execute the second query, the setCommand() method is called again to create an executable Command object with the second query string as the argument.

I. The setString() method is called to set up the positional parameter, student_id, for the second SQL query statement. The actual value for this parameter can be obtained from the Student ID text field, and we have gotten it from the first query.

J. The query is executed by calling the execute() method to perform the second query using the CachedRowSetImpl instance.

K. In order to pick up the second query result, which contains multiple rows with one column, we need to declare a String array Result[] and initialize it with a null value. This step is necessary, and otherwise a NullPointer exception may be encountered if this array has not been initialized as the project runs later.

L. A while loop is used with the next() method as the loop condition. Each time when the next() method is executed, the cursor in the ResultSet object is moved down one step to point to the next returned row. The getString() method is used to pick up that row and assign it to the local String variable sResult, and furthermore, to the String array Result[]. The index in the getString() method indicates the current column's number, and this process will be continued until all rows have been collected and assigned to the Result[] array.

M. All courses, exactly all course_id, collected and stored in the Result[] array, is assigned to the Course Selected listbox to be displayed in there. The setListData() method is a very useful method and the argument of this method must be an array when this method is used.

N. The CachedRowSetImpl object must be closed when it finished its mission. A close() method is used to perform this job.

O. The catch block is sued to track and monitor any possible exception during this data query process.

Next, let's add and display a student picture for the selected student.

```
A   import java.awt.*;

        ........
        catch(SQLException e){
            msgDlg.setMessage("RowSet is wrong!" + e.getMessage());
            msgDlg.setVisible(true);
            System.exit( 1 );
        } // end catch
      } // end if
B     if (!ShowStudent()){
C        msgDlg.setMessage("No matched student image found!");
         msgDlg.setVisible(true);
      }
  }
```

Figure 6.105. The added codes for displaying a student image.

6.4.6.6 Add and Display a Student Picture for the Selected Student

As we did for the FacultyFrame class, we can add a student picture as a part of student information to be displayed in the Canvas component. The coding is identical with that in Section 6.2.7.3.3, and refers to that section to get more detailed information about this piece of codes. Add the codes that are shown in Figure 6.105 into the Select button Click event handler, exactly add the codes after the catch block in the Select button Click event handler, and the new added codes have been highlighted in bold.

Let's have a closer look at this piece of new added codes to see how it works.

A. Import the java.awt.* package to this class since we need to use some classes and interfaces defined in that package to display a student image.

B. Change the name of the user-defined method from ShowFaculty() to ShowStudent().

C. Change the faculty image to the student image.

Now let's make some modifications to the ShowFaculty() method to make it our new method ShowStudent(). Refer to Section 6.2.7.3.3.2 for the detailed codes for that method, and perform the modifications shown in Figure 6.106 to this method. The modified parts have been highlighted in bold. Let's have a closer look at this piece of modified codes to see how it works.

A. The name of this method is changed to ShowStudent().

B. Since we have only five students in our Student table in our sample database; therefore, the maximum number of the students' images is 4, not 5, because the index of the student image array starts from 0.

C. Add all five students' names into the student name array fname[].

D. Add all five students' images into the student image array fimage[].

At this point, we have almost finished the coding for this StudentFrame class. Before we can run the project to test the function of this piece of codes, we need to finish the

```
A  private boolean ShowStudent(){
       Image img;
B      int imgId = 1, maxNumber = 4, timeout = 1000;
       MediaTracker tracker = new MediaTracker(this);
       String fImage = null;
C      String[] fname = {"Erica Johnson", "Ashly Jade", "Holes Smith", "Andrew Woods", "Blue Valley"};
D      String[] fimage = {"Erica.jpg", "Ashly.jpg", "Holes.jpg", "Andrew.jpg", "Blue.jpg"};
       for (int i=0; i<=maxNumber; i++){
          if (fname[i].equals((String)ComboName.getSelectedItem())){
             fImage = fimage[i];
             break;
          }
       }
       if (fImage != null){
          img = this.getToolkit().getImage(fImage);
          Graphics g = ImageCanvas.getGraphics();
          tracker.addImage(img,imgId);
          try{
             if(!tracker.waitForID(imgId,timeout)){
                msgDlg.setMessage("Failed to load image");
                msgDlg.setVisible(true);
                }//end if
          }catch(InterruptedException e){
             msgDlg.setMessage(e.toString()); msgDlg.setVisible(true);}
             g.drawImage(img, 0, 0, ImageCanvas.getWidth(), ImageCanvas.getHeight(), this);
             return true;
       }
       else{
          return false;
       }
   }
```

Figure 6.106. The codes for the ShowStudent() method.

```
private void cmdExitActionPerformed(java.awt.event.ActionEvent evt) {
     // TODO add your handling code here:
     this.setVisible(false);
     this.dispose();
}
```

Figure 6.107. The coding for the Exit button Click event handler.

coding for the Exit button, exactly for the Exit button Click event handler. Open this event handler and enter the codes that are shown in Figure 6.107 into this event handler.

The function of this piece of codes is very simple. The StudentFrame Form window will be closed and removed from the screen as this button is clicked by the user.

One point to be noted is that you need to copy all students' image files into our current project folder, which is `C:\Chapter 6\SQLSelectObject`, before you can run this StudentFrame class. All student image files can be found from the folder `Image` that is located at the accompanying ftp site (see Chapter 1).

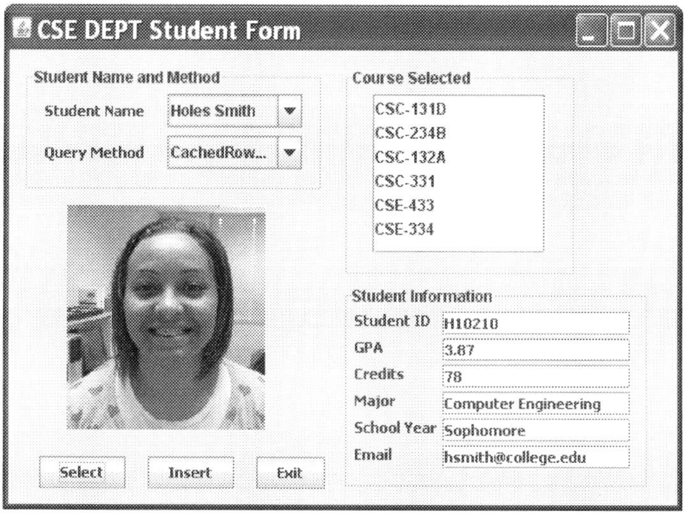

Figure 6.108. A running sample of the StudentFrame Form window.

Now we have completed all coding job for this StudentFrame class. Now let's build and run our project. Click on the Clean and Build Main Project button from the toolbar to build the project. Then right click on the StudentFrame.java from the Projects window, and select the Run File item from the pop-up menu to run the project.

The running status of this StudentFrame object is shown in Figure 6.108.

Select a student from the Student Name combo box and make sure to select the CachedRowSet Method from the Query Method combo box. Then click on the Select button to try to retrieve all pieces of information related to the selected student. A sample running result is shown in Figure 6.108.

Click on the Exit button to close this running project.

A complete project SQLSelectObject can be found from the folder DBProjects\Chapter 6 that is located at the accompanying ftp site (see Chapter 1).

In the next section, we will discuss how to use JDBC API and the runtime object method to perform data query from Oracle databases.

6.5 CREATE A JAVA APPLICATION PROJECT TO ACCESS THE ORACLE DATABASE

Basically, there is no significant difference between a Java database application to access an SQL Server or an Oracle database. Because of the similarity in the coding process for both database applications, we only discuss those differences and highlight those parts in this section.

The following differences are existed between these two database applications:

1. The JDBC Driver
2. The JDBC API package used for the Oracle database interfaces

3. The JDBC database connection url, username and password
4. The protocol and cursor used in the CallableStatements method
5. The protocol used in the RowSet method

We will discuss these differences in more details in the following sections based on the coding process for each JFrame class.

First let's create a new Java Application project named OracleSelectObject using the NetBeans IDE 6.8. Go to the File|New Project menu item to start this process.

- Select the Java Application from the Projects pane, and then click on the Next button.
- Enter OracleSelectObject into the `Project Name` box and uncheck the Create Main Class checkbox, then click on the Finish button.

A new Java Application project OracleSelectObject is created.

6.5.1 Create Graphic User Interfaces

All five GUIs are identical with those we built in the last project SQLSelectObject. Refer to those sections to build these six JFrame classes, LogInFrame, SelectionFrame, FacultyFrame, CourseFrame, StudentFrame, and MsgDialog.

As an example, the steps of creating a LogInFrame class are shown here:

1. Right click on our new project OracleSelectObject from the Projects window.
2. Select the New|JFrame Form item from the pop-up menu.
3. Enter LogInFrame into the Class Name box and type OracleSelectObject in the Package box. Click on the Finish to create this new JFrame class and GUI.

Follow these steps and refer to Section 6.4.1 to finish these GUIs development.

6.5.2 Perform the Data Query for the LogIn Table

First, let's take care of loading and registering the JDBC Driver for Oracle database.

6.5.2.1 Add Oracle JDBC Driver to the Project

Before we can load and register a JDBC driver, first we need to add the Oracle JDBC Driver we downloaded and installed in Section 6.2.1.3 as a library file into our current project Libraries node to enable our project to locate and find it when it is loaded and registered. To do that, follow steps below to finish this adding process:

1. Right click on our project OracleSelectObject from the Projects window and select Properties item from the pop-up menu to open Project Properties pane.
2. In the Categories box, select the Libraries item by clicking on it.
3. Click on the Add JAR/Folder button and browse to the location in which we installed the Oracle JDBC Driver, which is C:\Temp. Click on the driver ojdbc6.jar and click on the Open and OK buttons to add this driver to our project Libraries node.

Next, let's begin to load and register the Oracle JDBC Driver in our project.

6.5.2.2 Load and Register Oracle JDBC Driver

Similar to general JDBC packages, the Oracle core JDBC implementation is involved in two packages:

- oracle.jdbc: this package contains the implementations and extended functions provided by the java.sql and javax.sql interfaces, such as OraclePreparedStatement and OracleCallableStatement.
- oracle.sql: this package includes classes and interfaces that provide Java mappings to SQL data types, such as OracleTypes.

The first step to build a Java database application is to load and register a JDBC driver. Two important components, DriverManager and Driver, are used for this process. As we discussed in Chapter 4, Driver class contains six methods, and one of the most important methods is the connect() method, which is used to connect to the database. When using this Driver class, a point to be noted is that most methods defined in the Driver class never be called directly; instead, they should be called via the DriverManager class methods.

The DriverManager class is a set of utility functions that work with the Driver methods together and manage multiple JDBC drivers by keeping them as a list of drivers loaded. Although loading a driver and registering a driver are two steps, only one method call is necessary to perform these two operations. The operational sequence of loading and registering a JDBC driver is:

1. Call class methods in the DriverManager class to load the driver into the Java interpreter.
2. Register the driver using the registerDriver() method.

When loaded, the driver will execute the DriverManager.registerDriver() method to register itself. The above two operations will never be performed until a method in the DriverManager is executed, which means that even both operations have been coded in an application; however, the driver cannot be loaded and registered until a method such as connect() is first executed.

To load and register an Oracle JDBC driver, two popular methods can be used;

1. Use Class.forName() method: Class.forName("oracle.jdbc.OracleDriver");
2. Create a new instance of the Driver class: Driver oraDriver = new oracle.jdbc.OracleDriver;

The Driver Class name oracle.jdbc.OracleDriver can be found from the Add New Driver process we did in Section 6.2.1.3 (Fig. 6.21).

Relatively speaking, the first method is more professional since the driver is both loaded and registered when a valid method in the DriverManager class is executed. The second method cannot guarantee that the driver has been registered by using the DriverManager. We prefer to use the first method in this application.

6.5.2.3 The JDBC Uniform Resource Locators (URLs)

As we discussed in Section 6.4.2.1.3, a JDBC url is a string used to define the address of the Oracle database to which we need to connect to our Java application. The protocol of this string has been discussed in detail in that section. To an Oracle database, this string can be represented as:

```
jdbc:oracle:driver_type:@database
```

where

- driver_type: indicates the type of a JDBC driver to be used for the database connection. Three options are existed in the Oracle JDBC drivers:
  - oci: is for the Oracle9i and 10g OCI drivers
  - thin: is for the Oracle thin driver
  - kprb: is for the Oracle intern driver
- database: indicates the address to which the database to be connected. The following options are existed:
  - *host:port:sid:* this option works for the thin and the OCI drivers. The host is the host name or IP address of a database server, and the port is the port number of the Oracle listener. Both are similar to those in the SQL Server database. The sid is the Oracle system identifier or Oracle service name of the database.
  - *Net service name:* this is only used for the OCI driver. It is a tnsnames.ora file entry that resolves to a connect descriptor.
  - *Connect descriptor:* this is only used for the OCI or the thin driver. It is the Net8 address specification.

In our application, the driver_type is thin since we are using a thin driver. The database is represented as: localhost:1521:XE. The database server is built in our host computer, therefore the name is localhost. The listener port number is 1521, which can be found from the Oracle database configuration file tnsnames.ora, which is located at the folder `C:\oraclexe\app\oracle\product\ 10.2.0\server\NETWORK\ADMIN` after the Oracle Database 10g XE R2 is installed in our host computer.

Now let's combine all points we discussed above to develop the codes to load and register the Oracle JDBC Driver in our LogInFrame class. Open the Code Window of the LogInFrame by clicking on the Source tab from the top of the window, and enter the codes that are shown in Figure 6.109 into this window. This coding is similar with that we developed for the SQL Server database in Section 6.4.2.1.2. You can copy those codes and paste them into this code window with the modifications that have been highlighted in bold and shown in Figure 6.109.

Let's have a closer look at this piece of modified codes to see how it works.

A. The Oracle driver class name oracle.jdbc.OracleDriver is used here to replace the SQL Server driver class name to perform the loading and registration of the Oracle JDBC Driver.

B. The Oracle database connection string is built to be ready for the database connection.

C. The getConnection() method is called to try to connect to our Oracle sample database CSE_DEPT with a valid username and password as arguments. Refer to Chapter 2 to get more detailed information about this username and password.

A point to be noted for this url is that unlike the url string used for the SQL Server database connection, there is no any semicolon ; at the end of this url string. A NullPointer

```
package OracleSelectObject;
import java.sql.*;

public class LogInFrame extends javax.swing.JFrame {
   static Connection con;
   MsgDialog msgDlg = new MsgDialog(new javax.swing.JFrame(), true);
   /** Creates new form LogInFrame */
   public LogInFrame() {
      initComponents();
      this.setLocationRelativeTo(null);
      try
      {
         //Load and register Oracle driver
A        Class.forName("oracle.jdbc.OracleDriver");
      }
      catch (Exception e) {
         msgDlg.setMessage("Class not found exception!" + e.getMessage());
         msgDlg.setVisible(true);
      }
B     String url = "jdbc:oracle:thin:@localhost:1521:XE";
      //Establish a connection
      try {
C         con = DriverManager.getConnection(url,"CSE_DEPT","reback");
      }
      catch (SQLException e) {
          msgDlg.setMessage("Could not connect!" + e.getMessage());
          msgDlg.setVisible(true);
          e.printStackTrace();
      }
  }
```

Figure 6.109. The modified codes in the LogInFrame class for the Oracle database.

exception may be encountered when the project runs if you did not pay attention to this point.

All other codes, including the codes for the LogIn button click event handler and the codes for the Cancel button Click event handler, are identical with those we developed for the project SQLSelectObject with no modifications.

6.5.3 Develop the Codes for the SelectionFrame Form

The codes for this class are identical with those we did for the SelectionFrame used in the last project SQLSelectObject with no modification at all. You can copy all codes from that class

And paste them into this class in this project.

6.5.4 Perform the Data Query for the Faculty Table

The only modifications we need to make to this class is the coding inside the block of the Java Callable Method, which needs us to build an Oracle package to perform this kind of data query. First, let's create an Oracle package FacultyInfo with a procedure SelectFacultyInfo() embedded in that package.

6.5.4.1 Create an Oracle Package FacultyInfo

As you know, the stored procedure is divided into two categories in the Oracle database: package and procedure, which are defined as:

- A stored procedure that never returns any data is called a procedure
- A stored procedure always returns something is called a package

In our application, we need to call a stored procedure to fetch a row from the Faculty table based on the selected faculty name. Therefore, we need to build an Oracle package since we need our procedure to return something.

Open the Oracle Database 10g XE home page by going to Start|All Programs|Oracle Database 10g Express Edition|Go To Database Home Page items. Log in as a user by entering CSE_DEPT into the Username box and the password reback into the Password box. Click the `Object Browser` and select the Create|Package item to open the `Create Package` window.

Each package has two parts: The definition or specification part and the body part. First, let's create the specification part by checking the Specification radio button, and click the Next button to open the Name page.

Enter the package name FacultyInfo into the name box and click the Next button to go to the specification page.

A default package specification prototype, which includes a procedure and a function, is provided in this page, and you need to use your real specifications to replace those default items. Since we don't need any function for our application, remove the default function prototype, and change the default procedure's name from the test to our procedure name—SelectFacultyInfo. Enter the codes that are shown in Figure 6.110 into this package.

The coding language we used in this section is called `Procedural Language Extension` for SQL or PL/SQL, which is a popular language and widely used in the Oracle database programming.

Refer to Figure 6.110; in line 3, we defined the returned data type as a CURSOR_TYPE by using:

```
TYPE CURSOR_TYPE IS REF CURSOR;
```

since we must use a cursor to return a group of data.

```
create or replace package FacultyInfo
AS
  TYPE CURSOR_TYPE IS REF CURSOR;
  procedure SelectFacultyInfo ( FacultyName IN VARCHAR2,
                                Faculty_Info OUT CURSOR_TYPE);
END;
```

Figure 6.110. The codes for the Oracle package FacultyInfo.

The prototype of the procedure SelectFacultyInfo() is declared in line 4. Two arguments are used for this procedure: input parameter FacultyName, which is indicated as an input by using the keyword IN followed by the data type of VARCHAR2. The output parameter is a cursor named Faculty_Info followed by a keyword OUT. Each PL/SQL statement must be ended with a semi-colon, and this rule is also applied to the END statement.

Click the Finish button to complete this step. You can click the Compile button to compile this specification block if you like. Next, we need to create the body block for this package. Click the Body tab to open the Body page, and click the Edit button to begin to create our body part. Enter the PL/SQL codes, which are shown in Figure 6.111, into this package as the package body.

The real body part starts from the BEGIN statement. The OPEN Faculty_Info FOR command is used to collect the queried result and assigns it to this CURSOR variable, which will be returned to the Java calling program. The real SQL statement follows the OPEN command to perform the data query.

Now let's compile our package by clicking the Compile button. A successful compiling information

```
PL/SQL code successfully compiled (22:20:06)
```

will be displayed if this package is bug free.

Next, let's close the Oracle Database 10g XE and return to our Java application to develop the codes to try to call this package to perform the data query using the CallableStatement method.

6.5.4.2 Develop the Codes to Perform the CallableStatement Query

Open the Select button click event handler in the FacultyFrame Form window, and move to the `Java Callable Method` block and perform the modifications that are shown in Figure 6.112 to this part. The modified parts have been highlighted in bold.

Let's have a closer look at this piece of modified codes to see how it works.

A. The SQL92 syntax is used to call an Oracle package we built in the last section with an embedded stored procedure. The stored procedure SelecteFacultyInfo() must be prefixed with the package name FacultyInfo, and this is required by Oracle databases. Two

```
create or replace package body FacultyInfo
AS
  procedure SelectFacultyInfo (FacultyName IN VARCHAR2,
                               Faculty_Info OUT CURSOR_TYPE)
  AS
  BEGIN
  OPEN Faculty_Info FOR
  SELECT faculty_id, faculty_name, title, office, phone, college, email FROM Faculty
  WHERE faculty_name = FacultyName;
  END;
END;
```

Figure 6.111. The codes for the body part of the Oracle package FacultyInfo.

```
    ................
    if (ComboMethod.getSelectedItem()=="Java Callable Method"){
       CallableStatement cstmt = null;
       try{
A         String cquery = "{call FacultyInfo.SelectFacultyInfo(?, ?)}";
          cstmt = LogInFrame.con.prepareCall(cquery);
          cstmt.setString(1, ComboName.getSelectedItem().toString());
B         cstmt.registerOutParameter(2, oracle.jdbc.OracleTypes.CURSOR);
          cstmt.execute();
C         ResultSet rs = (ResultSet)cstmt.getObject(2);
D         ResultSetMetaData rsmd = rs.getMetaData();
E         while (rs.next()){
            for (int i=1; i <=rsmd.getColumnCount(); i++) {
               f_field[i-1].setText(rs.getString(i));
            }
          }
       } catch (SQLException e){
          msgDlg.setMessage("Error in CallableStatement! " + e.getMessage());
          msgDlg.setVisible(true);
       }
    }
```

Figure 6.112. The modified codes for the Java Callable Method.

positional parameters, the first one is an input and the second is an output, are represented by two question marks as the arguments for this calling. Then the prepareCall() method is executed to create a CallableStatement object, and a setter method is used to set up the input parameter.

B. The second positional parameter, which is an output parameter, is registered with the registerOutParameter() method. The point is that the data type of this parameter is an Oracle Cursor, which is equivalent to a ResultSet, and it can be used to return a collection of queried data; exactly it can be considered as a data table in which the returned data are stored. An Oracle extension Java type, oracle.jdbc.OracleTypes.CURSOR, is used here to define this returned data type. This is a necessary step to register this output parameter. Then the CallableStatement object is executed to perform this data query.

C. The getObject() method is used to pick up the returned data and assigned to a ResultSet object rs.

D. The getMetaData() method is also called to get the detailed information about the returned data stored in the Cursor.

E. A while loop is executed with the next() method as the loop condition. The first next() method moves the cursor one step down to point to the current returned row (exactly only one row is returned). Inside the while loop, a for loop is used to repeatedly pick up each column and assign each of them to the associated text field to display them.

At this point, we have finished all modifications to the FacultyFrame class. Before we can build and run the project to test the functionality of this FacultyFrame object, make sure that all faculty and student image files have been stored in our project folder, which is C:\Chapter 6\ OracleSelectObject. You can copy all faculty and student image files from the folder Images that is located at the accompanying ftp site (see Chapter 1), and paste them to our project folder.

6.5.5 Perform the Data Query for the Course Table

The only modification to this class is the Java Callable Method block in the Select button click event handler. In Section 6.4.5.4, we discussed how to build an SQL stored procedure dbo.FacultyCourse and how to call it using a Java CallableStatement interface. In this section, since we are using an Oracle database, therefore, we need to discuss how to build an Oracle stored procedure. As you know, we need to build an Oracle package and a stored procedure since we need that stored procedure to return a Cursor in which the queried multiple course_id are stored and returned.

6.5.5.1 Create an Oracle Package FacultyCourse

Just as we did in Section 6.5.4.1, to build an Oracle package with a stored procedure embedded, open the Oracle Database 10g XE home page by going to Start|All Programs|Oracle Database 10g Express Edition|Go To Database Home Page items. Login as a user by entering CSE_DEPT into the Username box and the password reback into the Password box. Click the Object Browser and select Create|Package item to open the `Create Package` window.

Check the Specification radio button and click the Next button to open the `Name` page. Enter the package name FacultyCourse into the name box and click the Next button to go to the specification page.

Since we don't need any function for our application, so remove the default function prototype, and change the default procedure's name from the test to our procedure name—SelectFacultyCourse. Enter the codes that are shown in Figure 6.113 into this package.

The prototype of the procedure SelectFacultyCourse() is declared in line 4. Two arguments are used for this procedure: input parameter `FacultyName`, which is indicated as an input by using the keyword IN followed by the data type of VARCHAR2. The output parameter is a cursor named `Faculty_Course` followed by a keyword OUT. Each PL/SQL statement must be ended with a semicolon, and this rule is also applied to the END statement.

Click on the Finish button to complete this step. You can click the Compile button to compile this specification block if you like. Next, we need to create the body block for this package. Click the Body tab to open the `Body` page, and click the Edit button to begin to create our body part. Enter the PL/SQL codes, which is shown in Figure 6.114, into this package as the package body.

Two queries are included in this stored procedure: the first one is to query a faculty_id from the Faculty table based on the input faculty_name, and the second one is to

```
create or replace package FacultyCourse
AS
  TYPE CURSOR_TYPE IS REF CURSOR;
  procedure SelectFacultyCourse ( FacultyName IN VARCHAR2,
                                  Faculty_Course OUT CURSOR_TYPE);
END;
```

Figure 6.113. The codes for the Oracle package FacultyCourse.

```
create or replace package body FacultyCourse
AS
  procedure SelectFacultyCourse ( FacultyName IN VARCHAR2,
                                   Faculty_Course OUT CURSOR_TYPE)  IS
  facultyID VARCHAR2(10);
  BEGIN
  SELECT faculty_id INTO facultyID FROM Faculty
  WHERE faculty_name = FacultyName;
  OPEN Faculty_Course FOR
  SELECT course_id FROM Course
  WHERE faculty_id = facultyID;
  END;
END;
```

Figure 6.114. The codes for the body part of the Oracle package FacultyInfo.

query all course_id from the Course table based on the queried faculty_id from the first query. As we know, there is no faculty_name column available in the Course table, and the only relationship between each course_id, and the associated faculty is the faculty_id, which is a primary key in the Faculty table and foreign key in the Course table. In order to get all course_id related to a faculty, we have to perform two queries from two tables. The advantage of using a stored procedure is that we can combine these two queries into a single procedure to speed up these processes.

The procedure prototype is redeclared in line 3. An IS operator is attached at the end of this prototype, and it is used to replace the AS operator to indicate that this procedure needs to use a local variable facultyID, and this variable will work as an intermediate variable to hold the returned faculty_id from the first query that is located at line 7.

Starting from the BEGIN, our first SQL statement is included in lines 7 and 8. The first query is to get the faculty_id from the Faculty table based on the input parameter FacultyName, which is the first argument of this procedure. A SELECT . . . INTO statement is utilized to temporarily store the returned faculty_id into the local variable facultyID.

The OPEN Faculty_Course FOR command is used to assign the returned data columns from the following query to the cursor variable Faculty_Course. Starting from lines 10 and 11, the second query is declared, and it is to get all course_id taught by the selected faculty from the Course table based on the local variable's value, facultyID, which is obtained from the first query above. The queried results are assigned to the cursor variable Faculty_Course.

Now let's compile our package by clicking the Compile button. A successful compiling information

```
PL/SQL code successfully compiled (15:14:48)
```

will be displayed if this package is bug free, which is shown in Figure 6.115.

The development of our Oracle package is completed, and now let's return to our Java application program to call this package to perform our course query from our Course table.

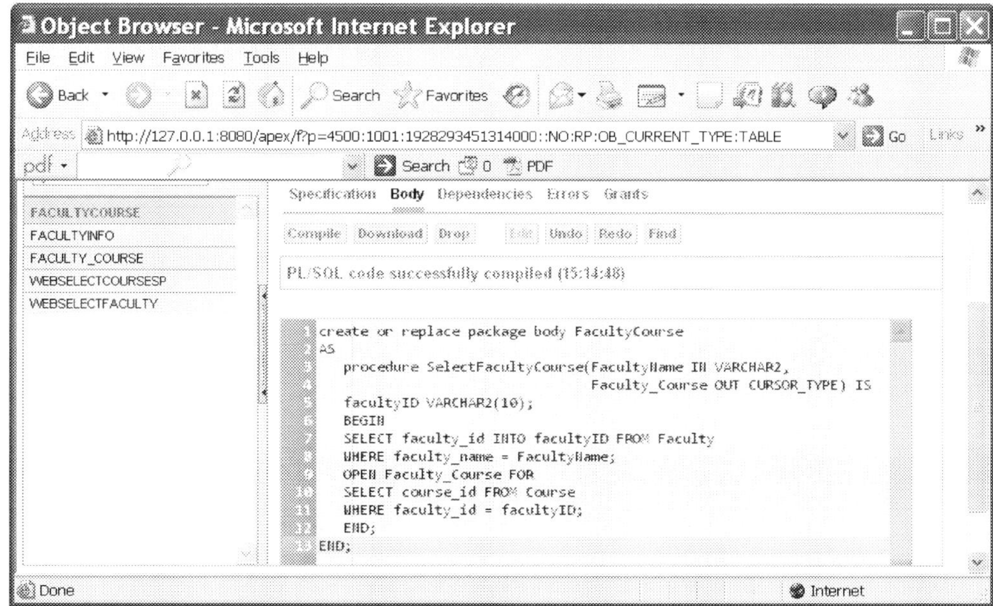

Figure 6.115. The completed Oracle package FacultyCourse.

6.5.5.2 Develop the Codes to Perform the CallableStatement Query

Open the Select button click event handler in the CourseFrame Form window, and move to the `Java Callable Method` block and perform the modifications that are shown in Figure 6.116 to this part. The modified parts have been highlighted in bold.

Let's have a closer look at this piece of modified codes to see how it works.

A. A SQL92 syntax is used to call an Oracle package FacultyCourse we built in the last section. The point to be noted is that the stored procedure SelectFacultyCourse() must be prefixed with the package name when this procedure is called. Two positional parameters are involved in this calling. The first one is an input, faculty_name, and the second is an output, a cursor in which all course_id are stored and returned.

B. The second parameter, which is an output cursor, is registered by calling the registerOutParameter() method. The data type of this parameter, as we mentioned, is a cursor, and this must be clearly indicated with an Oracle extension Java type, oracle.jdbc.OracleTypes.CURSOR.

C. The getObject() method is used to pick up the returned result that is stored in a returned cursor when this CallableStatement is done, and assign it to the ResultSet object.

D. A blank String array cResult[] is created, and this array is used to hold each column from the returned cursor.

E. A while loop is used with the next() method as the loop condition. First, the next() method moves the cursor one step down to point to the current or a valid row. The getString(1) method is used to pick up the returned row and assign it to one element in the blank String array cResult[]. Exactly, only one row is returned (this is indicated by the index of 1 in the

```
  private void cmdSelectActionPerformed(java.awt.event.ActionEvent evt) {
     // TODO add your handling code here:
     if (ComboMethod.getSelectedItem()=="Java Callable Method"){
        CallableStatement cstmt = null;
        try{
A             String query = "{call FacultyCourse.SelectFacultyCourse(?, ?)}";
              cstmt = LogInFrame.con.prepareCall(query);
              cstmt.setString(1, ComboName.getSelectedItem().toString());
B             cstmt.registerOutParameter(2, oracle.jdbc.OracleTypes.CURSOR);
              cstmt.execute();
C             ResultSet rs = (ResultSet)cstmt.getObject(2);
              int i = 0;
D             String cResult[] = {null, null, null, null, null, null, null, null, null};
E             while (rs.next()){
                 cResult[i] = rs.getString(1);
                 i++;
              }
F             CourseList.setListData(cResult);
         }
G        catch (SQLException e){
            msgDlg.setMessage("Error in CallableStatement! " + e.getMessage());
            msgDlg.setVisible(true);
         }
     }
  }
```

Figure 6.116. The modified codes for the Java Callable Method.

getString() method), and each next() method is used to move and point to each column until all columns have been selected and picked up.

F. All collected course_id is assigned to the Course ID List listbox by calling the method setListData() and all of them are displayed in there.

G. The catch block is sued to monitor and display any possible exception during the project runs.

Before we can build and run this project to test the functionality of the CallableStatement interface, we need to do one more thing, which is to develop the codes for the CourseListValueChanged() event handler to display detailed information for each selected course_id from the Course ID List listbox. To save time and space, you can copy those codes from the same event handler we developed in Section 6.4.5.5 and paste them into this event handler. Open the Design View of the CourseFrame Form window by clicking on the Design tab on the top of the window, and then right click on the Course ID List listbox and select the item Events|ListSelection|valueChanged to open this event handler. Now you can copy and paste those codes into this event handler. To access those codes, open the project SQLSelectObject, which can be found from the folder DBProjects\Chapter 6 that is located at the accompanying ftp site (see Chapter 1).

Now we can build and run our project. You may encounter some compiling errors, and that does not matter since all of those errors are coming from the StudentFrame class, and we will correct them in the following section. Just click on the Run Anyway button to continue to run the project.

6.5.6 Query Data from the Student Table Using the Java RowSet Object

The codes for this StudentFrame class are basically identical with those we did for the SQLSelectObject project in Section 6.4.6. The only modifications we need to make are the codes related to the Oracle JDBC Driver class name and connection url, since we need to use the RowSet object to access an Oracle database in this section.

Two event handlers contain the codes that involve with the JDBC Driver class name and the connection url: the constructor of the StudentFrame class and the Select button Click event handler. Let's first pay attention to the codes in the constructor.

6.5.6.1 Modify the Codes in the Constructor of the StudentFrame Class

Open the constructor of the StudentFrame class and perform the modifications that are shown in Figure 6.117. The modified parts have been highlighted with boldface.

The only modification is to change the JDBC Driver class name from an SQL JDBC Driver class name to the Oracle JDBC Driver class name oracle.jdbc.OracleDriver. This class name can be found when you add the Oracle JDBC Driver to our project in Section 6.5.2.1. Refer to that section to get more detailed information for this driver class name.

6.5.6.2 Modify the Codes in the Select Button Click Event Handler

Open the Select button Click event handler in the StudentFrame Form and perform the modifications that are shown in Figure 6.118 to this event handler. The modified parts have been highlighted in bold.

```
public class StudentFrame extends javax.swing.JFrame {
    MsgDialog msgDlg = new MsgDialog(new javax.swing.JFrame(), true);
    CachedRowSet rowSet = null;

    /** Creates new form StudentFrame */
    public StudentFrame() {
        initComponents();
        this.setLocationRelativeTo(null);
        ComboMethod.addItem("JPA Wizards Method");
        ComboMethod.addItem("Runtime Object Method");
        ComboMethod.addItem("CachedRowSet Method");
        ComboName.addItem("Erica Johnson");
        ComboName.addItem("Ashly Jade");
        ComboName.addItem("Holes Smith");
        ComboName.addItem("Andrew Woods");
        ComboName.addItem("Blue Valley");
        try
        {
            //Load and register SQL Server driver
A           Class.forName("oracle.jdbc.OracleDriver");
        }
        catch (Exception e) {
            msgDlg.setMessage("Class not found exception!" + e.getMessage());
            msgDlg.setVisible(true);
        }
    }
```

Figure 6.117. The modified codes for the constructor of the StudentFrame class.

```
private void cmdSelectActionPerformed(java.awt.event.ActionEvent evt) {
    // TODO add your handling code here:
    String strStudent = "SELECT student_id, gpa, credits, major, schoolYear, email FROM Student " +
                        "WHERE student_name = ?";
    String strStudentCourse = "SELECT course_id FROM StudentCourse WHERE student_id = ?";
    if (ComboMethod.getSelectedItem()== "CachedRowSet Method"){
      try{
A        String url = "jdbc:oracle:thin:@localhost:1521:XE";
         rowSet = new CachedRowSetImpl();
         rowSet.setUrl(url); // set database URL
B        rowSet.setUsername("CSE_DEPT"); // set username
C        rowSet.setPassword("reback"); // set password
         rowSet.setCommand(strStudent);
         rowSet.setString(1, ComboName.getSelectedItem().toString());
         rowSet.execute();
         while ( rowSet.next() ){
            StudentIDField.setText(rowSet.getString(1));
            GPAField.setText(rowSet.getString(2));
            CreditsField.setText(rowSet.getString(3));
            MajorField.setText(rowSet.getString(4));
            SchoolYearField.setText(rowSet.getString(5));
            EmailField.setText(rowSet.getString(6));
         } // end while
         rowSet.setCommand(strStudentCourse);
         rowSet.setString(1, StudentIDField.getText().toString());
         rowSet.execute();
         int i = 0;
         String Result[] = {null, null, null, null, null, null, null, null};
         while (rowSet.next()){
            String sResult = rowSet.getString(1);
            Result[i] = sResult;
            i++;
         }
         CourseList.setListData(Result);
         rowSet.close();
      } catch(SQLException e){
         msgDlg.setMessage("RowSet is wrong!" + e.getMessage());
         msgDlg.setVisible(true);
         System.exit( 1 );
      } // end catch
    } // end if
    if (!ShowStudent()){
      msgDlg.setMessage("No matched student image found!");
      msgDlg.setVisible(true);
    }
}
```

Figure 6.118. The modified codes for the Select button Click event handler.

Let's have a closer look at this piece of modified codes to see how it works.

A. The content of the connection url string has been changed to an Oracle url: jdbc:oracle:thin:@localhost:1521:XE. For detailed information about this url string, refer to Section 6.5.2.3, since we have provided a very detailed discussion about this string in there.

B. The CSE_DEPT is used as the username for our sample database and set up by using the setUsername() method. For more detailed information about this username, refer to Section 2.11.1 in Chapter 2, and we use it when we built our sample database.

C. The reback is used as the password to access to our sample database. Similarly, refer to Section 2.11.1 in Chapter 2 to get more detailed information about this password.

At this point, we have finished all modifications for the StudentFrame class. Now you can build and run this program by right clicking on the StudentFrame object from the Projects window, and select the Run File item from the pop-up menu.

Select CachedRowSet Method from the `Query Method` combo box and click on the Select button to try to perform a data query using the `CachedRowSet` method. Immediately, the selected information about a student is returned and displayed in all text fields. Also, a student image is displayed in the Canvas object. A running sample of this StudentFrame program is shown in Figure 6.119.

Click on the Exit button to terminate our project.

A complete Java application project OracleSelectObject can be found from the folder DBProjects\Chapter 6 that is located at the accompanying ftp site (see Chapter 1).

6.6 CHAPTER SUMMARY

Two Java database programming methods are discussed in detailed in this chapter: using JPA (JPA) Wizards and using Java runtime object to access relational databases and perform data queries. Unlike traditional professional Java database programming books, in which a huge block of codes starting from the first page and ending the last page is involved in the whole book, in this book, a new programming method—using JPA to map each relational database component to a class and perform the data query using that entity classes. By using this new method, the coding development process in the Java database programming can be significantly simplified. With a few lines of codes, a professional and practical Java database project can be built and executed in a so simple way!

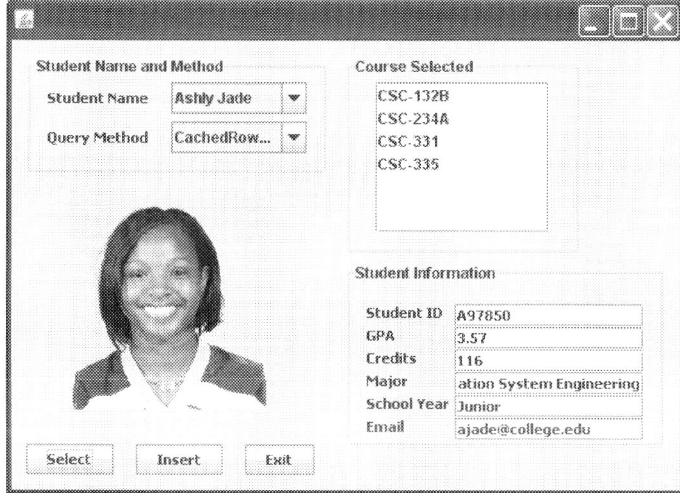

Figure 6.119. A running sample of the StudentFrame object.

The learning curve can be greatly reduced to the students and beginners in database programming, and the learning interests in this topic can also be improved significantly.

The JPA Wizards database programming technique is introduced first with two real sample projects: SelectQueryWizard and OracleSelectWizard. The coding development and building process are discussed in details, step by step and line by line, to provide readers a clear picture in how to build a JPA Wizard database project using the JPA components. The discussion in this part can be divided into the following sections:

- Architecture and Function of JPA
- Connect to Different Databases and Drivers Using JPA Wizards
- Query Data Using JPA Wizards

Some new and key techniques in using JPA to access popular databases, SQL Server and Oracle, to perform novel actions are discussed and covered in this section, which include:

1. Connect to the Microsoft SQL Server 2008 Express database
2. Connect to the Oracle Database 10g Express Edition database
3. Using JPA to create static and dynamic query strings to perform join column query

It looks like that both the first and the second techniques are not novel; however, so many technique difficulties and configuration challenges are involved in this connection topic, and no one can find these technique tricks from other similar books and sites.

For the third technique, any one-to-many or many-to-one relationship between tables, such as a primary key in a table, is connected to a foreign key in another table, and is always mapped to an object in a JPA mapped entity class. In order to perform a data query, we need to use the primary key as the query criterion. You have to figure out how to use that primary key that is an object, not a query string, to work as a query criterion. You cannot find a solution for this issue from any similar books or sites.

Starting from the second part, the Java runtime object method is discussed in detail with two real sample projects: SQLSelectObject and OracleSelectObject. With a lot of coding developments and dynamic parameters set ups, more complicated techniques in Java database programming are discussed and analyzed, which include:

- How to perform a dynamic data query using standard JDBC drivers, such as:
  1. Load and register database drivers
  2. Connect to databases and drivers
  3. Create and manage PreparedStatement object to perform dynamic query
  4. Use ResultSet object to pick up queried result
  5. Query data using JDBC MetaData interface
  6. The ParameterMetaData interface
  7. Use DatabaseMetaData interface
  8. Use ResultSetMetaData interface
  9. Query data using the CallableStatement method
- Query data using the Java RowSet object

The novel and key technique discussed in this part is the interface between an SQL stored procedure and a Java CallableStatement interface. Regularly, there is no mapped partner for the cursor data type in the JDBC data type; in other words, a cursor applied in the SQL Server stored procedure cannot be returned to a Java database application since the cursor cannot be mapped to a valid JDBC data type. In order to solve that problem, we developed a special SQL stored procedure to perform the conversion between a VARCHAR string and a cursor inside the SQL stored procedure, and returned a VARCHAR string to the Java database application.

Very detailed discussions in how to build SQL stored procedures and Oracle packages are provided in this part, too, to give readers a fully and clear picture in how to interface between a CallableStatement interface and a database stored procedure. Two popular databases are involved in this part: SQL Server and Oracle.

HOMEWORK

I. True/False Selections

____**1.** Java Persistence API is the standard API used for the management of the persistent data and object/relational mapping.

____**2.** The so-called persistence languages mean that those languages are non-Java programming languages.

____**3.** The Java Persistence API contains the following components: Java Persistence API, O-R mapping metadata, and persistence language.

____**4.** Each column in a data table in a relational database can be mapped to an entity class using the Java Persistence API.

____**5.** One does not need to change the TCP/IP port number when connecting to an SQL Server 2008 Express database since the default port number is 1434.

____**6.** Both JDBC Drivers for SQL Server and Oracle databases, Microsoft SQL Server JDBC Driver 2.0 and Oracle JDBC driver ojdbc6.jar, are type IV drivers.

____**7.** By using the JPA, each table in a relational database can be mapped to an entity class, and each column in that table can be mapped to a property in the entity class.

____**8.** After using the JPA to map all tables and columns in a relational database to entity classes and properties, one can still access those columns by using the original column names using Java Persistence Query language (JPQL).

____**9.** The Java Persistence Query Language (JPQL) is a platform-independent object-oriented query language that is defined as part of the Java Persistence API specification. JPQL is used to make queries against objects defined in the entity classes mapped from a relational database.

___**10.** A static query is called a Named Query and it is defined statically with the help of annotation or XML before the entity class is created.

___**11.** Dynamic queries belong to queries in which the query strings are provided at runtime or created dynamically. All callings to EntityManager.createQuery(queryString) are actually creating dynamic query objects.

___**12.** The java.awt package contains all basic and fundamental graphic user interface components. However, the javax.swing package contains extensions of java.awt, which means that all components in the javax.swing package have been built into a Model-View-Controller (MVC) mode.

___**13.** Only one way can be used to load and register a JDBC Driver during a project runs, which is to use the Class.forName() method.

___**14.** When using the getConnection() method in the DriverManager class to perform a database connection, the connection is made as soon as this instruction runs.

___**15.** The executeQuery() method will definitely return a query result, but the executeUpdate() method will never return any result.

___**16.** When a query is performed and a ResultSet is created, you need to retrieve the queried result from the ResultSet object by using a suitable getXXX() method.

___**17.** The advantage of using the getObject() method is that a returned datum, which is stored in a ResultSet object and its data type is unknown, can be automatically converted from its SQL data type to the ideal Java data type.

___**18.** The SQL92 syntax can only be used for calling an SQL stored procedure, not for an Oracle package or stored procedure.

___**19.** One has to use the registerOutParameter() method to register any output parameter in an SQL statement to allow the CallableStatement to know that there is an OUT parameter in that query and the returned value should be stored in that parameter.

___**20.** When using a Java RowSet object to query data, one has to create an instance of the RowSet Implementation class, not the RowSet class itself, since all RowSet classes are abstract classes.

II. Multiple Choices

1. The sequence to perform a data query from a database using a JDBC driver is _____

- **a.** Connect to database, load JDBC driver, perform the query, get result from ResultSet
- **b.** Perform the query, connect to database, load JDBC driver, get result from ResultSet
- **c.** Get result from ResultSet, connect to database, load JDBC driver, perform the query
- **d.** load JDBC driver, connect to database, perform the query, get result from ResultSet

2. Three components included in a JPA are ________

- **a.** Java Persistence API, O-R mapping metadata, Java Persistence query language
- **b.** Java Persistence API, JDBC metadata, Java Persistence query language
- **c.** Java Persistence API, O-R mapping metadata, Java Entity classes
- **d.** JDBC driver, O-R mapping metadata, Java Persistence query language

3. A data table can be mapped to a ______ by the JPA.

- **a.** Property
- **b.** Class
- **c.** Object
- **d.** Entity class

4. The difference between a JPQL and a standard SQL query string is that a(n) _______ is used and prefixed for each clause.

- **a.** Class name
- **b.** An abstract schema
- **c.** Property name
- **d.** A object schema

5. A named query can be considered as a ________ query.

- **a.** Dynamic
- **b.** Instance

c. Object
d. Static

6. One needs to use a ______ object as an image holder, a ______ object as a tool to display an image, and a _______ class as a monitor to coordinate the image processing.

   a. Canvas, MediaTracker, Graphics
   b. Graphics, MediaTracker, Canvas
   c. Canvas, Graphics, MediaTracker
   d. MediaTracker, Graphics, Canvas

7. Generally, a connection url contains three parts or three segments; _________, _________, and ________ for the database to be connected.

   a. Subname, subprotocol, subprotocol name
   b. Protocol name, subprotocol, subname
   c. Protocol name, subprotocol name, subname
   d. Protocol, subprotocol, subname

8. The execute() method can ____________.

   a. Not return any result
   b. Return some results
   c. Be used either to return a result or not return any result
   d. None of above

9. To distinguish or identify the data type returned by the execute() method, one needs to ________________.

   a. Use the getResultSet() method
   b. Use the getUpdateCount() method
   c. Use either of them
   d. Use both of them

10. The ResultSet object can be created by either executing the __________ or _________ method, which means that the ResultSet instance cannot be created or used without executing a query operation first.

    a. executeQuery(), getResultSet()
    b. getResultSet(), execute()
    c. createResultSet(), getResultSet()
    d. buildResultSet(), executeQuery()

11. The cursor in a ResultSet object can be moved by executing the __________ method.

    a. move()
    b. first()
    c. next()
    d. last()

12. A cursor in the Oracle database can be mapped to an ________________ data type.

    a. jdbc.oracle.CURSOR
    b. oracle.jdbc.OracleTypes.CURSOR
    c. oracle.jdbc.CURSOR
    d. jdbc.CURSOR

13. A __________ object, which contains all pieces of necessary information about the returned data stored in a ResultSet instance, is returned when the __________ method is executed.
    - **a.** getMetaData(), ResultSetMetaData
    - **b.** ResultSet, getMetaData()
    - **c.** getResultSet, ResultSet
    - **d.** ResultSetMetaData, getMetaData()
14. A CallableStatement can either return a ________ object and multiple ResultSet objects by using executeQuery() method or return nothing by using ________ method.
    - **a.** ResultSetMetaData, getResultSet()
    - **b.** Cursor, getCursor()
    - **c.** Object, getObject()
    - **d.** ResultSet, execute()
15. Two parts exist in an Oracle Package, and they are _____ and _____
    - **a.** Specification, body
    - **b.** Definition, specifications
    - **c.** Body, specification
    - **d.** Specification, execution

III. Exercises

1. Open the JPA mapped Entity class StudentCourse.java in the project SelectQueryWizard, answer and explain the following questions:
    - **a.** The column student_id and course_id have been mapped to studentId and courseId, respectively. What are the data types for these two mapped objects?
    - **b.** Why these two columns are mapped to this data type? Why all other columns are mapped to the Integer or the String data types?
    - **c.** How many static query methods have been created in this mapped entity class? What are they?
2. If we want to perform a query from the StudentCourse table using the StudentFrame class, how can we use the studentId and courseId as the query criteria and write them in the query statements (both of them are objects in the mapped entity class file, not String variables)?
3. List five steps to build a data query from a Java database application project to a relational database using the Java runtime object method.
4. Using Java JPA Wizards to perform the data query from the Student and StudentCourse tables with the StudentFrame class in the project SelectQueryWizard (the project file can be found from the folder DBProjects\Chapter 6 that is located at the accompanying ftp site [see Chapter 1]). The procedures to develop this data query include the steps listed below:
    - **a.** Refer to project SQLSelectObject, which can be found from the folder DBProjects\Chapter 6 that is located at the accompanying ftp site (see Chapter 1), to build the StudentFrame Form window.
    - **b.** Develop the codes for the StudentFrame class to perform the data query
    - **c.** Modify the codes in the SelectionFrame class to make a smooth switch from the SelectionFrame Form to the StudentFrame Form.
5. Using Java CallableStatement method to develop the data query from the Student and StudentCourse tables with the StudentFrame class in the OracleSelectObject project (the project file can be found from the folder DBProjects\Chapter 6 that is located at the accompa-

nying ftp site (see Chapter 1). The procedures to develop this data query include the steps listed below:

   a. Build an Oracle package StudentInfo using the Object Browser method in the Oracle Database 10g XE.

   b. Develop the codes for the StudentFrame class to perform the data query to that Oracle package (adding an else if block to the Select button Click event handler).

6. Develop a method by adding some codes into the LogIn button Click event handler in the LogInFrame class in the project OracleSelectObject to allow users to try the login process only three times. A warning message should be displayed and the project should be exited after three times of trying to login but all of them are failed.

7. Using Procedural Language Extension for SQL (PL-SQL) to create a Package GetStudent in the Object Browser page of Oracle Database 10g XE. The Package contains two stored procedures; the first one is used for query the student_id from the Student table based on the input student name, and the second is to query all course_id taken by the selected student from the StudentCourse table based on the student_id retrieved from the first stored procedure. Compile this package after it is created to confirm that it works.

8. Using JPA Wizards to call the package GetStudent developed in exercise 4 in the project OracleSelectWizard. The procedures to develop this data query include the steps listed below:

   a. Refer to project OracleSelectObject to build a StudentFrame Form window (the project OracleSelectObject can be found from the folder DBProjects\Chapter 6 that is located at the accompanying ftp site—see Chapter 1).

   b. Develop the codes for the StudentFrame class to perform the data query to that Oracle package (using CallableStatement interface).

Chapter 7

Insert, Update, and Delete Data from Databases

Similarly to manipulating data in Visual Studio.NET, when manipulating data in the Java NetBeans IDE environment, two manipulating modes or methods can be utilized: Java Persistence API (JPA) Wizards and runtime object method. Traditional Java codes (SDK 1.x) only allow users to access databases with a sequence of codes, starting from creating a DriverManager to load the database driver, setting up a connection using the Driver, creating a query statement object, running the `executeQuery` object, and processing the data using a ResultSet object. This coding is not a big deal to the experienced programmers; however, it may be a headache to the college students or beginners who are new to the Java database programming. In order to effectively remove the headache caused by the huge blocks of coding and reduce the learning curve, in this chapter, we introduce two methods to perform the database manipulations: JPA Wizards with the NetBeans IDE 6.8 and regular Java runtime object method.

In the following sections, we will concentrate on inserting, updating, and deleting data against our sample database using Java Persistence API.

If you check the JPQL library, you will find that the JPQL only provides the Update and Delete identifiers with no Insert identifier available. In fact, it is unnecessary to provide a mapping between a record and an entity class; instead, we can directly insert a new object into the different entity using the `persist()` method in JPQL.

SECTION I INSERT, UPDATE AND DELETE DATA USING JAVA PERSISTENCE API WIZARDS

In Chapter 6, we have provided a very detailed discussion and quite a few implementations on JPA and its wizards. In this chapter, we want to extend these knowledge and implementations to data manipulations against our sample database. You would find how easy it is to make database manipulations using the JPA in this Chapter, and I bet you that you will like it!

Generally, to perform data manipulation against a database using JPA wizards, we need to perform the following operations:

Practical Database Programming with Java, First Edition. Ying Bai.

1. Set a connection to our target database using JPA Wizards.
2. Use JPA to build entity classes from our target database.
3. Add the entity manager and JPA components into the our applications.
4. Use entity classes to build manipulating queries to perform data manipulations.
5. Use JPA wizards to check and validate data manipulation results.
6. Disconnect our target database.

Operational steps 1–3 have been discussed and illustrated in detail with a lot of real examples in Chapter 6. Please refer to associated sections in that chapter to get more detailed information for them. In this chapter, we will start from step 4 and use some finished projects we built in Chapter 6 as examples to illustrate how to

- Build data manipulating queries using entity classes.
- Use JPA wizards to check and validate data manipulation results.

Because the SQL Server and Oracle databases are most popular databases and widely implemented in most businesses, in this Chapter, we will concentrate on using these two kinds of databases.

To save the time and space, we can use some finished projects we built in Chapter 6 and modify some codes in certain Frames to perform data manipulations to our target databases. First, let's start with the data insertion manipulations to the SQL Server database.

7.1 PERFORM DATA MANIPULATIONS TO SQL SERVER DATABASE USING JPA WIZARDS

Let's take care of the data insertion to the SQL Server database using the JPA Wizards.

7.1.1 Perform Data Insertion to SQL Server Database Using JPA Wizards

We want to use and modify a finished project SelectQueryWizard we built in the last chapter to develop the data insertion function using the JPA wizards. Perform the following operations to complete this project transferring:

1. Open the Windows Explorer and create a new folder, such as JavaDBProject\Chapter 7.
2. Open a Web browser and go to the folder DBProjects\Chapter 6 that is located at the Wiley ftp site (refer to Figure 1.2 in Chapter 1).
3. Copy the project SelectQueryWizard from that folder and paste it to our new folder JavaDBProject\Chapter 7.

Now, we are ready to build our data insertion query to perform data manipulations to our SQL Server sample database CSE_DEPT.

In Section 6.2.7.1 in Chapter 6, we have created a FacultyFrame class and Faculty JFrame window FacultyFrame. Also, the following components have been added into that project:

- The Faculty Entity Manager has been added into the FacultyFrame class.
- The SQL Server sample database has been connected to our project.

In this section, we want to use the Insert button that has been added into the FacultyFrame window to perform this data insertion function.

7.1.1.1 Modify the FacultyFrame Window Form

First, let's modify the FacultyFrame form by adding three more Text Fields into this frame: two of them are added into the Faculty Information panel to enable us to insert a faculty record, and one them is added at the top of the faculty image box to allow us to insert a new faculty image (exactly the location of the faculty image).

Perform the following operations to open our pasted project SelectQueryWizard:

1. Launch the NetBeans IDE 6.8 and go to `File > Open Project` menu item to open the `Open Project` wizard.
2. Browse to the location where we copied and pasted our project SelectQueryWizard, which is JavaDBProject\Chapter 7. Make sure that the `Open as Main Project` checkbox has been checked, and select this project and click on the `Open Project` button to open it.
3. The point to be noted is that you now have two SelectQueryWizard projects in the NetBeans IDE, but they are different projects with different functions. The first SelectQueryWizard was built in Chapter 6 without data manipulation function, but this second project will be built in Chapter 7 with the data manipulation function.
4. Expand this project files to open the FacultyFrame.java file by double clicking on this file that is located under the `Source Packages\LogInFramePackage` node.
5. Click on the `Design` button at the top of this window to open the GUI window of this FacultyFrame class.

Perform the following operations to add three more Text Fields into this frame window:

- Enlarge the FacultyFrame window form and the `Faculty Information` panel.
- Add two more labels and two more Text fields into this `Faculty Information` panel, and one more label and the associated Text Field to the top of the Faculty Image box with the properties shown in Table 7.1.

Table 7.1. Objects and controls added into the faculty frame window

Type	Variable Name	Text	editable	Title
Label	Label1	Faculty ID		
Text Field	FacultyIDField		No check	
Label	Label2	Name		
Text Field	FacultyNameField		checked	
Label	Label3	Faculty Image		
Text Field	FacultyImageField		checked	

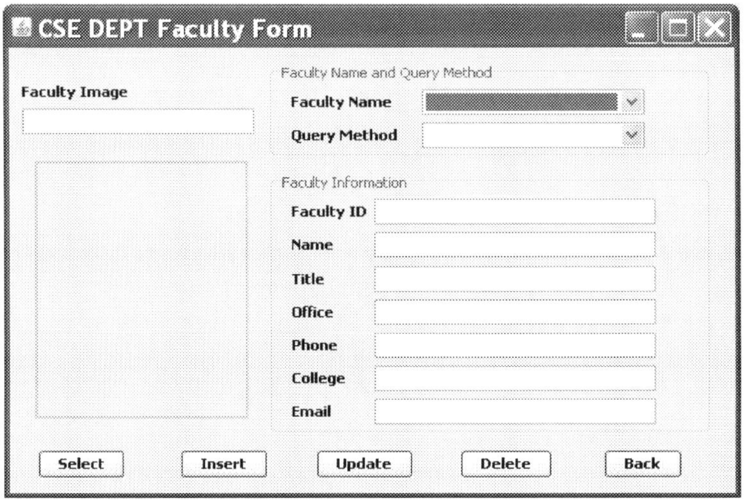

Figure 7.1. The modified FacultyFrame form window.

One point to be noted is the FacultyIDField, and its editable property is unchecked, which means that we do not want users to modify the faculty_id as the project runs because we will not update it during a faculty record updating process.

Your finished modified FacultyFrame form window is shown in Figure 7.1.

Now let's develop the codes for the Insert button click event handler to perform the data insertion function as the project runs. Before we can do that, first, let's take a closer look at the persist tool since the JPQL did not provide a direct Insert command, and therefore we have to use this tool to perform the data insertion function.

7.1.1.2 The Persist Method in the EntityManager Class

Persist is a Java-based Object Relational Mapping (ORM) and Data Access Object (DAO) tool. It provides only the minimal amount of functionalities necessary to map objects or maps from database queries and to statement parameters.

An EntityManager instance is associated with a persistence context. A persistence context is a set of entity instances in which for any persistent entity identity there is a unique entity instance. Within the persistence context, the entity instances and their lifecycle are managed. The EntityManager interface defines the methods that are used to interact with the persistence context. The EntityManager API is used to create and remove persistent entity instances, to find entities by their primary key, and to query over entities.

The set of entities that can be managed by a given EntityManager instance is defined by a persistence unit. A persistence unit defines the set of all classes that are related or grouped by the application, and which must be co-located in their mapping to a single database.

The EntityManager is the primary interface used by application developers to interact with the JPA runtime. The methods of the EntityManager can be divided into the following functional categories:

- **Transaction Association**
  Every EntityManager has a one-to-one relation with an EntityTransaction instance. In fact, many vendors use a single class to implement both the EntityManager and EntityTransaction interfaces. If an application requires multiple concurrent transactions, one will use multiple EntityManagers.
  One can retrieve the EntityTransaction associated with an EntityManager through the `getTransaction()` method. Note that most JPA implementations can integrate with an application server's managed transactions. If one takes advantage of this feature, one will control transactions by declarative demarcation or through the Java Transaction API (JTA) rather than through the EntityTransaction.
- **Entity Lifecycle Management**
  EntityManagers perform several actions that affect the lifecycle state of entity instances.

The `persist()` method, which belongs to the persistence unit, is used to add all necessary entities into the persistence context that can be managed by the EntityManager. For any data manipulation, such as Update, Delete, and even the execution of the `persist()` method, a Transaction Association must be started to monitor and execute this data manipulation. This is different with the data query, such as SELECT statement, in which no Transaction Association is needed.

Generally, to perform a data manipulation using the EntityManager and entities defined by the persistence unit, the following operational sequence should be executed:

1. An EntityManager instance that controls this data manipulation should be created.
2. A Transaction Association instance should be created using the `getTransaction()` method.
3. The created Transaction Association instance should be started by calling the `begin()` method.
4. Each entity instance involved in this data manipulation should be added into the persistence context by executing the `persist()` method one by one.
5. The data manipulation is performed by executing the `commit()` method.
6. The EntityManager instance should be closed after this data manipulation.

A piece of example codes used to insert two entities, magazine and publisher, into two entity classes that can be mapped to two tables, mag and pub, is shown in Figure 7.2.

```
A   Magazine mag = new Magazine("1B78-YU9L", "JavaWorld");

B   Company pub = new Company("Weston House");
C   pub.setRevenue(1750000D);
    mag.setPublisher(pub);
    pub.addMagazine(mag);

D   EntityManager em = emf.createEntityManager();

E   em.getTransaction().begin();
F   em.persist(mag);
    em.persist(pub);

G   em.getTransaction().commit();

    // or we could continue using the EntityManager...
H   em.close();
```

Figure 7.2. The operational sequence of perform a data manipulation using the EntityManager.

Let's have a closer look at this piece of codes to see how it works.

A. A new `Magazine` entity instance `mag` is created.

B. A new `Company` entity instance `pub` is created, too.

C. The entity instances are initialized using the `setXXX()` method to set all properties.

D. A new EntityManager instance is created that is used to manage this data manipulation.

E. A new Transaction Association instance is created and started using the `getTransaction()` and `begin()` method, respectively.

F. The `persist()` method is called two times to add these two entity instances into two entities.

G. The `commit()` method is called to execute this addition.

H. The EntityManager instance is removed if it is no longer to be used.

Now that we have a basic idea about the persistence unit, next, let's develop our codes for the Insert button click event handler to perform a data insertion using the persist tool.

7.1.1.3 Develop the Codes for the Insert Button Event Handler

The main function of this handler is to insert a new faculty record with a set of new faculty information, including the faculty id, faculty name, office, title, phone, graduated college, and email. A photo is an optional to a new faculty record. In this application, to make it simple, we assume that a default image Default.jpg has been created for this new faculty. When inserting a new faculty record into the Faculty table, you have the option to insert a new faculty image by entering the location of that image into the Faculty Image Text Field, or no faculty image by leaving that Text Field empty.

Double click on the Insert button to open its event handler and enter the codes that shown in Figure 7.3 into the opened Insert button's event handler.

```
  private void cmdInsertActionPerformed(java.awt.event.ActionEvent evt) {
      // TODO add your handling code here:
A     SelectQueryWizardPUEntityManager.clear();
B     final Faculty ft = new Faculty();
C     ft.setFacultyId(FacultyIDField.getText());
      ft.setFacultyName(FacultyNameField.getText());
      ft.setTitle(TitleField.getText());
      ft.setOffice(OfficeField.getText());
      ft.setPhone(PhoneField.getText());
      ft.setCollege(CollegeField.getText());
      ft.setEmail(EmailField.getText());
D     javax.persistence.EntityTransaction trr = SelectQueryWizardPUEntityManager.getTransaction();
E     if (!trr.isActive()){
         trr.begin();
      }
F     SelectQueryWizardPUEntityManager.persist(ft);
G     trr.commit();
H     ComboName.addItem(FacultyNameField.getText());
  }
```

Figure 7.3. The newly added codes to the Insert button click event handler.

Let's have a closer look at this piece of newly added codes to see how it works.

A. First, we need to clean up the entity manager SelectQueryWizardPUEntityManager by calling the `clear()` method to make sure it is clean and ready to create new queries. The point to be noted is that this new EntityManager instance has been created before when we created and configured this FacultyFrame form window.

B. Since the JPQL did not provide a direct Insert command, therefore, we have to use the `persist()` method to do this insertion. To do that, a new Faculty entity instance ft is created.

C. The different `setXXX()` methods defined in the entity class Faculty.java are used to set a new faculty record with the inputs coming from seven Text Fields in the Faculty Information panel in the FacultyFrame form window. The `getText()` method is used to pick up seven pieces of information related to a new faculty member.

D. A new Transaction Association instance is created by calling the `getTransaction()` method. This step is necessary, since any data manipulation performed in the JPA must be under the control of a Transaction Association instance, and this is a significant difference to the data query operation such as the Select query.

E. Before we can start this Transaction instance, we must check whether a valid Transaction instance has been started and active. If not, we can start this Transaction to begin the data manipulation operation by executing the `begin()` method.

F. The `persist()` method is executed to add this new entity ft into the Faculty entity class.

G. The `commit()` method is called to start this transaction.

H. Finally, this new inserted faculty name is added into the Faculty Name combo box to enable users to check and validate this data insertion later.

Before we can build and run this project to test our codes, we prefer to first finish the coding development for the validation of this data insertion.

7.1.1.4 Develop the Codes for the Validation of the Data Insertion

In fact, we can use the codes we built in the Select button click event handler to perform this data insertion validation. No modification is needed for the codes developed in that event handler except the `ShowFaculty()` method.

The reason for us to modify the codes in the `ShowFaculty()` method is that a new faculty photo may be inserted when a new faculty record is inserted into the Faculty table. In order to coordinate this situation, we need to break this method into two separate methods, `ShowFaculty()` and `DisplayImage()`.

The function of the `DisplayImage()` is used to only display a passed faculty image. The job of `ShowFaculty()` is to identify whether a new faculty image has been inserted with a data insertion, and perform the associated function based on this identification.

Open the `ShowFaculty()` method and perform the modifications shown in Figure 7.4. The modified part has been highlighted in bold.

Let's have a closer look at this piece of modified codes to see how it works.

A. First, we need to check whether a matched faculty image has been found or not. If a matched faculty image has been found, which means that the `fImage != null`, the matched faculty image is sent to the `DisplayImage()` method to be displayed.

```
  private boolean ShowFaculty(){
      int maxNumber = 7;
      String fImage = null;
      String[] fname = {"Ying Bai", "Black Anderson", "Satish Bhalla", "Steve Johnson",
                        "Jenney King", "Alice Brown", "Debby Angles", "Jeff Henry"};
      String[] fimage = {"Bai.jpg", "Anderson.jpg", "Satish.jpg", "Johnson.jpg",
                         "King.jpg", "Brown.jpg", "Angles.jpg", "Henry.jpg"};

      for (int i=0; i<=maxNumber; i++){
        if (fname[i].equals((String)ComboName.getSelectedItem())){
          fImage = fimage[i];
          break;
        }
      }
A     if (fImage != null){
        DisplayImage(fImage);
B       return  true;
      }
C     else if (FacultyImageField.getText() != null){
        fImage = FacultyImageField.getText();
        DisplayImage(fImage);
D       FacultyImageField.setText("");
E       return true;
      }
      else
F       return false;
  }
```

Figure 7.4. The modified codes for the ShowFaculty() method.

B. A true is returned to the calling method to indicate that the execution of the method `ShowFaculty()` is successful.

C. Next, we need to check whether a new faculty image has been inserted with this data insertion. If a valid faculty image has been inserted, which means that the content of the `FacultyImageField` is a valid location where a faculty image file is stored, that location is assigned to the local variable `fImage`, and it is sent to the `DisplayImage()` method to be displayed in the Faculty Image box.

D. Immediately, this FacultyImageField is cleaned up by calling the `setText()` method, since this faculty image is only used for this data insertion, and we do not want this faculty photo to be used again in the future.

E. A true is returned to the calling method to indicate that this `ShowFaculty()` method has been executed successfully.

F. If both above conditions are not satisfied, which means that no matched faculty image can be found, a false is returned to the calling method to indicate that this method is failed, and no matched faculty photo can be found.

The detailed codes for the method DisplayImage() is shown in Figure 7.5.

The detailed explanation for this piece of codes has been given in Section 6.2.7.3.3.2 and Figure 6.56 in Chapter 6. Refer to that section to get a clear and detailed picture about this coding.

Now that we have finished developing the codes for data insertion and the data validation, let's now build and run our project to test these functionalities.

```
private void DisplayImage(String facultyImage){
    Image img;
    int imgId = 1, timeout = 1000;
    MediaTracker tracker = new MediaTracker(this);
    MsgDialog msgDlg = new MsgDialog(new javax.swing.JFrame(), true);

    img = this.getToolkit().getImage(facultyImage);
    Graphics g = ImageCanvas.getGraphics();
    tracker.addImage(img, imgId);

    try{
       if(!tracker.waitForID(imgId,timeout)){
          msgDlg.setMessage("Failed to load image");
          msgDlg.setVisible(true);
       }//end if
    }catch(InterruptedException e){
       msgDlg.setMessage(e.toString()); msgDlg.setVisible(true);
    }
    g.drawImage(img, 0, 0, ImageCanvas.getWidth(), ImageCanvas.getHeight(), this);
}
```

Figure 7.5. The detailed codes for the method DisplayImage().

7.1.1.5 Build and Run the Project to Test the Data Insertion

Before you can run this project, the following conditions have to be met:

- The SQL Server sample database CSE_DEPT has been connected to this project. To check this connection, open the `Services` window and expand the `Databases` node to locate our sample database connection URL, jdbc:sqlserver://localhost\SQL2008EXPRESS: 5000;databaseName=CSE_DEPT [ybai on dbo]. Right click on this URL and select the `Connect` item to do this connection.
- A default faculty image Default.jpg has been saved to our project folder, which is C:\JavaDBProject\Chapter 7\SelectQueryWizard. You can find this image file from the folder Image that is located at the Wiley ftp site (refer to Figure 1.2 in Chapter 1). If you want to save your faculty image at any other folder you like, you need to enter the full name, which includes the path and the name of that image, into the Faculty Image Field as the project runs. You do not need to do this step if you do not want to insert any faculty image with the data insertion.

Now we are ready to build and run our project to test this data insertion and validation function.

Click on the Clean and Build Main Project button from the toolbar to build our project. Then click on the Run Main Project button to run the project.

Enter a suitable username and password, such as jhenry and test, to complete the login process and select the Faculty Information from the SelectFrame window to open the FacultyFrame window. The default faculty information is displayed.

Enter the following information into seven Text Fields inside the Faculty Information panel as a new faculty record, as shown in Figure 7.6.

1. **Faculty ID:** T56789
2. **Name:** Tom Jeff
3. **Title:** Associate Professor
4. **Office:** MTC-215

Figure 7.6. The newly inserted faculty record.

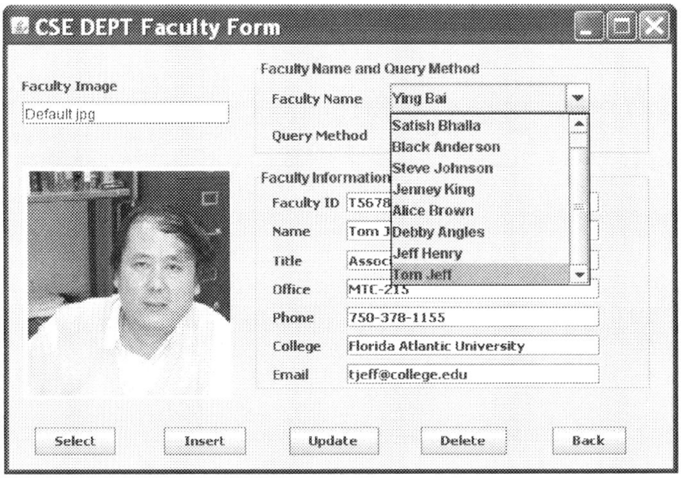

Figure 7.7. The newly added faculty name.

5. Phone: 750-378-1155
6. College: Florida Atlantic University
7. Email: tjeff@college.com

Also, enter `Default.jpg` into the Faculty Image Field, since we want to insert a default faculty image with this data insertion. Then click on the Insert button to perform this data insertion. Immediately, you can find that a new faculty `Tom Jeff` has been added into the Faculty Name combo box when you click on the drop-down arrow of that combo box, as shown in Figure 7.7.

To confirm and validate this data insertion, we have two ways to go: one way is to open our sample database CSE_DEPT using either the Microsoft SQL Server Management

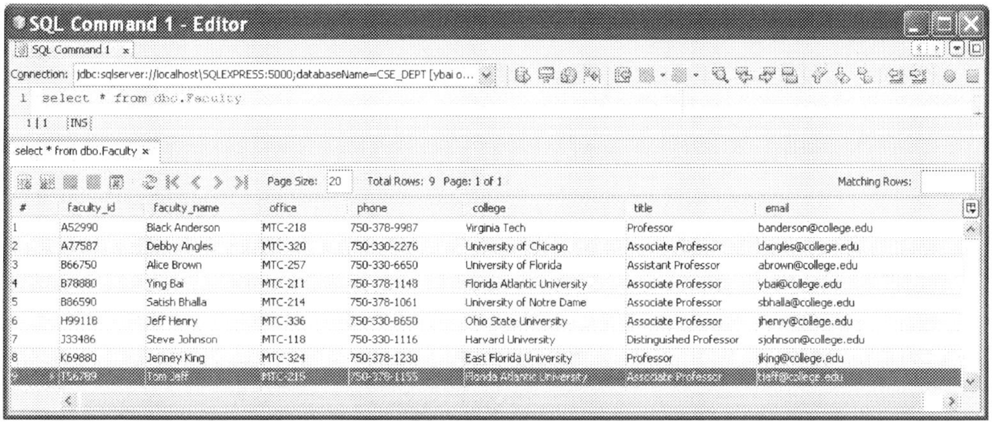

Figure 7.8. The opened Faculty table using the Services window in NetBeans IDE.

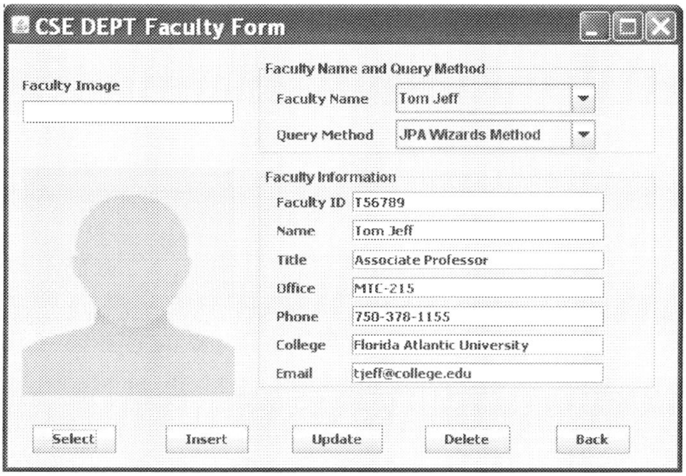

Figure 7.9. The retrieved inserted faculty information.

Studio Express or from the `Services` window in the NetBeans IDE, and another way is to click on the Select button on the FacultyFrame window to retrieve this inserted faculty record.

The opened Faculty table of our sample database CSE_DEPT is shown in Figure 7.8.

It can be found that a new faculty record, which is highlighted, has been added into the last row in our Faculty table.

Now select the new inserted faculty name Tom Jeff from the Faculty Name combo box and click on the Select button from the FacultyFrame window, seven pieces of newly inserted faculty information with the default faculty image is displayed on this form, as shown in Figure 7.9.

Click on the `Back` and `Exit` buttons to complete our project.

The running result of our project is successful, and a new faculty record has been inserted into our Faculty table successfully! It is highly recommended to remove this new inserted faculty record from our sample database since we want to keep our database clean and neat. You can use Microsoft SQL Server Management Studio Express to do this deletion.

Next, let's handle the data updating function to our Faculty table in our sample database.

7.1.2 Perform Data Updating to SQL Server Database Using JPA Wizards

Regularly, we do not need to update a faculty_id when we update a faculty record since a better way to do that is to insert a new faculty record and delete the old one. The main reason for this is that a very complicated operation would be performed if the faculty_id were updated since it is a primary key in the `Faculty` table and foreign keys in the `Course` and the `LogIn` tables. To update a primary key, one needs to update foreign keys first in the child tables and then update the primary key in the parent table. This will make our updating operation very complicated and easy to be confused. In order to avoid this confusion, in this sec tion, we will update a faculty record by changing any column except the faculty_id, and this is a popular way to update a table and widely implemented in most database applications.

7.1.2.1 Develop the Codes for the Update Button Event Handler

We want to use the Update button we built in this FacultyFrame form window to perform a faculty updating function; therefore, no modification to this FacultyFrame form window to be made. Now let's develop the codes for the Update button click event handler.

Open this event handler and enter the codes that are shown in Figure 7.10 into this event handler. Let's have a closer look at this piece of codes to see how it works.

- **A.** A local integer variable `numUpdated` is created, and it is used to hold the number of the updated rows when a data updating is performed.
- **B.** The query string with a JPQL identifier Update is created. The point to be noted is that here we used the Java Persistence Query Language (JPQL) to perform this data updating operation with the position holder as the positional parameters. The `facultyName`, which is a query criterion and followed the `WHERE` clause, is a named parameter. Refer to Section 6.2.5.4 in Chapter 6 to get a more detailed discussion about the positional and named parameters for a JPQL query. If you like, you can use the named parameters to replace those positional parameters, such as f.facultyName = :fname, f.title = : ftitle, and so on.
- **C.** The entity manager is first cleaned up to make it ready for our query.
- **D.** A new updating query is created by executing the `createQuery()` method with the query string as the argument.
- **E.** Six positional parameters involved in this updating query are initialized by using the `set-Parameter()` method. The input or argument for these methods are obtained by calling the `getText()` method of each associated Text Field object. The point to be noted is that the order of these positional parameters in these `setParameter()` methods must match to the order number in the query string.
- **F.** The query criterion, which is the selected faculty name from the Faculty Name combo box, is a named parameter. So this parameter is initialized with the named parameter format.

```
  private void cmdUpdateActionPerformed(java.awt.event.ActionEvent evt) {
    // TODO add your handling code here:
A   int numUpdated = 0;
B   String query = "UPDATE Faculty f SET f.facultyName=?1, f.title=?2, f.office=?3, f.phone=?4, " +
                  "f.college=?5, f.email=?6 WHERE f.facultyName=:FacultyName";
C   SelectQueryWizardPUEntityManager.clear();
D   facultyQuery = SelectQueryWizardPUEntityManager.createQuery(query);
E   facultyQuery.setParameter(1, FacultyNameField.getText());
    facultyQuery.setParameter(2, TitleField.getText());
    facultyQuery.setParameter(3, OfficeField.getText());
    facultyQuery.setParameter(4, PhoneField.getText());
    facultyQuery.setParameter(5, CollegeField.getText());
    facultyQuery.setParameter(6, EmailField.getText());
F   facultyQuery.setParameter("FacultyName", ComboName.getSelectedItem());
    // reserve the current faculty name
G   String cFacultyName = (String)ComboName.getSelectedItem();
H   javax.persistence.EntityTransaction tr = SelectQueryWizardPUEntityManager.getTransaction();
I   if (!tr.isActive()){
       tr.begin();
    }
J   numUpdated = facultyQuery.executeUpdate();
K   tr.commit();
L   System.out.println("The number of updated row is: " + numUpdated);
M   ComboName.addItem(FacultyNameField.getText());
N   ComboName.removeItem(cFacultyName);
  }
```

Figure 7.10. The developed codes for the Update button click event handler.

G. After this faculty record is updated, the current faculty name may also be updated. In order to update the Faculty Name combo box, we need to temporarily reserve this current faculty name. Therefore, a local String variable `cFacultyName` is created and used for this purpose.

H. A new Transaction Association instance is created by calling the `getTransaction()` method. Since this Transaction class is located at the javax.persistence package, so a full name is used here for this class. As we mentioned, unlike the data query, such as `SELECT` statement, all data manipulation queries, such as `UPDATE` and `DELETE`, must be under the control of a Transaction instance.

I. Before we can start this Transaction instance, we need to confirm whether this Transaction Association has been active. Then we can start it using the `begin()` method if this Transaction instance is inactive.

J. Now we can call the `executeUpdate()` method to perform this data updating transaction. The execution result of this method is an integer that indicates the number of rows that have been updated.

K. The `commit()`method is executed to trigger this data updating operation.

L. The execution result is printed out as a debug purpose.

M. The new updated faculty name stored in the `FacultyNameField` is added into the Faculty Name combo box to update that object and enable us to do the validation of this data updating later.

N. The current or old faculty name is removed from the Faculty Name combo box.

For the validation of this data updating, we can use the same codes we developed in Section 7.1.1.4.

Now let's build and run our project to test its data updating function. Make sure that a default faculty image file `Default.jpg` has been saved to our project folder in this application, which is C:\JavaDBProject\Chapter 7\SelectQueryWizard. Of course, you do not need this image file if you do not want to update any faculty image when you perform a faculty updating.

7.1.2.2 Build and Run the Project to Test the Data Updating

Before you can run this project, the following conditions have to be met:

- The SQL Server sample database CSE_DEPT has been connected to this project. To check this connection, open the `Services` window and expand the `Databases` node to locate our sample database connection URL, jdbc:sqlserver://localhost\SQL2008EXPRESS:5000;databaseName=CSE_DEPT [ybai on dbo]. Right click on this URL and select the `Connect` item to do this connection.

Click on the Clean and Build Main Project button from the toolbar to build our project. Then click on the Run Main Project button to run the project.

Enter a suitable username and password, such as jhenry and test, to complete the login process and select the Faculty Information from the SelectFrame window to open the FacultyFrame window. The default faculty information is displayed.

Enter the following information into six Text Fields (no Faculty ID Text Field) inside the Faculty Information panel as an updated faculty record, as shown in Figure 7.11.

1. Name: Susan Bai
2. Title: Professor
3. Office: MTC-215
4. Phone: 750-378-1111

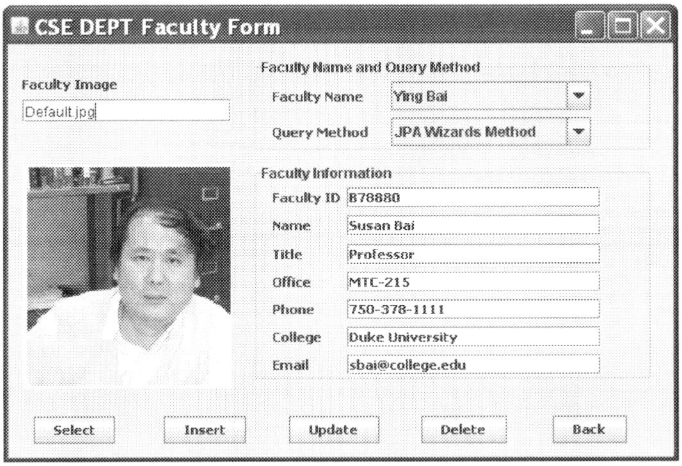

Figure 7.11. The updated faculty information.

5. College: Duke University
6. Email: sbai@college.com

Also, enter the name of a default faculty image file, `Default.jpg`, to the Faculty Image field, since we want to update this faculty's image with this data updating. Your finished updating window should match one that is shown in Figure 7.11.

Click on the **Update** button to perform this data updating. Immediately, you can find that the updated faculty name **Susan Bai** has been added into the Faculty Name combo box, and the original faculty member **Ying Bai** has been removed from this box when clicking on the drop down arrow of that box.

To test this data updating, open the **Output** window if it has not been opened. You can find that a running successful message is displayed in that window, as shown in Figure 7.12.

Similar to the data insertion operation, here we have two ways to validate this data updating. One way is to open our **Faculty** table to confirm this data updating, and the other way is to use the **Select** button (exactly the codes inside that button's click event handler) to do this validation.

To use the first method, open the **Services** window in the NetBeans IDE and open our **Faculty** table. You can find that the faculty member **Ying Bai** has been updated, as shown in Figure 7.13.

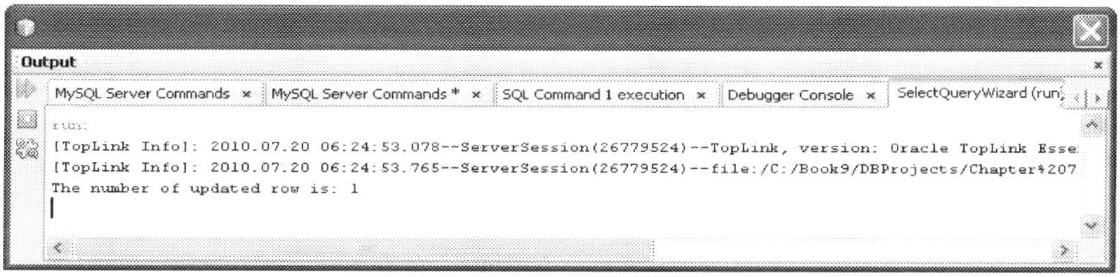

```
[TopLink Info]: 2010.07.20 06:24:53.078--ServerSession(26779524)--TopLink, version: Oracle TopLink Esse
[TopLink Info]: 2010.07.20 06:24:53.765--ServerSession(26779524)--file:/C:/Book9/DBProjects/Chapter%207
The number of updated row is: 1
```

Figure 7.12. A running successful message.

```
select * from dbo.Faculty
```

#	faculty_id	faculty_name	office	phone	college	title	email
1	A52990	Black Anderson	MTC-218	750-378-9987	Virginia Tech	Professor	banderson@college.edu
2	A77587	Debby Angles	MTC-320	750-330-2276	University of Chicago	Associate Professor	dangles@college.edu
3	B66750	Alice Brown	MTC-257	750-330-6650	University of Florida	Assistant Professor	abrown@college.edu
4	B78880	Susan Bai	MTC-215	750-378-1111	Duke University	Professor	sbai@college.edu
5	B86590	Satish Bhalla	MTC-214	750-378-1061	University of Notre Dame	Associate Professor	sbhalla@college.edu
6	H99118	Jeff Henry	MTC-336	750-330-8650	Ohio State University	Associate Professor	jhenry@college.edu
7	J33486	Steve Johnson	MTC-118	750-330-1116	Harvard University	Distinguished Professor	sjohnson@college.edu
8	K69880	Jenney King	MTC-324	750-378-1230	East Florida University	Professor	jking@college.edu
9	T56789	Tom Jeff	MTC-215	750-378-1155	Florida Atlantic University	Associate Professor	tjeff@college.edu

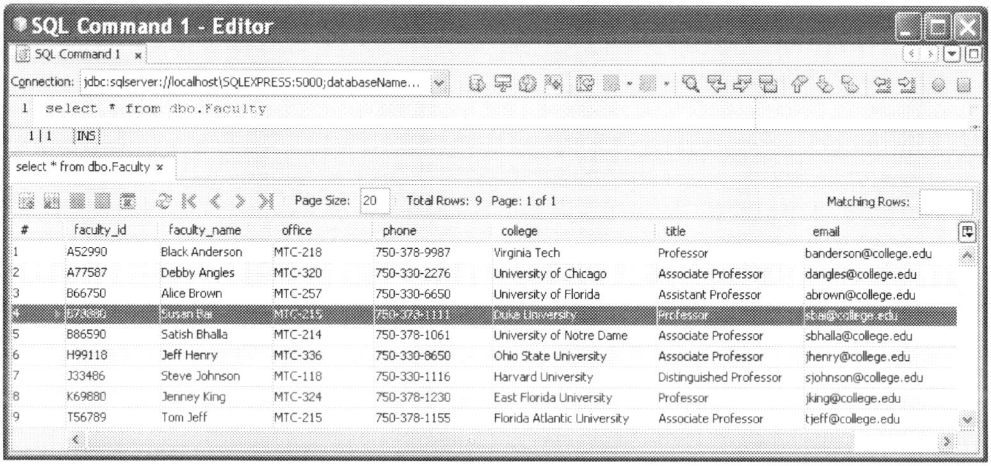

Figure 7.13. The updated faculty member Susan Bai.

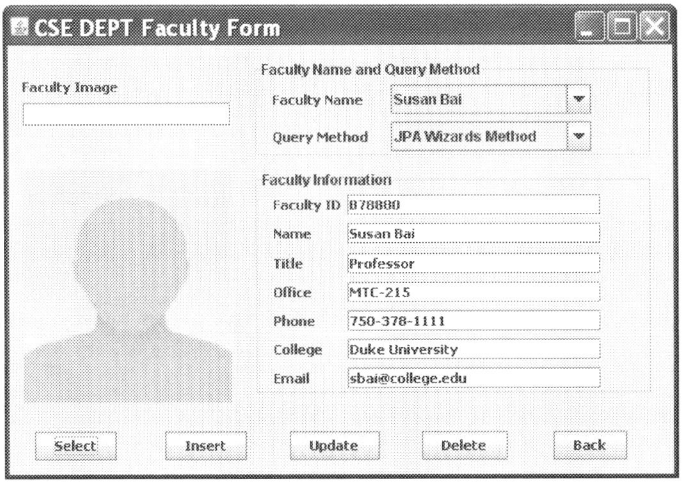

Figure 7.14. The updated faculty member.

To use the second way to do this data updating validation, select the updated faculty member Susan Bai from the Faculty Name combo box and click on the Select button to try to retrieve this updated faculty record from our sample database.

The retrieved updated faculty information is shown in Figure 7.14. Click on the Back and the Exit buttons to terminate our project.

Our data updating function is successful! It is highly recommended to recover the updated faculty record in the Faculty table since we want to keep our sample database clean and neat. You can do that recovery job by using the Microsoft SQL Server Management Studio Express. To open that Studio Express, go to `Start\All Programs\Microsoft SQL Server 2008\SQL Server Management Studio`.

Next, let's take care of the data deletion from our sample database using the JPA wizard.

7.1.3 Perform Data Deleting to SQL Server Database Using JPA Wizards

Basically, there is no significant difference between the data updating and deleting using JPA wizards. In this section, we try to use the Delete button we built in the FacultyFrame form window before to perform this data deletion operation.

To make this deleting simple, we want to just delete the selected faculty record without touching the associated faculty image.

7.1.3.1 Develop the Codes for the Delete Button Event Handler

Launch the NetBeans IDE 6.8 and open the SelectQueryWizard project and the FacultyFrame form window. Double click on the Delete button to open its click event handler. Enter the codes that are shown in Figure 7.15 into this event handler.

```
  private void cmdDeleteActionPerformed(java.awt.event.ActionEvent evt) {
      // TODO add your handling code here:
A     int numDeleted = 0;

B     String query = "DELETE FROM Faculty f WHERE f.facultyName=:FacultyName";
C     SelectQueryWizardPUEntityManager.clear();
D     facultyQuery = SelectQueryWizardPUEntityManager.createQuery(query);
E     facultyQuery.setParameter("FacultyName", ComboName.getSelectedItem());
F     String cFacultyName = (String)ComboName.getSelectedItem();

G     javax.persistence.EntityTransaction tr = SelectQueryWizardPUEntityManager.getTransaction();
H     if (!tr.isActive()){
         tr.begin();
      }
I     numDeleted = facultyQuery.executeUpdate();
J     tr.commit();
K     System.out.println("The number of deleted row is: " + numDeleted);
L     ComboName.removeItem(cFacultyName);
  }
```

Figure 7.15. The codes for the Delete button click event handler.

Let's have a closer look at this piece of codes to see how it works.

A. A local integer variable `numDeleted` is created and it is used to hold the number of the deleted rows when a data deleting is performed.

B. The query string with a JPQL identifier Delete is created. The point to be noted is that here we used the Java Persistence Query Language (JPQL) to perform this data deleting operation with the named parameter `FacultyName` as the query criterion.

C. The entity manager is first cleaned up to make it ready for our data deleting query.

D. A new data deleting query is created by executing the `createQuery()` method with the query string as the argument.

E. The query criterion, which is the selected faculty name from the Faculty Name combo box, is a named parameter. So this parameter is initialized with the named parameter format.

F. After this faculty record is deleted, the faculty name will be removed from the Faculty Name combo box later. In order to remember this deleted faculty name, we need to temporarily reserve this current faculty name. Therefore, a local String variable `cFacultyName` is created and used for this purpose.

G. A new Transaction Association instance is created by calling the `getTransaction()` method. Since this Transaction class is located at the javax.persistence package, so a full name is used here for this class. As we mentioned, unlike the data query such as SELECT statement, all data manipulation queries, such as UPDATE and DELETE, must be under the control of a Transaction instance.

H. Before we can start this Transaction instance, we need to confirm whether this Transaction Association has been active. Then we can start it using the `begin()` method if this Transaction instance is inactive.

I. Now we can call the `executeUpdate()` method to perform this data deleting transaction. The execution result of this method is an integer that indicates the number of rows that have been deleted.

J. The `commit()` method is executed to trigger this data deleting operation.

K. The execution result is printed out as a debug purpose.

L. The current or old faculty name is removed from the Faculty Name combo box.

At this point, we have finished developing the codes for this data deleting function. To confirm or validate this data deletion, we can still use the Select button, exactly the codes inside the Select button click event handler in this FacultyFrame form window.

Now let build and run our project to test and confirm this data deletion function.

7.1.3.2 Build and Run the Project to Test the Data Deletion

Make sure that our sample database CSE_DEPT has been connected to our project. To check this connection, open the Services window and expand the Databases node to locate our sample database connection URL, jdbc:sqlserver://localhost\SQL2008EXPRESS: 5000;databaseName= CSE_DEPT [ybai on dbo]. Right click on this URL and select the `Connect` item to do this connection.

Now click on the Clean and Build Main Project button from the toolbar to build our project. Then click on the Run Main Project button to run the project.

Enter a suitable username and password, such as jhenry and test, to complete the login process and select the Faculty Information from the SelectFrame window to open the FacultyFrame window. The default faculty information is displayed.

To test this data deletion function, we can try to delete one faculty member, such as Ying Bai, from our Faculty table. To do that, select this faculty member from the Faculty Name combo box, and click on the Delete button. Immediately, you can find that this faculty name has been removed from the Faculty Name combo box. Also, the running result is shown in the Output window, as shown in Figure 7.16.

To confirm this data deletion, click on the Back and the Exit button to stop our project. Then open our Faculty table by going to the `Services` window and expand the `Databases` node, and our connection URL, and finally our sample database CSE_DEPT. Expand our database schema dbo and right click on the Faculty table. Select the `View Data` item from the pop-up menu to open our Faculty table. On the opened Faculty table, you can find that the faculty member Ying Bai has been removed from this table.

Our data deletion function is successful!

To make our database clean and neat, it is highly recommended to recover this deletion. The point to be noted is that when we delete a faculty member from the Faculty table, which is a parent table relative to the Course and LogIn tables that are child tables, the related records to that deleted faculty in those child tables will also be deleted since

Figure 7.16. The running result of the data deletion query.

a cascaded deleting relationship has been set up between the parent and child tables when we built this database in Chapter 2. Therefore, the faculty login record in the LogIn table and all courses taught by that faculty in the Course table will be deleted when the faculty member is deleted from the Faculty table. Also because the Course table is a parent table relative to the StudentCourse table, all courses taken by students and taught by the deleted faculty will be deleted from the StudentCourse table. To recover these deleted records, one needs to recover all of those deleted records related to the deleted faculty in those four tables. An easy way to do this recovery job is to use the Microsoft SQL Server Management Studio Express. For your convenience, we show these original records in Tables 7.2–7.5 again, and you can add or insert them back to those four tables to complete this data recovery.

Table 7.2. The deleted faculty record in the faculty table

faculty_id	faculty_name	office	phone	college	title	email
B78880	Ying Bai	MTC-211	750-378-1148	Florida Atlantic University	Associate Professor	ybai@college.edu

Table 7.3. The deleted course records in the course table

course_id	course	credit	classroom	schedule	enrollment	faculty_id
CSC-132B	Introduction to Programming	3	TC-302	T-H: 1:00-2:25 PM	21	B78880
CSC-234A	Data Structure & Algorithms	3	TC-302	M-W-F: 9:00-9:55 AM	25	B78880
CSE-434	Advanced Electronics Systems	3	TC-213	M-W-F: 1:00-1:55 PM	26	B78880
CSE-438	Advd Logic & Microprocessor	3	TC-213	M-W-F: 11:00-11:55 AM	35	B78880

Table 7.4. The deleted login records in the login table

user_name	pass_word	faculty_id	student_id
ybai	reback	B78880	

Table 7.5. The deleted student course records in the studentcourse table

s_course_id	student_id	course_id	credit	major
1005	J77896	CSC-234A	3	CS/IS
1009	A78835	CSE-434	3	CE
1014	A78835	CSE-438	3	CE
1016	A97850	CSC-132B	3	ISE
1017	A97850	CSC-234A	3	ISE

A complete sample project SelectQueryWizard that can be used to perform data insertion, updating, and deletion actions against our SQL Server sample database can be found from the folder **DBProjects\Chapter 7** that is located at the Wiley ftp site (refer to Figure 1.2 in Chapter 1).

Next, let's take care of the data manipulations against the Oracle database using the JPA Wizards.

7.2 PERFORM DATA MANIPULATIONS TO ORACLE DATABASE USING JPA WIZARDS

Generally, there is no significant difference between the data manipulations for the SQL Server and the Oracle databases. The only differences are the protocol of the query string used in the data manipulations and the mapped data table name. In the following sections, we will emphasize the different points between the protocols of these query strings.

First, let's handle the data insertion query in the Oracle database.

7.2.1 Perform Data Insertion to Oracle Database Using JPA Wizards

To simplify this introduction, we can use a project OracleSelectWizard we developed in Section 6.2.9 in Chapter 6 and make some modifications to that project to make it as our new project. Perform the following operations to complete this project transferring:

1. Open the Windows Explorer and create a new folder, such as JavaDBProject\Chapter 7.
2. Open a Web browser and go to the folder DBProjects\Chapter 6 that is located at the Wiley ftp site (refer to Figure 1.2 in Chapter 1).
3. Copy the project OracleSelectWizard from that folder and paste it to our new folder JavaDBProject\Chapter 7.

Now we are ready to build our data insertion query to perform data manipulations to our Oracle sample database CSE_DEPT.

In Section 6.2.7.1 in Chapter 6, we have created a FacultyFrame class and Faculty JFrame window FacultyFrame. Also, the following components have been added into that project:

- The Faculty Entity Manager has been added into the FacultyFrame class.
- The Oracle sample database has been connected to our project.

In this section, we want to use the Insert button that has been added into the FacultyFrame window to perform this data insertion function.

7.2.1.1 Modify the FacultyFrame Window Form

First, let's modify the FacultyFrame form by adding three more Text Fields into this frame: two of them are added into the Faculty Information panel to enable us to insert a faculty record, and one them is added at the top of the faculty image box to allow us to insert a new faculty image (exactly the location of the faculty image).

Perform the following operations to open our pasted project OracleSelectWizard:

1. Launch the NetBeans IDE 6.8 and go to `File > Open Project` menu item to open the `Open Project` wizard.
2. Browse to the location where we copied and pasted our project OracleSelectWizard, which is JavaDBProject\Chapter 7. Make sure that the `Open as Main Project` checkbox has been checked, and select this project and click on the `Open Project` button to open it.

   The point to be noted is that you now have two OracleSelectWizard projects in the NetBeans IDE, but they are different projects with different functions. The first OracleSelectWizard was built in Chapter 6 without data manipulation function, but this second project will be built in Chapter 7 with the data manipulation function.
3. Expand this project files to open the FacultyFrame.java file by double clicking on this file that is located under the `Source Packages\LogInFramePackage` node.
4. Click on the `Design` button at the top of this window to open the GUI window of this FacultyFrame class.

Perform the following operations to add three more Text Fields into this frame window:

- Enlarge the FacultyFrame window form and the `Faculty Information` panel.
- Add two more labels and two more Text fields into this `Faculty Information` panel, and one more label and the associated Text Field to the top of the Faculty Image box with the properties shown in Table 7.6.

One point to be noted is the FacultyIDField, and its editable property is checked, which means that we want users to insert a new faculty_id as the project runs. However, this property should not be checked when we perform a data updating action because we will not update a faculty_id during a faculty record updating process.

Your finished modified FacultyFrame form window should match one that is shown in Figure 7.17.

Now let's develop the codes for the Insert button click event handler to perform the data insertion function as the project runs. As we did for the SQL Server database, we will use the JPQL `persist()` method to perform this data insertion.

7.2.1.2 Develop the Codes for the Insert Button Event Handler

As we mentioned, there is no significant difference in querying a SQL Server and an Oracle database using JPA Wizard in NetBeans 6.8. The whole project SelectQueryWizard

Table 7.6. Objects and controls added into the faculty frame window

Type	Variable Name	Text	editable	Title
Label	Label1	Faculty ID		
Text Field	FacultyIDField		checked	
Label	Label2	Name		
Text Field	FacultyNameField		checked	
Label	Label3	Faculty Image		
Text Field	FacultyImageField		checked	

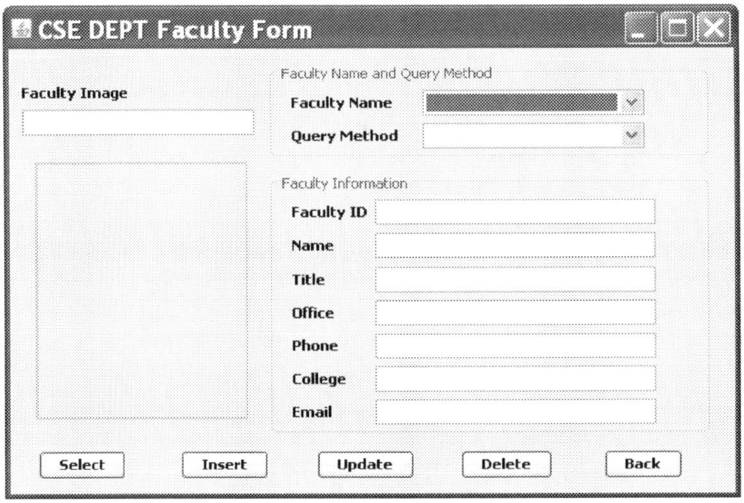

Figure 7.17. The modified FacultyFrame form window.

we built in Chapter 6 can be used to perform data manipulations to an Oracle database with a little modification. Exactly you can copy the codes in the Insert button click event handler we built in Section 7.1.1.3 and paste them into the Insert button click event handler in the FacultyFrame form in our current OracleSelectWizard project.

Four small modifications are important and necessary, and they are listed below:

1. The data table name used in the query strings. There is a little difference for the table names used in SQL Server database and Oracle database in the JPA mapped Entity classes. For example, the LogIn table in our sample SQL Server database CSE_DEPT is still mapped to LogIn in the LogIn.java Entity class; however, it is mapped to Login in the Login.java Entity class for the Oracle database. Make sure to check the Entity classes to confirm and use the correct table names when different databases are utilized.
2. The query components used in the data query operations. These is little difference in the names of the JPA query components used in SQL Server database and Oracle database when they are added into each Frame Form window. For example, the LogIn JPA query object used in SQL Server database is named logInQuery; however, it is named loginQuery when is created for the Oracle database. Make sure to check the added query components to confirm and use the correct query components for each Frame.
3. The entity manager class name used in the Oracle database is different with that in the SQL Server database. In the project OracleSelectWizard, the name of the mapped entity manager class is OracleSelectWizardPUEntityManager; therefore, you need to use this name to replace the SelectQueryWizardPUEntityManager, which is the name of the mapped entity manager for the SQL Server database, in all codes to perform a data manipulation to our Oracle sample database.

4. The ShowFaculty() method should be modified and divided into two submethods, ShowFaculty() and DisplayImage(), to coordinate the data manipulations. Refer to Section 7.1.1.4 to complete this modification.

One point to be remembered is that you can copy the codes from the Select button click event handler from the project SelectQueryWizard and paste them into the Select button click event handler in the FacultyFrame form in our current OracleSelectWizard project to perform the validation of this data insertion. The only modification is to replace the SQL Server entity manager SelectQueryWizardPUEntityManager with the Oracle entity manager OracleSelectWizardPUEntityManager in that piece of codes.

Another point to be noted is that you need to copy all image files, including both faculty and student image files, from the Image folder that is located at the site ftp://ftp.wiley.isbn/JavaDB, and paste them to your current project folder. In this case, it should be JavaDBProject\Chapter 7\OracleSelectWizard. You need also to remember to connect to our sample Oracle database we loaded in Section 6.2.1.3 when you create Entity classes for each tables in that Oracle database. Follow steps listed below to complete this database connection and mapping:

1. Click on the Services tab to open the `Services` window
2. Extend the Databases node and you can find our load-in Oracle sample database jdbc:oracle:thin:@localhost:1251:XE [CSE_DEPT on CSE_DEPT]
3. Right click on that load-in database node and select the Connect item from the pop-up menu to connect to this sample database

Now you can perform data insertion actions against our Oracle database. In order to keep our database clean and neat, it is highly recommended to delete this new inserted faculty record from our sample database after you finished this data insertion testing.

A complete sample project OracleSelectWizard that can be used to perform data insertion actions against Oracle Database 10g XE can be found from the folder **DBProjects\Chapter 7** that is located at the Wiley ftp site (refer to Figure 1.2 in Chapter 1).

Next, let's develop the codes to perform data updating actions against our Oracle database.

7.2.2 Perform Data Updating to Oracle Database Using JPA Wizards

Generally there is no difference between update data against a SQL Server and an Oracle database, and we can use almost all codes we developed in the Update button click event handler in Section 7.1.2.1 to perform a data updating action against our Oracle database. Therefore, you can copy those codes and paste them into the Update button click event handler in the FcaultyFrame form in our current OracleSelectWizard project.

The only point to be noted is that the FacultyIDField should be disabled since we do not want to update a faculty_id when we update a faculty record. Refer to Section 7.1.2 to get more details about the reason for this point.

To disable the faculty_id to be modified during a data updating action, open the Update button click event handler and add the codes that are shown in Figure 7.18 into this handler. The newly added codes have been highlighted in bold.

```
    private void cmdUpdateActionPerformed(java.awt.event.ActionEvent evt) {
        // TODO add your handling code here:
        int numUpdated = 0;
A       FacultyIDField.setEditable(false);
        String query = "UPDATE Faculty f SET f.facultyName=?1, f.title=?2, f.office=?3, f.phone=?4, " +
                       "f.college=?5, f.email=?6 WHERE f.facultyName=:FacultyName";
B       OracleSelectWizardPUEntityManager.clear();
C       facultyQuery = OracleSelectWizardPUEntityManager.createQuery(query);
        facultyQuery.setParameter(1, FacultyNameField.getText());
        facultyQuery.setParameter(2, TitleField.getText());
        facultyQuery.setParameter(3, OfficeField.getText());
        facultyQuery.setParameter(4, PhoneField.getText());
        facultyQuery.setParameter(5, CollegeField.getText());
        facultyQuery.setParameter(6, EmailField.getText());
        facultyQuery.setParameter("FacultyName", ComboName.getSelectedItem());
        String cFacultyName = (String)ComboName.getSelectedItem();
D       javax.persistence.EntityTransaction tr = OracleSelectWizardPUEntityManager.getTransaction();
        if (!tr.isActive()){
           tr.begin();
        }
        numUpdated = facultyQuery.executeUpdate();
        tr.commit();
        System.out.println("The number of updated row is: " + numUpdated);
        ComboName.addItem(FacultyNameField.getText());
        ComboName.removeItem(cFacultyName);
    }
```

Figure 7.18. The modified codes for the Update button click event handler.

Let's have a closer look at this piece of codes to see how it works.

A. To avoid the FacultyIDField to be modified, the setEditable() method is used to disable the editable ability of this text field.

B. In steps **B**, **C**, and **D**, we use the Oracle entity manager class to replace the SQL Server entity manager class to perform data manipulations against our Oracle database.

One point to be remembered is that you can copy the codes from the Select button click event handler from the project SelectQueryWizard and paste them into the Select button click event handler in the FacultyFrame form in our current OracleSelectWizard project to perform the validation of this data updating. The only modification is to replace the SQL Server entity manager SelectQueryWizardPUEntityManager with the Oracle entity manager OracleSelectWizardPUEntityManager in that piece of codes.

Now you can build and run the project to test the data updating action we build in this project.

In order to keep our database clean and neat, it is highly recommended to recover that updated record when you finished the testing of this updating action. Refer to Section 7.1.2.2 to complete this data recovery process.

A complete sample project OracleSelectWizard that can be used to perform data updating actions against our Oracle sample database can be found from the folder **DBProjects\Chapter 7** that is located at the Wiley ftp site (refer to Figure 1.2 in Chapter 1).

Next, let's develop the codes to perform data deletion actions against our Oracle database.

```
  private void cmdDeleteActionPerformed(java.awt.event.ActionEvent evt) {
      int numDeleted = 0;
      String query = "DELETE FROM Faculty f WHERE f.facultyName=:FacultyName";
A     OracleSelectWizardPUEntityManager.clear();
B     facultyQuery = OracleSelectWizardPUEntityManager.createQuery(query);
      facultyQuery.setParameter("FacultyName", ComboName.getSelectedItem());
      String cFacultyName = (String)ComboName.getSelectedItem();
C     javax.persistence.EntityTransaction tr = OracleSelectWizardPUEntityManager.getTransaction();
      if (!tr.isActive()){
         tr.begin();
      }
      numDeleted = facultyQuery.executeUpdate();
      tr.commit();
      System.out.println("The number of deleted row is: " + numDeleted);
      ComboName.removeItem(cFacultyName);
  }
```

Figure 7.19. The modified codes for the Delete button click event handler.

7.2.3 Perform Data Deleting to Oracle Database Using JPA Wizards

Because of the data manipulation similarity between the SQL Server and Oracle database, you can use the codes in the Delete button click event handler in the project SelectQueryWizard we built in Section 7.1.3 to perform the data deletion action against our Oracle sample database. The only modification is to replace the SQL Server entity manager SelectQueryWizardPUEntityManager with the Oracle entity manager OracleSelectWizardPUEntityManager in this piece of codes.

Open the Delete button click event handler, copy the codes from the Delete button in the project SelectQueryWizard we built in Section 7.1.3, and paste them into our current Delete button click event handler, as shown in Figure 7.19. The modified codes have been highlighted in bold.

The only modification to this piece of codes is to replace the SQL Server entity manager class with the Oracle entity manager class, as shown in steps A, B, and C in Figure 7.19.

Now you can build and run the project to test the data deletion action against our Oracle sample database by deleting a faculty member Ying Bai.

In order to keep our sample database clean and neat, it is highly recommended to recover the deleted faculty member and related records in our Faculty, LogIn, Course, and StudentCourse tables. Refer to Tables 7.2–7.5 in Section 7.1.3.2 to complete these data recoveries. An easy way to do this is to use the Oracle Database 10g Express Edition. To open this edition, go to Start\All Programs\Oracle Database 10g Express Edition\Go To Database Home Page, then enter the suitable username and password, such as CSE_DEPT and reback, to log in this page. Select the `Object Browser > Browse > Tables` to open the related four tables, click on the `Data` tab to modify or recover the desired records.

A complete sample project OracleSelectWizard that can be used to perform data deletion actions against our Oracle sample database can be found from the folder **DBProjects\Chapter 7** that is located at the Wiley ftp site (refer to Figure 1.2 in Chapter 1).

Now that we have finished the data manipulations using the JPA Wizards, we can move to the next part: Data manipulations using the Java runtime object method.

SECTION II INSERT, UPDATE AND DELETE DATA USING JAVA RUNTIME OBJECTS METHOD

7.3 PERFORM DATA MANIPULATIONS TO SQL SERVER DATABASE USING JAVA RUNTIME OBJECT

As we did for the data query operations, in this section, we will discuss how to perform data manipulations using the Java runtime object method. Relatively speaking, there are some limitations in using the JAPI wizards to do the data manipulations. For instance, after the mapped entity has been built and the entity manager object has been created, the data manipulation can only be performed to that specified entity object or that data table. In other words, a defined or mapped entity object cannot perform data manipulations to any other entity object or data table.

Compared with the Java runtime object method, the JPA Wizards have the following shortcomings:

1. The details of the Java database programming is not clear as that of the Java runtime object method we will discuss in this section. Since most codes are created by JPA Wizards, quite a few details would be hidden to the users, and a complete and clear picture of Java database programming, especially for the structure and organization, is hard to be obtained and understood.
2. It is not flexible as that of the Java runtime object method we will discuss in this section. All of the codes must be created and developed before the project runs, or, statically, no modification can be performed during the project runs.
3. The compatibility is not desired as we expected. Since all projects are built based on NetBeans IDE and J2EE 5, they are not easy to be run at different platform when other IDE is utilized.

A good solution to these limitations is to use the Java runtime object to perform the data manipulations, and this will provide much more flexibilities and controllabilities to the data manipulations against the database, and allow a single object to perform multiple data manipulations against the target database.

Let's first concentrate on the data insertion to our SQL Server database using the Java runtime object method.

7.3.1 Perform Data Insertion to SQL Server Database Using Java Runtime Object

We have provided a very detailed and clear discussion about the Java runtime object method in Section 6.3 in Chapter 6. Refer to that section to get more details for this topic. Generally, to use Java runtime object to perform data manipulations against our target database, the following six steps should be adopted:

1. Load and register the database driver using DriverManager class and Driver methods.
2. Establish a database connection using the Connection object.
3. Create a data manipulation statement using the `createStatement()` method.
4. Execute the data manipulation statement using the executeUpdate() or execute() method.
5. Retrieve and check the execution result of the data manipulations.
6. Close the statement and connection using the close() method.

Generally, SQL Server and Oracle databases are two popular database systems, and have been widely implemented in most commercial and industrial applications. In this and the following sections in this chapter, we will concentrate on these two database systems.

To save time and space, we can use and modify a project SQLSelectObject we built in Chapter 6 to perform data manipulations against our target database. Perform the following operations to complete this project transferring:

1. Open the Windows Explorer and create a new folder, such as JavaDBProject\Chapter 7.
2. Open a Web browser and go to the folder DBProjects\Chapter 6 that is located at the Wiley ftp site (refer to Figure 1.2 in Chapter 1).
3. Copy the project SQLSelectObject from that folder and paste it to our new folder JavaDBProject\Chapter 7.

Now we are ready to build our data insertion query to perform data manipulations to our SQL Server sample database CSE_DEPT.

In Section 6.4.1 in Chapter 6, we have created a FacultyFrame class and Faculty JFrame window FacultyFrame. Also, the following components have been added into that project:

- A JDBC driver for SQL Server database has been loaded and registered.
- A valid database connection to that project has been established.
- A PreparedStatement instance has been created and implemented in the Select button click event handler to perform the data query.

In this section, we want to use the Insert button that has been added into the FacultyFrame window to perform this data insertion function.

7.3.1.1 Modify the FacultyFrame Window Form

First, let's modify the FacultyFrame form by adding three more Text Fields into this frame: two of them are added into the Faculty Information panel to enable us to insert a faculty record, and one of them is added at the top of the faculty image box to allow us to insert a new faculty image (exactly the location of the faculty image).

Perform the following operations to open our pasted project SQLSelectObject:

1. Launch the NetBeans IDE 6.8 and go to `File > Open Project` menu item to open the `Open Project` wizard.
2. Browse to the location where we copied and pasted our project SQLSelectObject, which is JavaDBProject\Chapter 7. Make sure that the `Open as Main Project` checkbox has been checked, and select this project and click on the `Open Project` button to open it.

Table 7.7. Objects and controls added into the faculty frame window

Type	Variable Name	Text	editable	Title
Label	Label1	Faculty ID		
Text Field	FacultyIDField		checked	
Label	Label2	Name		
Text Field	FacultyNameField		checked	
Label	Label3	Faculty Image		
Text Field	FacultyImageField		checked	

The point to be noted is that you now have two SQLSelectObject projects in the NetBeans IDE, but they are different projects with different functions. The first SQLSelectObject was built in Chapter 6 without data manipulation function, but this second project will be built in Chapter 7 with the data manipulation function.

3. Expand this project files to open the FacultyFrame.java file by double clicking on this file that is located under the `Source Packages\SQLSelectObjectPackage` node.
4. Click on the `Design` button at the top of this window to open the GUI window of this FacultyFrame class.

Perform the following operations to add three more Text Fields into this frame window:

- Enlarge the FacultyFrame window form and the `Faculty Information` panel.
- Add two more labels and two more Text fields into this `Faculty Information` panel, and one more label and the associated Text Field to the top of the Faculty Image box with the properties shown in Table 7.7.

One point to be noted is that the FacultyIDField and its editable property is checked, which means that we need to modify the faculty_id as the project runs since we may insert a new faculty record, including a new faculty_id, as the project runs. However, this field should be disabled when a data updating is performed because we will not update it during a faculty record updating process.

Your finished modified FacultyFrame form window should match one that is shown in Figure 7.20.

Now let's develop the codes for the Insert button click event handler to perform the data insertion function as the project runs.

The function of this piece of codes is to insert a new faculty record into our SQL Server sample database CSE_DEPT using the Java runtime object method as this button is clicked.

7.3.1.2 Develop the Codes for the Insert Button Event Handler

In Section 6.4.2.4 in Chapter 6, we have given a detailed discussion about the dynamic data query using the PreparedStatement object method. Refer to that section to get more details about that method. In this section, we will use that object to perform a dynamic faculty member insertion to the Faculty table in our sample database.

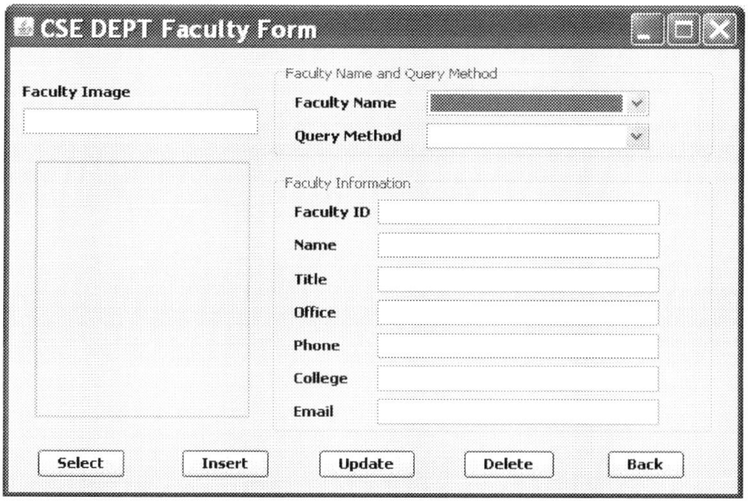

Figure 7.20. The modified FacultyFrame form window.

```
    private void cmdInsertActionPerformed(java.awt.event.ActionEvent evt) {
        // TODO add your handling code here:
A       int numInsert = 0;

B       String InsertQuery = "INSERT INTO Faculty (faculty_id, faculty_name, office, phone, " +
                             "college, title, email) VALUES (?, ?, ?, ?, ?, ?, ?)";
        try {
C           PreparedStatement pstmt = LogInFrame.con.prepareStatement(InsertQuery);
D           pstmt.setString(1, FacultyIDField.getText());
            pstmt.setString(2, FacultyNameField.getText());
            pstmt.setString(3, OfficeField.getText());
            pstmt.setString(4, PhoneField.getText());
            pstmt.setString(5, CollegeField.getText());
            pstmt.setString(6, TitleField.getText());
            pstmt.setString(7, EmailField.getText());
E           numInsert = pstmt.executeUpdate();
        }
F       catch (SQLException e) {
            msgDlg.setMessage("Error in Statement!" + e.getMessage());
            msgDlg.setVisible(true);
        }
G       System.out.println("The number of inserted row = " + numInsert);
H       ComboName.addItem(FacultyNameField.getText());
    }
```

Figure 7.21. The added codes to the Insert button click event handler.

Open the Insert button click event handler and enter the codes that are shown in Figure 7.21 into this handler.

Let's have a close look at this piece of codes to see how it works.

A. A local integer variable numInsert is created, and it is used to hold the returned number of inserted row as the data insert action is performed.

B. An insert query string is created with seven positional dynamic parameters, which are associated with seven pieces of inserted faculty information.

C. A try...catch block is used to initialize and execute the data insertion action. First, a `PreparedStatement` instance is created using the `Connection` object that is located at the LogInFrame class with the insert query string as the argument.

D. The setString() method is used to initialize seven pieces of inserted faculty information, which are obtained from seven text fields and entered by the user as the project runs.

E. The data insertion function is performed by calling the executeUpdate() method. The running result of this method, which is an integer that equals to the number of rows that have been inserted into the database, is assigned to the local variable numInsert.

F. The catch block is used to track and collect any possible exception encountered when this data insertion is executed.

G. The running result is printed out as a debug purpose.

H. The new inserted faculty name is attached into the Faculty Name combo box to enable users to validate this data insertion later.

Before we can build and run the project to test the data insertion function, we should first figure out how to validate this data insertion. As we mentioned, we want to use the codes we built in the Select button click event handler to do this validation. Now let's take care of this piece of codes to make it as our data insertion validation codes.

7.3.1.3 Develop the Codes for the Validation of the Data Insertion

To confirm and validate this data insertion, we can use the codes we built inside the Select button click event handler with some modifications. Two modifications are necessary:

1. Modify the codes inside the Select button click event handler to query two more columns, `faculty_id` and `faculty_name`, from the Faculty table.
2. Modify the `ShowFaculty()` method and divide it into two submethods, `ShowFaculty()` and `DisplayImage()`.

Let's do these modifications one by one.

During we developed the codes for the Select button click event handler in Chapter 6, we only query five columns without including the `faculty_id` and `faculty_name` columns. Now we need to add these two columns for this data query.

Open the Select button click event handler and perform the modifications shown in Figure 7.22. The modified parts have been highlighted in bold.

Let's have a closer look at this piece of modified codes to see how it works.

A. Two more columns, `faculty_id` and `faculty_name`, are added into the faculty text field array f_field since we need to query and display all columns from Faculty table to confirm the data insertion function.

B. Similarly, these two columns are added into the query string to enable them to be queried.

Now open the ShowFaculty() method and divide this method into two submethods, ShowFaculty() and DisplayImage(), which are shown in Figure 7.23. The modified parts have been highlighted in bold.

```
  private void cmdSelectActionPerformed(java.awt.event.ActionEvent evt) {
    // TODO add your handling code here:
A   javax.swing.JTextField[] f_field = {FacultyIDField, FacultyNameField, TitleField, OfficeField, PhoneField,
                                         CollegeField, EmailField};

B   String query = "SELECT faculty_id, faculty_name, title, office, phone, college, email " +
                   "FROM Faculty WHERE faculty_name = ?";

    if (ComboMethod.getSelectedItem()=="Runtime Object Method"){
      try{
            DatabaseMetaData dbmd = LogInFrame.con.getMetaData();
            String drName = dbmd.getDriverName();
            String drVersion = dbmd.getDriverVersion();
            msgDlg.setMessage("DriverName is: " + drName + ", Version is: " + drVersion);
            //msgDlg.setVisible(true);
            PreparedStatement pstmt = LogInFrame.con.prepareStatement(query);
            pstmt.setString(1, ComboName.getSelectedItem().toString());
            ResultSet rs = pstmt.executeQuery();
            ………
```

Figure 7.22. The modified codes for the Select button click event handler.

In Section 7.1.1.4, we have provided a detailed explanation about the modifications for this method, and refer to that section to get more information about this modification. The purpose of this modification is to allow the newly inserted faculty image to be displayed, either a new faculty image or a default one.

Now we are ready to build and run the project to test the data insertion function.

7.3.1.4 Build and Run the Project to Test the Data Insertion

Click on the `Clean and Build Main Project` button from the toolbar to build the project. Make sure that:

- All faculty and students' image files have been stored in the folder in which our project is located.
- Our sample SQL Server database CSE_DEPT has been connected to our project.

Now click on the Run Main Project button to run the project. Enter suitable username and password, such as `jhenry` and `test`, to the LogIn frame form and select the Faculty Information from the SelectFrame window to open the FacultyFrame form window. Make sure that the Runtime Object Method has been selected from the Query Method combo box. Then click on the Select button to query the default faculty information.

Modify seven text fields, which is equivalent to a piece of new faculty information, and enter the default faculty image file into the Faculty Image text field, as shown in Figure 7.24.

Click on the Insert button to try to insert this new faculty record into the Faculty table in our sample database. Immediately, you can find that a debug message is displayed in the Output window, as shown in Figure 7.25.

Also, you can find that the new inserted faculty name has been added into the Faculty Name combo box if you click on the drop-down arrow from that box.

```
private boolean ShowFaculty(){
      int maxNumber = 7;
      String fImage = null;
      String[] fname = {"Ying Bai", "Black Anderson", "Satish Bhalla", "Steve Johnson",
                        "Jenney King", "Alice Brown", "Debby Angles", "Jeff Henry"};
      String[] fimage = {"Bai.jpg", "Anderson.jpg", "Satish.jpg", "Johnson.jpg",
                         "King.jpg", "Brown.jpg", "Angles.jpg", "Henry.jpg"};
      for (int i=0; i<=maxNumber; i++){
         if (fname[i].equals((String)ComboName.getSelectedItem())){
            fImage = fimage[i];
            break;
         }
      }
      if (fImage != null){
         DisplayImage(fImage);
         return true;
      }
      else if (FacultyImageField.getText() != null){
         fImage = FacultyImageField.getText();
         DisplayImage(fImage);
         FacultyImageField.setText("");
         return true;
      }
      else
         return false;
}
private void DisplayImage(String facultyImage){
      Image img;
      int imgId = 1, timeout = 1000;
      MediaTracker tracker = new MediaTracker(this);
      MsgDialog msgDlg = new MsgDialog(new javax.swing.JFrame(), true);
      img = this.getToolkit().getImage(facultyImage);
      Graphics g = ImageCanvas.getGraphics();
      tracker.addImage(img, imgId);
      try{
          if(!tracker.waitForID(imgId,timeout)){
              msgDlg.setMessage("Failed to load image");
              msgDlg.setVisible(true);
          }//end if
      }catch(InterruptedException e){
          msgDlg.setMessage(e.toString()); msgDlg.setVisible(true);
      }
      g.drawImage(img, 0, 0, ImageCanvas.getWidth(), ImageCanvas.getHeight(), this);
}
```

Figure 7.23. The modified method ShowFaculty().

To confirm this data insertion, click on the new inserted faculty name from that combo box and click on the Select button to try to retrieve that newly inserted faculty record. The validation result is shown in Figure 7.26.

Our data insertion action is successful!

It is recommended to remove this inserted faculty from the Faculty table to keep our sample database neat and clean. Next, let's perform the data updating action against our sample database using the Java runtime object method.

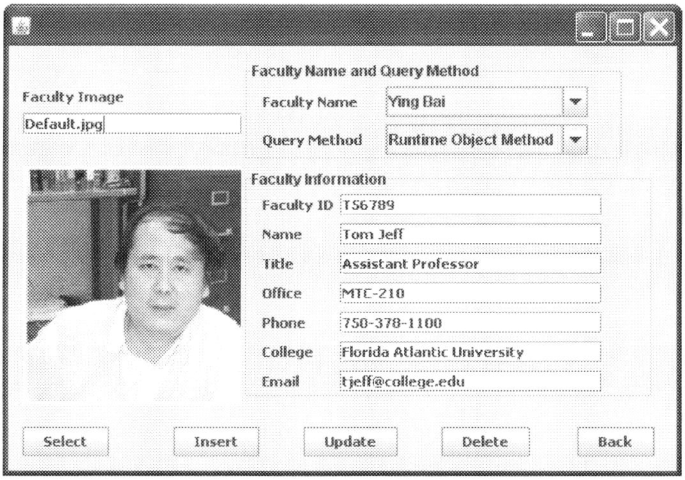

Figure 7.24. Insert a piece of new faculty information.

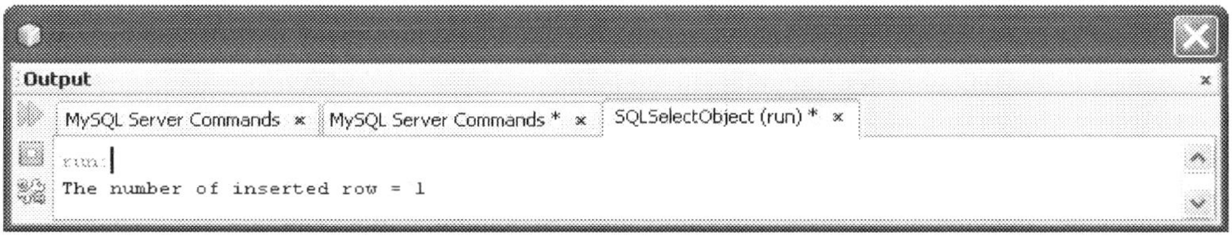

Figure 7.25. A successful data insertion message.

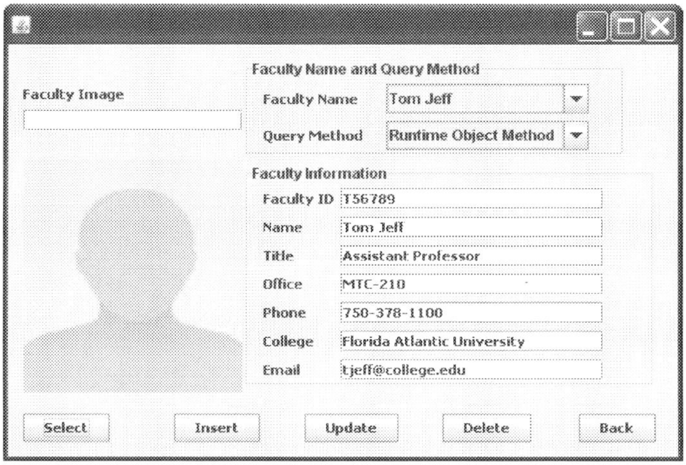

Figure 7.26. The data insertion validation result.

7.3.2 Perform Data Updating to SQL Server Database Using Java Runtime Object

Regularly, we do not need to update a faculty_id when we update a faculty record, since a better way to do that is to insert a new faculty record and delete the old one. The main reason for this is that a very complicated operation would be performed if the faculty_id were updated, since it is a primary key in the `Faculty` table and foreign keys in the `Course` and the `LogIn` tables. To update a primary key, one needs to update foreign keys first in the child tables and then update the primary key in the parent table. This will make our updating operation very complicated and easy to be confused. In order to avoid this confusion, in this section, we will update a faculty record by changing any column except the faculty_id, and this is a popular way to update a table and widely implemented in most database applications.

7.3.2.1 Develop the Codes for the Update Button Event Handler

We want to use the Update button we built in this FacultyFrame form window to perform the faculty updating function; therefore no any modification to this FacultyFrame form window to be made. Now, let's develop the codes for the Update button click event handler.

Open this event handler and enter the codes that are shown in Figure 7.27 into this event handler. Let's have a closer look at this piece of codes to see how it works.

A. Two local variables, numUpdated and cFacultyName, are created first, and these two variables are used to hold the running result of the data updating action and the current faculty name.

```
  private void cmdUpdateActionPerformed(java.awt.event.ActionEvent evt) {
    // TODO add your handling code here:
A   int numUpdated = 0;
    String cFacultyName = null;
B   String query = "UPDATE Faculty SET faculty_name=?, title=?, office=?, phone=?, college=?, email=? " +
                   "WHERE faculty_name= ?";
    try {
C       PreparedStatement pstmt = LogInFrame.con.prepareStatement(query);
D       pstmt.setString(1, FacultyNameField.getText());
        pstmt.setString(2, TitleField.getText());
        pstmt.setString(3, OfficeField.getText());
        pstmt.setString(4, PhoneField.getText());
        pstmt.setString(5, CollegeField.getText());
        pstmt.setString(6, EmailField.getText());
        pstmt.setString(7, ComboName.getSelectedItem().toString());
E       cFacultyName = (String)ComboName.getSelectedItem();
F       numUpdated = pstmt.executeUpdate();
    }
G   catch (SQLException e) {
        msgDlg.setMessage("Error in Statement!" + e.getMessage());
        msgDlg.setVisible(true);
    }
H   System.out.println("The number of updated row = " + numUpdated);
I   ComboName.addItem(FacultyNameField.getText());
J   ComboName.removeItem(cFacultyName);
  }
```

Figure 7.27. The developed codes for the Update button click event handler.

B. The updating query string is created with six positional parameters. The query criterion is the faculty name that is placed after the WHERE clause.

C. A try…catch block is used to assist this data updating action. First, a PreparedStatement instance is created using the Connection object that is located at the LogInFrame class with the updating query string as the argument.

D. The setString() method is used to initialize six pieces of updated faculty information, which are obtained from six text fields and entered by the user as the project runs.

E. After this faculty record has been updated, we need to remove the current or old faculty name from the Faculty Name combo box and add the updated faculty name into that box. In order to remember the current faculty name, we need to temporarily store it into our local string variable cFacultyName.

F. The data updating action is performed by calling the executeUpdate() method. The updating result, which is an integer number that is equal to the number of rows that have been updated by this data updating action, is returned and assigned to the local integer variable numUpdated.

G. The catch block is used to track and collect any possible exception encountered when this data updating is executed.

H. The running result is printed out as a debug purpose.

I. The updated faculty name is added into the Faculty Name combo box to enable the users to validate this data updating later.

J. The current or old faculty name is removed from this Faculty Name combo box.

Now, let's build and run the project to test the data updating action.

7.3.2.2 Build and Run the Project to Test the Data Updating

Before you can run this project, the following conditions have to be met:

- The SQL Server sample database CSE_DEPT has been connected to this project. To check this connection, open the Services window and expand the Databases node to locate our sample database connection URL, jdbc:sqlserver://localhost\SQL2008EXPRESS:5000;databaseName=CSE_DEPT [ybai on dbo]. Right click on this URL and select the Connect item to do this connection.

Click on the Clean and Build Main Project button from the toolbar to build our project. Then click on the Run Main Project button to run the project.

Enter a suitable username and password, such as jhenry and test, to complete the login process and select the Faculty Information from the SelectFrame window to open the FacultyFrame window. Make sure that the Runtime Object Method has been selected from the Query Method combo box. Then click on the Select button to query the default faculty information. The default faculty information is displayed.

Enter the following information into six Text Fields (no Faculty ID Text Field) inside the Faculty Information panel as an updated faculty record, as shown in Figure 7.28.

1. Name: Susan Bai
2. Title: Professor
3. Office: MTC-215
4. Phone: 750-378-1111

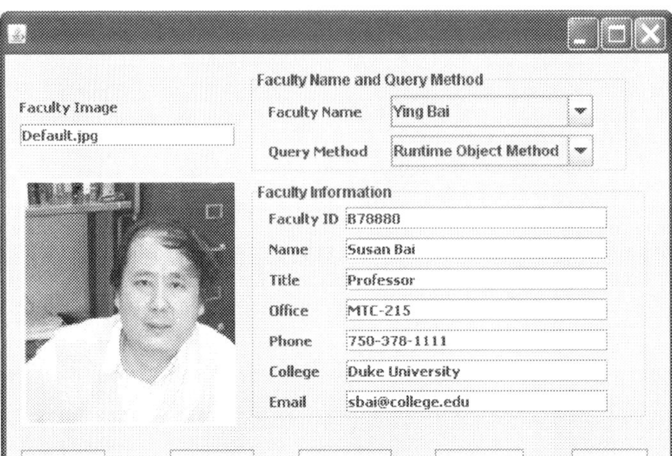

Figure 7.28. The entered faculty updating information.

Figure 7.29. The successful data updating message.

5. College: Duke University
6. Email: sbai@college.com

Also, enter the name of a default faculty image file, `Default.jpg`, to the Faculty Image field since we want to update this faculty's image with this data updating. Your finished updating window should match one that is shown in Figure 7.28.

Click on the **Update** button to perform this data updating. Immediately, you can find that the updated faculty name **Susan Bai** has been added into the Faculty Name combo box and the original faculty member **Ying Bai** has been removed from this box when clicking on the drop-down arrow of that box.

To validate this data updating, open the **Output** window if it has not been opened. You can find that a running successful message is displayed in that window, as shown in Figure 7.29.

Similar to the data insertion operation, here we have two ways to validate this data updating. One way is to open our **Faculty** table to confirm this data updating, and the other way is to use the **Select** button (exactly the codes inside that button's click event handler) to do this validation. We prefer to use the second way to do this validation. Click on the **Select** button to try to retrieve this updated faculty record, and the running result is shown in Figure 7.30.

Our data updating action is successful!

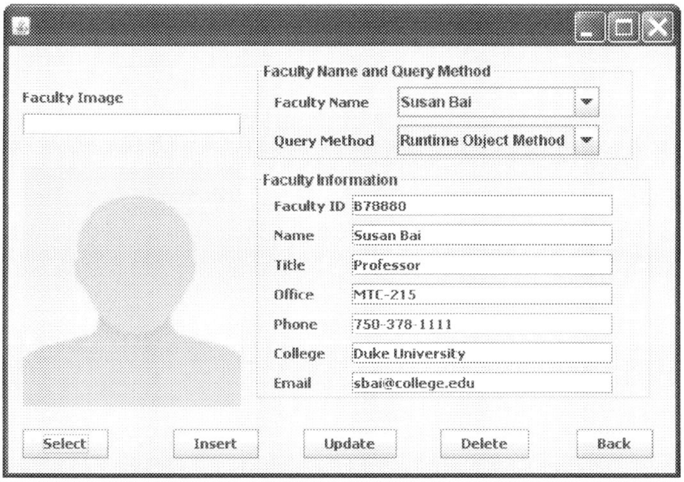

Figure 7.30. The data updated result.

It is highly recommended to recover that updated faculty record to keep our database clean and neat. Refer to Section 7.1.3.2 to do this recovery job. Of course, you can also perform this data recovering job using the codes in the Update button click event handler to do another data updating action again.

Next, let's handle the data deletion action against our sample database.

7.3.3 Perform Data Deleting to SQL Server Database Using Java Runtime Object

Basically, there is no significant difference between the data updating and deleting using Java runtime object method. In this section, we try to use the Delete button we built in the FacultyFrame form window to perform this data deletion operation.

To make this deleting simple, we want to just delete the selected faculty record without touching the associated faculty image.

7.3.3.1 Develop the Codes for the Delete Button Event Handler

Open the Delete button click event handler and enter the codes that are shown in Figure 7.31 into this event handler. Let's have a closer look at this piece of codes to see how it works.

A. Two local variables, numDeleted and cFacultyName, are created first, and these two variables are used to hold the running result of the data deleting action and the current faculty name.

B. The deleting query string is created with one positional parameter. The query criterion is the faculty name that is placed after the WHERE clause.

C. A try...catch block is used to assist this data deleting action. First, a `PreparedStatement` instance is created using the `Connection` object that is located at the LogInFrame class with the deleting query string as the argument.

```
  private void cmdDeleteActionPerformed(java.awt.event.ActionEvent evt) {
A     int numDeleted = 0;
      String cFacultyName = null;
B     String query = "DELETE FROM Faculty WHERE faculty_name = ?";
      try {
C           PreparedStatement  pstmt = LogInFrame.con.prepareStatement(query);
D           pstmt.setString(1, ComboName.getSelectedItem().toString());
E           cFacultyName = (String)ComboName.getSelectedItem();
F           numDeleted = pstmt.executeUpdate();
        }
G       catch (SQLException e) {
              msgDlg.setMessage("Error in Statement!" + e.getMessage());
              msgDlg.setVisible(true);
        }
H       System.out.println("The number of deleted row = " + numDeleted);
I       ComboName.removeItem(cFacultyName);
  }
```

Figure 7.31. The developed codes for the Delete button click event handler.

D. The setString() method is used to initialize the positional parameter, which is the faculty name to be deleted from the Faculty Name combo box.

E. After this faculty record has been deleted, we need to remove this faculty name from the Faculty Name combo box. In order to remember the current faculty name, we need to temporarily store it into our local string variable `cFacultyName`.

F. The data deleting action is performed by calling the executeUpdate() method. The deleting result, which is an integer number that is equal to the number of rows that have been deleted by this data deleting action, is returned and assigned to the local integer variable `numDeleted`.

G. The catch block is used to track and collect any possible exception encountered when this data deleting is executed.

H. The running result is printed out as a debug purpose.

I. The deleted faculty name is removed from this Faculty Name combo box.

Now we are ready to build and run the project to test the data deletion function.

7.3.3.2 Build and Run the Project to Test the Data Deleting

Make sure that our sample database CSE_DEPT has been connected to our project. To check this connection, open the Services window and expand the Databases node to locate our sample database connection URL, jdbc:sqlserver://localhost\SQL2008EXPRESS: 5000;databaseName= CSE_DEPT [ybai on dbo]. Right click on this URL and select the `Connect` item to do this connection.

Now click on the Clean and Build Main Project button from the toolbar to build our project. Then click on the Run Main Project button to run the project.

Enter suitable username and password, such as jhenry and test, to complete the login process and select the Faculty Information from the SelectFrame window to open the FacultyFrame window. Make sure that the Runtime Object Method has been selected

Figure 7.32. The successful data deletion message.

Table 7.8. The deleted faculty record in the faculty table

faculty_id	faculty_name	office	phone	college	title	email
B78880	Ying Bai	MTC-211	750-378-1148	Florida Atlantic University	Associate Professor	ybai@college.edu

from the Query Method combo box. Then click on the Select button to query the default faculty information. The default faculty information is displayed.

To test this data deletion function, we can try to delete one faculty member, such as Ying Bai, from our Faculty table. To do that, select this faculty member from the Faculty Name combo box, and click on the Delete button. Immediately, you can find that this faculty name has been removed from the Faculty Name combo box. Also, the running result is shown in the Output window, as shown in Figure 7.32.

To confirm this data deletion, click on the Back and the Exit button to stop our project. Then open our Faculty table by going to the `Services` window and expand the `Databases` node, and our connection URL, and finally our sample database CSE_DEPT. Expand our database schema dbo and right click on the Faculty table. Select the `View Data` item from the pop-up menu to open our Faculty table. On the opened Faculty table, you can find that the faculty member Ying Bai has been removed from this table. Our data deletion function is successful!

To make our database clean and neat, it is highly recommended to recover this deleted faculty member and related records in our Faculty, LogIn, Course, and StudentCourse tables. Refer to Tables 7.2–7.5 in Section 7.1.3.2 to complete these data recoveries. An easy way to do this is to use the Microsoft SQL Server 2008 Management Studio. For your convenience, we will show these deleted records in Tables 7.8–7.11 again, and you can add or insert them back to the related tables to complete this data recovery.

As we discussed in Section 6.4.2.3 in Chapter 6, in addition to using the executeUpdate() method to perform data manipulations, such as data insertion, updating, and deleting actions, one can use the execute() method to perform the similar data manipulations. I prefer to leave this optional method as a homework and allow students to handle this issue.

A complete sample project SQLSelectObject that can be used to perform data insertion, updating and deletion actions against our SQL Server sample database can be found from the folder **DBProjects\Chapter 7** that is located at the Wiley ftp site (refer to Figure 1.2 in Chapter 1).

Table 7.9. The deleted course records in the course table

course_id	course	credit	classroom	schedule	enrollment	faculty_id
CSC-132B	Introduction to Programming	3	TC-302	T-H: 1:00-2:25 PM	21	B78880
CSC-234A	Data Structure & Algorithms	3	TC-302	M-W-F: 9:00-9:55 AM	25	B78880
CSE-434	Advanced Electronics Systems	3	TC-213	M-W-F: 1:00-1:55 PM	26	B78880
CSE-438	Advd Logic & Microprocessor	3	TC-213	M-W-F: 11:00-11:55 AM	35	B78880

Table 7.10. The deleted login records in the login table

user_name	pass_word	faculty_id	student_id
ybai	reback	B78880	NULL

Table 7.11. The deleted records in the studentcourse table

s_course_id	student_id	course_id	credit	major
1005	J77896	CSC-234A	3	CS/IS
1009	A78835	CSE-434	3	CE
1014	A78835	CSE-438	3	CE
1016	A97850	CSC-132B	3	ISE
1017	A97850	CSC-234A	3	ISE

Next, let's take care of the data manipulations against the Oracle database using the Java runtime object method.

7.4 PERFORM DATA MANIPULATIONS TO ORACLE DATABASE USING JAVA RUNTIME OBJECT

Basically, there is no significant difference between a Java database application to access a SQL Server or an Oracle database. Because of the similarity in the coding process for both database applications, we only discuss those differences and highlight those parts in this section.

The following differences are existed between these two database applications:

1. The JDBC Driver
2. The JDBC API package used for the Oracle database interfaces
3. The JDBC database connection URL
4. The protocol and cursor used in the CallableStatements method
5. The protocol used in the RowSet method

The top three differences have been discussed in detailed in Sections 6.5.2.1–6.5.2.3, and the last two differences have also been discussed in Sections 6.5.4–6.5.6 in Chapter 6. To make this data manipulation simple, in this section, we only concentrate on the data manipulations to the Faculty table using the FacultyFrame class we built in Section 6.5.1 in Chapter 6.

To save time and space, we can use and modify a project OracleSelectObject we built in Chapter 6 to perform data manipulations against our target database. Perform the following operations to complete this project transferring:

1. Open the Windows Explorer and create a new folder, such as JavaDBProject\Chapter 7.
2. Open a Web browser and go to the folder DBProjects\Chapter 6 that is located at the Wiley ftp site (refer to Figure 1.2 in Chapter 1).
3. Copy the project OracleSelectObject from that folder and paste it to our new folder JavaDBProject\Chapter 7.

Now we are ready to build our data insertion query to perform data manipulations to our Oracle sample database CSE_DEPT.

7.4.1 Perform Data Insertion to Oracle Database Using Java Runtime Object

In Section 6.5.1 in Chapter 6, we have created a FacultyFrame class and Faculty JFrame window FacultyFrame. Also, the following components have been added into that project:

- A JDBC driver for Oracle database has been loaded and registered.
- A valid database connection to that project has been established.
- A PreparedStatement instance has been created and implemented in the Select button click event handler to perform the data query.

In this section, we want to use the Insert button that has been added into the FacultyFrame window to perform this data insertion function. First, let's do some modifications to this FacultyFrame form window to enable us to perform the data manipulations.

7.4.1.1 Modify the FacultyFrame Window Form

First, let's modify the FacultyFrame form by adding three more Text Fields into this frame: two of them are added into the Faculty Information panel to enable us to insert a faculty record, and one of them is added at the top of the faculty image box to allow us to insert a new faculty image (exactly the location of the faculty image).

Perform the following operations to open our pasted project OracleSelectObject:

1. Launch the NetBeans IDE 6.8 and go to `File > Open Project` menu item to open the `Open Project` wizard.
2. Browse to the location where we copied and pasted our project OracleSelectObject, which is JavaDBProject\Chapter 7. Make sure that the `Open as Main Project` checkbox has been checked, and select this project and click on the `Open Project` button to open it.

Table 7.12. Objects and controls added into the faculty frame window

Type	Variable Name	Text	editable	Title
Label	Label1	Faculty ID		
Text Field	FacultyIDField		checked	
Label	Label2	Name		
Text Field	FacultyNameField		checked	
Label	Label3	Faculty Image		
Text Field	FacultyImageField		checked	

The point to be noted is that you now have two OracleSelectObject projects in the NetBeans IDE, but they are different projects with different functions. The first OracleSelectObject was built in Chapter 6 without data manipulation function, but this second project will be built in Chapter 7 with the data manipulation function.

3. Expand this project files to open the FacultyFrame.java file by double clicking on this file that is located under the `Source Packages\OracleSelectObject` node.
4. Click on the `Design` button at the top of this window to open the GUI window of this FacultyFrame class.

Perform the following operations to add three more Text Fields into this frame window:

- Enlarge the FacultyFrame window form and the `Faculty Information` panel.
- Add two more labels and two more Text fields into this `Faculty Information` panel and one more label and the associated Text Field to the top of the Faculty Image box with the properties shown in Table 7.12.

One point to be noted is the FacultyIDField, and its editable property is checked, which means that we need to modify the faculty_id as the project runs since we may insert a new faculty record, including a new faculty_id, as the project runs. However, this field should be disabled when a data updating is performed, because we will not update it during a faculty record updating process. Your finished modified FacultyFrame form window should match one that is shown in Figure 7.33.

Now let's develop the codes for the Insert button click event handler to perform the data insertion function as the project runs. The function of this piece of codes is to insert a new faculty record into our Oracle sample database CSE_DEPT using the Java runtime object method as this button is clicked.

7.4.1.2 Develop the Codes for the Insert Button Event Handler

In fact, there is no difference in the coding part for data insertion to a SQL Server or an Oracle database. You can open the Insert button click event handler from the project SQLSelectObject we built in the last section, copy the codes from that handler, and paste them into our current Insert button click event handler in the project OracleSelectObject.

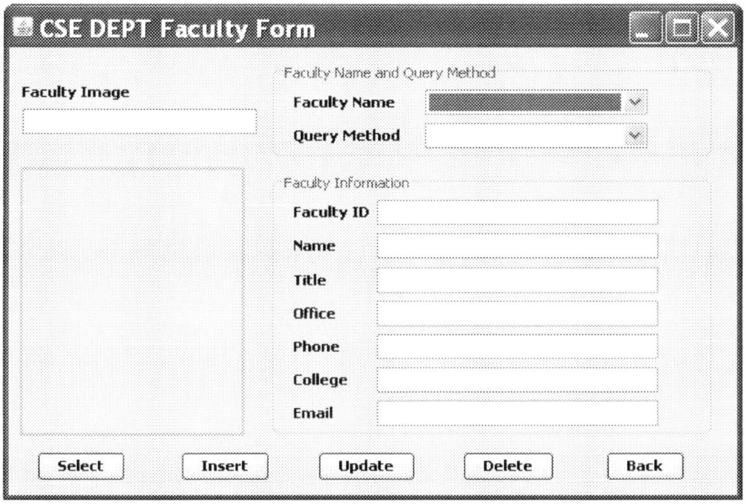

Figure 7.33. The modified FacultyFrame form window.

To confirm this data insertion, we can still use the codes inside the Select button click event handler, especially the codes inside the Runtime Object Method block. However, two important modifications need to be made to make them our desired validation methods:

1. Modify the codes inside the Select button click event handler to query two more columns, `faculty_id` and `faculty_name`, from the Faculty table.
2. Modify the `ShowFaculty()` method and divide it into two submethods, `ShowFaculty()` and `DisplayImage()`.

During the development the codes for the Select button click event handler in Chapter 6, we only query five columns without including the `faculty_id` and `faculty_name` columns. Now we need to add these two columns for this data insertion validation.

Open the Select button click event handler and perform the modifications shown in Figure 7.34. The modified parts have been highlighted in bold.

Let's have a closer look at this piece of modified codes to see how it works.

A. Two more columns, `faculty_id` and `faculty_name`, are added into the faculty text field array f_field since we need to query and display all columns from Faculty table to confirm the data insertion function.

B. Similarly, these two columns are added into the query string to enable them to be queried.

Now open the ShowFaculty() method and divide this method into two submethods, ShowFaculty() and DisplayImage(), which are shown in Figure 7.35. The modified parts have been highlighted in bold.

```
  private void cmdSelectActionPerformed(java.awt.event.ActionEvent evt) {
    // TODO add your handling code here:
A   javax.swing.JTextField[] f_field = {FacultyIDField, FacultyNameField, TitleField, OfficeField, PhoneField,
                                        CollegeField, EmailField};
B   String query = "SELECT faculty_id, faculty_name, title, office, phone, college, email " +
                   "FROM Faculty WHERE faculty_name = ?";
    if (ComboMethod.getSelectedItem()=="Runtime Object Method"){
      try{
           DatabaseMetaData dbmd = LogInFrame.con.getMetaData();
           String drName = dbmd.getDriverName();
           String drVersion = dbmd.getDriverVersion();
           msgDlg.setMessage("DriverName is: " + drName + ", Version is: " + drVersion);
           //msgDlg.setVisible(true);
           PreparedStatement pstmt = LogInFrame.con.prepareStatement(query);
           pstmt.setString(1, ComboName.getSelectedItem().toString());
           ResultSet rs = pstmt.executeQuery();
```

Figure 7.34. The modified codes for the Select button click event handler.

In Section 7.1.1.4, we have provided a detailed explanation about the modifications for this method, and refer to that section to get more information about this modification. The purpose of this modification is to allow the new inserted faculty image to be displayed, either a new faculty image or a default one.

Now we are ready to build and run the project to test the data insertion function.

Click on the Clean and Build Main Project button from the toolbar to build the project. Then click on the Run Main Project button to run the project.

Enter suitable username and password, such as `jhenry` and `test`, to the LogIn frame form and select the Faculty Information from the SelectFrame window to open the FacultyFrame form window. Make sure that the Runtime Object Method has been selected from the Query Method combo box. Then click on the Select button to query the default faculty information.

Modify seven text fields, which is equivalent to a piece of new faculty information, and enter the default faculty image file into the Faculty Image text field, as shown in Figure 7.36.

Click on the Insert button to try to insert this new faculty record into the Faculty table in our sample database. Immediately, you can find that a debug message is displayed in the Output window, as shown in Figure 7.37.

Also, you can find that the new inserted faculty name has been added into the Faculty Name combo box if you click on the drop-down arrow from that box.

To confirm this data insertion, click on the new inserted faculty name from that combo box and click on the Select button to try to retrieve that new inserted faculty record. The validation result will be displayed, and our data insertion action is successful!

To keep our database clean and neat, it is highly recommended to remove this newly inserted faculty record. You can do this data deletion using either the Object Browser in the Oracle Database 10g Express Edition or the Services window in NetBeans IDE 6.8.

Next, let's perform the data updating action against our sample Oracle database using the Java runtime object method.

```
private boolean ShowFaculty(){
      int maxNumber = 7;
      String fImage = null;
      String[] fname = {"Ying Bai", "Black Anderson", "Satish Bhalla", "Steve Johnson",
                        "Jenney King", "Alice Brown", "Debby Angles", "Jeff Henry"};
      String[] fimage = {"Bai.jpg", "Anderson.jpg", "Satish.jpg", "Johnson.jpg",
                         "King.jpg", "Brown.jpg", "Angles.jpg", "Henry.jpg"};
      for (int i=0; i<=maxNumber; i++){
         if (fname[i].equals((String)ComboName.getSelectedItem())){
            fImage = fimage[i];
            break;
         }
      }
      if (fImage != null){
         DisplayImage(fImage);
         return true;
      }
      else if (FacultyImageField.getText() != null){
         fImage = FacultyImageField.getText();
         DisplayImage(fImage);
         FacultyImageField.setText("");
         return true;
      }
      else
         return false;
}
private void DisplayImage(String facultyImage){
      Image img;
      int imgId = 1, timeout = 1000;
      MediaTracker tracker = new MediaTracker(this);
      MsgDialog msgDlg = new MsgDialog(new javax.swing.JFrame(), true);
      img = this.getToolkit().getImage(facultyImage);
      Graphics g = ImageCanvas.getGraphics();
      tracker.addImage(img, imgId);
      try{
         if(!tracker.waitForID(imgId,timeout)){
            msgDlg.setMessage("Failed to load image");
            msgDlg.setVisible(true);
         }//end if
      }catch(InterruptedException e){
         msgDlg.setMessage(e.toString()); msgDlg.setVisible(true);
      }
      g.drawImage(img, 0, 0, ImageCanvas.getWidth(), ImageCanvas.getHeight(), this);
}
```

Figure 7.35. The modified method ShowFaculty().

7.4.2 Perform Data Updating to Oracle Database Using Java Runtime Object

There is no difference in the coding part for data updating against a SQL Server or an Oracle database. You can open the Update button click event handler from the project SQLSelectObject we built in the last section, copy the codes from that handler, and paste them into our current Update button click event handler in the project OracleSelectObject. For your convenience, we list this coding again in Figure 7.38.

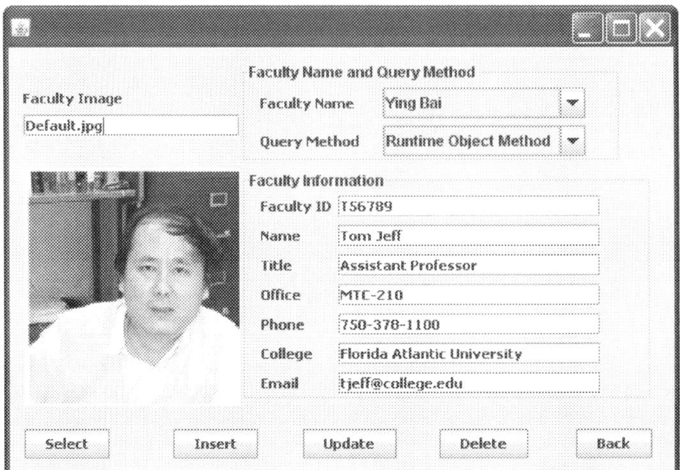

Figure 7.36. Insert a new faculty record.

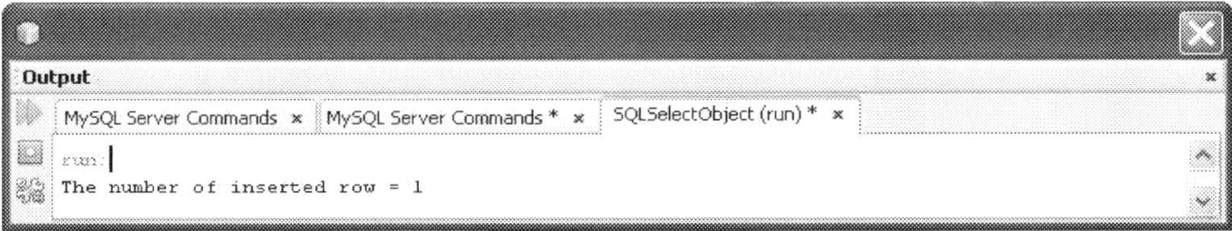

Figure 7.37. A successful data insertion message.

```
  private void cmdUpdateActionPerformed(java.awt.event.ActionEvent evt) {
    // TODO add your handling code here:
A   int  numUpdated = 0;
    String  cFacultyName = null;
B   String query = "UPDATE  Faculty SET faculty_name=?,  title=?,  office=?,  phone=?,  college=?,  email=? " +
                   "WHERE  faculty_name= ?";
    try {
C        PreparedStatement pstmt = LogInFrame.con.prepareStatement(query);
D        pstmt.setString(1, FacultyNameField.getText());
         pstmt.setString(2, TitleField.getText());
         pstmt.setString(3, OfficeField.getText());
         pstmt.setString(4, PhoneField.getText());
         pstmt.setString(5, CollegeField.getText());
         pstmt.setString(6, EmailField.getText());
         pstmt.setString(7, ComboName.getSelectedItem().toString());
E        cFacultyName = (String)ComboName.getSelectedItem();
F        numUpdated = pstmt.executeUpdate();
      }
G    catch (SQLException e) {
           msgDlg.setMessage("Error in Statement!" + e.getMessage());
           msgDlg.setVisible(true);
      }
H    System.out.println("The number of updated row = " + numUpdated);
I    ComboName.addItem(FacultyNameField.getText());
J    ComboName.removeItem(cFacultyName);
  }
```

Figure 7.38. The developed codes for the Update button click event handler.

For detailed explanations of this piece of codes, refer to Section 7.3.2.1 in this Chapter.

To confirm this data updating, we can still use the codes inside the Select button click event handler, especially the codes inside the Runtime Object Method block.

Now you can build and run the project to try to update a faculty member Ying Bai in our sample Oracle database. To keep our database clean and neat, it is highly recommended to recover the updated faculty member information. You can do that recovery job in two ways, using the Services window in the NetBeans IDE 6.8 or using the Object Browser in the Oracle Database 10g Express Edition. Refer to Table 7.2 in Section 7.1.3.2 to make this data recovery.

7.4.3 Perform Data Deleting to Oracle Database Using Java Runtime Object

Since no difference exists in the coding part for the data deleting from a SQL Server or an Oracle database, you can open the Delete button click event handler from the project SQLSelectObject we built in the last section, copy the codes from that handler, and paste them into our current Delete button click event handler in the project OracleSelectObject. For your convenience, we list this coding again in Figure 7.39.

For detailed explanations of this piece of codes, refer to Section 7.3.3.1 in this chapter.

Now you can build and run the project to try to delete a faculty member Ying Bai from our sample database. To make our database clean and neat, it is highly recommended to recover this deleted faculty member and related records in our Faculty, LogIn, Course, and StudentCourse tables. Refer to Tables 7.2–7.5 in Section 7.1.3.2 to complete this data recovery. An easy way to do this data recovery job is to use the Object Browser in the Oracle Database 10g Express Edition. To confirm this data deletion, we can still use the codes inside the Select button click event handler, especially the codes inside the Runtime Object Method block.

At this point, we have finished developing and building data manipulations to the Oracle database using the Java runtime object method. A complete sample project

```
  private void cmdDeleteActionPerformed(java.awt.event.ActionEvent evt) {
A     int numDeleted = 0;
      String cFacultyName = null;
B     String query = "DELETE FROM Faculty WHERE faculty_name = ?";
      try {
C         PreparedStatement  pstmt = LogInFrame.con.prepareStatement(query);
D         pstmt.setString(1, ComboName.getSelectedItem().toString());
E         cFacultyName = (String)ComboName.getSelectedItem();
F         numDeleted = pstmt.executeUpdate();
       }
G      catch (SQLException e) {
            msgDlg.setMessage("Error in Statement!" + e.getMessage());
            msgDlg.setVisible(true);
       }
H      System.out.println("The number of deleted row = " + numDeleted);
I      ComboName.removeItem(cFacultyName);
  }
```

Figure 7.39. The developed codes for the Delete button click event handler.

OracleSelectObject that can be used to perform data insertion, updating, and deletion actions against our Oracle sample database can be found from the folder **DBProjects\Chapter 7** that is located at the Wiley ftp site (refer to Figure 1.2 in Chapter 1).

Next, let's take care of the data manipulations against our sample database using the updatable ResultSet object method.

7.5 PERFORM DATA MANIPULATIONS USING UPDATABLE RESULTSET

As we discussed in Section 6.4.2.5 in Chapter 6, a ResultSet object can be considered as a table of data representing a database result set, which is usually generated by executing a statement that queries the database.

The ResultSet interface provides getXXX() methods for retrieving column values from the current row. Values can be retrieved using either the index number of the column or the name of the column. In general, using the column index will be more efficient. Columns are numbered from 1. For maximum portability, result set columns within each row should be read in left-to-right order, and each column should be read only once.

A default ResultSet object is not updatable and has a cursor that moves forward only. Thus, it is possible to iterate through it only once and only from the first row to the last row. New methods in the JDBC 2.0 API make it possible to produce ResultSet objects that are scrollable and/or updatable.

Before we can use the ResultSet object to perform data manipulations against our sample database, let's first have a clear picture about the ResultSet additional functionalities and categories supported in JDBC 2.0.

7.5.1 Introduction to ResultSet Enhanced Functionalities and Categories

ResultSet functionality in JDBC 2.0 includes enhancements for scrollability and positioning, sensitivity to changes by others, and updatability.

- **Scrollability:** the ability to move backward as well as forward through a ResultSet object. Associated with scrollability is the ability to move to any particular position in the ResultSet, through either relative positioning or absolute positioning.
- **Positioning:** the ability to move a specified number of rows forward or backward from the current row. Absolute positioning enables you to move to a specified row number, counting from either the beginning or the end of the ResultSet.
- **Sensitivity:** the ability to see changes made to the database while the ResultSet is open, providing a dynamic view of the underlying data. Changes made to the underlying columns values of rows in the ResultSet are visible.

Two parameters can be used to set up those properties of a ResultSet object when it is created, they are: ResultSet Type and Concurrency Type of a ResultSet.

Table 7.13 lists these types and their functions.

Table 7.13. The resultset type and concurrency type

ResultSet Type	**Functions**
Forward-only	This is an JDBC 1.0 functionality. This type of ResultSet is not scrollable, not positionable, and not sensitive
Scroll-sensitive	This type of ResultSet is scrollable and positionable. It is also sensitive to underlying database changes.
Scroll-insensitive	This type of result set is scrollable and positionable, but not sensitive to underlying database changes.
Concurrency type	Functions
Updatable	Data updating, insertion, and deleting can be performed on the ResultSet and copied to the database.
Read-only	The result set cannot be modified in any way.

Under JDBC 2.0, the Connection class has the following methods that take a ResultSet type and a concurrency type as input to define a newly created ResultSet object:

- `Statement createStatement(int resultSetType, int resultSetConcurrency)`
- `PreparedStatement prepareStatement(String sql, int resultSet-Type, int resultSetConcurrency)`
- `CallableStatement prepareCall(String sql, int resultSetType, int resultSetConcurrency)`

You can specify one of the following static constant values for ResultSet type:

- ResultSet.TYPE_FORWARD_ONLY
- ResultSet.TYPE_SCROLL_INSENSITIVE
- ResultSet.TYPE_SCROLL_SENSITIVE

And you can specify one of the following static constant values for concurrency type:

- ResultSet.CONCUR_READ_ONLY
- ResultSet.CONCUR_UPDATABLE

The following code fragment, in which conn is a valid Connection object and sql is a defined SQL query string, illustrates how to make a ResultSet that is scrollable and sensitive to updates by others, and that is updatable.

```
PreparedStatement pstmt = conn.prepareStatement
(sql, ResultSet.TYPE_SCROLL_SENSITIVE, ResultSet.CONCUR_UPDATABLE);
```

After we have a basic and fundamental understanding about the ResultSet and its enhanced functionalities, now we can go ahead to perform data manipulations against our sample database using the Updatable ResultSet object.

7.5.2 Perform Data Manipulations Using Updatable ResultSet Object

Generally, perform data manipulations using updatable ResultSet can be divided into the following three categories:

- Data insertion
- Data updating
- Data deleting

Different data manipulations need different operational steps, and Table 7.14 lists the most popular operational steps for these data manipulations.

It can be found from Table 7.14 that the data deleting is the easiest way to remove a piece of data from the database since it only needs one step to delete the data from both the ResultSet and the database. The other two data manipulations, data updating, and insertion, need at least two steps to complete that data manipulations.

The point to be noted is the data insertion action, in which the first step moveToInsertRow() is exactly moved to a blank row that is not a part of the ResultSet, but related to the ResultSet. The data insertion is exactly occurred when the insertRow() method is called and the next commit command is executed.

Let's start with the data insertion against our sample database first. Since there is no difference between data manipulation for SQL Server and Oracle database, in the following sections, we will use the Oracle database as our target database, and the same codes can be used for the SQL Server database as long as a valid database connection can be set up between our project and the target database.

7.5.2.1 Insert a New Row Using the Updatable ResultSet

To save time and space, we want to use and modify a project OracleSelectObject we built in Section 7.4 to make it as our new project to perform this data insertion action. Perform the following operations to make it as our project:

Table 7.14. The operational steps of data manipulations using updatable resultset

Manipulation Type	Steps
Data deleting	Single step: Using the deleteRow() method of the ResultSet class.
Data updating	Two steps: Update the data in the ResultSet using the associated updateXXX() methods. Copy the changes to the database using the updateRow() method.
Data insertion	Three steps: Move to the insert-row by calling the ResultSet moveToInsertRow() method. Use the appropriate updateXXX() methods to update data in the insert-row. Copy the changes to the database by calling the ResultSet insertRow() method.

```
public FacultyFrame() {
    initComponents();
    this.setLocationRelativeTo(null);   // set the faculty Form at the center
    ComboMethod.addItem("JPA Wizards Method");
    ComboMethod.addItem("Runtime Object Method");
    ComboMethod.addItem("Java execute() Method");
    ComboMethod.addItem("Java Callable Method");
    ComboMethod.addItem("Java Updatable ResultSet");
    ComboName.addItem("Ying Bai");
    ComboName.addItem("Satish Bhalla");
    ComboName.addItem("Black Anderson");
    ComboName.addItem("Steve Johnson");
    ComboName.addItem("Jenney King");
    ComboName.addItem("Alice Brown");
    ComboName.addItem("Debby Angles");
    ComboName.addItem("Jeff Henry");
}
```

Figure 7.40. The modified codes for the constructor of the FacultyFrame class.

1. Launch NetBeans IDE 6.8 and open the Projects window.
2. Right click on the project OracleSelectObject we built in Section 7.4 and select the `Set as Main Project` item from the popup menu.
3. Double click on the FacultyFrame.java to open the FacultyFrame class.
4. Click on the Design button to open the FacultyFrame form window.

Perform the following modifications to this form:

1. Open the constructor of this class and add one more statement shown below into this constructor,

   `ComboMethod.addItem("Java Updatable ResultSet");`

   Your modified codes in this constructor should match one that is shown in Figure 7.40. The modified part has been highlighted in bold.
2. Click on the Design button to switch back to the design view of the FacultyFrame form window, and double click on the Insert button to open its event handler. Enter the codes that are shown in Figure 7.41 into this handler to perform data insertion action against our Oracle database.

Let's have a closer look at this piece of modified codes to see how it works.

A. First, we add an `if` block to distinguish the `Runtime Object Method` and the `Java Updatable ResultSet` method to perform this data insertion.

B. An `else if` block is added with the same objective as step A.

C. The query string is created and it is used to help to use the Updatable ResultSet object to do this data insertion. One point to be noted is that because of the limitation for the Updatable ResultSet under JDBC 2.0, you cannot use a star (*) following the `SELECT` to query all columns from the target table, instead you have to explicitly list all columns for this query. An option is to use the table aliases, such as `SELECT f.* FROM TABLE f ......` to do this kind of query.

D. A try...catch block is used to perform this data insertion. A PreparedStatement is created with two ResultSet parameters, `TYPE_SCROLL_SENSITIVE` and `CONCUR_`

```
    private void cmdInsertActionPerformed(java.awt.event.ActionEvent evt) {
       int numInsert = 0;
A      if (ComboMethod.getSelectedItem()=="Runtime Object Method"){
          String InsertQuery = "INSERT INTO Faculty (faculty_id, faculty_name, office, phone, " +
                               "college, title, email) VALUES (?, ?, ?, ?, ?, ?, ?)";
          try {
               PreparedStatement pstmt = LogInFrame.con.prepareStatement(InsertQuery);
               pstmt.setString(1, FacultyIDField.getText());
               pstmt.setString(2, FacultyNameField.getText());
               pstmt.setString(3, OfficeField.getText());
               pstmt.setString(4, PhoneField.getText());
               pstmt.setString(5, CollegeField.getText());
               pstmt.setString(6, TitleField.getText());
               pstmt.setString(7, EmailField.getText());
               numInsert = pstmt.executeUpdate();
          }
          catch (SQLException e) {
               msgDlg.setMessage("Error in Statement!" + e.getMessage());
               msgDlg.setVisible(true);
          }
       }
B      else if (ComboMethod.getSelectedItem()=="Java Updatable ResultSet"){
C        String query = "SELECT faculty_id, faculty_name, title, office, phone, college, email  " +
                        "FROM Faculty WHERE faculty_name = ?";
         try {
D              PreparedStatement  pstmt = LogInFrame.con.prepareStatement(query,
                                  ResultSet.TYPE_SCROLL_SENSITIVE, ResultSet.CONCUR_UPDATABLE);
E              pstmt.setString(1, ComboName.getSelectedItem().toString());
F              ResultSet rs = pstmt.executeQuery();
G              rs.moveToInsertRow();
H              rs.updateString(1, FacultyIDField.getText());
               rs.updateString(2, FacultyNameField.getText());
               rs.updateString(3, TitleField.getText());
               rs.updateString(4, OfficeField.getText());
               rs.updateString(5, PhoneField.getText());
               rs.updateString(6, CollegeField.getText());
               rs.updateString(7, EmailField.getText());
I              rs.insertRow();
J              rs.moveToCurrentRow(); // Go back to where we came from...
           }
K          catch (SQLException e){
             msgDlg.setMessage("Error in Updatable ResultSet! " + e.getMessage());
             msgDlg.setVisible(true);
           }
        }
        System.out.println("The number of inserted row = " + numInsert);
        ComboName.addItem(FacultyNameField.getText());
    }
```

Figure 7.41. The modified codes for the Insert button click event handler.

UPDATABLE, to define the ResultSet object to enable it to be scrollable and updatable, and enable it to perform data manipulations.

E. The setString() method is used to initialize the positional parameter in the query string.

F. The executeQuery() method is called to perform this query and return the query result to a newly created ResultSet object.

G. In order to insert a new row into this ResultSet, the moveToInsertRow() method is executed to move the cursor of the ResultSet to a blank row that is not a part of the ResultSet but is related to that ResultSet.

H. A sequence of updateString() methods are executed to insert desired columns to the associated columns in the ResultSet. The point to be noted is that different updateXXX()

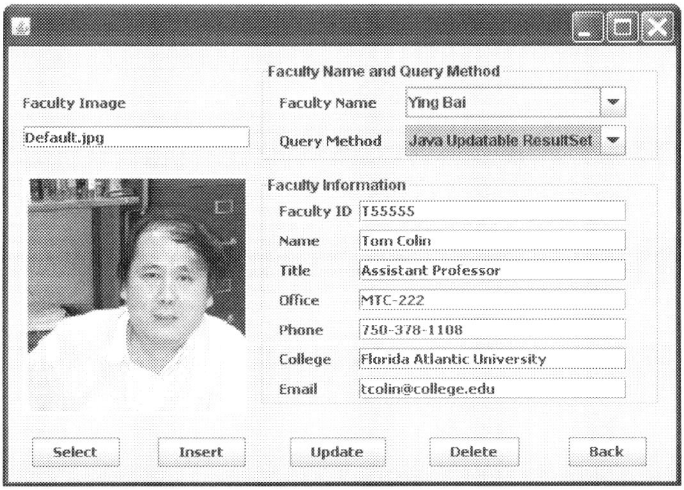

Figure 7.42. The newly inserted faculty record.

methods should be used if the target columns have the different data types, and the XXX indicate the associated data type, such as Int, Float, and Double.

I. The insertRow() method is executed to update this change to the database. Exactly, this data updating would not happen until the next Commit command is executed.

J. The moveToCurrentRow() method is an optional and it return the cursor of the ResultSet to the original position before this data insertion is performed.

K. The catch block is used to track and collect any possible exception for this data insertion action.

Now let's build and run the project to test this data insertion.

Click on the Clean and Build Main Project button to build the project, and click on the Run Main Project button to run it.

Enter suitable username and password, such as `jhenry` and `test`, to the LogIn frame form and select the Faculty Information from the SelectFrame window to open the FacultyFrame form window. Make sure that the Runtime Object Method has been selected from the Query Method combo box. Then click on the Select button to query the default faculty information.

Modify seven text fields, which is equivalent to a piece of new faculty information, and enter the default faculty image file into the Faculty Image text field. To test this data insertion using the Updatable ResultSet, select the Java Updatable ResultSet from the Query Method combo box, as shown in Figure 7.42. Then click on the Insert button to perform this data insertion.

To confirm and validate this data insertion, two ways are available. First, let's check this directly from this FacultyFrame form. Go to the Faculty Name combo box and you will find that new inserted faculty name Tom Colin has been added into this box. Select this new inserted faculty member from that box and select the Runtime Object Method from the Query Method combo box followed with a clicking on the Select button to try to retrieve this new inserted faculty record. The returned faculty record is displayed, as shown in Figure 7.43.

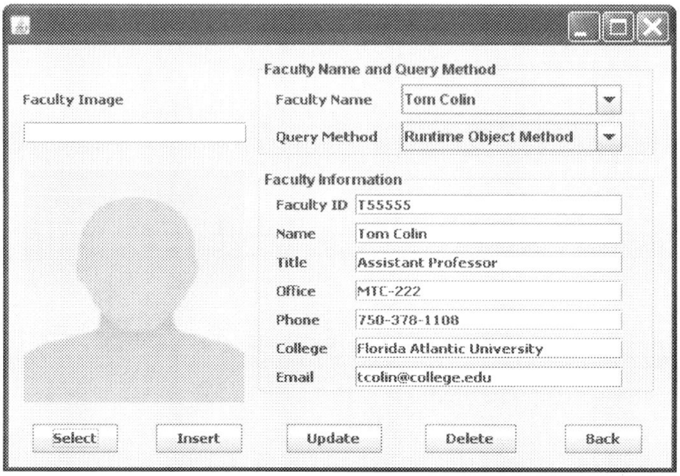

Figure 7.43. The retrieved newly inserted faculty record.

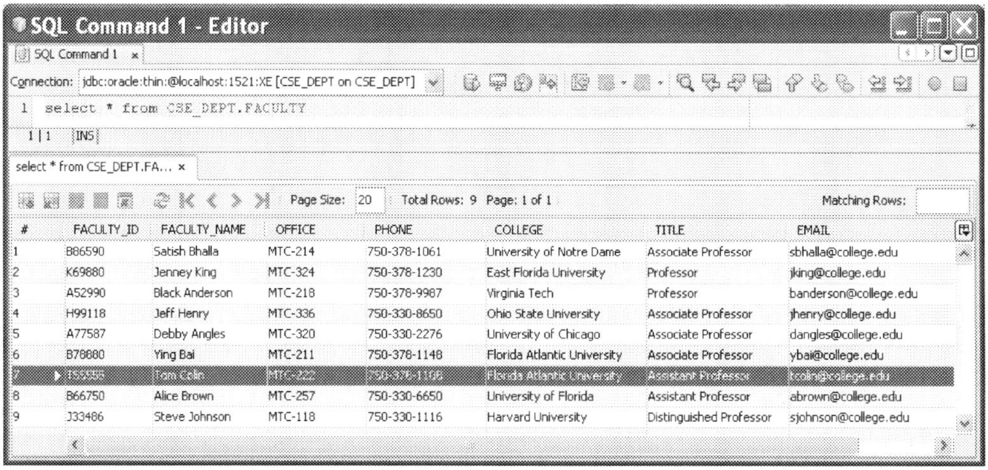

Figure 7.44. The newly inserted faculty member.

Now let's try to open the Faculty table to confirm this data insertion. Open the Services window in the NetBeans IDE, and expand the Databases node and connect our Oracle database using the connection URL, jdbc:oracle:thin:@localhost:1521:XE [CSE_DEPT on CSE_DEPT]. Then expand this connected database, the CSE_DEPT and the Tables node, and right click on the Faculty table and select the View Data to this table. On the opened Faculty table, you can find that the new inserted faculty member, which has been highlighted in the table, has been there as shown in Figure 7.44.

Click on the Back and the Exit buttons to terminate our project, and our data insertion function is successful. It is highly recommended to remove this newly inserted faculty record from our sample database to keep our database clean and neat.

Next, let's take care of the data updating action using the Updatable ResultSet object. As we did for the data insertion, we still want to use this FacultyFrame form window to update one of faculty members in the Faculty table in our sample database CSE_DEPT.

7.5.2.2 Update a Row Using the Updatable ResultSet

Double click on the Update button from the FacultyFrame form window to open its event handler, and modify the codes that are shown in Figure 7.45 to perform the data updating function using the Updatable ResultSet object.

```
  private void cmdUpdateActionPerformed(java.awt.event.ActionEvent evt) {
      int numUpdated = 0;
      String cFacultyName = null;
A     if (ComboMethod.getSelectedItem()=="Runtime Object Method"){
        String query = "UPDATE Faculty SET faculty_name=?, title=?, office=?, phone=?, college=?, email=? " +
                       "WHERE faculty_name= ?";
        try {
          PreparedStatement pstmt = LogInFrame.con.prepareStatement(query);
          pstmt.setString(1, FacultyNameField.getText());
          pstmt.setString(2, TitleField.getText());
          pstmt.setString(3, OfficeField.getText());
          pstmt.setString(4, PhoneField.getText());
          pstmt.setString(5, CollegeField.getText());
          pstmt.setString(6, EmailField.getText());
          pstmt.setString(7, ComboName.getSelectedItem().toString());
          cFacultyName = (String)ComboName.getSelectedItem();
          numUpdated = pstmt.executeUpdate();
        }
        catch (SQLException e) {
          msgDlg.setMessage("Error in Statement!" + e.getMessage());
          msgDlg.setVisible(true);
        }
      }
B     else if (ComboMethod.getSelectedItem()=="Java Updatable ResultSet"){
C       String query = "SELECT faculty_name, title, office, phone, college, email " +
                       "FROM Faculty WHERE faculty_name = ?";
        try {
D         PreparedStatement pstmt = LogInFrame.con.prepareStatement(query,
                              ResultSet.TYPE_SCROLL_SENSITIVE, ResultSet.CONCUR_UPDATABLE);
E         pstmt.setString(1, ComboName.getSelectedItem().toString());
F         ResultSet rs = pstmt.executeQuery();
G         if (rs.absolute(1)) {
            rs.updateString(1, FacultyNameField.getText());
            rs.updateString(2, TitleField.getText());
            rs.updateString(3, OfficeField.getText());
            rs.updateString(4, PhoneField.getText());
            rs.updateString(5, CollegeField.getText());
            rs.updateString(6, EmailField.getText());
H           rs.updateRow();
          }
I         cFacultyName = (String)ComboName.getSelectedItem();
        }
J       catch (SQLException e){
          msgDlg.setMessage("Error in Updatable ResultSet! " + e.getMessage());
          msgDlg.setVisible(true);
        }
      }
      System.out.println("The number of updated row = " + numUpdated);
      ComboName.addItem(FacultyNameField.getText());
      ComboName.removeItem(cFacultyName);
  }
```

Figure 7.45. The modified codes for the Update button click event handler.

Let's have a closer look at this piece of modified codes to see how it works.

A. First, we add an `if` block to distinguish the `Runtime Object Method` and the `Java Updatable ResultSet` method to perform this data updating action.

B. An `else if` block is added with the same objective as step **A**.

C. The query string is created, and it is used to help to use the Updatable ResultSet object to do this data updating action.

D. A try…catch block is used to perform this data updating action. A PreparedStatement is created with two ResultSet parameters, `TYPE_SCROLL_SENSITIVE`, and `CONCUR_UPDATABLE`, to define the ResultSet object to enable it to be scrollable and updatable, and enable it to perform data manipulations.

E. The setString() method is used to initialize the positional parameter in the query string.

F. The executeQuery() method is called to perform this query and return the query result to a newly created ResultSet object.

G. First, we need to identify the location of the row to be updated. Exactly, there is only one row that has been retrieved from our Faculty table and saved in the ResultSet, which is the default faculty member Ying Bai, and this row will be updated in this data updating action. Therefore, the absolute position for this row is 1. Then, a sequence of updateString() methods are executed to update desired columns to the associated columns in the ResultSet. The point to be noted is that different updateXXX() methods should be used if the target columns have the different data types, and the XXX indicate the associated data type, such as Int, Float, and Double.

H. The updateRow() method is executed to update this change to the database. Exactly, this data updating would not happen until the next Commit command is executed. Be aware that by default, the autocommit flag is set to true so that any operation run is committed immediately.

I. In order to update the selected faculty member, we need to remove the original faculty name and add the updated faculty name into the Faculty Name combo box when this data updating action is complete. To save the original faculty name, we need to temporarily store it to a local variable cFacultyName.

J. The catch block is used to track and collect any possible exception for this data updating action.

Now let's build and run the project to test this data updating function.

Click on the Clean and Build Main Project button to build the project, and click on the Run Main Project button to run it.

Enter suitable username and password, such as `jhenry` and `test`, to the LogIn frame form and select the Faculty Information from the SelectFrame window to open the FacultyFrame form window. Make sure that the Runtime Object Method has been selected from the Query Method combo box. Then click on the Select button to query the default faculty information.

Modify six text fields (without the Faculty ID field), which is equivalent to a piece of updated faculty information, and enter the default faculty image file into the Faculty Image text field. To test this data updating function using the Updatable ResultSet, select the Java Updatable ResultSet from the Query Method combo box, as shown in Figure 7.46. Then click on the Update button to perform this data updating.

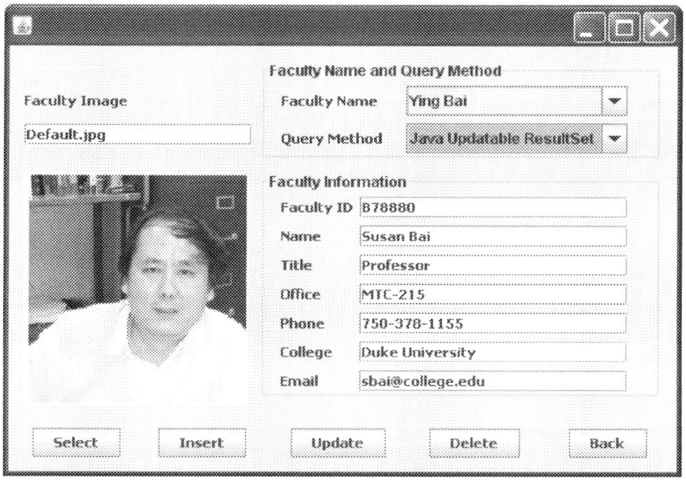

Figure 7.46. The updated faculty information.

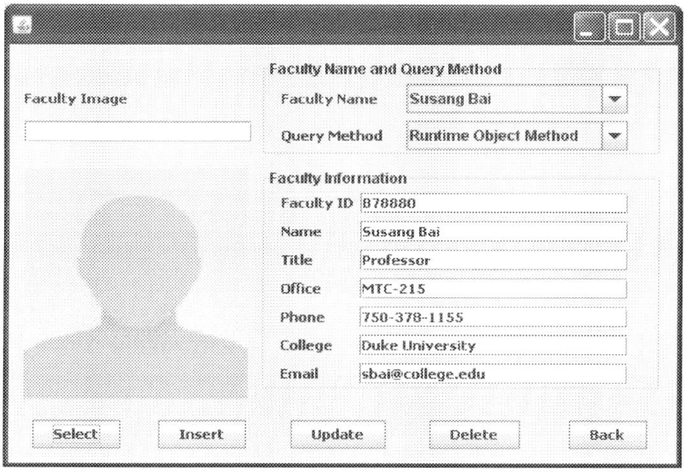

Figure 7.47. The retrieved updated faculty record.

To confirm and validate this data updating action, two ways are available. First, let's check this directly from this FacultyFrame form. Go to the Faculty Name combo box and you will find that updated faculty name Susan Bai has been added into this box. Select this new updated faculty member from that box and select the Runtime Object Method from the Query Method combo box followed with clicking on the Select button to try to retrieve this updated faculty record. The returned faculty record is displayed, as shown in Figure 7.47.

Now let's try to confirm this data updating in the second way, which is to open the Faculty table to confirm this data manipulation. Click on the Back and the Exit buttons to terminate our project. Then open the Services window in the NetBeans IDE, and expand the Databases node and connect our Oracle database using the connection URL,

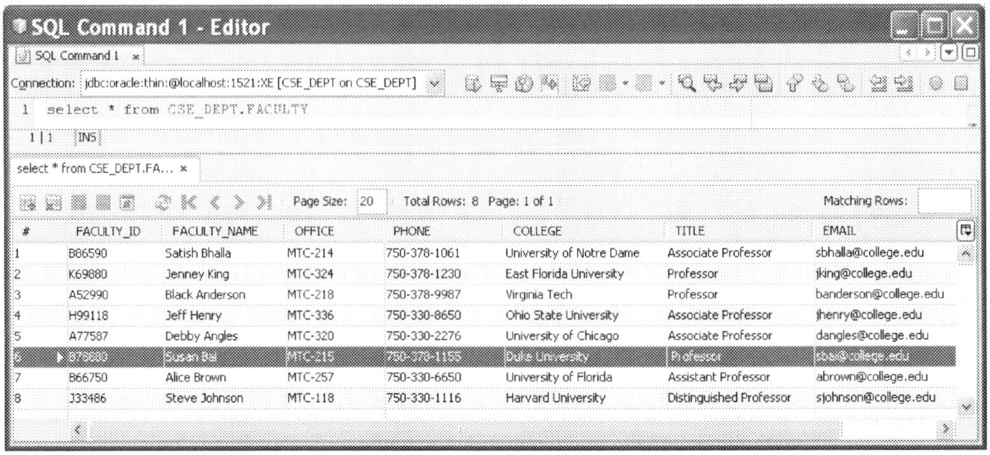

#	FACULTY_ID	FACULTY_NAME	OFFICE	PHONE	COLLEGE	TITLE	EMAIL
1	B86590	Satish Bhalla	MTC-214	750-378-1061	University of Notre Dame	Associate Professor	sbhalla@college.edu
2	K69880	Jenney King	MTC-324	750-378-1230	East Florida University	Professor	jking@college.edu
3	A52990	Black Anderson	MTC-218	750-378-9987	Virginia Tech	Professor	banderson@college.edu
4	H99118	Jeff Henry	MTC-336	750-330-8650	Ohio State University	Associate Professor	jhenry@college.edu
5	A77587	Debby Angles	MTC-320	750-330-2276	University of Chicago	Associate Professor	dangles@college.edu
6	B78880	Susan Bai	MTC-215	750-378-1155	Duke University	Professor	sbai@college.edu
7	B66750	Alice Brown	MTC-257	750-330-6650	University of Florida	Assistant Professor	abrown@college.edu
8	J33486	Steve Johnson	MTC-118	750-330-1116	Harvard University	Distinguished Professor	sjohnson@college.edu

Figure 7.48. The updated faculty record in the Faculty table.

jdbc:oracle:thin:@localhost:1521:XE [CSE_DEPT on CSE_DEPT] if it has not been connected. Then expand this connected database, the CSE_DEPT and the Tables node, and right click on the Faculty table and select the `View Data` to open this table. On the opened Faculty table, you can find that the updated faculty member, which has been highlighted, has been there as shown in Figure 7.48.

Our data updating function is successful.

It is highly recommended to recover this updated faculty record to the original one in our sample database to keep our database clean and neat. Refer to Table 7.8 in Section 7.3.3.2 to recover this updated faculty record.

Next, let's take care of the data deletion action using the Updatable ResultSet object. As we did for the data updating, we still want to use this FacultyFrame form window to delete one of faculty members in the Faculty table in our sample database CSE_DEPT.

7.5.2.3 Delete a Row Using the Updatable ResultSet

In this section, we try to delete a default faculty record from our Faculty table using the Updatable ResultSet.

Double click on the Delete button from the FacultyFrame form window to open its event handler, and modify the codes that are shown in Figure 7.49 to perform the data deleting function using the Updatable ResultSet object.

Let's have a closer look at this piece of modified codes to see how it works.

A. First, we add an `if` block to distinguish the `Runtime Object Method` and the `Java Updatable ResultSet` method to perform this data deletion action.

B. An `else if` block is added with the same objective as step **A**.

C. The query string is created, and it is used to help the Updatable ResultSet object to do this data deleting action. The point to be noted here is that a table aliases **f** is used to represent the Faculty table and enable this query to retrieve all columns from that table. You cannot directly use the star (*) to do this query since it is prohibited in this enhanced ResultSet.

```
  private void cmdDeleteActionPerformed(java.awt.event.ActionEvent evt) {
      int numDeleted = 0;
      String cFacultyName = null;
A     if (ComboMethod.getSelectedItem()=="Runtime Object Method"){
        String query = "DELETE FROM Faculty WHERE faculty_name = ?";
        try {
          PreparedStatement pstmt = LogInFrame.con.prepareStatement(query);
          pstmt.setString(1, ComboName.getSelectedItem().toString());
          cFacultyName = (String)ComboName.getSelectedItem();
          numDeleted = pstmt.executeUpdate();
        }
        catch (SQLException e) {
          msgDlg.setMessage("Error in Statement!" + e.getMessage());
          msgDlg.setVisible(true);
        }
      }
B     else if (ComboMethod.getSelectedItem()=="Java Updatable ResultSet"){
C       String query = "SELECT f.* FROM Faculty f WHERE f.faculty_name = ?";
D       try {
          PreparedStatement pstmt = LogInFrame.con.prepareStatement(query,
                                ResultSet.TYPE_SCROLL_SENSITIVE, ResultSet.CONCUR_UPDATABLE);
E         pstmt.setString(1, ComboName.getSelectedItem().toString());
F         ResultSet rs = pstmt.executeQuery();
G         rs.absolute(1);
H         rs.deleteRow();
I         cFacultyName = (String)ComboName.getSelectedItem();
          }
J       catch (SQLException e){
          msgDlg.setMessage("Error in Updatable ResultSet! " + e.getMessage());
          msgDlg.setVisible(true);
        }
      }
      System.out.println("The number of deleted row = " + numDeleted);
      ComboName.removeItem(cFacultyName);
  }
```

Figure 7.49. The modified codes for the Delete button click event handler.

D. A try...catch block is used to perform this data deleting action. A PreparedStatement is created with two ResultSet parameters, TYPE_SCROLL_SENSITIVE and CONCUR_UPDATABLE, to define the ResultSet object to enable it to be scrollable and updatable, and furthermore enable it to perform data manipulations.

E. The setString() method is used to initialize the positional parameter in the query string.

F. The executeQuery() method is called to perform this query and return the query result to a newly created ResultSet object.

G. We need first to identify the location of the row to be deleted. In fact, there is only one row that has been retrieved from our Faculty table and saved in the ResultSet, which is the default faculty member Ying Bai, and this row will be deleted from this data deleting action. Therefore, the absolute position for this row is 1.

H. The deleteRow() method is executed to delete this record from the ResultSet and the database. In fact, this data deleting would not happen until the next Commit command is executed. Be aware that by default, the autocommit flag is set to true so that any operation run is committed immediately.

I. In order to delete the selected faculty member, we need to remove that faculty name from the Faculty Name combo box when this data deleting action is complete. To save the original faculty name, we need to temporarily store it to a local variable cFacultyName.

J. The catch block is used to track and collect any possible exception for this data deletion.

Now let's build and run the project to test this data deleting function.

Click on the Clean and Build Main Project button to build the project, and click on the Run Main Project button to run it.

Enter suitable username and password, such as `jhenry` and `test`, to the LogIn frame form and select the Faculty Information from the SelectFrame window to open the FacultyFrame form window. Make sure that the Runtime Object Method has been selected from the Query Method combo box. Then click on the Select button to query the default faculty information.

To test this data deleting function using the Updatable ResultSet, select the Java Updatable ResultSet from the Query Method combo box. Then click on the Delete button to try to delete this default faculty member Ying Bai from our sample database.

Click on the Back and the Exit button to terminate our project.

To confirm and validate this data deleting action, open the Faculty table to confirm this data manipulation. To open the Faculty table, first open the Services window in the NetBeans IDE, and expand the Databases node and connect our Oracle database using the connection URL, jdbc:oracle:thin:@localhost:1521:XE [CSE_DEPT on CSE_DEPT] if it has not been connected. Then expand this connected database, the CSE_DEPT and the Tables nodes, and right click on the Faculty table and select the `View Data` to open this table. On the opened Faculty table, you can find that the faculty member Ying Bai with the faculty_id of B78880 has been deleted from this table.

Our data deleting function is successful.

To make our database clean and neat, it is highly recommended to recover this deleted faculty member and related records in our Faculty, LogIn, Course, and StudentCourse tables. Refer to Tables 7.2–7.5 in Section 7.1.3.2 to complete this data recovery. An easy way to do this data recovery job is to use the Object Browser in the Oracle Database 10g Express Edition.

A complete sample project OracleSelectObject that contains the data insertion, updating, and deleting functions using the Updatable ResultSet object can be found from the folder DBProjects\Chapter 7 located at the Wiley ftp site (refer to Figure 1.2 in Chapter 1).

Next, let's discuss how to perform the data manipulations using the Callable statement.

7.6 PERFORM DATA MANIPULATIONS USING CALLABLE STATEMENTS

In Sections 6.4.5 and 6.4.5.2 in Chapter 6, we have provided a very detailed discussion about the data query from the Course table in our sample database using the CallableStatement method. Some basic and fundamental ideas and techniques using the CallableStatement method and stored procedures have been given in detailed with some real sample projects. Refer to those sections to get clear pictures and understanding about the CallableStatement object. In this section, we will use this method to perform data manipulations against the Course table in our sample database CSE_DEPT.

7.6.1 Perform Data Manipulations to SQL Server Database Using Callable Statements

Since the similarity between data manipulations for the SQL Server and the Oracle databases, we start with the data manipulations against the SQL Server database. First let's take care of the data insertion to the Course table in our sample SQL Server database using the CallableStatement method.

7.6.1.1 Insert Data to SQL Server Database Using Callable Statements

In Section 6.4.1 in Chapter 6, we have built a project SQLSelectObject with some graphical user interface (GUI), including the CourseFrame form window, and we want to use that CourseFrame form window in that project with some modifications to make it as our GUI in this section. We will build the data insertion function with the CallableStatement method in the following procedures:

1. Modify the CourseFrame form window by adding one more Course ID text field to enable us to insert a new course record with this new course_id.
2. Build our stored procedure dbo.InsertNewCourse using the SQL Server Management Studio Express.
3. Develop the codes for the Insert button in the CourseFrame form window to execute the CallableStatement method to call our stored procedure dbo.InsertNewCourse to insert this new course record into the Course table in our sample database.
4. Confirm and validate this new course insertion using the codes we built for the Select button event handler.

Now let's start from the first step.

7.6.1.1.1 Modify the CourseFrame Form Window To save time and space, we want to use and modify a project SQLSelectObject we built in Section 7.3.1 to make it as our new project to perform this data insertion action.

Perform the following operations to make it as our project:

1. Launch NetBeans IDE 6.8 and open the Projects window.
2. Right click on the project SQLSelectObject we built in Section 7.3.1 and select the `Set as Main Project` item from the pop-up menu. If you cannot find this project, copy this project from the folder DBProjects\Chapter 7 located at the Wiley ftp site (refer to Figure 1.2 in Chapter 1) and paste it to your default project folder JavaDBProject\Chapter 7. Then in the NetBeans IDE, go to `File > Open Project` menu item to open this project.
3. Double click on the CourseFrame.java to open the CourseFrame class.
4. Click on the Design button to open the CourseFrame form window.

Perform the following modifications to this form:

- Add a Label and a Text Field into the Course Information panel with the properties shown in Table 7.15.
- Add two buttons, Update and Delete, with the properties shown in Table 7.15. Also, rearrange these five buttons to the bottom of the CourseFrame form.

Table 7.15. Objects and controls added into the courseframe window

Type	Variable Name	Text	editable	Title
Label	Label1	Course ID		
Text Field	CourseIDField		checked	
Button	cmdUpdate	Update		
Button	cmdDelete	Delete		

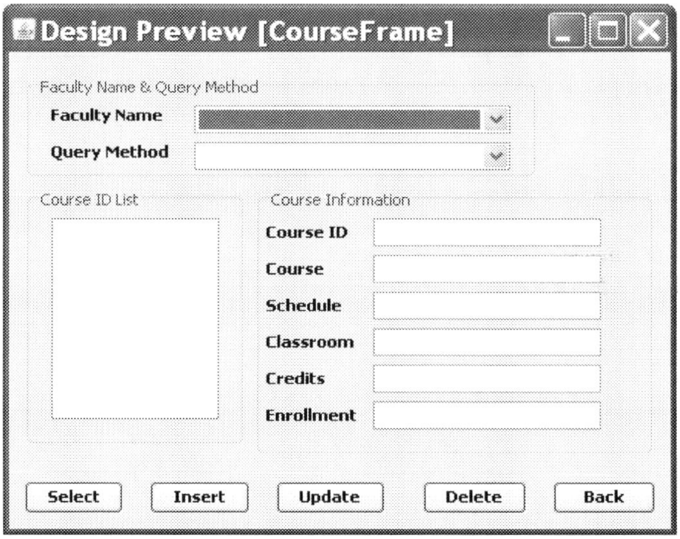

Figure 7.50. The modified CourseFrame form window.

Your finished CourseFrame form window should match one that is shown in Figure 7.50.

Before we can build the project using the CallableStatement method to perform the data manipulations, we need first to develop our stored procedure dbo.InsertNewCourse using the Microsoft SQL Server Management Studio Express.

7.6.1.1.2 Develop the Stored Procedure dbo.InsertNewCourse Recall that when we built our sample database CSE_DEPT in Chapter 2, there is no faculty name column in the Course table, and the only relationship that exist between the Faculty and the Course tables is the faculty_id, which is a primary key in the Faculty table, but a foreign key in the Course table. As the project runs, the user needs to insert a new course record based on the faculty name, not the faculty ID. Therefore, for this new course data insertion, we need to perform two queries with two tables: first, we need to make a query to the Faculty table to get the faculty_id based on the faculty name selected by the user, and second, we can insert a new course record based on the faculty_id we obtained from our first query. These two queries can be combined into a single stored procedure.

Launch the Microsoft SQL Server Management Studio Express by going to Start > All Programs > Microsoft SQL Server 2008 > SQL Server Management Studio. Click

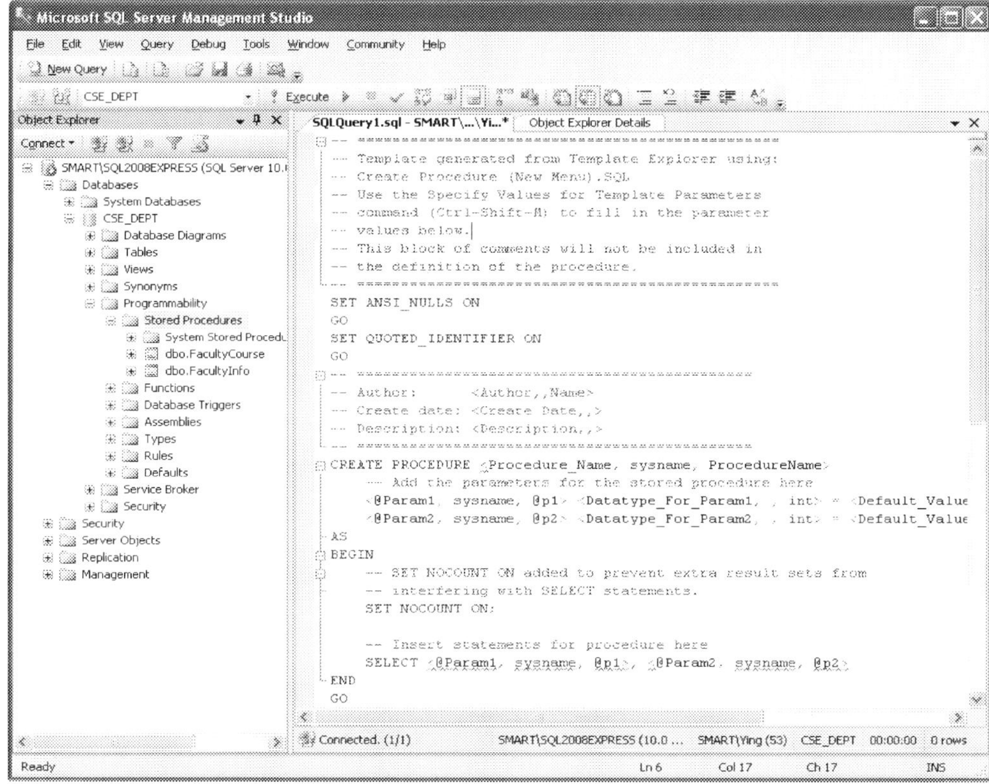

Figure 7.51. The newly stored procedure template.

the `Connect` button to open this studio server. On the opened studio, expand the **Databases** and our sample database **CSE_DEPT** nodes. Then expand the **Programmability** node and right click on the **Stored Procedures** node, and select the **New Stored Procedure** to open a new stored procedure template, as shown in Figure 7.51.

You can use the `Ctrl-Shift-M` combination keys to enter all parameters for this stored procedure. However, an easy way to do that is to directly enter all parameters manually. On the opened newly stored procedure template, enter the following codes that are shown in Figure 7.52 into this stored procedure template as the body of our new stored procedure. The newly added codes have been highlighted in bold and indicated in steps A, B, and C, respectively. The codes in green color are comments for this stored procedure.

Go to **File > Save SQLQuery1.sql** to save this stored procedure.

Right click on any location inside our new stored procedure and select the **Execute** item to try to run it. Then right click on the **Stored Procedures** node from the Object Explorer window and select the **Refresh** item to refresh it to get our newly created stored procedure **dbo.InsertNewCourse**. Right click on our newly stored procedure and select the **Execute Stored Procedure** to open the `Execute Procedure` wizard, which is shown in Figure 7.53.

```
USE [CSE_DEPT]
GO
/****** Object:  StoredProcedure [dbo].[InsertNewCourse]
        Script Date: 5/14/2010 17:12:23 ******/
-- ================================================
SET ANSI_NULLS ON
GO
SET QUOTED_IDENTIFIER ON
GO
-- ================================================
-- Author:          Y. Bai
-- Create date:     May, 2010
-- Description:     SQL Server stored procedure
-- ================================================
A  CREATE PROCEDURE dbo.InsertNewCourse
    -- Add the parameters for the stored procedure here
B   @FacultyName VARCHAR(50),
    @CourseID VARCHAR(50),
    @Course text,
    @Schedule text,
    @Classroom text,
    @Credit int,
    @Enroll int
AS
BEGIN
    -- SET NOCOUNT ON added to prevent extra result sets from
    -- interfering with SELECT statements.
SET NOCOUNT ON;
    -- Insert statements for procedure here
    DECLARE @FacultyID AS VARCHAR(50)
C   SET @FacultyID = (SELECT faculty_id FROM Faculty WHERE (faculty_name = @FacultyName))
    INSERT INTO Course(course_id, course, schedule, classroom, credit, enrollment, faculty_id)
    VALUES (@CourseID, @Course, @Schedule, @Classroom, @Credit, @Enroll, @FacultyID)
END
GO
```

Figure 7.52. The codes for our new stored procedure.

Enter a set of parameters shown in Figure 7.53 into the associated Value columns as a new course record, and click on the OK button to run this stored procedure to test its functionality.

The test result is shown in Figure 7.54. It can be found that a successful message, 1 row(s) affected, is displayed in the Output window.

It is highly recommended to delete this newly inserted course record from our Course table since we need to keep our sample database clean and neat. Another point is that we need to call this stored procedure later from our project to perform this data insertion. In order to avoid a duplicated data insertion, we need to remove this course record now. You can do this data deletion by opening the Course table from the NetBeans IDE or opening the Microsoft SQL Server Management Studio Express.

Now close the Microsoft SQL Server Management Studio Express, and we can continue to develop the codes for the CallableStatement method to call this stored procedure to perform a new course insertion action against our sample database.

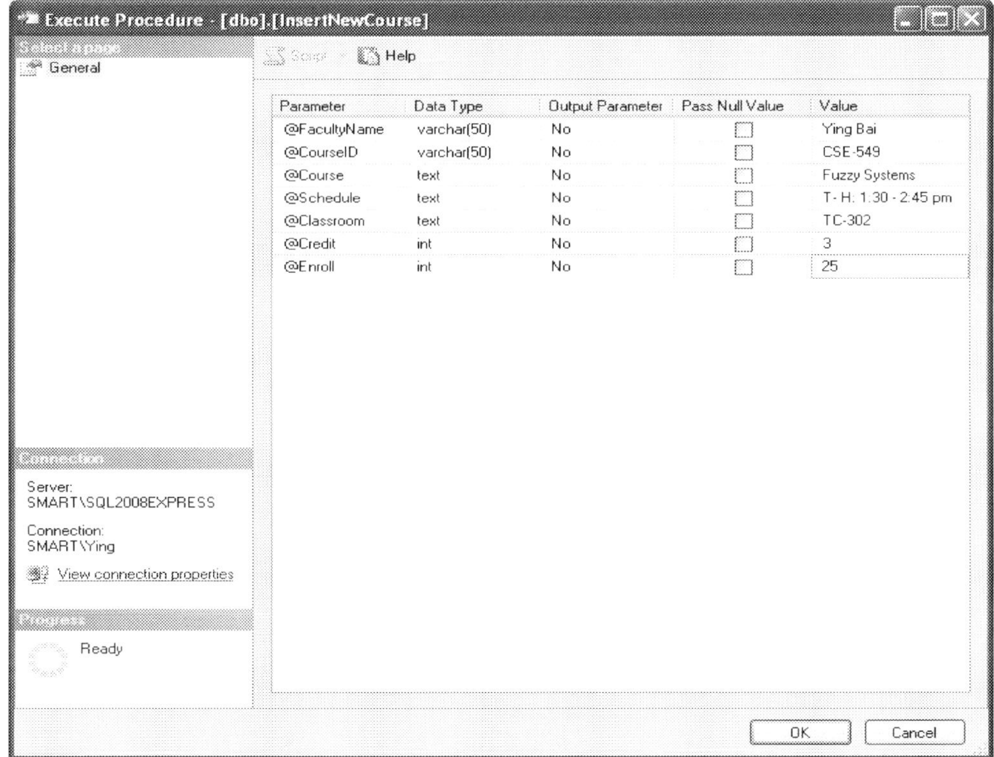

Figure 7.53. The opened Execute Procedure wizard.

7.6.1.1.3 Develop the Codes for the Insert Button Click Event Handler The function of this piece of codes is to call the stored procedure we built in the last section to perform a new course insertion to the Course table in our sample database. The insertion criterion is the faculty member selected from the Faculty Name combo box. The newly inserted course record can be retrieved and displayed in the CourseList listbox by clicking on the Select button to confirm this data insertion.

Generally, the sequence to run a CallableStatement to perform a stored procedure is:

1. Build and formulate the CallableStatement query string
2. Create a CallableStatement object
3. Set the input parameters
4. Register the output parameters
5. Execute CallableStatement
6. Retrieve the running result by using different getXXX() method

Since we do not have any output result to be returned from this stored procedure, therefore, we can skip steps 4 and 6.

Now let's develop the codes for this event handler to perform the calling of the stored procedure we built in the last section to perform this data insertion function.

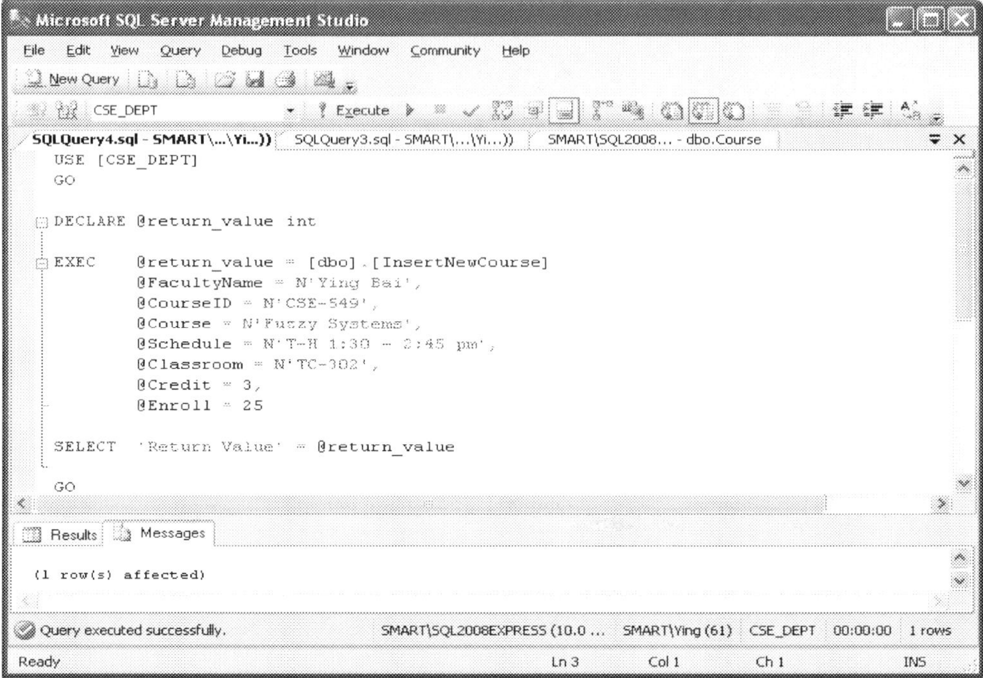

Figure 7.54. The running result of the stored procedure.

Double click on the Insert button on the CourseFrame form window to open its event handler and enter the codes that are shown in Figure 7.55 into this handler.

Let's have a closer look at this piece of codes to see how it works.

A. An `if` block is used to distinguish whether the Java Callable Method has been selected.

B. If it is, a new CallableStatement instance is declared.

C. A `try…catch` block is used to perform this data insertion using the CallableStatement method. The CallableStatement query string is created. Refer to Section 6.4.5.2 in Chapter 6 to get more detailed information about the structure and protocol of a CallableStatement query string. This is a dynamic query string with seven pieces of positional inserting information related to a new course; therefore, seven question marks are used as the position holders for those parameters.

D. A new CallableStatement instance is created by calling the prepareCall() method that is defined in the Connection class.

E. The dynamic query string is initialized with seven positional parameters, and the values of those parameters are entered by the user into the associated course-related text fields.

F. The CallableStatement instance is executed to call the stored procedure we built in the last section to insert a new course record into the Course table in our sample database.

G. The catch block is used to track and collect any possible exception for this data insertion process.

```
  private void cmdInsertActionPerformed(java.awt.event.ActionEvent evt) {
A     if (ComboMethod.getSelectedItem()=="Java Callable Method"){
B        CallableStatement cstmt = null;
      try{
C        String query = "{call dbo.InsertNewCourse(?, ?, ?, ?, ?, ?, ?)}";
D        cstmt = LogInFrame.con.prepareCall(query);
E        cstmt.setString(1, ComboName.getSelectedItem().toString());
         cstmt.setString(2, CourseIDField.getText());
         cstmt.setString(3, CourseField.getText());
         cstmt.setString(4, ScheduleField.getText());
         cstmt.setString(5, ClassroomField.getText());
         cstmt.setString(6, CreditField.getText());
         cstmt.setString(7, EnrollField.getText());
F        cstmt.execute();
        }
G     catch (SQLException e){
         msgDlg.setMessage("Error in CallableStatement! " + e.getMessage());
         msgDlg.setVisible(true);
        }
     }
  }
```

Figure 7.55. The codes for the Insert button click event handler.

Now let's build and run the project to test this data insertion function. Click on the Clean and Build Main Project button to build the project, and click on the Run Main Project button to run the project.

Enter suitable username and password, such as `jhenry` and `test`, to the LogIn frame form and select the Course Information from the SelectFrame window to open the CourseFrame form window. Make sure that the Java Callable Method has been selected from the Query Method combo box. Then click on the Select button to query the default course information for the selected faculty member Ying Bai.

Now enter the following data into seven text fields as a new course record for the selected faculty member:

Course ID: CSE-549

Course: Fuzzy Systems

Schedule: T-H: 1:30–2:45 pm

Classroom: TC-302

Credit: 3

Enrollment: 25

Then click on the Insert button to insert this course record into the Course table in our sample database.

To confirm and validate this data insertion, click on the Select button to try to retrieve all courses taught by the selected faculty member Ying Bai. The running result is shown in Figure 7.56, and you can see that the newly inserted course CSE-549 is indeed added to the database and displayed in the CourseList listbox.

Click on the Back and the Exit buttons to terminate our project.

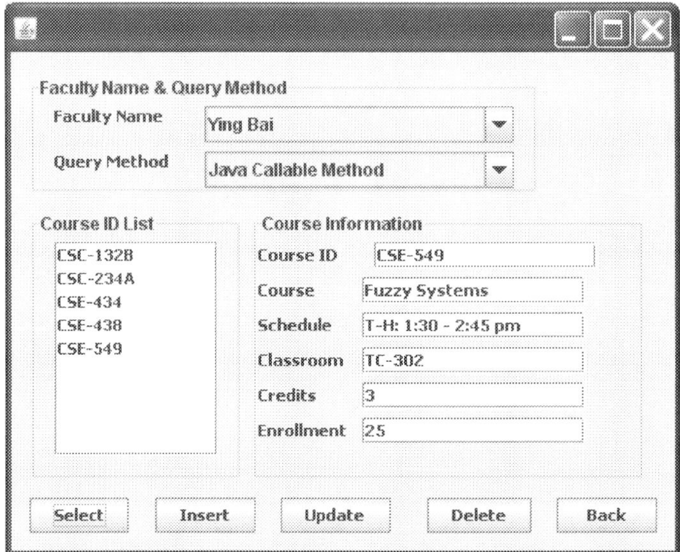

Figure 7.56. The running result for the data insertion validation.

Another way to confirm this data insertion is to open the Course table using the Services window in the NetBeans IDE. To do that, open the Services window and expand the Databases node and connect to our SQL Server database by right clicking on that URL and select the Connect item. Then expand that connected URL and our CSE_DEPT database node, dbo schema and Tables nodes. Right click on the Course table and select the View Data to open this table. Click on the `Next Page` tab, and you can find that the course CSE-549 has been inserted to the last line on this Course table, as shown in Figure 7.57.

Our data insertion using the CallableStatement object is successful.

Next, let's handle the data updating using the CallableStatement object method.

7.6.1.2 Update Data to SQL Server Database Using Callable Statements

Before we can build the project using the CallableStatement method to perform the data manipulations, we need first to develop our stored procedure dbo.UpdateCourse using the Microsoft SQL Server Management Studio Express.

7.6.1.2.1 Develop the Stored Procedure dbo.UpdateCourse Generally, we do not need to update a course_id when we update a course record in the Course table since a better way to do that is to insert a new course record and delete the old one. The main reason for this is that a very complicated operation would be performed if the course_id were updated, since it is a primary key in the `Course` table and foreign keys in the `StudentCourse` table. To update a primary key, one needs to update foreign keys first in the child tables and then update the primary key in the parent table. This will make our updating operation very complicated and easy to be confused. In order to avoid this confusion, in this section, we will update a course record by changing any other columns except the course_id, and this is a popular way to update a table and widely implemented in most database applications.

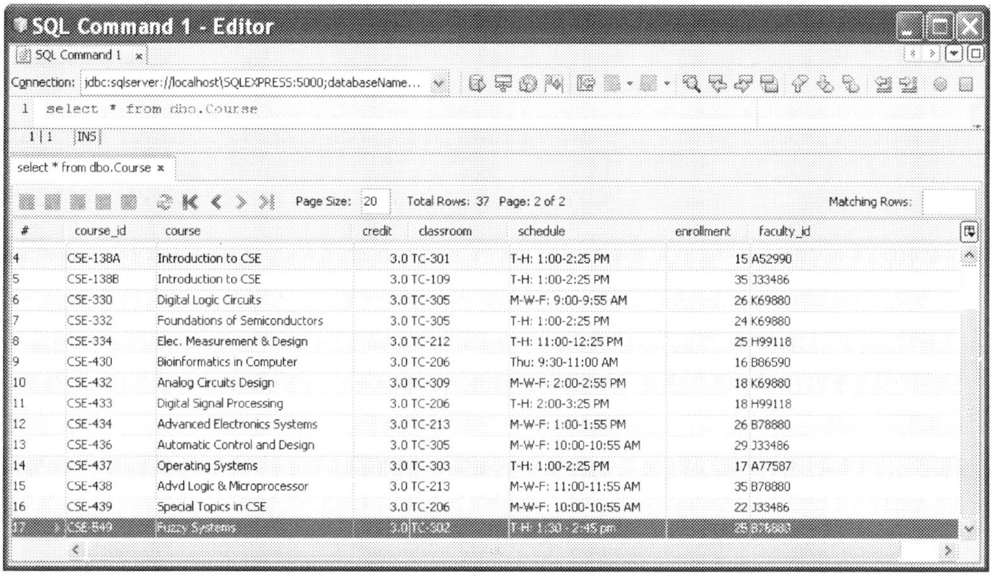

SQL Command 1 - Editor

Connection: jdbc:sqlserver://localhost\SQLEXPRESS:5000;databaseName...

```
select * from dbo.Course
```

Page Size: 20 Total Rows: 37 Page: 2 of 2 Matching Rows:

#	course_id	course	credit	classroom	schedule	enrollment	faculty_id
4	CSE-138A	Introduction to CSE	3.0	TC-301	T-H: 1:00-2:25 PM	15	A52990
5	CSE-138B	Introduction to CSE	3.0	TC-109	T-H: 1:00-2:25 PM	35	J33486
6	CSE-330	Digital Logic Circuits	3.0	TC-305	M-W-F: 9:00-9:55 AM	26	K69880
7	CSE-332	Foundations of Semiconductors	3.0	TC-305	T-H: 1:00-2:25 PM	24	K69880
8	CSE-334	Elec. Measurement & Design	3.0	TC-212	T-H: 11:00-12:25 PM	25	H99118
9	CSE-430	Bioinformatics in Computer	3.0	TC-206	Thu: 9:30-11:00 AM	16	B86590
10	CSE-432	Analog Circuits Design	3.0	TC-309	M-W-F: 2:00-2:55 PM	18	K69880
11	CSE-433	Digital Signal Processing	3.0	TC-206	T-H: 2:00-3:25 PM	18	H99118
12	CSE-434	Advanced Electronics Systems	3.0	TC-213	M-W-F: 1:00-1:55 PM	26	B78880
13	CSE-436	Automatic Control and Design	3.0	TC-305	M-W-F: 10:00-10:55 AM	29	J33486
14	CSE-437	Operating Systems	3.0	TC-303	T-H: 1:00-2:25 PM	17	A77587
15	CSE-438	Advd Logic & Microprocessor	3.0	TC-213	M-W-F: 11:00-11:55 AM	35	B78880
16	CSE-439	Special Topics in CSE	3.0	TC-206	M-W-F: 10:00-10:55 AM	22	J33486
17	CSE-549	Fuzzy Systems	3.0	TC-302	T-H: 1:30 - 2:45 pm	25	B78880

Figure 7.57. The newly inserted new course CSE-549.

Launch the Microsoft SQL Server Management Studio Express by going to Start > All Programs > Microsoft SQL Server 2008 > SQL Server Management Studio. Click the `Connect` button to open this studio server. On the opened studio, expand the Databases and our sample database CSE_DEPT nodes. Then expand the Programmability node and right click on the Stored Procedures node, select the `New Stored Procedure` to open a new stored procedure template.

You can use the `Ctrl-Shift-M` combination keys to enter all parameters for this stored procedure. However, an easy way to do that is to directly enter all parameters manually. On the opened new stored procedure template, enter the codes that are shown in Figure 7.58 into this stored procedure template as the body of our new stored procedure dbo.UpdateCourse.

An easy way to do the UPDATE statement coding part is to use the Design Query in Editor wizard. In this section, we try to use this wizard to build the UPDATE statement for this query.

To open this wizard, right click on any blank space in the opened new stored procedure template and select the Design Query in Editor item from the pop-up menu. Click on the Close button for the Add Table dialog box to close this dialog. Perform the following operations to build this UPDATE statement.

1. Select the `SELECT ... FROM` codes from the bottom pane to delete them.
2. Right click on the bottom pane and select the Change Type item and select the Update item from the pop-up menu.
3. Right click on the top pane and select the Add Table item. Select the Course table and click on the Add button. Click on the Close button to close this Add Table dialog.
4. Click on the row under the Column in the mid-pane and select the Course item.

```
-- ================================================
SET ANSI_NULLS ON
GO
SET QUOTED_IDENTIFIER ON
GO
-- =============================================
-- Author:                    Y. Bai
-- =============================================
CREATE PROCEDURE dbo.UpdateCourse
   -- Add the parameters for the stored procedure here
A  @CourseID VARCHAR(50),
   @Course text,
   @Schedule text,
   @Classroom text,
   @Credit int,
   @Enroll int
AS
BEGIN
  -- SET NOCOUNT ON added to prevent extra result sets from
  -- interfering with SELECT statements.
SET NOCOUNT ON;

   -- Insert statements for procedure here
B  UPDATE  Course
   SET course = @Course, schedule = @Schedule, classroom = @Classroom,
              credit = @Credit, enrollment = @Enroll
   WHERE  (course_id = @CourseID)
END
GO
```

Figure 7.58. The codes for the dbo.UpdateCourse stored procedure.

5. In the similar way to click on the row under the Course item and select the Schedule item in the Column. Continue in this way to select all other items, Classroom, Credit, Enrollment, and course_id.
6. Uncheck the check box for the row course_id in the Set column and type a question mark "?" in the Filter column for the course_id row, and then press the Enter key in your keyboard.
7. Modify the dynamic parameter's name from `@Param1` to `@CourseID`.
8. Enter the updated values to the associated New Value column. The point to be noted is that all of these updated values' names must be identical with those input parameters to the stored procedure we built in step **A** in Figure 7.58.

Your finished Query Designer wizard should match one that is shown in Figure 7.59. Click on the OK button to create this UPDATE statement codes that have been highlighted in the background color in step B in Figure 7.58.

Let's have a closer look at this piece of codes to see how it works.

A. Six input parameters to this stored procedure are declared first with the associated data types. These parameters must be identical with those parameters in the CallableStatement query string we will build later to enable the CallableStatement to recognize them when it is executed to perform the data updating action in our project.

B. The UPDATE statement we built using the Query Designer wizard is attached here, and the query criterion course_id is obtained from the CourseList listbox.

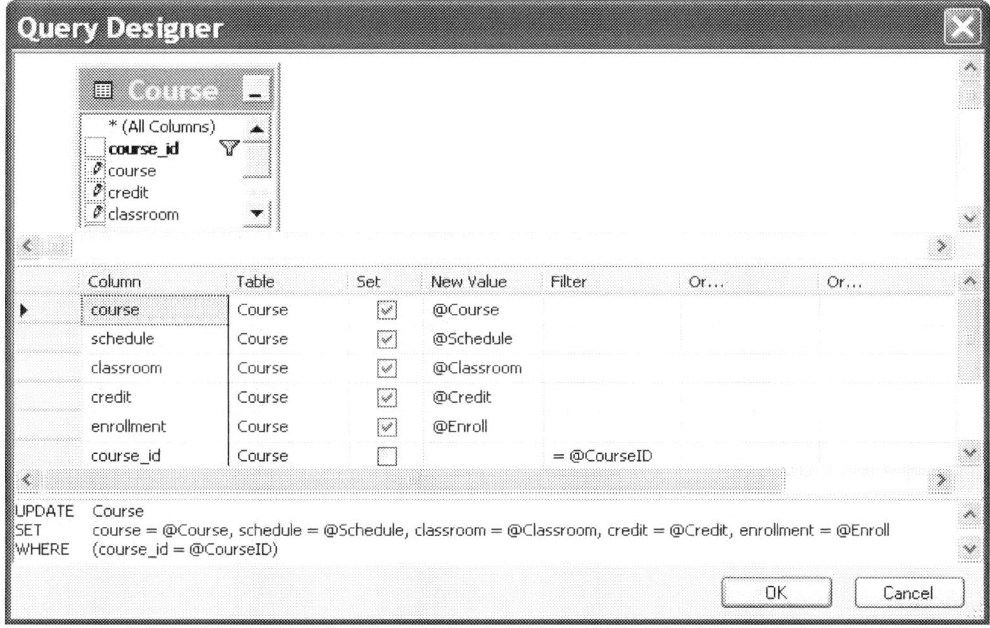

Figure 7.59. The Finished Query Designer wizard.

Save this stored procedure by going to the File > Save SQLQuery2.sql and click on the Save button. Right click on any location inside our new stored procedure and select the Execute item to try to run it. Then right click on the Stored Procedures node in the Object Explorer window and select the Refresh item to show our newly built stored procedure dbo.UpdateCourse.

Now let's run this stored procedure to test its functionality. Right click on our newly created stored procedure dbo.UpdateCourse from the Object Explorer window and select the Execute Stored Procedure item to open the Execute Procedure wizard. Enter the following data into the associated `Value` columns to this wizard:

- @CourseID: CSE-549
- @Course: Intelligent Controls
- @Schedule: M-W-F: 11:00–11:50 am
- @Classroom: TC-303
- @Credit: 3
- @Enrollment: 28

Click on the OK button to run this stored procedure. The running result is shown in Figure 7.60. It can be found that a successful running message is displayed in the Output windows (1 row(s) affected), and the Query executed successfully statement is also displayed in the status bar at the bottom of this window.

It is highly recommended to recover this updated course record to its original values since we need to call the CallableStatement object to run this stored procedure again when we test our project later. You can do this recovery job inside the Microsoft SQL

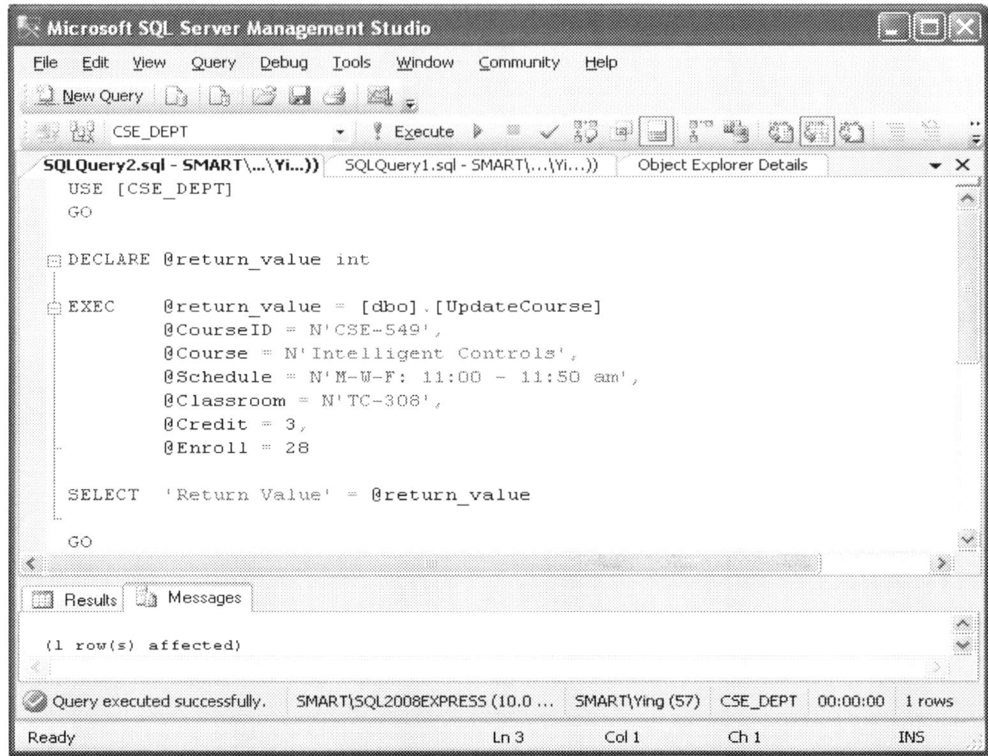

Figure 7.60. The running result of the stored procedure dbo.UpdateCourse.

Server Management Studio Express by opening the Course table. Close the Microsoft SQL Server Management Studio Express since we have finished building and testing the stored procedure.

Now let's build our codes for the Update button click event handler in the CourseFrame form to call this stored procedure to perform this data updating action.

7.6.1.2.2 Develop the Codes for the Update Button Click Event Handler

Double click on the Update button on the CourseFrame form window to open its event handler and enter the codes that are shown in Figure 7.61 into this handler.

Let's have a close look at this piece of codes to see how it works.

A. An `if` block is used to distinguish whether the Java Callable Method has been selected.

B. If it is, a new CallableStatement instance is declared.

C. A `try…catch` block is used to perform this data updating action using the CallableStatement method. The CallableStatement query string is created. Refer to Section 6.4.5.2 in Chapter 6 to get more detailed information about the structure and protocol of a CallableStatement query string. This is a dynamic query string with six pieces of positional updating information related to a new course; therefore, six question marks are used as the position holders for those parameters.

D. A new CallableStatement instance is created by calling the prepareCall() method that is defined in the Connection class.

```
  private void cmdUpdateActionPerformed(java.awt.event.ActionEvent evt) {
A   if (ComboMethod.getSelectedItem()=="Java Callable Method"){
B     CallableStatement cstmt = null;
      try{
C       String query = "{call dbo.UpdateCourse(?, ?, ?, ?, ?, ?)}";
D       cstmt = LogInFrame.con.prepareCall(query);
E       cstmt.setString(1, CourseList.getSelectedValue().toString());
        cstmt.setString(2, CourseField.getText());
        cstmt.setString(3, ScheduleField.getText());
        cstmt.setString(4, ClassroomField.getText());
        cstmt.setFloat(5, java.lang.Float.valueOf(CreditField.getText()));
        cstmt.setInt(6, java.lang.Integer.parseInt(EnrollField.getText()));
F       cstmt.execute();
      }
G     catch (SQLException e){
        msgDlg.setMessage("Error in CallableStatement! " + e.getMessage());
        msgDlg.setVisible(true);
      }
    }
H   CourseIDField.setText(CourseList.getSelectedValue().toString());
  }
```

Figure 7.61. The codes for the Update button click event handler.

E. The dynamic query string is initialized with six positional parameters, and the values of those parameters are entered by the user into the associated course-related text fields. The point to be noted is the last two parameters, which are credits (`float`) and enrollment (`integer`), respectively. Therefore, the associated setXXX() methods need to be used to initialize these two parameters. Since the `Float` and `Integer` classes belong to the java.lang package, here, a full name is used for these classes.

F. The CallableStatement instance is executed to call the stored procedure we built in the last section to update the selected course record in the Course table in our sample database.

G. The `catch` block is used to track and collect any possible exception for this data updating process.

H. Finally, the selected course_id from the CourseList listbox is assigned to the Course ID field to indicate this updated course.

Now let's build and run the project to test this data updating function. Click on the Clean and Build Main Project button to build the project, and click on the Run Main Project button to run the project.

Enter suitable username and password, such as `jhenry` and `test`, to the LogIn frame form and select the Course Information from the SelectFrame window to open the CourseFrame form window. Make sure that the Java Callable Method has been selected from the Query Method combo box. Then click on the Select button to query the default course information for the selected faculty member Ying Bai.

Now select the course CSE-549 from the CourseList listbox and enter the following data into six text fields as an updated course record for the selected course CSE-549:

Course: Intelligent Controls

Schedule: M-W-F: 11:00–11:50 am

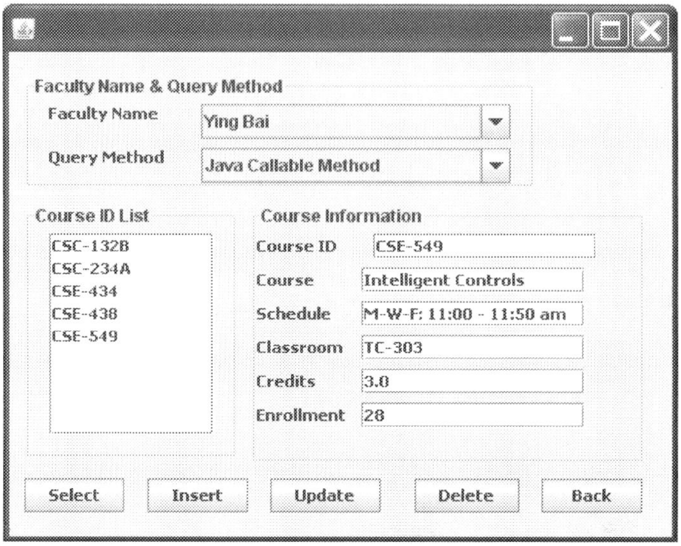

Figure 7.62. The running result of the data updating action.

Classroom: TC-303

Credit: 3

Enrollment: 28

Then click on the Update button to update this course record in the Course table in our sample database. To confirm and validate this data updating, click on the Select button to try to retrieve all courses taught by the selected faculty member Ying Bai. The running result is shown in Figure 7.62.

Another way to confirm this data updating action is to open the Course table using the Services window in the NetBeans IDE. To do that, open the Services window and expand the Databases node and connect to our SQL Server database by right clicking on that URL and selecting the Connect item. Then expand that connected URL and our CSE_DEPT database node, dbo schema and Tables nodes. Right click on the Course table and select the View Data to open this table. Click on the `Next Page` tab, and you can find that the course CSE-549 has been updated and displayed at the last line on this Course table, as shown in Figure 7.63.

Our data updating using the CallableStatement object is successful.

Next, let's handle the data deleting using the CallableStatement object method.

7.6.1.3 Delete Data from SQL Server Database Using Callable Statements

In this section, we try to delete a course record from our Course table using the CallableStatement object method. First, let's develop the stored procedure using Microsoft SQL Server Management Studio Express.

7.6.1.3.1 Develop the Stored Procedure dbo.DeleteCourse Launch the Microsoft SQL Server Management Studio Express by going to Start > All Programs > Microsoft

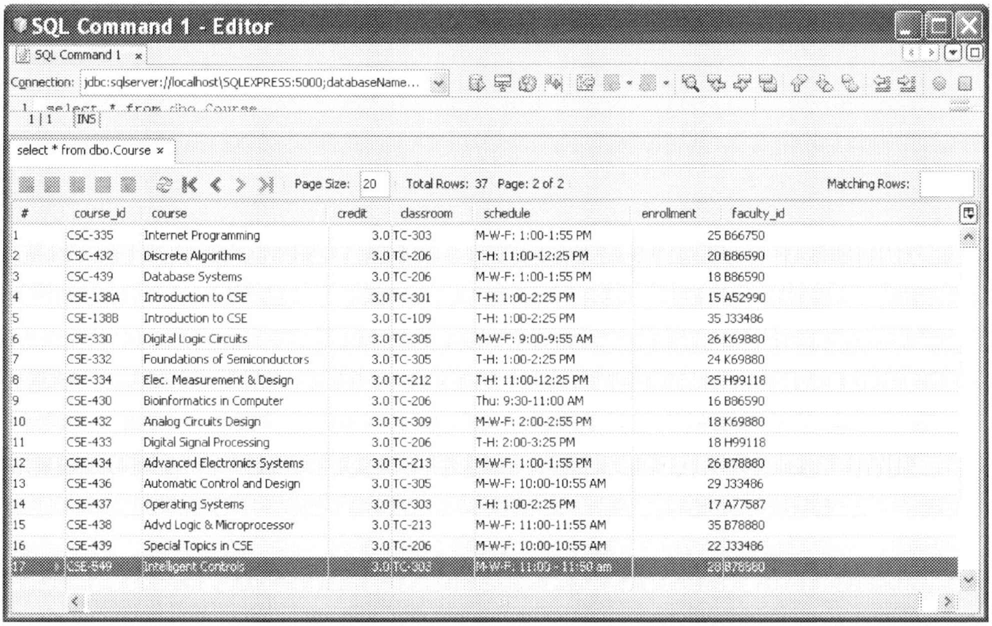
SQL Command 1 - Editor
SQL Command 1
Connection: jdbc:sqlserver://localhost\SQLEXPRESS:5000;databaseName...
1 select * from dbo.Course
1 | 1 INS
select * from dbo.Course
Page Size: 20 Total Rows: 37 Page: 2 of 2
Matching Rows:
course_id course credit classroom schedule enrollment faculty_id
1 CSC-335 Internet Programming 3.0 TC-303 M-W-F: 1:00-1:55 PM 25 B66750
2 CSC-432 Discrete Algorithms 3.0 TC-206 T-H: 11:00-12:25 PM 20 B86590
3 CSC-439 Database Systems 3.0 TC-206 M-W-F: 1:00-1:55 PM 18 B86590
4 CSE-138A Introduction to CSE 3.0 TC-301 T-H: 1:00-2:25 PM 15 A52990
5 CSE-138B Introduction to CSE 3.0 TC-109 T-H: 1:00-2:25 PM 35 J33486
6 CSE-330 Digital Logic Circuits 3.0 TC-305 M-W-F: 9:00-9:55 AM 26 K69880
7 CSE-332 Foundations of Semiconductors 3.0 TC-305 T-H: 1:00-2:25 PM 24 K69880
8 CSE-334 Elec. Measurement & Design 3.0 TC-212 T-H: 11:00-12:25 PM 25 H99118
9 CSE-430 Bioinformatics in Computer 3.0 TC-206 Thu: 9:30-11:00 AM 16 B86590
10 CSE-432 Analog Circuits Design 3.0 TC-309 M-W-F: 2:00-2:55 PM 18 K69880
11 CSE-433 Digital Signal Processing 3.0 TC-206 T-H: 2:00-3:25 PM 18 H99118
12 CSE-434 Advanced Electronics Systems 3.0 TC-213 M-W-F: 1:00-1:55 PM 26 B78880
13 CSE-436 Automatic Control and Design 3.0 TC-305 M-W-F: 10:00-10:55 AM 29 J33486
14 CSE-437 Operating Systems 3.0 TC-303 T-H: 1:00-2:25 PM 17 A77587
15 CSE-438 Advd Logic & Microprocessor 3.0 TC-213 M-W-F: 11:00-11:55 AM 35 B78880
16 CSE-439 Special Topics in CSE 3.0 TC-206 M-W-F: 10:00-10:55 AM 22 J33486
17 CSE-549 Intelligent Controls 3.0 TC-303 M-W-F: 11:00 - 11:50 am 28 B78880

Figure 7.63. The updated course CSE-549 in the Course table.

SQL Server 2008 > SQL Server Management Studio. Click the `Connect` button to open this studio server. On the opened studio, expand the **Databases** and our sample database **CSE_DEPT** nodes. Then expand the **Programmability** node and right click on the **Stored Procedures** node, select the `New Stored Procedure` to open a new stored procedure template.

You can use the `Ctrl-Shift-M` combination keys to enter all parameters for this stored procedure. However, an easy way to do that is to directly enter all parameters manually. On the opened newly stored procedure template, enter the codes that are shown in Figure 7.64 into this stored procedure template as the body of our newly stored procedure dbo.DeleteCourse. You can create this piece of codes manually or by using the Query Designer as we did in the last section for the stored procedure dbo. UpdateCourse.

Let's have a closer look at this piece of codes to see how it works.

A. The only input to this stored procedure is the course_id that is a primary key to the Course table. Here we use @CourseID as a dynamic parameter for this stored procedure.

B. The DELETE statement is created with the @CourseID as this deleting criterion.

Save this stored procedure by going to the `File > Save SQLQuery3.sql` and click on the **Save** button. Right click on any location inside our newly stored procedure and select the **Execute** item to try to run it. Then right click on the **Stored Procedures** node in the Object Explorer window and select the **Refresh** item to show our newly built stored procedure dbo.DeleteCourse.

Now let's run this stored procedure to test its functionality. Right click on our newly created stored procedure dbo.DeleteCourse from the Object Explorer window and

```
-- ================================================
SET ANSI_NULLS ON
GO
SET QUOTED_IDENTIFIER ON
GO
-- =============================================
-- Author:          Y. Bai
-- Create date:     Aug 3, 2010
-- =============================================
CREATE PROCEDURE dbo.DeleteCourse
        -- Add the parameters for the stored procedure here
A       @CourseID VARCHAR(50)
AS
BEGIN
      -- SET NOCOUNT ON added to prevent extra result sets from
      -- interfering with SELECT statements.
      SET NOCOUNT ON;
     -- Insert statements for procedure here
B     DELETE FROM Course
      WHERE (course_id = @CourseID)
END
GO
```

Figure 7.64. The codes for the stored procedure dbo.DeleteCourse.

select the Execute Stored Procedure item to open the Execute Procedure wizard. Enter the following data into the associated `Value` column to this wizard:

- @CourseID: CSE-549

Click on the OK button to run this stored procedure. The running result is shown in Figure 7.65. It can be found that a successful running message is displayed in the Output windows (1 row(s) affected), and the Query executed successfully statement is also displayed in the status bar at the bottom of this window.

It is highly recommended to recover this deleted course record to its original values since we need to call the CallableStatement object to run this stored procedure again when we test our project later. You can do this recovery job inside the Microsoft SQL Server Management Studio Express by opening the Course table. Refer to Table 7.16 to recover this deleted course record.

Now close the Microsoft SQL Server Management Studio, since we have finished building and testing the stored procedure.

Next, we need to build our codes for the Delete button click event handler in the CourseFrame form to call this stored procedure to perform this data-deleting action.

7.6.1.3.2 Develop the Codes for the Delete Button Click Event Handler Double click on the Delete button on the CourseFrame form window to open its event handler and enter the codes that are shown in Figure 7.66 into this handler.

Table 7.16. The deleted course record in the course table

course_id	course	credit	classroom	schedule	enrollment	faculty_id
CSE-549	Intelligent Controls	3	TC-303	M-W-F: 11:00 – 11:50 am	28	B78880

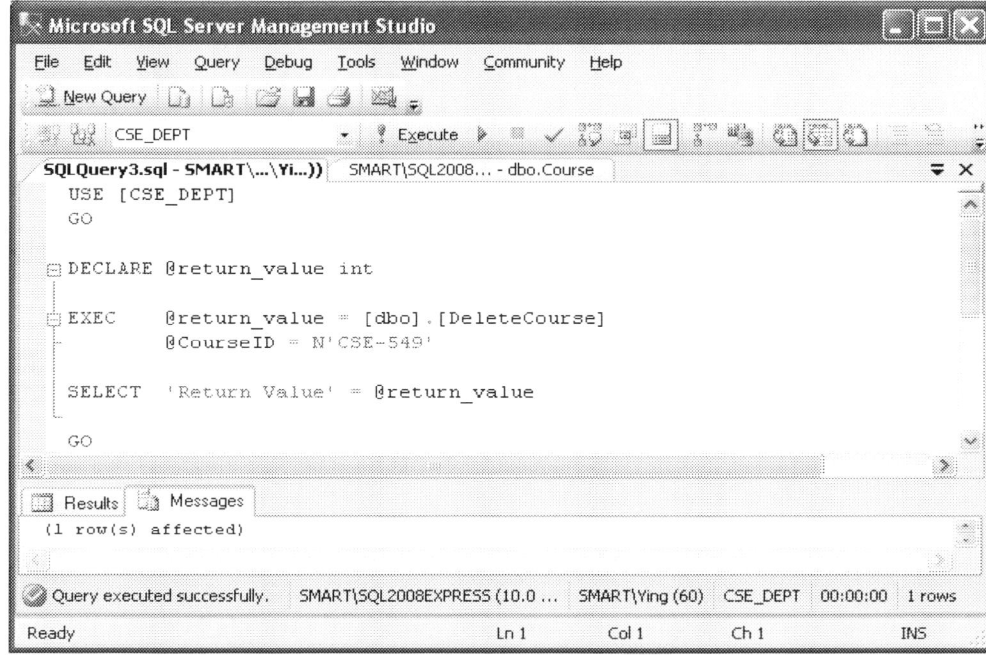

Figure 7.65. The running result of the stored procedure dbo.DeleteCourse.

```
  private void cmdDeleteActionPerformed(java.awt.event.ActionEvent evt) {
A     if (ComboMethod.getSelectedItem()=="Java Callable Method"){
B        CallableStatement cstmt = null;
         try{
C           String query = "{call dbo.DeleteCourse(?)}";
D           cstmt = LogInFrame.con.prepareCall(query);
E           cstmt.setString(1, CourseList.getSelectedValue().toString());
F           cstmt.execute();
         }
G        catch (SQLException e){
            msgDlg.setMessage("Error in CallableStatement! " + e.getMessage());
            msgDlg.setVisible(true);
         }
      }
H     CourseIDField.setText(null);
  }
```

Figure 7.66. The codes for the Delete button click event handler.

Let's have a close look at this piece of codes to see how it works.

A. An `if` block is used to distinguish whether the Java Callable Method has been selected.

B. If it is, a new CallableStatement instance is declared.

C. A `try...catch` block is used to perform this data deleting action using the CallableStatement method. The CallableStatement query string is created. Refer to Section 6.4.5.2 in Chapter

6 to get more detailed information about the structure and protocol of a CallableStatement query string. This is a dynamic query string with one positional parameter related to a new course; therefore, a question mark is used as the position holder for this parameter.

D. A new CallableStatement instance is created by calling the prepareCall() method that is defined in the Connection class.

E. The dynamic query string is initialized with a positional parameter, and the value of this parameter is selected by the user from the CourseList listbox.

F. The CallableStatement instance is executed to call the stored procedure we built in the last section to delete the selected course record in the Course table in our sample database.

G. The `catch` block is used to track and collect any possible exception for this data deleting.

H. The deleted course_id is removed from the Course ID field to indicate this deleting action.

Now let's build and run the project to test this data deleting function. Click on the Clean and Build Main Project button to build the project, and click on the Run Main Project button to run the project.

Enter suitable username and password, such as `jhenry` and `test`, to the LogIn frame form and select the Course Information from the SelectFrame window to open the CourseFrame form window. Make sure that the Java Callable Method has been selected from the Query Method combo box. Then click on the Select button to query the default course information for the selected faculty member Ying Bai.

Now select the course CSE-549 from the CourseList listbox and click on the Delete button to try to delete this course from the Course table in our sample database.

To confirm and validate this data deletion action, click on the Select button again to try to retrieve all courses taught by the default faculty Ying Bai. It can be found that there is no CSE-549 course in the CourseList listbox, and this means that the course CSE-549 has been deleted from the Course table. You can also confirm this data deleting action by opening the Course table using the Services window in the NetBeans IDE.

At this point, we have finished developing and building data manipulations project using CallableStatement object method. A complete project SQLSelectObject that contains all three data manipulation actions to SQL Server database can be found at the folder DBProjects\Chapter 7 that is located at the Wiley ftp site (refer to Figure 1.2 in Chapter 1).

Next, let's handle the data manipulations to Oracle database using the CallableStatement object method.

7.6.2 Perform Data Manipulations to Oracle Database Using Callable Statements

Basically, there is no significant difference between the data manipulations to SQL Server and Oracle databases using the CallableStatement object. The only differences are the connected database and stored procedures. As long as a valid connection to the selected database has been set up and all stored procedures are built using the Oracle Database 10g XE, all codes developed in Section 7.6.1 can be used for Oracle database without problem.

To save time and space, we can use and modify an Oracle project OracleSelectObject we built in Section 7.4 to make it as our new project to perform the data manipulations using the CallableStatement method.

In this section, we want to use the CourseFrame form to perform data manipulations, such as data insertion, updating, and deleting against the Course table in our Oracle sample database. The only modifications to this form are:

1. The CourseFrame form window
2. Three Oracle stored procedures

The first modification enables us to have all text fields and buttons in the CourseFrame form to allow us to perform all three kinds of data manipulations. The second modification enables us to call these Oracle stored procedures using the CallableStatement to perform the data manipulations. Let's start with the first modification.

7.6.2.1 Modify the CourseFrame Form Window

Refer to Section 7.6.1.1.1 to complete this CourseFrame form modification. Your modified CourseFrame form window should match one that is shown in Figure 7.67.

Now, you can open the project SQLSelectObject we built in the last section and copy the codes from the Insert, Update, and Delete button click event handlers in the CourseFrame form and paste them into the associated Insert, Update, and Delete button click event handlers in our current modified CourseFrame form one by one. To open the project SQLSelectObject, you can go to the folder DBProjects\Chapter 7 that is located at the Wiley ftp site (refer to Figure 1.2 in Chapter 1).

Now, let's do some modifications to these three event handlers to make them match to the data actions in Oracle database.

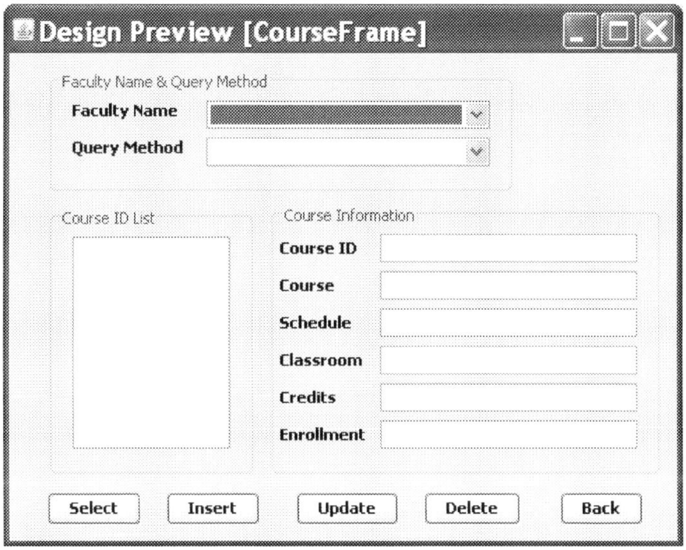

Figure 7.67. The modified CourseFrame form window.

The only modification we need to do is to remove the prefix dbo for each CallableStatement query string in three event handlers. As you remember, when we built our three stored procedures in Microsoft SQL Server Management Studio Express, dbo.InsertNewCourse, dbo.UpdateCourse and dbo.DeleteCourse, all of these stored procedures are prefixed with a prefix dbo, which is a SQL Server database schema. However, when we build those stored procedures in Oracle database, we do not need those prefixes anymore. Therefore, we need to remove these prefixes before each stored procedure in the CallableStatement query string.

Open these three event handlers and remove the prefix dbo from each query string in our pasted codes. After this deletion, our three stored procedures are named InsertNewCourse(), UpdateCourse(), and DeleteCourse(), respectively. Next, we will build three stored procedures with the identical names of those three stored procedures using the Object Browser in Oracle Database 10g Express Edition.

7.6.2.2 Build Three Oracle Stored Procedures

Recall in Section 6.5.4.1 in Chapter 6, we provided a very detailed discussion about the package and stored procedures in the Oracle database environment. Refer to that section to get more detailed information about how to create a package and stored procedure in Oracle database. In this section, we will provide some discussions about how to create Oracle stored procedures, InsertNewCourse(), UpdateCourse(), and DeleteCourse().

From Section 6.5.4.1, we got an idea about the difference between an Oracle stored procedure and an Oracle package. The key issue is that an Oracle stored procedure never return any data, but an Oracle package must return some data. For our course data insertion, updating, and deleting, we do not need to return any data. Based on this criterion, let's start to build our Oracle stored procedures to perform these three kinds of data actions against our sample Oracle database.

7.6.2.2.1 Create the InsertNewCourse Stored Procedure Open the Oracle Database 10g XE home page by going to Start|All Programs|Oracle Database 10g Express Edition|Go To Database Home Page items. Log in as a user by entering CSE_DEPT into the Username box and the password reback into the Password box. Click the Object Browser and select Create|Procedure to open the Create Procedure window.

Enter the procedure name, InsertNewCourse, into the `Procedure Name` field, and keep the `Include Arguments` checkbox checked, then click on the Next button.

In the Arguments page, enter seven pieces of new course information into seven Argument fields. Refer to Section 2.11.2.3 in Chapter 2 for data types of these seven data. Your finished Arguments page should match one that is shown in Figure 7.68.

Click on the Next button to go to the procedure-defining page.

Enter the codes that are shown in Figure 7.69 into this new procedure as the body of the procedure using the language that is called Procedural Language Extension for SQL or PL-SQL. Then click on the Next and the Finish buttons to confirm creating of this procedure.

Your finished Procedure-Define page is shown in Figure 7.70.

Seven input parameters are listed at the beginning of this procedure with the keyword **IN** to indicate that these parameters are inputs to the procedure. The intermediate parameter facultyID is obtained from the first query in this procedure from the Faculty table.

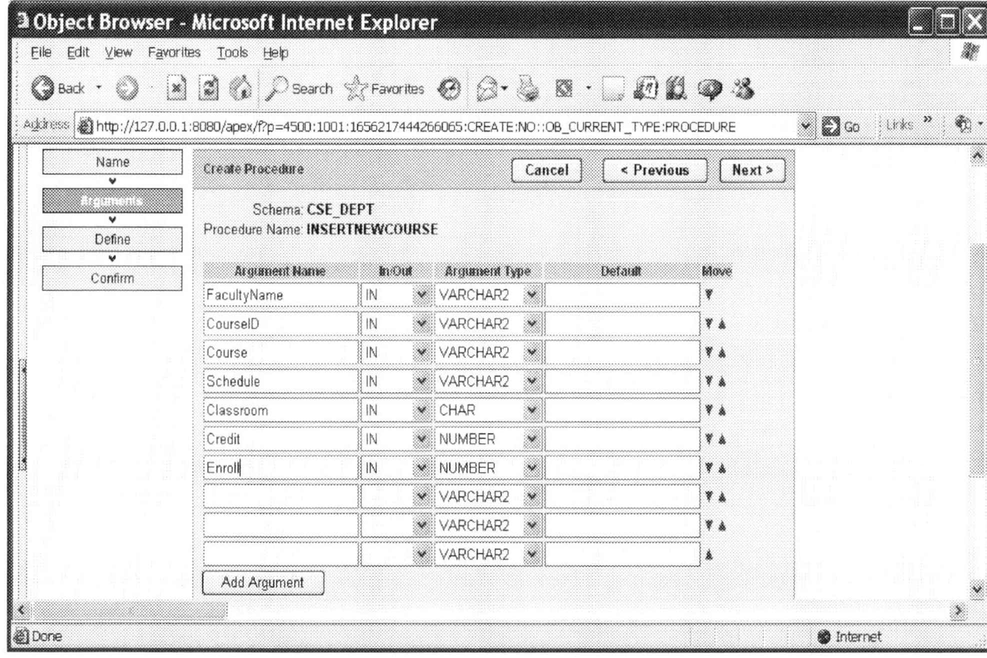

Figure 7.68. The finished Arguments page.

```
SELECT faculty_id INTO facultyID FROM Faculty
WHERE faculty_name = FacultyName;
INSERT INTO Course VALUES (CourseID, Course, Credit,
                           Classroom, Schedule, Enroll, facultyID);
```

Figure 7.69. The body of the stored procedure.

The data type of each parameter is indicated after the keyword **IN**, and it must be identical with the data type of the associated data column in the Course table. An **IS** command is attached after the procedure header to indicate that a query result, faculty_id, will be held by a local variable facultyID declared later.

Two queries are included in this procedure. The first query is used to get the faculty_id from the Faculty table based on the input parameter FacultyName, and the second query is to insert seven input parameters into the Course table based on the faculty_id obtained from the first query. A semicolon must be attached after each PL-SQL statement and after the command end.

One important issue is that you need to create one local variable `facultyID` and attach it after the **IS** command as shown in Figure 7.71, and this coding has been highlighted with the background color. Click the `Edit` button to add this local variable after the **IS** command. This local variable is used to hold the returned `faculty_id` from the execution of the first query.

Another important issue in distributing the input parameters or arguments in an INSERT command is that the order of those parameters or arguments must be identical

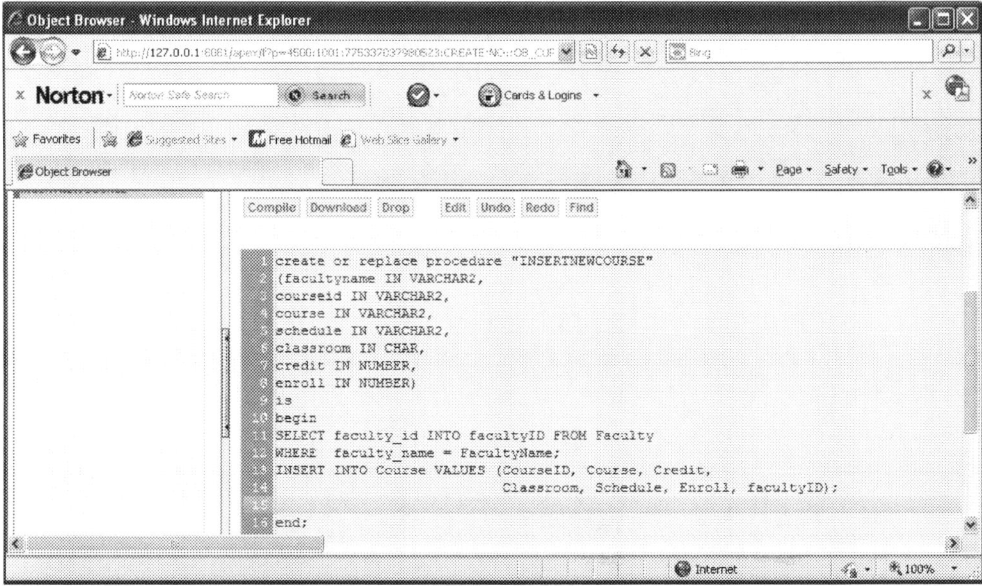

Figure 7.70. The finished procedure-define page.

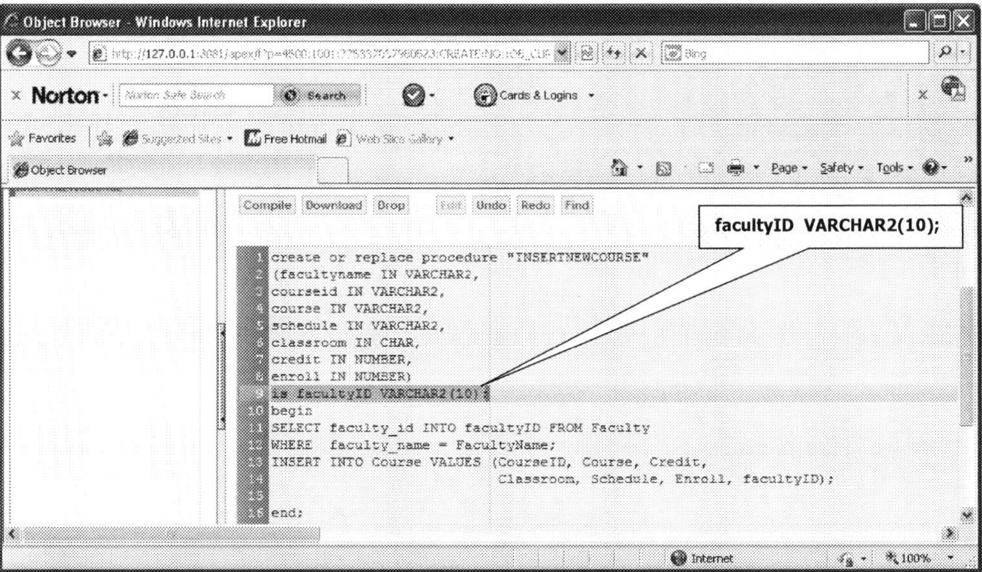

Figure 7.71. The modified stored procedure.

with the order of the data columns in the associated data table. For example, in the Course table, the order of the data columns is: course_id, course, credit, classroom, schedule, enrollment, and faculty_id. Accordingly, the order of input parameters placed in the INSERT argument list must be identical with the data columns' order displayed above.

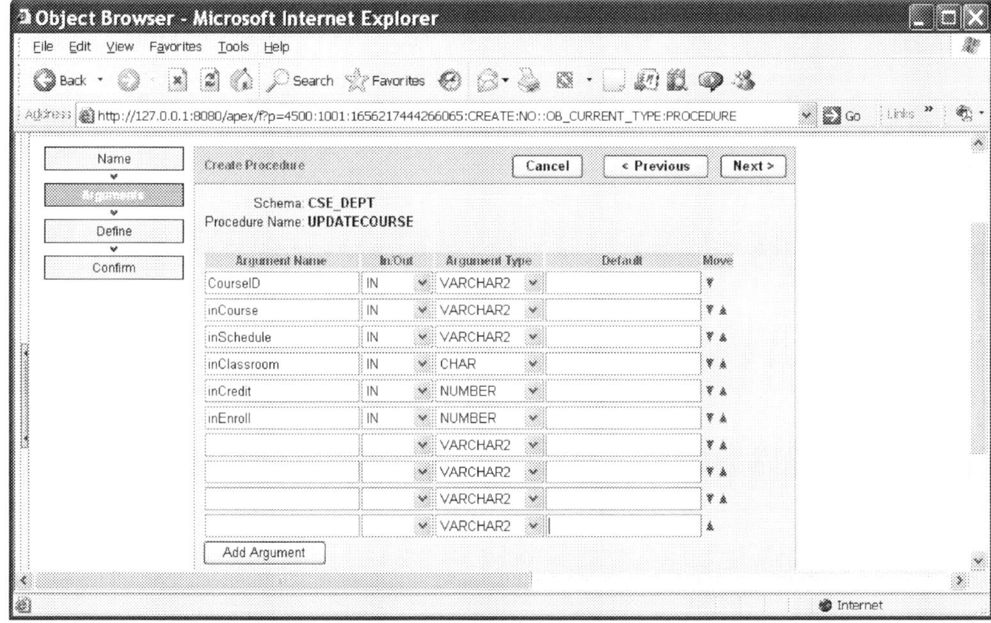

Figure 7.72. The finished Arguments page.

To make sure that this procedure is error free, we need to compile it first. Click the Compile button to compile and check our procedure. A successful compilation message should be displayed if our procedure is a bug-free stored procedure.

Next, let's continue to build our second stored procedure UpdateCourse().

7.6.2.2.2 Create the UpdateCourse Stored Procedure Click on the Create button located at the upper-right corner of this InsertNewCourse() procedure window and select the Procedure to open a new procedure page.

Enter UpdateCourse into the `Procedure Name` field and keep the `Include Arguments` checkbox checked, then click on the Next button.

In the Arguments page, enter six pieces of updated course information into six Argument fields. Refer to Section 2.11.2.3 in Chapter 2 for data types of these seven data. Your finished Arguments page should match one that is shown in Figure 7.72.

A point to be noted is that some input parameters, such as Course, Schedule, Classroom, Credit, and Enroll, are closely identical with the names of associated columns in our Course table. The only difference between them is that the first letters of those input parameters are capital, but the columns' names are not. However, as you know, the PL-SQL language is a case-insensitive language, and this difference would be removed when the stored procedure is executed. To avoid this confusion between the input parameters and names of columns in the Course table, we prefixed an in before those input parameters to distinguish them with the names of associated columns in our Course table.

Click on the Next button to go to the procedure-defining page.

Enter the codes that are shown in Figure 7.73 into this new procedure as the body of the procedure using the PL-SQL language. Then click on the Next and the Finish buttons to confirm creating of this procedure.

```
UPDATE Course
SET course = inCourse, credit = inCredit, classroom = inClassroom,
            Schedule = inSchedule, enrollment = inEnroll
WHERE course_id = CourseID;
```

Figure 7.73. The body of the stored procedure.

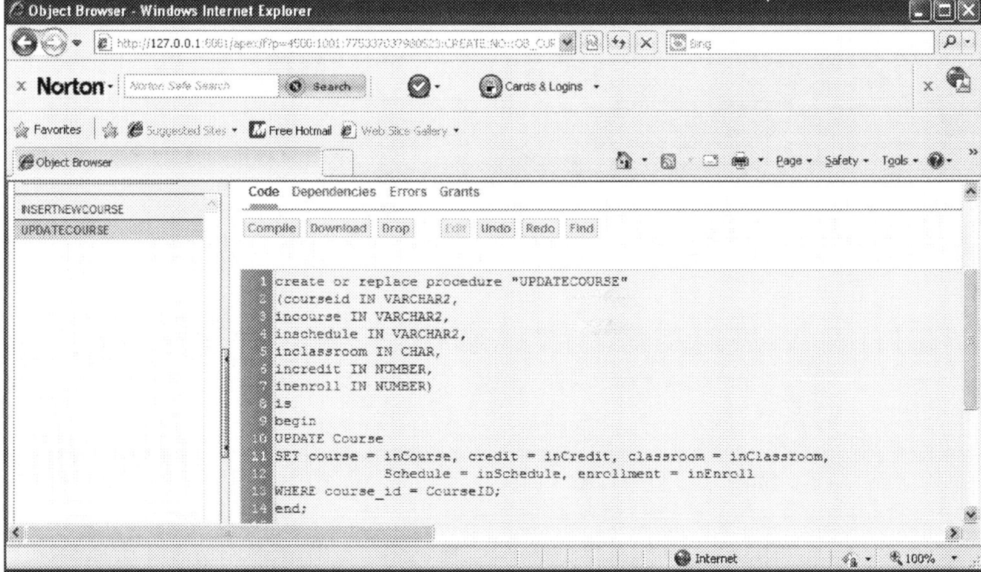

Figure 7.74. The finished UpdateCourse stored procedure.

Your finished Procedure-Define page is shown in Figure 7.74.

To make sure that this procedure is error free, we need to compile it first. Click the Compile button to compile and check our procedure. A successful compilation message should be displayed if our procedure is a bug-free stored procedure.

Next, let's continue to build our last stored procedure DeleteCourse().

7.6.2.2.3 Create the DeleteCourse Stored Procedure Click on the Create button located at the upper-right corner of this UpdateCourse() procedure window and select the Procedure to open a new procedure page.

Enter DeleteCourse into the `Procedure Name` field and keep the `Include Arguments` checkbox checked, then click on the `Next` button.

In the Arguments page, enter a CourseID for which the associated course will be deleted into the first Argument field. Refer to Section 2.11.2.3 in Chapter 2 to get this data type. Your finished Arguments page should match one that is shown in Figure 7.75.

Click on the Next button to go to the procedure-defining page.

Enter the codes that are shown in Figure 7.76 into this new procedure as the body of this procedure using the PL-SQL language. Then click on the Next and the Finish buttons to confirm creating of this procedure.

Your finished Procedure-Define page is shown in Figure 7.77.

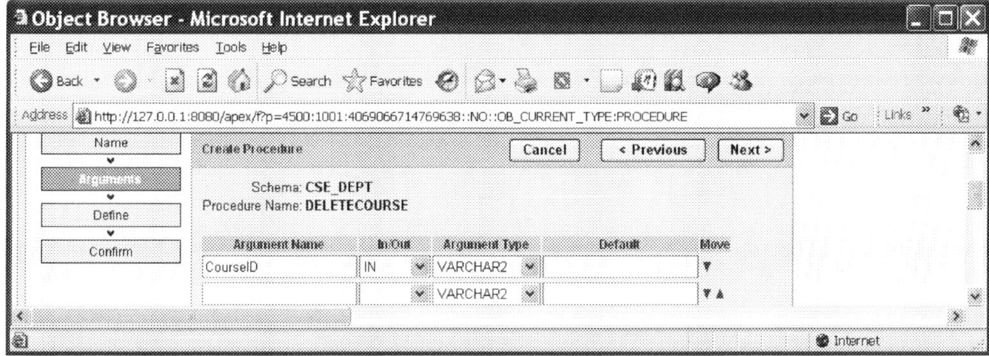

Figure 7.75. The finished Arguments page.

```
DELETE FROM Course WHERE course_id = CourseID;
```

Figure 7.76. The body of the stored procedure.

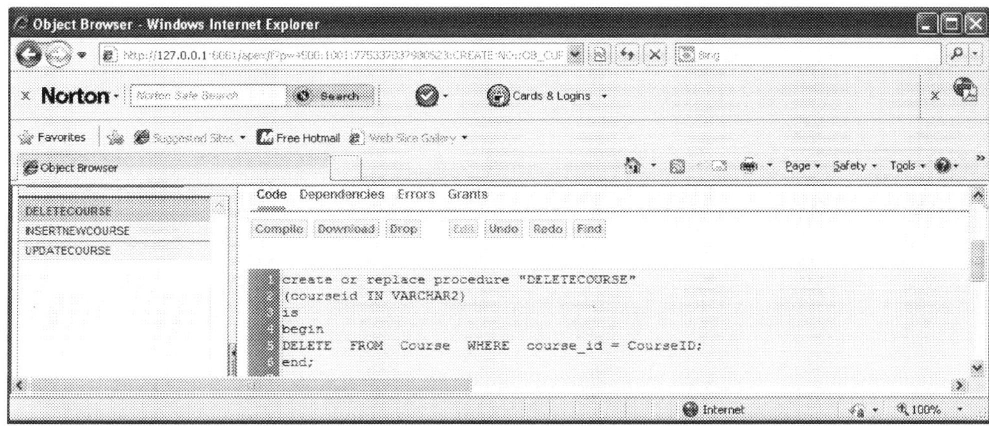

Figure 7.77. The finished stored procedure DeleteCourse().

To make sure that this procedure is error free, we need to compile it first. Click the Compile button to compile and check our procedure. A successful compilation message should be displayed if our procedure is a bug-free stored procedure.

At this point, we have finished building all three stored procedures in the Oracle database environment. Now close the Oracle Database 10g XE, and we can test the codes we made in Section 7.6.2.1 to call them to perform the associated data actions.

7.6.2.3 Build and Run the Project to Test the Data Manipulations

Launch NetBeans IDE 6.8 and our project OracleSelectObject. Click on the **Clean and Build Main Project** button to build the project. Then click on the **Run Main Project** button to run the project.

Enter suitable username and password, such as `jhenry` and `test`, to the LogIn frame form and select the Course Information from the SelectFrame window to open the CourseFrame form window. Make sure that the Java Callable Method has been selected from the Query Method combo box. Then click on the Select button to query the default course information for the selected faculty member Ying Bai.

Now enter the following data into seven text fields as a new course record for the selected faculty member:

Course ID: CSE-549
Course: Fuzzy Systems
Schedule: T-H: 1:30–2:45 pm
Classroom: TC-302
Credit: 3
Enrollment: 25

Then click on the Insert button to insert this course record into the Course table in our sample database.

To confirm and validate this data insertion, click on the Select button to try to retrieve all courses taught by the selected faculty member Ying Bai. The running result is shown in Figure 7.78, and you can see that the new inserted course CSE-549 is indeed added to the database and displayed in the CourseList listbox.

Now select the course CSE-549 from the CourseList listbox and enter the following data into six text fields as an updated course record for the selected course CSE-549:

Course: Intelligent Controls
Schedule: M-W-F: 11:00–11:50 a.m.

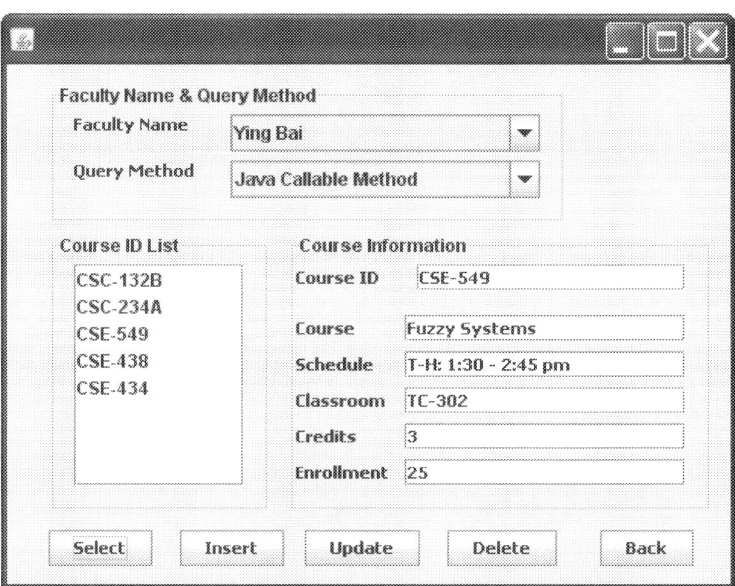

Figure 7.78. The running result for calling the InsertNewCourse() stored procedure.

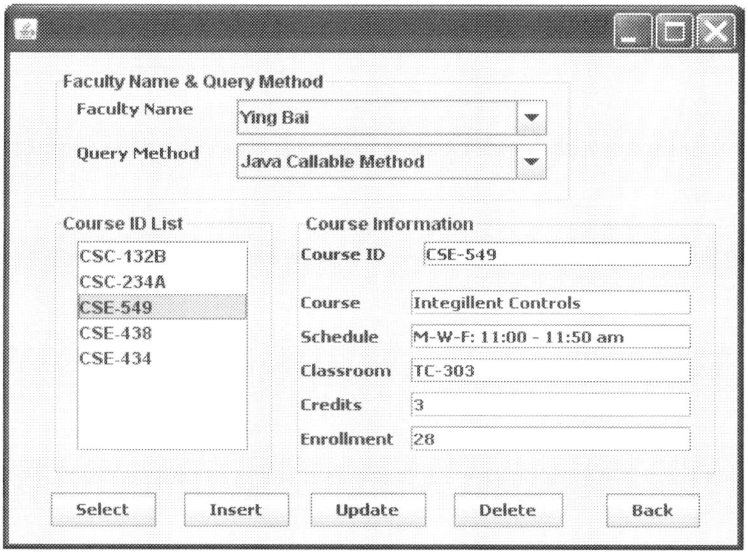

Figure 7.79. The running result for calling the UpdateCourse() stored procedure.

Classroom: TC-303

Credit: 3

Enrollment: 28

Then click on the Update button to update this course record in the Course table in our sample database. To confirm and validate this data updating, click on the Select button to try to retrieve all courses taught by the selected faculty member Ying Bai. The running result is shown in Figure 7.79.

Another way to confirm this data updating action is to open the Course table using the Services window in the NetBeans IDE. To do that, open the Services window and expand the Databases node and connect to our Oracle database by right clicking on that URL and select the Connect item. Then expand that connected URL and our CSE_DEPT database node and Tables nodes. Right click on the Course table and select the View Data to open this table. Click on the `Next Page` tab and you can find that the course CSE-549 has been updated and displayed at the last line on this Course table, as shown in Figure 7.80.

Now select the course CSE-549 from the CourseList listbox and click on the Delete button to try to delete this course from the Course table in our sample database.

To confirm and validate this data deletion action, click on the Select button again to try to retrieve all courses taught by the default faculty Ying Bai. It can be found that there is no CSE-549 course in the CourseList listbox, and this means that the course CSE-549 has been deleted from the Course table. You can also confirm this data deleting action by opening the Course table using the Services window in the NetBeans IDE.

At this point, we have finished developing and building data manipulations project to Oracle database using CallableStatement object method. A complete project OracleSelectObject that contains all three data manipulation actions to the Oracle

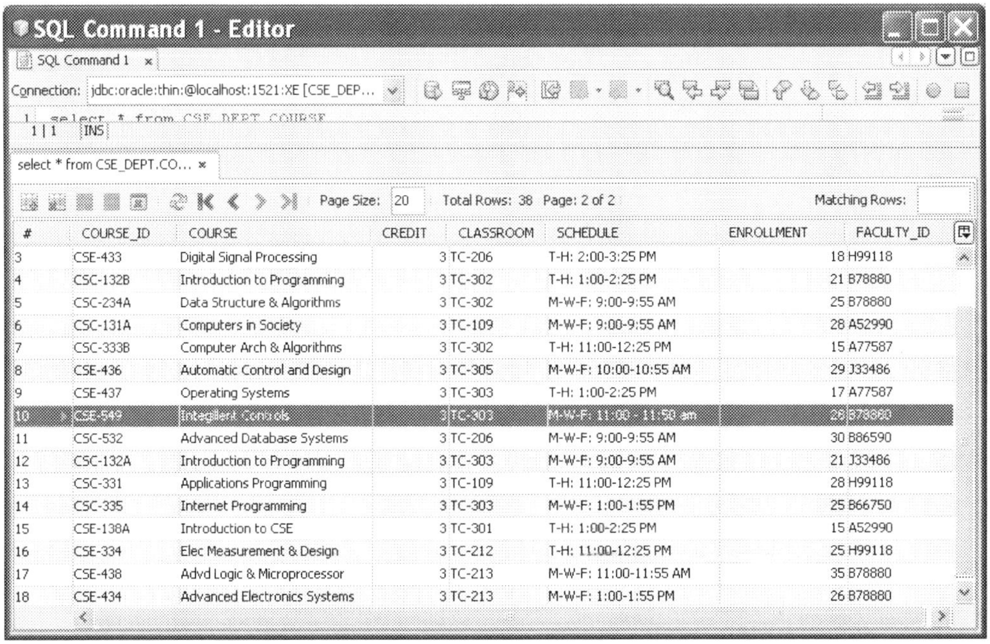

SQL Command 1 - Editor

SQL Command 1

Connection: jdbc:oracle:thin:@localhost:1521:XE [CSE_DEP...

select * from CSE_DEPT.CO...

Page Size: 20 Total Rows: 38 Page: 2 of 2 Matching Rows:

#	COURSE_ID	COURSE	CREDIT	CLASSROOM	SCHEDULE	ENROLLMENT	FACULTY_ID
3	CSE-433	Digital Signal Processing	3	TC-206	T-H: 2:00-3:25 PM	18	H99118
4	CSC-132B	Introduction to Programming	3	TC-302	T-H: 1:00-2:25 PM	21	B78880
5	CSC-234A	Data Structure & Algorithms	3	TC-302	M-W-F: 9:00-9:55 AM	25	B78880
6	CSC-131A	Computers in Society	3	TC-109	M-W-F: 9:00-9:55 AM	28	A52990
7	CSC-333B	Computer Arch & Algorithms	3	TC-302	T-H: 11:00-12:25 PM	15	A77587
8	CSE-436	Automatic Control and Design	3	TC-305	M-W-F: 10:00-10:55 AM	29	J33486
9	CSE-437	Operating Systems	3	TC-303	T-H: 1:00-2:25 PM	17	A77587
10	CSE-549	Integllent Controls	3	TC-303	M-W-F: 11:00 - 11:50 am	28	B78880
11	CSC-532	Advanced Database Systems	3	TC-206	M-W-F: 9:00-9:55 AM	30	B86590
12	CSC-132A	Introduction to Programming	3	TC-303	M-W-F: 9:00-9:55 AM	21	J33486
13	CSC-331	Applications Programming	3	TC-109	T-H: 11:00-12:25 PM	28	H99118
14	CSC-335	Internet Programming	3	TC-303	M-W-F: 1:00-1:55 PM	25	B66750
15	CSE-138A	Introduction to CSE	3	TC-301	T-H: 1:00-2:25 PM	15	A52990
16	CSE-334	Elec Measurement & Design	3	TC-212	T-H: 11:00-12:25 PM	25	H99118
17	CSE-438	Advd Logic & Microprocessor	3	TC-213	M-W-F: 11:00-11:55 AM	35	B78880
18	CSE-434	Advanced Electronics Systems	3	TC-213	M-W-F: 1:00-1:55 PM	26	B78880

Figure 7.80. The updated course CSE-549.

database can be found at the folder DBProjects\Chapter 7, which is located at the Wiley ftp site (refer to Figure 1.2 in Chapter 1).

7.7 CHAPTER SUMMARY

Three popular data manipulations against two kinds of databases, SQL Server and Oracle, have been discussed and analyzed in detailed with quite a few real project examples in this chapter.

This chapter is divided into two parts: Insert, update, and delete data to our sample database using JPA wizards, and insert, update, and delete data using the Java runtime object method. Relatively, the second method provides more flexibility and efficiency in data actions against different databases. In the second part, two more data manipulation methods, Updatable ResultSet and CallableStatement, are discussed with real projects for two popular databases, SQL Server and Oracle.

Detailed introduction and illustrations on building stored procedures under different database systems are provided with real and step-by-step examples. After finished this chapter, readers will be

- Able to design and build professional data actions against popular database systems using the JPA wizards.
- Able to design and build professional data actions against popular database systems using the Java runtime objects.
- Able to design and build popular stored procedures for different database systems.

- Able to design and build professional data actions against popular databases using Updatable ResultSet methods.
- Able to design and build professional data actions against popular databases using CallableStatement methods.

Starting from next chapter, we will discuss the Java Web database programming.

HOMEWORK

I. True/False Selections

____**1.** To use JPA to perform data manipulations against target databases, one needs first to set up a connection to the target database using JPA wizard.

____**2.** A persistence unit is used to hold a set of entities that can be managed by a given EntityManager instance.

____**3.** The `persist()` method, which belongs to the persistence unit, is used to add all necessary entities into the persistence context that can be managed by the EntityManager.

____**4.** For all kinds of data query, such as Select, Update, Delete, and even the execution of the `persist()` method, a Transaction Association must be started to monitor and execute this data query.

____**5.** In JPQL, no INSERT identifier is defined and implemented because we do not need this kind of identifier to do any mapping between a query string and an object, and we can directly insert a object using the `persist()` method.

____**6.** When using JPQL to create a dynamic data manipulation query string, one can only use the positional parameters in that query string.

____**7.** When using JPQL to perform data manipulations, the Transaction instance must be triggered and started by executing the `commit()` method.

____**8.** When perform data manipulations using Java runtime object method, one can use either `executeUpdate()` or `execute()` method.

____**9.** A default ResultSet object is updatable and has a cursor that can move either forward and backward.

___**10.** To insert a new record into a database using the Updatable ResultSet method, one needs first to move the cursor to an insert-row that is a blank row and is not a part of the ResultSet but related to the ResultSet.

II. Multiple Choices

1. When using JPA wizard to perform data manipulations, in order to create a Transaction Association instance, one need to use the __________ method.

   a. begin()
   b. getTransaction()
   c. persist()
   d. commit()

2. When using JPA wizard to perform data manipulations, the following data manipulations, such as ________________, need a Transaction Association instance.

   a. Update and Selection
   b. Delete and Selection

c. Update, Delete, and Select
d. Update and Delete

3. When using an Updatable ResultSet to perform data manipulations, two parameters can be used to set up properties of a ResultSet object, they are ________________.
   a. Forward-only, Updatable
   b. Scroll-sensitive, Read-only
   c. ResultSet Type, Concurrency Type of a ResultSet
   d. ResultSet Type, Updatable Type
4. Which of the following created ResultSet protocol is correct? _________
   a. Statement createStatement(int resultSetType, int resultSetConcurrency).
   b. PreparedStatement prepareStatement(String sql, int resultSetType, int resultSetConcurrency).
   c. CallableStatement prepareCall(String sql, int resultSetType, int resultSetConcurrency).
   d. All of them.
5. To update a record using the Updatable ResultSet, one needs to use ______ steps and they are: ________________________.
   a. 1, UpdateXXX()
   b. 2, UpdateXXX() and UpdateRow()
   c. 3, UpdateXXX(), UpdateCursor() and UpdateRow()
   d. 4, MoveToRow(), UpdateXXX(), UpdateCursor() and UpdateRow()
6. To insert a new record using the Updatable ResultSet, one needs to use ______ steps and they are: ________________________.
   a. 1, insertRow()
   b. 2, moveToInsertRow(), insertRow()
   c. 3, moveToInsertRow(),updateXXX(), insertRow()
   d. 4, moveToCursor(), moveToInsertRow(), updateXXX(), insertRow()
7. When building an Oracle stored procedure to perform data updating action, one needs to use the ____ input parameters to ______ them with the column names in the query string.
   a. Different, distinguish
   b. Same, identify
   c. Same, distinguish.
   d. Different, identify
8. By using which of the following static constant values, we can set an Updatable Result object that has a cursor that can move either forward and backward?
   a. ResultSet.TYPE_FORWARD_ONLY
   b. ResultSet.TYPE_SCROLL_INSENSITIVE
   c. ResultSet.CONCUR_UPDATABLE
   d. ResultSet.TYPE_SCROLL_SENSITIVE
9. By using which of the following static constant values can we set an Updatable Result object whose contents can be updated?
   a. ResultSet.TYPE_FORWARD_ONLY
   b. ResultSet.TYPE_SCROLL_INSENSITIVE
   c. ResultSet.CONCUR_UPDATABLE
   d. ResultSet.TYPE_SCROLL_SENSITIVE

10. Every EntityManager has a ________ relation with an EntityTransaction instance. If an application requires multiple concurrent transactions, one can use __________ EntityManager(s)

a. one-to-many, one
b. many-to-one, multiple
c. many-to-many, multiple
d. one-to-one, multiple

III. Exercises

1. Provide a brief description about the `persist()` method in the EntityManager class.
2. Provide a brief discussion about the Transaction Association object.
3. Figure 7.81 shows a piece of codes used to perform a data manipulation in JPA environment. Provide a clear and detailed explanation for each step and list them one by one.
4. List six steps to use Java runtime object to perform data manipulations against our target database.
5. List three steps to insert a new record into a target database using the Updatable ResultSet method. Convert the pseudo-codes shown below to the real Java codes (assume that a valid connection **conn** has been established).
   a. Create an Insert query.
   b. Create a PreparedStatement instance with two ResultSet parameters, `TYPE_SCROLL_SENSITIVE` and `CONCUR_UPDATABLE`, to define the ResultSet object to enable it to be scrollable and updatable, and enable it to perform data manipulations.
   c. The setString() method is used to initialize the positional parameter in the query string.
   d. The executeQuery() method is called to perform this query and return the query result to a newly created ResultSet object.
   e. The moveToInsertRow() method is executed to move the cursor of the ResultSet to a blank row that is not a part of the ResultSet but is related to that ResultSet.
   f. Two updateString() methods are executed to insert two desired columns to the associated columns in the ResultSet.
   g. The insertRow() method is executed to update this change to the database.

```
A   Book book = new Book("1B78-YU9L", "JavaWorld");
B   Company pub = new Company("Weston House");
C   pub.setRevenue(1750000D);
    book.setPublisher(pub);
    pub.addBook(mag);
D   EntityManager em = emf.createEntityManager();
E   em.getTransaction().begin();
F   em.persist(book);
    em.persist(pub);
G   em.getTransaction().commit();
    // or we could continue using the EntityManager...
H   em.close();
```

Figure 7.81. A piece of codes used to insert some data into two tables.

6. Refer to Section 7.3.1 to develop codes for the StudentFrame form window to insert a new student record into the Student table in our sample database using the Java runtime object method. The student's photo can be the Default.jpg.
7. Refer to Section 7.6.1.2 to develop codes for the FacultyFrame form class to update a faculty record for the Faculty table in our sample SQL Server database using CallableStatement method. The faculty's photo will be kept unchanged.

PART II
Building Three-Tier Client–Server Applications

Chapter 8

Developing Java Web Applications to Access Databases

As the rapid development of the Java Web application techniques, today, the Java Web applications are closely related to Java Enterprise Edition platform, and the latter provides rich and powerful APIs to support developers to build and develop more efficient and productive Web applications with less complexity and developing efforts.

The Java EE platform uses a simplified programming model. XML deployment descriptors are optional. Instead, a developer can simply enter the information as an annotation directly into a Java source file, and the Java EE server will configure the component at deployment and runtime. These annotations are generally used to embed in a program data that would otherwise be furnished in a deployment descriptor. With annotations, the specification information is put directly in your code next to the program element that it affects.

In order to have a clear and understandable idea about Java Web applications and their developments, let's first have a quick historical review on this topic, and this review is absolutely necessary for beginners who have never built and developed any Java Web application before. You are not required to understand all details on the codes in the following review sections, but we expect that you can understand them based on their functions.

8.1 A HISTORICAL REVIEW ABOUT JAVA WEB APPLICATION DEVELOPMENT

Java Web applications are based on Servlet technique, and the Servlet works as a Web server that provides all supports such as receiving requests from the client and sending responses back to the client. Exactly, a Servlet is a server class built in Java language with all functionalities of a server engine. A Servlet performs its job in the following ways:

- When a Servlet is created, the init() method is called to do the initialization jobs for the Web server.
- When a request is received by the Servlet, it creates two objects; request and response.

Practical Database Programming with Java, First Edition. Ying Bai.

- Then the Servlet sends these two objects to the service() method.
- The request object encapsulates the information passed from the HTTP request coming from the client.
- The service() method is a main responding body and will be used to process the request and send the response that has been embedded into the response object back to the client.

The conventional Web applications are built with a Servlet as a Web container and HTML pages as Web clients.

8.1.1 Using Servlet and HTML Web Pages for Java Web Applications

The main purpose of using the Servlet is to compensate the shortcoming of using a Common Gateway Interface (CGI). Unlike the CGI, the Servlet can be used to create dynamic web pages during the server–client communication processes. Two methods, doGet() and doPost(), are main channels to communicate between the server and clients.

General uses of Servlet include:

- Processing requests received from clients and responses back to clients
- Creating dynamic web pages
- Managing state information for applications
- Storing data and information for clients

Generally, the client pages can be divided into two categories: reading page and posting page. The former is used to read data from the user, and the latter is used for displaying feedback from the server. To interface to the client to get user's data, most of the time, the server calls the getParameter() method that belongs to the request object to do this job. To send feedback to the client, most of the time, the server uses println() method that belongs to the out object. With this pair of methods, a server can easily communicate with the client and transfer data between them.

By using an example that utilizes these methods to transfer the login information between a Servlet and a client Web page, we can get a much clearer picture and deeper understanding for this topic.

Open a Notepad and enter the following codes that are shown in Figure 8.1 to build the Login.html file.

Save this file with the name of "Login.html" to make it an HTML file. You have to use double quotation marks to enclose this file name with the .html extension to let Notepad know that you want to save it as an HTML file.

Double click on this file to run it and the running result is shown in Figure 8.2.

Two input text fields are used by users to enable them to enter the desired username and password. The key is the identifier for both text fields, username and password, which is the name property or attribute of these two text fields. When a server needs these two pieces of login information, it uses the getParameter() method defined in the request object with the names of two text fields as identifiers to get them. Figure 8.3 shows a piece of codes developed in the server side to perform this login information picking up operation.

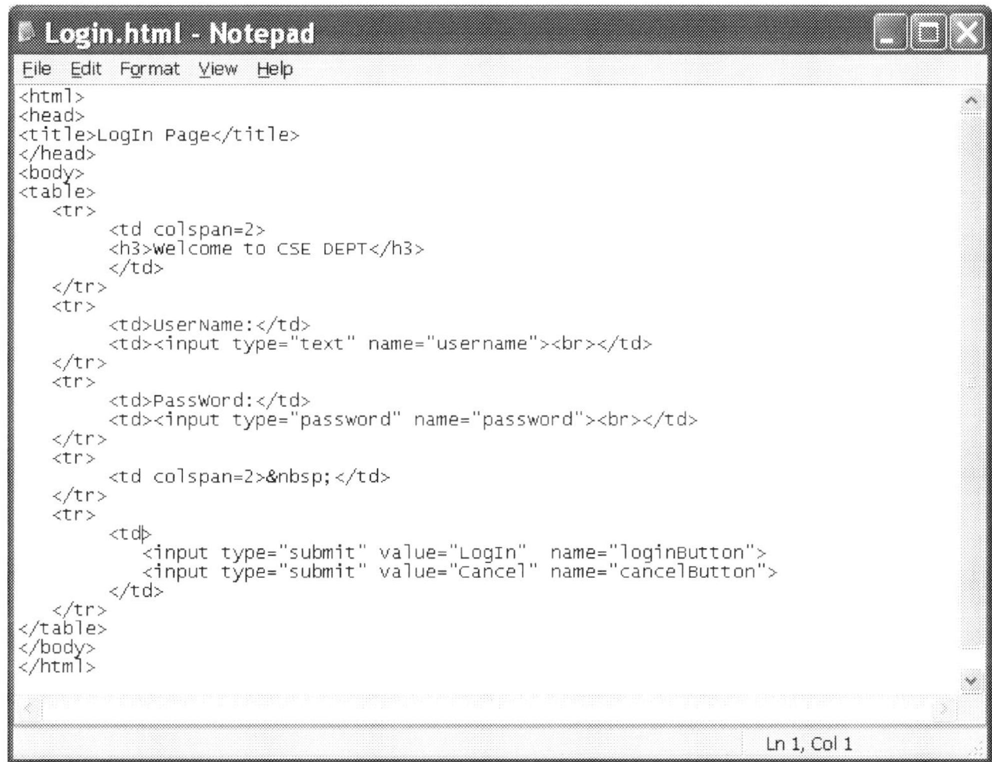

```
<html>
<head>
<title>LogIn Page</title>
</head>
<body>
<table>
   <tr>
        <td colspan=2>
        <h3>Welcome to CSE DEPT</h3>
        </td>
   </tr>
   <tr>
        <td>UserName:</td>
        <td><input type="text" name="username"><br></td>
   </tr>
   <tr>
        <td>PassWord:</td>
        <td><input type="password" name="password"><br></td>
   </tr>
   <tr>
        <td colspan=2> </td>
   </tr>
   <tr>
        <td>
           <input type="submit" value="LogIn"  name="loginButton">
           <input type="submit" value="Cancel" name="cancelButton">
        </td>
   </tr>
</table>
</body>
</html>
```

Figure 8.1. The finished Login.html file.

Figure 8.2. The Login.html running result.

```
public void doGet(HttpServletRequest request, HttpServletResponse response)
{
    response.setContentType("text/html");
    PrintWriter out = new PrintWriter(response.getWriter());

    String uname = request.getParameter("username");
    String pword = request.getParameter("password");

    // process the received uname and pword
```

Figure 8.3. Using getParameter() method to get data from the client.

Two variables, uname and pword, are used in the server side to hold the picked up username and password entered by the user from the client Web page. The getParameter() method is used to do this picking up operation. The identifiers for these two parameters are the names of two text fields in the HTML page.

With this simple example, you can see how easy it is for server and client to communicate for each other. The server can send feedback or post any desired information in the client by using the out object that is obtained from creating a new PrintWriter instance at the first two coding lines in this piece of codes.

Ok, now we have a clear picture about the module of using a Servlet and a client to build and implement a Java Web application in the early days. To deploy this login Servlet, we need to locate the Servlet class file to the suitable directory.

One of shortcomings for this kind of application is that the server and the client use two different languages, and a converter or a render is necessary to perform this conversion between these two languages. This will reduce the running speed and efficiency of the Web application. A solution to this issue is the Java ServerPage (JSP) technique, which was developed by Sun. With the help of the JSP, parts of server codes can be extended and embedded into the client side to facilitate the communications between a server and a client.

8.1.2 Using JavaServer Pages (JSP) Technology for Java Web Applications

In fact, JSP technique provides a way of using Java code within an HTML page, which means that you can embed a piece of Java codes or a part of Servlet functions into the codes in the client side with appropriate tags. The embedded Java codes will be compiled and executed by the JSP engine in the server side as the application runs. From this point of view, the JSP can be considered as a part of a Servlet or as an extension of an application server located at the client side. Although the JSP provides a lot of advantages over Servlets, it is actually a subclass of the Servlet class and built based on Servlets technology.

The JSP can be implemented not only in the HTML files, but also in the following files:

- Script language files, which allow you to specify a block of Java codes.
- JSP directives, which enable you to control the JSP structure and environment.

- Actions, which allow you to specify the executing commands, such as loading a parameter from a client page.

The JSP provides some useful built-in or implicit objects to perform most interfacing functions with clients and server. The so-called implicit objects in JSP are objects that are automatically available in JSP. Implicit objects are Java objects that the JSP Container provides to a developer to access them in their applications using JavaBeans and Servlets. These objects are called implicit objects because they are automatically instantiated. Some popular implicit JSP objects include:

- request
- response
- out
- session
- application
- pageContext
- page
- exception

Among those objects, the request, response and session are most popular objects, and are often used in the interfacing between clients and servers. Some other objects, such as out and pageContext, are mainly used to write output to the client and to access most built-in objects.

Figure 8.4 shows an example of using the out and the pageContext objects to write some feedback to the client (the top section) and to get a session object (the bottom section).

Two popular tags used by JSP to distinguish with other languages are:

- <% . . . . %>
- **<jsp: . . . . />**

Between these two tags, you can put any Java codes as you want to improve the execution of the Servlet techniques for Java Web applications.

In fact, you can get a JSP file or page easily by just changing the extension of the Login.html file, such as from Login.html to Login.jsp. Yes, it is so easy to do this to get a JSP file.

An example of using a JSP file to display the received user login data is shown in Figure 8.5.

```
out.println("<HTML>");
out.println("<HEAD>Hello World</HEAD>");
out.println("</HTML>");
out.close();
```

```
HttpSession session = pageContext.getSession();
```

Figure 8.4. An example of using the out and the pageContext objects.

```
<HTML>
<HEAD>
<TITLE>Welcome to CSE DEPT LogIn Page</TITLE>
</HEAD>
<BODY>
<%@ Page language="java" %>
<%
    String uname = request.getParameter("username");
    String pword = request.getParameter("password");
%>
User Name = <%=uname%><br>
Pass Word  = <%=pword%><br>
</BODY>
</HTML>
```

Figure 8.5. An example of Java Server Page file.

Within the tags <% . . . %>, two lines of Java codes are written, and they are used to call the getParameter() method to pick up the username and password entered by the user from the client Web page. You can directly display these received login data in the client side with the Java local variables uname and pword enclosed with the JSP tags.

In fact, the JSP can handle more complicated jobs such as the business logic, JDBC-related database connections, data processing, and JSP pages switching. Generally, a main or controller JSP takes charge of passing parameters between the server and clients, forwarding the user to the other target JSP or web pages based on the running result of Servlet.

A piece of example codes shown in Figure 8.6 illustrate how to use a JSP to handle multiple jobs, including the parameters collections from the client page, database accessing, and data processing and forwarding from the current page to the target Java Server pages based on the running results of data processing.

Let's have a closer look at this piece of codes to see how it works.

A. The getParameter() method is called to pick up two pieces of login information, username and password, which are entered by the user from the client page, and assigned to two local variables uname and pword in the Servlet.

B. These two picked up login data are displayed in the client side with the JSP tags.

C. Starting from the JSP tag <%, a piece of Java codes is developed. An Oracle database driver is loaded, and this is a type IV JDBC driver.

D. The Oracle JDBC URL is assigned to the local variable url.

E. The getConnection() method is executed to establish this database connection.

F. A query string is created and it is used to query a matched username and password from the LogIn table.

G. The createStatement() method is called to create a Statement object.

H. The executeQuery() method is executed to perform this query, and the returned result is assigned to the ResultSet object rs.

I. A while loop is used to pick up any possible matched username and password. In fact, only one row is returned, and therefore this loop can run only one time.

```
  <HTML>
  <HEAD>
  <TITLE>Welcome to CSE DEPT LogIn Page</TITLE></HEAD>
  <BODY>
  <%@ Page language="java" %>
  <%
A     String uname = request.getParameter("username");
      String pword = request.getParameter("password");
  %>
B User Name = <%=uname%><br>
  Pass Word  = <%=pword%><br>
  <%
      try {
C         Class.forName("oracle.jdbc.OracleDriver");
      }
      catch (Exception e) {
        msgDlg.setMessage("Class not found exception!" + e.getMessage());
        msgDlg.setVisible(true);
      }
D     String url = "jdbc:oracle:thin:@localhost:1521:XE";
      try {
E     con = DriverManager.getConnection(url,"CSE_DEPT","reback");
      }
      catch (SQLException e) {
        msgDlg.setMessage("Could not connect!" + e.getMessage());
        msgDlg.setVisible(true);
        e.printStackTrace();
      }

      Statement  stmt = null;
      ResultSet  rs = null;
F     String query = "SELECT user_name, pass_word FROM LogIn " +
                     "WHERE user_name = '" + uname + "' " + " AND pass_word = '"+pword+"';";
G    stmt = con.createStatement();
H    rs = stmt.executeQuery(query);
I    while (rs.next()) {
       String c_uname = rs.getString("user_name");
       String c_pword = rs.getString("pass_word");
     }
J    if (c_uname.equals(uname) && c_pword.equals(pword)) {
        String  nextPage = "Selection.jsp";
     }
K    else {
        String  nextPage = "LoginError.jsp";
     }
  %>
L <jsp:forward  page = "<%=nextPage%>" />
```

Figure 8.6. A piece of example codes.

J. If a matched username and password pair is found, the nextPage is assigned to the Selection.jsp.

K. Otherwise, the nextPage is assigned to the LoginError.jsp.

L. The <jsp:forward /> is used to direct the page to an appropriate page based on the matching result.

A good point of using this JSP technique to handle a lot of JDBC-related codes or business logics in this JavaServer Page is that the Servlet processing speed and efficiency can be improved. However, you can find that at the same time, a shortcoming also comes with this benefit, which is the relative complexity in the coding development. Quite a few codes for the JDBC database accessing and data processing, as well as the business logics, are involved into this JSP, and therefore make it a big mess during the coding development.

To solve this mess problem and separate the business logics and JDBC-related database processing from the result displaying in web pages, and make our coding process easy and clear, four possible ways can be used:

1. Using a Java help class file to handle all business logics and database-related processing. In this way, we can separate this login process into two different parts: the data displaying Web page and JDBC-related database processing or business logics to make this process more objective and clear based on its functionality. This Java help class file works just like a bridge or an intermediate layer to help the JSP to perform business-related jobs in a separate file to allow the JSP to concentrate on the data displaying process. You will see that this Java help class file can be translated to a Java Bean later.
2. Using Java Persistence API to simplify the JDBC-related database accessing and data processing. Either Java Persistence API or Hibernate Persistence API can handle this issue.
3. Using the session implicit object provided by JSP to store and transfer data between clients and server. This method still belongs to the Java help class category. Exactly, the session objects are used in the Java help class to help the data storage and retrieving between clients and clients, and between clients and the server.
4. Using Java Beans techniques to cover and handle the JDBC-related database accessing, data processing, and business logics, such as data matching and comparison process. The main role of JSP is to provide a view to display the results. A JSP can also need to load the Java Beans, pass the necessary parameters between Servlet and clients, and forward users to the different targeting pages based on the running result.

Let's have a detailed discussion about these three methods one by one.

8.1.3 Using Java Help Class Files for Java Web Applications

To distinguish between the database-related data processing and running results displaying, we can separate a Java Web application into two parts: the JDBC-related database processing and the business logics, such as checking and confirming a pair of matched username and password located at a Java help class file, and the data and running results displaying at a Web or a JavaServer page.

Take a look at the codes in Figure 8.6, you can find that about 80% of those codes are JDBC-related database processing codes, and 10% are about the data processing codes. Totally about 90% codes are used to access the database and query for the data and perform data matching functions. Only 10% codes are HTML codes.

To separate these two kinds of codes into two different files, we can pick up all JDBC related-codes and put them in a Java help class file, LogInQuery.java, as shown in Figure 8.7.

Let's have a closer look at this piece of codes to see how it works.

A. Some member data or attributes are defined first inside this class, which include two private String member data user_name and pass_word, a class-level connection variable con, and a dialog box that is used to display some debug information.

```
  import java.sql.*;

  public class LogInQuery {
A     private String user_name = null;
      private String pass_word = null;
      static Connection con;
      MsgDialog msgDlg = new MsgDialog(new javax.swing.JFrame(), true);

      public LogInQuery() {
        try {
B           Class.forName("oracle.jdbc.OracleDriver");
        }
        catch (Exception e) {
          msgDlg.setMessage("Class not found exception!" + e.getMessage());
          msgDlg.setVisible(true);
        }
C       String url = "jdbc:oracle:thin:@localhost:1521:XE";
        try {
D          con = DriverManager.getConnection(url,"CSE_DEPT","reback");
        }
        catch (SQLException e) {
          msgDlg.setMessage("Could not connect!" + e.getMessage());
          msgDlg.setVisible(true);
          e.printStackTrace();
        }
      }
E   public String checkLogIn(String uname, String pword) {
F     String c_uname = null, c_pword = null;
      Statement stmt = null;
      ResultSet rs = null;
G     String query = "SELECT user_name, pass_word FROM LogIn " +
                     "WHERE user_name = '" + uname + "' " + " AND pass_word = '"+pword+"';";
H     stmt = con.createStatement();
I     rs = stmt.executeQuery(query);
J     while (rs.next()) {
        c_uname = rs.getString("user_name");
        c_pword = rs.getString("pass_word");
      }
K     if (c_uname.equals(uname) && c_pword.equals(pword)) {
        user_name = c_uname;
        pass_word = c_pword;
        return "Matched";
      }
L     else {
        return "UnMatched";
      }
    }
  }
```

Figure 8.7. The codes for the Java Web help class LogInQuery.java.

B. Inside the class constructor, an Oracle database driver is loaded, and this is a type IV JDBC driver.

C. The Oracle JDBC URL is assigned to the local variable url.

D. The getConnection() method is executed to establish this database connection.

E. The Java help method checkLogIn() is declared inside this help class. This method is a main function in performing the JDBC-related data query and data matching operations.

F. Some local variables used in this method are defined first, which include the Statement and the ResultSet objects.

G. A query string is created, and it is used to query a matched username and password from the LogIn table.

H. The createStatement() method is called to create a Statement object.

I. The executeQuery() method is executed to perform this query, and the returned result is assigned to the ResultSet object rs.

J. A while loop is used to pick up any possible matched username and password. In fact, only one row is returned, and therefore this loop can run only one time. The getString() method is used to pick up the queried username and password. A point to be noted is that the arguments of this method, user_name and pass_word, are the column names in the LogIn table in our sample database CSE_DEPT, and they are different with those member data declared at the beginning of this class even they have the same names. The retuned username and password are assigned to two local variables c_uname and c_pword, respectively.

K. If a pair of matched username and password is found, they are assigned to two member data username and password, and return a "Matched" string to indicate that this check Login() method is successful and the matched results are found.

L. Otherwise, an "Unmatched" string is returned to indicate that no matched login information can be found.

Now let's do a little modification to our Login.html file and break this file into two JSP files: index.jsp and LogInQuery.jsp. The reason for us to make it into two JSP files is that we want to process and display data in two separate files to make it clear and easy. Generally, the index.jsp can be considered as a starting or a home page as a Web application runs. Figure 8.8 lists the modified codes for our original Login.html file that will be renamed to index.jsp, and the modified parts have been highlighted in bold.

Let's have a closer look at this piece of modified codes to see how it works.

A. The first modification is that a Form tag is added into this page with a POST method and an action attribute. Generally, a Form tag is used to create a HTML form to collect user information and send all pieces of those collected information to the server when a submit button on this Form is clicked. Therefore, a Form and all submitting buttons on that Form have a coordinate relationship. If a button is defined as a submit button by its type attribute, all Form data will be sent to the server whose URL is defined in the action attribute on the Form tag when this submitting button is clicked by the user. Here, we use a Java Server Page, .\LogInQuery.jsp, as the URL for our target page. Exactly this target page is used to access our Java help class file to handle all JDBC and data-related processing and business logics. The .\ symbol is used to indicate that our JSP file is located at the relatively current folder, since this page is a part of the server functions and will be run at the server side as the whole project runs.

B. The second modification is to change the type of our Cancel button from submit to button, and add one more attribute onclick for this button. The reason for us to do this modification is that we want to close our Login.jsp page when this Cancel button is clicked as the project runs, but we do not want to forward this button-click event to the server to allow the server to do this close action. Therefore, we have to change the type of this button to button (not submit) to avoid triggering the action attribute in the Form tag. We also need to add a self.close() method to the onclick attribute of this button to call the system close() method to terminate our application. The self means the current page.

C. The Form close tag is also added when the form arrived to its bottom.

```
  <html>
   <head>
        <meta http-equiv="Content-Type" content="text/html; charset=UTF-8">
        <title>LogIn Page</title>
   </head>
    <body>
    <%@page language="java" %>
A   <form method="POST" action=".\LogInQuery.jsp">
    <table>
     <tr>
          <td colspan=2>
          <h3>Welcome to CSE DEPT</h3>
          </td>
     </tr>
     <tr>
          <td>UserName:</td>
          <td><input type="text" name="username"><br></td>
     </tr>
     <tr>
          <td>PassWord:</td>
          <td><input type="password" name="password"><br></td>
     </tr>
     <tr>
          <td colspan=2> </td>
     </tr>
     <tr>
          <td>
            <input type="submit" value="LogIn"  name="loginButton">
B           <input type="button" value="Cancel" name="cancelButton" onclick="self.close()">
          </td>
     </tr>
    </table>
C   </form>
    </body>
  </html>
```

Figure 8.8. The modified Login.html file (now it is index.jsp).

Now let's build our LogInQuery.jsp page, which works as a part of server, to receive and handle the Form data, including the login information sent by the index.jsp page. Figure 8.9 shows the codes for this page.

Let's have a closer look at this piece of codes to see how it works.

A. A JSP directive tag is used to indicate that this page uses the Java language and it is a JSP file.

B. Some local variable and object are declared first. The string variable nextPage is used to hold the URL of the next page, and the lquery is a new instance of our Java help class LogInQuery we built at the beginning of this section.

C. The getParameter() method is used to pick up the login information entered by the user in the index.jsp page. The collected login information, including the username and password, is assigned to two local string variables u_name and p_word, respectively.

D. The checkLogIn() method defined in our Java help class file is called to perform the database query and the login matching processing. The collected login information is used as arguments and passed into this method. The running result of this method is a string, and it is assigned to the local string variable result.

```
  <html>
    <head>
      <meta http-equiv="Content-Type" content="text/html; charset=UTF-8">
      <title>LogIn Query Page</title>
    </head>
    <body>
A   <%@page language="java" %>
    <%
B     String nextPage = null;
      LogInQuery lquery = new LogInQuery();
C     String u_name = request.getParameter("username");
      String p_word = request.getParameter("password");
D     String result = lquery.checkLogIn(u_name, p_word);
E     if (result.equals("Matched")) {
        nextPage = "Selection.jsp";
        }
F     else { out.println("LogIn is failed"); }
    %>
G   <jsp:forward page = "<%=nextPage%>" />
    </body>
  </html>
```

Figure 8.9. The codes for the LogInUuery.jsp page.

E. An if block is used to check the running result of the checkLogIn() method. The program will be forwarded to a successful page (Selection.jsp) if a matched login record is found from our LogIn table.

F. Otherwise, an error message is printed to indicate that this login process has failed.

G. A JSP forward directive is used to direct the program to the next page.

In summary, to use a JavaServer Page to assistant a Java Web application, the following components should be considered and adopted:

1. The whole Web application can be divided into two parts:
   A. The JDBC and database processing-related functions and business logics—Java help class file (LogInQuery.java).
   B. The user data input and running result output functions—HTML or JSP (index.jsp and LogInQuery.jsp).
2. The relationships between these three pages are:
   A. The index.jsp, which runs on the client side, works as a starting or a homepage as the Web application runs, and it is used to collect the user information and sends it to the Web server.
   B. The LogInQuery.jsp, which can be considered as a part of the application server and runs at the server side, provides the information passing or transformation functions between the home page and other target pages to collect the user information, call the Java help class to perform the data and business logic processing, and direct the program to the different target pages based on the data processing results.
   C. The Java help class file LogInQuery.java, which provides the JDBC and database processing functions and business logics processing abilities, and works as an intermediate

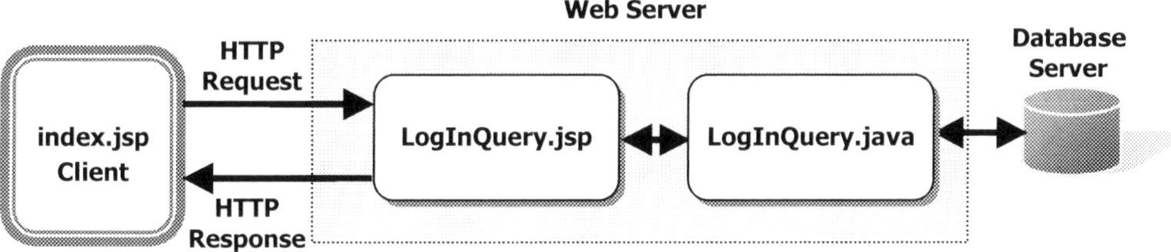

Figure 8.10. The components and their relationships in a JSP Web application.

layer between the server and clients to support above two JSP files. Since this help class file will be called by the LogInQuery.jsp, it also belongs to the server side software.

These components and their relationships can be expressed and illustrated in Figure 8.10.

Compared with our first Java Web application that utilized the Java Servlet and HTML page, the Web application that used the JSP techniques has a great improvement on simplification of data collection and processing by using different function-related pages and help class file. However, one defect is that the JDBC and database-related functions makes the Java help class file LogInQuery.java very complicated because too many database-related functions must be involved and executed, such as loading database driver, connecting to the database, creating query-related objects, building the data query, and collecting the queried results; all of these operations makes this file longer and increases the complex in operations. A good solution to this is to use the Java Persistence API to simplify these operations and make the file short and simple.

8.1.4 Using Java Persistence APIs for Java Web Applications

Two Java Persistence APIs are involved in NetBeans IDE, Java Persistence API and Hibernate API, and both provide good functions and controllabilities on database accessing and data processing. In this section, we want to use the Hibernate API to illustrate how to use this API to simplify the database accessing and data operations in our Java help class file.

In Section 5.3.6.2 in Chapter 5, we have provided a very detailed discussion about the Hibernate technique. In fact, Hibernate is an object-relational mapping (ORM) library for the Java language, and it provides a framework for mapping an object-oriented domain model to a traditional relational database. Unlike the Java Persistence API, Hibernate solves object-relational impedance mismatch problems by replacing direct persistence-related database accesses with high-level object handling functions.

To use the Hibernate technique to build a Web application in NetBeans IDE, perform the following operations:

1. Select the Hibernate framework when create a new Web application.
2. Modify the Hibernate Configuration file to include the desired database.
3. Create the HibernateUtil.java helper file to access the session object.
4. Generate Hibernate Mapping Files and Java Classes for all data tables in our sample database.

We will discuss these topics in more details in the following sections.

Suppose now we have installed the Hibernate frameworks and complete all of these operations listed above, now let's use the Hibernate frameworks to simplify the codes in our Java help class file LogInQuery.java. The modified LogInQuery.java file that used the Hibernate technique is shown in Figure 8.11.

Let's have a closer look at this piece of modified codes to see how it works.

A. All necessary packages related to components and library files used in this help class file are declared first.

B. A new instance of Hibernate session object is created and initialized. The purpose of creating this session instance is that we need to use it to perform all data actions to our sample database later.

C. The getCurrentSession() method is executed to get the default session object.

D. The detailed definition of the checkLogIn() method starts from here with the method header.

```
A  import csedept.entity.Login;
   import csedept.util.HibernateUtil;
   import java.util.List;
   import org.hibernate.Query;
   import org.hibernate.Session;

   public class LogInQuery {
      private String user_name = null;
      private String pass_word = null;
B     public Session session = null;

      public LogInQuery() {
C        this.session = HibernateUtil.getSessionFactory().getCurrentSession();
      }

D     public String checkLogIn(String uname, String pword) {
E        List<Login> loginList = null;
         MsgDialog msgDlg = new MsgDialog(new javax.swing.JFrame(), true);

         try {
F           org.hibernate.Transaction tx = session.beginTransaction();
G           Query q = session.createQuery ("from Login as lg where lg.userName like '"+uname+"'
                                         and lg.passWord like '"+pword+"'");
H           loginList = (List<Login>) q.list();
I        } catch (Exception e) {
            msgDlg.setMessage("Query is failed and no matched found!");
            msgDlg.setVisible(true);
            e.printStackTrace();
         }
J        user_name = loginList.get(0).getUserName();
         pass_word = loginList.get(0).getPassWord();

K        if (user_name.equals(uname) && pass_word.equals(pword)) {
            return "Matched";
         }
L        else {
            return "Nomatched";
         }
      }
   }
```

Figure 8.11. The Java help class with the Hibernate frameworks support.

E. A new java.util.List instance is created and initialized since we need this object to pick up and hold our queried login result.

F. A try…catch block is used to perform our data query. First, a new Transaction instance tx is created with the beginTransaction() method being executed.

G. Then a query string built with the Hibernate Query Language (HQL) is created, and this query string will be used to perform the login information query later.

H. The list() method is executed to perform a query to the LogIn table in our sample database to try to retrieve a pair of matched username and password. The query result is assigned to and held in a local variable loginList that has a List<LogIn> data type.

I. The catch block is used to track and collect any possible exception during this query process. An error message will be displayed if this query encountered any problem.

J. The loginList.get(0).getUserName() and loginList.get(0).getPassWord() methods are called to pick up the matched username and password. The first part, loginList.get(0), returns the first matched row in which a match username and a password are stored. The second part, getUserName() and getPassWord(), are used to pick up the matched username and password columns from that first matched row. Since in our database, exactly in our LogIn table, there is only one record or one row existed in there, therefore, only one row or the first row can be returned. The returned username and password are assigned to two member data or two properties of the help class, user_name and pass_word, respectively.

K. A business logic is performed to check whether the queried login information is matched to the login information entered by the user. If it is, a Matched string is returned to the LogInQuery.jsp file.

L. Otherwise a Nomatched string is returned.

Comparing the codes in Figure 8.7 with the codes in Figure 8.11, it can be found that the JDBC- and database-related process, as well as the business logics in the latter has been simplified by using the Hibernate API.

The components and their relationships used in this JSP Web application with the help of the Hibernate persistence API are basically identical with those used in the JSP Web applications without Hibernate persistence API. The only difference between them is that the coding processing has been greatly simplified in the former Web applications.

These components and their relationships used in this JSP Web application with the help of the Hibernate persistence API can be expressed and illustrated in Figure 8.12.

An alternative way is to use the Java Persistence API to replace this Hibernate API to perform an object-relational database mapping to execute data actions against our sample database for Web applications.

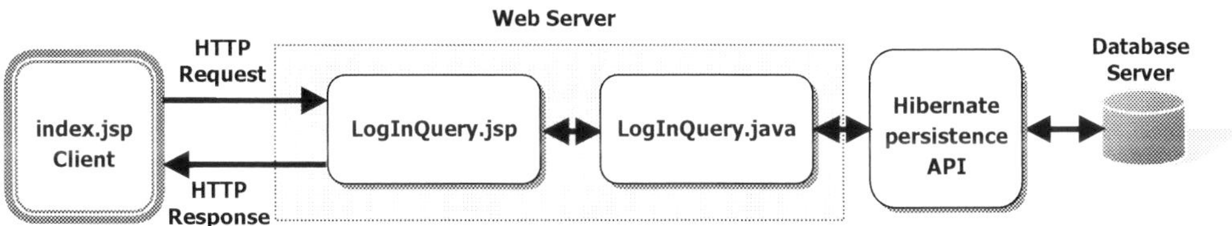

Figure 8.12. The components and relationships in a JSP Web application with Hibernate API.

After using the Java help class to handle the JDBC- and database-related processing, as well as business logics, the Java Web applications can be developed and built more objectively, simply and clearly. Next, let's discuss how to convert this help class to a former Java technique way, or a Java bean, to do these kinds data operations and business logics.

8.1.5 Using the JSP Implicit Object Session for Java Web Applications

As we mentioned in Section 8.1.2, the session is a JSP implicit object used to facilitate developers to build professional Java Web applications. The implicit means that those objects, including the session object, can be created automatically as a new JSP is executed. The specific property of using a session object is that you can save user data in some web pages and retrieve them from other web pages. This provides a great and convenient way to transfer data between clients and clients, and also between clients and a server.

In this section, we will use this session object to help us to build our Faculty page to query and display the desired faculty information from the Faculty table in our sample database. The structure or architecture of using the session object to coordinate the data query from the Faculty table is shown in Figure 8.13.

Basically, this structure is identical with that we discussed in the last section, and the only difference is that we use a new Java help class file FacultyBean.java that is not a real Java Bean class but is very similar to one JavaBean. The reason we did this is that we do not want to have a big jump between the help class and JavaBean to make this design difficult.

The FacultyPage.jsp that is our Web client page is shown in Figure 8.14. Because of its complexity in HTML and JSP codes, we will leave the building and coding of this page in our real project later. In fact, we need to use Microsoft Office Publisher 2007 to build a FacultyPage.html file first and then convert it to a FacultyPage.jsp file. Now we just assume that we have built this page and want to use it in our Faculty table query process.

Now let's modify this FacultyPage.jsp to use session object to perform data storage and retrieving functions between this page and the help class file FacultyQuery.jsp.

8.1.5.1 Modify the FacultyPage JSP File to Use the Session Object

Perform the modifications shown in Figure 8.15 to this FacultyPage.jsp file to use the session object to store and pick up data between client pages. All modified codes have been highlighted in bold.

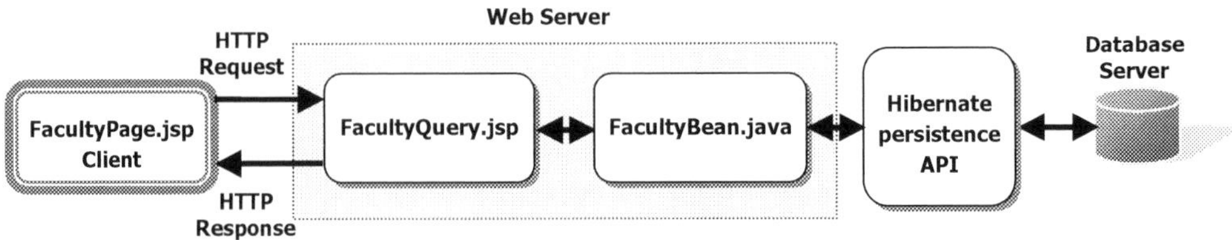

Figure 8.13. The architecture of using session object in Web applications.

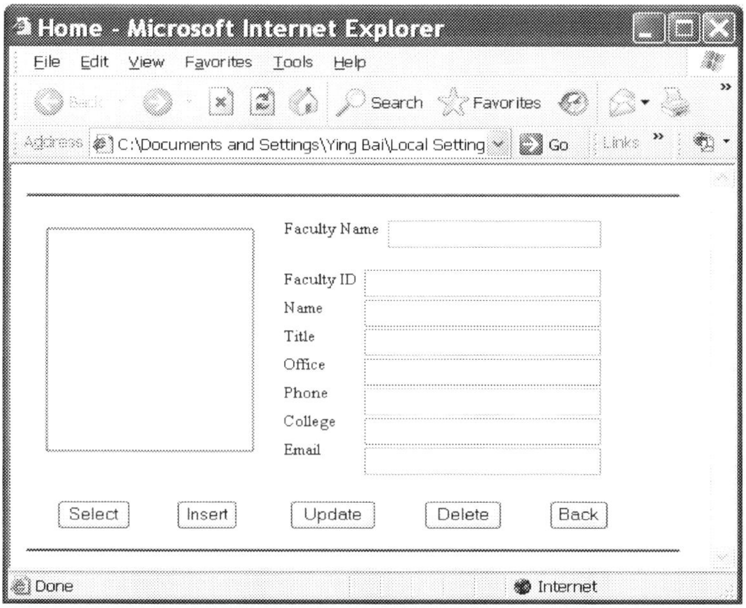

Figure 8.14. The preview of the FacultyPage.jsp page.

```
  <html>
    <head>
      <meta http-equiv="Content-Type" content="text/html; charset=UTF-8">
      <title>LogIn Query Page</title>
    </head>
    <body>
    <%@page language="java" %>
A   <form method=post action=".\FacultyQuery.jsp">
    <input name=FacultyNameField maxlength=255 size=24
B    value="<%=session.getAttribute("facultyName") %>" type=text v:shapes="_x0000_s1109">
    .........
    <input name=FacultyIDField maxlength=255 size=26
C    value="<%=session.getAttribute("facultyId") %>" type=text v:shapes="_x0000_s1110">
    .........
    <input name=NameField maxlength=255 size=26
D    value="<%=session.getAttribute("facultyName") %>" type=text v:shapes="_x0000_s1106">
    .........
    <input name=OfficeField maxlength=255 size=26
E    value="<%=session.getAttribute("office") %>" type=text v:shapes="_x0000_s1104">
    .........
    <input name=PhoneField maxlength=255 size=26
F    value="<%=session.getAttribute("phone") %>" type=text v:shapes="_x0000_s1116">
    .........
    <input name=CollegeField maxlength=255 size=26
G    value="<%=session.getAttribute("college") %>" type=text v:shapes="_x0000_s1117">
    .........
    <input name=EmailField maxlength=255 size=26
H    value="<%=session.getAttribute("email") %>" type=text v:shapes="_x0000_s1118">
    .........
    </body>
  </html>
```

Figure 8.15. The modifications to the FacultyPage.jsp file.

In step **A**, we add an `action` attribute to forward all information collected from this page to our model and controller page FcaultyQuery.jsp that will call our FacultyBean file to perform the faculty data query process.

Starting from step **B** until step **H**, we use the embedded JSP codes to assign the real queried faculty columns from our Faculty table to the `value` tag of each text field in the Facultypage.jsp using the getAttribute() method of the session class. In this way, as long as the queried faculty row has any change, this modification will be immediately updated and reflected to each text field in our FacultyPage.jsp page. In this way, a direct connection or binding between the text fields in our Facultypage.jsp page and the queried Faculty columns in our help class is established.

Now let's take a look at our model and controller page FacultyQuery.jsp.

8.1.5.2 Build the Transaction JSP File FacultyQuery.jsp

The purpose of this file is to transfer data and information between our main displaying page FacultyPage.jsp and our working help class file FacultyBean that performs all JDBC- and database-related operations and business logics. The codes for this file are shown in Figure 8.16.

Let's take a closer look at this piece of codes to see how it works.

A. You can embed any import directory using the JSP directive in a HTML or a JSP file. The format is <%@ page import="java package" %>. In this page, we embed two packages: one is java.util.*, since we need to use the List class and JavaWebHibDBOraclePackage.*, since we built our FacultyBean help class in that package.

```
A   <%@ page import="java.util.*" %>
    <%@ page import="JavaWebHibDBOraclePackage.*" %>
    <html>
      <head>
        <meta http-equiv="Content-Type" content="text/html; charset=UTF-8">
        <title>FacultyQuery JSP Page</title>
      </head>
      <body>
        <h1>This is the FaculrtQuery JSP Page!</h1>
        <%
B       String fname = request.getParameter("FacultyNameField");
C       FacultyBean fBean = new FacultyBean();
D       List fList = fBean.QueryFaculty(fname);
E       session.setAttribute("facultyId", fBean.getFacultyID());
        session.setAttribute("facultyName", fBean.getFacultyName());
        session.setAttribute("office", fBean.getOffice());
        session.setAttribute("title", fBean.getTitle());
        session.setAttribute("college", fBean.getCollege());
        session.setAttribute("phone", fBean.getPhone());
        session.setAttribute("email", fBean.getEmail());
F       response.sendRedirect("FacultyPage.jsp");
        %>
      </body>
    </html>
```

Figure 8.16. The codes for the model and controller page FacultyQuery.jsp.

B. The getParameter() method is executed to get the faculty name entered by the user to the Faculty Name text field in the FacultyPage.jsp page, and this faculty name is assigned to a local String variable fname.

C. A new instance of our help class FacultyBean is created.

D. The main help method QueryFaculty() we built in the FacultyBean is called to query a faculty record based on the faculty name we obtained from step **B**.

E. The setAttribute() method in the session class is executed to store each column of queried faculty row from the Faculty table with a given name. The getter() methods defined in the FacultyBean class are executed to pick up each queried column. The point to be noted is that later on, when we need to pick up these queried columns from the session object in other pages, we need to use the identical names we used here for each column, such as `facultyId`, `facultyName`, title, and so on.

F. Finally, since we need to display all queried columns to the associated text field in the FacultyPage.jsp page, we use the sendRedirect() method to return to that page.

Finally, let's take care of the help class file FacultyBean.

8.1.5.3 Build the Help Class FacultyBean

This class is a help class, but is very similar to a real Java bean class. The codes of this class are shown in Figure 8.17.

Let's have a closer look at this piece of codes to see how it works.

A. At the beginning of this class, seven member data or properties of this class are defined. This is very important in a Java bean class since all data-related transactions between the client pages and Java bean are dependent these properties. In other words, all clients could pick up data from a Java bean using those properties, and a one-to-one relationship exists between each property in the Java bean class and each queried column in the data table. According to the convention, all of these properties should be defined in private data type and can be accessed by using the getter() methods provided in this Java bean class.

B. A new instance of the Hibernate session class is created and initialized. The point to be noted is that this Hibernate session object is different with that JSP implicit session object.

C. The getCurrentSession() method is executed to get the default Hibernate session object.

D. The detailed definition of the QueryFcaulty() method starts from here with the method header.

E. A new java.util.List instance is created and initialized since we need this object to pick up and hold our queried faculty result. The MsgDislog instance is used to display error information in case any exception was encountered during this query operation.

F. A try...catch block is used to perform our data query. First, a new Transaction instance tx is created. with the beginTransaction() method being executed.

G. Then a query string built with the Hibernate Query Language (HQL) is created, and this query string will be used to perform the faculty information query later.

H. The list() method is executed to perform a query to the Faculty table in our sample database to try to retrieve a matched faculty record based on the selected faculty name fname. The query result is assigned to and held in a local variable facultyList that has a List<Faculty> data type.

```
  @Stateless
  public class FacultyBean {
A    private String facultyID;
     private String facultyName;
     private String office;
     private String title;
     private String phone;
     private String college;
     private String email;
B    public Session session = null;
     public FacultyBean() {
C       this.session = HibernateUtil.getSessionFactory().getCurrentSession();
     }
D    public List QueryFaculty(String fname) {
E       List<Faculty> facultyList = null;
        MsgDialog msgDlg = new MsgDialog(new javax.swing.JFrame(), true);
        try {
F          org.hibernate.Transaction tx = session.beginTransaction();
G          Query f = session.createQuery ("from Faculty as f where f.facultyName like '"+fname+"'");
H          facultyList = (List<Faculty>) f.list();
I       } catch (Exception e) {
           msgDlg.setMessage("Query is failed and no matched found!");
           msgDlg.setVisible(true);
           e.printStackTrace();
        }
J       facultyID = facultyList.get(0).getFacultyId();
        facultyName = facultyList.get(0).getFacultyName();
        office = facultyList.get(0).getOffice();
        title = facultyList.get(0).getTitle();
        phone = facultyList.get(0).getPhone();
        college = facultyList.get(0).getCollege();
        email = facultyList.get(0).getEmail();
        return facultyList;
     }
K    public String getFacultyID() {
        return this.facultyID;
     }
     public String getFacultyName() {
        return this.facultyName;
     }
     public String getOffice() {
        return this.office;
     }
     public String getTitle() {
        return this.title;
     }
     public String getPhone() {
        return this.phone;
     }
     public String getCollege() {
        return this.college;
     }
     public String getEmail() {
        return this.email;
     }
  }
```

Figure 8.17. The codes for the FacultyBean help class.

I. The catch block is used to track and collect any possible exception during this query process. An error message will be displayed if this query encountered any problem.

J. The facultyList.get(0) method is used to retrieve the first matched row from the query result. In fact, only one faculty row should be queried and retrieved, since all faculty names are unique in our sample database. A sequence of getter() methods is used to pick up the associated columns and assign them to the associated properties in this FacultyBean class. Finally, the query result is returned to the FacultyQuery.jsp page.

K. Seven getter() methods are defined at the bottom of this class, and they can be used to pick up all properties defined in this class.

An operational sequence and data transformation structure of the Faculty Name is shown in Figure 8.18.

In Figure 8.18, the faculty name is used as an example to illustrate how to transfer this data between client and the help class. The operational sequence is:

1. First, a desired faculty name is entered by the user into the Faculty Name text field in the FacultyPage.jsp page. This piece of data will be transferred to the FacultyQuery.jsp page as the Select button is clicked by the user.
2. In the FcaultyQuery.jsp page, the getParameter() method is used to pick up this transferred Faculty Name.
3. Then, the help method QueryFaculty() in the help class FacultyBean is called to query a matched faculty record from the Faculty table based on the transferred faculty name fname.
4. When the getter() method in the FacultyBean class is executed, the queried faculty name is returned to the FacultyQuery.jsp page.
5. One of session method, setAttribute(), is called to store this queried faculty name into the JSP implicit object session.
6. The getAttribute("facultyName") method that is assigned to the `value` tag of the `FacultyName` text field will pick up the queried faculty name and display in this text field in step 7.

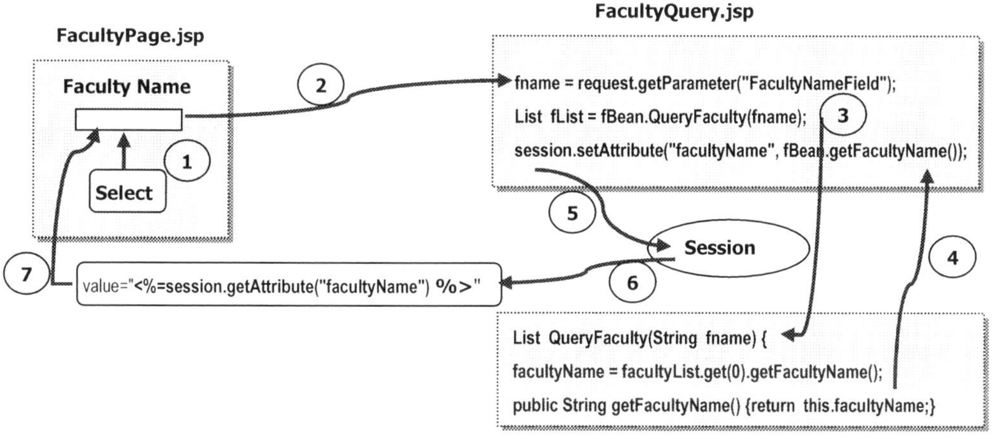

Figure 8.18. The operational sequence and data transfer structure using the session object.

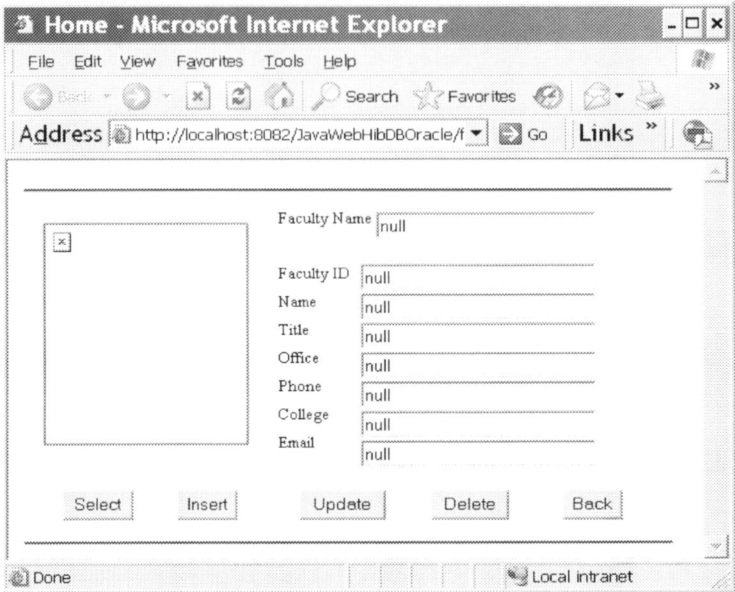

Figure 8.19. The running status of the FacultyPage.jsp.

By referring to Figure 8.18, we can get a clear and complete picture about the data storage and transferring between different pages.

Now if you compile and run these three files, FacultyPage.jsp, FacultyQuery.jsp, and FacultyBean.java, you can get the start page shown in Figure 8.19.

Enter a desired faculty name, such as Ying Bai, into the Faculty Name text field, and click on the Select button; the running result is shown in Figure 8.20.

As we mentioned at the beginning of this chapter, Java EE provides a set of powerful tools and supports to Java Web applications to access and manipulate databases. One of the most important components provided by Java EE is the Java bean that works as a separate component to perform database-related operations and business logics. By combining the JavaServer Faces techniques and Java beans, a professional Java Web database application can be divided into two separate parts: the GUIs that are built with JSF tags in JSP are used for data presentations and results displaying, and Java managed beans used for database-related operations and business logics. By dividing a Web application into these two sections, it has greatly reduced the development efforts and complexities in the coding development and organizations of the whole application.

Now let's take care of using Java beans technology for Java Web applications.

8.1.6 Using Java Beans Technology for Java Web Applications

In recent years, the Java bean technique has been widely applied in Java Web applications. In fact, a Java bean can be considered as an extended Java help class as we discussed in the previous sections, and the main purpose of a Java bean is to handle the JDBC- and database-related operations, as well as business logics in a Web application.

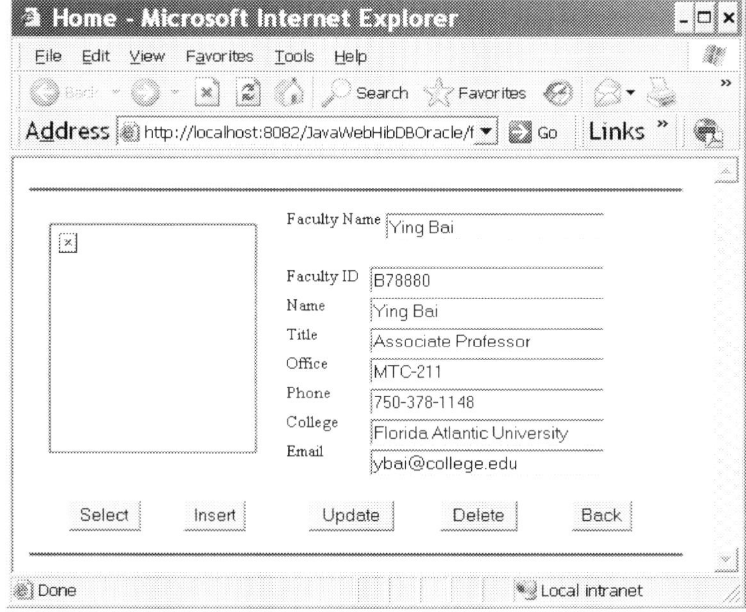

Figure 8.20. The running result of the FacultyPage.jsp.

In fact, Java beans are reusable components, and the main purpose of using Java beans is to separate business logics from the presentations.

Exactly, a Java bean is just an instance of a class.

Once a JavaBean is created and loaded, it can be used by all parts of your applications based on its scope. The so-called scope defined the section or part of you applications can access and use this bean. Generally, there are four popular scopes available to a Java Bean object and the default scope is page scope.

- **page scope:** The bean is accessible within a JSP page with the <jsp: useBean> tag, or any page's static include files until the page sends response to the client or forward a request to another page. In other words, as long as the process happened in the current page, the bean can be accessed and used until the process has been transferred to other pages.
- **request scope:** The bean is accessible from any JSP page as long as the same request is processed in that page until a JSP page sends a response to the client or forward the request to another page. In other words, the bean can be used until a different request has been forwarded or a response for that request has been received, which means that the life time or the scope of that request has been completed.
- **session scope:** The bean is accessible from any JSP page in the same session as the JSP page that creates the bean. A session can be considered as common place where many JSP pages can exist and share. The JSP page in which you create the Java bean must have a JSP page directive <%@ page %> with the session = true.
- **application scope:** The bean can be accessed from any JSP page in the same application as the JSP page that creates the bean. In other words, any JSP page can use the bean as long as that page is included in the application in which the JSP page that creates the bean is included.

It is no difference between creating a help class and creating a Java bean class. In fact, the help class FacultyBean.java we created in the last section is exactly a Java bean class.

To use a Java bean, the JSP provide three basic tags for working with beans.

```
<jsp:useBean id="bean name" class="bean class" scope = "page |
 request | session |application "/>
```

The definitions for these three tags are:

1. The bean name is just a given name to refer to the used Java bean. You can use any valid name for this tag.
2. The bean class is a full name of the Java bean class you created. The so-called full name means that you need to use both the bean class's name and the package's name in which the bean is located. For example, this bean class should be: mypackage.mybeanclass if the bean class named mybeanclass is located at the package mypackage.
3. The scope indicates the range or the life time the bean can be used. Refer to those four scopes we discussed above to get more detailed information about them.

A very useful JSP directive used for Java bean class is <jsp:setProperty />. The protocol of this directive is:

```
<jsp:setProperty name = "id" property = "someProperty" value =
 "someValue" />
```

Three arguments for this directive are:

1. The id is the bean name as we discussed in step 1 above.
2. The someProeprty is exactly the property's name defined inside the Java bean class, such as facultyId and facultyName we defined in our FacultyBean.java class in the last section.
3. The someValue is the initialized value assigned to a property in the bean class.

A variant for this tag is the property attribute, which can be replaced by an "*". What this does is that it accepts all the form parameters and thus reduces the need for writing multiple setProperty tags. The only point to be remembered when you are using this variant is that the form parameters' names must be the same as those of the bean properties' names.

An example of using this setProperty tag is:

```
<jsp:setProperty name="dbFaculty" property="*" />
```

In this setProperty tag, the id of the Java bean class is dbFaculty. The * in the property value means that all parameters transferred from another page can be assigned to the associated properties in the Java bean class.

Now let's modify the FacultyBean.java to make it a Java bean class to replace the help class file FacultyBean.java we built in the last section.

8.1.6.1 Modify the Help Class FacultyBean to Make it a Java Bean Class

First, we need to create a new Java Session Bean class named FacultyBean in the NetBeans IDE. Then, we need to add seven setter() method into this bean class. Your finished Java

```
@Stateless
public class FacultyBean {
    private String facultyID;
    private String facultyName;
    private String office;
    private String title;
    private String phone;
    private String college;
    private String email;

    public Session session = null;
    public FacultyBean() {
        this.session = HibernateUtil.getSessionFactory().getCurrentSession();
    }
    public List QueryFaculty(String fname) {
        List<Faculty> facultyList = null;
        MsgDialog msgDlg = new MsgDialog(new javax.swing.JFrame(), true);
        .........
        return facultyList;
    }
    public String getFacultyID() {
        return this.facultyID;
    }
    .........
A   public void setFacultyID(String facultyID) {
        this.facultyID = facultyID;
    }
B   public void setFacultyName(String facultyName) {
        this.facultyName = facultyName;
    }
C   public void setOffice(String office) {
        this.office = office;
    }
D   public void setTitle(String title) {
        this.title = title;
    }
E   public void setPhone(String phone) {
        this.phone = phone;
    }
F   public void setCollege(String college) {
        this.college = college;
    }
G   public void setEmail(String email) {
        this.email = email;
    }
}
```

Figure 8.21. The modified help class—now it is a Java bean class.

bean class FacultyBean.java is shown in Figure 8.21. All modified codes have been highlighted in bold.

Let's have a closer look at this piece of modified codes to see how it works.

Starting from step **A** until step **G**, seven setter() methods are added into this Java bean class. All of these setter() methods are used to set up the initial values for seven properties in this bean.

Next, we need to create a new transaction JSP page FacultyBeanQuery.jsp to make it to transfer data between our new starting page FacultyBeanPage.jsp and our Java bean class FacultyBean.java. Basically, this FacultyBeanQuery.jsp file has no significant

```
  <%@ page import="java.util.*" %>
  <%@ page import="JavaWebHibDBOraclePackage.*" %>
  <%@ page import="csedept.entity.Faculty" %>

  <html>
     <head>
        <meta http-equiv="Content-Type" content="text/html; charset=UTF-8">
        <title>FacultyBeanQuery Page</title>
     </head>
     <body>
        <h1>This is the FacultyBeanQuery Page</h1>
A       <jsp:useBean id="dbFaculty" scope="session" class="JavaWebHibDBOraclePackage.FacultyBean" />
B       <jsp:setProperty name="dbFaculty" property="*" />
        <%
C          String fname = request.getParameter("FacultyNameField");
D          List<Faculty> facultyList = dbFaculty.QueryFaculty(fname);
E          response.sendRedirect("FacultyBeanPage.jsp");
        %>
     </body>
  </html>
```

Figure 8.22. The codes for the FacultyBeanQuery.jsp page.

difference with the FacultyQuery.jsp we built in the last section. The only different part is the way to execute the JDBC- and database related queries or business logics. In FacultyQuery.jsp file, we called a Java help class FacultyBean.java to do those functions. However, in FacultyBeanQuery.jsp, we will call a modified help class that has been converted to a Java bean FacultyBean.java to perform these functions.

The codes of the FacultyBeanQuery.jsp file are shown in Figure 8.22.

Now let's have a closer look at this piece of codes to see how it works.

Some system-related or user-related packages are imported at the beginning of this page. The JSP directive <%@ page /> is used to convert those packages and embedded into this page. Three packages are imported here: the java.util.* package contains the List class, the JavaWebHibDBOraclePackage contains our Java bean class FacultyBean, and the csedept.entity.Faculty is a Hibernate class mapping for the Faculty table in our sample database CSE_DEPT.

A. The Java bean class is declared with the JSP tag <jsp:useBean /> with three tags we discussed at the beginning of this section. The referenced name for this bean is dbFaculty, which is assigned to the id of the bean. The scope of this bean is session. and the full name of this bean class is JavaWebHibDBOraclePackage.FacultyBean.

B. The setProperty tag is used to set up all parameters passed from the FacultyBeanPage.jsp page to the associated properties in the bean class FacultyBean.

C. The Java codes are starting from a JSP tag, and the faculty name parameter is retrieved by using the getParanmeter() method and assigned to a local String variable fname.

D. The main bean method QueryFaculty() is executed to query a faculty record based on the retrieved faculty name from the FacultyBeanPage.jsp page. The result is assigned to a local List variable. In fact, this result is not important in this application since the columns in the query result have been assigned to the associated properties in the bean class, and later on we can pick up those columns by calling the getter() methods in the bean class.

E. Since we want to fill those text fields in our starting page FacultyBeanPage.jsp with the queried result, we used the sendRedirect() method to return the process back to that page.

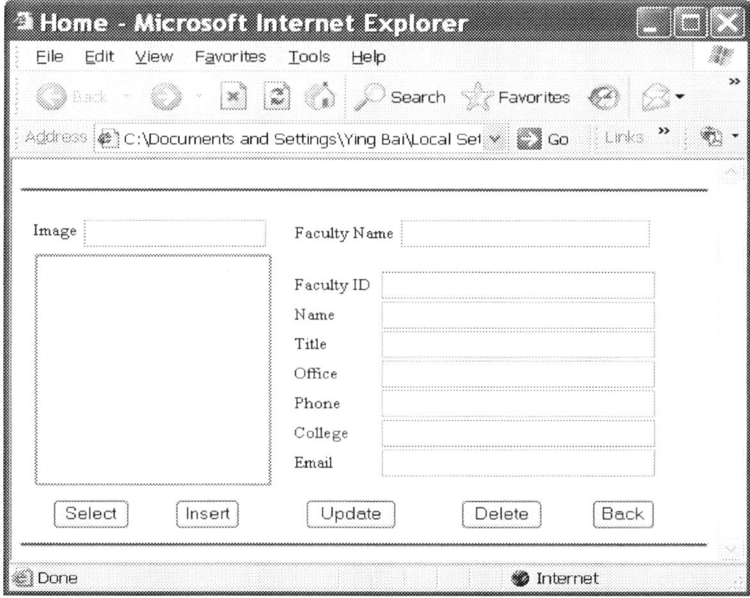

Figure 8.23. The new starting Web page FacultyBeanPage.jsp.

Now let's take a look at a new starting page FacultyBeanPage.jsp that will be used to call the transaction JSP page and Java bean to perform the faculty data query and display query result in this page. Because of the complex in building this page with HTML codes, we leave this coding job to our project development stage later.

8.1.6.2 Build a New Starting Web Page FacultyBeanPage

The preview of this page is shown in Figure 8.23.

The difference between this starting page and the starting page FacultyPage.jsp we built in the last section is: in the FcaultyPage.jsp, we used a JSP built-in or implicit object session to transfer data between this page and the help class. However, in the new starting page FacultyBeanPage.jsp, we need to use the properties defined in the Java bean class to do this data transferring jobs.

Exactly, we need to use the Java bean's getter() method to replace those session.getAttribute() methods embedded in the `value` tag of each text field to retrieve and display the associated column queried from the Faculty table in our sample database in each text field in this new starting page.

The codes for this new starting page are shown in Figure 8.24. The modified parts have been highlighted in bold.

Let's have a closer look at this piece of codes to see how it works.

A. A JSP tag that declared to use a Java bean is put in the beginning of this page to indicate that a Java bean will be called to perform JDBC- and database-related queries or business logics, and the result will be retrieved and reflected in this starting page.

```
A <jsp:useBean id="dbFaculty" scope="session" class="JavaWebHibDBOraclePackage.FacultyBean" />
  <html>
    <head>
      <meta http-equiv="Content-Type" content="text/html; charset=UTF-8">
      <title>Faculty Query Page</title>
    </head>
    <body>
    <%@page language="java" %>
B   <form method=post action=".\FacultyBeanQuery.jsp">
    <input name=FacultyNameField maxlength=255 size=24
C     value="<%=dbFaculty.getFacultyName() %>" type=text v:shapes="_x0000_s1109">
    .........
    <input name=FacultyIDField maxlength=255 size=26
D     value="<%=dbFaculty.getFacultyID() %>" type=text  v:shapes="_x0000_s1110">
    .........
    <input name=NameField maxlength=255 size=26
E     value="<%=dbFaculty.getFacultyName() %>" type=text  v:shapes="_x0000_s1106">
    .........
    <input name=OfficeField maxlength=255 size=26
F     value="<%=dbFaculty.getOffice() %>"  type=text  v:shapes="_x0000_s1104">
    .........
    <input name=PhoneField maxlength=255 size=26
G     value="<%=dbFaculty.getPhone() %>"  type=text  v:shapes="_x0000_s1116">
    .........
    <input name=CollegeField maxlength=255 size=26
H     value="<%=dbFaculty.getCollege() %>" type=text  v:shapes="_x0000_s1117">
    .........
    <input name=EmailField maxlength=255 size=26
I     value="<%=dbFaculty.getEmail() %>" type=text  v:shapes="_x0000_s1118">
    .........
    </body>
  </html>
```

Figure 8.24. The new starting page FacultyBeanPage.jsp.

B. The next page is changed to FacultyBeanQuery.jsp in the `action` tag of the form, which means that the page and all data in this starting page will be forwarded to the next page if any submit button is clicked by the user from this page.

C. Starting from step **C** until step **I**, the different Java bean's getter() methods are executed to retrieve the matched columns from the queried result and display them one by one in each associated text field.

From this piece of codes, you can find how easy it is to transfer data between the starting Web page written in either HTML or JSP and Java bean class by using the Java bean's properties.

From examples discussed above, it can be found that the JSP technology did provide a good communication and data passing ways between the Servlet and client web pages; however, they did not provide a direct binding and mapping between the Web page's components and the server side codes. This kind of binding and mapping plays more important roles in today's complicated and multi-tier Web applications. To meet this need, a new technology has been introduced in recent years, which is the JavaServer Faces (JSF) technology.

With this new technology, all Web components can be installed and distributed in a Web page by using the JSF tags. Also, more important, all of these components can be bound to the server side properties and functions using the so-called backing beans or

Java managed beans. By using a Unified Expression Language (EL) value expression, the value of the property of a mapped or bound Web component can be easily picked up from a backing bean in the server side.

8.1.7 Using JavaServer Faces Technology for Java Web Applications

JavaServer Faces (JSF) provides new techniques and components for building User Interfaces (UI) for server-side applications. In fact, JSF is a server-side technology for developing Web applications with rich user interfaces. Before JavaServer Faces, developers who built Web applications had to rely on building HTML user interface components with Servlets or JSP. This is mainly because HTML user interface components are the lowest common denominator that Web browsers support. One of the defects of using HTML or JSP techniques to build Web applications is that such Web applications do not have rich user interfaces, compared with standalone fat clients, and therefore less functionality and/or poor usability are involved in those Web applications. One of possible solutions is to use Applets to develop rich user interfaces; however, in most cases, Web application developers do not always know whether those Applets are signed or unsigned applets, and whether they can access the local database files or not. This will greatly limit the roles and implementations of Applets in Java Web database applications.

A good solution is to use JavaServer Face technique that provides a set of rich GUI components and can be installed and run in the server side. The GUI components provided by JSF are represented by a collection of component tags. All component tags are defined and stored in the `UIComponent` class. A model-view-controller (MVC) mode is applied to the JSF technique.

The JSF technology consists of following main components:

- JSF APIs used to represent UI components, manage state, handle events, and validate input. The UI components are represented and implemented using JSF tags. The API has support for internationalization and accessibility.
- A special Servlet class `FacesServlet` that is located at the server side and works as a controller to handle all JSF-related events.
- JSP pages that contain rich user interface components represented by customer tags and work as views. The GUI of a JSF page is one or more JSP pages that contain JSF component tags.
- Two JSP custom tag libraries used for expressing the JSF user interface (UI) components within a JSP page, and for wiring components to server-side objects. Page authors can easily add UI components to their pages.
- Java bean components used to work as model objects.
- Application configuration resource file faces-config.xml used to define the navigation rules between JSP pages and register the Java backing beans.
- Web deployment descriptor file web.xml used to define the FaceServlet and its mapping.

JavaServer Face technology is basically built based on JavaServer Page and Servlet techniques. It uses JSP pages as the GUI and FacesServlet as the Web container. A high-level architecture of JSF is shown in Figure 8.25.

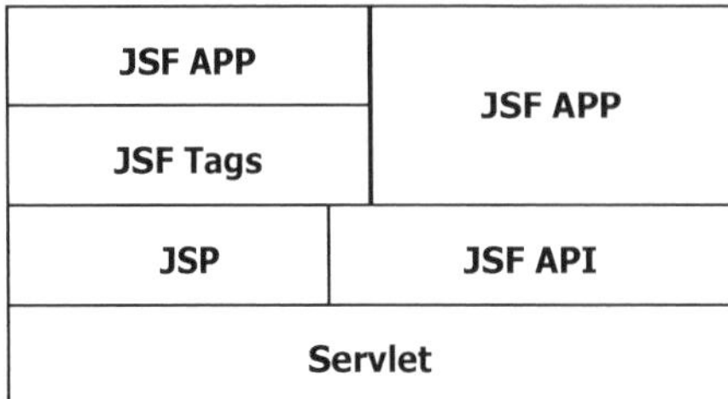

Figure 8.25. High-level architecture of JSF.

It can be found from Figure 8.25 that a JSF Web application is composed of JSP pages representing the user interface components using the JSF custom tag library and FacesServlet Web container, which can be considered as a part of Servlet class and takes care of the JSF related events.

JSF defines two standard tag libraries (Core and HTML) that you have to declare in your JSP pages with the <%@taglib%> directive. Two tag libraries are:

- html_basic.tld: A JSP custom tag library for building JSF applications that render to an HTML client.
- jsf_core.tld: A JSP custom tag library for representing core actions independent of a particular render kit.

The JSF core library contains tags that do not depend on any markup language, while the JSF HTML library was designed for pages that are viewed in a Web browser. The standard prefixes of the two tag libraries are f for the JSF Core and h for the JSF HTML. All JSF tags must be nested inside a <f:view> element. The <f:view> tag allows the JSF framework to save the state of the UI components as part of the response to a HTTP request.

To use these customer tags to represent JSF components in JSP pages, one needs to indicate them by using the following two `taglib` directive on the top of each JSF file:

- <%@ taglib uri="http://java.sun.com/jsf/html" prefix="h" %>
- <%@ taglib uri="http://java.sun.com/jsf/core" prefix="f" %>

The uri is used to indicate the locations of the customer tag libraries.

JavaServer Face (JSF) pages are just regular JSP pages that use the standard JSF tag libraries or other libraries based on the JSF API. When using JSF tag components to build a JavaServer Page, a component tree or a view is created in the server side memory, and this tree will be used by the JSF frameworks to handle the requests coming from the clients and send responses to the clients. Each JSF tag component is mapped to a component class defined in the `UIComponent` class. In fact, each tag is an instance of the mapped class in the `UIComponent`.

JSF utilized an MVCarchitecture, which means that it uses Java beans as models to stored application data, and JSF GUI as the view and the Servlet as the controller.

8.1.7.1 The Application Configuration Resource File faces-config.xml

The navigation from one page to another can be done in two ways. One way is directly to use the codes by writing the JSP tag such as <jsp:forward /> or the HTML hyperlink

```
<navigation-rule>
<from-view-id>/Current.jsp</from-view-id>
  <navigation-case>
  <from-outcome>clickAction</from-outcome>
  <to-view-id>/Next.jsp</to-view-id>
  </navigation-case>
</navigation-rule>
```

Figure 8.26. A part of application configuration resource file.

in the JSF file. Another way that is provided by JSF is to use the application configuration resource file faces-config.xml to build these navigation rules. The task of defining navigation rules involves defining which page is to be displayed after the user clicks on a button or a hyperlink. Each <navigation-rule> element defines how to get from one page as defined by the <form-view-id> to the other pages of the application. A <navigation-rule> element can contain any number of <navigation-case> elements that define the page to open next using the <to-view-id> based on a logical outcome defined by the <from-outcome>. This outcome is defined by the action attribute of the component that submits the form (such as the commandButton).

An application configuration resource file, faces-config.xml, is used to define your Java managed beans, validators, converters, and navigation rules.

Figure 8.26 shows a part of an example of an application configuration resource file. The configuration resource file is composed of a sequence tags listed below:

Starting from <navigation-rule> tag, a new navigation rule is defined. The <from-view-id> tag is used to define the navigation source, which is the current page (Current.jsp). The <navigation-case> tag is used to define one of the navigation destinations defined by the <to-view-id> tag based on the output of some clicked buttons or links triggered by the action tag in the current page. Those outputs are defined by the <from-outcome> tag.

You can use the design tools such as `PageFlow` to do this navigation plan graphically and directly. Refer to Section 5.3.5.12 in Chapter 5 to get more detailed information about using the design tools to build this configuration file graphically.

8.1.7.2 Sample JavaServer Face Page Files

Two JSF files are shown in Figures 8.27 and 8.28. In Figure 8.27, a Current.jsp page that works as a receiving page to get the username is shown. In Figure 8.28, a Next.jsp that works as a responding page to select and return a matched password based on the username to the Current.jsp page.

The function of the Current.jsp page is:

A. In order to use JSF tags, you need to include the taglib directives to the html and core tag libraries that refer to the standard HTML renderkit tag library, and the JSF core tag library, respectively.

B. A body tag with the bgcolor attribute is defined.

C. A page containing JSF tags is represented by a tree of components whose root is the UIViewRoot, which is represented by the view tag. All component tags must be enclosed

```
  <html>
    <head>
      <title>Current Page</title>
    </head>
A   <%@ taglib uri="http://java.sun.com/jsf/html" prefix="h" %>
    <%@ taglib uri="http://java.sun.com/jsf/core" prefix="f" %>
B   <body bgcolor="white">
C       <f:view>
D       <h:form id="QueryForm" >
E       <h:inputText id="userName" value="#{QueryBean.userName}"
            validator="#{ QueryBean.validate}"/>
F       <h:commandButton id="Query" action="success"
            value="Query" />
G       <h:message style="color: red; font-family: 'New Century Schoolbook',
            serif; font-style: oblique; text-decoration: overline"
            id="QueryError" for="userName"/>
        </h:form>
       </f:view>
    </body>
  </html>
```

Figure 8.27. The codes for the Current.jsp page.

```
  <html>
    <head>
      <title>Next Page</title>
    </head>
    <%@ taglib uri="http://java.sun.com/jsf/html" prefix="h" %>
    <%@ taglib uri="http://java.sun.com/jsf/core" prefix="f" %>
    <body bgcolor="white">
        <f:view>
A       <h:form id="ResponseForm" >
B       <h:graphicImage id="ResponseImg" url="/Response.jpg" />
C       <h:outputText id="QueryResult" value="#{QueryBean.passWord}" />
D       <h:commandButton id="Back" action="success"
          value="Back" />
        </h:form>
       </f:view>
    </body>
  </html>
```

Figure 8.28. The codes for the Next.jsp page.

in the view tag. Other content such as HTML and other JSP pages can be enclosed within that tag.

D. A typical JSP page includes a form, which is submitted to the next page when a button is clicked. The tags representing the form components (such as textfields and buttons) must be nested inside the form tag.

E. The inputText tag represents an input text field component. The id attribute represents the ID of the component object represented by this tag, and if it is missing, then the implementation will generate one. The validator attribute refers to a method-binding expression pointing to a Java backing bean method that performs validation on the component's data. The Java backing bean's property userName is bound to the value attribute by using the Unified Expression Language (EL) value expression.

F. The commandButton tag represents the button used to submit the data entered in the text field. The action attribute helps the navigation mechanism to decide which page to open next. Exactly, the next page has been defined in the application configuration resource file faces-config.xml using the <to-view-id> tag above, which is the Next.jsp.

G. The message tag displays an error message if the data entered is not valid. The for attribute refers to the component whose value failed validation.

An interesting thing in step **E** in this piece of sample codes is that an embedded backing bean property userName has been bound to the value attribute of the inputText tag. Recall that we used either the getAttribute() method of a JSP implicit object session (session.getAttribute()) or the getProperty() method of a Java bean to hook to the value attribute of this text field tag in the previous sample codes to enable this text field's value to be updated automatically. However, in this JSF file, we directly bind one of backing bean's properties, userName, with the value attribute of this text field by using the `value-binding` expressions that is called expression language (EL) and have the syntax #{bean-managed-property} to do this data updating job. One point to be noted is that the JSF EL bindings are bidirectional when it makes sense. For example, the UI component represented by the inputText tag can get the value of a bean property userName and present it to the user as a default value. When the user submits the QueryForm data, the UI component can automatically update the bean property userName so that the application logic can process the new value. You can see how easy it is now to set up a connection between a component in a JSF page and the related property in the backing bean object when using this binding for a JSF file. In fact, you can bind not only the bean's properties, but also the bean's methods, to certain UI components in the JSP pages.

The codes for the Next.jsp file are shown in Figure 8.28.

The detailed function of this piece of codes is:

A. The form id is defined as a ResponseForm.

B. An image is added into this page with the image id and the image URL. The forward slash "/" before the image name Response.jpg indicates that this image is located at the current project folder.

C. An outputText tag is equivalent to a label in a Web page. The selected password is assigned to the value attribute using the value-binding expressions that have the syntax #{bean-managed-property}. In fact, this value has been bound with a property password in the backing bean QueryBean class.

D. The commandButton Back is used to direct the page to return to the Current.jsp page as it is clicked by the user. This returning function has been defined in the application configuration source file faces-config.xml we discussed above.

The real tracking issue is that there is no username–password matching process occurred in either of these two pages. Yes, that is true! All of those data matching processes, or as we called them, business logics, occured in the backing Java bean QueryBean class.

When a user entered a valid username into the input textbox and clicked the Submit button in the Current.jsp page, all input data are sent to the next page Next.jsp. Of course, you can handle this data matching in the Next.jsp page based on the passed username. However, in order to separate the presentations from business logics, JSF uses JSF pages as views and assigns the business logics to the Java beans who work as controllers to handle those data matching jobs. In fact, since the userName has been bound to the value attribute of the inputText tag by using the `value-binding` expressions that have the syntax #{bean-managed-property}, any change of this data item will be immediately reflected to the associated property userName defined in the Java bean QueryBean class. The Java bean will perform the password matching process based on that username and send the matched password to the passWord property in that bean class. As soon as the Java bean finished the password matching processing and sent the matched password to the passWord property, it can be immediately updated and displayed in the outputText QueryResult in the Next.jsp page using the `value-binding` expressions #{QueryBean.passWord}.

8.1.7.3 The Java Bean Class File

The java bean class used in JSF pages is very similar to the FacultyBean class we built in Section 8.1.5.3. Like most Java bean classes, it should contain setter and getter methods, as well as some special methods to process the business logics.

In addition, the Java beans need to be configured in the application configuration resource file faces-config.xml so that the implementation can automatically create new instances of the beans as needed. The <managed-bean> element is used to create a mapping between a bean name and class. The first time the QueryBean is referenced, the object is created and stored in the appropriate scope. You can use the code elements shown in Figure 8.29 to register a Java bean in the faces-config.xml file:

Besides to register the Java bean class, you also need to use this configuration file to configure and define all properties created inside this Java bean. In this example, only two properties, userName and passWord, have been defined in this Java bean. Therefore, you need to use the <managed-property> element to do this configuration, as shown in Figure 8.30.

```
<managed-bean-name>QueryBean</managed-bean-name>
<managed-bean-class>LogInQuery.QueryBean</managed-bean-class>
<managed-bean-scope>session</managed-bean-scope>
```

Figure 8.29. A piece of sample codes to register a Java bean.

```
<managed-property>
<property-name>userName</property-name>
<property-class>string</property-class>
<value>null</value>
</managed-property>

<managed-property>
<property-name>passWord</property-name>
<property-class>string</property-class>
<value>null</value>
</managed-property>
```

Figure 8.30. A piece of codes to define all properties in a Java bean class.

In fact, you do not need to worry about these configurations if you are using an IDE such as the NetBeans IDE, and the NetBeans IDE can do these configurations automatically for you as you built the Java bean class file.

Next, let's take a look at the Web deployment descriptor file.

8.1.7.4 The Web Deployment Descriptor File web.xml

Before you can use and access a Servlet such as FacesServlet in the server side from a Web browser, you need to map the FacesServlet to a path in your deployment descriptor file web.xml. By using this deployment descriptor file, you can register Servlet and FacesServlet, and register listeners and map resources to URLs. Figure 8.31 shows a piece of example codes used in the web.xml file for the FacesServlet class.

Most codes in this file will be created automatically if you are using the NetBeans IDE to build your Web applications.

As we discussed in Section 8.1.6.1, regularly, JSP pages use the <jsp:useBean> tag to instantiate JavaBeans. When using the JSF framework, you do not have to specify the Java bean class names in your web pages anymore. Instead, you can configure your bean instances in the application configuration resource file faces-config.xml using the <managed-bean> element. You may use multiple configuration files if you develop a large application. In that case, you must add a javax.faces.CONFIG_FILES parameter in the deployment descriptor file web.xml.

Now that we have worked through all main techniques of JSF, now let's have a full picture about the complete running procedure of JSF Web applications.

8.1.7.5 A Complete Running Procedure of JSF Web Applications

As we mentioned, a UI component represented by a JSF tag in a JSP page can be bound to a Java bean's property or a Java bean's method. To separate the presentations and business logics, we can use JSP pages to present our GUI and the Java beans to store our data to perform business related logics. Therefore, we can divide methods into two categories: data access methods (business methods) and action methods. The data access methods

```
<web-app>
<display-name>JSF LogIn Application</display-name>
<description>JSF LogIn Application</description>
<!-- Faces Servlet -->
<servlet>
<servlet-name>Faces Servlet</servlet-name>
<servlet-class>javax.faces.webapp.FacesServlet</servlet-class>
<load-on-startup> 1 </load-on-startup>
</servlet>
<!-- Faces Servlet Mapping -->
<servlet-mapping>
<servlet-name>Faces Servlet</servlet-name>
<url-pattern>/login/*</url-pattern>
</servlet-mapping>
```

Figure 8.31. An example coding for the Web deployment descriptor file.

should be located at the Java bean side, and the action methods should be located at the JSF page side. Each data access method defined in the Java bean can be called by an associated action method defined in an action attribute of a submit button tag in the JSP page if that submit button has been bound to the action attribute.

Here, we use a login process to illustrate the operational procedure using the JSF technique. Two JSP pages, the LogIn.jsp and Selection.jsp, and a Java bean class LogInBean.java, are involved in this procedure. Two JSP pages work as views and are used to display the input and output login information, and the Java bean works as a model to handle the database-related processing and business logics. The functional procedure of this example application is:

1. When the user entered a username/password pair into the Username/Password input text fields in the LogIn.jsp page, and clicked on the LogIn button, a query request is sent to the Web server with all form data (Username and Password) for processing.
2. After the server received the request, if the validation is passed, all form data (Username and Password) will be stored into the associated properties of the Java bean.
3. The action method that is bound to the LogIn button will call the data access method defined in the Java bean to perform the database query to find the matched login information in the LogIn table.
4. If the data access method is successful, the next page, Selection.jsp, should be displayed.

To run this procedure using JSF technique, we need to have a clear picture between the JSF pages and Java beans, and the page-to-page navigation schedule.

8.1.7.5.1 The Java Bean—JSF Page Relationship and Page Navigations Table 8.1 lists all data access methods and action methods used in this example.

A Java bean can be connected to a JSF page by using the value attribute of an UI component represented by a JSF tag in that page. Exactly, a property or a method defined in a Java bean class can be mapped to a value attribute of a UI component in a JSF page. This relationship can be triggered and set up when a submit button in the JSF page is clicked by the user and all form data will be sent to the Web server. Refer to Figure 8.32; the operational procedure of executing a request is:

1. The data access method LogInQuery() is defined in the Java bean class LogInBean and will be called by the action method LogInBean.LogInAction() defined in the JSF page LogIn.jsp as the user clicks the LogIn button. Since the action method LogInBean.LogInAction() has been bound to the LogIn command button, all form data including the Username and Password entered by the user to the JSF page will be submitted to the FacesServlet as the LogIn button is clicked by the user.
2. After the FacesServlet received the form data, it will validate them and return the form back to the client if any error encountered.

Table 8.1. The relationship between the data access method and the action method

Data Access Method	Action Method	JSF Page
LogInQuery()	LogInBean.LogInAction()	LogIn.jsp

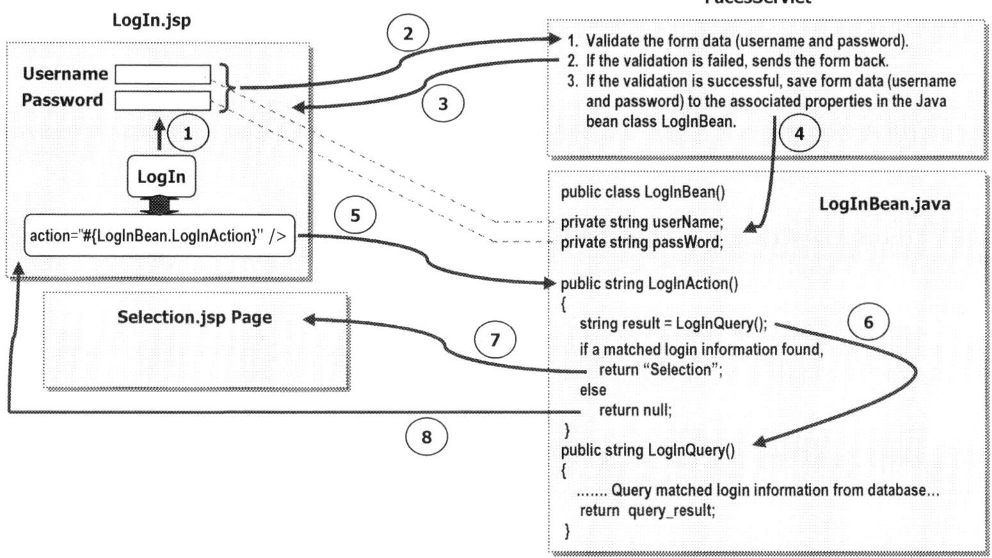

Figure 8.32. The operational procedure of executing a request using JSF.

3. Otherwise, the validated form data, including the Username and Password, will be stored to the associated properties in the Java bean class. Then JSF engine will call the action method LogInBean.LogInAction() that has been bound to the LogIn button, and in turn, to call the data access method LogInQuery() to perform database-related query to find matched login information.
4. After a piece of matched login information has been found, the associated properties, userName and passWord, which are defined inside the Java bean class, will be updated by assigning the matched username and password to them. These updating occurred in the Java bean side will be immediately reflected to the value attributes of the Username and Password inputText fields in the JSF page, since they have been bound together. Therefore, the content of each inputText tag will also be updated.
5. The action method LogInAction() defined in the `LogInBean` class will also be called when the `LogIn` button is clicked by the user, since it is bound to the `LogIn` button.
6. The data access method LogInQuery() will be executed to perform database-related queries and business logics.
7. Each action method returns a string called "outcome". JSF uses a navigation handler to determine what it is supposed to do for each outcome string. If an action method returns a null, which means that the execution of that method encountered some problems and the same page must be redisplayed. Otherwise, the desired next page should be displayed, depending on the returned outcome string. The default JSF navigation handler uses a set of navigation rules that are specified in the JSF application configuration file faces-config.xml, which is shown in Figure 8.33. In this example, if a piece of matched login information is found, the action method will return an outcome string "SELECTION" and the next page, Selection.jsp, should be displayed.
8. Otherwise, the query has failed, and no matched login user information can be found. The LogInAction() method returns a null to the JSF engine to redisplay the LogIn page.

```
  <faces-config version="2.0"
  <managed-bean>
A     <managed-bean-name>LogInBean</managed-bean-name>
B     <managed-bean-class>JavaWebDBApp. LogInBean</managed-bean-class>
C     <managed-bean-scope>session</managed-bean-scope>
  </managed-bean>
  <navigation-rule>
D     <from-view-id>/LogIn.jsp</from-view-id>
      <navigation-case>
E       <from-outcome>SELECTION</from-outcome>
F       <to-view-id>/Selection.jsp</to-view-id>
      </navigation-case>
  </navigation-rule>
  </faces-config>
```

Figure 8.33. The application configuration resource file faces-config.xml.

The detailed explanation on the codes shown in Figure 8.33 is listed below:

A. Our Java managed bean LogInBean is defined using the <managed-bean-name> tag.

B. The full class name, including the package name and the bean class name, is defined by the <managed-bean-class> tag.

C. The scope of this Java bean is defined by using the <managed-bean-scope> tag.

D. The current JSF page LogIn.jsp is defined by using the <from-view-id> tag.

E. The outcome string SELECTION, which is mapped to the next page Selection.jsp, is defined by using the <from-outcome> tag and should be returned by the action method LogInAction() if a matched login user has been found.

F. The name of the next page, Selection.jsp, is defined by using the <to-view-id> tag.

The points to be noted for this configuration file are:

1. Both outcome string and the next page should be defined inside the <navigation-case> tag, and all navigation pages should be defined inside the <navigation-rule> tag.
2. The forward-slash symbol "/" before each page name is used to indicate that those pages are located at the current location as the JSF project is located.
3. You can create and edit this configuration file using either the XML editor or the PageFlow design tool.

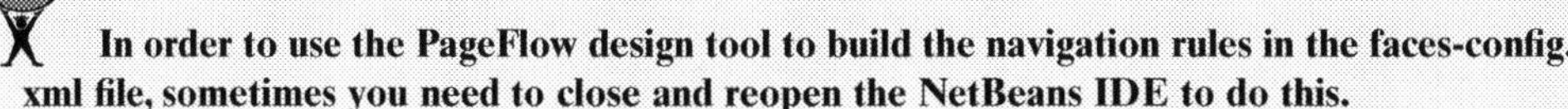

In order to use the PageFlow design tool to build the navigation rules in the faces-config.xml file, sometimes you need to close and reopen the NetBeans IDE to do this.

The codes for a sample LogIn.jsp page is shown in Figure 8.34. Let's have a closer look at this piece of codes to see how it works.

A. Two JSF standard customer tag libraries, one is for building JSF applications that render to an HTML client, and another is for representing core actions independent of a particular

```
  <html>
    <head>
      <meta http-equiv="Content-Type" content="text/html; charset=UTF-8">
      <title>LogIn Page</title>
    </head>
A   <%@ taglib uri="http://java.sun.com/jsf/html" prefix="h" %>
    <%@ taglib uri="http://java.sun.com/jsf/core" prefix="f" %>
    <body>
B     <f:view>
C       <h:form id="LogInForm">
D         <h:inputText id="userName" required="true" value="#{LogInBean.userName}"
          size="10" maxlength="40">
E         <f:validateLength minimum="1" maximum="40"/>
          </h:inputText>
F         <h:inputSecret id="passWord" required="true" value="#{LogInBean.passWord}"
          size="10" maxlength="20">
G         <f:validateLength minimum="6" maximum="20"/>
           </h:inputSecret>
H         <h:commandButton id="LogIn" action="#{LogInBean.LogInAction}"
          value="LogIn" />
        </h:form>
      </f:view>
    </body>
  </html>
```

Figure 8.34. The codes of a sample LogIn.jsp page.

render kit, are declared first at this page using the <%@taglib%> directive. The uri is used to indicate the valid sites where both libraries are located.

B. All of JSF tag components are represented by a tree of components whose root is the UIViewRoot, which is represented by the <f:view> tag. All JSF component tags must be enclosed in this <f: view> tag.

C. A JSP form, which is submitted to the Web server when a button is clicked, is represented by the <h:form> tag. The tags representing the form components, such as textfields and buttons, must be nested inside this form tag. The form is identified by its id, here it is a LogInForm.

D. An inputText tag is used to represent an input field to allow the user to enter one line of text string, such as a username in this example. This inputText tag is identified by its id, and the required attribute is set to true. This means that this inputText cannot be empty and must be filled something by the user as the project runs. The value attribute of this inputText tag is bound to the property userName in the Java bean class, LogInBean, by using the EL value expression. Two points to be noted for this tag is: (1) the value of this tag's id must be identical with the property name userName defined in the Java managed bean LogInBean, and (2) the value attribute of this tag must be bound to the same property userName defined in the Java managed bean LogInBean class, too. In this way, any updating made to this property userName in the Java bean can be immediately reflected to the value of this inputText tag, and furthermore, displayed in this input field.

E. A <f:validateLength> tag is used to make sure that the length of this username is in the range defined by the minimum and maximum attributes.

F. A similar tag is used for the `passWord` inputText, and it is bound to the passWord property defined in the Java-managed bean LogInBean class. The only difference between this tag and the `userName` inputText tag is that a <h:inputSecret> tag is used to replace the <h:inputText> tag since this is a way to present a password input style.

```
  @ManagedBean(name="LogInBean")
  @SessionScoped
  public class LogInBean {

     /** Creates a new instance of LogInBean */
     public LogInBean() {
     }
A    private String userName;
     private String passWord;

B    public String getPassWord() {
        return passWord;
     }
C    public void setPassWord(String passWord) {
        this.passWord = passWord;
     }
D    public String getUserName() {
        return userName;
     }
E    public void setUserName(String userName) {
        this.userName = userName;
     }
F    public String LogInAction()
     {
        String result=null;
        result = LogInQuery();
        return result;
     }
G    public String LogInQuery()
     {
        // query username from database and assign the queried value to the userName property
        // query password from database and assign the queried value to the passWord property
        return "SELECTION";
     }
  }
```

Figure 8.35. The codes for the Java bean class LogInBean.

G. A <f:validateLength> tag is also used to validate the length of the `passWord` to make sure that it is in the required range.

H. A <h:commandButton> tag is used to present a submit button component and its action attribute is bound to the action method defined in the Java managed bean LogInBean using the EL value expression "#{LogInBean.LogInAction}".

8.1.7.5.2 The Detailed Codes for the Java Bean Class The codes for the Java bean class LogInBean.java are shown in Figure 8.35. The functionality of each part of these codes is illustrated below.

A. Two properties, userName and passWord, are defined first, and these two properties must be identical with the id attributes defined in the inputText and inputSecret tags in the JSF page LogIn.jsp we discussed above.

B. The associated getter methods for these two properties are declared and defined in steps **B** and **D**, respectively.

C. The associated setter methods for these two properties are defined in steps **C** and **E**.

F. The action method LogInAction() is defined, and this method has been bound with the action attribute of the LogIn `commandButton` tag in the LogIn.jsp page. This method will be executed as the LogIn button is clicked by the user.

G. The data access method LogInQuery() is defined, and this method is used to perform the database-related query and business logics, and return a outcome string to the JSF page. The JSF page will use its handler to search the returned outcome string to determine the next page to navigate.

So far, we have provided a very detailed introduction and review about the development history of Java Web applications using different components, such as Java Servlet and HTML pages, JSP and help classes, JSP and Java beans, as well as JavaServer Faces and Java bean techniques. In the following sections, we will provide more detailed discussion for each component and techniques. Following these discussions, we will begin to build and develop real Java Web application projects to perform data actions against our sample databases.

8.2 JAVA EE WEB APPLICATION MODEL

The Java EE application model begins with the Java programming language and the Java virtual machine. The proven portability, security, and developer productivity they provide forms the basis of the application model. Java EE is designed to support applications that implement enterprise services for customers, employees, suppliers, partners, and others who make demands on or contributions to the enterprise. Such applications are inherently complex, potentially accessing data from a variety of sources and distributing applications to a variety of clients.

As we discussed in Chapter 5, most popular Java EE applications are built and implemented in a so-called three-tier architecture. To better control and manage these applications, the business functions to support these various users are conducted in the middle tier. The middle tier represents an environment that is closely controlled by an enterprise's information technology department. The middle tier is typically run on dedicated server hardware and has access to the full services of the enterprise.

The Java EE application model defines an architecture for implementing services as multitier applications that deliver the scalability, accessibility, and manageability needed by enterprise-level applications. This model partitions the work needed to implement a multitier service into two parts: the business and presentation logic to be implemented by the developer, and the standard system services provided by the Java EE platform. The developer can rely on the platform to provide solutions for the hard systems-level problems of developing a multitier service.

The Java EE platform uses a distributed multitiered application model for enterprise applications. Application logic is divided into components according to function, and the various application components that make up a Java EE application are installed on different machines depending on the tier in the multitiered Java EE environment to which the application component belongs.

Most Java Web database applications are three-tier client-server applications, which means that this kind of application can be built in three tiers or three containers: client container, Web server container, and database server container. Enterprise Java Beans (EJBs) plays an additional role in business data management and processing in this three-tier architecture. However, in recent years, because of its complexity and time-consuming development cycles, as well as undesired output performances, some researchers recommend to use Java EE without EJB.

In order to get a clearer picture about these two kinds of architectures, let's first concentrate on the difference between them.

8.2.1 Java EE Web Applications with and without EJB

In Section 5.3.5 in Chapter 5, we have provided a very detailed discussion about the Java Web application and Java Enterprise Edition Java EE 6, as well as their components. The relationship between Java Web applications and Java EE is that the latter provides rich and flexible tools and components to support Java Web applications and Web Services developments.

As shown in Figure 5.53 in Chapter 5, most Java Web applications can be divided into three tiers: client tier composed of client machines, Web tier consists of Java EE Server, and EIS tier made of Database server. The Java EJB also works as a business tier attached with the Java server layer. This relationship can be represented by different tiers shown in Figure 8.36.

In fact in recent years, because of undesired output results and complicated developing processes, some developers have changed their mind and moved to Java EE without EJB. This simplification can be illustrated by an architecture shown in Figure 8.37.

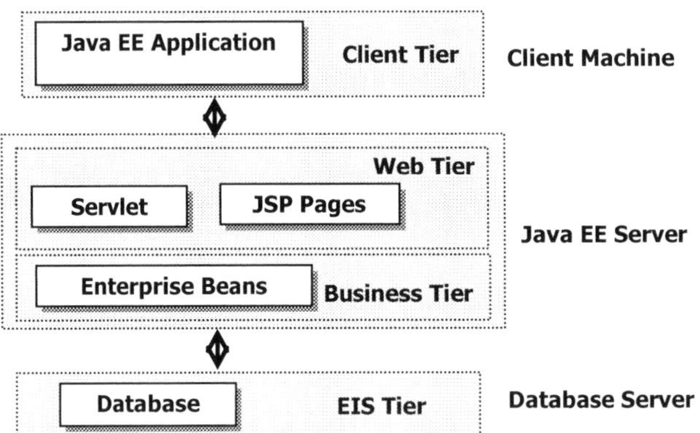

Figure 8.36. An illustration of Java EE three-tier application with EJB.

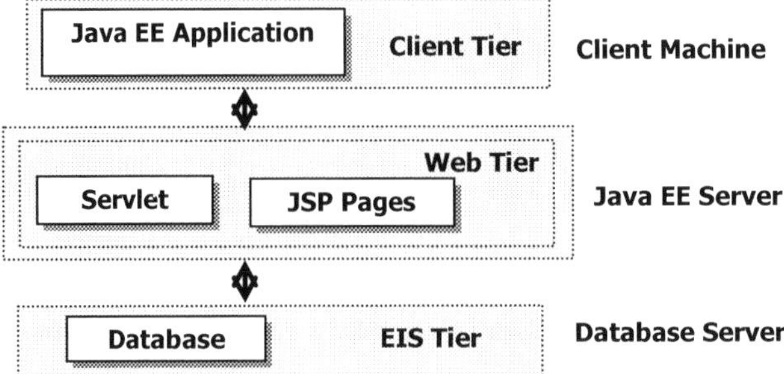

Figure 8.37. An illustration of Java EE three-tier application without EJB.

Compared with two architectures shown in Figures 8.36 and 8.37, it can be found that the business tier, EJB, has been removed from the Web layer, and this greatly simplifies the communications and data transformations between those related tiers. From the point of practical application view, this will also significantly reduces the coding development cycles and improve the efficiency of the program's executions in real time.

As we know, the popular Java EE components are:

- Application clients and Applets are components that run on the client machine.
- Java Servlet, JavaServer Faces, and JSP technology components are web components that run on the server.
- Enterprise JavaBeans (EJB) components are business components that run on the server.

As we build a Java Web application using the architecture shown in Figure 8.37, the third component, EJB, can be removed from this three-tier architecture.

When building a Java Web application, different modules can be adopted based on the different applications. A Java EE module consists of one or more Java EE components for the same container type, and, optionally, one component deployment descriptor of that type. An enterprise bean module deployment descriptor, for example, declares transaction attributes and security authorizations for an enterprise bean. A Java EE module can be deployed as a standalone module.

The four types of Java EE modules are:

1. EJB modules, which contain class files for enterprise beans and an EJB deployment descriptor. EJB modules are packaged as JAR files with a .jar extension.
2. Web modules, which contain Servlet class files, Web files, supporting class files, GIF and HTML files, and a Web application deployment descriptor. Web modules are packaged as JAR files with a .war (Web ARchive) extension.
3. Application client modules, which contain class files and an application client deployment descriptor. Application client modules are packaged as JAR files with a .jar extension.
4. Resource adapter modules, which contain all Java interfaces, classes, native libraries, and other documentation, along with the resource adapter deployment descriptor. Together, these implement the Connector architecture for a particular EIS. Resource adapter modules are packaged as JAR files with a .rar (resource adapter archive) extension.

Since we have provided some basic discussions about Java EE 6 with EJB in Chapter 5, in this chapter, we will concentrate on more deep discussions about Java EE Web application.

8.3 THE ARCHITECTURE AND COMPONENTS OF JAVA WEB APPLICATIONS

A Web application is a dynamic extension of a web or application server. There are two types of Web applications:

- **Presentation Oriented:** A presentation-oriented Web application generates interactive web pages containing various types of markup language (HTML, XHTML, XML, and so on) and dynamic content in response to requests. We will cover how to develop presentation-oriented Web applications in this chapter.

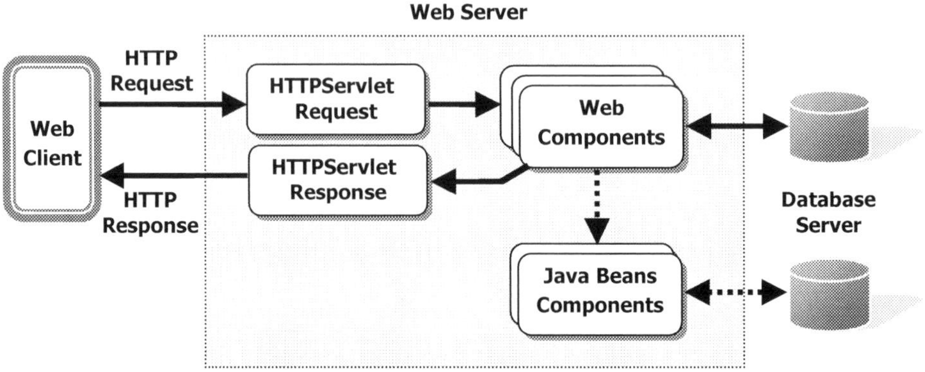

Figure 8.38. An illustration of the Java Web application.

- **Service Oriented:** A service-oriented Web application implements the end point of a Web service. Presentation-oriented applications are often clients of service-oriented Web applications. We will discuss how to develop service-oriented Web applications in the next chapter.

In the Java EE platform, Web components provide the dynamic extension capabilities for a Web server. Web components can be either Java Servlets, web pages, Web service end points, or JSP pages. The interaction between a Web client and a Web application is illustrated in Figure 8.38.

Based on Figure 8.38, a complete request-response message transformation for a Java Web application between a client and a Web server can be illustrated as below:

1. The client sends an HTTP request to the Web server.
2. A Web server that implements Java Servlet and JSP technology converts the request into an HTTPServletRequest object.
3. This object is delivered to a Web component, which can interact with either JavaBeans components or a database to generate dynamic content.
4. The Web component can then generate an HTTPServletResponse, or it can pass the request to another Web component.
5. Eventually, a Web component generates an HTTPServletResponse object.
6. The Web server converts this object to an HTTP response and returns it to the client.

The dash lines between the Web components and Java Beans components, between Java Beans components and Database, are alternative ways to interact with the database via business layer that is supported by the Java Beans components.

In order to get a clear and complete picture about how to control and transmit these request and response messages between Java EE Web Components, we need first to have a basic understanding about the Java EE Containers.

8.3.1 Java EE Containers

Java EE containers are the interfaces between a component and the low-level platform-specific functionality that supports the component. Before a Web, enterprise bean, or

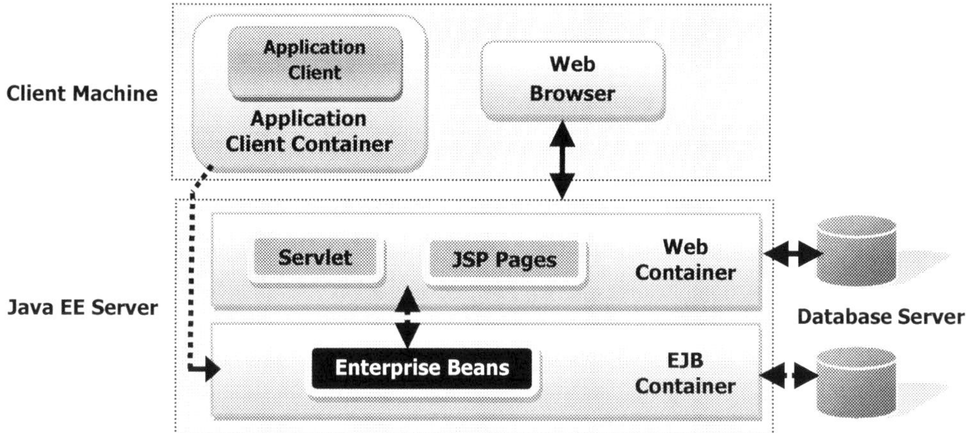

Figure 8.39. Java EE server and containers.

application client component can be executed, it must be assembled into a Java EE module and deployed into its container. Refer to Section 8.2 for a detailed discussion about four types of Java EE modules.

The assembly process involves specifying container settings for each component in the Java EE application and for the Java EE application itself. Container settings customize the underlying support provided by the Java EE server, including services such as security, transaction management, JavaNaming and Directory Interface (JNDI) lookups, and remote connectivity.

The deployment process installs Java EE application components in the Java EE containers as illustrated in Figure 8.39.

The function of each container is listed below:

- **Java EE Server:** The runtime portion of a Java EE product. A Java EE server provides EJB and web containers.
- **Enterprise JavaBeans (EJB) Container:** Manages the execution of enterprise beans for Java EE applications. Enterprise beans and their container run on the Java EE server.
- **Web Container:** Manages the execution of web pages, Servlets, and some EJB components for Java EE applications. Web components and their containers run on the Java EE server.
- **Application Client Container:** Manages the execution of application client components. Application clients and their container run on the client.

All Web components are under the control of the associated containers, and the containers take charge of collecting, organizing and transmitting requests and responses between those components.

Java EE Web components can be implemented with multiple APIs. Let's have a brief review about these APIs.

8.3.2 Java EE 6 APIs

In this section, we will give a brief summary of the most popular technologies required by the Java EE platform, and the APIs used in Java EE applications.

8.3.2.1 EJBs API Technology

An EJB component, or enterprise bean, is a body of code having fields and methods to implement modules of business logic. You can think of an enterprise bean as a building block that can be used alone or with other enterprise beans to execute business logic on the Java EE server.

There are two kinds of enterprise beans: *session beans* and *message-driven beans*. A *session bean* represents a transient conversation with a client. When the client finishes executing, the *session bean* and its data are gone. A *message-driven bean* combines features of a *session bean* and a message listener, allowing a business component to receive messages asynchronously. Commonly, these are JavaMessage Service (JMS) messages. Refer to Figure 5.58 in Chapter 5 to get more detailed information about the EJB.

In the Java EE 6 platform, new enterprise bean features include the following:

1. The ability to package local enterprise beans in a .WAR file
2. Singleton session beans, which provide easy access to shared state
3. A lightweight subset of EJBs functionality that can be provided within Java EE Profiles such as the Java EE Web Profile.

For more information about the EJB API technology, refer to Section 5.3.5 in Chapter 5.

8.3.2.2 Java Servlet API Technology

A Servlet is a class defined in Java programming language, and it is used to extend the capabilities of servers that host applications accessed by means of a request–response programming model. Although Servlets can respond to any type of request, they are commonly used to extend the applications hosted by Web servers. For such applications, Java Servlet API technology defines HTTP-specific Servlet classes.

The javax.servlet and javax.servlet.http packages provide interfaces and classes for writing Servlets. All Servlets must implement the Servlet interface, which defines life-cycle methods. When implementing a generic service, you can use or extend the GenericServlet class provided with the Java Servlet API. The HttpServlet class provides methods, such as doGet() and doPost(), for handling HTTP-specific services.

The life cycle of a Servlet is controlled by the container in which the Servlet has been deployed.

When a request is mapped to a Servlet, the container performs the following steps.

1. If an instance of the Servlet does not exist, the Web container
   - **A.** Loads the Servlet class.
   - **B.** Creates an instance of the Servlet class.
   - **C.** Initializes the Servlet instance by calling the init() method.
2. Invokes the service method, passing request, and response objects.

If the container needs to remove the Servlet, it finalizes the Servlet by calling the Servlet's destroy() method.

You can monitor and react to events in a Servlet's life cycle by defining listener objects whose methods get invoked when life-cycle events occur. To use these listener objects, you must define and specify the listener class.

8.3.2.3 JSP API Technology

JSP is a Java technology that helps software developers serve dynamically generated web pages based on HTML, XML, or other document types. Released in 1999 as Sun's answer to ASP and PHP, JSP was designed to address the perception that the Java programming environment didn't provide developers with enough support for the Web.

Architecturally, JSP may be considered as a high-level abstraction of Java Servlets. JSP pages are loaded in the server and operated from a structured specially installed Java server packet called a Java EE Web Application, often packaged as a .war or .ear file archive.

JSP allows Java code and certain pre-defined actions to be interleaved with static Web markup content, with the resulting page being compiled and executed on the server to deliver an HTML or XML document. The compiled pages and any dependent Java libraries use Java bytecode rather than a native software format, and must therefore be executed within a Java Virtual Machine (JVM) that integrates with the host operating system to provide an abstract platform-neutral environment.

JSP syntax is a fluid mix of two basic content forms: *scriptlet elements* and *markup*. Markup is typically standard HTML or XML, while scriptlet elements are delimited blocks of Java code that may be intermixed with the markup. When the page is requested, the Java code is executed and its output is added, *in situ*, with the surrounding markup to create the final page. Because Java is a compiled language, not a scripting language, JSP pages must be compiled to Java bytecode classes before they can be executed, but such compilation is needed only when a change to the source JSP file has occurred.

Java code is not required to be complete (self-contained) within its scriptlet element block, but can straddle markup content providing the page as a whole is syntactically correct (e.g., any Java if/for/while blocks opened in one scriptlet element must be correctly closed in a later element for the page to successfully compile). This system of split inline coding sections is called *step over scripting*, because it can wrap around the static markup by stepping over it. Markup which falls inside a split block of code is subject to that code, so markup inside an *if* block will only appear in the output when the *if* condition evaluates to true; likewise, markup inside a loop construct may appear multiple times in the output depending upon how many times the loop body runs.

The JSP syntax adds additional XML-like tags, called JSP actions, to invoke built-in functionality. Additionally, the technology allows for the creation of JSP tag libraries that act as extensions to the standard HTML or XML tags. JVM-operated tag libraries provide a platform independent way of extending the capabilities of a Web server. Note that not all commercial Java servers are Java EE specification compliant.

JSP technology lets you put snippets of Servlet code directly into a text-based document. A JSP page is a text-based document that contains two types of text: static data (which can be expressed in any text-based format such as HTML, WML, and XML) and JSP elements, which determine how the page constructs dynamic content.

The JavaServer Pages Standard Tag Library (JSTL) encapsulates core functionality common to many JSP applications. Instead of mixing tags from numerous vendors in your JSP applications, you employ a single, standard set of tags. This standardization allows you to deploy your applications on any JSP container that supports JSTL and makes it more likely that the implementation of the tags is optimized.

```
A <%@ page myPage="mypage.jsp" %>
  <%@ page import="com.foo.bar" %>

  <html>
  <head>
B <%! int serverInstanceVariable = 1;%>

  <% int localStackBasedVariable = 1; %>
  <table>
  <tr><td><%= toStringOrBlank( "expanded inline data " + 1 ) %></td></tr>
```

Figure 8.40. An example of JSP pages.

JSTL has an iterator and conditional tags for handling flow control, tags for manipulating XML documents, internationalization tags, tags for accessing databases using SQL, and commonly used functions.

JSP pages are compiled into Servlets by a JSP compiler. The compiler either generates a Servlet in Java code that is then compiled by the Java compiler, or it may compile the Servlet to bytecode which is directly executable. JSPs can also be interpreted on-the-fly, reducing the time taken to reload changes.

JSP simply puts Java inside HTML pages using JSP tags. You can take any existing HTML page and change its extension to .jsp instead of .html.

Regardless of whether the JSP compiler generates Java source code for a Servlet or emits the bytecode directly, it is helpful to understand how the JSP compiler transforms the page into a Java Servlet. For example, consider an input JSP page shown in Figure 8.40, and this JSP page can be compiled to create its resulting generated Java Servlet. The JSP tags <% . . . %> or <jsp . . . /> enclose Java expressions, which are evaluated at the runtime by JVM.

Refer to Figure 8.40. In step **A**, two JSP coding lines are created to declare a JSP page and an import component. Then in step **B**, two Java integer variables are created, one is an instance variable and the other one is the Stack-based variable.

8.3.2.4 JavaServer Faces API Technology

JavaServer Faces technology is a server-side component framework for building Java technology-based Web applications. JavaServer Faces technology consists of the following:

- An API for representing components and managing their state; handling events, server-side validation, and data conversion; defining page navigation; supporting internationalization and accessibility; and providing extensibility for all these features
- Tag libraries for adding components to web pages and for connecting components to server-side objects

JavaServer Faces technology provides a well-defined programming model and various tag libraries. These features significantly ease the burden of building and maintaining Web applications with server-side UIs. With minimal effort, you can complete the following tasks:

1. Create a Web page.
2. Drop components onto a Web page by adding component tags.

3. Bind components on a page to server-side data.
4. Wire component-generated events to server-side application code.
5. Save and restore application state beyond the life of server requests.
6. Reuse and extend components through customization.

The functionality provided by a JavaServer Faces application is similar to that of any other Java Web application. A typical JavaServer Faces application includes the following parts:

- A set of web pages in which components are laid out.
- A set of tags to add components to the Web page.
- A set of *backing beans* that are JavaBeans components that define properties and functions for components on a page.
- A Web deployment descriptor (web.xml file).
- Optionally, one or more application configuration resource files, such as a faces-config.xml file, which can be used to define page navigation rules and configure beans and other custom objects, such as custom components.
- Optionally, a set of custom objects created by the application developer. These objects can include custom components, validators, converters, or listeners.
- A set of custom tags for representing custom objects on the page.

Figure 8.41 describes the interaction between client and server in a typical JavaServer Faces application. In response to a client request, a Web page is rendered by the Web container that implements JavaServer Faces technology.

The Web page, Myface.xhtml, is built using JavaServer Faces component tags. Component tags are used to add components to the view (represented by MyUI in the diagram), which is the server-side representation of the page. In addition to components, the Web page can also reference objects such as the following:

1. Any event listeners, validators, and converters that are registered on the components
2. The JavaBeans components that capture the data and process the application-specific functionality of the components

On request from the client, the view is rendered as a response. Rendering is the process whereby, based on the server-side view, the Web container generates output such as HTML or XHTML that can be read by the browser.

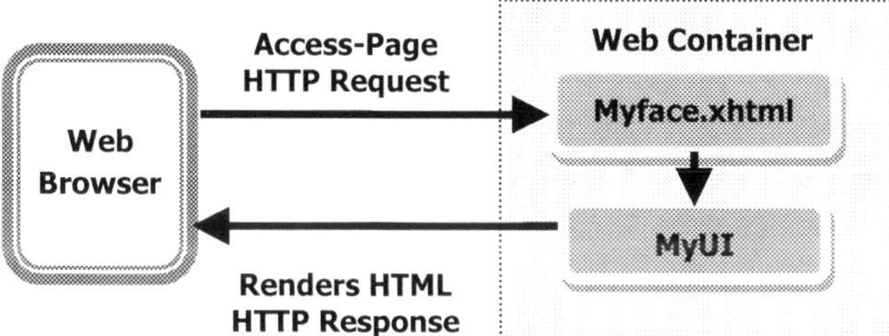

Figure 8.41. Responding to a client request for a JavaServer Faces page.

8.3.2.5 Java Persistence API

The Java Persistence API is a Java standards-based solution for persistence. Persistence uses an ORM approach to bridge the gap between an object-oriented model and a relational database. The Java Persistence API can also be used in Java SE applications, outside of the Java EE environment. Java Persistence consists of three areas:

- The Java Persistence API
- The query language
- Object/relational mapping metadata

The following three components and related functions are keys in Java Persistence API:

- Entities
- Manage Entities
- Query Entities

Let's have a closer look at these three components and their functions, as well as how to implement them in Java Persistence API in real Java programming applications.

Entities: An entity is a lightweight persistence domain object. Generally, an entity represents a table in a relational database, and each entity instance corresponds to a row in that table. The primary programming artifact of an entity is the entity class, although entities can use helper classes.
The persistent state of an entity is represented either through persistent fields or persistent properties. These fields or properties use object/relational mapping annotations to map the entities and entity relationships to the relational data in the underlying data store.

Manage Entities: Entities are managed by the entity manager. The entity manager is represented by javax.persistence.EntityManager instances. Each EntityManager instance is associated with a persistence context. A persistence context defines the scope under which particular entity instances are created, persisted, and removed.
A persistence context is a set of managed entity instances that exist in a particular data store. The EntityManager interface defines the methods that are used to interact with the persistence context.

Query Entities: There are two methods of querying entities using the Java Persistence API: The Java Persistence Query Language (JPQL) and the Criteria API. Relatively, the Java Persistence query language (JPQL) is a simple, string-based language similar to SQL used to query entities and their relationships. The Criteria API is used to create type-safe queries using Java programming language APIs to query for entities and their relationships. Each approach, JPQL and the Criteria API, has advantages and disadvantages.

We have provided a very detailed discussion about the Java Persistence API and JPQL in Sections 6.1 and 6.2 in Chapter 6. Refer to those sections to get more information for these components.

8.3.2.6 Java Transaction API

The Java Transaction API (JTA) provides a standard interface for demarcating transactions.

The Java EE architecture provides a default autocommit to handle transaction commits and rollbacks. An auto commit means that any other applications that are viewing data will see the updated data after each database read or write operation. However, if your application performs two separate database access operations that depend on each other, you will want to use the JTA API to demarcate where the entire transaction, including both operations, begins, rolls back, and commits.

In Section 7.1 in Chapter 7, we have provided a very detailed discussion about the Java Persistence API on Transaction mechanism and its implementation with some data manipulations in real projects, such as data insertion, updating, and deleting, using the JPA wizard. Refer to those parts to get more information for this API.

8.3.2.7 Java Message Service API

The JavaMessage Service (JMS) API is a messaging standard that allows Java EE application components to create, send, receive, and read messages. It enables distributed communication that is loosely coupled, reliable, and asynchronous.

Now that we have a basic and clear understanding about the Java EE architecture and components, let's take a look at the Java Web application life cycle.

8.3.3 Java Web Application Life Cycle

A Web application consists of Web components, static resource files such as images, and helper classes and libraries. The Web container provides many supporting services that enhance the capabilities of Web components and make them easier to develop. However, because a Web application must take these services into account, the process for creating and running a Web application is different from that of traditional stand-alone Java classes.

The process for creating, deploying, and executing a Web application can be summarized as follows:

1. Develop the Web component code.
2. Develop the Web application deployment descriptor.
3. Compile the Web application components and helper classes referenced by the components.
4. Optionally package the application into a deployable unit.
5. Deploy the application into a Web container.
6. Access a URL that references the Web application.

We will illustrate how to use this life cycle module to develop and build some professional Java Web applications in Section 8.4.

8.3.4 Java Web Modules

As we discussed in Section 8.2.1, four Java EE Web modules are available, and the Web module is one of them. In the Java EE architecture, Web components and static Web content files such as images are called web resources. A web module is the smallest deployable and usable unit of Web resources. A Java EE Web module corresponds to a Web application as defined in the Java Servlet specification.

In addition to Web components and Web resources, a Web module can contain other files:

- Server-side utility classes (database beans, shopping carts, and so on). Often these classes conform to the JavaBeans component architecture.
- Client-side classes (applets and utility classes).

A Web module has a specific structure. The top-level directory of a Web module is the document root of the application. The document root is where XHTML pages, client-side classes and archives, and static Web resources, such as images, are stored.

The document root contains a subdirectory named WEB-INF, which contains the following files and directories:

- web.xml: The Web application deployment descriptor.
- Tag library descriptor files.
- classes: A directory that contains server-side classes: servlets, utility classes, and JavaBeans components.
- tags: A directory that contains tag files, which are implementations of tag libraries.
- lib: A directory that contains JAR archives of libraries called by server-side classes.

If your Web module does not contain any Servlets, filter, or listener components, then it does not need a Web application deployment descriptor. In other words, if your Web module only contains XHTML pages and static files, you are not required to include a web.xml file.

You can also create application-specific subdirectories (that is, package directories) in either the document root or the WEB-INF/classes/directory.

A Web module can be deployed as an unpacked file structure, or can be packaged in a JAR file known as a Web archive (WAR) file. Because the contents and use of WAR files differ from those of JAR files, WAR file names use a .war extension. The Web module just described is portable; you can deploy it into any Web container that conforms to the Java Servlet Specification.

To deploy a WAR on the Enterprise Server, the file must also contain a runtime deployment descriptor. The runtime deployment descriptor is an XML file that contains information such as the context root of the Web application and the mapping of the portable names of an application's resources to the Enterprise Server's resources. The Enterprise Server Web application runtime DD is named sun-web.xml, and is located in the WEB-INF directory along with the Web application DD. The structure of a Web module that can be deployed on the Enterprise Server is shown in Figure 8.42.

To successfully build and implement a Java Web application, one needs to perform the following operations to make it a distributable application:

- Packaging Web Modules
- Deploying a WAR File

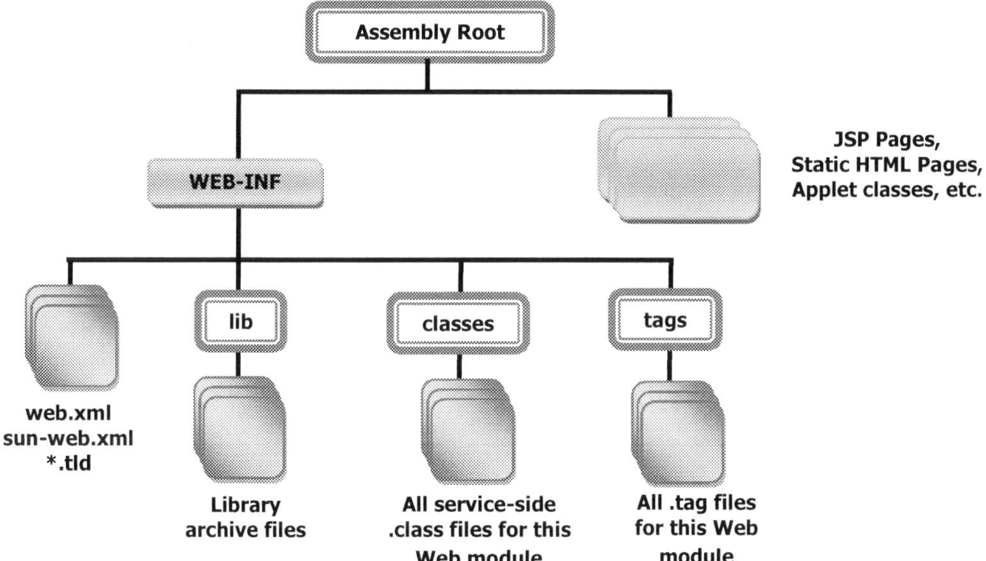

Figure 8.42. A Web module structure.

- Testing Deployed Web Modules
- Listing Deployed Web Modules
- Updating Web Modules
- Undeploying Web Modules

We will discuss these operations with more detailed in the following sections with some real Java Web application projects.

8.3.5 Java Web Frameworks

A Web application framework is a software framework that is designed to support the development of dynamic websites, Web applications, and Web services. The framework aims to alleviate the overhead associated with common activities performed in Web development. For example, many frameworks provide libraries for database access, template frameworks, and session management, and they often promote code reuse, too.

As we know, all Web components such as Java Servlets, web pages, or JSP pages, are under the control of the associated Web containers. The question is: who controls those Web containers? The answer is the Web frameworks. A Web framework is a software framework that provides all supports to develop and organize dynamic sites. Some main features provided by a Web framework include:

- Provide user-friendly graphical user interfaces (GUIs) to Web applications.
- Provide managements to Web containers to coordinate requests and responses transmission between Web server and clients.

- Provide security supports to Web servers.
- Provide supports to database accessing and mapping.
- Provide supports to URL mapping.
- Provide supports to update Web templates.

Almost all modern Web-development frameworks follow the MVC design. Business logic and presentation are separated, and a controller of logic flow coordinates requests from clients and actions taken on the server. This approach has become a popular style of Web development.

All frameworks use different techniques to coordinate the navigation within the Web application, such as the XML configuration file, java property files, or custom properties. All frameworks also differ in the way the controller module is implemented. For instance, EJBs may instantiate classes needed in each request, or Java reflection can be used to dynamically invoke an appropriate action classes. Also, frameworks may differ conceptually.

Java frameworks are similar in the way they structure data flow. After request, some action takes place on the application server, and some data-populated objects are always sent to the JSP layer with the response. Data are then extracted from those objects, which could be simple classes with setter and getter methods, java beans, value objects, or some collection objects. Modern Java frameworks also simplify a developer's tasks by providing automatic Session tracking with easy APIs, database connection pools, and even database call wrappers. Some frameworks either provide hooks into other J2EE technologies, such as JMS (Java Messaging Service) or JMX, or have these technologies integrated. Server data persistence and logging also could be part of a framework.

The most popular Web frameworks include:

- JavaServer Faces (JSF)
- Apache Wicket
- JBoss Seam
- Spring MVC & WebFlow
- Adobe Flex
- Hibernate
- PHP
- Perl
- Ruby
- ASP.NET
- Struts 2

Two popular Java frameworks used in NetBeans IDE 6.8 are JavaServer Faces and Hibernate.

Now that we have both a historical review and detailed discussion for each part of Java Web applications, let's concentrate on building and developing real Java Web database application projects starting from the next section.

8.4 GETTING STARTED WITH JAVA WEB APPLICATIONS USING NETBEANS IDE

Starting from this section, we will build some real Java Web database application projects using JSP, Java beans, and JavaServer Faces technologies we discussed in the previous sections in this chapter. We divide these discussions into the following parts:

1. First we create a new Java Web application project JavaWebDBJSPSQL to access our sample SQL Server database.
   - A. We discuss how to build a Web page to access and query the LogIn table using JSP and help class files.
   - B. Then we use JSP, JSP implicit Session object, JavaServer Faces and Java beans to develop different web pages to:
     - Access and query data from the Faculty table in our sample SQL Server database.
     - Insert new records to the Faculty table in our sample SQL Server database.
     - Update and delete records from the Faculty table in our sample database.
   - C. We then discuss how to use JSP, JavaServer Faces and Java beans techniques to build different web pages to:
     - Access and query data from the Course table in our sample SQL Server database.
     - Insert new records to the Course table in our sample SQL Server database.
     - Update and delete records from the Course table in our sample database.
   - D. Finally we discuss how to query data from the Student table in our sample database using JSP and Java beans techniques.
2. Then we create another new Java Web application project JavaWebDBJSPOracle to access our sample Oracle database.
   - A. We discuss how to use JavaServer Faces and Java beans techniques to develop different web pages to:
     - Access and query data from the LogIn table in our sample Oracle database.
     - Access and query data from the Faculty table in our sample Oracle database
     - Insert new records to the Faculty table in our sample Oracle database.
     - Update and delete records from the Faculty table in our sample Oracle database.
     - Access and query data from the Course table in our sample Oracle database.
     - Insert new records to the Course table in our sample Oracle database.
     - Update and delete records from the Course table in our sample Oracle database

Now let's start to build our first Java Web application project to access and manipulate data in our sample SQL Server database.

8.4.1 Create a Java Web Project

Launch NetBeans IDE and go to File > New Project item to open the New Project wizard. Select the Java Web from the `Categories` list and Web Application from the `Projects` list, as shown in Figure 8.43. Then click o the Next button to go to the next wizard.

Enter JavaWebDBJSPSQL into the `Project Name` field as this new project's name. Make sure that the desired folder in which you want to save this project is included in

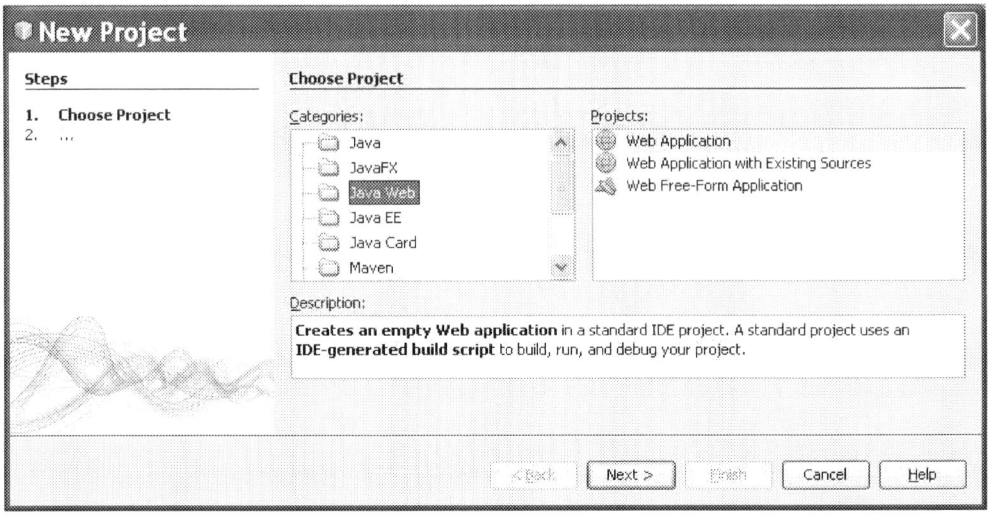

Figure 8.43. The opened New Project wizard.

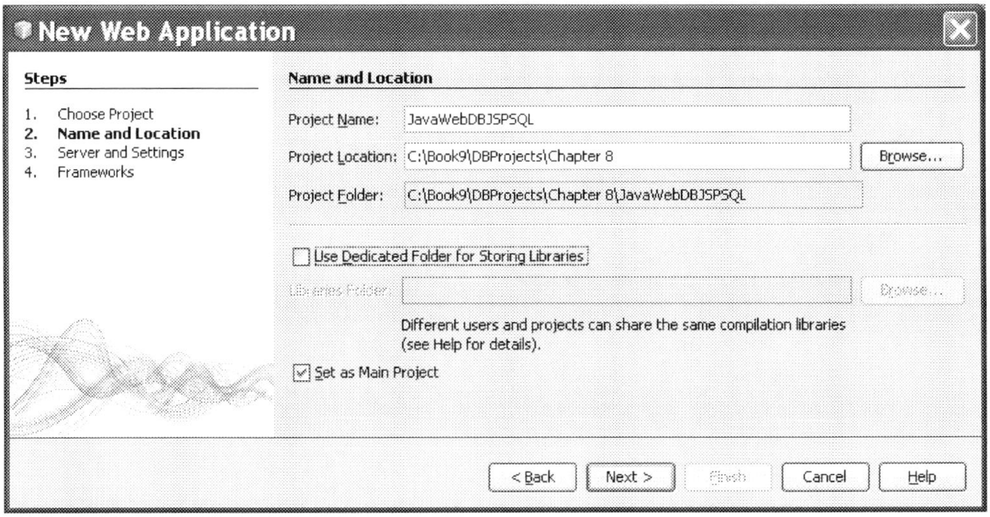

Figure 8.44. The Name and Location wizard.

the `Project Location` field and the `Set as Main Project` checkbox has been checked, as shown in Figure 8.44. Then click on the **Next** button.

In the opened `Server and Settings` wizard, you need to add the GlassFish v3 server as the Web server for this Web application. Refer to Section 5.3.5.2.2 in Chapter 5 to add this server to the NetBeans IDE if you have not done this. Your finished `Server and Settings` wizard should match one that is shown in Figure 8.45. Click on the **Next** button to continue.

Since we do not want to use any frameworks in this Web application, click on the **Finish** button in the next wizard to complete this new project creation process.

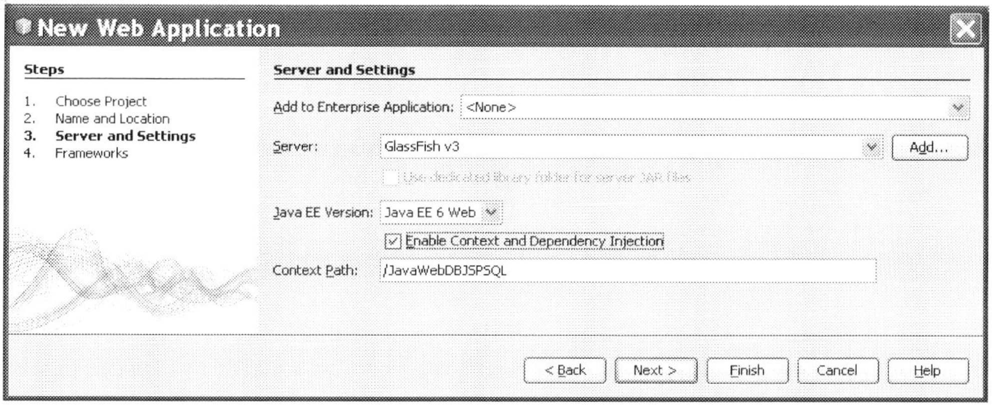

Figure 8.45. The finished Server and Settings wizard.

Because we need to use the Java Persistence API to help us to perform database-related queries and operations in this project, so next let's create an entity class for our sample SQL Server database CSE_DEPT.

8.4.2 Create the Entity Classes from the Database

Perform the following operations to create our entity classes for our sample database:

1. In the `Projects` window, right click on the JavaWebDBJSPSQL project and select the `New > Entity Classes from Database` item from the pop-up menu.
2. Click on the dropdown arrow of the `Data Source` combo box and select the `New Data Source` item. On the opened `Create Data Source` dialog box, enter CSE_DEPT into the JNDI Name field. Click on the drop-down arrow at the `Database Connection` combo box and select our SQL Server 2008 sample database URL: jdbc:sqlserver://localhost\SQL2008EXPRESS:5000;databaseName=CSE_DEPT [ybai on dbo]. Click on the OK button to continue.
3. Click on the Add All button to add all five tables to the `Selected Tables` list box. Your finished `New Entity Classes from Database` wizard should match one that is shown in Figure 8.46. Click on the Next button to continue.
4. In the opened Entity Classes wizard, enter JavaWebDBJSPSQLPackage into the `Package` field and use this as the package's name to store this entity class.
5. Click on the Create Persistence Unit button to create this entity class.
6. On the opened `Create Persistence Unit` wizard, select the TopLink item from the `Persistence Provider` combo box, which is shown in Figure 8.47, and click on the Create button to create this entity class.
   Your finished Entity Classes wizard should match one that is shown in Figure 8.48. Click on the Next button to go to the next wizard.
7. On the opened Mapping Options wizard, select java.util.List item from the `Collection Type` combo box since we need to use the List collection in this project. Your finished

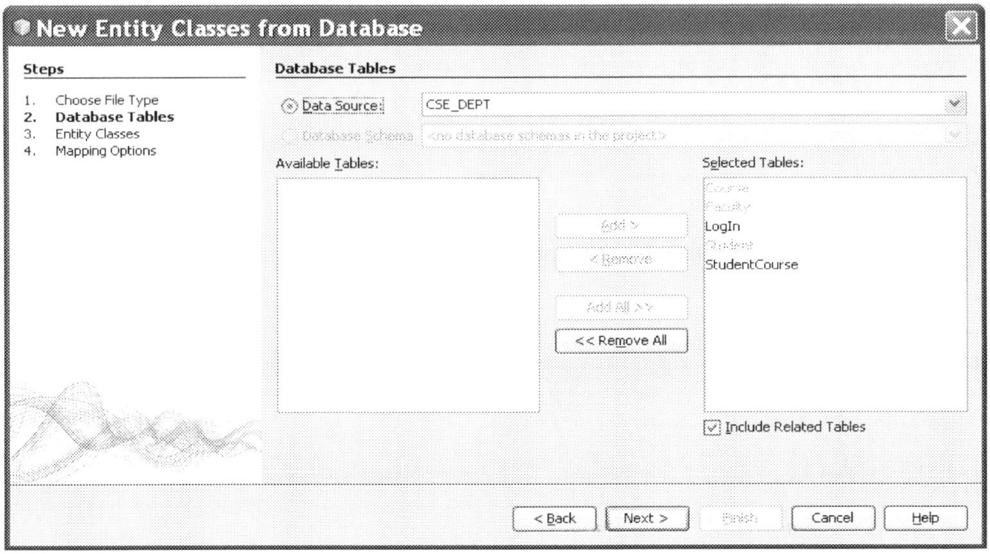

Figure 8.46. The finished Database Tables wizard.

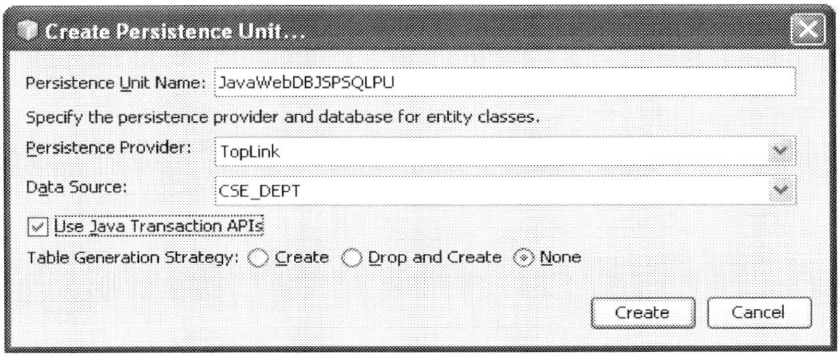

Figure 8.47. The finished Create Persistence Unit wizard.

Mapping Options wizard should match one this is shown in Figure 8.49. Click on the Finish button to complete this entity class creation process.

At this point, we have completed creating a new Web application project and installing the entity classes from our sample SQL Server database. Next, we will build five web pages as GUIs to query and manipulate data against our sample database via Web server and database server.

8.4.3 Create Five Web Pages Using Microsoft Office Publisher 2007

In this section, we will create five web pages, LogIn, Selection, Faculty, Course, and Student, as the GUIs to access and manipulate our sample database via Web server.

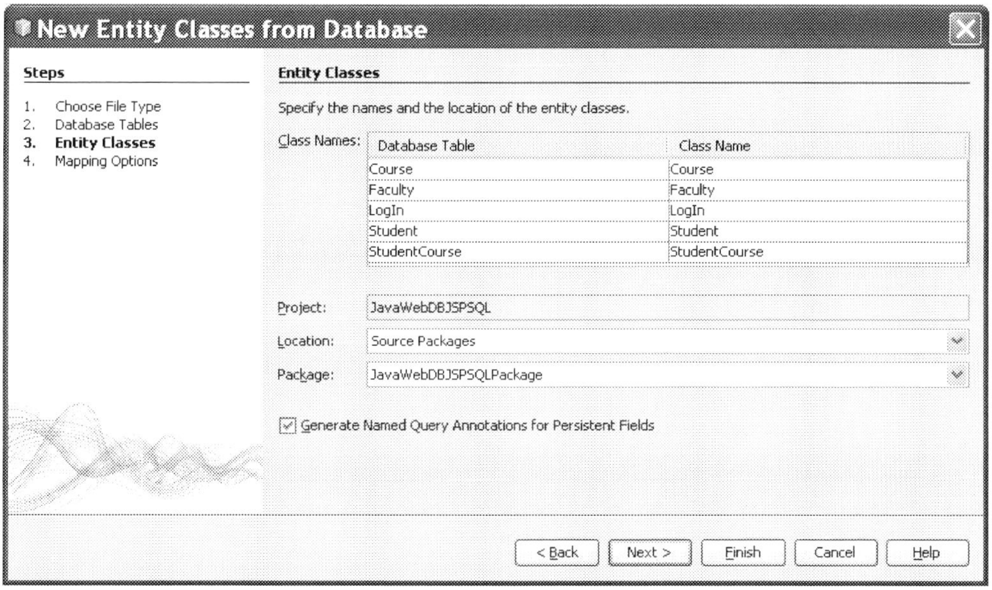

Figure 8.48. The finished Entity Classes wizard.

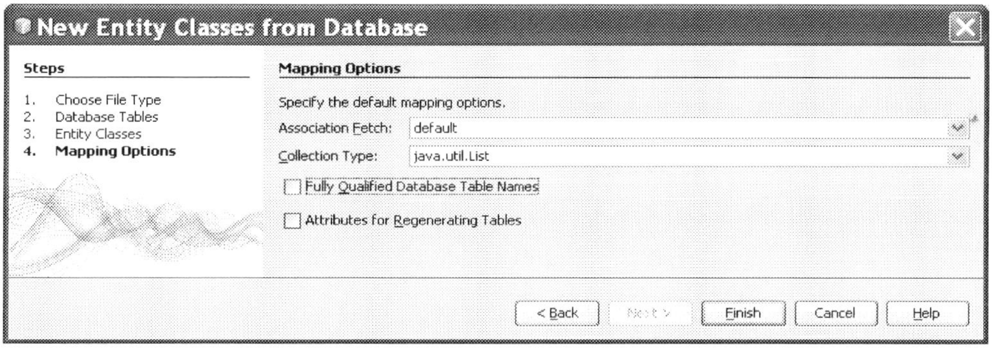

Figure 8.49. The finished Mapping Options wizard.

When a Web application starts, the default starting page is index.jsp. However, in this application, we want to use the LogIn.jsp page as our starting page. Because of the relative complexity in our five pages, we need to use Microsoft Office Publisher 2007 as a tool to help us to do this job.

Let's first handle the LogIn page.

8.4.3.1 Create the LogIn Page

The purpose of this page is to allow users to login to our sample SQL Server database to perform data actions to five tables in our sample database. Exactly this page is related to the LogIn table to enable users to login and enter this database.

Launch Microsoft Office Publisher 2007 and click on the Web Sites icon to open the `Web Sites` wizard. Scroll down to the bottom of this wizard and double click on the Web 984 × 4608px item under the `Blank Sizes` category as the template of this page. Perform the following operations to build this page:

1. Go to Insert > Text Box menu item to add a textbox to the top of this page. Enter Welcome to CSE DEPT LogIn Page into this textbox as a label for this page.
2. Highlight the text of the label and select the `Arial Black` as the font type and 12 as the font size.
3. Perform the similar operation as step 1 to create another two textboxes, and enter User Name and Pass Word as another two labels. Locate these two labels just under the top label as we did in step 1 above.
4. Go to Insert > Form Control > TextBox menu item to add two textboxes; align each of them after each of two labels, User Name and Pass Word, respectively.
5. Right click on the first textbox we added in step 4 above, and select the Format Form Properties item. Enter UserNameField into the text field under the `Return data with this label` as the name of this textbox. Click on the `OK` button to complete this naming process.
6. Perform the similar operation to the second textbox we added in step 4 above and name it as PassWordField.
7. Go to Insert > Form Control > Submit menu item to add a command button into this page. Uncheck the `Button text is same as button type` checkbox and enter LogIn into the `Button text` field. Locate this button under two textboxes we added in steps 4–6. Click on the `OK` button to close this dialog box.
8. Perform the similar operation to add another button, and use Cancel as the button text for this button.
9. Go to File > Save As item to save this page as an HTML file. On the opened `Save As` dialog, select the Web Page, Filtered (*.htm, *.html) from the `Save as type` combo box and enter LogIn.html to the `File name` field. Click on the Save button to save this HTML file to certain location in your root driver, such as C:\Temp. Click Yes to the message box and OK to the `Form Properties` dialog to complete this saving process.

Now go to File > Web Page Preview menu item to take a look at this LogIn page. Your finished LogIn page should match one that is shown in Figure 8.50.

To convert this HTML page to a JSP page, open the Notepad and perform the following operations:

1. On the opened Notepad, go to File > Open menu item to open the `Open` dialog box. Make sure to select All Files from the `Files of type` combo box at the bottom of this dialog.
2. Browse to the folder where you saved the LogIn.html file, such as C:\Temp; select it and click on the Open button to open this file.
3. Go to File > Save As menu item to open the `Save As` dialog box. Then enter "LogIn.jsp" into the `File name` field as the name of this page. The point to be noted is that you must use the double quotation marks to cover this file name to enable the Notepad to save it as a JSP file. Click on the Save button to save this JSP file to your desired folder, such as C:\Temp.
4. Close the Notepad and we have completed creating our LogIn.jsp file.

Next, let's handle to create our Selection JSP file.

Figure 8.50. The finished LogIn page.

8.4.3.2 Create the Selection Page

The purpose of this page is to allow users to choose other web pages to perform the related data actions with the different data tables in our sample database. Therefore, this page can be considered as a main or control page to enable users to browse to other pages to perform data actions against the related data table in our sample database.

Launch Microsoft Office Publisher 2007 and click on the Web Sites icon to open the `Web Sites` wizard. Scroll down to the bottom of this wizard and double click on the Web 984 × 4608px item under the `Blank Sizes` category as the template of this page. Perform the following operations to build this page:

1. Go to Insert > Text Box menu item to add a textbox to the top of this page. Enter Make Your Selection into this textbox as a label for this page.
2. Highlight the text of the label and select the `Arial Black` as the font type and 12 as the font size.
3. Go to Insert > Form Control > List Box menu item to add a listbox control. Locate this listbox just under the top label as we did in step 1 above.
4. Right click on the new added listbox and select Format Form Properties item to open `List Box Properties` dialog. Enter ListSelection into the `Return data with this label` field as the name of this listbox.
5. In the `Appearance` list, click on the Remove buttons three times to delete all default items from this list.
6. Click on the Add button to add the first item to this list. On the opened dialog, enter the Faculty Information into the `Item` field and check the Selected radio button. Make sure that the Item value is same as item text checkbox is checked. Your finished `Add/Modify List Box Item` dialog should match one that is shown in Figure 8.51. Click on the OK button to close this dialog box.
7. Click on the Add button to add our second item into this listbox. On the opened `Add/Modify List Box Item` dialog, enter Course Information into the `Item` field, and

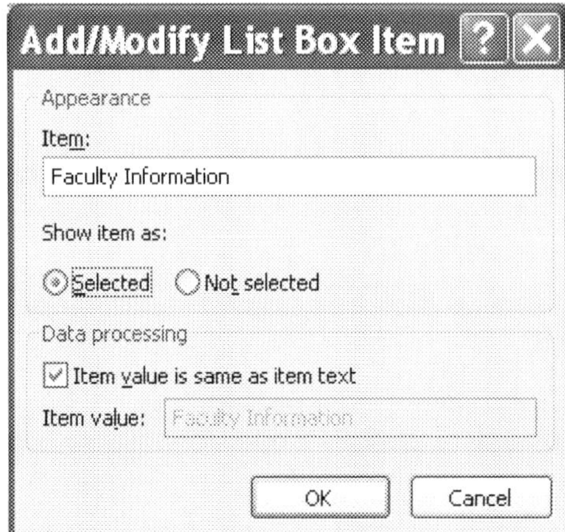

Figure 8.51. The finished Add/Modify List Box Item dialog box.

Figure 8.52. The finished List Box Properties dialog box.

make sure that both Not selected radio button and the Item value is same as item text checkbox are checked. Click on the OK button to close this dialog box.

8. Perform the similar operations as we did in step 7 above to add the third item, Student Information, into this listbox.
9. Your finished `List Box Properties` dialog should match one that is shown in Figure 8.52. Click on the OK button to complete this listbox setup process.
10. Go to Insert > Form Control > Submit menu item to add a command button into this page. Uncheck the `Button text is same as button type` checkbox and enter OK into the `Button text` field. Locate this button under the listbox we added above. Click on the `OK` button to close this dialog box.
11. Perform the similar operation to add another button and use Exit as the button text for this button.

Figure 8.53. The preview of the Selection page.

12. Go to File > Save As item to save this page as an HTML file. On the opened `Save As` dialog, select the Web Page, Filtered (*.htm, *.html) from the `Save as type` combo box and enter Selection.html to the `File name` field. Click on the Save button to save this HTML file to a certain location in your root driver, such as C:\Temp. Click Yes to the message box and OK to the `Form Properties` dialog to complete this saving process.
13. Now go to File > Web Page Preview menu item to take a look at this Selection page. Your finished Selection page should match one that is shown in Figure 8.53.

To convert this HTML page to a JSP page, open the Notepad and perform the following operations:

1. On the opened Notepad, go to File > Open menu item to open the `Open` dialog box. Make sure to select All Files from the `Files of type` combo box at the bottom of this dialog.
2. Browse to the folder where you saved the Selection.html file, such as C:\Temp, select it and click on the Open button to open this file.
3. Go to File > Save As menu item to open the `Save As` dialog box. Enter "Selection.jsp" into the `File name` field as the name of this page. The point to be noted is that you must use the double quotation marks to cover this file name to enable the Notepad to save it as a JSP file. Click on the Save button to save this JSP file to your desired folder, such as C:\Temp.
4. Close the Notepad and we have completed creating our Selection.jsp file.

Next let's handle to create our Faculty JSP file.

8.4.3.3 Create the Faculty Page

The purpose of this page is to allow users to access the Faculty table in our sample database to perform data actions via this page, such as data query, new faculty records

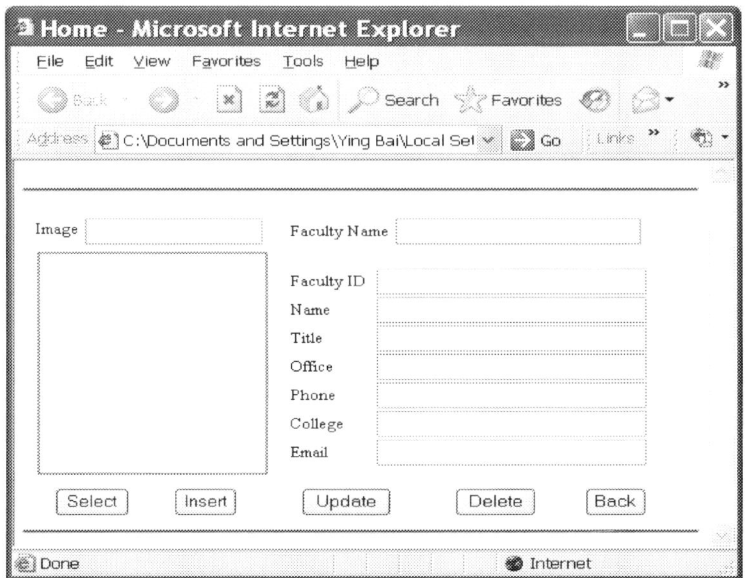

Figure 8.54. The preview of the Faculty page.

insertion, and faculty member updating and deleting. Because the HTML and JSP did not provide any combo box control, in this application, we have to use text box control to replace the combo box control and apply it in this page.

The preview of this Faculty page is shown in Figure 8.54.

Now let's start to build this page using Microsoft Office Publisher 2007.

Launch Microsoft Office Publisher 2007 and click on the Web Sites icon to open the `Web Sites` wizard. Scroll down to the bottom of this wizard and double click on the Web 984 × 4608px item under the `Blank Sizes` category as the template of this page. Perform the following operations to build this page:

1. Go to Insert > Text Box menu item to insert a textbox into this page and enter Image into this textbox as an image label.
2. Go to Insert > Form Control > Textbox menu item to insert a Textbox into this page and locate this textbox just to the right of the image label we added in step 1 above.
3. Right click on this inserted Textbox and select the `Format Form Properties` item to open the `Text Box Properties` dialog, as shown in Figure 8.55a. Then enter FacultyImageField into the `Return data with this label` field, as shown in Figure 8.55a. Click on the OK button to close this dialog.
4. Go to Insert > Picture > Empty Picture Frame menu item to insert a blank picture to this page. Locate this picture under the FacultyImageField textbox we added in step 2.
5. Go to Insert > Text Box to insert a new TextBox and move it to the right of the picture. Type Faculty Name in this inserted TextBox as the `Faculty Name` label.
6. Go to Insert > Form Control > Textbox menu item to insert a Textbox into this page and locate this textbox to the right of the `Faculty Name` label.
7. Right click on this inserted Textbox and select the `Format Form Properties` item to open the `Text Box Properties` dialog. Enter FacultyNameField into the `Return`

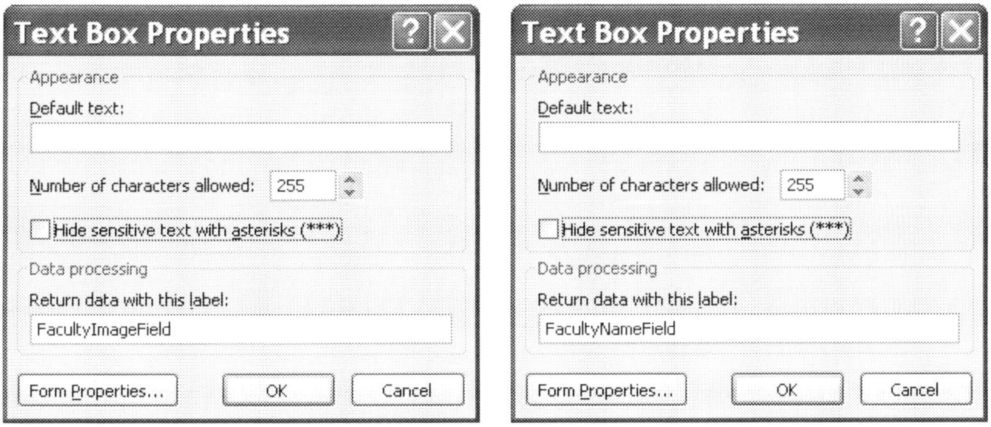

Figure 8.55. The FacultyImageField and FacultyNameField textboxes.

`data with this label` field, as shown in Figure 8.55b. Click on the OK button to close this dialog.

8. Go to Insert > Text Box menu item again to insert another TextBox and move it to the right of the picture under the Faculty Name TextBox. Type Faculty ID into this TextBox and use it as the `Faculty ID` label.
9. Go to Insert > Form Control > Textbox menu item to insert a Textbox into this page, and move this Textbox to the right of the `Faculty ID` label.
10. Change this Textbox's name to FacultyIDField as we did in step 7 above.
11. In a similar way, you can finish adding another six Textboxes and the associated labels, as shown in Figure 8.54. Use step 7 above to change these six Textboxes' names to:
    - **A.** NameField
    - **B.** TitleField
    - **C.** OfficeField
    - **D.** PhoneField
    - **E.** CollegeField
    - **F.** EmailField
12. You can use Format > Paragraph > Line spacing > Between lines menu property to modify the vertical distances between each label. In this application, set this distance to 0.6 sp.
13. Go to Insert > Form Control > Submit menu item to insert five buttons at the bottom of this page. In the opened `Command Button Properties` dialog, uncheck the `Button text is same as button type` checkbox, and enter
    - **A.** Select
    - **B.** Insert
    - **C.** Update
    - **D.** Delete
    - **E.** Back

    into the `Button text` field for these five buttons one by one. Click on the OK button to complete these five button creation process.

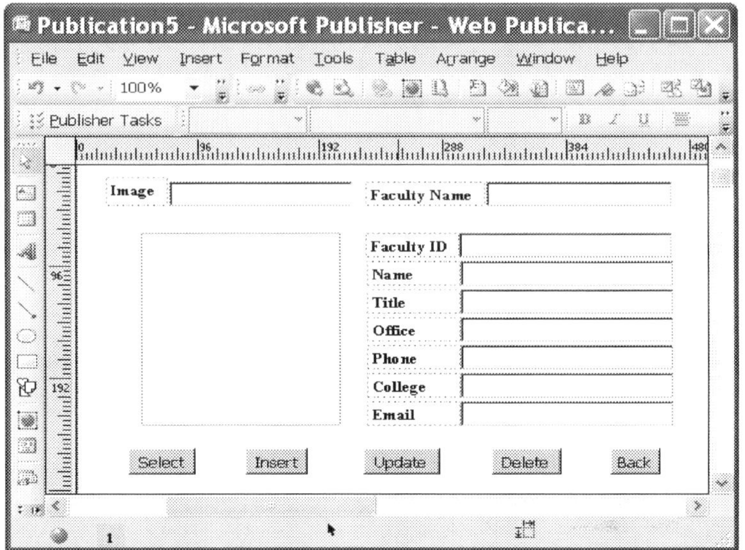

Figure 8.56. The finished Faculty page.

14. Your finished Faculty page in Microsoft Publisher 2007 should match one that is shown in Figure 8.56.
15. Go to File > Save As item to save this page as an HTML file. On the opened `Save As` dialog, select the Web Page, Filtered (*.htm, *.html) from the `Save as type` combo box and enter Faculty.html to the `File name` field. Click on the Save button to save this HTML file to a certain location in your root driver, such as C:\Temp. Click Yes to the message box and OK to the `Form Properties` dialog to complete this saving process.

To convert this HTML page to a JSP page, open the Notepad and perform the following operations:

1. On the opened Notepad, go to File > Open menu item to open the `Open` dialog box. Make sure to select All Files from the `Files of type` combo box at the bottom of this dialog.
2. Browse to the folder where you saved the Faculty.html file, such as C:\Temp, select it and click on the Open button to open this file.
3. Go to File > Save As menu item to open the `Save As` dialog box. Enter "Faculty.jsp" into the `File name` field as the name of this page. The point to be noted is that you must use the double quotation marks to cover this file name to enable the Notepad to save it as a JSP file. Click on the Save button to save this JSP file to your desired folder, such as C:\Temp.
4. Close the Notepad and we have completed creating our Faculty.jsp file.

Next, let's handle to create our Course JSP file.

8.4.3.4 Create the Course Page

The purpose of using this page is to allow users to access and manipulate data in the Course table in our sample database via the Web server, such as course query, new course

Figure 8.57. The preview of the Course page.

insertion, course updating and deleting, based on the selected faculty member from the Faculty Name textbox.

The preview of this Course page is shown in Figure 8.57.

Now let's start to build this page using Microsoft Office Publisher 2007.

Launch Microsoft Office Publisher 2007 and click on the Web Sites icon to open the `Web Sites` wizard. Scroll down to the bottom of this wizard and double click on the Web 984 × 4608px item under the `Blank Sizes` category as the template of this page. Perform the following operations to build this page:

1. Go to Insert > Picture > Clip Art menu item to open the `Clip Art` dialog box. Make sure to select the geometry in the `Search for` field and click on the Go button to display all clip arts related to geometry. Click on the first one and add it into the upper left corner of this page.
2. Go to Insert > Text Box menu item to insert a textbox into this page and enter Faculty Name into this textbox as the `Faculty Name` label.
3. Go to Insert > Form Control > Textbox menu item to insert a Textbox into this page and locate this textbox just to the right of the `Faculty Name` label we added in step 1 above.
4. Right click on this inserted Textbox and select the `Format Form Properties` item to open the `Text Box Properties` dialog. Then enter FacultyNameField into the `Return data with this label` field. Click on the OK button to close this dialog.
5. Go to Insert > Form Control > List Box menu item to add a listbox control. Locate this listbox just under the top label as we did in step 1 above.
6. Right click on the new added listbox and select Format Form Properties item to open `List Box Properties` dialog. Enter CourseList into the `Return data with this label` field as the name of this listbox.

7. In the Appearance list, click on the Remove buttons three times to delete all default items from this list.
8. Right click on the newly added listbox CourseList and select Format Form Properties to open the List Box Properties dialog. Click on the Add button to open the Add/Modify List Box Item dialog box. Enter Course ID into the Item field and check the Selected radio button, and click on the OK button.
9. Go to Insert > Text Box to insert a new TextBox and move it to the right of the listbox. Type Course Name in this TextBox as the Course Name label.
10. Go to Insert > Form Control > Textbox menu item to insert a Textbox into this page and locate this textbox to the right of the Course Name label.
11. Right click on this inserted Textbox and select the Format Form Properties item to open the Text Box Properties dialog. Enter CourseNameField into the Return data with this label field. Click on the OK button to close this dialog.
12. In a similar way, you can finish adding another four Textboxes and the associated labels, as shown in Figure 8.57. Use step 10 above to change these four Textboxes' names to:
    - **A.** ScheduleField
    - **B.** ClassroomField
    - **C.** CreditField
    - **D.** EnrollmentField
13. You can use Format > Paragraph > Line spacing > Between lines menu property to modify the vertical distances between each label. In this application, set this distance to 0.6 sp.
14. Go to Insert > Form Control > Submit menu item to insert five buttons at the bottom of this page. In the opened Command Button Properties dialog, uncheck the Button text is same as button type checkbox, and enter:
    - **A.** Select
    - **B.** Insert
    - **C.** Update
    - **D.** Delete
    - **E.** Back

    into the Button text field for these five buttons one by one. Click on the OK button to complete these five button creation process.
15. Your finished Faculty page in Microsoft Publisher 2007 is shown in Figure 8.58.

To convert this HTML page to a JSP page, open the Notepad and perform the following operations:

1. On the opened Notepad, go to File > Open menu item to open the Open dialog box. Make sure to select All Files from the Files of type combo box at the bottom of this dialog.
2. Browse to the folder where you saved the Course.html file, such as C:\Temp, select it, and click on the Open button to open this file.
3. Go to File > Save As menu item to open the Save As dialog box. Enter "Course.jsp" into the File name field as the name of this page. The point to be noted is that you must use the double quotation marks to cover this file name to enable the Notepad to save it as

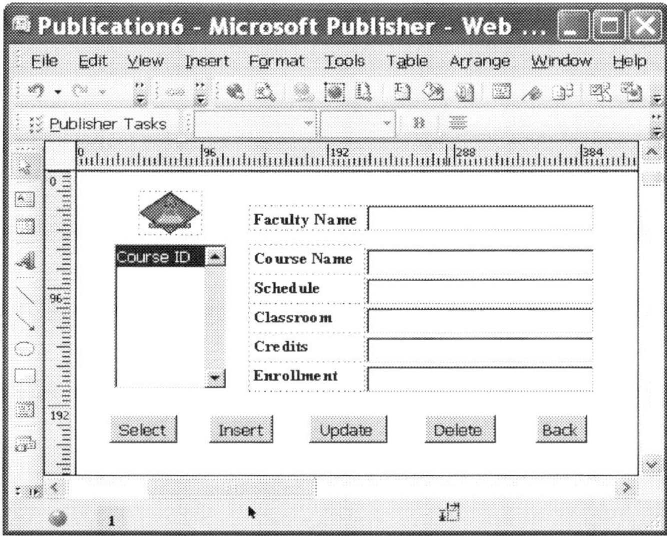

Figure 8.58. The finished Course page.

a JSP file. Click on the Save button to save this JSP file to your desired folder, such as C:\Temp.

4. Close the Notepad and we have completed creating our Course.jsp file.

Next, let's handle to create our last page, Student JSP file.

8.4.3.5 Create the Student Page

Because of the similarity between the Student page and all other pages we discussed above, here we only provide the necessary information for the names of those controls to be added to this page. A preview of this Student page is shown in Figure 8.59.

Table 8.2 lists the name of each control in the Student page.

Refer to discussions we made in the previous sections to build this Student page and convert it to the Student.jsp page.

At this point, we have finished all five web pages design and building process. Next we will begin to coding these web pages and the associated help class or Session object to perform data queries against our database.

8.5 BUILD JAVA WEB PROJECT TO ACCESS SQL SERVER DATABASE

First, let's use JSP and help class file to access and query data from the LogIn table in our sample SQL Server database CSE_DEPT via the LogIn.jsp page we built in Section 8.4.3.1 in this Chapter.

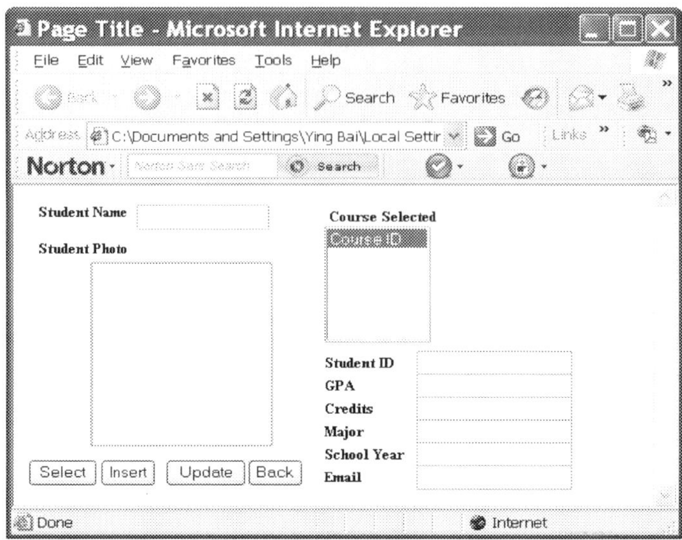

Figure 8.59. The preview of the Student page.

Table 8.2. All controls in the Student page

Control	Name
Student Name Textbox	StudentNameField
Course Selected Listbox	CourseList
The Item in the Course Selected Listbox	Course ID
Student ID Textbox	StudentIDField
GPA Textbox	GPAField
Credits Textbox	CreditField
Major Textbox	MajorField
School Year Textbox	SchoolYearField
Email Textbox	EmailField
Select Button	Select
Insert Button	Insert
Update Button	Update
Back Button	Back

We have provided a very detailed discussion about building and developing Java Web applications using JSP and Java help class file in Sections 8.1.2 and 8.1.3. Now let's follow those discussions to coding the LogIn page and creating the Java help class file LogInQuery.java to perform data query from the LogIn table.

8.5.1 Access and Query the LogIn Table Using JSP and Help Class Files

In Section 8.4.1, we have created a new Java Web application project, JavaWebDBJSPSQL, and added the entity class files into this new project. Now we will use this project to build our database application to perform the data actions against our sample SQL Server database.

First, let's add all five web pages we built in Sections 8.4.3.1–8.4.3.5 into this new project. Perform the following operations to complete this web pages addition process:

1. Launch the Windows Explorer and go to the folder where we stored those five web pages; in this application, it is C:\Temp. Copy all five pages including LogIn.jsp, Selection.jsp, Faculty.jsp, Course.jsp, and Student.jsp, and then paste them to our new Web project folder, which is C:\Chapter 8\JavaWebDBJSPSQL in this application.
2. Launch the NetBeans IDE and open our new Web project JavaWebDBJSPSQL. Click on the Files tab to open the `Files` window and browse to our Web project folder JavaWebDBJSPSQL. You can find that all five web pages have been added into this project. Select all of these five pages using the `Shift` key, right click on these five selected pages, and click on the Copy item from the popup menu.
3. Click on the Projects tab to open the `Projects` window, browse to our project folder and then the Web Pages folder, right click on this folder and select the Paste item to paste these five Web Pages to this Web Pages folder.

Next we need to do a little modification to our LogIn.jsp file and break this file into two JSP files: LogIn.jsp and LogInQuery.jsp. The reason for us to make it into two JSP files is that we want to process and display data in two separate files to make these operations clear and easy.

8.5.1.1 Modify the LogIn.jsp Page and Create LogInQuery.jsp File

Now let's first modify the LogIn.jsp page by double clicking on the LogIn.jsp to open it and perform the following modifications to this page. The modified parts have been highlighted in bold and are shown in Figure 8.60.

Let's have a closer look at these modifications to see how they work.

A. The first modification is to the `form` tag, and an action attribute has been added into this tag. Generally, a `form` tag is used to create a HTML form to collect user information and send all pieces of those collected information to the server when a submit button on this Form is clicked. Therefore, a `form` and all submitting buttons on that `form` have a coordinate relationship. If a button is defined as a submit button by its type attribute, all Form data will be sent to the server whose URL is defined in the action attribute on the `form` tag when this submitting button is clicked by the user. Here we use a Java Server Page, .\LogInQuery.jsp, as the URL for our target page. Exactly this target page is used to access our Java help class file to handle all JDBC- and database-related processing and business logics. The .\ symbol is used to indicate that our next JSP file is located at the relatively current folder, since this page is a part of the server functions and will be run at the server side as the whole project runs.

B. The second modification is to add a name attribute to the LogIn button in order for it to be identified in the server side later.

C. The third modification is to change the type of our Cancel button from submit to button, and add a name and an onclick attribute for this button. The reason for us to do these modifications is that we want to close our LogIn.jsp page when this Cancel button is clicked as the project runs, but we do not want to forward this button-click event to the

```
  <html xmlns:v="urn:schemas-microsoft-com:vml"
  .........
  <body style='margin:0'>
  <div style='position:absolute;width:10.-2040in;height:1.-1423in'>
  <![if !pub]>
A <form method=post action=".\LogInQuery.jsp">
  .........
  <input name=UserNameField maxlength=255 size=21 value="" type=text
   v:shapes="_x0000_s1028">
  .........
  <input name=PassWordField maxlength=255 size=21 value="" type=text
   v:shapes="_x0000_s1029">
  .........
B <input type=submit value=LogIn name="LogInButton" v:shapes="_x0000_s1030">
C <input type=button value=Cancel name="cancelButton" onclick="self.close()" v:shapes="_x0000_s1031">
  .........
  </form>
  </body>
  </html>
```

Figure 8.60. The modifications to the LogIn.jsp page.

server to allow the server to do this close action. Therefore, we have to change the type of this button to button (not submit) to avoid triggering the action attribute in the Form tag. We also need to add a self.close() method to the onclick attribute of this button to call the system close() method to terminate our application. The self means the current page.

Now let's create and build our LogInQuery.jsp page, which works as a part of a server, to receive and handle the Form data, including the login information sent by the LogIn.jsp page. Right click on our project JavaWebDBJSPSQL from the Projects window and select the New > JSP item from the pop-up menu to open the `New JSP File` wizard. If you cannot find the JSP item under the New menu item, go to Other item and select the Web from the `Categories` list, and the JSP item from the `File Types` list. Click on the Next button to open this wizard.

Enter LogInQuery to the `File Name` field in the opened `New JSP File` wizard and keep all other default settings unchanged. Then click on the Finish button to create this JSP file. Enter the codes that are shown in Figure 8.61 into the <body> . . . </body> tags in this page.

Let's have a closer look at this piece of codes to see how it works.

A. A JSP directive tag is used to indicate that this page uses Java language in this JSP page.

B. Some local variables and objects are declared first. The string variable nextPage is used to hold the URL of the next page, and the lquery is a new instance of our Java help class LogInQuery.java we will build in the next section.

C. The getParameter() method is used to pick up the login information entered by the user in the LogIn.jsp page. The collected login information, including the username and password, is assigned to two local string variables u_name and p_word, respectively.

```
  <html>
    <head>
      <meta http-equiv="Content-Type" content="text/html; charset=UTF-8">
      <title>LogIn Query Page</title>
    </head>
    <body>
A   <%@page language="java" %>
    <%
B     String nextPage = null;
      LogInQuery lquery = new LogInQuery();
C     String u_name = request.getParameter("UserNameField");
      String p_word = request.getParameter("PassWordField");
D     String result = lquery.checkLogIn(u_name, p_word);
E     if (result.equals("Matched"))
         nextPage = "Selection.jsp";
F     else
         out.println("LogIn is failed");
G     lquery.CloseDBConnection();
    %>
H   <jsp:forward page = "<%=nextPage%>" />
    </body>
  </html>
```

Figure 8.61. The codes for the LogInQuery.jsp page.

D. The checkLogIn() method defined in our Java help class file is called to perform the database query and the login matching processing. The collected login information is used as arguments and passed into this method. The running result of this method is a string, and it is assigned to the local string variable result.

E. An if block is used to check the running result of the checkLogIn() method. The program will be directed to a successful page (Selection.jsp) if a matched login record is found.

F. Otherwise, an error message is printed out to indicate that this login process has failed.

G. The CloseDBConnection() method defined in the help class is called to disconnect the connection to our sample database.

H. A JSP forward directive is used to direct the program to the next page.

Next, let's create and build our Java help class file LogInQuery.java to perform JDBC- and database-related operations and actions.

8.5.1.2 Create the Java Help Class File LogInQuery.java

The purpose of this help class file is to handle the JDBC-related operations and database-related actions. As we discussed in Section 8.1.3, to distinguish between the database-related data processing and running results displaying, we can separate a Java Web application into two parts: the JDBC-related database processing and the business logics, such as checking and confirming a pair of matched username and password located at a Java help class file, and the data and running results displaying at a Web or a JavaServer page.

It looks like that we can use the Java Persistence API to perform the database accessing and query to our LogIn table. However, because the Java Persistence API can only be implemented in a limited number of Java EE containers that provide the Resource Injection function, we cannot inject the Java persistence API into our normal Java help class file. Therefore, in this part, we have to use the Java runtime object method to perform database-related actions to check matched username and password from the LogIn table in our sample database. We can include these database related actions into this Java help class file.

Right click on our project JavaWebDBJSPSQL from the Projects window and select the New > Java Class item from the popup menu to open the `New Java Class` wizard. If you cannot find the Java Class item under the New menu item, go to Other item and select the Java item from the `Categories` list, and the Java Class item from the `File Types` list. Click on the Next button to open this wizard. On the opened wizard, enter LogInQuery into the `Class Name` field and select JavaWebDBJSPSQLPackage from the `Package` combo box, as shown in Figure 8.62. Click on the Finish button to create this help class file.

Before we can do the coding for this help class, we need first to create a dialog box in this project. This dialog box works as a message box to provide possible debug information during the project runs.

8.5.1.3 Create a Dialog Box as the Message Box

To create a new dialog box form window, perform the following operations:

1. Right click on our project JavaWebDBJSPSQL from the Projects window and select the New > Other item from the pop-up menu to open the `New File` wizard. Select the AWT GUI Forms from the `Categories` list and OK/Cancel Dialog Sample Form item from the `File Types` list. Click on the Next button to open a new dialog box form.

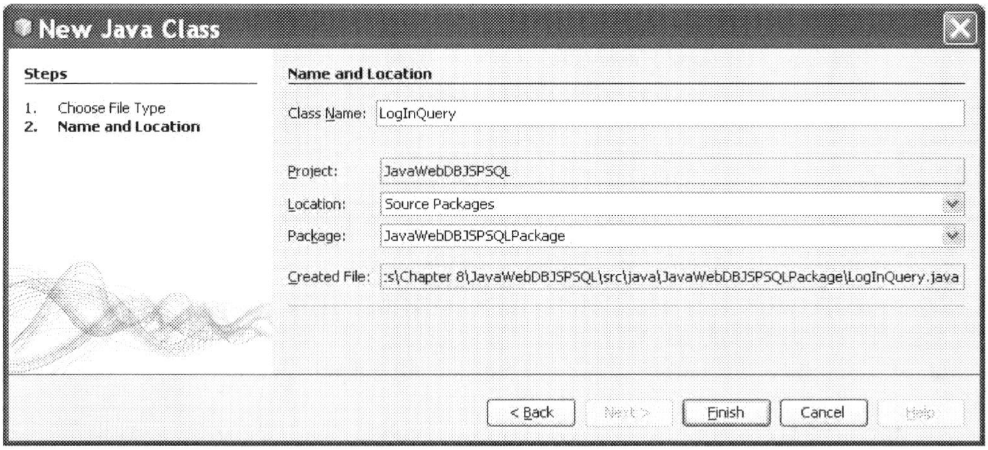

Figure 8.62. The completed New Java Class wizard.

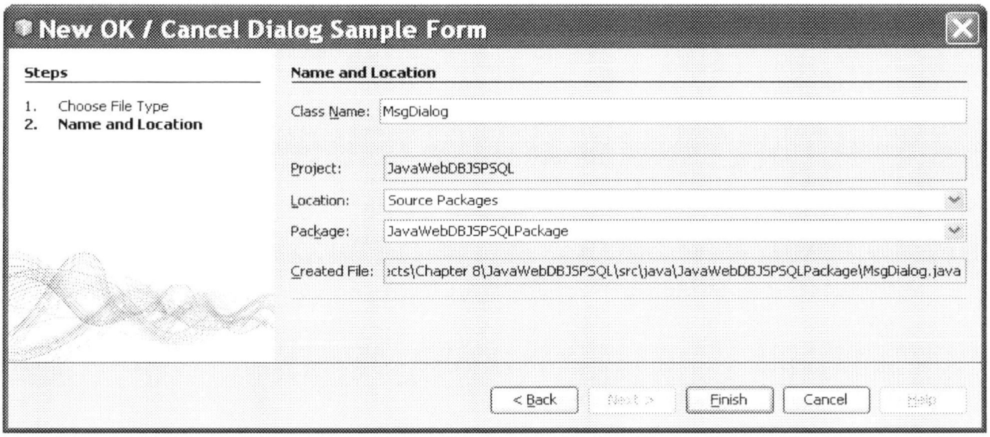

Figure 8.63. The finished New OK/Cancel Dialog Form wizard.

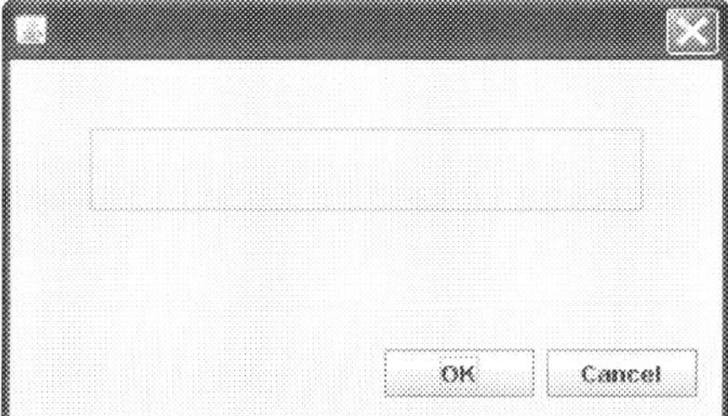

Figure 8.64. The preview of the dialog box.

2. Enter MsgDialog into the `Class Name` field and select the JavaWebDBJSPSQLPackage from the `Package` field. Your finished `New OK/Cancel Dialog Sample Form` wizard should match one that is shown in Figure 8.63. Click on the Finish button to create this new dialog box.
3. A new Java dialog box class file MsgDialog.java is created and located under the JavaWebDBJSPSQLPackage folder in the Projects window. Click on the Design button to open its dialog form window. Add a label to this dialog form window by dragging a Label control from the Palette window, exactly from the AWT subwindow, and placing it to the dialog form window.
4. Resize this label to an appropriate size, as shown in Figure 8.64. Right click on this label and select the Change Variable Name item from the pop-up menu to open the `Rename` dialog. Enter MsgLabel into the `New Name` field and click on the OK button.
5. Go to the text property and remove the default text label1 for this label.

Now click on the Source button to open the code window for this dialog box, and we need to add some codes to this class to enable it to display some necessary messages as the project runs.

```
public MsgDialog(java.awt.Frame parent, boolean modal) {
      super(parent, modal);
      initComponents();
      this.setLocationRelativeTo(null);
 }
public void setMessage(String  msg){
    MsgLabel.setText(msg);
}
```

Figure 8.65. The added codes to the MsgDialog.java class.

On the opened code window, add the codes that are highlighted in bold and shown in Figure 8.65.

The setLocationRelativeTo(null) instruction is used to set this dialog box at the center of the screen as the project runs. The method setMessage() is used to set up a user message by calling the setText() method.

Now we have finished creating and building our dialog box form, and let's begin to do the coding for our help class file.

8.5.1.4 Develop the Codes for the Help Class File

Double click on this help class LogInQuery.java from the Projects window to open its code window. Perform the following operations to complete the coding process for this class:

1. Import the SQL Server related package and create the constructor of this class.
2. Build the codes for the checkLogIn() method to access and query the LogIn table.
3. Build the codes for the CloseDBConnection() method to close the connection to our sample database when this login query is complete.

Let's do these one by one.

8.5.1.4.1 Import SQL Server Related Package and Create the Class Constructor Since we need to query our sample SQL Server database, therefore, we need to import the SQL Server-related package. The class constructor is used to build a valid connection to our sample database. The detailed codes are shown in Figure 8.66.

Let's have a closer look at this piece of codes to see how it works.

A. The JDBC SQL Server-related package is imported first since we need to use some JDBC classes defined in that package.

B. Some attributes or properties of this help class are defined first inside this class, which include two private String properties user_name and pass_word, a class-level connection variable con, and a dialog box that is used to display some debug information.

C. Inside the class constructor, a try….catch block is used to load the JDBC SQL Server driver, which is a type IV JDBC driver. Refer to Section 6.2.1.2.4 in Chapter 6 to get more detailed information about this driver name.

D. The catch block is used to collect any possible exceptions occurred during this driver loading process.

```
  package JavaWebDBJSPSQLPackage;
A import java.sql.*;
  public class LogInQuery {
B    private String user_name = null;
     private String pass_word = null;
     static Connection con;
     MsgDialog msgDlg = new MsgDialog(new javax.swing.JFrame(), true);
     public LogInQuery() {
C      try {
           Class.forName("com.microsoft.sqlserver.jdbc.SQLServerDriver");
        }
D       catch (Exception e) {
           msgDlg.setMessage("Class not found exception!" + e.getMessage());
           msgDlg.setVisible(true);
        }
E       String url = "jdbc:sqlserver://localhost\\SQL2008EXPRESS:5000;databaseName=CSE_DEPT;";
F       try {
           con = DriverManager.getConnection(url,"ybai","reback1956");
        }
G       catch (SQLException e) {
           msgDlg.setMessage("Could not connect!" + e.getMessage());
           msgDlg.setVisible(true);
           e.printStackTrace();
        }
     }
     .........
```

Figure 8.66. The codes of the class constructor.

E. The JDBC SQL Server URL is assigned to the local variable url. Refer to Section 6.2.1.2.4 in Chapter 6 to get more detailed information about this URL.

F. The getConnection() method that is embedded in a try block is executed to establish this database connection.

G. The catch block is used to collect any possible exceptions occurred during this database connection process.

Now let's build the codes for the checkLogIn() method to try to query the LogIn table to find a match username and password pair.

8.5.1.4.2 Build the Codes for the checkLogIn() Method The function of this method is to query the LogIn table in our sample database to try to find a matched username and password pair based on the username and password entered by the user from the LogIn.jsp page. A "Matched" string will be returned to the LogInQuery.jsp page if a matched username and password pair is found. Otherwise, an "Unmatched" string is returned. Based on this returned string, the LogInQuery.jsp will determine the next page to be opened. If a matched pair has been found, the Selection.jsp page will be displayed to allow users to select different information item to access and query different table in our sample database. Otherwise, an error message will be displayed to indicate that this login process has failed, since no matched login information can be found from our sample database.

In the opened code window of the help class LogInQuery.java, enter the codes that are shown in Figure 8.67 under the class constructor and make it the body of our checkLogIn() method.

```
  public String checkLogIn(String uname, String pword) {
A     String query = "SELECT user_name, pass_word FROM LogIn " +
                     "WHERE user_name = ? AND pass_word = ?";
      try{
B         PreparedStatement pstmt = con.prepareStatement(query);
C         pstmt.setString(1, uname);
          pstmt.setString(2, pword);

D         ResultSet rs = pstmt.executeQuery();
E         while (rs.next()){
             user_name = rs.getString(1);
             pass_word = rs.getString(2);
          }
      }
F     catch (SQLException e) {
         msgDlg.setMessage("Error in Statement! " + e.getMessage());
         msgDlg.setVisible(true);
      }
G     if (user_name.equals(uname) && pass_word.equals(pword))
         return "Matched";
H     else
         return "Nomatched";
  }
```

Figure 8.67. The codes for the checkLogIn() method.

Let's have a closer look at this piece of codes to see how it works.

A. The query string, which is a standard SQL statement, is created first with the actual column names as the query columns. The positional parameters are used for both username and password dynamic inputs.

B. Starting from a try block, the prepareStatement() method is called to create a PreparedStatement object pstmt.

C. The setter method is used to set two positional parameters in the positional order.

D. The executeQuery() method is executed to perform this query and the returned result is assigned to the ResultSet object rs.

E. A while loop is used to pick up any possible matched username and password. In fact, only one row is returned, and therefore this loop can run only one time. The getString() method is used to pick up the queried username and password. The retuned username and password are assigned to two properties, user_name and pass_word, respectively.

F. The catch block is used to collect any possible exceptions occurred during this database query process.

G. If a matched username/password pair is found, a "Matched" string will be returned to the LogInQuery.jsp page.

H. Otherwise, an "Unmatched" string is returned to indicate that this login query has failed.

Next, let's build the codes for the CloseDBConnection() method.

8.5.1.4.3 Build the Codes for the CloseDBConnection() Method This method is necessary when a data query is finished and no more data actions are needed for a database application. A possible running error may be encountered if one did not disconnect the established connection to a target database and exit the project.

```
    public void CloseDBConnection()
    {
A       try{
          if (!con.isClosed())
             con.close();
B       }catch (SQLException e) {
          msgDlg.setMessage("Error in close the DB! " + e.getMessage());
          msgDlg.setVisible(true);
        }
    }
```

Figure 8.68. The codes for the CloseDBConnection() method.

On the opened code window of the help class LogInQuery.java, enter the codes that are shown in Figure 8.68 under the checkLogIn() method to create our CloseDBConnection() method.

Let's have a closer look at this piece of codes to see how it works.

A. A try block is used to handle this database disconnection function. First we need to check whether a valid connection object exists, which means that the database is still being connected. The isClosed() method is executed to do this checking. A `false` will be returned if a valid connection object exists, which means that the database is still being connected. In that case, the close() method is called to disconnect this connection.

B. The catch block is sued to collect any possible exceptions occurred during this disconnection process.

Now we have finished all coding development for this login process. Before we can build and run our Web application project to test the login function using the LogIn.jsp and help class files, we need to first add the JDBC SQL Server driver into our project.

8.5.1.5 Add the JDBC Driver for the SQL Server Database into the Project

To enable our Java Web application project to load and connect to our sample SQL Server 2008 database, CSE_DEPT, which we built in Chapter 2, we need to:

1. Download this driver from the site http://msdn.microsoft.com/data/jdbc/
2. Configure the TCP/IP protocol and setup for the SQL server
3. Set up a SQL Server database connection using NetBeans 6.8 IDE
4. Add the JDBC SQL Server driver into our Web application project

Refer to Section 6.2.1.2 in Chapter 6 to complete the top three steps. Now let's perform the fourth step to add this JDBC driver into our project.

When we finished downloading this JDBC driver sqljdbc4.jar, the default location of this driver is at: C:\Program Files\Microsoft SQL Server JDBC Driver 2.0\sqljdbc_2.0\enu. To add this JDBC driver to our project, right click on our Web project JavaWebDBJSPSQL from the Projects window and select the `Properties` item from the pop-up menu. On the opened `Project Properties` dialog, select the Libraries item from the `Categories` list. Then click on the Add JAR/Folder button to open the `Add JAR/Folder` dialog, as shown in Figure 8.69.

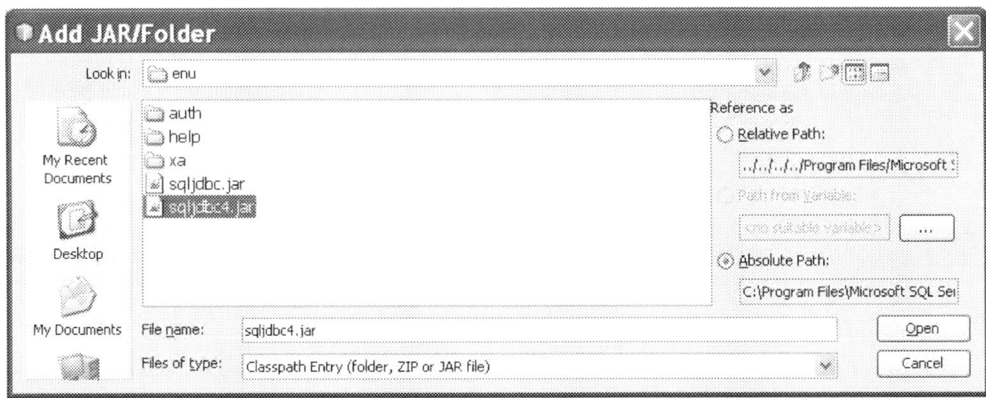

Figure 8.69. The opened Add JAR/Folder dialog box.

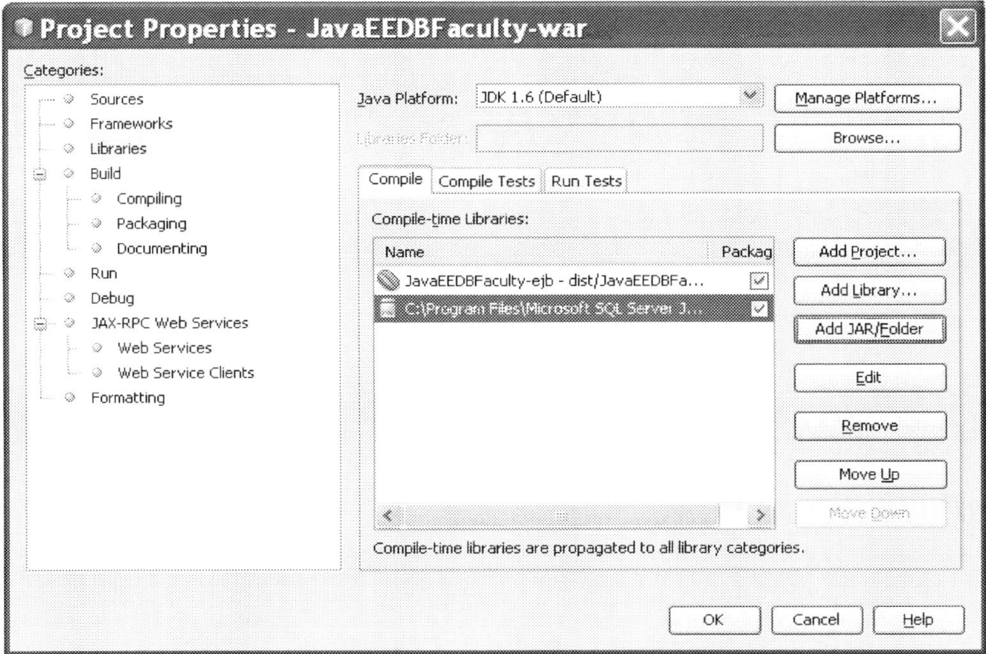

Figure 8.70. The finished Project Properties dialog box.

Click on the drop-down arrow in the `Look in` combo box and browse to the location where our downloaded JDBC driver sqljdbc4.jar is located, which is C:\Program Files\Microsoft SQL Server JDBC Driver 2.0lsqljdbc_2.0lenu. Then select this driver and click on the Open button. Your finished `Project Properties` dialog box should match one that is shown in Figure 8.70.

Click on the OK button to complete this JDBC driver adding process. Now we are ready to build and run our Web project to test the login function using the LogIn.jsp, LogInQuery.jsp, nd the help class file LogInQuery.java.

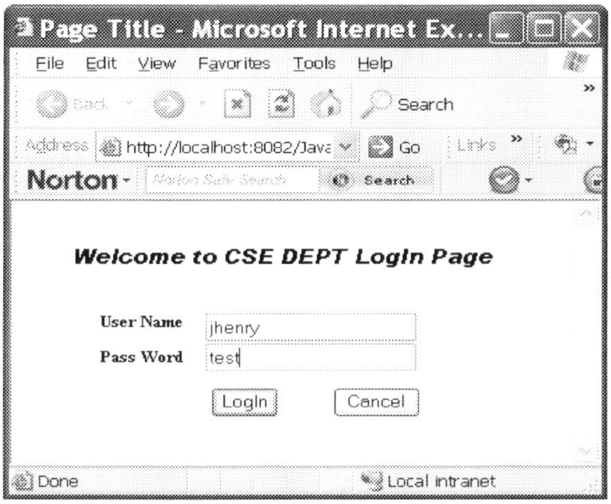

Figure 8.71. The displayed LogIn.jsp page.

Click on the Clean and Build Main Project button to build our project. Then right click on the LogIn.jsp file from the Projects window and select Compile File item from the pop-up menu to compile our web pages. Right click on the LogIn.jsp page again and select the Run File item from the popup menu to run our project. If the HTTP Port of the GlassFish server 8080 has been occupied and the page cannot be opened, refer to Appendix I to fix this Port number.

Enter `admin` and `reback` as the username and password to the Java Glassfish v3 Server to log in and start this Web server. Recall that we used these login data when we installed the Java Glassfish v3 Server in Section 5.3.5.2.1. Refer to that section to get more details for these login data. If the HTTP Port 8080 has been occupied and the browser cannot open the page, change the Port number to 8082 in the Address box in the Web page.

As the LogIn.jsp is displayed, enter a valid username and password, such as `jhenry` and `test`, into the associated fields, as shown in Figure 8.71.

Click on the LogIn button to call the checkLogIn() method to perform the login query to find a matched username and password pair. The Selection.jsp page is displayed to indicate that this login process is successful, and a matched username and password has been found, as shown in Figure 8.72.

Our login process using the JSP and help class file is successful.

Next, let's build and code for the Selection.jsp page. As we mentioned, this page can be considered as the control page, and it will direct users to the different pages to perform the different database query functions based on the users' choices.

8.5.2 Build the Selection Page

To handle the users' input and direct to the different target pages based on the users' input, we still want to use the MVC mode to build this page. We can use the Selection.jsp page as a `view` to display the input and output, and create another JSP page

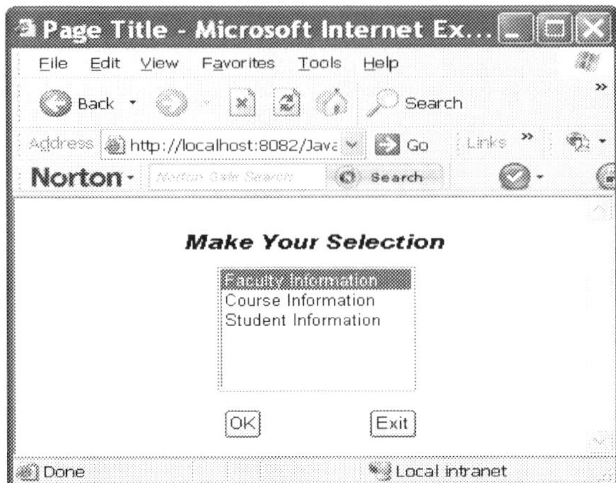

Figure 8.72. The successful page—Selection.jsp page.

```
  .........
  <div style='position:absolute;width:10.-2040in;height:2.047in'>
  <![if !pub]>
A <form method=post action=".\SelectionProcess.jsp">
  .........
  <input type=submit value=OK v:shapes="_x0000_s1028">
  .........
B <input type=button value=Exit onclick="self.close()"  v:shapes="_x0000_s1029">
  <![if !pub]></span><![endif]><![if !pub]>
  </form>
  .........
```

Figure 8.73. The coding modifications to the Selection.jsp page.

SelectionProcess.jsp as the `model` and `controller` to process the users' input and direct to the target page.

Of course, you can combine the MVC mode together to perform displaying and processing page at a single JSP page file. However, you need to add a hidden field to the page and use that hidden field as an identifier to indicate whether the page has been submitted or not. That will make the Selection.jsp page complex in the coding process.

We divide this page-building process into two steps: modify the Selection.jsp page and create the SelectionProcess.jsp page.

Let's first perform some necessary modifications to the Selection.jsp page.

Launch the NetBeans IDE and open the Selection.jsp page by double clicking on it from the Projects window, and perform the modifications shown in Figure 8.73 to this page. All modifications have been highlighted in bold.

Let's have a closer look at these modifications to see how they work.

A. An action attribute is added to the `Form` tag and the destination of this action is the SelectionProcess.jsp page. The '.\' operator is used to indicate to the Web controller that the next page, SelectionProcess.jsp, is located at the current folder.

B. The type of the second button, Exit, is changed from the submit to the button since we do not want to submit any form data to the next page when this button is clicked. Instead, we want a system method, self.close(), to be executed as this button is clicked to exit our project. Therefore an onclick attribute is used to direct the control to this method when this button is clicked.

Now, let's create the selection process page SelectionProcess.jsp.

Open our project JavaWebDBJSPSQL from the Projects window. Perform the following operations to create this page:

1. Right click on our project JavaWebDBJSPSQL from the Projects window and select the New > JSP item from the pop-up menu. If you cannot find the JSP item from the pop-up menu, go to the Other item to open the `New File` wizard. Select the Web from the `Categories` list and JSP from the File Types list to do this.
2. On the opened `New JSP File` wizard, enter SelectionProcess into the `File Name` field and click on the Finish button.

Now let's do the coding for this page. Double click on our newly created page SelectionProcess.jsp from the Projects window to open its code window. On the opened code window, perform the modifications shown in Figure 8.74 to this page. All modification parts have been highlighted in bold.

Let's have a closer look at this piece of codes to see how it works.

A. A JSP directive tag is used to indicate that this page uses the Java language and it is a JSP file.

B. A local string variable nextPage is declared first. This variable is used to hold the URL of the next page, which we will use later to direct the control to the associated page.

C. The getParameter() method is used to pick up the selected item by the user from the selection list in the Selection.jsp page. The argument of the getParameter() method is the name of the selection list in the Selection.jsp page. The selected item is then assigned to another local string variable userSel.

```
        <meta http-equiv="Content-Type" content="text/html; charset=UTF-8">
        <title>Selection Process Page</title>
      </head>
      <body>
A      <%@page language="java" %>
       <%
B        String nextPage = null;
C        String userSel = request.getParameter("ListSelection");
D        if (userSel.equals("Faculty Information"))
            nextPage = "Faculty.jsp";
         else if (userSel.equals("Course Information"))
            nextPage = "Course.jsp";
         else
            nextPage = "Student.jsp";
       %>
E      <jsp:forward  page = "<%=nextPage%>" />
      </body>
    </html>
```

Figure 8.74. The codes for the SelectionProcess.jsp page.

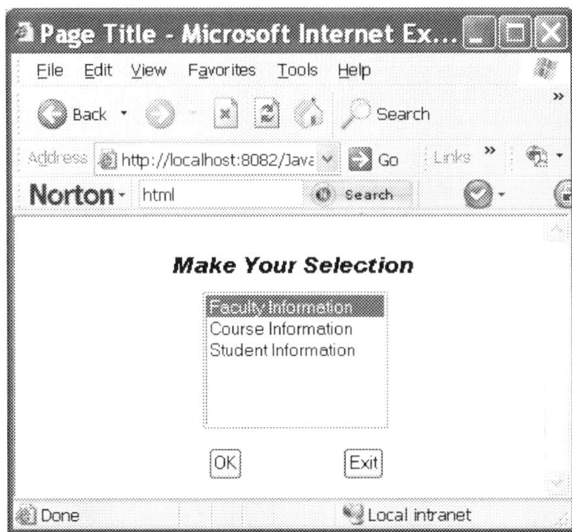

Figure 8.75. The running status of the Selection.jsp page.

D. An if selection structure is used to check the user's selection and assign the associated next page to the local variable nextPage.

E. Finally, a JSP forward directive is used to direct the program to the next page.

Now we can build and run this page to test its function.

Click on the Clean and Build Main Project button to compile and build our project. Then right click on the Selection.jsp page from the Projects window and select the `Run File` item from the pop-up menu to run the project. The Selection.jsp is displayed, as shown in Figure 8.75, when the project runs.

Select a desired item, such as `Faculty Information`, from the Selection listbox, and click on the OK button. You can find that the Faculty.jsp page is displayed. You can try to select other item from the listbox to open other related pages.

Click on the Exit button to terminate our project.

Our Selection page is successful!

8.5.3 Query the Faculty Table Using JSP and JSP Implicit Session Object

In this section, we will discuss how to access and query data from the Faculty table in our sample database using the JSP and JSP implicit session object.

In Section 8.1.5, we have provided a detailed discussion about how to use the JSP implicit session object to query our Faculty table. In this part, we will build a real project to perform this data query using this object. We divide this discussion into the following three parts:

1. Modify the Faculty.jsp page and use it as a view.
2. Create a new FacultyProcess.jsp page and use it as a model and controller page.

3. Create a help class file FacultyQuery.java to handle data query and related business logics.

First let's modify our view class, Fcaulty.jsp page.

8.5.3.1 Modify the Faculty.jsp Page

The Faculty.jsp page works as a view to provide the displaying function for input and output. We need to modify this page to enable it to forward the user's inputs to the model and controller page, and furthermore, to call the help class to process our data query. Also, the page needs to return to the Selection.jsp page if the user clicks on the Back button on this page.

Open this page by double clicking on it from the Projects window, and perform the modifications shown in Figure 8.76 to this page. All modified coding parts have been highlighted in bold.

```
A  <form method=post action=".\FacultyProcess.jsp">
   .........
B  <v:imagedata src="<%=session.getAttribute("facultyImage") %>" o:title="&lt;EMPTY&gt;"/>
    <v:shadow color="#ccc [4]"/>
   .........
   <input name=FacultyNameField maxlength=255 size=18
C   value="<%=session.getAttribute("facultyName") %>" type=text v:shapes="_x0000_s1029">
   .........
   <input name=FacultyIDField maxlength=255 size=21
D   value="<%=session.getAttribute("facultyId") %>" type=text v:shapes="_x0000_s1031">
   .........
   <input name=NameField maxlength=255 size=21
E   value="<%=session.getAttribute("facultyName") %>" type=text v:shapes="_x0000_s1033">
   .........
   <input name=TitleField maxlength=255 size=21
F   value="<%=session.getAttribute("title") %>" type=text v:shapes="_x0000_s1035">
   .........
   <input name=OfficeField maxlength=255 size=21
G   value="<%=session.getAttribute("office") %>" type=text v:shapes="_x0000_s1037">
   .........
   <input name=PhoneField maxlength=255 size=21
H   value="<%=session.getAttribute("phone") %>" type=text v:shapes="_x0000_s1039">
   .........
   <input name=CollegeField maxlength=255 size=21
I   value="<%=session.getAttribute("college") %>" type=text v:shapes="_x0000_s1041">
   .........
   <input name=EmailField maxlength=255 size=21
J   value="<%=session.getAttribute("email") %>" type=text v:shapes="_x0000_s1043">
   .........
K  <input type=submit value=Select name="Select" v:shapes="_x0000_s1044">
   .........
L  <input type=submit value=Insert name="Insert" v:shapes="_x0000_s1045">
   .........
M  <input type=submit value=Update name="Update" v:shapes="_x0000_s1046">
   .........
N  <input type=submit value=Delete name="Delete" v:shapes="_x0000_s1047">
   .........
O  <input type=submit value=Back name="Back" v:shapes="_x0000_s1048">
   .........
```

Figure 8.76. The modified codes for the Faculty.jsp page.

Let's have a closer look at this piece of modified codes to see how it works.

A. An `action` attribute is added to the Form tag to forward all information collected from this page to the model and controller page FcaultyProcess.jsp that will call our help class file FacultyQuery.java to perform the faculty data query process.

B. Starting from step **B** until step **J**, we use the embedded JSP codes to assign the selected faculty image and queried faculty columns from our Faculty table to the `src` and the `value` tags of the associated text field in the Facultypage.jsp using the getAttribute() method of the session class. In this way, as long as the queried faculty row has any change, this modification will be immediately updated and reflected to each text field in our Faculty.jsp page. In this way, a direct connection or binding between the text fields in our Faculty.jsp page and the queried Faculty columns in our help class is established.

K. From steps **K** to **O**, a `name` attribute is added into each Submit button tag. This attribute is very important since we need to use it to identify each submit button in the next page, our model and controller page, FacultyProcess.jsp, using the getParameter() method of the `request` object to direct the control to the different pages to handle different data query and data manipulation actions to the Faculty table in our sample SQL Server database CSE_DEPT.

In order to select the correct faculty image based on the faculty member selected by the user, we need to assign the session.getAttribute() method to the `src` attribute of the `imagedata` tag. The argument of this method should be defined as a property in our help class file, and a method, getFacultyImage() defined in that help class file, will be used to select the appropriate faculty image and assign it to this property.

Now let's take a look at our model and controller page FacultyProcess.jsp.

8.5.3.2 Create the FacultyProcess.jsp Page

The purpose of this page is to direct the control to the different help class files based on the button clicked by the user from the Faculty.jsp page. The following help class files will be triggered and executed based on the button clicked by the user from the Faculty.jsp page:

1. If the user selected and clicked the Select button, the control will be directed to the faculty data query help class file FacultyQuery.java to perform the faculty record query function.
2. If the user clicked the Insert button, the control will be directed to the faculty data insertion help class file FacultyInsert.java to do the faculty record insertion.
3. If the user clicked the Update or Delete button, the control will be directed to the faculty record updating help class file FacultyUpdate.java, or the faculty record deleting help class file FacultyDelete.java to perform the associated data manipulations.
4. If the user selected and clicked the Back button, the control will be returned to the Selection.jsp page to enable users to perform other information query operations.

Now let's create this FacultyProcess.jsp page.

Right click on our project JavaWebDBJSPSQL from the Projects window and select the New > JSP item from the pop-up menu to open the `New JSP File` wizard. Enter FacultyProcess into the `File Name` field and click on the Finish button.

Double click on our newly created FacultyProcess.jsp page from the Projects window, exactly under the Web Pages folder, to open this page. Enter the codes shown in Figure 8.77 into this page. The newly entered codes have been highlighted in bold.

Now let's have a close look at these codes to see how they work.

A. You can embed any import directory using the JSP directive in a HTML or a JSP file. The format is <%@ page import="java package" %>. In this page, we embed one package, JavaWebDBJSPSQLPackage.*, since we will build our Java help class file FacultyQuery.java in that package in the next section.

B. A new instance of our help class `FacultyQuery` that will be created in the next section, fQuery, is created, since we need to use properties and methods defined in that class to perform faculty record query and faculty image selection functions.

C. The getParameter() method defined in the session class is executed to identify which submit button has been clicked by the user in the Faculty.jsp page. As you know, in total, we have five buttons in the Faculty.jsp page. All Faculty.jsp form data, including all text fields, image box, and submit buttons, will be submitted to this FacultyProcess.jsp page when any of five buttons is clicked. If a button is clicked, the getParameter() method with the name of that clicked button as the argument of this method will return a non-null value. In this way, we can identify which button has been clicked. We use a sequence of `if ... else if` selection structures to check all five buttons to identify the clicked button.

D. If the Select button is clicked by the user, the getParameter() method with this button's name as argument will return a non-null value. This means that the user wants to perform a faculty record query from the Faculty table in our sample database. Again, the getParameter() method with the name of the faculty name field, FacultyNameField, is used to pick up a desired faculty name that is entered by the user from the Faculty.jsp page. The picked up faculty name is assigned to a local String variable fname.

E. Then the method QueryFaculty() defined in the help class file FacultyQuery.java will be called to execute this faculty data query based on the selected faculty name fname obtained from step **D** above.

F. If the QueryFaculty() method is executed unsuccessfully, which means that no matched faculty record has been found, a false is returned to indicate this situation. In this case, we need to reopen the Faculty.jsp page to enable the user to reenter new faculty data to do another query using the sendRedirect() method defined in the `response` class.

G. Otherwise, a matched faculty record has been found and the query is successful. The setAttribute() method defined in the session class is used to set up all properties defined in the help class file using the associated getter methods in that class.

H. The getFacultyImage() method, which is defined in the help class file FacultyQuery.java and will be developed in the next section, is executed to pick up the correct faculty image file, exactly the correct name of the faculty image file.

I. If the getFacultyImage() method returns a null, which means that no matched faculty image has been found. Then we will continue to check whether the user has entered a new faculty image in the `FacultyImageField` textbox in the Faculty.jsp page, and this is a normal case if the user wants to insert a new faculty record into the Faculty table with a new faculty image. If the getParameter() method returns a non-null value, which means that the user did enter a new faculty image, exactly the name of a new faculty image, into that field. In that case, we need to set up the `facultyImage` property with that name and later on display that new faculty image based on that property.

```
A  <%@ page  import="JavaWebDBJSPSQLPackage.*" %>
   <html>
      <head>
         <meta http-equiv="Content-Type" content="text/html; charset=UTF-8">
         <title>Faculty Process Page</title>
      </head>
      <body>
       <%
B       FacultyQuery fQuery = new FacultyQuery();
C       if (request.getParameter("Select")!= null) {
           //process the faculty record query
D          String fname = request.getParameter("FacultyNameField");
E          boolean res = fQuery.QueryFaculty(fname);
F          if (!res)
              response.sendRedirect("Faculty.jsp");
G          else {
              session.setAttribute("facultyId", fQuery.getFacultyID());
              session.setAttribute("facultyName", fQuery.getFacultyName());
              session.setAttribute("office", fQuery.getOffice());
              session.setAttribute("title", fQuery.getTitle());
              session.setAttribute("college", fQuery.getCollege());
              session.setAttribute("phone", fQuery.getPhone());
              session.setAttribute("email", fQuery.getEmail());
           }
H          String fimg = fQuery.getFacultyImage();
I          if (fimg == null) {
              if (request.getParameter("FacultyImageField")!= null)
                 session.setAttribute("facultyImage", request.getParameter("FacultyImageField"));
J             else
              session.setAttribute("facultyImage", "Default.jpg");
              }
K          else
              session.setAttribute("facultyImage", fimg);
L          fQuery.setFacultyImage(null);
M          response.sendRedirect("Faculty.jsp");
           }
N       else if (request.getParameter("Insert")!= null) {
           //process the faculty record insertion
           }
O       else if (request.getParameter("Update")!= null) {
           //process the faculty record updating
           }
P       else if (request.getParameter("Delete")!= null) {
           //process the faculty record deleting
           }
Q       else if (request.getParameter("Back") != null) {
           fQuery.CloseDBConnection();
           response.sendRedirect("Selection.jsp");
           }
       %>
      </body>
   </html>
```

Figure 8.77. The codes for the FacultyProcess.jsp page.

J. Otherwise, it means that no matched faculty image has been found, and the user did not want to enter a new faculty image. In that case, we need to display a default faculty image by assigning the name of that default faculty image to the `facultyImage` property.

K. If the getFacultyImage() method returns a non-null value, which means that a matched faculty image's name has been found, the setAttribute() method is executed to set up the `facultyImage` property with that faculty image's name.

L. The setFacultyImage() method is executed to clean up the content of the property of the help class, facultyImage, which is a static String variable and works as a global variable to store the current faculty image's name. When a new faculty image is inserted or updated with a faculty record insertion or updating, the name of that new faculty image will be assigned to the global variable facultyImage. To avoid displaying the same new faculty image in multiple times, we need to clean up this global variable each time when a faculty record has been retrieved and displayed.

M. The sendRedirect() method defined in the `response` class is executed to redisplay the Fcaulty.jsp page with the queried result on that page.

N. If the getParameter("Insert") method returns a non-null value, which means that the Insert button has been clicked by the user in the Faculty.jsp page, and the user wants to insert a new faculty record into the Faculty table in our sample database. We will build a Java bean class to handle this faculty data insertion later.

O. Similarly, if the getParameter("Update") method returns a non-null value, which means that the Update button has been clicked by the user in the Faculty.jsp page, and the user wants to update an existing faculty record in the Faculty table in our sample database. We will build a Java bean class to handle this faculty data updating action later.

P. If the getParameter("Delete") method returns a non-null value, which means that the Delete button has been clicked by the user in the Faculty.jsp page, and the user wants to delete an existing faculty record from the Faculty table in our sample database. We will build a Java bean class to handle this faculty data deleting action later.

Q. If the getParameter("Back") method returns a non-null value, which means that the Back button has been clicked by the user in the Faculty.jsp page, and the user wants to return to the Selection.jsp page to perform other data query operations. The CloseDBConnection() method is first executed to close the connection to our sample database, and then the sendRedirect() method is called to do this returning function.

Now let's build our Java help class file FacultyQuery.java to handle all data query actions, getter methods, class properties, and related business logics.

8.5.3.3 Create the Help Class File FacultyQuery.java

To create our Java help class file FacultyQuery.java to handle the faculty record query, right click on our project JavaWebDBJSPSQL from the Projects window and select the New > Java Class item from the pop-up menu to open the `New Java Class` wizard. Enter FacultyQuery into the `Class Name` field and select the JavaWebDBJSPSQLPackage from the `Package` combo box. Your finished `New Java Class` wizard should match one that is shown in Figure 8.78. Click on the Finish button to create this new Java help class file.

Now let's develop the codes for this new Java help class file. Double click on our new created Java help class file FacultyQuery.java from the Projects window to open this file, and enter the codes that are shown in Figure 8.79 into this file. Because of the large

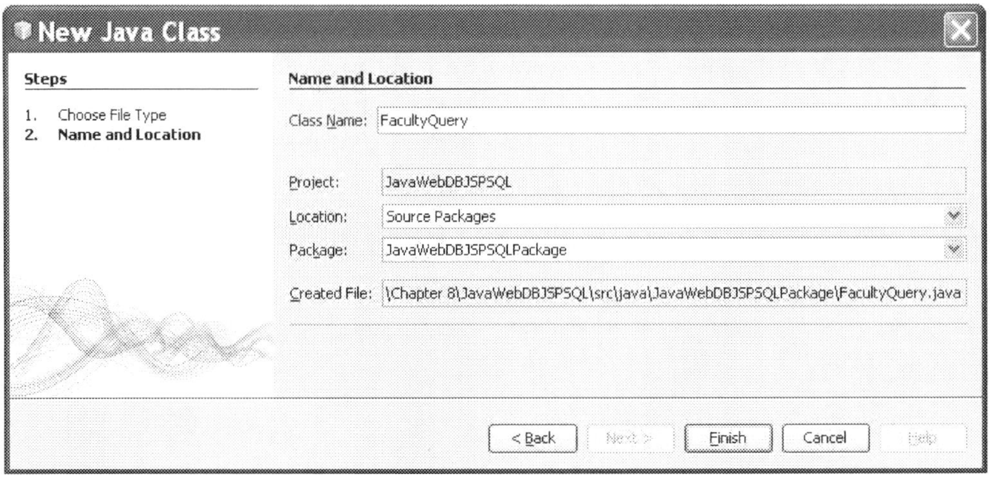

Figure 8.78. The finished New Java Class wizard.

size of this coding, we divide this coding process into two parts. The first part of the codes is shown in Figure 8.79, and the second part is shown in Figure 8.80. The new entered codes have been highlighted in bold.

Let's have a close look at these newly added codes in Figure 8.79 to see how they work.

- **A.** The java.sql.* package is imported first since all SQL Server database related classes and methods are defined in that package.
- **B.** Eight class properties related to the associated columns in the Faculty table in our sample database are declared first. These properties are very important since they are directly mapped to the associated columns in the Faculty table. All of these properties can be accessed by using the associated getter method defined at the bottom of this class.
- **C.** A class-level database connection object is created, and a Dialog object is also created. We will use the latter as a message box to display some debug information during the project runs.
- **D.** A try...catch block is used to load the database JDBC driver. The catch block is used to track and collect any possible exception during this database driver loading process.
- **E.** The database connection URL is defined. Refer to Section 6.2.1.2.4 in Chapter 6 to get more detailed information about this driver name.
- **F.** Another try...catch block is used to connect to our sample SQL Server database with the desired username and password. The catch block is used to track and collect any possible exception occurred during this database connection process.
- **G.** The main query method, QueryFaculty(), is defined with the selected faculty name as the argument. The SQL query statement is first created with the faculty name as the positional dynamic parameter.
- **H.** Starting from a try block, the prepareStatement() method is called to create a PreparedStatement object pstmt.
- **I.** The setter method is used to set the positional parameter in the positional order.

```
  package JavaWebDBJSPSQLPackage;
A import java.sql.*;
  public class FacultyQuery {
B    private static String facultyImage = null;
     private String facultyID;
     private String facultyName;
     private String office;
     private String title;
     private String phone;
     private String college;
     private String email;
C    static Connection con;
     MsgDialog  msgDlg = new  MsgDialog(new javax.swing.JFrame(), true);
  public FacultyQuery() {
D       try {
             Class.forName("com.microsoft.sqlserver.jdbc.SQLServerDriver");
          }
          catch (Exception e) {
              msgDlg.setMessage("Class not found exception!" + e.getMessage());
              msgDlg.setVisible(true);
          }
E         String url = "jdbc:sqlserver://localhost\\SQL2008EXPRESS:5000;databaseName=CSE_DEPT;";
F         try {
             con = DriverManager.getConnection(url,"ybai","reback1956");
          }
          catch (SQLException e) {
              msgDlg.setMessage("Could not connect!" + e.getMessage());
              msgDlg.setVisible(true);
              e.printStackTrace();
          }
     }
G public boolean QueryFaculty(String  fname) {
        String query = "SELECT faculty_id, title, office, phone, college, email  FROM Faculty " +
                       "WHERE faculty_name = ?";
H       try{
            PreparedStatement pstmt = con.prepareStatement(query);
I           pstmt.setString(1, fname);
J           ResultSet rs = pstmt.executeQuery();
K           while (rs.next()){
               facultyID = rs.getString(1);
               title = rs.getString(2);
               office = rs.getString(3);
               phone = rs.getString(4);
               college = rs.getString(5);
               email = rs.getString(6);
L              facultyName = fname;
            }
M           return true;
        }
N       catch (SQLException e) {
           msgDlg.setMessage("Error in Statement! " + e.getMessage());
           msgDlg.setVisible(true);
O          return false;
        }
     }
```

Figure 8.79. The first part of the codes for the Java help class file.

```
  public String getImage(String f_name) {
A      int maxNumber = 7;
       String fImage = null;
       String[] fname = { "Ying Bai", "Black Anderson", "Satish Bhalla", "Steve Johnson",
                          "Jenney King", "Alice Brown", "Debby Angles", "Jeff Henry"};
       String[] fimage = { "Bai.jpg", "Anderson.jpg", "Satish.jpg", "Johnson.jpg",
                           "King.jpg", "Brown.jpg", "Angles.jpg", "Henry.jpg"};
B      if (facultyImage != null)
         return facultyImage;
       else {
C        for (int i=0; i<=maxNumber; i++){
           if (fname[i].equals(f_name)){
             fImage = fimage[i];
             break;
           }
         }
D        facultyImage = fImage;
E        return fImage;
       }
     }
F    public void setFacultyImage(String img) {
       facultyImage = img;
     }
G    public void CloseDBConnection()
     {
       try{
         if (!con.isClosed())
           con.close();
       }catch (SQLException e) {
         msgDlg.setMessage("Error in close the DB! " + e.getMessage());
         msgDlg.setVisible(true);
       }
     }
H    public String getFacultyID() {
       return this.facultyID;
     }
I    public String getFacultyName() {
       return this.facultyName;
     }
J    public String getOffice() {
       return this.office;
     }
K    public String getTitle() {
       return this.title;
     }
L    public String getPhone() {
       return this.phone;
     }
M    public String getCollege() {
       return this.college;
     }
N    public String getEmail() {
       return this.email;
     }
O    public String getFacultyImage() {
       String result = getImage(facultyName);
       if (result != null)
         return this.facultyImage;
       else
         return null;
     }
  }
```

Figure 8.80. The second part of the codes for the Java help class file.

J. The executeQuery() method is executed to perform this query, and the returned result is assigned to the ResultSet object rs.

K. A while loop is used to pick up a matched faculty record. In fact, only one row is returned, and therefore this loop can run only one time. The getString() method is used to pick up each queried column and assign the associated property defined at the beginning of this help class. The index used for this getString() method should be matched to the order of the queried columns in the SQL query statement built in step **G**.

L. The passed argument fname, which is a faculty name entered by the user, is assigned to the property facultyName.

M. A `true` is returned to the FacultyProcess.jsp page to indicate that the execution of this query method is successful.

N. The catch block is used to collect any possible exception occurred during this query process.

O. A `false` is returned to the FacultyProcess.jsp page to indicate that this query has failed.

Now let's handle the second part of the codes of this help class file, which is shown in Figure 8.80. Let's have a closer look at these codes to see how they work.

A. A local method getImage() is defined inside the class file, and it is used to select the matched faculty image and returns the name of the matched faculty image. Some local variables are defined at the beginning of this method, such as the maximum number of faculty images maxNumber, the string variable fImage that is used to return the faculty image's name, and two string arrays, fname[] and fimage[], which contain all eight faculty members and the associated faculty images' names.

B. If the global variable facultyImage is not null, which means that a new faculty image has been assigned to this global variable when an insertion or an updating of a new faculty record has been executed, this new image's name will be returned.

C. Otherwise, a `for` loop is used to check all eight faculty members to try to find the matched faculty name and the associated faculty image's name. If a matched faculty name were found, the loop is broken, and the associated faculty image's name is assigned to the variable fImage.

D. Then the matched faculty image's name is assigned to the global variable facultyImage, which is a property defined at the beginning of this class.

E. The matched faculty image's name is returned to the calling method.

F. The setter method, setFacultyImage(), is used to assign a new faculty image's name to the global variable facultyImage. Since we are working in the Web server environment, we need to use this global variable to keep a record for our current faculty image's name.

G. The codes for the CloseDBConnection() method are identical with those we discussed in step **Q** in the last section.

H. Starting from step **H**, including steps **I–O**, all getter methods are defined, and they are used to pick up all related properties defined at the beginning of this class. A null will be returned from the method getFacultyImage() if no matched faculty image's name can be found.

Now we have finished all coding process for the Faculty information query operations. Before we can run the project to test the function of these codes, we need to store all faculty image files to our project. You can find all faculty and student image files at the folder Images that is located at the Wiley ftp site (refer to Figure 1.2 in Chapter 1). Perform the following operations to complete this image storage process:

1. Open the Windows Explorer and locate our project folder JavaWebDBJSPSQL.
2. Go to the `ftp` site shown above and copy all faculty and student image files from the Images folder and paste them into our current project folder JavaWebDBJSPSQL.
3. Launch the NetBeans IDE and open our project JavaWebDBJSPSQL.
4. Open the Files window and browse to our project folder where you can find all pasted faculty and student image files. Select all of them and right click on those selected image files, and select the Copy item from the pop-up menu.
5. Open the Projects window and browse to the Web Pages folder that is located under our project JavaWebDBJSPSQL. Right click on the Web Pages folder and select the Paste item from the pop-up menu to paste all faculty and student image files in this folder.

The reason we store all faculty and student image files in our Web Pages folder is that you can directly use those image's names to access and pick up them without needing to prefix any driver or folder in which those image files are located.

Now we can build and run our project to test its functions. Click on the Clean and Build Main Project button to build our project. Then right click on the LogIn.jsp file from the Projects window and select the Run File item to run our project.

In the opened LogIn page, enter an appropriate username and password, such as `jhenry` and `test`, and click on the LogIn button to perform the login process. If the login process is successful, select the `Faculty Information` from the Selection.jsp page to open the Faculty.jsp page. On the opened Faculty.jsp page, enter a desired faculty name, such as `Ying Bai`, into the `Faculty Name` field, and click on the Select button to try to query the detailed information for the selected faculty member.

If a matched faculty record is found, the detailed information about that faculty with a faculty image is displayed in seven fields and the photo box, as shown in Figure 8.81.

You can try to enter other desired faculty names, such as `Jenney King` or `Satish Bhalla`, into the `Faculty Name` field to query the information related to those faculty members. Also you can try to use a new faculty image by entering the name of that new faculty image into the `Image` field before you click on the Select button.

Click on the Back and then Exit button on the Selection.jsp page to terminate our Web project.

Our Web project and faculty information query are successful!

A complete Web application project JavaWebDBJSPSQL that includes the login, selection, and faculty information query processes can be found at the folder DBProjects\Chapter 8 at the Wiley ftp site (refer to Figure 1.2 in Chapter 1).

Next, let's handle to insert new records into the Faculty table using JSP and Java beans technologies.

8.5.4 Insert New Records to the Faculty Table Using JSP and Java Beans

To use the JSP and Java bean techniques to perform inserting new record into the Faculty table, we need to perform the following operations:

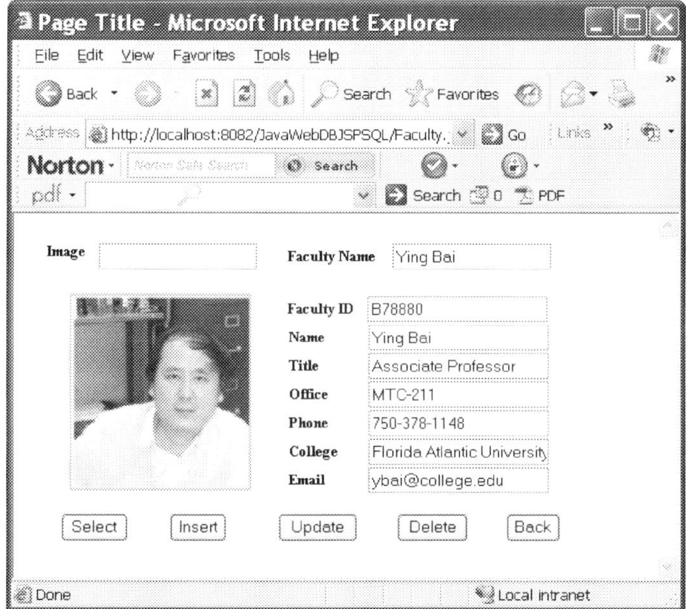

Figure 8.81. The running result of the Faculty.jsp page.

1. Modify the Java help class file FacultyQuery.java to make it our Java bean class file FacultyInsertBean.java to handle the new faculty record insertion actions.
2. Modify the model controller page FacultyProcess.jsp to handle the faculty data collection and insertion operations.

First, let's modify the Java help class file FacultyQuery.java to make it our Java bean class FacultyInsertBean.java to handle the new faculty record insertion actions.

8.5.4.1 Modify the Java Help Class FacultyQuery to Make it Java Bean Class

Double click on the Java help class file FacultyQuery.java from the Projects window to open it. Then go to File > Save As menu item to save this file as our new Java bean class file named FacultyInsertBean.java.

Perform the following modifications to this file to make it our Java bean class:

1. Change the class name and the constructor's name from the FacultyQuery to the FacultyInsertBean.
2. Remove the QueryFaculty() method and the getImage() method.
3. Remove the getFacultyImage() method and the facultyImage property.
4. Create a new method InsertFaculty() and enter the codes shown in Figure 8.82 into this method.

Let's have a close look at the codes for this method to see how they work.

A. A new InsertFaculty() method is created with a String array as the argument of this method. The String array contains all seven pieces of new faculty information.

```
A  public int InsertFaculty(String[] newFaculty) {
B       int numInsert = 0;
C       String InsertQuery = "INSERT INTO Faculty (faculty_id, faculty_name, office, phone, " +
                              "college, title, email) VALUES (?, ?, ?, ?, ?, ?, ?)";
D       try{
            PreparedStatement pstmt = con.prepareStatement(InsertQuery);
E           pstmt.setString(1, newFaculty[0]);
            pstmt.setString(2, newFaculty[1]);
            pstmt.setString(3, newFaculty[2]);
            pstmt.setString(4, newFaculty[3]);
            pstmt.setString(5, newFaculty[4]);
            pstmt.setString(6, newFaculty[5]);
            pstmt.setString(7, newFaculty[6]);
F           numInsert = pstmt.executeUpdate();
        }
G       catch (SQLException e) {
          msgDlg.setMessage("Error in Insert Statement! " + e.getMessage());
          msgDlg.setVisible(true);
        }
H       return numInsert;
   }
```

Figure 8.82. The codes for the new created method InsertFaculty().

- **B.** A local integer variable numInsert is created, and it is used to hold the returned data insertion result, which is regularly equal to the number of records that have been inserted into the Faculty table.
- **C.** The insert string is created with seven positional parameters represented by the question marks in the query string.
- **D.** A try...catch block is used to perform this faculty record insertion action. First, a PreparedStatement object is created with the query string as the argument.
- **E.** Then seven elements in the String array newFaculty[], which are equivalent to seven pieces of new faculty information, are assigned to seven positional parameters. The point to be noted is that the order of those seven elements must be identical with the order of columns represented in the query string.
- **F.** The executeUpdate() method is executed to perform this new record insertion action. The running result, which equals to the number of records that have been successfully inserted into the Faculty table, is returned and assigned to the local integer variable numInsert.
- **G.** The catch block is used to track and collect any possible exceptions during this data insertion action.
- **H.** Finally, the running result is returned to the calling method in the FacultyProcess.jsp page.

Next let's modify the model controller page FacultyProcess.jsp to handle the faculty data collection and insertion operations.

8.5.4.2 Modify the FacultyProcess.jsp Page to Handle Faculty Data Collection and Insertion

Double click on the FacultyProcess.jsp page from the Projects window, and perform the following modifications to this page to use Java bean FacultyInsertBean.java to perform new faculty record insertion actions:

Figure 8.83. The finished Insert Use Bean dialog box.

1. Move to the else if (request.getParameter("Insert")!= null) block, then open the `Palette` window by going to Window > Palette menu item. In the opened `Palette` window, browse to the `JSP` tab, drag the Use Bean icon, and place it inside the else if block.
2. On the opened `Insert Use Bean` dialog, enter InsertFaculty into the `ID` field, and JavaWebDBJSPSQLPackage.FacultyInsertBean into the `Class` filed. Select the session from the `Scope` combo box. Your finished `Insert Use Bean` dialog should match one that is shown in Figure 8.83. Click on the OK button to close this dialog box. A JSP directive that contains the bean id, bean scope, and class is added to this block.
3. Add a JSP directive to set up all properties on the Java bean class FacultyInsertBean.java shown below:

```
<jsp:setProperty name="InsertFaculty" property="*" />
```

4. Add the opening and ending JSP directives to enclose those two JSP directives we added above.

The codes related to steps 1–4 above are shown in the top on Figure 8.84. Add the codes shown in steps **A**–**I** in Figure 8.84 into this block.

Let's have a closer look at these codes to see how they work.

A. A local integer variable res is created, and it is used to hold the running result of executing the InsertFaculty() method in the Java bean class FacultyInsertBean with the bean id of InsertFaculty.

B. Seven getParameter() methods are used to pick up seven pieces of newly inserted faculty information stored in the seven fields in the Faculty.jsp page. The collected seven pieces of new faculty information are assigned to seven local String variables.

C. A new String array fnew is created, and it is used to hold seven pieces of new faculty information stored in the seven local String variables.

D. The InsertFaculty() method in our Java bean is executed to insert these seven pieces of faculty information as a new faculty record into the Faculty table. The seven pieces of new faculty information is stored in the String array fnew that works as the argument for this method. The running result of this method is returned and assigned to the local integer variable res.

E. If the running result is 0, which means that no record has been inserted into the Faculty table ,and this data insertion action has failed. In that case, we need to redisplay the Faculty.jsp page to enable users to reinsert that faculty record.

```
  else if (request.getParameter("Insert")!= null) {
        //process the faculty record insertion
     %>
1       <jsp:useBean id="InsertFaculty" scope="session"
2                     class="JavaWebDBJSPSQLPackage.FacultyInsertBean" />
3       <jsp:setProperty name="InsertFaculty" property="*" />
4    <%
A       int res = 0;
B       String fid = request.getParameter("FacultyIDField");
        String fname = request.getParameter("NameField");
        String office = request.getParameter("OfficeField");
        String phone = request.getParameter("PhoneField");
        String college = request.getParameter("CollegeField");
        String title = request.getParameter("TitleField");
        String email = request.getParameter("EmailField");
C       String[] fnew = {fid, fname, office, phone, college, title, email };
D        res = InsertFaculty.InsertFaculty(fnew);
E       if (res == 0) {
          response.sendRedirect("Faculty.jsp");
          }
F       else {
          request.setAttribute("FacultyIDField", null);
          request.setAttribute("NameField", null);
          request.setAttribute("OfficeField", null);
          request.setAttribute("PhoneField", null);
          request.setAttribute("CollegeField", null);
          request.setAttribute("TitleField", null);
          request.setAttribute("EmailField", null);
G         response.sendRedirect("Faculty.jsp");
H         fQuery.setFacultyImage(request.getParameter("FacultyImageField"));
           }
I       InsertFaculty.CloseDBConnection();
     }
     .........
```

Figure 8.84. The modified codes for the Insert block.

F. If the running result is nonzero, which means that at least one new faculty record has been inserted into the Faculty table. We need to clean up all seven fields that contain seven pieces of newly inserted faculty information in the Faculty.jsp page to enable users to either to test this insertion or insert the next faculty record.

G. Also, we need to redisplay the Faculty.jsp page to enable users to perform the next action.

H. We need to set the global variable facultyImage defined in the help class FacultyQuery.java, and assign the new faculty image's name to it in order to display this new faculty image later when we confirm a new faculty record's insertion or updating.

I. Finally, the CloseDBConnection() method is called to disconnect the connection to our database.

Now we can build and run our project to test this new faculty record insertion function. Click on the Clean and Build Main Project button to perform cleaning up and building our project. Then right click on the LogIn.jsp page from the Projects window to run our project. Enter the appropriate username and password to finish the login process, and select the `Faculty Information` item from the Selection.jsp page to

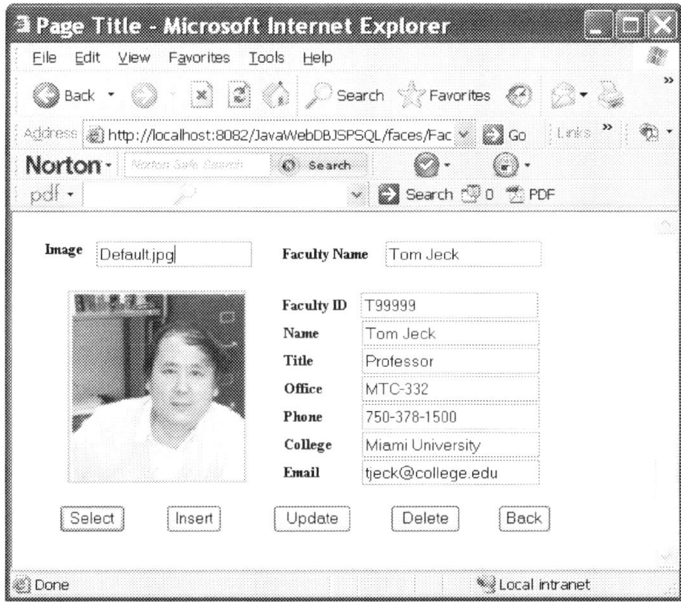

Figure 8.85. The entered new faculty information.

open the Fcaulty.jsp page. Enter seven pieces of information into the associated seven fields as a new faculty record, and enter the default faculty image's name, Default.jpg, into the `Image` field, since we want to use this default image as our new faculty image. The finished new faculty record is shown in Figure 8.85.

Click on the Insert button to try to insert this new faculty record into the Faculty table in our sample database. Immediately, you can find that the original faculty information is displayed, which means that this data insertion is successful.

To confirm this insertion, two ways could be used. The first way is to use the Select button in the Faculty.jsp page to retrieve this newly inserted record from the Faculty table. To do that, enter Tom Jeck to the `Faculty Name` field and click on the Select button. You can find that the new inserted record is retrieved and displayed in the seven fields with the default faculty image, as shown in Figure 8.86. Now click on the Back and Exit button to terminate our project.

The second way to confirm this data insertion is to open the Faculty table. Open the Services window, and expand the `Databases` node and our SQL Server database URL: jdbc:sqlserver://localhost\SQL2008EXPRESS:5000;databaseName=CSE_DEPT [ybai on dbo]. Right click on this URL and select the `Connect` item to connect to our sample database. Then expand our database CSE_DEPT, dbo, and Tables. Right click on the Faculty table and select the `View Data` item to open this table. You can find that the new faculty record has been inserted into this table at the last row.

Our data insertion using the JSP and Java bean is successful!

It is highly recommended to remove this newly inserted faculty record from the Faculty table, since we want to keep our database neat and clean.

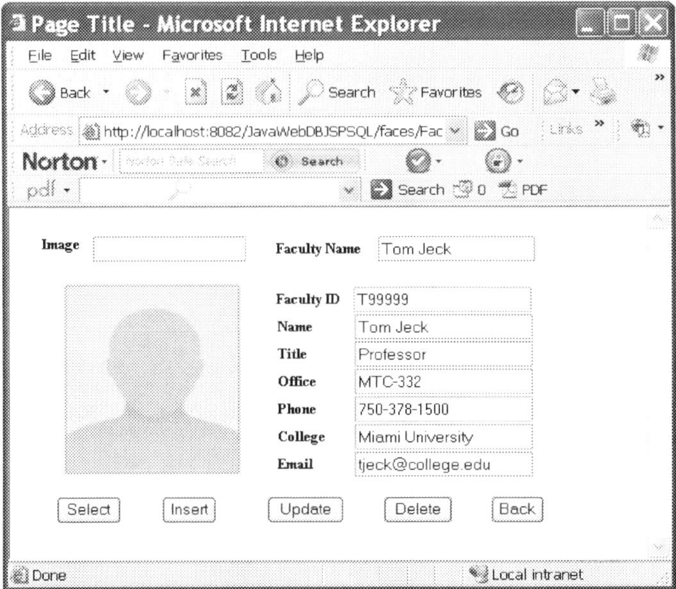

Figure 8.86. The new inserted faculty information.

8.5.5 Update and Delete Data from the Faculty Table Using JSP and Java Beans Techniques

To use the JSP and Java bean techniques to perform data updating and deleting actions against the Faculty table, we need to perform the following operations:

1. Create a new Java Session bean class FacultyUpdateDeleteBean.java to handle the data updating and deleting actions.
2. Modify the model controller page FacultyProcess.jsp to handle the faculty data collection and manipulations.

First let's create our Java session bean class FacultyUpdateDeleteBean.java to handle the data updating and deleting actions.

8.5.5.1 Create a New Java Session Bean Class

Perform the following operations to create a new Java session bean class:

1. Right click on our project JavaWebDBJSPSQL from the Projects window and select the New > Session Bean item to open the `New Session Bean` wizard.
2. Enter FacultyUpdateDeleteBean into the `EJB Name` field.
3. Select the JavaWebDBJSPSQLPackage from the `Package` combo box.
4. Keep all other default settings and click on the Finish button.

On the created FacultyUpdateDeleteBean.java class, we need to create two new methods UpdateFaculty() and DeleteFaculty(). These two methods are used to perform the data updating and deleting operations against our sample database. Figure 8.87

```
  package JavaWebDBJSPSQLPackage;
A import java.sql.*;
  import javax.ejb.Stateless;
  public class FacultyUpdateDeleteBean {
B    private String facultyID;
     private String facultyName;
     private String office;
     private String title;
     private String phone;
     private String college;
     private String email;
     static Connection con;
     MsgDialog  msgDlg = new  MsgDialog(new javax.swing.JFrame(), true);
     public FacultyUpdateDeleteBean() {
C       try {
             Class.forName("com.microsoft.sqlserver.jdbc.SQLServerDriver");
          }
          catch (Exception e) {
             msgDlg.setMessage("Class not found exception!" + e.getMessage());
             msgDlg.setVisible(true);
          }
D         String url = "jdbc:sqlserver://localhost\\SQL2008EXPRESS:5000;databaseName=CSE_DEPT;";
          try {
E              con = DriverManager.getConnection(url,"ybai","reback1956");
          }
          catch (SQLException e) {
             msgDlg.setMessage("Could not connect!" + e.getMessage());
             msgDlg.setVisible(true);
             e.printStackTrace();
          }
     }
     public int UpdateFaculty(String[] upFaculty) {
F       int  numUpdated = 0;
        String query = "UPDATE  Faculty SET faculty_name=?,  office=?,  phone=?,  title=?, college=?,
                        email=?  " + "WHERE  faculty_name= ?";
G    try {
          PreparedStatement pstmt = con.prepareStatement(query);
H         pstmt.setString(1, upFaculty[0]);          // NameField
          pstmt.setString(2, upFaculty[1]);          // OfficeField
          pstmt.setString(3, upFaculty[2]);          // PhoneField
          pstmt.setString(4, upFaculty[3]);          // TitleField
          pstmt.setString(5, upFaculty[4]);          // CollegeField
          pstmt.setString(6, upFaculty[5]);          // EmailField
          pstmt.setString(7, upFaculty[6]);          // FacultyNameField
I         numUpdated = pstmt.executeUpdate();
       }
J     catch (SQLException e) {
            msgDlg.setMessage("Error in Statement!" + e.getMessage());
            msgDlg.setVisible(true);
       }
K      return numUpdated;
     }
     .........
```

Figure 8.87. The first part of the codes of the Java bean class file.

shows the first part of the codes of this class, in which the UpdateFaculty() method is included.

Let's have a closer look at the codes for these two methods to see how they work.

A. The java.sql.* package is imported first, since all SQL Server database-related classes and methods are defined in that package.

B. Seven class properties related to the associated columns in the Faculty table in our sample database are declared first. These properties are very important since they are directly mapped to the associated columns in the Faculty table. All of these properties can be accessed by using the associated getter method defined in the second coding part of this class. A class level database connection object is created, and a Dialog object is also created. We will use the latter as a message box to display some debug information during the project runs.

C. In the constructor of this class, a try...catch block is used to load the database JDBC driver. The catch block is used to track and collect any possible exception during this database-driver loading process.

D. The database connection URL is defined. Refer to Section 6.2.1.2.4 in Chapter 6 to get more detailed information about this driver name.

E. Another try...catch block is used to connect to our sample SQL Server database with the desired username and password. The catch block is used to track and collect any possible exception occurred during this database connection process.

F. The main data updating method, UpdateFaculty(), is defined with the selected faculty updating information as the argument. This argument is exactly a String array that contains all seven pieces of updating faculty information. A local integer variable numUpdated and the SQL updating statement are first created with the faculty name as the positional dynamic parameter.

G. Starting from a try block, the prepareStatement() method is called to create a PreparedStatement object pstmt.

H. Seven setter methods are used to set the positional parameters in the SQL updating statement with the positional order. This order must be identical with that defined in the input argument upFaculty[], which is a String array.

I. The executeUpdate() method is executed to perform this data updating action, and the returned result, which is the number of the rows that have been successfully updated in the Faculty table, is assigned to the local integer variable numUpdated.

J. The catch block is used to track and collect any exceptions during this data updating operation.

K. The data updating result is returned to the calling method.

The second part of the codes for this Java bean class is shown in Figure 8.88. Let's have a closer look at this piece of codes to see how it works.

A. The codes for the CloseDBConnection() method are identical with those we discussed in the last section, and the purpose of this method is to close the connection between our Web application and our sample database.

B. Starting from step B, including steps **C** through **H**, seven getter methods are defined, and they are used to pick up all seven properties defined at the beginning of this class.

```
A    public void CloseDBConnection()
     {
       try{
         if (!con.isClosed())
           con.close();
       }catch (SQLException e) {
         msgDlg.setMessage("Error in close the DB! " + e.getMessage());
         msgDlg.setVisible(true);
       }
     }
B    public String getFacultyID() {
       return this.facultyID;
     }
C    public String getFacultyName() {
       return this.facultyName;
     }
D    public String getOffice() {
       return this.office;
     }
E    public String getTitle() {
       return this.title;
     }
F    public String getPhone() {
       return this.phone;
     }
G    public String getCollege() {
       return this.college;
     }
H    public String getEmail() {
       return this.email;
     }
   }
```

Figure 8.88. The second part of the codes of the Java bean class file.

In fact, the codes for this Java bean class file are basically identical with those we built in our Java help class file, which include the loading JDBC driver, defining the database connection URL, connecting to database, and executing the appropriate method to perform related data actions against our database.

Next, let's modify the FacultyProcess.jsp page to handle the faculty data collection and manipulations.

8.5.5.2 Modify the FacultyProcess Page to Handle Faculty Data Updating

Double click on the FacultyProcess.jsp page from the Projects window, and perform the following modifications to this page to use Java bean FacultyUpdateDeleteBean.java to perform the faculty record updating actions:

1. Move to the else if (request.getParameter("Update")!= null) block, then open the `Palette` window by going to the Window > Palette menu item. In the opened `Palette` window, browse to the `JSP` tab, drag the Use Bean icon, and place it inside the else if block.
2. On the opened `Insert Use Bean` dialog, enter UpdateFaculty into the `ID` field, and JavaWebDBJSPSQLPackage. FacultyUpdateDeleteBean into the `Class` filed. Select

```
  else if (request.getParameter("Update")!= null) {
     //process the faculty record updating
     %>
1        <jsp:useBean id="UpdateFaculty" scope="session"
2                          class="JavaWebDBJSPSQLPackage.FacultyUpdateDeleteBean" />
3        <jsp:setProperty name="UpdateFaculty" property="*" />
4     <%
A        int update = 0;
B        String fname = request.getParameter("NameField");
         String office = request.getParameter("OfficeField");
         String phone = request.getParameter("PhoneField");
         String college = request.getParameter("CollegeField");
         String title = request.getParameter("TitleField");
         String email = request.getParameter("EmailField");
         String f_name = request.getParameter("FacultyNameField");
C        String[] upf = {fname, office, phone, title, college, email, f_name };
D        update = UpdateFaculty.UpdateFaculty(upf);
E        if (update == 0)
           response.sendRedirect("Faculty.jsp");
F        else {
           session.setAttribute("FacultyIDField", null);
           session.setAttribute("NameField", null);
           session.setAttribute("OfficeField", null);
           session.setAttribute("PhoneField", null);
           session.setAttribute("CollegeField", null);
           session.setAttribute("TitleField", null);
           session.setAttribute("EmailField", null);
G          response.sendRedirect("Faculty.jsp");
H          fQuery.setFacultyImage(request.getParameter("FacultyImageField"));
           }
I        UpdateFaculty.CloseDBConnection();
         }
         ........
```

Figure 8.89. The modified codes for the Update block.

the session from the Scope combo box. A JSP directive that contains the bean id, bean scope, and class is added to this block.

3. Add a JSP directive to the Java bean class FacultyUpdateDeleteBean.java shown below:

```
<jsp:setProperty name="UpdateFaculty" property="*" />
```

4. Add the opening and ending JSP directives to enclose those two JSP directives we added above.

The codes related to steps 1–4 above are shown in the top on Figure 8.89. Add the codes shown in steps **A–I** in Figure 8.89 into this block.

Let's have a closer look at these codes to see how they work.

A. A local integer variable update is created, and it is used to hold the running result of executing the UpdateFaculty() method in the Java bean class FacultyUpdateDeleteBean with the bean id of UpdateFaculty.

B. Seven getParameter() methods are used to pick up seven pieces of updating faculty information stored in the seven fields in the Faculty.jsp page. The collected seven pieces of new faculty information are assigned to seven local String variables.

C. A new String array upf[] is created, and it is used to hold seven pieces of updating faculty information stored in the seven local String variables.

D. The UpdateFaculty() method in our Java bean is executed to update a faculty record with these seven pieces of faculty information in the Faculty table. The seven pieces of updating faculty information is stored in the String array upf[] that works as the argument for this method. The running result of this method is returned and assigned to the local integer variable update.

E. If the running result is 0, which means that no record has been updated in the Faculty table and this data updating action has failed. In that case, we need to redisplay the Faculty.jsp page to enable users to reupdate that faculty record.

F. If the running result is nonzero, which means that at least one faculty record has been updated in the Faculty table. We may clean up all seven fields that contain seven pieces of updated faculty information in the Faculty.jsp page to enable users to either to test this updating or update another faculty record.

G. We need to redisplay the Faculty.jsp page to enable users to perform the next action.

H. We need to set the global variable facultyImage defined in the help class FacultyQuery.java, and assign the updating faculty image's name to it in order to display this updated faculty image later when we confirm this faculty record's updating.

I. Finally, the CloseDBConnection() method is called to disconnect the connection to our database.

Now we can build and run our project to test this faculty record updating function. Click on the Clean and Build Main Project button to perform cleaning up and building our project. Then right click on the LogIn.jsp page from the Projects window to run our project. Enter the appropriate username and password, such as `jhenry` and `test`, to finish the login process and select the `Faculty Information` item from the Selection.jsp page to open the Fcaulty.jsp page.

To update a faculty record, first, let's perform a query operation to retrieve and display that faculty record. Enter a faculty name, such as Ying Bai, into the `Faculty Name` field and click on the Select button. All seven pieces of information related to that faculty are retrieved and displayed in this page. Now enter six pieces of updating information into the associated six fields (no `Faculty ID` field), and enter the default faculty image's name, Default.jpg, into the `Image` field, since we want to use this default image as our updating faculty image. The finished faculty updating record is shown in Figure 8.90.

Click on the Update button to try to update this faculty record in the Faculty table in our sample database. Immediately, you can find that the original faculty information is displayed, which means that this data updating is successful.

To confirm this updating action, two ways could be used. The first way is to use the Select button in the Faculty.jsp page to retrieve this updated record from the Faculty table. To do that, enter Susan Bai to the `Faculty Name` field and click on the Select button. You can find that the updated record is retrieved and displayed in the seven fields with the default faculty image, as shown in Figure 8.91. Now click on the Back and Exit button to terminate our project.

The second way to confirm this data updating is to open the Faculty table. Open the Services window, expand the `Databases` node and our SQL Server database URL: jdbc:sqlserver://localhost\SQLEXPRESS:5000;databaseName=CSE_DEPT[ybai

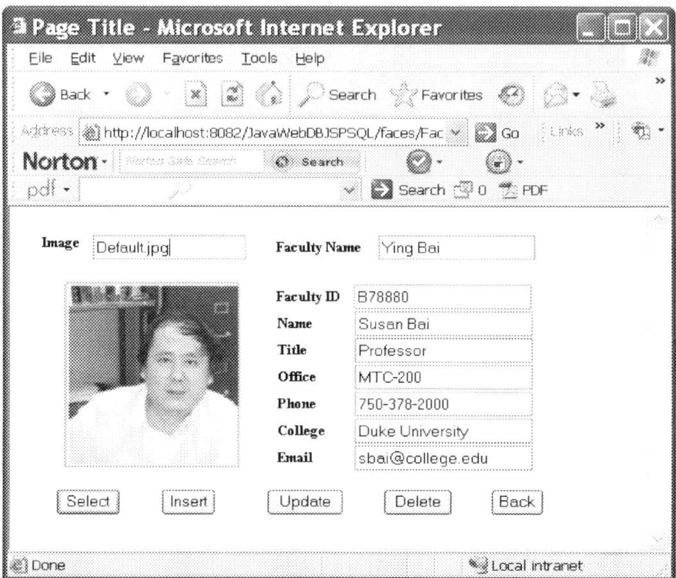

Figure 8.90. The entered faculty updating information.

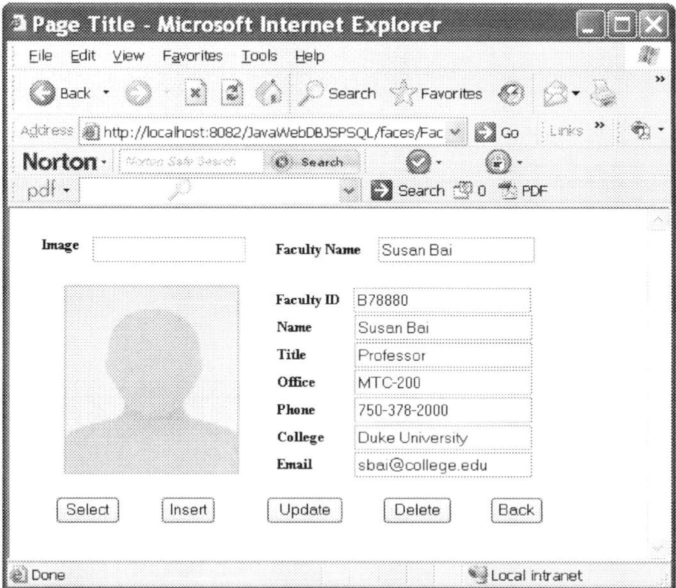

Figure 8.91. The updated faculty information.

Table 8.3. The original data for faculty member Ying Bai

faculty_id	faculty_name	office	phone	college	title	email
B78880	Ying Bai	MTC-211	750-378-1148	Florida Atlantic University	Associate Professor	ybai@college.edu

on dbo]. Right click on this URL and select the `Connect` item to connect to our sample database. Then expand our database CSE_DEPT, dbo and Tables. Right click on the Faculty table and select the `View Data` item to open this table. You can find that the faculty record with the faculty_id of B78880 has been updated.

Our data updating action using the JSP and Java bean is successful!

It is highly recommended to recover this updated faculty record in the Faculty table since we want to keep our database neat and clean. Apply the data shown in Table 8.3 to recover this faculty record. You can do this data recovery either in the NetBeans IDE or the Microsoft SQL Server Management Studio Express by opening the Faculty table.

8.5.5.3 Add a Method to the Session Bean to Perform Faculty Data Deleting

To perform the faculty record deleting action, we need to perform the following operations:

1. Add a new method to the Java session bean FacultyUpdateDeleteBean to handle the faculty record deleting actions.
2. Modify the FacultyProcess.jsp page to handle the faculty data collection and manipulations.

Let's first add a new method DeleteFaculty() into our Java session bean class FacultyUpdateDeleteBean to handle the faculty record deleting actions. Create a new method DeleteFaculty() and enter the codes shown in Figure 8.92 into this method.

Let's have a closer look at this piece of codes to see how it works.

A. A local integer variable numDeleted is created, and it is used to hold the running result of executing the DeleteFaculty() method in the Java bean class FacultyUpdateDeleteBean with the bean id of DeleteFaculty.

B. The SQL deleting statement is created with the faculty_name as the positional dynamic parameter.

C. A try...catch block is used to perform this data deleting action. The prepareStatement() method is called to create a PreparedStatement object pstmt.

D. The setter method is used to set up the positional dynamic parameter faculty_name.

E. The executeUpdate() method is executed to perform this data deleting action and the running result, which is the number of the rows that have been successfully deleted from the Faculty table, is assigned to the local integer variable numDeleted.

```
  ........
  public int DeleteFaculty(String fname) {
A       int numDeleted = 0;
B       String query = "DELETE FROM Faculty WHERE faculty_name = ?";
        try {
C         PreparedStatement pstmt = con.prepareStatement(query);
D         pstmt.setString(1, fname);
E          numDeleted = pstmt.executeUpdate();
        }
F       catch (SQLException e) {
          msgDlg.setMessage("Error in Statement!" + e.getMessage());
           msgDlg.setVisible(true);
        }
G       return numDeleted;
    }
    ........
```

Figure 8.92. The codes for the DeleteFaculty() method.

F. The catch block is used to track and collect any exceptions during this data deleting operation.

G. The data deleting result is returned to the calling method.

Now let's modify the FacultyProcess.jsp page to handle the faculty data collection and manipulations.

8.5.5.4 Modify the FacultyProcess Page to Handle Faculty Data Deleting

Double click on the FacultyProcess.jsp page from the Projects window to open this page, and perform the following modifications to this page to use the Java bean FacultyUpdateDeleteBean.java to perform the faculty record deleting actions:

1. Move to the else if (request.getParameter("Delete")!= null) block, then open the Palette window by going to the Window > Palette menu item. In the opened Palette window, browse to the JSP tab, drag the Use Bean icon, and place it inside the else if block.
2. On the opened Insert Use Bean dialog, enter DeleteFaculty into the ID field, and JavaWebDBJSPSQLPackage. FacultyUpdateDeleteBean into the Class field. Select the session from the Scope combo box. A JSP directive that contains the bean id, bean scope, and class is added to this block.
3. Add a JSP directive to the Java bean class FacultyUpdateDeleteBean.java shown below:

```
<jsp:setProperty name="DeleteFaculty" property="*" />
```

4. Add the opening and ending JSP directives to enclose those two JSP directives we added above.

The codes related to steps 1–4 above are shown in the top on Figure 8.93. Add the codes shown in steps **A–E** in Figure 8.93 into this block.

```
    .........
    else if (request.getParameter("Delete")!= null) {
        //process the faculty record deleting
        %>
            <jsp:useBean id="DeleteFaculty" scope="session"
                                 class="JavaWebDBJSPSQLPackage.FacultyUpdateDeleteBean" />
            <jsp:setProperty name="DeleteFaculty" property="*" />
        <%
A           int delete = 0;
B           String fname = request.getParameter("FacultyNameField");
C           delete = DeleteFaculty.DeleteFaculty(fname);
D           response.sendRedirect("Faculty.jsp");
E           DeleteFaculty.CloseDBConnection();
    }
    .........
```

Figure 8.93. The modified codes for the Delete block.

Let's have a closer look at these codes to see how they work.

A. A local integer variable delete is created, and it is used to hold the running result of executing the DeleteFaculty() method in the Java bean class FacultyUpdateDeleteBean with the bean id of DeleteFaculty.

B. The getParameter() method is used to pick up the name of the faculty to be deleted from the Faculty table. The retrieved faculty name is assigned to the local variable fname.

C. The DeleteFaculty() method in our Java bean is executed to delete a faculty record based on the selected faculty name from the Faculty table. The running result of this method is returned and assigned to the local integer variable delete.

D. We need to redisplay the Faculty.jsp page to enable users to perform the next action.

E. Finally, the CloseDBConnection() method is called to disconnect the connection to our database.

Now we can build and run our project to test this faculty record deleting function. Click on the Clean and Build Main Project button to perform cleaning up and building our project. Then right click on the LogIn.jsp page from the Projects window to run our project. Enter the appropriate username and password, such as `jhenry` and `test`, to finish the login process, and select the `Faculty Information` item from the Selection.jsp page to open the Fcaulty.jsp page.

To delete a faculty record, first, let's perform a query operation to retrieve and display that faculty record. Enter a faculty name, such as Ying Bai, into the `Faculty Name` field, and click on the Select button. All seven pieces of information related to that faculty are retrieved and displayed in this page. Now click on the Delete button to try to delete this record from our Faculty table.

To confirm this data deleting action, two ways could be used. The first way is to use the Select button in the Faculty.jsp page to try to retrieve this deleted record from the Faculty table. To do that, enter the deleted faculty name Ying Bai to the `Faculty Name` field and click on the Select button. You can find that all seven fields are displayed with nulls, as shown in Figure 8.94, which means that the faculty member Ying Bai has been

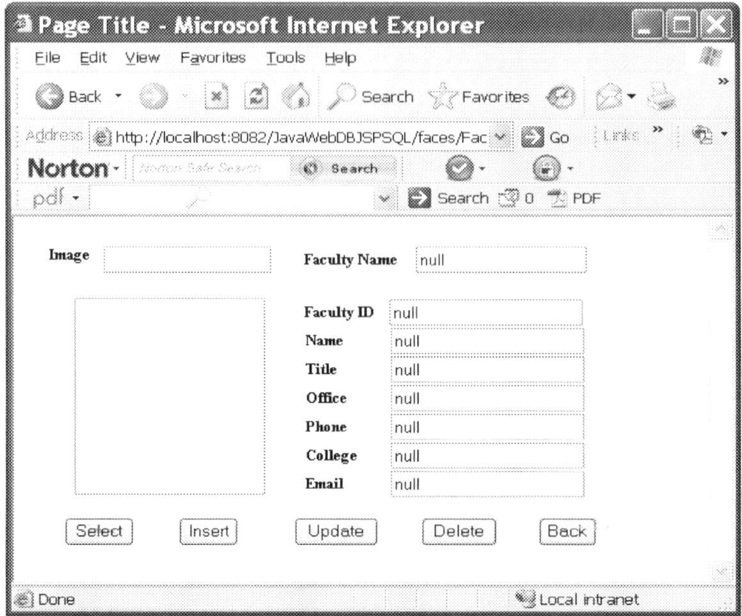

Figure 8.94. The confirmation of the faculty data deletion action.

deleted from the Faculty table. Now click on the Back and Exit button to terminate our project.

The second way to confirm this data deleting is to open the Faculty table in the NetBeans IDE environment. Open the Services window, expand the `Databases` node and our SQL Server database URL: jdbc:sqlserver://localhost\SQL2008EXPRESS:5000; databaseName=CSE_DEPT [ybai on dbo]. Right click on this URL and select the `Connect` item to connect to our sample database. Then expand our database CSE_DEPT, dbo, and Tables. Right click on the Faculty table and select the `View Data` item to open this table. You can find that the faculty record with the faculty_id of B78880 has been deleted.

Our data deleting action using the JSP and Java bean is successful!

It is highly recommended to recover this deleted faculty record in the Faculty table since we want to keep our database neat and clean.

The point to be noted is that when we delete a faculty member from the Faculty table, which is a parent table relative to the Course and LogIn tables that are child tables, the related records to that deleted faculty in those child tables will also be deleted, since a cascaded deleting relationship has been set up between the parent and child tables when we built this database in Chapter 2. Therefore, the faculty login record in the LogIn table and all courses taught by that faculty in the Course table will be deleted when the faculty member is deleted from the Faculty table. Also, because the Course table is a parent table relative to the StudentCourse table, all courses taken by students and taught by the deleted faculty will be deleted from the StudentCourse table. To recover these

Table 8.4. The deleted faculty record in the Faculty table

faculty_id	faculty_name	office	phone	college	title	email
B78880	Ying Bai	MTC-211	750-378-1148	Florida Atlantic University	Associate Professor	ybai@college.edu

Table 8.5. The deleted course records in the Course table

course_id	course	credit	classroom	schedule	enrollment	faculty_id
CSC-132B	Introduction to Programming	3	TC-302	T-H: 1:00-2:25 PM	21	B78880
CSC-234A	Data Structure & Algorithms	3	TC-302	M-W-F: 9:00-9:55 AM	25	B78880
CSE-434	Advanced Electronics Systems	3	TC-213	M-W-F: 1:00-1:55 PM	26	B78880
CSE-438	Advd Logic & Microprocessor	3	TC-213	M-W-F: 11:00-11:55 AM	35	B78880

Table 8.6. The deleted login records in the LogIn table

user_name	pass_word	faculty_id	student_id
ybai	reback	B78880	

Table 8.7. The deleted student course records in the StudentCourse table

s_course_id	student_id	course_id	credit	major
1005	J77896	CSC-234A	3	CS/IS
1009	A78835	CSE-434	3	CE
1014	A78835	CSE-438	3	CE
1016	A97850	CSC-132B	3	ISE
1017	A97850	CSC-234A	3	ISE

deleted records, one needs to recover all of those deleted records related to the deleted faculty in those four tables. An easy way to do this recovery job is to use either the Microsoft SQL Server Management Studio Express or the **Services** window in NetBeans IDE. For your convenience, we show these original records in Tables 8.4–8.7 again, and you can add or insert them back to those four tables to complete this data recovery.

Another point to be noted is that you must recover the Faculty table first, and then you can recover other records in other tables, since the **faculty_id** is a primary key in the Faculty table.

Next, let's discuss how to access and manipulate data in the Course table in our sample SQL Server database using JavaServer Faces and Java beans with Java Persistence API techniques.

8.5.6 Query Data from the Course Table Using JavaServer Faces and Java Beans

In this section, we will discuss how to perform data actions against our SQL Server 2008 sample database using JavaServer Faces, Java Bean, and Java Persistence API techniques. Generally, this three-tier Web application is composed of the following components:

- **Web container** includes the JSP or JSF pages as a view or an interface to collect the user inputs and display the output or query results from database via the Web server.
- **EJB** contains a Session Bean that works as an intermediate-level processor between the Web container and the Java Persistence API to handle the business logics and data-related operations. For complicated Web applications, more than one Java bean may be used to handle the different jobs and play the different roles.
- **Java Persistence API** works (1) as an interface between the Java Bean and database server, and performs a mapping between a relational database and a collection of mapped entity classes, and (2) handle all data actions and data translations between Java beans and database server.

First, let's modify the Course.jsp page to make it our JavaServer Face page.

8.5.6.1 Modify the Course Page to Make it JavaServer Face Page

As you know, there are some differences that exist between the JSP and JavaServer Faces pages; even the JavaServer Faces are built based on the JSP techniques. In fact, JavaServer Faces are built on JSP by inserting some JavaServer Faces tags into the JSP pages.

Perform the following operations to modify this Course page:

1. Launch the NetBeans IDE to open our project JavaWebDBJSPSQL.
2. Right click on our project folder and select the New > JSF Page item.
3. Enter CoursePage into the `File Name` field and check the JSP File radio button under the `Options` group.
4. Click on the Finish button to create a new JSF page.
5. On the created JSF page CoursePage, open the Palette window by going to Window > Palette item.
6. Drag the JSF Form icon under the `JSF` tag in the Palette window and place it under the `<body>` tag in the JSF page. A `<h:form> ... </h:form>` tag pair is created.
7. Open the Course.jsp page and copy the codes between the <form method=post action=".\CourseProcess.jsp"> tag and `</form>` tag, and paste them to the space between the `<h:form> ... </h:form>` tag pair in our new created JSF page CoursePage.
8. In the top part of the Course.jsp page, copy the codes between the `<style>` (under the `<title>` tag) and the `</head>` (exclude the `</head>` tag), and paste these codes to the space between the `<head>` and `</head>` tag pair in our new created JSF page CoursePage (under the `<title>` tag).
9. In the Course.jsp page, copy the `<![if !pub]>` tag (just under the `<div>` tag) and paste it to space between the `<body>` and the `<h:form>` tag in our new created JSF page CoursePage.

10. In the Course.jsp page, copy the <![endif]> tag (just under the </form> tag) and paste it to space just below the </h:form> tag in our new created JSF page CoursePage.

To make it the JSF page, perform the following modifications to the copied codes in the CoursePage file:

1. Add an id attribute to the JSF Form tag <h:form> and make it as
   ```
   <h:form id="CoursePage">.
   ```
2. Replace the <select name=CourseList ... ></select> tag pair with the <h:selectOneListbox> tag, and the result of this replacement is:
   ```
   <h:selectOneListbox id="courseList" value="#{CourseBean.
   selectedItem}" size="5" >
   <f:selectItems value="#{CourseBean.courseList}" />
   </h:selectOneListbox>
   ```
3. Replace the <input name=CourseNameField ... > tag with the <h:inputText> tag, and the result of this replacement is:
   ```
   <h:inputText id="courseName" value="#{CourseBean.courseName}"
   size="20" maxlength="60"></h:inputText>
   ```
4. Replace the <input name=ScheduleField ... > tag with the <h:inputText> tag, and the result of this replacement is:
   ```
   <h:inputText id="schedule" value="#{CourseBean.schedule}"
   size="20" maxlength="60"></h:inputText>
   ```
5. Replace the <input name=ClassroomField ... > tag with the <h:inputText> tag, and the result of this replacement is:
   ```
   <h:inputText id="classroom" value="#{CourseBean.classroom}"
   size="20" maxlength="20"></h:inputText>
   ```
6. Replace the <input name=CreditField ... > tag with the <h:inputText> tag, and the result of this replacement is:
   ```
   <h:inputText id="credit" value="#{CourseBean.credit}" size="20"
   maxlength="20"></h:inputText>
   ```
7. Replace the <input name=EnrollmentField ... > tag with the <h:inputText> tag, and the result of this replacement is:
   ```
   <h:inputText id="enrollment" value="#{CourseBean.enrollment}"
   size="20" maxlength="20"></h:inputText>
   ```
8. Replace the <input type=submit value=Select ... > tag with the <h:commandButton> tag, and the result of this replacement is:
   ```
   <h:commandButton id="Select" action="#{CourseBean.Select}"
   value="Select" />
   ```
9. Replace the <input type=submit value=Insert ... > tag with the <h:commandButton> tag, and the result of this replacement is:
   ```
   <h:commandButton id="Details" action="#{CourseBean.Details}"
   value="Details" />
   ```
10. Replace the <input type=submit value=Update ... > tag with the <h:commandButton> tag, and the result of this replacement is:
    ```
    <h:commandButton id="Update" action="#{CourseBean.Update}"
    value="Update" />
    ```

11. Replace the <input type=submit value=Delete ... > tag with the <h:commandButton> tag, and the result of this replacement is:

```
<h:commandButton id="Delete" action="#{CourseBean.Delete}"
value="Delete" />
```

12. Replace the <input type=submit value=Back ... > tag with the <h:commandButton> tag, and the result of this replacement is:

```
<h:commandButton id="Back" action="#{CourseBean.Back}"
value="Back" />
```

13. Replace the <input name=FacultyNameField ... > tag with the <h:inputText> tag, and the result of this replacement is:

```
<h:inputText id="facultyName" value="#{CourseBean.
facultyName}" size="20" maxlength="50"></h:inputText>
```

The modified JSF page CoursePage.jsp is shown in Figure 8.95. The modified parts have been highlighted in bold.

Although these modifications look a little complex, in fact, they are very simple, and the reason we need to perform these modifications is that we need to use Java bean class to handle the database-related operations, and to display the data action results by binding the value attribute of each inputText tag with the associated properties defined in our Java bean class CourseBean. Let's have a closer look at these modified codes to see how they work.

A. An id="CoursePage" attribute is added to the <h:form> tag to identify this form.

B. The <h:selectOneListbox> tag is used to redefine our CourseList box. In order to set up a binding relationship between this Listbox and a property in the Java bean CourseBean, the id of this Listbox, which is courseList, must be identical with a property courseList defined in our Java bean class CourseBean that will be created later. The value attribute of this courseList, which is the output of this courseList as the user clicks one item from this Listbox to select one, is bound to a property named selectedItem defined in our Java bean class CourseBean. The value attribute of the <f:selectItems> tag is bound to a property named courseList in our Java bean class CourseBean, and all queried course_id will be stored into this property and bound to the value attribute of this <f:selectItems> tag. The result of this binding is that all queried course_id will be displayed in this ListBox as the project runs. The point to be noted is that although both the id of the Listbox and the property has the same value, courseList, they are different in this application.

C. Starting from step **C** until step **G**, including steps **D** through to **F**, five inputText tags are defined, and they are used to display the detailed course information, such as the course name, schedule, classroom, credit, and enrollment, for a selected course_id from the courseList Listbox by the users as the project runs. Two points to be noted for these inputText tags are: (1) the id attribute of each inputText tag must be identical with the name of an associated property defined in our Java bean class CourseBean for binding purpose; and (2) the value attribute of each tag must be bound to an associated property defined in the Java bean CourseBean using the EL expression (#{...}). After this binding, the content of each inputText field will be equal to the value of the associated property in the Java bean, and, furthermore, they can be updated and displayed as the project runs.

H. From steps **H** through to **L**, the <h:commandButton> tags are used to define five buttons in this CoursePage. One point to be noted is that the action attribute of each button tag must be identical with an associated method defined in our Java bean class

```
  <%@page contentType="text/html" pageEncoding="UTF-8"%>

  <%@taglib prefix="f" uri="http://java.sun.com/jsf/core"%>
  <%@taglib prefix="h" uri="http://java.sun.com/jsf/html"%>

  <!DOCTYPE HTML PUBLIC "-//W3C//DTD HTML 4.01 Transitional//EN"
    "http://www.w3.org/TR/html4/loose.dtd">

  <f:view>
  <html>
  <head>
  <meta http-equiv="Content-Type" content="text/html; charset=UTF-8"/>
  <title>CoursePage Page</title>
  <style>
  ........
  </head>
  <body>
  <![if !pub]>
A <h:form id="CoursePage">
  .........
B <h:selectOneListbox id="courseList" value="#{CourseBean.selectedItem}" size="5" >
    <f:selectItems value="#{CourseBean.courseList}" />
  </h:selectOneListbox>
  .........
C <h:inputText id="courseName" value="#{CourseBean.courseName}" size="20" maxlength="60">
  </h:inputText>
  .........
D <h:inputText id="schedule" value="#{CourseBean.schedule}" size="20" maxlength="60">
  </h:inputText>
  .........
E <h:inputText id="classroom" value="#{CourseBean.classroom}" size="20" maxlength="20">
  </h:inputText>
  .........
F <h:inputText id="credit" value="#{CourseBean.credit}" size="20" maxlength="20">
  </h:inputText>
  .........
G <h:inputText id="enrollment" value="#{CourseBean.enrollment}" size="20" maxlength="20">
  </h:inputText>
  .........
H <h:commandButton id="Select" action="#{CourseBean.Select}" value="Select" />
  .........
I <h:commandButton id="Details" action="#{CourseBean.Details}" value="Details" />
  .........
J <h:commandButton id="Update" action="#{CourseBean.Update}" value="Update" />
  .........
K <h:commandButton id="Delete" action="#{CourseBean.Delete}" value="Delete" />
  .........
L <h:commandButton id="Back" action="#{CourseBean.Back}" value="Back" />
  .........
M <h:inputText id="facultyName" value="#{CourseBean.facultyName}" size="20" maxlength="50">
  </h:inputText>

  <![if !pub]></span><![endif]><![if !pub]>
  </h:form>
  <![endif]>
  </body>
  </html>
  </f:view>
```

Figure 8.95. The modified codes for the JSF page CoursePage.jsp.

CourseBean. In this way, we can bind the action attribute of each button to the associated method defined in our Java bean to enable that method to be triggered and executed as the button is clicked by the user.

M. Finally, another inputText tag is used to define and bind the facultyName field to an associated property named facultyName in our Java bean class CourseBean.

Next, let's build our Java Bean class CourseBean.java to handle the database-related operations and business logics.

8.5.6.2 Build the JavaServer Face Managed Bean CourseBean

We need to build a JavaServer Faces managed bean to handle the database-related operations and actions in this application. This JSF managed bean works as an intermediate-level process to handle business logics and database-related operations. In fact, the function of this bean is to:

- Query all courses, exactly course_id, from the Course table in our sample database based on the faculty name entered by the user, and display them in the CourseList box.
- Query five pieces of detailed course information based on the selected course_id from the CourseList box by the user, and display them in five text fields in the CoursePage.

As you know, there is no faculty_name column in our Course table, and the only selection criterion for the course is the faculty_id column. Therefore, we need to perform two queries for all course query operations: (1) query the faculty_id from the Faculty table based on the faculty name entered by the user, and (2) query all courses, exactly all course_id, from the Course table based on the faculty_id we queried in the first query.

Because of the coding complex in this section, we need to develop two Java bean classes to handle these queries: one is the JSF Managed Bean CourseBean that is used to control and coordinate all queries, and a Java Session Bean CourseFacade that is used to access our sample database to perform database related operations using Java Persistence API. Let's first handle the JSF Managed Bean CourseBean.

Perform the following operations to create this JSF managed bean class:

1. Launch the NetBeans IDE and open our Web application project JavaWebDBJSPSQL.
2. Right click on our project JavaWebDBJSPSQL from the Projects window and select the New > Other item to open the `New File` wizard.
3. Select JavaServer Faces from the `Categories` list, and JSF Managed Bean from the `File Types` list. Then click on the Next button.
4. Enter CourseBean into the `Class Name` field, and select the JavaWebDBJSPSQLPackage from the Package combo box. Select the session from the `Scope` combo box and click on the Finish button.

On the opened CourseBean class file, enter the first part of the codes, which is shown in Figure 8.96, into this managed bean. The newly added codes have been highlighted in bold.

Let's have a closer look at the codes in this part to see how they work.

A. First, seven properties, which should be bound to the associated attributes of tags in the CoursePage.jsp JSF page, are declared. The point to be noted is that the names of these properties must be identical with those of attributes defined in our View file, CoursePage.jsp

```
  package JavaWebDBJSPSQLPackage;

  import javax.faces.bean.ManagedBean;
  import javax.faces.bean.SessionScoped;

  @ManagedBean(name="CourseBean")
  @SessionScoped
  public class CourseBean {
A     private String courseName;
      private String schedule;
      private String classroom;
      private String credit;
      private String enrollment;
      private String courseID;
      private String facultyName;
      private List courseList;
      private String selectedItem = null;
B     MsgDialog  msgDlg = new  MsgDialog(new javax.swing.JFrame(), true);

      public CourseBean() {
      }
C     public void setSelectedItem(String cid) {
        selectedItem = cid;
      }
D     public String getSelectedItem() {
        return selectedItem;
      }
E     public void setCourseList(List cid) {
        courseList = cid;
      }
F     public List getCourseList() {
        return courseList;
      }
G     public String getFacultyName() {
        return facultyName;
      }
H     public void setFacultyName(String FacultyName) {
        this.facultyName = FacultyName;
      }
I     public String getCourseID() {
        return courseID;
      }
J     public void setCourseID(String CourseID) {
        this.courseID = CourseID;
      }
K     public String getEnrollment() {
        return enrollment;
      }
L     public void setEnrollment(String Enrollment) {
        this.enrollment = Enrollment;
      }
M     public String getCredit() {
        return credit;
      }
N     public void setCredit(String Credit) {
        this.credit = Credit;
      }
O     public String getClassroom() {
        return classroom;
      }
P     public void setClassroom(String Classroom) {
        this.classroom = Classroom;
      }
```

Figure 8.96. The first part codes of the CourseBean class.

file, including the cases since Java is a case-sensitive language. Also the List collection courseList, which is bound to the value attribute of the <f:selectItems> tag, and the selectedItem, which is bound to the value attribute of the <h:selectOneListbox> tag, are declared here, too.

B. The msgDlg is a new instance of our customer-built dialog box, and this is used to display our testing and debug information when we test the codes in this file later.

C. Starting from step **C** through step **P**, seven setter and getter methods are defined for seven properties we defined above. These methods are used to set or get each property defined in this Java bean class as the project runs.

Now, let's enter the second part of the codes into this Java bean class and locate them just below the first part codes, as show in Figure 8.97.

Let's have a closer look at the codes in this part to see how they work.

A. From steps **A** through to **D**, another two-set setter and getter methods are defined, and they are used to set and get two properties, schedule and courseName, defined in this bean class.

E. The Select() method, which is bound to the action attribute of the Select button on the CoursePage file, is defined here. This method will be called and executed as the Select button in the CoursePage.jsp is clicked by the user as the project runs. To use the List collection, first, a new ArrayList instance is created.

F. A new List instance, cList, is also created, and it is used to hold the queried result from calling the getCourseID() method that is defined in the session bean class CourseFacade that will be built in the next section. This method will return a List of course_id taught by the selected faculty by the user from the CoursePage as the project runs.

G. A for loop is utilized to pick up each course_id from the cList instance and assign it to a new instance of SelectItem class, courseid, and add it into the courseList property using the Add() method. A point to be noted is that the returned course_id must be converted to an instance of the class interface SelectItem that is in the package javax.faces.model, and then it can be added into the List collection.

H. Because the returned value is not important for this application, a null is returned when this method is done.

I. The Details() method, which is bound to the action attribute of the Details button on the CoursePage file, is defined here. This method will be called and executed as the Details button in the CoursePage.jsp page is clicked by the user as the project runs. This method will return five pieces of detailed information based on the selected course_id from the courseList box in the CoursePage as the project runs, and the returned five pieces of course information will be displayed in five inputText fields in that page. The selected course_id, which is stored in the selectedItem property in our JSF managed bean CourseBean and has been bound to the value attribute of the <h:selectOneListbox> tag in the CoursePage, will be checked first to make sure that a valid course_id has been selected by the user.

J. If the selectedItem property is non-null, which means that a valid course_id has been selected, the getCourseDetail() method defined in our session bean class CourseFacade that will be built in the next section, will be called to retrieve five pieces of detailed information for the selected course_id, and assign them to a List object courseDetail.

K. An enhanced for loop is used to retrieve the detailed course information from the query result list and assign them one by one to the associated properties defined in our JSF managed bean class CourseBean.

```
A      public String getSchedule() {
         return schedule;
       }
B      public void setSchedule(String Schedule) {
         this.schedule = Schedule;
       }
C      public String getCourseName() {
         return courseName;
       }
D      public void setCourseName(String CourseName) {
         this.courseName = CourseName;
       }
E      public String Select() {
         courseList = new ArrayList();
F        List cList = courseFacade.getCourseID(getFacultyName());
G        for (int i=0; i < cList.size(); i++) {
           SelectItem courseid = new SelectItem(cList.get(i).toString());
           courseList.add(courseid);
         }
H        return null;
       }
I      public Boolean Details() {
         if (selectedItem != null) {
J          List<Object[]> courseDetail = courseFacade.getCourseDetail(selectedItem);
K          for (Object[] result:courseDetail){
           courseName = (String)result[0];
           schedule = (String)result[1];
           classroom = (String)result[2];
           credit = result[3].toString();
           enrollment = result[4].toString();
           }
         }
L        else {
           msgDlg.setMessage("the selected courseID is invalid!");
            msgDlg.setVisible(true);
         }
M        return null;
       }
N      public Boolean Update() {
         return null;
       }
O      public Boolean Delete() {
         return null;
       }
P      public void Back() {
       }
     }
```

Figure 8.97. The second part codes of the CourseBean class.

L. If the selectedItem property contains a null value, which means that no valid course_id has been selected. A warning message is displayed for this situation using the msgDlg.

M. Since the returned value of this method is not important to us, therefore, a null is used.

N. Three other methods, Update(), Delete(), and Back(), which are bound to the action attributes of the associated buttons in the CoursePage file, are defined in steps **N**, **O**, and **P** in this Java bean class. We will develop the codes to execute the data updating and

```
package JavaWebDBJSPSQLPackage;

A  import java.util.*;
   import javax.faces.bean.ManagedBean;
   import javax.faces.bean.SessionScoped;
B  import javax.faces.model.SelectItem;
   .........
```

Figure 8.98. The modified import statements in the CourseBean class.

deleting actions against our sample database later using these methods. The Back() method is used to return to the Selection.jsp page.

After finishing the code development for this bean, you may encounter some real-time compiling errors indicated with either red or blue underscored lines. One reason for that is that some packages are missed when you try to use some classes or interfaces in this code development process. To fix that, right click on this coding window and select the Fix Imports item from the pop-up menu to add required packages. An example is the List class that is located at the java.util package, and an import java.util.List statement should have been added into this bean after you had performed the Fix Imports operation. Since we need to use the ArrayList class that is also located at the java.util package, we need to modify this import statement to import java.util.*.

Another package you may need to use for this bean is the javax.faces.model, since we need to use the SelectItem component as an element in the <h:selectOneListbox> tag. Therefore, add another import statement to this bean, import javax.faces.model.SelectItem. Your finished import package block should match one that is shown in Figure 8.98. The modified import statements have been highlighted in bold.

Next, let's develop and build our session bean class CourseFacade to handle database-related operations using the Java Persistence API.

8.5.6.3 Build the Session Bean for Entity Classes CourseFacade

The purpose of this session bean is to directly access our sample SQL Server 2008 database and perform all data queries and manipulations against our database via Java Persistence API. Recalled in Section 8.4.2, we have created an Entity class from our sample database and added it into this Web project. In this section, we will use that entity class to perform data actions against our sample database.

Perform the following operations to create a new session bean for entity classes CourseFacade:

1. Launch NetBeans IDE and open our Web project JavaWebDBJSPSQL.
2. Right click on our project JavaWebDBJSPSQL from the Projects window, and select New > Other to open the `New File` wizard.
3. Select Java EE from the `Categories` list and Session Beans For Entity Classes from the `File Types` list, and click on the Next button.
4. On the opened `New Session Beans for Entity Classes` wizard shown in Figure 8.99, select two entity classes, JavaWebDBJSPSQL.Course and JavaWebDBJSPSQL.Faculty from the `Available Entity Classes` list and click

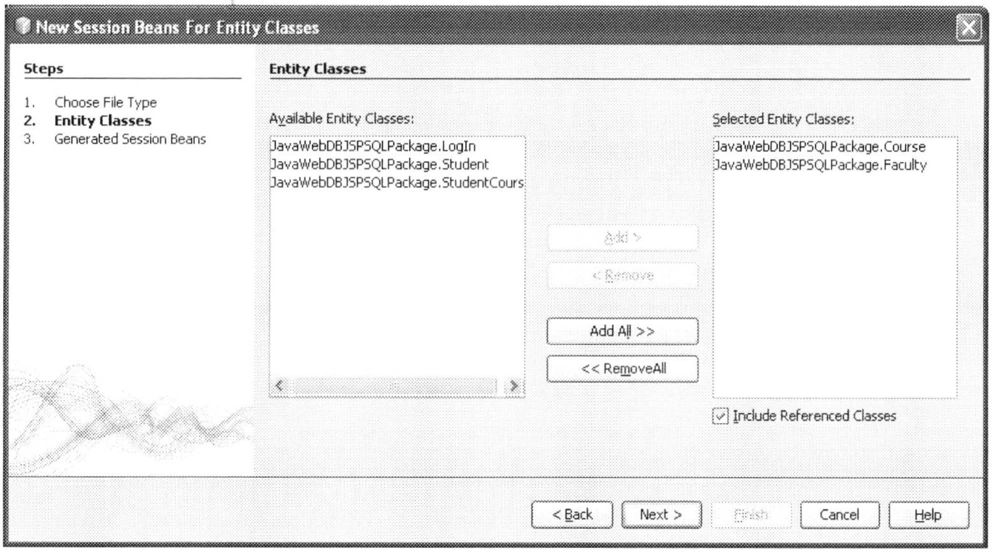

Figure 8.99. The Entity Classes wizard.

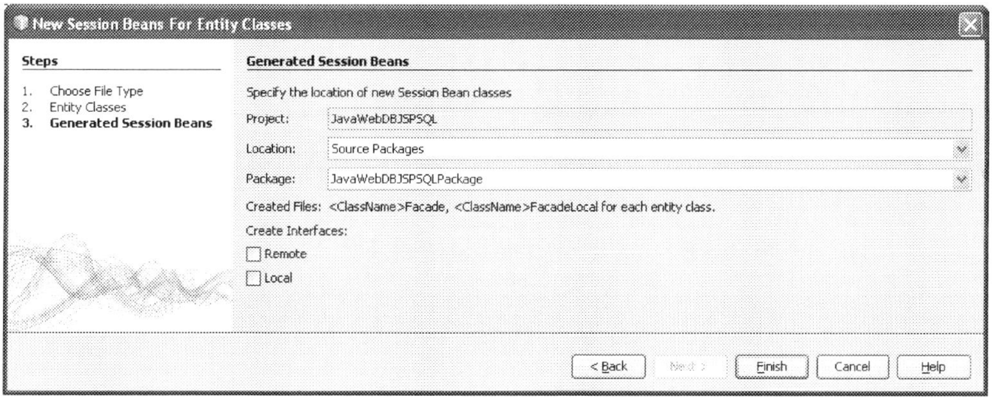

Figure 8.100. The Generated Session Beans wizard.

on the Add button to add them to the `Selected Entity Classes` list, as shown in Figure 8.99. Make sure to check the `Include Referenced Classes` checkbox and click on the Next button to continue.

5. In the opened `Generated Session Beans` wizard, which is shown in Figure 8.100, click on the Finish button to complete this creating new session beans for entity classes process.

The reason we only selected two entity classes, JavaWebDBJSPSQL.Course and JavaWebDBJSPSQL.Faculty, in step 4 above for this session bean is that we only need two tables, Course and Faculty, in our sample database to perform this course query operation. As you know, no faculty_name column is available in the Course table, and all course information is identified by using the faculty_id column in the Course table.

In order to get the faculty_id based on the selected faculty_name by the user, one needs to perform a query from the Faculty table to do that first. Therefore, we need these two tables to perform this course information query job.

Now, let's build the codes for this session bean class to perform data actions against our sample database using Java Persistence API technique.

Open the code window of this new Session Beans For Entity Class CourseFacade from the Projects window and enter the codes that are shown in Figure 8.101 into this class. The new added codes have been highlighted in bold.

Let's have a close look at these newly added codes to see how they work.

A. The javax.persistence.Query class is imported first since we need to use this component to perform the course information query in this class. All other packages are imported by the NetBeans IDE when this session class is created.

B. A user-defined property courseList is created since we need to use this property to store and return the queried result, which is a List component containing the queried course_id for the selected faculty member. The msgDlg is a JDialog object, and it is used to display the testing and debug information when this project is tested and debugged later.

C. The getCourseID() method is defined here, and this method is used to query all course_id taught by the selected faculty member by the user as the project runs. To perform this query, two queries needs to be performed. First, the faculty_id needs to be queried from the Faculty table based on the selected faculty_name, and then the course_id needs to be queried based on the faculty_id from the Course table. Here, a Java persistence query is created by using the createQuery() method to perform the first query. A named dynamic parameter :FacultyName is used for this query.

D. Steps **D**, **E** and **F** are used to set the named dynamic parameter :FacultyName for the first Java persistence query. First, a new Faculty instance fFaculty is created based on the Faculty entity class. Then the setFacultyName() method is executed with the selected faculty_name as the argument to make sure that the newly created Faculty instance has the selected faculty_name as the default faculty name. Finally, the setParameter() method is executed to set up the dynamic named parameter :FacultyName with the default faculty_name that is obtained by calling the getFacultyName() method as the argument. The reason we used these three steps to set up this named dynamic parameter is that the data type of the second argument for the setParameter() method is Object, not String. Therefore, we need to use a new Faculty instance to do that setup.

G. Similar to steps **D**, **E**, and **F**, we create another new Faculty instance cFaculty with the queried faculty_id as the argument to make it as an object for the setParameter() method in the second query. The getSingleResult() method that works as an argument for this newly created Faculty instance is used to execute the first query to get the faculty_id based on the faculty_name.

H. The second Java persistence query is created with the :facultyID as a named dynamic parameter.

I. The setParameter() method is executed to set up the named dynamic parameter :facultyID. The second argument of this method is a Faculty instance cFaculty that can be considered as an object, and it is created with the queried faculty_id in step G. This makes sure that the queried faculty_id will be set to that named dynamic parameter :facultyID.

J. The getResultList() method is executed to perform the second query to get all course_id, and the returned result is assigned to the bean's property courseList.

```
  package JavaWebDBJSPSQLPackage;

  import java.util.List;
  import javax.ejb.Stateless;
  import javax.persistence.EntityManager;
  import javax.persistence.PersistenceContext;
A import javax.persistence.Query;

  @Stateless
  public class CourseFacade {
     @PersistenceContext(unitName = "JavaWebDBJSPSQLPU")
     private EntityManager em;
B    private List courseList;
     MsgDialog msgDlg = new MsgDialog(new javax.swing.JFrame(), true);

     public void create(Course course) {
        em.persist(course);
     }
     public void edit(Course course) {
        em.merge(course);
     }
     public void remove(Course course) {
        em.remove(em.merge(course));
     }
     public Course find(Object id) {
        return em.find(Course.class, id);
     }
     public List<Course> findAll() {
        return em.createQuery("select object(o) from Course as o").getResultList();
     }
     public List<Course> findRange(int[] range) {
        Query q = em.createQuery("select object(o) from Course as o");
        q.setMaxResults(range[1] - range[0]);
        q.setFirstResult(range[0]);
        return q.getResultList();
     }
     public int count() {
        return ((Long) em.createQuery("select count(o) from Course as o").getSingleResult()).intValue();
     }
C    public List getCourseID(String fname) {
        Query fQuery = em.createQuery("SELECT f.facultyId FROM Faculty f " +
                                      "WHERE f.facultyName= :FacultyName");
D       Faculty fFaculty = new Faculty();
E       fFaculty.setFacultyName(fname);
F       fQuery.setParameter("FacultyName", fFaculty.getFacultyName());
G       Faculty cFaculty = new Faculty((String)fQuery.getSingleResult());
H       Query cQuery = em.createQuery("SELECT c.courseId FROM Course c WHERE c.facultyId = :facultyID");
I       cQuery.setParameter("facultyID", cFaculty);
J       this.courseList = cQuery.getResultList();
K       return courseList;
     }
L    public List<Object[]> getCourseDetail(String cid) {
        List<Object[]> courselist = null;
M       String strQuery = "SELECT c.course, c.schedule, c.classroom, c.credit, c.enrollment " +
                          "FROM Course c WHERE c.courseId = :courseid";
N       Query cQuery = em.createQuery(strQuery);
O       cQuery.setParameter("courseid", cid);
P       courselist = cQuery.getResultList();
Q       return courselist;
     }
  }
```

Figure 8.101. The codes for the session bean CourseFacade.

K. The queried result is returned to the JSF managed bean CourseBean for further process.

L. The getCourseDetail() method is defined here with the course_id as the argument. The purpose of this method is to query five pieces of detailed information from the Course entity based on the selected course_id, and return the result to the JSF managed bean. First, a new List instance courselist is created.

M. A Java persistence query is created with the courseid as a named dynamic parameter.

N. The query object cQuery is created by calling the createQuery() method.

O. The setParameter() method is executed to set up the named dynamic parameter :courseid.

P. The getResultList() method is executed to run this query to get five pieces of detailed information for the selected course_id, and the query result is assigned to the local List instance courselist.

Q. The query result is returned to the JSF managed bean CourseBean for future process.

Those codes that have not been highlighted in bold in this class are created by the NetBeans IDE automatically when this session bean is created.

If you encounter some real-time compiling errors for some codes in this window, right click on any place in this window and select the Fix Imports item to try to solve those errors. A typical error you may encounter is that you missed the java.util.List class in the import section.

Now, let's set up a calling relationship between the JSF managed bean CourseBean and the session bean CourseFacade.

8.5.6.4 Set Up Calling Relationship between the JSF Bean and the Session Bean

Perform the following operations to set up this calling relationship between the JSF managed bean CourseBean and the session bean CourseFacade:

1. Open the code window of the JSF managed bean class CourseBean.
2. Right click on this code window and select the Insert Code item from the pop-up menu.
3. Click on the Call Enterprise Bean item from the opened list.
4. On the opened `Call Enterprise Bean` wizard, as shown in Figure 8.102, select our session bean class CourseFacade from the list.
5. Keep the No Interface radio button checked since we do not need any interface, and we have built our Web page CoursePage as the interface for this project.
6. Click on the OK button to complete this setup.

Immediately, you can find that two coding lines, as shown below, have been added into the code window of our JSF managed bean class CourseBean. Exactly they are located under the class header:

```
@EJB
private CourseFacade courseFacade;
```

The @EJB is an injected source and added by the Java Enterprise Bean engine, and the new instance courseFacade is created as a new property in our JSF managed bean class CourseBean.

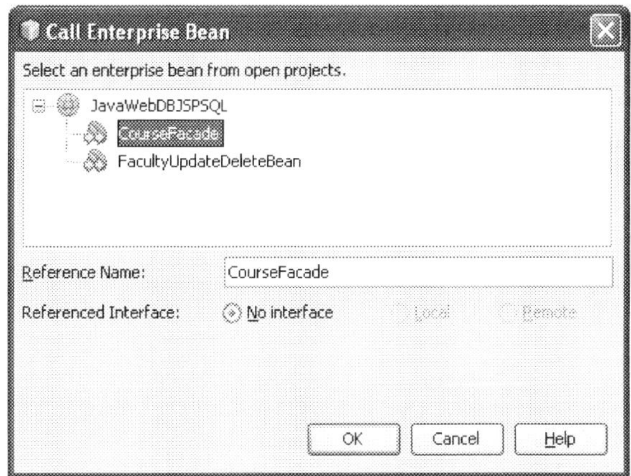

Figure 8.102. The finished Call Enterprise Bean wizard.

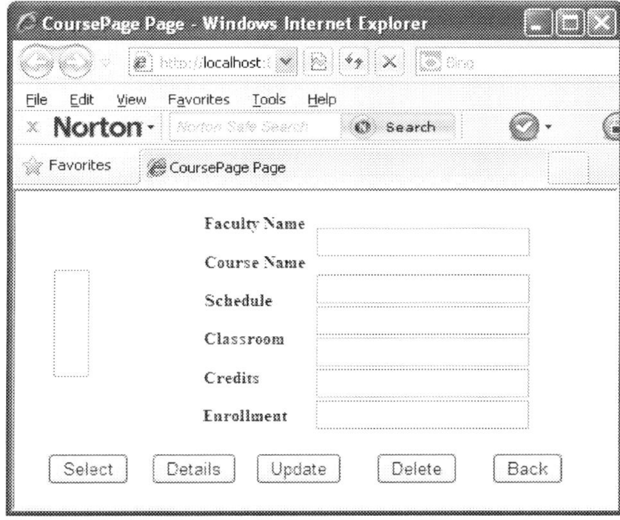

Figure 8.103. The running stage of the CoursePage.

At this point, we have finished all coding jobs for our project. Now let's build and run our project to test the codes we built in the previous sections for this project.

8.5.6.5 Build and Run the Project to Test the Course Information Query Functions

Now click on the Clean and Build Main Project button to build our project. If everything is fine, right click on our CoursePage.jsp from the Projects window and select the Run File item from the popup menu to run this page. The running page is shown in Figure 8.103.

Enter a faculty name, such as Jenney King, into the `Faculty Name` field, and click on the Select button to retrieve all courses, exactly all course_id, taught by the selected

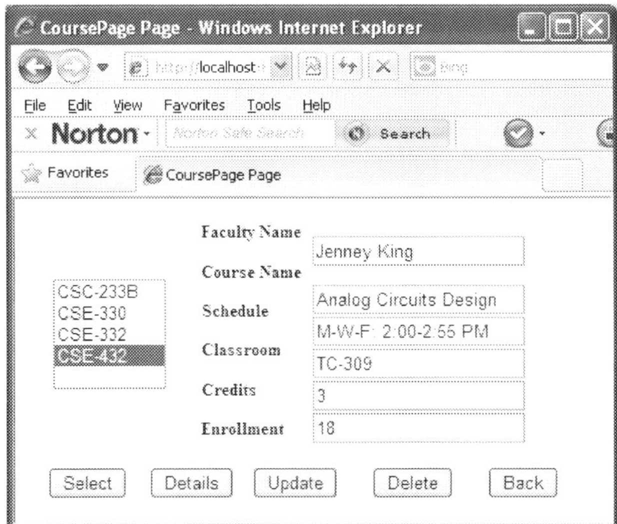

Figure 8.104. The queried results of the CoursePage.

faculty member. All four courses taught by the faculty member Jenney King are retrieved and displayed in the course listbox, as shown in Figure 8.104.

Click one course_id, such as CSE-432, from the course listbox, and click on the Details button to try to query and retrieve the details for that course. All five pieces of detailed information related to the selected course_id are displayed in five fields, as shown in Figure 8.104.

Our course information query using JSF pages and Java bean is successful.

Click on the Close button that is located at the upper-right corner of this page to close this page and project.

Next, we will discuss how to update and delete a record from the Course table in our sample database.

8.5.7 Update Records from the Course Table Using JavaServer Faces and Java Beans

In this section, we will discuss how to update a record for the Course table in our sample database using JSF page and Java beans techniques.

We will use the Update button on the CoursePage page to perform this data updating operation.

Recall that in Section 8.5.6.1, the Update button in the JSF page CoursePage is bound to the Update() method defined in the Java managed bean class CourseBean via the action attribute of that button. Now we can use this bound relationship to perform the course information updating operation against our sample database.

The key point to be noted is that in most real applications, all pieces of course information should be updated except the course_id, since it is much easier to insert a new course record with a new course_id than updating a record with an updated course_id.

```
  public Boolean Update() {
A     String[] newCourse = {null, null, null, null, null, null};
B     newCourse[0] = selectedItem;
      newCourse[1] = getCourseName();
      newCourse[2] = getSchedule();
      newCourse[3] = getClassroom();
      newCourse[4] = getCredit();
      newCourse[5] = getEnrollment();
C     courseFacade.UpdateCourse(newCourse);
D     return null;
  }
```

Figure 8.105. The codes for the Update() method.

Therefore, in this section, we will concentrate on the updating a course record based on an existing course_id.

As we did for the course information query in the last section, we still want to use the managed bean CourseBean as an intermediate-level controller to call a business method UpdateCourse() defined in the session bean CourseFacade to perform this course record updating.

First, let's create the codes for the Update() method in the JSF managed bean CourseBean to call the UpdateCourse() method that is defined in the session bean CourseFacade class and will be developed in the next section to do this course updating.

8.5.7.1 Create Codes for the Update() Method in the JSF Managed Bean

Open our project JavaWebDBJSPSQL from the Projects window and our managed bean class CourseBean. Browse to the Update() method and enter the codes that are shown in Figure 8.105 into this method.

Let's have a closer look at this piece of codes to see how it works.

A. In order to perform a course record updating, we need to collect and pass six pieces of updated course information into the UpdateCourse() method defined in the session bean CourseFacade to access the database to do this updating. So a string array newCourse[] that is used to hold those pieces of information with six elements is created first.

B. Then six pieces of collected course updating information are assigned to each element in the newCourse[] array using the getter methods. The point to be noted is the data process performed between the JSF page CoursePage and the JSF managed bean CourseBean. In fact, before the Update button in the CoursePage can be clicked by the user, all six pieces of course updating information should have been entered into six inputText field. Recall that the value attributes of these six inputText fields have been bound to the associated properties defined in the CourseBean class. The true story is that as the user clicks the Update button, all six pieces of course updating information stored in the six inputText fields will be submitted to the JSF managed bean CourseBean and assigned to the associated properties defined in that bean class. To get those properties, we need to use the associated getter method to do that and assign each of them to an element in the string array newCourse[]. The selectedItem property contains the course_id selected by the user from the <h:selectOneListbox> tag in the CoursePage.

```
  public void UpdateCourse(String[] nCourse) {
A     String query = "UPDATE Course c SET c.course=?1, c.schedule=?2, c.classroom=?3, " +
                     "c.credit=?4, c.enrollment=?5 WHERE c.courseId=:CourseID";
B     em.clear();
C     Query cQuery = em.createQuery(query);
D     cQuery.setParameter(1, nCourse[1]);
      cQuery.setParameter(2, nCourse[2]);
      cQuery.setParameter(3, nCourse[3]);
      cQuery.setParameter(4, Integer.parseInt(nCourse[4]));
      cQuery.setParameter(5, Integer.parseInt(nCourse[5]));
      cQuery.setParameter("CourseID", nCourse[0]);
E     cQuery.executeUpdate();
  }
```

Figure 8.106. The codes for the UpdateCourse() method.

C. The UpdateCourse() method defined in the session bean class CourseFacade is called with the newCourse[] array as the argument to perform this data updating action.

D. The returning value is not important to us since the data updating action has been performed by executing the UpdateCourse() method. To simplify the execution of this method, we did not use any returned value to check and confirm this action. You can use a returned integer or Boolean to do this confirmation if you like.

Next, let's develop the codes for the UpdateCourse() method in the session bean class to access our sample database to perform this data updating action.

8.5.7.2 Create Codes for the UpdateCourse() Method in the Session Bean

Open the code window of the session bean class CourseFacade and create a new method UpdateCourse() and enter the codes that are shown in Figure 8.106 into this method.

Let's have a closer look at this piece of codes to see how it works.

A. A dynamic JPA query statement with the positional parameters and named parameter is created first. The five pieces of course updating information are arranged in a sequence order with the attached number as the indicator, and the last parameter is a named parameter CourseID that works as a query criterion.

B. The EntityManager is first cleaned up to make this data updating ready.

C. The dynamic query object is created by calling the createQuery() method.

D. Five pieces of course updating information, including the query criterion course_id, are assigned to the associated positional and named parameters, and one by one defined in the query statement. Two points to be noted for these assignments are: first, the order of this assignment must be identical with the order of positional parameters defined in the query statement we created in step **A**. Second, the data types for parameters 4 and 5, or credit and enrollment, are both INTEGER (SMALLINT for credit and INTEGER for enrollment) when we created the Course table in our sample database. Therefore, you must use the parseInt() method defined in the Integer class to convert these two parameters from String to Integer, respectively, and then assign them to those dynamic parameters. Otherwise, you may encounter a compiling error during building the project later.

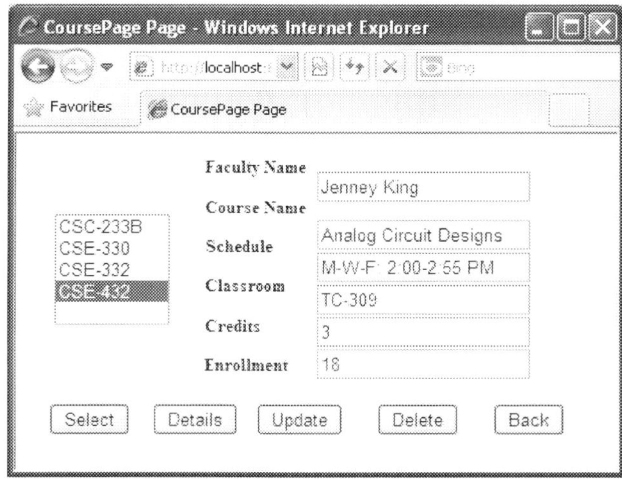

Figure 8.107. The running status of the CoursePage.

E. Finally the executeUpdate() method is executed to perform this data updating action. One point to be noted is that no Transaction object should be used for this data manipulation since JPA can handle this automatically.

At this point, we have completed all coding jobs for the course data updating operation. Now, let's build and run our project to test this data updating function.

Click on the Clean and Build Main Project button to build our project. If everything is fine, right click on our CoursePage.jsp from the Projects window and select the Run File item from the pop-up menu to run this page.

Enter a faculty name, such as Jenney King, into the `Faculty Name` field, and click on the Select button to retrieve and display all courses taught by this faculty in the CourseList box. Then select one course_id, such as CSE-432, from the CourseList box, and click on the Details button to get the details for this course. The running result is shown in Figure 8.107.

To update this course, enter the updating information shown in Figure 8.108 into the five inputText fields.

Click on the Update button to try to update this course.

To confirm this data updating action, two methods can be used: first, you can open the Course table from the NetBeans IDE environment to do this confirmation. To do that, open the Services window and expand to our Course table, right click on the Course table, and select the View Data item from the pop-up menu to open this table. Browse down to the course CSE-432, and you can find that the course has been updated, as shown in Figure 8.109.

The second way to confirm this updating action is to use the Details button to try to retrieve the details of this updated course. To do that, first select another course_id from the CourseList box and click on the Details button to get details for that course. Then select the CSE-432 from the list and click on the Details button again, You can find that the course CSE-432 has been updated based on the retrieved and displayed details for this course.

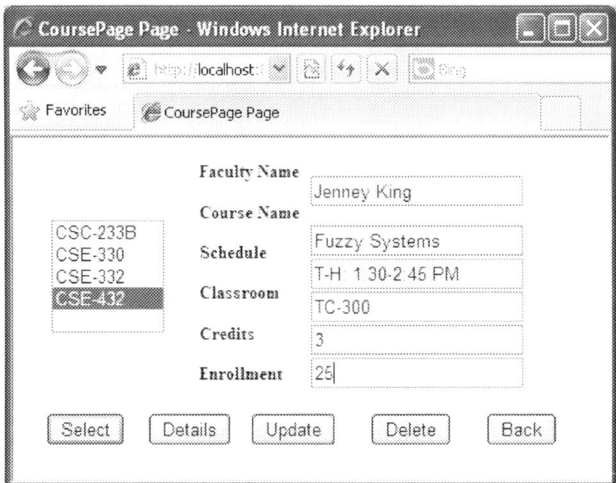

Figure 8.108. The updating information for the course CSE-432.

SQL Command 1 - Editor

Connection: jdbc:sqlserver://localhost\SQL2008...

```
select * from dbo.Course
```

select * from dbo.Course

Page Size: 20 Total Rows: 36 Page: 2 of 2 Matching Rows:

#	course_id	course	credit	classroom	schedule	enrollment	faculty_id
8	CSE-334	Elec Measurement & Design	3	TC-212	T-H: 11:00-12:25 PM	25	H99118
9	CSE-430	Bioinformatics in Computer	3	TC-206	Thu: 9:30-11:00 AM	16	B86590
10	CSE-432	Fuzzy Systems	3	TC-300	T-H: 1:30-2:45 PM	25	K69880
11	CSE-433	Digital Signal Processing	3	TC-206	T-H: 2:00-3:25 PM	18	H99118
12	CSE-434	Advanced Electronics Systems	3	TC-213	M-W-F: 1:00-1:55 PM	26	B78880
13	CSE-436	Automatic Control and Design	3	TC-305	M-W-F: 10:00-10:55 AM	29	J33486
14	CSE-437	Operating Systems	3	TC-303	T-H: 1:00-2:25 PM	17	A77587

Figure 8.109. The updated course CSE-432.

Before closing this project, it is highly recommended to recover this updated course. To do that recovery, just enter the following original details for the course CSE-432 into the five inputText fields, and then click on the Update button to complete this data recovery.

CourseID:	CSE-432
Course Name:	Analog Circuit Designs
Schedule:	M-W-F: 2:00–2:55 PM
Classroom:	TC-309
Credits:	3
Enrollment:	18

Now close the project by clicking on the Close button located at the upper-right corner of this page. Our data updating action using the JSF pages and Java bean is successful.

Finally, let's take care of the course data deleting action against our sample database using the JSF pages and Java bean techniques.

8.5.8 Delete Records from the Course Table Using JavaServer Faces and Java Beans

As we did for the course data updating action in the last section, we still want to use the Delete button defined in the CoursePage and the associated Delete() method defined in the managed bean CourseBean to perform this data deletion action.

First, let's build the codes for the Delete() method in our managed bean CourseBean class.

8.5.8.1 Build Codes for the Delete() Method in the JSF Managed Bean

Open the code window of the managed bean CourseBean and browse to the Delete() method, and enter the codes shown in Figure 8.110 into this method.

Let's have a closer look at this piece of codes to see how it works.

A. First, a returned boolean variable delete is created and initialized to false.

B. Then the DeleteCourse() method that is defined in the session bean CourseFacade and will be developed in the next section is called with the course_id as the argument to perform this course data deleting action.

C. If the returned value is `false`, which means that this action has failed, a warning message is displayed using our JDialog box to indicate this situation.

D. Otherwise, the course data deletion is successful. In fact, the returned value is not important to us and therefore a null is returned.

Now let's build the codes for the DeleteCourse() method in our session bean class to perform this data-deleting action.

```
    public Boolean Delete()  {
A        boolean  delete = false;
B        delete = courseFacade.DeleteCourse(selectedItem);
C        if (!delete) {
            msgDlg.setMessage("The course deleting is failed!");
            msgDlg.setVisible(true);
         }
D        return null;
    }
```

Figure 8.110. The codes for the Delete() method.

```
  public boolean DeleteCourse(String cid) {
A       int delete = 0;
B       String  query = "DELETE FROM Course c WHERE  c.courseId =:CourseID";
C       em.clear();
D       Query  cQuery = em.createQuery(query);
E       cQuery.setParameter("CourseID", cid);
F       delete = cQuery.executeUpdate();
G       if (delete != 0)
          return true;
H       else
          return false;
  }
```

Figure 8.111. The codes for the DeleteCourse() method.

8.5.8.2 Build Codes for the DeleteCourse() Method in the Session Bean

Open the code window for our session bean class CourseFacade and create a new method DeleteCourse(). Enter the codes shown in Figure 8.111 into this method.

Let's have a closer look at this piece of codes to see how it works.

A. A local integer variable delete is created, and it is used to hold the running result of the execution of the data deleting action.

B. The course deleting statement string is created with a named parameter CourseID.

C. The EntityManager is cleaned up to make it ready for this data deleting action.

D. The createQuery() method with the deleting query string as the argument is executed to create this deleting query object cQuery.

E. The setParameter() method is executed to initialize the named parameter CourseID with the input argument cid, which is the selected course_id.

F. The deleting action is performed by calling the executeUpdate() method, and the running result of this deleting action is assigned to the local integer variable delete.

G. The running result of this deletion is exactly an integer number indicating how many rows have been successfully deleted from the Course table. If this returned result is not equal to 0, which means that at least one row has been deleted from the Course table and this deleting action is successful, a `true` is returned to indicate this situation.

H. Otherwise, the deleting action has failed, and a `false` is returned.

Now let's build and run the project to test this data deleting action.

Click on the Clean and Build Main Project button to build our project. If everything is fine, right click on our CoursePage.jsp from the Projects window and select the Run File item from the pop-up menu to run this page.

Enter a faculty name, such as Jenney King, into the `Faculty Name` field, and click on the Select button to retrieve and display all courses taught by this faculty in the CourseList box. Then select one course_id, such as CSC-233B, from the CourseList box, and click on the Delete button to try to delete this course from our Course table.

To confirm this deleting action, two ways can be used. One way is to open the Course table from the Services window in the NetBeans IDE to check whether this course has

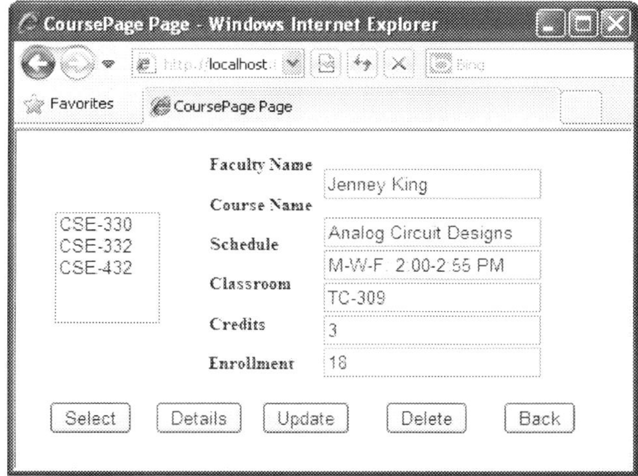

Figure 8.112. The running result of deleting course action.

Table 8.8. The course CSC-233B record in the Course table

course_id	course	credit	classroom	schedule	enrollment	faculty_id
CSC-233B	Introduction to Algorithms	3	TC-302	M-W-F: 11:00-11:55 AM	19	K69880

been removed. Another way is to use the Select button to try to retrieve all courses taught by the selected faculty from our Course table to confirm this deleting action. Now let's use the second way to do this checking since it is easy.

Make sure that the faculty member Jenney King is still in the `Faculty Name` field, and click on the Select button to try to retrieve all courses taught by this faculty. You can find that no course CSC-233B is displayed in the CourseList box, as shown in Figure 8.112, and this course has been deleted from the Course table successfully.

Now close the project by clicking on the Close button located at the upper-right corner of this page. Our data deleting action using the JSF pages and Java bean is successful.

It is highly recommended to recover this deleted course from the Course table to make our database clean and neat. Use the data shown in Table 8.8 to do this recovery job.

One easy way to recover this record is to open the Microsoft SQL Server 2008 Management Studio to insert a new row shown in Table 8.8 into our Course table. On the opened SQL Server 2008 Studio, expand to our dbo.Course table and right click on it, and select the Edit Top 200 Rows item to do this new row insertion.

The codes for the Back button in the CoursePage are not important in this application, and we'd like to leave this coding as a homework to the readers.

A complete Java Web application project JavaWebDBJSPSQL can be found from the folder DBProjects\Chapter 8 that is located at the Wiley ftp site (refer to Figure 1.2 in Chapter 1). You can download this project and test it in your computer if you like.

Next, let's handle building another Web application project to access and manipulate the data against Oracle databases.

8.6 BUILD JAVA WEB PROJECT TO ACCESS AND MANIPULATE ORACLE DATABASE

In this section, we will discuss how to access the Oracle database and perform related data manipulations against our sample Oracle database using JavaServer Faces, Java bean, and another Java persistence technique—Hibernate. The structure block diagram of this kind of application is shown in Figure 8.113.

As we discussed in Section 5.3.6.2 in Chapter 5, Hibernate is an ORM library for the Java language, and it provides a framework for mapping an object-oriented domain model to a traditional relational database. Unlike the traditional Java Persistence API, Hibernate solves object-relational impedance mismatch problems by replacing direct persistence-related database accesses with high-level object handling functions. Refer to Sections 5.3.6.2 and 5.3.6.6–5.3.6.7 in Chapter 5 to get more details about the configurations and implementations of Hibernate in Java database applications.

Based on Figure 8.113, we will build Java Web database applications to access and manipulate Oracle databases in the following structure:

1. Build and use JSF pages as the Web GUI or View to collect the users' inputs and display the querying results.
2. Build and use Java session bean classes as the model to process data collected from the JSF pages, perform queries to the database and return the query results to the JSF pages.
3. Build and use another JPA, Hibernate, to map the database and manipulate data against the mapped database.

The operational principle of three blocks above is:

1. The GUI components built in the JSF pages are bound to the associated properties or methods defined in the Java session bean class, and these binding can be divided into two categories:
   A. All value attributes for input and output tags are bound to the associated properties in the Java session bean class.
   B. All action attributes for button tags are bound to the associated methods defined in the Java session bean class.

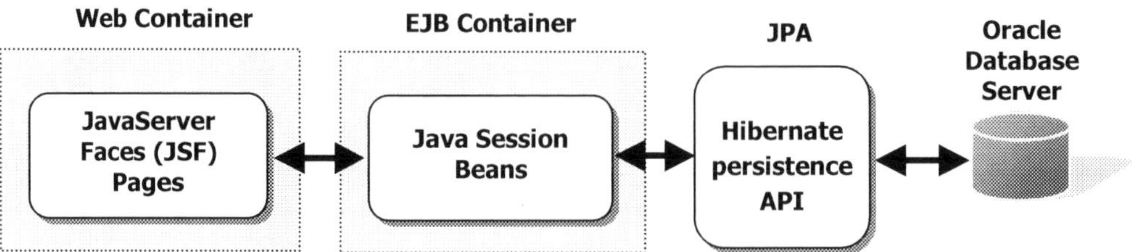

Figure 8.113. The structure of three-tier Web applications.

2. As the values of properties defined in the Java session bean are modified based on the queried result from the database, the bound values of the associated GUI components in the JSF pages are also modified immediately. Therefore, the input/output results can be collected and displayed between the JSF pages and Java beans through these binding relationships.
3. The navigations from one page to another page are based on the navigation rules defined in the faces-config.xml file.

Based on these structures and principles, now let's begin to build our Java Web database applications to access Oracle databases to perform desired data actions. First, let's create a new Java Web application project JavaWebDBJSPOracle.

8.6.1 Create a Java Web Application Project

Perform the following operations to create this new Java Web application project:

1. Launch NetBeans IDE and go to File > New Project menu item to open the `New Project` wizard. Select Java Web from the `Categories` list, and Web Application from the `Projects` list. Then click on the Next button to continue.
2. Enter JavaWebDBJSPOracle into the `Project Name` field and select the desired location to save this project by clicking on the Browse button. Your finished `Name and Location` wizard should match one that is shown in Figure 8.114. Click on the Next button to go to the next wizard.
3. Keep all default settings in the next wizard unchanged, which means that we need to use the Glassfish v3 as our application server and Java EE 6 as our platform in this project, and click on the Next button to continue.
4. In the Frameworks wizard, select the JavaServer Faces and Hibernate 3.2.5 from the list by checking them since we need to use both frameworks in this application. Also, click on the dropdown arrow from the `Database Connection` combo box, and select our

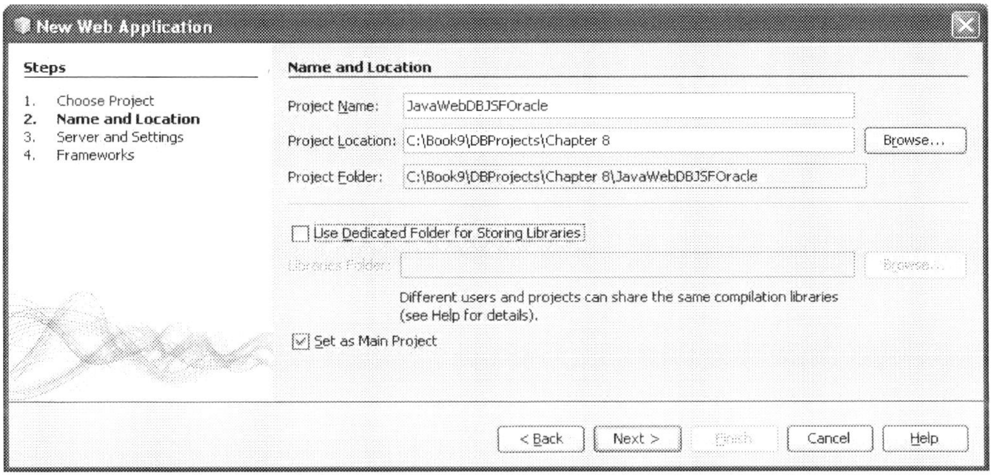

New Web Application

Steps

1. Choose Project
2. **Name and Location**
3. Server and Settings
4. Frameworks

Name and Location

Project Name: JavaWebDBJSFOracle

Project Location: C:\Book9\DBProjects\Chapter 8 [Browse...]

Project Folder: C:\Book9\DBProjects\Chapter 8\JavaWebDBJSFOracle

[ ] Use Dedicated Folder for Storing Libraries

Libraries Folder: [Browse...]

Different users and projects can share the same compilation libraries (see Help for details).

[✓] Set as Main Project

[< Back] [Next >] [Finish] [Cancel] [Help]

Figure 8.114. The finished Name and Location wizard.

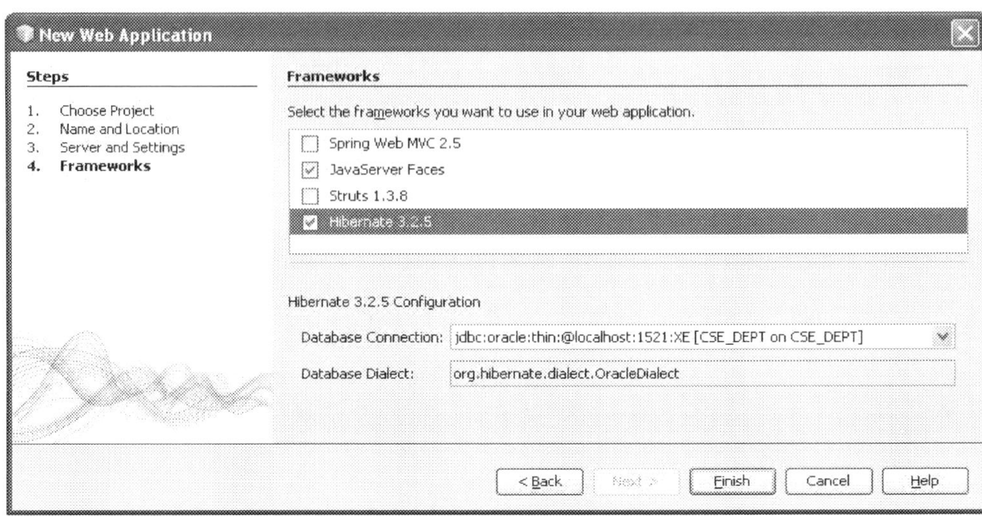

Figure 8.115. The finished Frameworks wizard.

sample Oracle database represented by its URL: jdbc:oracle:thin:@localhost:1521:XE [CSE_DEPT on CSE_DEPT], as shown in Figure 8.115. Click on the Finish button to complete this New Project creation process.

As soon as you create a new Web application project using the Hibernate framework, a Hibernate configuration file, hibernate.cfg.xml, will be automatically created by the NetBeans IDE at the root of the context classpath of the application, which is src/java in the Files window. The file is located in the `<default package>` under the Source Packages node in the Projects window. The configuration file contains information about the database connection, resource mappings, and other connection properties. You can edit the file using the multiview editor, or edit the XML directly in the XML editor.

To make our project work properly using the Hibernate tools, we need to do some modifications to this configuration file.

8.6.2 Modify the Hibernate Configuration File

Three modifications will be performed for this file; they are:

1. Add the hibernate.show_sql property to enables the debug logging of the SQL statements.
2. Add the hibernate.current_session_context_class property to enable Hibernate's automatic session context management.
3. Add the hibernate.query.factory_class property to enable the Hibernate to perform the factory translator query automatically.

Let's do those modifications one by one starting from the first one.

- Open the hibernate.cfg.xml in the `Design` tab. You can open the file by expanding Source Packages > <default package> in the Projects window and double clicking the configuration file hibernate.cfg.xml.

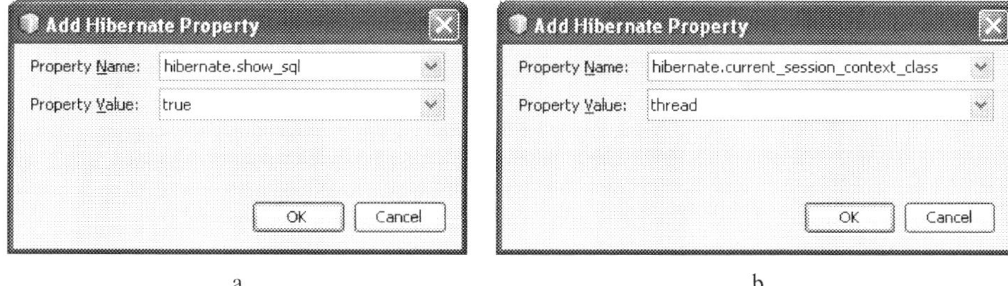

Figure 8.116. Modifications to the Hibernate configuration file.

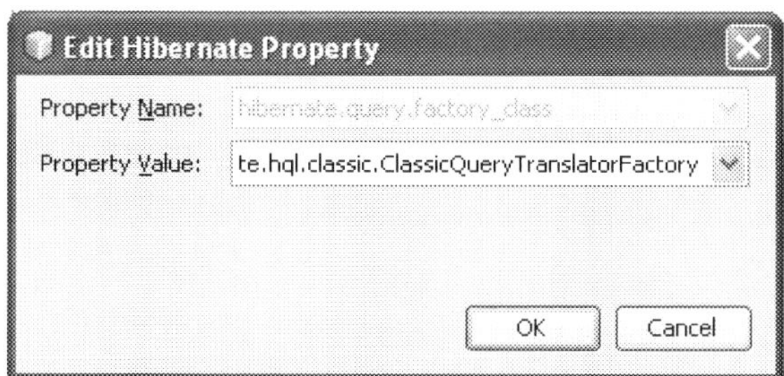

Figure 8.117. The third modified property for the Hibernate configuration file.

- In the multiview XML editor, expand the Configuration Properties node under the Optional Properties.
- Click on the Add button to open the `Add Hibernate Property` dialog box.
- In the dialog box, select the hibernate.show_sql property and set the value to true. The finished dialog box is shown in Figure 8.116a. This enables the debug logging of the SQL statements.

Perform the following operations to do the second modification:

- Expand the Miscellaneous Properties node and click on the Add button.
- In the opened dialog box, select the properties hibernate.current_session_context_class and set the value to thread to enable Hibernate's automatic session context management. Your finished modification for this property is shown in Figure 8.116b.

For the third modification, follow the operational sequence described below:

- Click on the Add button again under the Miscellaneous Properties node and select hibernate.query.factory_class in the `Property Name` drop-down list.
- Type org.hibernate.hql.classic.ClassicQueryTranslatorFactory as the `Property Value`, and then click on the OK button to complete this modification. Your finished modification for this property is shown in Figure 8.117.

Now click on the XML tab to open this modified configuration file in the XML format, and your modified file should match one that is shown in Figure 8.118.

In step **A**, the Oracle JDBC Driver is indicated by this driver class property, and the URL of our sample Oracle database is set by the url property. The username and

```
  <?xml version="1.0" encoding="UTF-8"?>
  <!DOCTYPE hibernate-configuration PUBLIC "-//Hibernate/Hibernate Configuration DTD 3.0//EN"
  "http://hibernate.sourceforge.net/hibernate-configuration-3.0.dtd">
  <hibernate-configuration>
    <session-factory>
      <property name="hibernate.dialect">org.hibernate.dialect.OracleDialect</property>
A     <property name="hibernate.connection.driver_class">oracle.jdbc.OracleDriver</property>
      <property name="hibernate.connection.url">jdbc:oracle:thin:@localhost:1521:XE</property>
B     <property name="hibernate.connection.username">CSE_DEPT</property>
      <property name="hibernate.connection.password">reback</property>
C     <property name="hibernate.show_sql">true</property>
      <property name="hibernate.current_session_context_class">thread</property>
      <property name="hibernate.query.factory_class">org.hibernate.hql.classic.ClassicQueryTranslatorFactory</property>
  </session-factory>
  </hibernate-configuration>
```

Figure 8.118. The modified Hibernate configuration file.

password of our sample database are set to the username and password properties of the Hibernate connection class in step **B**. Starting from step **C**, our three modifications are set to those three related properties on the Hibernate component.

Make sure that all properties defined in your Hibernate configuration file are identical with those shown in Figure 8.118. In case that the sample database is locked, please open our sample Oracle database and login with the administrator username and password (SYSTEM and reback) to unlock it.

Next let's create and configure the Hibernate components and related files since we need to use this component to perform database mapping and manipulations against our sample Oracle database in this application.

8.6.3 Create Hibernate Utility Files and Mapping Files

To correctly and smoothly implement the Hibernate component to map and access our sample database, we need to create some necessary utility files and mapping files for this component. First, let's create the utility files for this component.

8.6.3.1 Create the HibernateUtil.java Helper File

To use Hibernate framework, we need to create a helper class that handles startup and that accesses Hibernate's SessionFactory to obtain a Session object. The class will call Hibernate's configure() method, loads the hibernate.cfg.xml configuration file, and then builds the SessionFactory to obtain the Session object.

In this section, we will use the `New File` wizard to create the Hibernate helper class file HibernateUtil.java. Perform the following operations to create this helper class file:

1. Right click on the Source Packages node in the Projects window and select New > Other menu item to open the `New File` wizard.
2. Select Hibernate from the `Categories` list and HibernateUtil.java from the `File Types` list, and then click on the Next button.

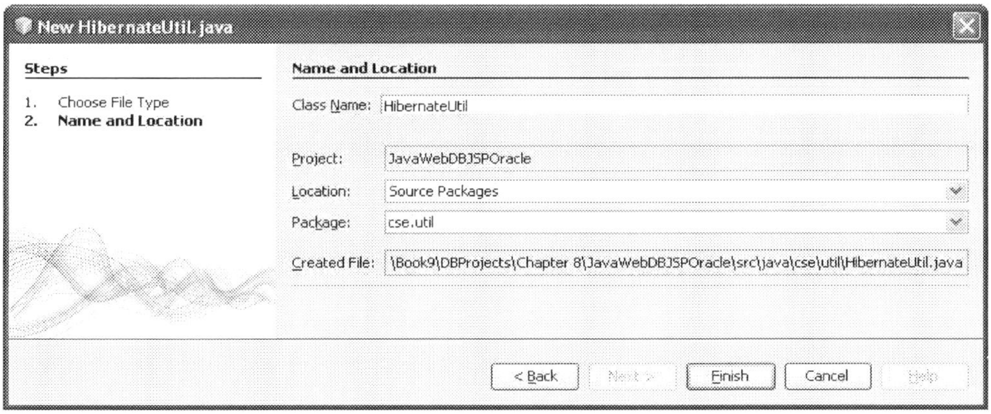

Figure 8.119. The finished New HibernateUtil.java dialog box.

3. Type **HibernateUtil** for the class name and **cse.util** as the package name, as shown in Figure 8.119. Click on the Finish button.

Next, let's create Hibernate mapping files and related Java classes to perform the data actions against our sample Oracle database.

8.6.3.2 Generate Hibernate Mapping Files and Java Classes

In this section, we will use a group of plain old Java object (POJO) files to represent the data in the five tables in our sample Oracle database. The classes specify the fields for the columns in tables and use simple setters and getters to retrieve and write the data. To map POJO files to the five tables, we can use a group of Hibernate mapping files or use annotations in the class.

We can use the `Reverse Engineering` wizard and the `Hibernate Mapping Files and POJOs from a Database` wizard to create multiple POJOs and mapping files based on database tables that we selected. Alternatively, we can use wizards provided by the NetBeans IDE to help us to create individual POJOs and mapping files from scratch.

A point to be noted is that if you want to create mapping files for multiple tables, you may most likely want to use the wizards. In this application, we need to create five POJOs and five mapping files so it is fairly easy to do that with the help of wizards.

To use the `POJOs and Mapping Files from Database` wizard, we need to first create the reveng.xml reverse engineering file in the src/java directory where we created and stored our hibernate.cfg.xml.

8.6.3.2.1 Create the Hibernate Reverse Engineering File Perform the following operations to create this reverse engineering file:

1. Right click on the `Source Packages` node from the Projects window and select New > Other menu item to open the `New File` wizard.
2. Select Hibernate from the `Categories` list and Hibernate Reverse Engineering Wizard from the `File Types` list. Click on the Next button to continue.

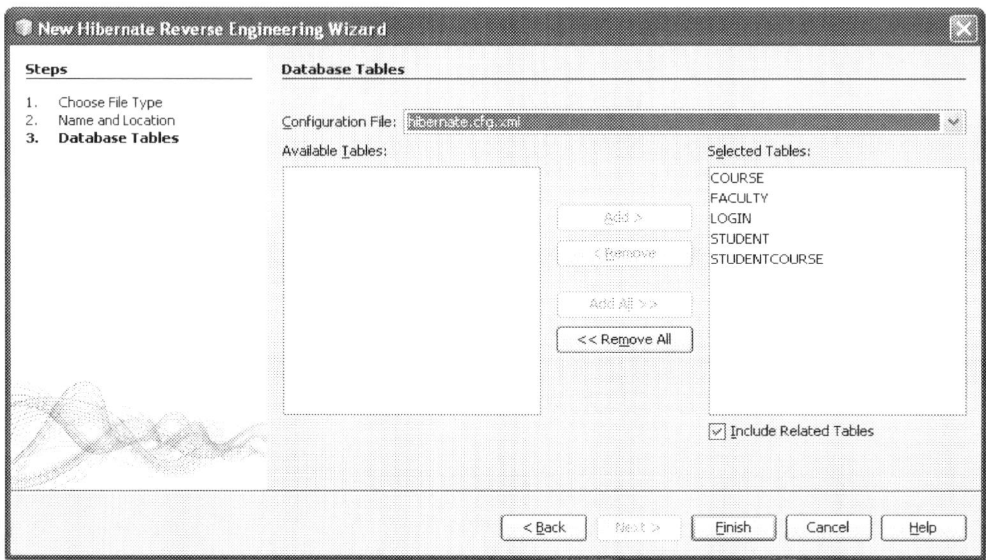

Figure 8.120. The finished Database Tables wizard.

3. Type `hibernate.reveng` for the file name.
4. Specify src/java as the `Folder` location, and then click on the Next button.
5. Select all five tables from the `Available Tables` list and click on the Add All button to add these data tables to our Hibernate class, as shown in Figure 8.120.
6. Click on the Finish button to complete this process.

The wizard generates a `hibernate.reveng.xml` reverse engineering file located at the default package in our project.

Now let's create Hibernate mapping files and POJOs from our sample Oracle database.

8.6.3.2.2 Create Hibernate Mapping Files and POJOs from Our Sample Database

The `Hibernate Mapping Files and POJOs from a Database` wizard generates files based on tables in the connected database. When using the wizard, the NetBeans IDE generates POJOs and mapping files for us based on the database tables specified in reverse engineering file `hibernate.reveng.xml`, and then adds the mapping entries to `hibernate.cfg.xml`. By using this wizard, we can choose the files that we want the NetBeans IDE to generate, for example, only the POJOs, and select code generation options,generate code that uses EJB 3 annotations.

Perform the following operations to create mapping files and POJOs:

1. Right click on the `Source Packages` node in the Projects window and choose New > Other menu item to open the `New File` dialog.
2. Select Hibernate from the `Categories` list and Hibernate Mapping Files and POJOs from a Database from the `File Types` list. Click on the Next button to continue.
3. Select hibernate.cfg.xml from the `Hibernate Configuration File` drop-down list, if this configuration file has not been selected.

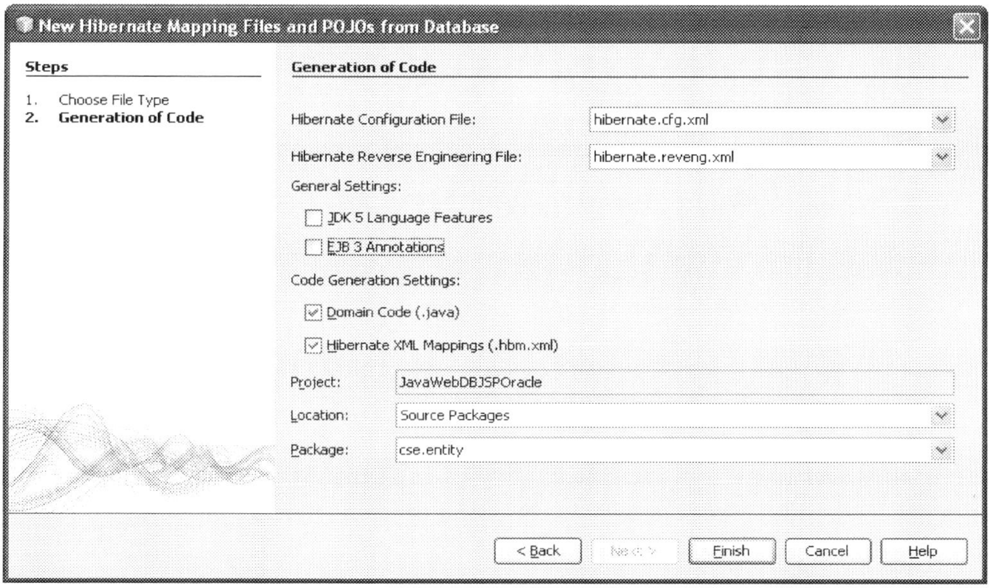

Figure 8.121. The finished Generation of Code wizard.

4. Select hibernate.reveng.xml from the `Hibernate Reverse Engineering File` dropdown list, if it has not been selected.
5. Ensure that the `Domain Code` and `Hibernate XML Mappings` options are selected.
6. Type cse.entity for the `Package` name. The finished New Hibernate Mapping Files and POJOs from Database wizard is shown in Figure 8.121.
7. Click on the Finish button to complete this creation process.

When clicking on the Finish button, the NetBeans IDE generates the POJO files with all the required fields in the `src/java/cse/entity` directory in the Files window. The NetBeans IDE also generates five Hibernate mapping files in the `src/java/cse/entity` directory and adds the mapping entries to the `hibernate.cfg.xml` configuration file.

Now that we have the POJOs and necessary Hibernate-related files, we can start to create our web pages and perform data operations for our application. We will also create and then add some Hibernate Query Language (HQL) queries that query from our sample database to retrieve and display the desired data. In that process, we need to use the HQL editor to build and test the queries. First, let's take care of the LogIn table query.

8.6.4 Query the LogIn Table Using JSF Pages and Java Beans

To save time and energy, we can modify the web pages we built in Sections 8.4.3.1–8.4.3.5 in this Chapter to make them as our JSF pages used in this project. We need to modify and change those pages from JSP to JavaServer Face pages. Let's start from the LogIn.jsp page.

8.6.4.1 Modify the LogIn.jsp Page to Make it JSF Page

In this section, we want to modify the LogIn.jsp page we built in our Web project JavaWebDBJSPSQL in Section 8.4.3.1 to make it our JSF page. You can find this project from the folder DBProjects\Chapter 8 that is located at the Wiley ftp site (refer to Figure 1.2 in Chapter 1).

Perform the following operations to create the JSF page based on the LogIn.jsp page:

1. Launch the NetBeans IDE and open our new project JavaWebDBJSPOracle. In the Projects window, right click on the Web Pages folder and select the New > JSF Page item from the pop-up menu.
2. On the opened `New JSF File` wizard, enter LogInPage into the `File Name` field and check the JSP File radio button under the `Options` panel. Then click on the Finish button to create this new JSF page.
3. On the opened new JSF page, open the Palette window by going to Window > Palette menu item. Then browse to the JSF Form that is located under the `JSF` group in the Palette window. Drag the JSF Form item from the Palette window and place it into the new JSF page, exactly between the <body> and </body> tag pair, as shown in Figure 8.122. Delete the original default label `<h1><h:outputText value="Hello World!"/></h1>` tag from this page, since we do not need this label in this application.

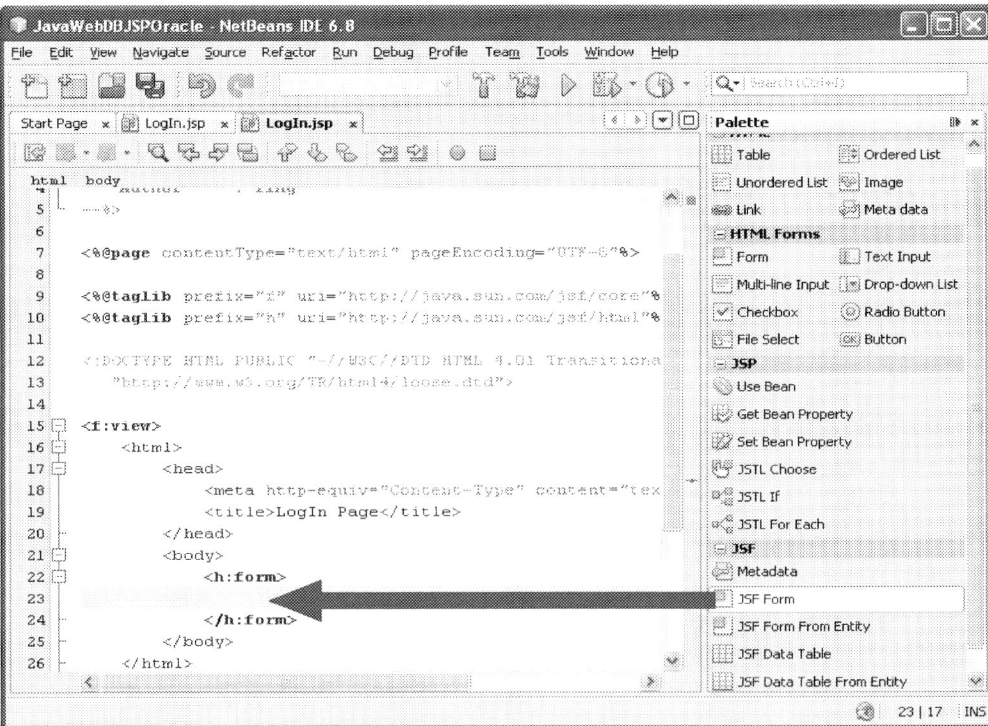

Figure 8.122. The new added JSF Form.

4. Open the project JavaWebDBJSPSQL we built in Section 8.4.3.1 and the LogIn.jsp page. Copy the codes between the <head> and </head> tag pair and paste them under the <head> tag in our new JSF page LogInPage.jsp.
5. Copy the <! [if !pub]> tag that is under the <div style...> tag and paste it to the new LogInPage.jsp page, just under the <body> tag.
6. Copy all codes between the <form> and </form> tag from the LogIn.jsp page and paste them into our new JSF page LogInpage.jsp, exactly between the <h:form> and </h:form> tag in the LogInPage.jsp file.
7. Copy the <! [endif]> tag from the LogIn.jsp file, which is located just under the </form> tag, and paste it to our new JSF page LogInPage.jsp, exactly just under the </h:form> tag.

Now perform the following modifications to the related attributes of tags to bind them to the associated properties or methods defined in the session bean class LogInBean.java that will be built in the following section.

A. Modify the margin and style of the labels displayed in this page by changing the following margins and text indent that are located under the /* Style Definitions */ group below the <style> tag:
    A. Change the text-indent from 0 pt to 45 pt. The result is text-indent:45 pt;
    B. Change the margin-top from 0 pt to 28 pt. The result is margin-top:28 pt;
    C. Change the margin-bottom from 0 pt to –22 pt. The result is margin-bottom:-22pt;
B. Add an new id attribute for the <h:form> tag and make this id equal to LogInPage. The modified <h:form> tag now becomes <h:form id="LogInPage">.
C. Replace the tag <input name=UserNameField maxlength=255 size=21 value="" type=text> with the tag <h:inputText id="userName" value="#{LogInBean.userName}"></h:inputText>.
D. Replace the tag <input name=PassWordField maxlength=255 size=21 value="" type=text> with the tag <h:inputText id="passWord" value="#{LogInBean.passWord}"></h:inputText>.
E. Replace the tag <input type=submit value=LogIn name="LogInButton"...> with the tag <h:commandButton id="LogIn" action="#{LogInBean.LogIn}" value="LogIn" />.
F. Replace the tag <input type=button value=Cancel name="cancelButton" onclick="self.close()"> with the tag <h:commandButton id="Cancel" value="Cancel" onclick="self.close()" />.

Your finished LogInPage.jsp file should match one that is shown in Figure 8.123. The modified parts have been highlighted in bold.

Now you can test this page by building and running this page. Right click on this page from the Projects window and select the Compile File item, and then right click on this page again and select the Run File item to run this page.

Refer to Figure 8.123; in steps C and D, the value attributes of the username and password inputText tags are bound to the associated properties in the Java managed bean LogInBean class that will be built in the next section. In step E, the action attribute of the LogIn commandButton tag is bound to the LogIn() method defined in the Java managed bean LogInBean. These binding relationships provide a convenient way to

```
  <%@page contentType="text/html" pageEncoding="UTF-8"%>

  <%@taglib prefix="f" uri="http://java.sun.com/jsf/core"%>
  <%@taglib prefix="h" uri="http://java.sun.com/jsf/html"%>

  <!DOCTYPE HTML PUBLIC "-//W3C//DTD HTML 4.01 Transitional//EN"
    "http://www.w3.org/TR/html4/loose.dtd">

  <f:view>
  <html>
  <head>
  .........
  /* Style Definitions */
  p.MsoNormal, li.MsoNormal, div.MsoNormal
     {margin-right:0pt;
A     text-indent:45pt;
      margin-top:28pt;
      margin-bottom:-22pt;
      text-align:left;
      .........
  </head>
  <body>
  <![if !pub]>
B <h:form  id="LogInPage">
  .........
C <h:inputText id="userName" value="#{LogInBean.userName}"></h:inputText>
  .........
D <h:inputText id="passWord" value="#{LogInBean.passWord}"></h:inputText>
  .........
E <h:commandButton id="LogIn"  action="#{LogInBean.LogIn}" value="LogIn" />
  .........
F <h:commandButton id="Cancel" value="Cancel" onclick="self.close()" />
  .........
  <![if !pub]></span><![endif]><![if !pub]>
  </h:form>
  <![endif]>
  </body>
  </html>
  </f:view>
```

Figure 8.123. The modified codes for the LogInPage.jsp file.

enable the values of each tag in the JSF page to be updated immediately as the associated properties in the Java bean class are modified.

Next, let's build the Java managed bean class LogInBean.java to handle data queries and actions against our LogIn table in our sample database using the Hibernate interface.

8.6.4.2 Create and Build the Java Managed Bean LogInBean Class

The purpose of this managed bean is to perform business logics and all database-related actions against our sample database using the Hibernate component.

Perform the following operations to create our Java managed bean class LogInBean.java:

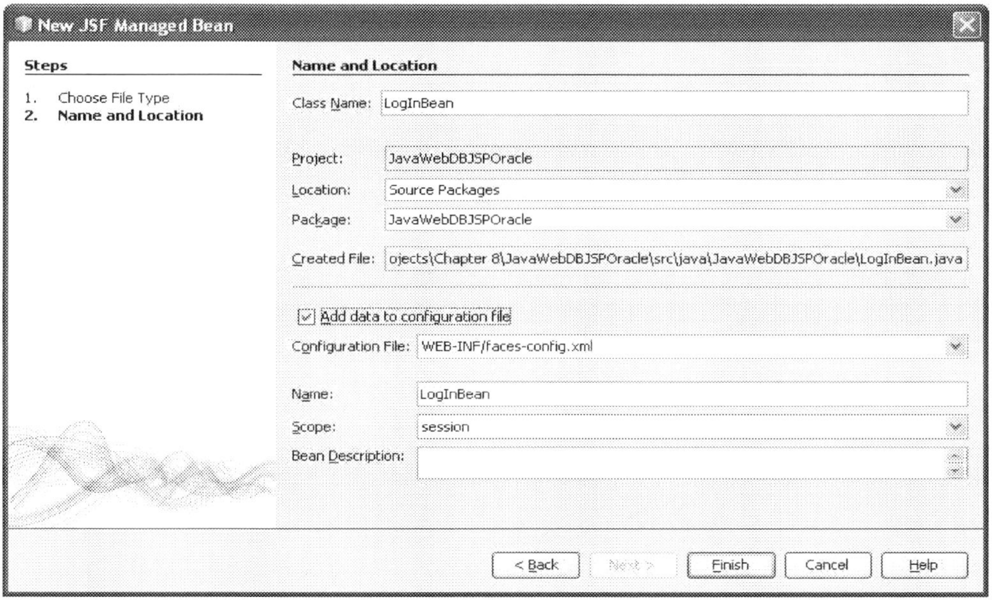

Figure 8.124. The finished Name and Location wizard.

1. Right click on our project JavaWebDBJSPOracle from the Projects window, and select the New > Other item to open the New File wizard.
2. Select JavaServer Faces from the Categories list and JSF Managed Bean from the File Types list, and then click on the Next button.
3. Enter LogInBean into the Class Name field. Type JavaWebDBJSPOracle into the Package combo box, and select the session from the Scope combo box. Make sure to check the Add data to configuration file checkbox since we need this configuration file. Your finished Name and Location wizard of this new managed bean is shown in Figure 8.124. Click on the Finish button to complete this managed bean creation process.

Now let's develop the codes for this managed bean class.

On the opened managed bean LogInBean.java, add two properties, userName and passWord, as shown in step **B** in Figure 8.125.

Then right click on any place inside this code window, select the Insert Code item and choose the Getter and Setter item to create two pairs of getter and setter methods for two properties we added in step **B** above. On the opened Generate Getters and Setters dialog box, check the userName and passWord two items and click on the Generate button to create these getter and setter methods.

Enter the rest of the codes as shown in Figure 8.125 into this class. Let's have a close look at this piece of codes to see how it works.

A. All necessary packages that contain classes and interfaces used in this class file are imported first. In fact, you do not need to specially do these imports by manual. When you finished all coding jobs in this file, just right click on any space inside this code window and select the Fix Imports item from the pop-up menu to enable the NetBeans IDE to do that automatically. The point is that you need to select the correct packages to fix these imports since some packages contain different classes with the same names.

```
  package cse.entity;
A import cse.util.HibernateUtil;
  import java.util.List;
  import javax.faces.bean.ManagedBean;
  import javax.faces.bean.SessionScoped;
  import org.hibernate.Query;
  import org.hibernate.Session;
  @ManagedBean(name="LogInBean")
  @SessionScoped
  public class LogInBean {
B    private String userName;
     private String passWord;
C    public Session session = null;
     public LogInBean() {
D      this.session = HibernateUtil.getSessionFactory().getCurrentSession();
     }
E    public String getPassWord() {
       return passWord;
     }
F    public void setPassWord(String passWord) {
       this.passWord = passWord;
     }
G    public String getUserName() {
       return userName;
     }
H    public void setUserName(String userName) {
       this.userName = userName;
     }
I    public String LogIn() {
       List<Login> loginList = null;
       MsgDialog msgDlg = new MsgDialog(new javax.swing.JFrame(), true);
       try {
J          org.hibernate.Transaction tx = session.beginTransaction();
K          Query q = session.createQuery ("from Login as lg where lg.userName like '"+userName+
                                          "' and lg.passWord like '"+passWord+"'");
L          loginList = (List<Login>) q.list();
M      } catch (Exception e) {
           msgDlg.setMessage("Query is failed and no matched found!");
           msgDlg.setVisible(true);
           e.printStackTrace();
       }
N      String username = loginList.get(0).getUserName();
       String password = loginList.get(0).getPassWord();
O      if (username.equals(userName) && password.equals(passWord))
         return "SELECTION";
P      else
         return "ERROR";
     }
  }
```

Figure 8.125. The codes for the Java managed bean LogInBean.

B. Two properties, userName and passWord, are created inside this bean and the names of these properties must be identical with those attributes of the tags defined in the JSF page LogInPage.jsp in this project to make sure that they are bound together.

C. A new Hibernate Session instance is created and initialized with a null value. The point to be noted is that this session object is different with those session beans defined in the JSF pages, and it is used to perform the Hibernate data actions.

D. The getCurrentSession() method is executed to obtain the current Hibernate session object and assign it to the new created session instance in step **C** above.

E. Starting from step E through to step **H**, two pair of getter and setter methods are created and coded.

I. The LogIn() method, which is bound to the action attribute of the LogIn commandButton in the JSF page LogInPage.jsp, is defined and coded here. Two local variables, a Login List and a JDialog instance, are created first inside the method. The former is used to query the login data from the LogIn table, and the latter is used to provide the debug information when the project is tested later. The point to be noted is that you have to copy the MsgDialog.java class file from our project JavaWebDBJSPSQL and paste it into this project, exactly into the cse.entity folder.

J. A try...catch block is used to perform the login data query using the Hibernate API. First, a Transaction instance is created to make it ready for the data actions.

K. Then, the createQuery() method is executed to create this login data query with a HQL statement. The point to be noted is that the names of columns used in this HQL query must be the Hibernate mapped names, not the original names defined in our LogIn table. Two dynamic parameters, userName and passWord, are properties defined in this class.

L. The query is performed by calling the list() method, and the result is returned and assigned to the Login List instance.

M. The catch block is used to track and collect any possible exception during this query and display the debug information using the MsgDialog.

N. The query result is further separate and assigned to two local string variables, username and password using the getUserName() and getPassWord() methods, respectively.

O. A comparison is performed between the properties of this class, userName and passWord, which are entered by the user from the JSF page LogInPage.jsp, and the query result. If a matching is found, a string "SELECTION" is returned to show the next page that is the Selection.jsp that will be built later to allow users to continue the project to query other information.

P. Otherwise, the program will be directed to an ERROR page, which will be built later, and it is used to display the exception information for this login data query.

Next, we need to set up the navigation relationship between the LogInPage and other pages, such as the SelectionPage and ErrorPage, to enable the program to switch to the appropriate next page. This switching relationship is dependent on the execution result of the login process. The SelectionPage should be the next page if the login is successful; otherwise, the ErrorPage should be displayed to indicate this situation.

In order to set up these relationships, we had better build the SelectionPage and the ErrorPage first. Then, we can use the faces configuration file, faces-config.xml, to set up these relationships.

8.6.5 Build the SelectionPage and the SelectionBean Class

To save time and energy, we can modify the Selection.jsp page we built in our previous project JavaWebDBJSPSQL to make it our JSF page. Perform the following operations to do this modification:

1. Right click on our current project JavaWebDBJSPOracle from the Projects window, and select New > JSF Page item from the pop up menu to open the `New JSF File` wizard.
2. Enter SelectionPage into the `File Name` field and check the JSP File radio button. Click on the Finish button to create this JSF page.
3. Remove the Hello World label from this page and go to the Window > Palette menu item to open the Palette window. Drag a JSF Form that is under the JSF group in the Palette window and place it into the space between the <body> and </body> tag.
4. Open the project JavaWebDBJSPSQL we built in Section 8.4.3.1 and the Selection.jsp page. Copy the codes between the <head> and </head> tag pair and paste them under the <head> tag in our new JSF page SelectionPage.jsp.
5. Copy the <![if !pub]> tag that is under the <div style...> tag and paste it to the new SelectionPage.jsp page, just under the <body> tag.
6. Copy all codes between the <form> and </form> tag from the Selection.jsp page and paste them into our new JSF page SelectionPage.jsp, exactly between the <h:form> and </h:form> tag in the SelectionPage.jsp file.
7. Copy the <![endif]> tag from the Selection.jsp file, which is located just under the </form> tag, and paste it to our new JSF page SelectionPage.jsp, exactly just under the </h:form> tag.

Now perform the following modifications to the related attributes of the tags to bind them to the associated properties or methods defined in the session bean class SelectionBean.java that will be built in the following section.

A. Modify the margin and style of the labels displayed in this page by changing the following margins and text indent that are located under the `/* Style Definitions */` group below the <style> tag:

a. Change the margin-right from 0pt to 90pt. The result is margin-right:90pt;

B. Add an new id attribute for the <h:form> tag and make this id equal to SelectionPage. The modified <h:form> tag now becomes <h:form id="SelectionPage">.

C. Replace the following tags

```
<select name=ListSelection size=6 v:shapes="_x0000_s1027">
<option selected value="Faculty Information">Faculty
Information</option>
<option value="Course Information">Course Information</option>
<option value="Student Information">Student Information
</option>
</select>
```

with the tags shown below:

```
<h:selectOneListbox id="selectionList" value="#{SelectionBean.
selectedItem}" size="5" >
<f:selectItem itemLabel="Faculty Information"
itemValue="Faculty Information" />
<f:selectItem itemLabel="Course Information" itemValue="Course
Information" />
```

```
<f:selectItem itemLabel="Student Information"
itemValue="Student Information" />
</h:selectOneListbox>
```

D. Replace the tag `<input type=submit value=OK v:shapes="_x0000_s1028">` with the tag `<h:commandButton id="OK" action="#{SelectionBean.OK}" value="OK" />`.

E. Replace the tag `<input type=button value=Exit onclick="self.close()" v:shapes=.....>` with the tag `<h:commandButton id="Exit" value="Exit" onclick="self.close()" />`.

Your finished SelectionPage.jsp file should match one that is shown in Figure 8.126. The modified parts have been highlighted in bold.

Next, we need to create and build the Java managed bean class SelectionBean.java to handle the page navigation process to direct the program to the different page based on the users' selection on the SelectionPage.

The bean class SelectionBean is used to process some business-related operations for the SelectionPage. Perform the following operations to create our Java managed bean class SelectionBean.java:

1. Right click on our project JavaWebDBJSPOracle from the Projects window, and select the New > Other item to open the `New File` wizard.
2. Select JavaServer Faces from the `Categories` list and JSF Managed Bean from the `File Types` list, and then click on the Next button.
3. Enter SelectionBean into the `Class Name` field. Select the JavaWebDBJSPOracle from the `Package` combo box, and select the session from the `Scope` combo box. Make sure to check the Add data to configuration file checkbox since we need to use this configuration file to build the page navigation rules later in this application. Click on the Finish button to complete this managed bean creation process.

Open the SelectionBean.java class file and perform the following operations to create the codes that are shown in Figure 8.127 for this file.

Let's have a closer look at this piece of codes to see how it works.

A. Some properties are created for this class, including a String variable selectedItem, which should be identical with the value attribute defined in the <h:selectOneListbox> tag in the SelectionPage.jsp file, and a JDialog instance msgDlg, which is used to display the debug and test information when the project runs.

B. The getter and setter methods are declared in steps **B** and **C**, respectively. To create these two methods, right click on any place inside this SelectionBean code window and select the Insert Code item from the pop-up menu. Then select the Getter and Setter item from the pop-up menu. On the opened wizard, check the selectedItem:String item and click on the Generate button.

D. Inside the OK() method, an if selection structure is used to identify the selected item from the selection list by the user. If the Faculty Information item has been selected, a "FACULTY" string is returned to indicate that the FacultyPage that will be developed in the following section will be opened to allow users to query the information related to faculty members in the sample CSE department. The point to be noted is that the name of this method should be identical with the action attribute defined in the <h:commandButton> tag in the SelectionPage.jsp page file to make sure that a binding

```
   <%@page contentType="text/html" pageEncoding="UTF-8"%>
   <%@taglib prefix="f" uri="http://java.sun.com/jsf/core"%>
   <%@taglib prefix="h" uri="http://java.sun.com/jsf/html"%>
   <!DOCTYPE HTML PUBLIC "-//W3C//DTD HTML 4.01 Transitional//EN"
     "http://www.w3.org/TR/html4/loose.dtd">
   <f:view>
   <html>
   <head>
   .........
   /* Style Definitions */
   p.MsoNormal, li.MsoNormal, div.MsoNormal
A  {margin-right:90pt;
    text-indent:0pt;
    margin-top:0pt;
    margin-bottom:0pt;
    text-align:left;
    .........
   </head>
   <body>
   <![if !pub]>
B  <h:form id="SelectionPage">
   .........
C  <h:selectOneListbox id="selectionList" value="#{SelectionBean.selectedItem}" size="5" >
     <f:selectItem itemLabel="Faculty Information"  itemValue="Faculty Information" />
     <f:selectItem itemLabel="Course Information"  itemValue="Course Information" />
     <f:selectItem itemLabel="Student Information"  itemValue="Student Information" />
   </h:selectOneListbox>
   .........
D  <h:commandButton id="OK"  action="#{SelectionBean.OK}" value="OK" />
   .........
E  <h:commandButton id="Exit" value="Exit" onclick="self.close()" />
   .........
   <![if !pub]></span><![endif]><![if !pub]>
   </h:form>
   <![endif]>
   </body>
   </html>
   </f:view>
```

Figure 8.126. The codes for the SelectionPage.jsp file.

relationship has been built between this method and the action attribute of the OK button in the JSF page. To correctly direct the program to the next selected page, we need to build the associated navigation rules in the JSF configuration file faces-config.xml in the following sections.

E. If the Course Information item has been selected, a "COURSE" string is returned to indicate that the CoursePage that will be developed in the following section will be opened to allow users to query the course information related to the selected faculty member in the sample CSE department.

F. If the Student Information item has been selected, a "STUDENT" string is returned to indicate that the StudentPage that will be developed in the following section will be opened

```
  package JavaWebDBJSPOracle;
  public class SelectionBean {
A     private String selectedItem;
      MsgDialog msgDlg = new MsgDialog(new javax.swing.JFrame(), true);
      /** Creates a new instance of SelectionBean */
      public SelectionBean() {
      }
B     public String getSelectedItem() {
         return selectedItem;
      }
C     public void setSelectedItem(String selectedItem) {
         this.selectedItem = selectedItem;
      }
      public String OK() {
D        if (selectedItem.equals("Faculty Information"))
            return "FACULTY";
E        else if (selectedItem.equals("Course Information"))
            return "COURSE";
F        else if (selectedItem.equals("Student Information"))
            return "STUDENT";
G        else
            return null;
      }
  }
```

Figure 8.127. The codes for the Java-managed bean SelectionBean class.

to allow the user to query the information related to the selected student in the sample CSE department.

G. If nothing has been selected, a null is returned.

Next, let's build an Error page to display any possible exception during the project running process.

8.6.6 Build the ErrorPage to Display any Error Information

Perform the following operations to create this Error page:

1. Right click on our project JavaWebDBJSPOracle from the Projects window and select the New > JSF Page item to open the New `JSF File` wizard.
2. Enter ErrorPage into the `File Name` field and check the JSP File radio button under the `Options` group.
3. Click on the Finish button to create this page.

On the opened code window of the ErrorPage file, change the value attribute of the <h:outputText> tag from "Hello World!" to "Some error occurred…". Your finished code window of the ErrorPage should match the one that is shown in Figure 8.128. The modified part has been highlighted in bold, as shown in step **A** in Figure 8.128.

```
<%@page contentType="text/html" pageEncoding="UTF-8"%>

<%@taglib prefix="f" uri="http://java.sun.com/jsf/core"%>
<%@taglib prefix="h" uri="http://java.sun.com/jsf/html"%>

<!DOCTYPE HTML PUBLIC "-//W3C//DTD HTML 4.01 Transitional//EN"
  "http://www.w3.org/TR/html4/loose.dtd">

<f:view>
   <html>
      <head>
         <meta http-equiv="Content-Type" content="text/html; charset=UTF-8"/>
         <title>JSP Page</title>
      </head>
      <body>
A        <h1><h:outputText value="Some error occurred......"/></h1>
      </body>
   </html>
</f:view>
```

Figure 8.128. The codes for the ErrorPage.jsp file.

So far, we have built the following JSF pages and the associated Java bean class files:

- LogInPage.jsp
- SelectionPage.jsp
- ErrorPage.jsp
- LogInBean.java
- SelectionBean.java

The LogInPage.jsp and the LogInBean.java is a pair of JSF page–Java bean, and the SelectionPage.jsp and the SelectionBean.java is another pair of JSF page–Java bean. For both pairs, the former is used to provide a Web interface to collect the user's inputs and display the querying results, which can be considered as a view, and the latter is used to perform business logics or database-related operations, which can be considered as a model. The data translations between this view and model are controlled by the Web server or the controller. This is a so-called MVC structure, or MVC operational mode.

We will use this mode to build other pages and beans in the following sections, such as FacultyPage.jsp and FacultyBean.java, CoursePage.jsp and CourseBean.java, as well as StudentPage.jsp and StudentBean.java to process the related queries or data actions against our sample database. However, before we can build these pages and beans; first, we need to set up the navigation rules for our existed pages to give readers a clear picture in how to perform the navigations between these different pages, such as between the LogInPage.jsp and the SelectionPage.jsp, as well as the ErrorPage.jsp.

8.6.7 Set Up the Navigation Rules for Existing Web Pages

To set up the correct navigation rules for our existing web pages, we need to use the JSF configuration file faces-config.xml. The function of the faces-config.xml file is to allow the JSF to configure the application, managed beans, convertors, validators, and naviga-

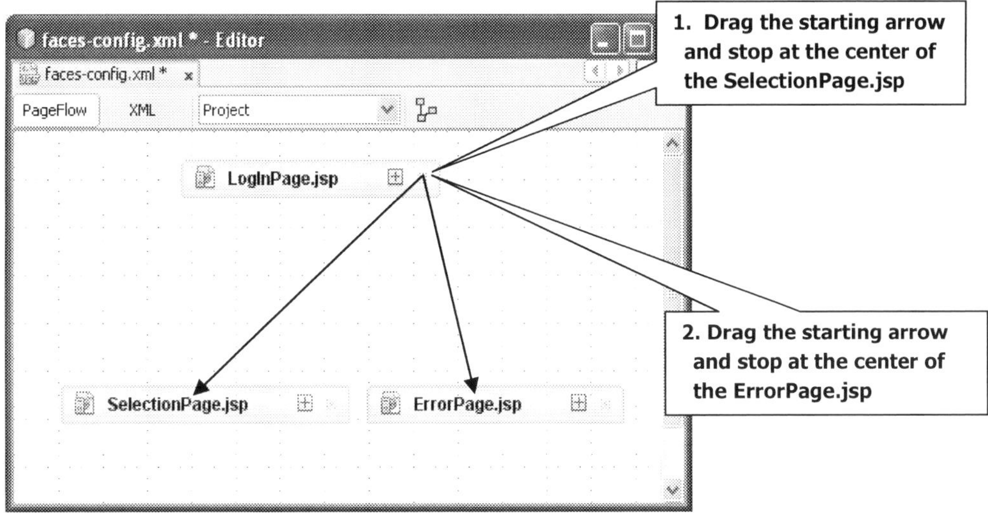

Figure 8.129. The opened PageFlow view of the faces-config.xml file.

tion rules. In Section 5.3.5.12 in Chapter 5, we have provided a detailed discussion about this configuration file. Refer to that section to get more details for this file.

The operational navigation rule is: if the login process is successful, the next page, SelectionPage.jsp, should be displayed to allow users to select different item from that page to perform related data query operations. Otherwise, if the login process has failed, the ErrorPage.jsp should be displayed to indicate this situation.

Now, let's use this configuration file to set up the navigation rules for our existing pages. Perform the following operations to set up the navigation rules for our existing pages:

1. Expand the Configuration Files node that is under our project node JavaWebDBJSPOracle from the Projects window and double click on the file faces-config.xml to open it.
2. Click on the PageFlow button on the top of this opened file to display the flow of the web pages built in this project, as shown in Figure 8.129.
3. Move your cursor to the starting arrow location as shown in Figure 8.129 until a square appears in the LogInPage.jsp page object. Then click on this square and drag this stating arrow and point to and stop at the center of the SelectionPage.jsp, as shown in Figure 8.129-1. A navigation link is established with the default name case1, as shown in Figure 8.129.
4. Double click on the default navigation link case1 and change its name to SELECTION.
5. Perform a similar operation to create another navigation link from the LogInPage.jsp to the ErrorPage.jsp, as shown in Figure 8.129-2.
6. Double click on the new established link and change its name to ERROR. Your finished PageFlow view of two JSF page objects should match the one that is shown in Figure 8.130.

Now if you click on the XML button to open the XML view of this faces-config.xml file, you can find that the navigation rules shown in Figure 8.130 have been added into this file. The new added codes have been shown in steps **A**, **B**, and **C** in Figure 8.131.

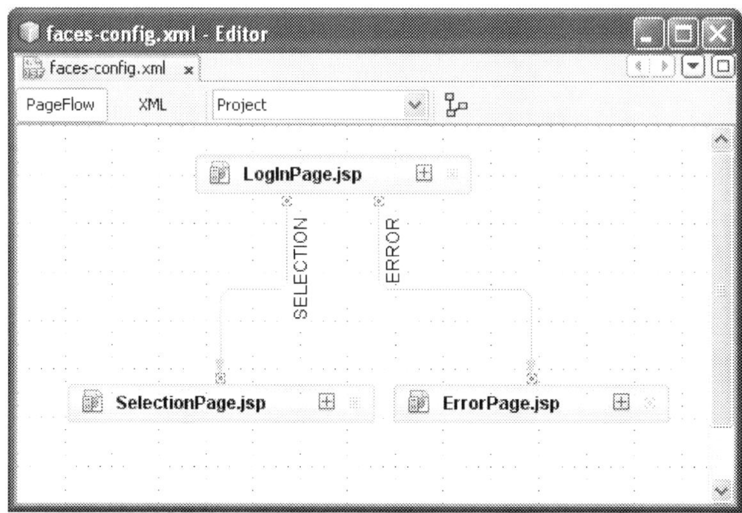

Figure 8.130. The finished PageFlow view of the JSF page objects.

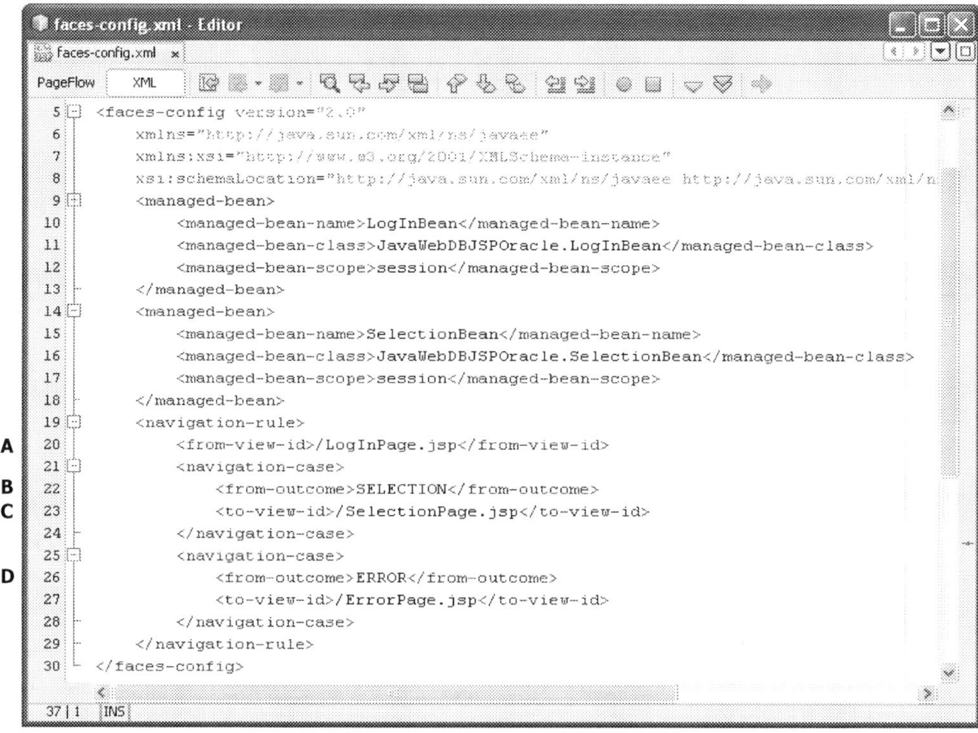

Figure 8.131. The XML view of the faces-config.xml file.

Let's have a closer look at this piece of newly created codes to see how it works.

A. Our source page, LogInPage.jsp, is added into the `<from-view-id>` tag that is located under the `<navigation-rule>` tag to indicate that this is the starting page.

B. Our next page for the login success processing, which is represented by a case String SELECTION, is added into the `<from-outcome>` tag.

C. Our next page SelectionPage.jsp has been added into the `<to-view-id>` tag to indicate that this is our destination page if the login is successful.

D. The ERROR String represented our ErrorPage.jsp is added into another `<from-outcome>` tag with the ErrorPage.jsp as the content of the `<to-view-id>` tag.

Now that we have set up the navigation rules for our pages, next, let's continue to build other pages and beans to perform the desired data queries. First, let's handle the data query from the Faculty table in our sample database.

8.6.8 Query the Faculty Table Using JavaServer Faces and Java Beans

First, let's build our Web page FacultyPage.jsp file.

Recalled that in Section 8.4.3.3, we discussed how to build the Faculty.jsp page and saved that page in the local folder, such as C:\Temp folder. Now we need to modify that page to make it our JSF page FacultyPage.jsp.

8.6.8.1 Modify the Faculty.jsp to Make it Our JSF Page FacultyPage.jsp

Open the Windows Explorer and browse to our Temp folder to locate the Faculty.jsp page file. Copy that file and save it to our current project folder JavaWebDBJSPOracle that should be located at the folder C:\Book9\Chapter 8. You can also find this page file from the folder JSP Files that is located at the Wiley ftp site (refer to Figure 1.2 in Chapter 1).

Then launch the NetBeans IDE and our project, JavaWebDBJSPOracle. Then open the Files window, find and copy the Faculty.jsp file from the Files window, and paste it to the Web Pages node in the Projects window.

Now perform the following operations to create our JSF page FacultyPage.jsp file and modify the Faculty.jsp file to make it our JSF page file.

1. Right click on our project JavaWebDBJSPOracle and select New > JSF Page item to open the `New JSF File` wizard.
2. Enter FacultyPage into the `File Name` field and check the JSP File radio button under the `Options` group.
3. Click on the Finish button to complete this JSF page creation process.
4. On the opened JSF page, remove the `<h:outputText value="Hello World!"/>` tag.
5. Open the Palette window by going to Window > Palette menu item.
6. Drag a JSF Form from the Palette window, which is located under the `JSF` group, and place it under the `<body>` tag in our newly created JSF page. Your JSF page should match the one that is shown in Figure 8.132.

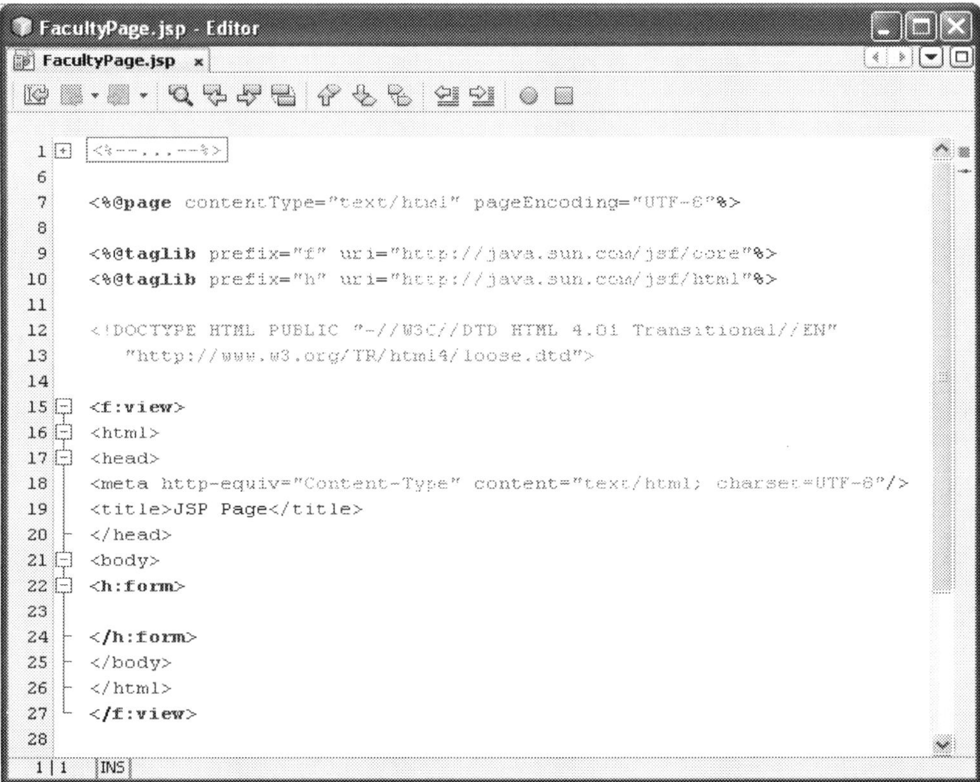

Figure 8.132. The code window of the JSF page FacultyPage.jsp.

7. Open the Faculty.jsp file and copy the codes between the <head> and </head> tag pair and paste them under the <head> tag in our new JSF page FacultyPage.jsp.
8. Copy the <![if !pub]> tag that is under the <div style…> tag in the Faculty.jsp file and paste it to the new FacultyPage.jsp page, just under the <body> tag.
9. Copy all codes between the <form> and </form> tag from the Faculty.jsp page and paste them into our new JSF page FacultyPage.jsp, exactly between the <h:form> and </h:form> tag in the FacultyPage.jsp file.
10. Copy the <![endif]> tag from the Faculty.jsp file, which is located just under the </form> tag, and paste it to our new JSF page FacultyPage.jsp, exactly just under the </h:form> tag.

Now perform the following modifications to the related attributes of the tags to bind them to the associated properties or methods defined in our managed bean class FacultyMBean.java that will be built in the following section.

A. Modify the margin and style of the labels displayed in this page by changing the following margins and text indent that are located under the /* Style Definitions */ group below the <style> tag:
   a. Change the margin-top from 0pt to –10pt. The result is margin-top:-10pt;
   b. Change the margin-bottom from 0pt to 10pt. The result is margin-bottom:10pt;

B. Add an new id attribute for the <h:form> tag, and make this id equal to FacultyPage. The modified <h:form> tag now becomes <h:form id="FacultyPage">.

C. Modify the tag

```
<div v:shape="_x0000_s1025" style='padding:2.88pt 2.88pt
2.88pt 2.88pt' class=shape> that is located under the
<table ... > tag and around line 108 to:
```

```
<div v:shape="_x0000_s1025" style='padding:20.88pt 2.88pt
2.88pt 2.88pt' class=shape>
```

D. Replace the following tag, which is located at line 130 in our new JSF page,

```
<v:imagedata src="Faculty_files/image295.emz" o:title="<EM
PTY>"/>
```

with the tag:

```
<h:graphicImage id="fImage" width="140" height="150"
value="#{FacultyMBean.facultyImage}"/>
```

E. Modify the tag <p class=MsoNormal><span lang=en-US style='font-weight:bold;language:en-US'>Faculty Name</span></p> that is around line 161 by removing the text label Faculty Name. The modified tag is:

```
<p class=MsoNormal><span lang=en-US style='font-
weight:bold;language:en-US'></span></p>
```

F. Modify the tag <p class=MsoNormal><span lang=en-US style='font-weight:bold;language:en-US'>Faculty ID</span></p> that is around line 191 by removing the text label Faculty ID. The modified tag is:

```
<p class=MsoNormal><span lang=en-US style='font-weight:
bold;language:en-US'></span></p>
```

G. In a similar way as we did in steps **E** and **F**, remove the text label Name (around line 221), Title (line 251), Office (line 281), Phone (line 311), College (line 341), and Email (line 371), respectively.

H. Replace the tag <input name=FacultyImageField maxlength=255 size=18 value="". . . . . . > with the tag:

```
<h:inputText id="facultyImageName" value="#{FacultyMBean.
facultyImageName}"></h:inputText>
```

I. Replace the tag <input name=FacultyNameField maxlength=255 size=18 value="". . . . . . > with the tags:

```
<h:outputLabel
style="position:absolute;left:-60pt;font-weight:bold;

font-size:10.0pt;language:en-US" value="Faculty Name"/>

<h:inputText id="facultyName" value="#{FacultyMBean.
facultyName}"></h:inputText>
```

J. Replace the tag <input name=FacultyIDField maxlength=255 size=21 value="" . . . . > with the tags:

```
<h:outputLabel
style="position:absolute;left:-50pt;font-weight:bold;

font-size:10.0pt;language:en-US" value="Faculty ID"/>

<h:inputText id="facultyID" value="#{FacultyMBean.
facultyID}"></h:inputText>
```

K. Replace the tag `<input name=NameField maxlength=255 size=21 value="" .........>` with the tags:

```
<h:outputLabel
style="position:absolute;left:-50pt;font-weight:bold;
font-size:10.0pt;language:en-US" value="Name"/>
<h:inputText id="name" value="#{FacultyMBean.
name}"></h:inputText>
```

L. Replace the tag `<input name=TitleField maxlength=255 size=21 value="" .........>` with the tags:

```
<h:outputLabel
style="position:absolute;left:-50pt;font-weight:bold;
font-size:10.0pt;language:en-US" value="Title"/>
<h:inputText id="title" value="#{FacultyMBean.
title}"></h:inputText>
```

M. Replace the tag `<input name=OfficeField maxlength=255 size=21 value="" .........>` with the tags:

```
<h:outputLabel
style="position:absolute;left:-50pt;font-weight:bold;
font-size:10.0pt;language:en-US" value="Office"/>
<h:inputText id="office" value="#{FacultyMBean.
office}"></h:inputText>
```

N. Replace the tag `<input name=PhoneField maxlength=255 size=21 value="" .........>` with the tags:

```
<h:outputLabel
style="position:absolute;left:-50pt;font-weight:bold;
font-size:10.0pt;language:en-US" value="Phone"/>
<h:inputText id="phone" value="#{FacultyMBean.
phone}"></h:inputText>
```

O. Replace the tag `<input name=CollegeField maxlength=255 size=21 value="" .........>` with the tags:

```
<h:outputLabel
style="position:absolute;left:-50pt;font-weight:bold;
font-size:10.0pt;language:en-US" value="College"/>
<h:inputText id="college" value="#{FacultyMBean.
college}"></h:inputText>
```

P. Replace the tag `<input name=EmailField maxlength=255 size=21 value="" .........>` with the tags:

```
<h:outputLabel
style="position:absolute;left:-50pt;font-weight:bold;
font-size:10.0pt;language:en-US" value="Email"/>
<h:inputText id="email" value="#{FacultyMBean.
email}"></h:inputText>
```

Q. Replace the tag `<input type=submit value=Select v:shapes="_x0000_s1044">` with the tag `<h:commandButton id="Select" action="#{FacultyMBean.Select}" value="Select" />`

R. Replace the tag `<input type=submit value=Insert v:shapes="_x0000_s1045">` with the tag `<h:commandButton id="Insert" action="#{FacultyMBean.Insert}" value="Insert" />`

S. Replace the tag `<input type=submit value=Update v:shapes="_x0000_s1046">` with the tag `<h:commandButton id="Update" action="#{FacultyMBean.Update}" value="Update" />`

T. Replace the tag `<input type=submit value=Delete v:shapes="_x0000_s1047">` with the tag `<h:commandButton id="Delete" action="#{FacultyMBean.Delete}" value="Delete" />`

U. Replace the tag `<input type=submit value=Back v:shapes="_x0000_s1048">` with the tag `<h:commandButton id="Back" action="#{FacultyMBean.Back}" value="Back" />`

Your finished FacultyPage.jsp file should match one that is shown in Figure 8.133. The modified parts have been highlighted in bold.

A complete JSF page FacultyPage.jsp, including the modified codes, can be found from the folder JSP Files that is located at the site: ftp://ftp.wiley.public.ISBN\BaiBook. You can directly use this page by downloading it from that site and saving that file to your project.

Next, we need to create and build the Java managed bean class FacultyMBean.java to handle the business logics and database-related actions against our sample Oracle database using the Hibernate component.

Because of the relatively complex in the faculty data queries, we divide this data action into two parts: the Java managed bean class FacultyMBean.java that is used to manage the data actions, and the Java session bean FacultySessionBean.java that is used to perform the data actions.

First, let's build the session bean class FacultySessionBean to perform the data query and actions against our sample Oracle database.

8.6.8.2 Build the Java Session Bean FacultySessionBean to Handle Data Actions

The Java session bean FacultySessionBean is used to perform the actual data query and actions against our database using the Hibernate API. Perform the following operations to create our Java session bean class FacultySessionBean.java:

1. Right click on our project JavaWebDBJSPOracle from the Projects window, and select the New > Other item to open the `New File` wizard.
2. Select Java EE from the `Categories` list and Session Bean from the `File Types` list, and then click on the Next button.
3. Enter FacultySessionBean into the `Class Name` field. Select the JavaWebDBJSPOracle from the `Package` combo box, and check the Stateless radio button from the `Session Type` group. Your finished `Name and Location` wizard should match one that is shown in Figure 8.134. Click on the Finish button to complete this session bean creation process.

On the opened FacultySessionBean.java class file, perform the following operations to create the codes for this file, which is shown in Figure 8.135.

```
  .........
  /* Style Definitions */
  p.MsoNormal, li.MsoNormal, div.MsoNormal
     {margin-right:0pt;
      text-indent:0pt;
A     margin-top:-10pt;
      margin-bottom:10pt;
      text-align:left;
      .........
  </head>
  <body>
  <![if !pub]>
B <h:form id="FacultyPage">
  .........
C <div v:shape="_x0000_s1025" style='padding:20.88pt 2.88pt 2.88pt 2.88pt' class=shape>
  .........
D <h:graphicImage id="fImage" width="140" height="150" value="#{FacultyMBean.facultyImage}"/>
  .........
E <p class=MsoNormal><span lang=en-US style='font-weight:bold;language:en-US'></span></p>
  .........
F <p class=MsoNormal><span lang=en-US style='font-weight:bold;language:en-US'></span></p>
  .........
G <p class=MsoNormal><span lang=en-US style='font-weight:bold;language:en-US'></span></p>
  .........
H <h:inputText id="facultyImageName" value="#{FacultyMBean.facultyImageName}">
  </h:inputText>
  .........
I <h:outputLabel style="position:absolute;left:-60pt;font-weight:bold; font-size:10.0pt;language:en-US"
                  value="Faculty Name"/>
  <h:inputText id="facultyName" value="#{FacultyMBean.facultyName}"></h:inputText>
  .........
J <h:outputLabel style="position:absolute;left:-50pt;font-weight:bold; font-size:10.0pt;language:en-US"
                  value="Faculty ID"/>
  <h:inputText id="facultyID" value="#{FacultyMBean.facultyID}"></h:inputText>
  .........
K <h:outputLabel style="position:absolute;left:-50pt;font-weight:bold; font-size:10.0pt;language:en-US"
                  value="Name"/>
  <h:inputText id="name" value="#{FacultyMBean.name}"></h:inputText>
  .........
L <h:outputLabel style="position:absolute;left:-50pt;font-weight:bold; font-size:10.0pt;language:en-US"
                  value="Title"/>
  <h:inputText id="title" value="#{FacultyMBean.title}"></h:inputText>
  .........
M <h:outputLabel style="position:absolute;left:-50pt;font-weight:bold; font-size:10.0pt;language:en-US"
                  value="Office"/>
  <h:inputText id="office" value="#{FacultyMBean.office}"></h:inputText>
  .........
N <h:outputLabel style="position:absolute;left:-50pt;font-weight:bold; font-size:10.0pt;language:en-US"
                  value="Phone"/>
  <h:inputText id="phone" value="#{FacultyMBean.phone}"></h:inputText>
  .........
O <h:outputLabel style="position:absolute;left:-50pt;font-weight:bold; font-size:10.0pt;language:en-US"
                  value="College"/>
  <h:inputText id="college" value="#{FacultyMBean.college}"></h:inputText>
  .........
P <h:outputLabel style="position:absolute;left:-50pt;font-weight:bold;  font-size:10.0pt;language:en-US"
                  value="Email"/>
  <h:inputText id="email" value="#{FacultyMBean.email}"></h:inputText>
  .........
Q <h:commandButton id="Select"  action="#{FacultyMBean.Select}" value="Select" />
  .........
R <h:commandButton id="Insert"  action="#{FacultyMBean.Insert}" value="Insert" />
  .........
S <h:commandButton id="Update"  action="#{FacultyMBean.Update}" value="Update" />
  .........
T <h:commandButton id="Delete"  action="#{FacultyMBean.Delete}" value="Delete" />
  .........
U <h:commandButton id="Back"  action="#{FacultyMBean.Back}" value="Back" />
  .........
```

Figure 8.133. The modified codes for the FacultyPage.jsp file.

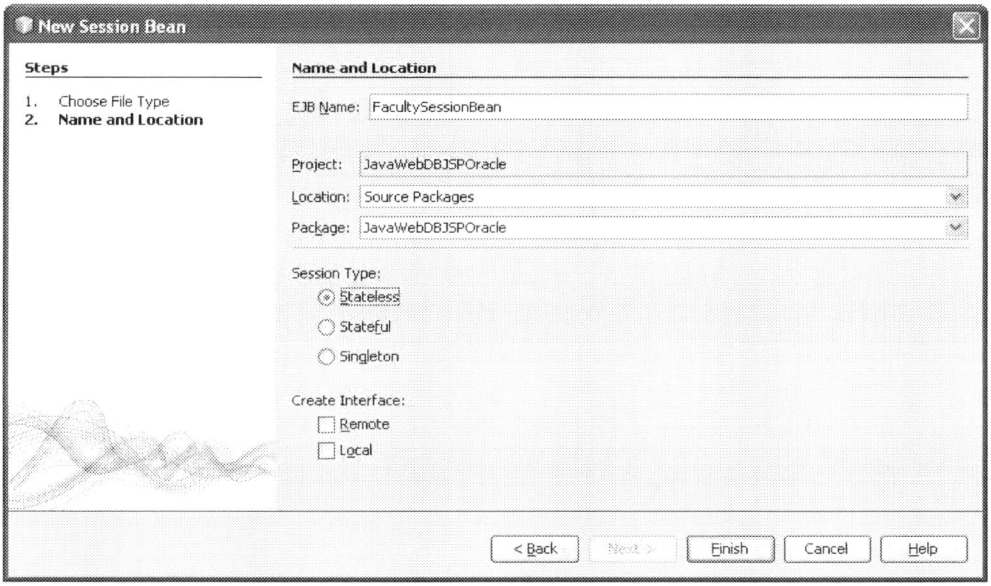

New Session Bean

Steps
1. Choose File Type
2. **Name and Location**

Name and Location
EJB Name: FacultySessionBean
Project: JavaWebDBJSPOracle
Location: Source Packages
Package: JavaWebDBJSPOracle
Session Type:
(•) Stateless
( ) Stateful
( ) Singleton
Create Interface:
[ ] Remote
[ ] Local

< Back | Next > | Finish | Cancel | Help

Figure 8.134. The finished Name and Location wizard.

```
  package JavaWebDBJSPOracle;
  import cse.entity.Faculty;
  import cse.util.HibernateUtil;
  import java.util.List;
  import javax.ejb.Stateless;
  import org.hibernate.Query;
  import org.hibernate.Session;
  @Stateless
  public class FacultySessionBean {
A     public Session session = null;
B     public FacultySessionBean() {
C       this.session = HibernateUtil.getSessionFactory().getCurrentSession();
      }
D     public List QueryFaculty(String  fname) {
E       List<Faculty> facultyList = null;
        MsgDialog msgDlg = new MsgDialog(new javax.swing.JFrame(), true);
F       this.session = HibernateUtil.getSessionFactory().getCurrentSession();
G       try {
          org.hibernate.Transaction tx = session.beginTransaction();
          Query  f = session.createQuery ("from Faculty as f where f.facultyName like '"+fname+"'");
H         facultyList = (List<Faculty>) f.list();
I         } catch (Exception e) {
          msgDlg.setMessage("Query is failed and no matched found!");
          msgDlg.setVisible(true);
          e.printStackTrace();
           return null;
         }
J      return facultyList;
      }
  }
```

Figure 8.135. The codes for the Java session bean class FacultySessionBean.

Let's have a closer look at this piece of codes to see how it works.

A. Add a new Session object as a property to this class since we need to create a new session object to perform the data query using the Hibernate later.

B. Right click on any space of this code window and select the Insert Code item. Select the `Constructor` item to create a constructor for this class.

C. Inside the class constructor, call the getCurrentSession() method to obtain the current session object and assign it to our session property created at step A above.

D. Right click on any space inside this code window and select the Insert Code from the pop-up menu. Then select the Add Business Method item to open the `Add Business Method` wizard. Enter QueryFaculty into the `Name` field and click on the Browse button to find the returning data type for this method. On the opened wizard, type List into the top field and select List (java.util) from the bottom list. Then click on the OK button, and the OK button again to create this new method. Add a String argument fname to this method.

E. Create two local variables for this method: facultyList, which is a `java.util.List` object, and a msgDlg, which is a JDialog object. The first is used to hold the returned queried result from the Faculty table, and the latter is used to display the debug information.

F. Before the query can be executed, the getCurrentSession() method is executed again to make sure that a valid session object has been opened.

G. A try...catch block is used to perform the faculty information query from our Faculty table. First, the beginTransaction() method is executed to create a new transaction object. Then the createQuery() method is called to perform this data query. A HQL statement works as an argument of this method and provides the query details.

H. The list() method is executed to perform this actual query operation. The queried result is returned and assigned to the local variable facultyList.

I. The catch block is used to track and detect any possible exception during this query operation, and display any error if any exception occurred. A `null` will be returned to the calling method if any exception occurred.

J. Finally, the queried result is returned to the calling method defined in our Java managed bean for further processing.

During the coding process, you may encounter some real-time compiling errors, which are indicated with some red underscores for the error sources. Most of these errors are related to the missed packages. To fix these errors, just right click on any space in this code window, and select the Fix Imports item to open the `Fix All Imports` wizard. The point to be noted is that you must select the correct packages for those real-time compiling error sources. For example, in this application, you need to select the following packages or classes for this file:

- org.hibernate.Query for the Query class
- org.hibernate.Session for the Session class
- java.util.List for the List collection class

Now we have completed the coding process for the faculty query operation with the Hibernate API. This piece of codes is only used for the faculty data query process, and the QueryFaculty() method will be called by our Java managed bean class FacultyMBean to execute this data query operation. We will add more methods and codes to perform other data actions, such as data insertion, updating, and deleting, against our sample database later in the following sections.

Next, let's build our Java managed bean class FacultyMBean.java to call some methods defined in the session bean to perform the actual data query and actions against our database.

8.6.8.3 Build the Java Managed Bean FacultyMBean to Manage Data Actions

The Java managed bean class FacultyMBean is used to manage and coordinate the faculty data queries and actions against our sample Oracle database. The session bean FacultySessionBean is under the control of this managed bean to perform the actual data actions against our database using the Hibernate API. Perform the following operations to create our Java managed bean class FacultyMBean.java:

1. Right click on our project JavaWebDBJSPOracle from the Projects window, and select the New > Other item to open the New File wizard.
2. Select JavaServer Faces from the Categories list and JSF Managed Bean from the File Types list, and then click on the Next button.
3. Enter FacultyMBean into the Class Name field. Select the JavaWebDBJSPOracle from the Package combo box, and select the session from the Scope combo box. Make sure to check the Add data to configuration file checkbox since we need to use this configuration file to build the page navigation rules later in this application. Your finished Name and Location wizard should match one that is shown in Figure 8.136. Click on the Finish button to complete this managed bean creation process.

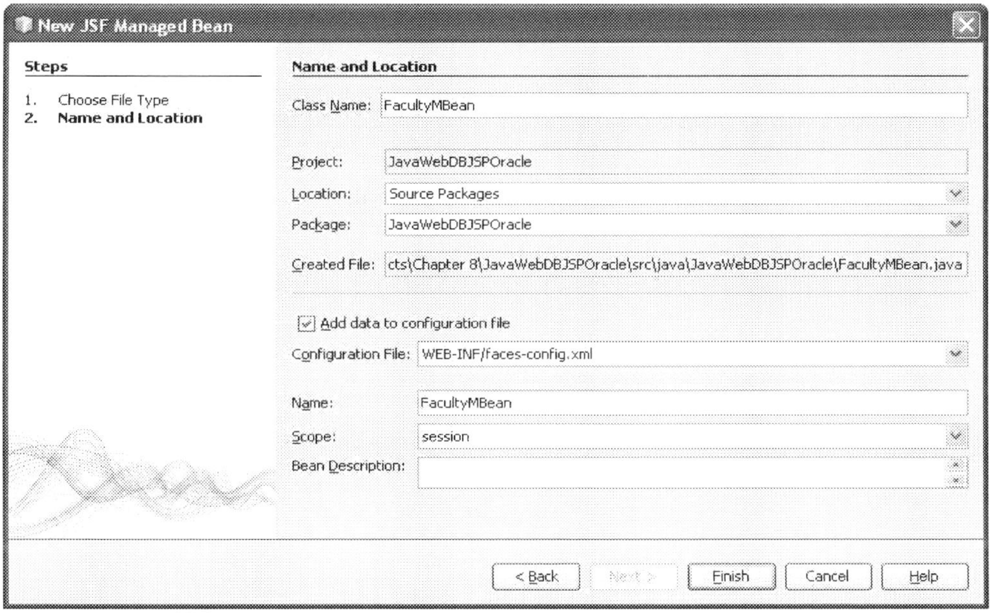

Figure 8.136. The finished Name and Location wizard.

Open the FacultyMBean.java class file and perform the following operations to create the first part of the codes of this file, which is shown in Figure 8.137.

Let's have a closer look at this piece of codes to see how it works.

A. Right click on any space inside this code window and select the Insert Code item. Then choose the Call Enterprise Bean item to open the `Call Enterprise Bean` wizard. Expand the package JavaWebDBJSPOracle from the list and select our Java session bean FacultySessionBean by clicking on it, and click on the OK button. Immediately, you can find that an object @EJB has been injected into our managed bean, and a new instance of our Java session bean class, facultySessionBean, has also been added into this class.

B. Add ten new properties into this class and the names of these properties should be identical with those value attributes defined in the associated tags in the FacultyPage.jsp file. For example, the facultyName property should be identical with the value attribute defined in the tag <h:inputText id="facultyName" value="#{FacultyMBean.facultyName}">. In this way, the property defined in the Java managed bean has been bound to the value attribute of the facultyName inputText tag or input field. The data type for the facultyImageName is `static` since we want to use this property as a global variable.

C. Right click on any space of this code window and select the Insert Code item. Select the Getter and Setter item to create 10 pairs of getter and setter methods for those 10 properties created in step **B** above. On the opened `Generate Getters and Setters` dialog box, check all 10 properties and click on the Generate button to create them.

D. Starting from step **C** until step **R**, eight pairs of getter and setter methods are created, and these methods are used to get and set the associated properties defined in this Java managed bean class.

Now let's continue to create the second part of the codes for this managed bean, which is shown in Figure 8.138. Let's have a closer look at this piece of codes to see how it works.

A. From steps **A** to **D**, another two pairs of getter and setter methods are defined, and they are used to pick up and set up the phone and the title properties in this managed bean class.

E. The Select() method is defined, and it is used to perform the data query operations from the Faculty table in our sample database using the Hibernate API. The point to be noted is that the name of this method must be identical with the value defined in the action attribute in the <h:commandButton> tag in our Java JSF page FacultyPage.jsp. In this way, the Select button in that JSF page can be bound to this Select() method defined in this managed class.

F. Two local variables are created first inside this method. The first one is the List collection instance, and it is used to hold the returned query result from the Faculty table. The second is a JDialog instance, and it is used to display debug information when the project runs.

G. The QueryFaculty() method defined in our session bean FacultySessionBean.java is executed to perform the faculty information query action. The property facultyName works as an argument for this query function. The returned query result is assigned to the List instance facultyList.

H. If the queried result is non-null, which means that the query is successful, and the get(0) method is executed to pick up each column from the List object and assign each of them

```
  package JavaWebDBJSPOracle;
  public class FacultyMBean {
A    @EJB
     private FacultySessionBean facultySessionBean;
B    private String facultyImage;
     private static String facultyImageName = null;
     private String facultyName;
     private String facultyID;
     private String name;
     private String title;
     private String office;
     private String phone;
     private String college;
     private String email;
C    public String getCollege() {
       return college;
     }
D    public void setCollege(String college) {
       this.college = college;
     }
E    public String getEmail() {
       return email;
     }
F    public void setEmail(String email) {
       this.email = email;
     }
G    public String getFacultyID() {
       return facultyID;
     }
H    public void setFacultyID(String facultyID) {
       this.facultyID = facultyID;
     }
I    public String getFacultyImage() {
       return facultyImage;
     }
J    public void setFacultyImage(String facultyImage) {
       this.facultyImage = facultyImage;
     }
K    public String getFacultyImageName() {
       return facultyImageName;
     }
L    public void setFacultyImageName(String facultyImageName) {
       this.facultyImageName = facultyImageName;
     }
M    public String getFacultyName() {
       return facultyName;
     }
N    public void setFacultyName(String facultyName) {
       this.facultyName = facultyName;
     }
O    public String getName() {
       return name;
     }
P    public void setName(String name) {
       this.name = name;
     }
Q    public String getOffice() {
       return office;
     }
R    public void setOffice(String office) {
       this.office = office;
     }
  .........
```

Figure 8.137. The first part of the codes for the Java managed bean FacultyMBean.

```
A     public String getPhone() {
        return phone;
      }
B     public void setPhone(String phone) {
        this.phone = phone;
      }
C     public String getTitle() {
        return title;
      }
D     public void setTitle(String title) {
        this.title = title;
      }
    /** Creates a new instance of FacultyMBean */
      public FacultyMBean() {
      }
E   public String  Select() {
F       List<Faculty>  facultyList = null;
        MsgDialog  msgDlg = new MsgDialog(new javax.swing.JFrame(), true);
G       facultyList = facultySessionBean.QueryFaculty(facultyName);
H       if (facultyList != null) {
          facultyID = facultyList.get(0).getFacultyId();
          name = facultyList.get(0).getFacultyName();
          office = facultyList.get(0).getOffice();
          title = facultyList.get(0).getTitle();
          phone = facultyList.get(0).getPhone();
          college = facultyList.get(0).getCollege();
          email = facultyList.get(0).getEmail();
        }
I       else {
          msgDlg.setMessage("The faculty query is failed!");
          msgDlg.setVisible(true);
        }
J       facultyImage = getFacultyImage();
K       return null;
      }
    }
```

Figure 8.138. The second part of the codes for the Java managed bean FacultyMBean.

to the associated property. Since only one row is returned, an index of 0 is used for the get() method.

I. Otherwise, this query has failed, and this exception information is displayed using the JDialog object.

J. The getter getFacultyImage() is executed to pick up the name of a matched faculty image file and assign it to the facultyImage property. Since this property is bound to the value attribute of the `<h:graphicImage>` tag in our JSF page FacultyPage.jsp, the matched faculty image will be displayed in that JSF page.

K. Because the returning value of this method is useless for this application, a null is returned.

If you encountered some real-time compiling exceptions, for example, the `List<Faculty>` item has been underscored with a red line. In most cases, it is the package or class missing-related errors. Just right click on any place inside this code window and select the Fix Imports item, then select the missed package or class such as java.util.List to fix them.

Now we can build and run our project to test this faculty information query operation.

8.6.8.4 Run the Project to Test the Faculty Information Query

Click on the Clean and Build Main Project button on the top to build our project. If everything is fine, right click on the FacultyPage.jsp from the Projects window and select the Compile File item from the pop-up menu to compile this page. Then right click on this FcaultyPage.jsp again and select the Run File item to run the project.

Enter the appropriate username and password, such as admin and reback, for our Web server GlassFish v3, and click on the OK button to continue. The point to be noted is that the username and password must be identical with those you created when downloading and installing the GlassFish v3 server in your machine.

On the opened FacultyPage.jsp page, enter a desired faculty name, such as Ying Bai, into the `Faculty Name` field. Then click on the Select button to query the related information for the selected faculty. Immediately, you can find the queried information is displayed in seven pieces of inputText fields, as shown in Figure 8.139.

Another way to test the project is to run a sequence of web pages we have built for this project, which starts from the LogInPage.jsp, and then SelectionPage.jsp and FacultyPage.jsp. To do that, we need to do some works to our SelectionBean.java class and the faces-config.xml file to set up the direction and page navigation rules between the SelectionPage and the FacultyPage.

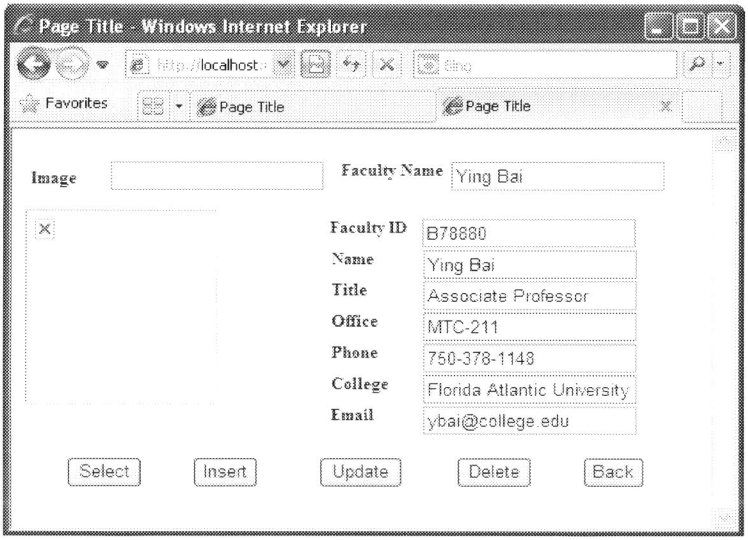

Figure 8.139. The running result of the project.

8.6.8.5 Modify the faces-config.xml File to Run Project in a Web Pages Sequence

Recall that in Section 8.6.5, we built the SelectionBean.java file to handle the Web page navigations in this project. Refer to Figure 8.127; the OK() method in that class takes charge of directing the project to the correct next page based on the user's selection from the selectionList box in the SelectionPage.jsp page. In addition to the OK() method, we also need to set up those navigation relationships between the LogInPage, SelectionPage, and ErrorPage using the faces-config.xml file in Section 8.6.7.

In this section, we also need to use this configuration file to set up another navigation rule between the SelectionPage and the FacultyPage. In fact, we need to set-up another two navigation rules, navigation between the SelectionPage and the CoursePage, and the navigation between the SelectionPage and the StudentPage. However, at this moment of the time, we have not built the CoursePage and the StudentPage; we can leave those jobs later when both pages have been built.

To set up a navigation rule between the SelectionPage and the FacultyPage, open the faces-config.xml file by expanding the `Configuration Files` node under our project from the Projects window and double clicking on this configuration file.

The opened PageFlow view of the faces-config.xml file is shown in Figure 8.140. Perform the following operations to set up this navigation rule:

1. Locate the starting point A from the SelectionPage.jsp page and drag to the ending point **B** at the FacultyPage.jsp page, as shown in Figure 8.140. Then double click on the label case1 and change it to FACULTY.
2. Locate the starting point **C** from the FacultyPage.jsp page and drag to the ending point **D** at the SelectionPage.jsp page, as shown in Figure 8.140. Then double click on the label case1 and change it to SELECTION.

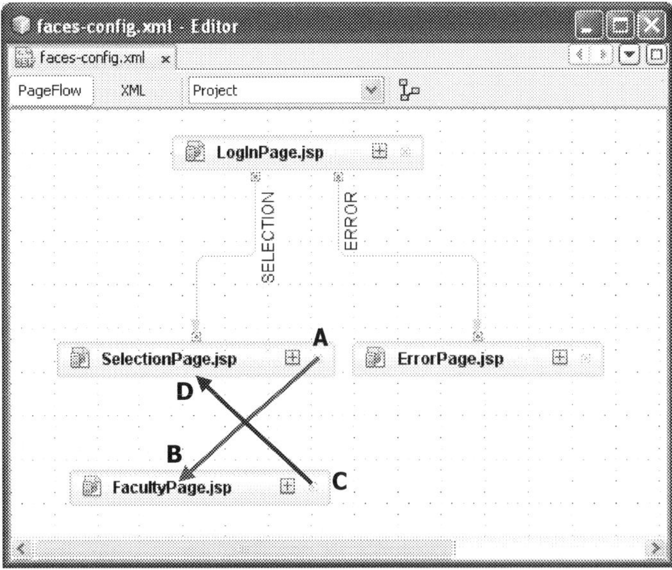

Figure 8.140. The opened faces-config.xml file.

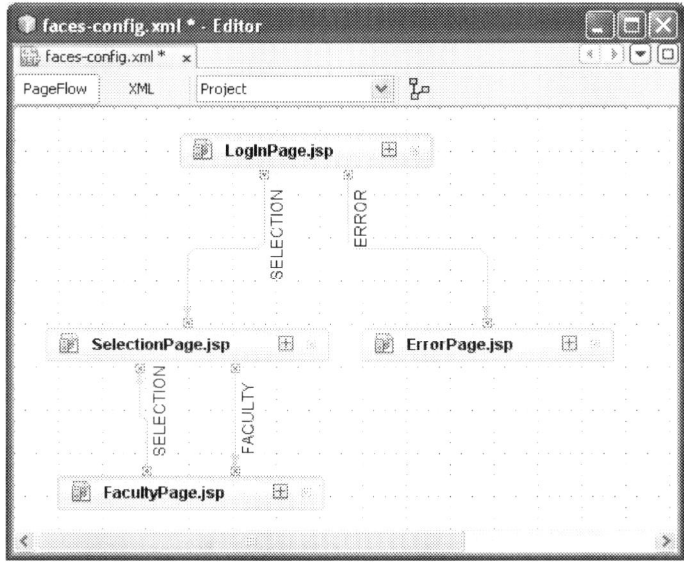

Figure 8.141. The finished faces-config.xml file.

Your finished faces-config.xml file should match one that is shown in Figure 8.141.

One point to be noted is that the contents of labels between web pages must be identical with those returned Strings defined in the OK() method in the SelectionBean.java file. Refer to Figure 8.127, you can find that the contents of labels in this faces-config.xml file are identical with those Strings inside the OK() method. For example, the label from the page SelectionPage.jsp to the page FacultyPage.jsp is FACULTY in the configuration file. The string returned in the first if block in the OK() method is also "FACULTY".

Now let's run the project to test it with a sequence of web pages we have built in this project. To do that, you need to right click on the LogInPage.jsp from the Projects window and select the Run File item to run the project.

On the opened LogInPage, enter a suitable username and password, such as jhenry and test, and click on the LogIn button to browse to the SelectionPage.jsp. Select the `Faculty Information` item from this page and click on the OK button to open the FacultyPage. Now you can test this faculty information query as we did above in the first test.

Our faculty information query using the Java JSF page and Java beans is successful! Next, let's add some codes into this project to improve this query by displaying a selected faculty image.

8.6.8.6 Add Codes to the Project to Display a Selected Faculty Image

First, let's modify the getter method, getFacultyImage(), in the FacultyMBean.java file to find and pick up a selected faculty image file, exactly a name of the faculty image file.

Open the Java managed bean class FacultyMBean.java and add the codes that are shown in Figure 8.142 into the getFacultyImage() method.

```
    getFacultyImage() {
A        if (facultyImageName != null) {
           facultyImage = facultyImageName;
           facultyImageName = null;
         }
B        else
           facultyImage = getImage(facultyName);
C        return facultyImage;
    }
```

Figure 8.142. The modified codes for the getter method.

```
    public String getImage(String f_name) {
A        int maxNumber = 7;
         String fImage = null;
B        String[] fname = { "Ying Bai", "Black Anderson", "Satish Bhalla", "Steve Johnson",
                            "Jenney King", "Alice Brown", "Debby Angles", "Jeff Henry"};
C        String[] fimage = { "Bai.jpg", "Anderson.jpg", "Satish.jpg", "Johnson.jpg",
                             "King.jpg", "Brown.jpg", "Angles.jpg", "Henry.jpg"};
D        for (int i=0; i<=maxNumber; i++) {
E          if (fname[i].equals(f_name)) {
             fImage = fimage[i];
             break;
           }
         }
F        facultyImage = fImage;
G        return fImage;
    }
```

Figure 8.143. The codes for the method getImage().

Let's have a closer look at these new added codes to see how they work.

A. First, we need to check whether the global variable facultyImageName contains a valid name of a new faculty image file. This situation will happen if the user wants to insert a new faculty record into the database with a new faculty image, and we will discuss this situation in Section 8.6.9 later. If this global variable did contain a valid name of a new faculty image file, we need to assign it to the property facultyImage and clean up this variable to make it ready for the next data insertion action.

B. If the facultyImageName did not contain any data, which means that this is not the data insertion action. The user defined method getImage() that will be built in the following part is executed to select and pick up a matched faculty image based on the faculty name, which works as an argument for this method.

C. The facultyImage property that contains a valid name of either a new or an existing faculty image file is returned. Another possibility is that this property may contain a null if a valid name of a faculty image file cannot be found.

Now let's build the getImage() method. In the opened FacultyMBean.java file, create a new method named getImage() and enter codes that are shown in Figure 8.143 into this method.

Let's have a closer look at this new method to see how it works.

A. Two local variables, maxNumber and fImage, are created first. The first one is used to define the maximum number of faculty members and associated faculty image files, and the second is used to hold the matched faculty image file's name.

B. A string array fname is created with all seven faculty members involved.

C. Another string variable fimage is declared with all seven matched faculty image file's names involved in this array. One point to be noted is that the orders in both array must be identical, which means that each faculty member in the fname array must be matched to a faculty image file's name fimage.

D. A for loop is used to scan all seven faculty members' names to try to find a matched faculty name with the input argument f_name.

E. If a matched faculty name has been found, the associated faculty image file's name is assigned to the local variable fImage, and the loop is terminated.

F. The matched faculty image file's name is assigned to the facultyImage property.

G. The matched faculty image file's name is returned.

Now we can build and run the project in a Web sequence to fetch the desired faculty information from the Faculty table in our sample database.

8.6.8.7 Run the Entire Project to Test the Faculty Information Query

Before we can run the project to test its function, first we must copy all faculty and student image files and paste them to the Web Pages node in our project. Perform the following operations to perform this copy and paste works:

1. Find all faculty and students' image files, which are located at the folder Images at the Wiley ftp site (refer to Figure 1.2 in Chapter 1).
2. Copy all image files from that location and paste them under the Web Pages node in our project folder JavaWebDBJSPOracle.

Click on the Clean and Build Main Project button on the top to build our project. If everything is fine, right click on the LogInPage.jsp from the Projects window and select the Run File item to run the project.

Enter the appropriate username and password, such as admin and reback, to our Web server, and click on the OK button to continue. The point to be noted is that the username and password must be identical with those you created when downloading and installing the GlassFish v3 server in your machine.

As the LogIn page opened, enter the desired username and password, such as jhenry and test, and click on the LogIn button. On the opened Selection page, select the `Faculty Information` item and click on the OK button to open the Faculty page.

To query a desired faculty record from the Faculty table in our sample Oracle database, enter a desired faculty name, such as Ying Bai, into the `Faculty Name` field, and click on the Select button to perform this query. Immediately, you can find that queried information for the selected faculty, and a matched faculty image are displayed in this page, as shown in Figure 8.144.

Figure 8.144. The running result of the project.

You can try to enter different faculty names, such as Jenney King and Jeff Henry, to query other faculty information. Click on the Close button that is on the upper-right corner of this page to close our project.

Our project for faculty information query is successful!

Next, let's discuss how to insert a new faculty record into our sample database using JavaServer Faces and Java beans.

8.6.9 Insert New Records to the Faculty Table Using JavaServer Faces and Java Beans

As we did for the faculty information query action in the last section, we can divide this new faculty insertion action into two Java beans: the Java managed bean FacultyMBean.java that is used to manage and control the data insertion, and the session bean FacultySessionBean.java that is used to perform the actual data insertion actions.

First, let's build the codes for the managed bean to manage this data insertion action.

8.6.9.1 Add the Codes to the Java Managed Bean to Manage Data Insertions

To begin this coding process, let's first add a new method Insert() into our managed bean FacultyMBean.java and bind it to the action attribute of the <h:commandButton id="Insert"> tag in our JSF page FacultyPage.jsp.

Open the code window of our managed bean FacultyMBean.java and add a new method Insert() into that file with the codes that are shown in Figure 8.145.

Recall that in Section 8.6.8.1, when we modified our JSF page FacultyPage.jsp file, we added one command tag shown below to that page:

```
<h:commandButton id="Insert" action="#{FacultyMBean.Insert}"
value="Insert" />
```

```
  public String Insert() {
A      boolean insert = false;
       MsgDialog msgDlg = new MsgDialog(new javax.swing.JFrame(), true);
       String[] fInsert = {facultyID, name, office, phone, college, title, email};
B      if (facultyImageName != null)
          facultyImage = facultyImageName;
C      insert = facultySessionBean.InsertFaculty(fInsert);
D      if (!insert) {
          msgDlg.setMessage("The faculty insertion is failed!");
           msgDlg.setVisible(true);
       }
E      return null;
  }
```

Figure 8.145. The codes for the new added method Insert().

With this tag, the Insert() method we just added into our managed bean has been bound to the action attribute of that tag, and this method will be called and executed as soon as the user clicks the Insert button on our JSF page FacultyPage.jsp as the project runs.

Let's have a closer look at this piece of new added codes to see how it works.

A. Some local variables are created first for this method. The insert is a boolean variable used to hold the running status of the InsertFaculty() method defined in the session bean class, and we will build this method in the next section. The msgDlg is a JDialog instance used to display the debug or exception information as the project runs. The fInsert[] is a string array used to hold seven pieces of new faculty information to be inserted into the Faculty table in our sample database. The point to be noted is that we used seven properties defined in this managed bean as seven pieces of new faculty information, since those properties have been bound to the associated value attributes of the <h:inputText> tags in our JSF page FacultyPage.jsp. Furthermore, those properties can be automatically updated as the users enter seven pieces of new faculty information into seven text fields related to those tags in our JSF page FacultyPage.jsp.

B. If the user entered a new faculty image into the Image field in the JSF page, the property facultyImageName defined in the managed bean should contain a valid faculty image file's name, and this name is assigned to the property facultyImage that will be used to display this new image later.

C. The InsertFaculty() method defined in our session bean, which will be developed in the next section, is called to perform this new faculty record insertion. The argument passed into that method is the string array fInsert[] that contains seven pieces of new faculty information. The running result of that method is returned and assigned to the local variable insert.

D. If the running result of the method InsertFaculty() is false, which means that the data insertion has failed, this situation is displayed by executing the setMessage() method in the msgDlg instance.

E. A null is returned since this returning value is not important to this application.

Next, let's develop the InsertFaculty() method in our session bean class FacultySessionBean.java to perform the data insertion using the Hibernate API.

```
  public boolean InsertFaculty(String[] newFaculty) {
A     Faculty ft = new Faculty();
B     org.hibernate.Transaction tx = session.beginTransaction();
C     if (!tx.isActive())
        tx.begin();
D     ft.setFacultyId(newFaculty[0]);
      ft.setFacultyName(newFaculty[1]);
      ft.setOffice(newFaculty[2]);
      ft.setPhone(newFaculty[3]);
      ft.setCollege(newFaculty[4]);
      ft.setTitle(newFaculty[5]);
      ft.setEmail(newFaculty[6]);
E     session.persist(ft);
F     tx.commit();
G     return true;
  }
```

Figure 8.146. The codes for the InsertFaculty() method.

8.6.9.2 Build the InsertFaculty() Method for the Session Bean to Perform Data Insertions

Open the code window for our session bean class FacultySessionBean.java, and enter the codes shown in Figure 8.146 into this file to create a new method InsertFaculty() and its codes.

Let's have a closer look at this piece of new codes to see how it works.

A. First, a new instance of the entity class Faculty is created, since we need this object to perform new faculty record insertion later.

B. A new Transaction object tx is created to help to perform this data insertion action.

C. If this new Transaction instance has not been active, the begin() method is executed to begin this transaction instance.

D. Seven setter methods are executed to set up seven pieces of new faculty information to the newly created Faculty entity object.

E. The insertion action is performed by executing the persist() method for the session object with the Faculty entity object as the argument of this method.

F. The commit() method is executed to actually trigger and perform this insertion action.

G. Finally, a true is returned to the calling method to indicate the success of this data insertion.

Now let's build and run the project to test this data insertion function.

8.6.9.3 Run the Project to Test the New Faculty Record Insertion

Click on the Clean and Build Main Project button to build our project. If everything is fine, right click on our JSF page FacultyPage.jsp from the Projects window and select the Run File item to run the project. Of course you can run the project by starting from the LogIn page.

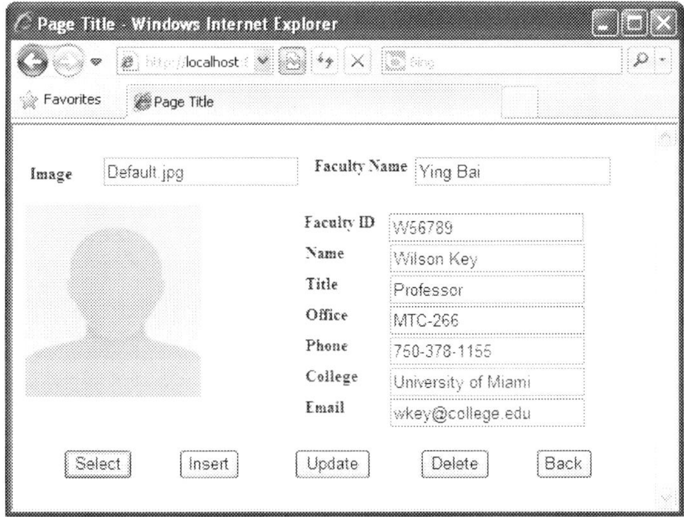

Figure 8.147. The newly inserted faculty record.

On the opened Faculty Page, type a desired faculty name such as Ying Bai into the `Faculty Name` field to perform a query for that faculty member. Then enter seven pieces of new faculty information shown in Figure 8.147 into the associated seven fields as a new faculty record. Also, enter the default faculty image file's name, Default.jpg, into the `Image` field as a new image for this new faculty, as shown in Figure 8.147. Then click on the Insert button to try to insert this new faculty record into the Faculty table in our sample database.

To check and confirm this new data insertion, open the Faculty table from our sample Oracle database by performing the following operations:

A. Open the Services window and expand the Databases node.

B. Right click on our Oracle database URL: jdbc:oracle:thin:@localhost:1521:XE [CSE_DEPT on CSE_DEPT], and select the Connect item to connect to our database.

C. Expand our sample database CSE_DEPT and Tables.

D. Right click on the Faculty table and select the View Data item.

Your opened Faculty table is shown in Figure 8.148.

It can be found that the new faculty record with the faculty_id of W56789, which is located at the first row and has been highlighted in dark color, has been successfully inserted into our database. Our data insertion action is successful!

It is highly recommended to remove this newly inserted faculty record from our database since we want to keep our database clean. To do this clean up, click and select the first row in this Faculty table, and click on the Delete Selected Record button that is the second button under the query statement: `select * from CSE_DEPT.FACULTY` at the top of this window. Click on the Yes button to the popup message box to confirm this deletion action.

Next, let's discuss how to update and delete an existing faculty record in our database using the JSF faces and Java beans.

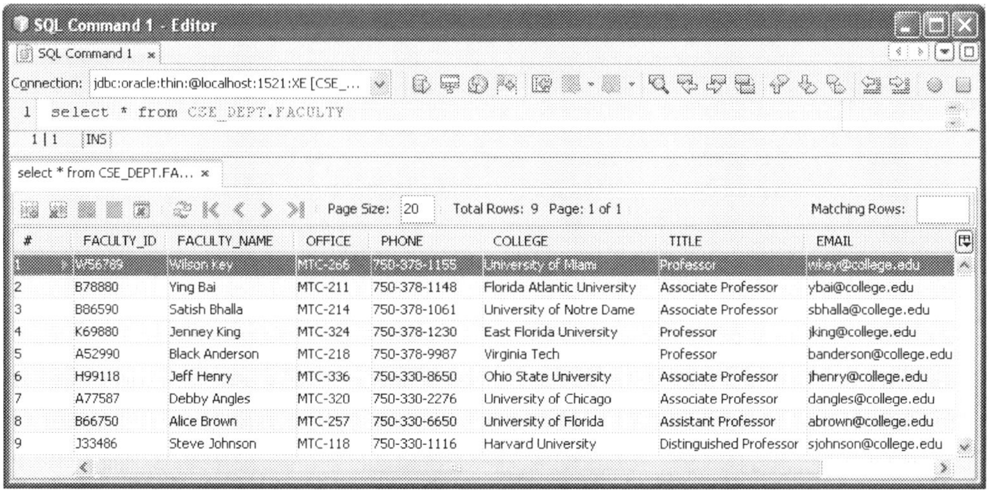

SQL Command 1 - Editor

Connection: jdbc:oracle:thin:@localhost:1521:XE [CSE_...

```
1  select * from CSE_DEPT.FACULTY
```

select * from CSE_DEPT.FA...

Page Size: 20 Total Rows: 9 Page: 1 of 1 Matching Rows:

#	FACULTY_ID	FACULTY_NAME	OFFICE	PHONE	COLLEGE	TITLE	EMAIL
1	W56789	Wilson Key	MTC-266	750-378-1155	University of Miami	Professor	wkey@college.edu
2	B78880	Ying Bai	MTC-211	750-378-1148	Florida Atlantic University	Associate Professor	ybai@college.edu
3	B86590	Satish Bhalla	MTC-214	750-378-1061	University of Notre Dame	Associate Professor	sbhalla@college.edu
4	K69880	Jenney King	MTC-324	750-378-1230	East Florida University	Professor	jking@college.edu
5	A52990	Black Anderson	MTC-218	750-378-9987	Virginia Tech	Professor	banderson@college.edu
6	H99118	Jeff Henry	MTC-336	750-330-8650	Ohio State University	Associate Professor	jhenry@college.edu
7	A77587	Debby Angles	MTC-320	750-330-2276	University of Chicago	Associate Professor	dangles@college.edu
8	B66750	Alice Brown	MTC-257	750-330-6650	University of Florida	Assistant Professor	abrown@college.edu
9	J33486	Steve Johnson	MTC-118	750-330-1116	Harvard University	Distinguished Professor	sjohnson@college.edu

Figure 8.148. The opened Faculty table in the NetBeans IDE.

8.6.10 Update and Delete Records from the Faculty Table Using JSF Page and Java Bean

First, let's handle the faculty record updating action.

Because of the complex in updating a faculty record with the primary key faculty_id, in this section, we still want to update a faculty record with an existing faculty_id. In other words, we will update a faculty record by changing all columns without touching the faculty_id column since one needs to update this faculty_id first in the child tables (LogIn and Course) before he can update it in the parent table (Faculty) if one wants to update this faculty_id column.

As we did for the new faculty record insertion in the last section, we can divide this faculty record updating action into two Java beans: the Java managed bean FacultyMBean.java that is used to manage and control the data updating, and the session bean FacultySessionBean.java that is used to perform the actual data updating actions.

First, let's build the codes for the managed bean to manage this data updating action.

8.6.10.1 Add the Codes to the Java Managed Bean to Manage Data Updating

To begin this coding process, let's first add a new method Update() into our managed bean FacultyMBean.java. Recall that in Section 8.6.8.1, we have bound this method to the `<h:commandButton id="Update">` tag in our JSF page FacultyPage.jsp.

Open the code window of our managed bean FacultyMBean.java and add a new method Update() into that file with the codes that are shown in Figure 8.149.

Recall that in Section 8.6.8.1, when we modified our JSF page FacultyPage.jsp file, we added one command tag shown below to that page:

```
<h:commandButton id="Update" action="#{FacultyMBean.Update}"
value="Update" />
```

```
  public String Update() {
A     boolean update = false;
      MsgDialog msgDlg = new MsgDialog(new javax.swing.JFrame(), true);
      String[] fUpdate = {name, office, phone, college, title, email, facultyID};
B     if (facultyImageName != null)
         facultyImage = facultyImageName;
C     update = facultySessionBean.UpdateFaculty(fUpdate);
D     if (!update) {
         msgDlg.setMessage("The faculty updating is failed!");
         msgDlg.setVisible(true);
      }
E     return null;
  }
```

Figure 8.149. The codes for the newly added method Update().

With this tag, the Update() method we just added into our managed bean has been bound to the action attribute of that tag, and this method will be called and executed as soon as the user clicks the Update button on our JSF page FacultyPage.jsp as the project runs.

Let's have a closer look at this piece of newly added codes to see how it works.

A. Some local variables are created first for this method. The update is a boolean variable used to hold the running status of the UpdateFaculty() method defined in the session bean class, and we will build this method in the next section. The msgDlg is a JDialog instance used to display the debug or exception information as the project runs. The fUpdate[] is a string array used to hold six pieces of updating faculty information for an existing record in the Faculty table in our sample database. The point to be noted is that we used six properties defined in this managed bean as six pieces of updating faculty information, since those properties have been bound to the associated value attributes of the <h:inputText> tags in our JSF page FacultyPage.jsp. Furthermore, those properties can be automatically updated as the users enter six pieces of updating faculty information into six text fields related to those tags in our JSF page FacultyPage.jsp. The seventh parameter in the fUpdate[] array is the property facultyID used to work as a query criterion.

B. If the user entered an updated faculty image's name into the Image field in the JSF page, the property facultyImageName defined in the managed bean should contain a valid faculty image file's name, and this name is assigned to the property facultyImage that will be used to display this updated image later.

C. The UpdateFaculty() method defined in our session bean, which will be developed in the next section, is called to perform this faculty record updating. The argument passed into that method is the string array fUpdate[] that contains six pieces of updated faculty information. The running result of that method is returned and assigned to the local variable update.

D. If the running result of the method UpdateFaculty() is false, which means that the data updating has failed, this situation is displayed by executing the setMessage() method in the msgDlg instance.

E. A null is returned since this returning value is not important to this application.

Next, let's develop the UpdateFaculty() method in our session bean class to perform the data updating using the Hibernate API.

```
  public boolean UpdateFaculty(String[] upFaculty) {
A     MsgDialog msgDlg = new MsgDialog(new javax.swing.JFrame(), true);
B     try {
         SessionFactory fact = new Configuration().configure().buildSessionFactory();
         session = fact.openSession();
C        org.hibernate.Transaction tx = session.beginTransaction();
D        if (!tx.isActive())
            tx.begin();
E        Faculty ft = (Faculty)session.get(Faculty.class, upFaculty[6]);
F        ft.setFacultyName(upFaculty[0]);
         ft.setOffice(upFaculty[1]);
         ft.setPhone(upFaculty[2]);
         ft.setCollege(upFaculty[3]);
         ft.setTitle(upFaculty[4]);
         ft.setEmail(upFaculty[5]);
G        session.update(ft);
H        tx.commit();
I        session.close();
J        return true;
      }
K     catch(Exception e) {
         msgDlg.setMessage(e.getMessage());
         msgDlg.setVisible(true);
L        return false;
      }
  }
```

Figure 8.150. The codes for the UpdateFaculty() method in the session bean.

8.6.10.2 Build the UpdateFaculty() Method in the Session Bean to Perform Data Updating

Open the code window for our session bean class FacultySessionBean.java and enter the codes shown in Figure 8.150 into this file to create a new method UpdateFaculty() and its codes.

Let's have a closer look at this piece of new codes to see how it works.

A. A new instance of the JDialog class msgDlg is created since we need to use it to display some debug information during the project running.

B. A try catch block is used to perform this data updating action. First, a new SessionFactory object fact is created by executing the buildSessionFactory() method. Then the session object is opened by executing the openSession() method.

C. A new Transaction object tx is created to help to perform this data updating action.

D. If this new Transaction instance has not been active, the begin() method is executed to begin this transaction instance.

E. The get() method in the session class is first executed to perform a query to retrieve an existing faculty record from the Faculty table based on the faculty_id that is stored in the string array upFaculty[6]. The first argument of this get() method is the class type Faculty, and the second argument is the faculty_id. The returned query result is assigned to a new Faculty instance ft. A point to be noted is that the Faculty class must be casted before this method to make sure that the session object returns an appropriate object.

F. Six setter methods are executed to set up six pieces of updated faculty information to the newly created Faculty entity object ft.

G. The updating action is performed by executing the update() method for the session object, with the Faculty entity object ft as the argument of this method.

H. The commit() method is executed to actually trigger and perform this data updating action.

I. The close() method is executed to close this opened session object when this data updating is complete.

J. Finally, a true is returned to the calling method to indicate the success of this data updating action.

K. The catch block is used to track and detect any exception during this data updating action. The exception information will be displayed using the JDialog instance msgDlg.

L. A false is returned if any exception occurred during this data updating process.

Now let's build and run the project to test this data updating function.

8.6.10.3 Run the Project to Test the Faculty Record Updating Action

Click on the Clean and Build Main Project button to build our project. If everything is fine, right click on our JSF page FacultyPage.jsp from the Projects window and select the Run File item to run the project. Of course, you can run the project by starting from the LogIn page.

On the opened Faculty Page, type a desired faculty name, such as Ying Bai, into the `Faculty Name` field to perform a query for that faculty member. Then enter six pieces of updated faculty information shown in Figure 8.151 into the associated six fields as an updated faculty record. Also, enter the default faculty image file's name, Default.jpg, into the `Image` field as an updated image for this faculty, as shown in Figure 8.151. Then click on the Update button to try to update this faculty record against the Faculty table in our sample database.

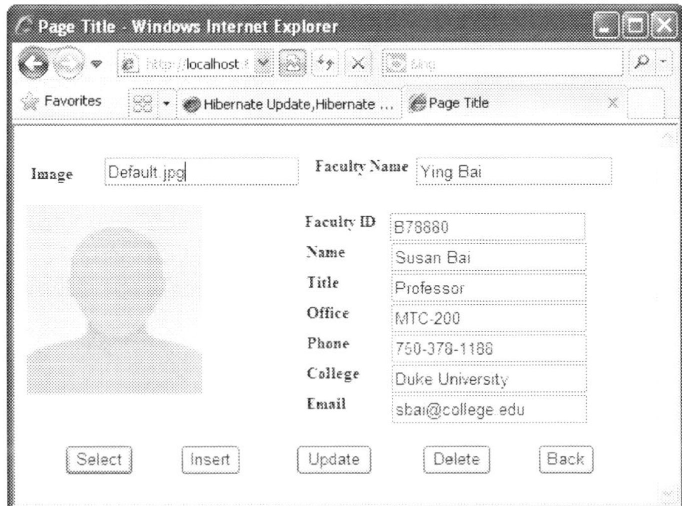

Figure 8.151. The updated faculty information.

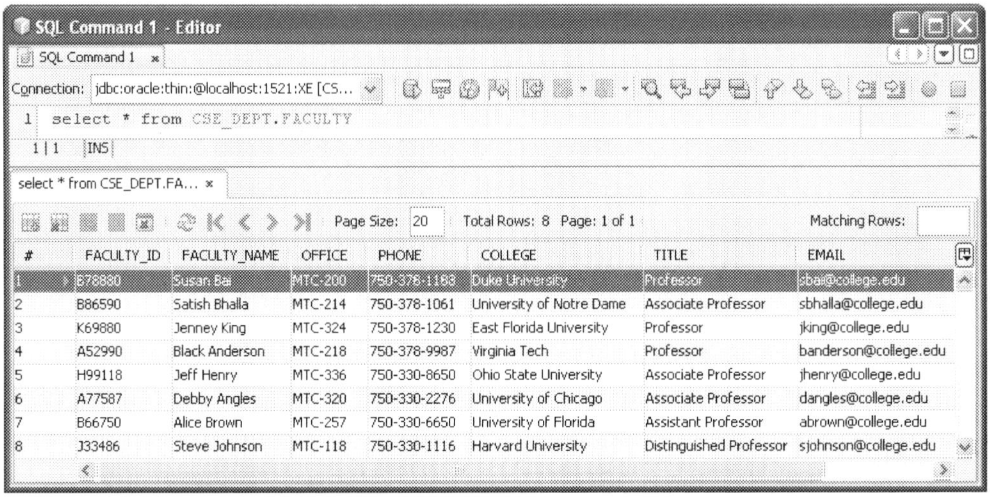

SQL Command 1 - Editor

Connection: jdbc:oracle:thin:@localhost:1521:XE [CS...

```
select * from CSE_DEPT.FACULTY
```

select * from CSE_DEPT.FA... Page Size: 20 Total Rows: 8 Page: 1 of 1 Matching Rows:

#	FACULTY_ID	FACULTY_NAME	OFFICE	PHONE	COLLEGE	TITLE	EMAIL
1	B78880	Susan Bai	MTC-200	750-378-1183	Duke University	Professor	sbai@college.edu
2	B86590	Satish Bhalla	MTC-214	750-378-1061	University of Notre Dame	Associate Professor	sbhalla@college.edu
3	K69880	Jenney King	MTC-324	750-378-1230	East Florida University	Professor	jking@college.edu
4	A52990	Black Anderson	MTC-218	750-378-9987	Virginia Tech	Professor	banderson@college.edu
5	H99118	Jeff Henry	MTC-336	750-330-8650	Ohio State University	Associate Professor	jhenry@college.edu
6	A77587	Debby Angles	MTC-320	750-330-2276	University of Chicago	Associate Professor	dangles@college.edu
7	B66750	Alice Brown	MTC-257	750-330-6650	University of Florida	Assistant Professor	abrown@college.edu
8	J33486	Steve Johnson	MTC-118	750-330-1116	Harvard University	Distinguished Professor	sjohnson@college.edu

Figure 8.152. The updated faculty record.

To check and confirm this data updating action, open the Faculty table from our sample Oracle database by performing the following operations:

A. Open the Services window and expand the Databases node.

B. Right click on our Oracle database URL: jdbc:oracle:thin:@localhost:1521:XE [CSE_DEPT on CSE_DEPT], and select the Connect item to connect to our database.

C. Expand our sample database CSE_DEPT and Tables.

D. Right click on the Faculty table and select the View Data item.

Your opened Faculty table is shown in Figure 8.152.

It can be found that the faculty record with the **faculty_id** of B78880, which is located at the first row on this table and has been highlighted in dark color, has been successfully updated with six pieces of updated faculty information. Our data updating action is successful!

It is highly recommended to recover this updated faculty record in our database, since we want to keep our database clean. To do this recovery, there are two ways to go.

The first and the easiest way is to use this JSF page FacultyPage.jsp to perform another updating action by entering the original information that is shown below for the faculty member Ying Bai and clicking on the Update button. Make sure that the Image field is empty when you use the first way to recover that faculty information since we do not want to update the image for the faculty Ying Bai.

The second way is that you can directly do this recovery by opening the Faculty table in the Services window and modifying the updated row with the original faculty information for faculty member Ying Bai, which is listed below:

- Name: Ying Bai
- Title: Associate Professor
- Office: MTC-211

- Phone: 750-378-1148
- College: Florida Atlantic University
- Email: ybai@college.edu

One point to be noted is that when you modify each column for the updated record, you must

1. Press the Enter key for each modified column to make it active.
2. Click on the Commit Record button on the top of this table to make the modification for the row effective after the entire row has been modified.

Next, let's discuss how to delete an existing faculty record from our database using the JSF faces and Java beans with the help of the Hibernate APIs.

8.6.10.4 Add the Codes to the Java Managed Bean to Manage Data Deleting

To begin this coding process, let's first add a new method Delete() into our managed bean FacultyMBean.java. Recall that in Section 8.6.8.1, we have bound this method to the action attribute of the <h:commandButton id="Delete"> tag in our JSF page FacultyPage.jsp.

Open the code window of our managed bean FacultyMBean.java and add a new method Delete() into that file with the codes that are shown in Figure 8.153.

Recall that in Section 8.6.8.1, when we modified our JSF page FacultyPage.jsp file, we added one command tag shown below to that page:

```
<h:commandButton id="Delete" action="#{FacultyMBean.Delete}"
value="Delete" />
```

With this tag, the Delete() method we just added into our managed bean has been bound to the action attribute of that tag, and this method will be called and executed as soon as the user clicks the Delete button on our JSF page FacultyPage.jsp as the project runs.

Let's have a closer look at this piece of newly added codes to see how it works.

A. Some local variables are created first for this method. The delete is a boolean variable used to hold the running status of the DeleteFaculty() method defined in the session bean

```
  public String Delete() {
A     boolean delete = false;
      MsgDialog msgDlg = new MsgDialog(new javax.swing.JFrame(), true);
B     delete = facultySessionBean.DeleteFaculty(facultyID);
C     if (!delete) {
        msgDlg.setMessage("The faculty deleting is failed!");
        msgDlg.setVisible(true);
      }
D     return null;
  }
```

Figure 8.153. The codes for the newly added method Delete().

class, and we will build this method in the next section. The msgDlg is a JDialog instance used to display the debug or exception information as the project runs.

B. The DeleteFaculty() method defined in our session bean, which will be developed in the next section, is called to perform this faculty record deleting action. The argument passed into that method is the faculty_id of the selected faculty that will be deleted. The running result of that method is returned and assigned to the local variable delete.

C. If the running result of the method DeleteFaculty() is false, which means that the data deleting has failed, this situation is displayed by executing the setMessage() method in the msgDlg instance.

D. A null is returned since this returning value is not important to this application.

Next, let's develop the DeleteFaculty() method in our session bean class to perform the data deleting action using the Hibernate API.

8.6.10.5 Build the DeleteFaculty() Method in the Session Bean to Perform Data Deleting

Open the code window for our session bean class FacultySessionBean.java, and enter the codes shown in Figure 8.154 into this file to create a new method DeleteFaculty() and its codes.

Let's have a closer look at this piece of new codes to see how it works.

A. A new instance of the JDialog class msgDlg is created, since we need to use it to display some debug information during the project running.

B. A try catch block is used to perform this data deleting action. First, a new SessionFactory object fact is created by executing the buildSessionFactory() method. Then, the session object is opened by executing the openSession() method.

```
  public boolean DeleteFaculty(String fid) {
A     MsgDialog msgDlg = new MsgDialog(new javax.swing.JFrame(), true);
B     try {
         SessionFactory fact = new Configuration().configure().buildSessionFactory();
         session = fact.openSession();
C        org.hibernate.Transaction tx = session.beginTransaction();
D        if (!tx.isActive())
            tx.begin();
E        Faculty ft = (Faculty)session.get(Faculty.class, fid);
F        session.delete(ft);
G        tx.commit();
H        session.close();
I        return true;
      }
J     catch(Exception e) {
         msgDlg.setMessage(e.getMessage());
         msgDlg.setVisible(true);
K        return false;
      }
  }
```

Figure 8.154. The codes for the DeleteFaculty() method in the session bean.

C. A new Transaction object tx is created to help to perform this data deleting action.

D. If this new Transaction instance has not been active, the begin() method is executed to begin this transaction instance.

E. The get() method in the session class is first executed to perform a query to retrieve an existing faculty record from the Faculty table based on the facultyID property. The first argument of this get() method is the class type Faculty, and the second argument is the facultyID property. The returned query result is assigned to a new Faculty instance ft. A point to be noted is that the Faculty class must be casted before this method to make sure that the session object returns an appropriate object.

F. The deleting action is performed by executing the delete() method for the session object with the Faculty entity object ft as the argument of this method.

G. The commit() method is executed to actually trigger and perform this data deleting action.

H. The close() method is executed to close this opened session object when this data deleting is complete.

I. Finally, a true is returned to the calling method to indicate the success of this data deleting action.

J. The catch block is used to track and detect any exception during this data deleting action. The exception information will be displayed using the JDialog instance msgDlg.

K. A false is returned if any exception occurred during this data deleting process.

Now let's build and run the project to test this data deleting function.

8.6.10.6 Run the Project to Test the Faculty Record Deleting Action

Click on the Clean and Build Main Project button to build our project. If everything is fine, right click on our JSF page FacultyPage.jsp from the Projects window and select the Run File item to run the project. Of course you can run the project by starting from the LogIn page.

On the opened Faculty Page, type a desired faculty name to be deleted, such as Ying Bai, into the `Faculty Name` field to first perform a query for that faculty member. Then click on the Delete button to try to delete this faculty record from the Faculty table in our sample database.

To check and confirm this data deleting action, open the Faculty table from our sample Oracle database in the NetBeans IDE by performing the following operations:

A. Open the Services window and expand the Databases node.

B. Right click on our Oracle database URL: jdbc:oracle:thin:@localhost:1521:XE [CSE_DEPT on CSE_DEPT], and select the Connect item to connect to our database.

C. Expand our sample database CSE_DEPT and Tables.

D. Right click on the Faculty table and select the View Data item.

It can be found from the opened Faculty table that the faculty record with the faculty_id of B78880 has been successfully deleted from the Faculty table. Our data deleting action is successful!

It is highly recommended to recover this deleted faculty record in our database since we want to keep our database clean. The point is that when we delete a faculty member from the Faculty table, the related records to that deleted faculty in those child tables will also be deleted since a cascaded deleting relationship has been set up between the parent and child tables when we built this database in Chapter 2. Therefore, the faculty login record in the LogIn table and all courses taught by that faculty in the Course table will be deleted when the faculty member is deleted from the Faculty table. Also, because the Course table is a parent table for the StudentCourse table, all courses taken by students and taught by the deleted faculty will also be deleted from the StudentCourse table. To recover these deleted records, one needs to recover all of those deleted records. You can directly do these recoveries in the NetBeans IDE environment by opening each table in the Services window and inserting the original information back as new rows to each table.

Refer to Tables 8.4–8.7 in Section 8.5.5.4 to recover these deleted records.

One point to be noted is that when you insert each column for a new record, you must

1. First click on the Insert Record button on the top of this table to open a new `Insert Record` wizard.
2. Enter the original faculty information piece by piece to each column.
3. Press the Enter key at the end of each inserted column to make it active.
4. Click on the Commit Record button on the top of this table to make the insertion effective after the entire row has been inserted.

Your finished Insert Record wizard should match one that is shown in Figure 8.155. Click on the Add Row button to insert this row into the Faculty table to complete this data recovery.

The final coding job is for the Back button. The function of this coding is that the program should be directed to the SelectionPage.jsp page to enable users to make other actions when this button is clicked by the user.

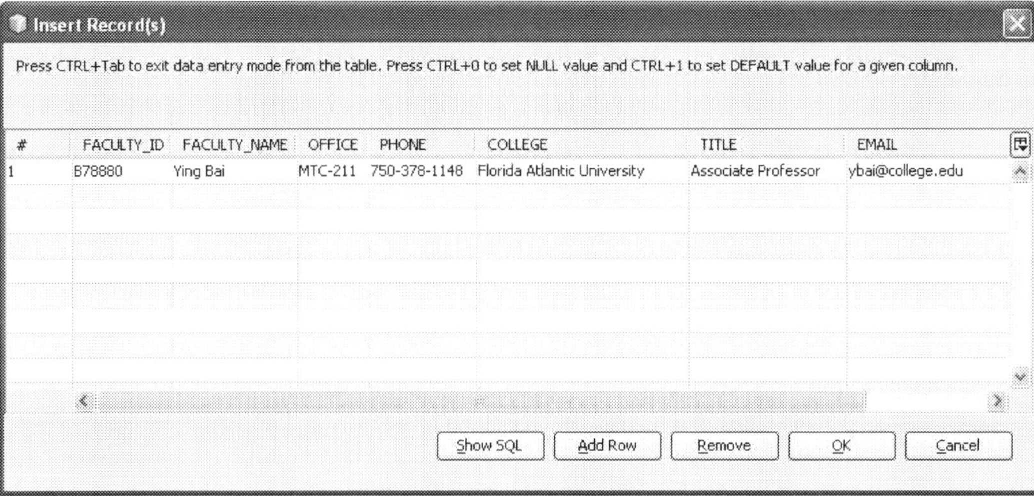

Figure 8.155. The finished Insert Record wizard.

```
  public String Back() {
A     return "SELECTION";
  }
```

Figure 8.156. The codes for the Back() method.

8.6.10.7 Build the Codes for the Back Button Action Attribute in JSF Page

First let's add a new method Back() to our managed bean class FacultyMBean.java.

Recall that in Section 8.6.8.1, when we modified our JSF page FacultyPage.jsp file, we added one command tag shown below to that page:

```
<h:commandButton id="Back" action="#{FacultyMBean.Back}"
value="Back" />
```

With this tag, the Back() method we just added into our managed bean has been bound to the action attribute of that tag, and this method will be called and executed as soon as the user clicks the Back button on our JSF page FacultyPage.jsp as the project runs.

Recall that when we built the navigation relationship between our LogIn, Selection, Error, and Faculty pages in Section 8.6.8.5, we have set up these navigation rules using the configuration file faces-config.xml. The relationship between the Faculty and the Selection pages has been determined by two rules, which is a round trip between these two pages. Refer to that section to get a detailed and clear picture for this relationship.

The coding job is very simple for this Back button. Open the code window of our managed bean FacultyMBean.java, and enter the codes shown in Figure 8.156 into the Back() method we just added into this class.

As shown in step **A** in Figure 8.156, this coding is very simple and a return "SELECTION" is executed as this Back button is clicked by the user. Refer to our Web configure file faces-config.xml, and you can find that the navigation rule from the Faculty page to the Selection page has been defined by a string "SELECTION". The point to be noted is that the returned string in this Back() method must be exactly identical with that string defined in the configuration file to enable this navigation rule effective.

Next, let's discuss how to query and manipulate data against the Course table in our database using the JSF faces and Java beans with the help of the Hibernate APIs.

8.6.11 Query Data from the Course Table Using JavaServer Faces and Java Beans

In Section 8.5, we discussed how to build a Web project JavaWebDBJSPSQL to access and manipulate our sample SQL Server database using different techniques. Especially in Section 8.5.6, we introduced how to access and manipulate data against the Course table using the JavaServer faces and Java beans. The only differences between that project and our current project are data sources and data manipulating tool. In our current project, the data source is Oracle database, and the manipulating tool is the Hibernate APIs.

Because of some similarity between the coding processes for these two projects, we will concentrate on these two different parts in the following development.

Recall that in Section 8.5.6.1, we modified our JSP page Course.jsp to a JavaServer Face page CoursePage.jsp when we built our project JavaWebDBJSPSQL. In this section, we want to use that page as our JSF page to perform data queries and actions against the Course table in our sample Oracle database. Perform the following operations to add this page into our current project:

1. Go to the Wiley ftp site (refer to Figure 1.2 in Chapter 1)
2. Open the folder JSP Files that is located in that site.
3. Copy the JSF file CoursePage.jsp from that folder.
4. Open our current project JavaWebDBJSPOracle and the Files window, and paste the copied JSF page CoursePage.jsp to the web folder under our opened project.

Now if you open the JSF page CoursePage.jsp, you can find that all inputText fields and commandButtons in that page have been bound to associated properties defined in a managed bean CourseBean.java class file.

As we did in Section 8.5, we still want to divide this course information query and manipulation into two parts: the Java managed bean CourseBean.java, which is used to control and manage the course data actions, and the Java session bean CourseSessionBean.java, which is used to perform the actual course data actions using the Hibernate API tool.

First, let's create our Java managed bean class CourseBean.java and use some codes from the JSF page CourseBean.java we built in Section 8.5.6.2 from the project JavaWebDBJSPSQL.

8.6.11.1 Build the JavaServer Face Managed Bean CourseBean

Perform the following operations to create this JSF managed bean class:

1. Launch the NetBeans IDE and open our Web application project JavaWebDBJSPOracle.
2. Right click on our project JavaWebDBJSPOracle from the Projects window and select the New > Other item to open the `New File` wizard.
3. Select JavaServer Faces from the `Categories` list and JSF Managed Bean from the `File Types` list. Then click on the Next button.
4. Enter CourseBean into the `Class Name` field, and select the JavaWebDBJSPOracle from the `Package` combo box.
5. Make sure to check the Add data to configuration file checkbox since we want to add this bean class into our Web configuration file to build a navigation rule later. Then select the session from the `Scope` combo box and click on the Finish button.

On the opened CourseBean class file, enter the first part of the codes, which is shown in Figure 8.157, into this managed bean. The new added codes have been highlighted in bold. In fact, most of codes are identical with those in the managed bean class CourseBean.java in the project JavaWebDBJSPSQL we built in Section 8.5, and you can copy and paste them in this class.

Let's have a closer look at the codes in this part to see how they work.

```
  package JavaWebDBJSPOracle;
A import java.util.*;
  import javax.faces.model.SelectItem;
  public class CourseBean {
B   private String courseName;
    private String schedule;
    private String classroom;
    private String credit;
    private String enrollment;
    private String courseID;
    private String facultyName;
    private List courseList;
    private String selectedItem = null;
C   MsgDialog  msgDlg = new  MsgDialog(new javax.swing.JFrame(), true);
    public CourseBean() {
    }
D   public void setSelectedItem(String cid) {
      selectedItem = cid;
    }
E   public String getSelectedItem() {
      return selectedItem;
    }
F   public void setCourseList(List cid) {
      courseList = cid;
    }
G   public List getCourseList() {
      return courseList;
    }
H   public String getFacultyName() {
      return facultyName;
    }
I   public void setFacultyName(String FacultyName) {
      this.facultyName = FacultyName;
    }
J   public String getCourseID() {
      return courseID;
    }
K   public void setCourseID(String CourseID) {
      this.courseID = CourseID;
    }
L   public String getEnrollment() {
      return enrollment;
    }
M   public void setEnrollment(String Enrollment) {
      this.enrollment = Enrollment;
    }
N   public String getCredit() {
      return credit;
    }
O   public void setCredit(String Credit) {
      this.credit = Credit;
    }
P   public String getClassroom() {
      return classroom;
    }
Q   public void setClassroom(String Classroom) {
      this.classroom = Classroom;
    }
    .........
```

Figure 8.157. The first part codes of the CourseBean class.

A. First, some useful Java packages are defined, since we will use some classes and components that are defined in those packages.

B. Then seven properties, which should be bound to the associated attributes of tags in the CoursePage.jsp JSF page, are declared. The point to be noted is that the names of these properties must be identical with those of attributes defined in our Web view file, CoursePage.jsp, including the cases since Java is a case-sensitive language. Also the List collection courseList, which is bound to the value attribute of the `<f:selectItems>` tag, and the selectedItem, which is bound to the value attribute of the `<h:selectOneListbox>` tag, are declared here, too.

C. The msgDlg is a new instance of our customer-built dialog box, and this is used to display our testing and debug information when we test the codes in this file later.

D. Starting from step **D** through step **Q**, seven setter and getter methods are defined for seven properties we defined above. These methods are used to set or get each property defined in this Java bean class as the project runs.

Now let's enter the second part of the codes into this Java bean class and locate them just below the first part codes, as show in Figure 8.158.

Let's have a closer look at the codes in this part to see how they work.

A. From steps **A** through to **D**, another two-set setter and getter methods are defined and they are used to set and get two properties, schedule and courseName, defined in this bean class.

E. The Select() method, which is bound to the action attribute of the Select button on the CoursePage file, is defined here. This method will be called and executed as the Select button in the CoursePage.jsp is clicked by the user as the project runs. To use the List collection, first, a new ArrayList instance is created.

F. A new List instance, cList, is also created, and it is used to hold the queried result from calling the getCourseID() method that is defined in the session bean class CourseSessionBean.java that will be built in the next section. This method will return a List of course_id taught by the selected faculty by the user from the CoursePage as the project runs.

G. A for loop is utilized to pick up each course_id from the cList instance and assign it to a new instance of SelectItem class, courseid, and add it into the courseList property using the Add() method. A point to be noted is that the returned course_id must be converted to an instance of the class interface SelectItem that is in the package javax.faces.model, and then it can be added into the List collection.

H. Because the returned value is not important for this application, a null is returned when this method is done.

I. The Details() method, which is bound to the action attribute of the Details button on the CoursePage file, is defined here. This method will be called and executed as the Details button in the CoursePage.jsp page is clicked by the user as the project runs. This method will return five pieces of detailed course information based on the selected course_id from the courseList box in the CoursePage as the project runs, and the returned five pieces of course information will be displayed in five inputText fields in that page. The selected course_id, which is stored in the selectedItem property in our JSF managed bean CourseBean and has been bound to the value attribute of the `<h:selectOneListbox>` tag in the CoursePage, will be checked first to make sure that a valid course_id has been selected by the user.

```
A     public String getSchedule() {
         return schedule;
      }
B     public void setSchedule(String Schedule) {
         this.schedule = Schedule;
      }
C     public String getCourseName() {
         return courseName;
      }
D     public void setCourseName(String CourseName) {
         this.courseName = CourseName;
      }
E     public String Select() {
         courseList = new ArrayList();
F        List cList = courseSessionBean.getCourseID(getFacultyName());
G        for (int i=0; i < cList.size(); i++) {
            SelectItem courseid = new SelectItem(cList.get(i).toString());
            courseList.add(courseid);
         }
H        return null;
      }
I     public Boolean Details() {
         if (selectedItem != null) {
J           List<Object[]> courseDetail = courseSessionBean.getCourseDetail(selectedItem);
K           for (Object[] result:courseDetail){
            courseName = (String)result[0];
            schedule = (String)result[1];
            classroom = (String)result[2];
            credit = result[3].toString();
            enrollment = result[4].toString();
            }
         }
L        else {
            msgDlg.setMessage("the selected courseID is invalid!");
             msgDlg.setVisible(true);
         }
M        return null;
      }
N     public Boolean Update() {
         return null;
      }
O     public Boolean Delete() {
         return null;
      }
P     public String Back() {
      }
   }
```

Figure 8.158. The second part codes of the CourseBean class.

J. If the selectedItem property is non-null, which means that a valid course_id has been selected, the getCourseDetail() method defined in our session bean class CourseSessionBean that will be built in the next section, will be called to retrieve five pieces of detailed information for the selected course_id, and assign them to a List object courseDetail.

K. An enhanced for loop is used to retrieve the detailed course information from the query result list and assign them one by one to the associated properties defined in our JSF managed bean class CourseBean.

L. If the selectedItem property contains a null value, which means that no valid course_id has been selected. A warning message is displayed for this situation using the msgDlg.

M. Since the returned value of this method is not important to us, a null is used.

N. Three other methods, Update(), Delete(), and Back(), which are bound to the action attributes of the associated buttons in the CoursePage file, are defined in steps **N**, **O**, and **P** in this Java bean class. We will develop the codes to execute the data updating and deleting actions against our sample database later using these methods. The Back() method is used to return to the Selection.jsp page.

After finishing the code development for this bean, you may encounter some real-time compiling errors indicated with either red or blue underscored lines. One reason for this is that some packages are missed when you try to use some classes or interfaces in this code development process. To fix that, right click on this coding window and select the Fix Imports item from the pop-up menu to add required packages. An example is the List class that is located at the java.util package, and an import java.util.List statement should have been added into this bean after you had performed the Fix Imports operation. Since we need to use the ArrayList class that is also located at the java.util package, so we need to modify this import statement to import java.util.*.

Another package you may need to use for this bean is the javax.faces.model, since we need to use the SelectItem component as an element in the <h:selectOneListbox> tag. Therefore, add another import statement to this bean, import javax.faces.model.SelectItem. Your finished import package block should match one that is shown in step A in Figure 8.157. The modified import statements have been highlighted in bold.

Next, let's develop and build our session bean class CourseSessionBean.java to handle database-related operations using the Hibernate APIs.

8.6.11.2 Build the Java Session Bean CourseSessionBean

The purpose of this session bean is to directly access our sample Oracle database and perform all course data queries and manipulations against our database via the Hibernate API.

Perform the following operations to create a new session bean class CourseSessionBean.java:

1. Right click on our project JavaWebDBJSPOracle from the Projects window, and select the New > Other item to open the `New File` wizard.
2. Select Java EE from the `Categories` list and Session Bean from the `File Types` list, and then click on the Next button.
3. Enter CourseSessionBean into the `Class Name` field. Select the JavaWebDBJSPOracle from the `Package` combo box, and check the Stateless radio button from the `Session Type` group. Your finished `Name and Location` wizard should match one that is shown in Figure 8.159. Click on the Finish button to complete this session bean creation process.

On the opened CourseSessionBean.java class file, perform the following operations to create the codes for this file, which is shown in Figure 8.160.

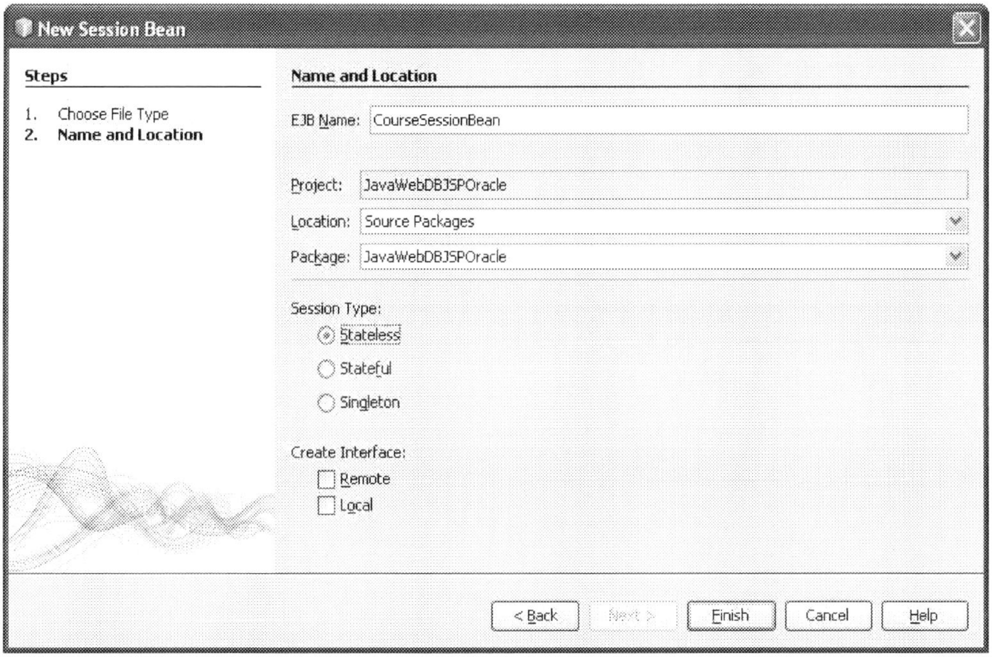

Figure 8.159. The finished Name and Location wizard.

Let's have a closer look at this piece of codes to see how it works.

A. Add a new Session object as a property to this class since we need to create a new session object to perform the course data query using the Hibernate API later.

B. Right click on any space inside this code window and select the Insert Code from the pop-up menu. Then select the Add Business Method item to open the Add Business Method wizard. Enter getCourseID into the Name field and click on the Browse button to find the returning data type for this method. On the opened wizard, type List into the top field and select List (java.util) from the bottom list. Then click on the OK button, and OK button again to create this new method. Add a String argument fname to this method.

C. Inside the getCourseID() method, the getCurrentSession() method is executed to obtain the current opened session object, and assign it to our session property session we created at step **A** above.

D. Two local variables for this method, courseList, which is a java.util.List object, and a msgDlg, which is a JDialog object, are created first. The courseList object is used to hold the returned queried result from the Course table, and the msgDlg is used to display the debug information as the project runs.

E. A combining HQL query that contains a subquery is created for this course_id query action. As you know, there is no faculty_name column available in the Course table, and the only relationship between each course (course_id) and the related faculty member is the faculty_id column in the Course table. Since the user's input is the selected faculty name, therefore, we need to perform two queries to get all course_id taught by the selected faculty member, (1) perform a query to the Faculty table to get the related faculty_id based on the input faculty name selected by the user, and (2) perform another query to

```
  package JavaWebDBJSPOracle;

  import cse.entity.Faculty;
  import cse.util.HibernateUtil;
  import java.util.List;
  import javax.ejb.Stateless;
  import org.hibernate.Query;
  import org.hibernate.Session;

  @Stateless
  public class CourseSessionBean {
A     public Session session = null;

B     public List getCourseID(String  fname) {

C       this.session = HibernateUtil.getSessionFactory().getCurrentSession();

D       List<Course> courseList = null;
        MsgDialog msgDlg = new MsgDialog(new javax.swing.JFrame(), true);

E       String query = "select c.courseId from Course c where c.facultyId like " +
                    "(select  f.facultyId  from Faculty as f  where f.facultyName  like '"+fname+"')";
        try {
F           org.hibernate.Transaction tx = session.beginTransaction();
            Query  c = session.createQuery (query);
G           courseList = (List<Course>) c.list();
H         } catch (Exception e) {
            msgDlg.setMessage("Query is failed and no matched course_id found!");
            msgDlg.setVisible(true);
            e.printStackTrace();
            return null;
          }
I       return courseList;
      }

J     public List<Object[]> getCourseDetail(String  cid) {

K       this.session = HibernateUtil.getSessionFactory().getCurrentSession();
        List<Object[]> courselist = null;

L       String strQuery = "select c.course, c.schedule, c.classroom, c.credit, c.enrollment " +
                        "from Course c WHERE c.courseId = :courseid";

M       org.hibernate.Transaction tx = session.beginTransaction();
N       Query cQuery = session.createQuery(strQuery);
O       cQuery.setParameter("courseid", cid);
P       courselist = (List<Object[]>)cQuery.list();

Q       return courselist;
      }
  }
```

Figure 8.160. The codes for the session bean class CourseSessionBean.java.

the Course table to get all course_id based on the faculty_id obtained from the first query. In order to simplify these two queries into one query, we need to use this combining query that contains a subquery that is used to perform the first query to the Faculty table to obtain the desired faculty_id based on the input faculty_name. The only point to be noted for this HQL subquery is that this subquery must be surrounded by parentheses.

F. A try...catch block is used to perform the course information query from our Course table. First, the beginTransaction() method is executed to create a new transaction object. Then the createQuery() method is called to perform this data query. The combining HQL query statement works as an argument of this method and provides the query details.

G. The list() method is executed to perform this actual query operation. The queried result is returned and assigned to the local variable courseList.

H. The catch block is used to track and detect any possible exception during this query operation, and display any error if any exception occurred. A `null` will be returned to the calling method if any exception occurred.

I. Finally, the queried result is returned to the calling method defined in our Java managed bean for further processing.

J. The getCourseDetail() method is defined here with the course_id as the argument. The purpose of this method is to query five pieces of detailed information from the Course entity based on the selected course_id and return the result to the JSF managed bean.

K. Inside the getCourseDetail () method, the getCurrentSession() method is executed to obtain the current opened session object and assign it to our session property session. Also, a new List instance courselist is created.

L. A HQL query is created with the courseid as a named dynamic parameter.

M. The beginTransaction() method is executed to create a new transaction object to help this course information query.

N. The query object cQuery is created by calling the createQuery() method.

O. The setParameter() method is executed to set up the named dynamic parameter :courseid.

P. The list() method is executed to run this query to get five pieces of detailed course information for the selected course_id, and the query result is assigned to the local List instance courselist.

Q. The query result is returned to the JSF managed bean CourseBean for future process.

During the coding process, you may encounter some real-time compiling errors, which are indicated with some red underscores for the error sources. Most of these errors are related to the missed packages. To fix these errors, just right click on any space in this code window, and select the Fix Imports item to open the `Fix All Imports` wizard. The point to be noted is that you must select the correct packages for those real-time compiling error sources. For example, in this application, you need to select the following packages or classes for this file:

- org.hibernate.Query for the Query class
- org.hibernate.Session for the Session class
- java.util.List for the List collection class

Now we have completed the coding process for the course query operation with the Hibernate API. This piece of codes is only used for the course data query process, and the getCourseID() and getCourseDetail() methods will be called by our Java managed bean class CourseBean to execute these data query operations. We will add more methods and codes to perform other course data actions, such as data updating and deleting against our sample database later in the following sections.

8.6.11.3 Set Up Calling Relationship between the Managed Bean and the Session Bean

Next, let's add this session bean object into our Java managed bean class CourseBean.java to enable the managed bean to recognize this session bean and call some methods defined in the session bean to perform the actual course data query and actions against our database.

Right click on any place inside the code window of the managed bean class CourseBean.java and select the Insert Code item and select the Call Enterprise Bean item from the pop-up menu to open the `Call Enterprise Bean` wizard. Expand our project JavaWebDBJSPOracle from the opened wizard and select our session bean CourseSessionBean class, and click on the OK button to complete this session bean addition process. Immediately, you can find that our session bean class has been injected into this managed bean with the following two objects:

```
@EJB
private CourseSessionBean courseSessionBean;
```

The @EJB is an injected source and added by the Java Enterprise Bean engine, and the new instance CourseSessionBean is created as a new property in our JSF managed bean class CourseBean.

At this point, we have finished all coding jobs related to course information query for our project. Now, let's build and run our project to test the codes we built in the previous sections for our project.

There are two ways to run our project. One way is to run and test the partial project starting from the CoursePage and only test this page. Another way is to run the whole project in a sequence: starting from the LogInPage, SelectionPage, and the CoursePage. Let's run and test the project in the first way.

8.6.11.4 Run and Test the Single Page—CoursePage.jsp

Now click on the Clean and Build Main Project button to build our project. If everything is fine, right click on our CoursePage.jsp from the Projects window and select the Run File item from the pop-up menu to run this page.

Enter a faculty name, such as Jenney King, into the `Faculty Name` field, and click on the Select button to retrieve all courses, exactly all course_id, taught by the selected faculty member. All four courses taught by the faculty member Jenney King are retrieved and displayed in the course listbox, as shown in Figure 8.161.

Click on one course_id, such as CSE-432, from the course listbox, and click on the Details button to query the details for that course. All five pieces of detailed course information related to the selected course_id are displayed in five fields, as shown in Figure 8.161.

Our course information query using JSF pages and Java bean is successful.

Click on the Close button that is located at the upper-right corner of this page to close this page and project.

Next, we will discuss how to run and test the project in the second way.

To run the project in the second way, we need to first set up the navigation rules between the CoursePage and the SelectionPage using the Web configuration file faces-config.xml as we did in Section 8.6.7.

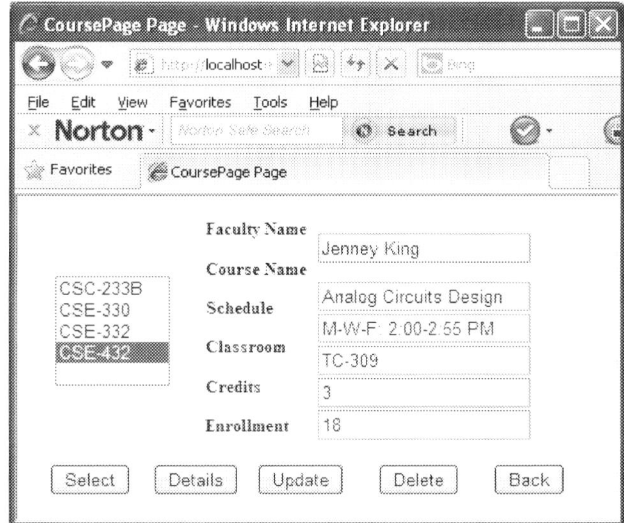

Figure 8.161. The queried results of the CoursePage.

8.6.11.5 Set Up the Navigation Rules for the CoursePage and the SelectionPage

As we did in Section 8.6.7, in this part, we will set up navigation relationships between the SelectionPage and the CoursePage to enable us to run and test the project in a sequential way.

To set up the correct navigation rules for these two web pages, we need to use the JSF configuration file faces-config.xml. The function of the faces-config.xml file is to allow the JSF to configure the application, managed beans, convertors, validators, and navigation rules. In Section 5.3.5.12 in Chapter 5, we have provided a detailed discussion about this configuration file. Refer to that section to get more details for this file.

The operational navigation rule is: if the login process is successful, the next page, SelectionPage.jsp, should be displayed to allow users to select different item from that page to perform related data query operations. If the user selected the Course Information item from the listbox, the CoursePage.jsp should be displayed to enable users to perform course related information queries. When the user clicks on the Back button on the CoursePage.jsp page, the SelectionPage should be displayed to enable users to perform other data actions.

Now, let's use this configuration file to set up the navigation rules for our SelectionPage and CoursePage pages. Perform the following operations to set up the navigation rules for these two pages:

1. Expand the Configuration Files node that is under our project node JavaWebDBJSPOracle from the Projects window and double click on the file faces-config.xml to open it.
2. Click on the PageFlow button on the top of this opened file to display the flow of the web pages built in this project, as shown in Figure 8.162.
3. Move your cursor to the starting arrow location as shown in Figure 8.162 until a square appears in the SelectionPage.jsp page object. Then click on this square and drag this

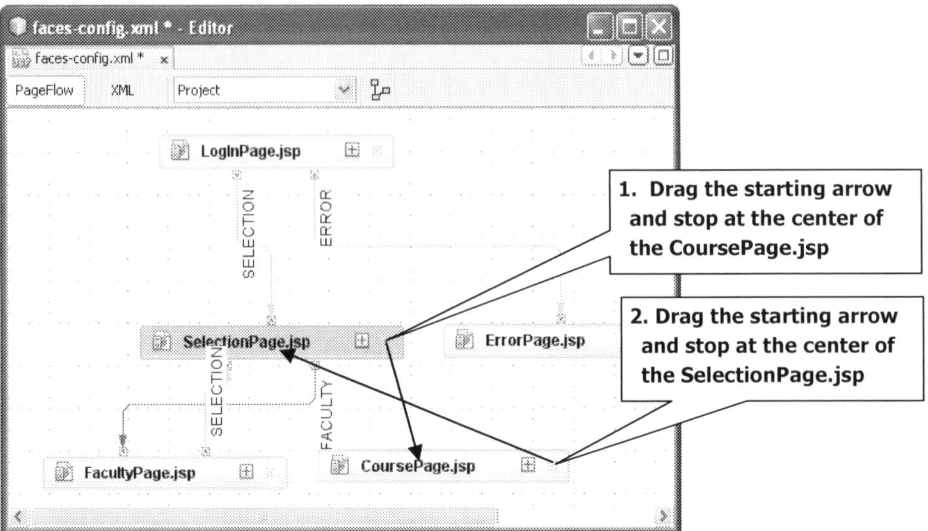

Figure 8.162. The opened PageFlow view of the faces-config.xml file.

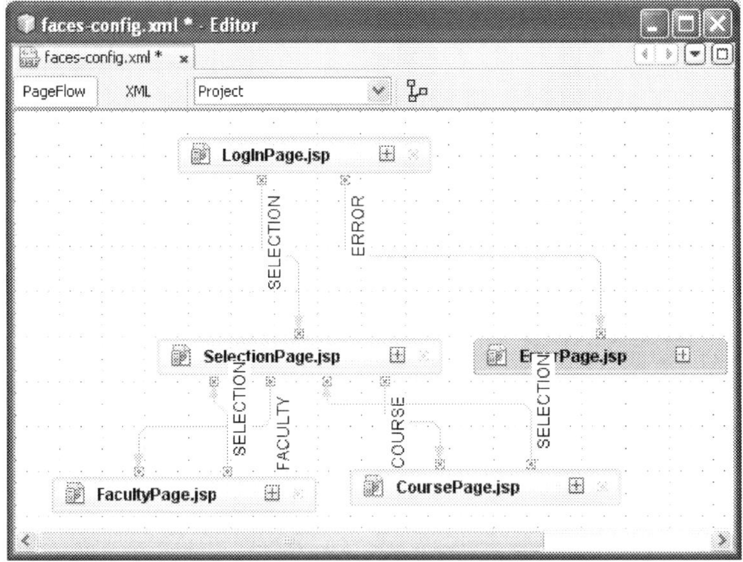

Figure 8.163. The finished PageFlow view of the JSF page objects.

stating arrow and point to and stop at the center of the CoursePage.jsp, as shown in Figure 8.162-1. A navigation link is established with the name case1, as shown in Figure 8.162.

4. Double click on the default navigation link case1 and change its name to COURSE.
5. Perform a similar operation to create another navigation link from the CoursePage.jsp to the SelectionPage.jsp, as shown in Figure 8.162-2.
6. Double click on the new established link and change its name to SELECTION. Your finished PageFlow view of two JSF page objects should match one that is shown in Figure 8.163.

```
  <?xml version='1.0' encoding='UTF-8'?>
  .........
   <navigation-rule>
A     <from-view-id>/SelectionPage.jsp</from-view-id>
      <navigation-case>
B        <from-outcome>FACULTY</from-outcome>
         <to-view-id>/FacultyPage.jsp</to-view-id>
      </navigation-case>
      <navigation-case>
C        <from-outcome>COURSE</from-outcome>
         <to-view-id>/CoursePage.jsp</to-view-id>
      </navigation-case>
   </navigation-rule>
   <navigation-rule>
D     <from-view-id>/CoursePage.jsp</from-view-id>
      <navigation-case>
E        <from-outcome>SELECTION</from-outcome>
         <to-view-id>/SelectionPage.jsp</to-view-id>
      </navigation-case>
   </navigation-rule>
  </faces-config>
```

Figure 8.164. The XML view of the faces-config.xml file.

Now if you click on the XML button to open the XML view of this faces-config.xml file, you can find that the navigation rules shown in Figure 8.163 have been added into this file. The new added codes have been shown in steps **A**, **C**, **D**, and **E** in Figure 8.164.

Let's have a closer look at this piece of newly created codes to see how it works.

A. Our source page, SelectionPage.jsp, is added into the <from-view-id> tag that is located under the <navigation-rule> tag to indicate that this is the starting page.

B. If the user selected the Faculty Information item from the listbox in the SelectionPage, our next page FacultyPage.jsp, which is indicated by the <to-view-id> tag and is represented by a case String FACULTY, is added into the <from-outcome> tag.

C. If the user selected the Course Information item from the listbox in the SelectionPage, our next page CoursePage.jsp, which is indicated by the <to-view-id> tag and is represented by a case String COURSE, is added into the <from-outcome> tag to indicate that this is our destination page.

D. Similarly, if the CoursePage.jsp has been opened, it then will work as a source page. Therefore, the CoursePage.jsp has been added to the <from-view-id> tag.

E. If the user clicked on the Back button on the CoursePage.jsp, our next page should be the SelectionPage. Therefore, the SelectionPage.jsp has been added to the <to-view-id> tag, and it is represented by a case String SELECTION, which is added into the <from-outcome> tag.

Now that we have set up the navigation rules for our pages, now we can run and test the project in a sequential way, which means starting from the LogInPasge, SelectionPage, and then either the FacultyPage or CoursePage.

8.6.11.6 Run and Test the Project in a Sequence Way

Now let's run the project in a sequence way starting from the LogInPage.

Right click on the LogInPage.jsp from the Projects window and click on the Run File item to start our project from the LogInPage.

Enter the appropriate username and password, such as admin and reback, to our Web server, and click on the OK button to continue. The point to be noted is that the username and password must be identical with those you created when downloading and installing the GlassFish v3 server in your machine.

As the LogIn page opened, enter the desired username and password, such as jhenry and test, and click on the LogIn button. On the opened Selection page, select the `Course Information` item and click on the OK button to open the Course page.

On the opened CoursePage.jsp, you can test the course information query function as we did in Section 8.6.11.4. Click on the Close button that is located at the upper-right corner of this page to close this page when the test is done.

Our course information query using the JSF pages and Java beans are successful. Next, let's handle the course information updating and deleting actions using the JSF pages and Java beans.

8.6.12 Update and Delete Records for the Course Table Using JSF Pages and Java Beans

First, let's handle the course record updating action.

Because of the complexity in updating a course record with the primary key course_id, in this section, we still want to update a course record with an existing course_id. In other words, we will update a course record by changing all columns without touching the course_id column, since one needs to update this course_id first in the child table (StudentCourse table) before he can update it in the parent table (Course) if one wants to update this course_id column.

As we did for the course information query in the last section, we can divide this course record updating action into two Java beans: the Java managed bean CourseBean.java that is used to manage and control the data updating, and the session bean CourseSessionBean.java that is used to perform the actual data updating actions.

First, let's build the codes for the managed bean to manage this data updating action.

8.6.12.1 Add the Codes to the Java Managed Bean to Manage Data Updating

Recall that in Section 8.6.11.1, when we built our managed bean CourseBean.java; in total, we created five user-defined methods, Select(), Details(), Update(), Delete(), and Back() in that bean class. All of these five methods have been bound to the action attributes of the associated <h:commandButton> tags in our JSF page CoursePage.jsp. We have developed and built the codes for the first two methods Select() and Details() in the previous sections to perform the course information queries. Now let's build the codes for the Update() method to perform the course information updating actions.

Open the code window of our managed bean CourseBean.java and add the codes that are shown in Figure 8.165 into this method.

```
    public Boolean Update() {
A       boolean update = false;
        String[] cUpdate = {courseName, schedule, classroom, credit, enrollment, selectedItem};
B       update = courseSessionBean.UpdateCourse(cUpdate);
C       if (!update) {
          msgDlg.setMessage("The course updating is failed!");
          msgDlg.setVisible(true);
        }
D       return null;
    }
```

Figure 8.165. The codes for the method Update().

Let's have a closer look at this piece of newly added codes to see how it works.

A. Some local variables are created first for this method. The update is a boolean variable used to hold the running status of the UpdateCourse() method defined in the session bean class, and we will build this method in the next section. The cUpdate[] is a string array used to hold five pieces of updating course information for an existing record in the Course table in our sample database. The point to be noted is that we used five properties defined in this managed bean as five pieces of updating course information since those properties have been bound to the associated value attributes of the <h:inputText> tags in our JSF page CoursePage.jsp. Furthermore, those properties can be automatically updated as the users enter five pieces of updating course information into five text fields related to those tags in our JSF page CoursePage.jsp. The sixth parameter in the cUpdate[] array is the property courseID selected by the user from the course listbox, and it is used to work as a query criterion.

B. The UpdateCourse() method defined in our session bean, which will be developed in the next section, is called to perform this course record updating. The argument passed into that method is the string array cUpdate[], which contains five pieces of updated course information, and the query criterion courseID. The running result of that method is returned and assigned to the local variable update.

C. If the running result of the method UpdateCourse() is false, which means that the data updating has failed, this situation is displayed by executing the setMessage() method in the msgDlg instance.

D. A null is returned since this returning value is not important to this application.

Next, let's develop the UpdateCourse() method in our session bean class to perform the course data updating using the Hibernate API.

8.6.12.2 Build the UpdateCourse() Method in the Session Bean to Perform Data Updating

Open the code window for our session bean class CourseSessionBean.java and enter the codes shown in Figure 8.166 into this file to create a new method UpdateCourse() and its codes.

Let's have a closer look at this piece of new codes to see how it works.

A. Two packages are added into this session bean class. The first is used for components to configure the session factory, and the second is used for the data conversion.

```
A  import org.hibernate.cfg.Configuration;
   import java.math.BigDecimal;
   .........
   public boolean UpdateCourse(String[] nCourse) {
B      MsgDialog msgDlg = new MsgDialog(new javax.swing.JFrame(), true);
       try {
C          SessionFactory fact = new Configuration().configure().buildSessionFactory();
           session = fact.openSession();

D          org.hibernate.Transaction tx = session.beginTransaction();
E          if (!tx.isActive())
              tx.begin();
F          Course cs = (Course)session.get(Course.class, nCourse[5]);
G          cs.setCourse(nCourse[0]);
           cs.setSchedule(nCourse[1]);
           cs.setClassroom(nCourse[2]);
H          BigDecimal decCredit = new BigDecimal(nCourse[3]);
           cs.setCredit(decCredit);
I          BigDecimal decEnroll = new BigDecimal(nCourse[4]);
           cs.setEnrollment(decEnroll);
J          session.update(cs);
K          tx.commit();
L          session.close();
M          return true;
       }
N      catch(Exception e) {
           msgDlg.setMessage(e.getMessage());
           msgDlg.setVisible(true);
           return false;
       }
   }
```

Figure 8.166. The codes for the UpdateFaculty() method in the session bean.

B. A new instance of the JDialog class msgDlg is created since we need to use it to display some debug information during the project running.

C. A try catch block is used to perform this data updating action. First, a new SessionFactory object fact is created by executing the buildSessionFactory() method. Then the session object is opened by executing the openSession() method.

D. A new Transaction object tx is created to help to perform this data updating action.

E. If this new Transaction instance has not been active, the begin() method is executed to begin this transaction instance.

F. The get() method in the session class is first executed to perform a query to retrieve an existing course record from the Course table based on the course_id that is stored in the string array nCourse[5]. The first argument of this get() method is the class type Course, and the second argument is the course_id. The returned query result is assigned to a new Course instance cs. A point to be noted is that the Course class must be casted before this method to make sure that the session object returns an appropriate object.

G. Five setter methods are executed to set up five pieces of updated course information to the new created Course entity object cs.

H. Two points to be noted for this step is the data type conversions between the Java.lang. String and the java.meth.BigDecimal. The required data type of the arguments for the setCredit() and setEnrollment() methods are java.meth.BigDecimal. However, the updating parameters stored in the nCourse[] array are java.lang.String. Therefore, it is necessary to perform a conversion between these two different data types. In steps **H** and **I**, we created two new instances of the BigDecimal class and used the constructor of this class to complete this conversion. This is an easy and convenient way to do this conversion.

J. The updating action is performed by executing the update() method for the session object with the Course entity object cs as the argument of this method.

K. The commit() method is executed to actually trigger and perform this data updating action.

L. The close() method is executed to close this opened session object when this data updating is complete.

M. Finally, a true is returned to the calling method to indicate the success of this data updating action.

N. The catch block is used to track and detect any exception during this data updating action. The exception information will be displayed using the JDialog instance msgDlg, and a false is returned if any exception occurred during this data updating process.

Now let's build and run the project to test this course data updating function.

8.6.12.3 Run the Project to Test the Course Record Updating Action

Click on the Clean and Build Main Project button to build our project. If everything is fine, right click on our JSF page CoursePage.jsp from the Projects window and select the Run File item to run the project. Of course, you can run the project by starting from the LogIn page.

On the opened Course Page, type a desired faculty name, such as Ying Bai, into the `Faculty Name` field to perform a course information query for that faculty member. Then select the first course_id from the course listbox, which is CSC-132B, and click on the Details button to pick up the detailed information for this course. To update this course, just enter five pieces of updated course information shown in Figure 8.167 into

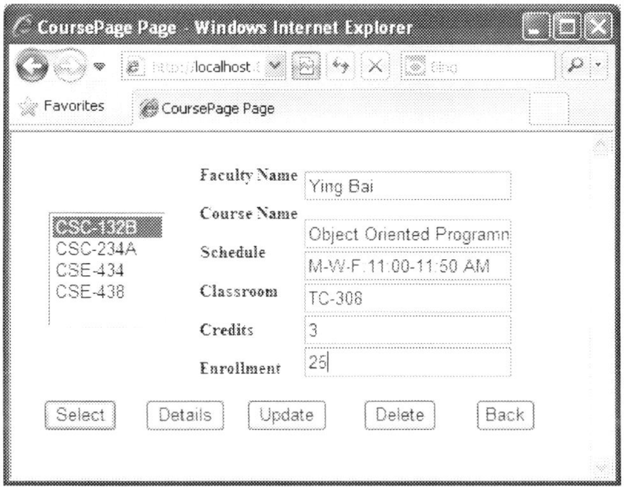

Figure 8.167. The updated course information.

the associated five fields as an updated course record. Then click on the Update button to try to update this course record against the Course table in our sample database.

To check and confirm this data updating action, you have two ways to go. The first and easiest way is to try to retrieve this updated course record. To do that, select another course_id, such as CSE-438, from the course listbox, and click on the Details button to query and display detailed information for that course. Then select the course CSC-132B from the course listbox and click on the Details button again to try to retrieve this updated course. You can find that this course has been successfully updated.

Another way to do this confirmation is to open the Course table from our sample Oracle database by performing the following operations:

A. Open the Services window and expand the Databases node.

B. Right click on our Oracle database URL: jdbc:oracle:thin:@localhost:1521:XE [CSE_DEPT on CSE_DEPT], and select the Connect item to connect to our database.

C. Expand our sample database CSE_DEPT and Tables.

D. Right click on the Course table and select the View Data item.

Your opened Course table is shown in Figure 8.168.

It is found that the course record with the course_id of CSC-132B, which is located at the sixth row on this table and has been highlighted in dark color, has been successfully updated with five pieces of updated course information. Our course data updating action is successful!

It is highly recommended to recover this updated course record in our database since we want to keep our database clean. To do this recovery, there are two ways to go.

The first and the easiest way is to use this JSF page CoursePage.jsp to perform another course updating action by entering the original course information that is shown below for the course_id CSC-132B and clicking on the Update button.

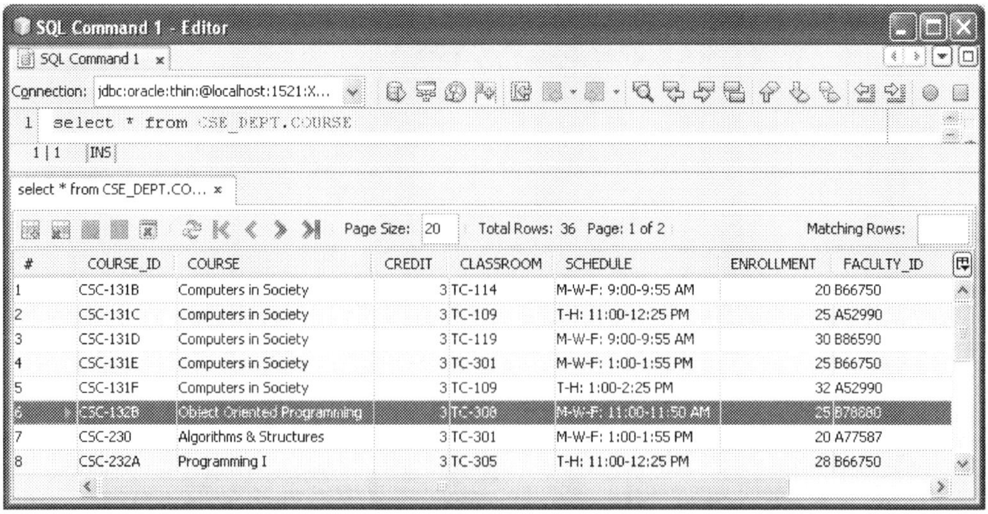

#	COURSE_ID	COURSE	CREDIT	CLASSROOM	SCHEDULE	ENROLLMENT	FACULTY_ID
1	CSC-131B	Computers in Society	3	TC-114	M-W-F: 9:00-9:55 AM	20	B66750
2	CSC-131C	Computers in Society	3	TC-109	T-H: 11:00-12:25 PM	25	A52990
3	CSC-131D	Computers in Society	3	TC-119	M-W-F: 9:00-9:55 AM	30	B86590
4	CSC-131E	Computers in Society	3	TC-301	M-W-F: 1:00-1:55 PM	25	B66750
5	CSC-131F	Computers in Society	3	TC-109	T-H: 1:00-2:25 PM	32	A52990
6	CSC-132B	Object Oriented Programming	3	TC-308	M-W-F: 11:00-11:50 AM	25	B78880
7	CSC-230	Algorithms & Structures	3	TC-301	M-W-F: 1:00-1:55 PM	20	A77587
8	CSC-232A	Programming I	3	TC-305	T-H: 11:00-12:25 PM	28	B66750

Figure 8.168. The updated course record.

The second way is that you can directly do this recovery by opening the Course table in the Services window and modifying the updated row with the original course information for the course_id CSC-132B, which is listed below:

- Course: Introduction to Programming
- Credit: 3
- Classroom: MTC-302
- Schedule: T-H: 1:00–2:25 p.m.
- Enrollment: 21
- faculty_id: B78880

One point to be noted is that when you modify each column for the updated record, you must

1. Press the Enter key for each modified column to make it active.
2. Click on the Commit Record button on the top of this table to make the modification of the row effective after the entire row has been modified.

Next, let's discuss how to delete an existing course record from our database using the JSF faces and Java beans with the help of the Hibernate APIs.

8.6.12.4 Add the Codes to the Java Managed Bean to Manage Data Deleting

Recall that in Section 8.5.6.1, we have bound this method to the action attribute of the <h:commandButton id="Delete"> tag in our JSF page CoursePage.jsp. With this tag, the Delete() method in our managed bean has been bound to the action attribute of that tag, and it will be called and executed as soon as the user clicks the Delete button on our JSF page CoursePage.jsp as the project runs.

Open the code window of our managed bean CourseBean.java and add the codes that are shown in Figure 8.169 into this method.

Let's have a closer look at this piece of newly added codes to see how it works.

A. A local variable delete is created and initialized first for this method. This is a boolean variable used to hold the running status of the DeleteCourse() method defined in the session bean class, and we will build this method in the next section.

B. The DeleteCourse() method defined in our session bean, which will be developed in the next section, is called to perform this course record deleting action. The argument passed

```
  public Boolean Delete() {
A     boolean delete = false;
B     delete = courseSessionBean.DeleteCourse(selectedItem);
C     if (!delete) {
         msgDlg.setMessage("The course deleting is failed!");
         msgDlg.setVisible(true);
      }
D     return null;
  }
```

Figure 8.169. The codes for the method Delete().

into that method is a course_id that is stored in the selectedItem property, and will be deleted from our Course table. The running result of that method is returned and assigned to the local variable delete.

C. If the running result of the method DeleteCourse() is false, which means that the data deleting has failed, this situation is displayed by executing the setMessage() method in the msgDlg instance.

D. Otherwise, if a true returned, which means that this course data deleting is successful, a null is returned since this returning value is not important to this application.

Next, let's develop the DeleteCourse() method in our session bean class to perform the course data deleting action using the Hibernate API.

8.6.12.5 Build the DeleteCourse() Method in the Session Bean to Perform Data Deleting

Open the code window for our session bean class CourseSessionBean.java and enter the codes shown in Figure 8.170 into this file to create a new method DeleteCourse() and its codes.

Let's have a closer look at this piece of new codes to see how it works.

A. A new instance of the JDialog class msgDlg is created since we need to use it to display some debug information during the project running.

B. A try . . . catch block is used to perform this data deleting action. First, a new SessionFactory object fact is created by executing the buildSessionFactory() method. Then, the session object is opened by executing the openSession() method.

C. A new Transaction object tx is created to help to perform this data deleting action.

```
    public boolean DeleteCourse(String cid) {
A       MsgDialog msgDlg = new MsgDialog(new javax.swing.JFrame(), true);
B       try {
           SessionFactory fact = new Configuration().configure().buildSessionFactory();
           session = fact.openSession();
C          org.hibernate.Transaction tx = session.beginTransaction();
D          if (!tx.isActive())
              tx.begin();
E          Course cs = (Course)session.get(Course.class, cid);
F          session.delete(cs);
G          tx.commit();
H          session.close();
I          return true;
        }
J       catch(Exception e) {
           msgDlg.setMessage(e.getMessage());
           msgDlg.setVisible(true);
K          return false;
        }
    }
```

Figure 8.170. The codes for the DeleteCourse() method in the session bean.

D. If this new Transaction instance has not been active, the begin() method is executed to begin this transaction instance.

E. The get() method in the session class is first executed to perform a query to retrieve an existing course record from the Course table based on the courseID that is stored in the input argument cid. The first argument of this get() method is the class type Course, and the second argument is the courseID property. The returned query result is assigned to a new Course instance cs. A point to be noted is that the Course class must be casted before this method to make sure that the session object returns an appropriate object.

F. The deleting action is performed by executing the delete() method for the session object with the Course entity object cs as the argument of this method.

G. The commit() method is executed to actually trigger and perform this data deleting action.

H. The close() method is executed to close this opened session object when this data deleting is complete.

I. Finally, a true is returned to the calling method to indicate the success of this data deleting action.

J. The catch block is used to track and detect any exception during this data deleting action. The exception information will be displayed using the JDialog instance msgDlg.

K. A false is returned if any exception occurred during this data deleting process.

Now let's build and run the project to test this course data deleting function. You can run the project in two ways: either run the single page CoursePage.jsp, or run the entire project starting from the LogInPage.jsp. Let's first run the project in the first way.

8.6.12.6 Run the Project to Test the Course Record Deleting Action

Click on the Clean and Build Main Project button to build our project. If everything is fine, right click on our JSF page CoursePage.jsp from the Projects window and select the Run File item to run the project.

On the opened Course Page, first, we need to perform a course information query based on a desired faculty. Type a faculty name, such as Jenney King, into the `Faculty Name` field and click on the Select button to retrieve all courses (course_id) taught by that selected faculty.

To delete a course, select a course_id from the course listbox, such as CSC-233B, and click on the Delete button to try to delete it from the Course table in our sample database.

To check and confirm this data deleting action, open the Course table from our sample Oracle database in the NetBeans IDE by performing the following operations:

a. Open the Services window and expand the Databases node.

b. Right click on our Oracle database URL: jdbc:oracle:thin:@localhost:1521:XE [CSE_DEPT on CSE_DEPT], and select the Connect item to connect to our database.

c. Expand our sample database CSE_DEPT and Tables.

d. Right click on the Course table and select the View Data item.

It can be found from the opened Course table that the course record with the course_id of CSC-233B has been successfully deleted from the Course table. Our data deleting action is successful!

It is highly recommended to recover this deleted course record in our database since we want to keep our database clean. You can directly do this recovery in the NetBeans IDE environment by opening the Course table in the Services window and insert a new row with the original course information for the faculty member Jenney King, which is listed below:

- course_id: CSC-233B
- course: Introduction to Algorithms
- credit: 3
- classroom: MTC-302
- schedule: M-W-F: 11:00-11:55 AM
- enrollment: 19
- faculty_id: K69880

The reason we selected the course CSC-233B as a deleting example is to make the data recovery process simpler. As you know, we have set up a cascaded deleting relationship between the parent table, Course table, and the child table, StudentCourse table, in our sample database in Chapter 2. If you want to delete any other course from the parent table Course, the same course with the identical course_id in the child table, StudentCourse, will also be deleted because of this cascaded deleting relationship. Since the course CSC-233B is the only course that has not been selected by any student in the StudentCourse table, therefore, we only need to recover this course in the Course table when a recovery job is needed after this course has been deleted.

One point to be noted is that when you insert each column for a new record, you must

1. First click on the Insert Record button on the top of this table to open a new `Insert Record` wizard.
2. Enter the original course information shown above piece by piece to each column.
3. Press the Enter key at the end of each inserted column to make it active.
4. Click on the Commit Record button on the top of this table to make the insertion effective after the entire row has been inserted.

Your finished Insert Record wizard should match one that is shown in Figure 8.171. Click on the Add Row button to insert this row into the Course table to complete this data recovery.

The final coding job is for the Back button. The function of this coding is that the program should be directed to the SelectionPage.jsp page to enable users to make other actions when this button is clicked by the user.

8.6.12.7 Build the Codes for the Back Button Action Attribute in JSF Page

Recall that in Section 8.5.6.1, when we modify our JSF page CoursePage.jsp., we added one command tag shown below to that page:

```
<h:commandButton id="Back" action="#{CourseBean.Back}"
value="Back" />
```

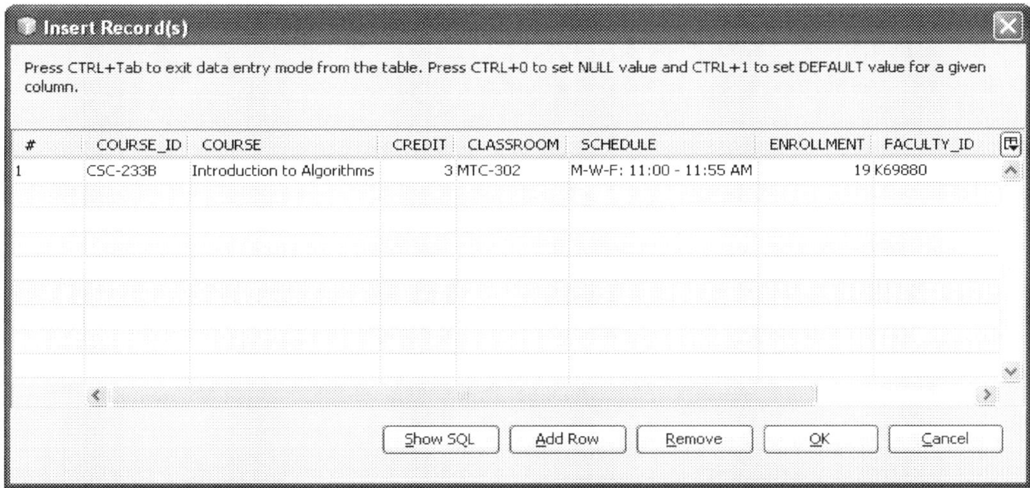

Figure 8.171. The finished Insert Record wizard.

```
    public String Back() {
A       return "SELECTION";
    }
```

Figure 8.172. The codes for the Back() method.

With this tag, the Back() method in our managed bean has been bound to the action attribute of that tag, and this method will be called and executed as soon as the user clicks the Back button on our JSF page CoursePage.jsp as the project runs.

Recall that when we built the navigation relationship between the Selection and Course pages in Section 8.6.11.5, we have set up these navigation rules using the configuration file faces-config.xml. The relationship between the Course and the Selection pages has been determined by two rules, which is a round trip between these two pages. Refer to that section to get a detailed and clear picture for this relationship.

The coding job is very simple for this Back button. Open the code window of our managed bean CourseBean.java and enter the codes shown in Figure 8.172 into the Back() method in this class.

As shown in step **A** in Figure 8.172, this coding is very simple, and a return "SELECTION" is executed as this Back button is clicked by the user. Refer to our Web configure file faces-config.xml, and you can find that the navigation rule from the Course page to the Selection page has been defined by a string "SELECTION". The point to be noted is that the returned string in this Back() method must be exactly identical with that string defined in the configuration file to enable this navigation rule effective.

Now you can run the project to test the function of this Back button on the CoursePage.jsp page.

At this point, we have finished all coding developments for this project. A complete Java Web application project using the Oracle database, JavaWebDBJSPOracle, can be found from the folder DBProjects\Chapter 8 that is located at the Wiley ftp site (refer to Figure 1.2 in Chapter 1). You can download this project and test it in your computer if you like. Also, in order to make it easy and convenient to readers, we have collected all JSP and JSF pages, such as LogInPage.jsp, SelectionPage.jsp, FacultyPage.jsp and CoursePage.jsp, and save them in a folder JSP Files that is located at the same ftp site. You can directly copy and use those pages in your projects.

8.7 CHAPTER SUMMARY

Most key techniques and knowledge in Java Web database programming are fully discussed and analyzed in this chapter with real project examples. The most popular and important techniques in Java Web database programming, such as JSP, JSF, EJB, and Java Persistence API, including the persistence and Hibernate APIs, are introduced and discussed in details in different sections in this chapter.

Starting from an introduction to the fundamental Java Web server Servlets and HTML web pages, a comprehensive historical review about Java Web application development and implementations are provided with some example codes. Then an introduction about the development of JSP and Java help classes to improve the Java Web database applications are given with some pieces of coding examples. The use of Java Persistence APIs and JSP implicit object session for Java Web applications are discussed with a few examples.

To effectively improve and enhance the efficiency and quality of Java Web database applications, the Java core techniques, Java beans, and Java enterprise edition (Java EE 6), are discussed and analyzed in details with a few of coding examples.

Following a quick introduction to the Java EE Web application models, two actual Java Web database projects are introduced and discussed in detail. The first project JavaWebDBJSPSQL, which is built based on the different techniques listed above, is used to access and manipulate the SQL Server 2008 database with the help of runtime object method and Persistence APIs. Four popular web pages, LogInPage.jsp, SelectionPage.jsp, FacultyPage.jsp, and CoursePage.jsp, which work as Web views, are built and developed with JSP techniques. The Glassfish v3 that works as a Web server, and the Java help classes and Java beans that work as models, are developed and implemented to provide users a global and detailed picture in the process of Java Web database application building and development.

The second project JavaWebDBJSPOracle, which is built based on the JSF pages and Java EJB techniques, is used to access and manipulate the Oracle database with the help of Hibernate APIs techniques. The binding relationships between each attribute of tags in the JSF pages and the associated property in the Java bean class are built and illustrated in details with actual example codes and step-by-step explanations in the coding process.

Some important techniques and points in developing and building a successful Web database application are emphasized and highlighted as below:

- Different data actions are performed and illustrated by using the coding process and line-by-line explanations, which include the data query, data insertion, data updating, and deleting.
- The Web project structure and navigation process are developed with the help of the Web configuration file, faces-config.xml, with actual examples and step-by-step illustrations.

- The relationships between the Java managed beans and the Java session beans are fully discussed and analyzed using the actual example codes and line-by-line explanations.
- The mapping relationships between each attribute in the tags on our JSF pages and the associated property in the Java managed beans are explicitly illustrated with the real coding process.

After finishing this chapter, readers can have a solid understanding, a clear and a full picture about the Java Web database application, including the Web structures, components, navigation, and mapping relationships between different objects, as well as the connections among those components.

It hard to find a similar book that contains so much details and so clear illustrations on these topics about the Java Web applications in the current market.

HOMEWORK

I. True/False Selections

____**1.** When a Servlet is created, the init() method is called to do the initialization jobs for the Web server.

____**2.** When a request is received by the Servlet, it creates two objects: request and response. Then the Servlet sends these two objects to the service() method, in which these two objects are further to be processed.

____**3.** The conventional Web applications are built with a Servlet as a Web container and JSF pages as Web clients.

____**4.** Unlike a Common Gateway Interface (CGI), a Servlet can be used to create dynamic web pages during the server–client communication processes.

____**5.** To interface to the client to get user's data, most of the time, the Web server calls the getParameter() method that belongs to the request object to do this job.

____**6.** The so-called implicit objects in JSP are objects that are automatically available in JSP because they are automatically instantiated as the project runs.

____**7.** Among those implicit objects, the request, response, and session are the most popular objects, and are often used in the interfacing between clients and servers.

____**8.** To use a Java bean, the JSP provide three basic tags for working with beans,

```
<jsp:useBean id="bean name" class="bean class" scope = "page|request
|session|application"/>
```

____**9.** To embed any Java codes into a HTML page, the JSP directive <%@ page /> must be used.

____**10.** The navigation from one page to another can be done in two ways. One way is to directly use the codes by writing the JSP tag such as <jsp:forward /> or the HTML hyperlink in the JSF file. Another way that is provided by JSF is to use the application configuration resource file faces-config.xml to build these navigation rules.

II. Multiple Choices

1. The <from-view-id> tag is used to define a navigation ____________.

- **a.** Source
- **b.** Terminal

c. Destination
d. None of above

2. To bind a Java bean's property to an associated attribute of a tag in the JSF page, one needs to use the _______________.
   a. Expression language (EL) with the syntax #(managedbean.property)
   b. Expression language (EL) with the syntax #{managedbean.property}
   c. Expression language (EL) with the syntax #[managedbean.property]
   d. Expression language (EL) with the syntax ${managedbean.property}
3. A typical Java bean class should contain _________________.
   a. All properties
   b. All properties, setter methods
   c. All properties, setter and getter methods
   d. All properties, setter and getter methods, as well as user-defined methods
4. Java beans need to be configured in the Web configuration file faces-config.xml so that the implementation can automatically create a new ________ of the beans as needed.
   a. Statement
   b. Method
   c. Instance
   d. Project
5. Before you can use a Servlet such as FacesServlet in the server side from a Web browser, you need to map the FacesServlet to a path in your deployment descriptor file _______.
   a. Web pages
   b. WEB INF file
   c. Web configuration file
   d. web.xml
6. To separate the presentations and business logics, we can use _______ pages to present our GUI and the __________ to store our data to perform business-related logics.
   a. HTML, Java help class
   b. XML, JSF pages
   c. JSP, Java beans
   d. JSF, JSP pages
7. All JSF tag components are represented by a tree of components whose root is the UIViewRoot, which is represented by the ________ tag. All JSF component tags must be enclosed in this ________ tag.
   a. UIComponent
   b. UITree
   c. <h:form>
   d. <f:view>
8. A JSP form, which is submitted to the Web server when a button is clicked, is represented by the ________ tag. The tags representing the form components, such as textfields and buttons, must be nested inside this tag.
   a. <f:form>
   b. <h:form>
   c. <h:view>
   d. <f:view>

9. If the required attribute is set to true, this means that the inputText ______________.

a. Cannot be empty

b. Must be filled something by the user

c. Both of above

d. Neither of above

10. A Web application is a dynamic extension of a web or application server. There are two types of Web applications: _____________ and _____________.

a. Dynamic, static

b. Single-tier, multi-tier

c. Web server, web client

d. Presentation-oriented, service-oriented

III. Exercises

1. Provide a brief description about the Java EE three-tier Web application with EJB.

2. What is the difference between a Java EE with EJB and a Java EE without EJB?

3. What are popular Java EE components?

4. Provide a brief description to illustrate the interaction between a Web client and a Web application.

5. Provide a brief description about the Java EE containers.

6. Refer to Section 8.5.3.3 to develop a Java bean class FacultyBean.java to replace the Java help class FacultyQuery.java to improve the faculty information query.

7. Refer to Section 8.5.4 to use a JSF page FacultyPage.jsp to replace the JSP page Faculty.jsp to improve this faculty data insertion.

Chapter 9

Developing Java Web Services to Access Databases

We provided a very detailed discussion about the Java Web applications in the last chapter. In this chapter, we will concentrate on another Java Web related topic—Java Web Services.

Unlike Java Web applications in which the user needs to access the Web server through the client browser by sending requests to the server to obtain the desired information, the Java Web Services provide an automatic way to search, identify, and return the desired information required by the user through a set of methods installed in the Web server, and those methods can be accessed by a computer program, not the user, via the Internet. Another important difference between the Java Web applications and Java Web Services is that the latter do not provide any graphic user interfaces (GUIs), and users needs to create those GUIs themselves to access the Web services via the Internet.

When finished this chapter, you will

- Understand the basic and popular Java Web Services models
- Understand the structure and components of **SOAP/WSDL-based** Java Web Services, such as Simple Object Access Protocol (SOAP), Web Services Description Language (WSDL), and Universal Description, Discovery and Integration (UDDI)
- Create correct SOAP Namespaces for the Web Services to make used names and identifiers unique in the user's document
- Create suitable security components to protect the Web methods
- Build the professional Java Web Service projects to access our sample database to obtain required information
- Build client applications to provide GUIs to consume a Web Service
- Build the professional Java Web Service projects to access our sample database to insert new information into that database
- Build the professional Java Web Service projects to access our sample database to update and delete information against that database

In order to help readers to successfully complete this chapter, first, we need to provide a detailed discussion about the Java Web Services and their components.

Practical Database Programming with Java, First Edition. Ying Bai.

9.1 INTRODUCTION TO JAVA WEB SERVICES

Web services are distributed application components that are externally available. You can use them to integrate computer applications that are written in different languages and run on different platforms. Web services are language and platform independent because vendors have agreed on common Web service standards.

Essentially, Web services can be considered as a set of methods installed in a Web server and can be called by computer programs installed on the clients through the Internet. Those methods can be used to locate and return the target information required by the computer programs. Web Services do not require the use of browsers or HTML, and therefore Web Services are sometimes called *application services*.

A complete Web services stack Metro, which is developed by the Sun Microsystems, covers all of a developer's needs, from simple Java Web Services demonstrations to reliable, secured, and transacted Web services. Metro includes Web Services Interoperability Technologies (WSIT). WSIT supports enterprise features such as security, reliability, and message optimization. WSIT ensures that Metro services with these features are interoperable with Microsoft .NET services. Within Metro, Project Tango develops and evolves the codebase for WSIT.

Several programming models are available to Web service developers. These models can be categorized into two groups, and both are supported by the NetBeans IDE:

- **REST Based**: **RE**presentational State Transfer is a new way to create and communicate with Web services. In REST, resources have Uniform Resource Identifiers (URIs) and are manipulated through HTTP header operations.
- **SOAP/WSDL Based**: In traditional Web service models, Web service interfaces are exposed through Web Services Description Language (WSDL) documents (a type of XML), which have URLs. Subsequent message exchange is in Simple Object Access Protocol (SOAP), another type of XML document.

Let's have a little more discussion about these two kinds of Web services.

9.1.1 REST-Based Web Services

REST-based or RESTful Web services are collections of Web resources identified by URIs. Every document and every process is modeled as a Web resource with a unique URI. These Web resources are manipulated by the actions that can be specified in an HTTP header. Neither SOAP, nor WSDL, nor WS-* standards are used. Instead, message exchange can be conducted in any format—XML, JavaScript Object Notation (JSON), HTML, etc. In many cases, a Web browser can serve as the client.

HTTP is the protocol in REST. Only four methods are available: GET, PUT, POST, and DELETE. Requests can be bookmarked and responses can be cached. A network administrator can easily follow what is going on with a RESTful service just by looking at the HTTP headers.

REST is a suitable technology for applications that do not require security beyond what is available in the HTTP infrastructure and where HTTP is the appropriate protocol. REST services can still deliver sophisticated functionality. NetBeans IDE Software as a

Service (SaaS) functionality lets you use Facebook, Zillow, and other third party-provided services in your own applications.

Project Jersey is the open source reference implementation for building RESTful Web services. The Jersey APIs are available as the RESTful Web Services plug-in for NetBeans IDE.

RESTful Web services are services built using the RESTful architectural style. Building Web services using the RESTful approach is emerging as a popular alternative to using SOAP-based technologies for deploying services on the Internet, due to its lightweight nature and the ability to transmit data directly over HTTP.

The NetBeans IDE supports rapid development of RESTful Web services using Java Specification Requests (JSR 311), a Java API for RESTful Web services (JAX-RS), and Jersey, the reference implementation for JAX-RS.

In addition to building RESTful Web services, the NetBeans IDE also supports testing, building client applications that access RESTful Web services, and generating code for invoking Web services (both RESTful and SOAP-based.)

Here is the list of RESTful features provided by the NetBeans IDE:

1. Rapid creation of RESTful Web services from JPA entity classes and patterns.
2. Rapid code generation for invoking Web services such as Google Map, Yahoo News Search, and StrikeIron Web services by drag-and-dropping components from the RESTful component palette.
3. Generation of JavaScript client stubs from RESTful Web services for building RESTful client applications.
4. Test client generation for testing RESTful Web services.
5. Logical view for easy navigation of RESTful Web service implementation classes in the project.
6. Fully integrated Spring framework, providing Spring transaction handling.

A structure and architecture of using a RESTful model to build a Web service is shown in Figure 9.1.

Next, let's take a look at the SOAP-based Web services.

9.1.2 SOAP-Based Web Services

In SOAP-based Web services, Java utilities create a WSDL file based on the Java code in the Web service. The WSDL is exposed on the net. Parties interested in using the Web service create a Java client based on the WSDL. Messages are exchanged in SOAP format. The range of operations that can be passed in SOAP is much broader than what is available in REST, especially in security.

SOAP-based Web services are suitable for heavyweight applications using complicated operations and for applications requiring sophisticated security, reliability, or other WS-* standards-supported features. They are also suitable when a transport protocol other than HTTP has to be used. Many of Amazon's Web services, particularly those involving commercial transactions, and the Web services used by banks and government agencies, are SOAP-based.

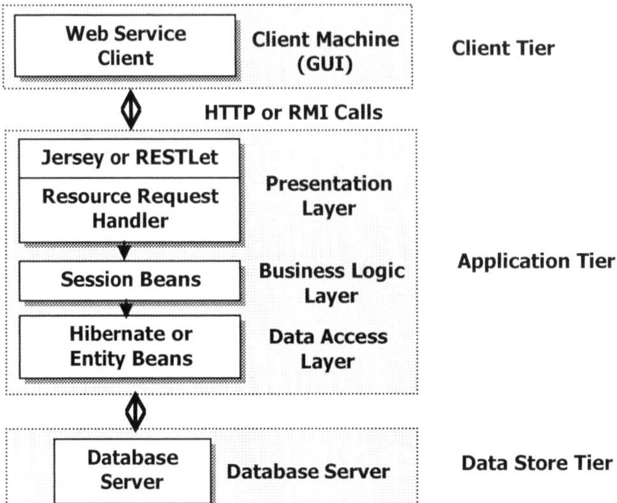

Figure 9.1. The architecture of a multitier Web services.

The Java API for XML Web Services (JAX-WS) is the current model for SOAP-based Web services in Metro. JAX-WS is built on the earlier Java API for XML Remote Procedure Call (JAX-RPC) model but uses specific Java EE 5 features, such as annotations, to simplify the task of developing Web services. Because it uses SOAP for messaging, JAX-WS is transport neutral. It also supports a wide range of modular WS-* specifications, such as WS-Security and WS-ReliableMessaging.

When you create a Web service client, you have the option of using either the JAX-WS or JAX-RPC model. This is because some older JAX-RPC services use a binding style that is not supported by JAX-WS. These services can only be consumed by JAX-RPC clients.

Metro Web services are interoperable with Apache Axis2 Web services. Apache Axis2 is an open-source implementation of the SOAP submission to the W3C. Two popular implementations of the Apache Axis2 Web services engine are Apache Axis2/Java and Apache Axis2/C. In addition, Axis2 not only supports SOAP 1.1 and SOAP 1.2, but it also has integrated support for RESTful Web services.

Because the SOAP-based Web services are suitable for heavyweight applications using complicated operations and for applications requiring sophisticated security and reliability, in this chapter, we will concentrate on this kind of Web services.

9.2 THE STRUCTURE AND COMPONENTS OF SOAP-BASED WEB SERVICES

To effectively find, identify, and return the target information required by computer programs, a SOAP-based Web Service needs the following components:

1. XML (Extensible Markup Language)
2. SOAP (Simple Object Access Protocol)

3. UDDI (Universal Description, Discovery and Integration)
4. WSDL (Web Services Description Language)

The functionality of each component is listed below:

XML is a text-based data storage language, and it uses a series of tags to define and store data. Exactly the so-called tags are used to "mark up" data to be exchanged between applications. The "marked up" data then can be recognized and used by different applications without any problem. As you know, the Web Services platform is XML + HTTP (Hypertext Transfer Protocol), and the HTTP protocol is the most popular Internet protocol. However, the XML provides a kind of language that can be used between different platforms and programming languages to express complex messages and functions. In order to make the codes used in the Web Services to be recognized by applications developed in different platforms and programming languages, the XML is used for the coding in the Web Services to make them up line by line.

SOAP is a communication protocol used for communications between applications. Essentially, SOAP is a simple XML-based protocol to help applications developed in different platforms and languages to exchange information over HTTP. Therefore, SOAP is a platform-independent and language-independent protocol, which means that it can be run at any operating systems with any programming languages. Exactly SOAP works as a carrier to transfer data or requests between applications. Whenever a request is made to the Web server to request a Web Service that request is first wrapped into a SOAP message and sent over the Internet to the Web server. Similarly, as the Web Service returns the target information to the client, the returned information is also wrapped into a SOAP message and sent over the Internet to the client browser.

WSDL is an XML-based language for describing Web Services and how to access them. In WSDL terminology, each Web Service is defined as an abstract end point or a Port and each Web method is defined as an abstract operation. Each operation or method can contain some SOAP messages to be transferred between applications. Each message is constructed by using the SOAP protocol as a request is made from the client. WSDL defines two styles for how a Web Service method can be formatted in a SOAP message: Remote Procedure Call (RPC) and Document. Both RPC and Document style messages can be used to communicate with a Web Service using a RPC.

A single end point can contain a group of Web methods, and that group of methods can be defined as an abstract set of operations called a Port Type. Therefore, WSDL is an XML format for describing network services as a set of end points operating on SOAP messages containing either document-oriented or procedure-oriented information. The operations and messages are described abstractly, and then bound to a concrete network protocol and message format to define an end point.

UDDI is an XML-based directory for businesses to list themselves on the Internet, and the goal of this directory is to enable companies to find one another on the Web and make their systems interoperable for e-commerce. UDDI is often considered as a telephone book'' yellow and white pages. By using those pages, it allows businesses to list themselves by name, products, locations, or the Web services they offer.

Summarily, based on these components and their roles discussed above, we can conclude:

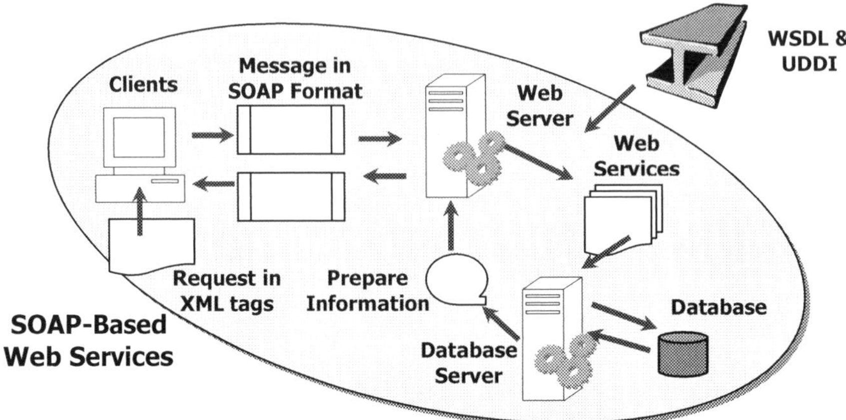

Figure 9.2. A typical process of a SOAP-based Web Service.

- The XML is used to tag the data to be transferred between applications.
- SOAP is used to wrap and pack the data tagged in the XML format into the messages represented in the SOAP protocol.
- WSDL is used to map a concrete network protocol and message format to an abstract end point, and describe the Web services available in a WSDL document format.
- UDDI is used to list all Web Services that are available to users and businesses.

Figure 9.2 shows a diagram to illustrate these components and their roles in a Java Web Service process.

By now we have obtained the fundamental knowledge about the SOAP-based Web Services and their components, next let's see how to build a Web Service project.

9.3 THE PROCEDURE OF BUILDING A TYPICAL SOAP-BASED WEB SERVICE PROJECT

Different methods and languages can be used to develop different Web Services, such as the C# Web Services, Java Web Services, and Perl Web Services. In this section, we only concentrate on developing the Java Web Services using the NetBeans IDE. Before we can start to build a real Web Service project, let's first take a closer look at the procedure of building a Java Web Service project.

Unlike ASP.NET Web services applications, a Java SOAP-based Web service project is involved in a Java Web application project in which the Web service can be deployed based on an appropriate container. Once a Java Web application project has been created with a desired container, you can create a new Java Web service project in that Web application project.

Regularly, to build and implement a Java SOAP-based Web service project, you need to follow the procedures listed below:

1. Create a new Java Web application project with an appropriate container.
2. Create a new Java SOAP-based Web service project.

3. Add desired operations (methods) to the Web service to build the desired functions for the Web service.
4. Deploy and test the Web service on the selected container.
5. Create Web service clients to consume the developed Java Web service.

Next, let's use a real simple Web service example WSTestApplication to illustrate these steps.

9.3.1 Create a New Java Web Application Project WSTestApplication

Before we can create a new Web service application project, we need to select our desired container to deploy our Web service. Generally, we can either deploy our Web service in a Web container or in an EJB container. This depends on our choice of implementation. If we are creating a Java EE 6 application, we had better use a Web container in any case since we can put EJBs directly in a Web application. However, if we plan to deploy our Web service project to the Tomcat Web Server, which only has a Web container, we need to create a Web application, not an EJB module.

After a container has been determined, next, we can create a new Java Web application project with the selected container. Perform the following operations to create this new Web application project WSTestApplication:

1. Launch NetBeans IDE and choose File > New Project (Ctrl-Shift-N). Select Web Application from the `Java Web` category.
2. Name the project WSTestApplication and click on the Browse button to select a desired location for the project. In this application, we used the C:\Chapter 9 as our project location. Click on the Next button to continue.
3. Select GlassFish v3 as our Web container and Java EE 6 Web as the Java EE version. Your finished Server and Settings wizard should match the one that is shown in Figure 9.3. Click on the Finish button to complete this new application creation process.

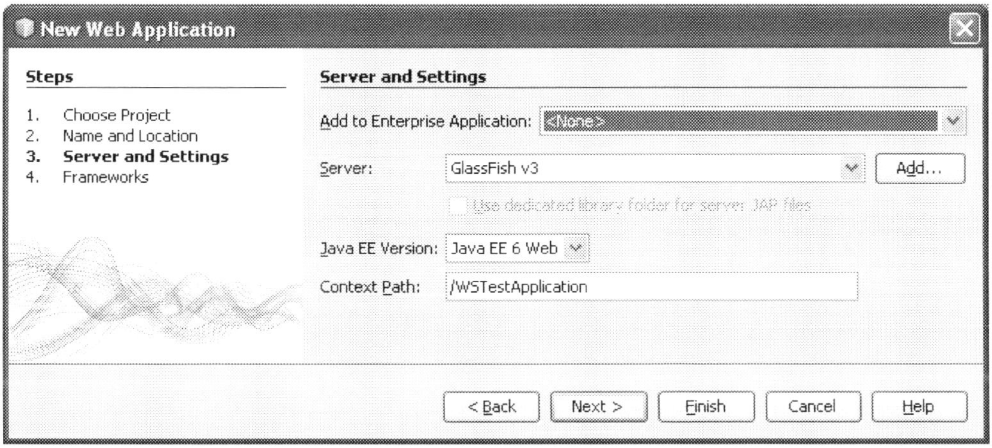

Figure 9.3. The finished Server and Settings wizard.

Now that a Web application has been created with a selected Web container, next, we can create our new Web service project WSTest.

9.3.2 Create A New Java SOAP-Based Web Service Project WSTest

The function of this Web service is to add two integers together and return the result. Perform the following operations to create this new Web service project WSTest:

1. In the opened Projects window, right click on our newly created project WSTestApplication, and select the New > Other menu item to open the `New File` wizard.
2. Select Web Services from the `Categories` list and Web Service from the `File Types` list, and click on the Next button.
3. Name the Web service WSTest and type org.wstest into the `Package` field. Leave Create Web Service from Scratch selected.
4. Check the Implement Web Service as Stateless Session Bean checkbox if we want to use Java beans in this Web service.

Your finished Name and Location wizard should match the one that is shown in Figure 9.4. Click on the Finish button to complete this process.

After a new Web service project WSTest is created, the following components are added into our Web application WSTestApplication:

1. A new node named org.wstest with a new Java class WSTest.java has been added to the Source Packages node in our application. This Java class file WSTest.java is the main body of this Web service, and all functions of this Web service should be performed by adding operations or methods into this class.

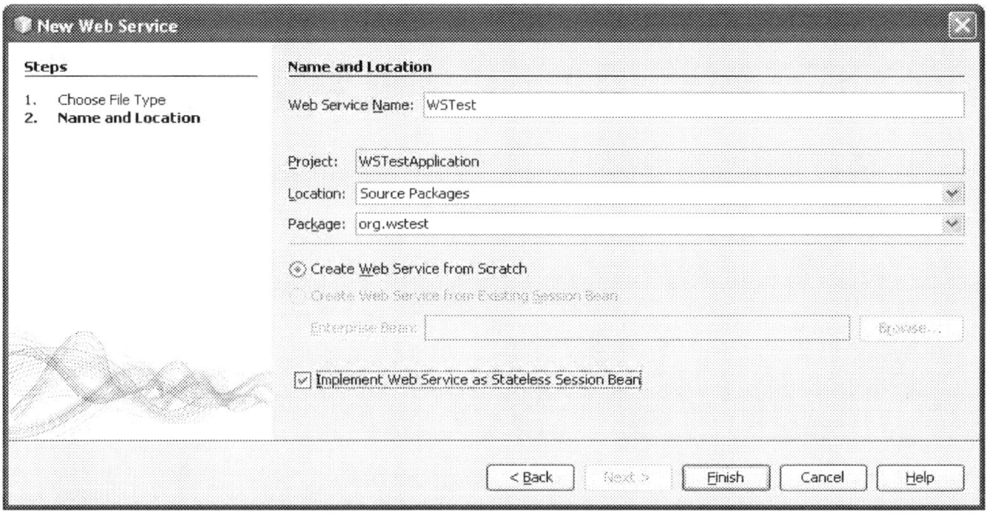

Figure 9.4. The finished Name and Location wizard.

Figure 9.5. New added components for our new Web service project.

2. A new node named Web Services with a new icon WSTest has been added into our Web application. This WSTest icon is our target Web service output file that can be tested later when it is built.
3. A new file named web.xml has been added into the Configuration Files node in our project. This file is called the Web deployment descriptor file, and it is used to define and describe how to deploy our Web service on a server.
4. Some Metro Web service libraries have also been added into the Libraries node in our project to provide all supports and assistances to our Web service developments.
5. A new node named Enterprise Beans with a newly added bean class WSTest has been added into our project, and this enables us to use any Java beans in our Web service project.

All of these newly added components are shown in Figure 9.5.

Now we can add new operations or methods into our main body class WSTest.java to build our Web service to perform the addition function for two integers input by users via a client.

9.3.3 Add Desired Operations to the Web Service

The goal of this project is to add to the Web service an operation that adds two integer numbers received from a client. The NetBeans IDE provides a dialog for adding an operation or a method to a Web service. You can open this dialog either in the Web service visual designer or in the Web service context menu.

To open this dialog using the Web service visual designer,

- Open our Web service main body file WSTest.java by double clicking on it from the Projects window.

- Click on the Design button on the top of this window.

To open this dialog using the Web service context menu,

- Find our target Web service output file WSTest from the Web Services node in the Projects window.
- Right-click on that node to open the context menu.

Click on Add Operation menu item in either the visual designer or the context menu. A dialog box appears where you can define the new operation.

Perform the following operations to add a new addition operation or new method:

1. In the upper part of the Add Operation dialog box, type Add into the Name field and type int into the Return Type drop-down list. In the lower part of the Add Operation dialog box, click on the Add button and create a parameter of type int named input1. Then click on the Add button again and create the second parameter of type int called input2. Your finished Add Operation dialog should match the one that is shown in Figure 9.6.
2. Click on the OK button to close this dialog. The newly added operation is displayed in the visual designer, as shown in Figure 9.7.
3. Click on the Source button on the top of this window to open the code window of this Web service main body file, and you can find that our new Web operation or method Add() has been added into this class, as shown in Figure 9.8.
4. In the opened WebMethod Add(), enter the codes shown below into this method:

```
int result = input1 + input2;
return result;
```

5. Your finished codes for this new operation method, which have been highlighted, are shown in Figure 9.9. The function of this operation is simple, and it only adds two input numbers entered by users via a client and returns the result to the client.

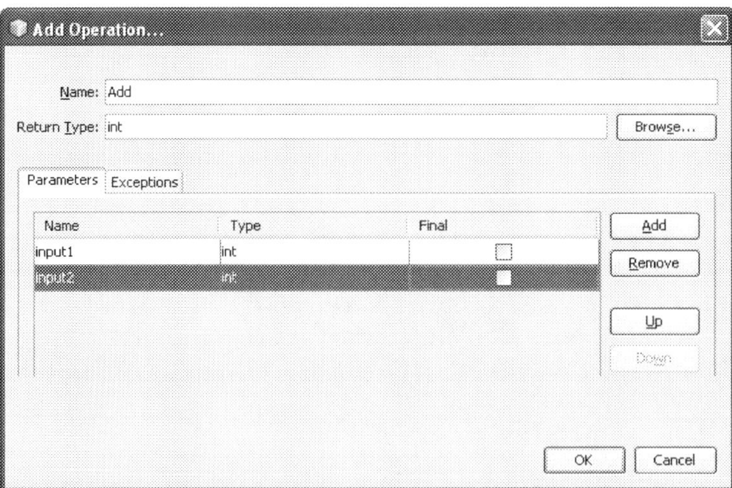

Figure 9.6. The finished Add Operation dialog.

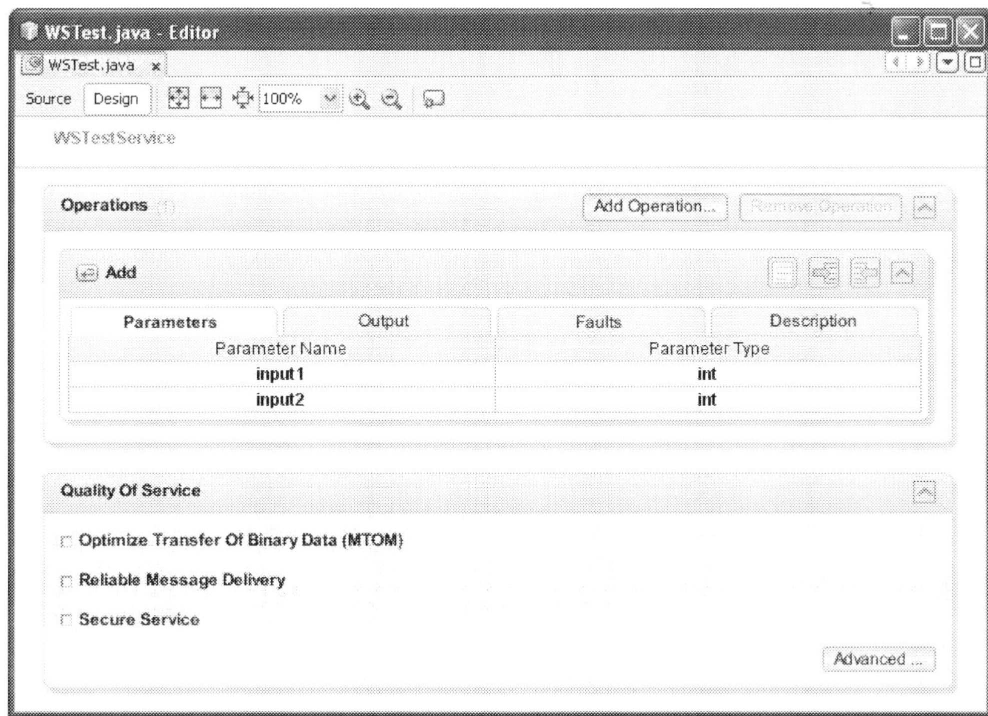

Figure 9.7. The opened visual designer.

```
/*...*/
package org.wstest;

import javax.jws.WebMethod;
import javax.jws.WebParam;
import javax.jws.WebService;
import javax.ejb.Stateless;

/**...*/
@WebService()
@Stateless()
public class WSTest {

    /**...*/
    @WebMethod(operationName = "Add")
    public int Add(@WebParam(name = "input1")
    int input1, @WebParam(name = "input2")
    int input2) {
        //TODO write your implementation code here:
        return 0;
    }
}
```

Figure 9.8. The codes created for the new added operation.

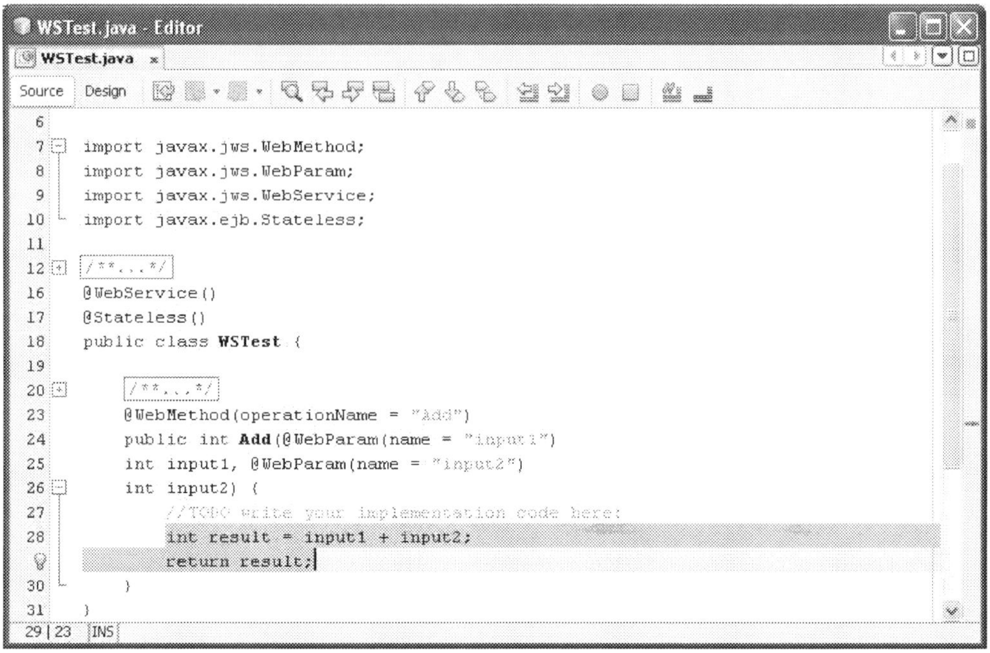
WSTest.java - Editor
WSTest.java
Source
Design
import javax.jws.WebMethod;
import javax.jws.WebParam;
import javax.jws.WebService;
import javax.ejb.Stateless;
/**...*/
@WebService()
@Stateless()
public class WSTest {
/**...*/
@WebMethod(operationName = "Add")
public int Add(@WebParam(name = "input1")
int input1, @WebParam(name = "input2")
int input2) {
//TODO write your implementation code here:
int result = input1 + input2;
return result;
}
}
29 | 23
INS

Figure 9.9. The finished codes for the new operation method.

At this point, we have finished developing our Web service project, and next, we need to deploy it to the selected Web container and test it with some consuming projects.

9.3.4 Deploy and Test the Web Service on the Selected Container

The NetBeans IDE provides a server's test client to assist us to test our Web service after it has been successfully deployed. Perform the following operations to deploy our Web service to our Web container GlassFish v3:

1. Right-click on our project WSTestApplication from the Projects window and choose the Deploy item. The NetBeans IDE will start the application server, build the application, and deploy the application to the server. You can follow the progress of these operations in the WSTestApplication (run-deploy) and the GlassFish v3 server in the Output window view.
2. Enter `admin` and `reback` as the username and password to the Java Glassfish v3 Server to login and start this Web server. Recall that we used these login data when we installed the Java Glassfish v3 Server in Section 5.3.5.2.1 in Chapter 5. Refer to that section to get more details for these login data.
3. If everything is fine, a successful deploy result should be obtained and displayed in the Output window, as shown in Figure 9.10.

To test our Web service, perform the following operations:

1. In the opened Projects window, expand the Web Services node of our project ,and right-click on our target Web service output file WSTest, and choose the Test Web Service item.

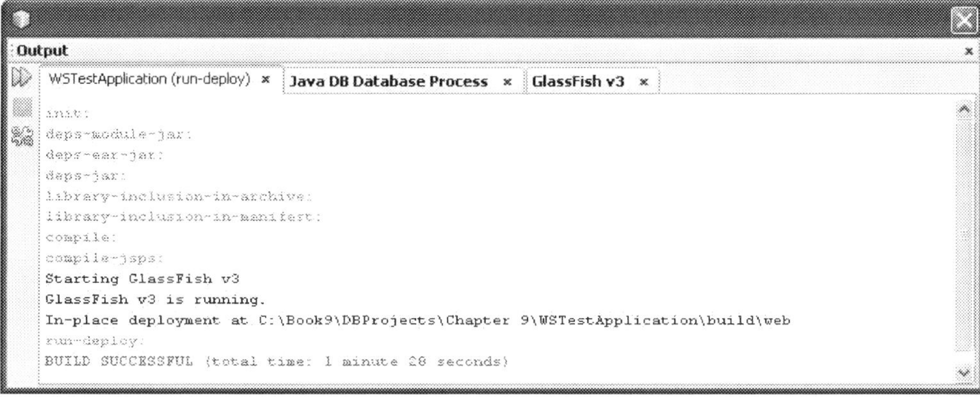

Figure 9.10. The deployment result.

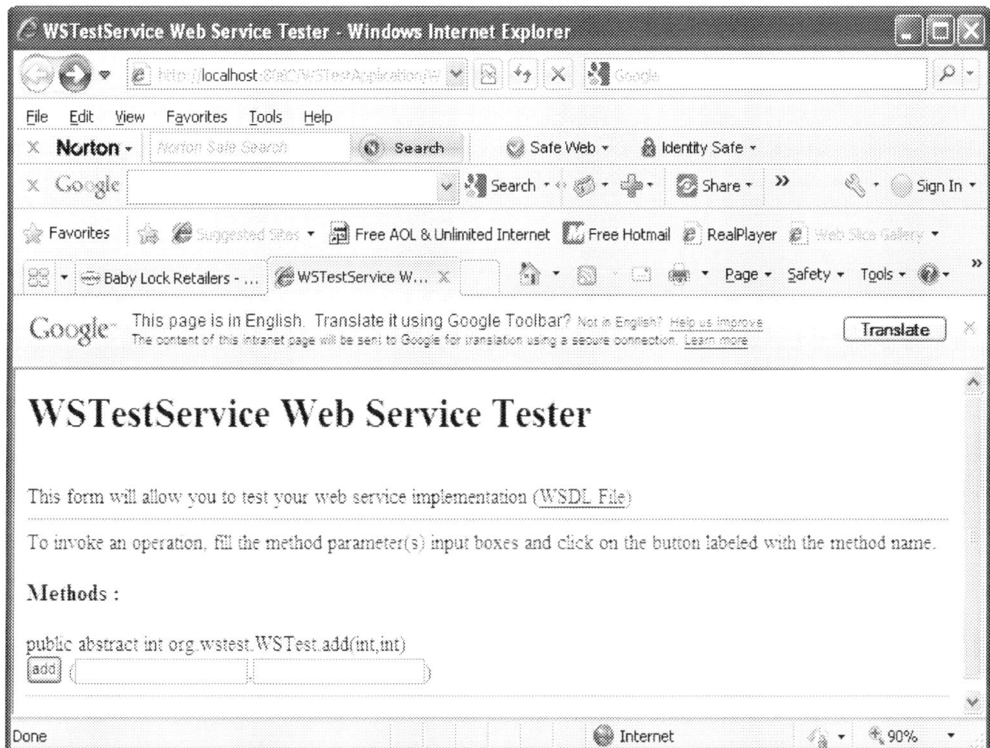

Figure 9.11. The Web service testing page.

2. The NetBeans IDE will display a tester page in your browser if everything is fine, which is shown in Figure 9.11.

To test our Web service project, enter 5 and 3 to the two input boxes, and click on the **add** button. You can find that a successful running result of our Web service is displayed with an addition result of 8, which is shown in Figure 9.12.

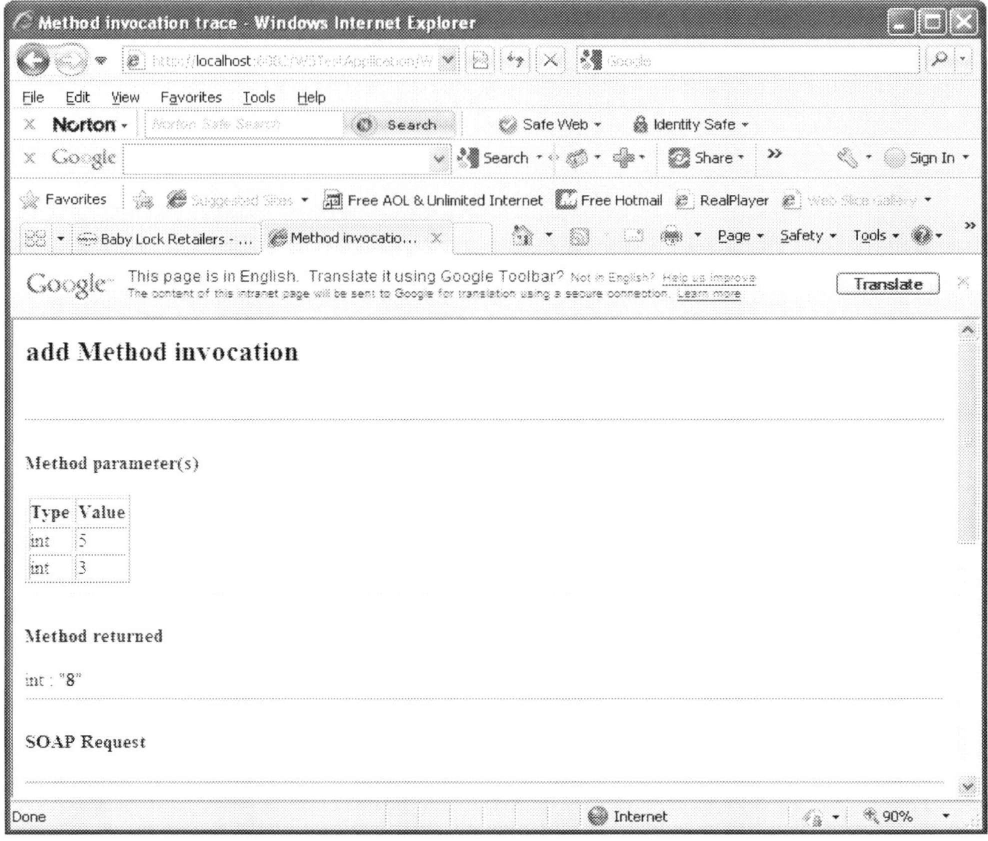

Figure 9.12. The Web service testing result.

One point to be noted is that if you are using the Tomcat Web Server as your application server, you would not find this tester page, and only a testing successful page is displayed without the page testing ability available. Also, if you are deploying a Web service built with EJB module, you cannot find this tester page either, since the NetBeans IDE will not support this testing function to any EJB module.

Next, let's build a Web service consuming project to consume our Web service.

9.3.5 Create Web Service Clients to Consume the Web Service

In fact, you can develop any kind of Java applications as a consuming project to consume a Web service, such as a general desktop Java application project, a Java servlet, or a JSP page in a Web application.

To make this client project simple, we prefer to build a simple Java desktop application project WSTestClient to consume this Web service.

Perform the following operations to create our client project:

1. Choose File > New Project menu item to open `New Project` wizard. Select Java from the `Categories` list and Java Application from the `Projects` list, and click on the Next button.
2. Name the project WSTestClient and select an appropriate location for this client project. Leave Create Main Class checkbox checked and accept all other default settings. Your finished `Name and Location` wizard should match the one that is shown in Figure 9.13. Click on the Finish button to complete this new project creation process.
3. Right click on our new client project WSTestClient node from the Projects window and choose New > Web Service Client item to open the `New Web Service Client` wizard.
4. Click on the Browse button that is next to the `Project` radio button to browse to our Web service project WSTest, as shown in Figure 9.14. Click on our Web service WSTest and click on the OK button.

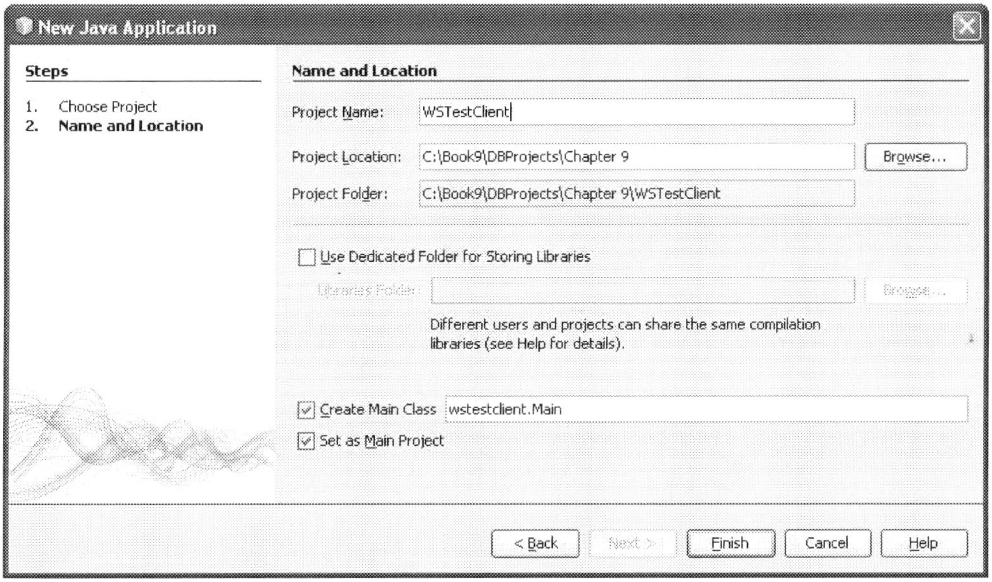

Figure 9.13. The finished Name and Location wizard.

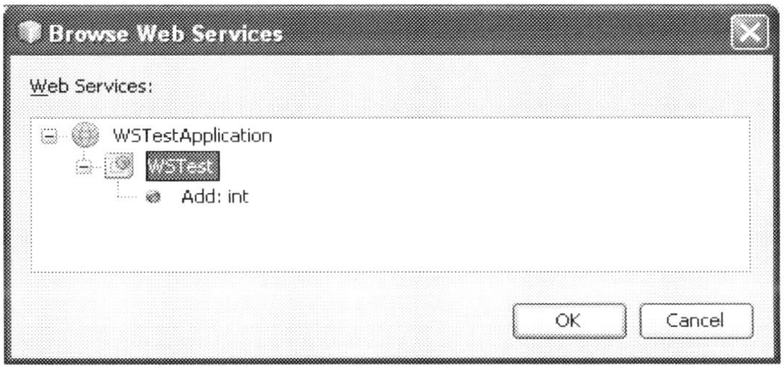

Figure 9.14. The Web service browse wizard.

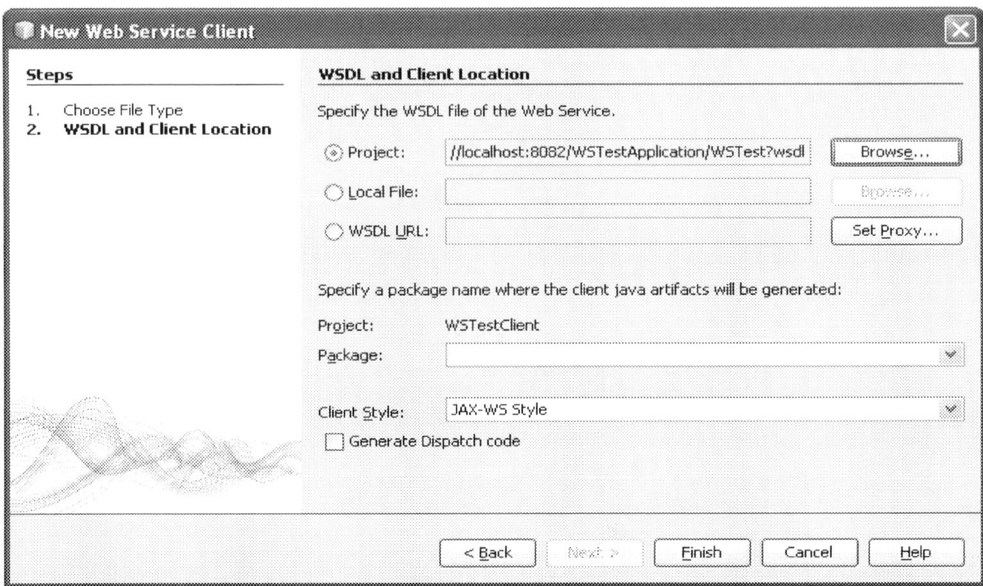

Figure 9.15. The finished New Web Service Client wizard.

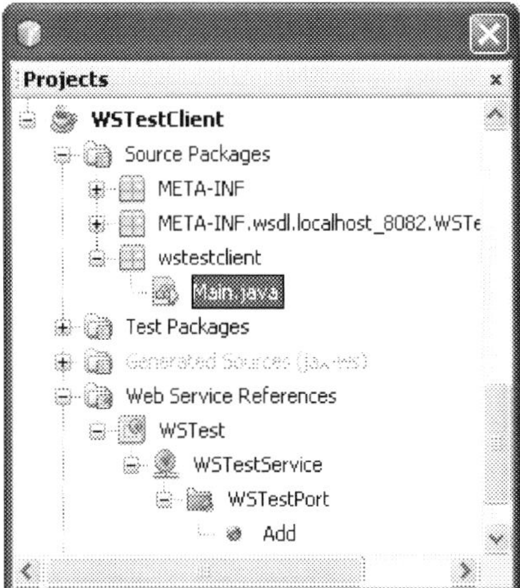

Figure 9.16. The new added Web Service References node and components.

5. Your finished `New Web Service Client` wizard should match the one that is shown in Figure 9.15. Click on the Finish button to complete this new consuming project creation process.
6. A new node named Web Service References with the following components has been added into our client project WSTestClient, as shown in Figure 9.16:

   A. Our target Web service output file WSTest

   B. Our Web service class file WSTestService

```
  public class Main {
     /**
      * @param args the command line arguments
      */
     public static void main(String[] args) {
        // TODO code application logic here
A       try {
B          org.wstest.WSTestService sevice = new org.wstest.WSTestService();
C          org.wstest.WSTest port = sevice.getWSTestPort();
D          int a = 5, b = 7;
E          int result = port.add(a, b);
F          System.out.println("Result = "+result);
        }
G       catch (Exception ex){
           System.out.println("exception" + ex);
        }
     }
  }
```

Figure 9.17. The codes for the main() method.

C. Our Web service port file WSTestPort

D. Our operation Add() method

Now let's build the codes for this consuming project to consume our Web service. Perform the following operations to build the codes for this consuming project:

1. Double click on our main class file Main.java that is located at the Source Packages\wstestclient node to open the code window of this file.
2. Enter the codes that shown in Figure 9.17 into the main() method on this file.

Let's have a closer look at this piece of codes to see how it works.

A. A try . . . catch block is used to call our Web service to perform a two-integer addition operation.

B. A new Web service instance service is created based on our Web service class WSTestService.

C. The getWSTestPort() method is executed to get the current port used by our Web service. This port is returned and assigned to a new Port instance port.

D. Two testing integers are created and initialized with 5 and 7, respectively.

E. The operation method Add() in our Web service is called to perform this addition operation. The running result of this method is assigned to a local variable named result.

F. The result is displayed on the Output window.

G. Any exception during this Web service calling process will be tracked and displayed on the Output window, too.

Now let's build and run our client project to call the Add() method built in our Web service to perform this two-integer addition operation.

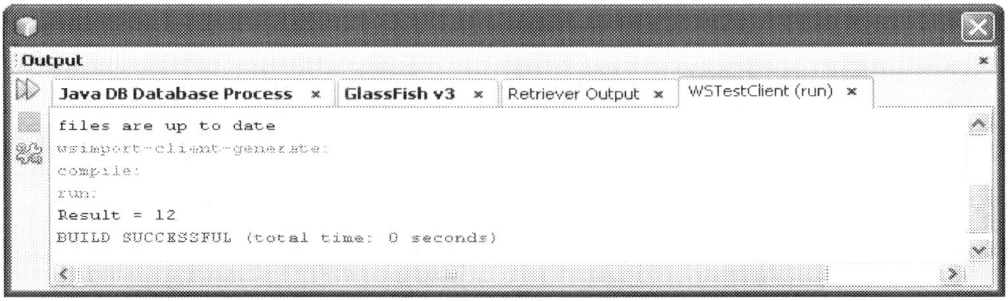

```
Output
Java DB Database Process | GlassFish v3 | Retriever Output | WSTestClient (run)
files are up to date
wsimport-client-generate:
compile:
run:
Result = 12
BUILD SUCCESSFUL (total time: 0 seconds)
```

Figure 9.18. The running result of calling our Web service.

Click on the Clean and Build Main Project button to build our client project. Then right click on our project WSTestClient and select the Run menu item from the pop-up menu. The running result is shown in Figure 9.18.

It can be found that the calling of our Web service is successful, and the addition result of 12 has been returned. Our first Web service project is successful.

At this point, we have gotten a fundamental knowledge and basic understanding about Java Web Services. Now let's start building some real Java Web Services projects to perform database query and manipulation operations against our sample database.

9.4 GETTING STARTED WITH JAVA WEB SERVICES USING NETBEANS IDE

In the following sections, we will develop and build different Java Web Services projects based on two main database systems, SQL Server 2008 and Oracle Database 10g XE, and different database operations.

Two kinds of real Java Web service projects will be developed and built:

1. Web services project to access and manipulate data against the SQL Server database.
2. Web services project to access and manipulate data against the Oracle database.

With the following data actions by adding the different operations or methods to those two Web service projects, respectively (because of the space limitations, we will concentrate on accessing and manipulating data against the Faculty table in our sample SQL Server 2008 database, and accessing and manipulating data against the Course table in our sample Oracle database):

1. Query data from the SQL Server 2008 database with QueryFaculty() operation.
2. Insert data into the SQL Server 2008 database with InsertFaculty() operation.
3. Update and delete data against the SQL Server database with UpdateFaculty() and DeleteFaculty() operations.
4. Query data from the Oracle database with QueryCourse() operation.
5. Query detailed course information from the Oracle database with DetailCourse() operation.

6. Update and delete data against the Oracle database with UpdateCourse() and DeleteCourse() operations.

For each Web services project, we need to build an associated Web client project to consume the Web services project we built to test its function. The following client projects will be built:

1. Web client project to consume the Web service to access the SQL Server database
2. Web client project to consume the Web service to insert data into the SQL Server database
3. Web client project to consume the Web service to update and delete data against the SQL Server database
4. Web client project to consume the Web service to access the Oracle database
5. Web client project to consume the Web service to query course details from the Oracle database
6. Web client project to consume the Web service to update and delete data against the Oracle database

As we know, we can develop any kind of client project to consume a Web service, either a standard Java desktop application, a JSP page or a JSF page. We will develop and build different client projects to consume our Web services to enable our projects to meet the actual needs in our real world.

Let's start from the SQL Server database.

9.5 BUILD JAVA WEB SERVICE PROJECTS TO ACCESS SQL SERVER DATABASE

In this section, we will discuss how to access and perform queries and manipulations against SQL Server 2008 database using Java Web Services. To make our Web Services project simple, we will use the following components to fulfill this query and manipulation:

- Build different operations or methods in our Web services as interfaces to communicate with Web clients that will be built in the future to perform desired data actions.
- Use runtime object method to actually access and query our sample SQL Server 2008 database.

The structure and components used in our Web services are shown in Figure 9.19.

Now let's create our first Web service project WebServiceSQL to perform data query and manipulation against our sample database.

9.5.1 Create a New Java Web Application Project WebServiceSQLApp

When creating a new Web service application project, we need to select a desired container to deploy our Web service. Generally, we can either deploy our Web service in a

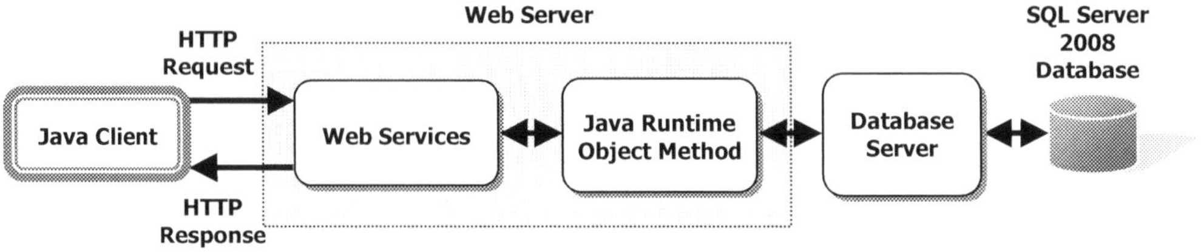

Web Server
HTTP Request
HTTP Response
Java Client
Web Services
Java Runtime Object Method
Database Server
SQL Server 2008 Database

Figure 9.19. The structure and components used in our Web services.

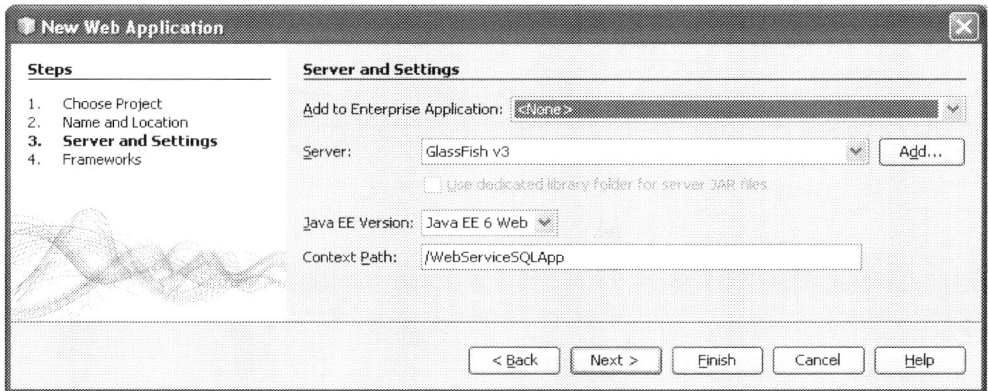

Figure 9.20. The finished Server and Settings wizard.

Web container or in an EJB container. In this application, we prefer to use a Web container since we are creating a Java EE 6 application.

Perform the following operations to create our Web application project WebServiceSQLApp:

1. Launch NetBeans IDE and choose File > New Project (Ctrl-Shift-N). Select Web Application from the `Java Web` category.
2. Name the project WebServiceSQLApp and click on the Browse button to select a desired location for the project. In this application, we used the C:\Chapter 9 as our project location. Click on the Next button to continue.
3. Select GlassFish v3 as our Web container and Java EE 6 Web as the Java EE version; your finished Server and Settings wizard should match the one that is shown in Figure 9.20. Click on the Finish button to complete this new application creation process.

Now that a Web application has been created with a selected Web container, next, we can create our new Web service project WebServiceSQL.

9.5.2 Create a New Java SOAP-Based Web Service Project WebServiceSQL

The function of this Web service is to perform data queries and manipulations to our sample SQL Server 2008 database and return the result. Perform the following operations to create this new Web service project WebServiceSQL:

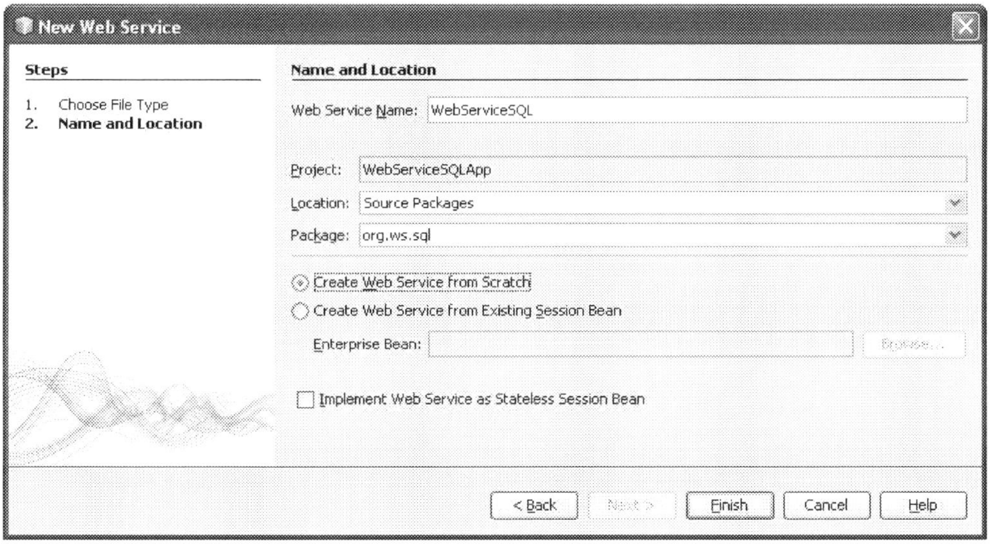

Figure 9.21. The finished Name and Location wizard.

1. In the opened Projects window, right click on our new created project WebServiceSQLApp and select the New > Other menu item to open the `New File` wizard.
2. Select Web Services from the `Categories` list and Web Service from the `File Types` list, and click on the Next button.
3. Name the Web service WebServiceSQL and type org.ws.sql into the `Package` field. Leave Create Web Service from Scratch selected.

Your finished Name and Location wizard should match the one that is shown in Figure 9.21. Click on the Finish button to complete this process.

Before we can add any operation to this Web service project, we need first to add a JDialog class into our project, and we need to use this component to display the debug information during the testing process for our Web service project.

9.5.3 Add Desired Operations to the Web Service

Now let's handle adding a JDialog component into our Web service project.

To save time, you can copy a JDialog class MsgDialog.java from most projects we built in the previous sections. For example, you can copy this JDialog class from our Web application project, JavaWebDBJSPSQL, and paste it into our current Web service, exactly, into the org.ws.sql node in our Web service project.

To do this copy and paste action, right click on this MsgDialog.java node from the project JavaWebDBJSPSQL and choose Refactor > Copy item. Select our current project WebServiceSQLApp from the `Project` combo box, select org.ws.sql from the `To Package` combo box, and click on the Refactor button to paste this JDialog into our project. The project JavaWebDBJSPSQL can be found at the folder DBProjects\Chapter 8 that is located at the Wiley ftp site (refer to Figure 1.2 in Chapter 1).

Next, let's handle the addition of new operations and coding for the newly added operations or methods in our Web service.

9.5.4 Add New Operations to Our Web Services to Perform Data Query

The main purpose of using the Web service in this section is to query data from the Faculty table in our sample database; therefore, we need to add one new operation QueryFaculty() to the Web service project.

Perform the following operations to add a new operation QueryFaculty() into our Web service project:

1. Click on the Design button on the top of the window to open the Design View of our Web service project WebServiceSQL.
2. Click on the Add Operation button to open the `Add Operation` wizard.
3. Enter QueryFaculty into the `Name` field and click on the Browse button that is next to the `Return Type` combo box. Type ArrayList into the `Type Name` field, and select the item ArrayList (java.util) from the list, and click on the OK button.
4. Click on the Add button and enter fname into the `Name` parameter field. Keep the default type java.lang.String unchanged and click on the OK button to complete this new operation creation process.

Your finished `Add Operation` wizard should match the one that is shown in Figure 9.22.

Click on the Source button on the top of this window to open the code window of our Web service project. Let's perform the coding for this newly added operation.

On the opened code window, enter the codes that are shown in Figure 9.23 into this newly added operation. Let's have a closer look at this piece of codes to see how it works.

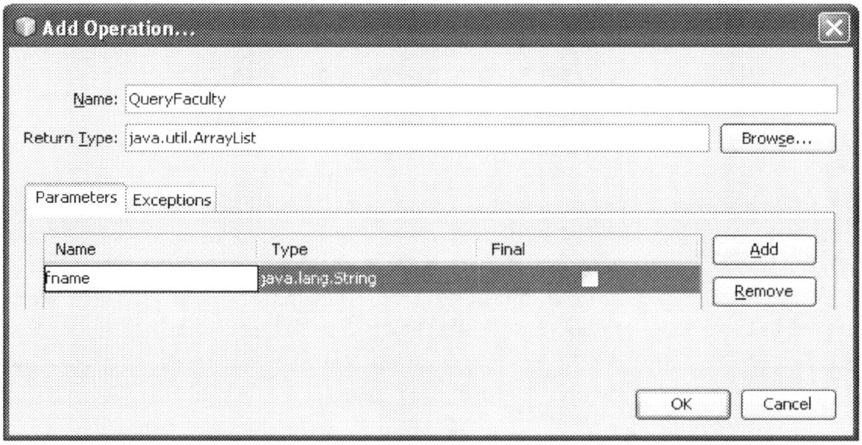

Figure 9.22. The finished Add Operation wizard.

```
  @WebService()
  public class WebServiceSQL {
A     Connection con = null;
      MsgDialog msgDlg = new MsgDialog(new javax.swing.JFrame(), true);

      public class WebServiceSQL {
      @WebMethod(operationName = "TestQuery")
      public ArrayList TestQuery(@WebParam(name = "fname")
      String fname) {
         //TODO write your implementation code here:
B        ArrayList<String> result = new ArrayList<String>();

C        String query = "SELECT * FROM Faculty WHERE faculty_name = ?";
         try {
D           con = DBConnection(con);
E           PreparedStatement pstmt =con.prepareStatement(query);
F           pstmt.setString(1, fname);
G           ResultSet rs = pstmt.executeQuery();
H           ResultSetMetaData rsmd = rs.getMetaData();
I           while (rs.next()){
               for (int colNum = 1; colNum <= rsmd.getColumnCount(); colNum++)
                  result.add(rs.getString(colNum));
            }
J           con.close();
K           return result;
         }
L        catch (Exception ex) {
            msgDlg.setMessage("exception is: " + ex);
            msgDlg.setVisible(true);
            return null;
         }
      }
  }
```

Figure 9.23. The codes for the new operation QueryFaculty().

- **A.** First, two class-level variables, con and msgDlg, are created. The first variable is used to hold the connection instance to our sample database, and the second is used to track and display the debug information when this Web service project is tested later.
- **B.** An ArrayList instance result is created, and this is an array list instance used to collect and store our query result, and return to the consumption project. The reason we used this ArrayList, not List is because the former is a concrete class, but the latter is an abstract class, and a runtime exception may be encountered if an abstract class is used as a returned object to the calling method.
- **C.** The SQL query statement is created with a positional parameter as the dynamic parameter for the query criterion faculty_name.
- **D.** The user-defined method DBConnection() that will be built later is called to set up a connection between our Web service and our sample database. A connection instance con is returned after the execution of this method.
- **E.** A new PreparedStatement instance pstmt is declared and created to perform the query.
- **F.** The setString() method is used to set up the actual value that is our input faculty name for the positional parameter faculty_name.
- **G.** The query is performed by calling the executeQuery() method, and the query result is returned and stored in a ResultSet object rs.

H. To get more related information about the queried database, the getMetaData() method is executed, and the result is stored in a ResultSetMetaData instance rsmd.

I. A `while` and a `for` loop are used to pick up each column from the queried result that is stored in the ResultSet object rs. In fact, the `while` loop only runs one time since only one matched faculty row will be returned. The getColumnCount() method is used as the upper-bound of the for loop, since it returns the total number of queried columns in the matched faculty row.

J. The close() method is executed to disconnect the connection to our database.

K. The queried result is returned.

L. The catch block is used to track and display any exception occurred during this data query process, and a null will be returned if this situation really happened.

During the coding process, you may encounter some in-time compiling errors. The main reason for those errors is that some packages are missed. To fix these errors, just right click on any space inside this code window, and select the **Fix Imports** item to find and add those missed packages.

Now let's build our user-defined method DBConnection() to set up a connection to our sample database from our Web service project.

9.5.5 Build the User-Defined Method DBConnection()

To make our Web service project simple, we will use the Java runtime object method to perform this database connection function. In the opened code window of our Web service project, enter the codes that are shown in Figure 9.24 into this service to create and define this connection method DBConnection().

```
  private Connection DBConnection(Connection conn) {
A     try
      {
        //Load and register SQL Server driver
        Class.forName("com.microsoft.sqlserver.jdbc.SQLServerDriver");
      }
B     catch (Exception e) {
        msgDlg.setMessage("Class not found exception!" + e.getMessage());
        msgDlg.setVisible(true);
      }
C     String url = "jdbc:sqlserver://localhost\\SQL2008EXPRESS:5000;databaseName=CSE_DEPT;";
D     try {
        conn = DriverManager.getConnection(url,"ybai","reback1956");
      }
E     catch (SQLException e) {
        msgDlg.setMessage("Could not connect! " + e.getMessage());
        msgDlg.setVisible(true);
        e.printStackTrace();
      }
F     return conn;
  }
```

Figure 9.24. The codes for the user-defined method DBConnection().

Let's have a closer look at this piece of codes to see how it works.

A. A try catch block is used to perform this database connection function. First, the SQL Server JDBC driver is loaded using the forName() method.

B. The catch block is used to track and detect any possible exception for this JDBC driver loading process. The debug information will be displayed using the msgDlg object if any exception occurred.

C. Our sample SQL Server database connection URL is defined, and it is used to set up a connection to our sample database. Refer to Section 6.2.1.2.4 in Chapter 6 to get more details about this connection URL.

D. Another try block is used to set up a connection to our sample database using the getConnection() method that belongs to the DriverManager class with the username and password as arguments.

E. The catch block is used to detect and display any possible exception during this connection process.

F. The established connection object is returned to the calling method.

At this point, we have finished all coding development for our Web service used to perform queries to our Faculty table. Now let's build and deploy our Web service project.

9.5.6 Deploy the Web Service Project and Test the Data Query Function

Perform the following operations to build and deploy our Web service project:

1. Click on the Clean and Build Main Project button to build our Web service.
2. Right click on our Web application WebServiceSQLApp and select the Deploy item to deploy our Web service. If everything is fine, a successful deployment result should be displayed, as shown in Figure 9.25.

Figure 9.25. The deployment result of our Web service project.

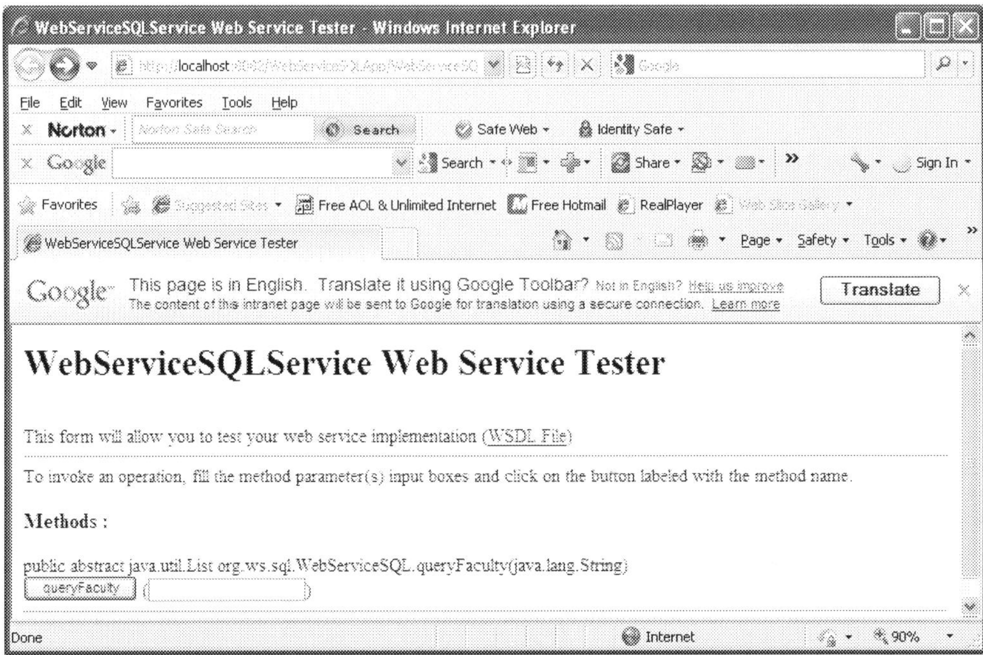

Figure 9.26. The tested page for our Web service.

3. To test this Web service, right click on our target service output file WebServiceSQL under the Web Services node in our project, and select the Test Web Service item.
4. Enter the appropriate username and password to our GlassFish v3 server, such as admin and reback, which are the username and password we used when we load and install our GlassFish v3 server in Section 5.3.5.2.1 in Chapter 5. Click on the OK button to finish this GlassFish v3 server login process.
5. The tested page is opened and displayed as shown in Figure 9.26.
6. Enter a desired faculty name such as Ying Bai into the text field and click on the query-Faculty button to call our Web service. The running result is shown in Figure 9.27.

It can be found that the all seven pieces of queried faculty information for the selected faculty member have been retrieved, and the data query for our Faculty table is successful using our Web service.

Next, we can develop some Web client projects to consume this Web service to perform data query from the Faculty table in our sample database. In fact, as we discussed in Section 9.3.5, we can develop different kinds of Web client projects to consume a Web service. In the following sections, we will discuss two popular client projects, Windows-based and Web-based clients, to consume our Web service to perform queries to our Faculty table.

First, let's discuss how to build a Windows-based client project to consume our Web service.

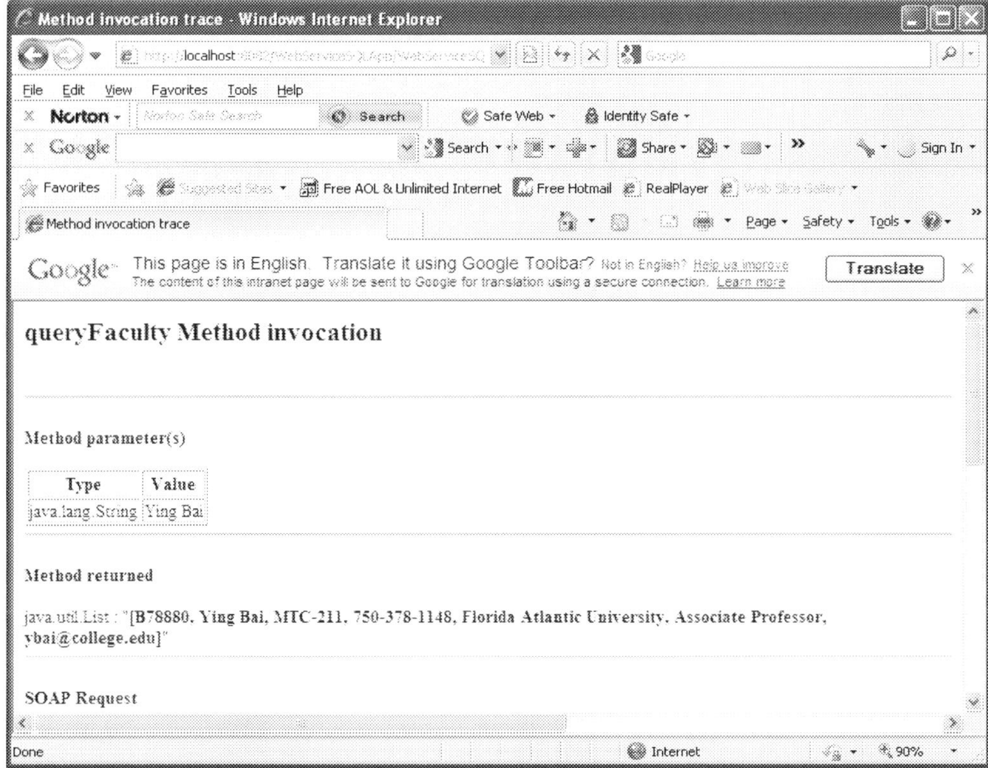

Figure 9.27. The testing result of our Web service project.

9.6 BUILD A WINDOWS-BASED WEB CLIENT PROJECT TO CONSUME THE WEB SERVICE

To save time and space, we can use a Windows-based project SQLSelectObject we developed in Section 6.4 in Chapter 6 to build this client project. The project can be found from the folder DBProjects\Chapter 6 that is located at the Wiley ftp site (refer to Figure 1.2 in Chapter 1).

9.6.1 Copy the FacultyFrame and MsgDislog Components as GUIs

Perform the following operations to create a GUI for our Windows-based client project WinClientSQL to consume our Web service:

1. Launch NetBeans IDE and choose the File > New Project item.
2. Select Java and Java Application from the `Categories` and the `Projects` lists, respectively. Click on the Next button.

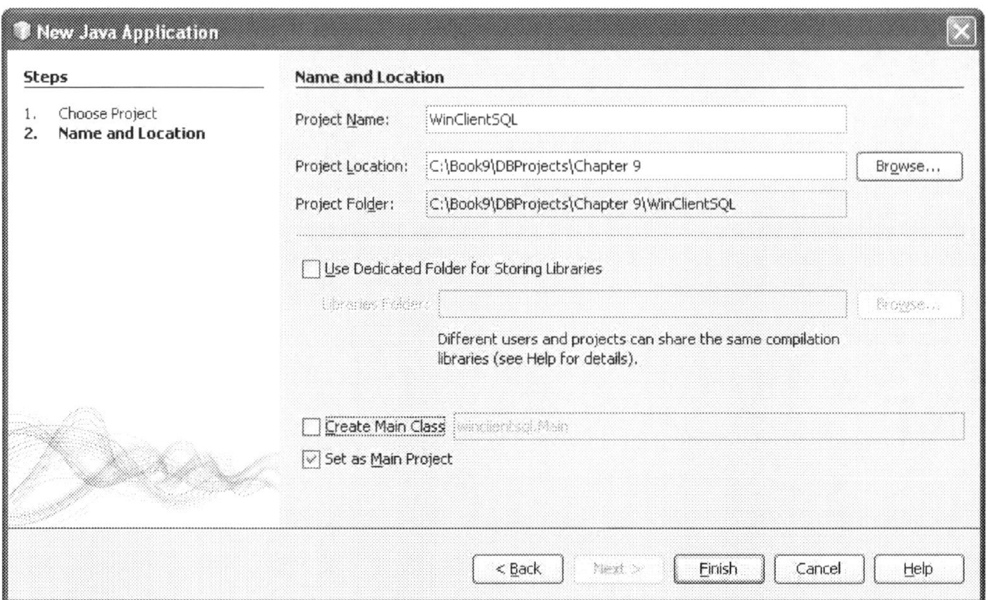

Figure 9.28. The finished Name and Location wizard.

3. Name the project as WinClientSQL and select a desired folder to save this project. Uncheck the Create Main Class checkbox. Your finished `Name and Location` wizard should match the one that is shown in Figure 9.28.
4. Go to the Wiley ftp site (refer to Figure 1.2 in Chapter 1), load and open the project SQLSelectObject from the folder DBProjects\Chapter 6.
5. On the opened project, right click on the Faculty Frame file FacultyFrame.java under the project package node, and select the Refactor > Copy item to copy this form file.
6. On the opened Copy Class—FacultyFrame wizard, select our new project WinClientSQL from the `Project` combo box and remove the 1 after the FacultyFrame from the `New Name` field.
7. Your finished Copy Class—FacultyFrame wizard should match the one that is shown in Figure 9.29.
8. Click on the Refactor button to make a refactoring copy for this frame file.
9. Return to our new project WinClientSQL, and you can find that a copied FacultyFrame.java file has been pasted in the default package in our project.

Since we may need to use this form to test the faculty data query, insertion, updating, and deleting actions via our Web service project, now let's perform some modifications to our copied FacultyFrame form window to make it as our desired GUI in this project.

Open our copied FacultyFrame form window and perform the following modifications to make this form as our desired GUI:

1. Remove the Query Method combo box and its label.
2. Add two more Text Fields and the associated labels shown in Table 9.1.

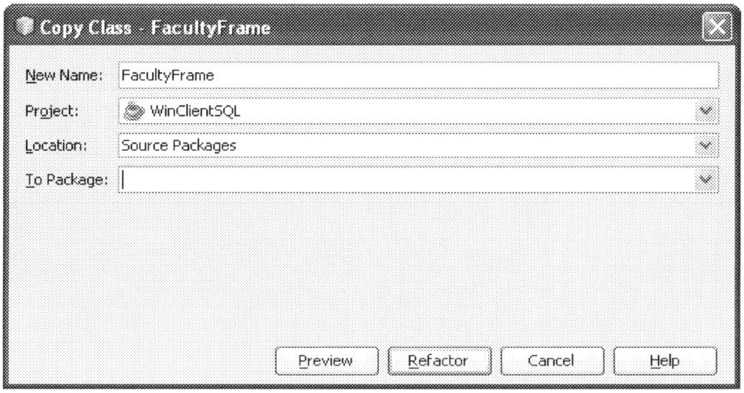

Figure 9.29. The finished Copy Class wizard.

Table 9.1. Newly added objects in the FacultyFrame form

Type	Variable Name	Text
Label	Label1	FacultyID
Text Field	IDField	
Label	Label2	Name
Text Field	NameField	

Your modified FacultyFrame form window should match the one that is shown in Figure 9.30.

Perform a similar operation to copy the MsgDialog.java file and paste it into our new client project. Next, let's develop the codes to call our Web service to perform this faculty data query. However, before we can begin the coding process, we must first set up or create a Web service reference for our WinClientSQL project to enable our project to recognize that Web service and to call it when it is instructed to do that.

9.6.2 Create a Web Service Reference for Our Windows-Based Client Project

Perform the following operations to set up a Web service reference for our client project:

1. Right click on our client project WinClientSQL from the Projects window, and select the New > Other item to open the `New File` wizard.
2. On the opened `New File` wizard, select Web Services from the `Categories` and Web Service Client from the `File Types` list, respectively. Click on the Next button to continue.
3. Click on the Browse button for the Project field, and expand our Web application project WebServiceSQLApp, and click on our Web service project WebServiceSQL to select it.

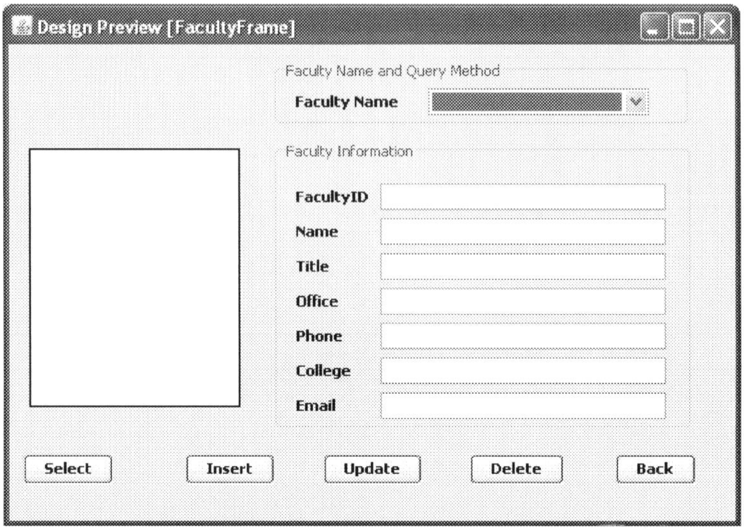

Figure 9.30. The modified FacultyFrame form window.

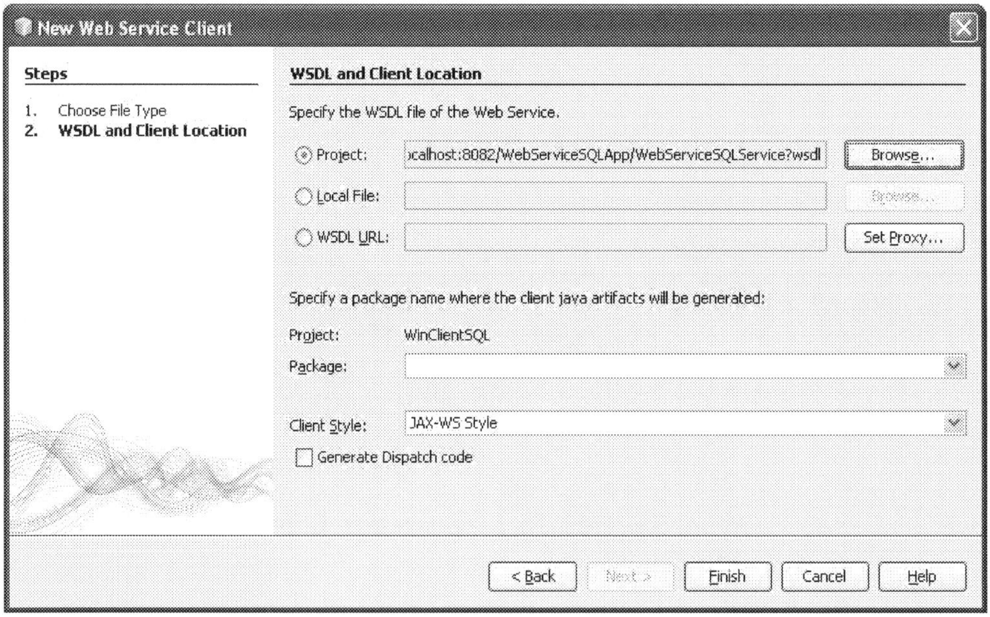

Figure 9.31. The finished New Web Service Client wizard.

Then click on the OK button to select this Web service. Your finished Web Service Client wizard should match the one that is shown in Figure 9.31.

4. Click on the Finish button to complete this Web service reference set up process.

Immediately, you can find that a new node named Web Service References has been created and added into our client project. Expand this node and you can find the associated Web service port and our Web service operation QueryFaculty() under that node.

Now let's develop the codes for this project to call the Web service to perform the data query from the Faculty table in our sample database.

9.6.3 Develop the Codes to Call Our Web Service Project

The coding process is divided into two parts: the modification to the original codes and creation of new codes. First, let' do some modifications to the original codes in this FacultyFrame class. Perform the following code modifications to make this project as our Web consuming project:

1. Double click on our new copied FacultyFrame.java file from our project to open it.
2. Click on the Source button on the top to open the code window.
3. Go to the constructor of this class, and remove all four query methods from the ComboMethod object.
4. Open the cmdSelectActionPerformed() method and remove all codes inside this method except the first coding line and the codes in the last if block.
5. Add two more items, IDField and NameField, into the beginning of the f_field[] JTextField array located at the first coding line. Also, change the order of the rest of items in this array to the order listed below:

   OfficeField, PhoneField, CollegeField, TitleField, EmailField

   to make them identical with the order of the columns in our Faculty table.

Now, let's develop some new codes to perform the faculty data query by calling our Web service project.

On the Design view of the FacultyFrame form window, double click on the Select button to open its event method cmdSelectActionPerformed(). Then enter the codes that are shown in Figure 9.32 into this method. The newly added and modified codes have been highlighted in bold.

Let's have a closer look at this piece of codes to see how it works.

A. Two more items, IDField and NameField, have been added into the beginning of the JTextField[] array. The order of the rest of items should also be modified to make them identical with the order of the columns in our Faculty table.
B. A new ArrayList instance al is created to receive and hold the query result.
C. A try catch block is used to call our Web service to perform the faculty data query operation. First, a new Web service instance service is created based on our Web service class WebServiceSQLService.
D. The getWebServiceSQLPort() method is executed to get the current port used by our Web service. This port is returned and assigned to a new Port instance port.
E. Before we can call our Web service, make sure that our ArrayList object al is empty by executing the clear() method.
F. The queryFaculty() method defined in our Web service is called to perform this faculty data query. Two points to be noted are: (1) the argument of this method is a selected

```
  private void cmdSelectActionPerformed(java.awt.event.ActionEvent evt) {
    // TODO add your handling code here:
A   javax.swing.JTextField[] f_field = {IDField, NameField, OfficeField, PhoneField, CollegeField, TitleField, EmailField};
B   ArrayList al = new ArrayList();

    try {
C       org.ws.sql.WebServiceSQLService service = new org.ws.sql.WebServiceSQLService();
D       org.ws.sql.WebServiceSQL port = service.getWebServiceSQLPort();
E       al.clear();
F       al = (ArrayList)port.queryFaculty(ComboName.getSelectedItem().toString());
G       for (int col = 0; col < al.size(); col++)
          f_field[col].setText(al.get(col).toString());
    }
H   catch (Exception ex){
      System.out.println("exception: " + ex);
    }
    if (!ShowFaculty()){
      msgDlg.setMessage("No matched faculty image found!");
      msgDlg.setVisible(true);
    }
  }
```

Figure 9.32. The modified codes for the cmdSelectActionPerformed() method.

faculty name obtained from the getSelectedItem() method from the Faculty Name combo box ComboName. Since this method returns an object, a toString() method must be attached to convert it to a string. (2) An ArrayList cast must be used to make sure that the returned query result is in this ArrayList type, since an ArrayList<String> type is used in our Web service project. The query result is assigned to our ArrayList instance al.

G. A for loop is used to pick up each column from the query result using the get() method. Two points to be noted are: (1) the argument of the get() method indicates the index of each column in the returned query result that is a single row, and that the data type of this method is an object. Therefore, a toString() method must be attached to convert it to a string. (2) To assign each column to each item in the f_field array, the setText() method must be used.

H. The catch block is used to track and display any possible exception during this Web service calling process.

During the coding process, you may encounter some real-time compiling errors. Most of these errors are introduced by missing some packages that contain classes or components used in this file. To fix these errors, just right click on this code window and select the Fix Imports item to load and import those missed packages to the top of this code window.

Now we have finished all coding process for this faculty data query action. Before we can build and run our project to test its function, we need to copy and save all images used in this project, including both faculty and students' image files, to our current project folder. Perform the following actions to finish this image files processing:

1. Open the Images folder that is located at the Wiley ftp site (refer to Figure 1.2 in Chapter 1), copy all image files from that folder.

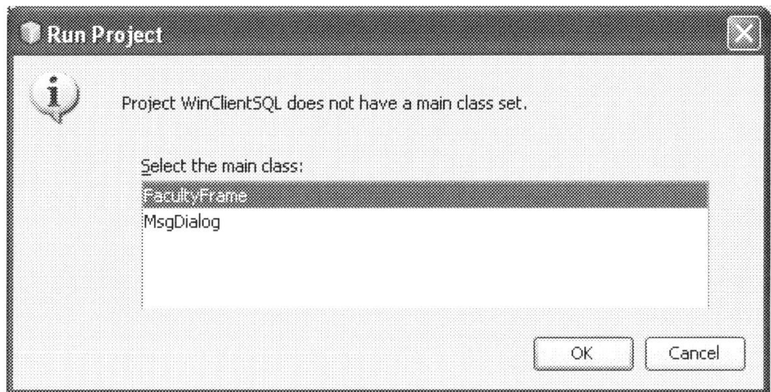

Figure 9.33. The Run Project dialog.

2. In the NetBeans IDE, open our project WinClientSQL and click on the Files button to open the Files window. Then right click on our project WinClientSQL and select the Paste item to paste all image files into our current project node WinClientSQL.

Now we are ready to build and run our client project to test its function to call our Web service to perform the faculty data query.

9.6.4 Build and Run Our Client Project to Query Faculty Data via Web Service

Click on the Clean and Build Main Project button to build our client project. If everything is fine, click on the Run Main Project button to run our client project.

A message box may be pup up to ask the main starting class, which is shown in Figure 9.33. Select our FacultyFrame class as the starting class, and click on the OK button to run the project.

The FacultyFrame form window is displayed, as shown in Figure 9.34.

Select a desired faculty member, such as Ying Bai, from the Faculty Name combo box, and click on the Select button to query the detailed information for this faculty via our Web service WebServiceSQL. The queried result is displayed in this form, as shown in Figure 9.34.

Our Web service and client projects are very successful!

Next, let's build a Web-based client project to consume our Web service WebServiceSQL to perform the faculty data query action.

9.7 BUILD A WEB-BASED CLIENT PROJECT TO CONSUME THE WEB SERVICE

To save time and space, we can use some components in a Web application project JavaWebDBJSPOracle we developed in Chapter 8 to build our Web-based client

Figure 9.34. The running result of our client project.

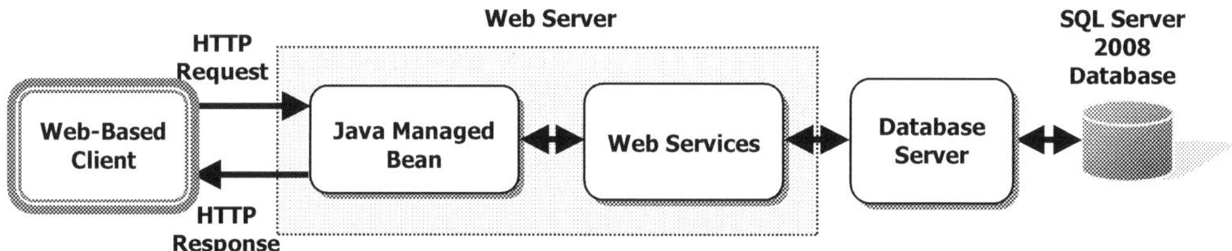

Figure 9.35. The architecture of our Web-based client project.

consuming project WebClientSQL in this section. In fact, we will use the FacultyPage.jsp file and a Java managed bean class in that project to query faculty data from our sample SQL Server database.

The structure of this Web-based client project is shown in Figure 9.35.

9.7.1 Create a Web-Based Client Project WebClientSQL

Perform the following operations to create a new Web application project WebClientSQL:

1. Launch NetBeans IDE and go to File > New Project item to open the `New Project` wizard. Select the Java Web from the `Categories` list and Web Application from the `Projects` list, then click on the Next button to go to the next wizard.
2. Enter WebClientSQL into the `Project Name` field as this new project's name. Make sure that the desired folder in which you want to save this project is included in the `Project Location` field and the `Set as Main Project` checkbox has been checked, then click on the Next button.
3. In the opened `Server and Settings` wizard, make sure that the GlassFish v3 server has been selected as the Web server for this Web application, and the Java EE 6 Web has been selected for this application. Refer to Section 5.3.5.2.2 in Chapter 5 to add this server to the NetBeans IDE if you have not done this. Click on the Next button to continue.

4. Select the JavaServer Faces as the Framework for this application, and click on the Finish button to complete this new Web application creation process.

Since we need a JavaServer Face as a view to query data from the Faculty table in our sample database, we need to add the FacultyPage.jsp we built in the project JavaWebDBJSPOracle in Chapter 8 into our current project. Perform the following operations to complete this Web page addition process:

1. Open the JSP Files folder that is located at the Wiley ftp site (refer to Figure 1.2 in Chapter 1), and copy the FacultyPage.jsp file from that folder.
2. In the NetBeans IDE, open our project WebClientSQL and click on the Files button to open the Files window. Then right click on the web node under our project WebClientSQL and select the Paste item to paste this JSF page into our current project.

Next, we need to create a Java managed bean class FacultyBean.java and copy the codes from the managed bean FacultyMBean.java we built in the Web application project JavaWebDBJSPOracle, and paste them into our managed bean class FacultyBean.java in our Web-based client project.

9.7.2 Create a Java Managed Bean FacultyMBean and Add the JDialog Class MsgDialog

Perform the following operations to create this Java managed bean and add a MsgDialog class into our current project:

1. Right click our Web-based client project WebClientSQL from the Projects window and select New > Other item to open the `New File` wizard.
2. On the opened wizard, select JavaServer Faces from the `Categories` and JSF Managed Bean from the `File Types` list, respectively. Then click on the Next button.
3. Name this managed bean as FacultyMBean, enter webclient into the `Package` field and select the session from the `Scope` combo box. Then click on the Finish button to complete this JSF managed bean creation process.
4. Double click on our newly created managed bean FacultyMBean.java to open its code window.
5. Now open the Web application project JavaWebDBJSPOracle we built in Chapter 8. You can find and download this project from the folder DBProjects\Chapter 8 at the Wiley ftp site (refer to Figure 1.2 in Chapter 1).
6. Expand the package JavaWebDBJSPOracle and copy all codes inside the managed bean class FacultyMBean (exclude the imported packages at the top of this file).
7. In our opened managed bean FacultyMBean.java, paste all copied codes inside this class.

Perform the following operations to add the MsgDialog class into our current project:

1. Launch the NetBeans IDE and open the Web application project JavaWebDBJSPSQL. You can find and download this project from the folder DBProjects\Chapter 8 at the Wiley ftp site (refer to Figure 1.2 in Chapter 1).

2. Expand the package JavaWebDBJSPSQL and copy the file MsgDialog.java.
3. Open our Web-based client project WebClientSQL and right click on the webclient node, and select the Paste item to paste this class into our project.

Next, let's do some modifications to the Java managed bean class to make it our bean class. Perform the following modifications to this class:

1. Remove the first EJB injection line @EJB from this file.
2. Remove the second line, which is the session bean declaration statement private FacultySessionBean facultySessionBean; from the class file.
3. Remove all codes inside the following methods except the last line return null:
   A. Select()
   B. Insert()
   C. Update()
   D. Delete()
4. Add an import statement, import java.util.List;, to the top of this file.
5. Remove the default constructor public FacultyMBean() {}.
6. Click on the Clean and Build Main Project button to compile the project.

Before we can develop the codes for the Java managed bean to perform faculty data query, we need first to add a Web reference to our current Web-based client project to enable our client to recognize our Web service and its operations.

9.7.3 Create a Web Service Reference for Our Web-Based Client Project

Perform the following operations to set up a Web service reference for our client project:

1. Right click on our client project WebClientSQL from the Projects window, and select the New > Other item to open the `New File` wizard.
2. On the opened `New File` wizard, and select Web Services from the `Categories` and Web Service Client from the `File Types` list, respectively. Click on the Next button to continue.
3. Click the Browse button for the Project field and expand our Web application project WebServiceSQLApp, and click on our Web service project WebServiceSQL to select it. Then click the OK button to select this Web service. Your finished Web Service Client wizard should match the one that is shown in Figure 9.36.
4. Click the Finish button to complete this Web service reference setup process.

Immediately, you can find that a new node named Web Service References has been created and added into our client project. Expand this node and you can find the associated Web service port and our Web service operation QueryFaculty() under that node.

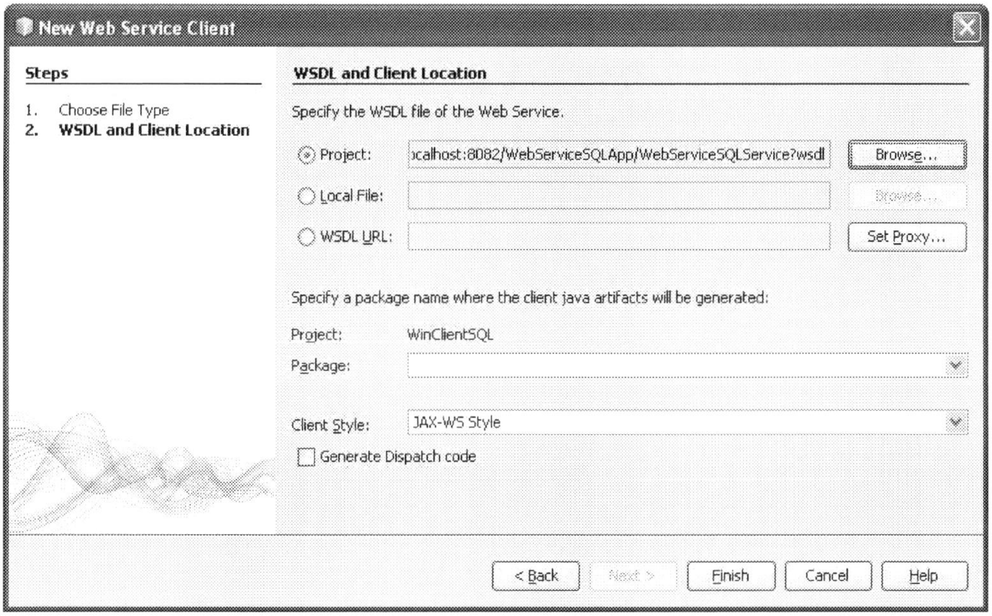

Figure 9.36. The finished New Web Service Client wizard.

A point to be noted is that you must deploy our Web service project first before you can add this Web Reference to any client project.

Now let's develop the codes to the different methods defined in the Java managed bean FacultyMBean one by one to perform data actions against the Faculty table in our sample database by calling the associated operations defined in our Web service project.

9.7.4 Build the Codes to Call the Web Service to Perform Data Query

First, let's concentrate on the Select() method. The function of this method is to:

1. Call our Web service operation QueryFaculty() to pick up a matched faculty record from the Faculty table in our sample database.
2. Assign each queried column to the associated property defined in our Java managed bean class FacultyMBean.java.

Each queried column will be reflected and displayed in the associated text field in our JSF page FacultyPage.jsp since they have been bound together.

There are two ways available to develop the codes inside the Select() method to call our Web service operation QueryFaculty() to perform the faculty data query: (1) drag the Web service operation node from the Projects window, and drop it to inside the

```
  public String Select() {
      try { // Call Web Service Operation
A        org.ws.sql.WebServiceSQLService service = new org.ws.sql.WebServiceSQLService();
B        org.ws.sql.WebServiceSQL port = service.getWebServiceSQLPort();
         // TODO initialize WS operation arguments here
C        java.lang.String fname = "";
         // TODO process result here
D        java.util.List<java.lang.Object> result = port.queryFaculty(fname);
         System.out.println("Result = "+result);
E     } catch (Exception ex) {
         // TODO handle custom exceptions here
      }
      return null;
  }
```

Figure 9.37. The automatically added codes by dragging the operation node.

Select() method, and (2) right click on any place inside the Select() method, and select the Insert Code item and choose the Call Web Service Operation item from the pop-up menu.

Let's use the first method as an example to add the codes to call our Web service operation.

1. Expand the Web Service References node under our Web-based client project WebClientSQL, and continue to expand the subservice port until our operation QueryFaculty node.
2. Open the code window of our Java managed bean class FacultyMBean.java, and browse to the Select() method.
3. Drag our Web service operation QueryFaculty node and place it inside the Select() method in our managed bean.

A piece of codes is automatically created and added into this method, which has been highlighted in bold and shown in Figure 9.37.

It is unnecessary to explain the function of this piece of codes line by line since all of coding lines have been illustrated by the built-in comments.

Now let's do some modifications to this piece of codes and add some codes to meet our data query requirements. Perform the following operations to make this piece of codes to perform our desired faculty data query:

A. An ArrayList instance al and a MsgDialog instance msgDlg are created first. The first local variable al is used to hold the returned query, and the second is used to display some debug information during the project runs.

B. Remove the code line java.lang.String fname = "";.

C. Replace the rest of the codes with a piece of codes that are shown in steps **C**, **D**, **E**, and **F** in Figure 9.38. First, the queryFaculty() operation in our Web service is executed to perform the faculty data query, and the result is returned and assigned to the local variable al. One point to be noted is that this returned result must be casted with ArrayList class, since the ArrayList<String> data type is used for this query result in our Web service operation.

```
  public String Select() {
A       ArrayList al = new ArrayList();
        MsgDialog msgDlg = new MsgDialog(new javax.swing.JFrame(), true);
        try { // Call Web Service Operation
            org.ws.sql.WebServiceSQLService service = new org.ws.sql.WebServiceSQLService();
            org.ws.sql.WebServiceSQL port = service.getWebServiceSQLPort();
B           // TODO process result here
C           al = (ArrayList)port.queryFaculty(facultyName);
D           facultyID = al.get(0).toString();
            name = al.get(1).toString();
            office = al.get(2).toString();
            phone = al.get(3).toString();
            college = al.get(4).toString();
            title = al.get(5).toString();
            email = al.get(6).toString();
E           facultyImage = getFacultyImage();
F       } catch (Exception ex) {
            // TODO handle custom exceptions here
            msgDlg.setMessage("Exception in Query Faculty Table: " + ex);
            msgDlg.setVisible(true);
        }
        return null;
  }
```

Figure 9.38. The modified codes for the method Select().

D. Seven returned columns are assigned to the associated properties defined in this managed bean FacultyMBean.java class, and will be displayed in the associated text field in our JSF page FacultyPage.jsp, since each of those tags has been bound to each associated property. The get() method is used to pick up each column from the returned query result, and a toString() method is used to convert each column to a String and assigned each of them to the associated property.

E. The getter method getFacultyImage() is executed to pick up a matched faculty image and display it in the faculty image box in our JSF page FacultyPage.jsp. Refer to that getter method to get the detailed codes for this method defined in this Java managed bean.

F. The catch block is used to track and display any possible exception during this Web service operation calling process.

During the coding process, you may encounter some real-time compiling errors. Most of these errors are introduced by missing some packages that contain classes or components used in this file. To fix these errors, just right click on this code window and select the Fix Imports item to load and import those missed packages to the top of this code window.

Now we have finished all coding process for this faculty data query action. Before we can build and run our project to test its function, we need to copy and save all images used in this project, including both faculty and students' image files, to our current project folder. Perform the following actions to finish this image files processing:

1. Open the Images folder that is located at the Wiley ftp site (refer to Figure 1.2 in Chapter 1), copy all image files from that folder.

2. In the NetBeans IDE, open our project WebClientSQL and click on the Files button to open the Files window. Then, right click on the web node under our project WebClientSQL and select the Paste item to paste all image files into our current project node WebClientSQL.

Now we are ready to build and run our client project to test its function.

9.7.5 Build and Run Our Client Project to Query Faculty Data via Web Service

Click on the Clean and Build Main Project button to build our client project. If everything is fine, right click on our JSF page FacultyPage.jsp from the Projects window and choose the Run File item to run our client project.

On the opened JSF page, which is shown in Figure 9.39, enter a desired faculty name, such as Ying Bai, into the `Faculty Name` field. Then click the Select button to perform a query for this selected faculty member. The query result is returned and displayed in this page, as shown in Figure 9.39.

Our Web client project to consume our Web service WebServiceSQL is successful! A complete Web client project WebClientSQL can be found from the folder DBProjects\Chapter 9 that is located at the Wiley ftp site (refer to Figure 1.2 in Chapter 1).

Next, let's discuss how to build a Web service to perform data insertion into our sample SQL Server database.

9.8 BUILD JAVA WEB SERVICE TO INSERT DATA INTO THE SQL SERVER DATABASE

To perform a faculty record insertion action using our Web service, we need to add another operation or method called InsertFaculty() into our Web service project WebServiceSQL.

Figure 9.39. The testing result for our Web client project.

9.8.1 Add a New Operation InsertFaculty() into Our Web Service Project

Perform the following operations to add this operation into our Web service:

1. Launch NetBeans IDE and open our Web service project WebServiceSQLApp, and select our Web service main class file WebServiceSQL.java from the Projects window.
2. Click on the Design button on the top of the window to open the Design View of our Web service project WebServiceSQL.
3. Click on the Add Operation button to open the `Add Operation` wizard.
4. Enter InsertFaculty into the `Name` field and click on the Browse button that is next to the `Return Type` combo box. Type boolean into the `Type Name` field and select the item Boolean (java.lang) from the list, and click on the OK button.
5. Click on the Add button and enter fdata into the `Name` parameter field. Then click on the drop-down arrow of the Type combo box, and select the Choose item to open the `Find Type` wizard. Type arraylist into the top field, and select the ArrayList (java.util) data type, and click on the OK button to select an ArrayList as the data type for the input parameter.

Your finished `Add Operation` wizard should match the one that is shown in Figure 9.40. Click on the OK button to complete this new operation creation process.

Click on the Source button on the top of this window to open the code window of our Web service project. Let's perform the coding for this newly added operation.

On the opened code window, enter the codes that are shown in Figure 9.41 into this newly added operation InsertFaculty().

Let's have a closer look at this piece of codes to see how it works.

A. First, a local integer variable numInsert is created, and it is used to hold the running result of inserting a new faculty record into our sample database.

B. The SQL inserting query statement is created with seven positional parameters as the dynamic parameters for seven pieces of new faculty information to be inserted.

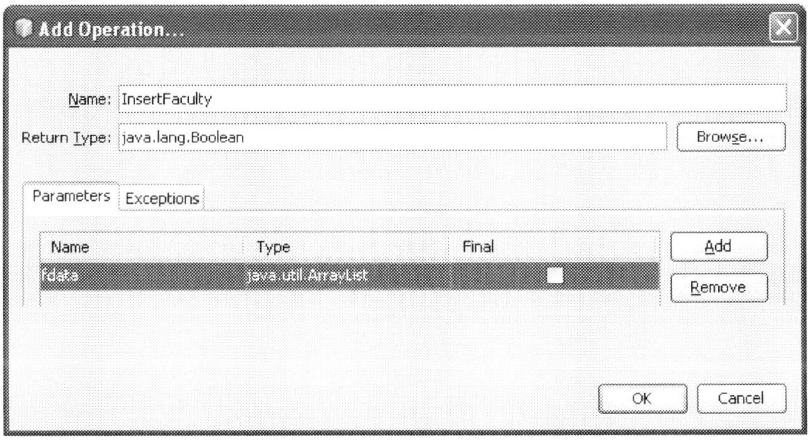

Figure 9.40. The complete Add Operation wizard.

```
  @WebMethod(operationName = "InsertFaculty")
    public Boolean InsertFaculty(@WebParam(name = "fdata")
    ArrayList fdata) {
      //TODO write your implementation code here:
A     int numInsert = 0;
B     String query = "INSERT INTO Faculty (faculty_id, faculty_name, office, " +
                      "phone, college, title, email) VALUES (?, ?, ?, ?, ?, ?, ?)";
      try {
C       con = DBConnection(con);
D       PreparedStatement pstmt =con.prepareStatement(query);
E       pstmt.setString(1, fdata.get(0).toString());
        pstmt.setString(2, fdata.get(1).toString());
        pstmt.setString(3, fdata.get(2).toString());
        pstmt.setString(4, fdata.get(3).toString());
        pstmt.setString(5, fdata.get(4).toString());
        pstmt.setString(6, fdata.get(5).toString());
        pstmt.setString(7, fdata.get(6).toString());
F       numInsert = pstmt.executeUpdate();
G       con.close();
H       if (numInsert != 0)
          return true;
I       else
          return false;
      }
J     catch (Exception ex) {
        msgDlg.setMessage("exception is: " + ex);
        msgDlg.setVisible(true);
        return false;
      }
  }
```

Figure 9.41. The codes for the new operation InsertFaculty().

C. The user-defined method DBConnection() is called to set up a connection between our Web service and our sample database. A connection instance con is returned after the execution of this method.

D. A new PreparedStatement instance pstmt is created to perform this insertion query.

E. Seven setString() methods are used to set up the actual values for seven positional dynamic parameters in the inserting query statement. One point to be noted is that the order of these setString() methods must be identical with the order of columns in our Faculty table.

F. The inserting action is performed by calling the executeUpdate() method, and the inserting result is returned and stored in the local integer variable numInsert.

G. The database connection is closed by executing the close() method, since we have completed our data insertion action and need to disconnect with our database.

H. The executeUpdate() method will return an integer to indicate whether this data insertion is successful or not. If a nonzero value is returned, which means that at least one row has been inserted into our Faculty table, then this data inserting action is successful, and a `true` is returned to the client project.

I. Otherwise, no row has been inserted into our sample database, and this data insertion has failed. A `false` is returned for this situation.

J. The catch block is used to track and display any exception occurred during this data insertion process, and a `false` will be returned if this situation is really happened.

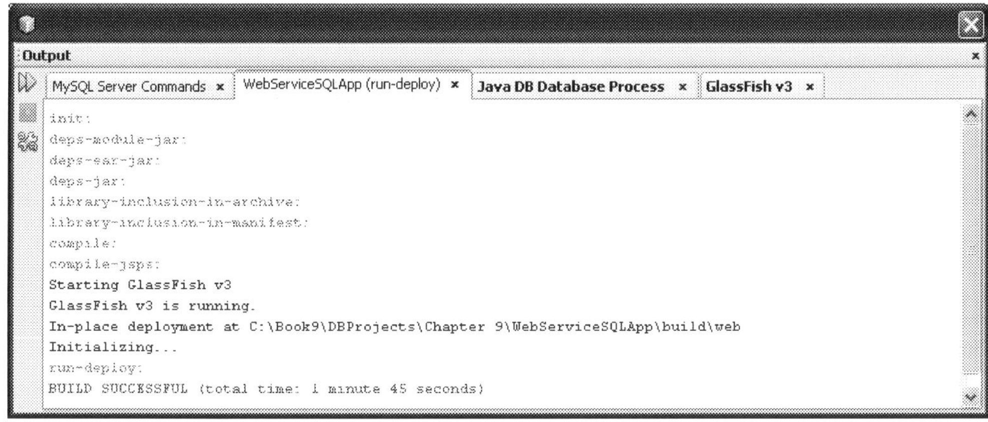

Figure 9.42. The deployment result of our Web service project.

At this point, we have completed all coding development for the data insertion action. Now let's build and run our Web service project to test its function.

9.8.2 Deploy the Web Service Project

Perform the following operations to build and deploy our Web service project:

1. Click on the Clean and Build Main Project button to build our Web service.
2. Right click on our Web application WebServiceSQLApp and select the Deploy item to deploy our Web service. If everything is fine, a successful deployment result should be displayed, as shown in Figure 9.42.

A problem arises when testing this Web service project using the tester page, which is the input parameter array fdata. As we know, the fdata has a data type of ArrayList, and it needs to (1) create an ArrayList instance, and then (2) assign a group of faculty information to that ArrayList object to call this Web service operation InsertFaculty() to perform the faculty data insertion. However, it is difficult to do those two operations manually by using this tester page. Therefore, we need to create some Web client projects to consume and test this Web service project.

Next, we can develop some Web client projects to consume this Web service to perform data insertion to the Faculty table in our sample database. First, let's discuss how to build a Windows-based client project to consume our Web service.

9.9 BUILD A WINDOWS-BASED WEB CLIENT PROJECT TO CONSUME THE WEB SERVICE

We can still use the Windows-based client project WinClientSQL we built in Section 9.6 to consume the Web service to perform faculty data inserting action. One point to be noted is that although a Web reference to our Web service has been established in Section 9.6, we still need to refresh this Web reference, since our Web service project has been modified by adding one more operation InsertFaculty() in our Web service. Otherwise, we would still use the old Web service that does not include this InsertFaculty() operation.

9.9.1 Refresh the Web Service Reference for Our Windows-Based Client Project

In order to call this InsertFaculty() operation in our Web service project WebServiceSQL, we need to refresh the Web reference in our Windows-based client project to use the updated Web service project. Perform the following operations to refresh the Web service reference:

1. Open our Windows-based client project WinClientSQL and expand the Web Service References node.
2. Right click on our Web service WebServiceSQLService and choose the Delete item to remove this old Web reference.
3. Right click on our Windows-based client project WinClientSQL and select the New > Web Service Client item to open the `New Web Service Client` wizard.
4. On the opened wizard, click on the Browse button that is next to the Project field and expand our Web application WebServiceSQLApp. Then choose our Web service WebServiceSQL by clicking on it, and click on the OK button.
5. Click on the Finish button to complete this Web service reference refreshing process.

Now that we have refreshed or updated the Web service reference for our Windows-based client project WinClientSQL, next, let's develop the codes in our client project to call that Web service operation InsertFaculty() to perform faculty data insertion.

9.9.2 Develop the Codes to Call Our Web Service Project

Open the Windows-based client project WinClientSQL and double click on our main class FacultyFrame.java to open it. Click on the Design button to open the graphic user interface. In this client project, we want to use the Insert button in this form as a trigger to start the faculty data insertion action. Therefore, double click on the Insert button to open its event method cmdInsertActionPerformed() and enter the codes that are shown in Figure 9.43 into this method.

Let's have a closer look at this piece of codes to see how it works.

- **A.** First, a new ArrayList instance al is created and initialized. This variable is used to pick up and reserve the input new faculty data array.
- **B.** The add() method is used to pick up and add seven pieces of new faculty information into this new ArrayList instance al. Seven pieces of new faculty information are entered by the user and stored in seven text fields in this FacultyFrame window form. The toString() method is used to convert each piece of new faculty information obtained using the getText() method that returns an object data type to a String. The index is necessary since it is used to indicate the position of each parameter in this ArrayList. One point to be

```
  void cmdInsertActionPerformed(java.awt.event.ActionEvent evt) {
      // TODO add your handling code here:
A     ArrayList al = new ArrayList();
      al.clear();
B     al.add(0, IDField.getText().toString());
      al.add(1, NameField.getText().toString());
      al.add(2, OfficeField.getText().toString());
      al.add(3, PhoneField.getText().toString());
      al.add(4, CollegeField.getText().toString());
      al.add(5, TitleField.getText().toString());
      al.add(6, EmailField.getText().toString());
C     try {
        org.ws.sql.WebServiceSQLService service = new org.ws.sql.WebServiceSQLService();
        org.ws.sql.WebServiceSQL port = service.getWebServiceSQLPort();
D       Boolean insert = port.insertFaculty(al);
E       if (!insert) {
          msgDlg.setMessage("The data insertion is failed!");
          msgDlg.setVisible(true);
        }
F       else
          ComboName.addItem(NameField.getText());
      }
G     catch (Exception ex){
        System.out.println("exception: " + ex);
      }
  }
```

Figure 9.43. The codes for the Insert button event method.

noted is the order of adding these text fields, which must be identical with order of columns in our Faculty table.

C. A try catch block is used to perform the calling of our Web service operation InsertFaculty() to perform this faculty data inserting action. First, a new Web service instance service is created based on our Web service class WebServiceSQLService. Then the getWebServiceSQLPort() method is executed to get the current port used by our Web service. This port is returned and assigned to a new Port instance port.

D. The Web service operation InsertFaculty() is executed with the ArrayList instance al that has been filled with seven pieces of new faculty information as the argument of this method. The running result of that operation is returned and assigned to a Boolean variable insert.

E. If the value of the variable insert is `false`, which means that no row has been inserted into our Faculty table, and this insertion has been failed, the msgDlg instance is used to show this situation.

F. Otherwise, if the value of the insert variable is true, which means that this data insertion is successful, the newly inserted faculty name will be added into the Faculty Name combo box ComboName using the addItem() method.

G. The catch block is used to track and display any possible exception during this Web service operation execution.

Now let's build and run our client project to call and test our Web service to perform faculty data inserting action.

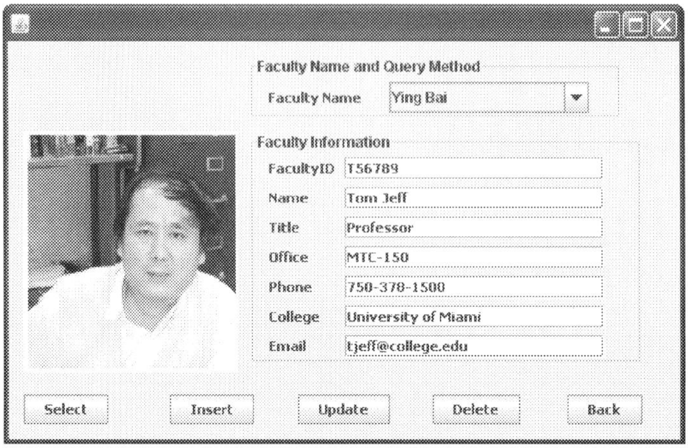

Figure 9.44. The seven pieces of newly inserted faculty information.

9.9.3 Build and Run Our Client Project to Insert Faculty Data via Web Service

Click on the Clean and Build Main Project button to build our client project. If everything is fine, click on the Run Main Project button to run our client project.

The FacultyFrame form window is displayed. First, let's perform a faculty query action. Select a desired faculty member, such as Ying Bai, from the Faculty Name combo box, and click on the Select button to query the detailed information for this faculty via our Web service WebServiceSQL. The queried result is displayed in seven text fields.

Now, enter a new faculty record with seven pieces of new faculty information shown below into seven text fields, which is shown in Figure 9.44.

- Faculty ID: T56789
- Name: Tom Jeff
- Title: Professor
- Office: MTC-150
- Phone: 750-378-1500
- College: University of Miami
- Email: tjeff@college.edu

Click on the Insert button to try to call our Web service operation InsertFaculty() to insert this new faculty record into the Faculty table in our sample database.

To confirm this data insertion, two methods can be used. First, we can open our Faculty table using either the Services window in the NetBeans IDE or the SQL Server 2008 Management Studio to check whether this new faculty record has been inserted. To do that using the Services window in the NetBeans IDE, perform the following operations:

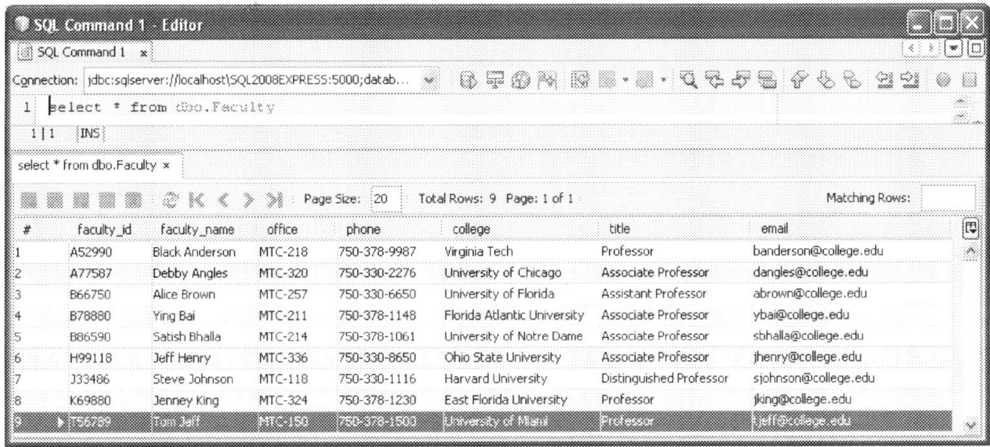

Figure 9.45. The opened Faculty table in the NetBeans IDE.

1. Open the Services window and expand the Databases node.
2. Right click on our SQL Server database URL: jdbc:sqlserver://localhost\SQL2008EXPRESS: 5000; databaseName=CSE_DEPT [ybai on dbo], and select the Connect item to connect to our database.
3. Expand our sample database CSE_DEPT and Tables.
4. Right click on the Faculty table and select the View Data item.

Your opened Faculty table is shown in Figure 9.45.

It can be found that the new faculty record with the faculty_id of T56789, which is located at the last row and has been highlighted in dark color, has been successfully inserted into our database.

The second way to confirm this data insertion, which is simpler, is to use the Select button in this form to perform a query to try to retrieve the inserted faculty record.

To do this checking in second way, go to the Faculty Name combo box, and you can find that the new faculty name Tom Jeff has been added into this box. Click it to select it, and click on the Select button. Do not worry about the exception message for the faculty image, since we did not insert any image for this newly inserted faculty. Just click on the OK button for that message box, and you can find that seven pieces of newly inserted faculty information have been retrieved and displayed in this form window. Our data insertion is successful!

It is highly recommended to remove this newly inserted faculty record from our database since we want to keep our database clean. You can delete this record by opening the SQL Server 2008 Management Studio to do it.

Next, let's build a Web-based client project to consume our Web service to insert a new faculty record into the Faculty table in our sample database.

9.10 BUILD A WEB-BASED CLIENT PROJECT TO CONSUME THE WEB SERVICE

We can still use a Web-based client project WebClientSQL we built in Section 9.7 to consume our Web service to perform the faculty data insertion action. First, let's refresh the Web service reference used for our Web-based client project to allow it to use the updated Web service operations.

9.10.1 Refresh the Web Service Reference for Our Web-Based Client Project

In order to call the InsertFaculty() operation in our Web service project WebServiceSQL, we need to refresh the Web reference in our Web-based client project WebClientSQL to use the updated Web service project. Perform the following operations to refresh the Web service reference:

1. Open our Web-based client project WebClientSQL and expand the Web Service References node.
2. Right click on our Web service WebServiceSQLService and choose the Delete item to remove this old Web reference.
3. Right click on our Web-based client project WebClientSQL and select the New > Web Service Client item to open the `New Web Service Client` wizard.
4. On the opened wizard, click on the Browse button that is next to the Project field and expand our Web application WebServiceSQLApp. Then choose our Web service WebServiceSQL by clicking on it, and click on the OK button.
5. Click on the Finish button to complete this Web service reference refreshing process.

Now that we have refreshed or updated the Web service reference for our Web-based client project WebClientSQL, next, let's develop the codes in our client project to call that Web service operation InsertFaculty() to perform faculty data insertion.

9.10.2 Develop the Codes to Call Our Web Service Project

The main coding process is in the Java managed bean class FacultyMBean.java.

As we know, a binding relationship between the action attribute of the Insert commandButton in our JSF page FacultyPage.jsp and the Insert() method in our Java managed bean class FacultyMBean.java has been established. Therefore, we can concentrate on the coding for the Insert() method in our Java managed bean.

Open our Web-based client project WebClientSQL and double click on the FacultyMBean.java from the Projects window to open this managed bean class file. Let's do the coding for the Insert() method in this class to fulfill this data insertion function.

Browse to the Insert() method and drag the Web service operation InsertFaculty under the WebService References node and place it inside the Insert() method. A piece of codes is created and added into this method, as shown in Figure 9.46.

It is unnecessary to explain the function of this piece of codes line by line since all of coding lines have been illustrated by the built-in comments.

Now let's do some modifications to this piece of codes and add some codes to meet our data insertion requirements. Enter the codes that are shown in Figure 9.47 into this method.

Let's have a closer look at this piece of new added codes to see how it works.

A. First, a new ArrayList instance al is created and initialized. This variable is used to pick up and reserve the input new faculty data array.

```
  public String Insert() {
A       try { // Call Web Service Operation
B         org.ws.sql.WebServiceSQL port = service.getWebServiceSQLPort();
          // TODO initialize WS operation arguments here
C         java.util.List<java.lang.Object> fdata = null;
          // TODO process result here
D         java.lang.Boolean result = port.insertFaculty(fdata);
          System.out.println("Result = "+result);
E       } catch (Exception ex) {
          // TODO handle custom exceptions here
        }
        return null;
  }
```

Figure 9.46. The automatically created codes by dragging the operation node.

```
  public String Insert() {
A       ArrayList al = new ArrayList();
        MsgDialog msgDlg = new MsgDialog(new javax.swing.JFrame(), true);

B       al.clear();
C       al.add(0, facultyID);
        al.add(1, name);
        al.add(2, office);
        al.add(3, phone);
        al.add(4, college);
        al.add(5, title);
        al.add(6, email);

        try { // Call Web Service Operation
          org.ws.sql.WebServiceSQL port = service.getWebServiceSQLPort();
          // TODO initialize WS operation arguments here
D         Boolean insert = port.insertFaculty(al);
E         if (!insert) {
            msgDlg.setMessage("The data insertion is failed!");
            msgDlg.setVisible(true);
          }
F       } catch (Exception ex) {
          // TODO handle custom exceptions here
          msgDlg.setMessage("exception: " + ex);
          msgDlg.setVisible(true);
        }
G       return null;
  }
```

Figure 9.47. The modified codes for the Insert() method.

B. The clear() method is executed to make sure that the ArrayList instance is clean before a new faculty record is collected.

C. The add() method is used to pick up and add seven pieces of new faculty information into this new ArrayList instance al. Seven pieces of new faculty information are entered by the user in the JSF page FacultyPage.jsp, and stored in seven properties defined in this managed bean.

D. The InsertFaculty() operation in our Web service is called with the ArrayList instance that contains seven pieces of new faculty information as the argument. The execution result of this faculty data insertion is returned and assigned to the local Boolean variable insert.

E. If the returned Boolean variable insert is false, which means that this data insertion has failed, the msgDlg instance is used to indicate this situation.

F. The catch block is used to catch any possible exception during this data insertion process.

G. Finally a null is returned since it is not important to our application.

Now let's build and run our Web client project to call our Web service operation to perform the faculty data inserting action.

9.10.3 Build and Run Our Client Project to Insert Faculty Data via Web Service

Click on the Clean and Build Main Project button to build our client project. If everything is fine, right click on our JSF page FacultyPage.jsp from the Projects window and choose the Run File item to run our client project.

On the opened JSF page, first, let's perform a faculty record query by entering a desired faculty name, such as Ying Bai, into the `Faculty Name` field, and then click on the Select button to get details for this selected faculty member. To insert a new faculty record, enter seven pieces of new faculty information shown below into the associated seven text fields, as shown in Figure 9.48.

- Faculty ID: T56789
- Name: Tom Jeff
- Title: Professor
- Office: MTC-150
- Phone: 750-378-1500
- College: University of Miami
- Email: tjeff@college.edu

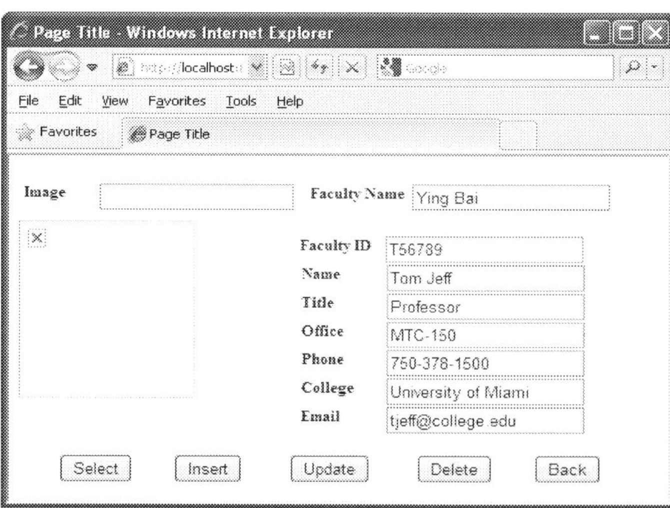

Figure 9.48. Seven pieces of new inserted faculty information.

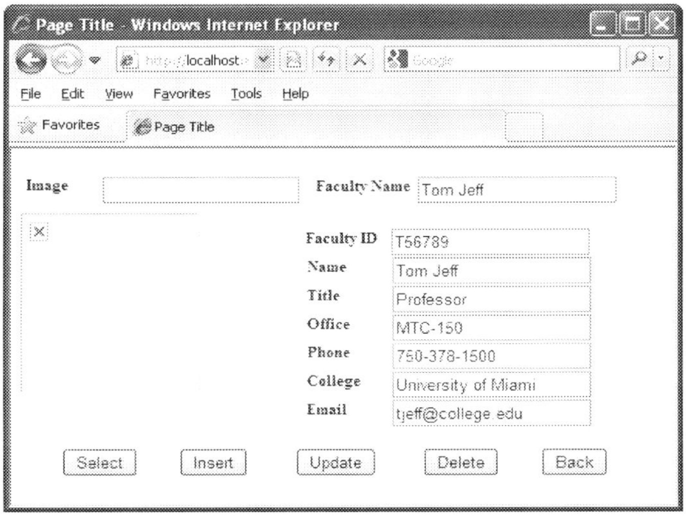

Figure 9.49. The confirmation of a new faculty record insertion.

Click on the Insert button to try to call our Web service operation InsertFaculty() to insert this new faculty record into the Faculty table in our sample database.

To confirm this data insertion, two ways can be used. The first way is to open our Faculty table using either the Services window in the NetBeans IDE or the SQL Server 2008 Management Studio to check whether this new faculty record has been inserted. The second way to confirm this data insertion, which is simpler, is to use the Select button in this form to perform a query to try to retrieve the inserted faculty record.

The second way to do this checking, first, you can perform another query for the selected faculty, such as Ying Bai, and then go to the `Faculty Name` combo box and type the new inserted faculty name Tom Jeff into this box. Click on the Select button to try to retrieve it. Now you can find that seven pieces of new inserted faculty information have been retrieved and displayed in this page, as shown in Figure 9.49.

It is highly recommended to remove this new inserted faculty record from our database since we want to keep our database clean. You can delete this record by opening the SQL Server 2008 Management Studio to do it.

Our Web client project to consume our Web service WebServiceSQL is successful! A complete Web client project WebClientSQL can be found from the folder DBProjects\Chapter 9 that is located at the Wiley ftp site (refer to Figure 1.2 in Chapter 1).

Next, let's discuss how to build a Web service to perform data updating and deleting against our sample SQL Server database.

9.11 BUILD JAVA WEB SERVICE TO UPDATE AND DELETE DATA FROM THE SQL SERVER DATABASE

To perform data updating and deleting actions against our sample SQL Server database via Web service is straightforward, and we can add two more new operations

UpdateFaculty() and DeleteFaculty() into our Web service project WebServiceSQL we built in the previous sections. First, let's concentrate on the faculty data updating action.

As we discussed in the previous sections, the key point to perform a faculty data updating is that in most real applications, all pieces of faculty information should be updated except the faculty_id, since it is much easier to insert a new faculty record with a new faculty_id than updating a record with an updated faculty_id because of the complexity in cascaded updating relationships we built in Chapter 2 when we create our sample database. Therefore, in this section, we will concentrate on the updating a faculty record based on an existing faculty_id.

9.11.1 Add a New Operation UpdateFaculty() to Perform the Faculty Data Updating

Perform the following operations to add a new operation UpdateFaculty() into our Web service project WebServiceSQL:

1. Launch NetBeans IDE and open our Web service project WebServiceSQLApp, and select our Web service main class file WebServiceSQL.java from the Projects window.
2. Click on the Design button on the top of the window to open the Design View of our Web service project WebServiceSQL.
3. Click on the Add Operation button to open the `Add Operation` wizard.
4. Enter UpdateFaculty into the `Name` field and click on the Browse button that is next to the `Return Type` combo box. Type boolean into the `Type Name` field and select the item Boolean (java.lang) from the list, and click on the OK button.
5. Click on the Add button and enter fdata into the `Name` parameter field. Then click on the drop-down arrow of the Type combo box, select the Choose item to open the `Find Type` wizard. Type arraylist into the top field and select the ArrayList (java.util) data type, and click on the OK button to select an ArrayList as the data type for the input parameter.

Your finished `Add Operation` wizard should match the one that is shown in Figure 9.50. Click on the OK button to complete this new operation creation process.

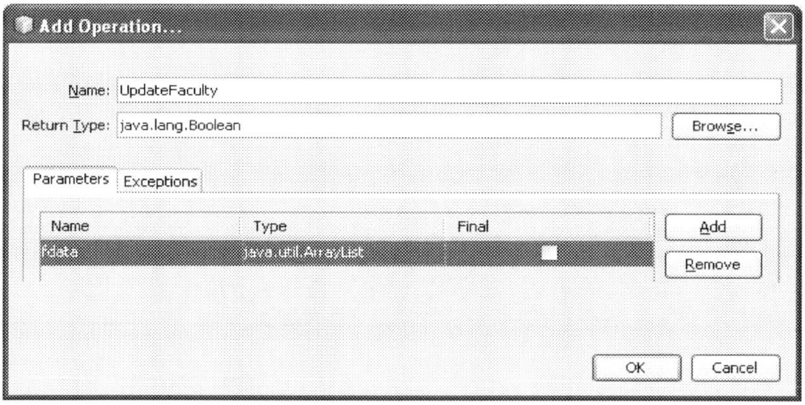

Figure 9.50. The complete Add Operation wizard.

```
  @WebMethod(operationName = "UpdateFaculty")
    public Boolean UpdateFaculty(@WebParam(name = "fdata")
    ArrayList fdata) {
     //TODO write your implementation code here:
A    int numUpdated = 0;
B    String query = "UPDATE Faculty SET faculty_name=?, office=?, phone=?, college=?, title=?, email=? " +
                      "WHERE faculty_name= ?";
     try {
C        con = DBConnection(con);
D        PreparedStatement pstmt =con.prepareStatement(query);
E        pstmt.setString(1, fdata.get(0).toString());
         pstmt.setString(2, fdata.get(1).toString());
         pstmt.setString(3, fdata.get(2).toString());
         pstmt.setString(4, fdata.get(3).toString());
         pstmt.setString(5, fdata.get(4).toString());
         pstmt.setString(6, fdata.get(5).toString());
         pstmt.setString(7, fdata.get(6).toString());
F        numUpdated = pstmt.executeUpdate();
G        con.close();
H        if (numUpdated != 0)
            return true;
I        else
            return false;
     }
J    catch (Exception ex) {
         msgDlg.setMessage("exception is: " + ex);
         msgDlg.setVisible(true);
         return false;
     }
  }
```

Figure 9.51. The codes for the new operation UpdateFaculty().

Click on the Source button on the top of this window to open the code window of our Web service project. Let's perform the coding for this newly added operation.

On the opened code window, enter the codes that are shown in Figure 9.51 into this newly added operation UpdateFaculty().

Let's have a closer look at this piece of codes to see how it works.

A. A local integer variable numUpdated is created first, and this variable is used to hold the running result of execution of the data updating operation.

B. The updating query string is created with six positional parameters. The query criterion is the faculty name that is the seventh positional parameter and placed after the WHERE clause.

C. The user-defined method DBConnection() is called to set up a connection between our Web service and our sample database. A connection instance con is returned after the execution of this method.

D. A new PreparedStatement instance pstmt is created to perform this updating query.

E. Seven setString() methods are used to set up the actual values for seven positional dynamic updated parameters in the updating query statement. One point to be noted is that the order of these setString() methods must be identical with the order of columns in our Faculty table.

F. The updating action is performed by calling the executeUpdate() method, and the updating result is returned and stored in the local integer variable numUpdated.

G. The database connection is closed by executing the close() method, since we have completed our data updating action and need to disconnect with our database.

H. The executeUpdate() method will return an integer to indicate whether this data updating is successful or not. If a nonzero value is returned, which means that at least one row has been updated in our Faculty table and this data updating action is successful, a `true` is returned to the client project.

I. Otherwise, no row has been updated in our sample database, and this data updating has failed. A `false` is returned for this situation.

J. The catch block is used to track and display any exception occurred during this data updating process, and a `false` will be returned if this situation is really happened.

Next, let's take care of the data deleting action against our sample database using Web service operation DeleteFaculty().

9.11.2 Add a New Operation DeleteFaculty() to Perform the Faculty Data Deleting

Perform the following operations to add a new operation DeleteFaculty() into our Web service project WebServiceSQL:

1. Launch NetBeans IDE and open our Web application project WebServiceSQLApp, and select our Web service main class file WebServiceSQL.java from the Projects window.
2. Click on the Design button on the top of the window to open the Design View of our Web service project WebServiceSQL.
3. Click on the Add Operation button to open the `Add Operation` wizard.
4. Enter DeleteFaculty into the `Name` field and click on the Browse button that is next to the `Return Type` combo box. Type boolean into the `Type Name` field, and select the item Boolean (java.lang) from the list, and click on the OK button.
5. Click on the Add button and enter fname into the `Name` parameter field to add a new parameter for this operation. Keep the default data type java.lang.String unchanged for this new added parameter fname.

Your finished `Add Operation` wizard should match the one that is shown in Figure 9.52. Click on the OK button to complete this new operation creation process.

Click on the Source button on the top of this window to open the code window of our Web service project. Let's perform the coding for this newly added operation.

On the opened code window, enter the codes that are shown in Figure 9.53 into this newly added operation DeleteFaculty().

Let's have a closer look at this piece of codes to see how it works.

A. A local integer variable numDeleted is created first, and this variable is used to hold the running result of execution of the data deleting operation.

B. The deleting query string is created with one positional parameter, which is the original faculty name that works as the query criterion and is placed after the WHERE clause.

C. A try catch block is used for this data deleting action. First, the user-defined method DBConnection() is called to set up a connection between our Web service and our sample database. A connection instance con is returned after the execution of this method.

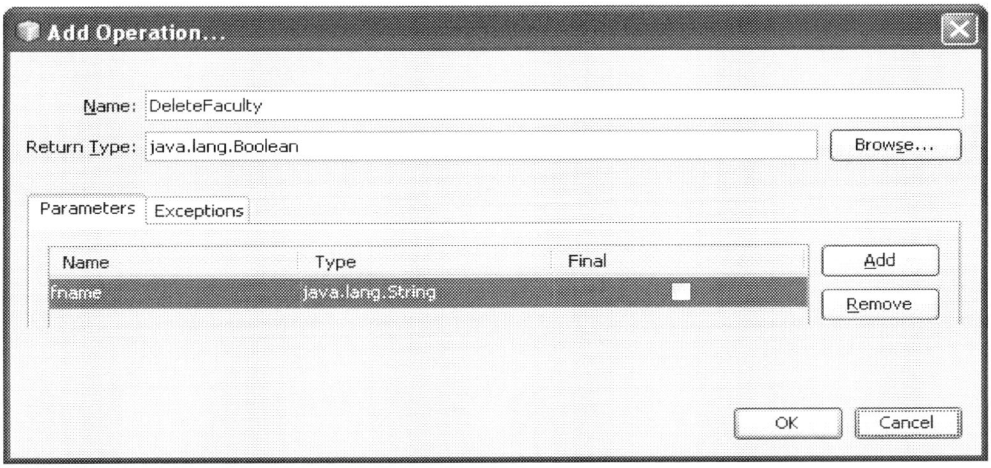

Figure 9.52. The complete Add Operation wizard.

```
  @WebMethod(operationName = "DeleteFaculty")
    public Boolean DeleteFaculty(@WebParam(name = "fname")
    String fname) {
      //TODO write your implementation code here:
A     int numDeleted = 0;
B     String query = "DELETE FROM Faculty WHERE faculty_name = ?";
      try {
C       con = DBConnection(con);
D       PreparedStatement pstmt =con.prepareStatement(query);
E       pstmt.setString(1, fname);
F       numDeleted = pstmt.executeUpdate();
G       con.close();
H       if (numDeleted != 0)
          return true;
I       else
          return false;
      }
J     catch (Exception ex) {
        msgDlg.setMessage("exception is: " + ex);
        msgDlg.setVisible(true);
        return false;
      }
  }
```

Figure 9.53. The codes for the new operation DeleteFaculty().

D. A new PreparedStatement instance pstmt is created to perform this deleting query.

E. The setString() method is used to set up the actual value for the positional dynamic parameter in the deleting query statement.

F. The deleting action is performed by calling the executeUpdate() method, and the deleting result is returned and stored in the local integer variable numDeleted.

G. The database connection is closed by executing the close() method, since we have completed our data deleting action and need to disconnect with our database.

H. The executeUpdate() method will return an integer to indicate whether this data deleting is successful or not. If a nonzero value is returned, which means that at least one row has been deleted from our Faculty table and this data deleting action is successful, a `true` is returned to the client project.

I. Otherwise, no row has been deleted from our sample database, and this data deleting has failed. A `false` is returned for this situation.

J. The catch block is used to track and display any exception occurred during this data deleting process, and a `false` will be returned if this situation is really happened.

At this point, we have completed all coding development for the data updating and deleting actions. Now let's build and run our Web service project to test its functions.

9.11.3 Deploy and Test the Web Service Project

Perform the following operations to build and deploy our Web service project:

1. Click on the Clean and Build Main Project button to build our Web service.
2. Right click on our Web application WebServiceSQLApp and select the Deploy item to deploy our Web service. If everything is fine, a successful deployment result should be displayed.

A problem arises when testing the UpdateFaculty() operation of this Web service using the tester page, which is the input parameter array fdata. As we know, the fdata has a data type of ArrayList, and it needs to (1) create an ArrayList instance, and then (2) assign a group of updated faculty information to that ArrayList object to call this Web service operation UpdateFaculty() to perform the faculty data updating. However, it is difficult to do those two operations manually by using this tester page. Therefore, we need to create some Web client projects to consume and test this updating operation later.

To test the DeleteFaculty() operation, just right click on our Web service output file WebServiceSQL under the Web Services node from the Projects window, and choose the Test Web Service item to open the tester page, which is shown in Figure 9.54.

Enter a desired faculty name to be deleted from the Faculty table in our sample database, such as Ying Bai, into the text field that is next to the deleteFaculty button, and click on the deleteFaculty button to perform this faculty data deleting action.

The testing result is shown in Figure 9.55. A `true` is returned, and this indicates that our data deleting action is successful.

To confirm this data deleting action, open our Faculty table by going to the Services window and expand the Databases node, and our connection URL, and finally our sample database CSE_DEPT. Expand our database schema dbo and right click on the Faculty table. Select the View Data item from the pop-up menu to open our Faculty table. On the opened Faculty table, you can find that the faculty record with the faculty name of Ying Bai has been removed from this table.

Recall that when we built our sample SQL Server database CSE_DEPT in Chapter 2, we set up a cascaded updating and deleting relationships among our five tables. Therefore, not only is a single faculty record whose name is Ying Bai has been deleted

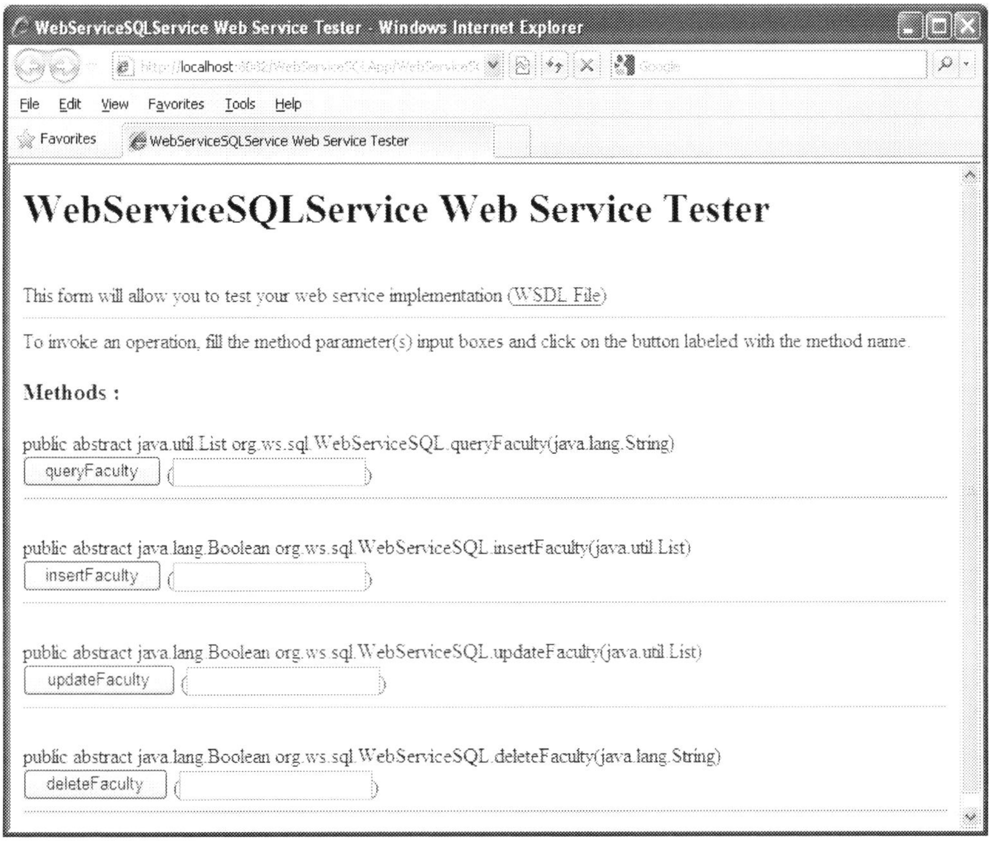

WebServiceSQLService Web Service Tester

This form will allow you to test your web service implementation (WSDL File)

To invoke an operation, fill the method parameter(s) input boxes and click on the button labeled with the method name.

Methods :

public abstract java.util.List org.ws.sql.WebServiceSQL.queryFaculty(java.lang.String)
queryFaculty ( )

public abstract java.lang.Boolean org.ws.sql.WebServiceSQL.insertFaculty(java.util.List)
insertFaculty ( )

public abstract java.lang.Boolean org.ws.sql.WebServiceSQL.updateFaculty(java.util.List)
updateFaculty ( )

public abstract java.lang.Boolean org.ws.sql.WebServiceSQL.deleteFaculty(java.lang.String)
deleteFaculty ( )

Figure 9.54. The tester page for our Web service project WebServiceSQL.

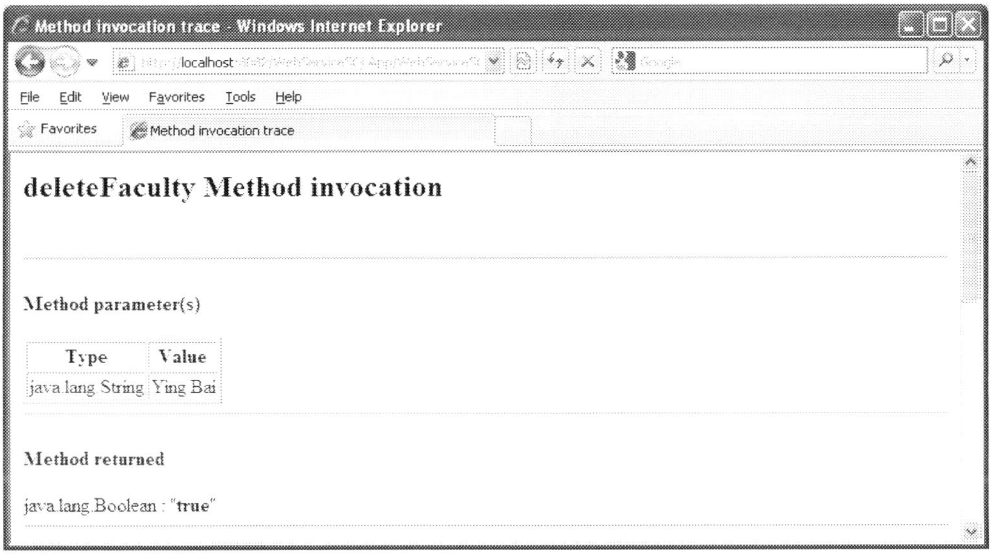

deleteFaculty Method invocation

Method parameter(s)

Type	Value
java.lang.String	Ying Bai

Method returned

java.lang.Boolean : "true"

Figure 9.55. The testing result of the deleting operation.

from the Faculty table when we perform this data deleting action, but also all columns related to this faculty member in other tables, such as the LogIn, Course, and StudentCourse, have also been deleted because of this cascaded relationship.

To make our sample database clean and neat, it is highly recommended to recover this deleted faculty member and related records in our Faculty, LogIn, Course, and StudentCourse tables. An easy way to do this recovery is to use the Microsoft SQL Server 2008 Management Studio. For your convenience, we show these deleted records in Tables 9.2–9.5, and you can add or insert them back to the related tables to complete this data recovery.

Next, we can develop some Web client projects to consume this Web service to perform data updating and deleting actions to the Faculty table in our sample database. First, let's discuss how to build a Windows-based client project to consume our Web service.

Table 9.2. The deleted record in the Faculty table

faculty_id	faculty_name	office	phone	college	title	email
B78880	Ying Bai	MTC-211	750-378-1148	Florida Atlantic University	Associate Professor	ybai@college.edu

Table 9.3. The deleted records in the Course table

course_id	course	credit	classroom	schedule	enrollment	faculty_id
CSC-132B	Introduction to Programming	3	TC-302	T-H: 1:00-2:25 PM	21	B78880
CSC-234A	Data Structure & Algorithms	3	TC-302	M-W-F: 9:00-9:55 AM	25	B78880
CSE-434	Advanced Electronics Systems	3	TC-213	M-W-F: 1:00-1:55 PM	26	B78880
CSE-438	Advd Logic & Microprocessor	3	TC-213	M-W-F: 11:00-11:55 AM	35	B78880

Table 9.4. The deleted records in the LogIn table

user_name	pass_word	faculty_id	student_id
ybai	reback	B78880	NULL

Table 9.5. The deleted records in the StudentCourse table

s_course_id	student_id	course_id	credit	major
1005	J77896	CSC-234A	3	CS/IS
1009	A78835	CSE-434	3	CE
1014	A78835	CSE-438	3	CE
1016	A97850	CSC-132B	3	ISE
1017	A97850	CSC-234A	3	ISE

9.12 BUILD A WINDOWS-BASED WEB CLIENT PROJECT TO CONSUME THE WEB SERVICE

We can still use the Windows-based client project WinClientSQL we built in Section 9.6 to consume the Web service to perform faculty data updating and deleting actions. One point to be noted is that although a Web reference to our Web service has been established in Section 9.6, we still need to refresh this Web reference, since our Web service project has been modified by adding two more operations UpdateFaculty() and DeleteFaculty() in our Web service. Otherwise, we would still use the old Web service that does not include these two operations.

9.12.1 Refresh the Web Service Reference for Our Windows-Based Client Project

In order to call the UpdateFaculty() and DeleteFaculty() operations in our Web service project WebServiceSQL, we need to refresh the Web reference in our client project to use the updated Web service project. Perform the following operations to refresh the Web service reference:

1. Open our Windows-based client project WinClientSQL and set it as our current project by right clicking on it and choosing the Set as Main Project item. Then expand the Web Service References node under our current project.
2. Right click on our Web service WebServiceSQLService and choose the Delete item to remove this old Web reference.
3. Right click on our Windows-based client project WinClientSQL and select the New > Web Service Client item to open the `New Web Service Client` wizard.
4. On the opened wizard, click on the Browse button that is next to the Project field, and expand our Web application WebServiceSQLApp. Then choose our Web service WebServiceSQL by clicking on it, and click on the OK button.
5. Click on the Finish button to complete this Web service reference refreshing process.

Now that we have refreshed or updated the Web service reference for our Windows-based client project WinClientSQL, next, let's develop the codes in our client project to call that Web service operations UpdateFaculty() and DeleteFaculty() to perform faculty data updating and deleting actions.

9.12.2 Develop the Codes to Call Our Web Service Project

First let's build the codes to perform the faculty data updating action.

9.12.2.1 Build the Codes to Call the UpdateFaculty() Operation

Open our Windows-based client project WinClientSQL and double click on our main class FacultyFrame.java to open it. Click on the Design button to open the graphic user interface. In this client project, we want to use the Update button in this form as a trigger

```
  private void cmdInsertActionPerformed(java.awt.event.ActionEvent evt) {
       // TODO add your handling code here:
A      ArrayList al = new ArrayList();
B      al.clear();
C      al.add(0, NameField.getText().toString());
       al.add(1, OfficeField.getText().toString());
       al.add(2, PhoneField.getText().toString());
       al.add(3, CollegeField.getText().toString());
       al.add(4, TitleField.getText().toString());
       al.add(5, EmailField.getText().toString());
       al.add(6, ComboName.getSelectedItem());
       .........
```

Figure 9.56. The newly added codes for the cmdUpdateActionPerformed() method.

to start the faculty data updating action. Therefore, double click on the Update button to open its event method cmdUpdateActionPerformed(), and enter the codes that are shown in Figure 9.56 into this method.

Let's have a closer look at this piece of codes to see how it works.

A. First, a new ArrayList instance al is created and initialized. This variable is used to pick up and reserve the input-updated faculty data array.

B. Then, the ArrayList instance al is cleaned up by calling the clear() method to make sure that this object is clean before the updated parameters can be added into this instance.

C. The add() method is used to pick up and add six pieces of updated faculty information into this new ArrayList instance al. These six pieces of updated faculty information are entered by the user and stored in six text fields in this FacultyFrame window form. The toString() method is used to convert each piece of these updated faculty information obtained using the getText() method that returns an Object data type to a String. The last or the seventh parameter is the original faculty name stored in the ComboName combo box. The index is necessary since it is used to indicate the position of each parameter in this ArrayList. One point to be noted is the order of adding these six text fields, which must be identical with order of columns in our Faculty table.

Now let's add the codes that are related to calling the UpdateFaculty() operation in our Web service and created automatically by the NetBeans IDE by dragging this operation node into this method. Perform the following operations to complete this code creation process:

1. Expand the Web Service References node in our client project WinClientSQL and all subnodes under this node until the WebServiceSQLPort.
2. Drag the UpdateFaculty operation under this node and place it into our opened method cmdUpdateActionPerformed(), exactly under the codes we created in Figure 9.56.
3. A piece of codes shown in Figure 9.57 has been automatically created and added into this method.

It is unnecessary to explain the function of this piece of codes line by line since all of coding lines have been illustrated by the built-in comments.

```
      .........
      try { // Call Web Service Operation
A         org.ws.sql.WebServiceSQLService service = new org.ws.sql.WebServiceSQLService();
B         org.ws.sql.WebServiceSQL port = service.getWebServiceSQLPort();
          // TODO initialize WS operation arguments here
C         java.util.List<java.lang.Object> fdata = null;
          // TODO process result here
D         java.lang.Boolean result = port.updateFaculty(fdata);
          System.out.println("Result = "+result);
      } catch (Exception ex) {
          // TODO handle custom exceptions here
      }
      .........
```

Figure 9.57. The automatically created codes by NetBeans IDE.

```
  private void cmdUpdateActionPerformed(java.awt.event.ActionEvent evt) {
      // TODO add your handling code here:
      ArrayList al = new ArrayList();
      al.clear();
      al.add(0, NameField.getText().toString());
      al.add(1, OfficeField.getText().toString());
      al.add(2, PhoneField.getText().toString());
      al.add(3, CollegeField.getText().toString());
      al.add(4, TitleField.getText().toString());
      al.add(5, EmailField.getText().toString());
      al.add(6, ComboName.getSelectedItem().toString());
      try { // Call Web Service Operation
          org.ws.sql.WebServiceSQLService service = new org.ws.sql.WebServiceSQLService();
          org.ws.sql.WebServiceSQL port = service.getWebServiceSQLPort();
          // TODO initialize WS operation arguments here
A         Boolean update = port.updateFaculty(al);
B         if (!update) {
              msgDlg.setMessage("The data updating is failed!");
              msgDlg.setVisible(true);
          }
C         else
              ComboName.addItem(NameField.getText());
      }
D     catch (Exception ex){
          System.out.println("exception: " + ex);
      }
  }
```

Figure 9.58. The complete codes for the cmdUpdateActionPerformed() method.

Now let's do some modifications to this piece of codes and add some codes to meet our data updating requirements. Enter the codes that are shown in Figure 9.58 into this method. The modified codes have been highlighted in bold.

Let's have a closer look at this piece of codes to see how it works.

A. The Web service operation UpdateFaculty() is executed with the ArrayList instance al, which has been filled with six pieces of updated faculty information as the argument of this method. The running result of that operation is returned and assigned to a Boolean variable update.

B. If the value of the variable update is `false`, which means that no row has been updated in our Faculty table and this data updating has been failed, the msgDlg instance is used to show this situation.

C. Otherwise, if the value of the update variable is `true`, which means that this data updating action is successful, the updated faculty name will be added into the Faculty Name combo box ComboName using the addItem() method.

D. The catch block is used to track and display any possible exception during this Web service operation execution.

Next, let's build the codes to perform the faculty data deleting action.

9.12.2.2 Build the Codes to Call the DeleteFaculty() Operation

Open our Windows-based client project WinClientSQL and double click on our main class FacultyFrame.java to open it. Click on the Design button to open the graphic user interface. In this client project, we want to use the Delete button in this form as a trigger to start the faculty data deleting action. Therefore, double click on the Delete button to open its event method cmdDeleteActionPerformed().

Now let's insert the codes that are related to calling the DeleteFaculty() operation in our Web service and created automatically by the NetBeans IDE by dragging this operation node into this method. Perform the following operations to complete this code creation process:

1. Expand the Web Service References node in our client project WinClientSQL and all subnodes under this node until the WebServiceSQLPort.
2. Drag the DeleteFaculty operation under this node and place it into our opened method cmdDeleteActionPerformed(). A piece of codes shown in Figure 9.59 has been automatically created and added into this method.

It is unnecessary to explain the function of this piece of codes line by line since all of coding lines have been illustrated by the built-in comments.

```
      .........
      try { // Call Web Service Operation
A         org.ws.sql.WebServiceSQLService service = new org.ws.sql.WebServiceSQLService();
B         org.ws.sql.WebServiceSQL port = service.getWebServiceSQLPort();
          // TODO initialize WS operation arguments here
C         java.lang.String fname = "";
          // TODO process result here
D         java.lang.Boolean result = port.deleteFaculty(fname);
          System.out.println("Result = "+result);
      } catch (Exception ex) {
          // TODO handle custom exceptions here
      }
      .........
```

Figure 9.59. The automatically created codes by NetBeans IDE.

```
  private void cmdDeleteActionPerformed(java.awt.event.ActionEvent evt) {
      // TODO add your handling code here:
      try { // Call Web Service Operation
          org.ws.sql.WebServiceSQLService service = new org.ws.sql.WebServiceSQLService();
          org.ws.sql.WebServiceSQL port = service.getWebServiceSQLPort();
          // TODO initialize WS operation arguments here
A         Boolean delete = port.deleteFaculty(ComboName.getSelectedItem().toString());
B         if (!delete) {
              msgDlg.setMessage("The data deleting is failed!");
              msgDlg.setVisible(true);
          }
      }
C     catch (Exception ex){
          System.out.println("exception: " + ex);
      }
  }
```

Figure 9.60. The complete codes for the cmdDeleteActionPerformed() method.

Now let's do some modifications to this piece of codes and add some codes to meet our data deleting requirements. Enter the codes that are shown in Figure 9.60 into this method. The modified codes have been highlighted in bold.

Let's have a closer look at this piece of codes to see how it works.

A. The Web service operation DeleteFaculty() is executed with the selected faculty name as the argument of this method. The running result of that operation is returned and assigned to a Boolean variable delete.

B. If the value of the variable delete is `false`, which means that no row has been deleted from our Faculty table and this data deleting has failed, the msgDlg instance is used to show this situation.

C. The catch block is used to track and display any possible exception during this Web service operation execution.

At this point, we have completed all coding development for our Windows-based client project for the data updating and deleting actions. Now let's build and run our client project to call and test our Web service to perform faculty data updating and deleting actions.

9.12.3 Build and Run Our Client Project to Update and Delete Faculty Record via Web Service

Click on the Clean and Build Main Project button to build our client project. If everything is fine, click on the Run Main Project button to run our client project.

The FacultyFrame form window is displayed. First, let's perform a faculty query action. Select a desired faculty member, such as Ying Bai, from the Faculty Name combo box, and click on the Select button to query the detailed information for this faculty via our Web service WebServiceSQL. The queried result is displayed in seven text fields.

Now enter an updating faculty record with six pieces of updated faculty information shown below into six text fields, which is shown in Figure 9.61.

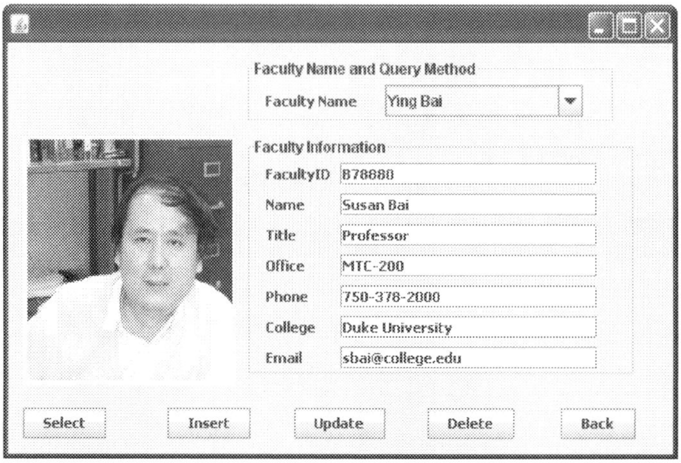

Figure 9.61. Six pieces of updated faculty information.

- Name: Susan Bai
- Title: Professor
- Office: MTC-200
- Phone: 750-378-2000
- College: Duke University
- Email: sbai@college.edu

Click on the Update button to try to call our Web service operation UpdateFaculty() to update this faculty record in the Faculty table in our sample database.

To confirm this data updating action, two methods can be used. First, we can open our Faculty table using either the Services window in the NetBeans IDE or the SQL Server 2008 Management Studio to check whether this faculty record has been updated. To do that using the Services window in the NetBeans IDE, perform the following operations:

1. Open the Services window and expand the Databases node.
2. Right click on our SQL Server database URL: jdbc:sqlserver://localhost\SQL2008EXPRESS: 5000; databaseName=CSE_DEPT [ybai on dbo], and select the Connect item to connect to our database.
3. Expand our sample database CSE_DEPT and Tables.
4. Right click on the Faculty table and select the View Data item.

Your opened Faculty table is shown in Figure 9.62. It can be found that the faculty record with the faculty_id of B78880, which is located at row 4, and has been highlighted in dark color, has been successfully updated in our database.

The second way to confirm this data updating, which is simpler, is to use the Select button in this form to perform a query to try to retrieve the updated faculty record.

A second way to check this is to go to the Faculty Name combo box, and you can find that the updated faculty name Susan Bai has been added into this box. Click it to

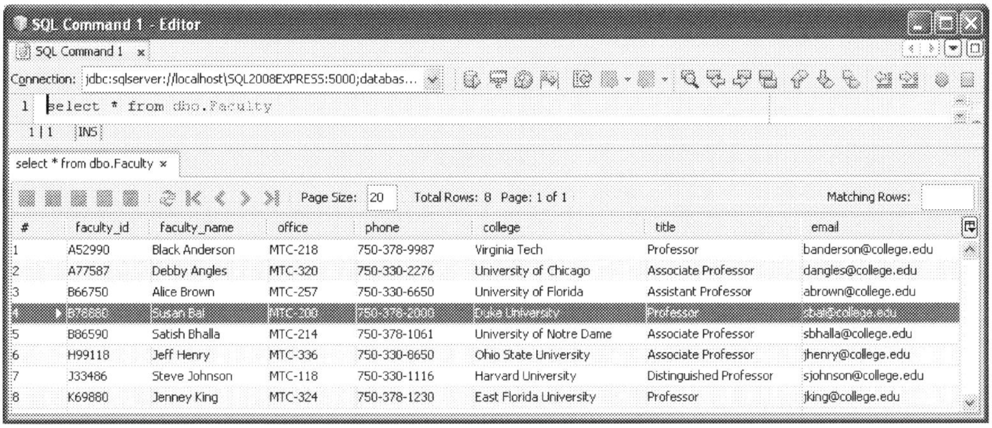

SQL Command 1 - Editor

SQL Command 1

Connection: jdbc:sqlserver://localhost\SQL2008EXPRESS:5000;databas...

```
1 select * from dbo.Faculty
```

1 | 1 INS

select * from dbo.Faculty

Page Size: 20 Total Rows: 8 Page: 1 of 1 Matching Rows:

#	faculty_id	faculty_name	office	phone	college	title	email
1	A52990	Black Anderson	MTC-218	750-378-9987	Virginia Tech	Professor	banderson@college.edu
2	A77587	Debby Angles	MTC-320	750-330-2276	University of Chicago	Associate Professor	dangles@college.edu
3	B66750	Alice Brown	MTC-257	750-330-6650	University of Florida	Assistant Professor	abrown@college.edu
4	B78880	Susan Bai	MTC-200	750-378-2000	Duke University	Professor	sbai@college.edu
5	B86590	Satish Bhalla	MTC-214	750-378-1061	University of Notre Dame	Associate Professor	sbhalla@college.edu
6	H99118	Jeff Henry	MTC-336	750-330-8650	Ohio State University	Associate Professor	jhenry@college.edu
7	J33486	Steve Johnson	MTC-118	750-330-1116	Harvard University	Distinguished Professor	sjohnson@college.edu
8	K69880	Jenney King	MTC-324	750-378-1230	East Florida University	Professor	jking@college.edu

Figure 9.62. The opened Faculty table in the NetBeans IDE.

Table 9.6. The original faculty record in the Faculty table

faculty_id	faculty_name	office	phone	college	title	email
B78880	Ying Bai	MTC-211	750-378-1148	Florida Atlantic University	Associate Professor	ybai@college.edu

select it and click on the **Select** button. Do not worry about the exception message for the faculty image, since we did not insert any image for this new inserted faculty. Just click on the **OK** button for that message box and you can find that six pieces of updated faculty information have been retrieved and displayed in this form window. Our data updating is successful!

It is highly recommended to recover this updated faculty record to the original one in our database since we want to keep our database clean. Refer to Table 9.6 to recover this original faculty record. You can recover this record by opening the SQL Server 2008 Management Studio to add it or performing another updating action in this form to recover it.

Next, let's test the faculty record deleting action via our Web service operation DeleteFaculty(). First, let's perform another updating action to recover the updated faculty member **Ying Bai** using the data shown in Table 9.6. Enter these six pieces of original faculty information into those six text fields and click on the **Update** button.

Then keep the faculty member **Ying Bai** selected in the Faculty Name combo box, and click on the **Delete** button to try to call our Web service operation DeleteFaculty() to delete this faculty record from our sample database.

To confirm this data deleting action, two ways can be used. First, you can perform a faculty data query operation by selecting the deleted faculty member **Ying Bai** from the `Faculty Name` combo box, and clicking on the **Select** button to try to retrieve this faculty record from our database. You can find that the querying faculty record cannot be found from our sample database and cannot be displayed in this form, and this means that our data deleting is successful.

Another way to confirm this data deleting is to open the Faculty table in our sample database.

A point to be noted is that as you perform reupdating actions, you must perform the both updating actions in a short period of time, which means that you have to perform the second updating within a short period of time after you do the first updating action.

To make our sample database clean and neat, it is highly recommended to recover this deleted faculty member and related records in our Faculty, LogIn, Course, and StudentCourse tables. An easy way to do this recovery is to use the Microsoft SQL Server 2008 Management Studio. Refer to deleted records shown in Tables 9.2–9.5 in Section 9.11.3 to add or insert them back to the related tables to complete this data recovery.

A point to be noted is that as you perform data recovery, the recovery order is very important. It means that you have to first recover the faculty data in the Faculty table, and then the data in other tables, since the Faculty table is a primary table.

A complete Windows-based client project WinClientSQL can be found from the folder DBProjects\Chapter 9 that is located at the Wiley ftp site (refer to Figure 1.2 in Chapter 1).

Next let's build a Web-based client project to consume our Web service to insert a new faculty record into the Faculty table in our sample database.

9.13 BUILD A WEB-BASED CLIENT PROJECT TO CONSUME THE WEB SERVICE

We can still use a Web-based client project WebClientSQL we built in Section 9.7 to consume our Web service to perform the faculty data updating and deleting actions. First, let's refresh the Web service reference used for our Web-based client project to allow it to use the updated Web service operations.

9.13.1 Refresh the Web Service Reference for Our Web-Based Client Project

In order to call the UpdateFaculty() and DeleteFaculty() operations in our Web service project WebServiceSQL, we need to refresh the Web reference in our Web-based client project WebClientSQL to use the updated Web service project. Perform the following operations to refresh the Web service reference:

1. Open our Web-based client project WebClientSQL and expand the Web Service References node.
2. Right click on our Web service WebServiceSQLService and choose the Delete item to remove this old Web reference.

3. Right click on our Web-based client project WebClientSQL and select the New > Web Service Client item to open the New Web Service Client wizard.
4. On the opened wizard, click on the Browse button that is next to the Project field and expand our Web application WebServiceSQLApp. Then choose our Web service WebServiceSQL by clicking on it, and click on the OK button.
5. Click on the Finish button to complete this Web service reference refreshing process.

Now that we have refreshed or updated the Web service reference for our Web-based client project WebClientSQL, next, let's develop the codes in our client project to call that Web service operations UpdateFaculty() and DeleteFaculty() to perform faculty data updating and deleting actions.

First, let's take care of the data updating operation UpdateFaculty().

9.13.2 Develop the Codes to Call Our Web Service Operation UpdateFaculty()

The main coding process is in the Java managed bean class FacultyMBean.java.

As we know, a binding relationship between the action attribute of the Update command Button in our JSF page FacultyPage.jsp and the Update() method in our Java managed bean class FacultyMBean.java has been established. Therefore, we can concentrate on the coding for the Update() method in our Java managed bean.

Open our Web-based client project WebClientSQL, and double click on the FacultyMBean.java from the Projects window to open this managed bean class file. Let's do the coding for the Update() method in this class to fulfill this data updating function.

Browse to the Update() method and drag the Web service operation UpdateFaculty under the Web Service References node and place it inside the Update() method. A piece of codes is created and added into this method, as shown in Figure 9.63.

It is unnecessary to explain the function of this piece of codes line by line since all of coding lines have been illustrated by the built-in comments.

Now let's do some modifications to this piece of codes and add some codes to meet our data updating requirements. Enter the codes that are shown in Figure 9.64 into this method.

```
  public String Update() {
A       try { // Call Web Service Operation
B          org.ws.sql.WebServiceSQL port = service.getWebServiceSQLPort();
           // TODO initialize WS operation arguments here
C          java.util.List<java.lang.Object> fdata = null;
           // TODO process result here
D          java.lang.Boolean result = port.updateFaculty(fdata);
           System.out.println("Result = "+result);
E       } catch (Exception ex) {
           // TODO handle custom exceptions here
        }
        return null;
  }
```

Figure 9.63. The automatically created codes by dragging the operation node.

```
  public String Update() {
A     ArrayList al = new ArrayList();
      MsgDialog msgDlg = new MsgDialog(new javax.swing.JFrame(), true);
B     al.clear();
C     al.add(0, name);
      al.add(1, office);
      al.add(2, phone);
      al.add(3, college);
      al.add(4, title);
      al.add(5, email);
      al.add(6, facultyName);
      try { // Call Web Service Operation
         org.ws.sql.WebServiceSQL port = service.getWebServiceSQLPort();
         // TODO initialize WS operation arguments here
D        Boolean update = port.updateFaculty(al);
E        if (!update) {
            msgDlg.setMessage("The data updating is failed!");
            msgDlg.setVisible(true);
         }
F     } catch (Exception ex) {
         // TODO handle custom exceptions here
         msgDlg.setMessage("exception: " + ex);
         msgDlg.setVisible(true);
      }
G     return null;
  }
```

Figure 9.64. The modified codes for the Update() method.

Let's have a closer look at this piece of newly added codes to see how it works.

A. First, a new ArrayList instance al is created and initialized. This variable is used to pick up and reserve the input updating faculty data array.

B. The clear() method is executed to make sure that the ArrayList instance is clean before a updating faculty record is collected.

C. The add() method is used to pick up and add six pieces of updating faculty information into this new ArrayList instance al. Six pieces of updating faculty information are entered by the user in the JSF page FacultyPage.jsp and stored in six properties defined in this managed bean. The last parameter, the seventh one, is the original faculty name.

D. The UpdateFaculty() operation in our Web service is called with the ArrayList instance that contains six pieces of updated faculty information as the argument. The execution result of this faculty data updating is returned and assigned to the local Boolean variable update.

E. If the returned Boolean variable update is false, which means that this data updating has failed, the msgDlg instance is used to indicate this situation.

F. The catch block is used to catch any possible exception during this data updating process.

G. Finally, a null is returned since it is not important to our application.

Next, let's build the codes for the Delete() method in our managed bean FacultyMBean.java to call our Web service operation DeleteFaculty() to perform the faculty data deleting action.

9.13.3 Develop the Codes to Call Our Web Service Operation DeleteFaculty()

As we know, a binding relationship between the action attribute of the Delete command Button in our JSF page FacultyPage.jsp and the Delete() method in our Java managed bean class FacultyMBean.java has been established. Therefore, we can concentrate on the coding for the Delete() method in our Java managed bean.

Open our Web-based client project WebClientSQL and double click on the FacultyMBean.java from the Projects window to open this managed bean class file. Let's do the coding for the Delete() method in this class to fulfill this data deleting function.

Browse to the Delete() method and drag the Web service operation DeleteFaculty under the Web Service References node and place it inside the Delete() method. A piece of codes is created and added into this method, as shown in Figure 9.65.

It is unnecessary to explain the function of this piece of codes line by line since all of coding lines have been illustrated by the built-in comments.

Now let's do some modifications to this piece of codes and add some codes to meet our data deleting requirements. Enter the codes that are shown in Figure 9.66 into this method.

Let's have a closer look at this piece of new added codes to see how it works.

- **A.** First a MsgDialog instance msgDlg is created, and this instance is used to track and display any possible exception during the data deleting action.
- **B.** The DeleteFaculty() operation in our Web service is called with the original faculty name as the argument. The execution result of this faculty data deleting is returned and assigned to the local Boolean variable delete.
- **C.** If the returned Boolean variable delete is false, which means that this data deleting has failed, the msgDlg instance is used to indicate this situation.
- **D.** The catch block is used to catch any possible exception during this data deleting process.
- **E.** Finally, a null is returned since it is not important to our application.

Now, let's build and run our Web client project to call our Web service operations to perform the faculty data updating and deleting actions.

```
  public String Delete() {
A     try { // Call Web Service Operation
B        org.ws.sql.WebServiceSQL port = service.getWebServiceSQLPort();
         // TODO initialize WS operation arguments here
C        java.lang.String fname = "";
         // TODO process result here
D        java.lang.Boolean result = port.deleteFaculty(fname);
         System.out.println("Result = "+result);
E     } catch (Exception ex) {
         // TODO handle custom exceptions here
      }
      return null;
  }
```

Figure 9.65. The automatically created codes by dragging the operation node.

```
  public String Delete() {
A     MsgDialog msgDlg = new MsgDialog(new javax.swing.JFrame(), true);
      try { // Call Web Service Operation
        org.ws.sql.WebServiceSQL port = service.getWebServiceSQLPort();
        // TODO initialize WS operation arguments here
B       Boolean delete = port.deleteFaculty(facultyName);
C       if (!delete) {
          msgDlg.setMessage("The data deleting is failed!");
          msgDlg.setVisible(true);
        }
D     } catch (Exception ex) {
        // TODO handle custom exceptions here
        msgDlg.setMessage("exception: " + ex);
        msgDlg.setVisible(true);
      }
E     return null;
  }
```

Figure 9.66. The modified codes for the Delete() method.

9.13.4 Build and Run Our Client Project to Update and Delete Faculty Record via Web Service

Click on the Clean and Build Main Project button to build our client project. If everything is fine, right click on our Web-based client project WebClientSQL from the Projects window and choose the Deploy item to deploy our Web application. Then, right click on our JSF page FacultyPage.jsp from the Projects window and choose the Run File item to run our client project.

On the opened JSF page, first, let's perform a faculty record query by entering a desired faculty name such as Ying Bai into the `Faculty Name` field, and then click on the Select button to get details for this selected faculty member. To update this faculty record, enter six pieces of updating faculty information shown below into the associated six text fields, as shown in Figure 9.67.

- Name: Susan Bai
- Title: Professor
- Office: MTC-200
- Phone: 750-378-2000
- College: Duke University
- Email: sbai@college.edu

Click on the Update button to try to call our Web service operation UpdateFaculty() to update this faculty record in the Faculty table in our sample database.

To confirm this data updating action, two methods can be used. First, we can open our Faculty table using either the Services window in the NetBeans IDE or the SQL Server 2008 Management Studio to check whether this faculty record has been updated. The second way to confirm this data updating, which is simpler, is to use the Select button in this form to perform a query to try to retrieve the updated faculty record.

Figure 9.67. Six pieces of updated faculty information.

Page Title - Windows Internet Explorer
http://localhost
File Edit View Favorites Tools Help
Favorites
Page Title
Image
Faculty Name
Susan Bai
Faculty ID
B78880
Name
Susan Bai
Title
Professor
Office
MTC-200
Phone
750-378-2000
College
Duke University
Email
sbai@college.edu
Select
Insert
Update
Delete
Back

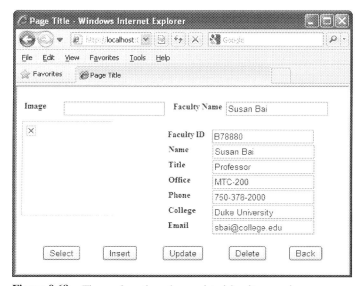

Figure 9.68. The confirmation of an updated faculty record.

The second way to do this checking is to, first, perform another query for the selected faculty such as Jenney King, and then go to the `Faculty Name` field and type the updated faculty name Susan Bai into this field. Click on the Select button to try to retrieve it. Now you can find that six pieces of updated faculty information for the updated faculty member Susan Bai have been retrieved and displayed in this page, as shown in Figure 9.68.

Now let's test the faculty deleting action by calling our Web service operation DeleteFaculty(). First, let's perform another faculty updating action to recover the faculty

Table 9.7. The original faculty record in the Faculty table

faculty_id	faculty_name	office	phone	college	title	email
B78880	Ying Bai	MTC-211	750-378-1148	Florida Atlantic University	Associate Professor	ybai@college.edu

member Ying Bai's record. Enter six pieces of original information shown in Table 9.7 into six associated fields in this page, and click on the Update button to complete this data updating.

Now type the updated faculty name Ying Bai into the `Faculty Name` field and click on the Select button to retrieve this updated faculty record. Then click on the Delete button to try to delete this faculty record.

To confirm this data deleting action, click on the Select button again to try to retrieve this faculty record from our sample database. An exception message is displayed to indicate that no matched faculty can be found from our sample database. Our data deleting is successful!

Sometimes, the execution of this deleting action seems to be still executed without completion. This means that an exception occurred. To watch this exception message, just minimize all current opened windows and forms, and then you can find this message.

To make our sample database clean and neat, it is highly recommended to recover this deleted faculty member and related records in our Faculty, LogIn, Course, and StudentCourse tables. An easy way to do this recovery is to use the Microsoft SQL Server 2008 Management Studio. Refer to deleted records shown in Tables 9.2–9.5 in Section 9.11.3 to add or insert them back to the related tables to complete this data recovery.

Our Web client project to consume our Web service WebServiceSQL is successful! A complete Web client project WebClientSQL can be found from the folder DBProjects\Chapter 9 that is located at the Wiley ftp site (refer to Figure 1.2 in Chapter 1).

Next, let's discuss how to build a Web service to access and manipulate data against our sample Oracle database.

9.14 BUILD JAVA WEB SERVICE PROJECTS TO ACCESS ORACLE DATABASES

We have provided a detailed discussion about the accessing and manipulating data in an SQL Server database via Web services using the runtime object method in the last section. In this section, we will discuss how to access and manipulate data in the Oracle database via Web services using Java beans and entity classes.

The structure and architecture of using Java beans and entity classes to access and manipulate data in an Oracle database via Web services is shown in Figure 9.69.

The advantages of using Java session beans and Java persistence APIs to access Oracle database are (1) all database-related operations are integrated into JAPIs and managed by the entity manager via entity classes, and (2) all interfaces and operations related to the business logic and database are controlled and managed by the session beans. The role of the Web service is exactly an interface to pass all requests coming from the clients to the associated operations or methods in the session beans, and the latter

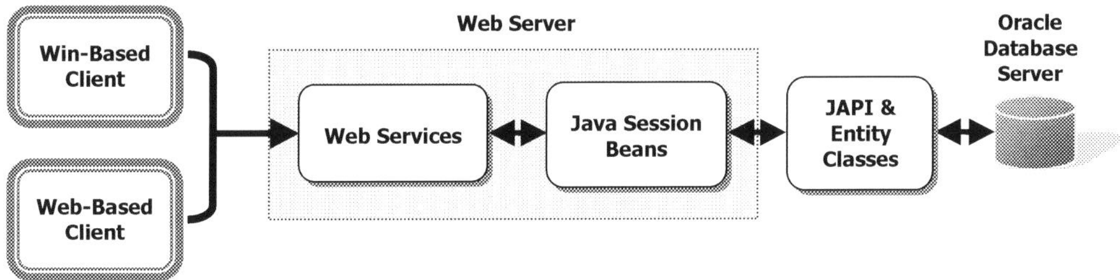

Figure 9.69. Architecture of accessing Oracle database via Web services.

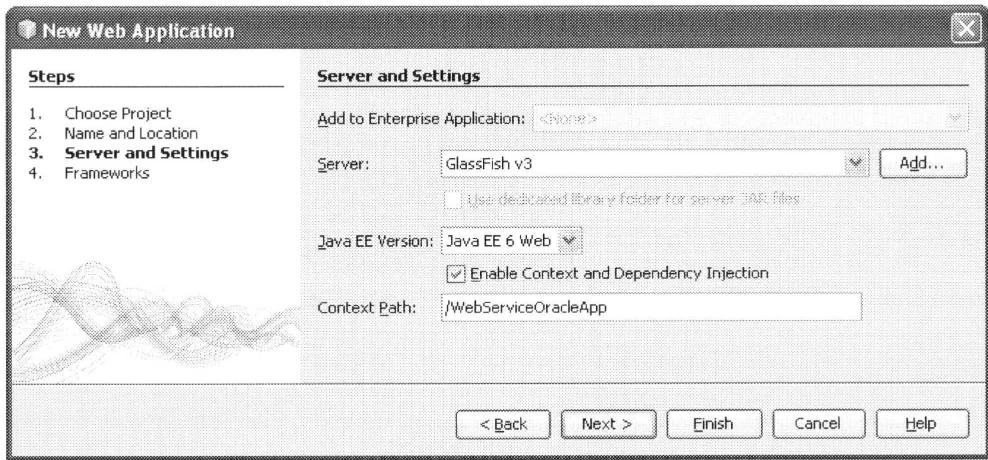

Figure 9.70. The finished Server and Settings wizard.

just passes those queries to the Java persistence APIs that access the Oracle database server to process those queries.

Let's begin our discussion by creating a new Web application WebServiceOracleApp and a Web service project WebServiceOracle.

9.14.1 Create a New Java Web Application Project WebServiceOracleApp

Perform the following operations to create our new Web application WebServiceOracleApp:

1. Launch NetBeans IDE and choose File > New Project (Ctrl-Shift-N). Select Web Application from the `Java Web` category.
2. Name the project WebServiceOracleApp and click on the Browse button to select a desired location for the project. In this application, we used the C:\Chapter 9 as our project location. Click on the Next button to continue.
3. Select GlassFish v3 as our Web container and Java EE 6 Web as the Java EE version; your finished Server and Settings wizard should match the one that is shown in Figure 9.70. Click on the Next button to go to the next wizard.

4. In the opened Frameworks wizard, you may select the JavaServer Faces as the framework for this application. Click on the Finish button to complete this new application creation process.

Now that a Web application has been created with a selected Web container, next, we can create our new Web service project WebServiceOracle.

9.14.2 Create a New Java SOAP-Based Web Service Project WebServiceOracle

The function of this Web service is to execute related operations in this Web service, and furthermore, to call the associated methods defined in our Java session beans to perform data queries and manipulations to our sample Oracle database via Java Persistence APIs and return the results.

Perform the following operations to create this new Web service project WebServiceOracle:

1. In the Projects window, right click on our newly created project WebServiceOracleApp and select the New > Other menu item to open the `New File` wizard.
2. Select Web Services from the `Categories` list and Web Service from the `File Types` list, and click on the Next button.
3. Name the Web service WebServiceOracle and type org.ws.oracle into the `Package` field. Leave Create Web Service from Scratch selected.

Your finished Name and Location wizard should match the one that is shown in Figure 9.71. Click on the Finish button to complete this process.

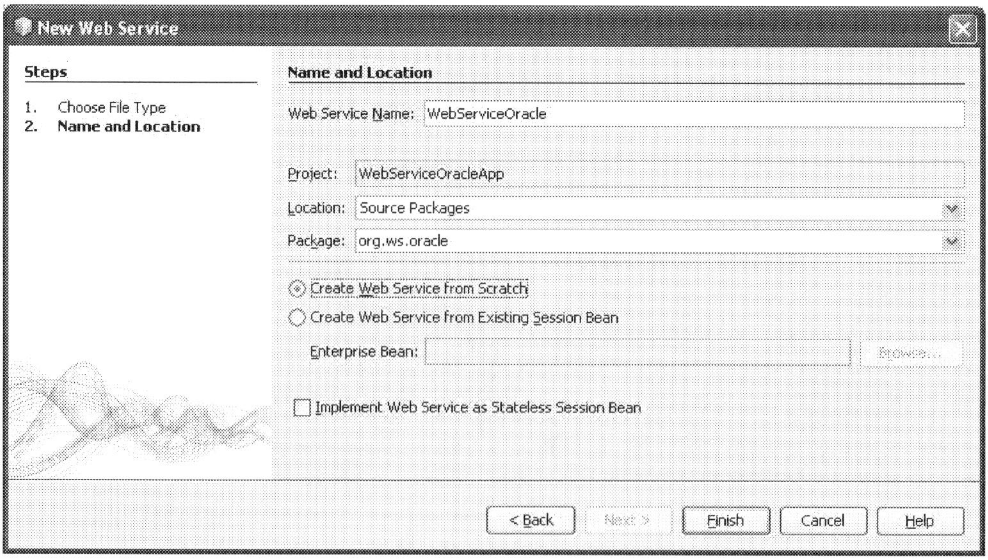

Figure 9.71. The finished Name and Location wizard.

Before we can add any operation to this Web service project, we need first to add a JDialog class into our project, and we need to use this component to display the debug information during the testing process for our Web service project.

9.14.3 Add a JDialog Class into the Web Services Project

Now let's handle adding a JDialog component into our Web service project.

To save time, you can copy a JDialog class MsgDialog.java from most projects we built in the previous sections. For example, you can copy this JDialog class from our Web application project, JavaWebDBJSPSQL, and paste it into our current Web service, exactly, into the org.ws.oracle node in our Web service project.

Perform the following operations to complete this copy and paste process:

1. Right click on this MsgDialog.java node from the project JavaWebDBJSPSQL and choose Refactor > Copy item.
2. Select our current project WebServiceOracleApp from the `Project` combo box, and select org.ws.oracle from the `To Package` combo box.
3. Make sure that the name of the copied JDialog is MsgDialog in the `New Name` field. Delete the 1 that is attached to this MsgDialog, since the default name is MsgDialog1.
4. Click on the Refactor button to paste this JDialog into our project.

The project JavaWebDBJSPSQL can be found at the folder DBProjects\Chapter 8 that is located at the Wiley ftp site (refer to Figure 1.2 in Chapter 1).

Next, let's handle the adding new operations and coding for the newly added operations or methods in our Web service to perform data query actions from our sample Oracle database. Since we have discussed how to access and manipulate data in the Faculty table in our sample SQL Server database in the last section, in this section, we will concentrate on the data queries and actions against the Course table in our sample Oracle database.

Since we need to use JAPI to perform data operations to our Oracle database, we need first to add all required entity classes into this Web service project.

9.14.4 Add Java Persistence API and Entity Classes from Database

Perform the following operations to add a new entity class from our sample Oracle database into this Web service project:

1. Right click on our Web application project WebServiceOracleApp and choose the New > Other item.
2. On the opened `New File` wizard, select Persistence from the `Categories` list and Entity Classes from Database from the `File Types` list, respectively. Click on the Next button.
3. Click on the drop-down arrow on the `Data Source` combo box, and choose the New Data Source item.
4. Enter CSEDEPT into the `JNDI Name` field as the name of our Oracle data source (since we have used CSE_DEPT as the name for our SQL Server data source), and click on the drop-down arrow of the `Database Connection` combo box. Then select the URL of

our sample Oracle database, jdbc:oracle:thin:@localhost:1521:XE [CSE_DEPT on CSE_DEPT], as shown in Figure 9.72. Click on the OK button to continue.

5. On the opened Connect wizard, enter the username and password for our sample Oracle database. In our application, they are CSE_DEPT and reback, which should be identical with those we used when we built this sample Oracle database in Chapter 2. Your finished Connect wizard is shown in Figure 9.73. Click on the OK button to continue.
6. In the opened `New Entity Classes from Database` wizard, click on the Add All button to add all our five tables into this Web service project, as shown in Figure 9.74. Then click on the Next button.
7. In the next opened wizard, click on the Create Persistence Unit button to create our Java persistence API. The opened `Create Persistence Unit` wizard is shown in Figure 9.75. Keep all default settings unchanged and click on the Create button to create this Persistence API unit.
8. In the opened `Entity Classes` wizard, enter org.ws.entity into the `Package` field as the package to store these entity classes. Your finished `Entity Classes` wizard should match the one that is shown in Figure 9.76. Click on the Next button to continue.
9. In the opened `Mapping Options` wizard, click on the drop-down arrow on the Collection Type combo box and select the java.util.List item, since we need to use this kind of List as the collection type for our data.

The finished Mapping Operations wizard is shown in Figure 9.77. Click on the Finish button to complete this Entity Classes from Database creation process.

Now in our Web application project, you can find that five entity classes, LogIn.java, Faculty.java, Course.java, Student.java, and StudentCourse.java, have been created and added into the org.ws.entity package in our project.

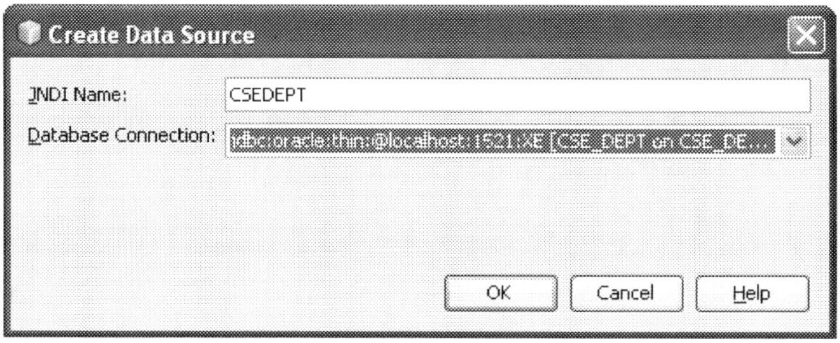

Figure 9.72. The Create Data Source wizard.

Figure 9.73. The finished Connect wizard.

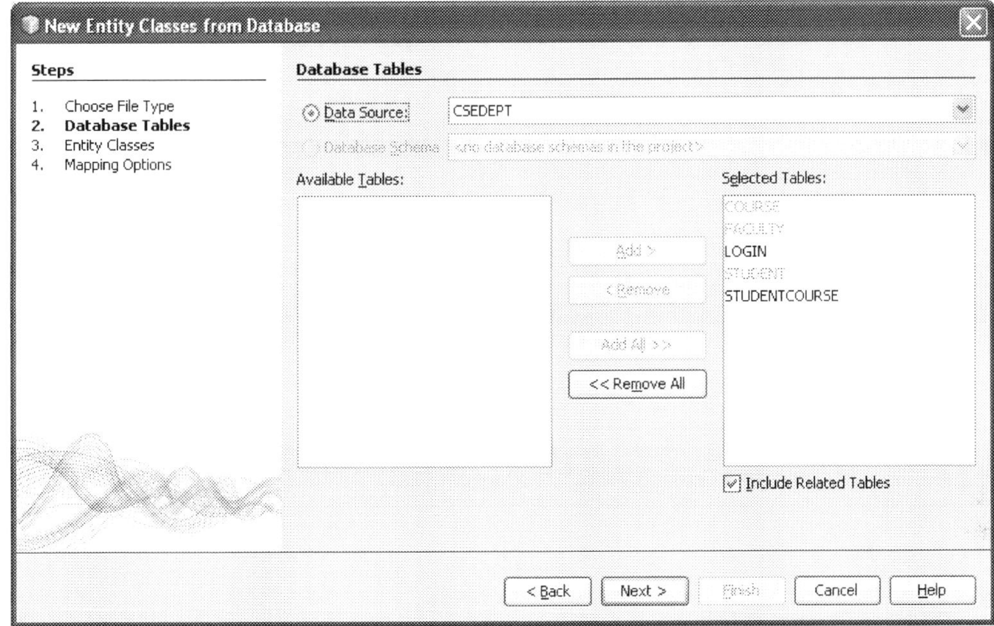

Figure 9.74. The added five tables.

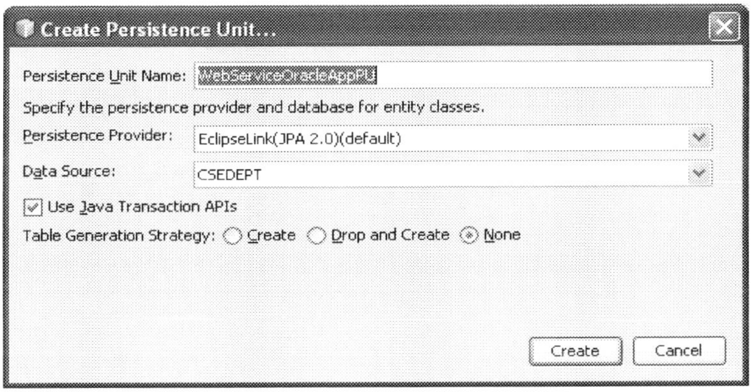

Figure 9.75. The finished Create Persistence Unit wizard.

Next, let's handle adding the Java session beans for entity classes into our Web service, since we want to use session beans to process database related operations and business logics.

9.14.5 Add Java Session Beans for Entity Classes

Perform the following operations to add a session bean for entity classes into our Web service project:

1. Right click on our Web application project WebServiceOracleApp and choose the New > Other item.

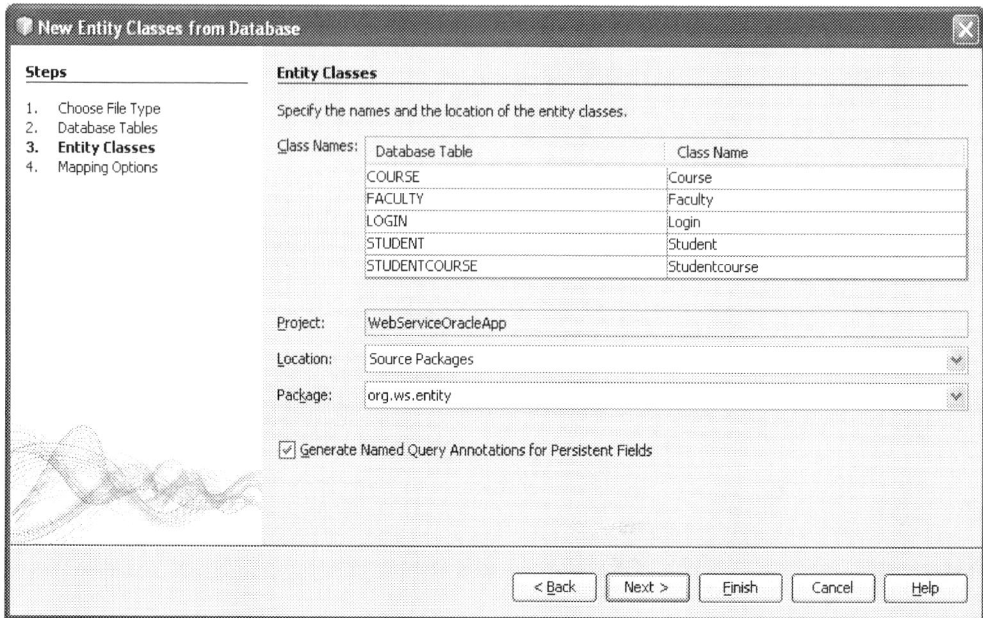

Figure 9.76. The finished New Entity Classes from Database wizard.

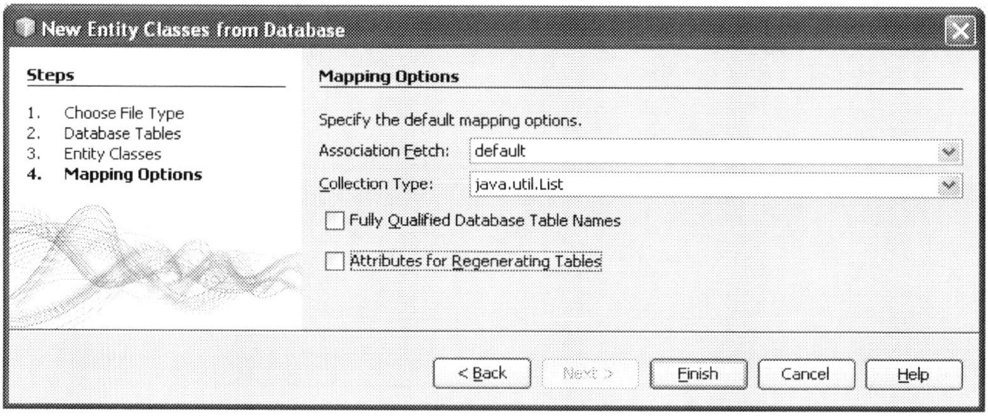

Figure 9.77. The finished Mapping Operations wizard.

2. On the opened `New File` wizard, select Java EE from the `Categories` list and Session Beans for Entity Classes from the `File Types` list, respectively. Click on the Next button.
3. In the opened `Entity Classes` wizard, click on the Add All button to add all five entity classes we added in the last section into our project. Your finished `Entity Classes` wizard is shown in Figure 9.78. Click on the Next button to continue.
4. In the opened `Generated Session Beans` wizard, click on the drop-down arrow from the Package combo box and choose org.ws.oracle as the package to save this session bean class. Your finished `Generated Session Beans` wizard should match the one

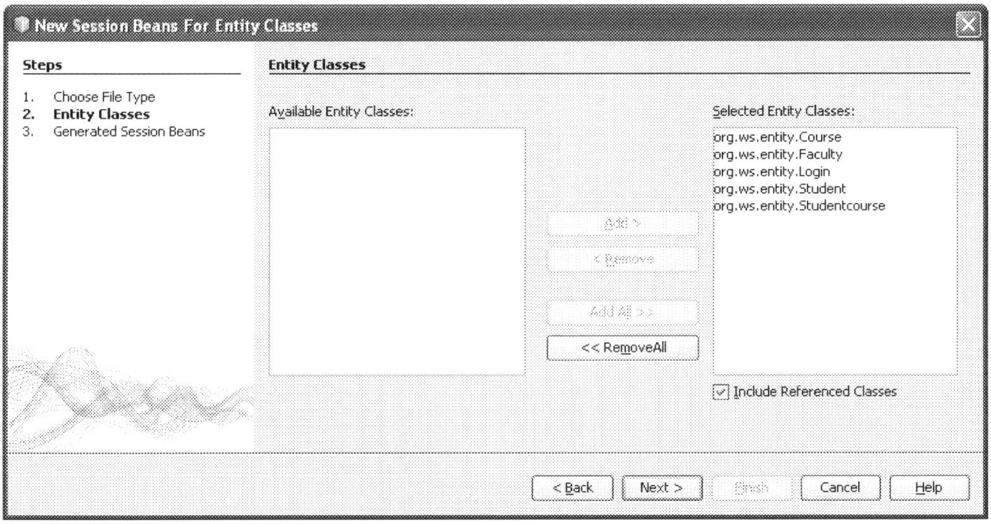

Figure 9.78. The finished Entity Classes wizard.

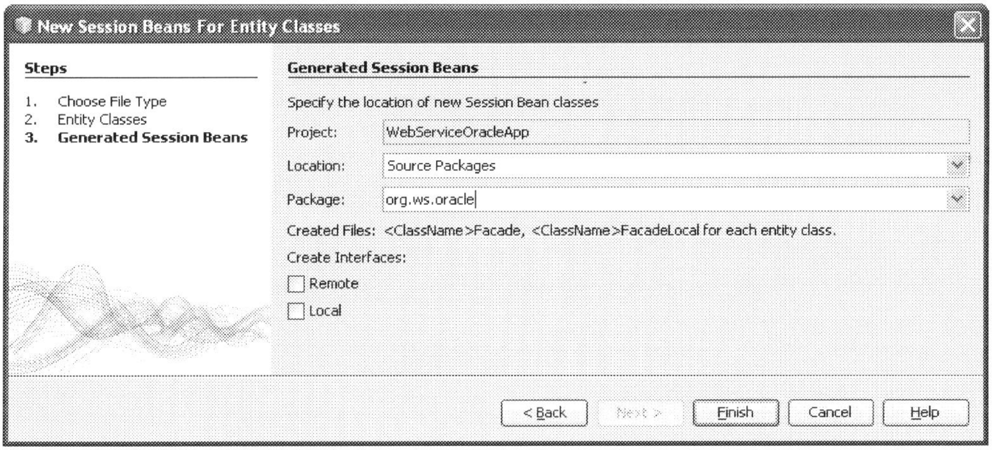

Figure 9.79. The finished Generated Session Beans wizard.

that is shown in Figure 9.79. Click on the Finish button to complete this session beans for entity classes creation process.

Now on our opened project, you can find that five session beans for entity classes, LoginFacade.java, FacultyFacade.java, CourseFacade.java, StudentFacade.java, and StudentcourseFacade.java, have been created and added into the org.ws.oracle package in our Web service project.

Now that we have finished adding Java persistence API, entity classes, and Java session beans for entity classes into our project, we are now ready to build the operations or methods in our Web service project to perform related Course information query actions.

9.14.6 The Organization of Web Service Operations and Session Bean Methods

The main purpose of using our Web service is to query and manipulate data from the Course table in our sample database. Therefore, we need to add some new operations to the Web service project. We will add five new operations based on the sequence of five operational tasks listed in section 9.14.3. This means that we will add the following five operations into this Web service project to perform related Course information query and manipulations:

- QueryCourseID(): Query all course_id taught by the selected faculty member.
- QueryCourse(): Query detailed information for selected course_id.
- InsertCourse(): Insert a new course record into the Course table.
- UpdateCourse(): Update an existing course record in the Course table.
- DeleteCourse(): Delete a course record from the Course table.

Generally, each operation listed above needs an associated method defined in our session bean to perform the actual database-related actions. Table 9.8 shows this one-to-one relationship between each operation in our Web service and each method in our session bean.

Based on this table, we will divide the coding process into two parts:

- Coding for the Web service operations.
- Coding for the associated methods defined in the Java session bean classes.

The relationship between each operation in our Web service and each user-defined method in our session bean is one-to-one. The function of each operation in our Web service is to: (1) call the associated method in our session bean class to perform the actual data query and actions against our sample Oracle database, (2) collect and process the queried data and send back to the client projects that will be used to consume the Web service and will be developed later. The function of each method defined in our session bean is to handle real database-related operation and business-related logics via Java persistence and entity classes.

Table 9.8. The relationship between each operation and each method

Web Service Operation	Session Bean Method	Function
QueryCourseID()	**getCourseID()**	Query all **course_id** taught by the selected faculty
QueryCourse()	**getCourse()**	Query detailed information for selected **course_id**
InsertCourse()	**newCourse()**	Insert a new course record into the Course table
UpdateCourse()	**setCourse()**	Update an existing course record in the Course table
DeleteCourse()	**removeCourse()**	Delete a course record from the Course table

Because each actual database-related action is performed inside each associated session bean method. Therefore, in this project, in order to provide readers with an understandable and sequential coding process, we will develop and build our data actions in the following ways:

1. Create each session bean method and develop the codes for that method to perform actual course data operations.
2. Create each Web service operation and develop the codes to call the associated session bean method to query and manipulate data.
3. Deploy and test each Web service operation to confirm its function.
4. After all Web service operations have been developed and deployed, some client projects will be built to consume our whole Web service project.

Before we can do the coding for any session bean method and Web service operation, we need first to add or inject the related session bean class, CourseFacade.java, into our Web service project to enable each operation to recognize this session bean and to call related method that is defined inside this session bean and will be developed later to perform desired data query or actions.

9.14.7 Add the Session Bean Classes CourseFacade into Our Web Service

Perform the following operations to add our Java session bean class CourseFacade.java into our Web service project:

1. Click on the Source button on the top of this window to open the code window of our Web service project.
2. Right click on any place inside our Web service class and choose Insert Code item, then select Call Enterprise Bean item.
3. Expand our Web service application WebServiceOracleApp, and choose our session bean class CourseFacade. Click on the OK button to complete this process.

Immediately, you can find that the session bean CourseFacade has been injected into our Web service project with the following two statements:

```
@EJB private CourseFacade courseFacade;
```

Now we are ready to create and build each session bean method and the associated Web service operation to perform the desired data query and data action.

9.14.8 Create and Build the Session Bean Methods and Web Service Operations

Let's start to create each session bean method and develop the codes for each of them. First, let's start from the getCourseID() method.

Recall that when we built our sample database in Chapter 2, especially when we built the Course table, there is no faculty_name column available in the Course table, and the only relationship between each course_id and each faculty member is the faculty_id column in the Course table. This is a many-to-one relationship between the course_id and the faculty_id in this table, which means that many courses (course_id) can be taught by a single faculty (faculty_id). However, in the Faculty table, there is a one-to-one relationship between each faculty_name and each faculty_id column.

Therefore, in order to query all courses, exactly all course_id, taught by the selected faculty member, exactly the faculty_name, we need to perform two queries from two tables.

- First, we need to perform a query to the Faculty table to get a matched faculty_id based on the selected faculty member (faculty_name).
- Then we need to perform another query to the Course table to get all course_id taught by the selected faculty_id that is obtained from the first query.

Based on this discussion, now let's perform the following operations to add a new method getCourseID() into our session bean CourseFacade.java to perform this course_id query:

9.14.8.1 Create and Build Session Bean Method getCourseID()

Perform the following operations to create a new method getCourseID() in our session bean class CourseFacade.java:

1. Open our Web service application project WebServiceOracleApp and double click on our session bean class CourseFacade.java from the Projects window to open it.
2. Right click on any place inside our session bean class body, then choose the Insert Code item and select the Add Business Method item to open the Add Business Method wizard.
3. Enter getCourseID into the Name field and click on the Browse button that is next to the Return Type combo box. On the opened Find Type wizard, type list into the top field and select the List (java.util) from the list and click on the OK button.
4. Click on the Add button to add one argument for this method. Enter fname into the Name column and keep the default data type java.lang.String unchanged. Your finished Add Business Method wizard should match the one that is shown in Figure 9.80. Click on the OK button to complete this business method creation process.

Now let's develop the codes for this method.

Click on the Source button on the top of this window to open the code window of our session bean class CourseFacade.java. Enter the codes that are shown in Figure 9.81 into this code window and the new method getCourseID().

Let's have a closer look at this piece of codes to see how it works.

A. First, an MsgDialog instance msgDlg is created since we need to use this object to track and display some debugging information as we test our Web service later.

B. A List instance courseList is created and initialized, and we need to use it to hold the query result, which are all course_id taught by the selected faculty member.

C. Two queries should be performed to get all course_id taught by the selected faculty member, (1) query to the Faculty table to get a matched faculty_id based on the selected faculty name, and (2) query to the Course table to get all course_id based on the faculty_

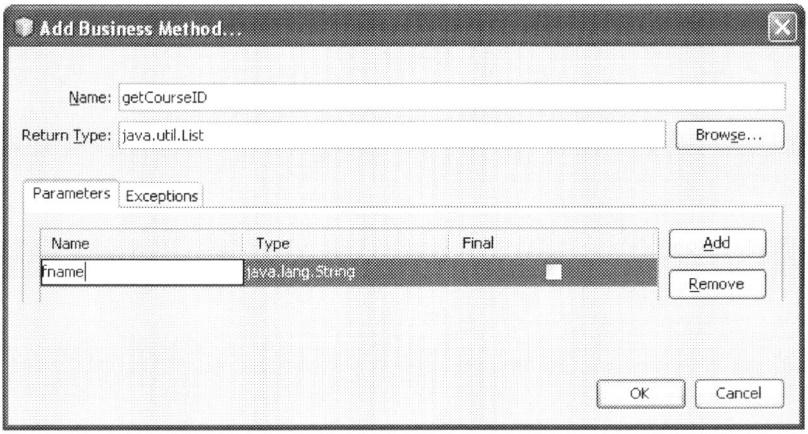

Figure 9.80. The finished Add Business Method wizard.

```
  @Stateless
  public class CourseFacade {
     @PersistenceContext(unitName = "WebServiceOracleAppPU")
     private EntityManager em;
A    MsgDialog msgDlg = new MsgDialog(new javax.swing.JFrame(), true);
     .........
     public List getCourseID(String fname) {
B       List courseList = null;

C       String f_query = "SELECT f.facultyId FROM Faculty f WHERE f.facultyName = :FacultyName";
D       Query  fQuery = em.createQuery(f_query);
E       fQuery.setParameter("FacultyName", fname);
F       String fid = fQuery.getSingleResult().toString();
G       String c_query = "SELECT c.courseId FROM Course c WHERE c.facultyId = :FacultyID";
H       Query cQuery = em.createQuery(c_query);
I       Faculty f = new Faculty(fid);
J       cQuery.setParameter("FacultyID", f);
K       courseList = cQuery.getResultList();

L       return courseList;
     }
  }
```

Figure 9.81. The codes for the method getCourseID().

id obtained from the first query. The query statement of the first query is created at this step.

D. The createQuery() method is executed to create the first query object fQuery based on the query statement created in step **C**.

E. Since the query statement in the first query contains a named dynamic parameter FacultyName, the setParameter() method is executed to set up this parameter with an actual value fname, which is the input argument of this method.

F. Then the getSingleResult() method is called to perform the first query to get a matched faculty_id and return it to a local variable fid.

G. The second query statement is created with a named dynamic parameter FacultyID.

H. The createQuery() method is executed to create the second query object cQuery based on the query statement created in step **G**.

I. A tricking issue arises in the next step. As we know, the data type for the second argument in the setParameter() method should be an Object. However, the data type for the queried faculty_id, or fid, from the first query is a String. In order to enable the setParameter() method to be executed correctly, we must create a new Faculty object with the queried faculty_id as the argument in this step.

J. Then the setParameter() method is executed to set up this correct faculty_id that is involved in the newly created Faculty object in step **I**.

K. The getResultList() method is executed to perform the second query and return the query result to the local variable courseList we created in step B.

L. Finally, the query result is returned to the calling method or operation.

During the coding process, you may encounter some real-time compiling errors. Most of these errors are introduced by missing some packages that contain classes or components used in this file. To fix these errors, just right click on this code window and select the Fix Imports item to load and import those missed packages to the top of this code window.

To save this piece of codes, click on the Clean and Build Main Project button on the top to build our project.

Next let's create and build our first Web service operation QueryCourseID() to call this session bean method getCourseID() to query all course_id taught by the selected faculty.

9.14.8.2 Create and Build Web Service Operation QueryCourseID()

Now let's begin the coding process for operations in our Web service project. First let's create the first operation in our Web service to query all course_id from the Course table.

Perform the following operations to add a new operation QueryCourseID() into our Web service project to perform this course_id query:

1. Double click on our Web service project WebServiceOracle.java from the Projects window to open it.
2. Click on the Design button on the top of the window to open the Design View of our Web service project WebServiceOracle.
3. Click on the Add Operation button to open the `Add Operation` wizard.
4. Enter QueryCourseID into the `Name` field and click on the Browse button that is next to the `Return Type` combo box. Type arraylist into the `Type Name` field and select the item ArrayList (java.util) from the list, and click on the OK button.
5. Click on the Add button and enter fname into the `Name` parameter field. Keep the default type java.lang.String unchanged and click on the OK button to complete this new operation creation process.

Your finished `Add Operation` wizard should match the one that is shown in Figure 9.82.

Click on the Source button on the top of this window to open the code window of our Web service project. Let's perform the coding for this newly added operation.

On the opened code window, enter the codes that are shown in Figure 9.83 into this code window and this newly added operation.

Let's have a closer look at this piece of codes to see how it works.

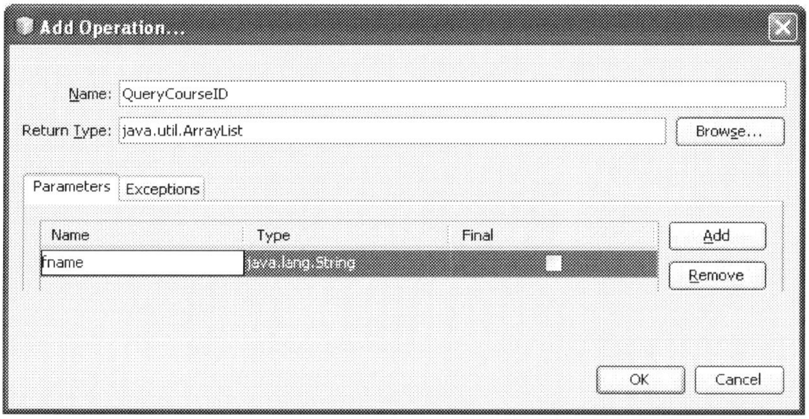

Figure 9.82. The finished Add Operation wizard.

```
  @WebService()
  public class WebServiceOracle {
     @EJB
     private CourseFacade courseFacade;
A    MsgDialog msgDlg = new MsgDialog(new javax.swing.JFrame(), true);
     @WebMethod(operationName = "QueryCourseID")
     public ArrayList QueryCourseID(@WebParam(name = "fname")
     String fname) {
        //TODO write your implementation code here:
B       ArrayList<String> al = new ArrayList<String>();
        List courseList = null;
C       courseList = courseFacade.getCourseID(fname);
D       for (int col = 0; col < courseList.size(); col++) {
           al.add(courseList.get(col).toString());
        }
E       return al;
     }
  }
```

Figure 9.83. The codes for the Web service operation QueryCourseID().

A. First, a class-level variable msgDlg is created. This variable is used to track and display the debug information when this Web service project is tested later.

B. An ArrayList instance al and a List instance courseList are created. The first variable is an array list instance used to collect and store our query result, and return to the consuming project. The second variable is used to hold and store the query result from the execution of the session bean method getCourseID().

C. The session bean method getCourseID() is called to query all course_id taught by the selected faculty member fname that works as an argument of that method. The query result is returned and assigned to the local variable courseList.

D. A for loop is used to pick up each queried course_id and add it into the ArrayList instance al. The reason we used an ArrayList, not a List instance, as the returned object is that the former is a concrete class but the latter is an abstract class, and a runtime exception may be encountered if an abstract class is used as a returned object to the calling method.

E. The queried result is returned to the consuming project.

During the coding process, you may encounter some in-time compiling errors. The main reason for those errors is that some packages are missed. To fix these errors, just right click on any space inside this code window, and select the Fix Imports item to find and add those missed packages.

At this point, we have finished all coding process for the course_id query. Now let's build and test our Web service to test this course_id query function.

9.14.8.3 Build and Run the Web Service to Test the course_id Query Function

Click on the Clean and Build Main Project button on the top of the window to build our Web service project. Then right click on our Web service application project WebServiceOracleApp and choose the Deploy item to deploy our Web service.

Enter the appropriate username and password to the Glassfish v3 server, such as admin and reback, which are used for this application, and click on the OK button to start the application server.

If everything is fine, expand the Web Services node under our Web service project and right click on our Web service target file WebServiceOracle, and choose the Test Web Service item to run our Web service project. The running status of our Web service is shown in Figure 9.84.

Enter a desired faculty name, such as Jenney King, into the text field, and click on the queryCourseID button to test this query function. The testing result is shown in Figure 9.85.

It can be found from Figure 9.85 that all course_id taught by the selected faculty member Jenney King have been retrieved and displayed at the bottom of this page, and our course_id query via Web service is successful!

Next, let's handle creating and coding process for the second session bean method getCourse() and Web service operation QueryCourse() to query details for a selected course_id.

Figure 9.84. The running status of our Web service operation QueryCourseID().

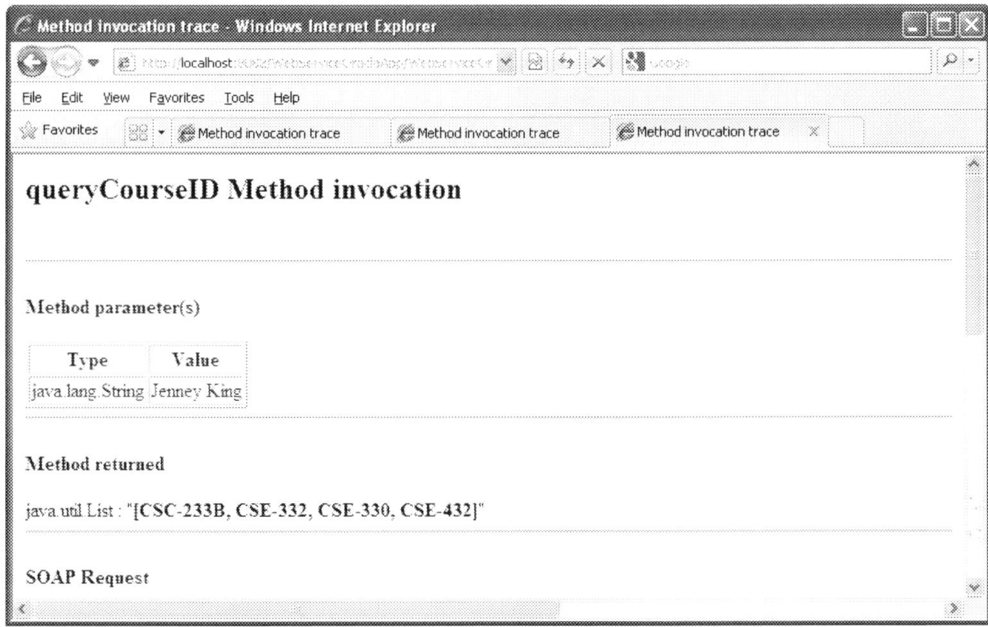

Figure 9.85. The running result of our Web service operation QueryCourseID().

9.14.8.4 Create and Build Session Bean Method getCourse()

Perform the following operations to create a new method getCourse() in our session bean class CourseFacade.java:

1. Open our Web service application project WebServiceOracleApp and double click on our session bean class CourseFacade.java from the Projects window to open it.
2. Right click on any place inside our session bean class body, choose the Insert Code item, and select the Add Business Method item to open the Add Business Method wizard.
3. Enter getCourse into the Name field and click on the Browse button that is next to the Return Type combo box. On the opened Find Type wizard, type course into the top field and select the Course (org.ws.entity) from the list and click on the OK button.
4. Click on the Add button to add one argument for this method. Enter cid into the Name column and keep the default data type java.lang.String unchanged. Your finished Add Business Method wizard should match the one that is shown in Figure 9.86. Click on the OK button to complete this business method creation process.

Now let's develop the codes for this method.

Click on the Source button on the top of this window to open the code window of our session bean class CourseFacade.java. Enter the codes that are shown in Figure 9.87 into this new method getCourse(). The newly added codes have been highlighted in bold.

The codes for this method is very simple since we utilized a built-in method find() that is created and added into this session bean class automatically when this session bean is created. Let's have a closer look at this piece of codes to see how it works.

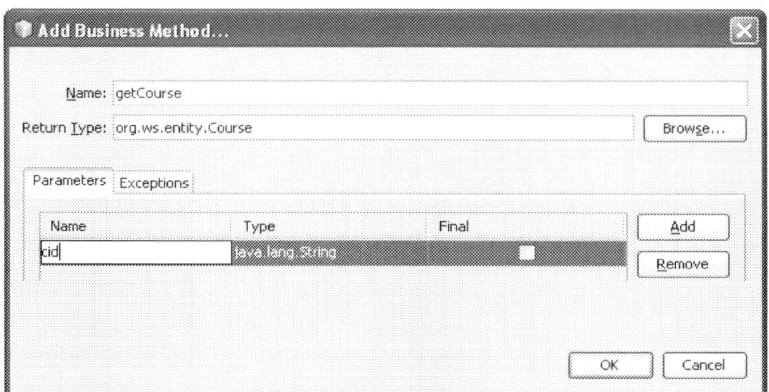

Figure 9.86. The finished Add Business Method wizard.

```
@Stateless
public class CourseFacade {
    @PersistenceContext(unitName = "WebServiceOracleAppPU")
    private EntityManager em;
    MsgDialog msgDlg = new MsgDialog(new javax.swing.JFrame(), true);
    .........
    public Course find(Object id) {
        return em.find(Course.class, id);
    }
    public Course getCourse(String  cid) {
A       Course  result = find(cid);
B       return  result;
    }
}
```

Figure 9.87. The codes for the method getCourse().

A. The built-in method find() is called with the given course_id as the argument. The function of the find() method is to try to find a course record whose primary key is the given course_id. The query result is returned and assigned to a local Course object result.

B. The query result is returned to the associated Web operation.

The point to be noted is that the returned object of this method is a Course instance, whose protocol is the entity class Course defined in our entity class Course.java.

During the coding process, you may encounter some real-time compiling errors. Most of these errors are introduced by missing some packages that contain classes or components used in this file. To fix these errors, just right click on this code window and select the Fix Imports item to load and import those missed packages to the top of this code window.

To save this piece of codes, click on the Clean and Build Main Project button on the top to build our project.

Next, let's create and build our second Web service operation QueryCourse() to call this session bean method getCourse() to query the details for a given course_id.

9.14.8.5 Create and Build Web Service Operation QueryCourse()

Perform the following operations to add a new operation QueryCourse() into our Web service project to perform this course details query:

1. Double click on our Web service project WebServiceOracle.java from the Projects window to open it.
2. Click on the Design button on the top of the window to open the Design View of our Web service project WebServiceOracle.
3. Click on the Add Operation button to open the `Add Operation` wizard.
4. Enter QueryCourse into the `Name` field and click on the Browse button that is next to the `Return Type` combo box. Type arraylist into the `Type Name` field, and select the item ArrayList (java.util) from the list, and click on the OK button.
5. Click on the Add button and enter courseID into the `Name` parameter field. Keep the default type java.lang.String unchanged and click on the OK button to complete this new operation creation process.

Your finished `Add Operation` wizard should match the one that is shown in Figure 9.88.

Click on the Source button on the top of this window to open the code window of our Web service project. Let's perform the coding for this newly added operation.

On the opened code window, enter the codes that are shown in Figure 9.89 into this newly added operation.

Let's have a closer look at this piece of codes to see how it works.

A. An ArrayList instance al is created and this variable is an array list instance used to collect and store our query result, and return to the consuming project.

B. Before we can call the session bean method getCourse() to query the course details, we need first to clean up the ArrayList instance al to make sure that it is empty.

C. The session bean method getCourse() is called to query the details for a given course_id. The courseID, which is an input parameter, works as the argument for that method. The query result is returned and assigned to the local variable result.

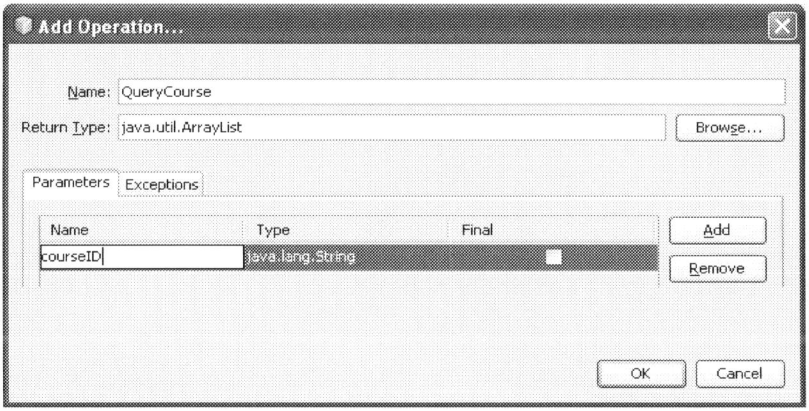

Figure 9.88. The finished Add Operation wizard.

```
  @WebMethod(operationName = "QueryCourse")
    public ArrayList QueryCourse(@WebParam(name = "courseID")
    String courseID) {
      //TODO write your implementation code here:
A     ArrayList<String> al = new ArrayList<String>();

B     al.clear();
C     Course result = courseFacade.getCourse(courseID);
D     al.add(0, result.getCourseId());
      al.add(1, result.getCourse());
      al.add(2, result.getCredit().toString());
      al.add(3, result.getClassroom());
      al.add(4, result.getSchedule());
      al.add(5, result.getEnrollment().toString());

E     return al;
  }
```

Figure 9.89. The codes for the Web service operation QueryCourse().

D. Six add() methods are used to add six pieces of detailed course information into the local ArrayList instance al. The point to be noted is that the data types of the credit and the enrollment columns in the Course table are numbers, therefore, a toString() method is needed to convert them to String before they can be added into the ArrayList object al.

E. The queried result is returned to the consuming project.

During the coding process, you may encounter some in-time compiling errors. The main reason for those errors is that some packages are missed. To fix these errors, just right click on any space inside this code window, and select the Fix Imports item to find and add those missed packages.

At this point, we have finished all coding process for the course details query. Now let's build and test our Web service to test this course query function.

9.14.8.6 Build and Run the Web Service to Test the Course Query Function

Click on the Clean and Build Main Project button on the top of the window to build our Web service project. Then right click on our Web service application project WebServiceOracleApp and choose the Deploy item to deploy our Web service.

Enter the appropriate username and password to the Glassfish v3 server, such as admin and reback, which are used for this application, and click on the OK button to start the application server.

If everything is fine, expand the Web Services node under our Web service project and right click on our Web service target file WebServiceOracle, and choose the Test Web Service item to run our Web service project. The running status of our Web service is shown in Figure 9.90.

Enter a desired course_id, such as CSE-432, into the text field, and click on the queryCourse button to test this query function. The testing result is shown in Figure 9.91.

It can be found from Figure 9.91 that the detailed course information for the given course_id of CSE-432 has been retrieved and displayed at the bottom of this page, and our course details query via Web service is successful!

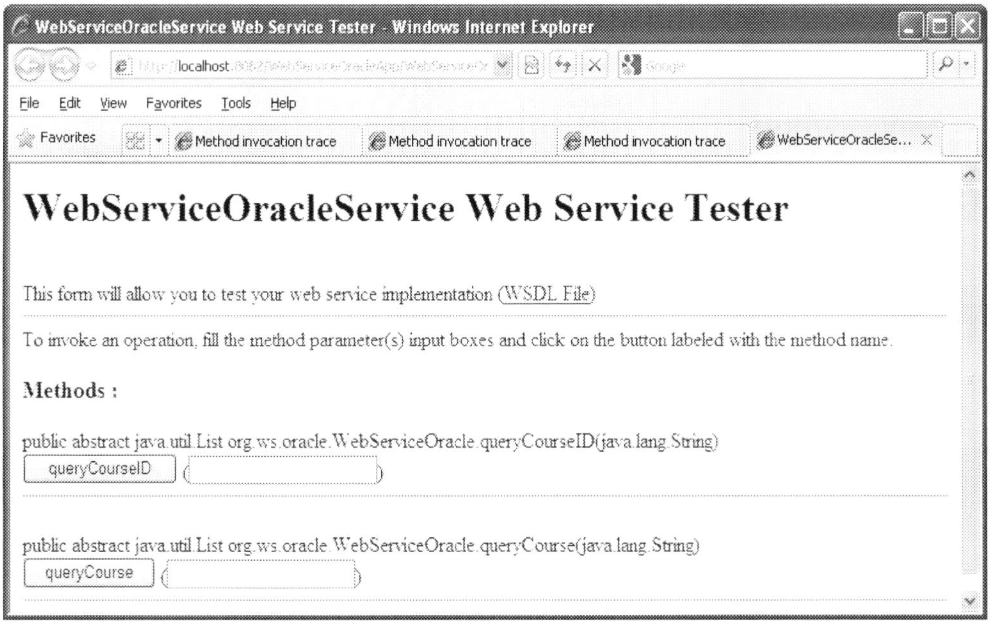

Figure 9.90. The running status of our Web service.

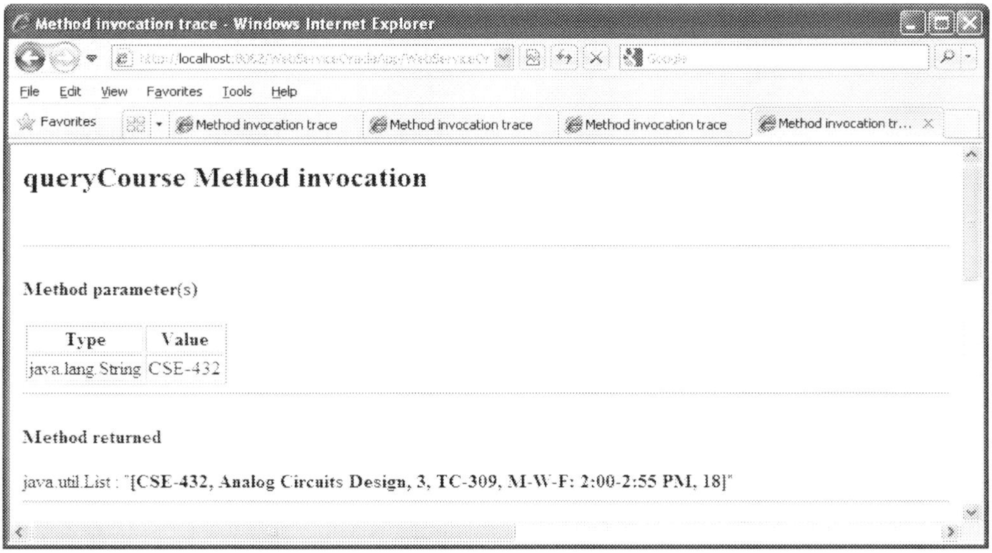

Figure 9.91. The running result of our Web operation QueryCourse().

Next let's handle creating and coding process for the third session bean method newCourse() and Web service operation InsertCourse() to insert a new course record into the Course table in our sample Oracle database.

9.14.8.7 Create and Build Session Bean Method newCourse()

Perform the following operations to create a new method newCourse() in our session bean class CourseFacade.java:

1. Open our Web service application project WebServiceOracleApp and double click on our session bean class CourseFacade.java from the Projects window to open it.
2. Right click on any place inside our session bean class body, choose the Insert Code item, and select the Add Business Method item to open the Add Business Method wizard.
3. Enter newCourse into the Name field and click on the Browse button that is next to the Return Type combo box. On the opened Find Type wizard, type boolean into the top field and select the Boolean (java.lang) from the list and click on the OK button.
4. Recall that in Chapter 2, when we built our sample database, the Course table contains seven columns. Therefore, in order to insert a new course record, we need to pass seven new values for those seven columns. We need to use an ArrayList object to store those parameters. Click on the Add button and enter cdata into the Name parameter field. Then click on the drop-down arrow of the Type combo box, and select the Choose item to open the Find Type wizard. Type arraylist into the top field and select the ArrayList (java.util) data type, and click on the OK button to select an ArrayList as the data type for the input parameter. Your finished Add Business Method wizard should match the one that is shown in Figure 9.92. Click on the OK button to complete this business method creation process.

Now let's develop the codes for this method.

Click on the Source button on the top of this window to open the code window of our session bean class CourseFacade.java. Enter the codes that are shown in Figure 9.93 into this new method newCourse(). The newly added codes have been highlighted in bold.

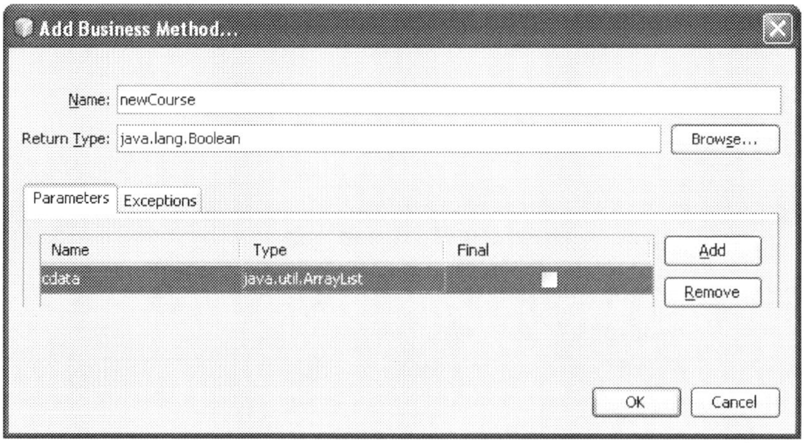

Figure 9.92. The finished Add Business Method wizard.

```
  public void create(Course course) {
        em.persist(course);
  }
  public Boolean newCourse(ArrayList cdata) {
A       Course c = new Course();
B       String f_query = "SELECT f.facultyId FROM Faculty f WHERE f.facultyName = :FacultyName";
        Query fQuery = em.createQuery(f_query);
        fQuery.setParameter("FacultyName", cdata.get(6).toString());
        String fid = fQuery.getSingleResult().toString();
C       c.setCourseId(cdata.get(0).toString());
        c.setCourse(cdata.get(1).toString());
D       c.setCredit(new BigInteger(cdata.get(2).toString()));
        c.setClassroom(cdata.get(3).toString());
        c.setSchedule(cdata.get(4).toString());
E       c.setEnrollment(new BigInteger(cdata.get(5).toString()));
F       c.setFacultyId(new Faculty(fid));
G       create(c);
H       return true;
  }
```

Figure 9.93. The codes for the method newCourse().

The codes for this method is a little complicated since we utilized a built-in method create() that is created and added into this session bean class automatically when this session bean is created.

As you know, when we built our Course table in Chapter 2, there is no faculty_name column available in the Course table, and the only relationship between each course_id and each faculty member is the faculty_id column in the Course table. This is a many-to-one relationship between the course_id and the faculty_id in this table, which means that many courses (course_id) can be taught by a single faculty (faculty_id). However, in the Faculty table, there is a one-to-one relationship between each faculty_name and each faculty_id column.

Therefore, in order to insert a new course record into the Course table based on a selected faculty member, exactly the faculty_name, we need to perform two queries from two tables.

- First, we need to perform a query to the Faculty table to get a matched faculty_id based on the selected faculty member (faculty_name).
- Then we need to perform another action to the Course table to insert a new course record including the faculty_id that is obtained from the first query.

Based on this discussion, let's have a closer look at this piece of codes to see how it works.

A. First, a new Course object **c** is created since we want to call a built-in method create() to perform this new course insertion, and that method needs a Course object as the argument.

B. Then the first query is executed to get a matched faculty_id based on the selected faculty_name, which is the sixth input parameter stored in our ArrayList instance cdata. The queried faculty_id is returned and assigned to a local variable fid.

C. Seven setter methods are executed to pick up seven input parameters that represent a new course record and set each of them to the associated column in the new Course object **c**.

D. Points to be noted are steps D and E. Since the data types for the 2nd and 5th parameters, credit and enrollment, in the input ArrayList instance are BigInteger, we must convert both data into that data type by creating a new instance of BigInteger class.

F. Since the setFacultyId() method needs a Faculty class as the argument data type, we need to create a new Faculty instance with the queried faculty_id as the argument to meet this requirement.

G. The built-in method create() is called with the built Course instance **c** as the argument. The function of the create() method is to create and insert a new course record into the Course table. No query result is returned for this method.

H. A `true` is returned to the associated Web operation to indicate that this data insertion is successful.

During the coding process, you may encounter some real-time compiling errors. Most of these errors are introduced by missing some packages that contain classes or components used in this file. To fix these errors, just right click on this code window and select the Fix Imports item to load and import those missed packages to the top of this code window.

To save this piece of codes, click on the Clean and Build Main Project button on the top to build our project.

Next, let's create and build our third Web service operation InsertCourse() to call this session bean method newCourse() to insert a new course record into our Course table.

9.14.8.8 Create and Build Web Service Operation InsertCourse()

Perform the following operations to add this operation into our Web service:

1. Launch NetBeans IDE and open our Web service project WebServiceOracleApp, and double click on our Web service main class file WebServiceOracle.java from the Projects window to open it.
2. Click on the Design button on the top of the window to open the Design View of our Web service project WebServiceOracle.
3. Click on the Add Operation button to open the `Add Operation` wizard.
4. Enter InsertCourse into the `Name` field and click on the Browse button that is next to the `Return Type` combo box. Type boolean into the `Type Name` field and select the item Boolean (java.lang) from the list, and click on the OK button.
5. Click on the Add button and enter cdata into the `Name` parameter field. Then click on the drop-down arrow of the Type combo box, and select the Choose item to open the `Find Type` wizard. Type arraylist into the top field and select the ArrayList (java.util) data type, and click on the OK button to select an ArrayList as the data type for the input parameter.

Your finished `Add Operation` wizard should match the one that is shown in Figure 9.94. Click on the OK button to complete this new operation creation process.

Click on the Source button on the top of this window to open the code window of our Web service project. Let's perform the coding for this newly added operation.

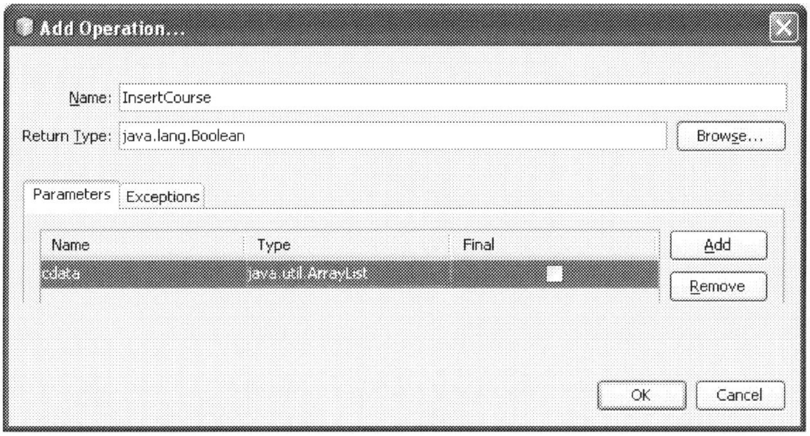

Figure 9.94. The complete Add Operation wizard.

```
  @WebMethod(operationName = "InsertCourse")
    public Boolean InsertCourse(@WebParam(name = "cdata")
    ArrayList cdata) {
      //TODO write your implementation code here:
A     Boolean insert = false;

B     insert = courseFacade.newCourse(cdata);
C     return insert;
  }
```

Figure 9.95. The codes for the Web service operation InsertCourse().

On the opened code window, enter the codes that are shown in Figure 9.95 into this newly added operation InsertCourse().

Let's have a closer look at this piece of newly added codes to see how it works.

A. A local Boolean variable insert is created and initialized to false. This local variable is used to hold the running result of execution of the session bean method newCourse() that performs a new course insertion action to the Course table in our sample database.

B. The session bean method newCourse() is called to perform a new course insertion action via Java persistence API and entity classes.

C. The running status of the session bean method is returned to the consuming project.

At this point, we have finished all coding processes for the course insertion action. Now we can build and deploy our Web service to save these codes.

9.14.8.9 Build and Deploy the Web Service Project

Perform the following operations to build and deploy our Web service project:

1. Click on the Clean and Build Main Project button to build our Web service.
2. Right click on our Web application WebServiceOracleApp and select the Deploy item to deploy our Web service. If everything is fine, a successful deployment result should be displayed, as shown in Figure 9.96.

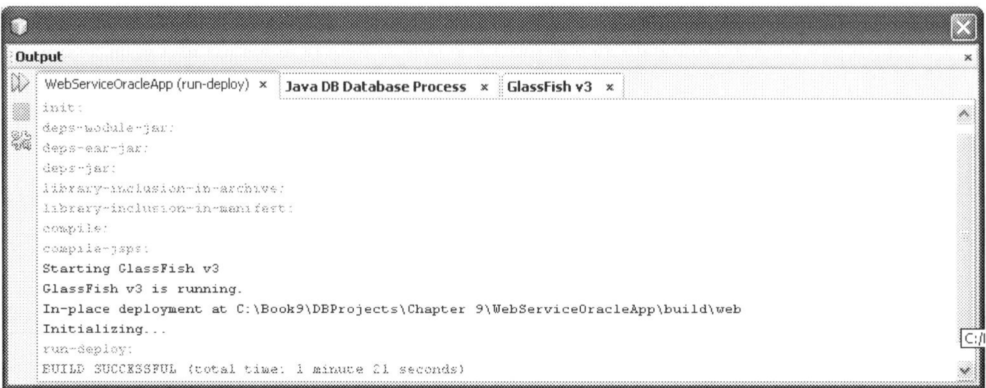

Figure 9.96. The deployment result of our Web service project.

A problem arises when testing this Web service project using the tester page, which is the input parameter array cdata. As we know, the cdata has a data type of ArrayList, and it needs to (1) create an ArrayList instance, and then (2) assign a group of new course information to that ArrayList object to call this Web service operation InsertCourse() to perform the course data insertion. However, it is difficult to do those two operations manually by using this tester page. Therefore, we need to create some Web client projects to consume and test this Web service project in the later sections.

Next, let's discuss how to update a course record using the Web service operations.

As we discussed in the previous sections, the key point to perform a course data updating is that in most real applications, all pieces of course information should be updated except the course_id, since it is much easier to insert a new course record with a new course_id than updating a record with an updated course_id because of the complexity in cascaded updating relationships we built in Chapter 2 when we create our sample database. Therefore, in this section, we will concentrate on the updating a course record based on an existing course_id.

As we discussed in Section 9.14.6, to update an existing course record in the Course table, we need to build a Web service operation UpdateCourse() and a session bean method setCourse(), respectively. First, let's take care of creating the session bean method setCourse() in our session bean class CourseFacade.java.

9.14.8.10 Create and Build Session Bean Method setCourse()

Perform the following operations to create a new method setCourse() in our session bean class CourseFacade.java:

1. Open our Web service application project WebServiceOracleApp and double click on our session bean class CourseFacade.java from the Projects window to open it.
2. Right click on any place inside our session bean class body, and choose the Insert Code item and select the Add Business Method item to open the Add Business Method wizard.
3. Enter setCourse into the Name field and click on the Browse button that is next to the Return Type combo box. On the opened Find Type wizard, type boolean into the top field and select the Boolean (java.lang) from the list and click on the OK button.

4. Recall that in Chapter 2, when we built our sample database, the Course table contains seven columns. Therefore, in order to update an existing course record based on a selected course_id, we need to pass six updated course columns' values with the seventh value that is the selected course_id. We like to use an ArrayList object to store those parameters. Click on the Add button and enter cdata into the Name parameter field. Then click on the drop-down arrow of the Type combo box, select the Choose item to open the Find Type wizard. Type arraylist into the top field and select the ArrayList (java.util) data type, and click on the OK button to select an ArrayList as the data type for the input parameter.

Your finished Add Business Method wizard should match the one that is shown in Figure 9.97. Click on the OK button to complete this business method creation process.

Now let's develop the codes for this method.

Click on the Source button on the top of this window to open the code window of our session bean class CourseFacade.java. Enter the codes that are shown in Figure 9.98 into this new method setCourse(). The newly added codes have been highlighted in bold.

Figure 9.97. The finished Add Business Method wizard.

```
  public void edit(Course course) {
       em.merge(course);
  }
  public Boolean setCourse(ArrayList cdata) {
A      Course c = new Course();
B      String f_query = "SELECT f.facultyId FROM Faculty f WHERE f.facultyName = :FacultyName";
       Query fQuery = em.createQuery(f_query).setParameter("FacultyName", cdata.get(6).toString());
C      c.setCourseId(cdata.get(0).toString());
       c.setCourse(cdata.get(1).toString());
D      c.setCredit(new BigInteger(cdata.get(2).toString()));
       c.setClassroom(cdata.get(3).toString());
       c.setSchedule(cdata.get(4).toString());
E      c.setEnrollment(new BigInteger(cdata.get(5).toString()));
F      c.setFacultyId(new Faculty(fQuery.getSingleResult().toString()));
G      edit(c);
H      return true;
  }
```

Figure 9.98. The codes for the method setCourse().

The codes for this method is similar to those we built for the newCourse() method, and we also utilized a built-in method edit() that is created and added into this session bean class automatically when this session bean is created.

Similar to our discussions in Section 9.14.8.7, in order to update an existing course record in the Course table based on the existing course_id and a selected faculty member, exactly the faculty_name, we need to perform two queries from two tables.

- First, we need to perform a query to the Faculty table to get a matched faculty_id based on the selected faculty member (faculty_name).
- Then, we need to perform another action to the Course table to update an existing course record including the faculty_id that is obtained from the first query.

Based on this discussion, let's have a closer look at the codes shown in Figure 9.93 to see how it works.

A. First, a new Course object **c** is created, since we want to call a built-in method edit() to perform this course data updating, and that method needs a Course object as the argument.

B. Then, the first query is executed to get a matched faculty_id based on the selected faculty_name, which is the sixth input parameter stored in our ArrayList instance cdata. A combination command is used to perform the named parameter setup operation.

C. Seven setter methods are executed to pick up seven input parameters that represent an updated course record and set each of them to the associated column in the new Course object **c**.

D. Points to be noted are steps D and E. Since the data types for the 2nd and 5th parameters, credit and enrollment, in the input ArrayList instance are BigInteger, we must convert both data into that data type by creating a new instance of BigInteger class.

F. Since the setFacultyId() method needs a Faculty class as the argument data type, we need to create a new Faculty instance with the queried faculty_id as the argument to meet this requirement. Here, we did not assign the first query result to a local variable as we did in the newCourse() method; instead we directly use the query result of the first query as an argument for this new Faculty instance.

G. The built-in method edit() is called with the built Course instance c as the argument. The function of the edit() method is to update an existing record and merge it to that original record in the Course table. No query result is returned for this method.

H. A `true` is returned to the associated Web operation to indicate that this data updating is successful.

During the coding process, you may encounter some real-time compiling errors. Most of these errors are introduced by missing some packages that contain classes or components used in this file. To fix these errors, just right click on this code window and select the Fix Imports item to load and import those missed packages to the top of this code window.

To save this piece of codes, click on the Clean and Build Main Project button on the top to build our project.

Next, let's create and build our fourth Web service operation UpdateCourse() to call this session bean method setCourse() to update an existing course record in our Course table.

9.14.8.11 Create and Build Web Service Operation UpdateCourse()

Perform the following operations to add this new operation into our Web service:

1. Launch NetBeans IDE and open our Web service project WebServiceOracleApp, and double click on our Web service main class file WebServiceOracle.java from the Projects window to open it.
2. Click on the Design button on the top of the window to open the Design View of our Web service project WebServiceOracle.
3. Click on the Add Operation button to open the `Add Operation` wizard.
4. Enter UpdateCourse into the `Name` field and click on the Browse button that is next to the `Return Type` combo box. Type boolean into the `Type Name` field and select the item Boolean (java.lang) from the list, and click on the OK button.
5. Click on the Add button and enter cdata into the `Name` parameter field. Then click on the drop-down arrow of the Type combo box, and select the Choose item to open the `Find Type` wizard. Type arraylist into the top field and select the ArrayList (java.util) data type, and click on the OK button to select an ArrayList as the data type for the input parameter.

Your finished `Add Operation` wizard should match the one that is shown in Figure 9.99. Click on the OK button to complete this new operation creation process.

Click on the Source button on the top of this window to open the code window of our Web service project. Let's perform the coding for this newly added operation.

On the opened code window, enter the codes that are shown in Figure 9.100 into this newly added operation UpdateCourse().

Let's have a closer look at this piece of new added codes to see how it works.

A. A local Boolean variable update is created and initialized to false. This local variable is used to hold the running result of execution of the session bean method setCourse() that performs a course record updating action to the Course table in our sample database.

B. The session bean method setCourse() is called to perform a course record updating action via Java persistence API and entity classes.

C. The running status of the session bean method is returned to the consuming project.

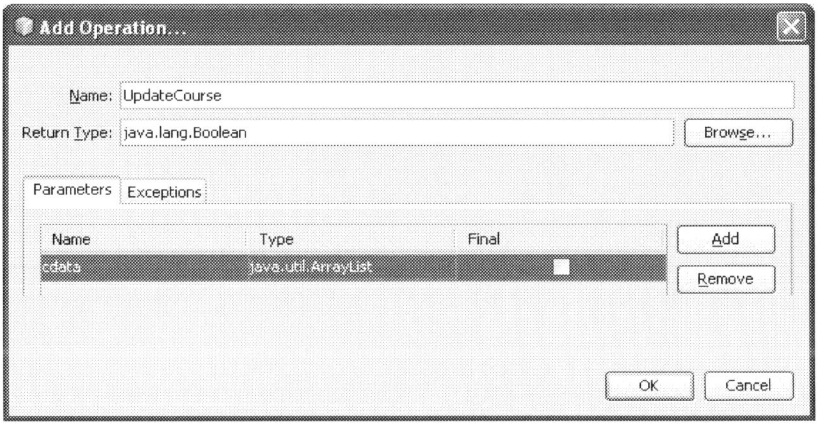

Add Operation...

Name	Type	Final
cdata	java.util.ArrayList	

Name: UpdateCourse
Return Type: java.lang.Boolean
Browse...
Parameters | Exceptions
Add
Remove
OK | Cancel

Figure 9.99. The complete Add Operation wizard.

```
  @WebMethod(operationName = "UpdateCourse")
    public Boolean UpdateCourse(@WebParam(name = "cdata")
    ArrayList cdata) {
      //TODO write your implementation code here:
A     Boolean update = false;

B     update = courseFacade.setCourse(cdata);
C     return update;
  }
```

Figure 9.100. The codes for the Web service operation UpdateCourse().

At this point, we have finished all coding processes for the course data updating action. Now we can build and deploy our Web service to save these codes.

9.14.8.12 Build and Deploy the Web Service Project

Perform the following operations to build and deploy our Web service project:

1. Click on the Clean and Build Main Project button to build our Web service.
2. Right click on our Web application WebServiceOracleApp and select the Deploy item to deploy our Web service. If everything is fine, a successful deployment result should be displayed.

A problem arises when testing this Web service project using the tester page, which is the input parameter array cdata. As we know, the cdata has a data type of ArrayList, and it needs to (1) create an ArrayList instance, and then (2) assign a group of updated course information to that ArrayList object to call this Web service operation UpdateCourse() to perform the course data updating. However, it is difficult to do those two operations manually by using this tester page. Therefore, we need to create some Web client projects to consume and test this Web service project in the later sections.

Next, let's discuss how to delete a course record using the Web service operations.

9.14.8.13 Create and Build Session Bean Method removeCourse()

Perform the following operations to create a new method removeCourse() in our session bean class CourseFacade.java:

1. Open our Web service application project WebServiceOracleApp and double click on our session bean class CourseFacade.java from the Projects window to open it.
2. Right click on any place inside our session bean class body, choose Insert Code item and select the Add Business Method item to open the Add Business Method wizard.
3. Enter removeCourse into the Name field and click on the Browse button that is next to the Return Type combo box. On the opened Find Type wizard, type boolean into the top field and select the Boolean (java.lang) from the list and click on the OK button.
4. Click on the Add button to add one argument for this method. Enter cid into the Name column and keep the default data type java.lang.String unchanged. Your finished Add Business Method wizard should match the one that is shown in Figure 9.101. Click on the OK button to complete this business method creation process.

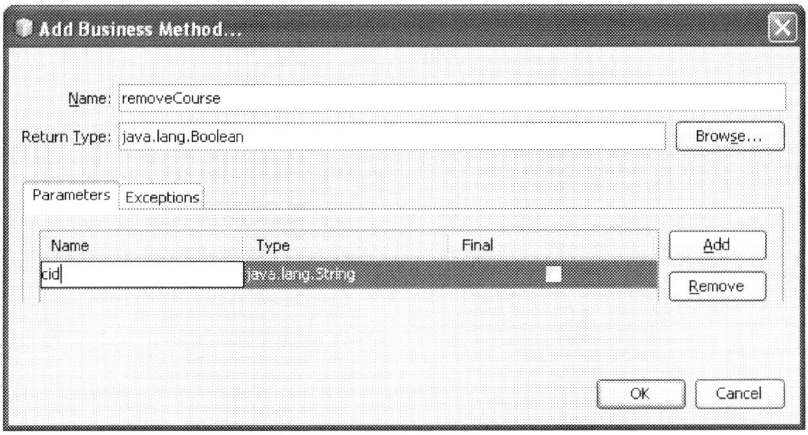

Figure 9.101. The finished Add Business Method wizard.

```
  public void remove(Course course) {
        em.remove(em.merge(course));
   }
   public Boolean removeCourse(String cid) {
A      Course c = new Course(cid);

B      remove(c);
C      return true;
  }
```

Figure 9.102. The codes for the method removeCourse().

Now let's develop the codes for this newly added method.

Click on the Source button on the top of this window to open the code window of our session bean class CourseFacade.java. Enter the codes that are shown in Figure 9.102 into this new method removeCourse(). The new added codes have been highlighted in bold.

The codes for this method is very simple since we utilized a built-in method remove() that is created and added into this session bean class automatically when this session bean is created.

Let's have a closer look at this piece of codes to see how it works.

A. A new Course instance is created first with the course_id as the argument since we need to call a built-in method remove() to perform this course record deleting action, and that method needs a Course object as the argument.

B. The built-in method remove() is called to try to delete a course record with the course_id as the deleting criterion. The function of this built-in method is to find the target course record and remove it from the Course table in our sample database.

C. A `true` is returned to the associated Web operation.

To save this piece of codes, click on the Clean and Build Main Project button on the top to build our project.

Next, let's create and build our last Web service operation DeleteCourse() to call this session bean method removeCourse() to delete an existing course record from our Course table.

9.14.8.14 Create and Build Web Service Operation DeleteCourse()

Perform the following operations to add this new operation into our Web service:

1. Launch NetBeans IDE and open our Web service project WebServiceOracleApp, and double click on our Web service main class file WebServiceOracle.java from the Projects window to open it.
2. Click on the Design button on the top of the window to open the Design View of our Web service project WebServiceOracle.
3. Click on the Add Operation button to open the `Add Operation` wizard.
4. Enter DeleteCourse into the `Name` field and click on the Browse button that is next to the `Return Type` combo box. Type boolean into the `Type Name` field, and select the item Boolean (java.lang) from the list, and click on the OK button.
5. Click on the Add button and enter cid into the `Name` parameter field. Keep the default data type java.lang.String unchanged.

Your finished `Add Operation` wizard should match the one that is shown in Figure 9.103. Click on the OK button to complete this new operation creation process.

Click on the Source button on the top of this window to open the code window of our Web service project. Let's perform the coding for this new added operation.

On the opened code window, enter the codes that are shown in Figure 9.104 into this new added operation DeleteCourse().

Let's have a closer look at this piece of newly added codes to see how it works.

A. A local Boolean variable delete is created and initialized to false. This local variable is used to hold the running result of execution of the session bean method removeCourse() that performs a course record deleting action from the Course table in our sample database.

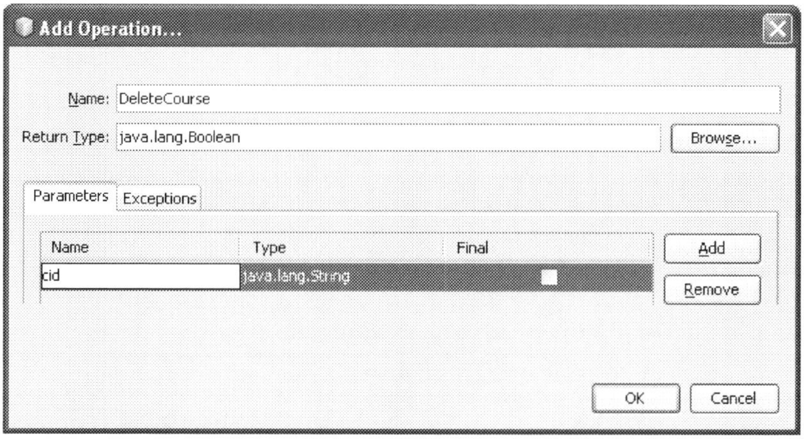

Figure 9.103. The complete Add Operation wizard.

```
  @WebMethod(operationName = "DeleteCourse")
    public Boolean DeleteCourse(@WebParam(name = "cid")
    String cid) {
      //TODO write your implementation code here:
A     Boolean delete = false;

B     delete = courseFacade.removeCourse(cid);
C     return delete;
  }
```

Figure 9.104. The codes for the Web service operation DeleteCourse().

B. The session bean method removeCourse() is called to perform a course record deleting action via Java persistence API and entity classes.

C. The running status of the session bean method is returned to the consuming project.

At this point, we have finished all coding processes for the course data deleting action. Now we can build, deploy, and test our Web service to save these codes.

9.14.8.15 Build and Test the Web Service Project

Perform the following operations to build and deploy our Web service project:

1. Click on the Clean and Build Main Project button to build our Web service.
2. Right click on our Web application WebServiceOracleApp and select the Deploy item to deploy our Web service. Enter the appropriate username and password to the Glassfish v3 server, such as admin and reback, which are used for this application, and click on the OK button to start the application server. If everything is fine, a successful deployment result should be displayed.
3. Expand the Web Services node under our Web service project and right click on our Web service target file WebServiceOracle, and choose the Test Web Service item to run our Web service project. The running status of our Web service is shown in Figure 9.105.
4. Enter a course_id to be deleted from the Course table, such as CSC-233B, into the text field and click on the deleteCourse button to test this course record deleting function. Immediately, you can find that a `true` is returned for this deleting action, which means that our data deleting is successful.

To confirm this course record deleting, open the Course table from the Services window in the NetBeans IDE. It can be found that the course CSC-233B has been deleted from the Course table.

The reason we selected the course CSC-233B as a deleting example is that this course has no relationship with the child table StudentCourse since no student has enrolled to that course. Recall that in Chapter 2, when we built our sample database, a one-to-many relationship has been set up between the primary table Course and the child table StudentCourse. Also, a cascaded deleting relationship has been set up for these two tables, which means that if a course in the Course table is deleted, the same course taken by students in the StudentCourse table will also be deleted. Since CSC-233B has not been taken by any student, therefore, no cascaded deleting relationship is existed for this course, and no deleting action will be performed for the StudentCourse table.

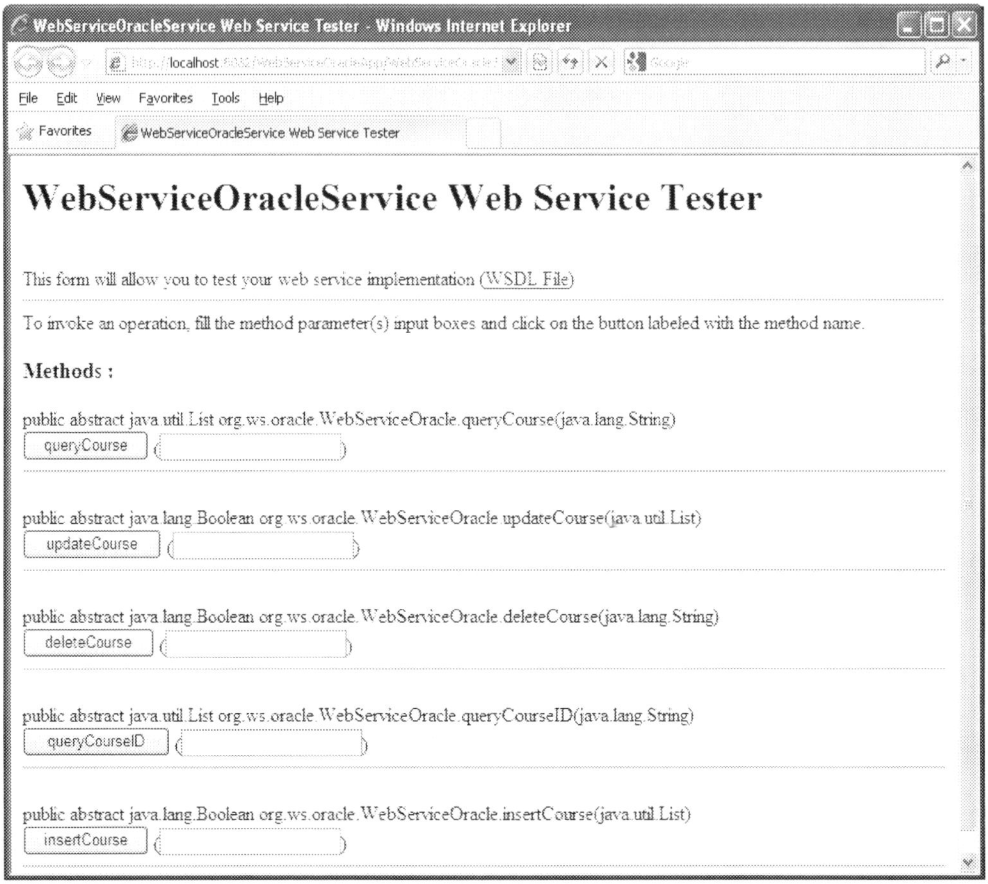

WebServiceOracleService Web Service Tester - Windows Internet Explorer

File Edit View Favorites Tools Help

Favorites WebServiceOracleService Web Service Tester

WebServiceOracleService Web Service Tester

This form will allow you to test your web service implementation (WSDL File)

To invoke an operation, fill the method parameter(s) input boxes and click on the button labeled with the method name.

Methods :

public abstract java.util.List org.ws.oracle.WebServiceOracle.queryCourse(java.lang.String)
queryCourse ( )

public abstract java.lang.Boolean org.ws.oracle.WebServiceOracle.updateCourse(java.util.List)
updateCourse ( )

public abstract java.lang.Boolean org.ws.oracle.WebServiceOracle.deleteCourse(java.lang.String)
deleteCourse ( )

public abstract java.util.List org.ws.oracle.WebServiceOracle.queryCourseID(java.lang.String)
queryCourseID ( )

public abstract java.lang.Boolean org.ws.oracle.WebServiceOracle.insertCourse(java.util.List)
insertCourse ( )

Figure 9.105. The running status of our Web service project.

Table 9.9. The original course record CSC-233B in the Course table

course_id	course	credit	classroom	schedule	enrollment	faculty_id
CSC-233B	Introduction to Algorithms	3	TC-302	M-W-F: 11:00-11:55 AM	19	K69880

It is highly recommended to recover this deleted course CSC-233B from our Course table in order to keep our sample database neat and complete. Refer to Table 9.9 to add this course into our Course table. You can do this data recovery using either the Oracle Database 10g XE or the opened Course table in the Services window in the NetBeans IDE.

At this point, we have finished developing and building our Web service project to access and manipulate data against our Oracle database. A complete Web service application project WebServiceOracleApp can be found from the folder DBProjects\Chapter 9 that is located at the Wiley ftp site (refer to Figure 1.2 in Chapter 1).

Next, let's build some Windows-based and Web-based client projects to consume this Web service. First, let's build a Windows-based client project WinClientOracle.

9.15 BUILD A WINDOWS-BASED WEB CLIENT PROJECT TO CONSUME THE WEB SERVICE

To save time and space, we can use some components we built in one Windows-based project SQLSelectObject in Section 6.4 in Chapter 6 to build this client project. The project can be found from the folder DBProjects\Chapter 6 that is located at the Wiley ftp site (refer to Figure 1.2 in Chapter 1).

9.15.1 Create a New Windows-Based Web Client Project WinClientOracle

Perform the following operations to create a new Windows-based Web client project WinClientOracle to consume our Web service:

1. Launch NetBeans IDE and choose File > New Project item.
2. Select Java and Java Application from the `Categories` and the `Projects` lists, respectively. Click on the Next button.
3. Name the project as WinClientOracle and select a desired folder to save this project. Uncheck the Create Main Class checkbox. Your finished `Name and Location` wizard should match the one that is shown in Figure 9.106.

Click on the Finish button to create this new project.

Next, let's copy some components from the project SQLSelectObject we built in Section 6.4 in Chapter 6, and paste them into this new project as our GUIs.

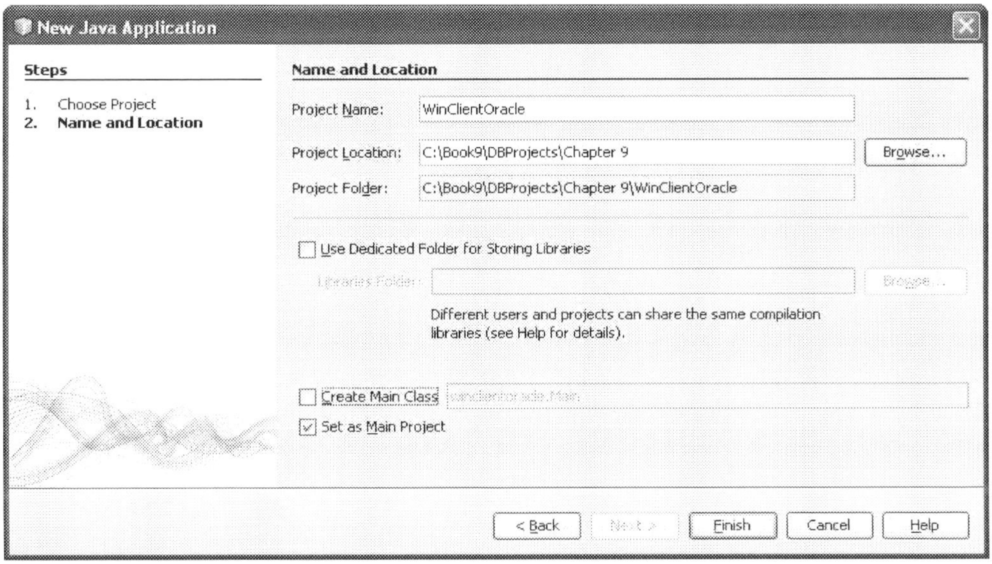

Figure 9.106. The finished Name and Location wizard.

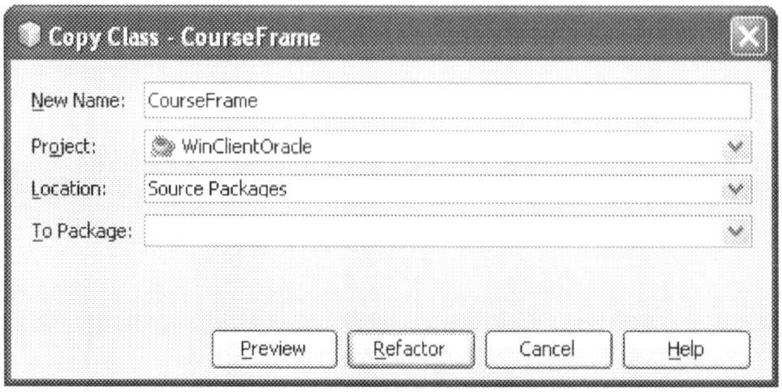

Figure 9.107. The finished Copy Class wizard.

9.15.2 Copy the CourseFrame and MsgDislog Components as GUIs

Perform the following operations to complete these copy-and-paste actions:

1. Go to the Wiley ftp site (refer to Figure 1.2 in Chapter 1), load and open the project SQLSelectObject from the folder DBProjects\Chapter 6.
2. On the opened project, right click on the Course Frame file CourseFrame.java under the project package node, and select the Refactor > Copy item to copy this form file.
3. On the opened Copy Class—CourseFrame wizard, select our new project WinClientOracle from the `Project` combo box and remove the 1 after the CourseFrame from the `New Name` field.
4. Your finished Copy Class—CourseFrame wizard is shown in Figure 9.107.
5. Click on the Refactor button to make a refactoring copy for this frame file.
6. Perform a similar operation to copy the MsgDialog.java GUI and paste it into our new project WinClientOracle.

Now return to our new project WinClientOracle; you can find that a copied CourseFrame.java and a MsgDialog.java file have been pasted in the default package in our new project.

Next, let's open the code window of the CourseFrame.java class file and perform some modifications to the copied codes for this file to make it as our client testing project:

1. Remove all codes from the cmdSelectActionPerformed() method.
2. Remove all codes from the CourseListValueChanged() method.

Since we need to use this form as our main GUI to interface to our Web service to perform five course data related actions, we need to modify this form by adding some buttons and fields to allow us to do those actions. Perform the following operations to modify this form:

1. Click on the Design button to open the CourseFrame form window.
2. Add a Label and a Text Field into the `Course Information` panel with the properties shown in Table 9.10.

Table 9.10. Objects and controls added into the CourseFrame window

Type	Variable Name	Text	editable	Title
Label	Label1	Course ID		
Text Field	CourseIDField		checked	
Button	cmdUpdate	Update		
Button	cmdDelete	Delete		

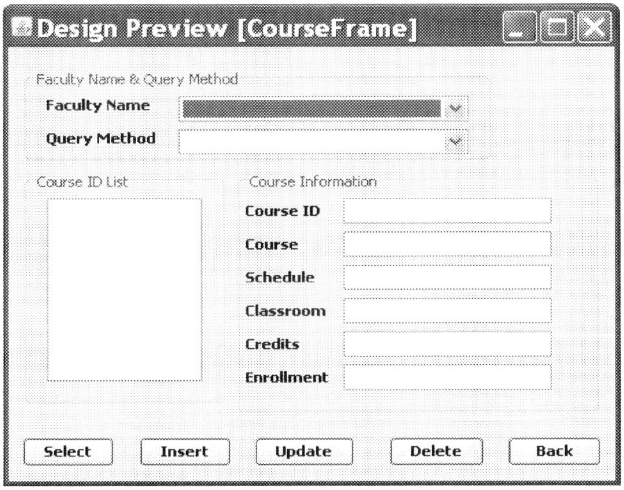

Figure 9.108. The modified CourseFrame form window.

3. Add two buttons, Update and Delete, with the properties shown in Table 9.10. Also, rearrange these five buttons to the bottom of the CourseFrame form.

Your finished CourseFrame form window should match the one that is shown in Figure 9.108.

Click on the Clean and Build Main Project button to build and save our project. Before we can build the codes for these methods, first we need to add our Web service reference into this new client project to enable our client to recognize our Web service and its operations.

9.15.3 Create a Web Service Reference for Our Windows-Based Client Project

Perform the following operations to set up a Web service reference for our client project:

1. Right click on our client project WinClientOracle from the Projects window, and select the New > Other item to open the `New File` wizard.

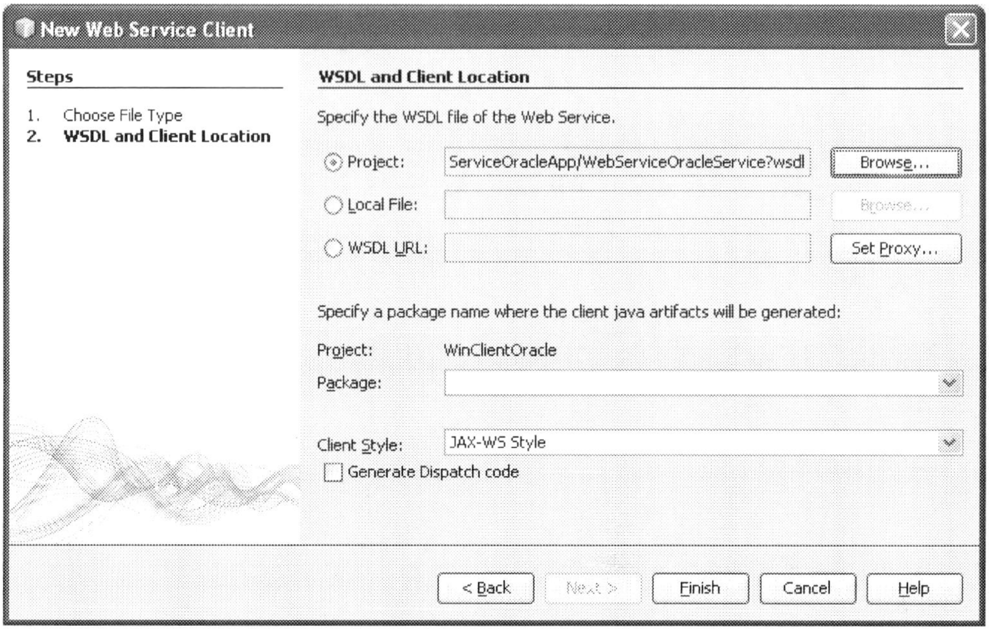

Figure 9.109. The finished New Web Service Client wizard.

2. On the opened New File wizard, select Web Services from the Categories and Web Service Client from the File Types list, respectively. Click on the Next button to continue.
3. Click on the Browse button for the Project field and expand our Web application project WebServiceOracleApp, and click on our Web service project WebServiceOracle to select it. Then click on the OK button to select this Web service. Your finished Web Service Client wizard should match the one that is shown in Figure 9.109.
4. Click on the Finish button to complete this Web service reference setup process.

Immediately, you can find a new node named Web Service References has been created and added into our client project. Expand this node and you can find the associated Web service port and our five Web service operations under that node.

Now let's develop the codes for this project to call the Web service to perform the data query and manipulations against the Course table in our sample database.

9.15.4 Develop the Codes to Call Our Web Service Project

In our Web service project WebServiceOracle, we built five operations with five different data actions against the Course table in our sample database. We need to develop the codes for five buttons, exactly five methods related to those five buttons, in our new client project WinClientOracle to call those five operations in our Web service to perform the desired data actions to the Course table. Table 9.11 shows these relationships

Table 9.11. The relationship between each button's method and each operation

Client Button & Method	Web Service Operation	Function
Select cmdSelectActionPerformed()	QueryCourseID()	Query all **course_id** taught by the selected faculty
CourseListValueChanged()	QueryCourse()	Query detailed information for selected **course_id**
Insert cmdInsertActionPerformed()	InsertCourse()	Insert a new course record into the Course table
Update cmdUpdateActionPerformed()	UpdateCourse()	Update an existing course record in the Course table
Delete cmdDeleteActionPerformed()	DeleteCourse()	Delete a course record from the Course table

between each button's method in our client project and each operation defined in our Web service.

Let's start our coding process from the first button Select in our client project and its method cmdSelectActionPerformed().

9.15.4.1 Build Codes for the Select Button Method to Query CourseIDs

The function of this method is to query all course_id taught by the selected faculty member as the Select button is clicked by the user. The queried result will be added and displayed in the Course ID List box in this CourseFrame form.

On the opened Design view of the CourseFrame form window, double click on the Select button to open this method. Perform the following operations to add the Web service operation QueryCourseID() into this method:

1. Browse to the Web Service References node under our client project WinClientOracle.
2. Expand our Web service and its port until all our five Web service operations have been exposed.
3. Drag the QueryCourseID operation and place it inside the cmdSelectActionPerformed() method.
4. A piece of codes is automatically created and added into this method, as shown in Figure 9.110.

It is unnecessary to explain the function of this piece of codes line by line since all of coding lines have been illustrated by the built-in comments.

Now let's do some modifications to this piece of codes and add some codes to meet our course_id query requirements. Enter the codes that are shown in Figure 9.111 into this method, and the modified codes have been highlighted in bold.

Let's have a closer look at this piece of newly added codes to see how it works.

A. Two local variables, al and cResult, are created first. The first is an ArrayList instance that is used to hold the query result, and the second is a String array used to convert the query result and display it in the `Course ID List`.

B. The Web service operation QueryCourseID() is called to perform this course data query to collect all course_id taught by the selected faculty member that is obtained from the

```
  private void cmdSelectActionPerformed(java.awt.event.ActionEvent evt) {
      // TODO add your handling code here:
      try { // Call Web Service Operation
A         org.ws.oracle.WebServiceOracleService service = new org.ws.oracle.WebServiceOracleService();
B         org.ws.oracle.WebServiceOracle port = service.getWebServiceOraclePort();
          // TODO initialize WS operation arguments here
C         java.lang.String fname = "";
          // TODO process result here
D         java.util.List<java.lang.Object> result = port.queryCourseID(fname);
          System.out.println("Result = "+result);
E     } catch (Exception ex) {
          // TODO handle custom exceptions here
      }
  }
```

Figure 9.110. The automatically created and added codes.

```
  private void cmdSelectActionPerformed(java.awt.event.ActionEvent evt) {
      // TODO add your handling code here:
A     ArrayList<String> al = new ArrayList<String>();
      String[] cResult = new String[6];
      try { // Call Web Service Operation
          org.ws.oracle.WebServiceOracleService service = new org.ws.oracle.WebServiceOracleService();
          org.ws.oracle.WebServiceOracle port = service.getWebServiceOraclePort();
          // TODO process result here
B         al = (ArrayList)port.queryCourseID(ComboName.getSelectedItem().toString());
C         for (int col = 0; col < al.size(); col++)
              cResult[col] = al.get(col).toString();
D         CourseList.setListData(cResult);
E     } catch (Exception ex) {
          msgDlg.setMessage("exception is: " + ex);
          msgDlg.setVisible(true);
      }
  }
```

Figure 9.111. The modified codes for the cmdSelectActionPerformed() method.

ComboName combo box. The query result is returned and assigned to the local ArrayList instance al.

C. A `for` loop is used to pick up each course_id and assign it to each element in the cResult[] array.

D. The converted query result is sent to the Course ID List variable, CourseList, to have it displayed in there using the setListData() method.

E. The `catch` block is used to track and display any possible exception during this course_id query process.

Now we have finished the coding process for calling the Web service operation QueryCourseID() to query all course_id based on the selected faculty member. Click on the Clean and Build Main Project button to build our project.

Click on the Run Main Project button to run our client project to test this course_id query function. Select the CourseFrame as our main class and click on the OK button to the `Run Project` dialog to run our project.

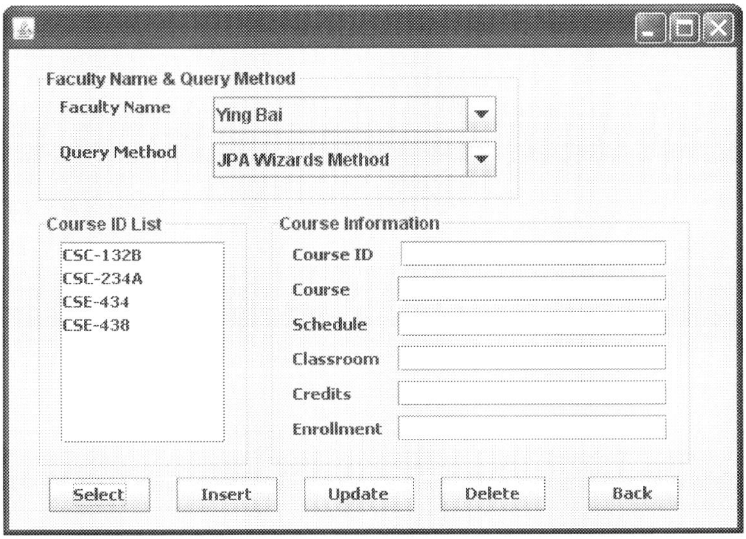

Figure 9.112. The running result of the course_id query.

On the opened client project, keep the default faculty member Ying Bai unchanged and click on the Select button to query all course_id taught by this selected faculty. Immediately, you can find that all four courses or four course_id taught by this faculty have been returned and displayed in the `Course ID List` box, as shown in Figure 9.112.

You can try to query course_id for other faculty members. Our client project in querying course_id is successful.

Next, let's take care of the coding for the CourseListValueChanged() method to query the detailed course information for a selected course_id from the Course ID List.

9.15.4.2 Build Codes for the CourseListValueChanged() Method to Get Course Details

The function of this method is that when a user clicks a course_id from the Course ID List box, the detailed course information, such as the course title, credit, classroom, schedule, and enrollment for the selected course_id, will be retrieved and displayed in six text fields in this CourseFrame form window.

Perform the following operations to build the codes for this method to perform this function:

1. Open our client project WinClientOracle if it has not been opened, and open our main GUI CourseFrame.java by double clicking on it.
2. Click on the Design button on the top of the window to open the GUI window, and right click on our `Course ID List` Listbox and select Events > ListSelection > valueChanged item to open this method.
3. Go to the Projects window and browse to our Web Service References node; expand this node until all of our five Web service operations are exposed. Drag the QueryCourse operation and place it into this method.
4. A piece of codes is created and added into this method, as shown in Figure 9.113.

```
  private void CourseListValueChanged(javax.swing.event.ListSelectionEvent evt) {
      // TODO add your handling code here:
      try { // Call Web Service Operation
A        org.ws.oracle.WebServiceOracleService service = new org.ws.oracle.WebServiceOracleService();
B        org.ws.oracle.WebServiceOracle port = service.getWebServiceOraclePort();
         // TODO initialize WS operation arguments here
C        java.lang.String courseID = "";
         // TODO process result here
D        java.util.List<java.lang.Object> result = port.queryCourse(courseID);
         System.out.println("Result = "+result);
E     } catch (Exception ex) {
         // TODO handle custom exceptions here
      }
  }
```

Figure 9.113. The automatically created and added codes.

```
  private void CourseListValueChanged(javax.swing.event.ListSelectionEvent evt) {
     // TODO add your handling code here:
A    ArrayList<String> al = new ArrayList<String>();
B    JTextField[] cField = {CourseIDField, CourseField, CreditField, ClassroomField, ScheduleField, EnrollField};
C    if(!CourseList.getValueIsAdjusting() ) {
        String courseid = (String)CourseList.getSelectedValue();
D       if (courseid != null){
           try { // Call Web Service Operation
                org.ws.oracle.WebServiceOracleService service = new org.ws.oracle.WebServiceOracleService();
                org.ws.oracle.WebServiceOracle port = service.getWebServiceOraclePort();
               // TODO initialize WS operation arguments here
E              al = (ArrayList)port.queryCourse(courseid);
F              for (int col = 0; col < al.size(); col++)
                  cField[col].setText(al.get(col).toString());
G          } catch (Exception ex) {
               msgDlg.setMessage("exception is: " + ex);
               msgDlg.setVisible(true);
           }
        }
     }
  }
```

Figure 9.114. The modified codes for the CourseListValueChanged() method.

It is unnecessary to explain the function of this piece of codes line by line since all coding lines have been illustrated by the built-in comments.

Now let's do some modifications to this piece of codes and add some codes to meet our course query requirements. Enter the codes that are shown in Figure 9.114 into this method, and the modified codes have been highlighted in bold.

Let's have a closer look at this piece of new added codes to see how it works.

A. An ArrayList instance al is created first, and it is used to collect the query result stored in an ArrayList object that is returned from the execution of the Web service operation QueryCourse().

B. A JTextField array cField[] is created and initialized with six text fields in this CourseFrame form. The purpose of this array is to store queried course details and display them in these six text fields.

C. Since the JList component belongs to the javax.swing package, not java.awt package, therefore, a clicking on an entry in the CourseList box causes the itemStateChanged() method to fire twice. Once when the mouse button is depressed, and once again when it is released. Therefore, the selected course_id will be appeared twice when it is selected. To prevent this from occurring, the getValueIsAdjusting() method is used to make sure that no item has been adjusted to be displayed twice. Then the selected course_id is assigned to a local String variable courseid by calling the getSelectedValue() method of the CourseList Box class.

D. Before we can proceed to the course query operation, first we need to confirm that the selected courseid is not a null value. A null value would be returned if the user did not select any course_id from the CourseList box; instead, the user just clicked on the Select button to try to find all courses taught by other faculty members. Even the user only clicked on the Select button without touching any course_id in the CourseList box; however, the system still considers that a null course_id has been selected and thus a null value will be returned. To avoid that situation from occurring, an `if` selection structure is used to make sure that no null value has been returned from the CourseList box.

E. The Web service operation QueryCourse() is called to perform this course data query to collect detailed course information for the selected course_id. The query result is returned and assigned to the local ArrayList instance al. A cast `(ArrayList)` is necessary for this assignment since the data type of al is an ArrayList<String> in this method.

F. A `for` loop is used to pick up each piece of detailed course information and assign it to each text field in the cField[] array using the setText() method.

G. The `catch` block is used to track and display any possible exception during this course_id query process.

During the coding process, you may encounter some real-time compiling errors. Most of these errors are introduced by missing some packages that contain classes or components used in this file. To fix these errors, just right click on this code window and select the Fix Imports item to load and import those missed packages to the top of this code window.

Now we have finished the coding process for calling the Web service operation QueryCourse() to query detailed course information based on the selected course_id. Click on the Clean and Build Main Project button to build our project.

Click on the Run Main Project button to run our client project to test this course query function.

On the opened client project, keep the default faculty member Ying Bai unchanged and click on the Select button to query all course_id taught by this selected faculty. Immediately, you can find that all four courses or four course_id taught by this faculty have been returned and displayed in the `Course ID List` box. To get course details for a selected course_id, just click on that course_id from the Course ID List. Figure 9.115 shows an example of course details for a course_id that is CSE-438.

You can try to click the different course_id to get related detailed course information. Our client project in querying detailed course information is successful.

A point to be noted is that before you can run any client project to consume a Web service, make sure that the Web service has been successfully deployed and the Glassfish v3 server is running. To confirm this, just build and deploy the Web service one more time before you run the client project to consume it, especially if you just start or restart the NetBeans IDE since the server will be stopped when the IDE is exited.

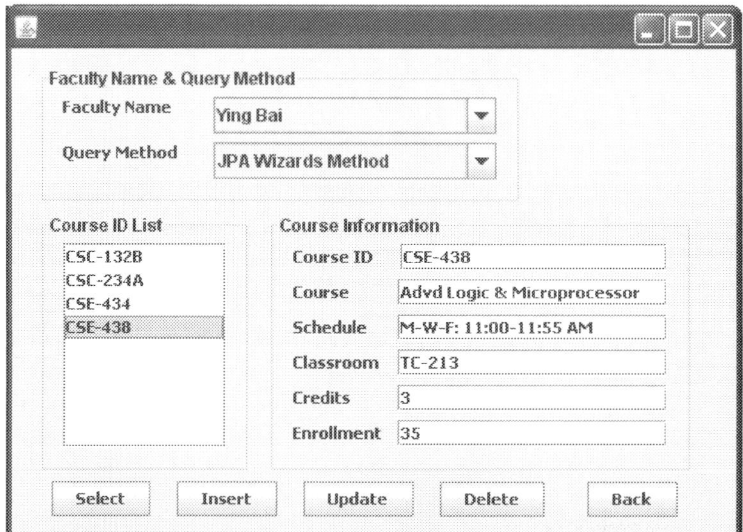

Figure 9.115. Running result for an example course_id CSE-438.

Next, let's take care of the coding for the cmdInsertActionPerformed() method to insert a new course record into the Course table in our sample database.

9.15.4.3 Build Codes for the Insert Button Method to Insert Courses

The function of this method is to insert a new course record as the Insert button is clicked by the user. The new course record will be inserted into the Course table in our sample Oracle database when this method is complete.

On the opened Design view of the CourseFrame form window, double click on the Insert button to open this method. Perform the following operations to add the Web service operation InsertCourse() into this method:

1. Browse to the Web Service References node under our client project WinClientOracle.
2. Expand our Web service and its port until all our five Web service operations have been exposed.
3. Drag the InsertCourse operation and place it inside the cmdInsertActionPerformed() method.
4. A piece of codes is created and added into this method, as shown in Figure 9.116.

It is unnecessary to explain the function of this piece of codes line by line since all of coding lines have been illustrated by the built-in comments.

Now let's do some modifications to this piece of codes and add some codes to meet our new course record insertion requirements. Enter the codes that are shown in Figure 9.117 into this method, and the modified codes have been highlighted in bold.

Let's have a closer look at this piece of new added codes to see how it works.

A. Two local variables, insert and al, are created first. The first one is a Boolean variable used to hold the running result of the execution of the Web service operation InsertCourse(),

```
  private void cmdInsertActionPerformed(java.awt.event.ActionEvent evt) {
      // TODO add your handling code here:
      try { // Call Web Service Operation
A         org.ws.oracle.WebServiceOracleService service = new org.ws.oracle.WebServiceOracleService();
B         org.ws.oracle.WebServiceOracle port = service.getWebServiceOraclePort();
          // TODO initialize WS operation arguments here
C         java.util.List<java.lang.Object> cdata = null;
          // TODO process result here
D         java.lang.Boolean result = port.insertCourse(cdata);
          System.out.println("Result = "+result);
E     } catch (Exception ex) {
          // TODO handle custom exceptions here
      }
  }
```

Figure 9.116. The automatically created and added codes.

```
  private void cmdInsertActionPerformed(java.awt.event.ActionEvent evt) {
      // TODO add your handling code here:
A     Boolean insert = false;
      ArrayList al = new ArrayList();
B     al.clear();
C     al.add(0, CourseIDField.getText());
      al.add(1, CourseField.getText());
      al.add(2, CreditField.getText());
      al.add(3, ClassroomField.getText());
      al.add(4, ScheduleField.getText());
      al.add(5, EnrollField.getText());
      al.add(6, ComboName.getSelectedItem().toString());
      try { // Call Web Service Operation
          org.ws.oracle.WebServiceOracleService service = new org.ws.oracle.WebServiceOracleService();
          org.ws.oracle.WebServiceOracle port = service.getWebServiceOraclePort();
D         insert = port.insertCourse(al);
E         if (!insert)
             System.out.println("Error in course insertion...");
F     } catch (Exception ex) {
          msgDlg.setMessage("exception is: " + ex);
          msgDlg.setVisible(true);
      }
  }
```

Figure 9.117. The modified codes for the cmdInsertActionPerformed() method.

and the second is an ArrayList instance used to store a new course record to be inserted into the Course table in our sample database.

B. The ArrayList instance al is cleaned up using the clear() method to make sure that the al is empty before it can store any data.

C. A group of add() methods are used to add seven pieces of new course information into the ArrayList instance. One point to be noted is that the order in which to add these course parameters must be identical with the order of assigning these parameters to the Course object in the session bean method newCourse() in our Web service project WebServiceOracle. Refer to that method to make sure that both orders are identical. An optional way to do this assignment is to create a `JTextField` array and use a `for` loop.

D. The Web operation InsertCourse() is called to insert this new course record stored in the argument al into the Course table via our Web service. The execution result that is a Boolean variable is returned and assigned to the local variable insert.

E. If a `false` is returned, which means that this course data insertion has been failed, the system println() method is used to indicate this situation.

F. The catch block is used to track and display any possible exception during this data insertion process.

Now we have finished the coding process for calling the Web service operation InsertCourse() to insert a new course record into the Course table based on the selected faculty member. Click on the Clean and Build Main Project button to build our project. Click on the Run Main Project button to run our client project to test this course data insertion function.

On the opened client project, keep the default faculty member Ying Bai unchanged and click on the Select button to query all course_id taught by this selected faculty. Immediately, you can find that all four courses or four course_id taught by this faculty have been returned and displayed in the `Course ID List` box. To insert a new course, enter six pieces of new course information shown below into six text fields.

- Course ID: CSE-549
- Course: Fuzzy Systems
- Schedule: T-H: 1:30–2:45 PM
- Classroom: TC-302
- Credit: 3
- Enrollment: 25

Your finished CourseFrame window is shown in Figure 9.118.

Click on the Insert button to insert this new course record into the Course table in our sample database.

To test this new course insertion, there are more than one way can be used. The first way is to open the Course table to confirm this new course insertion. But the second way,

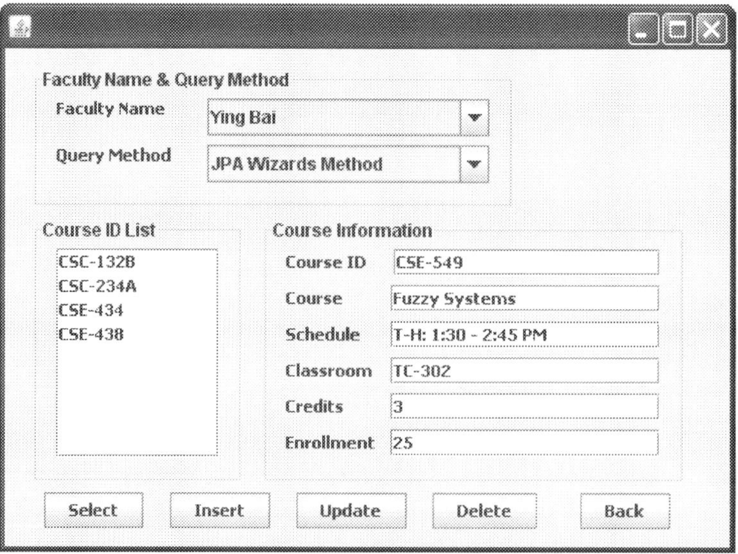

Figure 9.118. The new course record to be inserted.

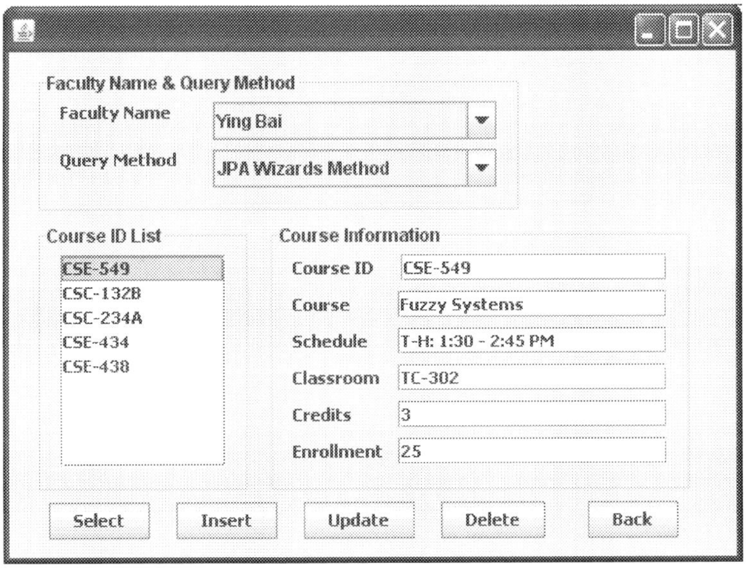

Figure 9.119. The confirmation of new inserted course CSE-549.

which is to use the Select button to perform a course query for the selected faculty, is an easy way. To use the second way to confirm this course insertion, keep the selected faculty member Ying Bai in the `Faculty Name` combo box unchanged, and just click on the Select button to query all course_id taught by this faculty. Immediately, you can find that our new inserted course CSE-549 has been retrieved and displayed in the Course ID List Listbox, which is shown in Figure 9.119.

To get detailed course information for this new inserted course, first click on any other course_id from this Listbox, then click on CSE-549 from the Course ID List Listbox. Six pieces of new inserted course information for the course CSE-549 are retrieved and displayed in six text fields, as shown in Figure 9.119.

Our new course insertion using Web service is successful.

Generally, it is recommended to remove this new inserted course from the Course table in our sample database to keep our database neat and clean. However, we will keep this inserted course right now since we need to use this record to perform the course updating and deleting actions in the following sections.

Next, let's discuss how to perform a course updating action to update an existing course in our sample database via Web service.

9.15.4.4 Build Codes for the Update Button Method to Update Courses

The function of this method is to update an existing course record as the Update button is clicked by the user. The existing course record will be updated in the Course table in our sample Oracle database when this method is complete.

On the opened Design view of the CourseFrame form window, double click on the Update button to open this method. Perform the following operations to add the Web service operation UpdateCourse() into this method:

1. Browse to the Web Service References node under our client project WinClientOracle.
2. Expand our Web service until all our five Web service operations have been exposed.
3. Drag the UpdateCourse operation and place it inside the cmdUpdateActionPerformed() method.
4. A piece of codes is automatically created and added into this method, which is shown in Figure 9.120.

It is unnecessary to explain the function of this piece of codes line by line since all of coding lines have been illustrated by the built-in comments.

Now let's do some modifications to this piece of codes and add some codes to meet our course record updating requirements. Enter the codes that are shown in Figure 9.121 into this method, and the modified codes have been highlighted in bold.

```
    private void cmdUpdateActionPerformed(java.awt.event.ActionEvent evt) {
        // TODO add your handling code here:
        try { // Call Web Service Operation
A           org.ws.oracle.WebServiceOracleService service = new org.ws.oracle.WebServiceOracleService();
B           org.ws.oracle.WebServiceOracle port = service.getWebServiceOraclePort();
            // TODO initialize WS operation arguments here
C           java.util.List<java.lang.Object> cdata = null;
            // TODO process result here
D           java.lang.Boolean result = port.updateCourse(cdata);
            System.out.println("Result = "+result);
E       } catch (Exception ex) {
            // TODO handle custom exceptions here
        }
    }
```

Figure 9.120. The automatically created and added codes.

```
    private void cmdUpdateActionPerformed(java.awt.event.ActionEvent evt) {
        // TODO add your handling code here:
A       Boolean update = false;
        ArrayList al = new ArrayList();

B       al.clear();
C       al.add(0, CourseIDField.getText());
        al.add(1, CourseField.getText());
        al.add(2, CreditField.getText());
        al.add(3, ClassroomField.getText());
        al.add(4, ScheduleField.getText());
        al.add(5, EnrollField.getText());
        al.add(6, ComboName.getSelectedItem().toString());

        try { // Call Web Service Operation
            org.ws.oracle.WebServiceOracleService service = new org.ws.oracle.WebServiceOracleService();
            org.ws.oracle.WebServiceOracle port = service.getWebServiceOraclePort();
D           update = port.updateCourse(al);
E           if (!update)
                System.out.println("Error in course updating...");
F       } catch (Exception ex) {
            msgDlg.setMessage("exception is: " + ex);
            msgDlg.setVisible(true);
        }
    }
```

Figure 9.121. The modified codes for the cmdUpdateActionPerformed() method.

This piece of codes is very similar to that we built for the Insert button's method. Let's have a closer look at this piece of new added codes to see how it works.

A. Two local variables, update and al, are created first. The first one is a Boolean variable used to hold the running result of the execution of the Web service operation UpdateCourse(), and the second is an ArrayList instance used to store a updating course record to be updated in the Course table in our sample database.

B. The ArrayList instance al is cleaned up using the clear() method to make sure that the al is empty before it can store any data.

C. A group of add() methods are used to add six pieces of updated course information into the ArrayList instance (The first parameter is a course_id that works as an updating criterion and will not be updated.). One point to be noted is that the order in which to add these course parameters must be identical with the order of assigning these parameters to the Course object in the session bean method setCourse() in our Web service project WebServiceOracle. Refer to that method to make sure that both orders are identical. An optional way to do this assignment is to create a `JTextField` array and use a `for` loop.

D. The Web operation UpdateCourse() is called to update this existing course record via our Web service. The execution result, which is a Boolean variable, is returned and assigned to the local variable update.

E. If a `false` is returned, which means that this course data updating has failed; the system println() method is used to indicate this situation.

F. The catch block is used to track and display any possible exception during this data updating process.

Now, we have finished the coding process for calling one of our Web service operations, UpdateCourse(), to update an existing course record in the Course table based on the selected faculty member. Click on the Clean and Build Main Project button to build our project. Click on the Run Main Project button to run our client project to test this course data updating function.

On the opened client project, keep the default faculty member Ying Bai unchanged, and click on the Select button to query all course_id taught by this selected faculty. Immediately, you can find that all four courses or four course_id taught by this faculty have been returned and displayed in the `Course ID List` box. To update an existing course CSE-549, enter six pieces of updated course information shown below into six text fields.

- Course ID: CSE-549
- Course: Modern Controls
- Schedule: M-W-F: 11:00–11:50 AM
- Classroom: TC-206
- Credit: 3
- Enrollment: 18

Your finished CourseFrame window is shown in Figure 9.122.

Click on the Update button to update this course record in the Course table in our sample database.

To test this course record updating action, there are more than one way that can be used. The first way is to open the Course table to confirm that this course has been

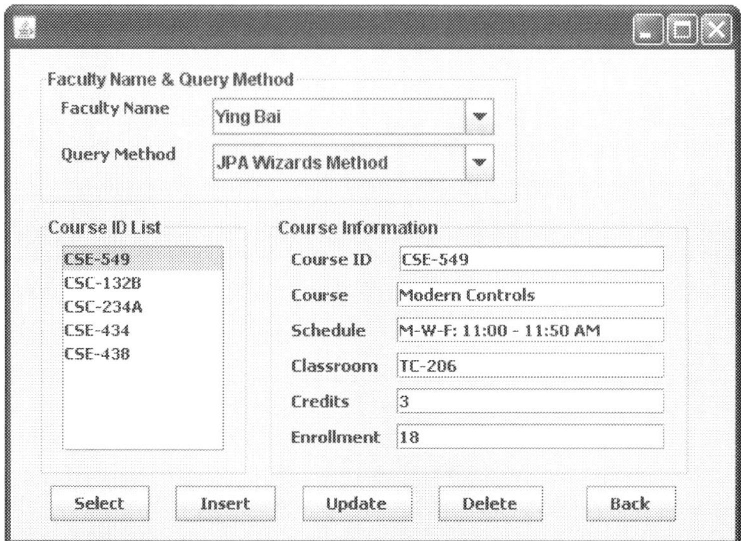

Figure 9.122. The updated course information for the course CSE-549.

updated. But the second way, which is to select the course_id whose course details have been updated from the Course ID List Listbox to get course details, is an easy way to confirm this course data updating.

Now let's use the second way to test this course data updating. Just click any other course_id, such as CSC-132B, from the Course ID List Listbox. Then click on the course_id CSE-549 whose details have been updated, to retrieve all course details. It can be found that this course is really updated based on the updating information shown in Figure 9.122.

Our course data updating using Web service is successful.

Generally it is recommended to recover this updated course in the Course table in our sample database to keep our database neat and clean. However, we will keep this course right now since we need to use this record to perform the course deleting action in the following section.

9.15.4.5 Build Codes for the Delete Button Method to Delete Courses

The function of this method is to delete an existing course record from our Course table as the Delete button is clicked by the user. The existing course record will be permanently deleted from the Course table in our sample Oracle database when this method is complete.

On the opened Design view of the CourseFrame form window, double click on the Delete button to open this method. Perform the following operations to add the Web service operation DeleteCourse() into this method:

1. Browse to the Web Service References node under our client project WinClientOracle.
2. Expand our Web service until all our five Web service operations have been exposed.
3. Drag the DeleteCourse operation and place it inside the cmdDeleteActionPerformed() method.

```
  private void cmdDeleteActionPerformed(java.awt.event.ActionEvent evt) {
      // TODO add your handling code here:
      try { // Call Web Service Operation
A         org.ws.oracle.WebServiceOracleService service = new org.ws.oracle.WebServiceOracleService();
B         org.ws.oracle.WebServiceOracle port = service.getWebServiceOraclePort();
          // TODO initialize WS operation arguments here
C         java.lang.String cid = "";
          // TODO process result here
D         java.lang.Boolean result = port.deleteCourse(cid);
          System.out.println("Result = "+result);
E     } catch (Exception ex) {
          // TODO handle custom exceptions here
      }
  }
```

Figure 9.123. The automatically created and added codes.

```
  private void cmdDeleteActionPerformed(java.awt.event.ActionEvent evt) {
      // TODO add your handling code here:
A     Boolean delete = false;
      try { // Call Web Service Operation
          org.ws.oracle.WebServiceOracleService service = new org.ws.oracle.WebServiceOracleService();
          org.ws.oracle.WebServiceOracle port = service.getWebServiceOraclePort();
B         delete = port.deleteCourse(CourseIDField.getText());
C         if (!delete)
              System.out.println("Error in course deleting...");
D     } catch (Exception ex) {
          msgDlg.setMessage("exception is: " + ex);
          msgDlg.setVisible(true);
      }
  }
```

Figure 9.124. The modified codes for the cmdDeleteActionPerformed() method.

4. A piece of codes is automatically created and added into this method, which is shown in Figure 9.123.

Now let's do some modifications to this piece of codes and add some codes to meet our course record deleting requirements. Enter the codes that are shown in Figure 9.124 into this method, and the modified codes have been highlighted in bold.

Let's have a closer look at this piece of newly added codes to see how it works.

A. A local variable delete is created first, and this variable is a Boolean variable used to hold the running result of the execution of the Web service operation DeleteCourse().

B. The Web service operation DeleteCourse() is called to delete an existing course record from our Course table based on the selected course_id. The running result is returned and assigned to the local variable delete.

C. If a `false` is returned, which means that this course data deleting has failed, the system println() method is used to indicate this situation.

D. The catch block is used to track and display any possible exception during this data deleting process.

Now we have finished the coding process for calling and executing our last Web service operation DeleteCourse() to delete an existing course record from the Course table based on the selected course_id. Click on the Clean and Build Main Project button to build our project. Click on the Run Main Project button to run our client project to test this course data deleting function.

On the opened client project, keep the default faculty member Ying Bai unchanged and click on the Select button to query all course_id taught by this selected faculty. Immediately, you can find that all four courses or four course_id taught by this faculty have been returned and displayed in the `Course ID List` box. To delete an existing course CSE-549, just click on this course_id from the Course ID List Listbox and click on the Delete button.

To confirm this course deleting action, two ways can be utilized. First, you can open our Course table to check whether this course has been deleted from our database. Another way, which is easy, is to use the Select button to try to retrieve this deleted course from our database. To do that, just keep the selected faculty member Ying Bai in the `Faculty Name` combo box unchanged and click on the Select button. It can be found from the returned courses, exactly all course_id taught by the selected faculty, that no CSE-549 is existed.

Our course record deleting using Web service is successful.

Generally, it is recommended to recover any deleted record from our database to keep our sample database neat and clean. However, since this course CSE-549 is added by us for testing purposes, therefore, we do not need to recover this course from our Course table.

At this point, we have finished all developing and building processes to consume our Web service using a Windows-based client project. A complete Windows-based client project that is used to consume our Web service to query and manipulate data against our Oracle database, WinClientOracle, can be found from the folder DBProjects\Chapter 9 that is located at the Wiley ftp site (refer to Figure 1.2 in Chapter 1).

Next, let's build a Web-based client project to consume this Web service.

9.16 BUILD A WEB-BASED WEB CLIENT PROJECT TO CONSUME THE WEB SERVICE

To save time and space, we can use some components in a Web application project JavaWebDBJSPOracle we developed in Chapter 8 to build our Web-based client consuming project WebClientOracle in this section. In fact, we will use the CoursePage.jsp file in that project and a Java managed bean class to query and manipulate course data in our sample Oracle database.

The structure of this Web-based client project is shown in Figure 9.125.

First, let's create our Web-based client project WebClientOracle.

9.16.1 Create a Web-Based Client Project WebClientOracle

Perform the following operations to create a new Web application project WebClientOracle:

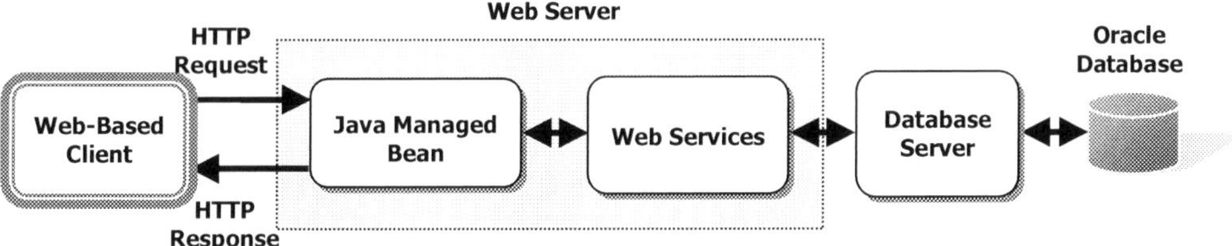

Figure 9.125. The architecture of our Web-based client project.

1. Launch NetBeans IDE and go to File > New Project item to open the `New Project` wizard. Select the Java Web from the `Categories` list and Web Application from the `Projects` list, then click o the Next button to go to the next wizard.
2. Enter WebClientOracle into the `Project Name` field as this new project's name. Make sure that the desired folder in which you want to save this project is included in the `Project Location` field and the `Set as Main Project` checkbox has been checked, then click on the Next button.
3. In the opened `Server and Settings` wizard, make sure that the GlassFish v3 server has been selected as the Web server for this Web application, and the Java EE 6 Web has been selected for this application. Refer to Section 5.3.5.2.2 in Chapter 5 to add this server to the NetBeans IDE if you have not done this. Click on the Next button to continue.
4. Select the JavaServer Faces as the Framework for this application and click on the Finish button to complete this new Web application creation process.

Since we need a JavaServer Face as a view to query and manipulate data against the Course table in our sample database, we need to add the CoursePage.jsp we built in the project JavaWebDBJSPOracle in Chapter 8 into our current project. Perform the following operations to complete this Web page addition process:

1. Open the JSP Files folder that is located at the Wiley ftp site (refer to Figure 1.2 in Chapter 1), copy the CoursePage.jsp file from that folder.
2. In the NetBeans IDE, open our project WebClientOracle and click on the Files button to open the Files window. Then right click on the web node under our current project WebClientOracle and select the Paste item to paste this JSF page into our current project.

Next, we need to create a Java managed bean class CourseBean.java and copy the codes from the managed bean CourseBean.java we built in the Web application project JavaWebDBJSPOracle, and paste them into our managed bean class CourseBean.java in our Web-based client project.

9.16.2 Create a Java Managed Bean CourseBean and Add the JDialog Class MsgDialog

Perform the following operations to create this Java managed bean and add a MsgDialog class into our current project:

1. Right click our Web-based client project WebClientOracle from the Projects window and select New > Other item to open the `New File` wizard.

2. On the opened wizard, select JavaServer Faces from the Categories and JSF Managed Bean from the File Types list, respectively. Then click on the Next button.
3. Name this managed bean as CourseBean, enter webclient into the Package field, and select the session from the Scope combo box. Then click on the Finish button to complete this JSF managed bean creation process.
4. Double click on our new created managed bean CourseBean.java to open its code window.
5. Now open the Web application project JavaWebDBJSPOracle we built in Chapter 8. You can find and download this project from the folder DBProjects\Chapter 8 at the Wiley ftp site (refer to Figure 1.2 in Chapter 1).
6. Expand the package JavaWebDBJSPOracle and copy all codes inside the managed bean class CourseBean (exclude the imported packages at the top of this file).
7. In our opened managed bean CourseBean.java, paste all copied codes inside this class.

Now perform the following operations to add an MsgDialog class into our current project:

1. Launch the NetBeans IDE and open the Web application project JavaWebDBJSPSQL. You can find and download this project from the folder DBProjects\Chapter 8 at the Wiley ftp site (refer to Figure 1.2 in Chapter 1).
2. Expand the package JavaWebDBJSPSQL and copy the file MsgDialog.java.
3. Open our Web-based client project WebClientOracle and right click on the webclient node and select the Paste item to paste this class into our project.

Next, let's do some modifications to the Java managed bean class to make it our bean class.

Perform the following modifications to this class:

1. Remove the first EJB injection line @EJB from this file.
2. Remove the second line, which is the session bean declaration statement private CourseSessionBean courseSessionBean; from the class file.
3. Remove all codes inside the following methods except the last line return null:
   - **A.** Select()
   - **B.** Details()
   - **C.** Update()
   - **D.** Delete()
4. Remove the default constructor public CourseBean() {}.
5. Add an import statement, import java.util.List;, to the top of this file.
6. Click on the Clean and Build Main Project button to compile the project.

Before we can develop the codes for the Java managed bean to perform course data query and manipulation, we need first to add a Web service reference to our current Web-based client project to enable our client to recognize our Web service and its operations.

9.16.3 Create a Web Service Reference for Our Web-Based Client Project

Perform the following operations to set up a Web service reference for our client project:

1. Right click on our client project WebClientOracle from the Projects window, and select the New > Other item to open the `New File` wizard.
2. On the opened `New File` wizard, select Web Services from the `Categories` and Web Service Client from the `File Types` list, respectively. Click on the Next button to continue.
3. Click on the Browse button for the Project field and expand our Web application project WebServiceOracleApp, and click on our Web service project WebServiceOracle to select it. Then click on the OK button to select this Web service. Your finished Web Service Client wizard should match the one that is shown in Figure 9.126.
4. Click on the Finish button to complete this Web service reference setup process.

Immediately, you can find that a new node named Web Service References has been created and added into our client project. Expand this node and you can find the associated Web service port and all our five Web service operations under that node.

A point to be noted is that you must deploy our Web service project first before you can add this Web Reference to any client project.

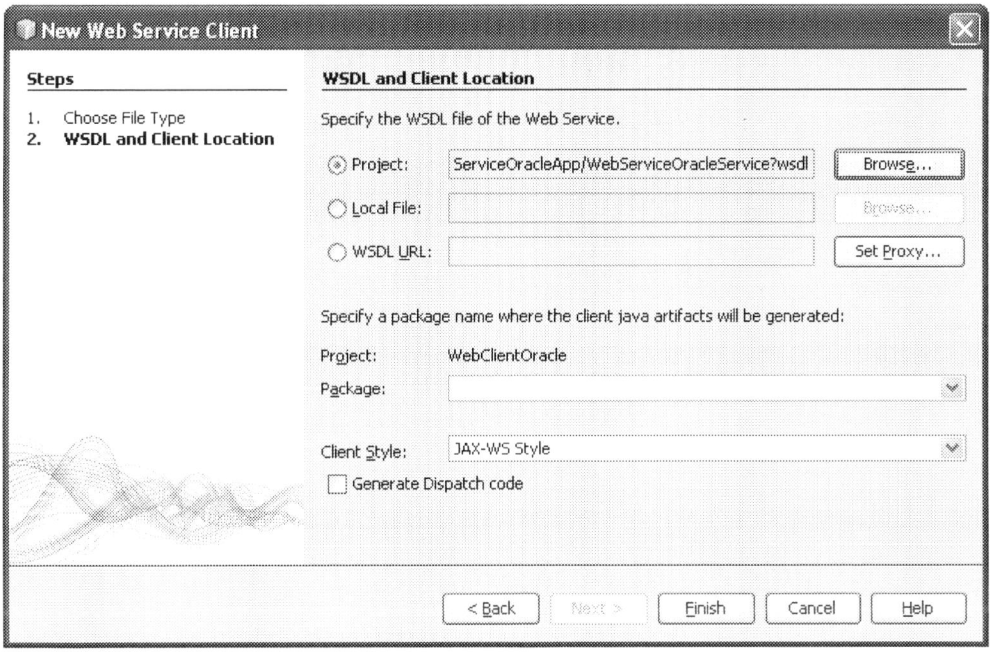

New Web Service Client

Steps

1. Choose File Type
2. **WSDL and Client Location**

WSDL and Client Location

Specify the WSDL file of the Web Service.

(•) Project: ServiceOracleApp/WebServiceOracleService?wsdl [Browse...]

( ) Local File: [Browse...]

( ) WSDL URL: [Set Proxy...]

Specify a package name where the client java artifacts will be generated:

Project: WebClientOracle

Package:

Client Style: JAX-WS Style

[ ] Generate Dispatch code

[< Back] [Next >] [Finish] [Cancel] [Help]

Figure 9.126. The finished New Web Service Client wizard.

Since the action and value attributes of all tags in our CoursePage.jsp have been bound to the associated properties and methods defined in our Java managed bean CourseBean, we only need to develop the codes for those methods defined in the Java managed bean CourseBean one by one to perform data actions against the Course table in our sample database by calling the associated operations defined in our Web service project.

9.16.4 Develop the Codes to Call Our Web Service Project

The relationship between each method defined in our Java managed bean and each operation in our Web service is shown in Table 9.12.

Let's start from the first method Select() defined in our managed bean CourseBean to query all course_id based on the selected faculty member.

9.16.4.1 Build Codes for the Select Button Method to Query CourseIDs

The function of this method is to query all course_id taught by the selected faculty member from the Course table when the Select button is clicked by the user. The queried result is returned and displayed in a Select-One-Listbox in the CoursePage.jsp page.

First, let's add our Web service operation QueryCourseID() into this Select() method by performing the following operations:

1. Open the code window of our Java managed bean CourseBean.java and browse to the Select() method.
2. Browse to the Web Service References node under our client project WebClientOracle.
3. Expand our Web service until all our five Web service operations have been exposed.
4. Drag the QueryCourseID operation and place it inside the Select() method.
5. A piece of codes is automatically created and added into this method, which is shown in Figure 9.127.

It is unnecessary to explain the function of this piece of codes line by line since all of coding lines have been illustrated by the built-in comments.

Now let's do some modifications to this piece of codes and add some codes to meet our course record query requirements. Enter the codes that are shown in Figure 9.128 into this method, and the modified codes have been highlighted in bold.

Table 9.12. The relationship between each bean method and each operation

Method in CourseBean	Web Service Operation	Function
Select()	QueryCourseID()	Query all **course_id** taught by the selected faculty
Details()	QueryCourse()	Query detailed information for selected **course_id**
Update()	UpdateCourse()	Update an existing course record in the Course table
Delete()	DeleteCourse()	Delete a course record from the Course table

```
  public String Select() {
A     try { // Call Web Service Operation
B        org.ws.oracle.WebServiceOracle port = service.getWebServiceOraclePort();
         // TODO initialize WS operation arguments here
C        java.lang.String fname = "";
         // TODO process result here
D        java.util.List<java.lang.Object> result = port.queryCourseID(fname);
         System.out.println("Result = "+result);
E     } catch (Exception ex) {
         // TODO handle custom exceptions here
      }
      return null;
  }
```

Figure 9.127. The automatically created and added codes.

```
  public String Select() {
A     ArrayList<String> cList = new ArrayList<String>();
      courseList = new ArrayList();
      try { // Call Web Service Operation
         org.ws.oracle.WebServiceOracle port = service.getWebServiceOraclePort();
         // TODO process result here
B        cList = (ArrayList)port.queryCourseID(getFacultyName());
C        for (int col = 0; col < cList.size(); col++) {
            SelectItem courseid = new SelectItem(cList.get(col).toString());
            courseList.add(courseid.getValue());
         }
D     } catch (Exception ex) {
         msgDlg.setMessage("exception is: " + ex);
         msgDlg.setVisible(true);
      }
E     return null;
  }
```

Figure 9.128. The modified codes for the Select() method.

Let's have a closer look at this piece of modified codes to see how it works.

A. Two ArrayList instances are created first since we need to use them to perform the course_id query and store queried result.

B. The Web service operation QueryCourseID() is called to get all course_id taught by the selected faculty member that works as an argument for this operation. The queried result is returned and assigned to the first ArrayList instance cList.

C. A `for` loop is used to pick up each queried course_id and add it into the courseList Listbox in our CoursePage.jsp page. Here, a tricking issue is that you must convert the courseList that is a List instance to an ArrayList object, and then you can use the add() method to add all queried course_id into this courseList since the List is an abstract class. Otherwise, you may encounter some null reference exception when your project runs.

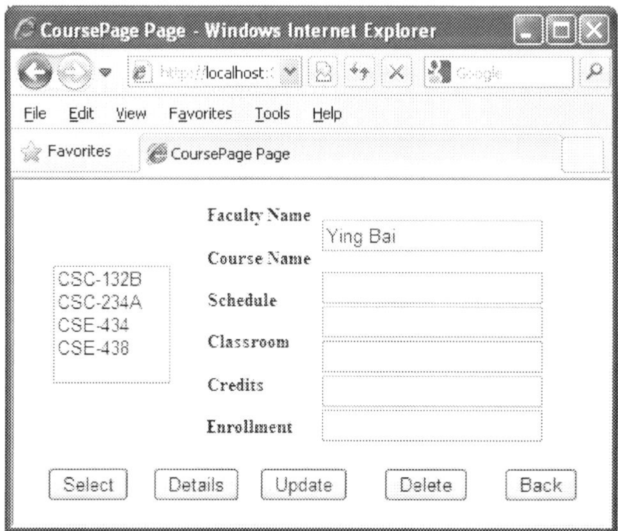

Figure 9.129. The course_id queried result for the selected faculty member.

D. The catch block is used to track and display any possible exception during this course_id query process.

E. Finally, a null is returned. Since we never use this returning value in this application, it is not important to us.

During the coding process, you may encounter some real-time compiling errors. Most of these errors are introduced by missing some packages that contain classes or components used in this file. To fix these errors, just right click on this code window and select the Fix Imports item to load and import those missed packages to the top of this code window.

Now we have finished all coding process for the course_id query action. Let's build and run our Web-based client project to test its function. Click on the Clean and Build Main Project button to build our client project. If everything is fine, deploy our client project by right clicking on our client project WebClientOracle and choose the Deploy item.

Run our client project by right clicking on our JSF page CoursePage.jsp from the Projects window and choose the Run File item.

On the opened JSF page, which is shown in Figure 9.129, enter a desired faculty name, such as Ying Bai, into the `Faculty Name` field. Then click the Select button to query all course_id taught by this selected faculty member. The query result is returned and displayed in the courseList Listbox on this page, as shown in Figure 9.129.

Our Web client project to consume our Web service operation QueryCourseID() is successful! A complete Web client project WebClientOracle can be found from the folder DBProjects\Chapter 9 that is located at the Wiley ftp site (refer to Figure 1.2 in Chapter 1).

Next, let's discuss how to consume the Web service operation QueryCourse() to get detailed course information for a given course_id from our sample Oracle database.

9.16.4.2 Build Codes for the Detail Button Method to Get Course Details

Now let's do the coding for the Details() method in our Java managed bean CourseBean.java to call a Web service operation QueryCourse() to get detailed course information for a given course_id.

The function of this method is to query detailed course information for a given course_id via the Web service operation QueryCourse() as the Details button in our JSF page CoursePage.jsp is clicked by the user. The queried result is returned and displayed in five text fields in that page.

First, let's add our Web service operation QueryCourse() into this Details() method by performing the following operations:

1. Open the code window of our Java managed bean CourseBean.java and browse to the Details() method.
2. Browse to the Web Service References node under our client project WebClientOracle.
3. Expand our Web service until all our five Web service operations have been exposed.
4. Drag the QueryCourse operation and place it inside the Details() method.
5. A piece of codes is automatically created and added into this method.

It is unnecessary to explain the function of this piece of codes line by line since all of coding lines have been illustrated by the built-in comments.

Now let's do some modifications to this piece of codes and add some codes to meet our course details query requirements. Enter the codes that are shown in Figure 9.130 into this method, and the modified codes have been highlighted in bold.

Let's have a closer look at this piece of modified codes to see how it works.

A. An ArrayList instance al is created first since we need to use it to collect and store the result of querying the detailed course information from our Course table.

B. We need to check whether a valid course_id has been selected by the user from the CourseList Listbox in our JSF page. If a valid course_id has been chosen, the Web service

```
    public Boolean Details() {
A       ArrayList<String> al = new ArrayList<String>();
        try { // Call Web Service Operation
            org.ws.oracle.WebServiceOracle port = service.getWebServiceOraclePort();
B           if (selectedItem != null) {
                al = (ArrayList)port.queryCourse(selectedItem);
C               courseName = al.get(1).toString();
                credit = al.get(2).toString();
                classroom = al.get(3).toString();
                schedule = al.get(4).toString();
                enrollment = al.get(5).toString();
            }
D       } catch (Exception ex) {
            msgDlg.setMessage("exception is: " + ex);
            msgDlg.setVisible(true);
        }
E       return null;
    }
```

Figure 9.130. The modified codes for the Details() method.

operation QueryCourse() is called to get detailed course information for that selected course_id (whose value has been bound to the selectedItem property) that works as an argument for this operation. The queried result is returned and assigned to the ArrayList instance al.

C. A group of get() methods is used to pick up each piece of course information and assign it to the associated property in this managed bean. Since each property has been bound to the associated value attributes of each inputText field in our JSF page CoursePage.jsp, each piece of detailed course information will be displayed in each of those inputText fields. The first element whose index is 0 in the returned query result is course_id.

D. The `catch` block is used to track and display any possible exception during this course details query process.

E. Finally, a null is returned. Since we never use this returning value in this application, it is not important to us.

Now we have finished all coding process for the course details query. Let's build and run our Web-based client project to test its function. Click on the Clean and Build Main Project button to build our client project. If everything is fine, deploy our client project by right clicking on our client project WebClientOracle and choose the Deploy item.

Run our client project by right clicking on our JSF page CoursePage.jsp from the Projects window and choose the Run File item.

On the opened JSF page, which is shown in Figure 9.131, enter a desired faculty name, such as Ying Bai, into the `Faculty Name` field. Then click the Select button to query all course_id taught by this selected faculty member. Then click on any course_id for which you want to get detailed information from the CourseList Listbox. The detailed course information for the selected course_id is retrieved and displayed in five inputText fields, as shown in Figure 9.131.

Our Web client project to consume our Web service operation QueryCourse() is successful!

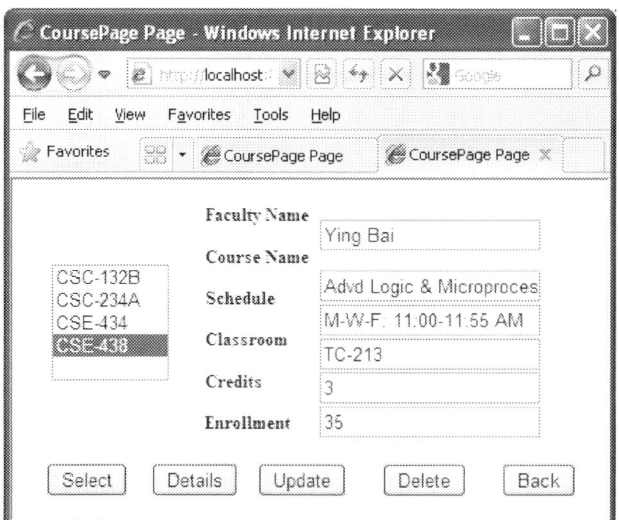

Figure 9.131. The running result of querying details for the course CSE-438.

Next, let's discuss how to consume the Web service operation UpdateCourse() to update an existing course record in our Course table for a given faculty member.

9.16.4.3 Build Codes for the Update Button Method to Update Courses

Now let's do the coding for the Update() method in our Java managed bean CourseBean.java to call a Web service operation UpdateCourse() to update an existing course record for a given faculty member.

The function of this method is to update a course record for a given faculty member via the Web service operation UpdateCourse() as the Update button in our JSF page CoursePage.jsp is clicked by the user.

First, let's add our Web service operation UpdateCourse() into this Update() method by performing the following operations:

1. Open the code window of our Java managed bean CourseBean.java and browse to the Update() method.
2. Browse to the Web Service References node under our client project WebClientOracle.
3. Expand our Web service until all our five Web service operations have been exposed.
4. Drag the UpdateCourse operation and place it inside the Update() method.
5. A piece of codes is automatically created and added into this method.

It is unnecessary to explain the function of this piece of codes line by line since all of coding lines have been illustrated by the built-in comments.

Now let's do some modifications to this piece of codes and add some codes to meet our course updating requirements. Enter the codes that are shown in Figure 9.132 into this method, and the modified codes have been highlighted in bold.

```
    public Boolean Update() {
A       boolean update = false;
        ArrayList al = new ArrayList();
B       al.clear();
C       al.add(0, selectedItem);
        al.add(1, courseName);
        al.add(2, credit);
        al.add(3, classroom);
        al.add(4, schedule);
        al.add(5, enrollment);
        al.add(6, getFacultyName());
        try { // Call Web Service Operation
          org.ws.oracle.WebServiceOracle port = service.getWebServiceOraclePort();
D         update = port.updateCourse(al);
E         if (!update)
            System.out.println("Error in UpdateCourse()...");
F       } catch (Exception ex) {
          msgDlg.setMessage("exception is: " + ex);
          msgDlg.setVisible(true);
        }
G       return null;
    }
```

Figure 9.132. The modified codes for the Update() method.

Let's have a closer look at this piece of modified codes to see how it works.

A. Two local variables, update and al, are created first. The first one is a Boolean variable used to hold the running result of the execution of the Web service operation UpdateCourse(), and the second is an ArrayList instance used to store a updating course record to be updated in the Course table in our sample database.

B. The ArrayList instance al is cleaned up using the clear() method to make sure that the al is empty before it can store any data.

C. A group of add() methods are used to add six pieces of updated course information into the ArrayList instance (The first parameter is a course_id whose value is stored in the selectedItem property that works as an updating criterion and will not be updated). One point to be noted is that the order in which to add these course parameters must be identical with the order of assigning these parameters to the Course object in the session bean method setCourse() in our Web service project WebServiceOracle. Refer to that method to make sure that both orders are identical.

D. The Web operation UpdateCourse() is called to update this existing course record via our Web service. The execution result that is a Boolean variable is returned and assigned to the local variable update.

E. If a `false` is returned, which means that this course data updating has been failed, the system println() method is used to indicate this situation.

F. The catch block is used to track and display any possible exception during this data updating process.

G. Finally, a null is returned. Since we never use this returning value in this application, it is not important to us.

Now we have finished all coding process for the course data updating action. Let's build and run our Web-based client project to test its function. Click on the Clean and Build Main Project button to build our client project. If everything is fine, deploy our client project by right clicking on our client project WebClientOracle and choose the Deploy item.

Run our client project by right clicking on our JSF page CoursePage.jsp from the Projects window and choose the Run File item.

On the opened JSF page, which is shown in Figure 9.133, enter a desired faculty name, such as Jenney King, into the `Faculty Name` field. Then click the Select button to query all course_id taught by this selected faculty member. Immediately, you can find that all four courses or four course_id taught by this faculty have been returned and displayed in the `CourseList` Listbox. Click on the Details button to get details for this selected course_id. To update an existing course CSC-233B, keep this course_id selected from the `CourseList` Listbox and enter five pieces of updated course information shown below into five text fields.

- Course: Network Theory
- Schedule: T-H: 9:30–10:45 AM
- Classroom: TC-206
- Credit: 3
- Enrollment: 26

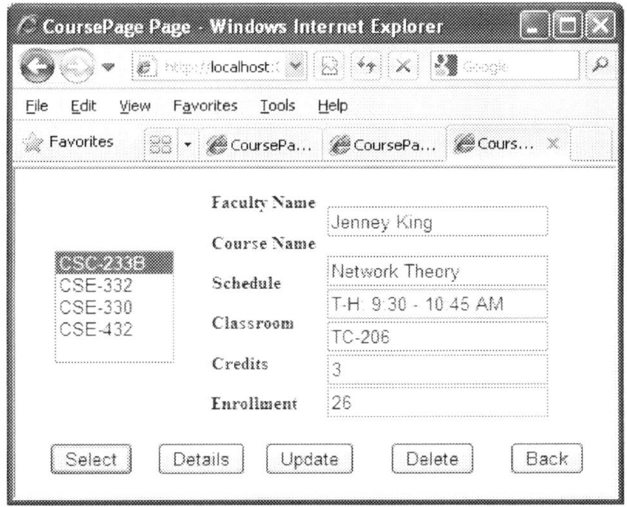

Figure 9.133. The running result of updating a course CSC-233B.

Your finished JSF page CoursePage.jsp is shown in Figure 9.133.

Click on the Update button to update this course record in the Course table in our sample database.

To test this course record updating action, there are more than one way can be used. The first way is to open the Course table to confirm that this course has been updated. But the second way, which is to select the course_id whose course details have been updated from the `CourseList` Listbox to get course details, is an easy way to confirm this course data updating.

Now let's use the second way to test this course data updating. Just click any other course_id, such as CSE-330, from the `CourseList` Listbox. Then click on the course_id CSC-233B whose details have been updated, and click on the Details button to retrieve all course details. It can be found that this course is really updated based on the updating information shown in Figure 9.133.

Generally, it is recommended to recover this updated course in the Course table in our sample database to keep our database neat and clean. However, we will keep this course right now since we need to use this record to perform the course deleting action in the following section.

Our Web client project to consume our Web service operation UpdateCourse() is successful!

Next, let's discuss how to consume the Web service operation DeleteCourse() to delete an existing course record from our Course table for a given faculty member.

9.16.4.4 Build Codes for the Delete Button Method to Delete Courses

Now let's do the coding for the Delete() method in our Java managed bean CourseBean.java to call a Web service operation DeleteCourse() to delete an existing course record from our Course table for a given course_id.

The function of this method is to delete a course record for a given course_id via the Web service operation DeleteCourse() as the Delete button in our JSF page CoursePage.jsp is clicked by the user.

First, let's add our Web service operation DeleteCourse() into this Delete() method by performing the following operations:

1. Open the code window of our Java managed bean CourseBean.java and browse to the Delete() method.
2. Browse to the Web Service References node under our client project WebClientOracle.
3. Expand our Web service until all our five Web service operations have been exposed.
4. Drag the DeleteCourse operation and place it inside the Delete() method.
5. A piece of codes is automatically created and added into this method.

It is unnecessary to explain the function of this piece of codes line by line since all of coding lines have been illustrated by the built-in comments.

Now let's do some modifications to this piece of codes and add some codes to meet our course deleting requirements. Enter the codes that are shown in Figure 9.134 into this method, and the modified codes have been highlighted in bold.

Let's have a closer look at this piece of modified codes to see how it works.

A. A local variable delete is created and this is a Boolean variable used to hold the running result of the execution of the Web service operation DeleteCourse().

B. The Web operation DeleteCourse() is called to delete an existing course record via our Web service. The execution result that is a Boolean variable is returned and assigned to the local variable delete.

C. If a `false` is returned, which means that this course data deleting has failed, the system println() method is used to indicate this situation.

D. The catch block is used to track and display any possible exception during this data deleting process.

E. Finally, a null is returned. Since we never use this returning value in this application, it is not important to us.

```
    public Boolean Delete() {
A       boolean delete = false;
        try { // Call Web Service Operation
            org.ws.oracle.WebServiceOracle port = service.getWebServiceOraclePort();
B           delete = port.deleteCourse(selectedItem);
C           if (!delete)
                System.out.println("Error in DeleteCourse()...");
D       } catch (Exception ex) {
            msgDlg.setMessage("exception is: " + ex);
            msgDlg.setVisible(true);
        }
E       return null;
    }
```

Figure 9.134. The modified codes for the Delete() method.

Now we have finished all coding process for the course data deleting action. Let's build and run our Web-based client project to test its function. Click on the **Clean and Build Main Project** button to build our client project. If everything is fine, deploy our client project by right clicking on our client project **WebClientOracle** and choose the **Deploy** item.

Run our client project by right clicking on our JSF page **CoursePage.jsp** from the **Projects** window and choose the **Run File** item.

On the opened JSF page, enter a desired faculty name, such as **Jenney King**, into the `Faculty Name` field. Then click the **Select** button to query all **course_id** taught by this selected faculty member. Immediately, you can find that all four courses or four **course_id** taught by this faculty have been returned and displayed in the `CourseList` Listbox. Click on the **Details** button to get details for this selected **course_id**.

To delete the course CSC-233B, keep this **course_id** selected from the `CourseList` Listbox, and click on the **Delete** button.

To confirm this course deleting action, two ways can be utilized. First, you can open our Course table to check whether this course has been deleted from our database. Another way, which is easy, is to use the **Select** button to try to retrieve this deleted course from our database. To do that, just keep the selected faculty member **Jenney King** in the `Faculty Name` combo box unchanged and click on the **Select** button. It can be found from the returned courses, exactly all **course_id** taught by the selected faculty, that no CSC-233B existed, as shown in Figure 9.135.

Our course record deleting using Web service is successful.

It is highly recommended to recover this deleted record from our database to keep our sample database neat and clean. You can recover this course using either the `Insert Record` method in the opened Course table via **Services** window in NetBeans IDE or Oracle Database 10g XE Object Browser. Refer to the data shown in Table 9.13 to recovery this course CSC-233B.

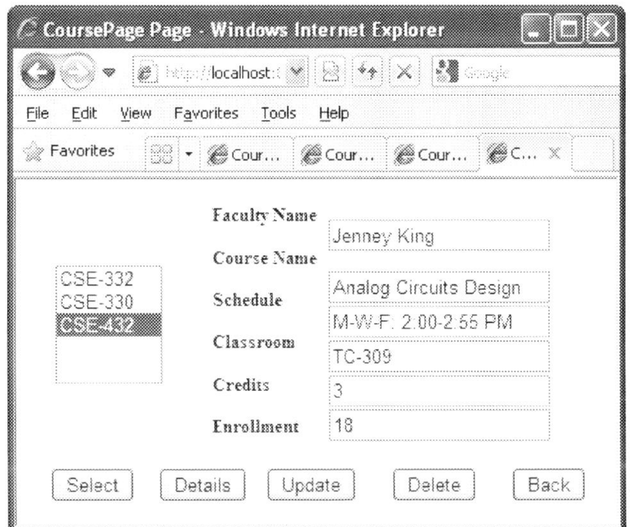

Figure 9.135. The running result of deleting a course CSC-233B.

Table 9.13. The original course record CSC-233B in the Course table

course_id	course	credit	classroom	schedule	enrollment	faculty_id
CSC-233B	Introduction to Algorithms	3	TC-302	M-W-F: 11:00-11:55 AM	19	K69880

At this point, we have finished all developing and building processes to consume our Web service using a Web-based client project. A complete Web-based client project that is used to consume our Web service to query and manipulate data against our Oracle database, WebClientOracle, can be found from the folder DBProjects\Chapter 9 that is located at the Wiley ftp site (refer to Figure 1.2 in Chapter 1).

9.17 CHAPTER SUMMARY

A detailed discussion and analysis of the structure and components about Java Web Services are provided in this chapter. Two popular Java Web Services, REST-Based and SOAP-Based services, are discussed in detail with illustrations. The procedure of building a typical SOAP-Based Web service project is introduced with a real project example.

Starting from Section 9.5, two typical SOAP-Based Web service projects, WebServiceSQL, which is used to access and manipulate data against a SQL Server 2008 database, and WebServiceOracle, which is used to access and manipulate data against an Oracle database, are discussed and analyzed in detail with two real project examples.

To consume these two kinds of Web services, four real client projects are developed and built with detailed coding processes and illustrations:

- **WinClientSQL**: a Windows-Based Web client project to consume the Web service WebServiceSQL to perform data query and manipulations to the Faculty table in our sample SQL Server 2008 database.
- **WebClientSQL**: a Web-Based Web client project to consume the Web service WebServiceSQL to perform data query and manipulations to the Faculty table in our sample SQL Server 2008 database.
- **WinClientOracle**: a Windows-Based Web client project to consume the Web service WebServiceOracle to perform data query and manipulations to the Course table in our sample Oracle database.
- **WebClientOracle**: a Web-Based Web client project to consume the Web service WebServiceOracle to perform data query and manipulations to the Course table in our sample Oracle database.

A console-based testing project OracleTest to test the data insertion and updating actions against our sample Oracle database is also included in this chapter.

All of these real projects have been tested and debugged, and can be used without modifications. To use these project examples, one needs to install

- Glassfish v3 Web application server
- Microsoft SQL Server 2008 Express database and management studio
- Microsoft SQL Server JDBC Driver

- Oracle Database 10g XE
- Oracle JDBC Driver

All of these software tools and drivers can be downloaded and installed on the users' computer with free of charge. Refer to Appendices to finish these downloading and installation processes.

HOMEWORK

I. True/False Selections

____**1.** Unlike Java Web applications, the Java Web Services provide an automatic way to search, identify, and return the desired information required by the user through a set of methods installed in the Web server.

____**2.** Java Web Services provide graphic user interfaces (GUIs) to enable users to access the Web services via the Internet.

____**3.** Web services can be considered as a set of methods installed in a Web server, and can be called by computer programs installed on the clients through the Internet.

____**4.** Two popular Java Web Services are: REST-based and SOAP-based services, and both are supported by NetBeans IDE.

____**5.** Both Web service models, JAX-WS and JAX-RPC, are popular and updated models used in Web service developments.

____**6.** Compared with REST-based service, SOAP-based Web Services are more suitable for heavyweight applications using complicated operations and for applications requiring sophisticated security and reliability.

____**7.** Unlike ASP.NET Web Services, a Java SOAP-based Web service project is involved in a Java Web application project in which the Web service can be deployed based on an appropriate container.

____**8.** To access a Web service, one does not have to call any operation defined in the Web service.

____**9.** Before one can call a Web service operation, a Web service reference must have been established for the client project.

____**10.** It is unnecessary to update a Web service each time when consuming it in a client project; however one must deploy that Web service each time when start it from NetBeans IDE.

II. Multiple Choices

1. **In a SOAP-Based** Java Web Service, the SOAP means __________.
   a. Statement Object Access Protocol
   b. Simplified Object Access Protocol
   c. Simple Object Access Protocol
   d. Structure Object Access Protocol
2. **In a REST-Based** Java Web Service, the REST means __________.
   a. **RE**presentational **S**tate **T**ransfer
   b. **RE**presentational **S**tate **T**ransmitter
   c. **RE**presentational **S**tatus **T**ransfer
   d. **Rapid E**ssential **S**tate **T**ransfer

3. When using a REST-Based Web service, only four methods are available: __________.
   - a. INPUT, OUTPUT, POST, and DELETE
   - b. SAVE, PUT, POST, and DELETE
   - c. GET, EXECUTE, POST, and DELETE
   - d. GET, PUT, POST, and DELETE
4. The protocol used in the REST-Based Web Services is __________.
   - a. FTP
   - b. XML
   - c. HTTP
   - d. TCP/IP
5. To effectively find, identify and return the target information required by computer programs, a SOAP-based Web Service needs the following components, __________.
   - a. XML and WSDL
   - b. SOAP, UDDI and WSDL
   - c. UDDI, XML and SOAP
   - d. WSDL, XML, UDDI and SOAP
6. SOAP is a simple __________-based protocol to help applications developed in different platforms and languages to exchange information over __________.
   - a. HTML, HTTP
   - b. XML, HTTP
   - c. FTP, TCP/IP
   - d. XML, Internet
7. In WSDL terminology, each Web service is defined as a __________, and each Web method is defined as an abstract __________.
   - a. Method, function
   - b. Service, operation
   - c. End point, function
   - d. Port, operation
8. SOAP is used to wrap and pack the data tagged in the __________ format into the messages represented in the __________ protocol.
   - a. XML, SOAP
   - b. HTML, HTTP
   - c. FTP, TCP/IP
   - d. SOAP, XML
9. When building a Java Web service, a __________ that contains a Web container for the __________ must be built first.
   - a. Web service, Web application
   - b. Web client, Web consuming project
   - c. Web service, Web client project
   - d. Web application, Web service
10. To consume a Web service, a __________ must be established in the client project.
   - a. Web service reference
   - b. Web service operation

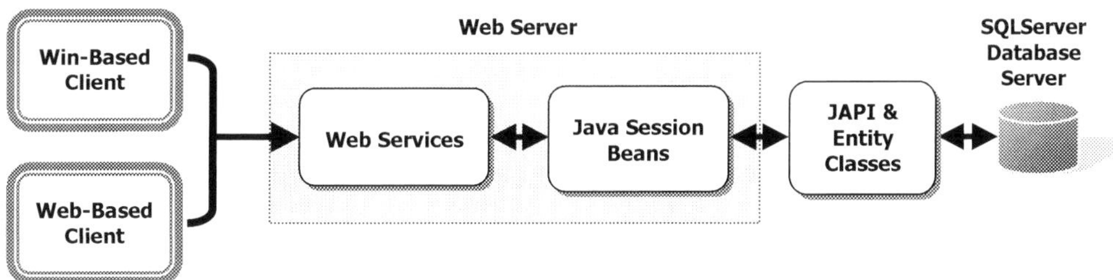

Figure 9.136. The structure of building a new Web service project.

c. Web service directory

d. All of them

III. Exercises

1. Provide a brief description about the advantages of using a SOAP-based Web service.
2. Illustrate the structure and components of SOAP-based Web services.
3. Provide a brief description about procedures of building a typical SOAP-based Web service project.
4. Provides a brief description about how to establish a Web service reference for a given client project to enable the latter to consume that Web service.
5. Explain the operational sequence of adding a Web service operation into a method in a client project to enable the latter to call that operation.
6. Using the structure shown in Figure 9.136 to build a Web service project WSSQLBean and replace the Java runtime object with the Java managed bean to perform data actions against the Faculty table in our SQL Server 2008 database.
7. Develop a similar Web service to access and manipulate data against the Student table in our sample SQL Server 2008 database.

Index

Practical Database Programming with Java, First Edition. Ying Bai.

D

About the Author

DR. YING BAI is a Professor in the Department of Computer Science and Engineering at Johnson C. Smith University, Charlotte, North Carolina. His special interests include soft computing, software engineering, mix-language programming, database programming, classical and fuzzy logic controls, robotic controls, and robot calibrations, as well as fuzzy multicriteria decision making. His industry experience includes positions as software and senior software engineers at companies such as Motorola MMS, Schlumberger ATE Technology, Immix TeleCom, and Lam Research. Dr. Bai has published some 30 academic research papers in IEEE Transactions Journals and international conferences. He has also written eight other books, mostly on multilanguage programming, fuzzy logic technologies, and database programming.

Practical Database Programming with Java, First Edition. Ying Bai.

Printed in the United States
By Bookmasters